THE ROUGH GUIDE TO

Turkey

This ninth edition updated by

Terry Richardson, Zoë Smith, Lizzie Williams
and Martin Zatko

ROUGH
GUIDES

roughguides.com

Contents

Introduction to
Turkey

A mesmerizing mix of the exotic and the familiar, Turkey is much more than its clichéd image of a "bridge between East and West". Invaded and settled from every direction since the start of recorded history, it combines influences from the Middle East and the Mediterranean, the Balkans and Central Asia. Mosques coexist with churches, Roman theatres and temples crumble near ancient Hittite cities, and dervish ceremonies and gypsy festivals are as much a part of the social landscape as classical music concerts or football matches.

The friendliness of the **Turkish people** makes visiting a pleasure; indeed, you risk causing offence by declining invitations, and find yourself making friends through the simplest of transactions. At the big resorts and tourist spots, of course, this can merely be an excuse to sell you something, but elsewhere, despite a history in which outsiders have so often brought trouble, the warmth and generosity are genuine.

Politically, modern Turkey was a grand experiment, largely the creation of one man – **Kemal Atatürk**. With superhuman energy, he salvaged the Turkish state from the wreckage of the Ottoman Empire and defined it as a modern, secular nation. Despite three military coups between 1960 and 1980, Turkey has maintained a reasonably successful multi-party democracy for over sixty years, and has managed to blend secularism and global capitalism with Islam. Challenges remain, however, with signs that the conservative, Islam-orientated **AKP** (Justice and Development Party) government are seeking to consolidate their rule through the introduction of a strongly presidential system led by one of their own, former prime minister **Recep Tayyip Erdoğan**. The meltdown of two countries bordering Turkey's southeast, Syria and Iraq, is also a major cause for concern.

When the Ottoman Empire imploded in the early twentieth century, refugees streamed into Anatolia, including Muslim Slavs, Greeks, Albanians, Crimean Tatars, Daghestanlis, Abkhazians and Circassians. There they joined an already mixed population that included

ABOVE GÖREME

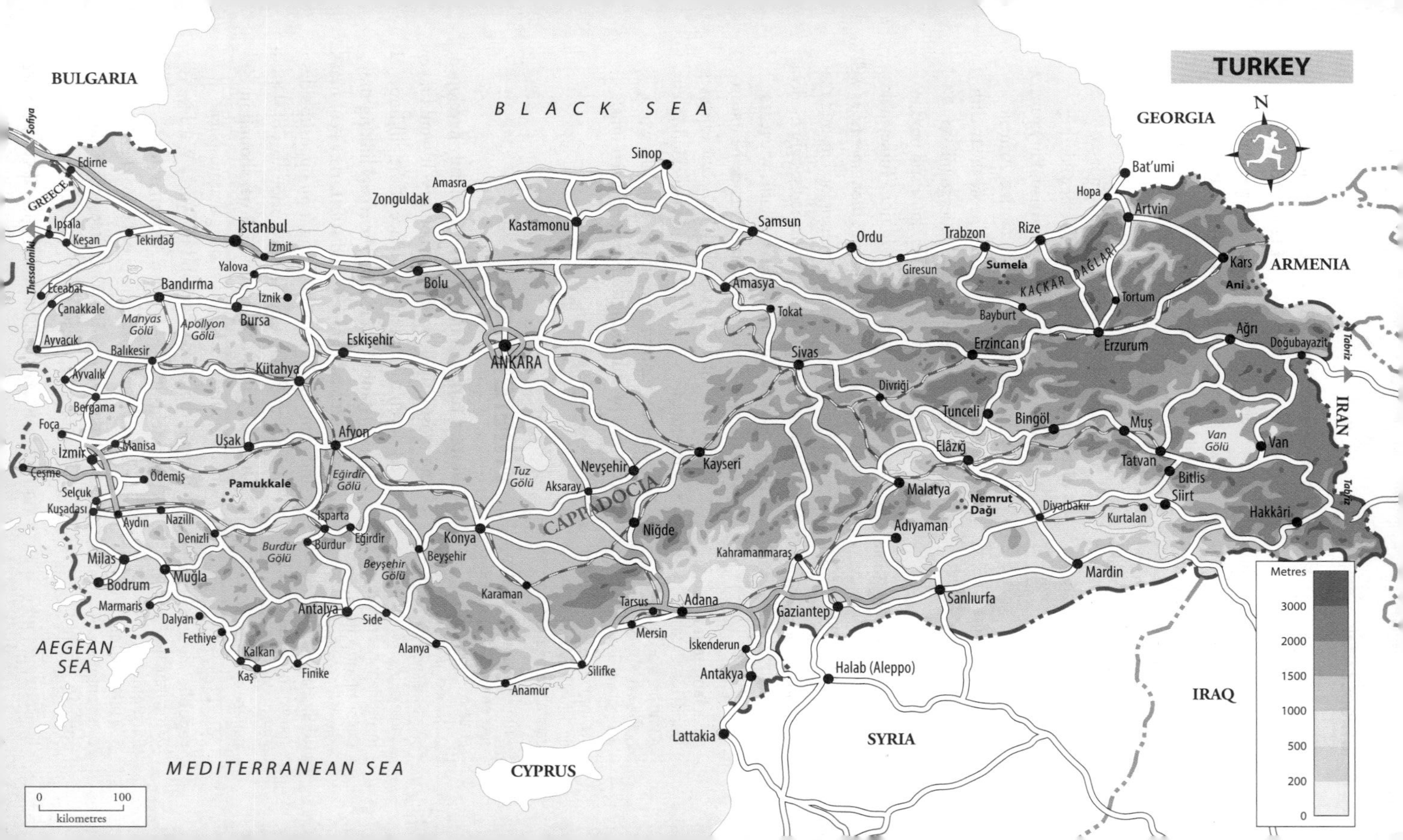
TURKEY
N
BLACK SEA
MEDITERRANEAN SEA
AEGEAN SEA
BULGARIA
GREECE
GEORGIA
ARMENIA
IRAN
IRAQ
SYRIA
CYPRUS
Sofiya
Thessaloniki
Tabriz
Tabriz
Edirne
İpsala
Keşan
Tekirdağ
İstanbul
İzmit
Yalova
Eceabat
Çanakkale
Bandırma
İznik
Bursa
Manyas Gölü
Apollyon Gölü
Ayvacık
Balıkesir
Ayvalık
Bergama
Foça
Manisa
İzmir
Çeşme
Ödemiş
Selçuk
Kuşadası
Aydın
Nazilli
Denizli
Pamukkale
Milas
Bodrum
Muğla
Marmaris
Dalyan
Fethiye
Kalkan
Kaş
Finike
Antalya
Side
Alanya
Anamur
Silifke
Burdur
Burdur Gölü
Isparta
Eğirdir
Eğirdir Gölü
Beyşehir
Beyşehir Gölü
Uşak
Afyon
Kütahya
Eskişehir
Bolu
Zonguldak
Amasra
Kastamonu
Sinop
Samsun
Amasya
Tokat
ANKARA
Tuz Gölü
Aksaray
Konya
Karaman
Nevşehir
CAPPADOCIA
Niğde
Kayseri
Sivas
Tarsus
Mersin
Adana
İskenderun
Antakya
Lattakia
Halab (Aleppo)
Gaziantep
Kahramanmaraş
Malatya
Adıyaman
Nemrut Dağı
Şanlıurfa
Mardin
Diyarbakır
Kurtalan
Siirt
Bitlis
Tatvan
Van
Van Gölü
Hakkâri
Muş
Bingöl
Elâzığ
Tunceli
Divriği
Erzincan
Erzurum
Ağrı
Doğubayazit
Kars
Ani
Tortum
Bayburt
KAÇKAR DAĞLARI
Sumela
Ordu
Giresun
Trabzon
Rize
Hopa
Artvin
Bat'umi
Metres
3000
2000
1500
1000
500
200
0
0
100
kilometres

FACT FILE

• Turkey covers a vast 814,578 sq km (97 percent in Asia, 3 percent in Europe). Four seas lap its 8333-km **coastline**: the Mediterranean, the Aegean, the Marmara and the Black Sea. Numerous **peaks** exceed 3000m, the highest being Ararat (Ağrı Dağı; 5165m). Turkey's three longest **rivers** – the Kızılırmak, Yeşilırmak and Sakarya – flow into the Black Sea, while its largest lake is Lake Van (3713 sq km).

• The population of 77 million is 99 percent **Muslim** (Sunni or Alevi), with dwindling **minorities** of the Armenian Apostolic or Catholic, Greek Orthodox, Syrian Orthodox and Jewish faiths. Besides standard Turkish, two dialects of Kurdish are widely spoken; other **languages** include Arabic, Laz, Circassian, Albanian, Macedonian, Bulgarian, Romany and Greek. Well over half the inhabitants live in cities; the four largest are İstanbul, Ankara (the capital), İzmir and Adana.

• Turkey's **economy**, rated seventeenth in the world in 2014, has undergone sustained growth in recent years. Inflation has fallen to single digits, inward investment has rocketed, major infrastructure projects have been realized at an astonishing rate, and the Turkish lira has generally held its own with the major currencies.

• Since 1922 Turkey has been a **republic**. The single-chamber Grand National Assembly (Büyük Meclis) in Ankara has 550 seats, and elects the president.

a very sizeable minority of Kurds. Thanks to recent arrivals from former Soviet or Eastern Bloc territories, that diversity endures. Another surprise may be Turkey's sheer **youthfulness**: more than half the population is under thirty, with legions of young people working in coastal resorts, and shoals of schoolkids surging through the city streets.

A huge part of Turkey's appeal lies in its **archeological sites**, a legacy of the bewildering succession of states – Hittite, Urartian, Phrygian, Greek, Hellenistic, Roman, Byzantine, Armeno-Georgian – that held sway here before the twelfth century. From grand Classical cities to hilltop fortresses and remote churches, some still produce exciting new finds today. In addition, Turkey holds a vast number of graceful **Islamic monuments**, as well as intriguing **city bazaars**, still hanging on amid the chain stores and shopping malls. Sadly, ugly modern architecture spoils most coastal resorts, where it's often hard to find a beach that matches the tourist-board hype. **Inland Turkey**, with its Asiatic expanses of mountains, steppes, lakes, and even cloud-forests, may leave a more vivid memory, especially when accented by crumbling *kervansaray* (desert inns), mosques and castles.

Where to go

Western Turkey is the most economically developed, and most visited, part of the country. It would take weeks even to scratch the surface of the old imperial capital, **Istanbul**, straddling the straits linking the Black and Marmara seas, and still Turkey's cultural and commercial hub. Flanking it on opposite sides of the Sea of Marmara, the two prior seats of the Ottoman Empire, **Bursa** and **Edirne**, abound in monumental attractions and regal atmosphere. Beyond the Dardanelles and its World War I battlefields lie Turkey's two **Aegean islands**, Gökçeada and Bozcaada, popular for their excellent beaches, lingering Greek-ethnic identity and (except in midsummer) tranquillity.

CLOCKWISE FROM TOP KEKOVA ISLAND; TURKISH COFFEE; CARPET SHOP IN ISTANBUL

Further south, the olive-swathed landscapes around Bergama and Ayvalık epitomize the Classical character of the **North Aegean**. Ancient Sardis, and the old Ottoman princely training ground of Manisa, also make a fine pair, although İzmir serves merely as a functional introduction to the **central and southern Aegean**. Celebrated Ephesus tends to overshadow the equally deserving ancient Ionian sites of Priene and Didyma, or the intriguing ruins of Aphrodisias and Labranda – and don't overlook evocative hill towns such as the lovely Şirince. Also inland are tranquil, islet-dotted Bafa Gölü and the compelling geological oddity of Pamukkale, where travertine formations abut Roman Hierapolis. While the coast itself is heavily developed, its star resorts – Datça is the quietest, Bodrum the most characterful – make comfortable bases.

Beyond the huge natural harbour at Marmaris, the Aegean gradually becomes the Mediterranean. Coastal cruises make popular pastimes in brazen Marmaris or more manageable Fethiye, the principal town of the **Turquoise Coast**, while fine beaches stretch at Dalyan and Patara, near eerie ancient Lycian tombs. Further east, Kaş and Kalkan are busy resorts, good for resting up between explorations of the mountainous hinterland. Beyond relatively untouched Çıralı beach, at ancient Olympos, fast-growing Antalya sprawls at the start of the **Mediterranean coast** proper. This is graced by extensive sands and archeological sites – most notably Termessos, Perge, Side and Aspendos – though its western parts get swamped in season. Beyond castle-topped Alanya, however, tourist numbers diminish; points of interest between Silifke and Adana include Roman Uzuncaburç and the romantic offshore fortress at Kızkalesi. Further east, Arab-influenced Antakya is the heart of the **Hatay**, culturally part of Syria.

Inland in **South Central Anatolia**, the rock-hewn churches, subterranean cities and tuff-pinnacle landscapes of **Cappadocia** await. The dry, salubrious climate, excellent wine, artistic and architectural treasures, plus horseriding or hot-air ballooning could occupy you for ten days, including a stop in Kayseri on the way north. You might also

TURKEY'S TOP FIVE BEACHES

With over 8000km of coastline, it's hardly surprising that Turkey has some excellent **beaches**. Below is a round up of some of the very best:

Patara Stretching for 15km along the beautiful Lycian coastline, Patara Beach is one of the longest and finest beaches in the entire Mediterranean. It's home to the atmospheric, dune-set ruins of ancient Patara, and a favoured nesting site of endangered turtles (see p.322).

İztuzu Best reached by a delightful thirty-minute boat ride downriver from the charming riverside resort of Dalyan, the soft golden sands of İztuzu Beach are as popular with visitors as they are with nesting loggerhead turtles (see p.310).

Çıralı This pebble-and-course-sand beach is book-ended by dramatic limestone spurs, backed by the snowcapped hulk of Mount Olympos and fronted by the Gulf of Antalya. A protected turtle nesting site, Çıralı is home to the overgrown ruins of ancient Olympos and the eternal flames of the Chimaera (see p.345).

Phaselis The ancient site of Phaselis sits grandly among pines right by the shore. The southern beach here shelves gently into the turquoise waters, while the small western beach fronts onto a shallow, lake-like lagoon (see p.348).

İskele Few foreign visitors make it out to low-key İskele, the beach-front offspring of nearby Anamur. Walk east along the beach to the fairy-tale medieval castle of Mamure, or west to the remote beachside ruins of ancient Anemurium (see p.380).

pause at the historic lakefront towns of Eğirdir or Beyşehir, or in Konya, renowned for its Selçuk architecture and associations with the Mevlevî dervishes.

Ankara, Turkey's capital, is a planned city whose contrived Western feel indicates the priorities of the Turkish Republic; it also features the outstanding Museum of Anatolian Civilizations. Highlights of surrounding **North Central Anatolia** include the bizarre temple of Aezani, near Kütahya; the Ottoman museum-town of Safranbolu; exquisitely decorated early Turkish monuments in Divriği; and remarkable Hittite sites at Hattuşaş and Alacahöyük. As you travel north, pause in the Yeşilırmak valley towns of Sivas, Tokat and Amasya. The lush shoreline of the Black Sea beyond holds little more than a chain of Byzantine-Genoese castles; the oldest, most interesting towns are Sinop, Anatolia's northernmost point, and Amasra. Fabled Trabzon, east of Sinop and once the seat of a Byzantine sub-empire, is now convenient for Aya Sofya and Sumela monasteries.

The Ankara–Sivas route positions you to head along the Euphrates River into the "back half" of Turkey. First stop in **northeastern Anatolia** is likely to be Erzurum, Turkey's highest and bleakest major city, a base for visits to the temperate,

OPPOSITE EGYPTIAN BAZAAR, ISTANBUL

WHO ARE THE TURKS?

Today's Turks are descended from nomadic pastoralist Turkic tribal groups that originated in Siberia, China and Central Asia, went on to conquer the Anatolian landmass, and have subsequently intermarried on a large scale with the region's already extremely heterogeneous population. Although historical records can trace them as a readily identifiable people as far back as the sixth century BC, only during the sixth century AD were they first recorded (by the Chinese) as "Tu-keh" or, to the west, **Turks**.

From around 1000 AD onwards, the Turks gradually migrated southwards and westwards. By the time they reached Anatolia, which would eventually become the heartland of the mighty Ottoman Turkish Empire, most had converted to **Islam**. Turks still maintain ethnic, linguistic and cultural links with Turkic peoples in Central Asia, the Caucasus, northwest Iran, northern Iraq, southern Russia, and Xinjiang in western China.

church-studded valleys of southern medieval Georgia, or treks in the Kaçkar Mountains. Kars is mainly visited for the sake of nearby Ani, the ruined medieval Armenian capital.

The **Euphrates and Tigris basin** have a real Middle Eastern flavour. Booming Gaziantep offers world-class Roman mosaics, an atmospheric old quarter and Turkey's spiciest cuisine. Further east, biblical Urfa is distinguished by its colourful bazaar and sacred pool, while cosmopolitan Mardin overlooks the vast Mesopotamian Plain. The major attraction, however, is a dawn or sunset trip to Nemrut Dağı's colossal ancient statues. Between Mardin and Nemrut Dağı, teeming, ethnically Kurdish Diyarbakır nestles inside medieval basalt walls. The terrain becomes increasingly mountainous towards the Iranian frontier, an area dominated by the unearthly blue, alkaline expanse of Lake Van. Urartian, Selçuk and Armenian monuments abound within sight of the water, in particular the exquisite, restored Armenian church on Akdamar islet. The east-shore city of Van is notable for its massive camel-shaped rock punctured with ancient tombs. Beyond Van looms the fairy-tale Kurdish castle of Hoşap, while just outside Doğubeyazıt, another isolated folly, the İshak Paşa Sarayı, stands in the shadow of Mount Ararat at the very end of Turkey.

A REAL TURKISH DELIGHT: YOGHURT

Only two genuinely Turkish words (as opposed to those loaned from Arabic or Farsi) have found their way into the English language. One is kiosk, from the Turkish *köşk*, which refers properly to an ornate wood-built mansion and informally to a raised seating area. The other is **yoghurt**, from the Turkish *yoğurt* (pronounced yo-urt). Given their origins as nomadic pastoralists in the steppes bounded by the Altai mountains, Lake Baikal and the Gobi desert, it's hardly surprising that yoghurt, relatively easily produced from the Turks' vast, mobile herds of sheep and goats, became a staple part of their diet.

Today yoghurt remains a prominent feature of Turkish meals, though it's as likely to be made from cow's milk as from that produced by sheep or goats. Although sweetened fruit concoctions have crept onto supermarket shelves in recent years, the vast majority of yoghurt is still purchased in its basic, pure, white and simple form. It forms the "sauce" for many of Turkey's most tempting *meze* (appetizers), is used in soups, slathered over kebabs and *mantı* (Turkish ravioli) as well as, when mixed with water and salt, drunk as *ayran*.

When to go

Among coastal areas, Istanbul and the Sea of Marmara shores have a relatively damp, Balkan climate, with muggy summers and cool, rainy (though seldom snowy) winters. These areas get crowded between late June and early September. The popular Aegean and Mediterranean coasts can be uncomfortably hot during July and August, especially between İzmir and Antakya; in spring or autumn, the weather here is gentler and the crowds thinner, while late October and early November see the idyllic *pastırma yazı* or "Indian summer". Even during winter, the Turquoise and Mediterranean coasts are – except for rainy periods in January and February – still fairly pleasant. The Black Sea is an anomaly, with exceptionally mild winters for so far north, and rain likely during the nine coolest months, lingering as mist and subtropical humidity during summer.

Cut off from the coast by mountains, Central Anatolia is mostly semi-arid steppe, with a bracing climate – warm but not unpleasant in summer, cool and fairly dry in winter, from late November to late March. Cappadocia makes a colourful, quiet treat during spring and autumn – or even December, when its rock formations are dusted with snow. As you travel east, into northeast Anatolia and around Lake Van, the altitude increases and conditions become deeply snowy between October and April, making late spring and summer by far the best time to visit. In the lower Euphrates and Tigris basin, a pronounced Middle Eastern influence exerts itself, with winters no worse than in Central Anatolia but torrid summers, without the compensation of a nearby beach.

CLIMATE

Average midday temperatures in °C & °F and monthly rainfall in mm

	Jan	Feb	Mar	Apr	May	Jun	Jul	Aug	Sep	Oct	Nov	Dec
ISTANBUL												
Temp (°C)/(°F)	6/43	6/43	7/45	12/54	17/63	21/70	24/75	24/75	20/68	16/61	12/54	8/47
Rainfall in mm	57.6	69.5	61.8	48.5	39.6	24.6	31	37	43.7	100.1	85.7	102
ANTALYA												
Temp (°C)/(°F)	11/52	12/54	13/56	17/63	21/70	23/77	29/84	29/84	25/77	21/70	16/61	12/54
Rainfall in mm	178	110.4	111.6	75.7	33	3	1	1	2	89.3	174.9	277.5
ANKARA												
Temp (°C)/(°F)	1/34	1/34	5/41	12/54	17/63	20/68	24/75	24/75	19/66	13/56	8/47	3/37
Rainfall in mm	14	15	20.5	25.1	24.9	16.5	22.3	7.1	25.2	19.1	26.1	30.9
TRABZON												
Temp (°C)/(°F)	8/47	8/47	9/48	12/54	16/61	20/68	23/73	24/75	20/68	17/63	14/57	10/50
Rainfall in mm	76	65.7	62.7	60.4	65	44.7	45.6	60.7	111.1	153.2	108.1	82.6
DİYARBAKIR												
Temp (°C)/(°F)	2/35	4/39	9/48	14/57	20/68	26/79	31/88	31/88	25/77	18/65	10/50	5/41
Rainfall in mm	57.3	72.5	62.4	52.4	42.6	20.2	1	5.4	2	48.5	55.4	67.4

Author picks

Our authors have traversed every corner of Turkey, from the bazaars of Istanbul to the resorts of the Turquoise Coast and the summit of Mount Nemrut. Here are some of their favourite experiences:

A big night out, Istanbul-style The Beyoğlu quarter (see p.104) of Turkey's leading city is a party animal's dream on a Friday and Saturday night. Warm up with a multi-course, rakı-infused spread at a lively *meyhane* (see p.126) before heading off to a pulsating club (see p.128).

Birthplace of the Ottoman dynasty Bursa, recently declared a World Heritage Site and an easy target from Istanbul via fast ferry across the Sea of Marmara, is packed with intriguing early Ottoman monuments (see p.167).

Çiğ köfte Most forms of Turkish sustenance are familiar to Western travellers, but this little lunchtime pick-me-up may be new to you: a *dürüm* wrap filled with spicy paste and vegetables, all given a little lemon zing. It's also super-cheap at around ₺5 (see p.252).

Get wet Make the most of Turkey's Aegean and Mediterranean coast by scuba diving off Kalkan or Kaş (see p.324 & p.328), windsurfing from hip Alaçatı (see p.235) or chilled Gümüşlük (see p.268), or kayaking around the Lycian shore (see p.324).

Turkey's Wild West Cappadocia's dusty plains, wildflower-covered slopes and weathered tuff chimneys provide an adventurous backdrop for a horseriding trek (see p.438).

Take tea in Sivas Well off the tourist trail, this charming little city is home to a couple of enchanting thirteenth-century Selçuk buildings whose table-filled courtyards are perhaps Turkey's most atmospheric places to take tea (see p.502).

Ride a cable car Several new *teleferiks* have been built on strategic mountaintops, offering Black Sea panoramas at Ordu (see p.518) and Samsun (see p.510); taking up skiers and hikers at Uludağ (see p.179); and whisking sightseers up to Pergamon's acropolis at Bergama (see p.212).

Our author recommendations don't end here. We've flagged up our favourite places – a perfectly sited hotel, an atmospheric café, a special restaurant – throughout the guide, highlighted with the ★ symbol.

27

things not to miss

It's not possible to see everything Turkey has to offer in one trip – and we don't suggest you try. What follows is a selective and subjective taste of the country's highlights: outstanding buildings and historic sites, natural wonders and exciting activities. All highlights are colour-coded by chapter and have a page reference to take you straight into the guide, where you can find out more.

1

1 HOT-AIR BALLOONING OVER CAPPADOCIA

Page 439

A lighter-than-air float gives an unrivalled perspective on the "fairy chimneys" and other features of the landscape.

2 İSHAK PAŞA SARAYI

Page 640

Strategically set astride the Silk Route, this architecturally eclectic seventeenth-century palace is one of eastern Turkey's most emblematic sites.

3 MONASTERY OF SUMELA

Page 528

Dramatically built into the side of the Pontic mountains, this Byzantine monastery is adorned with beautiful frescoes.

4 WHIRLING DERVISHES

Page 424

Members of a sect founded by the Konya-based Sufi mystic Celaleddin Rumi conduct "turning" ceremonies to effect union with God.

11 MUSEUM OF ANATOLIAN CIVILIZATIONS, ANKARA

Page 471

Home to finds of native cultures from the Stone Age onwards, this superb museum is the capital's one must-see attraction.

12 ANI RUINS

Page 566

Medieval Armenian capital in a superb setting at the Turkish border, scattered with fine churches.

13 ROMAN THEATRE AT ASPENDOS

Page 368

Anatolia's largest and best-preserved Classical theatre hosts an opera and ballet festival in summer.

14 MARDİN

Page 607

Medieval houses, historic mosques and churches, and boutique hotels mingle in this hilltop eyrie, high above the Mesopotamian plain.

15 HAGHIA SOPHIA, ISTANBUL

Page 72

The seemingly unsupported dome of Haghia Sophia is one of the architectural marvels of the world.

16 HITTITE CAPITAL OF HATTUŞA

Page 490

The ancient capital of the Hittites still impresses, with its extensive perimeter walls.

Itineraries

By European standards, Turkey is a huge country, the size of the UK and France combined; it's impossible to see it all in a single trip. Lovers of the beach, mountains and Greco-Roman sites will be attracted to the beautiful southwest Mediterranean coast. With a little longer you can combine vibrant İstanbul with Cappadocia's fairy-tale landscape, while adventurers with more time to spare will be drawn to the spectacular "wild east".

THE TURQUOISE COAST

Allow a minimum of ten days to enjoy the best of Turkey's Mediterranean coast.

❶ **Dalyan** This small resort, well served by Dalaman international airport, is unusually but beautifully situated on a reed-fringed river, opposite a superb ancient site and handy for the turtle-nesting beach at İztuzu. **See p.306**

❷ **Patara** A superb coastal retreat, with low-key accommodation in the village of Gelemiş, a Roman site peeking from the dunes, and Turkey's longest beach. **See p.322**

❸ **Kaş** Turkey's self-styled adventure capital, located at the feet of towering mountains, makes an excellent base to try scuba diving, sea kayaking, paragliding, canyoning or hiking the Lycian Way – or just chill. **See p.326**

❹ **Çıralı** A relaxed resort hidden in citrus groves, backed by mountains and home to the romantic Roman ruins at adjoining Olympos, the eternal flames of the Chimaera, and a great sweep of shingle beach. **See p.345**

❺ **Antalya** This bustling city is home to a superb archeological museum as well as the old walled quarter of Kaleiçi, which offers characterful accommodation, great nightlife and a tiny but pretty beach. **See p.354**

INTO ANATOLIA

With fifteen days at your disposal, you can get to know Istanbul; explore the wonders of Cappadocia; and visit the ancient treasures of the Mediterranean coast.

❶ **Istanbul** Truly one of the world's great cities, straddling Europe and Asia, Istanbul is blessed with fascinating Byzantine churches, curvaceous Ottoman mosques and bustling bazaars. It also boasts a buzzing nightlife scene. **See p.66**

❷ **Cappadocia** A unique landscape of weird rock pinnacles and deep valleys is enhanced by rock-cut, frescoed churches and entire underground cities. Two full days is an absolute minimum. **See p.428**

❸ **Konya** Once home to the founder of the mystical Whirling Dervish order, the city captivates the spiritually inclined. **See p.420**

❹ **Eğirdir** A welcome respite from a surfeit of sightseeing; most visitors to lakeside Eğirdir stay on the tiny island and simply admire the mountains, swim and eat. **See p.414**

❺ **Pamukkale** Glistening white travertine basins and hot springs form a geological wonder to match Cappadocia. The Greeks and Romans would agree; their ruined spa-city, Hierapolis, remains integral to the experience. **See p.278**

ABOVE PAMUKKALE

❻ Bodrum This former Greek fishing town is now an all-white architectural treat of a resort. Famed in ancient times for the Mausoleum of Halikarnassos, today it's better known for its club of (nearly) the same name, *Halikarnas*. **See p.260**

❼ Selçuk Charming little town with welcoming places to stay, a good museum, the Basilica of St John and the remnants of the Temple of Artemis. It's also handy for both iconic Ephesus and İzmir International Airport. **See p.237**

WAY OUT EAST

To do justice to Turkey's stunning "wild east", you'll need at least three weeks.

❶ Gaziantep The perfect gateway to Turkey's east. Explore Gaziantep's Arab-like bazaars, taste some of the country's finest cuisine, and admire the fantastic Roman mosaics at the state-of-the-art Zeugma Mosaic Museum. **See p.577**

❷ Nemrut Dağı The colossal Hellenistic statues that dominate this remote mountaintop fully reward the effort it takes to reach them. **See p.594**

❸ Şanlıurfa Famed for its pool of sacred carp, this traditional bazaar city makes the perfect base to visit the unique Neolithic temple sanctuary of Göbeklitepe, and the beehive houses at Harran. **See p.584**

❹ Mardin Honey-coloured medieval houses cluster beneath an ancient citadel, looking out over the chequerboard fields of the impossibly flat Mesopotamian plain. **See p.607**

❺ Midyat The old quarter of this venerable town makes a compelling place to kick back before or after exploring the Syrian Orthodox monasteries of the captivating Tör Abdin plateau. **See p.613**

❻ Hasankeyf Going but not yet gone, this incredible medieval ruined city, perched above the Tigris, will soon disappear beneath the waters of a controversial dam. **See p.615**

❼ Van Explore the vivid blue-soda Lake Van and its high-mountain hinterland, studded with unique Urartian sites and atmospheric Armenian churches – notably on Akdamar island. **See p.620**

❽ Doğubeyazıt This scruffy town, close to Iran, is the base for assaults on nearby Mt Ararat, and more sedate visits to the fairy-tale palace of a Kurdish chieftain, İshak Paşa Sarayı. **See p.640**

❾ Kars Set in vast, rolling tablelands, this city was brought to life in Orhan Pamuk's *Snow*. Take a day-trip to the long-abandoned Armenian city of Ani. **See p.562**

❿ Erzurum An upland city that holds fascinating Islamic monuments and is the gateway to Turkey's best ski resort, Palandöken. **See p.543**

⓫ Kaçkar Mountains This beautiful, green alpine range, dominated by Mt Kaçkar, spangled with *yaylas* (alpine pastures), glacier lakes and flowers, is perfect for trekking. **See p.554**

⓬ Trabzon Ancient Trebizond, a fiercely proud Black Sea port, has a superbly frescoed Byzantine church, the Aya Sofya, and is the base for day-trips to the spectacular cliff-hanging monastery of Sumela. **See p.519**

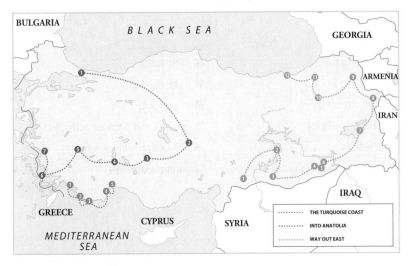

PIDE, ISTANBUL

Basics

Getting there

The wide range of flights to Turkey from the UK (fewer from Ireland) take between 3hr 30min and 5hr, depending on your start and end point. Turkish Airlines (THY) flies direct from North America to Turkey, but North American airlines reach Turkey via a European gateway airport. Travellers from Australia and New Zealand usually go via the Middle East or Asia, or use a Round-the-World (RTW) ticket that includes Istanbul. There are direct flights from South Africa to Istanbul.

Airfares from Europe and North America are at their highest during Easter week and from June to early September. They're lower in April and May, and from late September into October, while you'll get the best prices of all between November and March (excluding Christmas and New Year, when seats are at a premium). While the price of flights from Europe and to some extent North America are affected by Turkey's high or summer season, for flights from the southern hemisphere, early booking rather than time of year is the most important criterion for bagging a cheap seat. Flight comparison sites like Ⓦskyscanner.net and Ⓦexpedia.com are a good way to search for the cheapest option.

Flights from the UK and Ireland

You can **fly direct from the UK** to Istanbul (both airports), İzmir, Bodrum, Dalaman and Antalya. Reaching any other destination in Turkey involves a change in Istanbul.

Direct, **scheduled flights** are provided by Turkish Airlines (THY; Ⓦturkishairlines.com) and British Airways (Ⓦbritishairways.com). THY links London (Gatwick or Heathrow) with Istanbul (Atatürk or Sabiha Gökçen) year-round, with less frequent flights from Edinburgh, Manchester and Birmingham. Return flight prices range from £150 in winter to £350 in summer, with London generally the cheapest departure airports. BA has three daily services from Heathrow (from around £350 return

in July & Aug). Information on onward domestic flights with either THY or their low-cost division Anadolujet, or competitors such as Atlasjet, Onur Air or Pegasus can be found on p.35.

Budget and charter flights

Among **budget airlines**, **easyJet** (Ⓦeasyjet.com) no longer flies to Istanbul but does offer summer flights from Gatwick to İzmir; from Gatwick, Luton and Manchester to Antalya; from Bristol, Edinburgh, Liverpool, Luton, Gatwick or Stansted to Bodrum; and from Bristol, Gatwick, Manchester, Edinburgh or Stansted to Dalaman. Advance low-season fares can be under £40 each way, though this can rise to £200 for late bookings.

Pegasus (Ⓦflypgs.com) links Gatwick and Stansted to Istanbul Sabiha Gökçen all year, from where they have a far-reaching network of domestic flights (see p.35). **Jet2** (Ⓦjet2.com) has summer-only flights to Antalya, Dalaman and Bodrum from Glasgow, Edinburgh, Leeds-Bradford, Manchester, East Midlands and Newcastle. **Atlasjet** (Ⓦatlasjet .com) fly year-round from Luton to Istanbul Atatürk.

The widest choice of **charter flights** to Turkish coastal resorts is offered by Thomas Cook (Ⓦthomas cookairlines.com) and Thomson (Ⓦthomsonfly .com). With Thomas Cook, you can choose different departure and return airports and book one-way tickets. There are year-round charters to Antalya and Dalaman, while services to İzmir and Bodrum usually operate from late April/early May to late October. Peak-season prices can be as high as scheduled flights, but in winter they may drop as low as £100 return.

Flights from Ireland

From Belfast, British Airways offer year-round daily scheduled services, involving a stop in London or Manchester, but prices are high (in excess of £500 return in July and Aug). From Dublin, Turkish Airlines have a direct daily flight to Istanbul Atatürk, starting at €400 return. Usually the cheapest option is to use a budget carrier from either Dublin or Belfast to one of the UK cities, and connect with easyJet, Atlasjet or Pegasus to Turkey from there.

A BETTER KIND OF TRAVEL

At Rough Guides we are passionately committed to travel. We believe it helps us understand the world we live in and the people we share it with – and of course tourism is vital to many developing economies. But the scale of modern tourism has also damaged some places irreparably, and climate change is accelerated by most forms of transport, especially flying. All Rough Guides' flights are carbon-offset, and every year we donate money to a variety of environmental charities.

Flights from the US and Canada

The cheapest way to reach Turkey from North America is to buy a bargain transatlantic fare to Europe, and arrange your onward flight separately.

THY has expanded significantly in the US recently and now offers direct flights between Istanbul Atatürk and Atlanta, Austin, Boston, Chicago, New York (JFK), Los Angeles, and Washington DC. American Airlines (Waa.com), United Airlines (Wunited.com) and Delta (Wdelta.com) partner up with European airlines: American Airlines stopping flights go via London; United via Frankfurt or London; and Delta via Amsterdam. European carriers route through their **hubs**: British Airways (Wba.com) via London; Air France (Wairfrance.com) via Paris; KLM (Wklm.com) via Amsterdam; Lufthansa (Wlufthansa.com) via Frankfurt; and Swiss (Wswiss.com) via Zürich.

One-month return **fares** out of New York start from US$680 in winter and US$1200 in peak season. From LA, prices range $800–1350.

There is only one direct flight **from Canada** to Turkey: THY and Air Canada (Waircanada.com) partner daily flights between Toronto and Istanbul, with return fares from CAN$880. Otherwise, several airlines fly to Istanbul via major European hubs.

Flights from Australia, New Zealand and South Africa

There are no direct flights **from Australia or New Zealand** to Turkey. However, several options will get you there after either a plane change or short stopover in the airline's hub city. The most straightforward routes are through the Middle East: Emirates via Dubai (Wemirates.com); Etihad Airways via Abu Dhabi (Wetihad.com); or Qatar Airways via Doha (Wqatarairways.com). Other options include Malaysia Airlines via Kuala Lumpur (Wmalaysiaairlines.com); Singapore Airlines via Singapore (Wsingaporeair.com); or South African Airways (Wflysaa.com) and Qantas (Wqantas.com) via Johannesburg in South Africa. THY (Wturkishairlines.com) also fly to Istanbul from Kuala Lumpur, Singapore and Johannesburg. A marginally less expensive but far more time-consuming strategy would involve taking a flight to London and proceeding from there with one of the low-cost airlines. One-stop itineraries from **Sydney** start from around AUS$1500; **from Auckland**, fares start from NZ$2300.

Round-the-World (RTW) tickets including Turkey use combinations of airlines, and could be worth considering for a long trip taking in many destinations; generally, some free stopovers are allowed. Fares vary enormously, but start at AUS$2200 for options which include Istanbul.

From South Africa, THY has direct flights **from Johannesburg, Durban and Cape Town** to Istanbul, with prices starting at around R9000. The other options from South Africa (with changes) are with Emirates, Etihad Airways or Qatar Airways. South African Airways (Wflysaa.com) flies daily to Frankfurt, Munich, London and Zürich, from where you can connect on to Istanbul.

Trains

Travelling to Turkey **by train** is slow and expensive. It only makes sense if you are a rail buff or wish to visit several other countries en route. The best route **from the UK** begins with the Eurostar (Weurostar.com) from London to Paris, then a high-speed service to Munich, followed by a sleeper to Budapest, and finally two more nights aboard sleepers to Istanbul (including a change in Bucharest), making a total journey of five days and four nights. At the time of writing, the final leg, between the Bulgarian–Turkish border and Istanbul, was closed for line upgrading, with a replacement bus service in operation. Check the excellent Wseat61.com for more information. As each leg is booked separately, you can stop off in any of the cities where you change trains.

InterRail passes

The best train deal is provided by an **InterRail pass** (Winterrailnet.eu), which offers unlimited travel (except for express train supplements and reservation fees) on a zonal basis within thirty European rail networks. These passes are only available to European residents, and you must provide proof of residency to purchase one. To reach Turkey via the route described above, you need a Global Pass. For under-25s, a pass valid for one month's second-class travel covering thirty countries, including Turkey, costs €461 (£341); the price for over-25s is €983 (£728). A cheaper alternative is their five-days-travel-within-ten-days option – €192 (£142) for under-25s, or €403 (£299) for over-25s.

InterRail passes do not allow free travel between Britain and the Continent, although InterRail pass holders are eligible for discounts on rail travel in Britain and Northern Ireland, the cross-Channel ferries, and the London to Paris or Brussels Eurostar service.

By car from Europe

You can **drive from the UK** to Turkey in three to four days. However, this allows little time for stopping and sleeping, and most travellers prefer to do it more slowly, taking in a few places en route. Customs formalities and car insurance once in Turkey are covered in "Getting around" (see p.30).

The all-land itinerary goes via Belgium, Germany, Austria, Hungary, Romania and Bulgaria, though a more relaxing (if less direct) route is through France, Italy and Greece.

Ferries

Ferries no longer run **from Italy** direct to Turkey, but it's possible to take a ferry from either Ancona, Brindisi or Bari to Patras, in **Greece**, and make your way by road or rail to Athens (Piraeus). Regular ferries sail from there to several Greek islands which are linked by further ferries to Turkey (see below). Useful websites for information on Italy–Greece services include ⓦ feribot.net and ⓦ directferries.co.uk.

Ferries and catamarans from Greece

Many travellers take the short-hop ferries or catamarans over **from the Greek islands** to Turkish ports. These include Lésbos–Ayvalık, Chíos–Çeşme, Sámos–Kuşadası, Meis/Kastellerizo–Kaş, Kós–Bodrum and Rhodes–Marmaris and Fethiye. Services are daily in season (early May to early Oct), with much reduced sailings in winter. Fares are overpriced for the distances involved; full details of every service are given at the relevant points in this book. All the above have car-shuttle services (though Kuşadası has only one car ferry weekly), bar those serving Fethiye and Kaş.

AGENTS AND OPERATORS

Avro UK ☎ 0161 209 4259, ⓦ avro.co.uk. Seat-only sales of charter flights to Antalya and Dalaman from various regional airports.
North South Travel UK ☎ 01245 608291, ⓦ northsouthtravel .co.uk. Friendly, competitive flight agency, offering discounted fares – profits are used to support projects in the developing world.
Turkish Tursan Travel US ☎ 212 888 1180. Turkish specialist consolidator, based in New York.

Package tours and special-interest holidays

Scores of companies in the UK offer Turkish **package deals**. Most of these target Istanbul and the coast between Çeşme and Alanya, but most outfits also feature fly-drive plans. Coastal yachting (*gulet*) packages are available from May to October, while winter breaks are increasing in popularity. Inland holidays concentrate on Cappadocia, while special-interest programmes include trekking, bird-spotting, yoga retreats, whitewater rafting and battlefield tours.

Three- or four-night Istanbul city breaks start at around £230 off season for three-star bed-and-breakfast accommodation (including flights and transfers), £1000-plus for boutique or five-star hotels.

Prices for a cheap-and-cheerful two-week **beach package** start at around £240 per person (double occupancy) in low season, including flights; staying in a four-star hotel will set you back £500–800. Quality self-catering villas tend to cost £1000 per person per week, flights included, increasing to £1400 per person at peak periods. A seven-day **yachting or cruising** holiday will cost £550–850 per person (double occupancy basis) depending on season, booked in the UK through an agent, less if arranged in Turkey directly with skippers. **Cycling/hiking/multi-activity** trips vary from £300–350 for seven to eight days along the Lycian coast if arranged locally, or around £750 for a higher-quality adventure booked in the UK.

Specialist holidays, relying on the services of expert natural history/archeological guides, are priciest of all, from £1700 (1 week) to over £3000 (2 weeks), including flights.

The best of the **US-based cultural or adventure tours** don't come cheap either – expect to pay at least US$3600 for an eleven-day tour. The price will include all meals (excluding drinks), guides and ground transport, but not flights.

GENERAL TOUR OPERATORS

Anatolian Sky UK ☎ 0121 764 3553, ⓦ anatoliansky.co.uk. Mid-range to upmarket hotels and apartments on the southwest coast (particularly Kalkan, Dalyan, Akyaka, the Loryma peninsula, Antalya and Ölüdeniz), classic hotels in Istanbul, and a tailor-made programme.
Cachet Travel UK ☎ 020 8847 8700, ⓦ cachet-travel.co.uk. Small selection of villas and hotels along the Turquoise Coast, plus guided, low-season special-interest tours, and select Istanbul/Cappadocia hotels.
Discerning Collection UK ☎ 0178 481 7720, ⓦ discerningcollection .com. Limited but carefully selected portfolio of hotels and villas along the Turquoise Coast, as well as boutique hotels in Cappadocia and Istanbul.
Elixir Turkish Collection UK ☎ 020 7722 2288, ⓦ elixirholidays .com. Boutique hotels and villas in Kaş, Kalkan, Patara, Faralya and Datça, aiming for the luxury market, plus *gulet* cruises along the Lycian coast.
Turkish Collection (Ilios Travel) UK ☎ 01444 225633, ⓦ iliostravel.com. Top-quality (and thus pricey) villas-with-pool on the Bodrum and Datça peninsulas, plus rather more conventional accommodation at Akyaka, Kalkan and Kaş.

SAILING AND YACHTING

Cavurali ☎ +90 (0)242 419 2441, ⓦ cavurali.com. Turkish-American guide Enver Lucas and his father-in-law Tosun Sezen, both with years of local experience, offer bespoke sailing (and scuba) itineraries along the Turquoise Coast in a *gulet*-dive boat.

Day Dreams UK ☎ 01884 849200, ⓦ turkishcruises.co.uk. Large fleet of *gulets* or schooners hosting "house parties" for singles and couples; also makes on-land arrangements in unusual areas like Kazdağı.

Nautilus Yachting UK ☎ 01732 867445, ⓦ nautilusyachting.com. Bare-boat charters out of Marmaris, Bodrum, Fethiye and Göcek, plus set flotilla itineraries from Bodrum or Fethiye.

ScicSailing UK ☎ 0758 300 1766, ⓦ scicsailing.eu. Bodrum-area-based small fleet of wooden *gulets* specially adapted so that you actually travel under sail power rather than (as normally on such craft) with merely decorative rigging.

Setsail UK ☎ 01787 310445, ⓦ setsail.co.uk. Flotilla holidays from Göcek and Marmaris; also bare-boat charter.

Sunsail UK ☎ 020 3553 8353, ⓦ sunsail.co.uk. Flotilla holidays from Göcek, Gulluk and Turgutreis, taking in the Turquoise Coast and the peninsulas between Bodrum and Marmaris.

TREKKING AND ADVENTURE OPERATORS

Exodus UK ☎ 0845 287 7533, ⓦ exodus.co.uk. Offers an eight-day mountain-biking and hiking trip along the Lycian Way, plus kayaking on the Turquoise Coast and Cappadocia walking holidays staying in small hotels and village houses.

Explore UK ☎ 01252 883 814, ⓦ explore.co.uk. Selection of eight- or fifteen-day active trips, mostly in Cappadocia, the east and Lycia (including a cruising section), plus standard historical and "best of" tours.

G Adventures UK ☎ 0344 272 2060, ⓦ gadventures.com. Good choice of "comfort" and "budget" tours including sailing holidays, classic sightseeing itineraries, and active trips such as cycling and kayaking along the Lycian Way.

Imaginative Traveller UK ☎ 01728 862230, ⓦ imaginative -traveller.com. Long-established and quality overland group-tour operator with a vast assortment of tours, many pitched at families, taking in all the Turkish highlights as well as a number of lesser-known spots, plus some Turkey-and-Georgia combos.

World Expeditions UK ☎ 020 8875 5060, ⓦ worldexpeditions .com. Probably the most interesting Antipodean trekking operator for Turkey, with half a dozen itineraries, including a trip to Toros Mountains and Cappadocia region and a sightseeing "Best of Turkey" holiday, including hiking and cruising.

SPECIAL-INTEREST HOLIDAYS

Andante Travels UK ☎ 01722 713 800, ⓦ andantetravels.co.uk. Award-winning company with a very comprehensive selection of itineraries covering most of this archeologically fascinating country, covering all the major (and many minor) sites, led by experts in their fields.

Cultural Folk Tours US ☎ 1800 935 8875, ⓦ culturalfolktours .com. US-based company offering up to nine annual tours (accompanied by company founder and Turkish musician Bora Ozkok) that give a real insight into seldom-visited regions of the country.

Fairy Chimneys Travel Australia ☎ 1300 766 595, ⓦ fairychimneys.com.au. Small group and special interest tailor-made tours with an emphasis on luxury accommodation and good food, plus *gulet* and yacht arrangements.

Geographic Expeditions US ☎ 1888 570 7108, ⓦ geoex.com. Offers a thirteen-day "Tribute to Turkey" itinerary taking in the major historical sites, plus customized tailor-made trips to fit customers' interests.

Gölköy Centre UK ☎ 020 8699 1900, ⓦ yogaturkey.co.uk. Yoga retreat on Bodrum peninsula offering week-long courses May to October, encompassing shiatsu and assorted personal growth themes. Accommodation is in a nearby village or small coastal hotels.

Greentours UK ☎ 01298 83563, ⓦ greentours.co.uk. Several annual, one- or two-week natural-history holidays (emphasis on wildflowers), typically inland from the Turquoise or Mediterranean coasts. Enthusiastic English and Turkish guides know their subjects in incredible depth.

Huzur Vadisi ⓦ huzurvadisi.com. One-week yoga programmes from April to October at three secluded retreats; *Huzur Vadisi*, *Suleyman's Garden* and *The Pomegranate*, all a short distance inland from the Turquoise Coast.

Wilderness Travel US ☎ 1800 368 2794, ⓦ wildernesstravel .com. A fourteen-day combination Greek Island and Turquoise Coast cruise itinerary, plus tailor-made historical tours and multi-country Black Sea cruises with a focus on archeological interests.

Getting around

Virtually the whole of Turkey is well covered by public transport, including long-distance buses, domestic flights, minibuses and ferries. The aged train network is being overhauled, with new high-speed lines linking the capital, Ankara, with Istanbul and Konya. Late booking is the norm for public transport users in Turkey, but reserve well in advance for major public holidays – especially for flights and trains. Car rental rates are reasonable if you shop around, and low-season rentals usually consider- ably cheaper than in high season.

By train

Turkey's train network is run by **Turkish State Railways** (TCDD; ⓦ tcdd.gov.tr). A high-speed route (Yüksek Hızlı Tren or YHT) links the Istanbul suburb of Pendik with Ankara, taking a little over three and a half hours. When transport infrastructure works are completed, the line will terminate closer to the city centre and link in with Istanbul's metro system, allowing passengers to cross the city to Halkalı, in Europe, and join the line running through European Turkey and on into the Balkans. A YHT line also connects Ankara with Konya. It's possible to reach İzmir by rail by taking the high-speed ferry (see p.35) from the Istanbul suburb of Yenikapı to Bandırma, then the 6 Eylül Ekspres on to İzmir.

More high-speed lines are under construction. In the meantime, the remainder of the rail network is fairly antiquated, but is a cheap and cheerful way to reach provincial centres such as Adana, Kayseri, Erzerum, Kars and Diyarbakır. These trains are slow – the mountainous terrain has resulted in circuitous routes. As a result, journeys can sometimes take double the time they would by road. The advantages are the chance to stretch your legs, unwind and watch the scenery unfold at leisure. To get accurate schedule **information**, especially with the delays and re-schedulings caused by the network overhaul, go to the station in person, read the placards and then confirm departures with staff. Several choices of **seats** are available on most routes, including first-class, reclining Pullman seats; first-class standard seats (usually in a six-seater compartment); and second-class seats (generally in an eight-seater compartment). For long distances, though, it's advisable to get a **sleeper**. Cheapest are *küşetli* (couchettes), with either four or six bunks in a compartment depending on the route, and two-bedded *yataklı* (sleeping cars) with a basin, soap, towel and air conditioning. All *yataklı* beds come with sheets, pillows and blankets provided, as do *örtülü küşetli* beds; for standard *küşetli* beds you'll need to bring your own bedding. For maximum privacy, and for women travelling without male companions, it's probably best to book a *yataklı* berth to avoid having to share. There are always (usually helpful but tip expected) porters on hand to make up beds. Note that all beds fold away in the day to convert the compartment into a seating area.

All long-distance services should have a licensed *büfe* wagon, offering simple meals at surprisingly reasonable prices, but it's a good idea to check in advance (note that most wayside stations offer some sort of snacks). On major train routes it's essential to **reserve ahead**, but unfortunately this cannot be done earlier than two weeks in advance – and it's almost impossible to arrange sleeper facilities from a station that's not your start point. It's possible to book online, and the rail site ⓦseat61.com has a step-by-step guide on this. One drawback is that tickets for some services can only be bought within thirty days of departure, fifteen days on others, and ten days for YHT trains. It is also possible to buy tickets from some travel agencies for a small supplement.

Fares and passes

To give some idea of **prices**, a Pullman seat for the lengthy 28-hour, 1076km journey from Ankara to Kars (close to the Armenian border) costs ₺43, while a bed in a two-berth *yataklı* compartment costs ₺98. An economy seat on the YHT (High-Speed Train) for the 450km journey between Istanbul and Ankara costs ₺70, and a Pullman seat on the Bandirma to İzmir (334km) train is ₺23. Buying a return ticket brings each single-journey fare down by twenty percent, while foreign **students** (with appropriate ID) and children also get twenty percent off. InterRail passes (see p.28) are valid, though a better bet for Turkey-only travel is the one-month **TrenTur** card, available at major stations, which costs ₺210 a month for unlimited second-class travel, or ₺550 for any class of sleeping car.

By long-distance bus

Long-distance buses are a key part of the Turkish travel experience and, despite keen competition from domestic flights and relatively high road accident rates, look set to remain so. Major *otogars* (bus stations) are veritable hives of activity, with dozens of separate companies vying for business and a plethora of places to eat, drink, souvenir shop or have your shoes shined.

The vehicles used by many companies are luxurious coaches, complete with air conditioning, though without on-board toilets. Journeys are sometimes accompanied by loud Turkish music or film soundtracks, though increasingly the better (and more expensive) companies use coaches with aeroplane-style screens set in the back of the seat in front, along with headsets. There's a choice of TV channels and films, though very seldom in English. Several companies also have free wi-fi on-board, which is of far more use to the non-Turkish-speaking traveller. Traditional services remain, however, with attendants dishing out free drinking water and cologne for freshening up. In addition, most companies serve free coffee/tea/soft drinks and cakes on board. Every couple of hours or so there will be a fifteen-minute **rest stop** (*mola*) for tea, as well as less frequent half-hour pauses for meals at purpose-built roadside cafeterias.

As bus companies are private, there's no comprehensive national bus **timetable**, although individual companies often provide their own. **Prices** vary considerably between top- and bottom-drawer companies, though convenience of departure and on-board service are equally important criteria. If in doubt, inspect the vehicle out in the loading bay (*peron* in Turkish) and ask at the ticket office how long the trip will take.

Bear in mind that **long-haul journeys** (over 10hr) generally take place at night, and that because of rest stops, buses never cover more than 60km per hour on average. As a broad example of fares, Istanbul–Antalya (a 450km trip) costs around ₺65 with a standard bus company, ₺75 with a premium company. The 1240km journey from Istanbul to Hopa, on the Black Sea near the Georgian border, costs ₺110 with a premium company; the popular 753km run between Istanbul and Nevşehir (Cappadocia) is around ₺75.

Buying tickets

Most bus companies have **ticket booths** both at the *otogars* (bus terminals) and in the city centre. One of the big advantages of coach over plane travel is that, national holidays apart, you can usually just turn up at the bus station and find a seat. If you do this, it's worth checking out various companies to see what offers the best price and most convenient departure – touts that work for particular companies will not necessarily take you to the office of the company that has the cheapest or soonest departure.

Unacquainted women and men are not usually allowed to sit next to each other, and you may be asked to switch your assigned seat to accommodate this convention. If you buy your ticket at a sales office in the centre of town, ask about free *servis* (service) **transfer buses** to the *otogar*, especially if (as most now are) it's located a few kilometres out. These buses will often also take passengers from *otogars* into town centres, but that system is more erratic. Of the country's two **premium coach companies**, Ulusoy (W ulusoy.com.tr) and Varan (W varan.com.tr), Ulusoy offer by far the most comprehensive network. Their seats are more comfortable than most and they don't segregate single passengers by sex. Kamil Koç (W kamilkoc.com.tr) also has a very good reputation. All three companies have online booking systems in English. Another very reliable operator, Pamukkale (W pamukkaleturizm.com.tr), has yet to introduce an online system in English.

By dolmuş

A **dolmuş** (literally "stuffed") refers to a car or small van (*minibüs* in Turkish) that runs along set routes, picking passengers up (give a normal taxi hand signal) and dropping them off along the way (just say *inecek var* or *müsait bir yerde* to be set down). Few cities have car-type dolmuşes left – these include Bursa and Trabzon. On busy **urban routes** it's better to take the dolmuş from the start of its run, at a stand marked by a blue sign with a black-on-white-field "D", sometimes with the destination indicated – though usually you'll have to ask to learn the eventual destination, or look at the dolmuş' windscreen placard. The **fare** is invariably a flat rate (usually ₺3), making it very good value for cross-city journeys, not so great for a one-stop hop. In some cities (eg Antalya), dolmuşes have been banned because pulling in at random is dangerous and slows traffic. Locals, confusingly, still refer to the minibuses that replaced them (and stop only at fixed points) as dolmuşes.

Inter-town and village services are always provided by twelve- or fifteen-seater minibuses, and in these instances the term "*dolmuş*" is seldom used. For the remotest villages there will only be two services a day: to the nearest large town in the morning and back to the village in mid-afternoon. Generally, though, minibuses run constantly between 7am or 8am and 7pm in summer, stopping at sunset in winter or extending until 10pm or 11pm (or even later) near popular resorts.

By city bus and taxi

In larger towns, the main means of transport are **city buses**, which usually accept only pre-purchased tickets or smart travel cards, available from kiosks near the main terminals, newsagents, or from kerbside touts (at slightly inflated prices). This is certainly the case in Istanbul, where you have to use a pre-purchased token (*jeton*) or the *Istanbulkart* smart travel card (see p.113).

Yellow city **taxis** are everywhere, with ranks at appropriate places. Hailing one in the street is the best way to get a cab, but in suburban areas you can call them from useful street-corner telephones; sometimes you just press a buzzer and wait for a cab to turn up. City cabs all have working, digital-display

---

SEATING PLAN TIPS

When buying tickets, ask to see the **seating plan** so that you can choose window or aisle, a front seat (better views) or avoid certain less comfortable seats, such as those above the wheels and immediately behind the central door, which have less legroom. Even more important, if you're making a daytime trip in the heat of summer, work out the general direction of travel and try to get a seat on the shady side of the bus – a powerful sun beating down on the windows of even an air-conditioned bus makes quite a difference.

meters, and **fares** are reasonable. Each town sets its own rates, which includes the minimum charge and a unit charge for the distance covered. In Istanbul, for example, there's a ₺3.2 opening charge, plus a ₺2 per km fare rate. The main problem with using a cab is that few drivers – even in tourist areas – speak much English, so you may have to write down your destination on a piece of paper. Overcharging of foreigners in Istanbul and major resorts is, unfortunately, not uncommon – make sure that the driver turns his meter on and (trickier) that he doesn't take you all around the houses to reach your destination.

By car

While the excellent intercity bus network makes travel between major centres easy, having a **car** allows you to visit off-the-beaten-track sites. But be warned – the standard of driving in Turkey is often poor and attitudes aggressive, while the enforcement of traffic rules arbitrary. All these factors have contributed to the **high road-accident rate**, with over four thousand fatalities per year. Driving during public holidays, especially the religious Şeker and Kurban *bayrams*, and an hour or so prior to the *iftar* (fast-breaking meal) during Ramadan, is especially dangerous. In 2015, 74 people were killed and 446 injured in accidents in the notoriously risky few days preceding the Şeker Bayramı holiday, as families criss-crossed the country to visit relatives.

Rules of the road

You **drive on the right**, and yield to those approaching from the right. **Speed limits** are 50km/h within towns (40km/h if towing a trailer or caravan); open road limits are 90km/h for cars, 80km/h for vans (70km/h if towing); motorway (*otoyol* in Turkish) limits are 120km/h for cars, 100km/h for vans and small trucks. **Drink-driving laws** are in line with those of the EU: 50mg of alcohol per 100ml of blood – and drink-driving carries a fine of ₺800, reduced to ₺600 with early payment. Even so, drink-driving is a major problem; in 2010, almost 140,000 Turkish drivers had their licences seized for the offence. Front seat belts are mandatory and it's a fineable (₺88 or ₺66 with early payment) offence not to buckle up – though few drivers do.

Traffic control points at the approaches to major cities are common. You'll probably be waved through simply upon showing your foreign ID, especially if it's a rental car. Make sure the rental company provides the insurance certificate, the pollution compliance certificate (*eksoz muayene tasdiknamesi*) and the vehicle registration, or certified copies thereof.

Speeding fines, levied on a sliding scale according to how far above the limit you were, are heavy, with penalties of up to ₺392 (₺294 if the fine is paid within ten days). Usually you'll be given a ticket, which you take to a designated bank to pay. Jumping a red light carries a fine of ₺189.

If you have an **accident** serious enough to immobilize you and/or cause major damage to other people's property, the traffic police will appear and administer alcohol tests to all drivers, results of which must also be submitted along with an official accident report (*kaza raporu*) in order to claim insurance cover. It used to be an offence to move a vehicle involved in a car crash before the police showed up, but if there is only minor damage it is now OK to do so providing you have exchanged details with the other driver.

Heed the signposted **no-parking zones**, especially in resorts, as towing is common and, although the fines aren't too heavy, the hassle of finding the pound and negotiating language barriers is considerable. Generally, it's wisest to patronize the covered (*katlı*) or open *otoparks*. In open car parks you may well be required to leave your keys so the attendant can move your car. If you leave your car in the street in some towns and cities, you may return to find a chit on your windscreen (typically ₺10), to be paid to the roving attendant.

Road conditions

Road conditions have improved enormously over the last few years, with **better surfaces** and more and more **dual carriageways**. On both single and dual carriageways there's usually a hard-shoulder area to the right of the driving lane, and often slower-moving vehicles pull into this to allow impatient drivers to overtake. Be very wary of doing this, especially at night, as you might find yourself ploughing into pedestrians or parked/broken-down vehicles. With continual road improvements being made country-wide, road works are often a (sometimes dangerous) nuisance – especially in the southeast. Sizeable archeological sites are usually marked by large white-on-brown-field signs, but side roads to minor sites or villages are often poorly signposted.

Typical **hazards** include drivers overtaking right, left and centre, failure to signal, and huge trucks. Small-town driving hazards include suicidal pedestrians, horse-carts, speeding scooters and motorcycles (often with the entire family astride one vehicle) and tractors.

Toll highways, marked with white-on-green signs, are well worth the modest fees, but to use them you'll need to be enrolled in the **HGS** (Hızlı

ROAD SIGNS

Dur	Stop
Tek yön	One-way
Çıkmaz sokak	Dead end/cul-de-sac
Yol kapalı	Road closed
Yol boyunca	Road narrows
Tırmanma şeridi	Overtaking lane
Araç çıkabilir	Vehicles exiting
Yaya geçidi	Pedestrian crossing
Yol yapımı	Roadworks
Bozuk satıh	Rough surface
Düşük banket	Abrupt verge/ shoulder
Şehir merkezi	City centre
Park yapılmaz/ edilmez	No parking
Araç giremez	No entry
Aracınız çekilir	Your car will be towed
Giremez	No entry
Askeri bölge	Military zone
Heyelan bölgesi, heyelanlı bölge	Landslide zone

Geçis Systemi or Fast Transit System) first, as tollbooths accept neither cash nor credit cards. Many rental outlets offer cars with the requisite electronic chip sticker/registration card already fixed to the window – check before hiring a car if you intend using toll roads – and it's obligatory for rental agencies to provide one in and around Istanbul. With your own vehicle, it's possible to purchase the electronic chip sticker/registration card from a PTT (post office) for ₺10. Many Shell and OPET service stations also sell the HGS stickers. You must also "charge" it with a minimum of ₺30 and keep it topped up at "*HGS dolum noktası*" machines at many motorway service stations.

Main toll roads include Istanbul–Ankara, Istanbul–Edirne; Adana–Gaziantep; Adana–Pozanti, through the Cilician Gates; İzmir–Çeşme; and İzmir–Denizli.

Night driving is best not attempted by beginners – be prepared for unlit vehicles, glare from undipped lights, speeding intercity coaches and trucks and, in rural areas, flocks of sheep and goats and unlit tractors. Warning triangles are obligatory; make sure you put it on the road behind your vehicle following a flat tyre, breakdown or accident, and ensure your rental car has one.

Fuel and repairs

Filling stations are commonplace and open long hours, so it's difficult to run out of fuel. Fuel costs are high, and even diesel (*mazot or dizel*) is around ₺4

per litre. Petrol (*benzin*), available in four-star (*süper*) and lead-free (*kurşunsuz*) grades, goes for around ₺4.6 per litre. Rental cars generally use unleaded.

In western Turkey, roadside **rest-stop culture** conforming to Italian or French notions is the norm. You can eat, pray, patch a tyre, phone home, shop at mini-marts and, sometimes, even sleep at what amount to small hamlets (essentially the descendants of the medieval *kervansarays*) in the middle of nowhere. In the east you'll find more basic amenities.

Credit and debit cards (Visa Electron, Visa and MasterCard but also American Express) are widely honoured for fuel purchases in much of Turkey (chip-and-PIN protocol is the norm), but carry cash in more remote rural areas and the east.

Car **repair workshops** are located in industrial zones called *sanayis* at town outskirts. To repair a punctured tyre (a common event in Turkey) head to a *lastıkçı* (tyre workshop); new tyres for small cars start from ₺120. Always check that the spare and toolkit are sound and complete before leaving the rental agency.

Car rental

To rent a car you need to be at least 21 with a **driving licence** held for at least one year. Your home country licence should be enough, but it is very helpful, especially at traffic-control points, to be able to show an **international driver's permit** (IDP). A compact car rented from a major chain on the Aegean and Mediterranean coast will cost around €55 per day or €320 per week in high season (April–Oct), less in low season. Rent a car from a local firm and you may be able to find something for around €180 a week, even in high season. Diesel-fuelled rental cars are becoming more widely available at a premium, but are well worth considering if you intend travelling large distances. If you pick up a car at one of Istanbul's two airports (and think carefully before you do so – the city traffic is horrendous, parking and route-finding difficult and accidents commonplace), you will pay extra for the HGS sticker/registration card (at least ₺30) affixed to the screen, as you must use a toll road immediately.

Some rental companies allow rental in one town and drop-off in another – at a premium. The international players like Europcar have outlets at many of Turkey's airports as well as downtown/resort offices; local outfits (some of which also offer advance, online booking services) may not have an office in the airport, but with advance booking will bring the car to the airport and have someone meet you outside arrivals. Be warned: tanks are sometimes near empty so you need to fill up right away.

When checking any car out, agency staff should make a thorough note of any **blemishes** on the vehicle – go around the vehicle with them when they do this as you may be liable for scratches and dents not noted at the time of rental. Basic **insurance** is usually included, but CDW (Collision Damage Waiver) is not, and given typical driving conditions taking this out is virtually mandatory. Along with KDV (Value Added Tax), all these extras can push up the final total considerably. Rental insurance never covers smashed windscreens or ripped tyres.

By bike and motorbike

Touring Turkey by **bike** is a great experience for experienced cyclists, though you should try to avoid the hottest months and the busiest roads, and don't expect any kind of deference from motorists. On the plus side, the scenery is magnificent, many roads delightfully quiet and the local people you'll meet incredibly hospitable. Be prepared to do your own repairs as local mechanics experienced in working on state-of-the-art bikes are thin on the ground and confined to big cities such as Ankara, Antalya, Istanbul and İzmir. There is a well-developed home-grown mountain-bike industry, and spares by such as Shimano are readily found in the big cities. Indeed, unless you're passing through Turkey or are a real bicycle freak, it's worth considering buying a home-grown model here, as that way the spares and repairs will be less problematic. Reasonable bikes start from ₺350, though imported models are likely to be far more expensive than you could buy at home. In cities, lock your bike; in rural areas theft is not likely to be a problem, even if the curious stares of incredulous locals could be. **Bike-rental facilities** are few and far between in Turkey; a notable exception is Cappadocia, particularly Göreme (see p.434), and there are outlets in bigger resorts such as Antalya (see p.354).

Given Turkey's road conditions, only confident, experienced **motorcyclists** should consider driving here. Plenty of visitors risk a day or two on a **scooter** in resort areas. In larger resorts and big cities there will be at least one motorbike **rental agency**, or a car-rental company that also rents out motor-scooters and mopeds (*mobilet*). You'll need an appropriate driving licence, and most companies insist that it has been held for at least a year. As with cars, always check the bike for scratches and dents before renting it. Helmets are mandatory, despite the countless helmet-less riders you'll see.

By ferry

Turkey's domestic **ferry network** is confined to Istanbul and the Sea of Marmara. Şehir Hatları (Ⓦ sehirhatlari.com.tr) operates ferries along the Bosphorus, between the European and Asian sides of the same strait, and to the Princess Islands. Longer runs across the Sea of Marmara to Yalova (for Termal & İznik), Mudanya (for Bursa) and Bandırma (for the Aegean coast) are the preserve of Istanbul Deniz Ötobüsleri (Ⓦ ido.com.tr) sea buses. Any of the trans-Marmara car-ferry links save time compared to the dreary, circuitous road journey, but are relatively expensive with a vehicle.

Private companies offer services from the Mediterranean town of Taşucu to Girne in North Cyprus year-round, and catamarans run from the resort of Alanya in the summer months.

By plane

Travel by air is becoming the norm in what is a very big country, and makes sense for those on a tight schedule or who wish to visit far-flung places like Van or Erzurum. **Turkish Airways** (Türk Hava Yolları or THY; ☏ 0212 225 0566, Ⓦ thy.com), and its budget wing **Anadolujet** (☏ 444 2538, Ⓦ anadolujet.com.tr), offer the most comprehensive domestic flight network, though many flights from the west of the country are routed through either Istanbul or Ankara. This partnership faces stiff competition from private airlines such as Atlasjet, Onur Air, Pegasus and Sunexpress.

Atlasglobal (☏ 0850 222 0000, Ⓦ atlasglb.com) offers flights to Antalya, Bodrum, Dalaman, Gaziantep, and İzmir. **Onur Air** (☏ 0212 663 2300, Ⓦ onurair.com.tr) has direct flights from Istanbul to the following destinations: Adana, Antalya, Bodrum, Dalaman, Diyarbakır, Erzerum, Gaziantep, İzmir, Kayseri, Malatya, Samsun, Şanlıurfa and Trabzon.

Pegasus (☏ 444 0737, Ⓦ flypgs.com) covers Adana, Ankara, Antalya, Bodrum, Dalaman, Erzurum, Gaziantep, İzmir, Kayseri, Konya, Malatya, Mardin, Nevşehir (Cappadocia), Şanlıurfa, Trabzon and Van, while **Sunexpress** (☏ 444 0797, Ⓦ sunexpress.com), runs direct flights from the Mediterranean gateway resort of Antalya to Adana, Diyarbakir, Gaziantep, Hatay (Antakya), Istanbul, İzmir, Kayseri, Trabzon and Van.

Fares with THY are reasonable – for example, promotional one-way fares from Istanbul to Antalya (tax inclusive) are ₺94, though more usual prices are from ₺124. THY also offers variable student, youth and family discounts. Fares with Atlas, Onur,

Pegasus and Sunexpress also start from as low as ₺35 when there are special offers on.

The key to finding cheap economy fares is **early booking** – generally six weeks to a month prior to departure, except at peak holiday periods when even earlier booking is advised. These fares are often comparable to, if not cheaper than, intercity bus fares, though getting to and from some airports by cab adds to the cost considerably. If you have trouble booking online, try a travel agent, as most will book for you for a small fee.

You're told to appear at the airport 1hr 30min before your departure, but an hour is usually adequate leeway for completing security procedures. Baggage allowances vary between companies – usually it's either 15 or 20kg, but make sure you check to avoid unwanted extra charges.

Be sure to remember that Istanbul has two airports (see p.111), Sabiha Gökçen on the Asian side and Atatürk on the European. Some carriers use both airports, though Sunexpress only uses Sabiha Gökçen.

Accommodation

Simply turning up and finding a bed for the night is generally not a problem in Turkey, except in high season at the busier coastal resorts and in Istanbul. Most places have internet booking services, so you can reserve ahead. Prices are generally good value by most Western European standards, though Istanbul can be very expensive. In most of the larger coastal resorts, the big cities and touristy inland areas such as Cappadocia, a wide range of accommodation is available, from humble *pansiyons* (guesthouses) to five-star hotels. However, in towns of the interior, with fewer tourists, there's often little choice between fleapits or four-star luxury.

Rates are generally lower in winter (Nov–March) than high summer (June–Aug) but shoot up at Christmas/New Year and for religious festivals such as the Şeker and Kurban *bayrams* (see p.48), when many Turks take their holidays. Spring and autumn rates fall somewhere between the two, except in Istanbul, where prices are high during this period. Many establishments peg their rates to the euro as, after years of stability, the inflation rate has crept back to around ten percent. All but the most basic hotels **include breakfast**. Note that many pensions and hotels in coastal resorts close for the winter.

Rooms are generally on the small side by European standards, some have inadequate lighting and many have barely enough power points. To avoid **noise**, pick a room away from main thoroughfares and/or an adjacent mosque. You won't cause offence by asking to see another room, and never agree on a price for a room without seeing it first. Though break-ins aren't the norm in Turkey, **security** should be at least a consideration.

Plumbers quite frequently pipe the taps up the wrong way round, so check that the tap that should be hot is not the cold. Bathtubs and sinks seldom have plugs, so bring a universal plug from home. Especially on the south and southwest coast, **air conditioning** (a/c) is found in most accommodation, even *pansiyons*. **Double beds** for couples are becoming more popular; the magic words are *Fransiz yatak* ("French" bed).

Touts can be a nuisance in places on the backpacker trail (for example Cappadocia, Selçuk and Eğirdir), greeting weary travellers off the long-distance bus with offers of accommodation. It's best to ignore them and use the recommendations in this guide. If you do decide to check out the accommodation offered by a tout, make sure it's up to standard before accepting – there will be plenty more choice available.

Lift/elevator buttons can be a source of potential confusion. "Ç" stands for "call", a lit-up "K" means the lift is already on your floor; an illuminated "M" means "in use"; "Z" stands for ground floor; and "A" means the mezzanine floor.

Hotels

Turkish hotels are graded on a scale of one to five stars by the Ministry of Tourism; there is also a lower tier of unstarred establishments rated by municipalities. At the **four- and five-star** establishments expect to pay from €110–200 at the lower end of the scale to €200–800 for restored palaces or very upmarket boutique hotels. **Two- or three-star** outfits (€50–90) are more basic; no tubs in bathrooms and more spartan breakfasts, though in resort areas they may have a small pool, terrace and bar. The walk-in price of three-star and up hotels is always much higher than if it is prebooked, but if the hotel is slack you may be able to negotiate a much better deal.

Boutique hotels are popping up all over the place, especially in restored old mansions in such places as Amasya, Cappadocia, Gaziantep, Istanbul, Mardin, Safranbolu and Urfa. However, the term is overused to market any accommodation that has been done up in a minimalist or modernist style, and prices vary widely accordingly.

The **unrated hotels** licensed by municipalities can be virtually as good as the lower end of the one-star class, and most have en-suite bathrooms, televisions and phones (€35–45). Others though, at the very bottom end of the market, will have a basin in the room but shared showers and (squat) toilet down the hall, with prices ranging between €20 and €30. Most solo female travellers will feel uncomfortable in unstarred and even many one- and two-star hotels, especially in less touristy parts of the country.

Pansiyons and apartments

Often the most pleasant places to stay are **pansiyons** (pensions), small guesthouses common in touristy areas, where charges generally start at around €25 and go up to €40, including breakfast. Many offer home-cooked evening meals at modest prices. These usually have en-suite facilities, and many feature common gardens or terraces where breakfast is served. Rooms tend to be spartan but clean, furnished in one-star hotel mode and always with two sheets (*çarşafs*) on the bed. Hot water is always available, though with solar-powered systems, not always when you want it. Many have air conditioning, often for a supplement.

Particularly when it comes to family-run pensions, you may well find that the proprietor has links with similar establishments in other towns; often he/she will offer to call ahead to arrange both a stay and a transfer from the *otogar* for you. This informal network is a good way of avoiding the hassle with touts and a late-night search for a comfy bed.

Self-catering apartments are widespread in coastal resorts, and are mostly pitched at vacationing Turks or foreigners arriving on pre-arranged packages. Some are available to walk-in trade – local tourist offices maintain lists. Apart from the weekly price, the major (negotiable) outlay will be for the large gas bottle feeding the stove. Ensure, too, that kitchens are equipped well enough to make them truly self-catering.

Hostels, lodges and treehouses

While there are only a handful of internationally affiliated, foreigner-pitched hostels in the country, this gap has been amply filled by **backpackers' hostels**, found most notably in Istanbul, Çanakkale, Selçuk, Köyceğiz and Fethiye. Often 1970s *pansiyons* that have been adapted to feature multi-bedded rooms, laundry and internet facilities, self-catering kitchen, tours and lively bars, they can be fair value

– costs vary €10–18 per head in a large dorm, but double rooms are often more expensive than *pansiyons* or cheap hotels.

In recent years, a large number of **trekkers' lodges** have sprung up in the foothills of the Kaçkar Mountains, especially on the south slope, and along the Lycian Way. These generally offer a choice between communal sleeping on mattresses arrayed on a wooden terrace, or more enclosed double to quadruple rooms without en-suite facilities – strangely, cooking facilities may often also be absent. Costs are generally comparable to the backpackers' hostels, though some are far more expensive.

So-called "**treehouses**", usually just elevated shacks, are found principally on the southwest coast between Antalya and Fethiye. Some have dorm rooms while an increasing number are designed for two people and have doors, windows, electricity, air conditioning and, occasionally, en-suite facilities.

Campsites

In areas frequently visited by independent travellers, *pansiyons* and hostels with gardens will often allow **camping**. Charges run from a couple of euros to €7 per head in a well-appointed site at a major resort; you may also be charged to park your vehicle. The most appealing campsites are those run by the **Ministry of Forestry**, open April to October inclusive; look for brown wooden signs with yellow lettering. Twenty of them are sited in shady groves at strategic locations (mostly coastal) across the west of the country, and they make an ideal choice if you have your own transport, especially a combi-van or car and caravan.

Camping rough is not illegal, but hardly anybody does it except when trekking in the mountains, and, since you can expect a visit from curious police or even nosier villagers, it's not a good option for those who like privacy.

Food and drink

Turkish food is sometimes ranked alongside French and Chinese as one of the world's three great cuisines. Many venerable dishes are descended from Ottoman palace cuisine. The quality of produce is exceptional, with most ingredients available locally. Eating out is often very good value and many locals

do so frequently. The cheapest sit-down meals are to be found in establishments which do not serve alcohol (*içkisiz*), where it's possible to find a hearty three-course meal for ₺25 (€8). However, you'll often pay considerably more in resorts which aren't so frequented by Turkish tourists. It's easy to get stuck in a kebab rut, but show a little adventure and there are plenty of dishes available – more than enough to satisfy all but the strictest vegetarians.

Places to eat and specialities are summarized below, and at the back of this guide you'll find a **menu reader** (see p.704). Generic "Mediterranean" restaurants and burger/pizza/coffee chains, needing no translation, are almost everywhere.

Breakfast

The standard "Turkish" **breakfast** (*kahvaltı*) served at modest hotels and *pansiyons* usually comprises a basket of soft white bread, a pat of butter, a slice or two of feta-style cheese and salami, a dab of pre-packed jam, a scattering of black olives, a boiled egg and a few slices of tomato and cucumber. Only tea is likely to be available in quantity, and extras such as *omelette* will probably be charged for.

Things are far more exciting in the better hotels, where you can expect a range of breads and pastries, fresh fruit slices, a choice of olive and cheese types, delicious fresh yoghurt, dried fruits and nuts, and an array of cold and hot meats, plus eggs in various styles, though freshly squeezed orange or pomegranate juice will be extra. Turks are

---

BARGAIN BREAKFAST BITES

The classic budget breakfast is the national dish of **simit**, a bread ring coated in sesame seeds. These are usually sold by street vendors for ₺1.4, and can be enlivened by a processed cheese triangle – a surprisingly good combo. Another favourite is **börek**, a rich, flaky, layered pastry containing bits of mince or cheese, often available from specialist *büfes* (snack-cafés) for ₺4 and up. Bakers (*fırıncı*) are a great source of **poğça** (soft rolls usually filled with either cheese, olive spread or a spicy potato mixture) for ₺1 and up. A winter warmer favourite is a bowl of **çorba** (soup), invariably lentil and served with a lemon wedge, for around ₺5.

---

very fond of their breakfast, and often on a Sunday invite friends or family round for a big spread. Alternatively, they head out en masse to cafés that offer a full Turkish-style breakfast deal for around ₺18.

Street food

Unlike in Britain, **kebabs** (*kebap* in Turkish) are not generally considered takeaway food unless wrapped in *dürüm*, a tortilla wrap-like bread; more often you'll find *döner* or *köfte* in takeaway stalls, served on a baguette. A **sandwich** (*sandviç*) is a baguette chunk with various fillings (often *kokoreç* – stuffed lamb offal – or fish). In coastal cities, deep-fried **mussels** (*midye tava*) are often available, as are *midye dolması* (mussels stuffed with rice, pine nuts and allspice) – best avoided during summer because of the risk of food poisoning. In Istanbul and some other cities, look out for vendors (often street-carts) selling *nohutlu pilav* (pilau rice with chickpeas) and roast chestnuts.

A flat, pizza-like bread stuffed with various toppings, **pide** is served to diners in a *pideci* or *pide salonu* from 11am onwards. Its big advantage is that this dish is always made to order: typical styles are *kaşarlı* or *peynirli* (with cheese), *yumurtalı* (with egg), *kıymalı* (with mince) and *sucuklu* (with sausage).

Other specialities worth seeking out include **mantı** – the traditional Central Asian, meat-filled ravioli, served drenched in yoghurt and spice-reddened oil – and **gözleme**, a stuffed-*paratha*-like delicacy cooked on an upturned-wok-style dish.

Restaurants

A "**restoran**", denoting anything from a motorway-bus pit stop to a white-tablecloth affair, will provide *ızgara yemek* or meat dishes grilled to order. **Kebapcıs** traditionally specialize in kebabs, and at their most basic offer only limited side dishes – sometimes just salad, yoghurt and a few desserts. Many today, however, are veritable palaces, where you'll get a free flatbread to tear, share and mop up a few simple dips, then choose from a menu including soups, all kinds of kebabs, *köfte* (meatballs), *lahmacun* (a flatbread "pizza" topped with spicy mincemeat) and *pide*. A **lokanta** is a restaurant emphasizing *hazır yemek*, pre-cooked dishes kept warm in a steam-tray. Here also can be found *sulu yemek*, "watery food" – hearty meat or vegetable stews. Despite their often clinical appearance, the best *lokantas* may well provide your most memorable taste of Turkish cooking. Some *lokantas* are moderately upmarket, others, often referred to as *esnaf lokantas* (tradesmens' restaurants) are more down to earth. **İskembe salonus** are aimed at revellers emerging from clubs or taverns in the early hours, and open until 5am or 6am. Their stock-in-trade is tripe soup laced liberally with garlic oil, vinegar and red pepper flakes, an effective hangover cure. A **çorbacı** is a soup kitchen.

Another kind of place that has become very popular over the last few years is **Ev Yemekleri** (home-cooked foods) cafés. Typically these are run by women who dish up good-value meals more typical of those you'd find in a Turkish home rather than a standard restaurant, with *hazır* and *sulu yemek*, *börek*, *dolma* (stuffed vegetables) and *mantı* all usually figuring. Many feature excellent-value three-course lunches for as little as ₺8.

At an **ocakbaşı**, the grill and its hood occupy centre stage, as diners watch their meat being prepared. Even more interactive is the **kendin pişir kendin ye** (cook-it-and-eat-it-yourself) establishment, where a *mangal* (barbecue with coals), a specified quantity of raw meat, plus *kekik* (oregano) and *kimyon* (cumin) are brought to your outdoor/indoor table.

Meyhanes are taverns where eating is on a barely equal footing to tippling. Once almost solely the preserve of men, the fancier Istanbul ones, as well as some in the bigger cities and resort towns of western Turkey, are frequented by "respectable" Turkish (and foreign) women. They can be great fun, as well as dishing up excellent food. Plenty of *meyhanes* are not really suitable for foreign couples or female travellers, however, so examine the place before making your choice. **Balık Restoran** (fish restaurants) are ubiquitous in western Turkey, made viable by the fish-farming industry, which produces an endless supply of sea bass and sea bream.

Prices vary widely according to the type of establishment. Expect to pay from ₺10 for a hearty *pide* in a *pideci*, ₺15 and up for a kebab or *köfte*. A simple grill or kebab in a licensed restaurant is likely to be twenty percent more expensive than in an unlicensed *kebabcı*. A *meyhane* meal is likely to set you back ₺45–60 for the food, plus whatever you drink. Many have set deals, typically involving an array of cold and hot *meze*, a grilled-fish main and fruit dessert for around ₺100 – which includes as many local drinks as you desire. A main course in a *hazır yemek* joint usually costs around ₺7 for a vegetable dish, ₺10 and up for meat. A meal in a flashy fish restaurant serving wild-caught rather than farmed fish may set you back well over ₺130 without drinks.

WAITER TRICKS

Fancy, and not so fancy, restaurants sometimes levy both a *küver* (cover charge) *and* either a *garsoniye* ("waiter" charge) or *servis ücreti* (service charge, typically ten percent), though if it's not documented in writing on the menu, technically you don't have to pay this. At places without **menus** (which is common), you'll need to ascertain prices beforehand and review bills carefully when finished. Waiting staff are adept at bringing you items (pickles, garlic bread, *çiğ börek*, mini-*meze*, bottled water, etc) that you haven't specifically ordered – but which you will definitely pay for unless announced by the magic words *ıkramızdır* (with our compliments).

Dishes and specialities

The most common **soups** (*çorbas*) are mercimek (lentil), *ezo gelin* (a thick rice and vegetable broth – an appetizing breakfast) and *işkembe* (tripe). Çoban (shepherd's) *salatası* means the ubiquitous, micro-chopped cucumber, tomato, onion, pepper and parsley **salad** (approach the peppers with caution); *yeşil* (green) salad, usually just some *marul* (lettuce), is less often available. The more European *mevsim salatası* ("seasonal" salad) – perhaps tomato slices, watercress, red cabbage and lettuce hearts sprinkled with cheese and drenched in dressing – makes a welcome change from "shepherd's" salad.

Meze and vegetable dishes

Turkey is justly famous for its **meze** (appetizers). Found in any *içkili restoran* (licensed restaurant) or *meyhane* – and some unlicensed places too – they are the best dishes for vegetarians, since many are meat-free.

Common platters include *patlıcan salatası* (aubergine mash), *piyaz* (white haricot vinaigrette), *semizotu* (purslane weed, usually in yoghurt), *mücver* (courgette fritters), *sigara böreği* (tightly rolled cheese pastries), *imam bayıldı* (cold baked aubergine with onion and tomato) and *dolma* (any stuffed vegetable, but typically peppers or tomatoes).

In *hazır yemek* restaurants, *kuru fasulye* (haricot bean stew), *taze fasulye* (French beans), *sebze turlu* (vegetable stew) and *nohut* (chickpeas) are the principal **vegetable dishes**. Although no meat may be visible, they're almost always made with lamb or chicken broth; even bulgur and rice may be cooked in meat stock. Vegetarians might ask *İçinde et suyu var mı?* (Does it contain meat stock?).

Bread and cheese

The standard Turkish loaf is delicious hot out of the oven, but soon becomes stale. Flat, unadorned *pide* is served with soup at *kebapcıs* year-round (and daily throughout Ramadan), as is delicious *lavaş*, a flatbread brought hot to the table puffed-up like a balloon. *Kepekli* (wholemeal) or *çavdar* (rye bread; only from a *fırın* or bakery) afford relief in larger towns. In villages, cooked *yufka* – the basis of *börek* pastry – makes a welcome respite, as does *bazlama* (similar to an Indian *paratha*).

Beyaz peynir (like Greek feta) is the commonest Turkish **cheese**, but there are many others. *Dil peynir* ("tongue" cheese), a hard, salty cheese comprised of mozzarella-like filaments, and the plaited *oğru peynir*, can both be grilled or fried like Cypriot halloumi. *Tulum peynir* is a strong goat's cheese cured in a goatskin; it is used as *börek* stuffing, although together with walnuts, it makes a very popular *meze*. *Otlu peynir* from the Van area is cured with herbs; cow's-milk *kaşar*, especially *eski* (aged) *kaşar* from the Kars region, is also highly esteemed.

Meat dishes

Grilled meat dishes – normally served simply with a few *pide* slices and raw vegetable garnish – include several variations on the kebab. *Adana kebap* is spicy, with sprinkled purple sumac herb betraying Arab influence; *İskender kebap*, best sampled in Bursa, is heavy on the flatbread, tomato sauce and yoghurt; *sarmı beyti* is a ground-beef kebab wrapped in *dürüm* bread and baked in the oven. Chicken kebab (*tavuk* or *piliç şiş*) is ubiquitous, and chicken is also served as *şiş*, *pırzola* (grilled breast) or *kanat* (grilled wings). Offal is popular, particularly *böbrek* (kidney), *yürek* (heart), *ciğer* (liver), and *koç yumurtası* (ram's egg) or *billur* (crystal) – the last two euphemisms for testicle.

More elaborate **meat-and-veg combinations** include *mussaka* (inferior to the Greek rendition), *karnıyarık* (a much better Turkish variation), *güveç* (clay-pot fricassee), *tas kebap* (stew), *hunkar beğendi* (lamb, puréed aubergine and cheese), *saray kebap* (beef stew topped with bechamel sauce and oven-browned), *macar kebap* (fine veal chunks in a spicy sauce with tomatoes and wine) and *saç kavurma*, an Anatolian speciality of meat, vegetables and spices fried up in a *saç* (the Turkish wok). *Şalgam*, a fiery drink made from fermented turnip and carrot, is an acquired taste that makes the best accompaniment to *Adana kebab*.

Fish and seafood

Fish and seafood is good. Usually sold by weight, per-portion prices of about ₺15–20 prevail for fish-farmed and less-valued species such as *istavrit* (whitebait). Prized wild-caught species can be very expensive. Choose with an eye to what's in season (as opposed to farmed, frozen and imported), and don't turn your nose up at humbler varieties, which will likely be fresher. Budget mainstays include *sardalya* (grilled sardines), *palamut* (autumn tuna), *akya* (liche in French; no English name) and *sarıgöz* (black bream). *Çipura* (gilt-head bream) and *levrek* (sea bass) are usually farmed. Fish is invariably served simply, with just a garnish of spring onion (*soğan*) and rocket (*roka*).

Desserts and sweets

Turkish chefs pander shamelessly to the sweet-toothed, who will find a huge range of sugary treats at a **pastane** (sweet shop).

Turkish delight and baklava

The best-known Turkish sweet, *lokum* or "**Turkish delight**", is basically solidified sugar and pectin, flavoured (most commonly) with rosewater, often stuffed with pistachios or other nuts and finally sprinkled with powdered sugar. There are also numerous kinds of **helva**, including the tahini-paste chewy substance synonymous with the concoction in the West. *Yaz halvası* (summer *helva*) is made from semolina flour – the chocolate and nut-stuffed version is delicious.

Of the syrup-soaked **baklava**-type items – all permutations of a sugar, flour, nut and butter mix – the best is *antep fıstıklı sarması* (pistachio-filled *baklava*), though it's pricey at ₺8–12 per serving. Other *baklava* tend to be *cevizli* (walnut-filled) and slightly cheaper. *Künefe* – the "shredded wheat" filaments of *kadayif* perched atop white cheese, baked and then soaked in syrup – has become a ubiquitous dessert in kebab and *lahmacun* places; both *baklava* and *künefe* are often served with large dollops of glutinous Maraş ice cream (see opposite).

Puddings, ice cream and fruit

Less sweet and healthier than Turkish delight and *baklava* are the **milk-based** dishes, popular everywhere. *Süpangile* ("süp" for short, a corruption of *soupe d'Anglais*) is an incredibly dense, rich chocolate pudding with sponge or a biscuit embedded inside. More modest are *keşkül* (vanilla and nut-crumble custard) and *sütlaç* (rice pudding) – one dessert that's consistently available in ordinary restaurants. The most complicated dish is *tavukgöğsü*, a cinnamon-topped morsel made from hyper-boiled and strained chicken breast, semolina starch and milk. *Kazandibi* (literally "bottom of the pot") is *tavukgöğsü* residue with a dark crust on the bottom – not to be confused with *fırın sütlaç*, which is actually *sütlaç* pudding with a scorched top baked in a clay dish.

Aşure is a sort of rosewater jelly laced with pulses, wheat berries, raisins and nuts. It supposedly contains forty ingredients, after a legend claiming that after the Biblical Ark's forty-day sail during the Flood, and the first sighting of dry land, Noah commanded that a stew be made of the forty remaining kinds of food on board.

Traditional Turkish ice cream (*dondurma*) is an excellent summer treat, provided it's genuine *Maraşlı döşme* (whipped in the Kahraman Maraş tradition – a bit like Italian gelato). The outlandishly costumed *dondurma* street-sellers of yore have been overtaken by upmarket parlours selling every conceivable flavour; the best chain of these is Mado, with high prices but equally high quality.

Summer fruit (*meyve*) generally means *kavun* (Persian melon, honeydew) or *karpuz* (watermelon). Autumn choices include *kabak tatlısı* (candied squash with walnut chunks and *kaymak*, or clotted cream) or *ayva tatlısı* (stewed quince served with nuts or dried fruit, topped with *kaymak* and dusted with grated pistachio).

Slightly more healthy options include *cezeriye*, a sweetmeat made of carrot juice, honey and nuts; the east Anatolian snack of **peştil** (dried fruit), most commonly apricot and peach, pressed into sheets; and **tatlı sucuk**, a fruit, nut and molasses roll.

Coffee and tea

The Ottomans introduced **coffee** – and the notion of the coffee house – to the West during the seventeenth century. Intermittently banned as hotbeds of sedition and vice by the religious authorities, coffee houses had nonetheless become fixtures of Istanbul society by the mid-sixteenth century. The coffee was prepared, as it still is today, using finely ground coffee brewed up in a small pan and served, in tiny cups, *sade* (without sugar), *orta şekerli* (medium sweet) or *çok şekerli* (very sweet). Coffee fell out of favour during the early Republican period as, following the loss of the coffee-producing Arab territories, it had to be imported. But after decades of being both exorbitantly expensive and hard to find, coffee has made a major comeback. Traditional Turkish coffee is widely available today, and in the big cities and resorts there are plenty of cafés serving filter, latte and other types of coffee, though in more remote areas the usual standby is (invariably over-strong) instant coffee.

Tea has, however, become the national drink, especially in rural areas and among the less well off, as it's still much cheaper than coffee. Home-grown in the eastern Black Sea region since the 1920s, it's an essential social lubricant. The drink is prepared in a *çaydanlık* or *demlik*, a double-boiler apparatus, with a larger water chamber underneath the smaller receptacle containing dry leaves, to which a small quantity of hot water is added. After a suitable (or unsuitably long) wait, the tea is decanted into tulip-shaped glasses, then diluted with more water to taste: *açık* is weak, *demli* or *koyu* steeped on the side; milk is never added.

Herbal **teas** are also popular, particularly *ıhlamur* (linden flower), *kuşburnu* (rose hip), *papatya* (camomile) and *ada çay* ("island" tea), an infusion of a sage common in coastal areas. The much-touted **apple tea** (*elma çay*) contains chemicals and not a trace of real apple essence.

Soft drinks

Fruit juices (*meyva suyu*) nowadays usually come in cardboard cartons or cans, and are refreshing but high in added sugar. Flavours include *kayısı* (apricot), *şeftali* (peach) and *vişne* (sour cherry). Fresh orange juice is widely available in tourist areas and big cities, as is *nar suyu* (pomegranate juice).

Bottled **spring water** (*memba suyu*) or fizzy **mineral water** (*maden suyu* or *soda*) are restaurant staples, but cheaper establishments usually offer free potable tap water in a glass bottle or a jug. *Meşrubat* is the generic term for all types of carbonated **soft drinks**.

Certain beverages accompany particular kinds of food or appear at set seasons. *Sıcak süt* (hot milk) is the traditional complement to *börek*, though in winter it's fortified with *salep*, made from the ground tubers of a phenomenally expensive wild orchid (*Orchis mascula*) gathered in coastal hills near İzmir. **Salep** is a good safeguard against colds (and also reputedly an aphrodisiac), though most packages sold are heavily adulterated with powdered milk, starch and sugar. **Ayran** (watered-down yoghurt) is always on offer at *pidecis* and *kebapcıs*, and is an excellent accompaniment to spicy food. In autumn and winter, stalls sell **boza**, a delicious, mildly fermented millet drink.

Alcoholic drinks

Since the accession of the nominally Islamist AK Party in 2002, the price of **alcoholic drinks** has risen sharply – mainly because of the eighty percent tax levied. Alcoholic beverages are still widely available, however, especially in the big cities of western Turkey and all resort areas. It's much scarcer in provincial and conservative towns in central and eastern Anatolia, such as Afyon, Konya, Erzerum or Diyarbakır.

Wine

Wine (*şarap*) comes from vineyards scattered across western Anatolia between Cappadocia, the Euphrates Valley, Thrace and the Aegean. Fine wine now has a local audience, with expensive imported labels available in most upmarket town-centre or hotel restaurants and the bigger supermarkets. Local wines are also now better distributed, resulting in a huge variety in trendy resorts, though quality remains inconsistent. Red wine is *kırmızı*, white *beyaz*, rose *roze*. In shops, count on paying ₺18–35 per bottle of basic to mid-range wine. In restaurants, a standard table wine will set you back a minimum of ₺50, but more usually ₺70–80. Most places sell wine by the glass for ₺12–18.

The market is dominated by two large vintners: **Doluca** (try their Antik premium labels, or Moskado Sek) and **Kavaklıdere** (whose Çankaya white, Angora red and Lâl rose are commendable). Kavaklıdere also produces a sparkling white, İnci Damalası, the closest thing to local champagne. Other smaller, regional brands to watch for include Turasan, Narbağ, and Peribacası (Cappadocia). Feyzi Kutman red in particular is superb, though rarely found outside the largest centres. Another affordable Aegean producer worth sampling is Sevilen, which makes organic reds – Merlot and Cabernet – at premium prices, good whites and a palatable, MOR label, Tellibağ. Similarly confined to their areas of production are Majestik red, available only around İzmir, cheap-and-cheerful wines from Şirince, plus the vintners of Bozcaada (see box, p.200).

Rakı and other spirits

The Turkish national aperitif is **rakı**, not unlike Greek ouzo but stronger (45–48 percent alcohol), usually drunk over ice and topped up with bottled water. The *meyhane* routine of an evening is for a group to order a big bottle of rakı, a bucket of ice and a few bottles of water, and then slowly drink themselves under the table between bites of seafood *meze* or nibbles of *çerez* – the generic term for pumpkin seeds, roasted chickpeas, almonds etc, served on tiny plates. The best brand is reckoned to be Efe, particularly its green-label line. However, Burgaz is often better value and nearly as good (again in green-label variety). Tekirdağ, especially its "gold series", is also recommendable. Yeni is the most widely available at most establishments, with a double rakı in a *meyhane* running ₺12–16. A 70cl bottle of Yeni Rakı in a Turkish shop costs around ₺70, and all brands are much cheaper though duty-free.

Stronger **spirits** – *cin* (gin), *votka* (vodka) and *kanyak* (cognac) – exist as imported labels or cheaper but often nastier *yerli* (locally produced) variants. Avoid drinking spirits that are suspiciously cheap; several tourists have died in recent years from drinking bootleg liquor made from deadly methyl alcohol.

TURKISH BEER

Local brewery Efes Pilsen has a stranglehold on the Turkish beer (*bira*) market, sponsoring everything from a blues festival to one of the country's leading basketball teams. Luckily they produce a generally well-regarded pilsner-type brew, which comes in either 33cl or 50cl bottles or cans, plus in draught in many bars. From a supermarket or *bakkal* (small grocery store), expect to pay around ₺5 a bottle, slightly more for a can. **Efes Dark** is a sweeter, stronger stout-style brew, while **Efes-Xtra** is eight percent proof, though neither is widely available in bars or restaurants. Efes have added several more types of beer to their portfolio, the **Malt** being particularly good. Bottled **Efes Fıçı** (draught) also makes a nice change from the standard brew, as does **Bomonti**, a light wheat beer. **Tuborg**, of Danish origins, is the other major home-grown beer. It is less widely available than Efes, though some people swear by it. Their red-label beer is stronger than the standard green. **Carlsberg** is also brewed locally, while **Gusta** is a decent, dark, home-produced wheat beer.

Prices in bars and restaurants vary widely, with the cheaper places selling a 50cl beer for ₺9, trendier places for ₺15 and up. If the bar has draught (*fıçı*) beer, it's usually a little cheaper. If it's available, you'll pay at least a third more for the dubious privilege of drinking Corona, Fosters, Heineken or Becks.

Health

No special inoculations are required for Turkey, although jabs against tetanus, diptheria, polio, measles, mumps and rubella (MMR) and chickenpox are advisable. Cautious travellers might want typhoid and tetanus jabs, particularly for eastern Anatolia. Some visitors also get injections against hepatitis A and B, for which the risk is possibly greater in Istanbul than in rural areas. Malaria is theoretically a seasonal (April–July) problem between Adana and Mardin, especially in areas irrigated by the Southeastern Anatolia Project. However, for brief visits you shouldn't need prophylactic drugs. For up-to-date advice, consult a travel clinic.

Stomach upsets and drinking water

Many visitors experience bouts of **diarrhoea**, especially on longer stays. If you do get struck down, note that Lomotil or Imodium (trade names for diphenoxylate) are easily available in Turkey. They allow you to travel without constantly running to the bathroom, but do not kill the bug that ails you, as they slow down the process of flushing it out. Buscopan, also sold locally, is particularly good for stomach cramps, while Ge-Oral powder dissolved in pure water is an effective rehydration remedy. **Turkish tap water** is usually drinkable, but it tastes strongly of chlorine, so travellers usually prefer to stick to bottled water, especially in Istanbul where the water is particularly chlorinated. **Rural springs** are labelled *içilir*, *içilebilir* or *içme suyu* (all meaning "potable"), or *içilmez* (not drinkable).

Particularly during the hot summer months, serious **food poisoning** is a possibility – even in the biggest cities and resorts, and especially in southeastern Turkey. In restaurants, avoid dishes that look as if they have been standing around, and make sure meat and fish are well grilled. Don't, whatever you do, eat stuffed mussels in summer. If you're struck down, try to let the bug run its course and drink lots of fluids; eating plain white rice and yoghurt also helps. Stubborn cases will need a course of antibiotics or Flagyl (metronidazole), the latter effective against giardia and protozoans as well as certain bacteria; pharmacists are trained to recognize symptoms, and you don't need a prescription.

Bites and stings

Mosquitoes are sometimes a problem, and since no good topical repellents are available locally, you should bring your own. At night, mozzies are deterred with locally sold incense coils (*spiral tütsü*) or an *Esem Mat*, a small, electrified tray that slowly vaporizes an odourless disc. Hotels and *pansiyons* in heavily infested areas often have mosquito screens on the windows.

Jellyfish are an occasional hazard along the Aegean shore, and they are ubiquitous in the Bosphorus and Sea of Marmara (though they aren't such a problem around the Princes Islands). **Sea urchins**, whose spines easily detach if trodden on, are more common; the splinters must be removed to prevent infection. **Snakes** and **scorpions** can lurk among the stones at archeological sites, and in nooks and crannies of ground-floor accommodation. There are two kinds of vipers (*engerek* in Turkish): the deadly, metre-long Ottoman viper, fortunately rare, and the smaller, more common and less dangerous asp viper. Neither is particularly aggressive unless disturbed; both are most commonly seen during mild spring days.

Certain **ticks** in Turkey carry the Crimean-Congo haemorragic fever (**CCHF**) virus, with hundreds of cases (and fatalities in two figures) annually, though the danger seems confined to rural areas of several provinces between Ankara and the Black Sea.

Although rare (one to two cases per year), **rabies** is another potential danger. Be wary of any animal that bites, scratches or licks you, particularly if it's behaving erratically. If you do suspect you have been bitten by a rabid animal, wash the wound thoroughly (preferably with iodine) and seek medical attention immediately. Turkish cities are full of stray cats and dogs; dogs with a tag in their ear have been inoculated against rabies and other diseases and put back on the street with the blessing of the local authority.

Medical treatment

Minor complaints can be dealt with at a **pharmacy** (*eczane*); even the smallest town will have one. Turkish pharmacists may speak some English or German, and dispense medicines that would ordinarily require a prescription at home. Prices for locally produced medicines are low, but it may be difficult to find exact equivalents to your home prescription. Pharmacies are usually open Monday–Saturday 7am–7pm and closed on Sundays, but take turns to be a *Nöbet(ci)* (Duty) pharmacy. Each town or city will have one or more chemists open at night and on a Sunday; a duty roster is posted in Turkish in every chemist's front window. Note that there are usually several pharmacies near major hospitals, one of which is often the *Nöbet(ci)* pharmacy.

For more serious conditions, go to one of the **public clinics** (*sağlık ocağı*), or a **hospital** (*hastane*), indicated by a blue street sign with a large white "H" on it. Hospitals are either public (*Devlet Hastane* or *SSK Hastanesi*) or private (*Özel Hastane*). In terms of cutting bureaucracy and speed of treatment, a private hospital is far better, especially as many of the major ones have an English- (and often other languages) speaking assistant whose job is to deal with foreigners. Fees are lower than in northern Europe and North America but still substantial enough to make insurance cover essential (there are no reciprocal healthcare arrangements between Turkey and the EU). Expect to pay €35 and up to see a general doctor in a hospital, €90 and up to see a specialist consultant. The medical faculties of major universities – eg Istanbul, İzmir, Edirne, Antalya and Bursa – also have teaching hospitals, which are infinitely better than the state hospitals, but usually less expensive than the private ones. Summoning a doctor to your hotel room will cost about €50, plus medication delivered from a local pharmacy. If you're on a package tour, the better companies will have arrangements with competent, English-speaking doctors and dentists in or near the resort. In a medical **emergency**, summon an ambulance by dialling ☎112.

Contraception and female hygiene

International brands of **birth control** pills (*doğum kontrol hapıları*) are sold at pharmacies. **Condoms** (*preservatif*) are sold in most pharmacies and also supermarkets like Migros; don't buy off street-carts, where stock may be tampered with or expired. **Tampons** are available from pharmacies and supermarkets at UK prices; Orkid is the adequate domestic brand of sanitary towels.

Culture and etiquette

Many Turks, even in remote areas, have lived and worked abroad (mainly in Germany) or at tourist resorts in Turkey, and are used to foreign ways. But traditional customs matter, and although you're unlikely to cause offence through a social gaffe, it's best to be aware of prevailing customs. Also, many Turks are devout (or at least conservative) Muslims, so you should adhere to local dress codes – particularly away from resorts and when visiting mosques.

Invitations and meals

Hospitality (*misafirperverlik*) is a pillar of rural Turkish culture, so you're unlikely to leave the country without at least one invitation to **drink tea**, either in a *çayhane* (teahouse) or someone's home. If you really can't spare the time, mime "thanks" by placing one hand on your chest and pointing with the other to your watch and then in the direction you're headed. If you do stop, remember that drinking only one glass may be interpreted as casting aspersions on their tea. If offered a full meal, decline the first offer – if it's sincere it will be repeated at least twice and custom demands that you accept the third offer.

Being **invited for a meal** at a Turkish home is both an honour and an obligation. Always remove your shoes at the door. In urban, middle-class homes you'll sit at a table and eat with cutlery. In village houses, however, the meal is usually served at a low table with cushions on the floor; hide your feet under the table or a dropcloth provided for the purpose. (Feet, shoed or not, are considered unclean and should never be pointed at anyone.) When scooping food with bread sections from a communal bowl, **use your right hand** – the left is reserved for bodily hygiene. If you use toothpicks provided at restaurants, cover your mouth while doing so.

Dress and body language

What is acceptable dress-wise depends very much on which part of the country – or even which part of a city – you are visiting. Overall, though, Turkey is conservative regarding dress. **Beachwear** should be confined to the beach, while strolling shirtless around resort streets is offensive (though plenty of foreign men in resort areas do it). Revealing clothing such as miniskirts and skimpy shorts should be avoided away from heavily touristy areas. **Nude sunbathing** is not acceptable anywhere, though at any major Mediterranean/Aegean resort, discreet topless sunning takes place.

If you venture much off the tourist track, accept that being **stared at** is part of the experience and not considered rude. In some parts of the southeast, you may be mobbed by small children wishing to guide you around the local ruins and/or begging for pens, sweets or money.

Turks employ a variety of **body language** which is often not immediately obvious. Clicking the tongue against the roof of the mouth and simultaneously raising the eyebrows and chin means "no" or "there isn't any"; those economical of movement will rely on their eyebrows alone. By contrast, wagging the head rapidly from side to side means "Explain, I don't understand", while a single, obliquely inclined nod means "yes".

Black and Asian travellers

In remoter areas, **black and Asian people** may find themselves something of a curiosity, and may receive unsolicited comments – ranging from *Zenci!* (a Black!) to the notionally more appreciative *çok güzel* (very pretty!). Turkey is in fact one of the least racist countries around the Mediterranean. Many black footballers from Africa and South America play in Turkish teams, and you may also notice the country's black minority group, termed "Afro-Turks" (see box, p.230), particularly around İzmir.

Female travellers

While many **female travellers** encounter little more than some flirtatious banter while travelling in Turkey, a minority experience unwanted attention and more serious harassment in both resorts and rural areas. The key to avoiding trouble is to be aware of your surroundings, dress and behaviour and how it might be interpreted. If travelling alone, it's best to stick to mid-range hotels (particularly in the interior) and schedule transport to arrive during daylight hours. That said, the backstreets of most Turkish towns are a lot safer at night than those of many Western cities. This is partly due to a heavy police presence; do not hesitate to ask them for help. Away from the main resorts, **unaccompanied women** are a rare sight at night; when heading out for an evening, try to go as part of a group, preferably mixed-sex (all-female groups may still get some unwelcome attention). In restaurants,

WOMEN IN TURKEY

Acceptable behaviour and roles for **women** vary widely by class and region. In Istanbul and along the heavily touristy coastline, social freedom approximates that of Western Europe; in more traditional areas females act conservatively, with headscarves in abundance.

Turkish women have long held **jobs** in the professions and civil service as well as in the tourist sector, in hotels and for airlines. There are female police, and an increasing number of women can be found working in restaurants and bars – though only in resorts and some of the more westernized cities such as Antalya, Ankara, Istanbul and İzmir. Despite this, Global Gender Gap's 2015 figures revealed Turkey ranking a lowly 125th of 142 countries surveyed. In rural areas, women rarely have access to formal employment, and usually work the land. **Literacy rates** for girls are also significantly lower in rural areas despite compulsory education up to the age of fifteen.

In villages, parents still choose wives for their sons; in cities, more Western attitudes prevail and couples even live together unmarried. Despite the current AKP government openly calling for a ban, abortion is still legal, though many state hospitals refuse to carry out terminations. Contraceptives are readily obtainable; and a baby can be registered to unmarried parents. The average number of children per family is two, though there's a huge disparity between eastern and western Turkey, with families of up to twelve not uncommon in poorer southeastern (ethnically Kurdish) parts of the country. The law gives men considerable say over their children, though divorce law is fairly equitable.

Sadly, Turkey is also known for hundreds of annual "**honour**" **killings**, particularly in Kurdish areas. These occur for actual or suspected adultery, pregnancy out of wedlock or dating someone disapproved of by the family. While in the past this crime was carried out by a male relative, lately women have been forced to commit suicide instead. That said, the pro-Kurdish HDP (Peoples' Democracy Party) has, in fact, proportionally far more female MPs than any other party in Turkey.

Rates of **domestic violence** and **sexual abuse** are extremely worrying countrywide, highlighted by the fact that between 2003 and 2013 there was a 1400 percent increase in the number of women murdered. Some commentators attribute the rise to the "'value" of women declining in the decades of the Pro-Islamic AKP government; others put it down simply to more efficient recording and reporting of crimes against women.

unaccompanied women may be directed to the *aile salonu* (family parlour), usually upstairs, rather than be served with the male diners who tend to eat downstairs. While **public drunkenness** is unacceptable for both genders, this is especially true for women (see box, p.45).

Turkish women have, over the years, devised successful tactics to protect themselves from **harassment** – specifically, avoiding eye contact with men and looking as confident and purposeful as possible. When all else fails, the best way to neutralize harassment is to make a public scene. The words *Ayıp* ("Shame!") or *Beni rahatsız ediyorsun* ("You're disturbing me"), spoken very loudly, generally have the desired effect – passers-by or fellow passengers will deal with the situation for you. *Defol* ("Piss off!") and *Bırak beni* ("Leave me alone") are stronger retorts. In general, Turkish men back down when confronted, and cases of violent sexual harassment outside the home are rare.

Prostitution

Prostitution is thriving in Turkey, both in legal, state-controlled brothels and, illegally, on the streets and in certain bars and dubious hotels. Many prostitutes who work illegally come from Russia and former Soviet-bloc countries such as Moldova or Ukraine, and are known locally as "Natashas". Female travellers

---

HAMAMS (TURKISH BATHS)

The **hamam** (Turkish bath) once played a pivotal role in hygiene, social discourse and religious life (they were often part of a mosque complex) in Turkey, but as the standard of living has increased, its importance has diminished. As an exercise in nostalgia, however, it's well worth visiting one – Istanbul in particular boasts many historic hamams (see p.88, p.91, p.92 & p.93) worth experiencing for their architecture alone – and, of course, they make for a very relaxing end to a day of slogging around the sights.

Most Turkish towns have at least one hamam, usually signposted; otherwise look for the distinctive external profile of the roof domes. Ordinary hamams charge ₺10–15 basic **admission**, the price normally indicated by the front desk; those in coastal tourist resorts and Istanbul can be far more expensive (₺15–200 plus), with an optional scrub and/or massage adding to the cost. Most baths are either for men or women, or **sexually segregated** on a schedule, with women usually allotted more restricted hours, usually midweek during the day. Some larger hamams have both male and female sections.

HAMAM ETIQUETTE

On entering, leave your **valuables** in a small locking drawer, keeping the key (usually on a wrist thong) with you for the duration. Bring soap and shampoo, as it's not always sold in the foyer. Men are supplied with a *peştamal*, a thin, wraparound sarong, women generally enter in knickers but not bra; both sexes get *takunya*, awkward wooden clogs, and later a *havlu* (towel). Leave your clothes in the changing cubicle (*camekan* in Turkish).

The **hararet** or **main bath chamber** ranges from plain to ornate, though any decent hamam will be marble-clad at least up to chest height. Two or more *halvets*, semi-private corner rooms with two or three *kurnas* (basins) each, lead off from the main chamber. The internal temperature varies from tryingly hot to barely lukewarm, depending on how well run the baths are. Unless with a friend, it's one customer to a set of taps and basin; refrain from making a big soapy mess in the basin, which is meant for mixing pure water to ideal temperature. Use the scoop-dishes provided to sluice yourself. It's considered good etiquette to clean your marble slab with a few scoopfuls of water before leaving.

At the heart of the hamam is the **göbek taşı** or "**navel stone**", a raised platform positioned over the furnaces that heat the premises. The *göbek taşı* will be piping hot and covered with prostrate figures absorbing the heat. It's also the venue for (very) vigorous massages from the *tellâk* or masseur/masseuse. A *kese* (abrasive mitt) session from the same person, in which dead skin and grime are scrubbed away, will probably suit more people. Terms for the *tellâks'* services should be displayed in the foyer. Few hamams have a masseuse, so female visitors will have to think very carefully before accepting a massage from a masseur – though this is far from unknown. Scrubs and massages are charged extra, so make sure you know what you'll be paying. Upon return to your cubicle with its reclining couch(es) you'll be offered tea, soft drinks or mineral water – charged extra as per a posted price placard. Except in heavily touristed establishments, extra **tips** are not required or expected.

MOSQUE MANNERS

As you stroll around the tourist-thronged sites of Istanbul's Sultanahmet or the promenade of an Aegean or Mediterranean resort, it can at times be hard to remember that you are in a predominantly Muslim country – though even here the call to prayer echoes out five times daily: sunrise, midday, late afternoon, sunset and after dark.

Many of Turkey's inhabitants are, however, both conservative and devout. Bear this in mind particularly when **visiting a mosque**. All those likely to be of interest to a foreign visitor (and many more besides) display some kind of "conduct" notice at the door outlining the **entry rules** – which are simple:

- Cover your head (women) and shoulders/upper arms (both sexes).
- No shorts or miniskirts.
- Take off your shoes before entering. (Many mosques now provide a plastic bag for this – before entering, slip your shoes into the bag and carry them around with you. Alternatively, place your footwear on the shelves provided.)

Especially if you are in a very conservative part of the country (which includes most of inland Anatolia as well as conservative districts within the big cities, like Istanbul's Fatih) try to avoid your visit coinciding with **noon prayers** – particularly those on a **Friday**, the most important prayer session of the week. Once inside the mosque, you're free to wander around, take photographs and admire the interior – but keep your voice down (there are often people praying or reciting the Koran outside of the five daily prayer times) and don't take pictures of worshippers unless they give their permission. Although the imam is a state-paid official, upkeep of the building is down to charity, so you may want to put a **donation** in the collection box.

---

may be mistaken for prostitutes by local men assuming that any foreign woman out unaccompanied at night must be on the game. If you wander through **seedy districts** such as Aksaray in Istanbul, or stumble across known pick-up points on major highways, expect to be followed by kerb-crawlers; it's usually enough to explain that you're not a *natasha*. This guide doesn't recommend hotels used for prostitution, but management and clientele can change, so keep your antennae primed.

Gay and lesbian travellers

Turkish society has always been deeply ambivalent about male **homosexuality**, since the days of a rampantly bisexual Ottoman culture, when trans-vestite dancers and entertainers were the norm. That said, public attitudes are generally intolerant or closeted. The only place with a recognized gay scene is Istanbul, though the more liberal towns of Antalya and İzmir and the resorts of Bodrum, Marmaris and Alanya are considered gay-friendly.

Homosexual acts between adults over 18 are legal, but existing **laws** against "spreading homosexual information" in print – ie advocating the lifestyle – are sporadically enforced, Gay Pride festivals have been forcibly cancelled, and cruising is an offence. Advocating a gay lifestyle remains an offence. On a more positive note, in 2011 a major Gay Pride march down İstiklal Caddesi in Istanbul attracted over ten

thousand participants and passed without incident, though marchers in 2015 came under water-canon fire after chanting anti-government slogans. Despite the ambiguous official attitude to gays, there is a strong scene in Istanbul (see p.129).

In terms of **accommodation**, Ⓦturkey-gay-travel .com will help you find gay-friendly places to stay. The main pro-gay organisation, lambda, has a website, Ⓦlambdaistanbul.org, though in Turkish only.

Smoking

With over forty percent of the adult population (around 25 million) indulging in the nicotine habit, the old saying "smokes like a Turk" is a fairly accurate assessment. Yet things have changed dramatically in recent years. Smoking was **banned** on public transport and in airports, bus terminals and train stations back in 1997, and then further prohibited in 2009 in all public buildings, and all enclosed public spaces including bars, cafés, restaurants and clubs – including nargile (hookah) cafés. There was of course a major outcry, largely from the owners of *kahvehanes* (the basic, invariably all-male, tea-and-coffee dens) and bars and restaurants. The ban is widely flouted despite the steep fines for proprietors, many of whom have muddied the waters by erecting tent-like awnings at the front or rear of their establishment, warmed in winter by outdoor heaters.

Toilets

Western-style toilets are usual in many hotels, restaurants, cafés and bars. The only difference you're likely to notice is a small pipe fitted at the rear rim of the basin – which serves the same purpose as a bidet. The tap to turn it on is usually located on the wall behind the loo. Used toilet paper should go in the bins provided rather than in the toilet – blockages are not uncommon.

In rural areas (and less touristy parts of major cities), however, traditional **squat toilets** are still the norm, especially those attached to service stations, basic eateries and mosques. Mosque loos are often the only "public" toilet you'll be able to find in remote parts of big cities or in smaller towns. There's always a tap and plastic jug next to the toilet, but few provide paper, so it's a good idea to carry some around with you. An attendant at the entrance will divest you of a lira or so on your way out and, in return, give you a tissue and splash of cologne on your hands.

Festivals

Celebrations in Turkey include religious festivals, observed throughout the Islamic world on dates determined by the Muslim Hijra calendar, as well as annual cultural or harvest extravaganzas held in various cities and resorts across the country.

Religious festivals

The most important religious festival is **Ramadan** (*Ramazan* in Turkish), the Muslim month of daylight abstention from food, water, tobacco and sexual relations. Otherwise, life carries on as normal during Ramadan, despite the fact that half the population is fasting from sunrise to sunset. Some restaurants close for the duration or severely curtail their menus, others discreetly hide their salons behind curtains, but at most establishments you will be served with surprisingly good grace. The Koran allows pregnant and nursing mothers, the infirm and travellers to be excused from obligatory fasting; immediately after dark there's an orgy of eating (the *iftar yemeği*) by the famished in places public and private, and restaurants sell out of everything within an hour of sunset.

Kadir Gecesi (The Eve of Power), when Mohammed received the Koran from Allah, takes place between the 27th and 28th days of the month of Ramadan. Mosques – brilliantly illuminated for the whole month – are full all night, as it's believed that prayers at this time have special efficacy. On **Arife**, the last day of Ramadan, it is customary to go to the cemeteries and pay respects to departed ancestors; many rural restaurants close that evening.

The three-day **Şeker Bayramı** (Sugar Holiday) immediately follows Ramadan, celebrated by family reunions and the giving of presents and sweets to children, and restrained general partying in restaurants; on Arife eve, the night after Kadir Gecesi, you will have to book well in advance for tables at better establishments.

The four-day **Kurban Bayramı** (Festival of the Sacrifice), in which the sacrificial offering of a sheep represents Abraham's son Ishmael (a Koranic version of the Old Testament story), is marked by the massive slaughter of sheep and goats. Only wealthy families can afford to buy a whole animal, so part of the meat is distributed to the poor of the neighbourhood.

During the Şeker and Kurban festivals **travel** becomes difficult – reserve well in advance for a seat on any long-distance coach, train or plane. If you travel by road in national holiday periods, note that the already high traffic accident rate soars. Many shops and all banks, museums and government offices close during these periods (although corner grocery stores and most resort shops stay open) and when the festivals occur close to a national secular holiday, the whole country effectively grinds to a halt for up to a week.

Religious festival dates

As the Islamic calendar is lunar, the **dates** of the four important religious festivals drift backwards eleven days each year (twelve in a leap year) relative to the Gregorian calendar. Future dates of festivals given on Islamic websites are provisional.

2016 Şeker July 4–7; **Kurban** Sept 11–15
2017 Şeker June 24–27; **Kurban** Aug 31– Sept 4
2018 Şeker June 14–17; **Kurban** Aug 24–28
2019 Şeker June 4–7; **Kurban** Aug 10–14

Cultural festivals

Cultural festivals are most interesting in cities and resorts that have the resources to attract internationally renowned acts. Almost every town has some yearly bash, though many are of limited interest to outsiders. We've highlighted the best below, with fuller descriptions in the guide.

Folk-dance festivals provide an opportunity to see Turkey's best dance troupes perform a sample of the varied repertoire of Turkish dances in traditional costumes. In addition to the summary below there's a full festival calendar for Istanbul in chapter 1 (see box, p.130).

January

Camel wrestling Selçuk. The festival itself takes place on the last two weekends, though bouts occur throughout Aydın province from December onwards.

April

Istanbul International Film Festival Istanbul Ⓦ film.iksv.org /en. Full-length features and documentaries.

Tulip Festival Istanbul. Two-week festival honouring the national flower. Over fifteen million bulbs flower across the city, best seen in parks such as Emirgan and Gülhane early in the month.

May

Conquest Celebrations Istanbul Ⓦ ibb.gov.tr. Week-long celebration of the Ottoman conquest of old Constantinople – concerts by the Ottoman Mehter military band, fancy-dress processions and fireworks.

Ephesus Festival Ephesus. The ancient theatre hosts folk dancing plus more conventional acts.

Hıdırellez Gypsy festival Edirne. Celebration of the coming of spring, with gypsy bands performing, dancing in the street and jumping over bonfires. May 5–6.

International Theatre Festival Istanbul Ⓦ tiyatro.iksv.org. Biennial event (next up in 2016), showcasing the best Turkish and foreign theatre companies.

Takava Gypsy Festival Kırklareli. The same celebrations as at the Hıdırellez festival in Edirne. May 5–6.

June–July

Aspendos Opera and Ballet Festival Near Side, Antalya province Ⓦ aspendosfestival.gov.tr. The Mediterranean coast's big highbrow event runs mid-June to mid-Sept.

International İzmir Festival İzmir Ⓦ iksev.org. Month-long classical music, pop, ballet and jazz festival with many international names performing at Ephesus theatre and Çeşme castle.

Istanbul International Classical Music Festival Istanbul Ⓦ iksv .org. Performances by top soloists and orchestras, often in historic venues.

Istanbul Jazz Festival Istanbul Ⓦ iksv.org. Jazz as well as rock acts (see p.131). Early July.

Kafkasör Festival Artvin. Bullfighting between young beasts in a beautiful alpine setting, plus performances from folk-dance troupes and musical events – and lots of drinking. Late June.

Oil-wrestling Yağlı Güreş, near Edirne. Competitors from all over the country tangle with each other in the country's major, week-long oil-wrestling event, plus lots of music and dance events. Late June or early July.

One Love Istanbul Ⓦ oneloveistanbul.com. Moderately alternative city-centre weekend-long festival generally held at trendy Santrallstanbul, with plenty of DJ-led dance sets and performances from international and local bands.

Pir Abdal Musa *Tekke* village near Elmalı. Rites honouring the second most important Alevi saint after Hacı Bektaş Veli. Early June.

August

Chef's Contest Mengen, Bolu province. Cooking contest held in the region that purportedly produces the country's best cooks.

Hacı Bektaş Veli Commemoration Hacıbektaş village, Cappadocia. Bektaşis and their affiliates, the Alevis, meet for a weekend of ritual singing and dancing. Second half of Aug.

September–October

Akbank Jazz Festival Istanbul Ⓦ akbanksanat.com. A more traditional programme than Istanbul's other jazz festival in July.

Altın Portakal ("Golden Orange") Film Festival Antalya Ⓦ altin portakal.org.tr. A major fixture on the international film-festival circuit.

ArtInternational Istanbul Ⓦ artinternational-istanbul.com. Annual large-scale prestigious contemporary art fair established in 2013, attracting big players from around the globe.

Bodrum Festival Bodrum. Centred on the castle, and emphasizing ballet and opera. Early Sept.

Grape Harvest/Wine Festival Ürgüp, Cappadocia. Featuring some of the better local winery products.

Istanbul Biennial Istanbul Ⓦ iksv.org. Art exhibition, held odd-numbered years, with dozens of projects. Lasts into Nov.

Tourism and Handicrafts Festival Avanos. A celebration of the town's distinctive pottery.

Watermelon Festival Diyarbakır. A showcase for the region's most outsized fruit. Mid- to late Sept.

November

Istanbul Marathon Istanbul Ⓦ Istanbulmarathon.org. Runners from around the world compete in trans-continental marathon (see p.131).

December

Mevlâna Festival Konya. Whirling dervish performances at the home of the order. Dec 10–17.

The media

Newspapers and magazines were forbidden in Turkey until the mid-nineteenth century; now there are dozens of titles, representing the full gamut of public tastes. The airwaves were government-controlled until the late 1980s, but the advent of satellite dishes and cable has seen a huge growth in TV and radio stations of variable quality.

Turkish-language publications

Three titles – *Sabah*, *Hürriyet* and *Milliyet* – dominate the **newspaper** market. Conservative *Sabah* is the pro-Islamic AKP's government's mouthpiece, while the latter two are secular. Politically left of the main three papers stands *Radikal*, although another title,

Taraf, is far more radical than *Radikal* and frequently incurs establishment ire. *Cumhuriyet*, founded as the mouthpiece of the Turkish republic in 1924, mixes conservative nationalism with old-style socialism. Turkey's liberal-Islamist papers, *Yeni Şafak* and *Zaman*, give generally intelligent and thoughtful coverage.

Satirical weekly **comic strips** have a long history in Turkey. Look out for the distinctive artwork of L-Manyak, Le Man, Penguen and Uykusuz.

Television

Turkish channels include several **state-owned TRT** (Turkish Radio and Television) channels, with a mix of films, panel discussions, classical Turkish music shows and soaps. TRT-6, launched in 2009, broke a long-held Republican taboo by broadcasting in Kurdish. The most-watched **private channels** include Show, Star, ATV and Kanal D. For Turkish pop, the MTV-style Kral, Kral Pop and Power Turk lead the way.

The nation's leading digital company, Digiturk, has a number of English-language channels including CNBC-e and E2, both of which concentrate on re-runs of US TV shows and films. BBC Entertainment offers a mix of BBC comedies, dramas and soaps, while CNN, BBC World and Al Jazeera offer 24-hour news. Most high-end hotels subscribe to the Digiturk package screening these channels.

Digiturk also shows Turkish Premier League **football** on its Lig TV channel. English Premier League matches are shown on Premier League TV. Many bars and cafés subscribe to these and often have big screens showing Turkish matches. Bars in tourist areas usually have English and other European football games on.

Radio

Frequency-crowding means even popular channels are almost impossible to pick up without interfer-ence. Of the four **public radio stations**, Radyo Üç (the Third Programme or TRT-3), most commonly found at 88.2 MHz, broadcasts the highest propor-tion of Western music. NTV Radiyo (102.8) has the news in English at 6pm daily.

For Western music, try Açık Radyo (FM 94.9), Rock FM (94.5), Kiss FM (90.3) and Metro FM (97.2). Radyo Blue (94.5FM) specializes in dance, electronica and blues. Istanbul's coolest channel, Radyo Babylon (⑩radyobabylon.com; web only) is associated with its parent nightclub, Babylon (see p.128). For Turkish music, the best stations are Kral (92.0) and Best FM (98.4).

Cinema

With the exception of Istanbul's Beyoğlu district, where some period pieces date back to the 1920s, most cinemas are in shopping malls. **Films** are shown in the original language with Turkish subtitles, though kids' films are dubbed into Turkish. The volume is often excessively high, making the obligatory fifteen-minute interval a relief. There are often five screenings daily, generally at 11.30am or noon, then at around 3pm, 6pm and 9pm. **Tickets** in provincial cities cost ₺8–12, with reduced prices one or more days midweek; plusher cinemas charge ₺15 and up.

Shopping

Few visitors return from Turkey without some kind of souvenir; whether it's a pack of local herbs and spices or an expensive carpet depends on the budget of the traveller and the skill of the salesman. The best selection of good-quality wares is to be found in the major tourist centres: Istanbul, Cappadocia, Bursa and the coastal resorts. You won't

find a bargain at the production centres themselves; wholesalers and collectors have been there long before you.

How to bargain

Bargaining is a way of life in Turkey. In general it's acceptable to haggle over the price of souvenirs, which often lack price tags, so the vendor is able to adjust his asking price according to what he thinks you can or will pay. This applies to everything from expensive items such as carpets or kilims through to cheaper items like *lokum* (Turkish delight) and spices. As a guideline, begin at a figure lower than whatever you are prepared to pay, say half the shopkeeper's starting price. Once a price has been agreed, you are ethically committed to buy, so don't commence haggling unless you are reasonably sure you want the item.

"Assistance" from **touts**, whether in Istanbul, major resorts or even provincial towns, will automatically bump up the price thirty to fifty percent, as they will be getting a commission. Also, be prepared to hand over between three and seven percent extra if paying by credit card; your bargaining position is strongest with cash.

Don't bargain for bus, rail or air tickets, or for fruit or vegetables at street markets.

Bazaars, shops and markets

Several types of traditional bazaar continue to exist in Turkey. **Covered bazaars** are found in larger towns like Istanbul (see p.89), Bursa (see p.170) and Şanlıurfa (see p.586). Essentially medieval Ottoman shopping malls, they comprised several *bedestens* at which particular types of goods were sold, linked by covered arcades also originally assigned to a particular trade – though strict segregation has long since broken down.

Surrounding these covered bazaars are large areas of **small shops**, open-air extensions of the covered areas and governed by the same rules: each shop is a separate unit with an owner and apprentices, and successful businesses are not allowed to expand or merge.

Street markets are held in most towns and all cities, similar to those in northern Europe and selling cheap clothes, household utensils and most importantly fruit, vegetables, cheese, yoghurt, olives, nuts and the like. More exotic are the semi-permanent **flea markets** (*bit pazarı*, literally "louse markets"), ranging in quality from street stalls where old clothes are sold and resold among the homeless, to lanes of shops where you can buy antiques and bric-a-brac.

However, in many cities, particularly in Istanbul, everyday shopping is increasingly done in Western-style department stores, shopping malls and supermarkets.

Carpets and kilims

Turkish carpets and **kilims** (flat-weave rugs) are renowned for their quality and have a very long history (the designs on many kilims have their origins in the Neolitihic period). Rugs are no longer

CARPET AND KILIM BUYING TIPS

- **Do some research**, preferably before you leave home (check out some of the books reviewed in this guide; see p.699).
- Avoid buying in the first shop you visit, and **look around several**. You can always go back – preferably the next day, when you've had time to think about it.
- **Don't be embarrassed** at how many carpets the dealer is laying out for you – that's his (or usually his lowly assistant's) job.
- **Ask as many questions as you can** – this will test the dealer's worth, and could give you some interesting historical background should you make a purchase.
- **Check the pieces for flaws**, marks and the density of weave – hand-woven wool is preferable to machine as it is stronger, and the rug will last for longer.
- **Natural dyes** such as tobacco and saffron are the most highly prized and less likely to fade. You should be able to tell by opening up a section of the pile with your fingers. If the tint at the bottom of the pile is different to that at the top, it is a chemical dye.
- Even in the most reputable shop, **bargaining is essential**. Whatever you do, don't engage in the process if you've no intention of buying.
- You'll probably get a **better deal for cash** – this will also help overcome the temptation to credit-card splurge.
- Most important of all, **only buy the piece if you really like it** and are sure it'll look the part back home.

necessarily cheaper in Turkey than overseas, and many carpets have actually been made in places with cheap labour, such as Iran and China.

Most visitors will find themselves in a carpet shop at some point in their visit – willingly or unwillingly. It's very easy to be drawn into buying something you don't really want at a price you can barely afford once you've been smooth-talked and drip-fed with copious quantities of apple tea. However, it's still possible to get a good deal and enjoy the process (see box, p.51).

Carpets

Turkish carpets are single-sided, and knotted with a pile. They are either all-wool, wool pile on cotton warps and wefts, all-silk or – easily mistaken for silk – a glossy mercerized cotton pile on cotton warps and wefts. Needless to say, the higher the silk content, the more expensive the rug, with new, hand-woven wool carpets starting from around €150 per square metre, and pure silk ones starting at €550. Turkish carpets are made using the double-knot technique, making them more durable than their single-knot Persian counterparts. The most famous Turkish carpets are Hereke, named after their town of origin. Pure silk, they have an extremely high knot density. Larger Hereke take up to four years to weave and cost around €1010 per square metre, with prime examples going for tens of thousands of euros. Silk carpets woven in the central Anatolian province of Kayseri are usually a third cheaper. Other key carpet manufacturing areas are Bergama, Uşak and Milas – all near the Aegean coast. Be warned – any carpets that seem suspiciously cheap, especially silk ones, are almost certainly Chinese, not Turkish.

Kilims

A **kilim** is a pile-less, flat-woven wool rug. The better ones are double-sided (that is, the pattern should look much the same top or bottom). A cicim is a kilim with additional, raised designs stitched onto it. Traditionally woven by nomadic Anatolian tribal groupings such as the Turcomans and Kurds, kilims are generally much more affordable than carpets. Prices for newly woven examples (invariably woven by women and sold by men) start from around €30 per square metre, whereas a rare antique kilim can fetch thousands of euros. The vast majority of kilims are heavily patterned with geometric motifs – invariably stylized birds, animals, flowers or other images from the natural world that formed the backdrop to the nomads' lives. Originally they served as floor coverings, tent partitions and blankets or, stitched together, as storage/saddlebags and bolsters.

Clothes

Turkish designs are beginning to match the quality of local fabrics such as Bursa silk and Angora wool. You will pay near-Western prices for genuine locally designed items at reputable shops – local brands are aggressively protected from counterfeiting, if necessary by police raids.

However, many visitors find it hard to resist the allure of the cheap **fake designer clothing** available everywhere, with all the usual suspects (Armani, Diesel, Louis Vuitton et al) the victims. Genuine international designer wear is priced little differently to elsewhere.

Jewellery

Both in terms of design, quality and price, Turkey is a great country to buy **jewellery**, though gold prices in particular have rocketed in recent years. Gold and silver jewellery are sold by weight, with little regard for the disparate level of craftsmanship involved – at the time of writing, silver was a bargain at ₺1.3 per gram, gold ₺97 – and so too are semi-precious stones. One particularly intricate method is telkâri or wire filigree, most of which comes from eastern Turkey, particularly Mardin and nearby Midyat. Gold in particular can be very good value and is so pure (22 carat) that telkâri bangles bend easily. Also remember that sterling silver items should bear a hallmark.

Leather goods

Leather is still big business in Turkey. The industry was originally based in western Anatolia, where alum deposits and acorn-derived tannin aided the tanning process. Today, İzmir and Istanbul still have the largest workshops, though the retail business also booms on the Mediterranean coast, particularly in Antalya and Alanya. Jackets are the most obvious purchase, the prices of which vary from around €75 from a downmarket outlet to well over €350 from a branded "designer" shop such as Matraş, Desa or Derimod. Shoes are less good value and women's sizes rarely go over 40.

Miscellaneous souvenirs

A tavla takımı or **backgammon** set makes a good souvenir of Turkish popular culture. Mother-of-pearl inlaid sets are the most expensive, but fakes abound, so if in doubt go for one of the plain, wood-inlay sets. **Copperware** is still spun and hammered in the traditional way in some Turkish towns, notably Gaziantep in the southeast. The most popular items are lidded jugs, large serving trays and bowls. Mavi boncuk (blue bead) key rings,

<table><tr><td>

ANTIQUES AND SMUGGLING: A WARNING

Under Turkish law, it is an offence to buy, sell, export or even possess genuine **antiquities** (which includes fossils). Exact age limits are not specified, suggesting that decisions by customs officials are subjective, though a principal measure of antiquity is rarity. At popular archeological sites such as Ephesus, you may be offered "antiques" by hawkers, which are invariably fake.

In the case of **carpets** handled by established dealers, you run a very slight risk of investing a lot of money in a supposed "collector's item" that turns out to be collectable only by the Turkish Republic. If you're apprehensive about a proposed purchase, ask the dealer to prepare both a *fatura* (invoice) recording the exact purchase price – also necessary to satisfy customs – and a declaration stating that the item is not an antique. Expect a heavy fine and possibly imprisonment if you transgress these laws.

</td></tr></table>

lintel ornaments and animal collars are sold all over the place to ward off *nazar* (the evil eye).

Meerschaum **pipes**, carved from *lületaşı* stone quarried near Eskişehir, are available in all tourist areas. Less common are Karagöz puppets, representing the popular folk characters Karagöz and Hacıvat, preferably made from camel skin in Bursa. Towelling and silk goods, the best of which come from Bursa, are also good buys, as are the pure cotton *peştamals* (the usually striped cotton wraps used in Turkish baths), bathrobes and tablecloths woven in Denizli. Kütahya **ceramics** may not be the finest ever produced in Turkey, but the vases, bowls, plates and, in particular, tiles, churned out in this western-Anatolian town, are attractive enough and reasonable value as decorative items. Revived İznik ware is a cut above (see box, p.165). For more contemporary ceramics try the nationwide store Paşabahçe.

Musical instruments

Traditional Turkish **musical instruments** are sold all over the country. The most easily portable are the *ney*, the Mevlevî flute made from a length of calamus reed; the *davul* or drum; and the *saz/bağlama*, the long-necked Turkish lute. Rock and jazz musicians might like to score, a bit cheaper than abroad, a set of cymbals from one of two world-

famous brands – Istanbul and Zildjian – both made by Istanbul-based or Armenian companies.

If you've any interest in local recordings it's worth listening to a cross section of Turkish styles and making a purchase or two (CDs go for ₺18 and up). We list a discography of recommended items a the end of this guide (see p.690).

Spices and foodstuffs

Acknowledging the slight risk of having certain goods confiscated on return to the European Union or North America, locally produced **spices, condiments and foodstuffs** make for a compact, lightweight souvenir purchase. Low-grade saffron (*zafran*), the stamen of a particular kind of crocus, is still gathered in northern Anatolia. Sumac (*sumak*) is a ground-up purple leaf for sprinkling on barbecued meats and salad onions. Pine nuts (*çam fıstığı*), gathered in the coastal mountains, are excellent and, especially if purchased in northwest Turkey, are considerably cheaper than in Europe. *Pekmez* (molasses of grape, mulberry or carob pods) is nutritious and makes a splendid ice cream, muesli or yoghurt topping. Olive oil is a worthwhile purchase, as are the olives it's made from. Olive-oil soaps are also popular, especially Defne Sabunı, a laurel-scented soap from Antakya. Both hot and sweet peppers are made into concentrated pastes (*salçalar*), while dried aubergine/eggplant and pepper shells are convenient for stuffing. *Nar eksisi* is a sour-sweet pomegranate syrup widely used as a salad dressing or meat marinade. Turkish delight (*lokum*; see p.40) is a perennial favourite and comes in a bewildering variety of flavours.

Sports and outdoor activities

Whether you want to stand alongside some of the most passionate football fans in the world, hike a long-distance trail, climb up or ski down a mighty peak, raft the rapids of a mountain torrent, or paraglide over/dive beneath the warm waters of the Mediterranean, Turkey is the place to do it.

Football

Football is hugely popular in Turkey. Most Turks, no matter where they are from, profess allegiance to one of the "Big Three" Istanbul sides –

Galatasaray, Beşiktaş or Fenerbahçe (see p.107). The one exception is the Black Sea coastal town of Trabzon, whose citizens support their local team, Trabzonspor, which ranks up there with the Istanbul big boys.

Turkey has produced plenty of home-grown footballing talent (some now play in England, Germany and Spain), and many Turkish teams include international players, particularly from Africa and South America. The managers of the Istanbul "giants" are often recruited from abroad, though unusually in 2015 only one out of the "Big Three" managers was foreign (Fenerbahçe's Vitor Pereira). Although the teams qualifying for the Champions League often fall at the first hurdle, Galatasaray became the first Turkish team to win the UEFA Cup (in 2000; beating Arsenal 4–1 on penalties).

Matches are played between September and May. TV schedules mean that matches are spread over the weekend, and there's usually a match on Friday evening, then more on Saturday afternoons/evenings and Sunday afternoon. Obtaining **tickets** for provincial teams is usually both cheap and easy, with tickets available at the ground on match day for as little as ₺15, but prices can rise tenfold when one of the Istanbul "giants" is in town. Many bars show games on big screens, and can be very atmospheric, especially for derby games.

Football violence is common (in 2000, two English Leeds United fans were stabbed to death in Istanbul during street-fighting with Galatasaray fans), though the average foreigner is unlikely to get caught up in trouble. Turkish football was scarred by a big match-fixing scandal in 2012, which delayed the start of the new season and resulted in Fenerbahçe's chairman being jailed.

After big games, especially those involving the "Big Three", expect delirious celebrations, with flag-waving fans leaning on the horns of cruising cars embroiled in massive traffic jams.

Hiking and mountaineering

Turkey's wild **mountain ranges** are a treat for experienced hikers prepared to carry their own tents and food, and cope with few facilities. The lack of decent maps makes mountain exploration a real adventure, but the unspoiled countryside, the hospitality of rural Turks, the fascination of the *yaylas* (summer pastures), and the friendliness of other mountaineers more than compensate.

Several companies organize expeditions to the alpine **Kaçkar Dağları**, paralleling the Black Sea, and the most rewarding mountains in Turkey for trekking. Next up in interest are the limestone **Toros (Taurus) ranges**, especially the lofty Aladağlar mountains south of Cappadocia.

Aside from this, high-altitude **mountaineering** in Turkey consists mostly of climbing the volcanoes of the central plateau. All offer superb views from their summits. Most famous is 5137m **Ağrı Dağ**, or Ararat (see p.642) on the eastern borders of Turkey, though this requires a special permit due to its sensitive location. By contrast, 3916m **Erciyes Dağı** (see p.460) offers exhilarating climbing without any of the expense or bureaucracy prevalent at Ararat. **Süphan Dağı** (see p.628) Turkey's second-highest volcanic peak (4058m), stands in splendid isolation north of Lake Van. Unfortunately, the magnificent Cilo-Sat mountains south of Lake Van are sometimes a battleground between the Kurdish separatists and Turkish security forces, so are currently closed to outsiders.

WAYMARKED TRAILS

The exhilarating **Lycian Way** long-distance trail (see box, p.303) weaves its way through the westernmost reaches of the Toros, while the more challenging **St Paul Trail** (see box, p.418) crosses the range from south to north. Both trails are marked with red-and-white paint flashes and take in some stunning mountain and gorge scenery, remote ancient sites and timeless villages. Each has its own guidebook and map (see p.699); for more information check out ⓦ trekkinginturkey.com. Opened more recently, and coiling its way through some of southwest Turkey's most beautiful land and seascapes, is the 820km Carian Trail (ⓦ cariantrail.com), with its own guidebook (available from their website), complete with maps and GPS coordinates.

Other trails include the **Evliya Çelebi Way** in northwest Turkey, suitable for horseriders and walkers, the **Phrygian Way** and the **Hittite Trail**.

You can find more information on all these routes, and several others, at ⓦ cultureroutesinturkey.com, the website of the **Culture Routes Society**, a non-profit making organization which helps to set up, maintain and preserve walking routes in Turkey.

Hiking equipment and safety

Alpine huts are nonexistent, so you'll need to carry full **camping gear** to trek in the mountains. It's best to bring your own, as only Istanbul and Ankara have European-standard mountaineering shops. **Water** can be a problem in the limestone strata of the Toros, while on the volcanoes, detailed **maps** are very difficult to obtain and **trails** (when present) are seldom marked.

Rescue services are no match for those in more developed mountain areas in Europe and the US, but the local *jandarma* (see p.58) will turn out in an emergency. Voluntary NGO AKUT (Search and Rescue Association; Ⓦ akut.org.tr) has some 35 teams spread, patchily, across the country.

You'll find details on specific hiking routes through the Kaçkar Dağları, and a selection of walks on Bursa's Uludağ and along the Turquoise Coast, in the guide, but if you're daunted at the prospect of going alone, contact one of the adventure-travel companies listed in this chapter (see p.30). Except for the long-distance trails and the Kaçkar mountains (see p.554), it's virtually impossible to obtain large-scale **topographical maps** of specific areas for **trekking** (though usable-enough maps for the most popular trekking areas can be found in *Trekking in Turkey*, an unfortunately out-of-print guide that's still available secondhand).

Skiing

While few foreigners come to Turkey specifically to **ski**, the sport is growing in popularity, and if you're visiting between December and April it's well worth considering a day or more on the slopes. If you're willing to forego doorstep skiing, it's surprisingly easy and cheap to ski while based in towns like Erzurum or Bursa which are near to resorts. The Turkish State Meteorological Service gives information on snow heights at the various resorts (Ⓦ mgm.gov.tr).

Turkey's best-known ski resort is **Uludağ** (see p.180), above Bursa, with easy and intermediate runs, but the slopes are prone to mist and snow, and turn slushy after February. The **Saklıkent** complex in the Beydağları near Antalya would seem potentially ideal for an early spring sea-cum-ski holiday, but snow cover tends to be thin and the runs are limited. Close by is much better **Davraz**, near İsparta, where snow conditions are more reliable and there's plentiful accommodation in the nearby lakeside town of Eğirdir as well as at the resort (see box, p.416). Roughly midway between Istanbul and Ankara, near Bolu, **Kartalkaya** is better

than any of the aforementioned, despite a modest top altitude of 2223m; facilities now nearly match those of Uludağ, plus there are several red and black runs and, most importantly, in recent years there has been plentiful snow. The longest season and best snow conditions are usually at **Palandöken**, near Erzurum, where the top lift goes over 3000m and the Turkish Olympic team trains; there are three chair lifts, one T-bar and a 3km gondola car to service a mix of blue and red runs (see box, p.548). At **Tekir Yaylası**, on Erciyes Dağı near Kayseri, the season is nearly as long, the snow almost as powdery, with two chair lifts taking skiers to 2550m and 3000m respectively, plus six other lifts (see p.460). **Sarıkamış**, near Kars, has two chair lifts and one T-bar to service a handful of runs (mostly red and blue); the top lift is 2634m (see box, p.570). There are a number of hotels at each of the above resorts. For more information on Turkey's ski resorts, see Ⓦ skiingturkey.com.

Watersports

Most medium to large resorts offer **waterskiing** and its offspring, **parasailing**; the even more exciting thrill of **kitesurfing** is centred on Alaçatı, near Çeşme, while **windsurfers** head for the Bodrum peninsula. **Sea kayaking** makes a great way to explore the indented coastline, islets and shallow, clear waters in the environs of the southwest Mediterranean resort of Kaş.

For more thrills and spills but less skill (you just sit there unless you happen to be thrown – or pushed – into the torrent), there's also **whitewater rafting**. This is very popular on the Köprülü River near Antalya and the Dalaman River close to Fethiye, though for more serious outings the dam-threatened Çoruh in northeast Turkey is a world-class

---

BIRDWATCHING

Turkey stands astride several major bird migration routes and possesses some very bird-friendly habitat. Well-known **birdwatching sites** include the Göksu delta near Silifke (see box, p.384), the Belen Pass en route to Antakya (see p.398), and Lake Van (see p.620). On an active birdwatching holiday, you could expect to tick off nearly three hundred different species. For a database of bird species and distribution in Turkey, as reported by local and foreign birdwatchers, see Ⓦ kusbank.org.

rafting river. Another freshwater-based activity of a very different nature is **canyoning**, which involves abseiling down waterfalls, leaping into plunge pools and generally exploring precipitous gorges – trips are organized by outfits in Kaş (see p.330).

Scuba diving is one of the most popular water-based activities; outfits in Kaş, Kalkan and, further west, in Bodrum, Marmaris and Fethiye offer instruction and gear. There are underwater reefs and fish, wrecks and caves to explore, all in the (usually) clear, calm and warm waters of the Aegean/Mediterranean.

Other activities

With cheap flights, countless rock faces and ample winter sun, it's only a matter of time before Turkey begins to rival Spain on the itineraries of **climbers**. The best place to start is Geyikbayırı, conveniently located just 25km from the gateway Mediterranean resort of Antalya. Five hundred bolted routes track their way up a series of imposing limestone cliffs, and there are several camping/wooden chalet-style places to stay in the forest below. There's more climbing from beach level at the beautiful resort of nearby Olympos. For more information check out ⓦ climb-europe.com.

Cappadocia's bizarrely sculpted rock pinnacles and plunging valleys rank among the world's most striking landscapes. The best way to see this geological wonderland is to drift over it in an expertly piloted **hot-air balloon**, though the over-proliferation of operators has contributed to a number of fatal accidents in recent years. For more of an adrenaline rush, try **paragliding** (in tandem with a qualified pilot) from the mountains behind the bustling resorts of Kaş or Ölüdeniz.

Travelling with children

Turks adore children, and Turkish families tend to take their children with them wherever they go, thinking nothing of letting them run around restaurants until the early hours. In this sense, the country is a great place to visit with kids. And, of course, the coastal resorts offer a generally calm, warm sea and have pools, beaches (and sometimes waterparks) aplenty. On the down side, the number of play areas and children's attractions lags far behind Western Europe.

Turks have an uninhibited Mediterranean attitude towards children. Don't be surprised to find your child receive an affectionate pinch on the cheek by a passer-by, often accompanied by the word *maşallah*, which serves both to praise your offspring and ward off the evil eye, while waiters will sometimes unselfconsciously pick a kid up and waltz them off into the kitchen to show their workmates, often accompanied by cries all around of "how sweet" ("*çok tatlı*").

With a few honourable exceptions (eg Miniatürk and the Rahmi M. Koç Industrial Museum in Istanbul, and Minicity Antalya), there are few **attractions** aimed specifically at younger children, and few museums have kid-friendly displays or activities. And for buggy-pushing parents, the uneven surfaces and metre-high kerbs of the average Turkish pavement (where there is one) are a nightmare. For older kids there are plenty of outdoor activities on offer – kayaking and windsurfing at some coastal resorts, for example, and whitewater rafting, mountain biking and canyoning in the hinterland.

Turkish **food** should appeal to most kids – what's *köfte* but a (very) tasty burger, *pide* a pizza without the tomato paste, and *gözleme* a stuffed pancake? Maraş ice cream is just as delicious as Italian gelato and comes in myriad flavours. In general, restaurants are very welcoming to families – just don't expect highchairs. Disposable nappies are widely available from supermarkets and the larger *bakkals*.

Travel essentials

Archeological sites

Most **archeological sites** open daily 8am–7pm between April and October, and 9am–7pm between November and March, though there are some variations; exact times are listed in the relevant sections of the guide.

Don't pay **entrance fees** unless the wardens can produce a ticket, and keep it with you for the duration of your visit. Sites like Patara and Olympos straddle the route to a good beach. If you are staying nearby and want to visit the beach on several occasions, **smart PlajKarts** are available, allowing multiple site/beach entries.

Beaches

Except near major cities, where seawater is sometimes polluted, Turkish **beaches** are safe to swim at, though be prepared for occasional mountains of rubbish piled at the back of the beach. Tar can also be a problem on south-coast beaches that face Mediterranean shipping lanes; if you get tar on your feet, scrub it off with olive oil rather than chemical solvents. Virtually all beaches are free in theory, though luxury compounds that straddle routes to the sand will control access in various ways, and you'll pay for the use of beach-loungers and umbrellas.

Costs

Turkey is no longer the cheap destination it used to be; **prices** in the heavily touristed areas are comparable to many places in Europe. Exercise a little restraint, however, be prepared to live life at least occasionally at the local level (many Turks somehow survive on ₺700 a month) and you can still enjoy a great-value trip here.

Stay in a "treehouse" or backpackers' inn, eat in local workers' cafés or restaurants, travel around by train or bus, avoid alcohol and the most expensive sites, and you could get by on ₺90–120 (€30–40) a day. If that doesn't sound like much fun, double that and you could stay in a modest hotel, see the sights and have a beer or two with your evening meal. Equally, a night out on the town in Istanbul or one of the flasher coastal resorts could easily set you back over ₺150 (€50), and if you intend to see a lot of what is a very big country, transport costs could be a considerable drain on your budget – though taking night buses saves accommodation costs.

The more expensive tourist sites such as Ephesus, the Tokapı Palace and Haghia Sophia cost ₺30

KDV: TURKISH VAT

The Turkish variety of VAT (*Katma Değer Vergisi* or **KDV**), ranging from eight to 23 percent depending on the commodity, is included in the price of virtually all goods and services (except car rental, where the 18 percent figure is usually quoted separately). Look for the notice *Fiyatlarımız KDV Dahildir* (VAT included in our prices) if you think someone's trying to do you for it twice. There's a VAT refund scheme for large souvenir purchases made by those living outside Turkey, but it's such a rigmarole to get that it's probably not worth pursuing; if you insist, ask the shop to provide a *KDV İade Özel Fatura* (Special VAT Refund Invoice), assuming that it participates – very few do, and they tend to be the most expensive shops.

(€10), but there are many more sites varying between ₺3 and ₺15. There are no student discounts, and the *Müze Kart* (Museum Card), which gives admission to all state-run museums for ₺30 per annum, is only for Turkish citizens and foreigners with a resident permit.

Crime and personal safety

Turkey's **crime rate** remains lower than most of Europe and North America, although pickpocketing and bag-snatching are becoming more common in Istanbul (see box, p.72) and other major cities. Violent street crime is fortunately rare. Keep your wits about you and an eye on your belongings, just as you would anywhere else, and make sure your passport is secure at all times, and you shouldn't have any problems. Except for well-known "red-light" districts, and some eastern towns, female travellers (see p.45) are probably safer on their own than in other European countries.

Street demonstrations, which sometimes turn violent, have become a feature of an increasingly polarized Turkey, seen most clearly in 2013 at Gezi Park in Istanbul, when protests against the felling of trees to make way for a new mall turned into an anti-government occupation of the park and Taksim Square. Heavy-handed police tactics, with much use of tear gas and water cannon, exacerbated the situation; several protestors died as a result. Visitors should avoid demonstrations for obvious reasons – flash points include upper İstiklal Caddesi and Taksim Square in Istanbul, and central squares in other large cities. In October 2015, Turkey suffered its worst-ever atrocity when twin suicide bombers (with suspected links to ISIS), blew themselves up amid an anti-war demonstration in Ankara, resulting in 102 deaths and hundreds more wounded. Protests in the ethnically Kurdish southeast of the country should also be avoided (see p.59).

As well as the usual warnings on **drugs**, note that exporting antiquities is illegal (see box, p.53). Note, too, that it's an offence to **insult Atatürk or Turkey**, which can result in a prison sentence. Never deface, degrade or tear up currency or the flag; drunkenness will likely be considered an aggravating, not a mitigating, factor. Also, do not take **photographs** near the numerous, well-marked military zones.

The police, army and gendarmerie

Turkey's police service is split into several groups. The blue-uniformed **Polis** are the everyday security force in cities and towns with populations over two thousand; the white-capped **Trafik Polis** (traffic police) are a branch of this service. Istanbul and several other large towns have a rapid-response squad of red-and-black-uniformed motorbike police known as the *yunus* (dolphin) *polis*; they are generally courteous and helpful to tourists and may speak some English. The dark-blue-uniformed **Çevik Kuvvet Polis** are a rapid response team most likely seen at demonstrations, football matches and other events where large crowds are expected. In towns, **Belediye Zabitası**, the navy-clad market police, patrol the markets and bazaars to ensure that tradesmen aren't ripping off customers – approach them directly if you have reason for complaint. You're unlikely to come across plain-clothes police unless you wander off the beaten track in the ethnically Kurdish southeast.

In most rural areas, law enforcement is in the hands of the **jandarma** or gendarmerie, a division of the regular army charged with law enforcement duties. Gendarmes are usually kitted out in well-tailored green fatigues; most are conscripts who will be courteous and helpful if approached.

Note that it is obligatory to **carry ID** at all times – for locals and foreigners alike – so if you are concerned about having your passport stolen (or losing it) while out and about, at least carry a photocopy of the pages with your details and Turkish entry stamp.

Security and restricted areas

There is a noticeable security presence in the **Kurdish-dominated southeast** of the country, with firefights between Turkish security forces and the autonomy-minded **PKK** (Kurdish Workers Party) continuing at the time of writing. Security is tightest along the Iraqi, Iranian and Syrian borders, particularly south and east of Hakkari and around Şırnak in the mountains south of Lake Van. The civil war in Syria (with which Turkey shares a 900km border) that erupted in 2011 and had shown no sign of abating at the time of writing, is also problematic for Turkey, with foreign jihadist fighters en route to join **ISIS** (Islamic State of Iraq and Syria) in Syria and Iraq using the long, porous frontier between Turkey and Syria as a crossing point. Even worse, Turkey's biggest nightmare, a proto-Kurdish state run by Syria's Kurdish minority appeared to be developing across the frontier at the time of writing. Other areas which have seen sustained PKK activity include the rural hinterland of Diyarbakır and the mountainous region of Tunceli (the latter not covered in this guide). PKK attacks are mostly made in isolated rural areas, often targeting military vehicles with remotely detonated bombs. Occasional fully fledged assaults on military

outposts are made – inevitably followed by major reprisals by Turkish security forces. In 2015, a PKK affiliate took its struggle to the streets of some cities in the southeast, declaring certain areas autonomous zones and off-limits to the security forces. State reprisals led to week-long curfews in parts of Diyarbakır and other settlements in the region.

To add to the confusing picture, at the time of writing Turkey was launching cross-border **air-strikes** against PKK camps in the virtually autonomous region of Iraqi Kurdistan, and had just opened up an air base near the Syrian border to allow the US (under NATO auspices) to bomb ISIS in both Syria and Iraq. Turkey itself has also become embroiled in the anti-ISIS struggle and was launching aerial attacks on ISIS. One tragic consequence of Turkey's newfound determination to combat ISIS was a suicide bomb attack in Istanbul's historic heartland of Sultanahmet in January 2016, which resulted in the deaths of ten foreign visitors. this was an attack by ISIS that appeared to deliberately target Turkey's tourism industry.

What does this mean to the average traveller hoping to visit this beautiful region? At the time of writing, the British Foreign and Commonwealth Office (FCO; ⓦfco.gov.uk), for example, advised against all travel to within 10km of the Syrian border and against all but essential travel to the provinces of Diyarbakır, Şırnak, Mardin, Şanlıurfa, Gaziantep, Kilis, Siirt, Tunceli, Hakkari and the Hatay. The official line, then, is to **avoid the mountains south of Lake Van** that border the de facto Kurdish state in northern Iraq, and **stay well away from the Syrian border area** (where risk of kidnapping is a potential threat). However, note that places like Tunceli are a long, long way from the border.

The problem is compounded by the ever-fluctuating state of relations between the state and the PKK, with long ceasefires interrupted by violent flare-ups. At the time of writing, PKK attacks had resumed after a long, semi-official ceasefire, with over 120 security personnel killed between late July and early September 2015. However, in the Middle East things can change very quickly and it's quite possible the situation may have calmed down dramatically by the time you read this. In other words: read about what is happening in the press and on travellers' forums, and use your common sense and judgement before you travel.

Although there are fewer **checkpoints** on main roads than there used to be, you may be stopped if you attempt to travel to off-the-beaten-track sites and/or villages, and your presence may attract the attention of the *jandarma* (and quite possibly the plain-clothes secret police, who generally stand out a mile from the locals). This may involve, at most, a rather tedious, though polite, interrogation. Lone males especially may find themselves suspected of being journalists and/or having Kurdish/Armenian sympathies. **Avoid talking politics** with anyone unless you are absolutely sure you can trust them, and, if you are questioned, keep calm, smile a lot, and emphasize wherever possible that you are a *turist* (tourist). Of more concern to the average visitor are the violent **pro-Kurdish street demonstrations** that break out from time to time in southeastern cities such as Diyarbakır and Van – though major cities in the west of the country are not immune, especially Istanbul, Adana and Mersin, which have large and sometimes volatile Kurdish communities. One traditional spark for demonstrations is the Kurdish New Year or Nevruz (Newroz), on or around March 21. More information on the Kurdish problem is provided in Contexts (see p.678).

Electricity

Turkey operates on **220 volts**, **50 Hz**. Most European appliances should work as long as you have an adaptor for European-style two-pin plugs. American appliances will need a transformer as well as an adaptor.

Entry requirements

To enter Turkey, you'll need a passport with at least six months' validity, and tourist visas are required for citizens of several countries including the UK, USA, Ireland, Australia, Canada and South Africa; New Zealanders do not need advance visas. Prior to April 2014, visas were bought at the point of entry to Turkey. As of April 2014, visitors who require a visa should buy an electronic version in advance of their trip, available online from Ⓦ www.evisa.gov.tr. Filling in the online form is a simple process, and payment is by Mastercard or Visa debit/credit card (from the UK, USA and Ireland US$20; Australia and Canada US$60; South Africa free). Print out the e-visa and take it with you to the point of entry. **Visas** are multiple entry, and for most visitors, including citizens of the UK, US, Ireland, Canada, Australia and New Zealand, are valid for 90 days in 180 days from the date requested on your e-visa application (or from entry for New Zealanders). South African visas are valid 30 days in 180. It is usually possible to obtain a visa at the point of entry, but fees are higher and queues sometimes long. Note that entry requirements can and do change, so check what's

required well before your intended departure date at Ⓦ mfa.gov.tr.

If you want to stay in the country longer than a tourist visa allows, the best option is to apply for a six-month **residence permit** from the Security Division (*Emniyet Müdürlüğü*), preferably in a provincial capital that's used to foreigners. Do this well before your time expires, as it takes at least two weeks to process. You will need to complete an *"Ikamet izni beyanname formu"* application form and supply four passport-sized photographs, along with photocopies from your passport of the photo-page and the page showing your last entry into Turkey. The rub is that you also need to show that you have changed US$500 for each of the six months – showing change receipts from a bank or *döviz* will suffice. Residence permit rates vary according to nationality – UK citizens, for example, pay US$80 (payable in ₺, according to the exchange rate on the day you apply), but the cost of the "blue book" containing the permit is a steep ₺172. This is a one-off payment, however, as once you have the book you can keep renewing your permit for periods of between six months and ten years.

Turkish embassies and consulates abroad

Australia 60 Mugga Way, Red Hill, Canberra ACT 2603 Ⓣ 02 6295 0227.
Canada 197 Wurtemburg St, Ottawa, ON K1N 8L9 Ⓣ 613 789 4044.
Ireland 11 Clyde Rd, Ballsbridge, Dublin 4 Ⓣ 01 668 5240.
New Zealand 15–17 Murphy St, Level 8, Wellington Ⓣ 04 472 1290.
South Africa 1067 Church St, Hatfield 0181, Pretoria Ⓣ 012 342 5063.
UK 43 Belgrave Square, London SW1X 8PA Ⓣ 020 7393 0202.
US 2525 Massachusetts Ave NW, Washington, DC 20008 Ⓣ 202 612 6700.

Customs and border inspections

As Turkey is not yet an EU member, **duty-free limits** – and sales – for alcohol and tobacco are still prevalent. Limits are posted clearly at Istanbul's airports, and they apply for all frontiers.

Few people get stopped departing Turkey, but the guards may be on the lookout for **antiquities** and **fossils**. Penalties for trying to smuggle these out include long jail sentences, plus a large fine. What actually constitutes an antiquity is rather vague (see box, p.53), but it's best not to take any chances.

Insurance

It is essential to take out an **insurance policy** before you travel, to cover against illness or injury, as well as theft or loss. Some all-risks homeowners'

> ## ROUGH GUIDES TRAVEL INSURANCE
>
> Rough Guides has teamed up with WorldNomads.com to offer great **travel insurance** deals. Policies are available to residents of over 150 countries, with cover for a wide range of **adventure sports**, 24hr emergency assistance, high levels of medical and evacuation cover and a stream of **travel safety information**. Roughguides.com users can take advantage of their policies online 24/7, from anywhere in the world – even if you're already travelling. And since plans often change when you're on the road, you can extend your policy and even claim online. Roughguides.com users who buy travel insurance with WorldNomads.com can also leave a positive footprint and donate to a community development project. For more information go to ⓦ**roughguides.com/shop**.

or renters' insurance policies may cover your possessions when overseas, and many private medical schemes (such as BUPA and WPA) offer coverage extensions for abroad.

Most policies exclude so-called **dangerous sports** unless an extra premium is paid: in Turkey this can mean scuba diving, whitewater rafting, paragliding, windsurfing and trekking, though probably not kayaking or jeep safaris. Travel agents and package operators may require travel insurance when you book a holiday – you're not obliged to take theirs, though you have to sign a declaration saying that you already have another policy. Similarly, many no-frills airlines make a tidy sum from selling unnecessary insurance at the time of booking – beware, and opt out.

Internet

Most hotels, pensions and hostels have **wi-fi access**, as do an ever-increasing number of cafés. Access is usually free except in the more expensive international chain hotels. Rates in internet cafés, in decline since the advent of wi-fi and 4G phones, tend to be ₺2 per hour. The Turkish-character keyboard you'll probably be faced with may cause some confusion. The "@" sign is made by simultaneously pressing the "ALT" and "q" keys. More frustrating is the dotless "ı" (confusingly enough found right where you'll be expecting the conventional "i") – the Western "i" is located second key from right, middle row.

Mail

Post offices are easily spotted by their bold black-on-yellow **PTT** (Posta, Telegraf, Telefon) signs. Stamps are only available from the PTT, whose website (ⓦptt .gov.tr) has a (not necessarily up-to-date) English-language listing of services and prices. Post offices are generally open Monday to Friday 8.30am to 5.30pm and until noon on Saturday. Airmail (uçakla) rates to Europe are ₺2.5 for postcards, ₺2.5 for letters up to 20g, ₺31.25 for 2kg, the maximum weight for letters. Delivery to Europe or North America can take seven to ten days. A pricier express (acele) service cuts delivery times to the EU to about three days. When sending airmail, it's best to give your stamped letter/card to the clerk behind the counter, who will ensure it gets put in the right place; otherwise, place it in the relevant slot if one is available (yurtdışı for abroad; yurtiçi for elsewhere in Turkey).

Maps

Maps of Turkey are notoriously poor quality owing to the lack of survey-based cartography. Reasonable, easily obtainable choices include Insight's Turkey West and Turkey (both 1:800,000), both of which are easy to read and reasonably accurate, and the equally reliable Turkey Geocentre Euro Map (1:750,000) and Michelin's National Turkey (1:1000,000). Reise Know How's Turkey and the Mediterranean Coast and Cappadicia (both 1:700,000) are also good.

The best easily available regional touring maps are Sabri Aydal's 1:250,000 products for Cappadocia, Lycia, Pamphylia and Pisidia, available from bookshops and museums within Turkey. Kartographischer Verlag Reinhard Ryborsch (1:500,000; Frankfurt, Germany) Turkey maps, which cover the entire country in seven maps, are out of print but sometimes turn up in local shops or online.

Istanbul, Ankara, Antalya, Bursa and İzmir (as well as overseas) tourist offices stock reasonable, free **city street plans**. Sketch plans from provincial tourist offices vary widely in quality.

Among **Turkish-produced city maps**, Net's All of Istanbul (1:9000) is more comprehensive than Keskin Colour's Istanbul Street Plan (1:8500) and includes useful maps of the Prince's islands. The most detailed A–Z-style atlas for the European side, ideal for out-of-the-way monuments, is Mepmedya's Istanbul Avrupa Yakası (1:7500), though it's pricey (£32) and heavy. All are available in Istanbul, the latter also abroad.

For **trekking maps** see p.55.

Money

Turkey's currency is the **Turkish Lira** (Türk Lirası) or ₺ for short, divided into smaller units known as kuruş. Coins come in denominations of 1, 5, 10, 25, 50 kuruş and ₺1, with notes in denominations of ₺5, ₺10, ₺20, ₺50, ₺100 and ₺200. The symbol ₺, introduced in 2012, is phasing out the old system, where the price was suffixed by the letters TL, as in 10TL, but plenty of places still use the acronym.

At the time of writing the **exchange rate** was around ₺3.06 to the euro, ₺4.3 to the pound and ₺2.9 to the US dollar. As recently as 2004, hyper-inflation meant that millions of lira were needed to purchase the smallest everyday item. Many Turks still talk in millions, which can be confusing when you are asked for "*bir milyon*" or one million lira for a ₺1 glass of tea.

Rates for foreign currency are always better inside Turkey, so try not to buy much lira at home. Conversely, don't leave Turkey with unspent lira, as you won't get a decent exchange rate for them outside the country. It's wise to bring a fair wad of **hard currency** with you (euros are best, though US dollars and sterling are often accepted), as you can often use it to pay directly for souvenirs or accommodation (prices for both are frequently quoted in euros). **Travellers' cheques** are, frankly, not worth the bother, as exchange offices (see below) and some banks refuse them.

Changing money

All banks will change money, but the best rate is usually given by the **state-owned bank** Ziraat Bankası, which has dedicated *döviz* (exchange) counters – but despite the automated ticket/queuing system, queues can be long. **Döviz**, or exchange houses, are common in Turkey's cities and resorts. They buy and sell foreign currency of most sorts instantly, and have the convenience of long opening hours (usually 9/10am–8/10pm) and short or nonexistent queues. Most do not charge commission, but give a lower rate than the banks.

Remember to keep all foreign-exchange slips with you until departure, if only to prove the value of purchases made in case of queries by customs.

Credit/debit cards and ATMs

Credit cards are widely used in hotels, shops, restaurants, travel agencies and entertainment venues and with no commission (though many hotels and shops offer discounts for cash rather than credit-card payments). Don't expect, however, to use your card in basic eating places or small corner shops. Swipe readers plus **chip-and-PIN** protocol are now the norm in most of Turkey.

The simplest way to get hold of money in Turkey is to use the widespread **ATM** network. Most bank ATMs will accept any debit cards that are part of the Cirrus, Maestro or Visa/Plus systems. Screen prompts are given in English on request. You can also normally get cash advances at any bank displaying the appropriate sign, and in major cities and resorts some ATMs will give euros and dollars. It's safest to use ATMs attached to banks during normal working hours, so help can be summoned if your card is eaten (not uncommon). Turkish ATMs sometimes "time out" without disgorging cash, while your home bank may still debit your account – leaving you to argue the toss with them. ATM fraud is rife in Turkey – make sure you are not overlooked when keying in your PIN. You can also use Visa or Master-Card credit cards to get cash from ATMs, for a fee.

Opening hours and public holidays

Office workers keep conventional Monday–Friday 9am–6pm schedules, with a full lunch hour. Civil servants, including tourist offices and museum staff, in theory work 8.30am–5.30pm, but in practice hours can be much more erratic – don't expect to get official business attended to the same day after 2.30pm. Most state **banks** are open Monday–Friday 8.30am–noon and 1.30pm–5pm. Private banks such as Garanti Bankası and Köç operate throughout the day.

Ordinary **shops**, including large department stores and mall outlets, are open continuously from 8.30am or 9am until 7pm or 8pm (sometimes even later in major cities and resorts). Craftsmen and bazaar stallholders often work Monday–Saturday 9am–8/9pm,with only short breaks for meals, tea or prayers. Even on Sunday the trades-men's area may not be completely shut down – though don't count on this.

Museums hours vary quite considerably but are generally open from 8.30am or 9am until 4.30pm or 5pm in winter, later in the summer. Many museums in major tourist areas such as Istanbul have switched to being open 9am–7pm from April to October, and 9am–5pm November to March. Virtually all state, and some private, museums are closed on Monday, though in Istanbul closing days are staggered, so make sure you check the individual listings. All tourist sites and museums are closed on the mornings of public holidays (see p.61). Mosques are theoretically open all the time, but many of the less visited ones are kept locked outside of prayer times, and many do not encourage visitors at prayer times.

Public holidays

Secular **public holidays** are generally marked by processions of schoolchildren or the military, or by some demonstration of national strength and dignity, such as a sports display. Banks and government offices will normally be closed on these days (exceptions given below). See p.48 for religious holidays.

Jan 1 *Yılbaşı* – New Year's Day.

April 23 *Ulusal Egemenlik ve Çocuk Bayramı* – Independence Day, celebrating the first meeting of the new Republican parliament in Ankara, and Children's Day.

May 19 *Gençlik ve Spor Günü* – Youth and Sports Day, also Atatürk's birthday.

May 29 *İstanbul'un Fetih* İstanbul's capture by Mehmet the Conqueror in 1453 (İstanbul only).

July 1 *Denizcilik Günü* – Navy Day (banks and offices open).

Aug 26 *Silahlı Kuvvetler Günü* – Armed Forces Day (banks and offices open).

Aug 30 *Zafer Bayramı* – Celebration of the Turkish victory over the Greek forces at Dumlupınar in 1922.

Sept 9 *Kurtuluş Günü* – Liberation Day, with parades and speeches marking the end of the Independence War (İzmir only).

Oct 29 *Cumhuriyet Bayramı* – commemorates the proclamation of the Republic by Atatürk in 1923.

Nov 10 **Anniversary of Atatürk's death in 1938**. Observed at 9.05am (the time of his demise), when the whole country stops whatever it's doing and maintains a respectful silence for one minute. It's worth being on a Bosphorus ferry then, when all the engines are turned off, and the boats drift and sound their foghorns mournfully.

USEFUL TELEPHONE NUMBERS

EMERGENCY NUMBERS
Ambulance ☎ 112
Fire ☎ 110
Police ☎ 155
Tourist Police ☎ 0212 527 4503

ASSISTANCE
Directory assistance ☎ 118
International operator (reverse charges) ☎ 115
Intercity operator ☎ 131

INTERNATIONAL DIALLING CODES
Australia ☎ 61
Ireland ☎ 353
New Zealand ☎ 64
South Africa ☎ 27
UK ☎ 44
US & Canada ☎ 1

Phones

Most fixed-line **telecom services** are provided by TT (Türk Telekom); its website (🌐 turktelekom.com .tr) has an English-language page listing all services and tariffs. The best place to make phone calls is from either a PTT (post office) or a TT centre. Inside, or just adjacent, there is usually a row of card (*köntürlü* or *smartkart*) call boxes (TTs are blue and turquoise), and/or a *köntürlü* (metered, clerk-attended) phone, the latter sometimes in a closed booth. **Public phones** are to be found in squares and parks, outside many public buildings and at train stations and ferry terminals. The standard Turkish phone replies are the Frenchified *Allo* or the more local *Buyurun* (literally, "Avail yourself/at your service").

"Smart" **phonecards** are available from PTT or TT centres; when using these, wait for the number of units remaining to appear on the screen before you dial, and be aware that you will have little warning before being cut off. Cards are available for ₺5, ₺10 and ₺25. A number of phones have also been adapted to accept foreign **credit cards**. **Metered booths** inside PTTs or TTs, or at street kiosks or shops (look for signs reading *köntürlü telefon bulunur*), work out more expensive than cards, but are certainly far cheaper than hotels, and also tend to be quieter (plus you won't be cut off). Their disadvantage is that you can't see the meter ticking over, and instances of overcharging are not unknown.

Overseas calls

Overseas call rates are ₺0.25 per minute to Europe or North America. Try not to make anything other than local calls from a hotel room – there's usually a minimum 100 percent surcharge on phonecard rates. For extended chat overseas, it's best to buy an international phonecard. Best is the Alocard, available from PTT branches and usable in public phones. Reveal the 12-digit PIN by scratching; then call the domestic access number, followed by the destination number. Rates are low – for example, a ₺10 card allows 104 minutes to the UK or US. The cards can also be used for domestic calls, giving 140 minutes of calling time.

Turkey uses a system of eleven-digit **phone numbers** nationwide, consisting of four-digit area or mobile-provider codes (all starting with "0") plus a seven-digit subscriber number.

To call a number in Turkey **from overseas**, dial your country's international access code, then 90 for Turkey, then the area or mobile code minus the

GETTING MOBILE

Given the Turkish penchant for chatting, **mobile phones** are essential accessories here. Assuming that you have a roaming facility, your home mobile will connect with one of the local network providers – except those from the US, which don't work in Turkey. Charges, though, are high (up to £1.30/min to the UK), and you pay for incoming calls as well. Purchasing a **local SIM card** and pay-as-you-go package may be worth considering if you intend to make a lot of calls. The cheapest Turkcell SIM card package (which can take up to 24hr to activate) costs ₺51, which includes 100 minutes of domestic call time, 1000 domestic SMS messages and 2GB of internet use. Typically, calls cost ₺1 per min to Europe and North America, an SMS message to the UK the same. To purchase a SIM card, you'll need to sign an agreement form and present your passport for photocopying at a major Turkcell, Avea or Vodafone outlet where they'll fit the new card. All three companies have stands at arrivals in Istanbul's Atatürk and Sabiha Gökçen airports; Turkcell has the widest coverage. Note that the rules on bringing in mobiles from overseas and using them with a Turkish SIM card change regularly, mainly to avoid flooding the market with cheaply imported secondhand phones. At the time of writing, once-stringent rules had been relaxed, enabling a foreign mobile registered at a legitimate outlet to be used with a Turkish SIM for six months before it is blocked – though it needs to be topped up with a minimum of ₺15 credit at least once in that time. If you buy from one of the many smaller mobile phone stores and don't sign an agreement, you run the risk of your phone not being registered for use in Turkey, and it will be blocked within a matter of days.

initial zero, and finally the subscriber number. To call home **from Turkey**, dial ❶00 followed by the relevant international dialling code (see above), then the area code (without the initial zero if there is one), then the number.

Time

Turkey is two hours ahead of GMT in winter. As in Europe, daylight saving is observed between March and October – clocks change at 2am on the last Sunday in each of those months – so effectively Turkey remains two hours ahead of the UK year-round.

Tourist information

Most Turkish towns of any size will have a *Turizm Danışma Bürosu* or **tourist office** of some sort, often lodged inside the *Belediye* (city hall) in the smaller places. However, outside the larger cities and obvious tourist destinations there's often little hard information to be had, and world-weary staff may dismiss you with useless brochures. Lists of accommodation are sometimes kept at the busier offices; personnel, however, will generally not make bookings. On the other hand, staff in out-of-the-way places can be embarrassingly helpful. It's best to have a specific question – about bus schedules, festival ticket availability or museum opening hours – although in remote regions there is no guarantee that there will be anyone who can speak English.

Tourist offices generally adhere to a standard opening schedule of Monday–Friday 8.30am–2.30pm and 1.30–5.30pm. Between May and September in big-name resorts and large cities, these hours extend well into the evening and through much of the weekend. In winter, by contrast, many tourist offices in out-of-the-way spots will be shut most of the time.

Useful tourist websites

Ⓦ **biletix.com** A booking service for arts, cultural, music and sports events (mainly in Istanbul and Ankara), in both English and Turkish.

Ⓦ **cultureroutesinturkey.com** Umbrella site for the country's hiking, cycling and horseriding trails.

Ⓦ **goturkey.com** Turkey's official tourist information site.

Ⓦ **istanbuleats.com** Fascinating blog-cum-guide to Istanbul's food scene – especially off-the-beaten-track, salt-of-the-earth places, as well as general info on Turkish food.

Ⓦ **muze.gov.tr** Government website with information on the country's state-run museums, including the latest opening hours and admission fees.

Ⓦ **mymerhaba.com** Intended for long-term residents, and strongest on Istanbul, but nonetheless an authoritative, wide-ranging site with news of upcoming events and ticket-booking functions.

Ⓦ **turkeycentral.com** Useful information portal with links to a huge range of sites from scuba-diving operators to estate agents.

Ⓦ **turkeytravelplanner.com** This very useful site has loads of practical tips for journey planning, plus many links to vetted service providers.

Ⓦ **turkishculture.org** Not terribly innovative – but it does give a useful rundown on everything from architecture to ceramics, literature to music and lifestyles to cuisine – with plenty of photographs and illustrations.

Ⓦ **yabangee.com** The site of choice for young, literate expats, with listings, features and blogs.

Istanbul
and around

HAGHIA SOPHIA

1

Istanbul and around

Uniquely among the world's cities, Istanbul stands astride two continents, Europe and Asia. As if its spectacular geographical location were not enough, it can also boast of being the only city to have played capital to consecutive Christian and Islamic empires, a role that has shaped the region's history for more than 2500 years and bequeathed to Istanbul a staggering wealth of attractions; these range from the masterpiece Byzantine church of Haghia Sophia (Aya Sofya) to the formidable city walls, and the domes and minarets of the Ottoman mosques and palaces that dominate the city skyline. Although no longer its capital, the city remains the vibrant economic, cultural and intellectual heart of modern Turkey, a bustling, go-ahead city where east really does meet west.

In conservative districts such as Fatih, bearded men sporting skullcaps and baggy *shalwar*-style trousers devoutly heed the call to prayer, while women wouldn't dream of leaving the house with their heads uncovered. Yet across the water, the tidal wave of humanity sweeping down İstiklal Caddesi (Independence Street) includes young Turkish men and women in designer jeans and trainers who have rarely ever been to a mosque. In business districts such as Şişli, commuters arrive via the metro to work in high-rise office blocks, shop in state-of-the-art malls, and at weekends can be out clubbing until 6am.

Whether yours is the Istanbul of the Blue Mosque and the Topkapı Palace, or the Beyoğlu nightclubs and swish rooftop cocktail bars, the city takes time to get to know. Three to four days is enough to see the major historical sights in **Sultanahmet** and take a ferry trip on the **Bosphorus**. But plan on staying a week, or even two, if you want to fully explore the backstreets of the **old city** and the outlying suburbs and islands.

Brief history

In 2008, while digging the Yenikapı metro station, archeologists uncovered a Neolithic settlement dating back to circa 6500 BC. In popular tradition, however, the city was founded in the seventh century BC by **Byzas**, from Megara in Greece – hence the original name of **Byzantium**. Over the next thousand years, Byzantium became an important centre of trade and commerce, though not until the early fourth century AD did it reach the zenith of its wealth, power and prestige. For more than 350 years, it had been part of the Roman province of Asia. On Diocletian's retirement in 305, Licinius and **Constantine** fought for control of the empire. Constantine finally defeated his rival on the hills above Chrysopolis (Üsküdar) and chose Byzantium as the site for the new **capital of the Roman Empire** in 330 BC. The hilly promontory, commanding the Bosphorus and easily

TOPKAPI PALACE

Highlights

① Haghia Sophia The monumental Church of the Divine Wisdom is the ultimate expression of Byzantine architecture. **See p.72**

② Topkapı Palace Contemplate the majesty of the Ottoman sultanate in the fine buildings, gilded pavilions and immaculate gardens of this beautiful palace complex. **See p.76**

③ Kariye Museum Mosaics and frescoes portraying the life of Christ are among Istanbul's most evocative Byzantine treasures. **See p.99**

④ Galata Bridge Spanning the bustling waters of the Golden Horn, this landmark bridge, packed with simple fish restaurants and bars, is wonderful at sunset. **See p.100**

⑤ İstiklal Caddesi Lined with attractive nineteenth-century apartments, this lively street is the spine of the pulsating entertainment quarter of Beyoğlu. **See p.104**

⑥ Istanbul Modern This bold contemporary art gallery enjoys stunning views over the Bosphorus from a converted warehouse. **See p.106**

⑦ Cruise the Bosphorus Float past sumptuous villas, imposing fortresses, timeworn villages and two intercontinental bridges. **See p.115**

⑧ Princes' Islands One of the world's cheapest cruises takes you from the city's heaving streets to these tranquil, historic islands, in the sparkling Sea of Marmara. **See p.140**

HIGHLIGHTS ARE MARKED ON THE MAPS ON P.68 & PP.70–71

1

defensible on its landward side, was a superb choice. It was also well placed for access to the troublesome frontiers of both Europe and the Persian Empire.

In 395, the **division of the Roman Empire** between the two sons of Theodosius I left what was now named **Constantinople** as capital of the eastern part of the empire. It rapidly developed its own distinctive character, dissociating itself from Rome and adopting the Greek language and **Christianity**. Long and successful government was interrupted briefly, in Justinian's reign, by the Nika riots in 532. Half a century later, however, the dissolution of the Byzantine Empire had begun, as waves of Persians, Avars and Slavs attacked from the east and north. The empire was overrun by Arab invaders in the seventh and eighth centuries, and by Bulgars in the ninth and tenth. Only the city walls saved Constantinople, and even these could not keep out the **Crusaders**, who breached the sea walls in 1204 and sacked the city.

The Ottoman conquest

As the Byzantine Empire declined, the **Ottoman Empire** expanded. The Ottomans established first Bursa, then Edirne, as their capital, and Ottoman territory effectively surrounded the city long before it was taken. In 1453, **Mehmet II (the Conqueror)** – also known as Fatih Sultan Mehmet – besieged the city, which fell after seven weeks. Following the capture and subsequent pillage, Mehmet II began to rebuild the city, starting with a new palace and continuing with the Mosque of the Conqueror (Fatih Camii) and many smaller complexes. Tolerant of other religions, Mehmet actively encouraged Greek and Armenian Christians to take up residence in the city. His

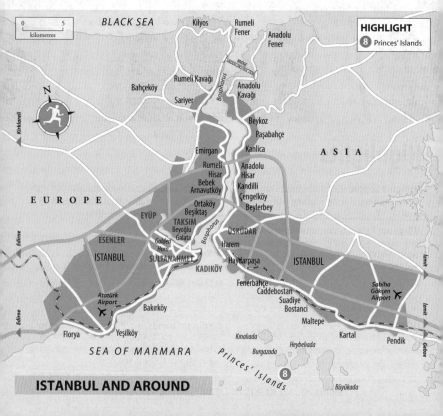

ISTANBUL AND AROUND

ISTANBUL ORIENTATION

1

Istanbul is divided in two by the **Bosphorus**, the narrow 30km strait that separates Europe from Asia and links the Black Sea and the Sea of Marmara. Feeding into the southern end of the strait from the European side, the **Golden Horn** is a 7km-long inlet of water that empties into the mouth of the Bosphorus. The European side of the city effectively has two **centres**, separated by the Golden Horn. The old city, centred on the **Sultanahmet district**, is Istanbul's historical core and home to the main sights, while **Beyoğlu/Taksim**, north of the Horn, form the fulcrum of the modern city. The two can easily be made out from the water, distinguished respectively by the landmarks of the Topkapı Palace and the Genoese Galata Tower.

A little way west of Sultanahmet, the massive Grand Bazaar (**Kapalı Çarşı**) is the focal point of a disparate area stretching from the shores of the Sea of Marmara in the south up to the hill overlooking the Golden Horn to the north. Above is the commanding presence of the impressive **Süleymaniye Camii**. Some 6km west of the old city, stretching between the Sea of Marmara and the Golden Horn, are the remarkably intact Byzantine **land walls**.

From Sultanahmet and the waterfront district just north of it, Eminönü, you're most likely to cross the Golden Horn by the Galata Bridge, entering the hip port area of **Karaköy**, then heading up the steep hill through the ancient **Galata** district. Near the northern end of Galata Bridge, the **Tünel**, the French-built underground funicular railway, chugs up to **Beyoğlu**, the city's elegant nineteenth-century European quarter. From the upper Tünel station, an antique tram runs the length of Beyoğlu's pedestrianized boulevard, **İstiklal Caddesi**, to **Taksim Square**, the twin focal points of the modern city's best hotels, bars, clubs and restaurants.

North of Taksim, on the M2 metro line, the city's newest business districts of Harbiye, Etiler, Nişantaşı and Şişli hold many airline offices and embassies. Downhill from Taksim, on the Bosphorus shore, lie Tophane, **Beşiktaş** and **Ortaköy**, inner-city districts with scenic waterside locations and a number of historic palaces and parks. Across the straits, in Asia, the main centres of **Üsküdar**, **Haydarpaşa and Kadıköy** form part of Istanbul's commuter belt, but also have a few architectural attractions and decent shops, restaurants and clubs.

successor Beyazıt II continued this policy, settling Jewish refugees from Spain into the city in an attempt to improve the economy.

In the century following the Conquest, the victory was reinforced by the great military achievements of **Selim the Grim** and by the reign of **Süleyman the Magnificent** (1520–66), "the Lawgiver" and greatest of all Ottoman leaders. His attempted conquest of Europe was only thwarted at the gates of Vienna, and the wealth gained in his military conquests funded the work of **Mimar Sinan**, the finest Ottoman architect.

From Ottoman Empire to Turkish Republic

A century after the death of Süleyman, the empire began to show signs of **decay**. Territorial losses abroad combined with corruption at home, which insinuated its way into the very heart of the empire, Topkapı Palace itself. Newly crowned sultans emerged, often insane, from the institution known as the Cage (see p.77), while others spent time in the harem rather than on the battlefield, consorting with women who increasingly became involved in grand-scale political intrigue.

As Ottoman territory was lost to the West, succeeding sultans became interested in Western institutional models. A short-lived parliament of 1876 was dissolved after a year by Abdülhamit II, but the **forces of reform** led to his deposition in 1909. The end of World War I saw Istanbul occupied by Allied troops as the victors procrastinated over how best to manage the rump of the once-great empire. After the War of Independence, Atatürk's declaration of the **Republic** in 1923 and the creation of a new capital in Ankara effectively solved the problem.

Istanbul today

The **population** of Greater Istanbul has increased twelvefold since the establishment of the Turkish Republic, and stands today at around 15 million. This rapid urban growth has

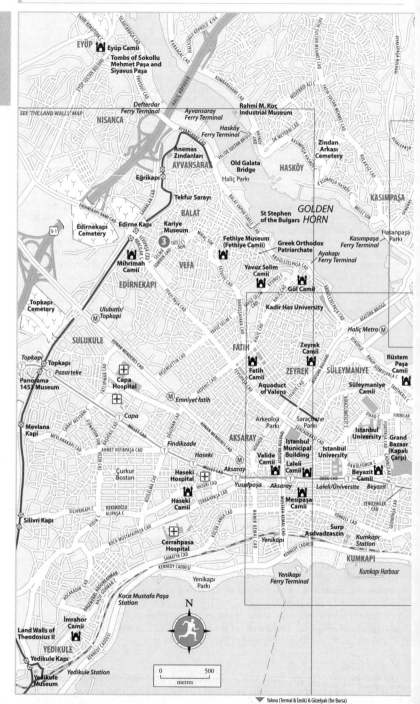

EYÜP

Eyüp Camii
Tombs of Sokollu
Mehmet Paşa and
Siyavuş Paşa

SEE THE LAND WALLS MAP

NISANCA

Defterdar
Ferry Terminal

Ayvansaray
Ferry Terminal

Rahmi M. Koç
Industrial Museum

Hasköy
Ferry Terminal

Zindan
Arkası
Cemetery

Anemas
Zindanları

AYVANSARAY

Eğrikapı

Old Galata
Bridge

HASKÖY

Haliç Parkı

KASIMPAŞA

Tekfur Sarayı

BALAT

St Stephen
of the Bulgars

GOLDEN
HORN

Kasımpaşa
Ferry Terminal

Hasanpaşa
Parkı

Edirnekapı
Cemetery

Edirne Kapı

Kariye
Museum

Fethiye Museum
(Fethiye Camii)

Greek Orthodox
Patriarchate

Ayakapı
Ferry Terminal

Mihrimah
Camii

VEFA

Yavuz Selim
Camii

Gül Camii

EDİRNEKAPI

Topkapı
Cemetery

Ulubatlı/
Topkapı

Kadir Has University

Haliç Metro

Rüstem
Paşa
Camii

SULUKULE

FATİH

Zeyrek
Camii

SÜLEYMANİYE

Topkapı

Topkapı

Pazarteke

Fatih
Camii

ZEYREK

Süleymaniye
Camii

Panorama
1453 Museum

Çapa
Hospital

Aquaduct
of Valens

FIRINLAR

Mevlana
Kapı

Çapa

Emniyet fatih

Arkeoloji
Parkı

Saraçhane
Parkı

Istanbul
University

Grand
Bazaar
(Kapalı
Çarşı)

Findikzade

AKSARAY

Istanbul
Municipal
Building

Istanbul
University

Beyazıt
Camii

Haseki

Valide
Camii

Laleli
Camii

Çurkur
Bostan

Haseki
Hospital

Aksaray

Yusufpaşa

Aksaray

Laleli/Üniversite

Beyazıt

Haseki
Camii

Mesipaşa
Camii

Silivri Kapı

Surp
Asdvadzaszin

Kumkapı
Station

Cerrahpaşa
Hospital

Yenikapı

KUMKAPI

Kumkapı Harbour

Koca Mustafa Paşa
Station

Yenikapı
Parkı

Yenikapı
Ferry Terminal

İmrahor
Camii

Land Walls of
Theodosius II

YEDİKULE

Yedikule Kapı

Yedikule
Museum

Yedikule Station

N

0   500
metres

▼ Yalova (Termal & İznik) & Güzelyalı (for Bursa)

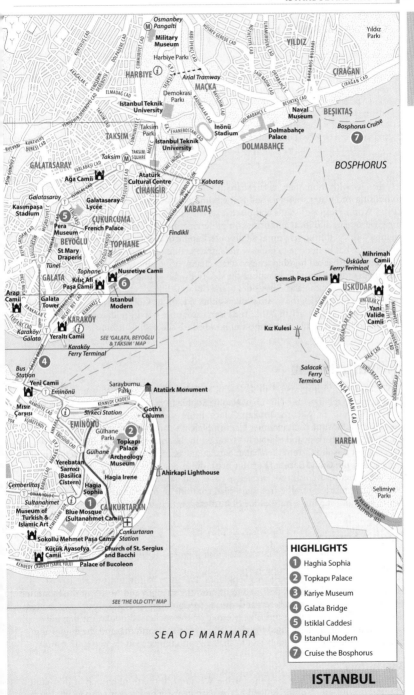

HIGHLIGHTS

1. Haghia Sophia
2. Topkapı Palace
3. Kariye Museum
4. Galata Bridge
5. Istiklal Caddesi
6. Istanbul Modern
7. Cruise the Bosphorus

ISTANBUL

CITY DANGER WATCH

Istanbul is safer than most European or North American cities, and cases of mugging and assault against tourists are rare.

For the average visitor, pickpocketing is the main cause for concern: be particularly careful around Sirkeci station, the Eminönü waterfront, the Galata Bridge, and around Taksim (especially at night). Also avoid being on or around the Byzantine land walls at dusk/night. Be very careful, too, on **public transport**, particularly when it is crowded. If you feel anyone is harassing or attempting to pickpocket you, try calling out *imdat!*, meaning "help!", and contact the tourist police (see p.136). Visitors should also be aware that political demonstrations sometimes turn into violent confrontations between police and protestors, as in the Gezi Park (part of Taksim Square) riots of 2013 (see p.105). Galatasary Meydanı, on busy İstiklal Caddesi, is the starting point for many protests.

---

left the city with more than its fair share of problems, from horrendous traffic congestion to housing and water shortages and rising crime rates. A UNESCO threat to revoke the city's "World Heritage" status and place it on the "In Danger" list focused the minds of the government and local authorities on preserving the city's glorious heritage, and Istanbul emerged from its year as a **European Capital of Culture** in 2010 with great credit.

Much else has been done to improve the infrastructure of one of the world's leading cities. A government-backed housing scheme offers quality, affordable housing to low-income families in order, eventually, to replace the shanty-dwellings that have long ringed the suburbs. The European and Asian sides of the city were linked by a rail tunnel under the Bosphorus in late 2013, the metro systems either side of the Golden Horn joined by a (controversial) bridge early in 2014. The Horn itself, once heavily polluted, has been cleaned up, and both anglers and cormorants can now be seen successfully fishing in its waters.

Sultanahmet

Most short-stay visitors spend all their time in **Sultanahmet**, home to Istanbul's main sightseeing attractions: the church of **Haghia Sophia** (Aya Sofya), the greatest legacy of the Byzantine Empire; the **Topkapı Palace**, heart of the Ottoman Empire; and the massive **Blue Mosque** (Sultanahmet Camii). Here also are the ancient **Hippodrome**, the **Museum of Turkish and Islamic Art** (housed in the former Palace of İbrahim Paşa), the eerily lit **Basilica Cistern** (Yerebatan Sarnıcı), a fascinating Byzantine underground cistern, and the **Grand Bazaar** (Kapalı Çarşı), the largest covered bazaar in the world. The monumental architecture, attractive parks and gardens, street-side cafés, and the benefits of a relatively traffic-free main road combine to make this area pleasant for both sightseeing and staying – but beware of **hustlers**, particularly the carpet-selling variety.

Haghia Sophia

Aya Sofya Müzesi • Daily: April–Oct 9am–7pm, last entry at 6pm, upper galleries close at 6.30pm; Nov–March 9am–5pm • ₺30; audioguide ₺10 • ⓦ ayasofyamuzesi.gov.tr

For almost a thousand years **Haghia Sophia**, or Aya Sofya in Turkish, was the largest enclosed space in the world, designed to impress the strength and wealth of the Byzantine emperors upon their own subjects and visiting foreign dignitaries alike. Superbly located between the Topkapı Palace and Blue Mosque on the ancient acropolis, the first hill of Istanbul, the church dominated the city skyline for a millennium, until the domes and minarets of the city's mosques began to challenge its eminence in the sixteenth century.

Brief history

Haghia Sophia, "the Church of the Divine Wisdom", is the third church of this name to stand on the site. Commissioned in the sixth century by Emperor Justinian after its predecessor had been razed to the ground in 532, its architects were **Anthemius of Tralles** and **Isidore of Miletus**. Prior to their pioneering design, most churches followed the pattern of the rectangular, pitch-roofed Roman basilica or meeting hall. Anthemius and Isidore were to create a building of a type and scale hitherto unknown to the Byzantine world. The mighty 30m-plus diameter **dome** was unprecedented, and no imitation was attempted until the sixteenth century. Constructed in five years, the building survived several earthquakes before, some twenty years later, the central dome collapsed. During reconstruction the height of the external buttresses and the dome was increased, and some of the windows blocked, resulting in an interior much

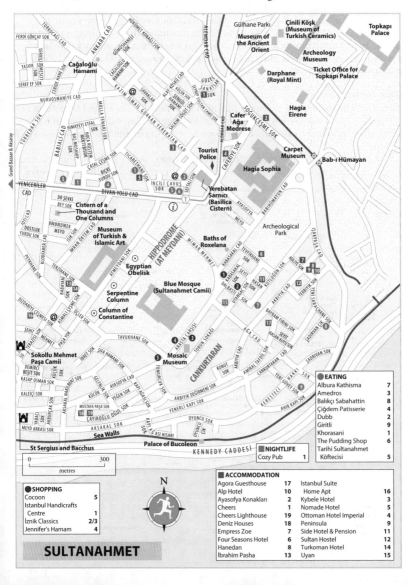

SULTANAHMET

● **EATING**
Albura Kathisma	7
Amedros	3
Balıkçı Sabahattin	8
Çiğdem Patisserie	4
Dubb	2
Giritli	9
Khorasani	1
The Pudding Shop	6
Tarihi Sultanahmet Köftecisi	5

■ **NIGHTLIFE**
Cozy Pub	1

■ **ACCOMMODATION**
Agora Guesthouse	17	Istanbul Suite Home Apt	16
Alp Hotel	10	Kybele Hotel	3
Ayasofya Konakları	2	Nomade Hotel	5
Cheers	1	Ottoman Hotel Imperial	4
Cheers Lighthouse	19	Peninsula	9
Deniz Houses	18	Side Hotel & Pension	11
Empress Zoe	7	Sultan Hostel	12
Four Seasons Hotel	6	Turkoman Hotel	14
Hanedan	8	Uyan	15
İbrahim Pasha	13		

● **SHOPPING**
Cocoon	5
Istanbul Handicrafts Centre	1
İznik Classics	2/3
Jennifer's Hamam	4

1

gloomier than originally intended. The dome collapsed again in 989 and was rebuilt in its final form by an Armenian architect, Tridat.

In 1204, Haghia Sophia was ransacked by Catholic soldiers during the **Fourth Crusade**. In 1452, far too late, the Byzantine Church reluctantly accepted union with the Catholics in the hope that Western powers would come to the aid of Constantinople against the Turks. On May 29, 1453, those who had said they would rather see the turban of a Turk than the hat of a cardinal in the streets of Constantinople got their way when the city was captured. **Mehmet the Conqueror** rode to the church of Haghia Sophia and stopped the looting that was taking place. He had the building cleared of relics and said his first prayer there on the following Friday; this former bastion of the Byzantine Christian Empire was now a mosque.

Extensive restorations were carried out on the mosaics in the mid-nineteenth century by the Swiss **Fossati brothers**, but due to Muslim sensitivities the mosaics were later covered over again. The building functioned as a **mosque** until 1932, and in 1934 it was opened as a **museum**.

The narthexes

Five large portals pierce the western wall of Haghia Sophia. The central **Orea Porta** or "Beautiful Gate" was reserved for the imperial entourage. Beyond it, the **outer narthex** or vestibule is a long cross-vaulted corridor where display boards outline the history of the site.

Five further doors lead through into the **inner narthex**, with a vaulted ceiling covered in gold mosaic and walls embellished with beautiful marble panels. The central portal

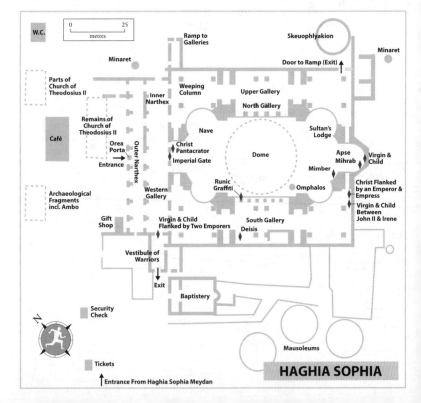

to the nave is the **Imperial Gate**, above which a superb mosaic depicts a seated **Christ Pantocrator** (the All Powerful) holding an open book showing a Greek inscription that reads "Peace be upon you, I am the light of the world". Grovelling to Christ's right, Emperor Leo IV begs forgiveness for having married more times than was permitted under Church law.

The nave

The nave awes by the sheer sense of space created by the heavenly dome, some 32m in diameter and 55m above floor level. Pierced by forty windows, its scale is cleverly exaggerated by the addition of half-domes to west and east. The tympanum walls to the south and north also emphasize the height of the building, especially as they are studded with rows of large, arched windows. At each corner of the nave are semicircular niches (*exedrae*). The galleries, which follow the line of these *exedrae* around the building, are supported by rows of columns and by four massive piers, which provide the main support for the dome.

In the northwest corner of the aisle is the **weeping column**. A legend dating from at least 1200 tells how St Gregory the Miracle-worker appeared here – the moisture subsequently seeping from the column has been believed to cure a wide range of conditions. Diagonally opposite, to the right of the apse, the circular marble-inlay panel in the floor is the **omphalos**, marking the spot where Byzantine emperors were crowned. The huge half-dome of the apse itself contains a ninth-century **mosaic of the Virgin Mary**, Christ seated on her lap.

When the building became a mosque, several new features were added to suit its new purpose. Still visible today are the *mihrab*, slightly offset in the apse, a *mimber* (pulpit), a sultan's loge, and the enormous wooden plaques that bear sacred Islamic names of God, the Prophet Mohammed, the first four caliphs and the Prophet's grandchildren Hasan and Hussein.

The upper galleries

To reach the **upper galleries** of Haghia Sophia, head up the sloping ramp at the northern end of the inner narthex. Proceed across the western gallery, past the circle of green Thessalian marble that marked the **throne of the empress**, then turn left and pass through the gap in a marble screen into the south gallery. All the **figurative mosaics** in Haghia Sophia date from after the Iconoclastic era (726–843). Among the finest is a **Deisis** scene to the right of the marble screen, depicting Christ, the Virgin and St John the Baptist. Opposite this, scratched into the balustrade running around the inside of the gallery, is some Viking **runic graffiti**.

The east wall of the south gallery holds a **mosaic of Christ flanked by an emperor and empress**. The inscriptions over their heads read "Zoë, the most pious Augusta" and "Constantine in Christ, the Lord Autocrat, faithful Emperor of the Romans, Monomachus". It is believed that the two figures are Constantine IX Monomachus and Empress Zoë. The other mosaic in the south gallery, dating from 1118, depicts the **Virgin and Child between Emperor John II Comnenus and Empress Irene**, and their son Prince Alexius, added later.

Carpet Museum

Halı Müzesi • Bab-ı Hümayün Caddesi • Tues–Sun 9am–4pm; ₺10 • ⓦ halimuzesi.com

Some three hundred years after the conversion of the Haghia Sophia into a mosque, an *imaret* (soup kitchen) was built at the northeast corner of the mosque complex, reached through an elaborate Baroque gateway. These splendid domed structures are now the well-organized, well-labelled Carpet Museum, displaying a collection of carpets and kilims woven as long ago as the fourteenth century and as recently as the twentieth.

1

MUSEUM PASS ISTANBUL

It's possible to make substantial savings on museum entry fees by purchasing a (Müzekart) issued by the Ministry of Culture and Tourism. The pass is valid for five days, costs ₺85 and gives entry to Haghia Sophia, Topkapı Palace and Harem, the Archeology Museum, Mosaic Museum, Museum of Turkish and Islamic Art, History of Science and Technology in Islam Museum, Kariye Museum and several others. Visit the first seven museums listed alone and the saving is ₺85. Another major advantage of a pass is fast-track entry to sites – a worthwhile consideration given the sometimes massive queues at Haghia Sophia and Topkapı. The passes are available from the first four museums listed above, and the Kariye Museum, from many big hotels as well as online from muze.gov.tr.

Caferağa Medresesi

Caferiye Sok, just west of Haghia Sophia • Daily 9am–6pm • ☎ 0212 528 0089

Built by the great Ottoman architect Sinan in the sixteenth century, the **Caferağa Medresesi** is a beautiful courtyard *medrese* that's now an artists' workshop-cum-traditional handicrafts shopping centre. It's a charitable foundation and a rare low-key shopping opportunity in Sultanahmet, with traditional wares for sale, plus workshops where visitors can join in and learn about painting miniatures.

Topkapı Palace

Topkapı Sarayı Müzesi • Mon & Wed–Sun: April–Oct 9am–7pm, last entry 6pm; Nov–March 9am–5pm • ₺30, free to enter the first court; ₺15 for Harem; audioguides ₺10 • ⓦ topkapisarayi.gov.tr

The **Topkapı Palace**, the symbolic and political centre of the Ottoman Empire for nearly four centuries, stands commandingly on the very tip of the promontory on which the old city of Istanbul is set. Its sheer opulence defies its origins in the tented encampments of nomadic Turkic warriors. Similar to the Alhambra of Granada, and every bit as unmissable, the palace consists of a collection of buildings arranged around a series of courtyards and attractive gardens.

The first courtyard and Haghia Eirene

The **first courtyard** of the Topkapı Palace, its service area, was always open to the general public. It's entered from the street through Mehmet the Conqueror's **Bab-ı Hümayün**, the great defensive imperial gate opposite the fountain of Ahmet III. The **palace bakeries** lie behind a wall to the right of the courtyard, while the buildings of the **imperial mint and outer treasury** are behind the wall north of the church of Haghia Eirene (Aya İrini in Turkish). In front of Haghia Eirene stood the quarters of the straw-weavers and carriers of silver pitchers, around a central courtyard in which the palace firewood was stored.

Haghia Eirene

Aya İrini • Mon & Wed–Sun 9am–4pm • ₺10

Haghia Eirene, "the Church of the Divine Peace", was one of the oldest in the city, but it was rebuilt along with Haghia Sophia after being burnt down in the Nika riots of 532. Inside this important church is the only **synthronon** (seating space for clergy in the apse of a church) in Istanbul. The interior is now plain, exposed brickwork. Most interesting is the simple mosaic in the apse, an Iconoclastic period black cross outlined against a gold background. Never converted to a mosque, it served as an arsenal for much of the Ottoman period.

Ortakapı and the second courtyard

To reach the **second courtyard** of the Topkapı Palace, you pass through the **Bab-üs Selam**, "the Gate of Salutations", otherwise known as the **Ortakapı**, or middle gate (where the entry fee is collected). Entering through Ortakapı, with the gateway to the third courtyard straight ahead of you, the Privy Stables of Mehmet II are on your immediate left, while beyond them are the buildings of the Divan and the Inner Treasury and the entrance to the Harem. Opposite the Divan, on the right side of the courtyard, is the kitchen area.

The gardens between the paths that radiate from the Ortakapı are planted with ancient cypresses and plane trees, rose bushes and lawns. Originally they would also have been resplendent with peacocks, gazelles and fountains. Running water was supplied in great quantity to the palace from the Byzantine Basilica Cistern (see p.84). This **second courtyard** would have been the scene of pageantry during state ceremonies, when the sultan would occupy his throne beneath the Bab-üs Saadet, "the Gate of Felicity".

The Divan

As you enter the buildings of the **Divan**, to the left of the second courtyard, you'll see a metal grille in the Council Chamber (the first room on the left), called "the Eye of the Sultan". Through this he could observe the proceedings of the Divan, where the eminent imperial councillors sat in session, and which took its name from the couch that ran around the room's three walls. The building dates essentially from the reign of Mehmet the Conqueror, while the Council Chamber was restored to its sixteenth-century appearance in 1945, with some of the original İznik tiles and arabesque painting.

The Armoury and Clock museums

Next to the Divan stands another building from Mehmet the Conqueror's original palace, the **Inner Treasury**, a six-domed hall that holds displays of Ottoman and European **armour**. Look out for Mehmet's curved sword, inscribed with the words "may the necks of the enemies of Sheriat become the scabbards of this sword", and all the usual paraphernalia of late medieval warfare, from maces and axes to bows and shields. Kids may be intrigued by the hologram room, with flickering 3-D representations of Ottoman janissaries and cavalry. Adjacent to the armoury museum is the fascinating **Clock Museum**, with some 380 exhibits spanning four centuries.

The kitchens

The **palace kitchens and cooks' quarters**, with their magnificent rows of chimneys, stand across the courtyard from the Armoury and Divan. Each of the ten kitchens, which had a staff of 1500, served a different purpose, including two just to make sweets and *helva*. The restored kitchen complex is home to the magnificent **Chinese and Japan Porcelain Collection**, which date from the thirteenth to the twentieth centuries, the former the largest outside of China itself.

The third courtyard

Pass through the **Bab-üs Saadet**, "the Gate of Felicity", and the **Throne Room** is immediately in front of you. This building, mainly dating from the reign of Selim I,

---

THE CAGE

The Cage or *Kafes* was the suite of rooms of the Harem where possible successors to the throne were kept incarcerated. The practice was adopted by Ahmet I as an alternative to the fratricide that had been institutionalized in the Ottoman Empire since the rule of Beyazıt II. After the death of their father, the younger princes would be kept under house arrest along with deaf mutes and a harem of concubines, while their eldest brother acceded to the throne. They remained here until such time as they were called upon to take power themselves. The concubines never left the Cage unless they became pregnant, in which case they were immediately drowned. The decline of the Ottoman Empire has been attributed in part to the institution of the Cage, as sultans who spent any length of time there emerged crazed, avaricious and debauched. The most infamous victim was "Ibrahim the Mad" (see p.80).

1

TOPKAPI PALACE

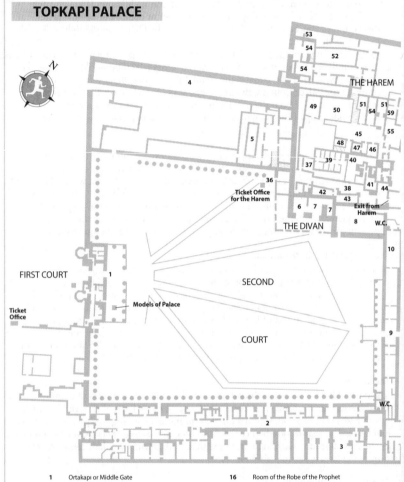

1	Ortakapı or Middle Gate	**16**	Room of the Robe of the Prophet
2	Kitchens and Cooks' Quarters	**17**	Rooms of the Relics of the Prophet
	(Chinese & Japanese Porcelain Collection)	**18**	Hall of the Treasury (Closed)
3	Reconstructed Kitchen		(Sultans' Portraits & Miniature Collection)
4	Stables and Harness Rooms	**19**	Hall of the Pantry (Museum Directorate)
5	Barrack of the Halberdiers of	**20**	Imperial Treasury (Pavilion of Mehmet II)
	the Long Tresses	**21**	Disrobing Chamber of Selim II Hamam
6	Hall of the Divan	**22**	Site of Selim II Hamam
7	Offices of the Divan	**23**	Site of Selim II Hamam Boilers
8	Inner Treasury (Arms, armour collection	**24**	Hall of the Expeditionary Force
	& Clock Museum)	**25**	Circumcision Köşkü
9	Gate of Felicity (Bab-üs Saadet)	**26**	Terrace and Bower
10	Quarters of the White Eunuchs	**27**	Pool
	(Costume collection)	**28**	Baghdad Köşkü
11	Throne Room	**29**	Pool
12	Ahmet III Library	**30**	Revan Köşkü
13	Library (Mosque of the School)	**31**	Tulip Gardens of Ahmet III
14	Harem Mosque	**32**	Mustafa Paşa Köşkü
15	Court of the Room of the Robe	**33**	Physician's Tower

34	Mecidiye Köşkü	53	Hospital Hamam
35	Third Gate	54	Hospital Kitchen Quarters
36	Entry to the Harem (Carriage Gate)	55	Sultan Ahmet Kiosk
37	Mosque of the Black Eunuchs	56	Harem Garden
38	Court of the Black Eunuchs	57	Valide Sultan's Court
39	Barrack of the Black Eunuchs	58	Valide Sultan's Dining Room
40	Princes' School	59	Valide Sultan's Bedroom
41	Quarters of the Chief Black Eunuchs	60	Valide Sultan's Hamam
42	Quarters of the Treasurer	61	Kadin's Quarters
43	Quarters of the Chamberlain	62	Golden Road
44	Aviary Gate (Kuşhane Kapisi)	63	Ahmet III Dining Room
45	Courtyard of the Women of the Harem	64	Throne Room Within
46	Kitchen of the Women	65	The Sultan's Hamam
47	Hamam of the Women	66	Osman III Terrace
48	Stairs to Bedrooms	67	Terrace of Selâmlik Garden
49	Laundry	68	Apartment of the Selamlik (Sultan's Rooms)
50	Women's Dormitory		
51	Apartments of Senior women		
52	Court of Women's hospital		

was where the sultan awaited the outcome of sessions of the Divan in order to give his assent or otherwise to their proposals. The restrained grey marble building at the centre of the third courtyard is the **Ahmet III Library**.

The room to the right of the gate and throne room and library, southwest of the courtyard, is the **Hall of the Expeditionary Force**. It houses a collection of embroidery and a very small assortment of imperial costumes.

The Treasury

The two-storey **Imperial Treasury** is housed in the rooms that once functioned as the Pavilion of Mehmet II, which takes up most of the southeast side of the third courtyard, to the right of the entrance. This two-storey building, with its colonnaded terrace, boasts the shell-shaped niches, stalactite capitals and pointed window arches so typical of the fifteenth century.

The first room contains a number of highly wrought and extremely beautiful objects, including a delicate silver model of a palace complete with tiny birds in the trees, a present to Abdülhamit II from Japan. The big crowd-puller in room two is the **Topkapı Dagger**, which starred alongside Peter Ustinov in the Sunday-matinée classic *Topkapi*. A present from Mahmut I to Nadir Shah that was waylaid and brought back when news of the shah's death reached Topkapı, the dagger is decorated with three enormous emeralds, one of which conceals a watch. The third room holds the **Spoonmaker's Diamond**, the fifth-largest diamond in the world.

The Pavilion of the Holy Mantle

Across the courtyard from the Treasury, the **Pavilion of the Holy Mantle** houses the **Rooms of the Relics of the Prophet**, holy relics brought home by Selim the Grim after his conquest of Egypt in 1517. The relics were originally viewed only by the sultan, his family and his immediate entourage on days of special religious significance. They include a footprint, hair and a tooth of the Prophet Mohammed, as well as his mantle and standard, swords of the first four caliphs, and a letter from the Prophet to the leader of the Coptic tribe.

The fourth courtyard

The **fourth courtyard** of the Topkapı Palace is entered through a passageway that runs between the Hall of the Treasury and the display of clocks and watches in the Silahdar Treasury. It consists of several gardens, each graced with pavilions, the most attractive of which are located around a wide marble terrace beyond the tulip gardens of Ahmet III.

The **Baghdad Köşkü**, the cruciform building north of the terrace, is the only pavilion currently open to the public. It was built by Murat IV to celebrate the conquest of Baghdad in 1638. The exterior and cool, dark interior are tiled in blue, turquoise and white, while the shutters and cupboard doors are inlaid with tortoiseshell and mother-of-pearl. The attractive pool and marble fountain on the terrace were the scene of debauched revels among İbrahim I and the women of his harem.

The **Circumcision Köşkü**, in the Portico of Columns above the terrace, also dates from the reign of İbrahim the Mad. The exterior is covered in prime-period İznik tiles of the sixteenth and early seventeenth centuries. At the other end of the Portico of Columns, the **Revan Köşkü** was built to commemorate the capture of Erivan (Yerevan) in the Caucasus by Mehmet IV.

The **Mecidiye Köşkü** – the last building to be erected at Topkapı – commands the finest view of any of the pavilions. It's been opened as the *Konyalı Café*, which has fine views across the Bosphorus but expensive, mediocre food.

The Harem

Mon & Wed–Sun April–Oct 9am–7pm; Nov–March 9am–4.30pm • ₺15

The **Harem** is usually relatively uncrowded because of the extra admission fee. The word "harem" means "forbidden" in Arabic; in Turkish it refers to a suite of apartments in a

1

THE WOMEN OF THE HAREM

The **women of the harem** were so shrouded in mystery that they became a source of great fascination for the world in general. Many were imported from Georgia and Caucasia for their looks, or were prisoners of war, captured in Hungary, Poland or Venice. Upon entering the harem, they would become the charges of the *haznedar usta*, who would teach them how to behave towards the sultan and the other palace inhabitants. The conditions in which most of these women lived were dangerously unhygienic, and many died of disease, or from the cold of an Istanbul winter. Those women who were chosen to enter the bedchamber of the sultan, however, were promoted to the rank of imperial odalisque, given slaves to serve them, and pleasant accommodation. If they bore a child, they would be promoted again, to become a favourite or wife, and given their own apartments. If the sultan subsequently lost affection for one of these women, he could give her in marriage to one of his courtiers.

The most renowned of the harem women was Haseki Hürrem, or **Roxelana** as she was known in the West, wife of Süleyman the Magnificent. Prior to their marriage, it was unusual for a sultan to marry at all, let alone to choose a wife from among his concubines. This was the beginning of a new age of harem intrigue, in which women began to take more control over affairs of state, often referred to as the "Rule of the Harem".

palace or private residence where the head of the household lived with his wives, odalisques (female slaves) and children. Situated on the north side of the Second Court, it consisted of over four hundred rooms, centred on the suites of the sultan and his mother, the Valide Sultan.

The Carriage Gate

The Harem was connected to the outside world by means of the **Carriage Gate**, so called because the odalisques would have entered their carriages here when they went on outings. To the left of the Carriage Gate as you enter the Harem is the Barracks of the Halberdiers of the Long Tresses, who carried logs and other loads into the Harem. The Halberdiers, who also served as imperial guardsmen, were only employed at certain hours, and even then they were blinkered. Both the Carriage Gate and the Aviary Gate were guarded by black eunuchs, who were responsible for running the Harem.

The rooms of the Harem

The **Court of the Black Eunuchs** dates mainly from a rebuilding programme that started after the great fire of 1665 damaged most of the Harem, as well as the Divan. The tiles in the eunuchs' quarters date from the seventeenth century, suggesting that the originals were destroyed in the fire. The *Altın Yol* or **Golden Road** ran the entire length of the Harem, from the quarters of the Black Eunuchs to the fourth courtyard. Strategically located at the start of the Golden Road, the **apartments of the Valide Sultan** were also rebuilt after 1665. They include a particularly lovely domed dining room.

The apartments and reception rooms of the *selâmlik*, the sultan's own rooms, lie beyond the Valide Sultan's apartments. In the largest and grandest, the **Hünkar Sofrası** or Imperial Hall, the sultan would entertain visitors. Another important room in this section is a masterwork of the architect Sinan: the **bedchamber of Murat III**, covered in sixteenth-century İznik tiles.

The northernmost rooms of the Harem are supported by immense piers and vaults, creating capacious basements that were used as dormitories and storerooms. Below the bedchamber is a large indoor **swimming pool**, with taps for hot and cold water, where Murat is supposed to have thrown gold to women who pleased him. The light and airy **library of Ahmet I**, next to the bedchamber, has windows overlooking both the Bosphorus and the Golden Horn. Beyond it, the walls of the **dining room of Ahmet III** are covered in wood panelling painted with bowls of fruit and flowers, typical of the extravagant tulip-loving sultan.

1

Visitors leave the Harem by way of the **Aviary Gate**, or Kuşhane Kapısı, into the Third Court.

Gülhane Parkı

Surrounding Topkapı Palace on all sides, **Gülhane Parkı** was once the extended gardens of the sultans. It is now a public park with a relaxed atmosphere – the nesting heron colony in spring apart – that's primarily noteworthy as home to the three museums that form the **Archeology Museum complex**, and the separate **Istanbul History of Science and Technology in Islam Museum**. The park also holds a modest array of kids' play equipment, and is home to a decent tea garden, the *Set Üstü*, which gives fine views across the Bosphorus.

The Archeology Museum complex

Osman Hamdi Bey Yokuşu, Gülhane Parkı

The **Archeology Museum complex** is entered either through Gülhane Parkı or from the first courtyard of the Topkapı Palace. A moderately thorough exploration of its three separate buildings will take at least half a day, though ongoing earthquake-proofing renovations may mean various sections are closed. The largest building is the **Archeology Museum** (Arkeoloji Müzesi), while the much smaller **Museum of the Ancient Orient** lies just beyond the ticket barrier, and the **Museum of Turkish Ceramics** (Çinili Köşk) is opposite the Archeology Museum itself.

The Archeology Museum

Arkeoloji Müzesi • Osman Hamdi Bey Yokuşu, Gülhane Parkı • Tues–Sun: April–Oct 9am–7pm; Nov–March 9am–5pm • Combined entry with Museum of the Ancient Orient and Çinili Köşk ₺15, audioguides ₺10 • ⓦ Istanbularkeoloji.gov.tr

Built by a French architect in 1891, the impressive Neoclassical **Archeology Museum** (Arkeoloji Müzesi) centres on a marvellous collection of sarcophagi from Sidon, housed in two rooms to the left of the entrance on the ground floor. The most famous is the so-called **Alexander Sarcophagus** from the late fourth century. Covered with scenes of what is presumed to be Alexander the Great hunting and in battle, it cannot be Alexander's own tomb; he's known to have been buried in Alexandria. Instead it's ascribed variously to a ruler of the Seleucid dynasty, or to the Phoenician Prince Abdolonyme.

Rooms 13 to 20, to the right of the entrance, contain a comprehensive collection of statuary dating from the Archaic through to the Roman period, much of it of superb quality. Room 16 exhibits a vivid statue of the young Alexander the Great, carved in the stylized manner popular at Pergamon, on Turkey's Aegean coast, in the second century BC.

On the first floor, **Istanbul through the Ages** traces the history of the city from archaic to Ottoman times, and includes the chain used by the Byzantines to block entry to the strategically crucial Golden Horn. The next level up exhibits some of the fascinating finds made by Schliemann and Dorpfeld at **Troy**, including beautiful gold jewellery. Down in the basement are finds from the oft-neglected **Byzantine period**, with some lavishly carved capitals among the pick of the exhibits.

The Museum of the Ancient Orient

Osman Hamdi Bey Yokuşu, Gülhane Parkı • Tues–Sun: April–Oct 9am–7pm; Nov–March 9am–5pm • Combined entry with Archeology Museum and Çinili Köşk ₺15, audioguides ₺10 • ⓦ istanbularkeoloji.gov.tr

The **Museum of the Ancient Orient** contains a small but dazzling collection of Anatolian, Egyptian and Mesopotamian artefacts. These include the oldest peace treaty known to mankind, the **Treaty of Kadesh** (1280–1269 BC), which was signed after a battle fought between Pharaoh Ramses II and the Hittite king Muvatellish ended in a

FROM TOP BASILICA CISTERN (P.84); GRAND BAZAAR (P.89) >

1

stalemate. Uncovered during excavations at the site of the Hittite capital of Hattuşa (see p.490), the version of the treaty displayed here includes a ceasefire agreement and pledges of a mutual exchange of political refugees. A copy decorates the entrance to the UN building in New York.

The blue-and-yellow **animal relief** in the corridor beyond the first room dates from the reign of Nebuchadnezzar (604–562 BC), the last hero-king of Babylonia, where it would have lined the processional way in Babylon. Other exhibits were taken from the palace-museum of Nebuchadnezzar, located at the Ishtar Gate. Another massive relief, in Room 8, depicts the **Hittite king Urpalla** presenting gifts of grapes and grain to a vegetation god, who is three times his own size.

Museum of Turkish Ceramics (Çinili Köşk)

Osman Hamdi Bey Yokuşu, Gülhane Parkı • Tues–Sun: April–Oct 9am–7pm; Nov–March 9am–5pm • Combined entry with Archeology Museum and Museum of the Ancient Orient ₺15, audioguides ₺10 • ⓦ istanbularkeoloji.gov.tr

The graceful **Çinili Köşk**, or Tiled Pavilion, was built in 1472 as a kind of grandstand, from which the sultan could watch sporting activities such as wrestling or polo. It now houses the **Museum of Turkish Ceramics**, displaying tiles of a quality equal to those in Topkapı Palace and Istanbul's older mosques, along with well-written explanations of the different periods in the history of Turkish ceramics.

Istanbul History of Science and Technology in Islam Museum

Gülhane Parkı • Mon & Wed–Sun April–Oct 9am–7pm; Oct–March 9am–5pm • ₺10

Housed in former stables, within Gülhane Parkı, the **Istanbul History of Science and Technology in Islam Museum** is a generally successful attempt to show the contribution made to civilization by scientists and inventors from the Islamic world between the eighth and sixteenth centuries. Carefully constructed replicas illustrate everything from astronomical observatories to medical equipment. Highlights include a model of a planetarium based on the tenth-century works of the Islamic astronomer as-Sigzi, and a re-creation of a twelfth-century water-powered clock, shaped like an elephant.

Basilica Cistern

Yerebatan Sarnıcı • Yerebatan Cad 13 • Daily: April–Oct 9am–6.30pm; Oct–March 9am–5.30pm • ₺20, audioguide ₺10 • ⓦ yerebatan.com

The **Basılıca Cıstern** or Yerebatan Sarnıc, literally the "Sunken Palace", once formed an integral part of the old city's water supply. Buried beneath the very core of Sultanahmet, it's the first of several such underground cisterns to have been extensively excavated.

Probably built by the Emperor Constantine in the fourth century, and enlarged by Justinian in the sixth, the cistern was supplied by aqueducts with water from the Belgrade Forest. It in turn supplied the Great Palace and later Topkapı Palace. Having fallen into disuse after the Ottoman conquest, the cistern was rediscovered in 1545 by the Frenchman **Petrus Gyllius**. His interest was aroused when he found fresh fish being sold in the streets nearby, and he enquired at local houses. The residents let him in on their "secret" – wells sunk through into the cistern, and boats kept on the water from which they could fish its depths.

Restored in 1987, the cistern is now beautifully lit and access is made easier by specially constructed walkways. The largest covered cistern in the city, at 140m by 70m, Yerebatan held eighty thousand cubic metres of water. The small brick **domes** are supported by 336 columns, many of which have Corinthian capitals. Two of the columns are supported by **Medusa heads**, clearly relics of an earlier building.

The Hippodrome

The arena of the **Hippodrome**, formerly the cultural focus of the Byzantine Empire, is now a long paved municipal park known as At Meydanı, or Square of Horses. An

Egyptian Obelisk adorns what was once the *spina* or central barrier of the chariot-racing track, at the centre of the park. It originally stood 60m tall, but only the upper third survived shipment from Egypt in the fourth century. It was commissioned to commemorate the campaigns of Thutmose III in Egypt during the sixteenth century BC, but the scenes on its base commemorate its erection in Constantinople under the direction of Theodosius I.

The **Serpentine Column**, also on the line of the *spina*, came from the Temple of Apollo at Delphi, where it was dedicated to the god by the 31 Greek cities that defeated the Persians at Plataea in 479 BC. It was brought to Constantinople by Constantine the Great. Each of the three intertwining bronze serpents originally had a head; the sole survivor is on display in the Archeology Museum (see p.82).

The third ancient monument on the *spina* is the undistinguished, 32m-high **Column of Constantine**, almost certainly not erected by that emperor.

The Blue Mosque

Sultanahmet Camii • Mon–Thurs, Sat & Sun from 9am until one hour before dusk prayer call; Fri until midday prayers

The monumental **Blue Mosque**, more properly known as the **Sultanahmet Camii**, dominates the southeastern side of the Hippodrome. With its six minarets, imposing bulk and commanding position on the skyline of old Istanbul, it is one of the best known, most visited monuments in the city. Viewed from the all-important approach from the Topkapı Palace, it forms a striking mass of shallow domes, half-domes and domed turrets, but its most striking profile is from the Sea of Marmara where, elevated above the hillside, it totally dominates its surroundings.

Visiting the mosque

The mosque is best approached from the attractive and graceful northwest, Hippodrome-facing side, from where an elaborate portal leads into the beautiful **courtyard.** Surrounded by a portico of thirty small domes, this has the same dimensions as the mosque itself. It's also possible to enter the courtyard from the Haghia Sophia side of the mosque, through the northeast portal.

Only practising Muslims are permitted to enter the prayer hall itself via the main southwest-facing door. If you are not a Muslim, exit the courtyard of the mosque via the southwest portal, then bear left along the outside of the mosque to reach a side door, where there is often a sizeable queue. Here you must remove your shoes and put them in a plastic bag (provided).

Inside, four "**elephant foot**" **pillars**, so called because of their 5m diameter, impose their disproportionate dimensions on the interior – particularly the dome, which is smaller and shallower than that of Ottoman master architect Sinan's Istanbul masterpiece, the nearby Süleymaniye Camii. The name "Blue Mosque" derives from the over twenty thousand predominantly **blue İznik tiles** that adorn the interior, though much of the "blue" is, in fact, stencilled paintwork. Most of the glass in the numerous arched windows was originally coloured Venetian bottle glass, but this has now been replaced by poor-quality modern windows.

The richly decorated **royal pavilion**, approached by ramp at the northeast corner of the complex, gives access to the sultan's loge inside the mosque. The ramp enabled the sultan to ride his horse right up to the door of his chambers.

Tomb of Sultan Ahmet

Tues–Sat 9am–4pm • Free

Outside the precinct wall to the northwest of the mosque, the *türbe* or **tomb of Sultan Ahmet** is decorated, like the mosque, with seventeenth-century İznik tiles. Buried here along with the sultan are his wife and three of his sons, two of whom (Osman II and Murat IV) ruled in their turn.

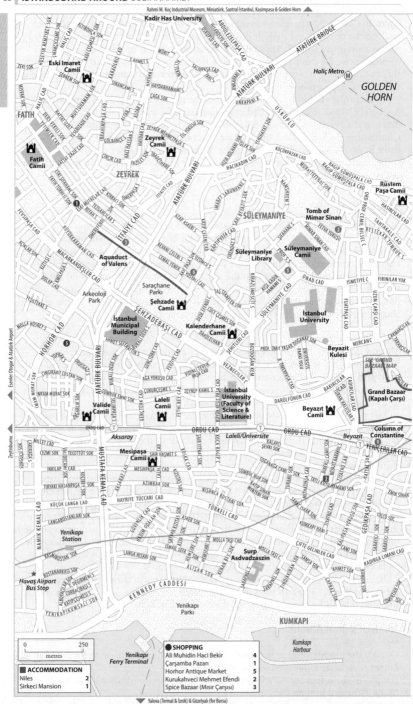

GOLDEN HORN

● SHOPPING	
Ali Muhidin Hacı Bekir	4
Çarşamba Pazarı	1
Horhor Antique Market	5
Kurukahveci Mehmet Efendi	2
Spice Bazaar (Mısır Çarşısı)	3

■ ACCOMMODATION	
Niles	2
Sirkeci Mansion	1

▼ Yalova (Termal & İzmik) & Güzelyalı (for Bursa)

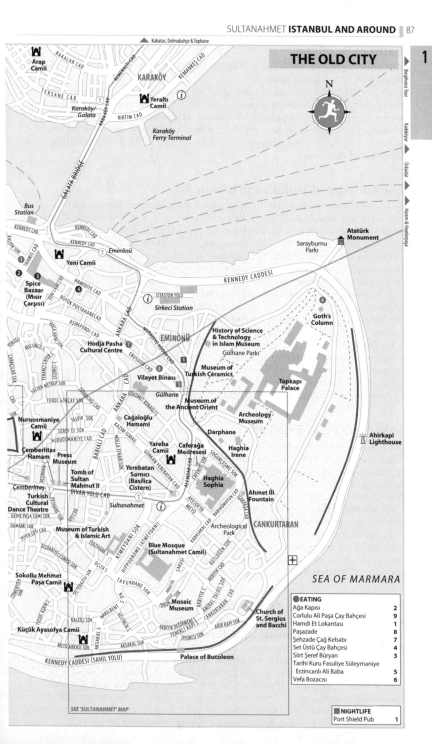

THE OLD CITY

1

Bosphorus Tour
Kadıköy
Üsküdar
Harem & Haydarpaşa

N

Kabataş, Dolmabahçe & Tophane

Arap Camii

BAKALAR CAD

KARAKÖY

KEMERALTI CAD

KEMANKEŞ CAD

TERSANE CAD

Yeraltı Camii

RIHTIM CAD

Karaköy/Galata

Karaköy Ferry Terminal

GALATA BRIDGE

Bus Station

KENNEDY CAD

KALON SOK

TAHMIS CAD

KENNEDY CAD

KENNEDY CAD

Atatürk Monument

Sarayburnu Parkı

Eminönü

Yeni Camii

KENNEDY CADDESI

Spice Bazaar (Mısır Çarşısı)

HAMIDIYE CAD

YENI CAMI CAD

BUYUK POSTAHANE CAD

ISTASYON YOLU

Sirceci Station

Goth's Column

AŞIREFENDI CAD

ANKARA CAD

MÜHENDİSHANE CAD

EMINÖNÜ

History of Science & Technology in Islam Museum

Hodja Pasha Cultural Centre

EBUSUUD CAD

Gülhane Parkı

HOCA PAŞA SOK

MACUNCU S

YORUK S

CARKCILAR SOK

TERACCI CIFTEH S

CEMES S S

S CEDIS S

SULTAN MEKTEP SOK

FERDI GÖKÇAY SOK

Museum of Turkish Ceramics

Vilayet Binası

Gülhane

Topkapı Palace

Museum of the Ancient Orient

ANKARA CAD

HÜKÜMET KONAĞI CAD

TASVIR SOK

Archeology Museum

Nuruosmaniye Camii

Çağaloğlu Hamamı

KAZIM ISMAIL

Darphane

SEREF EF SOK

NURUOSMANIYE CAD

BABIALI CAD

MOLLA FENARI SOK

Haghia Irene

Ahirkapi Lighthouse

Çemberlitaş Hamam

Press Museum

MEZHARCI

Yareba Camii

Caferağa Medresesi

SOGUKÇEŞME SOK

Tomb of Sultan Mahmut II

PEYHANE SOK

Yerebatan Sarnıcı (Basilica Cistern)

CAGALOGLU YEREBATAN CAD

Haghia Sophia

Ahmet III Fountain

Çemberlitaş

Turkish Cultural Dance Theatre

DIVAN YOLU CAD

Sultanahmet

GEDIK PAŞA CAMI SOK

AYES-OFTA MEYD

CAFERIYE SOK

ALEMDAR CAD

BASHUMAYUN CAD

BAHÇE KAPI CAD

CANKURTARAN

HAMAMI SOK

Museum of Turkish & Islamic Art

DIZDARIYECESMESI SOK

PIYER LOTI CAD

Archeological Park

KARASAKAL CAD

ATMEYDANI SOK

HIPPODROME (ATMEYDANI)

TERZIHANE S

UCLER S

Sokollu Mehmet Paşa Camii

SETTARAGASI SOK

YUSUF ASKIN S

TAVU KHANE SOK

Blue Mosque (Sultanahmet Camii)

ARASTA CARSISI

KUTLUGÜN SOK

AKBIYIK CAD

AMIRAL TAFDIL SOK

AKBIYIK CAD

KUTLUGÜN SOK

CANKURTARAN CAD

Mosaic Museum

KALEIÇI SOK

NAKILBENT SOK

AKSAKAL S

JOBUR SOK

ARKBIYE C

AKBIYIK DEGIRMENI SOK

TENEKELI KAPI S

Church of St. Sergius and Bacchi

Küçük Ayasofya Camii

MEYDARKASI SOK

AKSAKAL SOK

AHIR KAPI SOK

DUYUNCU SOK

Palace of Bucoleon

SEA OF MARMARA

KENNEDY CADDESI (SAHIL YOLU)

SEE 'SULTANAHMET' MAP

EATING

Ağa Kapısı	2
Çorlulu Ali Paşa Çay Bahçesi	9
Hamdi Et Lokantası	1
Paşazade	8
Şehzade Çağ Kebabı	7
Set Üstü Çay Bahçesi	4
Siirt Şeref Büryan	3
Tarihi Kuru Fasuliye Süleymaniye Erzincanlı Ali Baba	5
Vefa Bozacısı	6

NIGHTLIFE

Port Shield Pub	1

Baths of Roxelana

Ayasofya Hürrem Sultan Hamamı • Bab-ı Hümayün Cad 1 • Daily 7am–midnight • Bath packages €85–170; separate men and women's sections • ☎ 0212 517 3535, ⓦ ayasofyahamami.com

Built in 1556 by Mimar Sinan in honour of Süleyman the Magnificent's wife Roxelana, the opulent **Baths of Roxelana** (Ayasofya Hürrem Sultan Hamamı) reopened in 2011 after a lengthy restoration process. Virtually all its historical features – down to the marble squat toilets – have been preserved intact. It's the most expensive hamam experience in the city, but arguably worth it for the skill of the masseurs and the sheer loveliness of the interior.

The Museum of Turkish and Islamic Art

Türk ve Islam Eserleri Müzesi • Atmeydan Sok 6 • Tues–Sun: April–Oct 9am–7pm; Nov–March 9am–5pm • ₺20 • ☎ 0212 518 1805

The attractive **İbrahim Paşa Sarayı** (Palace of İbrahim Paşa) now holds the **Museum of Turkish and Islamic Art** (Türk ve İslam Eserleri Müzesi), containing one of the best-exhibited collections of Islamic artefacts in the world. The main concentration of exhibits deals with Selçuk, Mamluk and Ottoman Turkish art, though several important Timurid and Persian works are also on display. The **Selçuk Turks**, precursors of the Ottomans, are represented by some beautiful wall tiles and fine woodcarvings. Other impressive exhibits include sixteenth-century Persian miniatures and the tiny Sancak Korans, intended to be hung on the standard of the Ottoman imperial army in a *jihad* (holy war), so that the word of God would precede the troops into battle.

The **Great Hall** of the palace houses a wonderful collection of **Turkish carpets**. These range from tattered thirteenth-century remains to carpets that once adorned Istanbul's palaces, some weighing in at thousands of kilograms. On the basement floor, an ethnography section holds everything from the black goat-hair tents of the *Yörük* tribes of Anatolia, to a re-creation of the interior of a late Ottoman wooden house in Bursa.

Sokollu Mehmet Paşa Camii

Usually open; the imam should be around to unlock it during the day if not

The little-visited **Sokollu Mehmet Paşa Camii** ranks among the most attractive mosques in the city. A short walk downhill from the Hippodrome, it's one of Mimar Sinan's later buildings (1571), and was commissioned by Sokollu Mehmet Paşa, the last grand vizier of Süleyman the Magnificent.

The **interior** of the mosque is distinguished by the height of its dome and the impressive display of **İznik tiles** on its east wall. These date from the best period of Turkish ceramics: the white is pure, the green vivid, and the red intense. Calligraphic inscriptions are set against a jungle of enormous carnations and tulips, and the designs and colours are echoed all around the mosque and in the conical cap of the *mimber*, the tiling of which is unique in Istanbul.

Church of St Sergius and Bacchus

Küçük Ayasofya • 500m below the Blue Mosque, downhill on Küçük Ayasofya Cad • Daily 7am–dusk • Donations expected

Today a functioning mosque, the **Küçük Ayasofya Camii** (literally the "small mosque of Aya Sofya"), this building was, before its conversion following the Ottoman conquest of 1453, the important **Church of St Sergius and Bacchus**. Built between 527 and 536, it's actually older than Haghia Sophia up the hill. It was originally named after two Roman soldiers, **Sergius** and **Bacchus**, who were martyred for their faith and later became the patron saints of Christians in the Roman army, but was renamed in the Islamic period because of its resemblance to Haghia Sophia. The church was converted into a mosque early in the sixteenth century, during the reign of Beyazıt II.

Like most Byzantine churches of this era, its **exterior** is austere brick, and only inside can the satisfying proportions be properly appreciated. It is basically an octagon with semicircular niches at its diagonals, inscribed in a rectangle, but both these shapes are extremely irregular. A delicately carved frieze, honouring Justinian, Theodora and St Sergius, runs around the architrave under the gallery, and numerous columns sport ornate Byzantine capitals. The church was crucial to the development of Byzantine architecture as it was the first church in the city constructed with a dome.

Mosaic Museum

Büyük Saray Mozaikleri Müzesi Torun Sok, Sultanahmet • Daily: April–Oct 9am–7pm; Nov–March 9am–5pm; last entry 1hr before closing • ₺10

The mosaics displayed in the **Mosaic Museum** were originally a part of the Byzantine Great Palace, which stood on and around this area for many centuries. It is reached via the **Arasta Çarşısı** – a renovated street-bazaar selling tourist gifts, whose seventeenth-century shops were originally built to pay for the upkeep of the nearby Blue Mosque.

The building has been constructed to allow some of the mosaics, probably dating from Justinian's rebuilding programme of the sixth century, to be viewed from a catwalk as well as at floor level. Among them are portrayals of animals in their natural habitats, and domestic scenes. These include a vivid illustration of an elephant locking a lion in a deadly embrace with its trunk, and two children being led on the back of a camel.

Divan Yolu

The main approach from Sultanahmet to Beyazıt (see p.92) is **Divan Yolu**, a major thoroughfare that gained its name because it was the principal approach to the Divan from the Topkapı Gate. Hordes of people would pour along it three times a week to make their petitions to the court. In Roman and Byzantine times, this street was the Mese or "Middleway". It ran from a triumphal arch known as the **Milion**, a marked fragment of which remains at the eastern end of Divan Yolu, westwards through the city, and eventually linked in with the great Roman road system to reach as far as the Adriatic. It remains a crucial part of the city's transport network, though it is now given over to the trams that rattle their way from Zeytinburnu, through old Istanbul and over the Golden Horn to Kabataş.

The Grand Bazaar and around

Istanbul's Ottoman-era **Grand Bazaar** gets more than its fair share of souvenir-hungry visitors. The area around it, however, is relatively little explored, which is a shame as it holds some very worthwhile attractions, from the historic **Cembirlitaş Hamamı**, one of the best Turkish baths in the country, to the city's finest mosque, the hilltop **Süleymaniye Camii**. Throw in the ornate Baroque **Laleli Camii**, and it's easy to see how you can spend a day in this area alone. To get here from Sultanahmet, either walk or take the T1 tram.

The Grand Bazaar: Kapalı Çarşı

Kapalı Çarşı • Mon–Sat 9am–7pm

With 66 streets and alleys, more than four thousand shops, numerous storehouses, moneychangers and banks, a mosque, post office, police station, private security guards and its own health centre, Istanbul's **Grand Bazaar** is said to be the largest **covered bazaar** in the world. In Ottoman times it was based around two *bedestens* (domed buildings where foreign trade took place and valuable goods were stored): the İç Bedesten probably dates from the time of the Conquest, while the Sandal Bedesten

1

was added in the sixteenth century. The bazaar sprawls further, into the streets that lead down to the Golden Horn. This whole area was once controlled by strict laws laid down by the trade guilds, thus reducing competition between traders. Each shop could support just one owner and his apprentice, and successful merchants were not allowed to expand their businesses.

Visiting the bazaar

The best time to visit the bazaar is during the week, as it's very crowded with local shoppers on Saturday. Expect to get lost as most streets are either poorly marked, or their signs are hidden beneath goods hung on display. However, try finding Kavaflar Sok for **shoes**, Terlikçiler Sok for **slippers**, Kalpakçılar Başı and Kuyumcular caddesi for **gold**, and Tavuk Pazarı Sok, Kürkçüler Sok, Perdahçılar Caddesi and Bodrum Han for **leather clothing**. Carpet-sellers are just about everywhere, with more expensive collector's pieces on sale on Halıcılar Çarşısı, Takkeciler and Keseciler caddesi, and cheaper ones in the tiny Rubiye Han or İç Cebeci Han. **Ceramics** and leather and kilim **bags** can be found along Yağlıkçılar Caddesi, just off it in Çukur Han, and also along Keseciler Caddesi.

The old bazaar (İç Bedesten), located at the centre of the maze, was traditionally reserved for the most precious wares because it could be locked at night. These days, however, it's indistinguishable from the rest of the complex.

● EATING			● SHOPPING				
Bedesten Café	1		Abdulla	3	Dohko-Ethnicon	5	Şişko Osman	2
Havuzlu	2		Abdullah Şalabi	6	Koç Deri	8	Tradition	7
Subaşı Lokantası	3		Adnan & Hasan	4	Necdat Daniş	1	Yörük	9

A number of decent cafés in the bazaar (see p.122) enable shoppers to unwind and avoid the constant importuning of traders.

East of the Grand Bazaar

The landmark **Çembirlitaş** ("the hooped stone"), a burnt column of masonry also known as the **Column of Constantine**, stands on the north side of the tramline on the approach to the Grand Bazaar. Erected by Constantine the Great in 330 AD, it commemorated the city's dedication as capital of the Roman Empire. The column and baths opposite it to the east, the **Çemberlitaş Hamamı** (see below), mark the southern end of Vezirhanı Caddesi.

Turn north up here to reach the **Nuruosmaniye Camii**, just outside the bazaar to the east. Begun by Mahmut I in 1748 and finished seven years later by Osman III, this was the first and most impressive of the city's Baroque mosques.

Çemberlitaş Hamamı

Vezirhan Cad 8 • Daily 6am–midnight • ₺60, ₺95 with scrub and massage; separate men's and women's baths • ☎ 0212 522 7974, Ⓦ cemberlitashamami.com.tr

The four-hundred-year-old **Çemberlitaş Hamamı**, across Vezirhan Caddesi from the Column of Constantine, was founded in the sixteenth century by Nur Banu, one of the most powerful Valide Sultans. Architecturally it's among the finest Ottoman hamams in Istanbul, and well used to dealing with novice visitors.

The Süleymaniye Mosque Complex

Süleymaniye Külliyesi, Suleymaniye Mah, Fatih

Northwest of the Grand Bazaar, on the third hill of the old city, the **Sülemaniye Mosque Complex (Süleymaniye Külliyesi)** is an agglomeration of buildings that includes theological schools, a hospital, library, soup kitchen, caravanserai, shops and tombs. The centrepiece of the entire complex is a magnificent mosque, the **Süleymaniye Camii**. Built by the renowned architect **Mimar Sinan** (see box, p.92), in honour of his most illustrious patron, Süleyman the Magnificent, the complex is arguably his greatest achievement.

Süleymaniye Camii

Daily except for prayer times • Free

The beautifully restored **Süleymaniye Camii** is entered via the southwest portal, where plastic bags are provided for footwear. Once inside the mosque, the overwhelming impression is of light and uncluttered space, with a central dome 53m high (twice its diameter), surmounting a perfect square of 26.5m. The sense of space is further emphasized by the addition of supporting semi-domes to the northwest and southeast, while the monumental arched spaces to the southwest and northeast are filled with great tympana walls, pierced by windows through which the light pours. The four great rectangular piers that support the dome have been cleverly masked on two sides by linking them in with the arched colonnade walls. All in all, the mosque is a very successful take on the much earlier Haghia Sophia (see p.72).

A rope prevents non-worshippers from entering the main part of the prayer hall, but it's easy enough to admire the restrained arabesques and Koranic calligraphy that adorn the interior, along with the simple Proconnesian marble *mihrab*. The tiles here, used sparingly for effect, are top-notch İznik-ware, fired with flower motifs in blue, red and turquoise on a white ground.

The **Türbe (tomb) of Mimar Sinan** himself is located on the north side of the Sülemaniye Külliyesi complex, on Mimar Sinan Caddesi. Otherwise, the buildings of the complex served the usual functions. Despite its ornate design, the *imaret* (soup kitchen; today the *Darüzziyafe* restaurant) on Şifahane Sokak was constructed as a

1

MIMAR SINAN, MASTER BUILDER

Many of the finest works of Ottoman civil and religious architecture throughout Turkey can be traced to **Mimar Sinan** (1489–1588), who served as court architect to three sultans – Süleyman the Magnificent, Selim II and Murat III. Probably born to Greek or Armenian Christian parents, he was conscripted into the janissaries in 1513. As a military engineer, he travelled the length and breadth of southeastern Europe and the Middle East, giving him the opportunity to become familiar with the finest Islamic – and Christian – monumental architecture there. His bridges, siegeworks, harbours, and even ships, earned him the admiration of his superiors.

Sultan Süleyman appointed Sinan court architect in April 1536, and he completed his first major religious commission, Istanbul's Şehzade Camii, in 1548. Shortly thereafter, he embarked on a rapid succession of ambitious projects in and around the capital, including the waterworks leading from the Belgrade Forest and the Süleymaniye Camii. Competing with the Süleymaniye as his masterpiece was the Selimiye Camii, constructed between 1569 and 1575 in the former imperial capital of Edirne (see p.149). Despite temptations to luxury, he lived and died modestly, being buried in a simple tomb he made for himself in his garden in the grounds of the Süleymaniye Camii – the last of more than five hundred constructions by Sinan, large and small, throughout the empire.

public kitchen to supply food for the local poor. There's also a *kervansaray* (hotel), a *mektep* (primary school) and a library.

Tombs of Süleyman and Roxelana

Daily 5.30am–8pm • Free

The **cemetery** outside the southeast prayer-wall of Süleymaniye Camii holds the **tombs** of Süleyman the Magnificent and Haseki Hürrem, better known to the West as his powerful wife Roxelana. Süleyman's tomb is particularly impressive: its doors are inlaid with ebony, ivory, silver and jade, and his turban is huge. The spectacular inner dome has been faithfully restored in red, black and gold, inlaid with glittering ceramic stars.

Süleymaniye Hamamı

Mimar Sinan Cad 20 • Daily 10am–midnight, last entry 10pm • €40 for bath, scrub and massage • ☎ 0212 519 5569, ⓦ suleymaniyehamamı.com

The **Süleymaniye Hamamı** was built by Mimar Sinan in 1557, and legend has it that the great architect took all his baths here from 1557 to 1588. Today, however, it doesn't accept single males or females, only couples and families, and the bathing is mixed sex. It has been beautifully restored and is very atmospheric.

The Aqueduct of Valens

The magnificent **Aqueduct of Valens** spans Atatürk Bulvarı around 300m southwest of the Süleymaniye complex, here reaching a height of 18.5m. Originally built during the late fourth century, as part of a waterworks programme carried out by the emperor Valens, the aqueduct belonged to a distribution network that included reservoirs in the Belgrade Forest and various cisterns located around the city centre. It was used right up to the end of the nineteenth century, having been kept in good repair by successive rulers, who maintained a constant supply of water to the city in the face of both drought and siege.

Beyazıt Meydanı

Beyazıt Meydanı, just west of the Grand Bazaar, is the main square of Beyazıt. On the north side of the square, the principal approach to Istanbul University is marked by a magnificent portal, while a monumental nineteenth-century fire tower, Beyazıt Kulesi, stands behind it in the university grounds.

On the east of the square, **Beyazıt Camii**, completed in 1506, is the oldest surviving imperial mosque in the city. Its sombre courtyard is full of richly coloured marble, including twenty columns of verd antique, red granite and porphyry. Inside, the building is a perfect square of exactly the same proportions as the courtyard (although the aisles make it feel elongated). Just behind the mosque, on the approach to the Grand Bazaar, the famous **Sahaflar Çarşısı**, is a secondhand booksellers' market that dates back to the Byzantine era.

On the south side of the T1 tramline, opposite the southwest corner of the *meydan*, a jumble of fallen marble columns is decorated with curious teardrop patterns. These formed part of the famed triumphal **Arch of Theodosius**, erected in 393.

Laleli Camii

Ordu Cad, 1min walk from the Laleli/Üniversite tram stop

Perching above busy Ordu Caddesi, the attractive **Laleli Camii** was built in the Ottoman Baroque tradition. The main Baroque elements in the mosque complex are the use of ramps (including one that the reigning sultan would have used to ride up to his loge), the grand staircases, and the exquisite detail, noticeable in the window grilles of the tomb and in the carved eaves of the *sebil* (drinking fountain).

Eminönü

Heading north from Sultanahmet brings you to the waterfront district of **Eminönü**. Once the maritime gateway to the city, it remains a large and convenient transport hub, where buses, ferries, trams and trains converge. The latter arrive at **Sirkeci station**, once the last stop on the famed Orient Express, today merely a stop on the Marmaray metro line. Sights within this district include the **Cağaloğlu Hamamı** and the landmark **Yeni Cami** complex, which includes the ornate Ottoman-era **Spice Bazaar**.

Cağaloğlu Hamamı

Kazım İsmail Gürkan Cad 34 • Daily: men 8am–10pm; women 8am–8.30pm • €30 for self-service bath, €45 for bath and scrub, €50 for bath, scrub and massage • ☎ 0212 522 2424, ⓦ cagalogluhamami.com.tr

The very popular **Cağaloğlu Hamamı** is famous for its beautiful *hararet*s or steam rooms – open cruciform chambers with windowed domes, supported on a circle of columns. The baths were built in 1741 by Mahmut I to pay for the upkeep of his library in Haghia Sophia, and the arches, basins and taps of the hot room, and also the entries to the private cubicles, are all magnificently Baroque. Florence Nightingale is said to have bathed here, and the hamam has appeared in several films, including *Indiana Jones and the Temple of Doom*.

Yeni Cami

The **Yeni Cami**, or "new mosque", is a familiar city landmark, sited across the busy road from Eminönü's bustling waterfront. Completed in 1663, it was the last of Istanbul's imperial mosques to be built, erected for the powerful Valide Sultan, Safiye, mother of Mehmet III.

Spice Bazaar

Daily 9am–7pm

The most intriguing part of the Yeni Cami mosque complex is the **Spice Bazaar**, known in Turkish as the **Mısır Carşısı** or "Egyptian Bazaar". Completed a few years before Yeni Cami, the L-shaped bazaar has been the city's premier spice outlet for several centuries.

1

> ## THE GOLDEN HORN
>
> The **Golden Horn** (*Haliç* or "estuary" in Turkish) is one of the finest natural harbours in the world and has figured prominently in the city's history. In 1203–04, the Crusaders took the Horn and proceeded to besiege the city for ten months, until they breached the walls separating the inlet from the city. In April 1453 Mehmet the Conqueror, prevented from entering the Horn by a chain fastened across it, carried his ships overland at night and launched them into the inlet from its northern shore. Mehmet then constructed a pontoon across the top of the Horn, over which he transported his army and cannons in preparation for the siege of the land walls, which were finally breached in May 1453. For the Ottoman Empire, the Horn was a vital harbour, supplying the Genoese, Venetian and Jewish trading colonies on its northern shore.
>
> To make the most of the Golden Horn take the Sehirhatları Haliç ferry (w sheirhatlari.com.tr), which departs from a dock west of the Galata Bridge in Eminönü, up to Eyüp (see p.100). Boats depart hourly and views of the old city skyline en-route are spectacular.

Endowed with customs duties from Cairo – hence its name – it has 88 vaulted rooms and chambers above the entryways at the ends of the halls. Far more manageable than the Grand Bazaar, it sells a wide range of herbs, spices and Turkish delight. It's very touristy and expensive, however; the shops that line the exterior of the Spice Bazaar, and in the narrow streets between it and the **Rüstem Paşa Camii** (see below), sell the same goods at cheaper prices.

Rüstem Paşa Camii

A short walk northwest of the spice bazaar

Rüstem Paşa Camii is one of the most attractive smaller mosques in Istanbul. Built for Süleyman the Magnificent's grand vizier Rüstem Paşa in 1561, it's decorated inside and out by some of the finest İznik **tiles** in Turkey. Designs covering the walls, piers and pillars, and decorating the *mihrab* and *mimber*, include famous panels of tulips and carnations and geometric patterns. Built by Sinan on an awkward site, the mosque is easy to miss as you wander the streets below. At ground level on the Golden Horn side, an arcade of shops occupies the vaults, from where a flight of steps leads up to the mosque's terrace. Through an attractive entrance portal is a wide courtyard and a tiled double portico along the west wall.

The northwest quarter

Catch #99 bus from Eminönü to the Atatürk Bridge, and walk up to Zeyrek and Fatih, or stay on the bus to Fener and Balat; you can also walk up from the Aksaray stop on the T1 tramline, or take a ferry from Eminönü or Karaköy to Ayvansaray

One of the least visited but most fascinating areas of the old city, the **northwest quarter** is bounded on the west by the major thoroughfare of Fevzi Paşa Caddesi, to the north by the land walls of Theodosius, to the east by the Golden Horn, and on the south by traffic-choked Atatürk Bulvarı. Once home to a cosmopolitan population of Muslims, Christians and Jews, it's now a devoutly Muslim area, particularly in the district of **Fatih**, where you'll notice many women in chadors and bearded men in *şalvar* pants, long baggy shirts and skullcaps (dress appropriately).

The most notable sights are a former Byzantine church, now the **Zeyrek Camii**; two notable Ottoman mosques, the **Fatih** and **Yavuz Selim**; the magnificent Byzantine mosaics in the **Fethiye Museum**, the spiritual centre of the Orthodox Christian world; the **Greek Orthodox Patriarchate**; and the curious cast-iron church of **St Stephen of the Bulgars**. A spiritual centre of a different order awaits a couple of kilometres up the Golden Horn from the Patriarchate, the **Eyüp** area, sacred to Muslims worldwide as it boasts the tomb of Eyüp Ensari, standard-bearer of the Prophet Mohammed.

Zeyrek Camii

Nestling in the heart of Zeyrek, **Zeyrek Camii**, the former Church of the Pantocrator, was built in the twelfth century and converted into a mosque at the time of the Conquest. It originally consisted of two churches and a connecting chapel, built between 1118 and 1136 by John II Comnenus and Empress Irene. Restoration of this important building, today a mosque, was approaching completion at the time of writing.

Fatih Camii

Just over 300m east of Zeyrek Camii

Work on the **Fatih Camii**, or "Mosque of the Conqueror", started in 1463 on the site of the famous Byzantine Church of the Holy Apostles, but was not completed until 1470. Much rebuilt following a devastating earthquake in 1766, the **inner courtyard** contains green antique marble and highly polished porphyry columns supporting a domed portico, while an eighteenth-century fountain is surrounded by four enormous poplar trees. The architect was supposedly executed because the dome wasn't as large as that of Haghia Sophia. The whole complex has been restored to its former glory.

Yavuz Selim Camii

Yavuz Selim Cad, Fatih

Also called the Selimiye Camii, the **Yavuz Selim Camii** ranks among Istanbul's most attractive mosques. Recently beautifully restored, it's built on a terrace on the crest of one of the city's seven hills (the fifth, counting from Topkapı). The mosque of Yavuz Selim, or Selim the Grim, was probably begun in the reign of Selim and completed by Süleyman the Magnificent. It is much more basic than the other imperial mosques, with just a single large dome atop a square room with a walled courtyard in front of it. The *avlu* (courtyard) in front of the prayer hall is quite beautiful, with a central fountain surrounded by tall cypress trees.

The interior of the mosque is stunning in its simplicity, its shallower than usual dome emphasizing the sense of space. Light floods in through a series of windows in the tympanum arches and from the 24 stained-glass windows that pierce the dome. The interior of the mosque falls well short of the austere, though; gorgeous blue-and-white İznik tiles fill the lunettes above the lower windows, and gilt-work highlights the beautiful geometry of the stalactite carving above the *mihrab*.

Fethiye Museum

Fethiye Cad, Katip Mustehattın Mah, Fatih • Daily: April–Oct 9am–7pm; Nov–March 9am–5pm • ₺5

A major, but little-visited, Byzantine gem, the **Fethiye Camii** was once the **Church of Theotokos Pammakaristos**. This medium-sized church, attractively set on a terrace overlooking the Golden Horn, was built during the twelfth century and conforms to the usual cross-in-a-square design, its large central dome enhanced by four smaller, subsidiary domes. Despite the Ottoman conquest of Constantinople in 1453, it remained a Christian place of worship. Indeed, between 1456 and 1587 it served as the seat of the **Greek Orthodox Patriarch** (now situated nearby, in the district of Fener). It finally became a mosque in 1573, when it was renamed the Fethiye Camii or "Mosque of the Conquest". The southwest wing – originally a side chapel or *parecclesion* of the main church, added in 1310 – now serves as a **museum**. Helpful display boards in the entry to the chapel locate and give information on each of the mosaics, superb examples of the renaissance of Byzantine art, including, in the dome, Christ Pantocrator, encircled by the twelve prophets of the Old Testament. Other notable scenes show Christ with the Virgin Mary, the baptism of Christ and St John the Baptist.

The Greek Orthodox Patriarchate

Sadrazam Ali Paşa Cad 35, Fener • Daily 9am–5pm • Free

The **Greek Orthodox Patriarchate**, north of the Yavuz Selim Camii almost on the shores of the Golden Horn, has been the spiritual centre of the Orthodox world since 1599. It remains so today – despite the fact that the Greek Orthodox community in the city is now meagre (around 2500), and that a Turkish court controversially ruled that the authority of the Patriarch (currently Bartholomew I) was confined solely to Turkey's remaining Greek Orthodox Christians, rather than to the Orthodox Christian community worldwide.

St Stephen of the Bulgars

Mürsel Paşa Cad 85–8, Fener • Daily 8am–5pm • Free

St Stephen of the Bulgars is a curious, neo-Gothic white-painted church, stranded on a massive traffic-island-cum-park area. Built in 1896, it is made entirely from iron, cast in Vienna and carted all the way to Istanbul. Signs of rust betray the chosen building material, and the church was undergoing restoration at the time of writing.

The land walls

To reach the north end of the walls take the ferry from Eminönü or Karaköy to Ayvansaray İskelesı on the Golden Horn, or bus #99 from Eminönü; for the southern end of the walls take the Marmaray metro from Yenikapı to Kazlıçeşme, bus #80/T from Taksim, or bus #80 from Eminönü to Yedikule. Alternatively ride the T1 tram to Pazartekke, a little north of the mid-point of the walls

Theodosius II's **land walls** are among the most fascinating Byzantine remains in Turkey. Well-preserved remnants can still be found along the whole of their 6.5km length, though purists (and UNESCO) decry the fact that much of the recent work done on the walls looks like new-build rather than restoration.

The land walls were named after Theodosius II, and construction started in 413 AD. Stretching from the Marmara to Tekfur Saray, 2km further out than the previous walls of Constantine, they were built to accommodate the city's expanding population. All citizens, regardless of rank, were required to help in the rebuilding following their collapse in the earthquake of 447 AD, in the light of the imminent threat of attack by Attila the Hun. The completed construction consisted of the original wall, 5m thick and 12m high, plus an outer wall of 2m by 8.5m, and a 20m-wide moat, all of which proved sufficient to repel Atilla's assault.

Walking along the walls takes a little over two hours, though a full day allows time to enjoy it, and the adjacent sites, fully. Most of the outer wall and its 96 towers are still standing; access is restricted on some of the restored sections, though elsewhere there's the chance to scramble along the crumbling edifice. As there are still plenty of run-down **slums** in this area, it's best avoided at dusk (especially Topkapı).

The three principal sights can also be visited independently. The **Yedikule fortifications**, towards the southern terminus of the walls, are best reached by walking up from the Marmaray metro stop at Kazlıçeşme. The **Kariye Museum**, a former Byzantine church containing some of the best-preserved mosaics and frescoes in the world, just in from Edirnekapı and around 750m north of the Golden Horn, is easily accessed from the Ulubatlı M1 metro stop or the Pazartekke T1 tram stop, the **Mihrimah Camii** likewise – or take #28, #38E or #336E bus from Eminönü to Edirnekapı.

Yedikule and around

The run-down but attractive old quarter of **Yedikule** (Seven Towers), around 5km from the west of Sultanahmet, is ripe for gentrification. Its most impressive sight is the **Yedikule Museum** (Yedikule Müzesi; Tues–Sun 9am–6pm; ₺10), a massive fortification

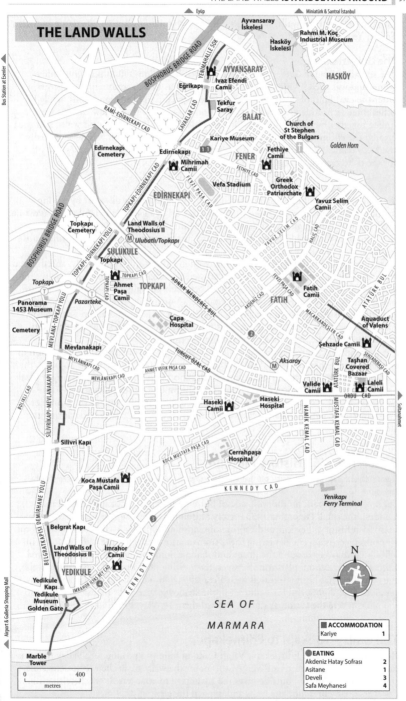

THE LAND WALLS

Eyüp

Miniatürk & Santral İstanbul

Bus Station at Esenler

Ayvansaray İskelesi

Rahmi M. Koç Industrial Museum

Hasköy İskelesi

BOSPHORUS BRIDGE ROAD

YENİMAHALLE SOK

AYVANSARAY

HASKÖY

İvaz Efendi Camii

Eğrikapı

SAVAKLAR CAD

Tekfur Saray

BALAT

Church of St Stephen of the Bulgars

Golden Horn

RAMI-EDİRNEKAPI CAD

Kariye Museum

FENER

Fethiye Camii

Edirnekapı

Edirne Cemetery

Mihrimah Camii

FETHİYE CAD

Greek Orthodox Patriarchate

Yavuz Selim Camii

FEVZİ PAŞA CAD

TOPKAPI-EDİRNEKAPI CAD

EDİRNEKAPI

Vefa Stadium

YAVUZ SELİM CAD

HALİÇ CAD

Topkapı Cemetery

Land Walls of Theodosius II

Ⓜ Ulubatlı/Topkapı

Fatih Camii

FEVZİ PAŞA CAD

MACARKARDEŞLER CAD

ATATÜRK BUL

BOSPHORUS BRIDGE ROAD

SULUKULE

Topkapı

ADNAN MENDERES BUL

AKDENİZ CAD

FATİH

Aquaduct of Valens

Topkapı

Ahmet Paşa Camii

TOPKAPI CAD

TOPKAPI

ŞEHZADEBAŞI CAD

Panorama 1453 Museum

Pazarteke

Çapa Hospital

Şehzade Camii

MEVLANA-TOPKAPI YOLU

Cemetery

Aksaray

Ⓜ

Taşhan Covered Bazaar

ORDU CAD

Sultanahmet

Mevlanakapı

TURGUT ÖZAL CAD

Valide Camii

ATATÜRK BUL

Laleli Camii

SİLİVRİKAPI-MEVLANAKAPI YOLU

MEVLANAKAPI CAD

AHMET VEFİK PAŞA CAD

MUSTAFA KEMAL CAD

BOZLU CAD

Silivri Kapı

Haseki Camii

Haseki Hospital

NAMIK KEMAL CAD

Airport & Galleria Shopping Mall

KOCA MUSTAFA PAŞA CAD

Cerrahpaşa Hospital

BELGRATKAPISI DEMIRHANE YOLU

Koca Mustafa Paşa Camii

KENNEDY CAD

Yenikapı Ferry Terminal

Belgrat Kapı

Land Walls of Theodosius II

İmrahor Camii

N

YEDİKULE

İMRAHOR İLYAS BEY CAD

Yedikule Kapı

KENNEDY CAD

Yedikule Museum Golden Gate

SEA OF

Marble Tower

MARMARA

0   400
metres

■ ACCOMMODATION	
Kariye	1

● EATING	
Akdeniz Hatay Sofrası	2
Asitane	1
Develi	3
Safa Meyhanesi	4

1

astride the line of the walls, situated southwest of İmrahor Camii on Yedikule Meydanı Sokak, Yedikule Caddesi.

The Golden Gate

The so-called **Golden Gate**, constructed by Theodosius I in 390, is actually made of stone, and was used by important visitors of state, as well as conquering emperors, to enter the city. Four of Yedikule's towers once formed part of the land walls, while the other three were added by Mehmet the Conqueror. These three "new" towers were linked together by curtain walls, which extended to the line of the land walls, and thus created the enclave that can be seen today. Despite its design, this was never actually used as a castle; two of the towers served as prisons, and others as treasuries and offices for the collection of revenue of the *Vakıf* or pious foundation.

The walls – Yedikule to Mevlanakapı

To walk along one of the best-preserved sections of the land walls, start by exiting Yedikule and heading north, then turn sharply west to a gate in the land walls, **Yedikule Kapı**. Go out of that, and head north along the outside of the walls, which here have not been overly restored (as are some sections further north), though the former moat is now in use as market gardens.

The next gate, **Belgrat Kapı**, was originally intended for military use only, and differed from a public gateway in that no bridge crossed the moat beyond the outer walls. The walls here, which are floodlit at night, have been substantially renovated, and it's now one of the best places to walk along the parapet. North from Belgrat Kapı to **Silivri Kapı**, the walls are largely untouched, though the sections around Silivri Kapı itself have been extensively renovated. There is more restoration work at the **Mevlanakapı**, where the outer wall holds some interesting inscriptions.

A road system dominates the outer side of the 1km Mevlanakapı–Topkapı section of wall, and a pavement has been constructed along the moat. Just south of Topkapı, the walls have been destroyed to make way for the enormous thoroughfare of Turgut Özal Caddesi, complete with its central tram track. Beyond it is the **Topkapı** (the "Gate of the Cannonball"), named after the most powerful cannon of Mehmet the Conqueror (see p.652), the famed **Orban**, which was trained on this part of the walls during the siege of 1453.

Panorama 1453 History Museum

Topkapı/Edirnekapı Cad • Daily 8am–6pm • ₺10, audioguide ₺5 • ⓦ panoramikmuze.com • T1 tram from Sultanahmet to the Topkapı stop

Set in a pleasant park on the west side of horrendously busy Topkapı/Edirnekapı Caddesi, the small **Panorama 1453 History Museum** pays homage to a landmark date in Turkish history, the siege and capture of Constantinople by Mehmet the Conqueror. Its centrepiece is a scene depicting the Ottoman army besieging the walls, painted in a 360-degree sweep around the drum and shallow dome of the building, and viewed from a circular central platform. Between the viewing platform and the painted scene, the battlefield has been re-created with a realistic tableau of models and mannequins. It's all the more powerful for being set in the shadow of the walls themselves, close to the point where the Ottomans first breached them on May 29, 1453.

The walls – Topkapı to Edirnekapı

Between Topkapı and Edirnekapı, Vatan Caddesi follows a pronounced valley that was once the course of the Lycus River. At this point the walls are at their least defensible, since the higher ground outside gives the advantage to attackers. It was here that the besiegers finally breached the walls and entered the city.

The gate of **Edirnekapı** takes its name from the route to modern Edirne. Close by, the beautifully restored sixteenth-century **Mihrimah Camii** stands on the highest of Istanbul's seven hills. It was named after Mihrimah, the favourite daughter of Süleyman the Magnificent, whose passion for architecture was as great as that of her husband Rüstem Paşa.

Kariye Museum

Kariye Cami Sok 26 • Daily: April–Oct 9am–7pm; Nov–March 9am–5pm • ₺15 • ⓦ choramuseum.com • Take M1 metro to Topkapı/Ulubatlı and walk, or catch a bus to Edirnekapı: #28 from Beşikta, #36/V and #37/Y from Vezneciler, #38 from Beyazıt, #38/E from Eminönü, or #55/EB from Beyazıt

Formerly the church of St Saviour in Chora, the **Kariye Museum** (Kariye Müzesi) is decorated with a superbly preserved series of **frescoes and mosaics** portraying the life and miracles of Christ. Arguably the most evocative of all the city's Byzantine treasures, it's thought to have been built in the early twelfth century on the site of a much older church far from the centre: hence "in Chora", meaning "in the country". Between 1316 and 1321, the statesman and scholar Theodore Metochites rebuilt the central dome and added the narthexes and mortuary chapel.

The mosaics

Inside the church, the most prominent of the mosaics is that of **Christ Pantocrator**, bearing the inscription "Jesus Christ, the Land of the Living". Opposite is a depiction of the Virgin and angels, with the inscription "Mother of God, the Dwelling Place of the Uncontainable". The third in the series, located in the inner narthex, shows Metochites offering a model of the building to a seated Christ. Saints Peter and Paul are portrayed on either side of the door leading to the nave, and to the right of the door are Christ with his Mother and two benefactors, Isaac (who built the original church), and the figure of a nun.

The two domes of the inner narthex hold medallions of **Christ Pantocrator** and the Virgin and Child, while in the fluting of the domes there's a series of notable figures – starting with Adam – from the **Genealogy of Christ**. The **Cycle of the Blessed Virgin** is located in the first three bays of the inner narthex. Episodes depicted here include the first seven steps of the Virgin; the Virgin caressed by her parents, with two beautiful peacocks in the background; the Virgin presented as an attendant at the temple, the Virgin receiving a skein of purple wool, as proof of her royal blood; Joseph taking the Virgin to his house, in which is also depicted one of Joseph's sons by his first wife; and Joseph returning from a trip to find his wife pregnant.

The next cycle, found in the arched apertures of the outer narthex, depicts the **Infancy of Christ**. The mosaics can be followed clockwise, starting with Joseph dreaming, the Virgin and two companions, and the journey to Bethlehem. Apart from well-known scenes such as the Journey of the Magi and the Nativity, there are depictions in the seventh bay of the Flight into Egypt. In the sixth bay is the Slaughter of the Innocents, complete with babies impaled on spikes.

The **Cycle of Christ's Ministry** fills the vaults of the outer narthex and parts of the south bay of the inner narthex. It includes wonderful scenes of the Temptation of Christ, with dramatic dialogue (Matthew 4: 3–10) that could almost be in speech bubbles, beginning "Devil: If thou be the Son of God, command that these stones be made bread. Christ: It is written, Man shall not live by bread alone, but by every word that proceedeth out of the mouth of God."

The frescoes

The main frescoes in the nave of St Saviour echo the mosaics, featuring the death of the Virgin over the door and, to the right, a depiction of Christ. The best known of all the works in the church, however, are the frescoes in the **funerary chapel** to the south of the nave.

1

The most spectacular of these is the **Resurrection**, also known as the Harrowing of Hell. It depicts Christ trampling the gates of Hell underfoot, and forcibly dragging Adam and Eve from their tombs. A black Satan lies among the broken fetters at his feet, bound at the ankles, wrists and neck. To the left, animated onlookers include John the Baptist, David and Solomon, while to the right Abel is standing in his mother's tomb; behind him is another group of the righteous.

Other frescoes in the chapel, in the vault of the east bay, depict the **Second Coming**, while in the east half of the domical vault Christ sits in judgement.

Eyüp

If you're coming from Eminönü, the conservative district of **Eyüp** is most easily reached by boat – it's the last ferry stop before the Golden Horn peters out into two small streams. The main sights here are **Eyüp mosque**, the tombs of various Muslim notables, and the hilltop cemetery.

The hills above the mosque are covered in plain modern stones interspersed with beautiful Ottoman tombs. This is the **Eyüp cemetery**, at its best at sunset with an arresting view of the Golden Horn. A twenty-minute walk from Eyüp Camii will bring you to the romantic *Pierre Loti Café* (daily 8am–midnight) overlooking the Horn, or take the new cable car (₺4) from the shores of the Golden Horn.

Eyüp Camii

Camii Kebir Cad • 10min walk from ferry terminal, or catch bus #39/A or #99

Eyüp owes its status as one of the holiest places in Islam to the fact that its mosque, **Eyüp Camii**, is the site of the tomb of **Eyüp Ensari** (674–678), the Prophet Mohammed's standard-bearer who was killed in the first Arab siege of Constantinople. Muslims come here from all over the Islamic world on pilgrimage. Try not to visit on Fridays, out of respect for conservative worshippers.

Originally built by Mehmet the Conqueror in honour of Eyüp Ensari, the mosque was destroyed by an earthquake in the eighteenth century. Its Baroque replacement, filled with light, gold, pale stone and white marble, was completed in 1800 and later used in the investiture ceremonies of the Ottoman sultans.

The adjoining **tomb of Eyüp Ensari** (Tues–Sun 9.30am–4.30pm), with its tile panels from many different periods, is more compelling than the mosque.

Galata and around

Immediately across the **Galata Bridge** from Eminönü and the old city, the up-and-coming port area of **Karaköy** is dominated by its cruise liner dock. Further inland is **Galata** proper, once a Genoese city-state within Istanbul and now a tourist-orientated district full of bars and restaurants.

The Galata Bridge

The first bridge to span the Golden Horn was completed in 1845. It was rebuilt three times before its most recent incarnation, the **Galata Köprüsü** (Galata Bridge), was erected in the late 1980s. While this latest version may lack grace, its stunning location and supreme importance in linking the old and new Istanbuls more than make up for its lack of architectural merit. A walkway follows either side of the bridge close to water level, backed by a myriad of lively cafés, bars and restaurants. The tram rumbles across the upper level, and the bridge's guardrails are invisible behind a solid wall of expectant anglers. To discover more about this landmark bridge and the people whose lives revolve around it, read Geert Mak's *The Bridge* (see p.698).

Karaköy

The once rough-and-ready port area of **Karaköy**, at the northern end of the Galata Bridge, has become the city's latest hip neighbourhood, with a rash of cool cafés, clubs and even hotels springing up among the vehicle repair shops, hardware shops and fish markets. From here you can either walk up to Galata/Beyoğlu on the steep Yüksek Kaldırım Caddesi, past the Galata Tower, or take the **Tünel** underground train/funicular (daily 7am–10pm; ₺4). Karaköy's port and Ottoman shipyard was once enclosed within the walls of the Castle of Galata. In 1446 the Byzantines stretched a great chain across the mouth of the Horn to prevent enemy ships from entering. At the far end of the port area is the **Kılıç Ali Paşa Camii**, constructed in 1580 by Sinan.

Jewish Museum

Meydanı Perçemli Sok • Mon & Thurs 10am–4pm, Fri & Sun 10am–2pm • ₺10 • ⓦ muze500.com

The Zülfaris Synagogue, west of the Galata Bridge, is home to Istanbul's **Jewish Museum**. Its small but fascinating display includes documents and photographs donated by local Jewish families, chronicling Turkish Jews since they first came to the country over seven hundred years ago.

SALT and the Ottoman Bank Museum

Bankalar Cad 35, Karaköy • Tues–Sat noon–8pm, Sun 10.30am–6pm• Free • ⓦ obmuze.com

Karaköy's Bankalar Caddesi (Street of Banks) is home to the former head office of the Ottoman Bank, designed by the renowned French architect Alexander Vallaury in 1890. In late 2011, the building became a part of the Garanti Bank's **SALT** contemporary arts project, complete with a public library, rooms dedicated to research, and exhibition space. It also contains the fascinating **Ottoman Bank Museum**, which relates the story of the bank's history through to the 1930s.

Kamondo Steps

The sculptural **Kamondo Steps** run up from Bankalar Caddesi towards the Galata Tower, from close to the Ottoman Bank Museum. Gracefully curving twin staircases, they were commissioned and paid for by the wealthy Jewish Kamondo family, and photographed by Henri Cartier-Bresson in the 1960s.

The Galata Tower and around

Galata Meydan Daily 9am–8pm • €6.50 or equivalent ₺ • ⓦ galatatower.net

In 1261, the Byzantine emperor Michael Paleologus granted the area of **Galata** to the **Genoese**, as a reward for supporting his attempts to drive out the Crusaders. Built by the Genoese in 1349, the **Galata Tower** (Galata Kulesi) sits on the site of a former tower constructed by Justinian in 528. Originally known as the Tower of Christ, it stood at the apex of the several sets of fortifications that surrounded the Genoese city-state. It has had a number of functions over the centuries, including turns as a jail, fire tower and even a springboard for early adventurers attempting to fly. Nowadays, there's a restaurant on the top floor. At 61m high, the tower's **viewing gallery** – reached by elevator – offers magnificent panoramas of the city and views across the Sea of Marmara and Golden Horn.

A short walk south of the tower, at Galata Kulesi Sok 61, is the **British prison**. Under the capitulations granted by the Ottomans, Western powers had the right to try their citizens under their own law, so consulates possessed their own courthouses and prisons. The court originated in the 1600s, but the current building dates from 1904 and today houses the *Galata House* restaurant-café (see p.125).

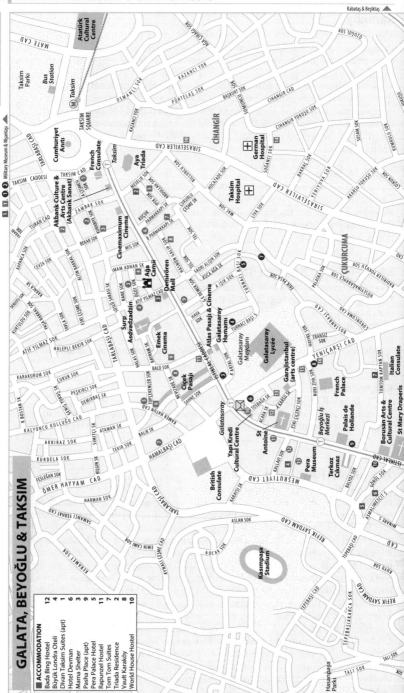

GALATA, BEYOĞLU & TAKSIM

ACCOMMODATION

Bada Bing Hostel	12
Büyük Londra Oteli	4
Divan Taksim Suites (apt)	1
Hotel Devman	6
Mama Shelter	3
Pasha Place (apt)	9
Pera Palace Hotel	5
Rapunzel Hostel	11
Tom Tom Suites	7
Triada Residence	2
Vault Karaköy	8
World House Hostel	10

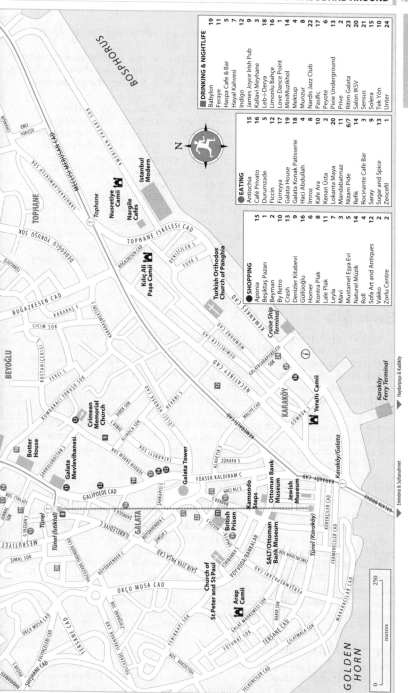

BOSPHORUS

TOPHANE

BEYOĞLU

KARAKÖY

GALATA

GOLDEN HORN

■ DRINKING & NIGHTLIFE

Babylon	19
Feraye	11
Haspa Cafe & Bar	5
Hayal Kahvesi	7
Indigo	12
James Joyce Irish Pub	9
Kallavi Meyhane	3
Leb-i-Derya	18
Limonlu Bahçe	16
Love Dance Point	1
MiniMüzikhol	14
Mektup	4
Munzur	8
Nardis Jazz Club	22
Pasific	17
Peyote	6
Pixie Underground	13
Ritim Galata	23
Salon IKSV	20
Sensus	21
Solera	15
Tek Yön	10
Unter	24

● EATING

Antiochia	15
Café Privato	16
Durumzade	5
Ficcin	12
Fürreyya	17
Galata House	19
Galata Konak Patisserie	18
Haci Abdullah	4
Imroz	6
Kafe Ara	10
Kenan Usta	8
Lokanta Maya	20
Mandabatmaz	11
Nizam Pide	6/7
Refik	14
Rocinante Cafe Bar	3
Saray	9
Sugar and Spice	13
Zencefil	1

● SHOPPING

Aponia	15
Beşiktaş Pazarı	2
Beyman	1
By Retro	10
Crash	13
Denizler Kitabevi	9
Güllüoğlu	16
Homer	6
Kontra Plak	8
Lale Plak	11
Leyla	3
Mavi	7
Mustamel Eşya Evi	5
Naturel Müzik	14
Roll	4
Sofia Art and Antiques	12
Vakko	2
Zorlu Centre	2

Haydarpaşa & Kadıköy

Eminönü & Sultanahmet

0 — 250 metres

1

The Galata Mevlevihanesi

Galipdede Caddesi • Daily except Tues 9.30am–5pm • ₺10 • *Sema* dances usually held every Sunday May–Sept 5pm, twice-monthly Oct–April 3pm • ₺40

An unassuming doorway on Galipdede Caddesi, on the right if you're heading up from the Galata Tower, leads to the tranquil courtyard of the **Galata Mevlevihanesi**. A former *tekke* (monastery) containing a *semahane* (ceremonial hall) of the **whirling dervishes**, the building now serves as a museum to the Mevlevî Sufi sect.

Constructed in the late fifteenth century, this is the oldest surviving dervish monastery in Istanbul, though it has been rebuilt several times. The downstairs rooms, which you should go around clockwise, hold well-signed displays dealing with the dervish life, and covering everything from musical instruments to traditional dress, and from utensils used in the lodge's kitchen to the begging bowls of wandering dervishes. Upstairs is the star of the show, the *semahane*, a beautifully restored, high-ceilinged room complete with wooden dancefloor where the dervishes whirl.

The **Mevlevî Sufi order** is one of the many mystical sects of Islam, once rife across Anatolia, that were banned by Atatürk because of their supposed political affiliations and religious conservatism. The founder of the sect, Mevlâna, was an iconoclast who, in the thirteenth century, repudiated the strictures and hypocrisy of mainstream Sunni Islam. Preaching love, charity and tolerance, he believed that union with God was possible through contemplation, meditation, dance and music (hence the "whirling" ceremonies in which the disciples engage).

Beyoğlu

North and uphill from the sprawl of Galata and Karaköy, the district of **Beyoğlu** is the beating heart of modern Istanbul. Locals head in droves to İstiklal Caddesi in particular, to shop, wine and dine, take in a film, club, gig or gallery – or simply promenade. So, too, do an ever-increasing number of visitors, who base themselves here to take advantage of the nightlife.

Beyoğlu's pedestrianized main boulevard, **İstiklal Caddesi**, boasts a cute antique tramway (see p.114), and bustles with life virtually twenty-four hours a day. Massive **Taksim Square**, at its northern end, is regarded as a symbol of the secular Turkish Republic, and holds numerous hotels as well as convenient bus and metro terminals. Side streets hereabouts are host to scores of lively bars, clubs and restaurants, many of which stay open until six in the morning.

Brief history

What's now **Beyoğlu** used to be known as **Pera** (Greek for "beyond" or "across"). By the mid-nineteenth century, Pera was where the main European powers chose to build their ambassadorial palaces, and this imported **architecture** still dominates today. The completion of the Orient Express Railway in 1889 encouraged an influx of tourists, catered for in luxurious hotels like the splendid *Pera Palace*.

The **nightlife** of the quarter was notoriously riotous even in the seventeenth century. By the nineteenth and early twentieth centuries, the area had become fashionable for its operettas, music halls, inns, cinemas and restaurants. Only after the gradual exodus of the Greek population from Istanbul following the establishment of the Turkish Republic in 1923 did Galata and Pera begin to lose their cosmopolitan flavour.

Along İstiklal Caddesi

The exit from the upper **Tünel station** in Beyoğlu is fronted by a small square from which **İstiklal Caddesi** (known as the "Grand Rue de Pera" prior to Independence) heads 1.5km north towards Taksim Square.

Not far up İstiklal Caddesi on the right, the **Botter House**, a fine Art Nouveau apartment building with a carved stone facade and wrought-iron balcony designed by the Italian architect Raimondo D'Aronco, was under renovation (it will be a hotel) at the time of writing. Further up on the right is the **Palais de Hollande**. Built in 1858 on the site of the home of Cornelis Haga, the first Dutch diplomat in Constantinople during the fifteenth century, it now houses the Consulate to the Netherlands.

The oldest church in the area is **St Mary Draperis** at no. 429, which dates from 1789, although the Franciscans built their first church on the site in the early fifteenth century. Better known is the Franciscan **church of St Antoine** at no. 325, a fine example of red-brick neo-Gothic architecture. Originally founded in 1725, it was demolished to make way for a tramway at the start of the twentieth century, and rebuilt in 1913.

The famous **Çiçek Pasajı** (Flower Passage) enjoyed its heyday in the 1930s, when the music and entertainment was supplied courtesy of anti-Bolshevik Russian émigrés. These days it's home to an assortment of attractive but rather overpriced and touristy restaurants. Far better is **Nevizade Sokak**, a street dedicated to fish restaurants (all with outside tables) and incredibly lively bars and clubs.

Pera Museum

Meşrutiyet Cad 25, Tepebaşı • Tues–Thurs & Sat 10am–7pm, Fri 10am–10pm & Sun noon–6pm • ₺10 • ⓦ peramuzesi.org

Housed in an artfully restored nineteenth-century building that was formerly the prestigious *Bristol Hotel*, the wonderful **Pera Museum** (Pera Müzesi) is home to an impressive collection of European Orientalist works, painted between the seventeenth and nineteenth centuries, as well as ceramics from Küthaya and an interesting collection of historic weights and measures. It's also the most convenient place in the city to see temporary exhibitions of works by major international artists.

Museum of Innocence

Masümiyet Müzesi • Çukurcuma Caddesi, Dalgıç Çıkmazı 2 • Tues–Wed & Thurs–Sun 10am–6pm, Thurs 10am–9pm • ₺25 • ⓦ masumiyetmuzesi.org

The Museum of Innocence is the brainchild of Turkey's best-known author, Orhan Pamuk (see p.694). Downstairs, a glass case contains the butts of the 4213 cigarettes smoked by the main character of Pamuk's novel of the same name between 1976 and 1984, while engaged in a doomed affair with a woman of lower social status, Füsun. It helps to have the read the book before visiting – not least because if you present the book for stamping on the relevant page you get in free – but even if you haven't, lovers of nostalgia will enjoy the videos of period Turkish adverts and glass cases with collections of kitsch pot dogs, vintage costumes and the like. All the exhibits are things the novel's lovers wore, used, saw or experienced during their affair, artily laid out in a converted 1920s townhouse.

Taksim Square and around

Taksim in Turkish means "distribution"; **Taksim Square** takes its name from the low **stone reservoir** on its south side. The reservoir was constructed in 1732 to distribute water brought from the Belgrade Forest by aqueduct. The green area on the south side of the square, with a pleasant tea garden and some kids' play equipment, is **Gezi Parkı**. Here, in the late Spring of 2013, demonstrators protesting government plans to cut down the trees and redevelop the area as a shopping mall occupied the square. Heavy-handed police tactics soon led to the anti-government protests which were filmed and beamed globally, with mainly young, secular-minded Turks coming under fire from water canons and tear gas. Redevelopment plans have stalled, but the iconic **Atatürk Cultural Centre** (Atatürk Kültür Merkezi or AKM), east of Taksim Square, remains closed.

1

Military Museum

1.5km north of Taksim • Wed–Sun 9am–5pm • ₺4 • Walk or catch a bus north along Cumhuriyet Cad to the Istanbul Radyoevi (radio building), or take the M2 metro to Osmanbey

Istanbul's **Military Museum** (Askeri Müzesi) is housed in the military academy where Atatürk received some of his training. Its comprehensive collection of memorabilia is proudly displayed and labelled in English. The most striking exhibits are the cotton- and silk-embroidered tents used by campaigning sultans, and a rich collection of Ottoman armour and weaponry. A traditional Ottoman military band known as the Mehter performs daily between 3pm and 4pm.

Tophane

The mixed dockland area of **Tophane** is named after the Imperial Armoury – now housing a university – that churned out cannonballs for the Ottoman war machine. It's dotted with venerable Ottoman buildings, most notably the **Kılıç Paşa Camii**, dating from 1780, and the more recent **Nusretiye Camii** (1822), both recently restored.

Istanbul Modern

Meclis-i Mebusan Caddesi • Tues–Sun 10am–6pm, Thurs 10am–8pm • ₺17 • ⓦ istanbulmodern.org • From Sultanahmet, take the T1 tramway to the Tophane stop just west of Nusretiye Camii, from where it's a 3min walk

Turkey's leading contemporary arts gallery, **Istanbul Modern**, is housed in a revamped warehouse on the edge of the Bosphorus, just in front of the Nusretiye Camii. The interior is all big, blank white walls and exposed ventilation pipes, with picture windows giving views across the Bosphorus to the Topkapı Palace. The collection includes the best of modern Turkish art, as well as some intriguing video installations from foreign artists. There's a reference library, a cinema showing arts and independent movies, and a trendy café with a terrace overlooking the Bosphorus.

Beşiktaş

Bus #25/T or #40 from Taksim or #28 or #28/T from Eminönü

Most visitors to the district of **Beşiktaş** are here to see the **Dolmabahçe Palace**, successor to Topkapı as the residence of the Ottoman sultans. However, it's worth spending a few more hours in the neighbourhood if you can, to visit the city's excellent **Naval Museum**, as well as **Yıldız Parkı** and palace. It's also home to one of Istanbul's three major football teams (see opposite).

Dolmabahçe Palace

Dolmabahçe Caddesi • Tues, Wed & Fri–Sun: Nov–March 8.30am–4pm; April–Oct 8.30am–5pm • Selamlık/administrative section ₺30, harem ₺20, combined ticket ₺40 (no combined tickets sold after 3pm) • No cameras allowed inside • ⓦ millisaraylar.gov.tr

The **Dolmabahçe Palace** is the largest and most extravagant of all the palaces on the Bosphorus, with an impressive 600m waterside frontage. Flanked by symmetrical flower-lined gardens, with a magnificent clover-shaped pond and fountain at its heart, the exterior of the palace is arguably more beautiful than the interior. It was built in the mid-nineteenth century by Armenian architect Karabet Balian and his son Nikoğos, and its brazen riches suggest that good taste suffered along with the fortunes of the Ottoman Empire. The modern European stylings opt for flamboyance over flair, with crystal-lined staircases and chandeliers, dazzling upholstery and such profuse lashings of gold that the effect is a virtual assault on the senses.

1

With groups of up to fifty people ushered through at a rapid pace, the tour experience is more akin to herding cattle; the friendly, multilingual guides spend more time dealing with crowd control than dealing out choice snippets of information about the key rooms.

The first half of the tour consists of shuffling down corridors, peeking into the cordoned-off rooms and trundling single-file through exhibition rooms that display semi-interesting collections of delicate tea cups and ornate household items. The second floor holds a few more impressive highlights – the **Sultan's reception room** is a Venetian-style boudoir with an outrageously decadent gold-plated ceiling; the antiquated **Abdülmecit Library** offers an intriguing glimpse into the past; and the hamam and bathing quarters feature possibly the world's most luxurious squat toilet, made of exquisite marble. In the dining hall, the handmade parquet floors – an intricate puzzle design carved from ebony, rosewood and mahogany – are an incongruously delicate masterpiece.

The masterful 36m-high **ceremonial hall** (double the height of the rest of the rooms), held up by 56 elaborate columns, is the crown jewel of the tour. Its centrepiece, a 4.5tonne crystal chandelier glittering with 664 bulbs, is among the largest ever made – a lavish present from Queen Victoria.

The harem section provides little stylistic deviation from the main building; its main attraction is Atatürk's bedroom, where the founder of the Turkish Republic died in 1938. The room itself, with its enormous Turkish flag adorning the bed, is a little disappointing except for Atatürk-loving Turkish visitors. The clock in the room is still set at 09.05 – the hour of his death.

The Naval Museum

Barbaros Hayrettin Paşa İskelesi Sok, off Beşiktaş Caddesi • Tues–Sun 9am–5pm (summer weekends 10am–6pm) • ₺6 • Ⓦ denizmuzesi.tsk.tr

The revamped **Naval Museum** (Deniz Müzesi) is housed in a large, well-designed building completed in 2013. On the entrance floor are temporary exhibitions, a café and a kids' play area. Reached by a gently graded ramp, a huge room, lit by glass picture windows looking onto the strait, contains a magnificent collection of restored

---

FEVER PITCH

Istanbul's three leading football teams **Beşiktaş**, **Fenerbahçe** and **Galatasaray** receive fanatical support – match times remain one of the few occasions when the city streets fall silent – and dominate the Turkish league. While there are sporadic outbreaks of football violence, the chances of a foreigner getting caught up in it are slim. There are two Turkish daily newspapers, *Fotomaç* and *Fanatik*, devoted almost entirely to the three Istanbul heavyweights, while matches (Aug–May) are staggered over each weekend in season so television coverage of the three doesn't clash.

Beşiktaş's (☎0212 236 7202, Ⓦ bjk.com.tr) old İnönü Stadium was under reconstruction at the time of writing. The stadium has been re-branded the Vodafone Arena. It's on Kadırgalar Cad, between Taksim and Beşiktaş, opposite the Dolmabahçe Palace; walk down the hill, or take bus #23/B from Taksim Square or #30 from Sultanahmet or Eminönü.

Fenerbahçe, the wealthiest club (☎0216 449 5667, Ⓦ fenerbahce.org), play at the 52,000-capacity Şükrü Saracoğlu Stadyium on Bağdat Cad in Kızıltoprak on the Asian side of the Bosphorus; take a ferry to Kadıköy, then a dolmuş marked "Cadde Bostan".

Galatasaray (☎0212 251 5707, Ⓦ galatasaray.org) play at the Türkcell Arena Stadyumu in Aslantepe (Şişli); catch the M2 metro from Taksim to Sanayı then the branch line to Seyrentepe.

Tickets are sold at the stadiums two days before a match. Regular fixtures cost from ₺35. Tickets are also available online from Biletix (Ⓦ biletix.com) and Biletix outlets. For information in English see Ⓦ www.budgetairlinefootball.co.uk.

1

caïques, one complete with life-like mannequins. These elegant boats were once used to row the sultans to and from their homes along the Bosphorus. The oarsmen – the *Bostanci* – reputedly barked like dogs while they rowed so as not to overhear the sultans talking. The largest of these caïques, dating from 1648, needed an incredible 144 oarsmen to power it. Downstairs is an exhibition devoted to woodcarving in the Ottoman navy, which has some superb figureheads. Further rooms have exhibits and information on important milestones in Ottoman naval history, right up to the Çanakkale/Gallipoli campaigns (see p.192) of WWI.

Yıldız Parkı

Public entrance opposite the Çırağan Sarayı on Çırağan Cad • Daily 8am–11pm • Free

Yıldız Parkı is a vast wooded area, dotted with mansions, pavilions, lakes and gardens, which was the centre of the Ottoman Empire for thirty years during the reign of Abdülhamid II. Its superb hillside location makes this one of the most popular places in Istanbul for city-dwellers.

Yıldız Chalet Museum

Şale Köşkü • Tues, Wed & Fri–Sun: March–Sept 9.30am–5pm; Oct–Feb 9.30am–4pm • ₺4

The most important surviving building in Yıldız Parkı is the Yıldız Chalet Museum, or Şale Köşkü. Like the Dolmabahçe Palace (see p.106), it was designed partly by the Armenian Balian brothers and partly by the Italian D'Aronco. The first of the pavilion's three separate sections was modelled on a Swiss chalet, while the other two were built to receive Kaiser Wilhelm II on his first and second state visits, in 1889 and 1898. The inside of the *köşk* belies its peeling exterior – the most impressive room, the **Ceremonial Hall**, takes up the greater part of the third section, with a Hereke carpet so big (approximately 400 square metres) that part of a wall was knocked down to install it. In the attractive dining room, at the top of the central stairway in the central section, the dining chairs were carved by the reclusive Abdülhamit himself, who lived here after deciding that the Bosphorus-front Dolmabahçe and Çırağan palaces were too open to potential assassins.

Ortaköy

1km northeast of Beşiktaş, beyond Yıldız Parkı and the Çırağan Palace • Bus #40 or #42T from Taksim or #30 from Eminönü; or T1 tram from the old city to Kabataş, then bus #22 or #25/E to Ortaköy; or take a bus or ferry to Beşiktaş and walk 15min

The former Bosphorus backwater of **Ortaköy** was traditionally an area of tolerance – a mosque, church and synagogue have existed side by side for centuries. While it remains cosmopolitan, its erstwhile character has been hijacked by flash nightclubs, trendy eateries, and the overwhelming presence of the first Bosphorus suspension bridge, completed in 1973, just to the north.

There's a lively Sunday market, and daily market stalls sell trendy silver jewellery and sunglasses on the waterfront. That's also the location of the attractive, Baroque **Büyük Mecidiye Camii**, built in 1855 and much photographed in juxtaposition with the suspension bridge towering behind.

The Golden Horn

Northwest of Beyoğlu, along the newly spruced-up north shore of the once heavily polluted **Golden Horn**, a couple of sights are well worth a look, especially if you're fed up with historic buildings and/or have kids in tow: the **Rahmi M. Koç Industrial Museum** and **Miniatürk**.

The Rahmi M. Koç Industrial Museum

Hasköy Cad 27 • April–Sept Tues–Fri 10am–5pm, Sat & Sun 10am–8pm; Oct–March Tues–Fri 10am–5pm, Sat & Sun 10am–6pm • ₺12.5 • ⓦ www.rmk-museum.org.tr • Catch bus #47 from Eminönü, on the opposite side of the Horn, or the #54/HT from Taksim; or it's a short walk from Hasköy ferry terminal, a stop for ferries between Eminönü and Eyüp

Formerly home to a substantial Jewish community, **Hasköy**, a couple of kilometres up the Golden Horn from Karaköy, was also the location of an Ottoman naval shipyard and royal park. Today it's noted for the excellent **Rahmi M. Koç Industrial Museum**, an old factory restored by Rahmi M. Koç, one of Turkey's most famous – and wealthiest – industrialists, to house his private collection of models, machines, vehicles and toys. Upstairs, the starboard main engine of the *Kalender* steam ferry, made in Newcastle-upon-Tyne in 1911, is the main exhibit. Downstairs holds a number of old bikes, from penny-farthings to an early Royal Enfield motorbike, and much else besides.

Miniatürk

İmrahor Cad • April–Oct Mon–Fri 9am–7pm; Nov–April daily 9am–5pm • ₺10 • ⓦ www.miniaturk.com • Bus #47, #47Ç, #47E, #47N from Eminönü, or #54/HT from Taksim

Upstream of Hasköy in dull Sütlüce, on the north side of the monumental Haliç Bridge, **Miniatürk** is one of those attractions you'll either love or hate. It displays over a hundred 1:25 scale models of Turkey's most impressive sights, spaced out along a 1.8km signed route. Istanbul itself is home to 45 of the attractions – from mundane Sirkeci Post Office through to the Blue Mosque – while another 45 cover sights in Anatolia. Not all the well-detailed models are buildings – if you've ever wanted to see Cappadocia's fairy chimneys or the travertine cascades of Pamukkale in miniature, then this is the place to do so.

Asian Istanbul

The best single reason to head across to the **Asian shore** of the city is to experience the ferry ride. The views from the Bosphorus are superb, with domes and minarets dominating the skyline of the old city, and skyscrapers the business districts beyond Beyoğlu – and where else in the world can you cruise from one continent to another for just over a euro? The three Asian neighbourhoods, **Üsküdar**, **Haydarpaşa** and **Kadıköy**, all hold some interesting sites, including fine Ottoman mosques and a British war cemetery – not to mention a handful of eating places of some repute.

Üsküdar

Üsküdar's main square is the first stop on the Asian side of the Marmaray metro line; alternatively, catch a ferry from Eminönü; buses run from in front of İskele Camii on Paşa Liman Cad in Üsküdar up the Bosphorus, as far as Anadolu Kavağı

Üsküdar holds some notable Islamic monuments. Its most obvious mosque, **İskele** or **Mihrimah Camii**, sits on a high platform, fronted by an immense covered porch, opposite the ferry landing on İskele Meydanı. Designed by Mimar Sinan and built in 1547–48, it's the only Ottoman mosque with three semi-domes (as opposed to two or four), thanks to the requirements of a difficult site against the hillside behind.

Directly across the square is the **Yeni Valide Camii**, which was built between 1708 and 1710 by Ahmet III in honour of his mother. It's most readily identified by the Valide Sultan's green, birdcage-like tomb, whose meshed roof was designed to keep birds out while allowing rain in to water the garden tomb below.

1

Kız Kulesi

Museum Tues–Sun noon–7pm • Free • **Restaurant** Daily 7.30pm–1am • **Kız** Boats from Salacak (on the main coast road between Üsküdar and Harem) 9am–6.45pm (₺5) • A private boat service operates for those who are eating and/or drinking at the tower from 8.30pm–12.30am; see Ⓦ kizkulesi.com.tr

South of Üsküdar, on an island in the Bosphorus, the small white **Kız Kulesi** (Maiden's Tower) is also known as Leander's Tower. Many myths are associated with it: in one a princess, who was prophesied to die from a snakebite, came here to escape her fate, only to succumb to it when a serpent was delivered to her retreat in a basket of fruit. The tower also featured in the 1999 James Bond film, *The World Is Not Enough*. Now open to visitors, it doubles as an expensive restaurant in the evening.

Haydarpaşa

Ferries to Kadıköy depart regularly from Eminönü and Karaköy; take a taxi from Kadıköy to the station building

South of Üsküdar and across the bay from Kadıköy, the serried ranks of enormous nineteenth- and early twentieth-century buildings in **Haydarpaşa** make quite an impact. The palace-like **Haydarpaşa train station**, jutting into the Bosphorus, was completed in 1908 by a German architect as part of Germany's grandiose plans for a Berlin-to-Baghdad railway. It was presented to Sultan Abdülhamit II by Kaiser Wilhelm II; its stained glass is particularly impressive. The station has been made defunct by the Marmaray metro line and its future uncertain.

Directly north of the station, between the sea and Tıbbiye Caddesiare, is the Marmara University and the **British War Cemetery** (daily 7am–7pm), a beautifully kept spot sheltering the dead of the Crimean War and the two world wars.

The Florence Nightingale Museum

Kavak Iskele Cad • By appointment only, Mon–Fri 9am–5pm; fax a photocopy of the identity page of your passport – plus desired visiting date and time – and phone number to the museum's military guardians, several weeks before your intended visit • Free • ☎ 0216 553 8000 or ☏ 0216 310 7929

The imposing **Selimiye Barracks**, whose northwest wing was used as a hospital by the British during the Crimean War (1854–56), today houses the **Florence Nightingale Museum**. Florence Nightingale lived and worked in the northern tower, where she reduced the death toll among patients from twenty percent to two percent, and established universally accepted principles of modern nursing. The museum contains two of her famous lamps, and you can see the rooms where she lived and worked.

Kadıköy

The suburb of **Kadıköy** makes for a surprisingly enjoyable outing from the European side of the city. It's a lively place, with some great shops, restaurants, bars and cinemas. Towards the end of the nineteenth century, when the introduction of steam-driven ferries made it feasible to commute across the Bosphorus, Kadıköy became a popular residential area for foreign businesspeople and wealthy Greeks and Armenians. Their most visible legacy is the **churches** southeast of the ferry terminal. There's a scattering of older constructions amid the concrete: look out for the tall, narrow curves of the cream Art Deco-style **Kuru Kahveci Mehmet Efendi building**, home to the famous purveyor of Turkish Coffee, and the beautifully restored **Süreyya Opera House** on Bahariye Caddesi (see below); dating back to 1927, its ornate Neoclassical facade is adorned with relief-work pilasters, cherubs and classical-style theatre masks.

Most sites of interest in Kadıköy are located between the waterfront **Sahil Yolu** (coast road) and **Bahariye Caddesi**, a right turn off Söğütlüçeşme Caddesi, the steep, wide street that leads uphill from the ferry terminal. The two latter streets have their own tram, a grittier version of İstiklal Caddesi; indeed, the area bounded by Söğütlüçeşme

Caddesi to the north, Bahariye and Emın Bey caddesis to the east and south and the Bosphorus waterfront to the west is becoming a mini-Beyoğlu, with a similar mix of alternative-clothing outlets, bookstores and bric-a-brac shops dotted among the cafés and restaurants that spill out onto jam-packed pedestrianized streets. It's also a great area for shopping, especially for spices, coffee, olives, dried fruit, nuts, Turkish delight and other goodies, in the colourful permanent market centred on **Guneşlibahçe Sokak.**

ARRIVAL AND DEPARTURE   ISTANBUL

Istanbul's main points of arrival by air are **Atatürk airport** on the European side of the Bosphorus, and **Sabiha Gökçen airport** across the strait in Asia. A major third airport northwest of the city is under construction. Most buses come into **Esenler bus station**, in the suburbs on the European side, and trains into the centrally located **Sirkeci station**. Taxis and public transport run from all these transport hubs to the main accommodation areas, in Sultanahmet and Taksim/Beyoğlu.

BY PLANE

Atatürk airport 24km west of the centre at Yeşilköy, near the Sea of Marmara (Atatürk Hava Lımani; ☎0212 465 5555, ⓦ ataturkairport.com). The international (*dışhatları*) and domestic (*içhatları*) terminals are in linked buildings.

Sabiha Gökçen airport Near Pendik on the Asian side of the city (☎0216 585 5000, ⓦ sgairport.com).

Destinations Adana (at least 17 daily; 1hr 30min); Ankara (at least 25 daily; 1hr 5min); Antalya (at least 22 daily; 1hr 5min); Bodrum (at least 11 daily; 1hr); Dalaman (at least 6 daily; 1hr 10min); Denizli (2 daily; 1hr 10min); Diyarbakır (at least 10 daily; 1hr 45min); Erzurum (at least 4 daily; 1hr 50min); Gaziantep (at least 6 daily; 1hr 40min); İzmir (at least 18 daily; 1hr); Kars (direct 2 daily; 2hr; via Ankara 3 daily; at least 3hr 25min); Kayseri (at least 4 daily; 1hr 25min); Konya (at least 7 daily; 1hr 15min); Malatya (at least 4 daily; 1hr 30min); Mardin (at least 3 daily direct; 2hr; 3 daily via Ankara; at least 4hr 10min); Samsun (at least 6 daily; 1hr 15min); Şanlıurfa (at least 3 daily; 1hr 50min); Trabzon (at least 10 daily; 1hr 35min); Van (at least 4 daily; 2hr 5min).

TRANSFERS FROM ATATÜRK

By bus The Havataş bus service (☎444 2656, ⓦ havatas .com) runs from both the international and the domestic terminals to Taksim Square (every 30min, daily 4am–1am; 30–40min; ₺11). The bus drops old city bound visitors at Aksaray, 200m from Yenikapı train station; walk up the hill to the Aksaray T1 tram stop for trams into Sultanahmet or Eminönü. To return to Atatürk airport, Havataş buses depart from Taksim Square, picking up at Aksaray (every 30min, daily 4am–1am; ₺11).

By metro The M1 metro (*hafif metro*; see p.115) runs from the airport to the city centre (every 10min, daily 6am–midnight). To catch it, follow signs for "Hafif Metro/Rapid Transit", and buy two tokens or *jetons* (₺4 each) from the kiosk; alternatively and much cheaper in the long run, buy the *Istanbulkart* (see p.113), for ₺10, also from a vending-machine near the barriers, and top it up with travel credit at another machine. Get off at Zeytinburnu and follow the signs a short distance to the Zeytinburnu T1 tram stop, which is where you need the second *jeton*. The T1 tram runs to the centre of the old city, Sultanahmet, where many visitors stay. For visitors heading across the Golden Horn to the Galata/Beyoğlu/Taksim areas, take the M1 metro to Yenikapı. Change here onto the M2 metro and get off at Şişhane (for Galata and the south part of Beyoğlu) or Taksim (for Taksim Square or the northern part of Beyoğlu).

By taxi A taxi from Atatürk airport to Sultanahmet or Taksim should cost around ₺50. Many hotels, and several travel agents on Divan Yolu Cad, can arrange airport taxi collections and drop-offs (on request) for around ₺40.

TRANSFERS FROM SABIHA GÖKÇEN

By bus Havataş shuttle buses run into Taksim Square (every 30min, daily 4am–1am; journey time 1hr 30min; ₺14); return trips from Taksim run longer hours (every 30min, daily 3.30am–1am). You can also buy an *Istanbulkart* (see p.113) from the kiosk outside the airport, and catch the green #E10 bus to Kadiköy (journey time 45min; ₺4). The bus terminates opposite the Turyol ferry, which will whisk you across the Bosphorus to either Eminönü (for Sultanahmet) or Karaköy (for Beyoğlu) for

THE MARMARAY PROJECT

In the autumn of 2013 a tunnel under the Bosphorus was completed, and an **underwater link** between European and Asian Istanbul – an idea that first hit the drawing board back in the Ottoman period – finally became a reality. Visitors can now hop on a metro train at iconic Sirkeci station and be whisked under the Bosphorus to Üsküdar in Asia in a couple of minutes. When the Marmaray line is completed (slated, optimistically, for 2016) it will link the termini of the European and Asian rail networks, theoretically opening up the possibility of direct rail travel between the Atlantic and Pacific seaboards.

1

ISTANBUL BUS COMPANIES

The following reputable bus companies are based at Esenler *otogar*.
Adıyaman Ünal (bay 29; ☎0146 216 1112, ⓦadiyamanunalturizm.com.tr) for Nemrut Dağı.
Göreme Turizm (bay 18; ☎0212 658 1213) for Cappadocia.
Has Diyarbakır (☎444 1121, ⓦhasdiyarbakir.com.tr) for southeast Anatolia.
Kamil Koç (bays 144–146; ☎0212 658 2000, ⓦkamilkoc.com.tr) to Ankara and Aegean and Mediterranean resorts.
Mersin (bay 8; ☎0212 658 3535) for the east.
Metro (bays 51–52; ☎444 3455, ⓦmetroturizm.com.tr) for the Black Sea coast.
Nevtur (bay 24; ☎444 5050) for Cappadocia.
Nevşehir Seyahat (☎444 5050, ⓦnevsehirlilerseyahat.com.tr) for Cappadocia.
Özdiyarbakır (bay 152; ☎0212 658 0475, ⓦozkaymak.com.tr) for southeast Turkey, Konya and the southwest Mediterranean.
Pamukkale (bays 41–42; ☎0212 658 2222, ⓦpamukkale.com.tr) to the west and southern coasts.
Ulusoy (bay 127; ☎444 1818, ⓦulusoy.com.tr) to major cities and the Black Sea coast.
Vangölü (bays 47–48; ☎0432 2231545, ⓦvangoluturizm.com.tr) to Van and eastern Turkey.
Varan (bays 1–2; ☎444 8999, ⓦvaran.com.tr) for western and southern destinations including nonstop luxury services to Ankara, İzmir and south-coast resorts.
Yeşil Artvin Ekspres (bays 71–72; ☎0466 2126161, ⓦyesilartvinekspres.com.tr) to Black Sea and northeast Turkey.

₺34 – note that the Turyol service only operates 6.45am–8.30pm. Alternatively there's an IDO ferry a short walk south, with the last ferry to Eminönü at 8.30pm, and a useful later ferry to Karaköy at 11pm.
By taxi A taxi into town from Sabiha Gökçen will cost at least ₺70.

AIRLINES

Most airlines have their offices around Taksim Square, Elmadağ and the business districts of Şişli/Levent further north. Major world player THY (Turkish Airlines; ☎444 0849, ⓦturkishairlines.com) offers the widest range of domestic and international flights; its subsidiary Anadolujet (☎444 2538, ⓦanadolujet.com.tr) offers budget flights throughout Turkey but all are routed via Ankara. Other budget carriers, which also offer a limited number of international flights, include Atlas Jet (☎444 3387, ⓦatlasjet.com), Pegasus Airlines (☎444 0737, ⓦflypgs.com), Onur Air (☎0212 233 3800, ⓦonurair.com.tr) and Sunexpress (☎444 0797, ⓦsunexpresss.com).

BY TRAIN

The city's two traditional main-line train stations –Sirkeci in Europe and Haydarpaşa in Asia, have been made redundant by massive transport infrastructure projects both within Istanbul and in European Turkey and Anatolia. For the moment, to head into Anatolia by rail travellers must head for the Asian-side suburb of Pendik, 25km from the city centre, using a combination of ferry, metro and taxi, then take the new high-speed train to Ankara, which connects with much of the rest of Turkey's rail network. Works on the line to the west, linking Istanbul with Europe, mean passsengers are ferried out by bus to the Turkish/

Bulgarian border, where they board the train for Bucharest (Bosfor Ekspresi; daily departures). Keep an eye out for any updates on ⓦseat61.com.

BY BUS

Istanbul has two major *otogars* (bus stations): Esenler, 10km northwest of the centre, and Harem, on the Asian side between Üsküdar and Kadıköy. Most national bus services stop at both, regardless of destination, and both are open 24hr.

ESENLAR OTOGAR

Esenler bus station is well organized. Some 150 companies have numbered ticket stands; most run free service buses to and from Taksim, or can arrange for you to travel with another company. To get to Sultanahmet from Esenler, take the M1 metro (every 15min, daily 6am–midnight) from the station in the centre of the *otogar* to Aksaray, and then switch to the T1 tram to Sultanahmet. After midnight, your only option is to take a taxi into town (around ₺30). Travelling from the city centre to Esenler by metro, remember to get off at Otogar, not Esenler station. For tickets booked through a travel agent or bus company's city offices, a (free) shuttle service runs from Taksim or Sultanahmet to Esenler (usually an hour before departure).

HAREM OTOGAR

Arriving in Istanbul by bus from Asia, it's worth disembarking at Harem, thus saving a tedious journey to Esenler through terrible traffic snarl-ups. From Harem, regular (car) ferries cross the Bosphorus to Eminönü (every hour, daily 7.30am–9.30pm), while private boats run to Beşiktaş and Kabataş. Dolmuşes run every few minutes to

Kadıköy and to Üsküdar, leaving from the south side of the complex, beyond the ticket offices. From either of these suburbs, ferries cross to Eminönü (daily 7am–8.40pm), or from Üsküdar to Beşiktaş (daily 7am–8.30pm) for Taksim.

DOMESTIC BUS SERVICES

Although distances are long, bus travel in Turkey is generally very comfortable, and still usually works out cheaper than taking an internal flight (see p.35).

Black Sea coast Artvin (daily; 21hr); Hopa (3 daily; 18hr); Rize (4 daily; 18hr); Samsun (4 daily; 9hr); Trabzon (9 daily; 17hr).

Cappadocia Göreme (5 daily; 11hr); Nevşehir (5 daily; 11hr); Ürgüp (5 daily; 11hr 30min).

Eastern Turkey Diyarbakır (3 daily; 19hr); Doğubeyazıt (daily; 24hr); Erzurum (3 daily; 24hr); Gaziantep (several daily; 16hr); Konya (7 daily; 10hr); Mardin (daily; 22hr); Urfa (daily; 21hr).

Mediterranean and Aegean coasts Adana (several daily; 13.5hr); Alanya (12 daily; 15hr); Antakya (2 daily; 17hr); Antalya (several in the evening from 6pm; 12hr); Ayvalık (hourly; 8hr); Bodrum (hourly; 12hr); Datça (daily; 17hr); Fethiye (3 daily in the evening; 14hr); İzmir (hourly; 10hr); Kuşadası (5 daily; 9hr); Marmaris (4 daily; 13hr); Side (several in the evening from 6pm; 14hr).

Western Turkey Ankara (several hourly; 6hr); Bandırma (hourly; 5hr); Bursa (hourly; 4hr); Çanakkale (hourly; 6hr); Denizli (3 daily; 11hr); Edirne (hourly; 2hr 30min); Kütahya (6 daily; 5hr 30min).

INTERNATIONAL BUS SERVICES

Onward travel by bus to neighbouring countries can make sense – especially if you want to be flexible. Buses depart from the Esenler *otogar*.

Bulgaria With Alpar and Metro: Sofya (several daily; 12hr).

Georgia With Mahmudoğlu: Tiflis (2 daily; 24hr).

Greece With Ulusoy: Thessaloniki (daily; 10hr).

Russia With Ortadoğu: Moscow (2 weekly; 36hr).

BY FERRY

Passenger-only sea bus (*deniz otobüsleri*) and high-speed car/passenger ferries (*hızlı feribotları*) operated by IDO (Istanbul Deniz Otobüsleri; ☏ 0212 444 4436, ⓦ ido.com .tr), run from Yalova and Bandırma (on the İzmir–Istanbul route), arriving at the Yenikapı ferry terminal, off Kennedy Caddesi in Kumkapı, just south of Aksaray. From here, catch the Marmaray metro to Sirkeci, from where it's a short walk to Sultanahmet, or across the Golden Horn to Galata/ Beyoğlu/Taksim. There are also IDO car ferries across the Bosphorus from Harem to Eminönü (daily 7.30am–9.30pm).

Destinations Bandırma (*hızlı feribotları* 3 daily, more at weekends; 2hr; many connect with the train to İzmir; *deniz otobüsleri* 2 weekly); Güzelyalı (for Bursa; *hızlı feribotları* at least 4 daily; *deniz otobüsleri* 6 weekly mid-June to end Aug); Yalova (*hızlı feribotları* at least 7 daily; 1hr; *deniz otobüsleri* daily).

CRUISE SHIPS

Passengers arriving on cruise ships go through customs and immigration procedures at Karaköy International Maritime Passenger Terminal, across the Galata Bridge from Eminönü. From here, you can either take the T1 tram to Sultanahmet; the Tünel up to Beyoğlu; the funicular from Kabataş to Taksim Square; or a taxi.

GETTING AROUND

Istanbul has a wide range of transport, from ferry to high-speed tram. Traffic jams are unavoidable, so where possible either walk or travel by tram, metro, suburban train or ferry, though all can be jam-packed at peak times. The newly extended metro and tramway links most parts of the city that you're likely to want to visit, while the bus system is daunting, but manageable on certain routes. Dolmuşes (shared taxis) and minibuses are occasionally useful and cheap and

---

ISTANBULKART – THE SMARTCARD WAY TO TRAVEL

An **Istanbulkart** is a must for anyone staying in Istanbul for a few days who wants to explore the city on public transport. A credit-card-sized smartcard, it can be purchased for ₺10 from machines at Atatürk and Sabiha Gökçen airports on arrival. This fee includes ₺4 credit. It can also be purchased for ₺6 (sometimes there is a mark-up of a further ₺1) in Eminönü, Sultanahmet, Sirkeci, Beyazıt/Grand Bazaar, Aksaray and many other major transport stops, and be "charged" to whatever value you require at the same places – or from machines labelled "Elektronik bilet ve dolum cihazı" (electronic ticket top-up machine), located close to major transport stops. These provide touch-screen instructions in English and German as well as Turkish. The passes are accepted on all municipal and some private buses, sea buses, ferries, the metro and the tram. Convenience aside, you also make a sizeable saving on each journey (1.95 kuruş) by using your card rather than a *jeton*, and bigger savings on Princes' Islands ferries, the antique tram and Tünel.

The entrances to tram, metro, train and ferry transport stops hold turnstiles; place the *Istanbulkart* against the receptor, and the journey cost (₺2.05) is deducted.

1

JETONS

If you don't want to buy the *Istanbulkart* (see p.113), you'll have to buy plastic tokens (*jetons*), which work on city buses, trams, metro, rail and ferries, from a *Jetonmatik* machine. Located next to many stops – including Eminönü, Sultanahmet and Sirkeci – the machines accept 5, 10 and ₺20 notes as well as 25 kuruş, 50 kuruş and ₺1 coins. You insert the *jetons* into the turnstiles at the entrance to tram, metro, train and ferry stops.

taxis very reasonably priced (assuming you're not over-charged). A great way to explore a city that, historically, has put its best face towards the water, is by ferry.

BY BUS

Istanbul's buses (*otobus* in Turkish) are usually the red-and-cream, green and green/blue municipality buses, all with "IETT" (Istanbul Elektrik Tramvay ve Tünel) written on them. For information on bus routes and numbers (which change regularly) see ⓦ iett.gov.tr/en. There are also some private buses, usually pale blue. Most buses run daily 6.30am–11.30pm. For all municipal buses, either use an *Istanbulkart* (see p.113) or buy a *jeton* (₺4; see above) in advance from a *Jetonmatik* machine.

BUS TERMINALS

The old city holds useful bus terminals at Beyazıt, Eminönü and Vezneciler, across the Golden Horn in Taksim Square, Beşiktaş and Kabataş and, on the Asian side, at Üsküdar and Kadıköy.

Eminönü From Eminönü bus station, three tram stops down the hill from Sultanahmet, buses run to Taksim; westbound to Aksaray and Topkapı; and to the Bosphorus shore through Beşiktaş, Ortaköy and Arnavutköy to Bebek, where you can change to continue through the suburbs as far as the village of Rumeli Kavaği.

Taksim Square Buses from Taksim Square head through Mecidiyeköy to the northern suburbs; down along the Bosphorus through Beşiktaş, Ortaköy and Aranvutköy; and across the Horn to Topkapı and Aksaray.

USEFUL ROUTES

#12 and #12/A Kadıköy to Üsküdar
#15 Üsküdar along the Bosphorus to Beylerbeyi, Kanlıca and Beykoz
#22 Kabataş up the Bosphorus to Beşiktaş, Ortaköy, Kuruçeşme, Arnavutköy, Bebek, Emirgan and İstinye
#25/A Levent Metro, Maslak, Sariyer and Rumeli Kavaği
#28T Topkapı to Beşiktaş via Fatih, Eminönü, Karaköy, Tophane and Kabataş
#36/V and #37/Y Vezneciler to Edirenkapı
#38 Beyazıt to Edirnekapı (city land walls)
#38/E Eminönü to Edirne Kapı via Unkapanı/Atatürk Bridge and Fatih
#40 Taksim up the Bosphorus including Beşiktaş, Kuruçeşme, Arnavutköy, Bebek, Emirgan, İstinye, Tarabya and Sariyer

#54HT Taksim to upper Golden Horn (for Miniatürk, Rami Koç Museum and Santralistanbul).

FUNICULARS AND THE CABLE CAR

Use your *Istanbulkart* or buy a *jeton* for both of these.
Tünel Known as the Tünel, the antique funicular between Karaköy and İstiklal Caddesi in Beyoğlu connects with the antique tram (see below) on İstiklal Caddesi.
F1 A modern funicular, F1 links Kabata, at the northern end of the tramline, with Taksim Square (and the M2 metro).
Cable car The cable car that links the southern shore of the Golden Horn in Eyüp with the *Pierre Loti* café and Eyüp cemetery may not connect with the rail or tram systems, but it does save your legs.

BY TRAM

T1 tram The main T1 tram service runs from Zeytinburnu via Topkapı Gate to Aksaray, Laleli, Beyazıt, Cemberlitaş, Sultanahmet, downhill to Eminönü, and across the Galata Bridge to Karaköy (for Beyoğlu/Galata), Tophane, Fındıklı and Kabataş (where it connects with the funicular to Taksim Square and the ferry terminal for boats to the Princes' Islands). Trams are frequent and operate 6am–midnight. Approaching trams signal their arrival with a bell, and passengers must wait on the concrete platforms, placed at regular intervals along the tracks. Note that the tram stops are marked, confusingly, by the same "M" sign as the metro. *Jetons* (₺4) can be bought at machines next to the platforms, and are put in turnstiles on entry, or you can use the *Istanbulkart*.
Antique tram The antique tram (with ticket collectors in appropriately antiquated uniforms) runs between the Tünel station, at the Beyoğlu end of İstiklal Caddesi, for 1.5km to Taksim Square (every 15min, daily 9am–9pm; ₺4). *Jetons* can be purchased from kiosks at either end of the route or at the one fixed stop halfway at Galatasaray School; *Istanbulkart* also accepted.

BY METRO

There are several metro lines in Istanbul, but only two are of interest to the vast majority of visitors. Trains run every 4 mins at peak times (6am–midnight); *jetons* (₺4) are inserted in turnstiles on entry, or use the *Istanbulkart*.

M1 The southern M1 metro line runs west from Yenikapı in the old city via the intercity *otogar* near Esenler, to Atatürk airport. Although it's called a metro, only short sections run underground.

M2 The M2 metro runs from Yenikapı underground across the old city, briefly emerging to cross the Golden Horn by bridge before disappearing back underground. First stop north of the Golden Horn is Şişhane (at the southern end of İstiklal Caddesi). The line then runs all the way out to Hacıosman via Taksim Square, Osmanbey, Şişli, Gayrettepe Levent and Levent 4.

BY DOLMUŞES AND MINIBUSES

Dolmuşes are shared taxis – either cabs or, more usually, minibuses – that run on fixed routes, departing only when full ("dolmuş" means "full"). Vehicles display their destination in the window, and charge a flat fare fixed by the municipality: watch what Turkish passengers are paying – usually a little more than a municipality bus – shout your destination to the driver and pay accordingly, passing the money via other passengers. Dolmuş and minibus stands at points of origin are denoted with a signposted "D".

Routes The only dolmuş routes of interest to most visitors are the yellow minibuses departing from the northern end of Tarlabaşı Bulvarı, just below Taksim Square, which run across into the old town and along the Sea of Marmara to the city land walls near Yedikule. Minibuses run up the Asian side of the Bosphorus between Kadıköy and Üsküdar and beyond.

BY TAXI

Taxis are ubiquitous, with over 19,000 legal *taksici* (taxi drivers) in Istanbul. They are invariably painted yellow. Fares are reasonable: an official rate of ₺2 per km plus a flat starting rate of ₺3.2, with an extra toll when crossing either of the Bosphorus bridges. All taxis are equipped with meters, but check that the driver switches it on to avoid arguments later. Check Ⓦtaksiyle.com/en for the latest information and a fare calculator. It's also worth noting that there are upward of ten thousand unregistered cabs in the city – be wary.

BY FERRY AND SEA BUS

ŞEHIR HATLARI

The main ferry company is the efficient Şehir Hatları (City Lines; ☎444 1851, Ⓦsehirhatlari.com.tr). Timings change seasonally; it's essential to get hold of the current timetable, available from the ferry terminals and from tourist offices as well as their website, so that you can be sure when the last ferry back departs. The busiest routes, such as Karaköy to Kadıköy, generally have three to five ferries per hour, 6am–11pm; all charge a flat fare of ₺4 each way. For both ferries and the faster sea buses (see p.35), buy a *jeton* and deposit it at the turnstile on entry, or use your *Istanbulkart*.

THE BOSPHORUS CRUISE

Taking a **boat trip** up the Bosphorus, from the bustling quays of Eminönü to the quiet fishing village of Anadolu Kavağı, is a highlight of any visit to Istanbul. The long **Bosphorus Cruise**, run by the Şehir Hatları company (☎444 1851, Ⓦsehirhatlari.com.tr), leaves from the Boğaz Ferry Terminal just east of the Galata Bridge in Eminönü (daily: May–Oct 10.35am & 1.35pm, Nov–April 10.35am; one-way ₺15, round trip ₺25).

In summer, especially at weekends, the queues to buy **tickets** can be very long, so allow at least half an hour, or, preferably, buy your ticket a day or two in advance. There are also often long queues to board, so late comers end up sitting in the worst seats. The ferries are rather antiquated but comfortable enough, and you can buy snacks, sandwiches and drinks on board. The round trip, including a 2hr 30min **lunch** stop at Anadolu Kavağı, takes about seven hours.

The boat **stops** at Beşiktaş, Kanlıca (Asia), Sariyer and Rumeli Kavağı (all Europe) and, finally, Anadolu Kavağı (Asia); the only stop on the return is Beşiktaş. You can leave the boat at any of the landings to explore the waterfront or hinterland, but most passengers do the return cruise. A shorter version is also available for ₺12.5, departing from the same ferry terminal and covering the same distance with no stops (other than to pick up more passengers at Üsküdar). The tour takes around two hours, departing Eminönü at 2.30pm (April–Oct daily; Nov–March Sun & public holidays).

On Saturday nights only, between early June and mid-September, a **night-time Mehtaplı cruise** (₺25) makes an attractive alternative, with the great suspension bridges lit up like Christmas trees, and the lights of Asia and Europe twinkling on either side. The boat departs Eminönü at 7pm, reaching Anadolu Kavağı at 8.30pm, where it moors for dinner, before arriving back in Eminönü around midnight.

The private Turyol company (see p.116) also runs tours up the Bosphorus, as far as the Fatih bridge. Boats depart every hour on the hour on weekdays, more frequently at weekends, and the 1hr 30min round trip costs ₺12.

1

TURYOL

The busiest routes are also served by several other small, privately run ferries, many under the umbrella of the cooperative Turyol. Most Turyol boats leave from a terminal just west of the Galata Bridge in Eminönü, or over the water in Karaköy, again just west of the Galata Bridge. The main destinations are Haydarpaşa and Kadıköy; tickets are sold at kiosks on the quayside.

CITY FERRY TERMINAL

The main City Ferry Terminal at Eminönü – between Sirkeci station and the Galata Bridge – holds a line of ferry quays or terminals (*iskelesi* in Turkish), which are listed below, from west to east. Be wary, however: at the time of writing, they were being reorganized, and the authorities may change the destinations from the new departure terminals.

Yemiş İskelesi On the west side of the Galata Bridge; Haliç Hattı (Golden Horn Lines) ferries up the Golden Horn to Eyüp via Kasımpaşa, Hasköy, Ayvansaray and Sütlüce (roughly hourly, daily 7am–8pm). The ferry actually originates across the Bosphorus in Üsküdar, so on the return journey make sure you get off at Eminönü.

Boğaz İskelesi The nearest terminal to the east side of the Galata Bridge; ferries run up the Bosphorus to Rumeli Kavağı (see p.115).

Hezarfen Ahmet Çelebi Ferries to Üsküdar (daily 6.35am–11pm).

Evliya Çelebi İskelesi Ferries across the Bosphorus to Kadıköy (daily 7.30am–9pm).

IDO terminal Car ferries to Harem (daily 8am–9.30pm).

OTHER FERRY TERMINALS

Karaköy On the north side of the Galata Bridge; regular Şehir Hatları ferries to Kadıköy (daily 6.30am–11pm).

Kabataş The last east-bound stop on the T1 tram, northeast of Galata/Beyoğlu. Ferries cross the Bosphorus to Kadıköy (Mon–Fri 7am–8pm), with a daily service (6.45am–9pm) from Beşiktaş to Kadıköy and Üsküdar. Also regular ferries to the Princes' Islands, as well as faster sea buses (*deniz otobüsleri*) run by IDO (Istanbul Deniz Otobüsleri; ☎ 0212 444 4436, ⊛ ido.com.tr; see p.115).

BY CAR

If you're determined to drive in this traffic-choked, accident-waiting-to-happen metropolis, note that the agencies below have pick-up points at Atatürk International Airport and (bar Europcar) Sabiha Gökçen, and offices elsewhere in Istanbul – check their websites for working hours. Expect to pay ₺70–190 a day for a week's rental (ten percent more for daily rental), depending on the car. Many of the major arteries around Istanbul are toll roads; they don't accept cash, so you have to buy a HGS toll card for ₺30 (₺35 from a rental agency).

INFORMATION

Tourist offices Istanbul's most helpful tourist office is on Divan Yolu Caddesi, in Sultanahmet, near the Hippodrome (daily 9am–5pm; ☎ 0212 518 8754). Others can be found in the international arrivals area of Atatürk airport (daily 24hr; ☎ 0212 573 4136); Sirkeci train station (daily 9am–5pm; ☎ 0212 511 5888); Karaköy International Maritime Passenger Terminal (Mon–Sat 9am–5pm; ☎ 0212 249 5776); and the Hilton Hotel arcade on Cumhuriyet Caddesi (Mon–Sat 9am–5pm; ☎ 0212 233 0592).

ACCOMMODATION

New hotels open in Istanbul on a seemingly daily basis, so it's nearly always possible to find a decent room with a modicum of advance planning – but bear in mind that spring and autumn are the busiest and most expensive times. For nightlife stay across the Golden Horn in Beyoğlu or Galata, while to be on the doorstep of the major historical sites base yourself in or around Sultanahmet. Virtually all but the most basic hotels have free wi-fi. Note that walk-in rack rates can often be unrealistically high, having been fixed in a busy season or for the benefit of tour companies, and many hotels will be happy to bargain. High season is mid-March to mid-November, and Christmas and New Year. Some establishments are a little cheaper in July and August, and most places offer discounts during the main low season, usually around fifteen to twenty percent.

SULTANAHMET

Some of Istanbul's best small hotels, *pansiyons* and hostels are in Sultanahmet, the historic heart of touristic Istanbul. Those around the Hippodrome are particularly well placed to offer a sense of history. Accommodation is especially concentrated in and around Akbıyık Caddesi and Cankurtaran, while the hotels off Divan Y olu Caddesi have the advantage of being handy for the tram.

AROUND THE HIPPODROME

★**Cheers Lighthouse** Çayıroğlu Sok 18 ☎ 0212 458 2324, ⊛ cheerslighthouse.com; map p.73. An imaginative offshoot of the excellent *Cheers* hostel (see opposite), this cosy hostel offers a wide range of accommodation for visitors who appreciate the communal hostel vibe yet want plenty of privacy, with both suites and dorms. On the ground floor is a great lobby, bar and terrace with views over the now defunct suburban railway line to the sea, and the attached restaurant offers outstanding food. There's free tea and coffee too. Dorm €18, suites €120

Deniz Houses Çayıroğlu Sok 14 ☎0212 518 9595, ⓦdenizhouses.com; map p.73. This very friendly establishment consists of a couple of adjacent townhouses on a characterful side street. The front rooms in A Blok have sea views but some noise from the railway, while all of the smallish rooms have funky kilims and wooden floors. Rooms in B Blok are plusher and more spacious, but lack sea views. €65

★**İbrahim Paşa** Terzihane Sok 5 Adliye Yani ☎0212 518 0394, ⓦibrahimpasha.com; map p.73. This lovingly converted pair of early twentieth-century townhouses forms arguably the most tasteful boutique hotel in Sultanahmet, successfully blending a stylish modern interior with Ottoman antiques. Views from the recently expanded roof terrace across the domes and minarets of Sultanahmet and down to the Sea of Marmara are superb, and the freshly prepared breakfast in the cosy and charming downstairs breakfast room is a delight. Ten percent discount for cash. €99

Turkoman Hotel Asmalı Çeşme Sok, Adliye Yanı 2 ☎0212 516 2956, ⓦturkomanhotel.com; map p.73. Converted house in nineteenth-century Turkish style, right on the Hippodrome and opposite the Egyptian obelisk, with fine views of the Blue Mosque from the roof terrace. Each attractive room is named after one of the old Turkoman tribes, and has a brass bed and wooden floors. Free airport transfers. €109

AROUND TOPKAPI PALACE

Ayasofya Konakları Soğukçeşme Sok ☎0212 513 3660, ⓦayasofyakonaklari.com; map p.73. Created from a series of ten nineteenth-century wooden houses on a cobbled street squeezed between the walls of the Topkapı Palace and the Haghia Sophia, this is one of the most atmospheric hotels in the city. Taking a room in the imposing Konuk Evi, a detached wooden mansion in its own garden opposite the main hotel, is about as close to period living as you can get, with original brass beds, parquet flooring adorned with Turkish carpets, and painted wooden ceilings. €170

AROUND DIVAN YOLU CADDESI

★**Cheers** Zeynepsultan Cami Sok 21 ☎0212 526 0200, ⓦcheershostel.com; map p.73. Set in an old house on a quiet side street just off the tramline below the Haghia Sophia, this hostel makes a refreshing change from the options clustered around Akbıyık Caddesi. In addition to four- and ten-bed dorms, a/c doubles and twins are available. Apart from the peaceful location, a real draw is the terrace bar, which looks over mature plane trees onto the west face of the Haghia Sophia, a view few visitors ever see. Dorm €16, double €70

Kybele Hotel Yerebatan Cad 35 ☎0212 511 7766, ⓦkybelehotel.com; map p.73. Atmospheric, unusual, late nineteenth-century rendered brick building, colourfully painted. Inside are over three thousand multi-hued antique-style light fittings and some great original Bakelite radios. The sixteen spacious rooms sport marbled wallpaper and old wood flooring. Breakfast is served in a courtyard full of candelabras, cushions, empty bottles and other knick-knacks. €110

★**Nomade Hotel** Ticarethane Sok 15 ☎0212 511 1296, ⓦhotelnomade.com; map p.73. Described as "ethnic trendy" by the French designer responsible for its chic interior, this hotel has white-floored rooms finished in bold colours, with rich coordinating fabrics and blonde-wood modernist furniture. The charming and sophisticated twin sisters who run it ensure excellent service. There's a great roof terrace, too, with stunning views across Sultanahmet. €100

Ottoman Hotel Imperial Caferiye Sok 6/1 ☎0212 513 6151, ⓦwww.ottomanhotelimperial.com; map p.73. Hard to believe this well-positioned, tastefully refurbished hotel was once the *Yücelt Hostel*, mainstay of the young and impecunious heading out to India in the 1970s (and some apparently came back). The best rooms, at a premium, have views over the Cafer Ağa Medresesi, big tubs and plasma TVs – all have tea- and coffee-making facilities. €125

Sirkeci Mansion Taya Hatun Cad 5 ☎0212 528 4344, ⓦsirkecimansion.com; map pp.86–87. Good old-fashioned comfort in a former nineteenth-century Ottoman *konak* (mansion), right next to the walls of Gülhane Parkı, with tea- and coffee-making facilities in the rooms, palatial en-suite bathrooms and comfy beds. There's a fitness centre and small pool in the basement, and free afternoon tea for guests. €170

SULTANAHMET (CANKURTARAN)

Agora Guest House Amiral Tafdil Sok 6 ☎0212 458 5547, ⓦagoraguesthouse.com; map p.73. Blurring the lines between hotel and guesthouse, this excellent budget choice is right in the heart of the old city. The tastefully furnished communal breakfast/lounge area has a massive flatscreen TV, a funky terrace and a great atmosphere. There are ten well-appointed doubles, and dorms range from four to ten beds. Dorm €17, double €80

Alp Hotel Akbıyık Cad, Adliye Sok 4 ☎0212 517 9570, ⓦalpguesthouse.com; map p.73. This fine establishment, with a dark-wood exterior, is situated down a quiet lane. Its smallish rooms (some with sea views) are immaculately furnished, some with four-poster beds, and have a/c, wooden floors and tidy bathrooms. The pretty breakfast terrace commands views of palaces, mosques and the sea. €80

★**Empress Zoe** Akbıyık Cad, Adliye Sok 10 ☎0212 518 2504, ⓦemzoe.com; map p.73. Owned by American Ann

1

Nevans, who has decorated throughout with her personal touch – the nineteen rooms are in dark wood with richly coloured textiles, accessed by a narrow spiral staircase. Parts of the basement walls belong to the remains of the Byzantine Palace, and the sun terrace has panoramic views of the Blue Mosque and Haghia Sophia. Ten percent discount for cash. €140

Four Seasons Hotel Tevfikhane Sok 1 ☎ 0212 638 8200, ⊛ fourseasons.com; map p.73. Until it was completely renovated as a five-star hotel in the early 1980s, this formidable building served as the Sultanahmet Prison. The watchtowers and exercise court are still evident beneath the flowers and vines, but the 54 beautiful high-ceilinged rooms are unrecognizable as former cells. Excellent, attentive service, as you'd expect. €490

★**Hanedan** Akbıyık Cad, Adliye Sok 3 ☎ 0212 516 4869/418 1564, ⊛ hanedanhotel.com; map p.73. Tucked away on a quiet side street off Akbıyık Cad, this friendly hotel, run by four friends, is great value for the quality of accommodation and service. The dark-wood floors in the rooms are offset by the pale plain walls, and the overall feel is of unfussy comfort. A roof terrace offers stunning views over the Haghia Sophia and the Sea of Marmara, while the great breakfast includes filter coffee. Discount for long stays. €60

★**Peninsula** Adliye Sok 6 ☎ 0212 458 6850, ⊛ hotelpeninsula.com; map p.73. Comfortable budget accommodation on a quiet side street, with the same owner as the *Hanedan* opposite. The eleven rooms are simply furnished but boast a/c, central heating and double glazing as well as flatscreen TVs. The smallest doubles are cheaper than doubles in many of the hostels, and the place is spotlessly clean and well managed. Rooms and bathrooms are on the small side, but at these prices that's to be expected; there's also a roof terrace with great views. €45

Side Hotel & Pension Utangaç Sok 20 ☎ 0212 517 2282, ⊛ sidehotel.com; map p.73. Owned by three charismatic brothers, this place is bright, spacious and friendly, and resists the pressure to go all modern or faux-Ottoman. Pricier en-suite rooms (a/c) on the hotel side, cheaper ones (some with shared bathroom) in the pension, both sharing the extensive breakfast terraces, which have great views of the Princes' Islands. Pension €40, hotel €80

Sultan Hostel Akbıyık Cad 21 ☎ 0212 516 9260, ⊛ sultanhostel.com; map p.73. This 160-bed hostel is very popular because of its convenient location, spotless rooms, comfy beds sporting gleaming white linen, and regularly cleaned shared bathrooms. Dorm prices vary according to the number of beds per room; some have en-suite showers and toilets. The doubles are not such good value. Dorm €12, double €46

★**Uyan** Utangaç Sok 25 ☎ 0212 518 9255, ⊛ uyanhotel.com; map p.73. Atmospheric 29-room hotel set in a beautifully renovated 1920s corner-plot building in the heart of the old city. The ground-floor rooms are a little gloomy, but the rest are light and airy, with light-wood floors scattered with oriental rugs, white walls and white bed linen. Different-sized rooms range from small doubles to a honeymoon suite. "Blue Mosque", room 405, has great views over the Blue Mosque and Haghia Sophia, as well as Scandinavian-style furniture and a jacuzzi. An added bonus is the breathtaking view from the roof terrace. €99

THE GRAND BAZAAR AND AROUND

A stay in this workaday quarter makes a refreshing change from the heavily touristed streets of Cankurtaran, but the main sites are still within easily walking distance, and the Beyazıt and Çemberlitaş tram stops are very convenient.

Niles Dibekli Cami Sok 13 ☎ 0212 517 3239, ⊛ hotelniles.com; map pp.86–87. Well-established hotel, offering better value than most of its competitors in nearby Sultanahmet. The standard rooms are well-appointed, with small but immaculately finished shower-bathrooms, while the suites, at just under twice the price, are more elaborately furnished and decorated in faux-Ottoman style, and boast marble, Turkish-bath-style bathrooms. There's a pretty ground-floor courtyard garden and a roof terrace with panoramic views over busy Yenikapı Harbour. €105

THE NORTHWEST QUARTER

Kariye Kariye Camii Sok 6, Erdirne Kapı ☎ 0212 534 8414, ⊛ kariyeotel.com; map p.97. Situated right next door to the Kariye Museum, arguably the finest Byzantine site in the city (see p.99), this nineteenth-century mansion has been restored with style and restraint. The rooms are kitted out in soft pastel colours, much of the furniture is ornate late nineteenth-century in style, and the polished honey-coloured parquet floor is enlivened by the odd tasteful kilim. The reasonable prices reflect the rather small, shower-only bathrooms and fans rather than a/c. €70

GALATA, BEYOĞLU AND AROUND

The heart of Beyoğlu, the former European quarter, is undoubtedly İstiklal Caddesi – lined with attractive nineteenth-century townhouses and arcades, it's Istanbul's premier entertainment area, home to the city's densest concentration of restaurants, bars and clubs. Tepebaşı, a mixed commercial/tourist district just west of İstiklal Caddesi's southern end, gives easy access to İstiklal but has charms of its own, from trendy rooftop bars and restaurants to the impressive Pera Museum. Galata and waterfront Karaköy have an ever-increasing number of hip places to stay.

GALATA AND KARAKÖY

★**Bada Bing Hostel** Serçe Sok 6, Karaköy ☎ 0212 249 4111, ⊕ badabinghostel.com; map pp.102–103. In the heart of an old dockland area of the city undergoing major gentrification, there's no shortage of trendy cafés, clubs and art galleries on the doorstep of this welcome addition to the Istanbul hostel scene. A/c dorm rooms range from four- to ten-bed, with an eight-bed female-only option. There are stylishly decorated private rooms as well, plus a massive lounge area and rooftop terrace complete with bean-bags for lounging and cool beers for sipping. Dorm €12, double €50

★**Rapunzel Guesthouse** Bereketzade Camii Sok 3 ☎ 0212 292 5034, ⊕ rapunzelistanbul.com; map pp.102–103. This quirky hostel has bags of character with its original nineteenth-century stone walls, artistically scattered curiosities and colourful artwork. A little pricier than other backpackers' in the area, it's the small things here that make the difference – the roomy six-bed dorms with sparkling-clean en suites, individual reading lights, hairdryers, a hearty breakfast and on-tap potable water. The team of young, attentive staff are keen to mingle with guests and always on hand with tips and recommendations for the area. Look out for the black-and-pink sign, as this place is easy to miss, and ring the doorbell. Dorm €20, double €70

Vault Karaköy Bankalar Cad 5, Karaköy ☎ 0212 244 3400, ⊕ thehousehotel.com; map pp.102–103. The latest addition to the upmarket House brand, the *Vault* occupies an imposing building dating back to 1863, once the HQ of the prestigious Credit General Ottoman Bank. Many of the south-facing rooms (carrying a substantial premium) have great views across the Golden Horn to the old city, all have high ceilings, period furniture, large LCD TVs, Ipod docks and chic bathrooms with Carrera marble floors. The German-made vaults in the basement have been preserved and are used to store the wine for the in-house restaurant; the original granite floors and Neoclassical pillars adds character to the public areas. €175

World House Hostel Galipdede Cad 85 ☎ 0212 293 5520, ⊕ worldhouseistanbul.com; map pp.102–103. This colourful ninety-bed hostel ticks all the boxes for a budget traveller – clean, modern and in a great location. Despite the nearby 24hr entertainment, it's quiet too, bar the prayer call from the adjacent mosque. The hostel also has a sister hostel *Liberta*, just off İstiklal Cad, as well as short/long-term apartments – check the website for details. Dorm €12, double €50

İSTIKLAL CADDESİ, TEPEBAŞI AND AROUND

Büyük Londra Oteli Meşrutiyet Cad 117, Tepebaşı ☎ 0212 249 1025, ⊕ londrahotel.net; map pp.102–103. Palatial, mid-nineteenth-century townhouse. Many of the rooms are timeworn and cluttered with battered

period furniture, which gives the hotel its retro-bohemian charm. Others that have been modernized have inevitably lost their raffishness. Ernest Hemingway stayed here in 1922, as a journalist covering the Turkish War of Independence, as did Alexander Hacke when shooting the definitive film of the city's music scene, *Istanbul: Crossing the Bridge*. €50

Hotel Devman Asmalımescit Sok 52 ☎ 0212 245 6212, ⊕ devmanhotel.com; map pp.102–103. Modern hotel in the arty nineteenth-century backstreets off İstiklal Cad, with spotless blue-tiled bathrooms with power shower, firm beds and a (meagre) open-buffet breakfast. Good value for the location and right next to the nightlife – try to bag a room at the rear to avoid the worst of the noise of carousing diners and music from the bars. €60

Mama Shelter İstiklal Cad 50–54, ☎ 0212 252 0100, ⊕ mamashelter.com; map pp.102–103. Situated on the top-floor of the Demirören shopping mall, the rooms in this concept hotel have bright white walls, bed linen and curtains. It's not all modernist minimalism though, as the fun animal cartoon masks draped over the bedside lamps attest. Downstairs is a very hip bar and restaurant run by a Michelin-starred Turkish chef, which attracts locals as well as guests, especially on the DJ set nights (Thurs–Sun). €79

Pera Palace Meşrutiyet Cad 52, Tepebaşı ☎ 0212 377 4000, ⊕ perapalace.com; map pp.102–103. A contender for the most atmospheric hotel in Istanbul (see p.104), the *Pera* was built in the nineteenth century to accommodate Orient Express passengers – its rooms are marked with the names of famous occupants such as Agatha Christie and Graham Greene. It reopened in 2010 following a lengthy restoration, and has managed to maintain much of its character. €230

★**TomTom Suites** Boğazkesen Caddesi, Tomtom Kaptan Sok 18 ☎ 0212 292 4949, ⊕ tomtomsuites.com; map pp.102–103. A designer hotel fashioned from an early nineteenth-century Franciscan nunnery, virtually opposite the ornate and historic Italian Consulate. The suites are spacious and soothingly decorated in soft whites and muted browns; bathrooms have underfloor heating, jacuzzis and rain showers. Tucked away on the slope below bustling İstiklal Caddesi this is, by Beyoğlu standards, an extremely quiet location. €189

Triada Residence İstıklal Cad, Meşelik Sok 4 ☎ 0212 251 0101, ⊕ triada.com.tr; map pp.102–103. Small but very stylish rooms in a lovely early twentieth-century townhouse on a quiet side street. All rooms have boldly grained wood-laminate floors, an American-style kitchen including a coffee-making machine and fridge, and there's a shared sauna. One of the few genuine boutique-style hotels in this part of town, with fabulous views from the roof terrace over the domes of the Greek Orthodox Aya Triada church. €120

1

APARTMENTS

Apartments are a good choice for many visitors, particularly if you are staying for a while or if you are a group or family. Even booked on a night by night basis, the price of a small apartment is often less than a hotel of a similar standard and for stays of a week or more the cost can drop substantially. The number of companies offering apartments for rent across the city has rocketed in recent years, with stiff competition offered by the controversial US-based Airbnb website (@ airbnb.com), which provides a listing service for private individuals who want to let a room, apartment or house, and a safe booking system for those who want to rent one. Below we list just a few of these companies, followed by some recommended individual properties (prices shown are per night).

RECOMMENDED LETTING COMPANIES

Arsu Living Istanbul Apartments Beyoğlu ☎ 0531 221 7156, @ living-istanbul.com. German-Turkish couple with five well-priced, nicely fitted out apartments in and around Beyoğlu.

Istanbul Apartments Tel Sok 27, Beyoğlu ☎ 0212 249 5065, @ istanbul.com. Professionally run Turkish operation with a good choice of apartments on İstiklal Caddesi and in Cihangir.

istanbul!place apartments ☎ +44 7729 251676, @ istanbulplace. Run by a friendly Anglo-Turkish couple, Tarkan and Julia, istanbul!place offers fifteen beautifully restored apartments, all housed in fine late nineteenth-century houses in and around the trendy Galata district.

Manzara İstanbul Tatarbeyi Sok 26b, Galata ☎ 0212 252 4600, @ manzara-stanbul.com. A reliable organization run by a German-born Turkish architect, with around forty carefully chosen properties, mainly in Galata and Beyoğlu.

THE OLD CITY

★**Istanbul Suite Home** Dizdariye Çeşmesi Sok 51 ☎ 0212 458 5255, @ istanbulsuitehome.com; map p.73. Situated in a tall, narrow townhouse on a quiet backstreet south of Divan Yolu, the five apartments here are extremely stylish and very good value. Three of them have two bedrooms, two just one bedroom; they're modish without being minimalist, all pale wood and white. All have a spacious dining area with attached kitchen. **€125**

GALATA, BEYOĞLU AND TAKSİM

Divan Taksim Suites Cumhuriyet Cad 49 ☎ 0212 254 7777, @ divan.com.tr; map pp.102–103. White blinds, white rugs, white furnishings, blonde-wood floors: this is Scandinavian-style minimalism in the heart of Taksim. The suites all work on an open-plan scheme, with nicely kitted-out kitchens off a spacious sleeping/dining/sitting area. All suites have large workstations plus a music system and TV. **€190**

★**Pasha Place** Serdar-I Ekrem Caddesi, Galata @ istanbulplace.com; map pp.102–103. *Pasha*, the flagship apartment of istanbul!place apartments, is located on the third floor of one of this fashionable street's most attractive nineteenth-century apartments. Facing south, the sitting-room and main bedroom have fantastic views across rooftops and the Golden Horn to the old city skyline. High ceilings, white walls, original wooden or antique tile flooring make this a perfect blend of period elegance and contemporary styling. There are three bedrooms (two doubles, one twin), a well-equipped and stylish kitchen, and separate shower room and w.c. **€300**

EATING

Istanbul is home to Turkey's best restaurants, including several that lavish time and skill on old Ottoman cuisine, and, thanks to the lengthy coastline, fish is a firm menu favourite. Snacks are ubiquitous, with kebab stands, pastry shops, fast-food outlets and cafés across the city catering to locals, workers and tourists alike. Restaurants around tourist honey-pot Sultanahmet tend to be of poorer quality, and are more expensive than elsewhere in the city.

ESSENTIALS

Opening hours Workers' cafés and *lokantas* open as early as 6am and serve until 4pm; other cafés generally open daily between 9am and 9pm. Restaurants open for lunch and dinner, with last orders at 10pm or 11pm, with those in more popular areas (such as Nevizade Sokak) and live music venues staying open until the early hours. In the more commercial districts, restaurants follow the shops and close on a Sunday.

Costs Prices vary depending on the establishment and location, but range from ₺1 for a *simit* to ₺4 or so for a takeaway chicken *dürüm* (slivers of *döner* chicken and salad in a flatbread wrap); a café latte or similar, by contrast, will

likely set you back at least ₺7. Main courses start from ₺10 at a cheap restaurant frequented by locals, and run up to ₺100 or more at a swish restaurant with all the trimmings. Some places serve set meals at ₺90–120, with a wide choice of *mezes* followed by a substantial main course, Turkish desserts and, usually, half a bottle of wine or rakı. Credit cards are widely accepted in all but the smallest restaurants.

CAFÉS AND BUDGET EATING

Today's Istanbul has a wide range of cafés, ranging from sophisticated continental cafés serving trendy coffees and imported alcoholic drinks to simple *lokantas* dishing up

CLOCKWISE FROM TOP LEFT ÇIYA SOFRASI (P.126); FISH MARKET, KARAKÖY (P.101); BAKLAVA (P.40); KURUKAHVECİ MEHMET COFFEE (P.134) >

cheap-and-cheerful stews from bains-maries. Budget options include *lokanta*-style buffets (where what you see is what you get), and *pide* or *kebap salonu* for cheap and filling meat- and bread-based staples. Barrow-boys all over the city offer *simits* and other snacks, and fishermen in Karaköy and Eminönü serve fish sandwiches off their boats, while booths and pushcarts in the more salubrious areas sell sizzling tangles of sheep innards (*kokoreç*), stuffed mussels (*midye dolması*), corn on the cob, roast chestnuts and *pilaf* rice.

SULTANAHMET AND EMINÖNÜ

Çiğdem Patisserie Divan Yolu Cad 62 ☎0212 526 8859; map p.73. For more than forty years, the *Çiğdem* has been offering a good selection of both Turkish and non-Turkish pastries and sweets – plus fresh juices, coffee (including lattes at ₺7) and tea (₺2). The *baklava* and *sutlaç* (rice pudding) are both reliable. Daily 8am–11pm.

The Pudding Shop (Lale Restaurant) Divan You Cad 6 ☎0212 522 2970, ⓦ puddingshop.com; map p.73. This Sultanahmet institution first opened its doors in 1957, and in the late 1960s became the meeting place for hippies and other travellers overlanding to India. Times have changed but the *Pudding Shop* is still dishing up its signature rice pudding (₺7) along with a wide array of traditional Turkish dishes. The food's not outstanding, but it's well located right on Divan Yolu, serves alcohol and has a unique place in the history of baby-boom-generation travel. Daily 8am–11pm.

Şehzade Çağ Kebabı Hocapaşa Sok 3/A ☎0212 520 3361; map pp.86–87. Like all the best local places to eat in Istanbul, *Şehzade Çağ Kebabı* specializes in just one thing and concentrates on doing it right. The eponymous *çağ kebabı* (from the mountainous Erzurum region) is said to be the forerunner of the more ubiquitous *döner*, but cooked on a horizontal rather than vertical spit. Order slices of the grilled meat as a portion or in a *dürüm* (wrap) for ₺14. The only other options on the menu are meant to be eaten as condiments; spicy tomato paste, salad, and buffalo yoghurt. Unlicensed. Mon–Sat 11.30am–8pm.

Set Üstü Çay Bahçesi Gülhane Parkı, Sirkeci ☎0212 513 9610; map pp.86–87. This open-air café, tucked away at the southern end of the park near the Goth's Column, with great views over the Bosphorus and back up to the walls of the Topkapı Palace, does excellent samovar-style Turkish tea and is a great place to rest up after sightseeing. Also has a simple snack-menu with toasted sandwiches (₺5). Unlicensed. Daily 9am–10pm.

★**Tarihi Sultanahmet Köftecisi** Divan Yolu 4 ☎0212 511 3960; map p.73. Longest established of the three *köfte* specialists at this end of Divan Yolu, and well frequented by Turkish celebrities (check out the framed newspaper clippings and thank-you letters on the tiled walls). A plate of tasty meatballs, haricot-bean salad, pickled peppers, fresh bread and a spicy tomato-sauce dip will set you back ₺16. Daily 11am–11pm.

GRAND BAZAAR AND AROUND

★**Ağa Kapısı** Nazir Izzet Efendi Sok 11 ☎0212 519 5176; map pp.86–87. Tucked away on a dead-end street just below the Süleymaniye Camii and frequented mainly by local traders, young headscarved women students and their lecturers, the *Ağa Kapısı* boasts the picture window beyond compare, giving a stunning panoramic view down over the Galata Bridge, the mouth of the Golden Horn and the Bosphorus beyond. Try the *gözleme* (a kind of paratha stuffed with goat's cheese) and a glass of tea, traditional Turkish style, or splash out on Ottoman-style sherbet drinks. Daily 8am–midnight.

★**Bedesten Café** Cevahir Bedesteni 143–151, Kapalı Çarşı ☎0212 520 2250; map p.90. The best café in the Grand Bazaar, an oasis of peace and tranquillity away from the main thoroughfares (look out for the two giant *alem* – the crescent- and star-topped finials that adorn mosque domes and minarets – and an even bigger portrait of Atatürk). The food is quality, with delicacies such as scrambled omelette *menemen* and Turkish ravioli (*manti*) in garlic and yoghurt sauce (₺18). There's also a great selection of cakes. Mon–Sat 9am–6.30pm.

Çorlulu Ali Paşa Çay Bahçesi Yeniçeriler Cad 36/38 ☎0212 528 3785; map pp.86–87. In the courtyard of a three-hundred-year-old *medrese* (religious school), Erlener Çay Bahçesi is a cheap and cheerful bazaar-worker-oriented nargile café with waterpipes for ₺12, tea for a lira and snacks like toasted sandwiches. Unlicensed. Daily: April–Oct 7am–3am; Nov–March 7am–midnight.

★**Subaşı Lokantası** Nuruosmaniye Cad 48, Çarşı Kapı ☎0212 522 4762; map pp.86–87. Behind Nuruosmaniye Camii, just inside the main entrance of the Grand Bazaar, this spit-and-sawdust place serves excellent lunchtime food to the market traders. Go early (noon–1pm), as it gets packed and food may run out. Mains cost ₺8–14 per portion, depending how much meat they contain – try the stuffed peppers or delicious *karnı yarık* (mince-topped aubergine). Mon–Sat 9am–6pm.

Tarihi Kuru Fasuliye Süleymaniye Erzincanlı Ali Baba Siddik Sami Onar Cad 11 ☎0212 513 6219; map pp.86–87. In the gorgeous Süleymaniye Camii complex, with tables set out on the precinct between the mosque and *medrese* behind, this simple place serves up some of the tastiest beans in town for a bargain ₺5 – though beware of the hot chilli pepper draped innocently atop your steaming bowl of buttery, tomato-sauce-drenched pulses. Daily 9am–7pm.

Vefa Bozacısı Katip Çelebi Cad 104/1 ☎0212 519 4922, ⓦ vefa.com.tr; map pp.86–87. Worth a look just to see the interior: old tiled floor, dark-wood shelves, ornate Victorian-style mirrors, 1920s light fittings, and bottles of vinegar with label designs unchanged for decades (Atatürk was here in 1937). The *boza* (₺3), a cloudy, viscous drink made by fermenting millet with sugar and water that's best drunk in winter, is an acquired taste but very healthy. Daily 7am–midnight.

GALATA AND BEYOĞLU

★**Café Privato** Tımarcı Sok 3B, Galata ☎ 0212/293 2055 ⓦprivatocafe.com; map pp.102–103. One of the best breakfasts in town. Cosy and quaint, the tables are bestowed with a staggering array of dishes; home-made organic jams, mini Georgian pancakes, five types of cheese, dressed olives and more. It's not cheap at ₺30 per serving but usually one full breakfast is enough for two people. Daily 9am–midnight.

Dürümzade Kamer Hatun Cad 26/A 0212/249 0147; map pp.102–103. On a busy side street, this tiny corner joint has become something of an institution. Serves up various *dürüms* (wraps) with perfectly chargrilled meats for an excellent value ₺6–10. The secret here is the chewy flatbread they use which is rubbed with spice mix before being toasted on the grill. Daily 8am–4am.

Galata Konak Patisserie Hacı Ali Sok 2 ☎0212 252 5346, ⓦgalatakonakcafe.com; map pp.102–103. Just down from the Galata Tower, this stylish café dishes up delicious lattes (with amaretti biscuits) and tempting cakes and desserts from ₺6. For something a little more substantial, head up the lantern-lit stairwell or take the antique lift to the rooftop terrace restaurant for a mix of Turkish and European fare and an expansive view over the Golden Horn. Popular with locals and tourists alike, it always seems to be packed. Unlicensed. Daily 9am–9pm.

★**Kafe Ara** Tosbağa Sok8/A, off Yeniçarşı Cad, Beyoğlu ☎0212 245 4105; map pp.102–103. Great place tucked away just off Galatasaray Meydanı, with a raft of tables out in the alley and a lovely dark-wood bistro-style interior lined with black-and-white photography by Ara Güler. A large, tulip-shaped glass of Turkish tea costs a reasonable ₺3, big bowls of salad ₺16–20. Mon–Thurs 8am–11pm, Fri 8am–midnight, Sat & Sun 10am–11pm.

★**Mandabatmaz** Olivia Geçidi off İstiklal Cad; map pp.102–103. This tiny Turkish coffee joint is more of an institution than a café. Open since 1967, you get the impression it hasn't changed a jot – impressive, in the face of the rampant development of the surrounding area. Pull up a stool in the cramped interior or on the street outside and, for ₺3, enjoy one of the best Turkish coffees in Istanbul – thick, velvety and chocolate-like – the result of its custom roasted coffee beans. Unlicensed. Daily 9am–midnight.

Nizam Pide İstiklal Cad, Büyükparmakkapı Sok ☎0212 249 7918; map pp.102–103. Offers excellent *pides* (₺10 and up). A second branch on Kalyoncu Kulluğu Cad, behind Nevizade Sok in the fish market, has framed articles from Turkish newspapers proclaiming it to be one of the top ten *pide* outlets in Turkey. Daily 24hr.

Saray İstiklal Cad 102–104, Beyoğlu ☎0212 292 3434, ⓦsaraymuhallebicisi.com; map pp.102–103. The emphasis at this place established in 1935, is on classic Turkish desserts such as *fırın sütlaç* (baked rice pudding), *irmik helvası* (semolina with nuts) and *baklava*-type sweets, including wonderful *fıstık sarma* (pistachios packed in a syrup-drenched pastry roll) – cakes cost ₺6 and up – though it also serves soups and grills. Daily 8am–11pm.

ASIAN ISTANBUL

Baylan Muvakkithane Cad 19, Kadiköy ☎0216 346 6350. This famous patisserie is a must for nostalgia freaks, with its 1950s dark-wood and chrome frontage. The trellis-shaded garden area is popular with mums and their offspring, many of whom tuck into traditional ice creams or plates of pastel-coloured macaroons. The liqueur chocolates demonstrate the café's Christian Armenian origins. Daily 10am–10pm.

RESTAURANTS

Generally the old city, including Sultanahmet, can't compare with the city's Beyoğlu entertainment hub for variety or quality, but there are a few honourable exceptions. Across the Golden Horn in Beyoğlu, Galata and Taksim restaurants cater for theatre- and cinema-goers and young people filling up before a night out, as well as for those who want to linger all evening over a meal and a bottle of rakı. The liveliest spot is undoubtedly Nevizade Sokak, where restaurants serve *mezes*, kebabs and fish, accompanied by the sound of serenading street musicians. Back in the old city Kumkapı boasts more than fifty fish restaurants and a lively weekend vibe. Though the food is generally mediocre, it remains a popular spot on a balmy summer evening, with candlelit tables spilling out on to the narrow, traffic-free streets. Otherwise you can try your luck in the cobbled streets around the ferry terminal in Ortaköy, where numerous trendy options rub shoulders with older, more traditional places, or across the Bosphorus in Üsküdar or Kadıköy.

SULTANAHMET

Albura Kathisma Akbıyık Cad 26 ☎0212 517 9031, ⓦalburakathisma.com; map p.73. Quite a few restaurants hereabouts now serve regional Anatolian-style dishes, but *Albura* was among the first and remains one of the best. Try the special *Kathisma Palace*, a lamb casserole with figs and almonds (₺50 for two). Angora wine is priced at a reasonable (for Istanbul) ₺50 per bottle. The dining room is a cavernous but stylish bare-brick affair, and there are plenty of outside tables on this bustling tourist street. Daily 10am–11pm.

★**Amedros** Hoca Rüstem Sok 7, Divan Yolu ☎0212 522 8356, ⓦamedroscafe.com; map p.73. A sophisticated café-restaurant with an interior that manages to be both stylish and homely. The food is good, too – a mixture of European (try the Flame Marmer steak) and traditional Anatolian (the *testi* kebab, a succulent lamb and vegetable stew slow-cooked in a sealed clay pot, is a good bet). The service is attentive without being obsequious, and the whole place is very professionally run. Mains from ₺20. Daily 11am–1am.

Balıkçı Sabahattin Seyit Hasan Koyu Sok 1, Cankurtan ☎0212 458 1824, ⓦbalikcisabahattin.com; map p.73. Fish restaurant by Cankurtan station, five minutes' walk but a world away from the tourist joints up the hill. While not cheap (it's *the* in place for moneyed locals), it's about as atmospheric as you can get, with vine-shaded tables set out in a narrow alley in summer, and a wood-floored dining room in an old wooden house in winter. Starters begin at ₺12, mains ₺30 and up, with every kind of locally caught fish on the menu. Daily 11am–1am.

★**Dubb** Incili Çavuş Sok ☎0212 513 7308, ⓦdubbindian.com; map p.73. A funky spot with one Indian and two Turkish chefs serving up authentic dishes from the subcontinent in a chic yet ethnic setting. Spread over several floors, the rooms are small, and there's a roof terrace and tables on the street. Delicious samosa and pakora, vegetable curries from ₺15. Owner Mehmet and

his Japanese wife also run *Dubb Ethnic* on Mimar Ağa Cad 25, just off Akbıyık Cad (same hours), with ethnic cuisine from Turkey to Japan. Daily noon–midnight.

★**Giritli** Keresteci Hakkı Sok, Ahırkapı ☎0212 458 2270, ⓦgiritliresrtoran.com; map p.73. Atmospheric fish restaurant set in a historic building near the *Armada Hotel*, specializing in Cretan dishes. For a no-holds-barred evening out, go for the fixed menu at ₺125, and enjoy a sea-food *pilaf*, 23 *meze* morsels, and three hot starters, followed by a choice of four or five fish – and as much beer, wine or rakı as you can drink. Daily noon–midnight.

Khorasani Ticarethane Sok 39/41, Divan Yolu ☎0212 519 5959, ⓦkhorasanirestaurant.com; map p.73. If you are staying in Sultanahmet, this is the nearest place to sample authentic southeastern Turkish cuisine, including hummus and the spicy walnut and pepper dip *muhamara* (₺8 a portion). The kebabs are wonderful, prepared *ocakbaşı* style over a charcoal grill (₺19–26). There are tables on the cobbled pedestrian street, and a stylish mezzanine-floor dining room for colder weather. Watch out for the ten percent service charge. Daily noon–1am.

GRAND BAZAAR AND AROUND

★**Akdeniz Hatay Sofrası** Ahmediye Cad 44/A, Aksaray ☎0212 531 3333, ⓦhataysofrasi.com; map

---

COOK LIKE A LOCAL, EAT LIKE A LOCAL

Istanbul is fast becoming as popular a destination for foodies as it is for history buffs. Yet while eating here gives visitors a chance to scratch the surface of the culinary diversity, there are opportunities to dig a little deeper and learn how to prepare some recipes as a lasting souvenir.

Cooking Alaturka ☎0212 458 5919, ⓦcookingalaturka.com. Cooking Alaturka runs fun and informative Turkish cookery classes from Akbıyık Cad 72/A, right in the centre of Sultanahmet. The courses are the concept of Eveline Zoutendijk, who opened the city's first cookery school back in 2003. For €65 per head, you can learn how to prepare a four-course Turkish meal, for either lunch or dinner, with Eveline and chef Feyzi Yıldırım – and then eat it. For ₺55 a head you can eat a fixed-menu four-course meal here without the hassle of cooking it yourself.

Istanbul Culinary Institute ☎0212 251 2214, ⓦistanbulculinary.com.tr. For a lesson in a professional culinary school environment, this is the best option. Check their website for their monthly programme of evening amateur workshops, which cost ₺80–110. Programmes are themed, with "Aegean Flavours" and "Mezes" among the many options. The three-hour classes end with dining on the results, accompanied by Turkish wine.

Istanbul Eats ⓦistanbuleats.com. To get to grips with Istanbul's vibrant food scene in a very different

way, Istanbul Eats run backstreet culinary adventures for small groups (2–6 people) of foodies who want to avoid the usual tourist haunts. There are different options available (US$75–125), so you can choose between Hidden Beyoğlu, Kebab Crawl, Culinary Secrets of the Old City and more. As well as trying a whole range of traditional Turkish fare, there's the chance to buy Turkish herbs, spices and deli-style favourites at the same prices the locals do. They also do a handy guidebook to the city's lesser-known places to eat entitled *Istanbul Eats: Exploring the Culinary Backstreets*.

Turkish Flavours ☎0532 218 0653, ⓦturkishflavours .com. Selin Rozanes is a colourful character with years of experience in the tourism and culinary industry. She offers food-tasting walks around the Spice Bazaar and Kadıköy market, stopping at *Çiya* (see p.126) for lunch, for US$145 or a cooking class that begins with a tasting session at the Spice Bazaar before heading to Selin's home on the Asian side to cook up a storm for US$125. The latter offers the chance to see the inside of a Turkish home, and learn some of the distinctive Sephardic Jewish dishes which reflect Selin's own background.

p.97. This spotless emporium serves up the best southeastern Turkish cuisine in the city. The hummus is served warm and liberally sprinkled with pistachios, and the dip *muhamara* (a spicy mix of breadcrumbs, walnuts, tomato and hot pepper) is delicious; the whole chicken roasted in salt (*tuzda tavuk*) has to be ordered a couple of hours ahead. To get here take the T1 tram to the Aksaray stop, then walk 500m along Vatan Cad; it's next to the Historia mall. Mon–Sat 9am–midnight, Sun 8am–1pm.

Havuzlu Gani Çelebi Sok 3, Kapalı Çarşı ☎ 0212 520 2250; map p.90. Appealing Grand Bazaar restaurant, with Ottoman-style decor and white tablecloths on dark-wood tables laid out beneath a barrel-vaulted ceiling. A good range of kebabs (the İskender is recommended) and *hazır yemek* (steam-tray food) dishes. Brisk service, tasty food and reasonable prices (kebabs around ₺15).Unlicensed. Mon–Sat 10am–5pm.

Siirt Şeref Büryan Kebap Salonu, İtfaye Cad 4, Fatih ☎ 0212 635 8085; map pp.86–87. Located in the shadow of the towering late Roman Aqueduct of Valens, this great establishment has been dishing up regional dishes from the Arab/Kurdish southeast of Turkey for decades. Best is the *perde pilaf*, a tasty concoction of rice, shredded chicken, almonds, pine nuts and various herbs cooked in a pot until the outside "burns" to a tasty crust (₺10). *Büryan* is spring lamb cooked in a deep clay *tandır* (tandoori) oven and served chopped on a bed of soft *pide* bread. Daily 11am–11pm.

NORTH OF SULTANAHMET

Hamdi Et Lokantası Kalçin Sok 17 Tahmis Cad, Eminönü ☎ 0212 528 0390; map pp.86–87. The uninspiring facade of this five-floor joint, fronting the square in Eminönü, belies the quality of the food on offer inside. Tender, charcoal-grilled kebabs of various kinds form the mainstay of the menu, but it's also a good place to try *lahmacun*, a thin, chapati-type bread smeared with spicy mincemeat. The clientele is a mix of local shopkeepers, businessmen and tourists – try to get a seat at the terrace, which offers great views over the Golden Horn. Kebabs from ₺23. Daily 11am–midnight.

Paşazade Sirkeci İbn-I Kemal Cad 13 ☎ 0212 513 3757; map pp.86–87. Well-run faux-Ottoman place. Though the interior may verge on twee, the service is good and the food (try the lamb blanquette with quince) tasty and good value (mains from ₺18). It's traditional Turkish cuisine with a twist, there's plenty of choice for vegetarians, and in warm weather the outside tables make for great people-watching. Daily noon–1am.

THE LAND WALLS AND AROUND

★**Asitane** Kariye Hotel, Kariye Camii Sok 18 ☎ 0212 534 8414, ⊛ asitanerestaurant.com; map p.97. Garden-restaurant next door to the Kariye Museum. It's expensive,

but you may feel like splashing out for good service and food in such a peaceful (if far-flung) location. The menu is described as nouvelle Ottoman cuisine – plenty of meat-and fruit-based stews (₺26–40), or try the *hükar beğendi* (tender lamb with aubergine purée). Meals served on a lovely terrace swamped by roses, accompanied by classical Turkish music. Daily 11.30am–11pm.

★**Develi** Gümüş Yüzük Sok 7, Samatya ☎ 0212 529 0833, ⊛ develikebap.com; map p.97. This posh (and unusually, licensed) joint, serving up the best food from Gaziantep in Turkey's southeast, is out of the way but easy enough to reach on the suburban train line from either Sirkeci or Cankurtaran – get off at the Kocamustafapaşa stop. Great kebabs from ₺22, but best are the starters (hummus with pastrami) and *baklava*-type desserts. Nice roof terrace overlooking a quaint square, with the Sea of Marmara beyond. Daily noon–midnight.

Safa Meyhanesi İlyasbey Cad 12, Yedikule ☎ 0212 585 5594, ⊛ safameyhanesi.com; map p.97. The chandelier taking centre stage of the long, narrow dining room sets the tone of this old school establishment; that and the copious rakı bottles lined up behind glass cabinets. This is probably the most atmospheric *meyhane* in town, with a nostalgic 1940s feel. The food here is standard *meyhane* fare but reasonably priced (mezes are ₺7–15), and it's well worth a trip to this very untouristy neighbourhood to sit among the local intelligentsia and soak up the charm. Daily 11am–midnight.

GALATA AND KARAKÖY

Fürreyya Serdar-ı Ekrem Sok 2B, Galata ☎ 0212 252 4853, ⊛ furreyyagalata.com; map pp.102–103. This tiny establishment, just a stone's throw from Galata Tower, is conveniently located at the entrance to chic, boutique-filled Serdar-ı Ekrem Sokak. A little gem of a fish restaurant, it's rather unusual in that it's not adjacent to the water. *Fürreya* serves up perfectly cooked seafood with a few modern touches, at very reasonable prices. The fish wrap, prawn casserole and fishcakes with basil sauce all come highly recommended. Mains from ₺12. Daily noon–11pm.

Galata House Galata Külesi Sok 61 ☎ 0212 245 1861, ⊛ thegalatahouse.com; map pp.102–103. This restaurant offers all the comfort of eating in your own living room, with small, cosy rooms, an outdoor terrace lit by fairy lights, and a menu of hearty Georgian cuisine (mains around ₺20) – try the house speciality *hindali* (meat-filled dumplings in a tomato sauce). History buffs can ogle the original prison fittings and try to decipher graffiti etched into the wall by prisoners. With only fifty seats, it's best to book ahead. Tues–Sun 3pm–midnight.

Lokanta Maya Kemankeş Cad 35/A, Karaköy ☎ 0212 252 6884, ⊛ lokantamaya.com; map pp.102–103. A modern and very stylish twist on a traditional *lokanta*, *Maya* is run by a Turkish woman, Didem, who studied at

1

the French Culinary Institute in New York. On the daily changing menu, soups such as cauliflower with cured beef croutons start at ₺12, a wonderful array of *meze* from just a little more. It's a block back from the waterfront hustle (and there's plenty here as this is where the behemoth cruise ships dock) in a comparatively peaceful location. Reservations a must. Mon–Sat noon–5pm & 7–11pm.

İSTİKLAL CADDESİ AND AROUND

Antiochia General Yazgan Sok 3, Asmalımescit ☎0212/292 1100, ⓦantiochiaconcept.com; map pp.102–103. One of the best options for enjoying tasty southeastern Turkish cuisine in the Beyoğlu area. Try the *zahter* (a tangy wild thyme salad) or the spicy walnut and pepper *muammara* dip (better yet, get a mixed *meze* plate for ₺25) followed by a marinated kebab served with paper-thin *lavaş* bread (kebabs from ₺19). One of the owners, Jale Balcı, has written a book about Antakya (ancient Antioch) cuisine, available here. Mon–Sat 11am–2am.

Fıccın İstiklal Cad, Kallavi Sok 13 ☎0212 293 3786, ⓦficcin.com; map pp.102–103. Unpretentious and great-value place on this quiet (by Beyoğlu standards) side street, offering some unusual and substantial dishes. Try the eponymous *ficcin*, a kind of hearty, Caucasian meat pie, or the *çerkez mantası*, a ravioli-style dish in which the pasta is stuffed with tomato and served in a yoghurt sauce (mains from ₺8). Soups include a tasty rocket-based one, wine and beer are both reasonably priced, and there's plenty of choice for vegetarians. Tues–Sat 8am–10pm.

Hacı Abdullah İstiklal Cad, Sakızağacı Cad 17 ☎0212 293 8051, ⓦhaciabdullah.com.tr; map pp.102–103. One of the best traditional restaurants in town, sporting a high-ceilinged atrium salon at the back. Main courses from ₺12 – try the *hunkar beğendili kebap* (beef stew on a bed of aubergine and cheese purée) and the *ayva tatlı* (stewed quince with clotted cream). Strictly no alcohol served. Daily 11am–10pm.

★İmroz Nevizade Sok 24 ☎0212 249 9073, ⓦkrependekiimroz.com.tr; map pp.102–103. This Greek-owned Istanbul institution has been dishing up reasonably priced fish dishes (mains around ₺16) since 1942. Spread over three floors, it's perhaps the liveliest of the fish restaurants in the Balık Pazarı area. Daily 11am–2am.

★Kenan Üsta Ocakbaşı Kurabiye Sok 18 ☎0212 293 5619; map pp.102–103. Watch master grillsman Kenan cook *lavaş* (tortilla-style bread) over his basement charcoal grill, smear it with olive oil, sprinkle it with pepper flakes, thyme and salt, then pop it back on the grill to finish. This bread is used as the "plate" to serve an astonishing array of kebabs and grilled meat to a loyal and virtually one hundred percent Turkish clientele. Mains from ₺20; licensed. Daily 10am–2am.

Refik Sofyalı Sok 10–12, Tünel ☎0212/245 7879; map pp.102–103. Modest *rakı*-infused Turkish joint, a meeting point for local intellectuals, specializing in Black Sea cuisine. *Kara lahana dolması* is a traditional stuffed cabbage dish, popular with the locals. Refik Baba, the good-natured owner, likes to chat in numerous languages, though he doesn't speak much of any. Set menu ₺100, including as many local alcoholic drinks as you desire. Mon–Sat noon–midnight, Sun 6.30pm–midnight.

Zencefil Kurabiye Sok 8 ☎0212/244 4082; map pp.102–103. The ever-changing menu includes vegetarian versions of various Turkish dishes, and Western-style meals such as vegetarian lasagne and quiche – from as little as ₺13 – plus great salads, home-made breads, herbal teas, mint lemonade and local wines. The courtyard area is a particularly enticing place to relax and enjoy your food. Mon–Sat 9am–midnight.

ASIAN ISTANBUL

★Çiya Sofrası & Kebapçi Güneşlibahçe Sok 43 ☎0216 349 1902, ⓦcıyasofrasi.com. "*Çiya*" means "mountain" in Kurdish, though the inspiration for the food here comes from many different corners of this vast country – and beyond to the Middle East and Balkans. There are actually three restaurants; the two on the right as you approach along pedestrianized Güneşlibahçe street are kebab-orientated, the one on the left focuses on salads, *meze* and stews. Choose your own selection of *meze* and salads and have your plate weighed to learn the price (around ₺12 for a substantial lunch). Daily 10am–midnight.

Kanaat Selmanipak Cad 25, Üsküdar ☎0216 341 5444, ⓦkanaatlokantasi.com.tr. One of the city's more famous *lokantas*, established in 1933, featuring copies of İznik-tile panels from the Selimiye Camii in Edirne and a copper chimneypiece. Mains start from ₺13 a head; no alcohol served. Daily 6am–11pm.

NIGHTLIFE

With such a youthful population, a booming economy and relentless Westernization, it is not surprising that Istanbul has established a reputation for **clubbing**. The best **bars** and **clubs** are in Beyoğlu, Taksim, Ortaköy and the richer Bosphorus suburbs such as Kadıköy. For a more traditional night out, head to a **meyhane** (tavern), where a *fasil* band might accompany your food and bottle of rakı. Alternatively, try a **Türkü bar**, where you can drink and listen to the plaintive sounds of Anatolian folk music. Both *meyhanes* and *Türkü* bars are enjoying something of a revival of late, but if you want something more familiar there are countless café-bars and modern nightclubs as well.

BARS

Away from conservative Islamic areas like Fatih and Eyüp, Istanbul takes drinkers in its stride, and you'll find bars ranging from the dangerously seedy to the chic and overpriced. Sultanahmet's bars are dull in comparison to buzzing Beyoğlu, where drinking goes on well into the early hours. There's a wide range of bars along the lively streets leading off İstiklal Caddesi, at the Taksim Square end – from jazz joints to student bars, sophisticated rooftop cafés to throbbing basement rock-bars. Kadıköy, on the Asian side of the Bosphorus, boasts several drinking haunts. To reach Kadıköy's studenty/arty Kadife Sokak, walk or take a taxi from the Kadıköy ferry terminal south down Moda Caddesi, until it turns into Doktor Esat Işık Caddesi – Kadife Sokak is on the left. The line between Istanbul's bars and cafés tends to blur, with most open during the day to serve food and coffee, becoming more alcoholic as the evening progresses. A cover charge is often introduced between 10pm and 2am if there is live music.

SULTANAHMET

Cozy Pub Divan Yolu Cad 66 ☎ 0212 520 0990; map p.73. Situated on a prominent corner plot, this pleasant dark-wood bar has tables out on the street in the warmer months – great for people-watching on hectic Divan Yolu. Beers a reasonable ₺8. Daily 10am–2am.

Port Shield Pub Ebusuud Cad 2 ☎ 0212 527 0931; map pp.86–87. Situated right opposite the Gülhane tram stop and just a short step downhill from the Haghia Sophia, this mock-English pub, part of a chain, is usually packed with sports addicts taking in big-screen football, rugby and cricket matches from around the world. Beers ₺14. Daily 11.30am–1.30am.

GALATA AND KARAKÖY

Ritim Galata Galata Kulesi Sok 3/C ☎ 0212 249 0252; map pp.102–103. Just down from the Galata Tower, this mellow bar attracts a more sophisticated crowd than many of the places up in Beyoğlu. In summer a few tables spill out onto the street, and the cosy interior, with a mezzanine floor and exposed brickwork, is great. Large beers cost ₺10, not bad considering the soothing sounds from the DJ, and the Turkish-fusion food menu. Daily 10am–2am.

Sensus Büyükhendek Cad 5, Galata ☎ 0212 245 5657, ⓦ sensuswine.com; map pp.102–103. Just a stone's throw from the tower (down a little side street and on the right), this "wine and cheese boutique" is reached down some steps, and has the feel of a boutique wine cellar. Service is chaotic at best, but the range of wines on display (from ₺9 a glass) and the atmospheric environment make it a pleasant stop-off (best avoided weekend evenings). Daily 10am–11pm.

Unter Kara Ali Kaptan Sok 4, Karaköy ☎ 0212 244 5151, ⓦ unter.com.tr; map pp.102–103. The hipster magnet of Karaköy is best known for its cool cafés. However, there are a few options for evening drinks and this is the most popular. Limited space (sometimes taken up by a DJ) inside means cool young Istanbulites spill out into the street. Tues–Sun 10am–midnight, Fri & Sat 10am–2am.

İSTİKLAL CADDESİ AND AROUND

James Joyce Irish Pub Irish Centre, Balo Sok 26 ☎ 0212 224 2013; map pp.102–103. Housed in a wonderfully ornate and rambling nineteenth-century apartment block, the Irish Centre's focal point is this lively pub. There's also a games bar with sports on TV that gets very crowded for big occasions, and live bands play most nights of the week. Daily 1pm–2am.

★ **Leb-i-Derya** Kumbaracı Yokuşu 115/7 ☎ 0212 293 4989; map pp.102–103. A great place for an early evening (or early morning) drink, with fabulous Bosphorus views and chilled-out sounds. It's not cheap, though, with wine ₺19 a glass and cocktails starting around ₺25 and you may be turned away if you look scruffy. There's also a decent food menu. Daily 11am–4am.

★ **Limonlu Bahçe** Yeniçarşı Cad 98, Galatasaray ☎ 0212 252 1094, ⓦ limonlubahce.com; map pp.102–103. Just a five-minute walk from İstiklal Caddesi, the "Lemon Garden" is a calm oasis providing a welcome retreat from the chaos of Beyoğlu. Reached via an impossibly long maze of corridors which open out onto this leafy space, usually bustling with a young professional crowd, it's a little pricey (beers ₺12, mojitos ₺25), but worth it if you need an escape from the bustle outside. Also has an extensive food and soft drinks menu. Daily 9am–1am.

Pasific Sofyalı Sok ☎ 0212 292 7642; map pp.102–103. Small, friendly bar with a good selection of rock music and well-priced beer (₺9 for draught). It's a struggle to find a seat on the alleyway tables in summer, though the *Kino Garden* next door is run jointly with *Pasific* and has a garden out back. Daily 10am–2am.

★ **Solera** Yeniçarşı Cad 44, Galatasaray ☎ 0212 252 2719; map pp.102–103. This tiny wine bar may be small, but it's also perfectly formed. Stocking over 1000 different Turkish and international wines, ranging from ₺8 per glass/₺34 a bottle up – it's also one of the cheapest places to get a decent wine in the city. Tasty snacks and *meze* are served, and owner Suleyman Er is always on hand to give advice. Daily 10am–1am.

ASIAN ISTANBUL

Isis Kadife Sok 26, Caferağa Mah ☎ 0216 349 7381. Kadıköy three-storey townhouse that's a café by day and bar-disco at night. Cutting-edge music and good food, plus a garden open during the summer months. Daily 11am–2am.

Karga Kadife Sok 16, Kadıköy ☎ 0216 449 1725. A self-consciously cool venue on the trendiest street in Asian Istanbul, this grungy/arty place is set in a tall, narrow

1

nineteenth-century townhouse. Part pub (the lower floors) and part art gallery (top floor), it also has a large, pleasant garden out back. Daily 11am–2am.

CLUBS AND LIVE MUSIC

Istanbul's best clubs are bang up to date in terms of design, lighting and atmosphere, while live music – jazz, rock, alternative, blues, R&B and even reggae – is plentiful around the backstreets of Beyoğlu. Expect to spend no less than you would in London, New York or Sydney on a night out. Most places have entry charges at weekends (anything from ₺10 to ₺70), and tend to be open from around 9pm until 2am or 4am. Local and visiting foreign bands also play at a welter of annual festivals (see box, p.130) – including two jazz festivals, a couple of rock festivals, an international music festival, plus separate dance and techno and blues events.

GALATA AND KARKÖY

★**Nardis Jazz Club** Galata Kulesi Sok 14, Galata ᴡ nardisjazz.com; map pp.102–103. Run by a couple of enthusiasts, this small, intimate venue is a great introduction to the city's jazz scene, with performances by both local and international artists. The emphasis is on the mainstream, but modern, fusion and ethnic get an airing from time to time. Advance booking recommended. Sets: Mon–Thurs 9.30pm–12.30am, Fri & Sat 8pm–2am.

Salon İKSV Sadi Konuralp Cad 5, Şişhane ☎ 0212 334 0752, ᴡ saloniksv.com; map pp.102–103. Trendy multi-purpose venue backed by the Istanbul Foundation for Culture and Arts (IKSV), hosting contemporary ambient, electronic, jazz and indie concerts, plus some theatrical performances. Tickets are available from Biletix (see p.63), or commission-free from the venue. Opening hours vary according to the act.

İSTİKLAL CADDESİ AND AROUND

Babylon Şehbender Sok 3, Asmalımescit ᴡ babylon .com.tr; map pp.102–103. Set in a modest-sized but atmospheric bare-brick vault, this is Istanbul's premier live music club with a regular programme of local and foreign groups playing jazz, world, indie and electronica. Ticket prices vary wildly according to the act (booking office across the street daily noon–6pm, or from Biletix); performances usually start around 10pm. In summer, the action moves to the Aegean coast near İzmir and the venue closes its doors; see website for details. A new, bigger venue has opened in a disused beer factory in Bomonti (check website for details). Tues–Thurs 9.30pm–2am, Fri & Sat 10pm–3am; closed in summer.

Hayal Kahvesi Büyükparmakkapı Sok 19 ☎ 0212/244 2558, ᴡ hayalkahvesi.com.tr; map pp.102–103. Attractive brick-and-wood joint with blues, rock and indie every night from 10pm. Mostly decent local bands, but they also book the occasional big name here. There's a sister

branch, *Çubuklu Hayal Kahvesi*, in Burunbahçe on the Asian side of the Bosphorus (☎ 0216 413 6880). There's a free boat service from İstinye across the strait. Admission varies. Daily 5pm–4am.

Indigo Akarsu Sok 1/2, off İstiklal Cad ᴡ livingindigo .com; map pp.102–103. This remains the venue of choice for electronica-lovers, though it has now embraced a more inclusive policy, and offers a wider range of musical styles. Bigger-name DJs and acts, many international, tend to play Fri and Sat. Mon–Thurs & Sun 10pm–4am, Fri & Sat 11pm–5am.

MiniMüzikhol Soğancı Sok 7, off Sıraselviler Cad ☎ 0212 245 1996, ᴡ minimuzikhol.com; map pp.102–103. This intimate club is a favourite with the city's late night hipsters and features both local and international DJs playing house, techno, hip-hop and dubstep. Cover charge is around ₺20 on weekends. Wed–Sat 10pm–4am.

Peyote Kameriye Sok 4, Balık Pazarı ᴡ peyote.com; map pp.102–103. The city's best place for alternative/indie types looking for an "underground" scene. In a band themselves, the owners give stage space to upcoming rivals from across the metropolis. There's a lively roof terrace with an eclectic mix of music, live bands play on the second floor, while the first floor is given over to electronica. Beers are a reasonable ₺9 and the (variable) entry charge is not too steep. Daily 10pm–4am.

Pixie Underground Toşbaşağa Sok 12; map pp.102–103. This small venue is musically one of the most cutting-edge clubs in Beyoğlu. Istanbul's only bass music club, the emphasis is on dubstep, drum'n'bass and jungle, and it's a chance to see some of the city's up-and-coming producers. Beers are a respectable price and entry is either free or ₺10. Daily 2pm–4am.

ORTAKÖY

Anjelique Salhane Sok 5, off Muallim Naci Cad ☎ 0212 327 2844, ᴡ anjelique.com.tr. One of Istanbul's most popular, mainstream clubs, in the heart of buzzing Ortaköy. Spread over three floors in a Bosphorus-facing mansion, reimagined by design company Autobahn. Each floor plays a different type of music from Turkish pop to house so you can choose according to your mood or pick the floor with the best crowd. No cover charge, but expensive drinks and you'll need to dress to impress if you want to get in. Daily 6pm–4am.

Kiki Osmanzade Sok 8 ☎ 0212/258 5524 ᴡ kiki.com.tr. Situated right in Ortaköy square, this is one of the least flashy clubs in the district – it's still very trendy but attracts a younger, less showy clientele, who come for the deep house DJs. Spread over three floors, the best action takes place on the roof terrace in the summer months. Entrance is usually free, drinks dear. Wed–Sat 8pm–4am.

Reina Muallim Naci Cad 120 ᴡ reina.com.tr. Summer drinking outside until dawn for the bright young things who manage to get through the door. There are dancefloors, video screens and bars all directly overlooking the Bosphorus, and overpriced sushi – early birds get thirty percent off drinks between 6pm and 8pm. Entry ₺50 including one drink. June–Sept daily 6pm–4am.

GAY BARS AND CLUBS

Istanbul is Turkey's gay capital, with the scene centred on Taksim and Beyoğlu. For information on the gay scene check out ⊚istanbulgay.com or ⊚gaysofturkey.com, which both give rundowns of the best gay bars and clubs, gay-friendly hotels and the like. Another good site in English is ⊚hipsultan.com, which is commercially run but does have some good tips. Otherwise, try the weekly *Time Out Istanbul* reviews of gay and lesbian venues.

CAFÉS

Rocinante Café Bar Oğut Sok 6/2, Sakızağcı Sok Cad, Beyoğlu ☎0212 244 8219; map pp.102–103. Behind the prominent Ağa Camii (mosque) on İstiklal Caddesi is this popular lesbian-friendly (the owner and many of her friends are lesbian) café-cum-meeting point. Daily 2pm–2am.

Sugar and Spice Sakalsalim Çıkmazı 3/A, off İstiklal Cad, Beyoğlu ☎0212 245 0096, ⊚sugar-cafe.com; map pp.102–103. Low-key meeting and hangout joint off the busy main drag, somewhere to grab a coffee or a beer and decide what you're going to do later on, with food on offer from 1pm–10pm. Daily 11am–1am.

BARS AND CLUBS

Haspa Café & Bar Küçük Parmakkapı, İpek Sok 18/2, off İstiklal Cad, Beyoğlu; map pp.102–103. A local pre-club favourite, popular with a fun young crowd, providing live music and entertainment some nights, and reasonably priced drinks. Daily 6pm–3.30am.

Love Dance Point Cumhuriyet Cad 349, Harbiye ☎0212 296 3358; map pp.102–103. Glitzy, hi-tech and spacious club opposite the Military Museum. DJs spin a wide range of sounds, from techno to Turkish pop. A proper club rather than a glorified café/bar, it also holds regular parties. Wed free admission; Fri & Sat ₺25 including one drink. Wed 11.30pm–4am, Fri & Sat 11.30pm–5am.

Prive Tarlabası Bul 28, Taksim ☎0212 235 7999; map pp.102–103. Gay-only dance club, with a devoted following due to its reputation as a pick-up place. The mix of electro and Turkish music will appeal to most punters. This street has a bad reputation in the city – and not just among straights – so take care if you decide to venture out here. Cover Fri & Sat only ₺20 including a drink. Daily 11pm–5am.

Tek Yön Siraselviler Cad 63/1 Beyoğlu ☎0212 233 0654, ⊚www.tekyonclub.com; map pp.102–103. Probably the most popular, long-standing mainstream club. The friendly staff perform occasional drag shows, and there's a garden out back to escape the noise. Daily 11.00pm–4am.

ARTS, ENTERTAINMENT AND FESTIVALS

Istanbul hosts a decent range of annual cultural **festivals**, and matches other European cities for the breadth of its **arts scene**. State-subsidized theatre, opera and ballet make performances affordable for all, and there's something going on almost every night at venues around the city. Music features heavily over the summer months, when international festivals draw musicians from all over the world. Information on many music and theatre events, and on the various cultural festivals, is available from the Istanbul Foundation for Culture and Arts (IKSV), Sadı Konuralp Cad 5, Şişhane, Beyoğlu (☎0212 334 0700, ⊚iksv.org).

Tickets Tickets for many cultural events, as well as sporting events, can be purchased online from Biletix (⊚biletix.com) or ⊚pozitif-ist.com.

FILM

Hundreds of cinemas (*sinema*) all over Istanbul show mainly Hollywood releases with Turkish subtitles. Many of the modern complexes are situated in large shopping malls, with the best old-style cinemas in Beyoğlu, once the centre of domestic film production. Most still have a fifteen-minute coffee and cigarette interval. Tickets cost from ₺10, but most cinemas have one or more day(s) midweek where tickets are discounted. The annual International Film Festival (mid-April to May) takes place mainly at cinemas in Beyoğlu.

Cinemaximum İstiklal Cad 24–26, Beyoğlu ☎0212 292 1111, ⊚afm.com.tr; map pp.102–103. Popular ten-screen cinema not far from Taksim Square, showing the

newest films. It's the smartest cinema in Beyoğlu, but lacks character.

City Life City's Mall, Teşvikiye Cad 162, Nişantaşı ☎0212 373 3535, ⊚citylifecinema.com. Seven-screen, state-of-the-art cinema housed in the retro-style City's Mall shopping centre in upmarket Nişantaşı, with trendy (and expensive) café-bars attached.

Kanyon, Mars Kanyon Mall, Büyukdere Cad 185, Levent ☎0212 353 0814, ⊚marssinema.com. Not surprisingly, given its location in this ultra-modern shopping mall, the ticket prices are above average, but probably worth it if you want the comfiest seats and best picture and sound quality in town.

Şafak Yeniçeriler Cad, Çemberlitaş ☎0212 516 2660, ⊚ozenfilm.com.tr. The closest cinema to Sultanahmet lies buried deep within the bowels of a shopping centre, with seven screens showing the latest Western and Turkish releases.

1

THEATRES AND CONCERT HALLS

There are regular classical music, ballet and opera performances in Istanbul. The main annual event is the International Music Festival during June and July, which includes jazz, classical and world music concerts, as well as performances by the Istanbul State Symphony Orchestra. Theatre is popular, but it's mostly Turkish plays that are performed on the thirty or so stages in the city. Information on all music and theatre events, and on the various cultural festivals, is available from the Istanbul Foundation for Culture and Arts (IKSV; ⓦ iksv.org).

Akbank Culture and Arts Centre (Akbanksanat) İstiklal Cad 8/A, Beyoğlu ☎0212 252 3500, ⓦ akbanksanat.com; map pp.102–103. Multi-purpose centre including a café, art gallery, dance studio, music room, library and theatre. The centre also hosts film festivals and organizes the annual Akbank Jazz Festival (see p.131). Tues–Sat 11am–7pm.

Borusan Arts and Cultural Centre İstiklal Cad 421, Tünel, Beyoğlu ☎0212 292 0655, ⓦ borusansanat .com; map pp.102–103. Home to the Borusan Philharmonic Orchestra, one of Turkey's most successful private orchestras, which performs two monthly concerts.

Also boasts one of the country's most extensive CD libraries.

Cemal Reşit Rey (CRR) Darulbedayi Cad 1, Harbiye ☎0212 231 5497, ⓦ crrks.org. Chamber, classical, jazz and Turkish music, plus regular performances by visiting international orchestras. Venue for the International Music Festival in June and the CRR Piano Festival in December. Oct–May daily 8pm.

Garajistanbul Kaymakan Reşit Bey Sok 11, off Yeniciler Cad, Beyoğlu ☎0212 244 4499, ⓦ garajistanbul.org; map pp.102–103. Trendy, stripped-down performing-arts venue in a former underground car park just off Galatasaray Meydanı. This is as cutting-edge as it gets in Istanbul, with workshops, films and art projects, modern dance, theatre and other performances. With seating limited to 250, it's worth booking for most things. Performances Sept–June only.

Süreyya Opera Bahariye Cad 29, Kadıköy ☎0216 346 1531, ⓦ www.sureyyaoperasi.org; tickets ⓦ dobgm .gov.tr. Set in a gorgeous, beautifully restored opera house built in 1924, this is a delightfully intimate place to watch opera, ballet and classical music, and a rare oasis of culture on the Asian side of the Bosphorus. Performances Oct–May only.

ISTANBUL FESTIVALS

The annual festival calendar is pretty full, especially between April and October. The most important modern art event is the **International Istanbul Biennial** (see below).

APRIL

International Film Festival ⓦ film.iksv.org/en. Turkish, European and Hollywood movies premiere at Istanbul's cinemas, mainly in Beyoğlu, plus the best of the non-English-speaking world's releases from the previous year.

Tulip Festival Two-week-long festival honouring the national flower, including concerts, arts events and competitions at different locations around the city. Over fifteen million bulbs flower across the city, best seen at Emirgan Park (see p.137).

MAY

Chill Out ⓦ chilloutfest.com. Dance and electronica festival held in the incongruous surroundings of ultra-posh Kemer Golf and Country Club in Belgrade Forest.

Conquest Celebrations ⓦ ibb.gov.tr. Week-long celebration of the Ottoman conquest of old Constantinople (May 29, 1453) – concerts by the Ottoman Mehter military band, fancy-dress processions and fireworks.

Freshtival ⓦ millerfreshtival.com. Held in Maçka's Küçükçiftlik Parkı, this festival mixes indie, dance and rock sounds, with both international and local acts and DJs.

International Theatre Festival ⓦ iksv.org. Biennial event on even years, showcasing the year's best Turkish plays and performances by visiting foreign theatres.

JUNE/JULY

One Love ⓦ eonelove.com. Moderately alternative city-centre weekend-long festival, usually held at Santralistanbul, with plenty of DJ-led dance sets and performances from international bands such as Röyksopp and Klaxons, plus assorted home-grown acts.

The International Music Festival ⓦ iksv.org. This hugely successful festival was launched in 1973 to celebrate Turkey's fifty years of independence and brings top-notch orchestras and soloists from all over the world to perform in such atmospheric venues as the church of Haghia Eirene.

TRADITIONAL TURKISH MUSIC

There are many different types of Turkish music and all may, initially at least, sound incongruous, off-key even, to the Western ear – largely because of the copious use of quarter-tones. If you really want to scratch beneath the surface of what makes this city tick, it's worth searching out a **traditional music** venue. The *Türkü* bar, where traditional Anatolian folk songs are played, tends to be drinking and music-orientated, though most serve food as well. The *meyhane* (tavern) experience is as much about the endless courses of food served as it is about the *fasil* music that is played. In the **Türkü bar**, the focus is on the *bağlama*, a kind of long-necked lute played with amazing dexterity by experts. On a typical evening, expect to sit around, beer in hand, listening to its plaintive sounds. As the evening progresses, the *bağlama* player, perhaps accompanied by fellow musicians playing the *deblek* (a kind of bongo-drum) and a *ney* (a type of flute) raises the tempo and the audience gets to their feet, links fingers and dances the *halay*, the country's national dance. It's great fun and very popular among young Istanbulites. *Fasil* music is quite different and played mainly by Roma (gypsy) bands. Visit virtually any **meyhane** (such as those on Nevizade Sokak or Asmalımescit) and you won't be able to escape it even if you wanted to, as the musicians serenade each and every table in search of tips.

FASIL AND TÜRKÜ VENUES

Feraye Balo Sok 1 First Floor, off İstiklal Cad ☎0212 244 7472, ⓦferaye.net; map pp.102–103. This smart *meyhane* is a favourite with local Turkish music-lovers who come for the live performances on weekends. Inevitably the whole restaurant is on their feet by the end of the night. Prices are a little higher than elsewhere (fixed menu including drinks ₺100), but the atmosphere makes it an experience. Daily noon–4am.

Kallavi Meyhane Kurabiye Sok 16, off İstiklal Cad ☎0212 245 1213, ⓦkallavi20.net; map pp.102–103. A small, traditional restaurant. The fixed menu (₺90) includes ten starters, four mains, a dessert and fruit, plus unlimited local drinks. With live *fasil* music every night, it's very popular with the locals, so best to book ahead. There's another branch at Şefikbey Sok in Kadıköy. Mon–Sat 11am–2am.

★**Mektup** İmam Adnan Sok 20, off İstiklal Cad ☎0212/251 0110, ⓦmektupbar.com; map

---

Sonisphere ⓦsonispherefestivals.com. Two-day head-banging event for (mainly Turkish) heavy-metal lovers.

JULY/AUGUST

International Jazz Festival ⓦiksv.org. Two weeks of gigs and jamming sessions from world-class performers (with the definition of jazz stretched to include rock artists such as Lou Reed and Marianne Faithful).

Rumeli Hisarı Fortress Concerts Nightly summer concerts within the walls of this Ottoman fortification overlooking the Bosphorus – a varied programme from classical to rock.

SEPTEMBER

ArtInternational ⓦistanbulartinternational.com. Epitomizing Istanbul's Importance on the international contemporary art scene, this large-scale annual art fair was established in 2013 and is held in the Haliç Congress Centre. Aiming to act as a bridge between the East and West it attracts some big players from around the globe.

International Istanbul Biennial ⓦiksv.org. Multimedia contemporary arts festival; usually runs mid-September to the first week in November. Held on odd years: 2013, 2015, etc.

OCTOBER/NOVEMBER

Akbank International Jazz Festival ⓦakbanksanat.com. Two-week festival concentrating on traditional jazz, with performers such as Dave Holland and Henry Threadgill. Events include film screenings, informal jamming sessions and drum workshops.

Efes Pilsen Blues Festival Two-day late-night blues festival – a showcase of new local talent and famous foreign bands.

International Puppet Festival ☎0212 232 0224, ⓦistanbulkuklafestivali.com. A celebration of Turkish Shadow Theatre, or karağöz – silent puppets tell their tale behind a two-dimensional screen.

Istanbul Marathon ⓦistanbulmarathon. Runners from around the world compete in trans-continental marathon.

1

pp.102–103. The food on offer here is limited in range but perfectly passable. More importantly, the *Türkü* music is of a very high standard– it has seen sets by notable artists such as Ebru Destan and Tuğbay Özay. Voted the best *Türkü* bar in the country by the *Hürriyet* newspaper, so booking is advisable – especially at weekends. Daily noon–4am.

Munzur Hasnün Galip Sok 21/A, off İstiklal Cad

☎0212 245 4669; map pp.102–103. The Munzur mountains, away to the east in the heartland of Turkey's Kurdish Alevi population (the Alevi have spawned the nation's best *bağlama* players), are the inspiration for this no-frills but lively *Türkü* bar. The food is okay, the drinks not too pricey, and when things get going there are plenty of linked bodies dancing around the tables. Daily 6pm–4am.

TRADITIONAL DANCE AND CULTURAL SHOWS

Folk dancing to traditional music has managed to survive into the modern day, as have the rituals of religious orders such as the Sufi Mevlevî (see p.104). The easiest way for visitors to sample some of the action is to attend a show. Those performed in the two places below are generally well regarded, though inevitably the entire audience will be fellow visitors.

Hodja Paşa Culture Centre Hodjapaşa Hamam Sok 3/B, Sirkeci ⓦ hodjapasha.com; map pp.86–87. Housed in a beautifully restored Ottoman hamam, with the dance area and seats atmospherically set beneath an exposed brick dome. A 70min show introduces the visitor to music and dances from all parts of the Ottoman Empire for ₺50, including an interval drink. There's also a more specialist whirling dervish ceremony put on by Sufis from the Galata Mevlevihanesi. Whirling dervish ceremony Mon, Wed &

Fri–Sun 7.30pm; regular show Tues & Thurs 8pm, Sat & Sun 9pm.

Turkish Cultural Dance Theatre Fırat Culture Centre, Divan Yolu Cad, Sultanahmet ☎0554 797 2646, ⓦ dancesofcolours.com; map pp.86–87. Presents a whirling dervish music and dance show in a restored house that once belonged to a distinguished *dede* (leader). This is purely theatre, with no dinner or the other trappings of a club. ₺50. Mon, Thurs & Sat.

SHOPPING

Shopping in Istanbul is an experience. Whether or not it's a pleasant one depends on your ability to ignore the hustlers when you're not in the mood, and to bargain hard when you are. Don't miss the **Grand Bazaar** (see p.89), a hive of over four thousand little shops. Equally interesting shopping districts scattered around the city include **İstiklal Caddesi** for clothes, **Nişantaşı** for upmarket international fashion; and the **Spice Bazaar** (Mısır Çarşısı) and its environs for spices and sweets. Out of the centre, **shopping malls** have taken off in a big way, good for homeware and clothes. The covered bazaar is credit-card-friendly, as are all shops except the smallest of grocers (*bakals*) or kiosks.

ANTIQUES AND BRIC-A-BRAC

If you're expecting to find bargain antiques, you'll probably be disappointed. The average Istanbullu may care little for the old and worn, but a city of over fifteen million holds enough who do to ensure buoyant prices. Bear in mind that you're supposed to have clearance from the Museums Directorate to take anything out of the country that's over one hundred years old (see p.53). The best places to find twentieth-century items, up to 1980s retro stuff, are the streets leading down from İstiklal Caddesi in Çukurcuma, or the Horohor Antiques market in Aksaray.

Abdullah Sandal Bedestan 6, Kapılı Çarşısı; map p.90. Established in 1880 and run by the fluent English-speaking Pol Şalabi, this small shop stocks a treasure-trove of icons, jewellery from 1800 to the 1950s, and much else besides. Mon–Sat 9am–7pm.

Horhor Antique Market Yorum Kırık Tulumba Sok 13/22, Aksaray; map pp.86–87. Over two hundred bric-a-brac and antique shops in a multistorey building in the drab suburb of Aksaray, a 15min walk from the Aksaray metro station. Daily 10am–8pm.

Kadıköy Antika Çarşısı Tellalzade Sok, Çakıroğlu İş Han, Kadıköy. Tellalzade Sokak has a number of small shops selling all kinds of retro and bric-a-brac items, plus some genuine antiques. An excursion here fits in well with food souvenir shopping and the wonderful *Çiya* restaurant (see p.126). Daily 10am–7pm.

Leyla Altıpatlar Sok 10, Çukurcuma; map pp.102–103. This well-established shop stocks all manner of antique clothing, from the late nineteenth century to the 1960s, plus all sorts of cloth-related items – including embroidered cushions and throws – collected by enthusiast Leyla Seyhanlı. Mon–Sat 10am–7pm.

Müstamel Eşya Evi Turancıbaşı Cad 38/1, off İstiklal Cad, Beyoğlu; map pp.102–103. Spread over two floors, this retro-orientated shop is run by friendly, architect-trained Aslıhan Kendiroğlu, and concentrates on the 1950s to the 1970s, from bakelite phones to chrome light-fixtures, and from furniture to clothes. Mon–Sat 9am–7pm.

Sofa Art and Antiques Nuruosmaniye Cad 53A, Nuruosmaniye and Serdar-ı Ekrem Sok 47, Galata ☎0212 292 3977, ⓦ kashifsofa.com; pp.102–103. With one store located just outside the Grand Bazaar, and one in trendy Galata, husband and wife team Kaşif and Dilek have all the bases covered – and are some of the most friendly and knowledgeable old hands in the business; their shops are treasure-troves of Ottoman and European finds. Mon–Sat 9am–7pm.

BOOKS, MAPS AND PRINTS

The most traditional place to buy books in the city is Sahaflar Çarşısı (old book market) at Beyazıt, between the Grand Bazaar and Beyazıt Camii, which stocks numerous new titles on both Istanbul and Turkey in general – in English – as well as some secondhand books. For the widest range of books, Beyoğlu is the best bet.

Denizler Kitabevi İstiklal Cad 395, Beyoğlu ☎ 0212/249 8893; map pp.102–103. Specialists in nautical books and charts, plus an extensive range of collectors' books on Turkey and the Ottomans. Mon–Sat 9.30am–7.30pm.

Galeri Kayseri Divan Yolu Cad 58, Sultanahmet ⓦ galerikayseri.com; map p.73. The biggest distributor of English-language books in Turkey, with a vast range of books on Ottoman history and all other imaginable Turkish topics. Daily 9am–8.30pm.

Greenhouse Bookshop Café Moda Cad 28, Kadiköy. The best bookshop on the Asian shore, managed by an English woman and stocking an excellent range of books in English, including an extensive children's department. Mon & Wed–Sat 10am–6.30pm.

Homer Yeni Çarşışı Cad 28, Beyoğlu; map pp.102–103. A wonderful selection of anything archeological, historical and cultural written on Turkey, plus the odd *Rough Guide*. Mon–Sat 10am–7.30pm.

CLOTHES

Many Western high-street stores produce their clothes in Turkey, and outlets across the city specialize in seconds and production overruns at bargain prices. Fakes abound, so check thoroughly before purchasing. The best places to look are the arcades off İstiklal Caddesi. Turkish stores (with multiple branches) to watch out for include: Beymen, Damat Tween, Homestore, Karaca, La Luna, Mudo City, Mudo, and Yargıcı. Vakko is one of the most reputable fashion chains in Istanbul; Vakkorama is its youth-market offshoot.

RETRO AND BARGAIN CLOTHES

Atlas Pasajı Off İstiklal Cad 209, Beyoğlu; map pp.102–103. This trendy and historic arcade behind the Atlas Cinema has bargain clothing – plus alternative/street-style clothes outlets, funky jewellery shops, piercing places and CD/DVD shops, and an amazing array of original film posters in a couple of the basement stores. Daily 9.30am–11pm.

Beyoğlu İş Merkezi İstiklal Cad 331–369; map pp.102–103. Three floors of bargain end-of-line and seconds clothing, with the odd genuine bargain for the persistent. Daily 10am–10pm.

By Retro Suriye Pasajı, İstiklal Cad, Beyoğlu ☎ 0212 245 6420, ⓦ byretro.com; map pp.102–103. Set in the basement of this historic arcade is what claims to be Europe's largest secondhand clothing shop. Owner Hakan Vardar scours Europe for vintage clothes and there are rails and rails of the results here. Daily 10am–10.30pm.

Terkoz Çıkmaz Off İstiklal Cad, Beyoğlu; map pp.102–103. This side street off İstiklal Cad – next to the Paşabahçe glass store, down towards Tünel – is crammed with stalls selling overruns that bear British, French and German high-street names. Daily 10am–10pm.

HIGH-STREET AND DESIGNER CLOTHES

Aponia Store Galipdede Caddesi 101/A ⓦ aponiastore .com; map pp.102–103. A quirky design store-cum-coffee shop where you can find original T-shirts, bags, hoodies and posters that make affordable and wearable souvenirs. Daily 10am–10pm.

Beyman Zorlu Center, Zincirlikuyu ☎ 0212 306 3300 ⓦ beymen.com; map pp.102–103. Quality chain shop for tailored men's and women's suits, dress shirts, silk ties and scarves, and other accessories. Daily 10am–10pm.

Crash Galip Dede Cad 35, Galata; map pp.102–103. A small, alternative outlet in up-and-coming Galata, with a good range of individually designed T-shirts, hoodies and shorts – plus some secondhand retro stuff. Mon–Sat 10am–9pm.

Mavi İstiklal Cad 117, Beyoğlu; map pp.102–103; and in all shopping malls. Gap-inspired jeans label, good-quality denimwear, T-shirts (including a good range of "cool" Istanbul designs), sweat tops and funky bags. Daily 10am–10pm.

Roll Turnacıbaşı Sok 13/1, off İstiklal Cad, Beyoğlu; map pp.102–103. The outlet of choice for indie types who want cutting-edge street fashion. Much of their output is generic, but look out for the range of tongue-in-cheek T's emblazoned with "legendary" Turkish cars such as the Murat 124 and the Anadol. Also stocks secondhand retro-style clothing. Daily 10am–10pm.

Vakko Zorlu Center, Zincirlikuyu ☎ 0212/708 3333, ⓦ vakko.com.tr; map pp.102–103. Classy 50-year-old Turkish fashion label renowned for its sense of style and use of fine fabrics. The clothes don't come cheap though, and you have to dress up a bit if you want to feel comfortable. Daily 10am–10pm.

Yargıcı Akmerkez Shopping Mall, Etiler and other branches. Turkey's answer to Marks & Spencer – well-made and reasonably priced clothing from work suits to sportswear and underwear. Daily 10am–10pm.

CARPETS AND KILIMS

Adnan & Hasan Halıcılar Cad 89–92, Grand Bazaar ⓦ adnanandhasan.com; map p.90. A wide range of modern and antique kilims and carpets from a reputable

1

dealership, established in 1978, with Ushak and Hereke carpets vying for shop space with Anatolian and Caucasian kilims. Mon–Sat 9am–7pm.

Dhoko-Ethnicon Takkeciler Sok 58–60, Grand Bazaar ☎0212 527 6841, ⊚ethnicon.com; map p.90. Fixed prices for kilims made in the traditional way (with natural dyes and no child labour) but with contemporary (often large, geometric blocks of colour) styling.

Şişko Osman Zincirli Han, Grand Bazaar ☎0212 528 3548, ⊚siskoosman.com; map p.90. Arguably the most knowledgeable dealer in the Grand Bazaar, reputable Şişko ("Fat") Osman's family origins are in the east of Turkey, but he has been flogging top-quality rugs to all-comers (including the rich and famous) here for many years. Over sixty percent of his clients are Turks, which gives some idea of the quality of the (mainly) dowry pieces on offer here. His kilims range from €400 to €2500 and carpets €500 to €2500 – excluding the more expensive genuine period pieces, some dating back to the eighteenth century, stocked in one of his four adjacent shops. Mon–Sat 9am–7pm.

Tradition Rubiye Han 11/12, Kürkçüler Sok, Grand Bazaar ☎0212 520 7907; map p.90. Opened in 1988 and co-run by French woman Florence Heilbron, this fine establishment has a very good reputation, lots of repeat customers (including a coterie of French diplomats and politicians) and sells pieces from €50 to €10,000. Mon–Sat 9am–7pm.

Yörük Kürkçüler Cad 17, Grand Bazaar; map p.90. Run by Ersoy, whose family came to the city from the Caucasus in 1864 via the Central Anatolian town of Kayseri. The stock runs from chemical-dyed pieces for as little as €80 to vintage dowry pieces up to €5000. Very reliable. Mon–Sat 9am–7pm.

FOOD AND SPICES

Istanbul is a great place to stock up on herbs and spices, most obviously in the Mısır Çarşısı (Spice Bazaar), though the streets roundabout it, and Güneşlibahçe Sokak in Kadıköy, are far better value. Dried fruits are also great value and delicious. Two specialities to look out for are *nar ekşisi*, the viscous pomegranate syrup used so liberally in many Turkish salads, sold in small bottles, and *pekmez*, a sweet topping for yoghurt, usually made from either grapes or mulberries. Turkish coffee (*Türk kahvesi*) is about as traditional a Turkish product as you can get, though you'll need to buy a small pan known as a *kahve tenceresi* if you want to make it properly back home. Then, of course, in all its glutinous splendour, there is *lokum*, known in the West as Turkish delight.

Ali Muhidin Haci Bekir Hamidiye Cad 83, Eminönü; map pp.102–103. Founded in 1777, this is the best place in the city to buy Turkish delight – choose from over twenty varieties – and more unusual delicacies such as *fındıklı ezmesi* (hazelnut marzipan). The interior is wonderful, with

an eye-catching array of sugary treats displayed on period wooden shelves and in glass-fronted cabinets. Daily 9am–9pm.

Güllüoğlu Mumhane Cad 171, Karaköy; map pp.102–103. Arguably the best *baklava* in the city, delicious, buttery and nut-filled. If you're looking to take some home, this is the place to buy it – not only is it the best, but it's not as syrupy as other brands and therefore less likely to leak over your hand luggage. Daily 10am–midnight.

Kurukahveci Mehmet Efendi Tahmis Sok 66, Eminönü; map pp.86–87. There are always big queues outside this wonderful paean to the aromatic coffee bean. Started in 1871, it's now housed in a rare (for this city) and impressive Art Deco building west of the Spice Bazaar. Sells beans and powder for Turkish and filter coffees, plus *sahlep*, the ground-orchid-root drink so popular in Istanbul in the winter. Mon–Sat 9am–7pm.

Spice Bazaar (Mısır Çarşısı) Eminönü; map pp.86–87. To choose between the myriad purveyors of different spices, herbs, herbal teas, Turkish delight, nuts and dried-fruits in the historic Spice Bazaar would be meaningless – don't be afraid to try a taste before you buy. Daily 9am–7pm.

GIFTS AND HANDICRAFTS

In their own way just as authentic as the traditional Ottoman crafts are the modern twists on old designs sold in upmarket household goods stores such as Paşabahçe – especially glassware.

Abdulla Halıcılar Cad 53, Kapalı Çarşı; map p.90. Restrained design is the key to this chic store selling handmade olive-oil-based soaps, bath wraps (*peştemal*), bed linen, fluffy towels and the like – it tweaks traditional products to fit the tastes of the city's new elite and Western visitors alike. Mon–Sat 9am–7pm.

Cocoon Küçük Aya Sofya Cad 13; map p.73. Four floors showcasing gorgeously hued and patterned felt hats, bags, animals and even jewellery, plus a wide range of traditional Central Asian textiles, carpets and kilims. It's all very tastefully done and the prices are not too unreasonable. There's a smaller shop in the Arasta Bazaar. Daily 9am–7pm.

Istanbul Handicrafts Centre Kabasakal Cad 5, Sultanahmet; map p.73. Restored *medrese* – an extension to the Yeşil Ev Hotel – where artists and craftsmen keep alive traditional skills such as *ebru* marbling, calligraphy, lace-making and embroidery. Daily 10am–7pm.

İznik Classics Arasta Çarşısı 67, Sultanahmet; map p.73. Some of the best examples of İznik tiles you'll see anywhere, beautifully displayed in this small shop in the Arasta Bazaar (there are other outlets in the Grand Bazaar and on nearby Utangaç Sokak). The tiles are handmade by different artists, and all reflect the high quality of the finest period of İznik pottery and are consequently expensive, with prices from ₺120 and up. Daily: April–Oct 9am–9pm; Nov–March 9am–7pm.

Jennifer's Hamam Arasta Bazaar, Sultanahmet; map p.73. All the textiles here are made from organic cotton, linen or silk, and woven by hand on traditional looms. Prices are a little above average because of this, but the product is top-notch, with a fabulous range of *pestemals*, fluffy towels and scarves on offer. The owner is a knowledgeable Canadian. Daily 9am–8pm.

Necdat Danış Yağlıkçılar Sok, Grand Bazaar; map p.90. This place has been selling hand-woven textiles for over forty years, and has an excellent reputation for its keen prices and wide range of scarves, *peştemals*, tablecloths and reams of gorgeous fabrics. They supplied the textiles used in the Hollywood film, *Troy*. Mon–Sat 9am–7pm.

LEATHER

Note that you run less chance of getting ripped off if you shop at one of the classier outlets listed below, rather than in the Grand Bazaar.

Derimod Akmerkez Mall, Nisbetiye Cad, Etiler. Excellent-quality leather goods – coats, jackets, bags, shoes and other accessories. Classic rather than cutting-edge, but then most people don't want to make a short-lived fashion mistake at these prices. Daily 10am–10pm.

Koç Deri Kürkçüler Cad 22/46, Grand Bazaar; map p.90. Established in 1960, this specialist leather shop in the Grand Bazaar runs up stuff for the likes of Armani and Dolce & Gabbana. Needless to say, it's not cheap, but it does have a good reputation – your wallet may be considerably lighter after a purchase, but you won't have been "done". Mon–Sat 9am–7pm.

Matraş Akmerkez Mall, Nisbetiye Cad, Etiler. Everything in leather from this quality Turkish store, including wallets, handbags, belts and briefcases. Daily 10am–8pm.

MUSIC AND MUSICAL INSTRUMENTS

Turkish music aside, you'll find a good general selection of world music, classical, pop and jazz in the music shops listed below, and in the many outlets on İstiklal Caddesi and in the shopping malls. Traditional musical instruments are on sale in the Grand Bazaar, though prices are much better at any one of the myriad instrument shops on and around Galipdede Caddesi, near the upper Tünel station in Beyoğlu.

D & R Kanyon Mall (see opposite). Chain that stocks a decent range of traditional and contemporary Turkish sounds, as well as foreign CDs, DVDs, computer accessories, books, magazines and games. Other branches across the city. Daily 10am–10pm.

Kontra Plak Yeni Çarşı Cad 60/A, Galatasary ☎0212/243 8680, ⓦ kontrarecords.com; map pp.102–103. One of a new breed of hip record stores, in Beyoğlu, this basement store has a cool feel and stocks an impressive range of records and CDs of all genres from Turkey and beyond. Daily 9am–10pm.

Lale Plak Galipdede Cad 1, Tünel, Beyoğlu; map pp.102–103. Funky old-style music store, the best place for traditional Turkish music CDs but even more so for jazz. The staff know their stuff – aided, no doubt, by the continuity of a business that's been going for nigh on fifty years. Daily 10am–7pm.

Naturel Müzik Galipdede Cad 103/B, Beyoğlu; map pp.102–103. A good choice on "music alley", stocked with reasonably priced quality guitars, *bağlama, saz, ud, darasbuka* and other traditional Turkish instruments. Daily 10am–7pm.

SHOPPING MALLS

Looked at in a positive way, an American-style mall is just a modern version of a bazaar – and while their food courts may boast a *McDonald's* or *Burger King*, they hold far more outlets knocking out traditional Turkish fare such as *pide*, *lahmacun* and *köfte*.

City's Mall Teşvikiye Cad 162, Nişantaşı ⓦ citysnisantasi.com. Upmarket addition to the city's mall scene, well designed, with sleek Art Deco lines. It's exclusive and mainly fashion-orientated – think Louis Vuitton, Dolce & Gabbana, Jean-Paul Gaultier and the like. There's an attached luxury multiscreen cinema and a few posh places to eat. Daily 10am–10pm.

Demirören İstiklal Cad, Beyoğlu ⓦ demirorenistiklal .com; map pp.102–103. This controversial mall (İstiklal Caddesi is lined with historic buildings) is likely to be the most convenient for the majority of visitors, and includes a Virgin Megastore, Mothercare and Gap among many other shops, as well as a cinema. Daily 10am–10pm.

Kanyon Büyükdere Cad 185, Levent ⓦ kanyon.com.tr. Take the metro to Levent for this "open-air" canyon-shaped, four-storey, state-of-the-art shopping mall. It features the most popular Western consumer chains and has an extremely plush cinema. Daily 10am–10pm.

Zorlu Center Zincirlikuyu ☎0212 336 9160, ⓦ zorlucenter.com; map pp.102–103. An impressive mixed use centre containing a shopping mall, hotel, residences and performing arts centre. Since opening in 2013, it has taken over from Kanyon as the city's most exclusive designer haven and also features international restaurant chains. Daily 10am–10pm.

STREET MARKETS

For a lively atmosphere it's worth heading out to one of the city's famous street markets. Most now concentrate on fresh fruit, vegetables, olives, cheese and other foodstuffs along with cheap (often fake designer-ware) clothing and household essentials.

Beşiktaş Pazarı Beşiktaş; map pp.102–103. Saturday bazaar held in a warren of streets to either side of Şair Nedim Cad (about 10min from the ferry terminal). It's pot luck what you'll find, as just about any kind of clothing can turn up here. Sat 9am–dusk.

1

Çarşamba Pazarı Fatih; map pp.86–87. Held every Wednesday and occupying the narrow streets close to Fatih Cami, this is the most authentic of the city's markets, but better for fruit, vegetables and the like than bargain clothing. Wed 8am–dusk.

DIRECTORY

Banks and exchange Exchange offices (*döviz*) around Eminönü, Sultanahmet and Taksim, and on most main city thoroughfares, change cash. Most don't charge commission, but check first to confirm; hours are generally daily 9am–8pm (sometimes later in peak season). There are also exchange offices at the airport (24hr), Esenler *otogar* (daily 8.30am–11pm) and Sirkeci station (daily 9am–5pm). Opening hours for banks are Mon–Fri 9am–12.30pm & 1.30–5pm, though the larger branches of Garanti Bankası stay open through lunch; major banks have ATMs, some of which also dispense euros. Bank rates are generally better than *döviz*, especially at the Ziraat Bankası.

Consulates Australia, Asker Ocağı Cad 15, Elmadağ, Şişli (☎ 0212 243 1333); Canada, Tekfen Tower, 209 Büyükdere Cad, Levent 4 (☎ 0212 385 9700); New Zealand, İnönü Cad 48/3, Taksim (☎ 0212 244 0272); South Africa (Honorary Consul), Alarko Centre, Musallim Naci Cad 113–115, Ortaköy (☎ 0212 260 378); UK, Meşrutiyet Cad 34, Tepebaşı, Beyoğlu (☎ 0212 334 6400); US, Kaplıcalar Mevkii Sok 2, İstinye (☎ 0212 335 9000).

Dentists The main alternatives to the practices in the German and American hospitals (see below), both with English-speaking staff, are Prodent-Can Ergene, Valikonağı Cad 109/5, Nişantaşı (☎ 0212 230 4635), and Reha Sezgin, Halaskargazi Cad 48/9, Harbiye (☎ 0212 240 3322).

Emergencies Ambulance ☎ 112; Fire ☎ 110; Police ☎ 155.

Hospitals The Taksim First Aid Hospital (Taksim İlkyardim Hastanesi), at Sıraselviler Cad 112, Taksim (☎ 0212 252 4300), is state-run and deals with emergencies only; patients are often referred on to one of the hospitals listed below. For emergencies, as well as regular doctor's appointments, private foreign hospitals are better, though more expensive than the state hospitals, which are understaffed and overcrowded. One of the city's best equipped is the American Hospital (Amerikan Hastanesi), Güzelbahçe Sok 20, Nişantaşı (☎ 0212 311 2000, ⊚ amerikanhastanesi.org). The German Hospital, at Sıraselviler Cad 119, Taksim (☎ 0212 293 2150; map pp.102–103), also has a dental and eye clinic.

Internet access Almost all Istanbul hotels and hostels have wi-fi and/or an internet terminal for guests to use. Many cafés also have wi-fi. As a result internet cafés are dwindling and most favoured by game-playing youngsters.

Left luggage Left-luggage offices (*Emanet* in Turkish) can be found at Atatürk airport (open 24hr; ₺20 standard-size bags, ₺30 large bags). Esenler and Harem *otogars* and Sirkeci and Haydarpaşa train stations also have left-luggage facilities.

Pharmacies Pharmacies (*Eczane*) are found everywhere and Turkish pharmacists are qualified to give injections, take blood pressure and treat minor wounds. In each Istanbul neighbourhood they take turns in providing a 24hr service called *Nöbetçi*. At night, the *Nöbetçi* rota is posted on the window of the other pharmacies.

Police Reports of theft or loss should be made to the Tourist Police, in a prominent blue wooden building at Yerebatan Cad 6, Sultanahmet (☎ 0212 527 4503); there are English-speaking officers on the premises 24hr daily. Any commercial misdealings should be reported to the *Zabita* (market police) offices found all over town, a handy one in Sultanahmet, at the far end of the Hippodrome.

Post offices The main post office (PTT) is on Büyük Posthane Cad in Sirkeci, not far from the train station (daily 8.30am–5.30pm for full postal services, 24hr section for stamps and phone calls). Other branch offices, including that Yeniçarşı Caddesi, off İstiklal Cad and that at Cumhuriyet Cad in Taksim Square, are open daily 8.30am–12.30pm & 1.30–5pm. Smaller branch offices are usually open Mon–Fri 8am–3pm.

Swimming pools For a substantial fee (₺50 up to well over ₺100 at weekends) visitors can use the pools in major hotels including *Ceylan Intercontinental*, Asker Ocağı Cad 1, Taksim, which has the great advantage of being centrally located in Taksim, with a large, heated outdoor pool and pool bar. The expensive *Ciragan Palace Hotel Kempinski*, Ciragan Cad 32, Beşiktaş, has indoor and outdoor pools; the *Hilton* on Cumhuriyet Cad, Harbiye, has a fitness centre as well; and the monstrous *Ritz Carlton* on Asker Ocağı Cad in Elmadağ has indoor and outdoor lap pools, plus stunning views over the Bosphorus and the rest of the city.

Telephones Istanbul has two phone-number prefixes, one for Europe, one for Asia, which must be used when calling the opposite shore; Europe ☎ 0212, Asia ☎ 0216. Local and international calls can be made from any public booth, at the PTTs (post offices) or TT (Türk Telekom) centres. Useful clusters of booths can be found in Sultanahmet, Taksim Square and Sirkeci train station. Most accept "Smart" phonecards, which can be bought at PTT counters, newsagent kiosks and shops.

Travel agents Travel agents are concentrated along Divan Yolu Cad in Sultanahmet and Cumhuriyet Cad in Taksim. Most can book destinations anywhere in Turkey, and arrange hotel stays, car rental and transfers to the airport or bus station: try the reliable Turista Travel, Divan Yolu Cad 16 (☎ 0212 518 6570, ⊚ turistatravel.com). For budget tours, bus tickets and backpacker travel, contact Backpackers Travel, Yeni Akbiyik Cad 22, Sultanahmet (☎ 0212 638 6343, ⊚ backpackerstravel.com).

Along the Bosphorus

1

The 30km strait known as the **Bosphorus** divides Europe and Asia and connects the Marmara and Black seas, its width varying from 660m to 4.5km. Its name derives from the Greek myth of Io, lover of Zeus, whom the god transformed into a cow to conceal her from his jealous wife Hera. She plunged into the straits to escape a gadfly, hence Bosphorus, or "Ford of the Cow".

Around eighty thousand cargo ships, oil tankers and ocean liners pass through the strait each year, while for residents and visitors alike the Bosphorus remains Istanbul's most important transport artery. The passenger ferries and sea buses that weave their way up and down from shore to shore provide one of the city's real highlights: along the way are imperial palaces and ancient fortresses interspersed with small fishing villages and wooden *yalıs* (waterside mansions). Despite its pollution the Bosphorus is also full of fish – from swordfish to *hamsi* (a small fish belonging to the anchovy family).

The European shore

The **European shore** is very built up, as far as the second Bosphorus bridge. The villages turned suburbs of **Arnavutköy** and **Bebek**, popular haunts of the rich, are pretty enough when viewed from a boat. Further north, the fish restaurants in the villages of **Sariyer** and **Rumeli Kavağı** make pleasant destinations for lunch or dinner. West of Sariyer, the **Belgrade Forest** is Istanbul's nearest tract of woodland, offering quiet, rural surroundings.

Arnavutköy

North of Ortaköy, the coast road runs under the 1km-long **Atatürk bridge**, completed in 1973. A couple of kilometres beyond, **ARNAVUTKÖY** is famous for its line of *yalıs*, wooden waterfront mansions with their boat moorings carved out beneath them. It's home to several trendy restaurants, while in the backstreets behind the waterfront, a sizeable Greek Orthodox church and the remains of a synagogue testify to the settlement's cosmopolitan past.

Bebek

Affluent **BEBEK** lies a fifteen-minute walk up the strait from Arnavutköy. If you arrive by boat, Bebek's most famous building stands to the left of the jetty: the beautifully restored waterfront **Hıdıv Sarayı** (Khedive's Palace), an Art Nouveau-style mansion belonging to the Egyptian consulate.

The impressive **fortress of Rumeli Hisarı** is another fifteen-minute walk along the promenade north of Bebek (Tues–Sun: April–Oct 9am–7pm; Nov–March 9am–7pm; ₺10). Grander than its counterpart, Anadolu Hisarı, across the strait, this Ottoman fortress was constructed in four months in 1452, before the Ottoman conquest of the city. It houses a small open-air theatre, providing a summer-evening venue for concerts and plays, particularly during the International Music Festival (see p.130). Like Arnavutköy, Bebek holds a number of upscale restaurants.

Fatih Sultan Mehmet bridge

The second Bosphorus bridge, the **Fatih Sultan Mehmet bridge**, looms high above the fortress of Rumeli Hisarı. Completed in 1988, it's among the world's longest suspension bridges, at 1090m, and spans the Bosphorus at the point where King Darius of Persia crossed the straits by pontoon bridge in 512 BC.

Emirgan

EMIRGAN is home to the excellent **Sakip Sabancı Museum** (Sakip Sabancı Müzesi; Tues, Fri, Sat & Sun 10am–6pm, Wed 10am–8pm; ₺10; ⑩muze.sakipsabancmuzesi.org). Located in a beautifully restored 1920s villa just behind the waterfront, the museum

1

boasts exquisite examples of Ottoman calligraphy, and hosts varied and prestigious temporary exhibitions; past subjects have included Picasso and Dalí.

A short walk north from the museum, **Emirgan Park** is the most attractive park in the city, with delightfully landscaped gardens and some quaint, pastel-hued *köşks* (pavilions).

Sarıyer

SARIYER, a stop on the Bosphorus Cruise, is around 5km north of Yeniköy. The main reason to visit is its **Sadberk Hanım Museum** (Sadberk Hanım Müzesi),

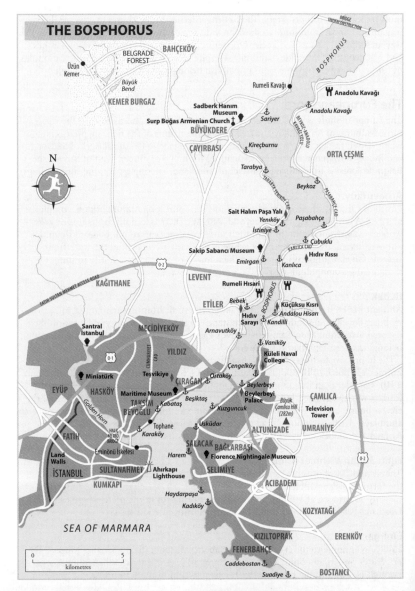

THE BOSPHORUS

Büyükdere Cad 27–29 (Mon, Tues & Thurs–Sun 10am–5pm; ₺7; ⓦsadber khanimmuzesi.org.tr), which holds a beautifully displayed assortment of archeological items, the vast majority found in Anatolia. Finds range from the Neolithic through to the Byzantine period, and there's also a splendid display of Ottoman-era ethnographical objects, collected by one of the nation's wealthiest families, Koç, displayed over three floors.

Rumeli Kavağı

The last village on the European Bosphorus shore is **RUMELI KAVAĞI**, a 2km dolmuş or short ferry ride from Sarıyer. Nicer than Sarıyer, with more of a village feel, it's no more than a string of houses, with some simple **fish restaurants** clustered around its ferry terminal.

The Asian shore

The **Asian side** of the Bosphorus holds vast suburbs and small villages, all virtually unknown to tourists. The Bosphorus Tour (see p.115) calls in at the suburb of Kanlıca on the way to its final stop Anadolu Kavağı, the last village on the Asian side.

Beylerbeyi Palace

Tues, Wed & Fri–Sun 9.30am–6pm • ₺5

Just 500m north of the first (Atatürk) Bosphorus bridge, the **Beylerbeyi Palace** is a nineteenth-century white marble summer residence and guesthouse of the Ottoman sultans. The interior decoration was designed by Sultan Abdülaziz himself, while some of the furniture, including the matching dining chairs in the harem and the *selâmlik*, was carved by Sultan Abdülhamit II during his six years of imprisonment here up to his death in 1918.

Anadolu Kavaği

The last call on the Bosphorus Tour from Eminönü is **ANADOLU KAVAĞI**, where the boat stops for a couple of hours. The village has a distinct, if dilapidated, charm – balconied houses with boat-mooring stations overlook the Bosphorus. The waterfront and main street have some decent **fish restaurants** and food stands, which is just as well as this is the longest stop on the Bosphorus Cruise. The Byzantine **fortress** from which the village takes its name sprawls across an overgrown hilltop above Anadolu Kavağı.

ARRIVAL AND DEPARTURE ALONG THE BOSPHORUS

Bosphorus Tour Most visitors prefer the ease of the Bosphorus Tour (see p.115). To ensure a good outside seat in summer, arrive at least half an hour before departure.

By ferry and bus While it's possible to explore the Bosphorus by ferry and bus, using the crowded and unfamiliar local buses is hard work. Make sure you have Şehır Hatları and IDO ferry timetables to hand, and have a topped-up *Istanbulkart* for the ferries and buses.

Along the European shore The #25/E bus runs from the Kabataş tram terminal along the coast to Rumeli Kavağı, the last stop on the European shore of the Bosphorus Cruise. Alternatively, take a #25/T or #40 from Taksim to Sarıyer, then a dolmüş or the #25/A on to Rumeli Kavağı. Another option is the Boğaz Hattı sea bus from Kabataş for İstinye then Sarıyer (Sat & Sun only, departs 8.15am, returns from Sarıyer at 6pm). The #22 and #22/RE from Kabataş are both useful for reaching Arnavutköy, Bebek and Emirgan (for the Sakıp Sabancı Museum). Şehir Hatları ferries run reasonably regularly from Sarıyer up to both Rumeli and (more frequently) Anadolu Kavağı.

Along the Asian shore From the best starting point, Üsküdar, bus #15 runs as far as Beykoz, the #15/A on to Anadolu Kavağı. A Şehir Hatları ferry zigzags between Cegelköy (Asia) and İstinye (Europe), taking in Bebek, Kanlıca and Emirgan.

The Princes' Islands

With their charming waterfront villages, *fin-de-siècle* architecture, wooded hills and rocky coves, the romantic **Princes' Islands** have always been a favourite retreat from the mainland. Set in the Sea of Marmara between 15km and 30km southeast of the city, the islands are easily accessible by ferry from Istanbul, and can get very crowded in summer, especially at weekends. Cars are banned on the islands, so **transport** is either by foot, phaeton (horse-drawn carriage), hired bike or donkey. Their proximity to the city makes them an easy, enjoyable and very cheap day-trip, but accommodation is surprisingly expensive, and, on summer weekends, hard to come by.

Brief history

The copper mines of Chalkitis (**Heybeliada**), famed in antiquity, are long since exhausted, but they remain visible near Çam Limanı. During the Byzantine era, numerous convents and monasteries were built on the islands, which soon became luxurious prisons for banished emperors, empresses and princes (often after they had been blinded). The islands were neglected by the conquering Ottoman Turks and became a place of refuge for Greek, Armenian and Jewish communities.

In 1846 a ferry service was established and the islands grew popular with Pera's wealthy merchants and bankers, becoming Istanbul's favourite summer resort after the establishment of the Republic in 1923. Mosques began to appear in the villages, and hotels and apartment buildings soon followed. A Turkish naval college was established on Heybeliada and Atatürk's private yacht was moored here as a training ship.

Kınalıada

Kınalıada, "Henna Island", takes its name from the red colouring of its eastern cliffs; in Greek it was known as *Proti*, as it's the nearest of the islands to the mainland. Like Heybeliada, Kınalıada's history is notable for exiles, including Romanus IV Diogenes, deposed after his disastrous defeat at the Battle of Manzikert by the Selçuk Turks. Today, its population is seventy percent Armenian, and their nineteenth-century **Surp Krikor Lusovoric** church, in the bustling village clustered around the ferry quay, is the

---

THE BEACHES OF THE PRINCES' ISLANDS

While beaches are by no means the only reason to visit the Princes' Islands, the most popular strands attract multitudes of visitors from the city in summer. In several instances, the best way to reach a particular beach is by catching a small boat from the island's ferry port, usually provided free by the pay beach owners themselves.

HEYBELIADA

Değirmen Burnu Plajı Northwest Heybeliada. This small, shingly curve of beach is set in pretty pine forest, at the foot of some small cliffs, on the south shore of a peninsula that projects from the northwest corner of the island. Mon–Fri ₺13, Sat & Sun ₺15. Daily 9am–dusk.

Green Beach Club On the opposite side of Heybeliada from the ferry terminal ⓦ green beachclub.com. A free service boat ferries customers to the beach, departing from just north of the island's quay. Mon–Fri ₺30, Sat & Sun ₺40. Late April to Sept daily 8am–sunset.

BÜYÜKADA

Halik Köyü Plajı Further south down the coast from the Yörükali Plajı. Although stony, this beach, looking across to the green, southern shores of the Sea of Marmara, has an Aegean island feel. Reached via a free boat from the ferry terminal, or a 20min bike ride. ₺15. Daily 8am–dusk.

Yörükali Plajı Halfway along the west coast of the island ⓦ yorukali.com. Sunbathing is accompanied by loud Turkish pop, but the beach is sandy and good for kids. Free boat transfers from the ferry terminal. ₺30 including lounger and umbrella. Mid-April to Sept daily 8am–sunset.

one notable site. The island is popular for swimming (there's a free Halk Plajı or "People's Beach" on the southeast shore), and bikes can be rented in the village for ₺15 per day.

Burgazada

Rising in tiers from the waterfront and ferry quay, the sleepy village of **BURGAZADA** is pretty enough, with a number of fine nineteenth- and early twentieth-century villas slumbering beneath fig, bay and oleander trees. Its most prominent landmark is the dome of its church of St John the Baptist. Across the square on which it stands, there's a small **museum**, at Burgaz Çayırı Sok 15 (Tues–Fri 10am–noon & 2–5pm, Sat 10am–noon; free), dedicated to the novelist **Sait Faik**, who's often described as the Turkish Mark Twain. Most people come here, however, to swim. The Kalpazankaya area (₺5) on the west side of the island (₺30 in a phaeton, or rent a bike for ₺15 a day) is a good bet, and has a nice restaurant attached.

Heybeliada

Most visitors come to **Heybeliada** to cycle around its charming hilly terrain – Heybeliada means "Island of the Saddlebag", a reference to its two hills, separated by a low saddle – or swim and/or sunbathe at one of the beach clubs.

The **Naval High School** (Deniz Harp Okulu), on the east shore, along the coast road from the main jetty, was originally the Naval War Academy, situated here since 1852. An Orthodox church, **Aya Nikola**, a prominent red-and-cream building with a curious clock tower, stands just behind the waterfront in the town centre.

Greek Orthodox School of Theology

Entry by appointment only Mon–Sat 10am–noon & 2–4pm • Free • ☎ 0216 351 8563

The nineteenth-century, hilltop **Greek Orthodox School of Theology**, the Aya Triada Manastiri, is a pleasant fifteen-minute walk through pine forest from the port, though you can also take a phaeton. The building is set in beautiful grounds, and encloses a pretty, eight-hundred-year-old church, with a stunning gilt iconostasis. Getting inside the compound is by appointment only, however, and permission is hard to obtain.

Büyükada

Büyükada (the "Great Island", the original *Prinkipo*, or "Prince's Island", in Greek) is the largest and by far the busiest of the islands, and has long been inhabited by minorities. Leon Trotsky lived here from 1929 to 1933, spending most of his time at **İzzet Paşa Köşkü**, a currently derelict mansion awaiting restoration on Çankaya Caddesi, just below the very impressive and newly restored Con Paşa Köşkü. Many of the island's mansions have beautiful gardens, filled with magnolia, mimosa and jasmine, and myrtle, lilac and rock roses grow wild in the surrounding forests.

The island consists of two hills, both surmounted by monasteries. The southernmost, **Yüce Tepe**, is home to the **Monastery of St George**, probably on the site of a twelfth-century building. To reach the monastery, take a phaeton to the small park on the main road that goes over the hill, from where a steep path leads up several hundred metres to the monastery. Alternatively, take a donkey from the stables at the bottom of this path.

The monastery on the northern hill, **İsa Tepe**, is a nineteenth-century building, formerly a Greek orphanage. Over on the east side of the island, the interesting Museum of the Princes' Islands (₺5; Tues–Sun 9am–5pm) tells the history of the island through old photographs, and has additional information on the islands' geology, flora and fauna.

1

ARRIVAL AND DEPARTURE

Sea buses The fastest way to reach the islands, IDO sea buses (*deniz otobüs*) sail from the Adalar terminal in Kabata, at the end of the T1 tramline run to Kınalıada. They go to Burgazada (9 daily), Heybeliada (12 daily) and Büyükada (12 daily); services are much less frequent in winter. Journeys take 25–45min; ₺9 each way, ₺7.10 with an *Istanbulkart*. Arrive early, as queues can be massive.

Şehir Hatları ferries Slower, cheaper Şehir Hatları ferries sail to the four larger islands – Büyükada, Heybeliada, Burgazada and Kınalıada – from both the Adalar terminal in Kabataş and from Kadıköy (sailings from both: summer 15 daily Mon–Sat from 6.50am, Sunday from 7.30am; less frequently in winter; ₺5 each way, ₺3.5 *Istanbulkart*). The journey time to Büyükada is around 1hr 30min.

THE PRINCES' ISLANDS

Island-hopping among the islands is easy, but check ferry times at the dock as the service is notoriously changeable. An *Istanbulkart* or a handful of *jetons* makes island-hopping easier.

HEYBELİADA
Ferries and sea buses arrive at Heybeliada ferry terminal on the main quayside of Rıhtım Caddesi.

BÜYÜKADA
Ferries and sea buses dock at two adjacent terminals on Büyük İskele Caddesi in Büyükada's main town, from where the main square and most of the hotels, restaurants and shops are just a short walk away.

GETTING AROUND

HEYBELİADA
Walking and cycling are good ways to enjoy Heybeliada, its pine forests and hills making for scenic rides and rambles.

Bike rental İmralı Sok 3, near the quayside; ₺5 an hour, ₺15 a day.

Phaeton tours Horse-and-carriage tours (for up to four

people; short tour ₺45, long tour ₺58) leave from the phaeton park off the main square on Isa Çelebi Sokak, 50m above the ferry terminal.

Donkey rides Donkey rides (about ₺12 per ride) up the hills start from a little park just up Kadayoran Caddesi from the centre of town.

ACCOMMODATION

BURGAZADA
Mehtap 45 On the northeast coast of the island ☎ 0216 381 2660. Though it's got all the mod cons, this is fairly spartan for a boutique hotel and might not seem incredibly good value, but the rooms are comfortable enough, the views northwest to the metropolis superb, and owner Abbas will proudly tell you how much England football legend Bobby Charlton enjoyed his four-day stay here. The island itself offers the best combination of beauty and peace, another major attraction of *Mehtap 45*. **€90**

HEYBELİADA
Heybeliada is lower-key, and offers cheaper accommodation, than neighbouring Büyükada, though booking in advance is recommended, particularly at weekends.

Özdemir Pansiyon Ayyıldız Cad 41 ☎ 0216 351 1866, ⊛ adalar-ozdemirpansiyon.com. The cheapest option on the island, with tiny chalet-type en-suite rooms with a shower over squat loos, plus larger rooms in the main block. Both are comfortable enough. Prices rise by fifty percent on Fri and Sat. No breakfast. **₺100**

BÜYÜKADA
Accommodation on Büyükada is uniformly expensive,

though the chance to stay in a grand restored mansion or boutique seafront hotel may be appealing. Rates rise at weekends.

Ayanikola Butik Aya Nikola Mevki 104 ☎ 0126 382 4143, ⊛ ayanikolabutikpansiyon.com. This eleven-room boutique hotel is a gem. Each room has a sea view and is individually furnished with antique furniture and fittings, which contrast wonderfully with the plain white walls, stripped floors and exposed brickwork. The "special" rooms have a bed right next to a picture window giving stunning views over to Asia. **₺330**

Naya Retreat Maden, Yılmaz Türk Cad 96 ☎ 0216 382 4598, ⊛ nayaistanbul.com. A fine 105-year-old wooden mansion set in lush gardens on the island's east coast, the unusual *Naya* is a hybrid yoga/alternative therapy/meditation centre-cum-semi-rural retreat offering rooms furnished in upmarket ethnic-hippy style, in the house, or tents in the rambling garden. **€110**

Splendid Palas Nisan Cad 23 ☎ 0216 382 6950, ⊛ splendidhotel.net. A few minutes west of the ferry terminal, the *Splendid Palas*, dating from 1908, once played host to Edward VIII and Mrs Simpson. It has serious *fin-de-siècle* grandeur, with cupolas, balconies and a swimming pool out back. It has gained in comfort and lost in character from a 2013 upgrade. Closed Nov–March. Sea-view rooms **US$145**, garden view **US$170**

EATING AND DRINKING

Barba Yani Yalı Cad 6, Burgazada ☎0216 381 2404. Located some 50m to the left of the jetty as you land, this Greek-run restaurant serves reasonably priced fish dishes and *meze* (expect to pay around ₺60 per person, including an alcoholic drink). With its natty chequered tablecloths and harbour-front location, it's an atmospheric spot to while away the time waiting for the next ferry back to the city.

Heyamola Ada Lokantası Yalı Cad, Heybeliada (opposite Mavi Marmara ferry port) ☎0216 351 1111, ⓦheyamolaadalokantasi.com. In a strip of outdoor restaurants facing the water, this stands out with its colourful, chintzy decor. The food here is also a cut above the rest. The *meze* have a distinctly Aegean leaning with some unusual creations and priced reasonably at ₺8 and up – try the delicious *cevizli kabak* (walnuts with courgettes). The wine list also offers some excellent lesser-known brands with surprisingly low prices. Mon–Fri 10am–midnight, Sat–Sun 8am–midnight.

★**Kalpazankaya Mevkii** Burgazada ☎0216 381 1111. Superbly situated on a headland overlooking a tiny beach on the west shore of the island, this casual place dishes up over thirty different delicious *meze* (₺5–25), fifteen different hot appetizers (₺6–35) and seasonal fish sold by the kilo. It's the ideal place for a quiet lunch, with the sound of the waves on the rocks and a breeze brushing through the canopy of olive trees, or for a more lively, rakı-infused evening. It's well worth making the effort to walk or cycle the 1.5km out here from the ferry pier, or if you're feeling lazy catch a phaeton, as it's a world away from the usual touristy island restaurants. Daily noon–midnight.

Yücetepe Kır Gazinosu Aya Yorgi, Yüce Tepe, Büyükada. Simple but excellent restaurant right on Yüce Tepe, the hilltop crowned by the Monastery of St George, offering superb views across the island and the Sea of Marmara. The food is basic but freshly prepared and hearty, with deep-fried, cheese and savoury salami-filled *paçanga böreği* (₺10) one of the highlights. The home-made chips are delicious, as is the yoghurt-drenched aubergine starter (all ₺6). Big beers are a reasonable ₺10. Daily 9am–11pm.

Around the Sea of Marmara

SELIMIYE CAMII

Around the Sea of Marmara

Despite their proximity to Istanbul, the shores and hinterland of the Sea of Marmara are neglected by most foreign travellers. While this may not be altogether surprising – Turkey here is at its most Balkan and, at first glance, least exotic – there are good reasons to visit. Above all, the exquisite early Ottoman centres of Edirne, İznik and Bursa are the real highlights, the latter now recognized as a UNESCO World Heritage Site for its importance as the birthplace of the Ottoman dynasty. While most of the Thracian coast is disappointing, and the scrappy beaches of the Marmara islands hold little interest, two bright spots stand out – the beach-and-fortress town of Kıyıköy on the Black Sea, and the Saros Gulf resort of Erikli. Crossing the Sea of Marmara is easy and efficient: fast ferries sail from Istanbul to Yalova, Mudanya and Bandırma, while at the Dardanelles end Gelibolu is linked by car ferry to Lapseki opposite.

In terms of evocative inland scenery in the southern Marmara, there are two shallow lakes, **Uluabat Gölü** and **Manyas Gölü**, which support a dwindling fishing community and a bird sanctuary respectively. The **Uludağ** range above Bursa attracts skiers in winter and hikers in summer, while **Cumalıkızık** at the base of the mountain is a showcase village.

Before the wars and population exchanges of the early twentieth century, much of the local population was Greek (or Bulgarian) Orthodox, though all the larger towns held substantial Jewish and Armenian communities. After the Turkish Republic was established, massive immigration – both internal and from abroad – changed the mix. The resultant ethnic stew includes people of Çerkez (Circassian), Artvinli and Greek Muslim descent, as well as a large settled Romany population, but consists predominantly of **Pomak**, **Bosnian** and **Macedonian Muslims**, plus **Bulgarian Turks**. All these groups had, in fact, been trickling in for decades before 1923, as Austro-Hungarian or Orthodox nationalist victories in the Balkans made their previous homes inhospitable to Turks or Slavic Muslims.

Thrace

Thrace (Trakya in Turkish), the historic territory bounded by the rivers Danube and Nestos and the Aegean, Marmara and Black seas, is today divided roughly equally among Turkey, Greece and Bulgaria. In the flatter terrain of **East Thrace** (Doğu Trakya, the European part of Turkey), much of the coast has fallen prey to estates of concrete holiday homes – seasonal barbecue pads for Istanbul's workers – while inland is staunchly agricultural and in summer a sea of yellow sunflowers, grown for oil, spreads for many kilometres. Further west, in the wetter lands around **Üzünköprü**, rice is predominant, and to the north, the rolling **Istranca hills** have dense forests of oak and conifers as well as myriad fish farms raising rainbow trout.

Kırkpınar oil-wrestling festival p.153
Thrace border crossings p.155
İznik tiles p.165
Koza Hanı and Bursa silk p.171

Burulaş p.176
Bursa cuisine p.178
Skiing at Uludağ p.180

OIL-WRESTLING, KIRKPINAR FESTIVAL

Highlights

❶ Selimiye Camii The jewel of Edirne and one of the finest mosques in Turkey. **See p.152**

❷ Kırkpınar festival Wrestlers slicked down head-to-toe in olive oil battle it out in a 650-year-old tournament at Edirne. **See p.153**

❸ Termal Get steamy at Termal's near-scalding hot springs, where people have taken the waters since Roman times. **See p.161**

❹ İznik Sleepy lakeside town nestled in an olive-mantled valley, famous for its beautiful sixteenth-century tiles used to decorate some of the country's finest buildings. **See p.162**

❺ Bursa's Koza Hanı Centrepiece of Bursa's atmospheric covered bazaar and its "quarter of hans", part of Bursa's World Heritage Site. See p.171

❻ Muradiye Külliyesi and the Royal Tombs Shaded by centuries-old trees, this tranquil complex houses an impressive mosque and the finely decorated Ottoman tombs. **See p.173**

❼ Cumalıkızık A finely preserved Ottoman village on the lowers slopes of the Uludağ range, its cobbled streets full of classic wooden houses. **See p.178**

❽ Uludağ A new state-of-the-art cable car or *teleferik* takes visitors up to this mountaintop national park and one of Turkey's top ski resorts. See p.179

HIGHLIGHTS ARE MARKED ON THE MAP ON P.148

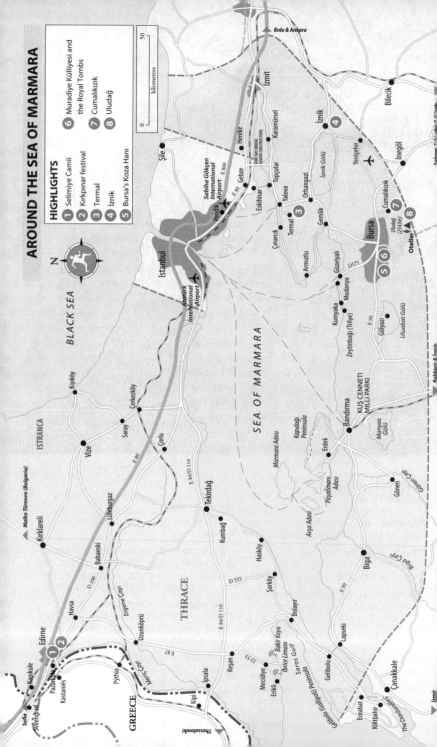

The E80 motorway from Istanbul to the main Thracian town of **Edirne** runs parallel to the route of the Roman and Byzantine road **Via Egnatia**, which later became the medieval route to the Ottoman holdings in Europe, and is now the D100 highway. Many towns along this road began life as Roman staging posts, a role continued under the Ottomans who endowed each with a civic monument or two. Few spots have much to detain you, though keep an eye out for fine **old bridges**, which like the road itself may be Ottoman reworkings of Roman or Byzantine originals. The best of these is the quadruple Büyükçekmece span, crossing the neck of an estuary west of Istanbul and built by the great architect Mimar Sinan in 1563.

2

Edirne

More than just the quintessential border town, **EDİRNE** – 235km northwest of Istanbul – is one of the best-preserved Ottoman cities, and makes an impressive, easily digestible introduction to Turkey. Unlike so many other towns in Thrace, it hasn't completely disappeared behind a wall of high-rise apartment blocks, and is instead a lively, attractive place of almost 150,000 people. It occupies a rise overlooking the mingling of the Tunca, Arda and Meriç rivers, very near the Greek and Bulgarian frontiers.

Downtown, teeming bazaars and elegant domestic architecture vie for attention with a clutch of striking **Ottoman monuments**. The best of these, crowning the town's central hillock and sufficient reason alone for a visit, is the **Selimiye Camii**, masterpiece of the imperial architect Mimar Sinan.

You can explore all Edirne's main sights on foot in a few hours, which means it's doable on a long day-trip from the capital (roughly 2hr 30min each way). Many of its Ottoman monuments lie north and west of town, deliberately rusticated by the early sultans to provide a nucleus for future suburbs. Because of depopulation since the 1700s, urban growth never caught up with some of the monuments, which have a rather forlorn atmosphere. Still, if the weather's fine, walking there is enjoyable, especially since you'll follow the willow-shaded banks of the **Tunca River** for some distance.

Brief history

The strategic point now occupied by Edirne has always held a settlement of some kind, destined to be repeatedly captured – and sometimes sacked for good measure – over the centuries. Thracian Uscudama became Hellenistic Oresteia, but the city really entered history as **Hadrianopolis**, designated the capital of Roman Thrace by Emperor Hadrian. Under the Byzantines it retained its significance, not least as a forward base en route to the Balkans – or, more ominously from the Byzantine point of view, first stop on the way to attempts on the imperial capital itself. Unsuccessful besiegers of Constantinople habitually vented their frustration on Hadrianopolis as they retreated, and a handful of emperors met their end here in pitched battles with Thracian "barbarians" of one sort or another.

In 1361, after Hadrianopolis surrendered to the besieging Murat I, the provisional **Ottoman capital** was effectively transferred here from Bursa. A century later, Mehmet the Conqueror trained his troops and tested his artillery here in preparation for the march on Constantinople; indeed, the Ottoman court was not completely moved to the Bosphorus until 1458. Because of its excellent opportunities for hunting and falconry, Edirne, as the Turks renamed it, remained a favourite haunt of sultans for three more centuries, earning the title *Der-I Saadet* or "Gate of Contentment" – during which it saw enough victory celebrations, circumcision ceremonies and marriages to rival Constantinople.

Decline set in after a 1751 **earthquake**, while Tsarist troops occupied and pillaged the city during the **Russo-Turkish wars** of 1829 and 1878–79. Worse followed, when the Bulgarians (with Serbian aid) besieged the city for 143 days from November 3, 1912 before taking it, thus ending the First Balkan War. The Greeks, as one of the victorious World War I Allies, annexed "**Adrianópoli**" along with the rest of Turkish Thrace from

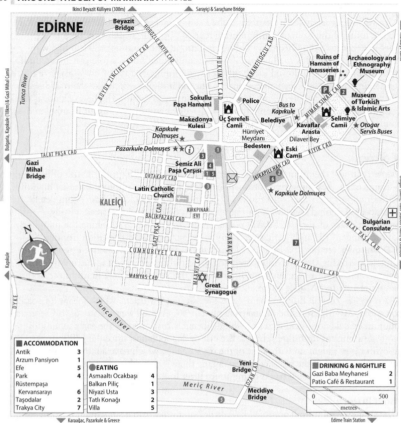

EDİRNE

1920 to 1922, and Turkish sovereignty over the city was only confirmed by the 1923 **Treaty of Lausanne**. Bulgarian, Latin Catholic and Greek Orthodox churches remain, along with elegant houses and a ruined synagogue in the former Jewish quarter, as evidence of the pre-1912, multicultural city, of which half the population was Turkish, and the remainder Greek, Bulgarian, Armenian and Jewish.

Eski Cami

Cnr Mimar Sinan and Talat Paşa cads

The logical starting point for explorations of Edirne is the boxy **Eski Cami**, the oldest mosque in town, with recycled Roman columns out front and some celebrated giant calligraphic inscriptions inside. Topped by nine vaults arranged three-square, and supported by four square pillars, it's a more elaborate version of Bursa's Ulu Cami (see p.170). Emir Süleyman, son of the luckless Beyazıt I, began it in 1403, but it was his younger brother Mehmet I – the only one of three brothers left alive after a bloody succession struggle – who dedicated it eleven years later.

Bedesten

Muaffiklarhane Sok

The fifteenth-century **Bedesten** was Edirne's first covered bazaar, a portion of whose rents helped maintain the nearby Eski Cami mosque. Constructed by Mehmet I, the barn-like structure with its fourteen vaulted chambers was restored in the 1980s, but shops with tatty wares let the interior down.

Semiz Ali Paşa Çarşısı
At the top of Saraçlar Cad

The six-gated, multi-domed covered bazaar of **Semiz Ali Paşa Çarşısı** was constructed by Mimar Sinan in 1568 at the behest of Semiz Ali, one of the most able and congenial grand viziers. Located at the top of Edirne's liveliest, mostly pedestrianized modern commercial street, renovations after a 1992 fire were administered with care, and the building far outshines the mostly dull merchandise sold inside.

Makedonya Kulesi
Talat Paşa Cad

Opposite the north entrance of Semiz Ali Paşa Çarşısı is the **Makedonya Kulesi** (Macedonia Tower), the sole remnant of the town's extensive Roman/Byzantine city walls; the Ottomans, in a burst of confidence after expanding the limits of empire far beyond Edirne, demolished the rest.

Kaleiçi

To the west and south of the bazaar is the district of **Kaleiçi** (which more or less means "inside the walls"), a rectangular grid of Byzantine-era streets lined with much-interrupted terraces of ornate eighteenth- and nineteenth-century wooden townhouses. The best roads for strolling are Maarif Caddesi, the parallel Gazi Paşa Caddesi, and their linking perpendicular Cumhuriyet Caddesi, once the heart of the **Jewish quarter**, where house dedication dates (in the Hebraic calendar) go up to 1912. When built in 1906 to replace thirteen others destroyed by fire, the recently restored (but closed to the public) **synagogue** at the bottom of Maarif Caddesi was the largest in the Balkans – an indication of how huge the community then was. Within a few decades, however, the new frontiers, populist pogroms (unusual in Turkey) and official harassment had compelled local Jews to flee to Europe, Istanbul or Israel.

Üç Şerefeli Cami
Hukumet Cad, on the north side of Hürriyet Meydanı

The **Üç Şerefeli Cami** replaced the Eski Cami as Edirne's Friday mosque in 1447. Ten years in the making, its conceptual daring represented the pinnacle of Ottoman religious architecture until overshadowed by the Selimiye Camii a short time later. Its name – "three-balconied" – derives from the three galleries for the muezzin on the tallest of its four whimsically idiosyncratic **minarets**; the second-highest has two balconies, the others one, and each of the multiple balconies is reached by a separate stairway within the minaret. The **courtyard**, too, was an innovation, centred on a *sadırvan* and ringed by porphyry and marble columns pilfered from Roman buildings. The mosque's experimental nature is further confirmed by its **interior**, much wider than it is deep and covered by a main dome 24m in diameter, with four flanking domes – the largest that the Turks had built at the time.

Sokullu Paşa Hamamı
Hukumet Cad, opposite the Üç Şerefeli Cami • Daily 8.30am–11pm (men); 9am–5pm (women) • Bath with massage ₺30 • ☎ 0284 225 2193

The sixteenth-century **Sokullu Paşa Hamamı** was built by master architect Mimar Sinan for Grand Vizier Sokullu Mehmet. An entrance of ornate columns and a triple-vaulted portico mirrors the Üç Şerefeli Cami over the road. One of Turkey's largest hamams, this is a traveller-friendly option with separate wings for men and women.

Selimiye Camii

Between Kiyik and Mimar Sinan cads • No photos in the interior

Designed by the eighty-year-old **Mimar Sinan** (see box, p.92) in 1569, at the command of Selim II, the masterly **Selimiye Camii** is one of Turkey's finest mosques. The work of a confident craftsman at the height of his powers, who is said to have thought of it as his greatest achievement, it's visible from some distance away on the Thracian plain. The mosque, together with its *külliye*, was inscribed as a UNESCO World Heritage Site in 2011.

The mosque **courtyard**, approached from the *arasta* up a flight of stone steps, is surrounded by a colonnaded portico with arches in alternating red and white stone, ancient columns, and domes of varying size above the arcades. Its delicately fashioned *şadırvan* (ablutions fountain) is the finest in the city. In a nod to his predecessors, Sinan gave each of the four identical, slender **minarets** three balconies.

It's the celestial **interior**, however, and specifically the dome, which impresses most (no photos allowed). Planned expressly to surpass that of Aya Sofya in Istanbul, it succeeds, at 31.5m in diameter, by a bare few centimetres, thus achieving Sinan's lifetime ambition. Held aloft by eight mammoth but surprisingly unobtrusive twelve-sided pillars, the cupola floats 44m above the floor, covered in calligraphy proclaiming the glory of Allah. The most ornate stone carving is reserved for the *mihrab* and *mimber*, backed by fine İznik faïence illuminated by sunlight streaming in through the many windows. Immediately below the dome, the muezzin's platform, supported on twelve columns, is an ideal place from which to contemplate the proportions of the mosque.

Kavaflar Arasta

The **Kavaflar Arasta** (Cobbler's Arcade), on the southwestern side of the square in front of Selimiye Camii, was built by Sinan's pupil Davut, originally as a home for a guild of shoemakers. Today it is used as a covered market, and is full of household goods, souvenirs and cheap clothing. Every day, beneath the market's prayer dome, the shopkeepers promise to conduct their business honestly.

Museum of Turkish and Islamic Arts

Eastern cnr of Selimiye Camii mosque precinct • Daily 9am–7pm, Nov–March till 5.30pm • ₺5 • ☎ 0284 225 3029, ⓦ muze.gov.tr

A former *medrese* of the Selimiye Camii, the **Museum of Turkish and Islamic Arts** (Türk İslam Eserleri Müzesi) consists of fourteen rooms around a central courtyard, which were originally used to house and educate Koranic pupils. Each displays assorted wooden, ceramic and martial knick-knacks, and while the collection is a little ad hoc, it is fairly diverting. One room is dedicated to Kırkpınar oil-wrestling (see opposite), one to artefacts decorated by Dervish calligraphers, and another, oddly, to hand-knitted woollen socks collected from different regions of the country.

Archeology and Ethnography Museum

Kadır Paşa Mektep Sok • Daily 9am–7pm, Nov–March till 5.30pm • ₺5 • ☎ 0284 225 0232, ⓦ muze.gov.tr

Northeast of Selimiye Camii, the good archeological section at the **Archeology and Ethnography Museum** (Arkeoloji ve Etnoğrafya Müzesi) holds bronze, glass and ceramic relics from ancient Hadrianopolis and Aenos at the mouth of the Meriç, while a Turkish-only ethnographic section features traditional carpet-weaving and colourful village bridal wear. In the grounds are some reproductions of the round wattle-and-daub huts popular with early Thracians, as well as some Ottoman tombstones belonging to the Selimiye Camii.

Muradiye Camii

Mimar Sinan Cad • Admission at prayer times only • 10min walk east from Selimiye Camii

According to legend, Celaleddin Rumi, founder of the Mevlevî dervish order, appeared in a dream to the pious Murat II at some date between 1426 and 1435, urging him to build a sanctuary for the Mevlevîs in Edirne. The result is the pleasing, T-shaped

Muradiye Camii, a *zaviye* or dervish convent crouched on a hill looking north over vegetable patches and the Tunca River; the grassy entry court lends a final bucolic touch. The interior is distinguished by the best İznik tiles outside Bursa, which cover the *mihrab* and walls up to eye level. The calligraphic frescoes that once adorned the higher surfaces have probably been missing since the catastrophic earthquake of 1751. The dervishes initially congregated in the *eyvans*, the ends of the T's cross-stroke; Murat later housed them in a separate *tekke* (lodge)in the garden.

Along the Tunca River

Only one bridge crosses the **Meriç**, the bigger of Edirne's two rivers: the graceful **Mecidiye**, completed in 1847 and now effectively Edirne's municipal logo. The narrower **Tunca River**, on the other hand, is spanned by a half-dozen fifteenth- or sixteenth-century bridges, and the best way to see them is to stroll along the east (city-side) bank.

The pair furthest upstream, the fifteenth-century **Saray (Kanûni)** and **Fatih bridges**, join the left and right banks of the Tunca to the river-island of **Sarayiçi**. The island takes its name from the *saray* or royal palace that formerly stood here, which was blown up by the Ottomans in 1877 to prevent munitions from falling into Russian hands. The Sarayiçi Er Meydani Stadium that hosts the Kırkpınar **oil-wrestling matches** (see box below) stands beside the ruins.

Following the riverbank west and downstream, past the **Saraçhane bridge**, brings you, after twenty minutes, to the double-staged **Beyazıt bridge**, across another small island in the Tunca, and its extension **Yalnızgöz** ("one-eyed" after its single hump) **bridge**.

KIRKPINAR OIL-WRESTLING FESTIVAL

Oil-wrestling (*yağlı güreş*) is popular throughout Turkey, but reaches the pinnacle of acclaim at the doyenne of tournaments, the three-day annual **Kırkpınar festival**, staged each summer (June or July) on Sarayiçi islet on the northeastern outskirts of Edirne (Ⓦ kirkpinar.com or Ⓦ turkishwrestling.com).

The origins of Kırkpınar, meaning "forty sources", date to the fourteenth century, when it is thought a group of forty **Ottoman raiders**, bored and in need of diversion, began wrestling in their camp. Two of the men fought through the night and eventually killed one another; they were buried by their comrades beneath a fig tree. Since then, wrestling matches have been held annually, except during war or Edirne's occupation, and it is said to be the longest-standing annual sporting event in the world.

Despite the less than atmospheric environment of the modern **Sarayiçi Er Meydani Stadium** where it now takes place, tradition still permeates the event (though thankfully bouts are no longer a fight to the death). The festival is launched by a procession carrying the golden prize belt through the streets of Edirne, accompanied by forty bands of musicians playing the *davul* (deep-toned drum) and *zurna* (single-reed Islamic oboe). This is followed by prayers at the Selimiye Camii before the contestants – up to two thousand – head to the stadium to start their warm-ups (*peşrev*). Wrestlers dress only in heavy leather knickers called *kisbet* and are slicked down head-to-toe in diluted olive oil. They are classed by height and ability rather than weight, from toddlers up to the *pehlivan* (full-size) category. The competitors are solemnly introduced by the *cazgır* (master of ceremonies), usually a former champion, and a match is started by the opponents shouting *Hayda bre pehlivan!* ("Bring it on, wrestler!"), before they grip one another.

Several **bouts** take place simultaneously. Each lasts anything from a few minutes to nearly an hour, until one competitor collapses or has his back pinned to the grass. Referees keep a lookout for the limited number of illegal moves or holds, and victors advance more or less immediately to the next round until only the *başpehlivan* (champion) remains. Despite the small prize purse donated by the *Kırkpınar ağaları* – the local worthies who put on the whole show – a champion benefits from appearance and endorsement fees, plus the furious on- and off-site betting. Gladiators tend mainly to be villagers from across Turkey who have won regional titles, starry-eyed with the prospect of fame and escape from the rut of rural poverty.

2

İkinci Beyazıt Külliyesi

Sağlık Müzesi, Yenimaret, across the Beyazıt and Yalnızgöz bridges • Museum daily 8.30am–5.30pm • ₺10

The vast **İkinci Beyazıt Külliyesi** was built in 1488 by Hayrettin, court architect to Beyazıt II. Within a single irregular boundary wall, and assembled beneath a hundred domes, the complex is comprised of a mosque, food storehouse, bakery, *imaret*, dervish hostel, medical school and mental asylum.

Apart from its handsome courtyard and the sultan's loge inside, the **mosque** itself is disappointing, and today most of the other buildings are under the custodianship of the Trakya Üniversitesi and are closed to the public; more interesting is the old **medical school** in the furthest northwest corner of the complex. This was conveniently linked to the **timarhane**, or madhouse, built around an open garden, which in turn leads to the magnificent **darüşşifa** (therapy centre). This hexagonal, domed structure consists of a circular central space onto which six *eyvans* open; the inmates were brought here regularly, so that musicians could play to soothe the more intractable cases. Strange five-sided rooms with fireplaces open off three of the *eyvans*. Also administered by the Trakya Üniversitesi, the *darüşşifa* now houses the **Sultan Bayezid II Health Museum** (Sultan II Bayezid Külliyesi Sağlık Müzesi), in which interesting displays chronicle Ottoman medical history.

Gazi Mihal bridge

Londra Asfaltı

The western entrance to Edirne crosses the Tunca River via the **Gazi Mihal bridge**, an Ottoman refurbishment of a thirteenth-century Byzantine span. Gazi Mihal was a Christian nobleman who became an enthusiastic convert to Islam – hence the epithet *Gazi*, "Warrior for the Faith".

ARRIVAL AND DEPARTURE | EDİRNE

By bus Edirne's *otogar* is just over 8km southeast of the centre on the access road to the E80; *servis* buses go to the cluster of the city offices of the bus companies just off Kıyık Cad southwest of Selimiye Camii, or take city bus #5 which runs to the centre around Hürriyet Meydanı.

Destinations Çanakkale (2 daily; 4hr); Istanbul (every 30min; 2hr 30min); Keşan (every 20min; 1hr 45min); Kapıkule (Bulgarian border; every 30min; 25min).

By train Edirne's train station is 4km southeast of the centre. However, at the time of writing all train services in Eastern Thrace – including the Bosphorus Express (Bosfor Ekspresi; see opposite) – were suspended while the Turkish railways were being upgraded.

INFORMATION

Tourist office On Talat Paşa Cad, just west of Hürriyet Meydanı (April–Sept daily, Oct–March Mon–Fri 8.30am–noon & 1–5.30pm; ☏ 0284 213 9208); there's also a booth at the Bulgarian (Kapıkule) frontier gate (daily 8.30am–5pm; ☏ 0284 238 2019). Both supply an excellent map of Edirne.

Hamam The huge Sokullu Paşa Hamamı on Hukumet Cad is a good option (see p.151).

ACCOMMODATION

Book accommodation at least a month in advance for the Kırkpınar Festival (June or July) when rates are at a premium. The cheaper central options line Maarif Caddesi, though a few serious dives here are worth avoiding, and all are beset by traffic noise – get a rear-facing room if possible.

★**Antik** Maarif Cad 6 ☏0284 225 1555, ⓦedirneantikhotel.com. Popular, conveniently located and well-priced hotel in a restored Neoclassical building, with three creaky floors' worth of large, plush en-suite rooms, and slightly kitsch antique decor. There's a pleasant courtyard garden restaurant and friendly staff. ₺160

Arzum Pansiyon Hamam Sok 9 ☏0284 213 1334, ⓦarzumpansiyon.net. Cheap and cheerful *pansiyon* on a side street opposite Selimiye Camii, with small and simply furnished but modern and spotlessly clean en-suite rooms with a/c; some are triples (₺110) and quads (₺130). Mosque-facing rooms come with balconies while those at the rear are, of course, quieter. Some street parking is available but no breakfast. ₺80

Efe Maarif Cad 13 ☏0284 213 6080, ⓦefehotel.com. Salubrious, if somewhat overpriced hotel where the cheerful, well-appointed rooms vary – those at the back are almost suite-sized, with double beds and fridges. Has

THRACE BORDER CROSSINGS

The **Bulgarian and Greek frontier posts** nearest Edirne are open 24 hours. For EU nationals and citizens of the US, Canada, Australia and New Zealand, no advance visas are necessary for entry to Greece or Bulgaria. South Africans, however, need to apply for a **Schengen Zone visa** in their home country before travelling from Turkey to Greece and other European countries in the Schengen Zone, which Bulgaria is due to join soon; for up-to-date requirements check ⓦschengenvisainfo.com.

TURKEY–BULGARIA

The vast Bulgarian border complex straddles the busy E80 expressway at **Kapıkule**, 18km northwest of Edirne (and 320km south of Sofia, Bulgaria's capital). Dolmuşes from Edirne to Kapıkule (every 30min; ₺7) leave from two stops on the north side of **Talat Paşa Cad**, one behind the *Hotel Rüstempaşa Kervansaray* (see below) and the other near the tourist office; a taxi will set you back ₺30. At the border itself are fast-food restaurants, duty-free shops and ATMs; there are no facilities in the nearest Bulgarian village, **Kapitan Andreevo**, but reasonable hotels in **Svilengrad**, the first proper town 9km beyond.

At the time of writing, no **trains** crossed the border here, as the line was being upgraded. For now, the daily international Bosphorus Express (Bosfor Ekspresi) – which ran from Sirkeci Station in Istanbul to Sofia and Bucharest – is replaced by a bus between Istanbul and Kapikule, departing Sirkeci daily at 10pm and arriving in Kapikule at around 2.30am. In theory, the connecting Bulgarian train then goes from Kapikule to Bucharest (11hr; change at Dimitrovgrad) and Sofia (6hr; change at Plovdiv), but in reality many of these services are also affected by long-term engineering works and buses often replace certain sections. For up-to-date information, check the TCDD website (ⓦtcdd.gov.tr) and that of Bulgarian State Railways (ⓦbdz.bg). **Buses** also run from Kapitan Andreevo to Sofia (daily at least every 4hr; 5hr 30min–7hr) via Svilengrad, with changes in Haskovo or Plovdiv.

TURKEY–GREECE

There are two Turkey-Greece borders in Thrace. The **Pazarkule** frontier post, separated from the Greek one at **Kastaniés** by a kilometre-wide no-man's-land, is 8km west of Edirne and 2km beyond the last Turkish village of **Karaağaç**. Dolmuşes to Karaağaç (every 30min; 15min; ₺3) depart from the south side of Talat Paşa Cad, near the tourist office, and most go the final 2km from Karaağaç to Pazarkule. A taxi to the border costs ₺20. Once through the Turkish post, you may have to take a Greek taxi to the Kastaniés post, as you're not usually allowed to walk across; this applies coming from Greece too – budget €4/₺8 per car for the 1km gap. From Kastaniés, on the Greek side, three TRAINOSE trains daily (4.11am, 12.08am & 7.05pm; ⓦtrainose.gr), and about as many buses, make the 2hr 30min run down to Alexandhroúpoli, the first major Greek city.

The far busier frontier post of **İpsala-Kipi** is on the E90/110 highway, 120km south of Edirne and 8km from the town of **İpsala**, 28km west of Keşan. Buses travelling from Istanbul to Greece use this border, where there's a 500m-wide military zone between the Turkish post and the Greek town of Kípi on the other side. Crossing on foot is forbidden; during daylight hours at least, it's fairly easy to hitch a ride over in either direction (ask at the duty-free shop or petrol station), though drivers will routinely refuse to take you further. From Kípi, several buses a day run further into Greece; at the Turkish post, without your own vehicle you'll need to get a taxi for the 8km run to İpsala town, from where there are dolmuşes to Keşan.

an English-style, street-side winter pub, plus a pleasant garden restaurant at the rear. ₺175
Park Aziziye Cad 6, corner of Maarif Cad ☎0284 213 4610, ⓦedirneparkotel.com. In a well-worn 1980s-built block, this business-class hotel is not quite as spruce as the *Efe*, though the ground-floor restaurant is more contemporary. The sixty bland but spacious a/c rooms with TV are good value if you can bargain them down a category, and there's a parking garage. ₺170

Rüstempaşa Kervansarayı İki Kapılı Han Cad 57 ☎0284 212 6119, ⓦedirnekervansarayhotel.com. A sympathetic restoration retained much of the exotic atmosphere of this sixteenth-century *kervansaray*, including a romantic, peaceful courtyard and thick walls that buffer most of the noise from the busy street outside. The cell-like rooms have original vaulted ceilings and the smallest of exterior windows, though they can disappoint with their cheap, spartan decor. ₺140

2

Taşodalar Hamam Sok 3, behind Selimiye Camii ☎0284 212 3529, ⓦtasodalar.com. One of Edirne's better hotels, this restored fifteenth-century building has nine rooms with dark-wood floors and trim throughout, though the decor – a mix of genuine antiques and kitsch – is in variable taste, to say the least. The upstairs rooms look towards the mosque – the best, no. 109, has a bay window – and there's a peaceful tea garden/restaurant (no

alcohol) and a car park. ₺275

Trakya City Sabuni Mahallesi Mehmetaga Sok 21 ☎0284 214 6575, ⓦtrakyacityhotel.com. Although a little tricky to find in the narrow lanes below Talat Paşa Cad, this smart, new place is quiet thanks to its soundproofing, and the 51 rooms are perfectly functional, if a little characterless. A 10–15min walk to Selimiye Camii and there's private parking. ₺190

EATING

Most of Edirne's restaurants are undistinguished, and licensed places are scarce in the centre – we've indicated all known options. The local speciality is *ciğer tava*, deep-fried slivers of calf's liver with tomato, onion and hot chilli garnish.

RESTAURANTS

Asmaaltı Ocakbaşı Saraçlar Cad 149 ☎0284 212 8712. Occupying two floors of an attractively restored old industrial building, this is the only meat-grill downtown serving alcohol, thus a bit bumped up in price. Allow ₺25 minimum a head for a heaped plate of *kebap*, *köftë*, chicken and chopped tomato and aubergine all cooked on skewers over open coals. Daily noon–3pm & 7–11pm.

Balkan Piliç Saraçlar Cad 14 ☎0284 225 2155. Popular *lokanta* with tables both inside and on the pavement of the busy pedestrian-only street. A helpful picture menu offers plenty of wholesome *lokanta* fare – not just chicken (*piliç*) but enticing vegetable dishes and good roast lamb – served by efficient waiters. Mains ₺6–14. Daily 9am–10pm.

★ **Niyazi Usta** Alipaşa Ortakapı Cad 9 ☎0284 213 3372, ⓦcigerciniyaziusta.com.tr. The best regarded of several *ciğercis* (liver purveyors) in this area, worth a slight price premium for their expert rendition of *ciğer tava* (₺14 or half-portion ₺8). The salubrious surroundings stretch over two floors, and are festooned with photos of founder

Niyazi and various celebrities. There's also an annexe a few doors up at no. 5. Daily 9.30am–9pm.

Tatlı Konağı İkikapılı Han Cad 24 ☎0282 651 0002. A tiny patisserie (the name means "sweet house"), on the same block as the *Rüstempaşa Kervansarayı* hotel (see p.155), specializing in three unusual desserts (₺5–9), which are particularly popular in the Thrace region: *peynir helvası*, an ultra-sugary halva made from cheese; *hayrabolu*, a vermicelli-like pastry stuffed with cheese and soaked in sugar-syrup; and *trileçe*, a sponge cake cooked in milk with a caramel topping. Order at the counter and sit at indoor or outdoor tables. Daily 8am–11pm.

Villa 1.5km south of town along Karaağaç Yolu, on the Meriç River ☎0284 223 4077, ⓦedirnevilla.com. Licensed restaurant specializing in meat and *meze*, plus sometimes *yayın* (catfish). While open all year, their *raison d'être* is a summer outdoor terrace overlooking the river and its elegant, honey-coloured bridge. You pay premium prices, of course, for the view. Mains ₺18–28. Daily 11am–11pm.

DRINKING AND NIGHTLIFE

Despite the large student contingent, nightlife is limited to a few venues on or around Saraçlar Caddesi, especially towards the old Jewish bazaar at the south end, and the area along Lozan Caddesi between the two river bridges, known as *Bülbül Adası* – "Nightingale Island".

BARS & CAFÉS

Gazi Baba Meyhanesi Zindan Altı Sok 139, off the southern end of Saraçlar Cad ☎0284 214 5050, ⓦgazibabameyhanesi.com. A traditional *meyhane* that has been going since 1967, in an atmospheric stone- and-wood building. The ground floor and pavement are more for drinking (including a choice of rakı; ₺11), while the upstairs resaurant serves the usual *mezes* and grills for around ₺7–12. Daily 10am–2am.

★ **Patio Café & Restaurant** Aziziye Cad 5, just off Maarif Cad near the Efe Hotel ☎0284 225 6767. Edirne's most contemporary café/bar is located in a restored wooden house, with sleek interiors and tables on a semi-covered courtyard patio. Serves proper European coffees, imported alcoholic drinks including a good choice of wine, and non-Turkish food like pasta, burgers, steaks and sandwiches, much of which is made from organic produce. Mains ₺12–20. Daily 10am–1am.

South of Edirne

Unless you're heading to or from Greece via İpsala (see box, p.155), there's little reason to stop at any point along the E87 highway as it heads south from **Havsa**, the junction 27km southeast of Edirne, until you reach the pleasant resorts of **İbrice Limanı** and **Erikli**.

Uzunköprü

Formerly called Plotinopolis, **UZUNKÖPRÜ**, off the E87 en route to Keşan, gets its current name, meaning "Long Bridge", from the 1400m-long, 174-arched **Ottoman bridge** that spans the Ergene River's water meadows at the north end of town. A remarkable feat of engineering, completed in 1443, the bridge remains entirely intact despite its location in an earthquake zone. For many years it was a notorious traffic bottleneck, clogged with heavy lorries and buses, but most drivers now use a new, four-lane bridge, which ends just south of the train station 2km east.

Keşan

KEŞAN, 53km south of Uzunköprü, is a nondescript place that most travellers don't even enter, as its *otogar* – with frequent connections to Istanbul, Edirne and Çanakkale, as well as İpsala for the Greece-bound – is out of town (see below). It's also a jumping-off point for Turkey's northernmost Aegean resorts, on the Gulf of Saros.

İbrice Limanı

Although the port of **İBRİCE LİMANI**, on the **Saros Körfezi** (Saros Gulf) 40km south of Keşan, amounts to little more than one fish **restaurant** and a few **scuba-dive** boats, it's home to a number of seasonal diving schools (see below). As well as being a popular spot for beginners, the gulf provides experienced divers with access to a dozen nearby sites. The best beach for non-divers is at **Bakirkoyu**, 3km east of the harbour.

Erikli

ERİKLİ, the only developed resort on the Saros Gulf coast, stands roughly 7km west of İbrice Limanı. With transport, it makes an excellent first or last stop en route from or to Greece.

While Erikli is a bit tatty at the edges, which border a small inland lake frequented by flamingoes, its glorious broad **beach**, over 1.5km long, compensates. You may see lots of jellyfish in the waters here, though the majority are harmless.

ARRIVAL AND DEPARTURE   SOUTH OF EDİRNE

KEŞAN

Keşan's *otogar* is on the E87 highway as it runs through the western side of town.

Destinations Çanakkale via Gelibolu and Eceabat (at least 10 daily; 2hr); İpsala (hourly; 25min); Istanbul (at least 14 daily; 3hr 45min); Tekirdağ (14 daily; 1hr 30min).

İBRİCE LİMANI AND ERİKLİ

By dolmuş There are regular services south from Keşan to Mecidiye (30min), from where you may have to swap vehicles to go the extra 5km to İbrice Limanı or the 10km to Erikli. More frequent direct dolmuşes link Keşan with İbrice Limanı and Erikli in summer, especially over weekends.

ACTIVITIES

DIVING

The diving season in the Saros Gulf usually runs from the end of April to early Nov.

İbrice Dalış Merkezi İbrice Limanı ☎0536 466 6690, ⓦibricedalismerkezi.com. A well-established PADI- and CMAS-certified set-up offering accompanied night dives as well as multi-day beginner courses.

Mavi Tutku Dalış Merkezi İbrice Limanı ☎0555 995 2322, ⓦmavitutkudalismerkezi.wordpress.com. PADI-certified dive school with an impressive twin-level boat, offering dives for all levels as well as first-aid certifications.

ACCOMMODATION AND EATING

İBRİCE LİMANI

★**Sığınak** Off the road to Mecidiye, 3km north of the port ☎0284 783 4310, ⓦsiginak.com. The closest accommodation to the coast, in a pleasant though isolated rural setting. Nine rustic wood-and-stone bungalows and rooms are tucked away in the Thracian maquis; there's a welcoming lounge with fireplace and a fish restaurant in

the main building which is open to passing trade for lunch, but you need to prebook for dinner. ₺260

ERİKLİ

Erikli Far western end of the beach, 400m from village centre ☎0284 737 3386, ⓦeriklihotel.com. Low-rise beachfront hotel with modern, airy en-suite a/c rooms;

most face the sea, but not all have balconies (for which you'll pay a higher rate). The restaurant serves reasonable buffet meals, while the large outdoor beach-bar-cum-lounge area, which serves snacks and is open to all (daily 8am–11pm), is very popular in summer. ₺290

İşçimen Aqua Resort Middle of the beach ☏ 0284 737 3148, ⓦ iscimenhotel.com.tr. Family-owned since the 1970s, this is the less salubrious of Erikli's two beachfront hotels. The 42 ageing a/c rooms are relatively small but nonetheless comfortable, and most have sea views. The fish restaurant (open to non-guests daily 11am–10pm) is highly regarded. The beach club (and its associated noise) here can last well into the night during summer. ₺175

Saros Balık Middle of the beach, next to İşçimen Aqua Resort ☏ 0544 961 4596. The menu at Erikli's best restaurant, as you'd expect, is biased towards seafood, some of which is bought to order from fishermen selling their catch in the adjacent car park. They also serve a good *kahvaltı*. A/c tables inside, plus outdoor tables on the beach. Licenced. Mains ₺12–25. Daily 9am–11pm.

Kıyıköy

The sleepy, walled citadel of **KIYIKÖY**, 165km northwest of Istanbul, occupies an idyllic location overlooking the Black Sea where headlands unfold into the distance, vaguely recalling the coastline of Cornwall in the UK. Flanked on both sides by the slow-moving Papuç and Kazandere rivers, and backing onto lushly forested spurs of the Istranca hills, the village was fortified by the Byzantines around the sixth century, though most of what remains dates from the thirteenth and fourteenth centuries. While Kıyıköy's pre-1923 Greek population was replaced by Balkan Muslims, many inhabitants still use the former name, "Midye" – a corruption of Medea – after the locally harvested mussels. Today, the village meanders quietly from one day to the next, and offers visitors a photogenic palette of gently crumbling half-timbered houses and quiet backstreets festooned with fishing nets – the small harbour here is the only deep-water anchorage on this part of the coast. The main approach into the walled citadel, **Kıyıkent Kalesi**, is via the narrow south gate, and within is a central, leafy square, from where all accommodation and restaurants are within walking distance.

Aya Nikola Manastırı

800m southwest of the village, signposted from the road to Kazandere River • Daily 24hr; unenclosed • Free

Kıyıköy's most conspicuous ancient monument is the Byzantine **Aya Nikola Manastırı** (St Nicholas Monastery). This extraordinary complex is carved into the rock of the hillside, deep inside which a rock-cut church – complete with colonnaded aisles, barrel vaulting and a semicircular apse of tiered seats where the clergy used to sit – remained in use until 1923. You can also see the remains of a sacred pool, where the ailing and diseased bathed in the hope of a cure; hundreds of tiny crosses etched into the walls near the entrance are a reminder of their visits.

Beaches

Alongside the river mouth of the Kazandere River, 1.5km west of Kıyıköy's south gate, **Belediye Plaji** is a long stretch of sandy **beach** that's backed by low cliffs oozing fossils. Sadly, during summer, the landscape here can be blighted by campers' rubbish and semi-permanent tents. With your own transport, however, several more almost-empty **beaches** – indeed, some of the most beautiful and undeveloped in Turkey – lie within reach roughly 5km north of Kıyıköy, near where the Pabuçdere meets the sea. There are scores of jellyfish in these waters, most of which don't sting.

ARRIVAL AND DEPARTURE	KIYIKÖY

By bus and dolmuş Buses from Istanbul run to sleepy Saray, 29km southwest (18 daily; 3hr), which is served by dolmuşes to Kıyıköy (every 2–3hr; 1hr).

ACCOMMODATION

Genç Cumhuriyet Cad, 50m west of square ☏ 0288 388 6568. Central budget hotel with two floors of ageing, sterile en-suite rooms that are nonetheless large and clean. There are restaurants and a supermarket across the road, and a quiet bar on the ground floor. ₺85

★ **Kıyıköy Resort** Orkide Sok 12, west of the citadel, signposted from the road to Vize ☎0288 388 6364, ⓦkiyikoyresort.com. An honourable attempt to inject a touch of class into Kıyıköy, and with distant views of the beach and river. The 24 contemporary, minimalist-styled a/c rooms have balconies or patios overlooking a large garden and wood-decked pool, and there's an excellent

restaurant (see below). Istanbul/Saray pick-ups and boat trips are available. Half board only. ₺250

Marina On the village's western fringe on the road to Vize ☎0544 368 0605, ⓦkiyikoyotel.com. A modern place just out of town, where the eight balconied rooms come with a fridge and TV. While the decor is a little haphazard, it's good value, and from the rooftop terrace and breakfast room there are fabulous views overlooking open fields to the sea. ₺110

EATING AND DRINKING

Kıyıköy Resort Restaurant Orkide Sok 12, west of the citadel, off the road to Vize ☎0288 388 6364, ⓦkiyikoyresort.com. Often still referred to as the *Endorfina*, the hotel's former name, the house speciality here is freshly grilled Black Sea turbot, but the menu also includes *meze*, chicken and grilled meat. Eat inside or on a shaded terrace looking out to the distant beach. Mains ₺13–25. Daily noon–3pm & 7–10pm.

Köşk 50m south of square ☎0536 475 8169. Cosy, all-wood restaurant run by a father-and-son team, with tables and a fireplace inside plus a few outdoor tables on a shaded

veranda with harbour views. Like the *Kıyıköy Resort* (see above), it's a good place to try turbot, but also serves other tasty seasonal seafood, as well as *mezes* and grilled meat dishes. Mains ₺6–17. Daily 9am–10pm.

Marina Cumhuriyet Cad ☎0542 586 0472. Not to be confused with the hotel of same name, this modern stone-and-wood restaurant is at the far end of the main road within the citadel, with a menu of mainly seafood dishes but also *koftë* and grilled chicken. As it's licensed, the wooden benches in the garden below are good for a relaxed drink overlooking the harbour. Mains ₺7–16. Daily 7am–1am.

The North Marmara coast

West of Istanbul, the city's straggling suburbs slowly dissipate into small, unattractive settlements squeezed between the main E80 highway and the north Marmara coast. Roughly halfway between Istanbul and the Gelibolu Peninsula, **Tekirdağ** is the largest port before the Dardanelles – although at the time of writing no passenger ferries were running and seemed unlikely to do so any time soon.

Tekirdağ

Enjoying a hilly setting at the head of a gently curving bay, **TEKİRDAĞ** – the ancient and medieval town of Rodosto – is a fairly pleasant settlement 145km west of Istanbul, with an attractive waterfront, and a few remaining, dilapidated wooden houses in the backstreets. One of these is the old, well-kept Ottoman-style Tekirdağ Vali Konağı (provincial governor's building, 1927), which is now the modest **Archeology and Ethnology Museum** (Tekirdağ Arkeoloji ve Etnografya Müzesi; Rákóczi Cad 1; Tues–Sun 9am–5pm; free; ☎0282 261 2082). Of note here is the fact that of all the statues of Atatürk in Turkey, the town centre of Tekirdağ holds the only one that was made exactly life-size.

Gelibolu

Strategically sited at the northwest entrance of the Dardanelles, **GELİBOLU** is a moderately inviting, if often windy, medium-sized town. Founded by the ancient Greeks as Kallipolis, it served as the Anglo-French headquarters during the Crimean War, and still holds an important naval base. As the Gallipoli battlefields (see p.190) are another 50km further southwest, the town is usually too far to be a practical base unless you have your own transport, or if there's no closer accommodation available, as can occur on Anzac Day (April 25).

The colourful, square **fishing harbour** at the heart of town is ringed by cafés and restaurants. Only a conspicuous tower remains of the fortifications of Byzantine Kallipolis. Held by an army of rebellious Catalan mercenaries for seven years in the early fourteenth century, the fortress later fell to the Ottomans (1354), who rebuilt and expanded it. A few sturdy but otherwise unremarkable Ottoman **tombs** lie inland from the port and around **Hamzaköy**, the resort district in the north of town, with its long, coarse-sand beach.

2

Piri Reis Museum

In Gelibolu's tower, in the harbour • 8.30am–noon & 1–5pm, closed Thurs • Free

The broad stone **tower** that separates the two pools of Gelibolu's harbour now holds the **Piri Reis Museum** (Piri Reis Müzesi). Intriguing displays trace the story of the legendary sixteenth-century Turkish cartographer, who prepared navigation charts of the Mediterranean and was the first man to accurately map the American coastline.

ARRIVAL AND DEPARTURE

TEKİRDAĞ

By bus Tekirdağ's *otogar* is 1km or a short dolmuş ride northeast of Cumhuriyet Meydanı (on the waterfront), though buses towards Çanakkale also pass along the waterfront.
Destinations Çanakkale via Gelibolu and Eceabat (at least 10 daily; 3hr 30min); Edirne (hourly; 2hr); Gelibolu (at least 10 daily; 2hr 30min); Istanbul (hourly; 2hr); Keşan (18 daily; 1hr 30min).

GELİBOLU

By ferry The jetty for car-and-passenger ferries to Lapseki

THE NORTH MARMARA COAST

is at the inner harbour entrance.
Destinations Lapseki (hourly 24hr; 30min).
By bus Gelibolu's *otogar* is 600m south of town on the Eceabat road, though a few dolmuşes to Eceabat or Çanakkale may pass by the harbour. To reach destinations along the southern Marmara shore, take a ferry to Lapseki, from where you can get buses to Bandırma (8 daily; 2hr 45min) and Bursa (5 daily; 3hr 30min).
Destinations Eceabat (hourly; 40min); Kilitbahir (hourly; 50min).

ACCOMMODATION

TEKİRDAĞ

Golden Yat Yali Sok 21 ☎0282 261 1054, ⊛goldenyat .com. A good three-star option in central Tekirdağ conveniently located 800m from the ferry terminal. The 52 comfortable rooms have a/c and TV, and the sea views are impressive, especially from the breakfast room on the fifth floor. There are a number of restaurants nearby, and the hotel has free parking. ₺170

GELİBOLU

Butik Hotel Gelibolu Across from the ferry terminal ☎0286 566 6600, ⊛butikhotelgelibolu.com. This small, elegantly furnished hotel makes a welcome contrast to Gelibolu's other tired hotels. However, while the eight rooms have all the latest facilities, they're remarkably small. The smart *Yonca Restaurant* offers buffet breakfasts and à la carte lunches and dinners, while the *Bulvar Café* serves a delightful afternoon tea. ₺250

EATING AND DRINKING

TEKİRDAĞ

A local speciality is pellet-shaped lamb meatballs served with tomato sauce known as *Tekirdağ köfteleri*. There are several *köftecis* along the waterfront and around Cumhuriyet Meydanı, the main square.
Meydan Köfte Çorba On the east side of the main square ☎0282 262 4910, ⊛meydankofte.com. This vast triple-storey eatery is a local favourite and offers a decent-sized plate of *köfteleri* as well as tasty soups, salads and desserts. The service is slick and there are good views of the square from the window tables. Mains ₺7–20. Daily 9am–11pm.

GELİBOLU

Be sure to try the locally caught fish, particularly *mezgit* (whitebait), *kanat* (baby bluefish) and mackerel, as well as grilled *sardalya* (sardines), the canned variety being the town's main commerce. The harbour pool is surrounded by half a dozen restaurants suitable for lunch.
Yelkenci Corner of the harbour ☎0286 566 4600. Reliable licensed restaurant, with indoor and outdoor tables. Fair-sized portions of seasonal fish, including grilled sardines and sea bass, plus other seafood. Mains ₺7–19. Daily 11am–1pm.

Southern Marmara

The best way to explore the **southern shoreline** of the Sea of Marmara is to use the fast car and foot-passenger **ferries** to Yalova, Mudanya, Bandırma and Güzelyalı. Instead of following the gulf shore via İzmit, most buses from Istanbul cross via the car ferries at Pendik or Eskihisar to Yalova and Topcular. However, before long they will use the new, impressive İzmit Körfez Köprüsü (İzmit Bay Bridge) over the Gulf of İzmit, which when completed in 2017 will be the fourth-longest suspension bridge in the world. Coming from Istanbul and using a combination of ferry and buses (see p.112) or your own vehicle, you could see all the sights in the region, particularly the attractive **İznik** and **Bursa**, in three to four days, and perhaps return to Istanbul via Bandırma (or vice verca).

Southern Marmara ports and resorts

While the coastal ports of **Yalova** and **Mudanyu** like to call themselves resorts, they hold few compelling attractions or beaches. The coastline here is mostly rocky, but the inland contours are softened by the ubiquitous olive groves and conifer forest.

2

Yalova

Little more than an hour's ferry ride from Istanbul, **Yalova** is a main transport hub for the Southern Marmara. Not many visitors hang around any longer than it takes to catch onward transport to Termal, Bursa and İznik. To the west of town is the striking (if sombre) **Yalova Deprem Anıtı** (Yalova Earthquake Monument), commemorating the devastating earthquake of August 1999, which killed an estimated 30,000 people – many of them victims of rogue builders who ignored construction regulations.

Termal

Although patronized by Byzantine and Roman emperors, the **hot springs** at **TERMAL** only became fashionable again in the 1890s, and most of the spa's Ottoman *belle époque* buildings date from that era. Atatürk used to come here to bathe in the health-giving waters, and his arboretum today boasts more than 1800 trees. The village itself, 12km southwest of Yalova, has unfortunately sprawled in recent years, and now holds several so-called luxury hotels, all offering spa treatments and wellness sessions.

Kurşunlu Banyo

In the central park • Daily 7.30am–10.30pm • ₺22 for 90min in pool, ₺25 for massage

The most popular of Termal's many bathing centres is the **Kurşunlu Banyo**. The water is supposedly beneficial for rheumatism and skin diseases, but temperatures reach 65°C, so the best time to take the plunge is in winter. Otherwise, there's an **open-air pool** at a more manageable 38°C at the nearby *Çamlık Hotel* (daily 7am–9pm; ₺12 for non-guests).

Mudanya

Now the ferry port for Bursa, **MUDANYA** is always busy with people on their way to and from Istanbul; waiting passengers can indulge in a *balık sandviç* or go for a quick trot by horse-and-carriage along the seafront.

Mütadele Evi

12 Eylül Cad 8, on the waterfront 1.2km north of the ferry terminal • Tues–Sun 8am–5pm • ₺5 • ☎ 0224 544 1068

The town's major moment in history was when the provisional armistice between Turkey and the Allies was signed on October 11, 1922, in a wooden waterside mansion. This now whitewashed and elegant **Mütadele Evi** (Armistice House) is today a small **museum**, and a fine furnished example of the seaside mansions built as summer retreats by Istanbul's wealthiest families in the early twentieth century.

ARRIVAL AND DEPARTURE   SOUTHERN MARMARA PORTS AND RESORTS

Bus tickets from Istanbul to Southern Marmara destinations include the ferry crossings; bus journey times will reduce significantly once the İzmit Körfez Köprüsü (İzmit Bay Bridge) is completed in 2017.

YALOVA

By ferry IDO car and passenger ferries (ⓦido.com.tr) connect Yenikapı in Istanbul with Yalova (at least 6 daily; 1hr 15min). From Sabiha Gökçen International Airport and the east side of Istanbul, you're best taking a ferry from Pendik to Yalova (at least 14 daily; 45min) or Eskihisar (20km southeast of Pendik) to Topçular (14km east of Yalova), near the new bridge (hourly; 45min). From Topçular you can hop in a minibus to Yalova (10min).

By bus and dolmuş Onward vehicles from Yalova go directly from the ferry terminal.

Destinations Bursa (every 30min; 45min); İznik (hourly; 1hr); Termal (every 30min; 20min).

TERMAL

By dolmuş The village is 12km southwest of Yalova, linked by a minor road which is frequented by regular dolmuşes. You'll need to return to Yalova for onward transport.

Destinations Yalova (every 30min; 20min).

MUDANYA

By ferry The two ferry companies operate from their own terminals; BUDO (ⓦburulas.com.tr; see box, p.176) fast passenger-only ferries go from the main ferry dock on the waterfront at Mudanya, to/from Kabataş in Istanbul (8 daily; 1hr 45min). IDO (ⓦido.com.tr) fast passenger-only ferries go from Güzelyalı, 3km east of Mudanya, to/from Kabataş (4–6 daily, up to 8 in summer; 2hr). IDO also operates car ferries between Güzelyalı and Yenikapı in Istanbul (2 daily; 1hr 35min). From both Mudanya and Güzelyalı, buses to the centre of Bursa and to the BursaRay (metro) connect with arriving boats (see above). If you're not going into Bursa proper, note that bus #1/F links both with Bursa's *otogar*, known as Terminal, which is 10km north of the city, for onward connections.

ACCOMMODATION AND EATING

TERMAL

Çınar ☎0226 675 7400, ⓦyalovatermal.com. The Yalova Thermal Hot Spring Resorts group manages three hotels in Termal, the smallest and nicest of which is the *Çınar* (Plane Tree), with seventeen well-appointed rooms with plush carpets and drapes, in a restored late nineteenth-century building. There are several private baths in the basement, and the courtyard is almost completely filled by a giant plane tree, its 200-year-old boughs supported by lampposts. ₺270

Limak Thermal Adnan Kahveci Cad ☎0226 675 7800, ⓦlimakhotels.com. Once a summer residence for Atatürk and now restored to its former 1930s glory, with a price tag to match. As you'd expect, the 48 rooms are palatial in size and furnishings, with individual jacuzzis fed by thermal waters, and there's a fine brasserie restaurant, café/bakery and in-house spa. ₺650

Çamlık ☎0226 675 7400, ⓦyalovatermal.com. Also run by Yalova Thermal Hot Spring Resorts, the *Çamlık* (Pine Grove) is less expensive than the *Çınar* (see above). The wooden-clad exterior of its 1980s-built block is attractive, though the eighty-odd rooms inside are fairly plain and old-fashioned. However, the hotel offers eighteen thermal baths in private cabins (open 24hr), and the two restaurants (fish and pizza) are shared with the *Çınar*. ₺155

MUDANYA

Montania Eski İstasyon Cad ☎0224 544 6000, ⓦmontaniahotel.com. Mudanya's best hotel, on the seaside esplanade with 32 rooms in a renovated 150-year-old train station – be sure to request the sea-view rooms. It has indoor and outdoor pools, a hamam and a restaurant-bar (*La Gare*) in what used to be the waiting room (open to non-guests; daily 6am–11.30pm). ₺180

İznik

It's hard to believe that **İZNİK** (ancient Nicaea), today a backwater among fruit orchards and olive groves at the east end of the eponymous lake, was once a seat of empire and scene of desperate battles. As you look around this fertile valley, however, you can understand its attraction for imperial powers needing a fortified base near the sea lanes of the Marmara. With its regular street plan, İznik's walled centre is easy to navigate on foot, and it's a popular long day or overnight trip out of Istanbul or Bursa. A day here is enough time to visit the monuments, perhaps have lunch at a lakeside café on a summer's day, and pick up souvenirs from the local ceramics workshops. During its sixteenth-century heyday, İznik produced Turkey's finest **tiles**; the tradition has recently been revived and the colourful patterned tiled souvenirs you'll find in bazaars across the country are İznik-inspired.

Brief history

Founded by Alexander's general Antigonos in 316 BC, İznik was seized and enlarged fifteen years later by his rival Lysimakhos, who named it **Nicaea** after his late wife. He also gave Nicaea its first set of walls and the grid plan typical of Hellenistic towns; both are still evident. When the Bithynian kingdom succeeded Lysimakhos, Nicaea alternated with nearby Nicomedia as its capital until bequeathed to Rome in 74 BC. After prospering as capital of the Roman province, the city continued to flourish during the Byzantine era.

FROM TOP KOZA HANI, BURSA (P.171); TILES FROM İZNİK (P.142) >

Nicaea played a pivotal role in early Christianity, hosting two important **ecumenical councils**. The first, convened by Constantine the Great in 325 AD, resulted in the condemnation of the Arian heresy – which maintained that Christ's nature was inferior to God the Father's – and the promulgation of the **Nicene Creed**, affirming Christ's divine nature, which remains central to Christian belief. Empress Irene presided over the second council to be held here (the seventh in all) in 787 AD, in which the Iconoclast controversy was settled by the pronouncement, widely misunderstood in the West, that icons had their proper place in the church so long as they were revered and not worshipped.

Nicaea's much-mended walls seldom repelled invaders. The Selçuks took the city in 1081, only to be evicted by a combined force of Byzantines and Crusaders sixteen years later. The fall of Constantinople to the Fourth Crusade in 1204 propelled Nicaea into the spotlight once more, for the Byzantine heir to the throne Theodore Laskaris retreated here, and made it the base of the improbably successful **Nicaean Empire**. The Laskarid dynasty added a second circuit of walls before returning to Constantinople in 1261, but these again failed to deter the besieging Ottomans, who, led by Orhan Gazi, the victor of Bursa, broke through in March 1331. Renamed İznik, the city embarked on a golden age of sorts, interrupted briefly by the pillaging of Tamerlane in 1402.

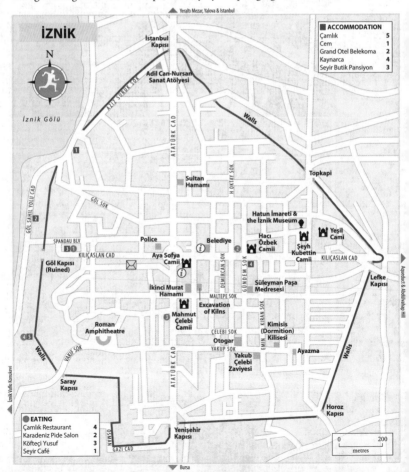

While virtually all the surviving monuments predate the Mongol sacking, the most enduring contribution to art and architecture – the celebrated **İznik tiles and pottery** – first appeared after Çelebi Mehmet I brought skilled potters from Persia to begin the local industry. This received another boost in 1514 when Selim the Grim took Tabriz and sent more craftsmen west as war booty, and by the end of the sixteenth century, ceramic production was at its height. This flowering was brief, however; in 1609 Sultan Ahmed I conscripted all İznik tile-makers to work on Istanbul's Sultanahmet Camii (it was İznik tiles that bestowed its nickname, the Blue Mosque), forbidding them to work on anything else. By the time the mosque was completed seven years later, the kilns in İznik had been reduced from three hundred to fewer than ten, and by the mid-eighteenth century the local industry had packed up completely. The town began a long, steady decline, hastened by near-total devastation during the 1920–22 war.

Aya Sofya Camii

On İznik's central roundabout

Originally the Byzantine Church of Holy Wisdom, the **Aya Sofya Camii** (Aya Sofya Müzesi) was founded by Justinian I. The present building was built after an earthquake in 1065. As the cathedral of the provisional Byzantine capital, it hosted the coronations of the four Nicaean emperors. The Ottomans converted it into a mosque directly upon taking the city, and Mimar Sinan restored it, but the premises were half ruined when razed to the ground in 1922. Recent restoration raised the walls to their former height and added a roof, and it has now reverted from a museum back to a functioning mosque. Inside, there's little to see except some damaged floor mosaics and a faint **fresco** of Christ, John the Baptist and Mary, at ground level behind a glass panel to the left as you enter.

Yeşil Cami

Yeşil Cami Cad

The **Yeşil Cami** (Green Mosque), erected toward the end of the fourteenth century, is a small gem of a building, where the highlight is the fantastic **marble relief** on the portico. The mosque takes its name from the green İznik tiles that once adorned its stubby minaret, which looks back to Selçuk models. Sadly, though, the tiles have long since been replaced by mediocre, tri-coloured work.

Nilüfer Hatun İmareti and the İznik Museum

Müze Cad • Tues–Sun 9am–1pm & 2–6pm • ₺3 • ☎ 0224 757 1027

The sprawling, T-form **Nilüfer Hatun İmareti**, with a huge main dome flanked by two smaller ones, is more accurately called a *zaviye* than a mere soup kitchen (*imaret*), and is

---

İZNİK TİLES

To watch **İznik tiles** being made, visit the **İznik Vakfı**, or İznik Foundation (Vakıf Sok 13, near Saray Kapisi; Mon–Fri 8am–5pm; ☎ 0224 757 6025, ⓦiznik.com), which was established in 1993 to restart production using traditional methods. It sells tiles of extremely high quality, and correspondingly high price – around ₺50 for a 20cm x 10cm border piece or a small bowl.

However, there are numerous other decent local **workshops** (*atölyes*), where the price is a more affordable ₺20 for a small tile, plus they offer discounts for bulk buys. The best reasonably priced one-stop shop is **Adil Can-Nursan Sanat Atölyesi**, just inside the Istanbul Kapısı (Aziz Sürük Sok 1; daily 9am–5pm; ☎ 0224 757 6529, ⓦadil-can.com). Other quality (as opposed to kitsch) shops cluster along **Demircan Sokağı** and inside the **Süleyman Paşa Medresesi**, the oldest (1332) Ottoman *medrese* in Turkey and the first one with an open courtyard, which here is surrounded by eleven chambers and nineteen domes.

The toughest, best, most waterproof – and most expensive – tiles are not ceramic-based but made primarily from locally quarried, finely ground **quartz**. Quartz-rich tiles are air-porous, have good acoustic qualities (hence their use in mosques), and make good insulators, as they contract slightly in winter and expand in summer.

one of the few that never doubled as a mosque. It was commissioned by Murat I in 1388 in honour of his mother, Nilüfer Hatun, the daughter of a Byzantine noble who was married off to Orhan Gazi to consolidate a Byzantine–Ottoman alliance. Her ability was soon recognized by Orhan, who appointed her regent during his frequent absences.

The *imaret* was originally the meeting place of the Ahi brotherhood, a guild drawn from the ranks of skilled craftsmen that also acted as a community welfare and benevolent society. It now contains the **İznik Museum**, where you can see genuine İznik pottery, including fourteenth-century tile fragments excavated from the town's kilns. Other exhibits include a bronze dancing Roman-era Pan, some Byzantine gold jewellery and, standing out amid the nondescript marble clutter, a sarcophagus in near-mint condition.

The walls

While only enthusiasts will want to walk the entire perimeter of İznik's double **walls**, now missing most of their hundred original watchtowers, two of the seven portals are worth some time. Heavy traffic has been rerouted through modern breaches in the fortifications to prevent vibration damage to the original openings, now restricted to tractors and pedestrians.

The closest gate to the Yeşil Cami, the eastern **Lefke Kapısı**, is a three-ply affair incorporating two towers erected by Emperor Hadrian between the two courses of walls. You can get up on the ramparts here for a stroll, as it is at the northerly **Istanbul Kapısı**, the best-preserved gate. It too is triple-layered, with the middle section a triumphal arch celebrating Hadrian's visit in 123 AD. The innermost gate is decorated by two stone-carved **masks**, probably taken from the city's Roman theatre.

Other traces of Roman Nicaea are evident in the southwestern quarter, including the so-called **Senatus Court** by the lakeshore, outside the **Saray Kapısı**, and the all-but-vanished **Roman theatre**, just inside the gate.

Abdülvahap hill

2.5km east of the Lefke Kapısı

If time permits, you might walk or drive past a Roman aqueduct to the obvious **Abdülvahap hill** for comprehensive views over İznik and its surroundings – a popular summer excursion for locals at sunset. The less compelling tomb on top is that of Abdülvahap, a semi-legendary figure in the eighth-century Arab raids.

From the hill you can also see the vast **İznik Gölü** (Lake İznik), which provides decent swimming in summer, though the shoreline near the town is uninviting. In order to reach the best beaches, located at its far western end between Gölyaka and Orhangazi, you really need a car.

ARRIVAL AND DEPARTURE   İZNİK

By bus and dolmuş İznik's tiny *otogar* is on Çelebi Sokağı, in the southeast quarter.

Destinations Bursa (every 30min; 1hr 15min); Yalova (hourly; 1hr).

Tourist office On the ground floor of the *Belediye* on Kılıçaslan Caddesi (Mon–Fri 8.30am–noon & 1–5.30pm; ☎0224 757 1933). There's also a seasonal wooden information booth by Aya Sofya.

ACCOMMODATION

Çamlık Göl Sahili Yolu 11 ☎0224 757 1362, ⓦiznik -camlikmotel.com. Lakeside motel, well positioned for sunset views, with 24 a/c rooms of varying sizes, some with little balconies (though these suffer more road noise). The decor is a tad 1980s, but the place is spotless and well maintained. Breakfast is served in the restaurant next door (see opposite). ₺**140**

Cem Göl Sahili Yolu 34 ☎0224 757 1687, ⓦcemotel .com. Well-run lakeside hotel with cheery

tan-and-earth-tone decor, modern though small bathrooms, mosaic-paved stairs and a competent ground-floor restaurant, the *Antik*. Set back a bit in a gap of the walls, so quieter than the nearby *Çamlık*. ₺**160**

Grand Otel Belekoma Göl Sahili Yolu 8 ☎0224 757 1407, ⓦiznikbelekomahotel.com. The most modern lakeside accommodation, with 48 rooms in a white block, all with TV, a/c and minibar but some on the ground floor are a little small and unremarkable. Opt for ones with balconies and lake views. There's a decent restaurant, large pool and car park. ₺190

Kaynarca Gündem Sok 1 ☎ 0224 757 1753. İznik's best budget *pansiyon*, run by English-speaking Ali and his charming family, with dorm beds as well as en-suite rooms with TV; breakfast (₺7.50 extra) is served on the rooftop terrace, and there's a guest kitchen with a gas cooker. No reservations. Dorm ₺35, double ₺85

★ **Seyir Butik Pansiyon** Kılıçarslan Cad 5 ☎ 0505 505 2250, ⓦ seyirbutik.com. Neat as a pin, this newly opened *pansiyon* is set in a renovated İznik mansion with nine delightful rooms above a café (see below). Each room has wooden floors, a TV and small but modern tiled bathrooms, and some have wrought-iron balconies overlooking the peaceful rose-filled garden and lake. ₺130

2

EATING

Maple-canopied Kılıçaslan Caddesi holds a few unlicensed restaurants of the *pide*-and-*köfte* variety, but most visitors choose to eat at licensed places by the lakeshore, where there are also shady tea gardens and *dondurma* parlours too.

Çamlık Restaurant Göl Sahili Yolu 11 ☎ 0224 757 1362, ⓦ iznik-camlikmotel.com. The nicest setting of the waterside restaurants, this is a good place to try the excellent local grilled or fried *yayın* (catfish) or some generous *mezes* accompanied by a cold beer at one of the peaceful garden tables. Staff can be rather brusque though, at times. Mains ₺7–20. Daily noon–3pm & 6–10pm.

Karadeniz Pide Salon Kılıçaslan Cad 149 ☎ 0224 757 0143. Popular local restaurant on the ground floor of an atmospheric 1935 building, serving fresh and cheap *pides* and pizzas washed down with *ayran*. Pide ₺3, mains ₺7–12. Daily 11am–11pm.

Köfteçi Yusuf Atatürk Cad 75 ☎ 0224 757 3597. A quick-serving, friendly (though unlicensed) carnivore heaven – not just *köfte* but chicken wings, kidneys, *şiş* and the like. A range of salads (such as *piyaz*) and desserts rounds off the menu; seating is on two levels, with an open terrace. Expect to pay around ₺20 for *köfte* with bread and salads; tea/coffee is complimentary. Daily 11am–3pm & 6–10pm.

★ **Seyir Café** Kılıçaslan Cad 5 ☎ 0505 505 2250, ⓦ seyircafem.com. Lovely café-restaurant with tables in pretty gardens right next to the city walls. They offer a more contemporary menu than most, with a number of tasty beef and chicken dishes including stir-fry and stroganoff, plus they serve pizzas and hot breakfasts. Mains ₺7–16. Daily 7am–10pm.

Bursa

Draped like a ribbon along the leafy lower slopes of Uludağ, which towers more than 2000m higher, the newly inscribed World Heritage Site of **BURSA** does more justice to its setting than any other Turkish city apart from Istanbul. Gathered here are some of the country's finest early Ottoman monuments, set within neighbourhoods that, despite being increasingly hemmed in by concrete tower blocks, remain appealing.

Straggling for some 20km either side of the E90 highway, and home to a population of 2.7 million, Bursa is now Turkey's fourth-largest city and no longer exactly elegant. Silk and textile manufacture, plus the local thermal spas, were for centuries its most important enterprises; they're now outstripped by automobile manufacture and canneries and bottlers that process the rich harvest of the plain. Vast numbers of settlers have been attracted by **factory jobs**, while the **students** of Uludağ University provide a necessary leavening in what might otherwise be a uniformly **conservative community**. Some of this atmosphere derives from Bursa's role as first capital of the Ottoman Empire and burial place of the first six sultans, their piety as well as authority emanating from the mosques, Ottoman/polic-welfare and the tombs built at their command.

There are fast **ferry routes** from Istanbul to Güzelyalı, Mudanya and Yalova on the southern shore of the Sea of Marmara, with excellent bus and metro links into central Bursa (see p.176). Though the city is sometimes touted as a long day-trip from Istanbul, it really merits a one- and preferably two-night stay, particularly to allow time to visit the slopes of Uludağ.

Brief history

Although the area had been settled at least a millennium previously, the first city on the site of modern Bursa was founded early in the second century BC by King

2

BURSA

Kültürpark, Çanakkale & Mudanya

DR. RÜŞTÜ BURLU CAD
MUDANYA CAD
ÇEKIRGE CAD

Yeni
Kaplıca

N

Merinos (M)

ANKARA YOLU CADESSI/D200

KIBRIS ŞEHITLER CAD

USLU SOK
USLU SOK

Osmangazi (M)

MERINOSLU SOK

Archeological
Museum

Kültür Parkı

DARMŞTAD CAD

J. SUMER SOK

RUSÇUKLU MUSTAFA CAD
İLKBAHAR CAD

KARAOSMAN SOK

Kültür Parkı
Açıkhava
Tiyatrosu
(Open Air Theatre)

Atatürk
Stadium

ÇEKIRGE CAD

ŞIRIN SOK
ALTINPARMAK SOK
DEĞIRMEN CAD

SAN SOK
SILI SOK

TABAK SOK
ÇIÇEK SOK
BAHÇELER SOK

BEŞICILER CAD

BURSALI TAHIR CAD

HAMZABEY CAD

Ottoman
House
Museum

SEDAT SOK

Murat
Hamamı &
Medresesi

Muradiye
Camii

Muradiye
Külliyesi &
The Royal Tombs

BURSALI TAHIR CAD

ALTIPARMAK CAD

BELKBEY SOK

J. MÜREKKEPÇI SOK

Hüsnü Züber Evi

Muradiye
Parkı

II MURAT CAD

KAPLICA CAD

YAYLA SOK

BOZKURT CAD

SAKARYA CAD

Geruş (7)

MURADIYE

KÖSK CAD

KIZLAR CAD

BAYIR SOK

AŞIKBEY CAD

HASTALARYURDU CAD

Devlet (State)
Hastanesi

ORHANELI CAD

ORTAPAZAR CAD

ACCOMMODATION

Artıç	3
Çeşmeli	2
Divan	5
Efehan	1
Gold Butik	6
Gönlüferah City	7
Güneş	4
Kitap Evi	9
Safran	8

HISAR
(TOPHANE)

Alâeddin
Camii

Zindan
Kapısı

KÖSK CAD

FERAH SOK

ALACAHIRKA CAD

Pinarbaşı
Kapısı

EATING

Arap Şükrü	7
Çiçek Izgara	2
Fayton Müze	9
Hacibey İskender	4
Kebapçı İskender	3/5
Mahfel	8
Maviyel Café	6
Üç Köfte	1

0 — 250
metres

BAYRAMYERI CAD

Cılımboz Deresi

SEYDI NASIR CAD

KESTANELIK CAD

ESKIYOL SOK

SEYDI NASIR CAD

LIVE MUSIC VENUES

Kültür Parkı Açıkhava Tiyatrosu	2
Tayyare Kültür Merkezi	1

(1) — Tramway line #1 stop
(3) — Tramway line #3 stop

Prusias I of Bithynia, who in typical Hellenistic fashion named the town **Proussa** after himself. Legend claims that Hannibal helped him pick the location of the acropolis, today's Hisar.

Overshadowed by nearby Nicomedia (modern İzmit) and Nicaea (İznik), the city stagnated until the **Romans**, attracted by its natural hot springs, spent lavish amounts on public baths and made it capital of their province of Mysia. Justinian introduced

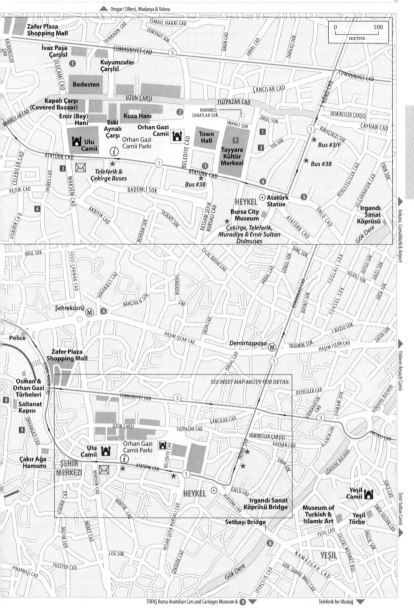

silkworm culture, and Byzantine Proussa flourished until Arab raids of the seventh and eighth centuries, and the subsequent tug-of-war for sovereignty between the Selçuks and Greeks, precipitated its decline.

The dawn of the fourteenth century saw a small band of nomadic Turks, led by **Osman Gazi**, camped outside the walls of Proussa. After almost a decade of siege, the city capitulated in 1326 to Osman's son, Orhan, and the **Ottomans** ceased to be a wandering tribe of marauders. Orhan marked the acquisition of a capital and the organization of an infant state by styling himself sultan and giving the city its present name. Bursa then embarked on a second golden age: the silk industry was expanded and the city, outgrowing the confines of the citadel, was graced with monuments.

Following Orhan's death in 1362, the imperial capital was gradually relocated to Edirne, but Bursa's place in history, and in the hearts of the Ottomans, was sealed; succeeding sultans continued to add buildings and were laid to rest here for another hundred years. Disastrous fires and earthquakes in the nineteenth century, and the 1919–22 War of Independence, only slightly diminished the city's splendour.

Şehir Merkezi

Bursa's historical heart is the **city centre** (Şehir Merkezi), which is surprisingly compact and particularly good for exploring on foot. It is centred along Atatürk Caddesi from the Gök Dere stream in the east, to the landmark blue glass pyramid of the modern Zafer Plaza shopping mall, which lies beneath the Hisar plateau in the west. The two focal points between these are **Heykel** (meaning statue), the plaza marked by the equestrian statue of Atatürk, and the shady **Orhan Gazi Parkı**, (also known as **Koza Parkı**), with its fountains, benches, strolling crowds and cafés.

Orhan Gazi Camii

Northeast corner of Orhan Gazi Parkı

Founded in 1336, the **Orhan Gazi Camii** is Bursa's second-oldest mosque, though it has been destroyed and rebuilt twice. Originally built as a *zaviye* for dervishes, it's the earliest example of the T-form mosque with *eyvans* flanking the main prayer hall. **Karagöz puppets**, the painted camel-leather props used in the Turkish national shadow-play, supposedly represent workers who were involved in building the Orhan Gazi Camii. According to legend, the antics of Karagöz and his sidekick Hacıvat so entertained their fellow workmen that Orhan had them beheaded to end the distraction. Later, missing the comedians and repenting of his deed, he arranged to immortalize the pair in the art form that now bears the name of Karagöz.

Ulu Cami

Cnr Atatürk Cad and Orhan Gazi Parkı

The vast tawny limestone **Ulu Cami** (Great Mosque) was built between 1396 and 1399 by Yıldırım Beyazıt I, using booty won from the Crusaders at Macedonian Nikopolis. Before the battle, Yıldırım (Thunderbolt) had vowed, if granted victory, to construct twenty mosques. Consisting of twenty domes supported by twelve freestanding pillars, the present building was his rather loose interpretation of this promise, but was still the largest and most ambitious Ottoman mosque of its time. The interior is dominated by a huge *şadırvan* pool in the centre, whose dome oculus (now glassed over) once stood open to the elements, as well as an impressive collection of exquisite calligraphy and an intricate walnut pulpit pieced together, it's claimed, without nails or glue.

The bazaars

From the north side of Orhan Gazi Parkı, several entrances lead into Bursa's vast, atmospheric and constantly busy **Kapalı Çarşı** (Covered Bazaar). The warren of narrow lanes is bisected by its main central thoroughfare, the roofed **Uzun Çarşı** (Long Bazaar). The Kapalı Çarşı and its assorted shops and galleries (under the World Heritage Site label of "Quarter of Hans") today sells all manner of goods from clothes, towels and bolts of cloth to fresh produce and local confectionary such as candied chestnuts.

Emir (Bey) Hanı, at the rear of the Ulu Cami, is the oldest part of the bazaar and one of more than a dozen hans built between the fourteenth and sixteenth centuries as inns for caravanning merchants peddling their wares along Asia's trade routes. As with most

KOZA HANI AND BURSA SILK

The centrepiece of the Kapalı Çarşı is the **Koza Hanı**, or "**Silk-Cocoon Hall**", which was built in 1491 by Sultan Bayezid II when Bursa was the final stop on the Silk Route from China. Centuries earlier, silkworm larvae from China had been introduced to this region by the Romans, as it was suitable for the cultivation of mulberry trees, a chief food source for silkworms. Craftspeople spun the silken thread from the cocoons and weaved it into high-quality fabric, and by the time of the Ottoman conquest, sericulture had become an important industry around Bursa. The Koza Hanı was built to capitalize on this thriving industry and to bolster the city's standing as a centre of the world silk trade. For five hundred years silk-breeders gathered to hawk their valuable produce at an annual cocoon auction, when the Koza Hanı became a lake of white torpedoes the size of a songbird's egg.

But by the 1990s, waves of cheaper silk imported from Asia had reduced Bursa's silk production to a slow trickle, and today, cocoon dealers no longer flood Koza Hanı's courtyard. However, there are still some **silk and brocade merchants** here selling scarves, neckties, table linen, and the like. Most are cheap imports brought in to satisfy price-conscious shoppers, but if you're willing to dig a little deeper into your pocket, real silk can be found; make sure the label says *ipek* (silk) and not *ithal ipek* (artificial silk). In any event, the hugely atmospheric **han** is worth a visit for its friendly mix of tea gardens and souvenir shops clustered around its minuscule *mescit* (small mosque), perched over a beautiful marble *şadırvan* (fountain).

traditional Ottoman *hans*, a main gate leads into a central courtyard containing a fountain or a domed *mesjid* (prayer chapel) and surrounded by double-storey inward-facing rooms for traders, livestock and merchandise.

The **bedesten**, with its fine vaulted ceiling, was built in 1400 by Sultan Bayezid II to store the city's valuables, and today is given over to the sale and warehousing of jewellery and precious metals. The **Eski Aynalı Çarşı**, formerly the **Bey Hamamı** of the Orhan Gazi complex (note the domes and skylights), is the place to go for more tourist-orientated goods.

Bursa City Museum

Atatürk Cad 8 • Tues–Sun 9.30am–5.30pm • ₺3 • ☏ 0224 220 2626, ⊚ bursakentmuzesi.com • Free audioguides available in English

In the old courthouse, behind Heykel's statue of Atatürk, lies the well-designed **Bursa City Museum** (Bursa Kent Müzesi). More contemporary and engaging than you might expect, it chronicles the city's **history**, from the life of the Ottoman sultans to the early Republic. The highlight, in the basement, is replicas of old shops, including a saddle-and-shoemaker, sweet shop, and a copper, lace and textile market.

Hisar (Tophane)

Bursa's original fortified nucleus, **Hisar**, also known as **Tophane**, looks over modern-day Bursa from atop a plateau on the western edge of the city centre. Some 300m downhill from Ulu Cami, on Cemal Nadir Caddesi, just before the **Zafer Plaza** shopping mall, you can climb up the ancient walls via pedestrian ramps, steps and, in some places, escalators. Alternatively, Orhangazi Caddesi allows access to vehicles.

The atmospheric old city retains clusters of dilapidated **Ottoman housing** within its warren of narrow lanes, enclosed by sections of medieval wall, including the impressively restored **Sultanat (or Hisar) Kapısı (gate)** on the east side. At the top of the old town is a pleasant clifftop **park**, where you can sit at one of the cafés and absorb the city views. The park sprawls around a six-storey clock tower and the **Osman and Orhan Gazi Türbeleri** – the tombs of the two men credited for founding the Ottoman Empire. Osman laid siege in 1317 to what was, at the time, a fully Byzantine city. Nine year later, in 1326, his son, Orhan, finally rode victorious into the city, named it Bursa and went on to expand the Ottoman dynasty as far as Constantinople. The tombs, resting on the site of a long-vanished Byzantine church, were all but levelled by the 1855 earthquake and given a mausoleum-style reconstruction in 1863.

Yeşil and around

A 15min walk east of Heykel via Atatürk Caddesi and over Setbaşı Bridge, the road forks at a Y-junction: take the left fork, Yeşil Caddesi, for Yeşil and Emir Sultan; you can also take the tram along Cumhuriyet Cad to the top end of Gökdere Bulvarı

Yeşil, Bursa's neighbourhood east of Heykel, spans out around the eponymous mosque and tomb. The immediate environs of the two monuments swarm with tour groups; competition has restrained prices at most of the nearby cafés, but also ensured that a clutch of garishly repainted old houses are glutted with souvenir dross. A little east of Yeşil, along Emir Sultan Caddesi, lies the suburb of **Emir Sultan**, another area named after its mosque.

Irgandı Sanat Köprüsü

Linking Heykel and Yeşil over the **Gök Dere** stream, the pedestrianized **Irgandı Sanat Köprüsü** (Irgandı Artisanry Bridge), 200m north of Setbaşı Bridge, was built in 1442 along with thirty shops and warehouses overlooking the river. Numerous facelifts since the 1855 earthquake have shaped the rows of cafés and tourist shops lining the bridge to look something like their Ottoman predecessors.

TOFAŞ Bursa Anatolian Cars and Carriages Museum

Kapıcı Cad, 500m south of the Setbaşı Bridge • Tues–Sun 10am–5pm • Free • ☏ 0224 329 3941, ⊛ tofasanadoluarabalarimuzesi.com • Follow signs down İpekçilik Cad

The surprisingly attention-grabbing **Bursa Anatolian Cars and Carriages Museum** (Bursa Anadolu Arabaları Müzesi), sponsored by car manufacturer **TOFAŞ**, is housed in a former silk-processing factory, surrounded by attractive gardens with a tremendous **café** (see p.178). The well-presented exhibits include a collection of old **horse-drawn carriages**, **oxcarts** and **buggies** from across Anatolia, as well as a number of TOFAŞ vehicles, including the 1971 **Murat 124** – one of Turkey's most popular cars ever.

The Umurbey Hamamı in the museum grounds has been restored into an unexpectedly good **clock exhibition** displaying over 1800 clocks and with interactive components demonstrating the development of the concept of time.

Yeşil Cami

Yeşil Cad

Designed by architect Hacı İvaz atop a slight rise, construction on the **Yeşil Cami** (Green Mosque) was started in 1413 by Çelebi Mehmet I, who won the civil war caused by the death of Beyazıt I. Although unfinished – work ceased in 1424, three years after Mehmet's death – and despite catastrophic damage from two nineteenth-century earth tremors, it's the most spectacular of Bursa's imperial mosques. The incomplete entrance (narthex), faced in a light marble, lacks a portico, and, beside the stalactite vaulting and relief calligraphy, you can see the supports for arches never built.

Pass through a foyer supported by pilfered Byzantine columns to reach the **interior**, a variation on the T-plan usually reserved for dervish *zaviyes*. A fine *şadırvan* occupies the centre of the "T", but your eye is monopolized by the hundreds of mostly blue and green **tiles** that line not just the dazzling *mihrab* but every available vertical surface up to 5m in height, particularly two recesses flanking the entryway. Above the portal, reached by a small staircase, and only accessible with permission from the imam, the **hünkâr mahfili** (**imperial loge**) is the most extravagantly decorated chamber of all. Several artisans from Tabriz participated in the tiling of Yeşil Cami, but the loge is attributed to a certain Al-Majnun, which means "madman" (due to the effects of excessive hashish-smoking) in Arabic.

Yeşil Türbe

Yeşil Cad • Daily 8am–noon & 1–5pm • Free

Located in a small park across from the Yeşil Cami, the tile-lined **Yeşil Türbe** of Çelebi Sultan Mehmet I and his assorted offspring is arguably one of the most beautiful structures in all of Bursa. It was built by his son and successor, Murad II, following the death of the sovereign in 1421. The exterior of the mausoleum is clad with green-blue tiles that give it its name, and inside, İznik tiles with flower patterns in blue, white and yellow adorn the portal, while the walls and Mehmet's tomb glisten with the glorious original Tabriz material.

Museum of Turkish and Islamic Arts

Yeşil Cad • Daily 9am–7pm, Nov–March till 5pm • ₺5 • ☎ 0224 220 9926, ⓦ muze.gov.tr

Originally the fifteenth-century *medrese* for the Yeşil Cami, the collection at Bursa's **Türk ve İslam Eserleri Müzesi** includes İznik ware, dervish paraphernalia, Beykoz glass, weapons, coins and antiquarian manuscripts. The exhibits are poorly labelled, but the building itself, set around a pleasant courtyard with fountain, has been recently restored to reveal its pretty turquoise tiles around the windows.

Emir Sultan Camii

Doyuran Cad, off Emir Sultan Cad, 300m east of Yeşil Cami

The **Emir Sultan Camii** lies amid extensive graveyards where every religious Bursan hopes to be buried. Endowed by a Bokharan dervish and trusted adviser to three sultans (the first of whom was Beyazıt I), the mosque was rebuilt from earthquake ruins in the Ottoman Baroque style during the early nineteenth century, and further restoration was done in the 1990s. The interior is fairly plain, but the building boasts the largest single-span dome of Bursa's mosques. From beneath the huge sycamore and cypress trees on the east side you can enjoy panoramic views of the city from the tea garden.

Yıldırım Beyazıt Camii

Yıldırım Cad, 1km north of Emir Sultan Camii • Dolmuşes also go from Heykel, marked "Heykel–Beyazit Yıldırım" (15min)

One of the oldest mosques in Bursa, the **Yıldırım Beyazıt Camii** is perched on a small hillock in the suburb of Yıldırım at the northeast edge of the city centre. Now a component of the World Heritage Site, the mosque was completed by **Beyazıt I** between 1390 and 1395 and features a handsome, five-arched portico defined by square columns. Its interior is unremarkable except for a gravity-defying arch that bisects the prayer hall, its lower supports apparently tapering away to end in stalactite moulding. The only other note of whimsy in this spare building is the use of elaborate niches out on the porch.

The associated **medrese**, exceptionally long and narrow because of its sloping site, huddles just downhill; today it houses a medical clinic. The **türbe** (tomb) of the luckless Beyazit, supposedly kept in an iron cage by the rampaging Tamerlane until his death in 1403, is usually locked. Perhaps the mosque custodians fear a revival of the Ottoman inclination to abuse the tomb of the most ignominiously defeated sultan.

Muradiye Külliyesi and around

2.5km west of Heykel • Catch a Çekirge-bound bus or dolmuş and alight at the junction of Altıparmak and Çekirge cads (10min), from where you can climb up II Murat Cad to Muradiye Parkı; the T1 tram also goes down Altıparmak Cad

The **Muradiye** neighbourhood developed around the hilltop **Muradiye Külliyesi** (Muradiye Complex), built by Murat II between 1425 and 1451. With its fine mosque, baths and tombs set around the shady **Muradiye Parkı**, it perfectly encapsulates Bursa's early Ottoman spirit, and the complex is now a component of the World Heritage Site. The surrounding narrow lanes of Muradiye exude a refined, cultured air thanks to the well-preserved dwellings of the later Ottoman period of the seventeenth to nineteenth centuries.

Muradiye Camii

Muradiye Külliyesi, Sedat Sok

Begun in 1424 by Murat II, the Muradiye Camii was completed in 1426 and is similar in plan to Orhan Gazi, but more impressive, with its profuse glazed tiling low on the walls, calligraphy higher up and two domes. On the western side of the mosque, the

Murat Hamami is today a skills training facility for the disabled, while the **Muradiye Medresesi** is a modern health centre.

Royal Tombs

Muradiye Külliyesi, Sedat Sok • Daily 8.30am–noon & 1–5.30pm; may close earlier in winter • Free

The twelve **Royal Tombs** are mostly the final resting places of Ottoman crown princes who fell victim to stronger, or smarter, relatives hell bent on power by any means. Added gradually during the century or so after Muradiye Camii, the tombs are set in lovingly tended and fragrant **gardens** whose serenity belies the tragic stories of those entombed.

The first tomb you come to holds **Şehzade Ahmet** and his brother Şehinşah, both murdered in 1513 by their cousin Selim I. The luxury of the two-tone blue İznik tiles within contrasts sharply with the adjacent austerity of **Murat II's tomb**, where Roman columns inside and a wooden canopy out front are the only superfluities. As much contemplative mystic as warrior-sultan, Murat was the only Ottoman ruler ever to abdicate voluntarily, though pressures of state forced him to leave his dervish order and return to the throne after just two years. The last sultan to be interred at Bursa, he's one of the few here who died in his bed; both the coffin and dome were originally open to the sky "so that the rain of heaven might wash my face like any pauper's".

Next along is the tomb of **Şehzade Mustafa**, Süleyman the Magnificent's unjustly murdered heir; perhaps indicative of his father's remorse, the tomb is done up in extravagant İznik tiles, with a top border of calligraphy. Nearby, the tomb of **Cem Sultan**, his brother Mustafa and two of Beyazıt II's sons is decorated with abstract, botanical and calligraphic paint strokes up to the dome, with turquoise tiles below. Cem, the cultured favourite son of **Mehmet the Conqueror**, was an interesting might-have-been. Following Mehmet's death in 1481, he lost a brief dynastic struggle with the successful claimant, brother **Beyazıt II**, and fled abroad. For fourteen years he wandered, seeking sponsorship from Christian benefactors who became his jailers: first the Knights of St John at Bodrum and Rhodes, later the papacy. At one point it seemed he would command a Crusader army to retake Istanbul, but all such plans came to nothing, as Beyazıt anticipated his opponents' moves and bribed them handsomely to desist, making Cem a lucrative prisoner. His usefulness as a pawn exhausted, Cem was probably poisoned in Italy by Pope Alexander VI in 1495, leaving reams of poems aching with nostalgia and homesickness.

Hüsnü Züber Evi

Uzunyol Sok 3 • Tues–Sun 10am–5pm • Free, but donations appreciated • ☎ 0224 221 3542 • 1min walk uphill behind Murat Hamami (follow signs)

A former Ottoman guesthouse, built in 1836 and once also used as the Russian Consulate, the **Hüsnü Züber Evi** sports a typical overhanging upper storey, wooden roof and garden courtyard. It now houses a collection of carved wooden musical instruments, spoons and farming utensils, many made by former owner Hüsnü Züber. The main exhibit, however, is the **house** itself, which, like the Osmanlı Evi (see below), is one of the few of its era to have been well restored and opened to the public.

Ottoman House Museum

Aralık Sok, just behind and north of Muradiye Camii • Tues–Sun 8am–noon & 1–5pm • Free • ☎ 0224 222 0868

Set in a restored seventeenth-century house, the **Ottoman House Museum** (Osmanlı Evi Müzesi) is worth a quick look to admire the building, with its open-sided verandas and lovely painted rooms. The upstairs room in particular has beautiful stencilled plant and flower motifs on its inlaid wooden cabinets and hexagonal ceiling.

Kültür Parkı

Çekirge Cad

Kültür Parkı is an oasis of green providing welcome shade and a sense of seclusion from the busy surrounding streets. Courting couples stroll along broad driveways dotted with park benches, while young families enjoy play areas and a small funfair. There's also a tea garden, a small boating lake and a few overpriced, licensed restaurants, while an open-air theatre hosts summer concerts. Bursa's **Archeological Museum** (Arkeoloji Müzesi) stands near the centre of the park, but at the time of writing it was closed for a lengthy refurbishment.

Çekirge

2km northwest of Kültür Parkı • About a 20min walk along Çekirge Cad from the southwest side of the park; buses, including 6/E, B/25 and 48/A, and dolmuşes shuttle to and from stops on Atatürk Caddessi in Heykel to Çekirge (20min)

The main incentive to visit the thermal centre of **Çekirge** – meaning "Grasshopper", presumably a reference to the natural soundtrack of a summer evening – is to enjoy a relaxing dip in one of its many **hot springs**.

Yeni Kaplıca

Yeni Kaplıca Cad, just west of Kültür Parkı • **Main baths and Kaynarca Hamamı** Daily 7am–11pm • ₺15; exfoliating mitt (*kese*) ₺15; massage ₺20 • ☎ 0224 236 6968, ⓦ yenikaplica.com.tr • **Kara Mustafa Hamamı** Daily 7am–11pm • ₺20; *kese* ₺20; massage ₺25 • ☎ 0224 236 6955

The water at the **Yeni Kaplıca** (New Baths) usually flows out at a whopping 84°C. Hardly "new", the spa itself dates from the mid-sixteenth century but was so called to distinguish it from the Old Baths (see below). According to legend, Süleyman the Magnificent was cured of gout after a dip in the Byzantine baths here. Fragments of mosaic paving stud the floor, and the walls are lined with once-exquisite, now blurred, İznik tiles. There is a women's section, though it is nothing like as splendid as the men's with its huge, deep central pool. Within the Yeni Kaplıca complex are two other baths; the women-only **Kaynarca Hamamı** and the **Kara Mustafa Hamamı** (54°C at source) for families; the latter is now accessed from the neighbouring *Kara Mustafa Hotel.*

Eski Kaplıca

Eski Kaplıca Sok, off Çekirge Cad, next to *Kervansaray Termal Hotel* • Daily 7am–10.30pm • ₺30; exfoliating mitt (*kese*) ₺20; massage ₺20 • ☎ 0224 233 9300

Bursa's most ancient baths, the **Eski Kaplıca** (Old Baths), is much the nicest public bath for women. Byzantine rulers Justinian and Theodora improved a Roman spa on this site, and Murat I had a go at the structure in the late fourteenth century. Huge but shallow keyhole-shaped pools dominate the *hararetler* (hot rooms) of the men's and women's sections, whose domes are supported by eight Byzantine columns. The baths are now managed by the hotel next door, hence the high admission cost.

Hüdavendigar (Birinci) Murat Camii

Junction of Çekirge and Murat cads

With its five-arched portico and alternating bands of brick and stone, the **Hüdavendigar (Birinci) Murat Camii** resembles a Byzantine church from Ravenna or Macedonia. Indeed, tradition asserts that the architect and builders were Christians, who dallied twenty years at the task because Murat I, whose pompous epithet literally means "Creator of the Universe", was continually off at war and unable to supervise the work. The interior plan, consisting of a first-floor *medrese* above a highly modified, T-type *zaviye* at ground level, is unique in Islam. Unfortunately, the upper storey is rarely open for visitors.

Türbe of Murat I

Junction of Çekirge and Murat cads, across the street from the Hüdavendigar (Birinci) Murat Camii • Open access

The body of **Murat I**, brought back from Serbia in 1389, lies in a much-modified **türbe**. In June of that year Murat was about to win his greatest triumph, over the Serbian king Lazar and his allies at the **Battle of Kosovo**, when he was stabbed to death in his tent by Miloš Obilić, a Serbian noble who had feigned desertion. Murat's son Beyazit, later styled as Yıldırım, immediately had his brother Yakub strangled and, once in sole command, crushed the Christian armies. Beyazit's acts had two far-reaching consequences: the

Balkans remained under Ottoman control until early in the twentieth century, and a gruesome precedent of fratricide was established for subsequent Ottoman coronations.

ARRIVAL AND DEPARTURE BURSA

By plane Bursa Yenisehir Airport (☎0224 781 8181, ⓦyenisehir.dhmi.gov.tr), 43km east of the city, is served by AndoluJet flights (☎0224 781 8015, ⓦanadolulujet.com). Taxis and Burulaş city buses meet the flights. You can also fly to/from Istanbul's Sabiha Gokcen International Airport, from where direct buses to Bursa via the car ferry at Yalova or Topçular depart every 30min (2hr 15min).

Destinations Ankara (1 daily; 55min); Erzurum (1 daily; 40min); Trabzon (1 daily; 1hr 30min).

By bus Bursa's vast *otogar* (☎0224 261 5400, ⓦbursaterminal .com.tr), more commonly called Terminal, complete with restaurants, 24hr left-luggage facility and a tourist information desk, is 10km north of the city centre on the Yalova road. City bus #38 runs straight to Atatürk Cad in Heykel, and #96 serves Çekirge; both take 30–50min depending on traffic.

Destinations Ankara (hourly; 5hr 30min); Ayvalık (5 daily; 5hr); Balıkesir (hourly; 2hr); Bandırma (18 daily; 2hr); Çanakkale (7 daily; 4hr); Eskişehir (every 30min; 2hr 15min); Gölyazı (12–16 daily; 40min); Istanbul, with ferry transfer (every 30min; 3hr); İzmir via Balıkesir and often Ayvalık (hourly; 6hr); Kütahya (8 daily; 3hr); Mudanya and Güzelyalı (every 30min; 30min); Yalova (every 30min; 45min).

By car International rental chains based in Çekirge include Avis, Çekirge Cad 143 (☎0224 236 5133, ⓦavis.com.tr), Europcar, Kürkütlü Cad 39 (☎0224 235 3270, ⓦeuropcar .com.tr), and Sixt, Kürkütlü Cad 33 (☎0224 233 6325,

ⓦsixt.com). Local operators include the city-owned Burulaş Car Rental (☎0224 452 5244, ⓦrent.burulas.com.tr).

By ferry Burulaş transport (ⓦburulas.com.tr) links the ferries arriving on the southern Marmara coast from Istanbul (see p.113). From the Mudanya BUDO ferry terminal, bus #3/F bus runs via Çekirge (40min), through Heykel (50min) and all the way to the *teleferik* (1hr) for Uludağ (see p.179). Alternatively, a Burulaş shuttle bus runs between Emek, the end of the M1 Line on the BursaRay (metro), and the Mudanya and Güzelyalı ferry terminals (both 25min), while bus #1/F links them with the *otogar* (Terminal; 30min).

By seaplane and helicopter The Burulaş 19-passenger seaplane flies between Istanbul's Balt ferry dock on the Golden Horn, and Gemlik on the Sea of Marmara, 24km north of Bursa's city centre and linked by *servis* bus (4 daily; 40min; one-way from ₺140). Burulaş helicopter-taxis (*Helitaksi*) go between the heliports in Bursa on Akpınar Cad, north of Kültür Parkı, and Kadıköy in Istanbul (at least 2 daily; 35min; one-way from ₺425).

By train The bus/TCDD high-speed train combination is a good option for getting to Ankara. Direct buses connect Bursa's *otogar* with the railway station at Eskişehir (every 30min; 2hr 10min) – ensure you get a bus to Eskişehir station (Gar TCDD), not to Eskişehir *otogar* – from where the train takes 1hr 25min to Ankara (ⓦtcdd.gov.tr). Eventually the high-speed railway will reach Bursa itself.

GETTING AROUND

By bus and dolmuş All vehicles run in an anticlockwise direction on the city-centre one-way system. There is a constant stream of buses along Atatürk Cad to most destinations; useful routes include #3/A and #3/F, linking Heykel with the Uludağ *teleferik*. The main city-centre dolmuş stop is behind the Bursa City Museum in Heykel; for other pick-up/set-down points, look for a large "D" sign

(fares from ₺3).

By metro The two BursaRay lines (M1 from Emek and M2 from Üniversite) merge on the west of the city centre and run through to the eastern areas of Kestel and Gürsü. The most useful stations for visitors are Şehreküstü and Demirtaşpaşa on the northern edge of the bazaar district, from where the M1 runs via several stations on the north side of Kültür Parkı

BURULAŞ

Bursa's remarkably sophisticated public transport system including all **buses** (Otobüs), **trams** (Burtram) and the **metro** (BursaRay), is run by the Bursa Büyükşehir Belediyesi (Bursa Metropolitan Municipality). It all falls under **Burulaş**, a conflation of the words Bursa and Ulaşım (transportation). Multifunctional **tickets** for these (**BuKart**) are sold at kiosks at the main bus stops and stations as well as many newsstands and small shops; look out for BuKart Satış Noktası (BuKart Sales Point) signs. **Fares** cost from ₺4 depending on distance, and BuKarts can be pre-loaded with credit. Burulaş also operates **sea buses** (BUDO: Bursa Deniz Otobüsleri; see above), **seaplanes** (Deniz Uçağı; see above) and **helicopter-taxis** (Helitaksi; see above) across the Sea of Marmara to Istanbul. They even have their own car hire (see above).

Burulaş produces its own **magazine** (English copies available) that can be picked up from main stops, stations and the ferry terminal, containing **transport information**, timetables and fares, all of which is also on the website: ⓦburulas.com.tr.

and Çekirge to Emek (for the ferry terminals).

By tram The Bursa tram network (Burtram) runs on two routes: the red T1 operates in a loop from Stadium to Gazcilar and back, and the green-and-white T3 runs in a straight line from Zafer Plaza shopping mall in the west,

along Cumhuriyet Cad and on to Davutkadı in the east – useful for getting to Yeşil and Emir Sultan (fares from ₺3).

By car Parking is a nightmare – there are never enough central street spaces to be had, and car parks are expensive. Park some way out, and use Burulaş transport or walk to the sights.

INFORMATION

Tourist office The helpful kiosk is on the southwest corner of Orhan Gazi Camii Parki, opposite Ulu Camii (Mon–Fri 8am–noon & 1–5pm, also open Sat in summer; ☎0224 220 1848, ⓦbursa.com.tr).

ACCOMMODATION

There's usually no shortage of reasonably priced hotel beds in Bursa. Wealthier foreigners gravitate towards the luxurious spa-hotels at Çekirge, which also has a cluster of modest establishments, around the Birinci Murat Camii. If your prime interest is monumental Bursa, staying in the bazaar or Hisar districts makes more sense.

BAZAAR DISTRICT

Artıç Atatürk Cad, Ulu Cami Karşısı 95 ☎0224 223 5505, ⓦartichotel.com. Set slightly back from Atatürk Cad, this standard business hotel has seventy rooms with all the usual amenities, though very small bathrooms; a few larger suites come with city views. The staff are friendly, and the plentiful breakfast is served in a glass-fronted restaurant looking directly across at the Ulu Cami. ₺185

Çeşmeli Gümüşçeken Cad 6 ☎0224 224 1511. Welcoming budget hotel, predominantly run by women, which takes it's name from the marble drinking fountain set into the outside wall. Offers spacious, comfortable rooms (if a little dated), with double-glazing to buffer the noise, a very good buffet breakfast, and there's a parking garage at the back. ₺130

Efehan Gümüşçeken Cad 34 ☎0224 225 2260, ⓦefehan.com.tr. This good value three-star hotel has tasteful rooms, some with mountain views and all with spacious bathrooms, TV and a/c. The top-floor breakfast room offers sweeping city panoramas, the lobby has quirky knick-knack decor, and there's parking nearby. ₺155

Güneş İnebey Cad 75 ☎0224 224 1404, ⓦhotelgunes .weebly.com. The closest thing to a hostel in Bursa, this slightly tatty but clean and friendly family-run budget *pansiyon* in a converted Ottoman house has laminate-floor rooms with shared bathrooms. A simple breakfast is ₺8 extra. Singles, triples and quads available. ₺70

HISAR

★**Kitap Evi** Burç Üstü 21, in from Saltanat Kapısı ☎0224 225 4160, ⓦkitapevi.com.tr. Bursa's only true boutique hotel was originally an avant-garde bookstore. Eclectically decorated throughout, there's a range of themed rooms (some old-fashioned, some contemporary

in design) and suites with dark-wood floors and (often) freestanding baths. The front rooms (and roof suite) have glorious city views but some noise; quieter units face the rear-garden breakfast café/restaurant. Limited street parking. ₺305

Safran Ortapazar Cad, Arka Sok 4, inside Saltanat Kapısı ☎0224 224 7216, ⓦsafranotel.com. A converted Ottoman wooden-house hotel with atmospheric common areas. The ten varying size a/c rooms themselves are blandly modern and a bit overpriced, but there are ample breakfasts and friendly, helpful staff. Limited parking on the front street available. ₺280

ÇEKİRGE

★**Divan** Dr. Rüştü Burlu Cad 11 ☎0224 234 265 1000, ⓦdivan.com.tr. Stylish, modern and well-priced hotel with 105 a/c rooms built in a tiered block, all with balconies, TV and neat glass-walled bathrooms. Good facilities include an outdoor pool, a vast indoor thermal pool with spa, restaurant, patisserie and car park. The BursaRay Kültürpark station is 300m away. ₺290

Gold Butik Brinici Murat Cami Arkasi 17 ☎0224 232 1964, ⓦhotelgold.com.tr. Also known as *Gold 2*, this much-altered eighteenth-century building is one of the few budget hotels in town, with laminate floor rooms, a creaky lift, pleasant breakfast/bar area, and some parking out front. Some top-floor rooms have balconies; no. 401 has a view of the mosque domes. ₺140

Gönlüferah City Murat Cad 20 ☎0224 233 9500, ⓦwww.gonluferah.com. Four-star hotel whose ninety well-equipped rooms have medium-dark veneer trim and marble sinks, some with great views over the city. There's an adjoining hamam and spa, as well as a decent terrace restaurant and secure parking. ₺280

EATING

Bursa's **cuisine** is solidly meat-oriented and served in a largely alcohol-free environment. For licensed restaurants, head to the pedestrianized **Sakarya Caddesi** between Altıparmak Caddesi and the walls of Hisar above – the former fish market and main commercial street of the **Jewish quarter** now make an atmospheric venue for an outdoor fish dinner on a summer's evening.

BURSA CUISINE

The most famous local recipes are **İskender kebabı** (essentially *döner kebap* soaked in a rich butter, tomato and yoghurt sauce) and **İnegöl köftesi** (rich little pellets of mince sometimes laced with cheese, when they're known as *kaşarlı köfte*). The city is also famous for its **kestane şekeri** (candied chestnuts), sold ubiquitously within a 50km radius. If you're sick of Turkish sponge-bread, look out for Bursan **kepekli** (whole bran) loaves at any bakery.

2

Arap Şükrü Sakarya Cad 6 & 27, Tophane. This cobblestoned lane is known locally as Arap Şükrü Sokağı, after the owner of the first restaurant here. The pedestrianized lane now offers a dozen restaurants all named after the original and owned by descendents of Arap Şükrü, all offering near-identical fish dishes (₺18–35) and *mezes* (from ₺5) displayed on trays, and beer, wine or rakı to wash it down. However, the bill may come as a bit of a surprise if you don't ask prices first. Daily noon–11pm.

Çiçek İzgara Belediye Cad 15 ☎0224 221 1288, ⓦcicekizgara.com. The original of what is now a popular Bursa chain, this overlooks the leafy square behind the town hall and is known for its signature meatball dish *kaşarlı köfte* (₺10), as well as *sütlü kadayıf*, a pudding of shredded wheat in a milk sorbet (₺7). Mon–Sat noon–3pm & 7–10pm.

★**Fayton Müze** TOFAŞ Bursa Anatolian Cars and Carriages Museum, Kapıcı Cad ☎0224 327 3777. Eat in the stylish interior or the flowering garden at this delightful restaurant in the TOFAŞ museum (see p.172). An excellent menu of both local and non-Turkish meals including cooked breakfasts, pizza, home-made pasta, club sandwiches and chicken schnitzel (mains ₺16–30), plus draught Efes beer (₺12) and an excellent choice of wine by the glass (₺20). Daily 9am–midnight.

Hacıbey İskender Taşkapı Sok 4, off Atatürk Cad, Heykel. This tiny, two-storey establishment claims to be the original *İskender* salon, with decor of old wood, fake Ottoman tiles and photos of Olde Bursa. Their *İskender* is good, though you pay extra for the ambience. Mains ₺20. Daily noon–11pm.

Kebapçı İskender Unlu Cad 7A, Heykel ☎0224 221 1076, ⓦiskender.com.tr. This fake Ottoman building is another local claimant as the inventor of the namesake dish, supposedly in 1867 – and that's about all they serve. It's always packed, even though it's moderately expensive (₺23 and up for smallish portions). Now a chain, there's another on Atatürk Cad, near the Kültür Merkezi. Daily 11am–9pm.

Mahfel Namazgah Cad 2, southeast side of Setbaşı Bridge ☎0224 326 8888. Supposedly Bursa's oldest café, serving slightly pricey Western snacks but lovely, reasonably priced puddings (₺6–8), and there are shady tables on its riverside terrace. Daily 8am–10pm.

Maviyel Café Tuğsa İş Merkezi, Haşim İşcan Cad 27 ☎0224 225 5724, ⓦmaviyelcafe.com. Outside the northeast exit of the Şehreküstü BursaRay (metro) station and on the thirteenth floor of an office block, this is worth coming to for the outstanding views – perhaps some of the best in Bursa – from its rooftop terrace of the old city sprawled across the foothills of Uludağ. The menu is nothing fancy, but there's a decent choice of burgers, *köfte*-style meals and desserts (₺6–12). Daily 1–11pm.

Üç Köfte Hacı İvaz Paşa Çarşısı 3 ☎0224 221 9205. The name of this long-established spot, in the north of the covered bazaar, means "three (*İnegöl*-style) meatballs", and that's what you get, served up three times so the food on your plate is always piping hot. Mains ₺10–15. Tues–Sun noon–9.30pm.

ENTERTAINMENT

Kültür Parkı Açıkhava Tiyatrosu (Open Air Theatre) Kültür Parkı; access off Çekirge Cad. The main venue (tickets ₺17–22) for musical performances of the annual Uluslarası Bursa Festival (May–June; ⓦbursafestivali.org), mostly showcasing popular Turkish acts but also with a token roster of foreign performers.

Tayyare Kültür Merkezi Atatürk Cad, Heykel ☎0224 220 8847. Built in 1932, this handsome, restored cultural centre hosts art exhibitions and occasional concerts. Bill-posters outside advertise what's on.

DIRECTORY

Hamams Try the baths at Çekirge (see p.175) or the central, historic Çakır Ağa Hamamı, located just below Hisar on Cemal Nadir Cad (men and women; 6am–midnight; ₺25; massage ₺15).

Hospitals Devlet (State) Hastanesi, Hasta Yurdu Cad, Hisar (☎0224 280 2800); Uludağ Üniversite Hastanesi, P. Tezok Cad, Hastane Sok, Çekirge (☎0224 295 0000).

Around Bursa

A couple of worthwhile targets for half-day or even overnight outings are located immediately around Bursa. The picturesque rural Ottoman village of **Cumalıkızık** is one of the components of the newly declared UNESCO World Heritage Site, which is further enhancing its tourism potential, while the mountain resort of **Uludağ** is a year-round attraction.

Further afield, the 120km route west from Bursa towards Bandırma port is enlivened by two large but shallow lakes, the largest inland bodies of water in the historical region of Mysia. The first, 36km from central Bursa, is **Uluabat Gölü**, home to the appealing village of **Gölyazı** built atop the ancient settlement of Apollonia, while the second lake, **Manyas Gölü**, southeast, supports a bird sanctuary.

2

Cumalıkızık

Buses stop in the village square; catch Buruleş bus #22 (every 90min; 45min) from Atatürk Caddesi in Heykel

The showcase village of **CUMALIKIZIK**, set on the lower slopes of Uludağ, and now practically a neighbourhood of Bursa, 17km from the city centre on the Ankara road (D200) – head east, then south – is the most attractive of several such *kizik* (valley) villages in the region. While the earliest records of the village mosque and hamam date from 1685, it's thought to be at least three centuries older. Cumalıkızık's cobbled streets are full of traditional dwellings, some restored and painted, others leaning brokenly into each other.

The narrow **alleys** that radiate from the village square, dominated by two enormous plane trees, are often only wide enough for pedestrians and pack animals. The ground and first floors of the **village houses** traditionally harboured the storerooms and stables, while the living quarters with their latticed bay windows were upstairs under tiled eaves. Many of the surviving double-front doors sport large-headed nails, wrought-iron strips and massive handles.

ACCOMMODATION	CUMALIKIZIK

★**Mavi Boncuk** Saldede Sok ☎0224 208 1055, ⓦmaviboncukkonukevi.com. This delightful *pansiyon* in a pair of old village houses exudes a welcoming, rustic charm, with creaky floorboards, granny-style embroidered pillows and home-made jams. The small but comfortable and private rooms sit upstairs, while downstairs is a quaint, lush garden and an open-sided veranda. The restaurant (daily 8am–8.30pm), open to non-guests, serves an excellent breakfast and other meals using fresh herbs, good olive oil and home-made bread (mains from ₺8). ₺140

Uludağ

The dramatic, often cloud-cloaked massif of 2543m-high **Uludağ** (or "Great Mountain") presides over Bursa, its northern reaches dropping precipitously into the city. In ancient times it was known as the Mount Olympos of Mysia, one of nearly twenty peaks around the Aegean so named (Olympos was possibly a generic Phoenician or Doric word for "mountain"). Locals insist this was the seat from which the gods watched the battle of Troy. Early in the Christian era the range became a refuge for monks and hermits, replaced after the Ottoman conquest by Muslim dervishes.

The teleferik

These days the upper reaches are designated as the **Uludağ Milli Parkı (Uludağ National Park)**, which is a popular winter sports destination, as well as a summer spot for picnics and hiking. Getting there is half the fun, especially if you opt for the **teleferik** (cable car; see p.180), which links the mountain with the Teleferüç borough of Bursa. It first travels up to the picnic grounds at **Sarıalan** (1635m), where a cluster of *et mangals* and *kendin pişin kendin ye* (cook-it-yourself establishments) await your custom. Since a 2014 extension of the *teleferik*, it now continues for another 6km from Sarıalan into the **skiing** area, known as **Oteller**, which lies at 1810m. If heights aren't your thing, you can take a taxi or dolmuş all the way from central Bursa to Oteller (see p.176).

Hiking

Out of ski season there are a few kilometres of marked **hiking** trails from the top of Oteller. A few hours' walking brings you to glacial **lakes** in a wild, rocky setting just

2

SKIING AT ULUDAĞ

The **ski season** runs from December to late March, though it's better earlier in the season when the snow is more powdery. Uludağ's slopes are not that steep – there are no "black" runs – and are generally fairly short, so are best (and fun) for beginners and families.

Oteller has a dense cluster of nearly thirty **hotels** (see below), as well as plenty of **restaurants**, **cafés** and **shops**, and skiers can make use of the eight chair lifts and several T-bars to access the 13 **ski runs**, which in total cover 28km. At the time of writing, **passes** for the public ski-lifts (daily in season 9am–4pm) cost ₺50 for four hours or ₺70 for the day, and are sold at booths or at the hotels. There are also a few private chair lifts run by hotels. You can rent ski equipment and clothes on the spot from **hire shops** are at the base of the slopes; expect to pay in the region of ₺30–50 for boots, skis and poles or snowboards and about ₺10 extra per item for the likes of helmets or ski-wear. Lessons go for about ₺80 for 50min–1hr.

---

below the summit and high above the trees, crowds and jeep tracks, you just might glimpse patches of the distant Sea of Marmara to the north. The best months for hiking are May and June, with wildflowers in bloom, or September and October, when the mist is less dense.

ARRIVAL AND DEPARTURE ULUDAĞ

By teleferik Bursa Teleferik connects Teleferüç in Bursa to Oteller on Uludağ (daily 8am–8pm; ₺20 one-way, ₺30 return, Burulaş BuKarts are also accepted; ☏0224 444 6345, ⓦteleferik.com.tr). You can reach the lower cable-car station in Teleferüç via dolmuş from the stop behind the Bursa City Museum or by a number of buses, including #3/A from Atatürk Caddesi in Heykel. Bus #94 goes straight from the *otogar*, and #3/F from the Mudanya BUDO ferry terminal. The cable cars are wheelchair-accessible, and the lower station has coffee shops and a car park. The price is the same whether you go to Sarıalan, Oteller or both, so you can break up your journey; each leg takes about 20min.

By dolmuş Dolmuşes from both Orhangazi Cad in Hisar and Kent Meydanı at the northern end of Fevzi Çakmak Cad go all the way to Oteller, along 32km of paved, twisty road (₺12; 1hr 30min).

By car The 32km road to Oteller from Bursa veers off above Çekirge and climbs rapidly through successive vegetation zones. It's 22km to the gate of Uludağ Milli Parkı (₺10/car), from where it's another 12km to Oteller; this final stretch of road beyond the gate is very rough cobble, designed to prevent drivers from skidding – or speeding – so allow nearly an hour for the trip. In bad weather, you may not be allowed to make the journey unless there are chains on your wheels.

ACCOMMODATION

The many **resorts** at the road's end in Oteller hold around 7500 hotel beds. There's little to distinguish each resort from the next; all are listed on ⓦturkeyskihotels.com. Summer rates can dip as low as ₺160/night, but expect to pay up to ₺500 (full board) in ski season. **Camping** is not recommended; the national park campsites are squalid and always full in summer.

Gölyazı

Bus #5/G links Gölyazı with Bursa's Küçük Sanayı metro station; if driving, look for an inconspicuous sign, 31km west of Bursa on the E90, that indicates the 5km side road to the village

Largely constructed on an island that's now lashed by a causeway to the shore of **Uluabat Gölü**, **GÖLYAZI** is an atmospheric community of storks' nests and a few surviving half-timbered houses daubed with rust-tint or ochre paint. Bits of Roman and Byzantine **Apollonia** have unconcernedly been pressed into domestic service, with extensive courses of wall ringing the island's shoreline.

In the smaller mainland neighbourhood, the huge **Saint Panteleimon** Greek church, large enough for a few hundred parishioners, has recently been restored. The lake itself, speckled with nine islets, is only 2m deep, murky and not suitable for swimming, though it does attract waterbirds and short (30min) boat trips can easily be negotiated with the local fishermen. There's a daily (11am) **fish auction** at the island end of the causeway, while women mending nets and rowing boats are much in evidence.

Gölyazı holds no reliable **accommodation**, but there are **teahouses** on either side of the causeway.

EATING   GÖLYAZI

Tarihi Gölyazı Hamam Cafe Right in the middle of the village, behind the mosque ☎0531 383 4178, ⓦgolyazihamamcafe.com. An attraction in its own right, this atmospheric café is in the village's old Byzantine bathhouse, with tables both inside (heated by a wooden stove) and outside in the pretty courtyard. The menu includes reasonably priced mains (₺7–16) including yayın (catfish) and turna (pike) from the lake, plus a generous buffet breakfast (₺15). Daily 8.30am–5.30pm.

Bandırma

Bandırma, the largest port on the Southern Marmara, 95km west of Bursa, makes an easy route between Istanbul and the North Aegean. All but flattened during battles in 1922, however, it lacks any atmospheric old quarter or architectural heritage, and in the absence of decent accommodation, it's best to avoid staying here if at all possible. Most services offered by the adjacent ferry and train terminals connect, while the edge-of-town *otogar* offers abundant departures to the major regional centres.

ARRIVAL AND DEPARTURE   BANDIRMA

By ferry The port is in the heart of town, and is served by IDO (ⓦido.com.tr) car and passenger ferries to and from Yenikapı in Istanbul.
Destinations Istanbul (2–4 daily; 2hr 30min).
By train The station adjoins the ferry port. The schedules connecting the ferries at Bandırma with TCDD trains (ⓦtcdd.gov.tr) to/from İzmir are not all well coordinated; it may be quicker to get the bus to İzmir (4hr).
Destinations İzmir (2 daily; 5hr 30min).

By bus and dolmuş The main *otogar* is on the southern outskirts of town, 1800m inland and uphill from the ferry terminal. Catch a taxi, or a city bus labelled "Garaj/600 Evler", from a marquee 200m east of the ferry terminal.
Destinations Bergama (4 daily; 4hr); Bursa (18 daily; 2hr); Çanakkale via Lapseki (8 daily; 2hr 45min); İzmir (17 daily; 4hr 30min); Lapseki (8 daily; 2hr 15min); Manisa (2 daily; 4hr 45min).

Kuş Cenneti Milli Parkı

Northeast corner of Manyas Gölü, off the E90, 19km southeast of Bandırma • Daily 9am–6pm • ₺5 • No public transport

The **Kuş Cenneti Milli Parkı** (**Bird Paradise National Park**) spreads for 160 acres across a stream delta and swamps at the northeast corner of the **Manyas Gölü** lake. Its small visitor centre is filled with dioramas, labelled in Turkish, and stocked with stuffed geese, orioles, spoonbills, herons, pelicans, ducks, egrets and owls. More interesting, though, is the wooden **observation tower** (bring your own binoculars), from where you can view pelicans (white and Dalmatian, nesting in May), smews, spoonbills, spotted eagles and night herons, with cormorants and grey herons also common. The best months to visit are October – during the first rains, and various species' southward migrations – and April and May, when the swamps are at their fullest and the birds are flying north. During these migrations, up to 178 species stop by, adding to the 80 or so already resident.

While there are no facilities in the park grounds, **Eski Sığırcı** village, 1.5km before the gate, has a simple roadside restaurant with a couple of *pansiyon* rooms.

The North Aegean

SARDIS

The North Aegean

In antiquity, Turkey's North Aegean was known as Aeolia, and provided the setting for the Trojan War. Civilization first bloomed here under the Phrygians, who arrived in Anatolia during the thirteenth century BC. Later, Greek colonists established coastal settlements, leaving the region rich in Classical and Hellenistic remains. These days, however, it sees far fewer visitors than the coastline further south. While there are some excellent sandy beaches surrounded by pine and olive-clad hills, the lower sea temperature has protected the region from widespread development. Most summer visitors are Turks from Istanbul, and away from the few resorts, farming, fishing and heavy industry (near İzmir) provide the main livelihoods.

While the sparse ruins of **Troy** don't quite live up to their literary and legendary reputation, ancient **Assos** and **Pergamon** (modern **Bergama**) display more tangible reminders of the power and wealth of the greater Greek cultural sphere. Less visited are the recently excavated ruins of **Alexandria Troas**, and the isolated Lydian city of **Sardis**, ancient capital of King Croesus, huddled at the foot of impressive mountains.

If you're coming from Istanbul or anywhere else in northwest Turkey, the most obvious entry point is **Çanakkale** – useful as a base for both Troy and the World War I battlefields on the **Gelibolu** (Gallipoli) peninsula. Offshore, the fine Turkish Aegean islands of **Gökçeada** and **Bozcaada** provide an easy escape. The road south from Çanakkale is wooded and gently hilly, giving way to a coastal strip backed by the mountains of the Kazdağı range that conceal idyllic villages like **Yeşilyurt** and **Adatepe**. Further south, the best stretches of beach lie near the long-established resort of **Ayvalık-Cunda**, but there are also pleasant sands north of **Foça**.

There's less to see **inland**, with a mountainous landscape and a few predominantly industrial cities. However, the **İzmir–Bandırma railway** provides an alternative approach to the region, passing through unremarkable Balıkesir (from where frequent buses run to Ayvalık), Soma (a short bus ride from Bergama), and **Manisa** – the only town worthy of prolonged attention. The other option is to approach the region by flying into İzmir, from where there's good transport north along the E87 coastal highway.

Çanakkale

Blessed with a superb setting on the Dardanelles straits, **ÇANAKKALE** is a vibrant harbour town with a multicultural past that held significant Greek, Jewish and Armenian populations, and even foreign consuls – the Italian one donated the clock tower in 1897. The name Çanakkale means "Pottery Castle", after the unique local brown, green and yellow glazed ceramics that were first popular in the nineteenth

BOZCAADA

Highlights

❶ Battlefield sites and cemeteries The Gelibolu (Gallipoli) peninsula was the scene of a major Allied defeat during World War I, commemorated each April on Anzac Day. **See p.195**

❷ Gökçeada Turkey's largest island is a scenic, rugged place, with idyllic beaches and a lingering ethnic-Greek presence. **See p.196**

❸ Bozcaada (Tenedos) This small, popular island has an elegant harbour town, fine wines and decent beaches. **See p.199**

❹ Assos The ancient site offers stunning views of Lésvos island: the hilltop medieval village and

picturesque harbour are built of the same volcanic stone. **See p.204**

❺ Ayvalık and Cunda Relax in these adjacent, former Greek olive-oil-processing ports, with their intriguing mix of restored Greek and Ottoman houses. **See p.207**

❻ Ancient Pergamon Both the Acropolis, with its sweeping views and restored temple, and the Asklepion downhill rank among the finest Roman ruins in the Aegean. **See p.213**

❼ Sardis With an evocative Artemis temple and restored baths, these remote ruins reward a detour inland. **See p.220**

HIGHLIGHTS ARE MARKED ON THE MAP ON P.186

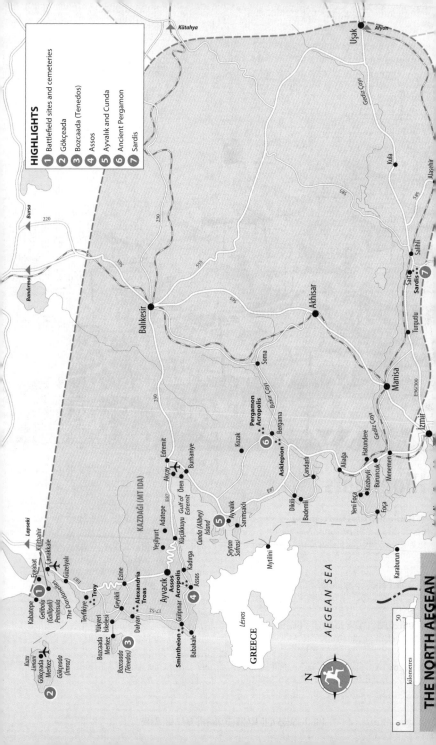

THE NORTH AEGEAN

AEGEAN SEA

GREECE

N

kilometres
0   50

THE WEARY WATERS OF THE DARDANELLES

The **Dardanelles** (Çanakkale Boğazı), the straits that connect the Aegean with the Sea of Marmara, have defined Çanakkale's history and its place in myth. The area's Classical name, **Hellespont**, derives from Helle, who, escaping from her wicked stepmother on the back of a winged ram, fell into the swift-moving channel and drowned. From Abydos on the Asian side, the youth **Leander** used to swim to Sestos on the European shore for trysts with his lover **Hero**, until one night he too perished in the currents; in despair, Hero drowned herself as well. In 1810, enthusiastic swimmer **Lord Byron** succeeded in crossing the channel only on his second attempt – a feat he often claimed as his greatest-ever achievement.

Persian hordes under **Xerxes** crossed these waters on their way to Greece in 480 BC, and in 411 and 405 BC the last two naval battles of the Peloponnesian War took place in the straits; the latter engagement ended in decisive defeat for the Athenian fleet. Twenty centuries later, **Mehmet the Conqueror** constructed the elaborate fortresses of Kilitbahir and Çimenlik Kale, across from each other, to tighten the stranglehold being applied to doomed Constantinople.

In March 1915, an Allied fleet attempting to force the Dardanelles and attack Istanbul was repulsed by Turkish shore batteries, with severe losses, prompting the even bloodier land campaign usually known as **Gallipoli**. These days the straits are still militarized, and modern Çanakkale is very much a navy town.

3

---

century and, which have found their way into the ethnographic section of every Turkish museum. While the town undeniably makes a convenient base for the World War I battlefields at Gallipoli, on the European side of the Dardanelles, Çanakkale itself deserves at least an overnight stop, with a couple of interesting sights and a nightlife scene that positively hums in the summer. The compact old quarter with its well-restored bazaar is a good place to poke around, and the busy seafront is home to a replica of the **Trojan horse** used in the 2004 film *Troy*. It's also the starting point for sea buses to the Turkish Aegean islands of Gökçeada and Bozcaada.

Çimenlik Park

Naval Museum • Çimenlik Sok • Tues–Sun 9am–noon & 1.30–5pm • ₺6.50 • ☏ 0286 217 1707

Çimenlik Park, beyond the bazaar, contains Sultan Mehmet II's castle, **Çimenlik Kale**, built in 1462, and an assortment of torpedoes and artillery from various countries. It's also home to the **Naval Museum** (Deniz Müzesi), which holds more military paraphernalia, as well as photos of Seddülbahir in ruins after Allied shelling, and of Atatürk's funeral.

Also within the park, there's a moored replica of the minelayer **Nusrat**, which stymied the Allied fleet in March 1915 by re-mining, at night, zones that the French and British had swept clean by day.

Archeological Museum

Barbaros Mahalessi, 100-Yil Cad; almost 2km south of the town centre along Atatürk Cad • Daily 8am–7pm, Nov–March till 5pm • ₺5 • ☏ 0286 217 2371, ⊛ muze.gov.tr • Served by any Atatürk Cad dolmuş labelled "Kepez" or "Güzelyalı"

The poorly labelled and badly lit collection in Çanakkale's **Archeological Museum** (Arkeoloji Müzesi) is strong on brass implements, delicate glass and glazed pottery, gold and jewellery, unfired lamps, and Hellenistic figurines from the nearby Bozcaada and Dardanos tumuli. The highlights, however, are two exquisite **sarcophagi**: the late Archaic "Polyxena", in perfect condition, with a procession on one side and the sacrifice (in grisly detail) of Priam's daughter on the other, and the fourth-century BC "Altıkulaç", more damaged but showing a finely detailed boar hunt and battle scene with a mounted warrior spearing a victim. The **garden** too is quite delightful, where pillars and amphorae are set among the rose bushes.

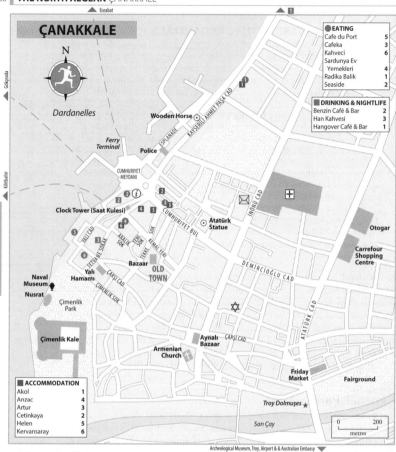

ARRIVAL AND DEPARTURE

ÇANAKKALE

By ferry Ferries run by Gestaş (☏ gestasdenizulasim.com.tr) from Eceabat, on the Gelibolu peninsula, or from Gökçeada, dock at the base of Cumhuriyet Bulvarı in Çanakkale; those from Kilitbahir dock a block southwest. Tickets for the Çanakkale–Eceabat car ferry are valid to continue the same day from Kabatepe to Gökçeada and vice versa.

Destinations Bozcaada (5 weekly; 55min; no cars); Eceabat (every 30min–1hr; 30min); Gökçeada (2 weekly; 1hr; no cars); Kilitbahir (every 30min–1hr; 15min).

By plane Çanakkale Airport, with domestic flights run by Borajet (☏ borajet.com.tr), is 3km southeast of town (☏ 0286 213 1021). Municipality service buses run between the airport and Cumhuriyet Meyd, in front of the main jetty (daily 7.30am–8pm), and taxis usually await incoming flights.

Destinations Ankara (daily; 1hr 30min); Istanbul (summer daily; 1hr 5min).

By bus or dolmuş Çanakkale's *otogar* is on Atatürk Caddesi, 1km east of the central seafront (15min walk), and is served by free shuttles from bus company offices near the tourist office. For buses crossing the straits, you can usually just board at the ferry docks. Dolmuşes to Troy run from a riverside terminal adjacent to the northern end of the bridge over the Sarı Çay, 1km southeast of the town centre.

Destinations Ayvalık (10 daily; 3hr 45min); Bandırma via Lapseki (8 daily; 2hr 45min); Bursa (8 daily; 4hr 30min); Edirne (3 daily; 3hr 30min); Istanbul (13 daily via Thrace; 6hr 30min); İzmir (11 daily; 5hr 30min); Yükyeri İskelesi via Geyikli (timed to meet Bozcaada ferry; 1hr).

INFORMATION

Tourist office You can pick up bus and ferry timetables plus an excellent, free, pocket-sized city guide at the tourist office

at Cumhuriyet Meyd, next to the main jetty (June–Sept daily 8am–noon & 1–7pm, Oct–May Mon–Fri 8am–noon &

1–5pm; ☎ 0286 217 1187).
Consulate The Australian Embassy has an honorary consul at the *Kolin Hotel*, 3.8km south of the town centre on Boğazkent Mevkii, off Atatürk Cad, near the university (☎ 0286 218 1721, ⓦ turkey.embassy.gov.au).

ACCOMMODATION

Akol Kayserili Ahmet Paşa Cad ☎ 0286 217 9456, ⓦ hotelakol.com.tr. Right on the waterfront, close to the town centre, this multistorey four-star hotel offers a decent level of comfort – albeit rather impersonal – in good-sized rooms with balconies (some with sea views). There's a pool and two restaurants, the better of which is *Radika Balik* (see below). ₺265

★ **Anzac** Saat Kulesi Meyd 8, opposite the clock tower ☎ 0286 217 7777, ⓦ anzachotel.com. A very friendly and welcoming mid-range hotel whose rather grim exterior belies the cheerful, good-value earth-tone rooms with TVs and big bathrooms. The on-site restaurant and separate café are decorated with mirror art, and the English-speaking staff are an excellent source of local information. ₺120

Artur Cumhuriyet Meyd 28 ☎ 0286 213 2000, ⓦ hotelartur.com. The brown, cream and ochre decor of the rooms at this three-star hotel don't quite match the lobby for splendour, but the bathrooms are modern and fair-sized, and there are some superior suites (without balcony, however). There's also a decent ground-floor restaurant, Cafeka (see below). ₺200

Cetinkaya Kızılay Sok 18 ☎ 0286 217 1069, ⓦ cetinkayahotel.com. Well located, with secure parking close by, this is one of the best-value hotels in town. The simply furnished rooms have wooden floors, TV and walk-in showers, accessed by a winding staircase (the one drawback). Not to be confused with *Cetinkaya 2 Hotel*, next door. ₺133

Helen Cumhuriyet Meyd 57 ☎ 0286 212 1818, ⓦ helenhotel.com. A good-value, well-located mid-range hotel. The clean and comfortable rooms have wood-panelled floors and modern bathrooms, but no balconies. There's a pleasant mezzanine where breakfast is taken, plus off-street parking and friendly management. ₺144

★ **Kervansaray** Fetvane Sok 13 ☎ 0286 217 8192, ⓦ canakkalekervansarayhotel.com. Justifiably popular hotel in a 1903 judge's mansion with a more recent rear annexe, with lots of atmosphere and good service. The mansion rooms are boutique-style, with mock *belle époque* furnishings and squeaky wooden floors and staircases; the front ones suffer from street noise, so ask for 206 or 207 facing the lovely central garden. The annexe rooms are less distinguished, perched over the area where the above-average breakfast is served. ₺188

EATING

★ **Cafe du Port** Limani Hotel, Yali Cad 12 ☎ 0286 217 2908. Across from the harbour, this offers elegant surroundings and an affordable, varied continental menu (such as chicken schnitzel, lamb chops and shrimp risotto), as well as a very good breakfast buffet with the likes of croque-monsieur or eggs florentine. It's licensed, with a wine list including local vintages, and the bar livens up in the evening. Breakfast ₺12, mains ₺10–30. Daily 8am–10.30pm.

★ **Cafeka** Cumhuriyet Meyd 28 ☎ 0286 217 4900. A welcoming dining space beneath the *Artur Hotel* (see above), with a jovial ambience and attentive service. The affordable Mediterranean bistro-style menu is a definite departure from local cuisine, with dishes such as salmon fettuccine, chicken fajitas and a marinated steak with parmesan. Mains ₺14–30. Licensed. Daily noon–11pm.

Kahveci Çarşı Cad 14, opposite the Yalı Camii ☎ 0286 217 6168. An inviting café with a small, rustic interior of wooden floors and exposed brick walls, and a few tables on the pavement. The young staff serve proper European cappuccinos and espressos – at European prices (coffee ₺8). Daily 9am–9pm.

Radika Balik Kayserili Ahmet Paşa Cad 1 ☎ 0286 217 9456. On the top floor of the *Akol Hotel* (see above), this has wonderful views from floor-to-ceiling windows over the waterfront and across the Dardenelles. The menu features excellent grilled octopus and fish, and a tasty *karides güveç* (shrimp, vegetable and cheese stew). Mains ₺15–30. Daily noon–10.30pm.

Sardunya Ev Yemekleri Fetvane Sok 11 ☎ 0286 213 9899. The most popular of several similar *ev yemekleri* (home-style cooking) places on this lane, where you can sit on the narrow, vine-shaded patio out back, or in the funky old house. Try the fried sardines or stews of the day. Mains ₺12–25. Licensed. Mon–Sat noon–10.30pm.

Seaside Eski Balikhane Sok 3 ☎ 0286 214 2726. Popular with locals and travellers alike, with designer interior, hovering waiters, outdoor tables and a Western soundtrack. The Mediterranean bistro menu offers pizza, pasta and delicious fish and calamari, perfectly cooked and presented. Breakfast buffet ₺14, mains ₺9–30. Licensed. Daily 9am–11pm.

DRINKING AND NIGHTLIFE

A major university town, Çanakkale has a lively student nightlife, especially along Fetvane Sokağı running south from the clock tower. Bars there change regularly – choose according to the soundtrack and the crowd.

Benzin Café & Bar Eski Balikhane Sok 11 ☎ 0286 212 2237. Consistently among the liveliest bar-cafés along the waterfront, with a few tables outside on the busy pavement and plenty of snug seating in the cosy, wooden interior. The beer (₺8) is always cold and there's also a good menu of light meals (₺5–15) and comfort food. Daily noon–late.

Han Kahvesi Fetvane Sok 28 ☎ 0286 212 2649. The courtyard of the historic *Yalı Hanı* caravanserai is the place for a well-priced tea, coffee (₺3), soft drink, beer (₺7) or nargile

at any hour. There's live music or DJs a few nights a week in the upstairs bar, when prices climb slightly and the student contingent attends in force. Daily 10.30am–midnight.

★ **Hangover Café & Bar** Gazi Bulvarı 32, 1km north of the ferry docks ☎ 0286 217 1393. Aimed at the visiting backpacker fraternity and trendy young Turks, with up-to-date European music and a vast and varied menu, plus cheaper bar snacks. If you're after a quieter meal, go upstairs to the lovely terrace with sea views. Beer ₺9, light meals ₺5–12, mains ₺9–20. Daily 9am–2am.

The Gelibolu peninsula

Burdened with a grim military history, but nonetheless endowed with fine scenery and beaches, the slender **Gelibolu (Gallipoli) peninsula** – roughly 60km long and from 4km to 18km wide – forms the northwest side of the **Dardanelles**. As the site of the 1915 **Gallipoli landings**, the peninsula is scattered with memorials, both Allied and Turkish.

The **World War I battlefields and cemeteries** are a moving sight, the past violence made all the more poignant by the present beauty of the landscape, which consists of fertile rolling country interspersed with thick scrub and pine forest, alive with birds. Much of the flatter land is farmed, and every year ploughing still turns up rusting equipment, fragments of shrapnel, human bones and even unexploded munitions.

The entire area southwest of Eceabat and Kabatepe is a protected **national historical park**. The Allied cemeteries and memorials, built in the early 1920s and mostly designed by Scottish architect Sir John Burnet, replaced and consolidated the makeshift graveyards of 1915. Over half the deceased were never found or identified, however – hence the massive cenotaphs.

The battlefields and cemeteries are also popular with Turkish visitors, many of whom venerate the Turkish fallen as *şehitler*, or martyrs for Islam – in pointed contrast to the secularist narrative spun around the eight-month Gallipoli campaign, which made famous a previously unknown lieutenant-colonel, Mustapha Kemal, later Atatürk.

Eceabat

Most buses arrive at the relevant ticket offices behind the jetty; regular car ferries from Çanakkale (every 30min–1hr; 30min) arrive at the jetty

ECEABAT, 40km south of Gelibolu and diagonally opposite Çanakkale, is a scruffy, quiet place. Without your own transport, however, it makes the most convenient base for touring the battlefields. Next to the ferry dock and hugging the waterfront promenade, is the **Respect for History Park** (Tarihe Saygı Parki), which has a scale model of the Gelibolu peninsula with the main features and battle sites marked.

ACCOMMODATION   ECEABAT

Boss Cumhuriyet Cad 14, on ferry plaza ☎ 0286 814 1464, ⊕ heyboss.com. One of three *Boss* hotels in town, this one overlooks the ferry plaza and offers good-value, modern en-suite rooms, with either wooden or newly carpeted floors; the cheaper singles are exceptionally small, but other rooms sleep up to five. Free parking. ₺105

★ **Crowded House** Huseyin Avni Sok 4, one block inland from ferry plaza ☎ 0286 810 0041, ⊕ hotelcrowdedhouse.com. This friendly, well-managed hotel is the best budget option by far. The 26 double, twin or triple small en-suite rooms are modern and clean and

have TV and a/c. Meals and drinks are available from a very pleasant lobby area that has a mezzanine-level with funky couches, and the hotel's tour company of the same name offers very good battlefields tours (see p.195). ₺88

★ **Gallipoli Houses** Kocadere village, 7km northwest of Eceabat, just off the Kabatepe road ☎ 0286 814 2650, ⊕ www.thegallipolihouses.com. State-of-the-art rooms in this Belgian/Turkish-run place are distributed over a restored main house (with roof terrace) and newer garden units: all have a/c, terraces or balconies, rain showers and under-floor heating. The evening meals (₺45) are a highlight, marrying

Turkish *mezes* with continental mains, plus there's an excellent regional wine and rakı cellar. Advance booking is essential; minimum two-night stay in summer. Closed mid-Nov to mid-March. No public transport to the village. ₺185

TJs Hotel Cumhuriyet Cad 5, just north of ferry plaza

📞 0286 814 3121, 🌐 tjshotel.com. Owned by a Turkish–Australian couple and renovated to good standards with sixteen spacious, modern rooms (one triple) with a/c and TV. There's also a generous breakfast buffet. You can arrange excursion and trips here too, with TJs Tours. ₺172

EATING AND DRINKING

Boomerang Bar Cumhuriyet Cad 102, on the water's edge at the town's northern entrance 📞 0286 814 2144. A scruffy beach shack that was legendary among

Antipodeans for its Anzac Day "celebrations" since owner Mesut opened up in the mid-1990s. The exuberant days have passed somewhat, given that many visitors come

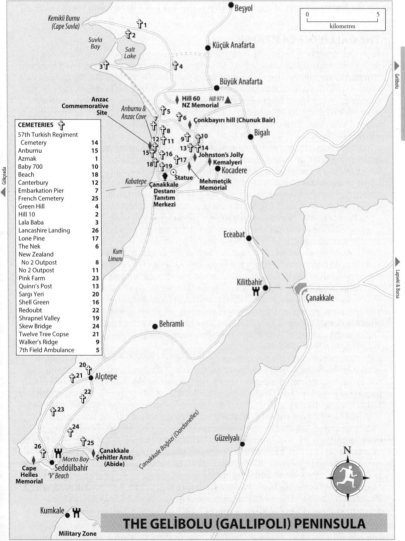

CEMETERIES

57th Turkish Regiment Cemetery	14
Arıburnu	15
Azmak	1
Baby 700	10
Beach	18
Canterbury	12
Embarkation Pier	7
French Cemetery	25
Green Hill	4
Hill 10	2
Lala Baba	3
Lancashire Landing	26
Lone Pine	17
The Nek	6
New Zealand No 2 Outpost	8
No 2 Outpost	11
Pink Farm	23
Quinn's Post	13
Sargı Yeri	20
Shell Green	16
Redoubt	22
Shrapnel Valley	19
Skew Bridge	24
Twelve Tree Copse	21
Walker's Ridge	9
7th Field Ambulance	5

THE GELİBOLU (GALLIPOLI) PENINSULA

to Gallipoli on quick tours from Istanbul, but the *Boomerang* is a welcoming and relaxed place to enjoy a beer (₺6) and Western (read: Aussie and Kiwi) music. Daily 11am–late.

Liman Atatürk Cad 1, at the end of the main street facing into the waterfront park ☎0286 814 2755.

Typical *balık* restaurant with pleasant terrace, well used to tourists on day-trips, with efficient and friendly service. Ask for the catch of the day and you might get sardines or sea bass, if you're lucky. The hot and cold appetizers are also tasty. Mains ₺12–25. Daily noon–10pm.

Kilitbahir

A peaceful, if slightly underwhelming, entry into "Europe" from "Asia", the tiny fishing village of **KILITBAHIR** is 5km south of Eceabat and accessible by ferry from Çanakkale across the narrowest part of the strait. This is the shortest distance and voyage time

---

THE GALLIPOLI CAMPAIGN

Soon after World War I began, the Allies realized that Russia could not be supplied by sea, nor a Balkan front opened against the Central Powers, unless Ottoman Turkey was eliminated. **Winston Churchill**, then the British First Lord of the Admiralty, decided that the quickest way to accomplish this would be to force the Dardanelles with a fleet, and bombard Istanbul into submission. A combined **Anglo-French armada** made several, repulsed attempts on the straits during November 1914, before returning in earnest on March 18, 1915, when they reached 10km up the waterway before striking numerous Turkish mines, losing several vessels and hundreds of crew.

The Allied fleet retreated and regrouped on the Greek island of Límnos to prepare an amphibious assault on Turkish positions along the peninsula. The plan involved an Anglo-French landing at Cape Helles, Seddülbahir and Morto Bay at the mouth of the straits, and a simultaneous **Anzac** (Australia-New Zealand Army Corps) assault at Kabatepe beach, 13km north. The Australians landed first at dawn on April 25, 1915, with the British and French landing an hour afterwards, followed by the New Zealanders later in the day.

This hare-brained scheme ran into trouble immediately. Anglo-French brigades at the southernmost cape were pinned down by Turkish fire, and the French contingent was virtually annihilated; after two days they had only penetrated 6.5km inland, just before Krithia (Alçıtepe) village, and never got any further. The fate of the Anzac landing was even more horrific: owing to a drifting signal buoy, the Aussies and Kiwis disembarked not on the broad sands of Kabatepe, with gentle terrain inland, but at a cramped cove by Arıburnu, 2km north, overlooked by Turkish-held cliffs. Despite heavy casualties (around 2000 on the first day alone), the Australians advanced inland, as the Turks initially retreated. The next day, the Australians threatened the stronghold of Çonkbayırı, where Turkish lieutenant-colonel **Mustafa Kemal** told his poorly equipped, illiterate troops: "I am not ordering you to attack, I am ordering you to die." Turkish reinforcements soon arrived, and the Anzac force never made it further than 800m inland.

A supplementary British landing at northerly Cape Suvla was followed by ferocious assaults on the summit in the middle of August, which the Turks repulsed. Otherwise, the confrontation consisted of stagnant trench warfare; neither side had sufficient artillery to gain a decisive advantage. Finally, in November 1915, the Allies gave up. The last troops left Seddülbahir on January 9, 1916. Churchill's career went into temporary eclipse, while that of Mustafa Kemal, later known as **Atatürk**, was only just beginning (see box, p.662).

At various times, half a million men were deployed at Gallipoli; over fifty percent were killed, wounded or missing. Allied deaths totalled around 46,000, while the Turkish dead are estimated at 86,000. Fatal **casualties** among the Anzacs in particular – around 11,500 – were severe compared to the island-nations' populations, but would be dwarfed by the 48,000 or so Anzacs killed on the western front later in the war.

However, this baptism by blood had several long-term effects for the Anzacs, including a sense that Australia and New Zealand had come of age as sovereign countries, and the designation of April 25 as Anzac Day, a solemn holiday in Australia and New Zealand to both remember Gallipoli and celebrate the nations' self-pride.

(see p.188) across the Dardanelles, but while there are a few teahouses along the shoreline in Kilitbahir, the nearest accommodation is in Eceabat, 5km north (see p.190).

Kilitbahir Kale

Yalı Cad, 1km south of the ferry terminal • Interior closed for refurbishment

Kilitbahir is dwarfed by Sultan Mehmet the Conqueror's massive, irregularly shaped **castle**, also known as *Kilitbahir Kalesi, "Lock on the Sea"*. Constructed in 1452, **Kilitbahir Kale** was built in conjunction with Çimenlik Kale across the strait in Çanakkale, to strengthen the siege on doomed Constantinople. It features a lobed, triangular keep and six steep and precarious stairways leading up to the curtain walls. The imposing seven-storey tower in the walls was built a century later, by Süleyman the Magnificent. At the time of writing, the interior was being refurbished and closed to visitors; in the meantime you can walk around the outside walls.

Namazgah Tabyası

Yalı Cad, on the seaward side of Kilitbahir Kale • Tues–Sun 8.30am–noon & 1.30–5pm • ₺2

The **Namazgah Tabyası** (Namazgah Bastion), a series of half-subterranean bunkers and shore batteries built in the 1890s, formed part of the Ottoman defence system against the Allied fleet during February and March 1915. A large bronze statue of an Ottoman soldier, bare-chested and carrying a massive artillery shell, pays tribute to the Turkish gunners who stood firm against shelling from Allied warships. A small **museum** houses interesting photographs from World War I.

ARRIVAL AND DEPARTURE

KILITBAHIR

By dolmuş Dolmuşes run the 4.5km from Eceabat to Kilitbahir dock (at least every 30min; 20min).

By ferry The fastest and, for drivers, cheapest ferry trip over the Dardanelles crosses its narrowest point, at 1300m, to Çanakkale.

Destinations Çanakkale (every 30min 6.30am–7pm, then hourly/according to demand till 12.15am; 15min).

Kabatepe

9km northwest of Eceabat and 4km south of Anzac Cove

KABATEPE port, the boarding point for the car ferry to the Turkish Aegean island of Gökçeada (see p.196). There's a broad **beach** north of the harbour – intended site of the Anzac landing – and another just south at a forestry picnic ground (admission ₺3). A third beach, 5km south at **Kum Limanı**, is the best of the lot, with warm, clean, calm sea, accessible via the large *Kum Hotel* (see p.194).

Çanakkale Destanı Tanıtım Merkezi

1km uphill and northeast of the ferry terminal in Kabatepe • Daily 8.30am–6pm • ₺10 • ☎ 0286 810 0050

Located on the site of the old **Kabatepe Museum**, the **Çanakkale Destanı Tanıtım Merkezi** (Çanakkale Epic Presentation Centre) reopened in 2012 after being completely rebuilt and now features eleven galleries on four floors. On display are archive photos, maps, weapons, trenching tools, uniforms, mess-kits, personal effects – such as touching letters home – and a few human remains, including a Turkish skull with a bullet lodged in it and a discarded shoe with parts of foot bones still in it. There are several audiovisual and interactive exhibits; refreshingly, the new facility tells the story from both Turkish and Anzac points of view.

ARRIVAL AND DEPARTURE

KABATEPE

By dolmuş Dolmuşes connect the ferry dock at Kabatepe with that of Eceabat (every 30min–1hr; 20min).

By ferry Tickets on the Çanakkale–Eceabat car ferry (see p.188) are valid to continue the same day from Kabatepe to Gökçeada, and vice versa.

Destinations Gökçeada (June–Sept 6–8 daily; Oct–May 3 daily at 10am, 3pm & 7pm; 1hr 20min).

ANZAC DAY

Anzac Day, April 25, is the busiest day of the year on the Gelibolu peninsula, when up to ten thousand Australians and New Zealanders arrive to commemorate the Allied defeat and remember ancestors who lost their lives.

The day begins with the 5.30am **Dawn Service** at Anzac Cove and the service features official speeches, prayers, and a member of the Australian or New Zealand forces playing a poignant "Last Post" at sunrise. **Wreaths** are laid at the British, French and Turkish memorials, and most Australians walk 3.1km up Artillery Road to the Lone Pine Memorial for the one-hour **service** at 11am; New Zealanders continue a further 3.3km uphill to Chunuk Bair for the one-hour service at 12.30pm.

The whole experience can be very special and moving but go prepared: you can expect to walk up to 10km during the commemorative period, so ensure you carry warm and wet weather gear and appropriate footwear, as it will be several hours before you get back to your vehicle again. Alcohol is strictly banned at all the cemeteries and memorials.

ACCOMMODATION

Kum Hotel Kum Limanı ☎ 0286 814 1455, ⓦ hotelkum .com. Average resort-style hotel with old, bland rooms in two-storey concrete blocks, plus various bars and swimming pools, and a restaurant that serves up repetitive buffet meals, but there's nowhere else to eat; room rates include half board. There's also a grassed site for caravans (₺40) and camper vans (no tents). There's a pleasant private beach, and this is the closest hotel to Anzac Cove. Closed Nov–March. **₺210**

West-coast cemeteries and memorials

The first sites along the coast road north of Kabatepe are the **Beach**, **Shrapnel Valley** and **Shell Green** cemeteries – the latter 300m inland up a steep track, suitable only for 4WD vehicles. Shrapnel Valley was the one perilous supply line up-valley from what's now the Beach Cemetery to the trenches.

These are followed by **Anzac Cove** and **Arıburnu**, site of the first, bungled Anzac landing. For many years these ceremonies were held at Arıburnu Cemetery, the resting place of 182 Australians, but the number of people attending grew so large that the Anzac Commemorative Site was opened in 2000, 300m to the north.

Looking inland, you'll see the murderous badlands – including the eroded pinnacle overhead nicknamed "The Sphinx" by the hapless Australians – that gave the defenders such an advantage (see box, p.491). Beyond Anzac Cove, the terrain flattens out and the four other cemeteries (Canterbury, No. 2 Outpost, New Zealand No. 2 Outpost and Embarkation Pier) are more dispersed.

Good dirt tracks lead north from Arıburnu to the beaches and salt lake at **Cape Suvla**, today renamed Kemikli Burnu ("bone-strewn headland"), location of four more cemeteries of August casualties, mostly English, Scottish, Welsh and Irish.

Central inland sites

A one-way road, roughly following what was the front line, leads uphill and northeast from the Kabatepe Museum to the former strongholds (now cemeteries) scattered around **Çonkbayırı** hill (Chunuk Bair).

Beside the road, a massive **statue** depicts a purported incident from the first day of landings – a Turk carrying a wounded Australian officer back to his lines – supposedly witnessed by another officer who later, as Lord Casey, became Governor-General of Australia. However, Casey didn't mention the incident in his memoirs, and wasn't even at that sector of the lines, so the statue is best viewed as an allegory of the chivalry that (sometimes) prevailed in the campaign.

Just beyond is **Lone Pine** (Kanlı Sırt), the lowest strategic position on the ridge and the largest graveyard-cum-memorial to those buried unmarked or at sea. Just above is the **Mehmetcik memorial** to the Turkish soldiers who perished, while at **Johnston's Jolly** (named after an artillery officer who liked to "jolly the Turks up" with his gun) there's a section of **trench** beneath the pine trees. All along the ridge, opposing trenches lay within a few metres of each other, but most are reconstructions; the modern road corresponds to the no-man's-land in between. British/Anzac ones followed a zigzag course, while the Turks adopted the German dogtooth pattern.

Further along, on the right, is the **57th Turkish Regiment Cemetery**, whose men Mustafa Kemal ordered to their deaths, thus buying time for reinforcements to arrive. Here the religious aspect of the campaign for contemporary Turks is made clear, with an inscription eulogizing martyrdom and a small open-air prayer area. To the right, a road goes uphill to **Baby 700** cemetery, marking the furthest Allied advance on April 25.

Back on the main road, the route continues uphill and left to the massive New Zealand memorial obelisk and the five-monolith Turkish memorial atop **Çonkbayırı hill** (Chunuk Bair). This also marks the spot where Atatürk's pocket-watch stopped a fragment of shrapnel, saving his life. Just beyond, **The Nek** is the scene of the futile charge and massacre of the Australian Light Horse Brigade.

3

VISITING THE BATTLEFIELDS AND CEMETERIES

Whether you visit the battlefields independently or on a tour, **Çanakkale**, and **Eceabat** in the south of the peninsula, make the best bases; modern Gelibolu town at the northern end of the peninsula is too far away.

The numerous open-air sites have **no admission fees** or fixed opening hours. Even with your own transport, you'll need a day – two for enthusiasts – to see the major cemeteries and cenotaphs. You'll also want time to wander a little, take in the natural beauty and, in season, swim. Outside the villages of Eceabat and Seddülbahir there are few amenities, so lunch stops must be carefully planned.

It's also possible to visit the sites using a combination of minibus rides and walking. Dolmuşes run from Eceabat to Kilitbahir and Kabatepe docks. You can walk around the main sites north of the museum in Kabatepe within a couple of hours. At Kilitbahir, minibuses meet the Çanakkale car ferries in summer and take passengers to Seddülbahir via Alçıtepe, from where you can tour the surrounding cemeteries and memorials on foot. It's also usually possible to **rent mountain bikes** in Eceabat (try *TJs Hotel*; see p.191), although some roads are steep, and secondary tracks can be rough and muddy in winter.

GUIDED TOURS

There's little to choose between the many companies that offer **guided tours** of the battlefields – all should have licensed, English-speaking guides with a thorough knowledge of the sites. All tours from Çanakkale or Eceabat tend to cost the same (around ₺120 per head), be the same length (5hr; in the afternoon), and visit identical sites, usually including lunch. Itineraries, with a strong Anzac emphasis, don't stray much from a core area just north of the park boundary, and visit – in this order – the Kabatepe Museum, several beach cemeteries nearby, the Lone Pine cemetery, Johnston's Jolly, the Turkish 57th Regiment cemetery, The Nek and Çonkbayırı hill.

Crowded House Huseyin Avni Sok 4, Eceabat ☎0286 814 1565, ⓦcrowdedhousegallipoli.com. By far the best of the conventional tours. For an additional ₺35, they offer a morning's add-on of snorkelling over the *Milo*, a partially sunk Allied ship. You need to be fit enough to swim the 75m from the shore to the wreck and back.

Hassle Free Travel Agency Çanakkale ☎0286 213 5969, ⓦanzachouse.com. Recommended operator offering the standard tour from Çanakkale, and return tours from Istanbul (snorkelling option ₺30 extra).

Kenan Çelik Çanakkale ☎0286 217 7468 or ☎0532 738 6675, ⓦkcelik.com. If you have your own transport, consider hiring the best private guide to the battlefields, Kenan Çelik, who leads 6hr standard tours or full-day tours which include the Turkish sites too.

Southern peninsula sites

Beyond the rural hamlet of **Alçıtepe**, at the entrance to the southern section of the peninsula, assorted cemeteries, consequences of the landing at Cape Helles, and the huge British **Cape Helles Memorial**, lie scattered towards Seddülbahir. The views are magnificent, with abundant **Ottoman fortifications** hinting at the age-old importance of the place. Tucked between the medieval bulwarks is the **V Beach** of the Allied expedition, behind which lies the largest of the local British cemeteries.

Alçıtepe

There's not much to **ALÇITEPE**, other than a few souvenir stands and teahouses, and its vague significance as the objective of the first day of the landing on April 25, 1915 (see box, p.195). War graves in the immediate vicinity include the British **Pink Farm** cemetery, named after the reddish soil on which the site lies, and the Turkish **Sargı Yeri** cemetery.

Seddülbahir

The sleepy village of **SEDDÜLBAHİR** ("Walls of the Sea"), at the far southern tip of the peninsula, consists of a few basic *pansiyons* and restaurants, and an Ottoman-era fortress overlooking a quaint harbour. A fine specimen of Ottoman military architecture from the early modern era, the **Seddülbahir Kale**, also known as Eski Kale ("Old Castle") – like its sister fortress, Kumkale, across the Dardanelles on the opposite shore – was built in 1658 by the mother of Sultan Mehmed IV, Hadice Turhan Sultan.

A southeast turning just before Seddülbahir leads to the striking **French Cemetery**, above the sandy Morto Bay, with its massive ossuaries, rows of black metal crosses (with North and West African troops disproportionately represented), and memorial to the sailors of the *Bouvet*, sunk on March 18, 1915. At the end of this road, the 41.7m-high Çanakkale Şehitler Anıtı, or **Çanakkale Martyrs' Memorial**, which resembles a stark, four-legged footstool, commemorates all the Ottoman dead.

ACCOMMODATION   **SEDDÜLBAHİR**

Helles Panorama Cape Helles road, at the northern edge of the village ☎ 0286 862 0035, ⊛ helles panorama.com.tr. The pleasant and friendly *Panorama pansiyon* offers simple but clean rooms with shared bathrooms, accessed through lovely gardens and with panoramic views of both the Çanakkale Martyrs' and Cape Helles memorials. **₺70**

The Turkish Aegean islands

Strategically straddling the Dardanelles, **Gökçeada** and **Bozcaada** were the only Aegean islands to revert to Turkey after the 1923 Treaty of Lausanne concluded the Greek-Turkish war. Although a formal population exchange was never instigated, most of the islands' Greek population had left by 1974, to be replaced by Turkish settlers. Nevertheless, there's still a strong Greek influence on the islands, particularly in the older architecture and the cuisine.

Both islands have **good beaches**: the smaller Bozcaada, with its flat and open landscapes, is fashionable with weekenders from Istanbul, thus expensive; larger, mountainous Gökçeada is cheaper and more dramatic, with fewer tourists.

Gökçeada (Imbros)

Measuring roughly 13km from north to south and 26km from east to west, **GÖKÇEADA** is Turkey's largest island. Unpretentious and for the most part unchanged, it makes a blissful escape from the often overdeveloped mainland Aegean coast. The island is scenic, fertile and volcanic, with healthy pine and kermes oak forests, fields of oleander and wild thyme, sandy beaches with mountain backdrops, and springs pure enough to drink from.

Known as Imbros until 1970, the island was taken by Greece in the 1912–13 **Balkan Wars**. During the Gallipoli campaign, it served as British commander Sir Ian Hamilton's HQ, and an important way station between Límnos and the battlefields. Handed over to Turkey in 1923, it remains an important military base, though its main claim to fame is its superb **organic produce**, especially olive oil, tomato jam, honey and cheese. Its summer tourist trade comprises some Romanians and Bulgarians, but mostly consists of thousands of returned Greek islanders and their descendants, especially around the main Orthodox *panayır* (festival) of August 14–16, when beds are at a premium.

Gökçeada's small inland capital is known as **GÖKÇEADA MERKEZ** (Panayiá). A modern settlement with little character, it's the island's business hub as well as a transit point for travel elsewhere.

Northeast of Gökçeada Merkez

Gökçeada's **northeast coast** is home to the island's small ferry harbour at **Kuzu Limanı**, 6km northeast of Gökçeada Merkez, and the seaside village of **KALEKÖY**, 5km north of Gökçeada Merkez. **Kaleköy Limanı** has a modern seafront with a small, unattractive beach and a quay dotted with fishing boats overlooked by accommodation and a few bars and restaurants, while the settlement reaches uphill to **Kaleköy Yukarı** (Kástro). This atmospheric original Greek village has a ruined Byzantine-Genoese castle, the Agios Nikolaos church, and the island's former cathedral, **Ayía Marína**, which has recently been renovated. Offshore, the **Gökçeada Su Altı Milli Parkı** (Gökçeada Marine Park) stretches between the island and the Saros Körfezi (Gulf of Saros), an inlet of the Aegean north of the Gelibolu peninsula; Turkey's only underwater national park, it's popular for diving and boat trips.

Western hilltop villages

Above the island's central valley, scenic **hilltop villages** hold rustic stone houses dotted among shrubs of pink oleander and shady fig trees. Historically, their elevated locations saved them from sea raiders, but they were also close to the island's natural springs. Many of the central cafés in **Zeytinliköy** (Áyii Theodhóri), 3km west of Gökçeada Merkez, are Greek-run and specialize in *dibek kahvesi* – coffee ground in a giant mortar and pestle. The pretty village of Agrídhia, the former name of hilltop **Tepeköy**, 10km west of Gökçeada Merkez, is exclusively Orthodox-inhabited, and said to be the only settlement in Turkey without a mosque. **Dereköy** (Skhinoúdhi), 15km west of Gökçeada Merkez, was once the island's largest village, with 1900 houses, shops, craftsmen and even a cinema, but today it's only home to about sixty residences. A track leads 7km north from its western edge, to **Marmaros** pebble cove, where there's a 38m **waterfall** 1km inland.

Aydıncık and the south-coast beaches

Arguably the best (and closest) of several **south-coast beaches**, just 10km from Gökçeada Merkez, is **Aydıncık**, 1500m of sugary blonde sand lapped by warm, pristine water. The salt lake just inland is a major habitat for migratory birds, especially flamingoes, and the entire area is supposedly a protected reserve – though this has neither prevented tourist development nor deterred Balkan tourists from wallowing in the shoreline's black mud, said to have healing properties. Kite- and windsurfing conditions are the best in the north Aegean, so schools cluster on the beach (see p.198).

A paved road heads west from here, mostly hugging the coast, for 15km to the long, unsigned **Kapıkaya** beach (no amenities); another 5km leads to the marked (1km) side road to **Lazköyü** (Ayía Káli), a 400m, scenic, protected sandy bay with just a summer snack-shack.

There's no public access to any beaches beyond before **Yuvalı**, a further 9km, and even there you must patronize the beach restaurants of the sprawling *Mavi Su Resort* (see opposite). The final beach, 3km west of little **Uğurlu** (Livoúnia) fishing port, is **Gizli Liman**, with no facilities but fine sand and a pine-grove backdrop. From Uğurlu, a paved road leads back to the western hill villages.

ARRIVAL AND INFORMATION GÖKÇEADA

By bus Truva Turizm (W truvaturizm.com) offers a direct service to Gökçeada from Istanbul's Esenler *otogar*, travelling by road to Kabatepe and then ferry to the island. The 7.5hr journey leaves Istanbul daily at 1pm, and Gökçeada Merkez at 6.30am (₺55 each way).

By ferry Gökçeada is easily accessible by car ferry from Kabatepe and sea bus (passenger only) from Çanakkale; services are run by Gestaş (W gestasdenizulasim.com.tr). In Aug, or any summer weekend, car spaces must be booked hours in advance, and south winds may cancel services. Boats dock at Kuzu Limani (Áyios Kírykos), 6km from Gökçeada Merkez. Tickets for the Çanakkale–Eceabat car

ferry are valid to continue the same day from Kabatepe to Gökçeada, and vice versa.
Destinations Çanakkale (twice weekly; 1hr); Kabatepe (3–8 daily; 1hr 20min).
By plane The tiny Çanakkale-Gökçeada airport is 6km west of Gökçeada Merkez, but at the time of writing there were no scheduled flights.
Tourist office Seasonal information booth on the central roundabout in Gökçeada Merkez (daily June–Sept 10.30am–7pm; T 0286 887 4642).
Banks and money The various ATMs in Gökçeada Merkez can run dry in summer, so come prepared.

GETTING AROUND

By car The easiest way to explore is by car. The only two rental agencies in Gökçeada Merkez are Gökçeada Rent A Car, at Soğuk Hava Deposu Yanı (T 0536 377 5602, W gokceada.com/gokceadarent) and Gökçeada Emre Property & Automotive, at Ataturk Cad 27 (T 0532 227 6098, W gokceadaarackiralama.com); small sedans cost

around ₺180 per day.
By bus and dolmuş Public transport between Kuzu Limani, Gökçeada Merkez and Kaleköy runs irregularly and only during the daytime.
By taxi Private taxis from Kuzu Limani to Gökçeada Merkez cost ₺15–20, and a further ₺25 to continue to Aydıncık.

ACCOMMODATION

GÖKÇEADA MERKEZ

Taşkin Çınarlı, Zeytinli Cad 3, 300m southwest of the main intersection T 0286 887 3266, W taskinotel.net. While the plain block of the *Taşkin* won't win any architectural awards, the 27 rooms are perfectly spacious and comfortable, with small balconies and some with three or four beds; those at the rear face open countryside. ₺85

KALEKÖY

★**Anemos** Kaleköy Yukarı, 15min uphill walk from Kaleköy Limani waterfront T 0554 541 4737, W anemos.com.tr. Opened in 2011, with discreet and exemplary service, *Anemos* is situated in peaceful, semi-rural surroundings and offers the quintessential getaway. Rooms are set in two-storey stone villas, and the best have balconies with either valley or sea views. Activity centres around the sizeable pool, where sunset cocktails are the norm. Rates drop by at least ₺100 out of season. ₺360
★**Imbros Organik Otel** Eski Bademli Koyü, 3km inland from Kaleköy Limani T 0286 887 4040, W gokceadaimbroshotel.com. Set up high near the old Greek village of Bademli, with stunning Aegean views from its wide terrace, this stone-and-wood hotel offers comfortable and spacious rooms, some with balconies. The restaurant is open to non-guests, and serves up healthy Mediterranean cuisine and delicious buffet breakfasts. You'll need your own transport or an expensive taxi to go

anywhere though. ₺265
Kale Motel Barbaros Cad 34, Kaleköy Limani T 0286 887 4404, W kalemotel.com. One of several waterfront hotels and *pansiyons*, the smallish and simple upstairs a/c rooms at *Kale* are bright; the best ones have balconies shrouded by the enormous vine growing on the front of the building. The waterfront restaurant (see opposite) is a great spot for people- and sunset-watching. ₺158

ZEYTINLIKÖY

Zeytindali Zeytinliköy 168, 200m from the main square T 0286 887 3707, W zeytindalihotel.com. The village's only accommodation (and formal restaurant; see opposite), is a superbly restored old inn that's accessed on foot by a narrow, cobbled lane. Two connecting stone buildings in the traditional Greek style house sixteen individually decorated en-suite rooms, simple without being spartan. Most have distant sea views or overlook the village. ₺280

TEPEKÖY

Barba Yorgo Tepeköy T 0286 887 4247, W barbayorgo.com. Accommodation in this idyllic village is available in rustic, three-bedroomed houses and family-friendly two-bedroomed villas, with en-suite or shared bathrooms and fitted kitchens, all restored and owner-managed by larger-than-life local Yorgos (George) Zarbuzanis. Closed early Sept to Easter. ₺220

AYDINCIK

Gökçeada Windsurf Club On the beach ☎0286 898 1022, ⓦsurfgokceada.com. The stone-clad bungalows of the beach's smartest option have contemporary earthtone decor, a/c, fridges and big bathrooms. Those facing the lake catch the stiff breeze, while those facing the sea suffer slightly from noise coming from the very good licensed restaurant and nearby beach bar. Rates include breakfast. Kite- and windsurfing lessons are on offer here too (equipment hire from ₺30/hr, 1hr lesson from ₺40).

EATING AND DRINKING

KALEKÖY

★**Kale** Barbaros Cad 34, Kaleköy Limani ☎0286 887 4404. The restaurant of the *Kale Motel* (see opposite) has tables spilling out onto the cobbles under a vine-covered trellis. Good seafood, including grilled octopus and fish wrapped in vine leaves, plus *mezes* and breakfast. Licensed. Mains ₺10–25. Daily 8am–10.30pm.

ZEYTINLIKÖY

Zeytindali Restaurant Zeytinliköy 168, Zeytinliköy ☎0286 887 3707, ⓦzeytindalihotel.com. The groundfloor restaurant of this atmospheric hotel (see p.198) opens onto a cobbled alleyway and, though pricey, is a perfect spot for a lazy brunch or lingering sunset dinner. Efficient staff preside over a Greek-slanted menu that's

Closed Nov–March. ₺232

YUVALI

Mavi Su Resort Yuvalı Plaj ☎0286 897 6090. This family-friendly resort has an all-inclusive buffet restaurant, overpriced bars, double rooms in a plain four-storey block and cheerier bungalows sleeping up to four (₺250). Although suffering from a slightly institutional 1980s feel, the resort offers long stretches of sandy beach and an almost exotic sense of isolation. Closed Nov–March. ₺180

big on local organic produce; the mainly vegetarian *meze* is a house speciality, as is the thyme-flavoured honey offered at breakfast. Mains ₺20–30. Daily 8–11am & 7–11pm.

TEPEKÖY

Barba Yorgo Taverna Tepeköy ☎0286 887 4247, ⓦbarbayorgo.com. Gökçeada's most authentic Greek taverna is run by the man himself, Barba Yorgo (Papa George). The menu features good *mezes* and well-priced mains (₺8–25), including goat and wild boar. More a vintner than a restaurateur, George makes the most of the island's (rather rough-and-ready) wine from *kundúra* or *kalambáki* grapes, available in copious amounts. Closed early Sept to Easter. Daily 11am–11pm.

Bozcaada (Tenedos)

Only seven nautical miles from the Turkish mainland, and a mere forty square kilometres in size, the windswept island of **BOZCAADA** (Tenedos) is more architecturally homogeneous than neighbouring Gökçeada. Its gently undulating countryside, covered in vineyards, leads to near-deserted sandy beaches and pebbly coves. Lacking great sights and the pretensions of other Aegean and Mediterranean islands, it's a charming place in which to wander.

That idyllic setting tempts well-heeled Turkish holiday-makers and second-home buyers alike, and the island can be quite overrun in summer.

Bozcaada Merkez

The only real settlement on the island, **BOZCAADA MERKEZ** centres on a single square, just inland from the taverna-lined quay and its neighbouring castle. Built on a grid plan along a slight slope, it's divided into cobbled Greek and Turkish quarters.

The castle

Daily 10am–8pm • ₺5

Among the largest citadels in the Aegean, the enormous **castle** that dominates the little fishing port and ferry jetty was once Genoese and Venetian, before being rebuilt in 1455 under Sultan Mehmet the Conqueror. There's not much to see inside its double walls, apart from remnants of two mosques and some Roman pillars, as well as various tombstones and an old army barracks. The ramparts offer great views of the Aegean, the town and the island.

BOZCAADA WINES

Thanks to its breezy climate and volcanic soil, **Bozcaada** has been famed for its **wine** ever since the days of Homer – a two-thousand-year-old silver coin struck here bears a bunch of grapes. Around one-third of the island is under vine, much of it the traditional grape varieties found only here and on Gökçeada, such as the whites Vasilaki and Çavuş, and the reds Karalahna, Kuntra and Karasakız. The white grapes are extremely sweet, so need to be fermented to almost thirteen percent alcohol. Local red wines tend to be rather tannic; the entire grape is left in the vats throughout the fermentation process.

The island's four vintners, Talay, Çamlıbağ, Ataol and Gülerada all have well-signed **tasting boutiques** in the Greek quarter. You can buy decent wines from ₺15–20 a bottle. The Talay winery, just off the main square (Lale Sok 3 ☎0286 697 8080; 8am–6pm) has its own wine bar and tasting centre upstairs.

The beaches

Small, quiet beaches surround the island, though strong winds often prevail. **Ayazma**, 6km southwest of town, is the most developed beach and offers watersports, sunbeds and restaurants. The next bay west, **Sulubahçe**, has good broad sand but no parking or facilities, other than a **campsite** well inland. Beyond, **Habbelle** is more cramped, with a single snack bar/sunbed franchise.

Inland from Ayazma and its abandoned monastery, another paved road leads southeast past secluded, sandy **Beylik** cove, and then above small **Aqvaryum** bay, tucked scenically to one side of the **Mermer Burnu** cape. Once past **Tuzburnu** with its lighthouse, wind turbines and sandy bay, the road swings north on its way back to the port.

ARRIVAL AND DEPARTURE   BOZCAADA

By ferry Gestaş (☎0286 444 0752, ⓦgestasdenizulasim .com.tr) run ferries to Bozcaada Merkez from both Çanakkale and Geyikli (Yükyeri) İskelesi, a tiny port 70km southwest of Çanakkale that's served by direct dolmuşes from Çanakkale's

otogar. If you're approaching from the south, head first to Ezine, then Geyikli. Book ahead to bring a car in high season. Destinations Çanakkale (5 weekly; 55min; no cars); Geyikli (summer hourly, low season 3 daily; 30min).

GETTING AROUND

By car The three petrol stations in Bozcaada Merkez can run empty in high season. The only free car parks in Bozcaada Merkez are behind the castle, and between the *Ege* and *Kale* hotels.

By minibus The only public transport is the summer-only minibuses, which leave town every 15min or so to Ayazma

and Habbele beaches. A couple also head out to Cape Polente, the westernmost point of the island, for sunset.

By scooter or mountain bike Both Ada (☎0286 0286 697 8795) and Akyüz (☎0545 541 9514) offer rentals from tented kiosks set up in various places in town (May–Oct).

INFORMATION

Tourist information Bozcaada Tourism Managers Association (☎0531 784 3173) usually mans a kiosk in summer on the ferry pier (daily 8am–5pm). Otherwise try the friendly café in Bozcaada Merkez, *Ada* (see opposite),

who run the helpful website ⓦbozcaada.info.
Banks and money The ATMs, on the main square in Bozcaada Merkez, can run out in high season, so come prepared.

ACCOMMODATION

Book accommodation in advance during summer months, when the island is at its busiest.

★**Aika** Alaybey Mah, Namzgah Cad 8 ☎0532 461 4255, ⓦaikahotel.com. The charming small boutique-style hotel in the Ottoman quarter has nine smallish but attractively decorated rooms with fresh flowers, a/c and TVs. Breakfast can be taken in the pretty garden courtyard. They also rent out a three-bed townhouse in the Greek

quarter. Closed Nov–May. ₺270
Ege Mektep Sok, behind the castle ☎0532 710 9162, ⓦegehotel.com. Set in a nineteenth-century Greek school, this hotel has well-appointed rooms over three floors – the smaller top-floor ones have balconies facing the castle. There's a pleasant garden bar, which serves a

tasty breakfast with local jams. ₺245

Kaikias Duvarlıkuyu Sok 1, behind the castle ☎ 0286 697 0250, ⓦ kaikias.com. Masonry fragments, nautical Greek antiques, faded hall frescoes and distressed wood floors make this rambling place seem older than its 2001 origins. The large rooms have vaulted ceilings and marble-clad bathrooms, and the upstairs front ones catch the sea breeze. Rates drop by ₺100 out of season. ₺350

Kale Cumhuriyet Mah 69 ☎ 0286 697 8640, ⓦ kalepansiyon.net. Professionally run *pansiyon* at the top of the Greek quarter, a 300m steep walk from the ferry. Lacking balconies but with views of the castle, the a/c, wooden-floor, en-suite rooms have recently been renovated by new owners. Tasty breakfasts are served at a shaded terrace opposite. ₺160

★ **Katina** Eylül Cad, Kısa Sok 1, 300m south of the ferry landing ☎ 0533 737 1924, ⓦ katinaas.com. One of the better boutique hotels, occupying two old houses in the Greek quarter. The eight warm and inviting designer-style rooms have large modern bathrooms and in-room tea and coffee. Drinks and meals, including an ample breakfast, are served in the lane under the vines, or in the ground-floor café. Significant reductions out of season. ₺345

Panorama Değirmenler Sok 24, on the southern ridge overlooking town ☎ 0286 697 0217, ⓦ panoramaotel .com. A welcoming family runs this quiet, luxurious inn where the six rooms benefit from a classy feminine touch, and blend antique furniture with modern finishes. The large ground-floor terrace, with great views and leather sofas, doubles as a good café. ₺360

Rengigül İstiklal Sok 12, below the church ☎ 0286 697 8171, ⓦ rengigul.net. This upmarket *pansiyon*, in an 1876 townhouse, has different-sized guestrooms (only one en suite) decorated with antiques and artwork by its charming and attentive female owner, a retired teacher. An impressive breakfast, including the island's delicious tomato jam, is served within a conservatory in the walled rear garden, shaded by a pomegranate tree. ₺215

EATING, DRINKING AND NIGHTLIFE

In the evening, the action migrates down to the quayside where the fish restaurants get packed to bursting. In high season, prices get ratcheted up to near Istanbul levels – make sure you check menu prices first.

★ **Ada** Çinalı Çarşı Cad 35, between the central square and the quay ☎ 0286 697 8795. This friendly café is known for its *gelincik şerbeti* (poppy syrup drink) and *sakızlı kurabiye* (mastic-flavoured biscuits), but also serves up a very good breakfast, tasty *mezes* and seafood. Licensed. Mains ₺9–20. Daily 8.30am–11pm.

★ **Café at Lisa's** Cami Sok 1, just inland from the quay ☎ 0286 697 0182. Charming little café, run by a former Aussie and now long-time Bozcaada resident. The menu is big on comfort food, such as breakfast muesli, mini-pizzas, pasta and home-made cakes (including Lisa's famous chocolate cake). Occasionally hosts exhibits by island-resident artists. Licensed. Mains ₺12–18. Daily 8.30am–midnight.

Eski Kahve Cumhuriyet Meyd ☎ 0286 697 0436. A town-square café where you can sit under the shaded veranda and sip the refreshing signature grape juice or local wines. The menu offers freshly baked pastries including beautiful chocolate éclairs and mini-cheesecakes, and light main meals such as stuffed ravioli or Greek salad. Licensed. Mains ₺6–17. Daily 8am–1am.

Polente Yali Sok 41, İskele Cad, between the town square and the quay ☎ 0286 697 8605. Bozcaada's most durable nightspot, with both local and foreign youngish holidaying clientele enjoying jazz (early on) and cutting-edge Greek and Latino music (later on). The jaunty blue-and-white tables on the cobbles are also good for a drink during the day. Beer ₺7. Daily 8pm–2am.

Sandal Cumhuriyet Mahallesi, Alsancak Sok ☎ 0286 697 0278. A pricey but always busy place, with outside tables and half a boat on the wall in homage to its name (meaning "rowboat"). The Greek appetizers, goat's cheese stew and the lamb are superb, although the seafood is better at the Turkish harbour restaurants. Licensed. Mains ₺10–30. Daily noon–2am.

Troy to İzmir

Squeezed between the azure blue waters of the North Aegean and a succession of largely untouched mountain ranges, the coastline and immediate hinterland between **Troy** and **İzmir** rewards the inquisitive traveller with an enticing palette of ancient ruins, historical towns, lively coastal villages and sleepy mountain hamlets.

Troy

While by no means Turkey's most spectacular archeological site, **Troy** – thanks to Homer – is probably the most celebrated. Known as Truva or Troia in Turkish, the

ALEXANDRIA TROAS

The ruins of **Alexandria Troas**, an ancient city founded by Alexander the Great's general Antigonos I in 300 BC, lie 30km south of Troy, and 2km south of Dalyan village. Excavated since 2000 by archeologists from the University of Münster, the site (unenclosed; free) consists of mostly Roman ruins surrounded by 8km of **city wall**. A sacred way linked it to Smintheion (see p.203), while another avenue lined with shops (now uncovered) served the ancient harbour at Dalyan. The modern road roughly bisects the city; just west of this are the site's most obvious features, including the **agora temple**, its columns and reliefs set aside for restoration; a huge structure of unknown function; and a partly dug-up **odeion** with two massive arched entrances. On the other side of the road are a **basilica** and one of several **baths**, with clay piping exposed. If the warden is present and you can understand Turkish, you may want the free guided tour: if not, you can wander the site at will.

remains of the ancient city lie 30km south of Çanakkale, 5km west of the main road. If you show up without expectations and use your imagination, you may well be impressed. An English-speaking guide also helps to bring the ruins alive, but modern excavation work has greatly clarified the site, making it easier for non-specialists to grasp the basic layout and different settlement periods.

Brief history

Troy was long believed to have existed in legend only. The Troad plain, where the ruins lie, was known to be associated with the Troy that Homer celebrated in the *Iliad*, but all traces of the city had vanished. Then, in 1871, **Heinrich Schliemann**, a German/American businessman turned amateur archeologist, obtained permission from the Ottoman government to start digging on a hill called **Hisarlık**, where earlier excavators had already found the remains of a Classical temple and signs of further, older ruins.

Schliemann's sloppy trenching work caused considerable damage to the site, only rectified by the first professional archeologist to work at Troy, Carl Blegen, who began excavations in 1932. Schliemann was also responsible for removing the so-called **Treasure of Priam**, a large cache of copper, silver and gold vessels, plus some fine jewellery, which he smuggled to Berlin where it was displayed until 1941. The hoard disappeared when the Red Army sacked the city in May 1945, but resurfaced in Moscow in 1993, and is now exhibited in the Pushkin Museum there. Germany and the Russian Federation continue to wrangle over legal ownership, and Turkey has put in a claim too.

Whatever Schliemann's shortcomings, his unsystematic excavations did uncover nine distinct layers of consecutive urban developments, spanning four millennia. The oldest, **Troy I**, dates to about 3600 BC and was followed by four similar settlements. Either **Troy VI** or **VII** is thought to have been the city described by Homer: the former is known to have been destroyed by an earthquake in about 1275 BC, while the latter shows signs of having been wiped out by fire a quarter of a century later, around the time when historians estimate the Trojan War took place. **Troy VIII**, which thrived from 700 to 300 BC, was a Greek foundation, while much of the final layer of development, **Troy IX** (300 BC to 300 AD), was built during the heyday of the Roman Empire.

Although there's no way to prove that the **Trojan War** did take place, circumstantial evidence suggests that the city was the scene of some kind of armed conflict, even if it wasn't the ten-year struggle described in the *Iliad*. Homer's epic may have been based on a number of wars fought between Mycenaean Greeks and the inhabitants of Troy, who were by turns trading partners and commercial rivals.

The site

Daily 8am–7.30pm, Nov–March till 5pm • ₺20 • ⓦ muze.gov.tr

A 1970s reconstruction of the Homeric **wooden horse** stands immediately beyond the entrance to the site of Troy. You can climb a ladder up into the horse's belly and look out of windows cut into its flanks (which presumably didn't feature in the original design). A few paces west, the city ruins cloak an outcrop overlooking the Troad plain, which extends about 8km to the sea. A circular trail takes you around the site, with twelve explanatory panels that go some way towards bringing the ruins to life. Standing on what's left of the ramparts and looking across the plain, it's not too hard to imagine a besieging army camped below.

The most impressive remains are the **east wall and gate** from Troy VI (1700–1275 BC), of which 330m survive, curving around the eastern and southern flanks of the city. Angled inwards, the walls, 6m high and over 4m thick, would have been surmounted by an additional brick section. A ramp paved with flat stones from Troy II (2500–2300 BC), which would have led to the citadel entrance, also stands out, as does the nearby partially reconstructed **Megaron Building** (protected beneath a giant canvas roof) from the same era, the bricks of which were turned a bright red when Troy II was destroyed by fire. Schliemann erroneously used the evidence of this fire to conclude that this had been Homer's Troy and that the hoard he discovered here made up "**Priam's treasure**".

The most important monument of Greco-Roman Troy VIII–IX, or Ilium, is the Doric **Temple of Athena**, rebuilt by Alexander the Great's general, Lysimakhos, after Alexander himself had visited the temple and left his armour as a gift. The most famous relief from the temple, depicting Apollo astride four pawing stallions, is now in Berlin. Troy was an important religious centre during Greek and Roman times, and another **sanctuary to the Samothracian deities** can be seen near the westernmost point of the site, outside the walls. East of this are a Greco-Roman odeion and bouleuterion (council hall).

ARRIVAL AND DEPARTURE   TROY

By bus or dolmuş Dolmuşes run from the terminal beside the river bridge in Çanakkale, the most sensible base for seeing Troy, to Tevfikiye village just outside the site entrance. If you're moving on further south, catch the Troy–Çanakkale minibus to the main road, then flag down a long-haul bus.

Destinations Çanakkale (hourly; 35min).
By car Troy is well signposted off the E87, 25km south of Çanakkale, from where it's another 5km down a winding country road to Tevfikiye. If you're coming from the Izmir direction, the turn-off is on the left, 22km after Ezine.

INFORMATION AND TOURS

Tourist information The on-site gift shop and the souvenir shops lining the approach road sell the map/guide *A Tour of Troia*, written by Dr Manfred Korfmann, the archeologist who oversaw the site's excavation for 17 years.
Tours Most travel agencies in Çanakkale and Eceabat offer

morning tours of Troy (around ₺105 or €35 per person), usually connecting with afternoon Gallipoli tours.
Guides English-speaking guides are usually available at the entrance, costing around ₺100 for a 1–2hr tour.

ACCOMMODATION AND EATING

Staying at Tevfikiye, 1km from the site entrance, gives you both a head start on the crowds, and the chance to experience a little slice of rural Turkey.

Hisarlık Hotel & Restaurant Near the minibus stop, 500m from Troy ☎ 0286 283 0026, ⓦ troyhisarlik.com. Veteran establishment associated with Mustafa Askin, a renowned local guide who has written books on Troy and conducts tours in English, German and Swedish. The restaurant caters lunch for tour groups and serves up a passable menu of Turkish standards. The eleven simple

upstairs rooms are neat and have a/c and hot showers, but, like the meals, are overpriced. ₺120
Varol Pansiyon Tevfikiye Merkez, village centre ☎ 0286 283 0828. Friendly family-run *pansiyon* with large, simply furnished rooms with clean bathrooms, a spacious living room, and a kitchen for guest use. There's a grocery store next door, but breakfast is included. ₺80

Smintheion

62km south of Troy, at the western edge of Gülpınar village • Temple daily 8am–5pm, summer till 7pm • ₺5 • ⓦ muze.gov.tr • With only scanty dolmuş service from Ezine, or Ayvacık via Behramkale (Assos), it's best to visit by bike or car

Within the ancient Greek and Roman settlement of **Smintheion** is a shrine dedicated to one of the more bizarre manifestations of the god Apollo, as Slayer of Mice. When the original Cretan colonists here were besieged by mice, they remembered an oracle advising them to settle where they were overrun by the "sons of earth". This they took to mean the rodents, so founded the ancient town of Khryse nearby. Coins excavated from the site depict Apollo treading on a mouse.

The surviving Hellenistic, Ionic **temple** has been partly restored and some columns re-erected, though its southwest corner has been re-clad in garish new stone. The Efes beer brewery has funded the renovation as well as the ongoing excavations at adjacent **Khryse**, which have so far exposed a square **reservoir** in the sacred precinct, an arcaded **baths** complex just below, and part of the **Sacred Way** from Alexandria Troas.

Assos

Situated on and around the eponymous ancient Greek city, the modern-day settlement of **ASSOS**, 25km south of Ayvacık, encompasses the charming late medieval village of **Behramkale**; the **Assos acropolis**, perched above it; and a tiny, attractive **harbour** below, known as İskele or Assos Liman. Aside from exploring the ruins and the village, you'll find that Assos is simply a place in which to unwind and gaze out over a perfectly blue sea.

Brief history

Assos dates from about 950 BC, when Greek colonists from Mithymna on neighbouring Lesbos (modern Lésvos) established a settlement. Hermias, a eunuch disciple of Plato, ruled here during the fourth century BC, attempting to put Plato's theories of the ideal city-state into practice. Between 348 and 345 BC, **Aristotle** lived in Assos as Hermias' guest before crossing to Lesbos, just before the Persians arrived and put Hermias to death. **St Paul** also passed through en route to Lesbos during his third evangelical journey (c.55 AD; Acts 20:13–14). The site was rediscovered and initially excavated in 1880–83 by a 25-year-old American, Francis Bacon.

Assos Acropolis

Behramkale • Daylight hours • ₺10 • ⓦ muze.gov.tr • Follow the string of tourist stalls lining the road from Behramkale's village square

The enclosed acropolis site contains the iconic **Temple of Athena**, dating back to 530 BC, which has sweeping views across the straits to Greek Lésvos. In an attempt to give visitors an idea of what it would have looked like in its heyday, the temple's Doric columns were re-erected during the 1980s using concrete, but remedial work is now under way to replace this with stone from the original quarries. While it is the most familiar relic of ancient Assos, other **ruins** (unenclosed) are scattered down the hillside towards the harbour, including a second-century BC theatre with another spectacular straits view, the sarcophagi of the necropolis and the remains of a Byzantine basilica, as well as a stretch of Roman road on the landward side of the street shortly after it starts its descent from Behramkale village.

Behramkale

The hilltop village of **Behramkale**, just below the Temple of Athena, has a central core of attractive old houses built in the same local volcanic stone (andesite) as the temple.

The single-domed **Hüdavendigar Camii** (closed), beside the temple entrance, is often overlooked in the rush to get to the temple. Built during the reign of Murat I Hüdavendigar (1359–89), it's an austere, square-plan fourteenth-century mosque that incorporates masonry taken from a sixth-century Byzantine church in its walls.

Assos Liman (İskele)

Summer weekends see Assos's few hundred metres of picturesque waterfront, **Assos Liman (İskele)**, stretching two hundred steep metres below Behramkale, overflowing with busloads of tour groups; however, out of season it can be idyllic. The cluster of old coastal stone buildings, once warehouses storing locally tanned leather, now hold sea-view hotels and restaurants.

ARRIVAL AND DEPARTURE · ASSOS

By dolmuş Regular dolmuşes connect Assos with Ayvacık to the north and Küçükkuyu to the southeast. Dolmuşes from Ayvacık usually continue to Assos Liman (İskele), where they wait for return custom. In summer, a shuttle bus connects the two all day, or it's a 30min walk.
Destinations Ayvacık (several daily; 20min); Küçükkuyu (several daily; 1hr).

By car At the road junction as you approach from Ayvacık or Gülpınar, turn left, uphill, to reach Behramkale, with the Assos acropolis above; alternatively, keep straight on, heading downhill, and you'll come to Assos Liman (İskele). There's almost no parking at the waterfront, so find a space on the final curve before the descent.

ACCOMMODATION

Popular with the Istanbul literati, Assos is anything but cheap. Most hotels insist on half board and have decks crammed with loungers and swimming platforms to make up for the lack of a beach. On summer weekends advance bookings are essential. Accommodation in Behramkale is far more relaxed and personal than down in the harbour.

BEHRAMKALE

★**Assos Alarga** Behramkale Köyü 88, east of the square ☎0286 721 7260, ⓦassosalarga.com. This family home turned designer *pansiyon* is as good as they come and exquisitely restored throughout. The three large, elegantly furnished rooms have modern bathrooms and gloriously large windows looking out over the pool and valley. The impeccable service includes delicious breakfasts, late brunches and home-style dinners. ₺290

Assos Nar Konak Behramkale Köyü 82, east end of the village ☎0533 480 9393, ⓦassosnarkonak.com. A charming B&B with stunning views across the valley from its high rocky perch. The five romantic and individually decorated rooms have stone walls, wooden floors and a/c. The friendly owners can lend you bikes, and breakfasts (plus sandwiches to send you on your way) are made from organic garden produce. ₺365

Assosyal Otel Alan Meyd 8, east end of the village ☎0286 721 7046, ⓦassosyalotel.com. A boutique hotel whose modern interior contrasts sharply with the 100-year-old stone exterior. Eclectically decorated throughout, the rooms are on the small side, but most have balconies with sweeping valley views. Breakfast is taken on the conservatory-terrace, and there's also a licensed restaurant. Half board available. ₺305

Biber Evi Behramkale Köyü 46, signposted just before the end of the road to the temple ☎0286 721 7410, ⓦbiberevi.com. The upmarket *Biber Evi*, right at the top of the village and with fine terrace views, is named for the twenty species of peppers (*biber*) growing in its garden. There are three rooms in the main house, built in 1860, and three more modest ones in the annexe. ₺275

Eris Pansiyon Behramkale Köyü 6, east end of the village ☎0286 721 7080, ⓦassos.de/eris. Owner-managed by a very hospitable American lady, this *pansiyon* offers three plain but tasteful en-suite B&B rooms with valley views. More a house than a hotel, *Eris*'s communal areas are sociable places, especially the garden terrace where a "high tea" of home-made bread and jams is served. ₺130

ASSOS LIMAN (İSKELE)

Assos Behram Assos İskele Mevkii ☎0286 721 7016, ⓦassosbehramhotel.com. Each of the a/c rooms at this converted harbour warehouse is named after a Greek god; some are small and tucked up in the rafters, while others have sea views. The waterside pier seafood restaurant is deservedly popular. Half board. ₺244

Assos Kervansaray Assos İskele 3 ☎0286 721 7093, ⓦassoskervansaray.com. Another converted nineteenth-century warehouse, the *Kervansaray* has "cosy" rooms which are nonetheless comfortable and equipped with antique wooden furniture; some have balconies with sea views. There are both indoor and outdoor pools, a restaurant on the water and private parking. Half board. ₺220

EATING, DRINKING AND NIGHTLIFE

All the hotels down in the harbour boast licensed restaurants, although the quality of their cuisine tends to reflect a captive market and can be expensive; ask for a menu with prices before ordering. Behramkale has humbler and more relaxed dining.

BEHRAMKALE

Assos Koyum Behramkale Köyü 51 ☎0286 721 7424. Overlooking the main square and with good views from the rooftop terrace, this simple village restaurant (no desserts or fancy coffees here, though there is beer) offers good seasonal meat, fish and vegetarian dishes; try the Turkish

3

ravioli or stuffed courgette flowers, if available. Mains ₺10–22. Daily 7am–1am.

Börek Evi Behramkale Köyü 19 ☎0286 721 7050. Popular with locals, central *Börek* offers standard *lokantasi* fare, pre-prepared and kept warm in steam trays. Choose between mainly chicken and lamb dishes, though there's usually also a good selection of hot and cold *mezes*. One of few licensed restaurants in the village. Mains ₺7–9. Daily 9am–7pm.

ASSOS LIMAN (İSKELE)

Uzun Ev Assos İskele 3 ☎0286 721 7007. One of the better fish restaurants in the harbour, *Uzun Ev*'s steamed

sea bass dish is a local speciality. With both waterfront tables and a terrace across the road, in summer it turns into the local nightspot, hosting live acoustic Turkish music some evenings. Try negotiating prices out of season. Mains ₺12–30. Daily 11am–11pm.

Yıldız Saray Assos İskele 6 ☎0286 721 7204, ⓦassosyildizsarayotel.com. The restaurant of this waterfront converted-warehouse hotel, far outranks the accommodation. Diners can choose from atmospheric indoor tables around a fireplace, or on a shaded floating pontoon on the water's edge. The menu offers a good selection of mainly fish dishes at reasonable prices, plus a good choice of local wines. Mains ₺9–30. Daily 11am–11pm.

3 | Along the Gulf of Edremit

The E87 Çanakkale–İzmir road bypasses the east of Ayvacık and descends in curves through pine-forested hills, allowing occasional glimpses over the **Gulf of Edremit**, and straightens out at the coastal town of **Küçükkuyu**. The other approach is to follow the coastal road from Assos via Kadırga Bay, a pleasant drive lined with olive trees.

Küçükkuyu
29km southeast of Ayvacık, 26km east of Assos

The clutch of small fishing boats lying off the olive-oil town of **KÜÇÜKKUYU** ("Little Well") is joined by dozens of fancy leisure craft during the summer, when the town swells with holidaying Turks. There are some atmospheric backstreets to wander, dotted with shops selling all manner of olive-oil products, but few visitors stay longer than it takes to have a seafood **meal** on the port quay.

Yeşilyurt and Adatepe

You can hike or drive from Küçükkuyu to the two traditional villages of **Yeşilyurt** and **Adatepe** in the foothills of the Kazdağı range (the ancient Mount Ida). Yeşilyurt, 3km west of Küçükkuyu on the E87, then 1km inland, is an attractive village of honey-coloured stone houses huddled around a picturesque main square. Adatepe, just over 4km northeast of Küçükkuyu, is most noteworthy for its "Zeus Altarı" (15min marked walk from the approach road), a carved rock platform with a cistern, from where Zeus was believed to have watched the fighting at Troy on the plains below; the views from the top of the steps are superb.

ACCOMMODATION AND EATING | ALONG THE GULF OF EDREMIT

KÜÇÜKKUYU

Alp Balık Evi Suleyman Sakalli Cad 49 ☎0286 752 5304. The most popular and well known of a number of quayside restaurants in Küçükkuyu, the *Alp* is big on fresh fish, with its own supplier stocking the fridges daily with sardines, whiting and sea bass. Good food, but the service sometimes wanes. No alcohol. Mains ₺11–30. Daily 11.30am–10.30pm.

YEŞİLYURT

Manici Kasrı Yeşilyurt Köyü 16 ☎0286 752 1731, ⓦmanicikasri.com. An all-stone villa with elegant rooms, in warm, colourful tones and stylishly furnished with antiques and large beds. The olde-worlde common area

has a fireplace and beamed ceilings, plus there's a terrace swimming pool and restaurant. Half board. ₺376

★**Öngen Country Otel** At the very top of Yeşilyurt Köyü (a steep drive) ☎0286 752 2434, ⓦongencountry.com. With a mix of standard rooms and larger suites and villas, this stone castle-like complex, in beautiful flowering gardens, climbs prettily up the hillside above the village. Rooms feature splashes of bright colours and antique furniture, most have balconies and some fireplaces, while the restaurant and pool terraces have sweeping sea views. ₺350

ADATEPE

Hünnap Han Adatepe Köyü 34 ☎0286 752 6581, ⓦhunnaphan.com. Adatepe's best accommodation, this welcoming owner-managed place is named after the jujube tree in its serene, walled main garden. Six stone-and-wood-trim rooms occupy a rambling, main *konak*, dating from 1750, with the *Taş Ev* annexe (sleeping eight) for groups, and a second annexe (*Palmiye*) downhill with two bedrooms and a pool. Half board. **₺320**

Ayvalık

Thanks to its charming old quarter of picturesque Greek houses, **AYVALıK**, 56km south of Edremit, has long been popular with Turkish and European visitors. The closest good beaches are at the mainstream resort of **Sarımsaklı**, with some remoter, rockier ones on **Cunda island** (see p.210), both easily reached from town. Ayvalık is also convenient for day-trips to ancient Pergamon, and the Greek island of Lésvos opposite, served by regular ferry (see p.208).

Brief history

Due to its excellent anchorages, the area has been inhabited since ancient times, but today's Ayvalık began as the **Ottoman Greek** settlement of Kydoníes during the early eighteenth century. Both Turkish and Greek names refer to the local quince orchards, now vanished.

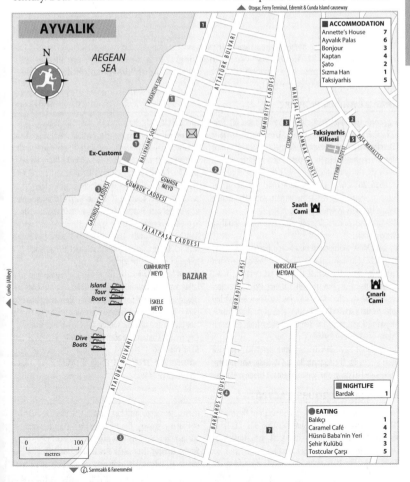

In the 1790s, the town was effectively granted autonomy by Grand Vizier Cezayırlı Hasan Paşa, who, as an Ottoman admiral, had been rescued in 1771 by the Greeks of Ayvalık following a disastrous defeat by the Russian navy. This soon became the most prosperous and imposing town on the Aegean coast after İzmir, boasting an academy, a publishing house and around twenty Orthodox churches, many of which still remain, albeit converted into mosques after 1923. Ironically, most of the people resettled here were Greek-speaking Muslims from Crete and Mytilini (Lésvos), and many of Ayvalık's older inhabitants still speak Greek.

Old quarter and waterfront

Almost uniquely for the Aegean, central Ayvalık is pretty much a perfectly preserved Ottoman market town, though few of the traditional trades are left. Converted nineteenth-century **churches** punctuate the warren of inland streets, riotously painted horse-carts still clatter through the cobbled **bazaar** (good for locally produced cotton garments), and the colourful boats of the fishing fleet bob up and down beside a lengthy waterfront promenade. Thursday is the **market day** for produce from the surrounding villages (although there is a smaller version on Saturday), with its epicentre at two *meydans* either side of *Annette's House pansiyon*.

Sarimsaklı

7km south of Ayvalık • Frequent dolmuşes from just south of İskele Meydanı

SARIMSAKLI ("Garlic Beach"), is home to the longest local **beach**. There are all the trappings you'd expect of a Turkish resort but with a slightly downmarket flavour; few would choose to stay overnight.

ARRIVAL AND DEPARTURE

AYVALIK

By plane The small Balıkesir Koca Seyit Airport (☎0266 372 2336, ⓦedremitairport.com) is 37km north of Ayvalık (5km from the city of Edremit). Borajet (ⓦborajet.com.tr) offer a free shuttle bus for its passengers to Edremit, from where you can get buses on to Ayvalık (hourly; 45min). Edo (☎0536 765 2671, ⓦedorentacar.com), an agent for Europcar, has an office at the airport and can arrange private transfers to Ayvalık.
Destinations Ankara (2 daily; 1hr 15min); Istanbul (2 weekly; 1hr).

By bus Most southbound buses drop passengers at the Ayvalık E87 highway junction, 5km northeast of town, and served by taxis. The *otogar* is 1.5km north of the town centre, but any city bus labelled "Çamlık" and most major-company *servis* vehicles will take you into town. Buses from İzmir usually pass through the central seafront İskele Meydanı, while those for Bergama collect from the main square on their way to/from the *otogar*.
Destinations Balıkesir (10 daily; 2hr); Bergama, some via Dikili (13 daily; 1hr 45min); Bursa (10 daily; 4hr 15min); Çanakkale (10 daily; 3hr 45min); Edremit (hourly; 45min);

Istanbul (16 daily; 8hr); İzmir (13 daily; 3hr 15min).
By ferry The morning ferries to Mytilini (Midilli in Turkish) in Lésvos depart from the terminal 1.5km north of the centre (100m south of the *otogar*), opposite ticket agencies Jale Tur (☎0266 331 3170, ⓦjaletour.com) and Turyol (☎0266 331 6700, ⓦturyolonline.com). Take your passport when booking (€20 one-way, €30 return, plus €55/65 per car). Boats to Cunda leave from the main quay in the town centre.
Destinations Cunda (June–Sept 2–3 hourly; 15min); Mytilini, Lésvos, Greece (May to mid-Oct 15 daily, mid-Oct to April 3 weekly; 1hr 30min).

By car In the old quarter, the network of narrow one-way lanes makes navigation especially difficult; most roads are closed on Thurs and Sat (market days). The easiest place to park is along the waterfront; drivers can also stay on Cunda (see p.210) and take the shuttle-ferry or bus into town.
Car rental Central agencies include Avis, Talatpaşa Cad 61/B (☎0266 312 2456); Duke Tour, Atatürk Cad 23/C (☎0266 312 3794); and Europcar, Atatütk Bul 186/A (☎0266 312 3446).

INFORMATION, TOURS & ACTIVITIES

Tourist office Atatürk Bulvarı, just south of the marina (Mon–Fri 8am–noon & 1–5pm; ☎0266 312 2122). In summer, there's also an information kiosk on the waterfront (July–Sept daily 8am–noon & 1–5pm).

Boat trips Day-trips around local islets leave from the

main quay, stopping off for swimming, sunbathing and a bit of island exploring. The trips run May–Oct, departing at 10am, returning at 4.30pm, and include lunch (₺70–100).

Scuba diving The Ayvalık area is noted for deep-growing red coral, submerged archeological artefacts and caves.

Dive outfit Körfez (Atatürk Bul Özeral Pasaji 617A; ☎0266 312 4966, ⓦkorfezdiving.com) pioneered many local sites off Ayvalık, and offers CMAS- and PADI-affiliated courses, as well as night dives (dives from around €35).

ACCOMMODATION

OLD QUARTER

Annette's House Neşe Sok 12 ☎0542 663 3193, ⓦannetteshouse.com. Owner-managed by its gentle German namesake, *Annette's House* is comprised of two linked houses in the maze-like old quarter. Rooms here are slightly "granny-like" but perfectly comfortable and have a good ratio of shared bathrooms, plus there's a top-floor en-suite quad room. No breakfast, though there are facilities for self-catering. Worth trying to negotiate the rate. Parking available except Thurs. ₺210

Bonjour Mareşal Çakmak Cad, Çeşme Sok 5 ☎0266 312 8085, ⓦbonjourpansiyon.com. Occupying a grand mansion with painted ceilings and antiques, this former French embassy (hence the name) – atmospheric, old and creaky – offers basic rooms and shared bathrooms, plus one en suite behind the courtyard where breakfast (₺15) is served. ₺133

Şato İsmet Paşa Mahalessi 100 ☎0266 312 2351. Hard to find, but wonderfully ensconced high in the old quarter, with antique- and art-filled rooms (some en suite) in two houses on the same street. The original century-old house has a Lésvos-view terrace and guest-friendly kitchen; a large breakfast is served in the shaded garden. ₺110

★**Taksiyarhis** İsmet Paşa Mahalessi 71 ☎0266 312 1494, ⓦtaksiyarhispension.com. One of the most characterful pensions on the Aegean coast, occupying two knocked-together Greek houses, eclectically decorated with antiques and curios from owner Yasemin's travels. The comfortable a/c rooms are spaced out over a number of floors, sharing spotless bathrooms, plus there's one dorm. There are also two terraces – breakfast (₺15) on the top one is a major highlight – and a kitchen for guest use. Dorm ₺35 double ₺120

THE WATERFRONT

Ayvalık Palas Gümrük Meyd ☎0266 312 1064. While definitely not a "palace", this serviceable waterfront hotel has decent if slightly bland rooms with TV and a/c, some with balconies offering exceptional sea views. The large on-site restaurant is only recommended for the buffet breakfast. Parking ₺15 per day. ₺205

Kaptan Balıkhane Sok 7 ☎0266 312 8834. The rooms at *Kaptan*, set in a restored waterfront olive-oil warehouse, are starting to age, but still offer a few comforts, with floor-to-ceiling windows and balconies, some with wonderful sea views. It's possible to swim just in front of the hotel in summer. Rates almost halve out of season. ₺160

★**Sızma Han** Gümrük Cad, İkinci Sok 49 ☎0266 312 7700, ⓦbutiksizmahan.com. Beautifully renovated olive-oil factory from 1908, where the compact rooms with original small windows are low-key modern with veneer floors and furniture, and exposed stone pointing. The lounge-with-fireplace is a focal point, the seafood-strong seaside terrace restaurant features Sevilen wines, and there's safe but limited street parking. Heavily reduced off-season rates. ₺247

EATING

The cheap local **seafood speciality** is *papalina* (fried sprat, a kind of whitebait) and fried mussels in a garlic, olive oil and white-wine sauce.

Balıkçı Balıkhane Sok 7 ☎0266 312 9099. Something of a local legend, *Balıkçı* offers the waterfront's best (and most expensive) seafood. Friendly waiters will explain the catches of the day, and you can dine on a lovely terrace or indoors, often to the accompaniment of live *fasıl* music. Mains ₺15–35. Daily 8am–11pm.

★**Caramel Café** Barbaros Cad 37/A ☎0266 312 8520. This tiny sky-blue café with wrought-iron tables in the alleyway offers a refreshingly inventive, home-cooked menu of Turkish standards and Mediterranean classics, such as seafood pasta, pesto penne, Turkish ravioli, an excellent chocolate mousse and the best cappucino in town. Owner-chef Yasemin is both a welcoming host and impressive chef. Mains ₺6–15. Mon–Sat 8am–10pm.

Hüsnü Baba'nin Yeri Tenekeçiler Sok 16 ☎0266 312 8714. One of very few restaurants in the bazaar, this welcoming *meyhane* specializes in *mezes* and seafood, including *papalina* and *deniz kestanesi* (sea urchin) in season, cooked in oil, from gregarious owner/chef Hüsnü's own olive grove. Tables inside and out on the cobbled lane, but no written menu; confirm prices in advance. Mains ₺6–18. Daily 7–11pm.

Şehir Kulübü Gazinolar Cad ☎0266 312 3676. Often busy with local office workers devouring seafood lunches, this place is a notch in presentation and price above most along the waterfront. Their *papalina* is usually not too greasy, and the wonderful sea views can be appreciated inside or outside. Mains ₺11–23. Daily 11am–11pm.

Tostcular Çarşı Nisan Sok 16. The popular "Toast-makers Market" is a huddle of small cafés serving *Ayvalık tostu*, a toasted sandwich packed solid with salami, pickles, tomatoes and pepper, and coated with liberal doses of mayonnaise and tomato sauce (₺2–5). Daily 8am–8pm.

3

NIGHTLIFE

Bardak Balıkhane Sok ☎ 0530 582 4062. Ayvalık's main nightlife option, within a cavernous brick-and-stone building near the waterfront, attracts a young crowd of both locals and travellers, with a Western–Turkish music mix (both DJs and live) and reasonably priced drinks (beer ₺7). Tues–Sat 8pm–late.

Cunda

Across the bay from Ayvalık, the island of **CUNDA**, also known as **Alibey Adası**, is accessible via a short ferry ride or a causeway and constitutes either a good day-trip or an overnight halt. It's a marginally quieter, less grand version of Ayvalık old town, with a lively main harbour and cobbled backstreets lined by restored stone houses – remnants of life before 1923, when Cunda was known as Moskhonísi to its Greek Orthodox inhabitants. The island has become popular with affluent Istanbulites bent on owning an Aegean retreat, though the dense ranks of tatty trinket and ice-cream stalls along the quay clash somewhat with its twee image. Northern Cunda, known as **Patriça**, holds some relatively deserted beaches accessed via a dirt road. Boat tours from Ayvalık quay visit two northern derelict **Greek monasteries**, Áyios Yórgis and Áyios Dhimítrios tou Sélina, accessible only by sea.

Taksiyarhis Church

Şeref Sok • The interior is currently closed for restoration by the Rahmi Koç Museum (ⓦ www.rmk-museum.org.tr)

Not to be confused with the church of the same name in Ayvalık itself, the Orthodox **Taksiyarhis Church** lies halfway up the slope from the waterfront, its huge basilica dome Cunda's main landmark. Built by the Greek Orthodox congregation in 1873, but heavily damaged by a 1944 earthquake, it is finally undergoing a welcome restoration.

ARRIVAL AND DEPARTURE   CUNDA

By boat Small bus-boats leave for Cunda from Ayvalık's main quay (June–Sept at least hourly; 15min).
By bus Hourly city buses from Ayvalık's İskele Meydanı cross the causeway that links Cunda to the mainland.
By foot The causeway from Ayvalık starts at the northern end of Yunus Emre Cad, an extension of Atatürk Bulvarı (roughly 8km to the Cunda waterfront). It's a very pleasant walk with fine sea views, and there are plenty of places to stop for refreshments en route.

ACCOMMODATION

Ada Camping 3km southwest of town ☎ 0266 327 1211, ⓦ adacamping.com. Good facilities at this large resort include an on-site restaurant and self-catering kitchen. The grassed sites have a little shade, and a number of a/c wooden bungalows overlook the sandy beach. Closed Dec–March. Camping ₺60, bungalow ₺250
Altay Butik Namık Kemal Mahallesi Cad 18 ☎ 0266 327 1024, ⓦ altaybutikotel.com. A friendly family-run affair and one of Cunda's oldest *pansiyons* (established 1960), located in the cobbled streets behind the waterfront.

Decorated with a quirky mix of retro objects, the simple, tiled en-suite rooms are set round a central shaded courtyard where breakfast is taken among the flowering pot plants. ₺260
Zehra Teyze'nin Evi Şeref Sok 7, Namık Kemal Mahallesi Cad ☎ 0266 327 2285, ⓦ cundaevi.com. In the grounds of Taksiyarhis Church, "Aunt Zehra's House" is the former priest's residence. Homely and cheerful rather than particularly smart, its comfortable en-suite rooms are accessed via a pleasant garden. ₺200

EATING AND DRINKING

Cunda Deniz Sahil Yolu 15 ☎ 0266 327 1685, ⓦ cundadeniz.com. One of the island's original fish restaurants, and still among the best. Popular with locals and tourists, the waterfront *Deniz* offers excellent, seasonal *mezes* to accompany a wide range of fresh fish and other seafood, including mussels in white wine. Mains ₺15–30. Daily 11.30am–11pm.

★**Son Vapur** Belediye Cad, Çarşı Sok 3 ☎ 0535 312 7260. Stylish spot with fisherman's decor and kilim-covered cushions at the tables on the cobbled street. Another good seafood venue, but super-welcoming owners Orkide and Arek will also advise on a good selection of non-fishy *mezes*. A little cheaper than most, too (mains ₺10–25). Daily 6–10pm.

FROM TOP AYVALIK (P.207); TROJAN HORSE, ÇANAKKALE (P.187) >

Taş Kahve Sahil Böyü 20 ☎ 0266 327 1166, ⓦ taskahve .com.tr. Cunda's most atmospheric café, where old men play cards and backgammon on rickety wooden chairs, in a church-like 200-year-old hall with high wooden ceilings and large stained-glass windows. Good breakfasts and *mezes* (₺7–12) accompanied by piping-hot tea and coffee, or beer (₺8) in the evenings. Daily 7am–1.30am.

Bergama

Although possible as a day-trip from Ayvalık, **BERGAMA**, 50km southeast, site of the ancient city of **Pergamon**, rates an overnight stop in its own right. Towering over modern Bergama, the stunning **Acropolis** of the Pergamene dynasty is the main attraction, but two lesser sights, the **Asklepion** and **Kızıl Avlu**, as well as the town's medieval quarter, are well worth exploring. Bear in mind that the two parts of ancient Pergamon, unshaded and extremely hot at midday in summer, are some distance from each other.

Brief history

Pergamon rose to prominence as the base of Lysimakhos, a successor to Alexander the Great who died in 281 BC. He left considerable treasure to his eunuch-steward Philetaeros who passed it on to his nephew Eumenes I, founder of the Pergamene dynasty. The city only achieved true greatness under **Eumenes II** (197–159 BC), who built its gymnasium, the Altar of Zeus, library, theatre and Acropolis wall. Eumenes' brother Attalos II ruled until 138 BC, followed by the five-year reign of the cruel but scholarly **Attalos III**, who perversely left the kingdom to the **Romans**. Under them Pergamon became an artistic and commercial centre of 150,000 people, but after the arrival of the Goths in 262 AD, it declined and fell into ruin.

The German engineer **Carl Humann** rediscovered ancient Pergamon in 1871, when some locals showed him a strange mosaic that turned out to be part of the relief from the Altar of Zeus. Humann bought the mosaic, and began excavating the Acropolis. Work was completed by 1886, but unfortunately most of the finds were carted off to Germany, including the Altar of Zeus reliefs, now in the Pergamon Museum in Berlin. Nevertheless, the magnificent site was deservedly inscribed as a UNESCO World Heritage Site in 2014.

In 1998 a second significant archeological site, the Roman spa and asklepion of **Allianoi**, was discovered 19km northeast of Pergamon. However, it had only been partly excavated before the Yortanlı irrigation dam flooded the site in 2011 despite domestic and international protest. The site was first "re-buried" under a protective layer of clay so that future generations may be able to excavate it once the dam's tenure (only 50 years, say some experts) is complete.

EXPLORING BERGAMA

Bergama is an uncharacteristically long and spread-out city, whose *otogar* is 7km from the modern centre, around the **Archeological Museum**. From there, it's about a further 1km north along the main street to the **Kızıl Avlu** in the **old town**, and then another 5km up to the summit of **Pergama's Acropolis**. You can either follow the steep switchback Akropol Caddesi, or take the footpath which starts on the far side of the second bridge, upstream from the Kızıl Avlu, angling obliquely up to the road – cross here and follow a steep incline into the lower agora. However, the easiest option to access the Acropolis is the cable car, **Bergama Akropol Teleferik** (daily 8am–5pm, summer till 7pm; ₺8 each way; ☎0232 631 0805, ⓦakropolisteleferik .com.tr), the lower station of which is at the base of Akropol Caddesi. You're swept to the top in under four minutes – most visitors choose to ride up and walk back down through the ruins.

The **Asklepion** is uphill, above the modern city centre, and accessible via the winding Asklepion Caddesi, which joins Atatürk Bulvarı almost a kilometre south of the museum, from where it's another 1.5km or so up to the ticket office. There's also a footpath which starts (and is signposted) next to the Kursunlu Cami.

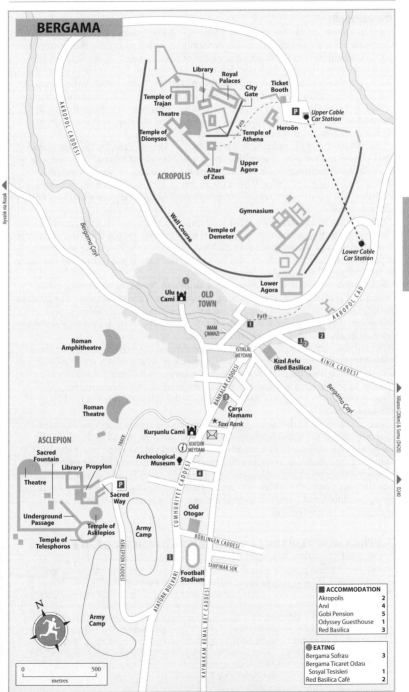

BERGAMA

Library
Royal Palaces
City Gate
Ticket Booth
Temple of Trajan
Theatre
Temple of Dionysos
Temple of Athena
Heroön
Upper Cable Car Station
ACROPOLIS
Altar of Zeus
Upper Agora
Gymnasium
Temple of Demeter
Lower Cable Car Station
Wall Course
Lower Agora
AKROPOL CADDESI
Bergama Çayı
Ayvalık via Kozak
Ulu Cami
OLD TOWN
IMAM ÇIKMAZI
Path
AKROPOL CAD
Roman Amphitheatre
ISTIKLAL MEYDANI
Kızıl Avlu (Red Basilica)
KINIK CADDESI
BANKALAR CADDESI
Bergama Çayı
Alibeyli (20km) & Soma (0420)
Roman Theatre
Çarşı Hamamı
Taxi Rank
ASCLEPION
Kurşunlu Cami
ATATÜRK MEYDANI
TRACK
Sacred Fountain
Library
Propylon
Archeological Museum
Theatre
CUMHURIYET CADDESI
Sacred Way
Underground Passage
Temple of Asklepios
Old Otogar
Temple of Telesphoros
Army Camp
BÖBLINGEN CADDESI
ASKLEPION CADDESI
TANPINAR SOK
ATATÜRK BULVARI
Football Stadium
Army Camp
KAYMAKAM KEMAL BEY CADDESI
D240

N

0   500
metres

■ ACCOMMODATION
Akropolis   2
Anıl   4
Gobi Pension   5
Odyssey Guesthouse 1
Red Basilica   3

● EATING
Bergama Sofrası   3
Bergama Ticaret Odası
 Sosyal Tesisleri   1
Red Basilica Café   2

Otogar (6km) and E87 for Aliağa & İzmir (south) or Ayvalık & Dikili (north)

The Acropolis

Akropol Cad • Daily: April–Oct 8.30am–7pm; Nov–March 8am–5pm • ₺25 • Ⓦ muze.gov.tr • Access on foot or by cable car (see box, p.212)

Once you enter the site of Pergamon's **Acropolis**, an uphill path from the former city gate leads southwest to the huge, square **Altar of Zeus**, standing in the shade of two large stone pines. Built by Eumenes II to commemorate his father's victory over the Gauls, the altar was decorated with reliefs depicting the battle between the Titans and the gods, symbolizing the triumph of order over chaos (and, presumably, that of Attalos I over the Gauls). Even today its former splendour is apparent, if much diminished by the removal of the reliefs to Berlin. The main approach stairway was on the west, now the most deteriorated side.

Directly northeast of, and exactly parallel to, the Altar of Zeus, on the next terrace up, lie the sparse remains of the third-century BC **Temple of Athena**. Only some of its stepped foundations survive *in situ*, although the entrance gate, with its inscribed dedication "King Eumenes to Athena the Bearer of Victories", has been reconstructed in Berlin. The scanty north stoa of the temple once housed Pergamon's famous **Library** (see box below).

A narrow staircase leads down from the Temple of Athena to the spectacular Hellenistic **theatre**, cut into the hillside and with capacity for ten thousand spectators. The wooden stage was removed after each performance – the holes into which the supporting posts were driven can still be seen on the stage terrace – to allow free access to the **Temple of Dionysos**, on the same terrace.

Still further north and uphill looms the Corinthian **Temple of Trajan**, where both Trajan and Hadrian were revered during Roman times – their busts were also taken to Berlin. German archeologists have re-erected some of the temple columns, plus much of the stoa that surrounded the shrine on three sides. The north architrave is lined with Medusa heads, two of them modern recastings.

Behind the temple are the remains of barracks and the highest reaches of the city's **perimeter wall**. Nearby yawns a cistern once fed by an **aqueduct**, traces of which are still visible running parallel to a modern one on the hillside to the northwest. Finally, as you begin your descent back down towards the main entrance, you'll pass – east of the library and Athena temple – the extensive but jumbled ruins of the **royal palaces**.

The terrace south of the Altar of Zeus now holds little more than Carl Humann's grave, though as the **upper agora** it was once the commercial and social focus of Pergamon. An ancient street descends past the **Temple of Demeter**, where the local variant of the Eleusinian Mysteries was enacted. Across the way lies the **gymnasium**, where the city's youth were educated. Its upper level, with its palaestra and lecture hall, was for young men, the middle was used by the adolescents, and the lower served as a playground for small boys. From the **lower agora**, the path back down to town is indicated by blue waymarks.

PERGAMON'S LIBRARY AND THE BIRTH OF THE MODERN BOOK

Founded by Eumenes II and enlarged by Attalos II, both fanatical collectors of books, Pergamon's **Library** grew to contain two hundred thousand titles – volumes by Aristotle and Theophrastos were paid for with their weight in gold. Eventually the Egyptian Ptolemies, alarmed at this growing rival to their own library in Alexandria, banned the export of papyrus, on which all scrolls were written, and of which they were sole producers.

In response to this bid to stem the library's expansion, the Pergamene dynasty revived the old practice of writing on specially treated animal skins, **parchment**. That led quickly to the invention of the **codex** or paged book, since parchment couldn't be rolled up like papyrus. The words "parchment" and the more archaic "pergamene" both derive from "Pergamon". The library was appropriated by Mark Antony, who gave it to Cleopatra as a gift, and many of its works survived in Alexandria until destroyed by the Arabs in the seventh century.

The Asklepion

Asklepion Cad • Daily: April–Oct 8.30am–7pm; Nov–March 8am–5pm • ₺20 • ⓦ muze.gov.tr

An uphill hike southwest of the modern town centre, either on a steep track or along a winding road, the ancient, sacred therapeutic centre of **Asklepion** is named after Asklepios, the god of healing, and was the world's first psychiatric hospital.

Healing methods at all asklepia combined the ritualistic and the practical. Patients were required to sleep in the temple so that Asklepios, semi-divine son of Apollo and god of healing, might appear in their dreams to suggest diagnosis and treatment. However, special diets, bathing in hot or cold water and exercise also figured in the therapeutic regimes. **Galen** (129–202 AD), the greatest physician of antiquity, whose theories dominated medicine until the sixteenth century, was born in Pergamon, and worked here as well as in Rome.

Much of what survives dates from the reign of **Hadrian** (117–38 AD), when the Asklepion functioned much like a spa and featured as part of elite social life.

The site

A long, colonnaded **sacred way**, originally lined with shops, leads from the site entrance to the **propylon**, or monumental entrance gate, rebuilt in the third century AD after an earthquake seriously damaged it in the previous century. North of the propylon, the square **library** housed the statue of Hadrian that's now in the local museum.

South of the propylon is the circular **Temple of Asklepios** (150 AD), which was modelled on Rome's Pantheon. Although only foundations remain today, when intact its graceful dome was 24m across, with an oculus for light and air to penetrate. The broad, open area to the west was originally enclosed by colonnaded stoas. At the western end of the re-erected, mostly Ionic northern colonnade, an over-restored **theatre** seated 3500 and entertained townspeople as well as patients. At the centre of the open area, the **sacred fountain** still trickles weakly radioactive water. Nearby, an 80m underground passage leads to the **Temple of Telesphoros** (the lesser deity of Accomplishment), where patients slept while awaiting dream diagnoses. Only its lower, vaulted level survives in good repair.

Archeological Museum

Cumhuriyet Cad 6 • Daily 8am–7pm, Nov–March till 5pm • ₺5 • ☎ 0232 631 2884

The **Archeological Museum** (Arkeoloji Müzesi), on Bergama's main street, holds a large collection of locally unearthed relics, including a statue of Hadrian from the Asklepion. Assorted fourth-century BC statues also display the naturalistic technique that was first developed in Pergamon, and later influenced European Baroque art. Incorporating accentuated body shape and muscle tone, the technique allowed a wider range of expressions to be shown than did the traditional, more abstract and grotesque style.

Kızıl Avlu

Kınık Cad • Daily 8am–7pm, Nov–March till 5pm • ₺5

Bergama's foremost attraction, the huge red-brick **Kızıl Avlu** or "**Red Basilica**", is on the river below the Acropolis. Originally built in the second century AD as a temple to the Egyptian gods Serapis, Harpokrates and Isis, it was used as a basilica by the Byzantines – who merely built a smaller church within the confines. It was also one of the Seven Churches of the Apocalypse addressed by St John the Divine, who referred to it in Revelation 2:13 as "the throne of Satan", perhaps a nod to the still-extant Egyptian cult. Now an attractive though crumbling ruin, with some sections roped or fenced off, it's in the throes of various stages of restoration.

Inside the walls, one of the towers holds the Kurtuluş Cami (mosque), while the ancient **Selinos River** (today the **Bergama Çayı**) passes beneath the basilica via two tunnels. Just downstream you'll see a handsome Ottoman bridge, built in 1384, with two equally well-preserved Roman bridges upstream.

3

The old quarter

Bergama's **old quarter**, north of the river uphill from Kızıl Avlu, is a jumble of Ottoman buildings, antique and carpet shops, mosques and maze-like streets. The antique stalls are full of very beautiful, overpriced copperware – too many coach tours have had their effect. Similarly, the reputation of Bergama carpets has been besmirched by too much synthetic dye and machine-weaving.

ARRIVAL AND INFORMATION   BERGAMA

By bus and minibus The new *otogar*, inconveniently located 7km south near the junction of the E87 highway, is linked to the old *otogar*, 500m south of the Archeological Museum, by dolmuşes and a free *servis* shuttle (6am–7pm every 30min). The last direct minibus to Ayvalık leaves the *otogar* at 5pm, but indirect services via Dikili run until 8pm. To get to Istanbul, one option is to take a bus to Bandırma and then a fast ferry; so-called "direct" night buses to

Istanbul tend to be slow and expensive.

Destinations Aliağa (hourly; 1hr); Ankara (1 nightly; 8hr 30min); Ayvalık (hourly; 1hr 15min); Bandırma (4 daily; 4hr); Istanbul (2 daily; 10hr); İzmir (every 30min; 1hr 45min); Soma (hourly; 1hr).

Tourist office Cumhuriyet Cad, near the Archeological Museum (Mon–Fri 8.30am–noon & 1–5.30pm; ☎ 0232 631 2851).

GETTING AROUND

By dolmuş During the day, dolmuşes travel along the main road through town, between the old *otogar* and Kızıl Avlu.

By taxi Taxi drivers offer to ferry passengers arriving at Bergama's *otogar* around the ruins for the extortionate sum

of ₺70–100, or slightly less in low season. This might make sense if you're in a group, or in a hurry, but it limits you to 1hr at the Acropolis, 10min at the Red Basilica and 30min at the Asklepion. The main taxi stand in central Bergama is beside the Çarşı Hamamı on Bankalar Cad.

ACCOMMODATION

Akropolis Guest House Kayalık Sok 3 ☎ 0232 631 2621, ⓦ akropolisguesthouse.com. The rooms of these two adjoining stone buildings, close to the cable car and Kızıl Avlu, look inward to a pleasant courtyard with a welcoming (in summer) pool. Standard rooms are a little dark – the airier deluxe rooms (₺30 extra) offer better views and more light. There's also parking and a well-priced restaurant. **₺140**

Anıl Hatuniye Cad 4 ☎ 0232 633 2153, ⓦ anilhotel bergama.com. While the futuristic, neon-lit theme at *Anıl* won't be to everybody's taste, the modern tower block is sensibly priced and well located in the town centre, near the Archeological Museum. The comfortable rooms have TV, a/c and fancy walk-in showers, and the management is super-helpful. **₺168**

★**Odyssey Guesthouse** Abacıhan Sok 13

☎ 0232 631 3501, ⓦ odysseyguesthouse.com. Traveller-friendly with a guaranteed warm welcome from the English-speaking managers, this consists of two linked century-old Greek houses with wooden floorboards and stairs, delightful views from roof-terraces-cum-reading rooms, a guest kitchen and heating in winter. All eleven rooms are high-ceilinged and very comfortable, but only some are en suite (₺20 extra). **₺90**

★**Red Basilica** Kınık Cad 77/B ☎ 0232 632 7601, ⓦ www.redbasilica.com. In the shadow of Kızıl Avlu, this stylish boutique hotel in beautifully restored old-quarter houses is a welcome surprise in Bergama. The seven rooms vary in size and price, but all are wonderfully decorated, and owner Fatih couldn't be more helpful or enthusiastic, plus there's a lovely café (see below). **₺175**

EATING AND DRINKING

Bergama Sofrası Bankalar Cad 44 ☎ 0232 631 5131. Easy to find on the edge of the old quarter, this simple *lokanta* is the best in Bergama. Choose from the likes of beef stew, lamb shanks in bechamel, and *köfte* in tomato sauce, as well as rice, lentil, chickpea and aubergine dishes (mains ₺8–15). Although not actually licensed, they can usually offer a glass of wine. Daily 10am–10pm.

Bergama Ticaret Odası Sosyal Tesisleri Uckemer Cad, 150m uphill from the Ulu Cami ☎ 0232 632 9641. One of very few licensed restaurants in town, this family-run place is set in a former Greek school. While the menu

doesn't quite match the fantastic views, the moderately priced grills (lamb, veal or chicken) and *mezes* are still decent. Mains ₺15–25. Daily 9am–11pm.

★**Red Basilica Café** Kınık Cad 77/B ☎ 0232 632 7601. At this bistro-café, on the street-side of the hotel of the same name (see above), you can choose from pavement tables offering excellent people-watching and views on to the red walls of the Kızıl Avlu, or an a/c interior full of local art. Relaxed and easy-going, with a range of organic, locally sourced options, from breakfast (₺12) to home-cooked cakes, crunchy salads and heartier meat dishes (₺9–25). Licensed. Daily 9am–late.

Foça

The small coastal resort of **FOÇA**, 86km north of İzmir, is an attractive and welcoming place, where the charming cobbled backstreets are lined with Greek fishermen's cottages and a few more opulent Ottoman mansions. A relaxing stopover, it's sometimes called Eski (Old) Foça to distinguish it from its smaller and less interesting neighbour 25km further north, **Yeni Foça**, which is increasingly the haunt of wealthy second-home owners from İzmir and unlikely to appeal to international visitors.

"Phokaia" derives from the ancient Greek for "seal" and refers to Mediterranean **monk** seals, so named because the grey of their backs against the brown of the rest of the body resembles a traditional monk's cowl. They are now highly endangered and thought to number fewer than six hundred – you're highly unlikely to spot any in the area.

Ancient Phokaia

Foça stands on the site of **ancient Phokaia**, founded around 1000 BC by Ionian colonists. Great seafarers, the Phokaians plied the Mediterranean as far as the Straits of Gibraltar, founding numerous colonies, including (around 600 BC) Massalia, now Marseilles.

Little now remains of the ancient town. The most striking remnant, 8km east of modern Foça, is the **Taş Ev**, an unusual tomb cut from the rock in the eighth century BC, squatting beside an Ottoman bridge and a modern cemetery. A small, much later **ancient theatre** marks the east entry to Foça, while some mosaic pavements from a Roman villa have been unearthed about 150m southwest.

Beşkapılar fortress

Aşıklar Cad • Interior is closed to the public but opens occasionally for art exhibitions and local events

The oldest intact structure in Foça itself is the waterfront **Beşkapılar fortress**. Originally Byzantine, it was much modified by successive occupiers, including the Genoese, who occupied the castle until the Ottomans seized it in the fifteenth century. Two interesting mosques from that era bracket Beşkapılar: the unheralded but beautiful **Fatih Camii**, and the **Kayalar Camii**, at the summit of the castle enclosure, sporting a distinctly lighthouse-like minaret.

The harbours

Foça's castle headland splits the bay into two smaller harbours. The northerly, more picturesque **Küçükdeniz** (**Little Sea**) is where most of the action takes place and is the more obvious centre for tourists, along seafront Reha Midilli Caddesi, while bleak, southerly **Büyükdeniz** (**Large Sea**) is of interest only as the point where ferries connect the town to the Karaburun peninsula and Lésvos in high season and the fishing fleet is anchored. Neither bay has a decent beach, though that doesn't stop bathers from establishing themselves on the slightly grubby shingle or launching themselves from platforms at rocky Küçükdeniz.

The beaches

Beach access around ₺20, sometimes more at weekends

Some excellent **beaches** are dotted along the scenic 20km of road that separates Foça from Yeni Foça. After the first 2km, the beach is dominated by the package-holiday resort *Neilson Phokaia Beachclub*. Beyond here, the nicest (and rubbish-free) beaches are accessible only by paying fees to the **campsites** that own them, such as *Camping Alanı*, 7km out, and *Acar Kamping* 3km beyond. Alternatively, there's *Mambo Beach Club* (☎0533 927 7545, ⊚mambobc.com), 17km from Foça and 5km short of Yeni Foça, who usually waive the fee if you patronize their snack bar.

ARRIVAL AND DEPARTURE

FOÇA

By plane İzmir's Adnan Menderes Airport (see p.231) is around 90km away (taxi 1.5hr drive; ₺200). Foça hotels or shuttle services at the airport can organize cheaper transfers from around ₺45 per head in six-seater minivans, depending on numbers. You can also get the İzmir metro İZBAN (🌐izban .com.tr) from the airport either to the centre for buses to Foça (see p.217), or to Hatundere on the Northern Line, from where there are regular dolmuşes to Foça (29km; around 35min) though you may have to swap vehicles at Buruncuk on the main road (E87), 3km from the Hatundere station.

By bus or dolmuş Direct buses from İzmir arrive just south of the seafront main square, behind Büyükdeniz. Long-haul buses on the E87 highway drop passengers at Buruncuk, 26km east of Foça, which is served by regular connecting dolmuşes.

Destinations Buruncuk/Hatundere (hourly; 35min); İzmir (hourly; 1hr 15min).

By ferry Ferries dock in Büyükdeniz harbour. Summer ferries to the Karaburun peninsula and Lésvos (Mytilini), Greece, are operated by Turyol (🌐turyol.com), whose agent is Ampuria Tour (Atatürk Mah, Ressam Avni Arbaş Sok 9, Eski Foça; ☎0232 812 5042, 🌐ampuriatour.com.tr).

Destinations Karaburun (June–Sept 8 weekly; 1hr); Lésvos (Mytilini), Greece (June–Sept 5 weekly; 2hr).

INFORMATION AND TOURS

Tourist office Cumhuriyet Meyd (May–Sept Mon–Fri 8.30am–noon & 1.30–5.30pm, Sat 10am–5.30pm; Oct–April Mon–Fri 8.30am–5.30pm; ☎0232 812 5534).

Boat trips Most excursions from Küçükdeniz to the small islets northwest of Foça follow similar itineraries, with stops for swimming and a grilled fish lunch included (May–Sept daily 10.30am–5pm; ₺3–50).

ACCOMMODATION

Foçantique Reha Midilli Cad 154 ☎0232 812 4313, 🌐focantiquehotel.com. Owned by two former tour guides, Foça's first boutique hotel is a restored old garden-house whose small rooms have exposed stonework and rather average bathrooms (except for one with a converted hamam). A modern extension at the front holds a terrace sea-view bar/breakfast area and an apartment to rent that sleeps four (₺565). **₺260**

Huzur 139 Sok 5, at the north end of Küçükdeniz ☎0232 812 1203, 🌐huzurpansiyon.com. The same friendly family have been operating this *pansiyon* since 1970. With direct sea frontage and a delightful, shaded breakfast terrace on the roof, *Huzur* offers simple, tiled en-suite rooms, some sleeping four, the pricier ones with balconies and sea views. **₺120**

★**İyon Pansiyon** Ismetpaşa Mahallesi, 198 Sok 8 ☎0232 812 1415, 🌐iyonpansiyon.com. Close to the action but on a quiet side street, *İyon* has a choice of basic rooms in a restored Greek house, and more spacious, comfortable ones in the rear garden annexe. Breakfast is served on the raised front deck, and the common lobby has a wood-burning stove. There's parking nearby. **₺120**

Karacama Ismetpaşa Mahallesi, Reha Midilli Cad 70 ☎0232 812 1416, 🌐hotelkaracam.com.tr. Juxtaposed with the plain modern blocks around it, Küçükdeniz's smartest waterside hotel is set in a brilliant-white restored Greek building dating to 1881. Most of the 21 rooms have balconies, timber floors and high airy ceilings, plus a/c and TV. The front entrance opens directly on to the pedestrianized wharf. **₺280**

★**Lola 38** Reha Midilli Cad 140, corner of 149 Sok ☎0232 812 3809, 🌐lola38hotel.com. Foça's best boutique hotel, built in 1891 as a Greek ship-owner's mansion, and once an Orthodox priest's residence, *Lola 38* has attentive hosts, sea frontage and a perfect blend of antique and contemporary decor throughout. The eight beautiful rooms are divided into the main house and the quaint stone buildings in the back garden, with its lawn-bar and small spa-pool. **₺371**

EATING, DRINKING AND NIGHTLIFE

The pedestrianized plaza at the head of Küçükdeniz harbour is crammed with **seafood restaurants**, none that exciting but packed on weekends. In the warren of bazaar lanes east of the seafront esplanade, noisy music bars provide the town's **nightlife**.

Çarşı Lokantası 187 Sok 43 ☎0232 812 2377. Down a shaded cobbled lane, the cheerful and busy *Çarşı* serves typical, well-priced *lokanta* home-cooked dishes, including a few vegetable-only options and pasta, as well as the usual rice. Pleasant (and popular) pavement tables. Mains ₺8–19. Daily 11am–midnight.

★**Fokai** Balık Atatürk Mah 121, Sok 8, behind the castle overlooking Büyükdeniz ☎0232 812 2186, 🌐fokaibalik.com. At this excellent licensed fish restaurant, the daily catch is the best and most reasonably priced in town, with fresh and farmed fish clearly distinguished. The menu also includes *mezes*, pizzas and meat, plus a delicious chocolate cake. Mains ₺12–28. Daily 11.30am–11pm.

★**Letafet** 197 Sok 3 ☎0232 812 1191. In the bazaar lanes east of the seafront esplanade, this offers a diverse and affordable menu of *mezes* and a good wine list, including local Chardonnay. Unlike the restaurants at the front, the staff are not pushy and give you time to peruse the menu and have a leisurely meal. There's often live guitar music and dancing in the pretty back courtyard decorated with fairy lights. Mains ₺8–25. Daily noon–11pm.

Nazmi Usta Girit Dondurmaları Reha Midilli Cad 82 ☎0232 812 5471. This small *dondurma* outlet on the Küçükdeniz seafront esplanade is easily the best in Foça, attracting long queues in summer. Fabulous ice cream (from ₺5) in dozens of flavours, including mastic gum, best slurped at a pavement table while watching the world go by. Daily 11am–late.

Manisa

Spilling out from the foothills of the Manisa Dağı range, the sprawling city of **MANISA** lies 38km east of Menemen along the E87highway. While most of its historic centre was torched by the Greek army during its 1922 retreat, a few fine Selçuk and Ottoman monuments survive, and it's now home to more than 280,000 people.

Brief history

The area was settled early in the first millennium BC, according to legend by veterans of the Trojan War, and the ancient town of Magnesia ad Sipylus was an important Roman centre. For a short time during the thirteenth century, after the Fourth Crusade sacked Constantinople, Manisa was capital of the Byzantine Empire. In 1313 it was captured by Selçuk chieftain Saruhan Bey, responsible for the earliest of the surviving local monuments. Later, the Ottomans sent heirs to the throne here to serve an apprenticeship as local governors, to prepare them for the rigours of Istanbul palace life.

Sultan Camii

Sultan Meyd, corner of İzmir Cad and İbrahim Gökçen Bul

Dominating the well-signed Sultan Meydanı is the **Sultan Camii**, which was built in 1522 for Ayşe Hafize, mother of Süleyman the Magnificent, who lived here with her son while he was serving as governor. It's a rectangular mosque, much wider than it is deep, with a single central dome flanked by two pairs of satellite domes. Late Ottoman Baroque paint decoration and a tiny wood-railed pulpit on the west enliven the porch – actually a *son cemaat yeri* (latecomers' praying place). Of the surrounding complex, which included a *medrese* and mental hospital, only the hamam continues in its original function.

Muradiye Camii

Murat Cad, 100m east of Sultan Meyd

Designed by the great imperial architect Mimar Sinan, the **Muradiye Camii** was eventually built by Mehmet Ağa (famed builder of Istanbul's Sultanahmet Camii) for the future Murat III, while he was governor here in 1583–85. The interior, with its stained-glass windows and walls decorated with exquisite İznik tiles, is impressive: the carved wooden *mimber*, or pulpit, and the sultan's loge are particularly fine. Unusually, a large women's gallery runs the full length of the cross-stroke of the reverse-T ground plan.

Manisa Archeological Museum

Murat Cad, next door to Muradiye Camii • Daily 8am–7pm, Nov–March till 5pm • ₺5 • ⓦ muze.gov.tr

The Muradiye Camii was originally part of a larger complex that included a *medrese* (theological school) and *imaret* (soup kitchen), the latter of which now holds the **Manisa Arkeoloji Müzesi**. Inside is an interesting collection of archeological and ethnological exhibits, including items retrieved from Sardis and fossilized footprints dating back to 20,000–25,000 BC, found in the nearby region of Salihli.

POWER-GUM FESTIVAL

Every year around the spring equinox, the *Mesir Macunu Şenlikleri*, or **Power-Gum Festival** – now well into its fifth century – takes place around the **Sultan Camii**, to commemorate local doctor Merkez Efendi's concoction of a special resin to cure Ayşe Hafize (see above) of an unspecified ailment. Re-created each year, the gum, or *mesir macunu*, containing 41 herbs and spices, is scattered from the minaret by the muezzin to crowds who use the paste as a remedy against aches, pains and snake or insect bites.

Ulu Cami

On a natural, landscaped terrace 250m above Manisa Museum, accessed by steps

Manisa's oldest surviving mosque, the Ulu Cami was built atop a Byzantine church in 1366 by Işak Çelebi, Saruhan Bey's grandson. The spectacular view north over town rewards the steep climb up. Entering the open-roofed courtyard via the ornate portal, you confront the glory of the place, a forest of **antique columns**, some "double" and others carrying Byzantine capitals, presumably recycled from the church that once stood here.

ARRIVAL AND DEPARTURE   MANISA

By bus Manisa's *otogar* is on İbrahim Gökçen Bulvarı, 2km (15min walk) north of Sultan Meyd; dolmuşes marked "Ulu Parkı" ply the route.

Destinations İzmir (every 15min; 1hr); Salihli via Sart/ Sardis (every 30min; 1hr 20min).

By train The station is 2km northwest of Sultan Meyd,

along Atatürk Bulvarı. Manisa sits on a major rail junction; services include the İzmir Mavi Tren (İzmir Blue Train) to Ankara and trains between İzmir and Bandirma.

Destinations Ankara (1 daily; 14hr): Balıkesir (2 daily; 2hr 30min); Bandirma (2 daily; 4hr 45min): İzmir (6 daily; 1hr 15min).

ACCOMMODATION

Arma Sekiz Eylül Cad 14, 1.5km from Manisa Archeological Museum ☎ 0236 231 1980, ⓦ hotelarma .com.tr. This central hotel holds no surprises. Its carpeted business-class rooms are starting to age but remain

spacious and clean, with thick windows buffering any noise from the busy street below. The in-house restaurant serves a decent buffet breakfast, and the reception staff are friendly and professional. **₺175**

EATING AND DRINKING

Gediz Kebap Mimar Sinan Mah, 8 Eylül Cad 19; follow İbrahim Gökçen Blv 800m north of Sultan Meyd ☎ 0236 231 2525. This popular restaurant serves up a carnivore's delight of *döner*, *pide* and *kebap*, including the local sausage-like version. Dessert offerings include the chicken-and-milk pudding *tavuk göğsü*, or less adventurous chocolate profiteroles. Mains ₺6–18. Daily 10am–11pm.

Yeni Han Corner of Dr Sadik Ahmet & Dumlupınar cads. This restored nineteenth-century *han* (inn) has half a dozen cafés lining the open coutryard with menus that offer pasta and stir-fry dishes, home-baked cakes, *tostlarımızı* (toasted sandwiches) and teas. The courtyard sometimes hosts live music and events, and there are craft shops upstairs. Mains ₺5–14. Daily 8am–10pm.

Sardis

Daily 8am–7pm, Nov–March till 5pm • ₺8 • ⓦ muze.gov.tr

Ancient **Sardis** (Sart in Turkish) is a large site divided by the İzmir–Uşak highway (E96/D300) and accessible from the small village of Sart, 65km southeast of Manisa and 85km east of İzmir. The surrounding countryside, on the lower slopes of the Bozdağ range, is dominated by sultana-producing vineyards. Capital of the ancient kingdom of Lydia, Sardis also saw Persian, Greek, Roman and Christian rule, and housed a prosperous Jewish community. While not as impressive as Ephesus – whose Temple of Artemis was paid for by Croesus – the partially restored ruins are pleasantly free of crowds and touts. Both its clusters of ruins are easily reached on foot from the main road in Sart, though the uphill one is a hot walk in summer.

Brief history

Sardis became incredibly wealthy thanks to the gold flecks that were washed down from Mount Tmolos (now Bozdağ) and caught in sheepskins by the locals. According to legend, the source of this wealth was the eighth-century BC Phrygian king **Midas**, whose touch turned everything to gold. Unable to eat, his curse was lifted when the gods bid him wash his hands in the River Paktolos, which flowed down to Sardis from the south.

Not surprisingly, perhaps, the Lydians invented coinage under Sardis's most celebrated king, Croesus (560–546 BC). When his wealth attracted the attention of the Persians under Cyrus, the Delphic oracle ambiguously advised a worried Croesus that should he attack first, a great empire would be destroyed. Croesus went to war and was defeated, and after a two-week siege Sardis fell; taken prisoner by Cyrus, Croesus was burned alive, though some accounts have him rescued from the pyre by a rainstorm.

As a Persian city, Sardis was sacked during the Ionian revolt of 499 BC. It revived under Alexander the Great, but was destroyed by an earthquake in 17 AD, and rebuilt by the Romans. Although Sardis ranked as one of the Seven Churches of Asia addressed by St John in Revelation (3:1–6), that didn't spare Byzantine Sardis from conquest by Saruhan and destruction at the hands of Tamerlane in 1401. The city only came to light again when American archeologists excavated here between 1904 and 1914.

Gymnasium and synagogue

The first of Sardis's two sites lies just north of the road on the eastern edge of Sart. Entry is via a partially revealed, marble-paved **Roman avenue**, which passes various shops, though low walls with discernible doorways are all that remain. A break in the shopping mall leads into the restored **synagogue**. The walls are covered with copies of the original coloured stonework, now housed in the Manisa Museum; the extensive floor mosaics are, however, original.

Adjacent to the synagogue, the **gymnasium and bath complex** was once the city's most prominent building. Its **Marble Court**, the entry from the palaestra to the baths, has been spectacularly restored to its appearance when first built in 211 AD. Behind the court are the remains of a plunge pool and rest area.

The Temple of Artemis

Reached along a paved lane leading 1200m south from Sart, the **Temple of Artemis** (**Artemis Tapınağı**) was once among the four largest temples in Asia Minor. It was built by Croesus, destroyed by Greek raiders during the Ionian revolt, and rebuilt by Alexander the Great. Today, fifteen massive Ionic columns remain standing, though only two are intact. However, enough of the foundations remain to suggest just how large the building – constructed to rival the temples of Ephesus, Samos and Didyma – used to be. The remnants of a small Byzantine church huddle beside the two complete columns. More than anything, it's the beauty of the setting, enclosed by wooded and vine-covered hills and accented by weird Cappadocia-like pinnacles, that leaves a lasting impression.

ARRIVAL AND DEPARTURE   SARDIS

By bus or dolmuş Dolmuşes from Manisa and buses from İzmir, both heading to Salihli, drop passengers at the petrol stations on the main highway in Sart; make sure you request to be let off at Sart, though Sardis is also usually understood.

Destinations İzmir (hourly; 1hr 25min); Manisa (10 daily; 1hr 50min); Salihli (at least hourly; 10min).

ACCOMMODATION AND EATING

Hotel Lidya Sardes Kursunlu Kaplicalari Yolu 107, Salihli ☎ 0236 715 5555, ⓦ lidyatermalotel.com. The nearest accommodation to Sardis, overlooking the mountainside town of Salihli, 8km east on the İzmir–Afyon road, this enormous hotel caters to tour buses, but also offers good-value rooms for independent travellers. Apartment-style suites (₺310) have kitchens and plenty of space, but are an uphill walk from the main hotel, where the carpeted rooms are also spacious, with subtle, Sardis-like decor. There are various dining and drinking options, plus a swimming-pool-thermal complex with good spa treatments. **₺240**

The central and southern Aegean

PAMUKKALE

The central and southern Aegean

The central and southern Aegean coast and its hinterland have seen foreign tourism for longer than any other part of Turkey. The territory between modern İzmir and Marmaris corresponds to the bulk of ancient Ionia and just about all of old Caria, and contains a concentration of Classical Greek, Hellenistic and Roman antiquities unrivalled in Turkey. Of these, Ephesus is usually first on everyone's list, but the understated charms of exquisitely positioned sites such as Priene and Labranda hold at least as much appeal. Of course, most visitors are drawn especially by the beaches – Kuşadası, Bodrum and Marmaris are among the largest resorts in all Turkey, bursting with cruise passengers and package tourists but rather likeable places nonetheless. Independent travellers may prefer to seek more secluded sections of coast: the resort of Çeşme is certainly not overblown, the Datça peninsula is unspoiled and quite spectacular, and the towns and villages on the Çeşme, Bodrum and Hisarönü peninsulas are highly popular with moneyed locals.

4

There's plenty to see once you get away from the coast, too. Sprawling **İzmir**, the third-largest city in Turkey, is an earthy place that attracts almost no foreign visitors – swing by to see how "real" Turkey functions, and for an excursion west along the peninsula to **Alaçatı**, a well-preserved former Greek village that's now a weekend magnet for affluent Turks. The territory of **ancient Ionia** begins to the south, bookended – in travel terms – by little **Selçuk**, most famed as the jumping-off point for **Ephesus** but a delightful place in its own right. South of here is **Kuşadası**, an unabashedly utilitarian resort that serves well for excursions to the major antiquities and the nearby **Dilek National Park**. Ruins spanning numerous eras pepper the former coast – now some way inland – as you head further south, including **Priene**, perhaps the most dramatic site of all the Ionian cities; sprawling **Miletus**; and **Didyma**, with its gargantuan temple.

South of the main Ionian sites, the southern Aegean begins with reminders of another ancient civilization – the **Carians**, a purportedly barbarous people indigenous to the area (a rarity in Anatolia) who spoke a language distantly related to Greek. The waters of **Bafa Gölü**, and ancient **Heracleia ad Latmos** on its northeast shore, make a suitably dramatic introduction to this once-isolated and mysterious region. From **Milas**, the nearest substantial town, a cluster of ancient sites provides tempting excursions. South again, party-hard **Bodrum** and its peninsula are the big event on this coast. While the tentacles of

EPHESUS

Highlights

❶ Alaçatı This marvellous little village has become one of the best places in which to sample the Aegean area's unique cuisine. **See p.234**

❷ Selçuk More than a mere base for visiting ancient ruins, this is one of Turkey's most pleasant small towns, and a great place to shack up for a few days. **See p.237**

❸ Ephesus Hot, crowded and exhausting it may be, but you simply can't miss Turkey's best-preserved ancient city – a magnificent monument to the wealth of Rome. **See p.239**

❹ Priene Scramble over the ruins of a superbly preserved Hellenistic town and gaze out over the Meander basin. **See p.249**

❺ Bodrum Spend a few days sampling the nightlife at Turkey's most fashionable and sophisticated beach resort. **See p.260**

❻ Pamukkale Visit the geological oddity that has found its way onto every Turkish tourism poster. **See p.278**

❼ Aphrodisias New excavations at this beautifully sited Roman city are revealing a site to rival Ephesus in grandeur and importance. **See p.283**

HIGHLIGHTS ARE MARKED ON THE MAP ON PP.226–227

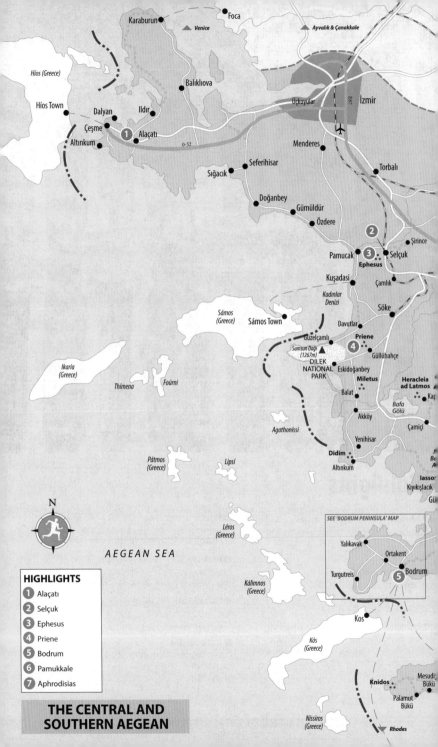

THE CENTRAL AND
SOUTHERN AEGEAN

HIGHLIGHTS

1. Alaçatı
2. Selçuk
3. Ephesus
4. Priene
5. Bodrum
6. Pamukkale
7. Aphrodisias

AEGEAN SEA

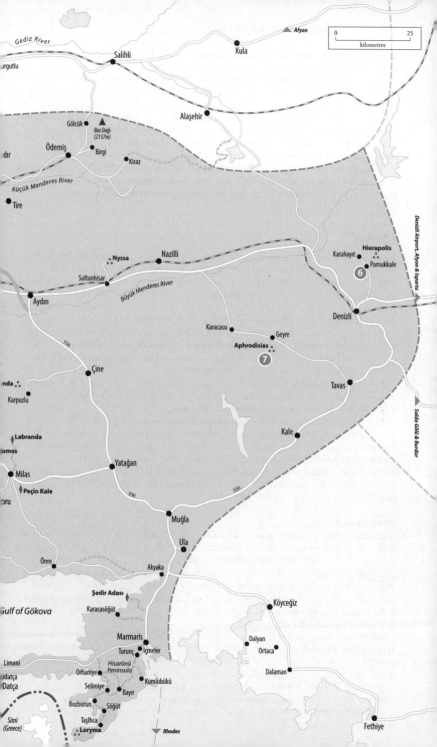

development creep over the surrounding land, the features that first attracted outsiders to the area still occasionally shine through. Next up is **Marmaris**, another big, rather overblown resort; the **Hisarönü peninsula** beyond, bereft of a sandy shoreline but blessed with magnificent scenery, offers the closest escape – **Datça** and the remote beaches nearby are more rewarding than the much-touted ruins of ancient **Knidos**. Lastly, inland you'll find the otherworldly travertine terraces that surround the hot springs of **Pamukkale** – picture-perfect proof that beaches are not the only natural attraction in this spellbinding region.

If you've been travelling in other parts of Turkey, the Aegean area's high **accommodation prices** may come as an unpleasant surprise – rates at the coastal resorts go through the roof in summer, though inland (including İzmir, Selçuk and Pamukkale) you can find budget rooms at any time of year. As for **Aegean cuisine**, it's unusual in placing far less emphasis on meat, and far more on fresh herbs and vegetables.

İzmir

Consistently ignored by those in search of beach life or ancient treasures further south, and derided by urban Turks from elsewhere, **İZMİR** is nevertheless worth at least a little of your time – not least because it boasts a long and illustrious history of its own, most pertinently its incarnation as the site of ancient **Smyrna** (see p.228). Secondly, there's İzmir's enviable position straddling the head of a 50km-long gulf – surrounded on all sides by mountains, the city is arrayed like a gigantic amphitheatre, with the **Ionian Sea** functioning as a sort of never-ending show. Finally, consider the alternating, occasionally dubious charms of its various neighbourhoods – most urbane of the lot is **Alsancak**, north of the centre, full of bars and cafés and surprisingly trendy for provincial Turkey. Heading south down the coastal road, you'll come to the fascinating **bazaar** area, busy with shoppers and spiked by minarets, and occupying a fair chunk of the city centre; to the south is **Konak**, a shopping area with a couple of worthwhile museums. Further inland, the small streets surrounding **Basmane** station have long been somewhat appealing in a scruffy way – at the time of writing, they also played temporary home to a substantial contingent of Syrian refugees awaiting sea transport to Europe, their predicament made painfully evident by the life jackets on sale outside many clothing stores. Lastly, the mazey alleys heading up to the **castle** – the **Kadifekale** – overlooking the city are tremendously atmospheric.

One negative point is that the **weather**, though mild for much of the year, gets stinking hot in the summer – there are no city beaches to escape to, but the Çeşme peninsula (see p.234) is not too far away.

Brief history

The site of modern İzmir was settled by aboriginal **Anatolians** as long ago as the third millennium BC. Around 600 BC, Lydian raids sent the area into a long decline; it was recovering tentatively when **Alexander the Great** appeared in 334 BC. Spurred by a timely dream corroborated by the oracle of Apollo at Claros, Alexander decreed the foundation of a new, better-fortified settlement on Mount Pagos, the flat-topped hill today adorned with the **Kadifekale**. His generals, Antigonus and Lysimachus, carried out Alexander's plan after his death, by which time the city bore the name – **Smyrna** – familiar to the West for centuries after.

Roman rule endowed the city with impressive buildings, but **Arab** raids in the seventh century AD triggered several centuries of turbulence. **Selçuk** Turks held the city for two decades prior to 1097, when the **Byzantines** recaptured it. The thirteenth-century Latin tenure in Constantinople provoked another era of disruption at Smyrna, with Crusaders, Genoese, Tamerlane's Mongols and minor Turkish emirs jockeying for position. Order was re-established in 1415 by Mehmet I, who finally incorporated the town into the **Ottoman Empire**, his successors repulsing repeated Venetian efforts to retake it.

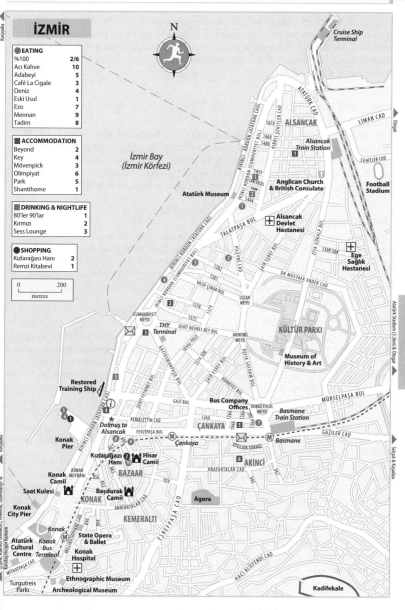

İZMIR

● EATING	
%100	2/6
Acı Kahve	10
Adabeyi	5
Café La Cigale	3
Deniz	4
Eski Usul	1
Ezo	7
Mennan	9
Tadim	8

■ ACCOMMODATION	
Beyond	2
Key	4
Mövenpick	3
Olimpiyat	6
Park	5
Shantihome	1

■ DRINKING & NIGHTLIFE	
80'ler 90'lar	1
Kırmızı	2
Sess Lounge	3

● SHOPPING	
Kızlarağası Hanı	2
Remzi Kitabevi	1

Following **World War I**, Greece was given an indefinite mandate over İzmir and its hinterland. Foolishly, a huge Greek expeditionary force pressed inland, inciting the resistance of the Turkish nationalists under Atatürk. The climactic defeat in the two-year struggle against Greece and her nominal French and Italian allies was the entry into Smyrna of the Turkish army on September 9, 1922. The secular republic not having yet been proclaimed, the **reconquest of the city** took on the character of a successfully concluded jihad, or holy Muslim war, with three days of murder and plunder. Almost seventy percent of the city burned to the ground and thousands of non-Muslims died. A quarter of a million refugees huddled at the quayside while British, American, French and Italian vessels stood idly by, refusing to grant them safe passage until the third day.

Restored Training Ship

Off Birinci Kordon • Tues–Sun 10am–6pm • Free

Permanently anchored off the İzmir waterfront, the **Restored Training Ship** is an old navy vessel that now functions as a museum of sorts – nothing special, but the most worthwhile target beside the water here. Inside you'll find some model boats, brass nautical fittings, photographs of İzmir in days of yore (yore having mostly been active in the 1960s), and the obligatory pictures of a certain Mustafa Kemal.

Archeological Museum

Turgutreis Parkı, just above Konak bus terminal and metro station • Tues–Sun 8am–5.30pm • ₺10

The **Archeological Museum** features an excellent collection of finds from all over İzmir province and beyond. The ground floor is largely given over to statuary and friezes of all eras, while the top floor focuses on smaller objects, with an emphasis on Bronze Age and archaic pottery – more exciting than it sounds.

Ethnographic Museum

Turgutreis Parkı, just above Konak bus terminal and metro station and alongside the Archeological Museum • Tues–Sun 8am–5.30pm • Free

Built in 1831 and originally functioning as a hospital, the **Ethnographic Museum** feels somewhat neglected. Exhibits on its lower floor concentrate on the two types of traditional İzmir house, the wooden Turkish residence and the more substantial "Levantine" (Christian and Jewish merchants) house; up the spiral staircase you'll find weaponry and woven ware.

Agora

Off Eşrefpaşa Cad; entrance at south of compound • Daily 8am–7pm • ₺5

The only surviving pre-Ottoman monument in the flatlands, the **Agora** is İzmir's most accessible ancient site. It probably dates back to the early second century BC, but what you see now are the remains of a later reconstruction, financed during the reign of the Roman Emperor Marcus Aurelius after the catastrophic earthquake of 178 AD. It's an impressive site, with water still coursing through ancient ducts and channels. Principal structures include a **colonnade** of fourteen Corinthian columns on the west side and the remains of, reputedly, the second-largest basilica in the Roman world.

AFRO-TURKS

Many travellers to western Turkey, and İzmir in particular, are surprised by the sight of **Africans** who are obviously not visitors. Often termed *Arap* or "Arabs" by other Turks, they are in fact descendants of the large numbers of Sudanese, Somalis, Algerians and Egyptians who were brought to Anatolia during the Ottoman Empire. Many arrived as slaves, forced to work in the tobacco and cotton fields or as household servants, particularly wet nurses.

Today there are about twenty thousand **Afro-Turks** (as they prefer to be known) in the western Aegean provinces, most of whom live in the mountains between İzmir and Mersin. Speaking fluent Turkish and devoutly Muslim, they are often proud of their Turkish heritage, though intermarriage with other Turks is rare.

A BOAT TRIP ACROSS İZMİR BAY

One of İzmir's best sights is the city itself, seen from the bay it surrounds – at ₺4.50 for a return trip, these are by far the Aegean's cheapest **boat trips**. Boats head from three docks – Konak, Pasaport and Alsancak – to the best destination, **Karşıyaka**. Leaving from Pasaport provides the most spectacular trip, crawling past İzmir's 1970s' tricolore of white-yellow-brown buildings to Alsancak before heading across the bay.

Karşıyaka itself is a pleasant part of İzmir, its pedestrianized central street – **Kemalpaşa Cad** – sporting a clutch of shops, restaurants and cafés. Try eating at *Alesta*, a small restaurant facing the local mosque, selling cheap seafood sandwiches, and itself sandwiched by two fishmongers.

Kadifekale

Rakım Erkutlu Cad, a 20min uphill walk from the agora • Daily 24hr • Free

Way up above the agora is the old acropolis of Smyrna, now known as the **Kadifekale**, or "Velvet Castle". Visible by night as well as by day thanks to skilful floodlighting, it's mainly worth visiting for the views over the city. However, the journey up is often just as enjoyable – labyrinthine alleys twist their way uphill through a series of pleasantly earthy neighbourhoods, some of which have noticeable Kurdish populations.

Asansör

Off Mithatpaşa Cad, 15min walk southwest of Konak • Daily 6am–midnight • Free

Offering views across most of the city, the old-fashioned **Asansör** – Turkish for "lift" – was constructed in 1907 in a 50m-high brick tower. Originally serving as a quick route to and from the mansions perched on the hill above, the elevator has since been completely refurbished; from the restaurant at the top, you can look down on narrow streets of crumbling houses and out over the bay.

4

ARRIVAL AND DEPARTURE   İZMİR

BY PLANE

Adnan Menderes airport (☎ 444 9828), 18km southeast of the city, hosts a growing number of domestic and international routes, with the regular – and often remarkably cheap – flights to and from Istanbul shaving hours and hours from the roundabout bus, train or ferry routes. The airport is linked by train to Basmane station in central İzmir (8 daily; ₺2.25; 20min); İZBAN light-rail trains also head to Alsancak in the north of the city (hourly; ₺2.25; 35min), and there are direct services to Denizli, for Pamukkale (see p.278) and Selçuk (see p.237). Havaş airport buses (hourly; 40min–1hr; ₺10) will deposit you in front of the *Swissôtel Grand Efes* on Gaziosmanpaşa Bul. The hourly city bus #202 (₺4.50) follows a similar route from the airport, terminating in Cumhuriyet Meydanı. Taxis cost around ₺60 to downtown İzmir.

Destinations Adana (3–4 daily; 1hr 25min); Ankara (3–4 daily; 1hr 15min); Antalya (2 daily; 1hr 5min); Gaziantep (1–2 daily; 1hr 40min); Hatay (3 weekly; 1hr 35min); Istanbul (every 30min; 1hr 10min); Kars (3 weekly; 2hr); Kayseri (4 weekly; 1hr 30min); Samsun (1–2 daily; 1hr 35min); Trabzon (1–2 daily; 1hr 50min); Van (1 daily; 2hr).

BY BUS

The main bus station, known as the *büyük otogar*, is 8km northeast of the centre. Many bus companies offer free *servis* buses to their offices in 9 Eylül Meydanı, just north of Basmane; otherwise, it's best to take a taxi (₺40) into the centre. Buses run to and from the Çeşme peninsula from the coastal suburb of Üçkuyular, 6km southwest of downtown (₺20 by taxi from Konak, or a short walk from Üçkuyular Fahrettin Atalay station on the blue metro line).

Destinations from otogar Ankara (hourly; 8hr 30min); Antalya (hourly; 7hr); Bodrum (hourly; 3hr); Bursa (hourly; 5hr); Çanakkale (10 daily; 5hr); Datça (6 daily; 5hr 15min); Denizli (hourly; 4hr); Fethiye (15 daily; 6hr); Istanbul (hourly; 9hr); Kuşadası (every 30min; 1hr 30min); Marmaris (hourly; 3hr 30min); Selçuk (every 20min; 1hr).

Destinations from Üçkuyular Alaçatı (7 daily; 1hr); Çeşme (7 daily; 1hr 30min); Foça (hourly; 1hr 15min).

BY TRAIN

Trains from the line to Denizli pull in at Basmane station, right in the centre of town, while longer-distance services use Alsancak station, to the north. To get to or from Istanbul you'll save time by using a train-ferry combination, via Bandırma.

Destinations from Alsancak Afyon (2 daily; 7hr 30min); Ankara (3 daily; 11–13hr); Bandırma (2 daily; 6hr).

Destinations from Basmane Denizli (6 daily; 4hr 15min); Selçuk (8 daily; 1hr 15min).

GETTING AROUND AND INFORMATION

On foot Walking is much the quickest and easiest way to explore the city. The level of city traffic means you're rarely better off taking a bus.

By public transport The underground metro line (daily 6am–midnight) provides a fast, useful transport link between Basmane station and the Konak district, with further extensions planned. Most of the municipality's numbered bus routes start from Konak bus terminal, though few tourists use these services. Lastly, ferries run along the coast and across the bay (see p.231). All run on prepaid card systems (₺2.25/ticket); you can buy individual tickets for metro and ferry rides, though for buses you're likely to need a Kent Card (₺6; available from kiosks and shops), which will also save you money on each journey if you're in town for a while.

By bike The city has several rental-bike stands (₺1 for 2hr) dotted along the shorefront, which makes a great cycling route – you can head clean around the bay, if you so desire. Getting hold of one without a Turkish phone number is tricky, though, and you'll have to register online beforehand (ⓦ nextbike.com.tr).

By tour bus Tourist buses run a convoluted figure-of-eight route from Alsancak to all the main sights (hourly 9am–2pm, or every 30min if a cruise ship is in town; ₺60). Tickets last all day, so you can hop on and off as you wish.

Tourist office There's an office in the airport arrivals hall (daily 9am–6pm; ☏ 0232 274 2214), and a central bureau at 1344 Sok 2, Pasaport district (daily 8am–5pm; ☏ 0232 483 5117). Both can suggest accommodation (mid-range and up), and hand out useful free city plans.

ACCOMMODATION

It's normally easy to find somewhere to stay, though street noise (particularly from car horns) is a nearly universal problem. The main area for **budget hotels** is immediately in front of the train station, which at the time of writing is facing an influx of refugees. For more upmarket digs, head for the streets around the seafront.

Beyond 1376 Sok 5 ☏ 0232 463 0585, ⓦ hotelbeyond .com. Contemporary boutique choice that's great for couples – think mood lighting, dangling lamps and elaborate bedheads. Rooms come in six colours: you're encouraged to choose according to your mood. ₺280

★**Key** 1379 Sok 55, Sevgi Yolu ☏ 0232 489 1940, ⓦ keyhotel.com. Formerly the city's central bank, this brazenly modern affair is now its most appealing hotel. Even the smallest of its 31 rooms is huge – get one on the waterfront and you may wake to find your ceiling a shimmer with reflected sunlight. Service is impeccable: you can, for example, be picked up from the airport in the hotel's own Silver Ghost Rolls-Royce. ₺500

Mövenpick Cumhuriyet Bul 138 ☏ 0232 488 1414, ⓦ moevenpick-hotels.com. The city's best-designed five-star hotel, offering all you'd expect of the chain. The 185 rooms share a chocolate colour scheme, and some have a partial view of the sea; facilities are excellent, especially the pleasing indoor pool. ₺800

Olimpiyat 1296 Sok 24 ☏ 0232 425 1269, ⓦ otelantikhan.com. Quirky place on an atmospheric road near Basmane station. Don't be put off by the lobby area; most of the rooms themselves are quite presentable, with all mod cons and good showers; the staff are also switched-on English-speakers. A good buffet breakfast rounds out the picture. ₺120

★**Park** 1366 Sok 6 ☏ 0232 425 3333, ⓦ parkhotelizmir .com. The Basmane area's token boutique hotel, and it's not half bad. Even after walking through the semi-swanky, Orient Express-style lobby, the rooms do not disappoint – large and well-appointed, with attractive flourishes. ₺160

★**Shantihome** 1464 Sok 15 ☏ 0546 235 0805, ⓦ shantihome.org. The city's first hostel is a bright, traveller-friendly place in the middle of the Alsancak action. The curtained-off bunks are a grand idea, the fully equipped kitchen is great for further penny-pinching, and there are bicycles for rent. Dorm ₺30

EATING

The budget options within sight of Basmane station have tables on the street and offer the usual range of kebabs, *pide* and stews. The **bazaar** holds another selection of inexpensive outfits, although its warren of streets can be confusing. **Alsancak** and the Birinci Kordon **waterfront** offer a step up in quality and price.

Adabeyi Konak Pier ☏ 0232 482 0470, ⓦ adabeyi.com .tr. Perfectly poised on a swish terrace at the tip of Konak Pier, this restaurant offers the best possible views of the bay. The menu has Turkish staples livened up with some intriguing additions; the stuffed sardines (₺25) are superb, as is the semolina *helva* with ice cream (₺12). Daily noon–11pm.

★**Café La Cigale** Fransız Kültür Merkezi, Cumhuriyet

Bul 152 ☏ 0232 421 4780. The French Cultural Institute's leafy gardens are the place to be on a sunny afternoon, with delectable French main courses and pasta dishes (all around ₺20) served up on chequered tablecloths. It's hard to say no to their lemon cheesecake (₺8.50). Daily 8.30am–10.30pm.

Deniz İzmir Palas Hotel, Atatürk Bul ☏ 0232 422 0601.

Somewhat pricey local favourite offering a sophisticated range of seafood dishes, including grilled fish (₺30–50) or mixed *meze* platters (₺35). Reservations advisable at weekend mealtimes. Daily 11am–11pm.

★ **Eski Usul** İfran Boyuer Sok 2 ☎ 0232 421 3570. Great-value Alsancak restaurant with decor arranged along Orient Express-style lines. Their grilled fish is superb (₺15–19), but most people are here for the *meze*, brought out on a platter and yours for about ₺7/plate; pick judiciously and, like an Anatolian Hannibal Lecter, you can have liver with fava beans and a nice rakı. Daily 8.30am–10.30pm.

Ezo 1366 Sok ☎ 0232 489 8953. The best of the Basmane area's kebab restaurants – popular enough, in any case, to have two outlets facing each other. Kebabs cost from ₺15/portion, and there's good *pide*, too. Daily 10am–11pm.

CAFÉS AND ICE CREAM PARLOURS

%100 Doktor Mustafa Bey Cad 18 ☎ 0232 422 5535, ⓦ yuzdeyuzcafe.com. The swankiest of the many cafés lining the city's most upper-class street, selling decent coffee (from ₺8) in a space lined with sleek, black-and-white floor tiles, and dotted with golden accoutrements. There's another branch on the end of Konak Pier. Mon–Sat 7am–10pm.

Acı Kahve Kızlarağası Hanı ☎ 0232 471 5593. The main part of this café is on the second floor of the bazaar, but head on up to the second floor and you'll be able to take your tea or lemonade (both ₺1.50) with a truly wonderful mosque view. Daily 8am–8pm; Sat & Sun second floor closed.

Mennan Bazaar. If you find yourself in the bazaar, hunt down this little ice-cream vendor, which sells little scoops of heaven for ₺2 and up. Mon–Fri 8am–6pm.

★ **Tadim** Fevzipaşa Bul. There's not too much to recommend this fast-food joint – bar the incredibly cheap juice bar tucked into its lower level. Just ₺0.50 will buy you a fresh orange juice; pay a little more and you can have an apple-carrot mix, melon, kiwi – or even pomegranate if you're there from late Aug. Daily 8am–10pm.

DRINKING AND NIGHTLIFE

Upper **Alsancak** has blossomed as the district for trendy **nightlife**, with bars and clubs tucked inland along pedestrianized side streets invisible from **Birinci Kordon**. As ownership and themes of each establishment tend to roll over on a two-year cycle, specific recommendations are subject to change, but each street has its own distinct atmosphere. Starting from the south, narrow **Cumbalı Sok** has an upbeat, indie feel. One street north and shaded by vines, **Can Yucel** attracts a slightly older crowd and offers a more refined atmosphere. North again, **1453 Sok** is a wider affair, boasting proper pubs and clubs in restored old houses. All the pricey bars on **Konak Pier** offer good sea views.

80'ler 90'lar 1453 Sok ☎ 0232 497 5414. İzmiris come over a bit retro in this club, bouncing their way through 80s and 90s hits (hence the name), interspersed with the odd Turkopop chart number. Bring energy. Daily 4pm–late.

Kırmızı Cumbalı Sok ☎ 0232 464 8416. Unassuming place that's typical of this part of Alsancak. The benefits are cheap drinks, and outdoor tables – a good spot from which to soak up the vibe and plot your next destination. Daily 1pm–late.

Sess Lounge South of Cumhuriyet Meyd. The quirkiest of the bars south of the Cumhuriyet roundabout, with old phones on the tables, black-and-white pictures behind iron grilles and music that generally fits into the pigeonhole marked "yesteryear". Beers ₺10; sea view free. Daily 9am–4am.

ENTERTAINMENT

Atatürk Cultural Centre Mithatpaşa Cad 92 ☎ 0232 483 8520. Home to the local symphony orchestra, which plays regularly on Fri and Sat and hosts occasional concerts by soloists.

Cinemaxium Konak Pier ☎ 0232 446 9040. Decent cinema on Konak Pier, showing a mix of Hollywood and Istanbul-made films for around ₺17 a ticket.

State Opera and Ballet Milli Kütüphane Cad ☎ 0232 489 0474, ⓦ dobgm.gov.tr. The pleasingly varied programme at this wonderful Ottoman Art Deco venue ranges from chamber music to pop and jazz.

THE INTERNATIONAL İZMIR FESTIVAL

The linchpin of İzmir's summer season – though it's a bit of a misnomer, since many events take place at restored venues at Ephesus or Çeşme castle – is the **International İzmir Festival**, running from mid-June to early July. Tickets run to ₺30–100 a head, but half-price student discounts are available and the acts featured are often world-class – past names have included the Moscow Ballet, Paco Peña and the late Ravi Shankar. Check the programme and find ticket vendors online (ⓦ iksev.org).

4

SHOPPING

The shops that fill the narrow lanes of İzmir's wonderfully atmospheric **Kemeraltı bazaar** sell all sorts, from spices to Chinese-made socks. For brand names, Alsancak and the wider Konak area are your best bets.

Kızlarağası Hanı Bazaar area ⓦ kizlaragasihani.com. If you're hitting Kemeraltı bazaar with a purchase in mind, rather than simply wandering, this is where to head – a restored *kervansaray* with dozens of places to buy waterpipes, jewellery, knives (check-in luggage only, remember) and traditional musical instruments. Most shops daily 9am–9pm.

Remzi Kitabevi Konak Pier ☎ 0232 489 5325. The best bookshop for a long way around, with an admirable array of English-language novels, guidebooks and magazines – not surprising, really, since many of the city's language academies are clustered on the other side of the main road. Daily 10am–10pm.

DIRECTORY

Hamam The cleanest and most secure is Karataş Hoşgör (☎ 0232 425 2093), on an alley inland from Mithatpaşa Cad 10 (daily: men 7–11am & 5pm–midnight; women 11am–5pm; ₺15).
Hospitals The most central state hospitals are Alsancak Devlet Hastanesi, on Ali Çetinkaya Bul (☎ 0232 463 6465), and the Konak Hospital (with dental section), across from

the ethnographic and archeological museums (☎ 0232 425 9480). Much better is the Ege Sağlık Hastanesi on 1399 Sok (☎ 0232 463 7700).
Post The main PTT office is at Cumhuriyet Meyd (Mon–Sat 8am–8pm, Sun 8.30am–5pm), but there are branches across the city. DHL (☎ 0232 422 1537), on Şehit Nevres Bul, is the best placed of the international couriers.

4   The Çeşme peninsula

A claw-like mass of land extending west from İzmir, the **Çeşme peninsula** is not just a quick escape from the city, but a highly tempting destination in its own right. The first place of note you'll come to is hip **Alaçatı**, which has blossomed from simple village to nouveau riche preening ground in the space of a decade. The peninsula terminates near the eponymous town of **Çeşme**, the least touristed and most relaxing of the central Aegean's main coastal resorts. Nearby **Altınkum** is the best of many nearby beaches.

Much of the Çeşme peninsula is green and hilly, with added colour from the deeply aquamarine sea and the white of the wind turbines on the approach to the peninsula. The **climate** here is noticeably drier, cooler and healthier than anywhere nearby on the Turkish coast, especially in comparison with occasionally hellish İzmir or muggy Kuşadası. These conditions, combined with the presence of several thermal springs, have made the peninsula a popular resort for more than a century.

Alaçatı

The architecturally stunning old Greek village of **ALAÇATI** is one of the most upmarket locales on the Aegean coast. With an undeniably Mediterranean air, it's one of those places that makes you question whether you're still in Turkey at all – the lone call to prayer is heeded by next to no one, while cafés, shops and wine bars run a brisk trade. However, this is no Brit-packed beach resort. Most of it is manifestly inland, for a start, while the overwhelming majority of visitors are Turkish – mainly cosmopolitan, moneyed sorts from Istanbul and İzmir, who pop by on weekend trips.

Things have changed considerably since 2001, when Alaçatı was just another charming peninsular village. Then one of the town's old stone houses opened up as a swish designer hotel; within a few years it had spawned a dozen tasteful imitators, and a similar number of gourmet restaurants. There are now well over two hundred hotels and one hundred restaurants, with numbers still rising; however, strict building regulations have ensured the rapid growth has had little effect on Alaçatı's architectural character. Its old lanes and cobbled streets, particularly on the main thoroughfare, **Kemalpaşa Caddesi**, are dotted with antique shops, art galleries and snazzy boutiques selling designer goods.

Most visitors head to the town's 300m-long sandy **beach**, 4km south, to take advantage of unique **wind- and kitesurfing** conditions. The strong, reliable "Meltemi" wind, combined with shallow water and lack of waves, makes the bay ideal for learners.

ARRIVAL AND DEPARTURE ALAÇATI

By bus or dolmuş Most buses between Çeşme and İzmir stop in Alaçatı; the former is also accessible by dolmuş. The largely pedestrianized town centre is a short walk south of the bus stop – just follow the crowd.
Destinations Çeşme (every 10min; 30min); İzmir (7 daily; 1hr).

ACTIVITIES

Bike rental The *Naciye Teyze* hotel rents out bikes from ₺10/hr or ₺30/day.
Hot springs and mud baths There are a few places offering spring-water pools and mud-bath treatments just north of town, around the village of Şifne; you'll pay around ₺20.
Kitesurfing Kite Turkey (www.kite-turkey.com) works with all levels, and can supply all gear. Ten-hour courses start at €300.

ACCOMMODATION

Though landlocked, Alaçatı's accommodation follows a coastal pattern: wildly expensive in summer, often full on weekends, and far cheaper out of season. Consult the main booking engines, though, and you may well pick up a bargain. Surfers generally **camp** out of town on the beach.

Çiprika Pansiyon 3005 Sok 5 ☎0232 716 7303, ciprika.com. One of the cheapest places in town – for all that's worth. Run by a local family, it almost feels more like a homestay, with rooms that are a little rough around the edges, yet possibly all the better for that. The garden's good for people-watching, too. **₺200**
★ **İncirliev** 3074 Sok 3 ☎0232 716 0353, incirliev.com. A relatively new boutique hotel, this is a superb place to stay, with eight splendidly decorated rooms. Guests gush about the breakfasts, which include more than twenty kinds of home-made jams and marmalades. There's no pool (just a pool table), but the regular wine evenings more than make up for that. **₺430**
La Vela 3024 Sok 13 ☎0232 716 0808, alacatilavela.com. Amid the glut of converted-house pensions in town, this Swiss-run establishment stands out as a little different. Rather than focus on the small and homely, they've made their place relaxing in a more spacious, airy sense – the generously sized pool in the garden certainly helps, while the rooms are marginally more hotel-like than many competitors. **₺380**
Morlimon Cemaliye Cad 6 ☎0232 716 0557, morlimonotel.com. This seven-room hotel underwent a thorough refreshing in 2014, and the end result is rather eye-catching. Each room has been individually designed, and most are equipped with balconies. Breakfast can be taken in the garden. **₺350**
★ **Alaçatı Taş Hotel** Kemalpaşa Cad 132 ☎0232 716 7772, tasotel.com. This hotel, made Alaçatı what it is today – its refurbishment kick-started the town's regeneration. Despite the copycats, it's still the best in town, set in a lovingly restored 1890s building with eight large, stylish rooms, all with balconies and a/c. Service is professional yet relaxed, and the tasty breakfast is best enjoyed by the pool. In the afternoon, guests can return for tea and cake. One of the nicest places to stay in Turkey. **₺470**

EATING AND DRINKING

There are plenty of snazzy places to eat in town, though on summer evenings it can be hard to find a table – ask at your hotel if you'd like to **book ahead** at a specific place. The venues listed below don't usually require reservations.

★ **Asma Yaprağı** 1005 Sok 50 ☎0232 716 0178, asmayapragi.com.tr. What the Taş did for hotels (see above), this did for restaurants. Their trick of filling out a large table with home-made Aegean-style *meze* has now been copied by umpteen places lining a road which has become the trendiest in town, but the pleasing garden here remains the best place to head – especially for lunchtime, since dinner bookings are often made weeks ahead. You'll pay around ₺7.50 for each small *meze* plate; offerings change with the seasons but usually include goodies such as artichoke, stuffed vine leaves and samphire. Daily 2–6pm & 8pm–midnight.
Avrasya Uğur Mumcu Sevgi Yolu 22 ☎0232 716 9144, avrasyarestaurant.com. Locals, and tourists bored with pretentious restaurants and high prices, tend to gravitate to this place near the bus stop – tasty Turkish cooking at regular Turkish prices. *Pide* go from ₺10, kebabs a little more. Daily 9am–11pm.

Badem Mantı 13002 Sok 2 ☎0232 716 0748. A fairly down-to-earth place (though still very attractive … this is still Alaçatı), selling simple comfort food – *mantı*, Turkey's answer to ravioli. They offer numerous takes on the usual minced-meat filling, including spinach, cheese, and even a fried version. You'll pay around ₺20/dish. Daily noon–2am.

★**Ferdi Baba** By the port ☎0232 717 2145, ⓦferdibababalik.com. For a fabulous fish blow-out, grab a cab south out of town to the port area's stretch of seafront terraces. Though pricey (figure on at least ₺60/diner, without drinks), the seafood is as exquisite as the location – try the stuffed squid or the octopus kebabs. They've also opened another branch on Alaçatı's main street. Daily noon–1am.

Imren Kemalpaşa Cad 65 ☎0232 716 8356, ⓦimrenhelvatatlievi.com. The most tempting of the town's many, many cafés, largely on account of the mouthwatering desserts laid out by the counter – take your pick from several milky puddings, or plump for the superlative lemon cheesecake (₺14), served with a crushed biscuit base in a tall glass. Daily 9am–11pm.

Roka Bahçe Kemalpaşa Cad 107a ☎0232 716 9659. Smart-looking restaurant, and one of the best places on the main road for one simple reason – they've put up small, cute barriers between their outdoor seats and the busy pedestrianized street, meaning that nobody will be brushing past you as you dine. The menu is largely "fusion" – Aegean specialities with a twist, for around ₺40/main. Daily noon–11pm.

Traktor 11005 Sok 25 ☎0232 716 0679. There are a bunch of great wine bars on "Meze Street", but many require dinner bookings too. Hooray, then, for this relatively small, simple place, where you can just grab a seat and order a cocktail (₺40) or bottle of wine (from ₺90). Also great for coffee and people-watching during the day. Daily 2–6pm & 8pm–midnight.

Çeşme and around

A picturesque, often sleepy town of old Greek houses wrapped around a Genoese castle, **ÇEŞME** ("drinking fountain" in Turkish) doubtless takes its name from the many Ottoman fountains, some still functioning, scattered around its streets. Getting around is easy. You'll soon find yourself on the main bazaar thoroughfare, **İnkilap Cad**, which ends at the sea; head left for the castle, and right to stroll the town's **esplanade**, which itself ends at a small crescent-shaped beach.

Çeşme Castle
Entrance off Çarşı Cad • Tues–Sun 8am–7pm • ₺8

Visitors are free to clamber about every centimetre of Çeşme's restored **castle**. Much repaired by the Ottomans, it's now home to a small **museum** containing an interesting collection of archeological finds from nearby Erythrae, as well as a permanent exhibition detailing a sea battle fought in the straits here in 1770, in which the Russian fleet annihilated the Ottoman navy. The castle's crumbling open-air theatre also hosts performances during the **International İzmir Festival** (see box, p.233).

Altınkum
9km southwest of Çeşme • Dolmuşes from Çeşme (every 20min; ₺3.50)

The best local **beaches** on the Çeşme peninsula lie along **Altınkum**, a series of sun-baked coves tucked away beyond the seaside township of Çiftlik. In fact, with multi-hued water lapping hundreds of metres of sand and dunes, this is probably the best beach between Bozcaada and the Turquoise Coast.

ARRIVAL AND DEPARTURE ÇEŞME

By bus or dolmuş Çeşme's small *otogar* is 1km south of the town centre, although local buses and dolmuşes serving most nearby destinations, including İzmir, Dalyan, Ilıca and Alaçatı, stop at the eastern end of İnkilap Cad.

By ferry Çeşme has ferry connections to Hios in Greece, which is known as Chios in Turkish (daily 9.30am & 6pm; 1hr; €26 return), to and from a ferry dock just across the bay. Three different operators have ticket booths below the castle.

INFORMATION AND TOURS

Tourist office There's a helpful tourist office by the Customs Office near the quayside (Mon–Fri 8.30am–5.30pm, Sat & Sun 9am–noon & 1–5pm; ☎0232 712 6653).

Car rental Uzun Rent-a-car, 16 Eylül Mah, 3010 Sok 3 (☎0232 712 0928), is about the cheapest; they also rent motorbikes, which are perfectly adequate for exploring the

peninsula.

Boat trips Daily boat trips leave from just north of Cumhuriyet Meydanı, heading along the coast to local beauty spots and nearby Donkey Island. They usually set off at 10.30am, returning at 5.30pm, and cost around ₺40, including lunch.

ACCOMMODATION

Çeşme's popularity as a summer bolthole for İzmiris means there's a plethora of accommodation, though **prices** go berserk in July and Aug. The most desirable options line the waterfront.

★**Kanuni Kervansaray** 1015 Sok ☎0232 712 0630. Dating back to the days of Süleyman the Magnificent, this restored *kervansaray* is now a suitably plush hotel, with a swimming pool and a couple of date palms in its courtyard. Its cave-style rooms are small but atmospheric (opt for the upper level), and there are great views from the rooftop seating area. **₺300**

Mandalin 1021 Sok 8 ☎0232 712 6305, ⍟otelmandalin .com. One of the cheaper options in town, tucked away by

the mosque. Rooms are decorated with an orange motif, and they charge per person, making it a good deal for single travellers (₺100), less so for pairs. **₺200**

Marin By the harbour ☎0232 712 7580. Relatively new hotel where many of the spick-and-span rooms have balconies and wonderful sea views – you can even spy Greece, if the weather agrees. There's a bar on the ground floor, though this can make things a little noisy. Prices halve out of season. **₺250**

EATING

★**Imren** İnkilap Cad 6 ☎0232 712 7620. This must be in the running for Turkey's best-looking *lokanta*, should such an award exist, eschewing as it does the usual canteen style for a splendidly verdant outdoor section and a highly attractive interior. You'll pay ₺20 for a mixed *meze* platter, and from ₺15 for hot plates or grills. Daily noon–11pm.

Mado On the harbour ☎0232 712 7810, ⍟mado .com.tr. Branches of this dessert chain are all over Turkey, but few are so magnificently located – right on the new harbour, the view all sea and sail-masts. Good *baklava* and ice cream (₺16 for a serving of both), as well as savoury brunch meals. Daily 9am–midnight.

Rıhtım Overlooking the fishing port ☎0232 712 7433. Simple affair that's the best place in town for fish, facing the boats that bring many of them in. Good-value set menus (₺26) include sea bream and bass. Daily 10am–10pm.

Rumeli Pastanesi İnkilap Cad 44 ☎0232 712 6759. A local legend, with some of the best ice cream on the Aegean (₺1.50/scoop), as attested by innumerable top-ten-in-Turkey accolades in local magazine articles. They also sell home-made fruit preserves, made with more or less the same list of fruits and nuts – fig, pistachio and the like. Daily 10am–midnight.

Selçuk and around

One has to admire little **SELÇUK**. No more than a farming town just a generation ago, it has been catapulted into the limelight of premier-league tourism by its proximity to the ruins of **Ephesus**, the second most visited site in Turkey after the Sultanahmet district of Istanbul. Despite this, and its status as the burial place of **St John the Evangelist**, Selçuk remains an incredibly relaxed, easy-going place – swallows squeal and wheel from eave to eave, storks build nests atop Roman columns, and life dawdles by at a snail's pace.

This laidback vibe is largely because Ephesus is also so near the coast – the overwhelming majority of visitors to the ruins are staying in nearby Kuşadası (see p.246), or visiting on day-trips from the other resorts. Unless you absolutely need to be by the sea (which, in any case, is less than half an hour away), Selçuk makes an excellent base, with super-cheap accommodation, good restaurants and a relaxed, backpacker-ish feel.

As for sightseeing, Ephesus is not the end of the story – stay a couple of days here and you'll be able to see the hill village of **Şirince**, the shrine at **Meryemana** and Selçuk's own array of antiquities, most pertinently those in its excellent **museum**.

Ayasoluk Hill

Entrance off St Jean Cad • Daily 8am–7pm; castle section only open until 5pm • ₺10

The obvious first spot to head for, **Ayasoluk Hill**, has been the focal point of settlement in every era. It's famed as the burial place of **St John the Evangelist**, who came to Ephesus in the middle of the first century and died there around 100 AD. Indeed, the hill's name is thought to be a corruption of Ayios Theologos, or "Divine Theologian". The sixth-century Byzantine emperor Justinian decided to replace two earlier churches sheltering John's tomb with a basilica worthy of the saint's reputation. Until its destruction by Tamerlane's Mongols in 1402, it was among the largest and most ornate of all Byzantine churches.

You'll enter the site through the **Gate of Persecution**, so called by the Byzantines because it was once adorned by a relief of Achilles in combat, mistakenly thought to depict Christians being martyred in the amphitheatre of Ephesus. Then come the re-erected colonnades and walls of the **Basilica of St John**; the purported tomb of the evangelist is marked by a slab on the former site of the altar. Beside the nave is the **Baptistry**, where tourists pose for photos in the act of dunking.

A restored **Byzantine castle** stands atop the hill, and makes for a fun clamber around. It was only reopened in 2014, after Byzantine houses unearthed on its south side caused two full years of delay. The basilica at the top of the rise may well have been the spot where St John penned (or quilled) his section of the bible; the building itself was constructed in his memory in the fifth century.

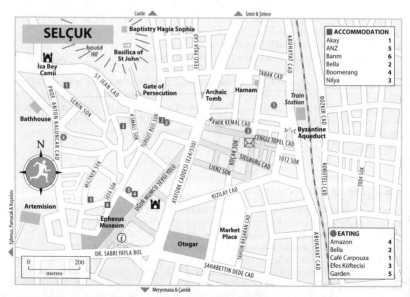

> ## SAVING MONEY SEEING SELÇUK'S SIGHTS
>
> There are numerous ways in which to save a few lira when visiting Selçuk's sights. Easiest are the **combination tickets** available at certain sight entrances – you'll pay ₺35 for Ephesus (see below) plus either Ayasoluk Hill (see opposite) or the Ephesus Museum (see below), or ₺40 for all three. Alternatively, you may wish to consider buying a **Müzekart** (⌾ muze.gov.tr), which will get you into museums and other sights clean across the Aegean (₺75 for a week) or all Turkey (₺105 for fifteen days).

İsa Bey Camii

Off 1054 Sok • Free

The **İsa Bey Camii** is the most distinguished of the Selçuk monuments that gave the town its name. A late fourteenth-century Aydınoğlu mosque, it represents a transition between Selçuk and Ottoman styles, with its innovative courtyard – where most of the congregation would worship – and stalactite vaulting over the entrance. Inside the main hall, you'll see a high, gabled roof supported by Roman columns and some fine tile-work in the south dome.

Ephesus Museum

Uğur Mumcu Sevgi Yolu • Daily 8.30am–6.30pm • ₺10 • ☎ 0232 892 6010

Always packed, the **Ephesus Museum** is well worth visiting. Arranged thematically rather than chronologically, its galleries present the ancient city as a living space rather than being just a repository of artefacts. Celebrated objects here include effigies of the phallic god Priapus; a bust of the Greek dramatist Menander; Eros riding a dolphin; and excellent miniatures from the Roman terrace houses at Ephesus. A large courtyard holds sarcophagi, column capitals and stelae.

Continuing through the main galleries, and a hall devoted to tomb finds and mortuary practices, you reach the famous **Artemis room**. This holds two renditions of the goddess studded with multiple bull's testicles (not breasts, as is commonly believed) and tiny figurines of real and mythical beasts, honouring her role as mistress of animals.

Artemision

300m west of the centre, off the Ephesus road • Daily 8.30am–5.30pm • Free

The scanty remains of the **Artemision**, or sanctuary of Artemis, lie on the outskirts of town. The archaic temple here replaced three predecessors dedicated to Cybele, and was itself burned down in 356 BC by Herostratus, a lunatic who (correctly) reckoned his name would be immortalized by the act. The massive Hellenistic replacement was considered to be one of the **Seven Wonders of the Ancient World**, though that's hard to believe today. After the Goths sacked it in 263 AD, the Byzantines carted off most of the remaining masonry to Ayasoluk and Constantinople, leaving just a lone column (re-erected in modern times) amid battered foundation blocks.

Ephesus

3km southwest of Selçuk Daily 8am–7pm • ₺30, terraced houses an extra ₺15; audioguides ₺20 • Selçuk hotels offer free drop-offs and pick-ups, while regular minibuses from Selçuk and Kuşadası drop passengers near the lower entrance; taxis cost ₺20 from Selçuk, ₺80 from Kuşadası

Of Turkey's superb array of ancient cities, **Ephesus** (known as Efes in Turkish) is by far the best preserved. In fact, with the possible exception of Pompeii, one could argue that it's the world's finest surviving example of a Greco-Roman **Classical city**. A big claim, but with so much to back it up – the ruins here are not merely rocks on the ground, but near-fully fledged incarnations of what life must have been like in ancient times.

The tantalizing prospect of delving back so many centuries in architectural time makes Ephesus a cast-iron must-see if you're in, or anywhere near, the area. As one would expect, the ruins are mobbed for much of the year, particularly with summer cruise-ship arrivals from nearby Kuşadası. However, with a little planning and initiative it's possible to tour the site in relative peace.

There are **two entrances** to Ephesus, both surrounded by stands selling souvenirs and overpriced snacks. The prevailing current of people heads downhill from the upper entrance – a particularly good idea in summer – and this is the route followed in the account that follows. You'll need two to three hours to see Ephesus, and in summer you'll need a **hat** – there's next to no shade, meaning that the acres of stone act as a grill in the heat of the day. Whatever the season, you'll probably need to carry **water** too; this is only sold at the entrances, where multilingual **audioguides** are also available.

Brief history

Legends relate that Ephesus was founded by **Androclus**, son of King Kodrus of Athens, who was advised by an oracle to settle at a place indicated by a fish and a wild boar. Androclus and his entourage arrived here to find natives roasting fish by the sea; embers from the fire set a bush ablaze, out of which charged a pig, and the city was on its way. The imported worship of Artemis melded easily with that of the indigenous **Cybele**, and the Ephesus of 1000 BC was built on the north slope of Mount Pion (Panayır Dağı), very close to the temple of the goddess.

Alexander the Great, on his visit in 334 BC, offered to fund the completion of the latest version of the Artemis shrine, but the city fathers tactfully demurred, saying that one deity should not support another. Following Alexander's death, his lieutenant **Lysimachus** moved the city to its present location – necessary because the sea had already receded considerably – and provided it with its first **walls**, traces of which are still visible on Panayır Dağı and Mount Koressos (Bülbül Dağı) to the south.

In subsequent centuries, Ephesus changed allegiance frequently and backed various revolts against Roman rule. Yet it never suffered for this lack of principle: during the Roman imperial period it was designated the **capital of Asia** and ornamented with magnificent public buildings – those on view today – by successive emperors. Ephesus' quarter-million population was swollen substantially at times by the right of sanctuary linked to the sacred precinct of Artemis, allowing shelter to large numbers of criminals. Of a somewhat less lurid cast was the more stable, mixed population of Jews, Romans, and Egyptian and Anatolian cultists.

The Christians arrive

Christianity took root early and quickly at Ephesus. St John the Evangelist arrived in the mid-first century, and **St Paul** spent the years 51–53 AD in the city, proselytizing foremost among the Jewish community. As usual, Paul managed to foment controversy even in this cosmopolitan environment, apparently being imprisoned for some time – in a tower bearing his name near the west end of the walls – and later provoking the famous silversmiths' riot, described in Acts 19:23–20:1.

Under the Byzantines, Ephesus was the venue for two **councils of the Church**, including one in 431 AD at which the Nestorian heresy (see p.638) was anathematized. However, the general tenor of the Byzantine era was one of decline, owing to the abandonment of Artemis worship, Arab raids and (worst of all) the final silting up of the harbour. The population began to siphon off to the nearby hill crowned by the tomb and church of St John, future nucleus of the town of Selçuk, and by the time the Selçuks themselves appeared the process was virtually complete.

Upper agora and around

Approaching from the **upper entrance**, you'll almost immediately find yourself in the large, overgrown **upper agora**, which lies opposite the civic heart of the Roman

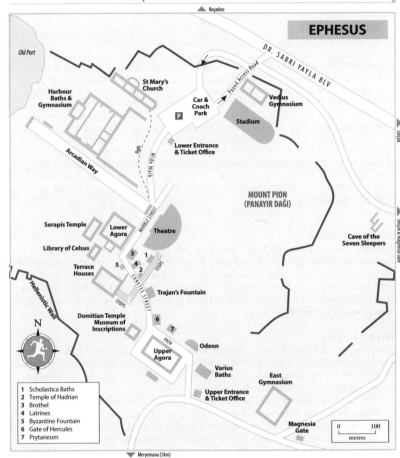

EPHESUS

1 Scholastica Baths
2 Temple of Hadrian
3 Brothel
4 Latrines
5 Byzantine Fountain
6 Gate of Hercules
7 Prytaneum

community – the **prytaneum**. This housed the inextinguishable sacred flame of Ephesus and two of the Artemis statues now in the Ephesus Museum in Selçuk (see p.239), even though Hestia (also known as **Vesta**) was the presiding goddess; it also served as the reception area for official guests. The adjacent **odeon**, once the local parliament, has been as insensitively restored as the main theatre (see p.244).

You'll soon find yourself heading down **Curetes Street**, which starts at the **Gate of Hercules**, where a remaining column relief depicts the hero wrapped in the skin of the Nemean lion. A little further down is **Trajan's Fountain**, whose ornamentation has been removed to the museum.

Temple of Hadrian

The so-called **Temple of Hadrian** was donated in 118 AD by a wealthy citizen in honour of Hadrian, Artemis and the city in general. Most of the relief works here are plaster copies of the originals, which reside in Selçuk's Ephesus Museum. The two small heads on the arches spanning the four columns out front are of Tyche and possibly Medusa, respectively installed for luck and to ward off evil influences. The public **latrines**, a little lower, provide evidence that ancient humans were human too, and are a favourite photo opportunity.

ANCIENT IONIA

The **Ionian coast** was first colonized by **Greek-speakers** in the twelfth century BC. The culture reached its zenith during the seventh and sixth centuries BC, when it was at the forefront of the newly emergent sciences, philosophy and the arts. Enormous advantages accrued to those who settled here: an amenable climate, fertile, well-watered terrain and a strategic location between the Aegean – with its many fine harbours – and inland Anatolia. Partly thanks to the silting up of local rivers, the coastline soon began to recede, and by mid-Byzantine times virtually all of the Ionian cities had been abandoned; with the declaration of **Christianity** as the state religion, religious centres and oracles met a similar fate.

Today's inhabitants have found the silver lining to the cloud of the advancing deltas, cashing in on the rich soil brought down from the hills. Vast tracts of cotton, tobacco, sesame and grain benefit from irrigation works, while groves of pine, olive and cypress, which need no such encouragement, adorn the hills and wilder reaches. And with the sea, though more distant than in former times, still beckoning when tramping the ruins begins to pall, **tourism** is now threatening to outstrip agriculture.

Scholastica Baths

The first-century **Scholastica baths**, sprawling behind and above the Temple of Hadrian, are named after the fifth-century Byzantine lady whose headless statue adorns the entrance, and who restored the complex. There was direct access from here to the latrines and thence the brothel, though it seems from graffiti that the baths, too, were at one stage used as a bawdy house. As at many points in Ephesus, clay drainage pipes remain visibly lodged in the floor.

Terrace houses

The 62 rooms of Ephesus' famous **terrace houses**, housed in a protective shelter, form one of the world's best-preserved Roman domestic environments. Since they're accessed on a separate ticket, many tour groups skip this incredible site – all the better for you to enjoy it relatively unobstructed.

Broken down into seven dwellings, Terrace House 2 was buried, and thus very well preserved, by earthquakes during the third century AD. Excavation teams continue to work as visitors are channelled through the complex via transparent glass walkways. At the time of writing, highlights include a basilica "wallpapered" with thin sheets of marble in Dwelling 6, underfloor heating in Dwelling 5, and the mosaics and murals in the Room of the Nine Muses in Dwelling 3. These are pointed out on signboards which, though moderately informative, are often in completely the wrong places.

Library of Celsus

Looming directly across the intersection of Ephesus' two major streets, the awe-inspiring **Library of Celsus** was erected by the consul Gaius Julius Aquila between 110 and 135 AD as a memorial to his father Celsus Polemaeanus, who is still entombed under its west wall. The elegant, two-storey facade is the classic image of Ephesus. It was fitted with niches for statues of the four personified intellectual virtues, today filled with plaster copies (the originals are in Vienna). Inside, twelve thousand scrolls were stored in galleries designed to forestall damp – the Goths burned them all when they sacked the area in 262 AD. Abutting the library, and designed to provide entry to the lower agora, stands the restored triple **gate of Mazaeus and Mithridates**.

Marble Street

The so-called **Marble Street** begins at the **lower agora** and ends near the base of the theatre; wheel-ruts in the road and the slightly elevated colonnade remnant to the right indicate that pedestrians and vehicles were kept neatly separated. Adjoining the agora is

FROM TOP ŞİRİNCE (P.244); BODRUM (P.260) >

the **Serapis Temple**, where the city's many Egyptian merchants would have worshipped. Across the road, metal stanchions protect alleged "signposting" – a footprint and a female head etched into the rock – for a **brothel**.

The Arcadian Way

Downhill from Marble Street, the ancient **theatre** has been somewhat brutally restored, although it's worth the climb for the views over the surrounding countryside. It faces the splendid **Arcadian Way**, named after the fifth-century Byzantine emperor Arcadius who renovated it. Currently roped off and the site of regular faux-gladiator performances, it was originally lined with hundreds of shops and illuminated at night. Its northern side is fringed by the **harbour baths** and **gymnasium**, though these are overgrown and difficult to explore.

St Mary's church

From the fenced-off end of the Arcadian Way, a small, little-trodden trail (signed "Meryem Kilisesi") leads to **St Mary's church**, an absurdly elongated hotchpotch constructed between the second and fourth centuries AD. The building, originally a Roman warehouse, was the venue of the ecumenical council in 431 AD; its baptistry is in good condition. Lastly – or your first view of the city if coming from the lower entrance – are the remains of the **Vedius gymnasium**, and a large **stadium** funded by Nero.

Meryemana

8km southwest of Selçuk, beyond Ephesus • Daily dawn–dusk • ₺10 • No public transport; come by private car or taxi

Meryemana is a monument to piety and faith. Though most Orthodox theologians maintain that the Virgin Mary died and was buried in Jerusalem, another school of thought holds that the mother of Jesus accompanied St John the Evangelist when he left Palestine in the middle of the first century on his way to Ephesus.

Bar its biblical history, however, Meryemana is not a particularly diverting place. Enclosed within a municipal park, the site is heavily commercialized. The **house** itself, now a chapel aligned unusually southwest to northeast, probably dates from early Byzantine times, though its foundations may indeed be first-century. It overlooks a beautiful wooded valley and two terraces where a spring gushes forth; nearby, tree branches are festooned with the votive rag-scraps left by Muslim pilgrims, for whom *Meryemana* (Mother Mary) is also a saint.

Cave of the Seven Sleepers

En route to Meryemana from Selçuk, between the upper and lower Ephesus entrances • Daily dawn–dusk • Free • Walkable from Ephesus, but best seen as part of a taxi-trip that includes Ephesus

Seven persecuted Christians are said to have fled to the **Cave of the Seven Sleepers**, en route to Meryemana, then been sealed inside by their pursuers; exposed by an earthquake two hundred years later, they sidled into town for a bite to eat. More prosaically, it's the site of a **Byzantine necropolis** whose tombs were cut into the surrounding rock. Fences mean that you can't get too close to them now, but the area is still rather pretty. Most visitors munch on *gözleme* from the excellent restaurant immediately outside.

Şirince

8km east of Selçuk • Regular dolmuşes (₺3; 20min) leave from Selçuk's *otogar*; taxis more like ₺40

Originally built by Greeks, the evocative, well-preserved **hill village** of **ŞIRINCE** is surrounded by lush orchards and vineyards – you can taste the wines, and buy bottles at many shops. Laden with pesky hawkers in season, and now rather overcrowded during the day thanks to its positioning on the Chinese tour-group trail, it's much more pleasant and relaxed outside summer and genuinely lives up to its reputation as one of the region's most idyllic villages – this despite being just a short cab ride from Selçuk.

The late nineteenth-century **church** at the edge of Şirince has a pebble-mosaic floor, plaster-relief work on the ceiling, and wooden vaulting, while the larger stone **basilica** nearer the centre dates from 1839. The main reason to visit, though, is the idyllic scenery and the handsome domestic architecture, which these days attracts wealthy urban Turks in search of characterful vacation homes.

ARRIVAL, INFORMATION AND TOURS   SELÇUK AND AROUND

By train Selçuk's train station, just east of the centre, has (incredibly cheap) connections to İzmir (8 daily; 1hr 15min) and Denizli, the jumping-off point for Pamukkale (7 daily; 3hr). At the time of writing, a new station was being built here to serve a new line, which will speed journey times up a tad.

By bus The simple *otogar* in Selçuk is conveniently located at the southern end of Atatürk Cad.

Destinations Istanbul (hourly; 10hr); İzmir (every 30min–1hr; 1hr); Kuşadası (every 20min; 30min); Pamukkale

(10 daily; 3hr 30min); Şirince (every 20min; 20min).

Tourist office On the corner of Selçuk's central park and Uğur Mumcu Sevgi Yolu – or "Love Street", as the sign proclaims (Mon–Fri 8.30am–noon & 1–5.30pm, Sat 8.30am–noon & 1–5pm; ☎ 0232 892 6328).

Tours Agencies all over Selçuk offer guided tours to Ephesus, but independent travellers can easily make their own way. Day-tours of Priene, Miletus and Didyma cost around ₺100/person.

ACCOMMODATION

SELÇUK

Most hotels offer free transport to Ephesus, as well as collection from the ferry in Kuşadası. Prices, already lower than they really should be, plummet even further off season. Camping is possible on Pamucak beach, a short bus ride away.

Akay 1054 Sok 3 ☎ 0232 892 3172, ⓦ hotelakay.com. Affordable boutique-style two-star spread over two properties, with standard and superior rooms. You'll be able to relax on deckchairs by the swimming pool – who needs the beach? **₺150**

ANZ 1064 Sok 12 ☎ 0232 892 6050, ⓦ anzguesthouse .com. Run by a returned Turkish-Australian, this *pansiyon* has basic rooms but a nice rooftop bar, where occasional barbecues are served. Dorm beds available. Rates for doubles include breakfast. Dorm **₺30**, double **₺90**

★**Barım** 1045 Sok 34 ☎ 0232 892 6923, ⓦ barimpension.com. One of the cheapest places in a uniformly cheap town, set in a restored, rambling old house complete with lush courtyard/garden. Rooms have traditional Turkish decor and stone-clad walls, with modern fixtures and fittings. **₺80**

★**Bella** St John Cad 7 ☎ 0232 892 3944, ⓦ hotelbella .com. Opposite the basilica gate, this veteran option is still Selçuk's best, and phenomenal value for the price. Service is friendly and informative, rooms are beautifully decorated, and there's a great restaurant – open to non-guests, too (see p.246). **₺120**

Boomerang 1047 Sok 10 ☎ 0232 892 4879, ⓦ boomerangguesthouse.com. This spick-and-span little guesthouse enjoys a quiet yet wonderfully central location. An extra ₺20 will get you a balcony, or a mini

garden area if you're on the ground floor; they've now got a large, spacious dorm room too. Finally, the on-site *Garden* restaurant (see p.246) is an excellent place to eat. Dorm **₺30**, double **₺120**

Nilya 1051 Sok 7 ☎ 0232 892 9081, ⓦ nilya.com. Owned by the same team as the *Bella* up the road, this hotel has an even quieter setting behind high walls, with charmingly cluttered kilim-strewn rooms (all en suite) laid out around a peaceful, tree-lined courtyard. Excellent breakfasts. **₺200**

ŞİRİNCE

Just before dusk, Şirince morphs from outdoor shopping mall to simple mountain village – locals pack up their goods, sit on the roadsides and chat until bedtime, making it tempting to stay overnight.

Güllü Konakları Up from the main square ☎ 0232 898 3131. Şirince's fanciest hotel, its gorgeous rooms spread out over a wide, flower-filled swathe of hillside. There's an excellent restaurant, as well as an outdoor jacuzzi, and all manner of places to unwind. **₺500**

Mystic Konak Downhill from the basilica ☎ 0232 898 3163. A cheap, characterful option, this *pansiyon* has pleasingly decorated rooms and a tranquil setting. The owners also have a cheaper place down the road. **₺150**

Nişanyan Evleri High above the town ☎ 0232 898 3208, ⓦ nisanyan.com. Run by a local writer, this restored mansion has serene views and superb singles and doubles. It's easily visible from Şirince, but unless you want to lug your bags uphill (really, you don't), drop into their café at the entrance to the village, or just call on arrival for a pick-up. **₺400**

EATING

SELÇUK

Much like the town's accommodation, Selçuk's restaurants are usually good value. Several hotels also have decent dining

rooms that are open to the public. Alcohol is easy to track down; many restaurants are licensed, and there are several noisy bars in the warren of streets around the train station.

4

Amazon Prof A. Kaluncur Cad 36 ☎0232 892 3215. On the western fringe of town, this good-looking restaurant has views of the Artemision from its outdoor tables, which are set in a niche across the road. The menu includes foreign meals such as pasta (₺11), schnitzel and the like, while their mixed *meze* sets (₺13) are up there with the best in town. Daily 10am–10pm.

★**Bella** St John Cad 7 ☎0232 892 3944, ⓦhotelbella .com. The best of the hotel restaurants, plonked up on the rooftop with views of the basilica, castle, surrounding countryside and – if you're in luck – storks alighting on their nearby nests. You'll pay ₺17 for a kebab-and-*meze* set, or ₺30 for a full meal including soup and more *meze*. Daily noon–10.30pm.

Café Carpouza On the north side of the aqueduct ☎0232 892 2665. Set in a glorious building dating back to 1875, this is the most atmospheric place in town for Turkish coffee (₺2.50), served at tables dotted around a garden so large it's basically a park. They also serve cheesecake (₺7) and other desserts, and cocktails in the evening. Daily 8am–1am.

Efes Köftecisi Cengiz Topel Cad. A *lokanta* that's more popular with locals than tourists – a good sign, and the English-language menu helps. They serve up good, simple and cheap steam-tray specials (from ₺6), as well as their signature meatballs (₺12). Daily 8am–11pm.

Garden 1047 Sok, ⓦboomerangguesthouse.com. Relatively elegant, and great value, offering good cooking in a leafy courtyard. The Chinese dishes (such as fried noodles, ₺20) are particularly recommended, as the proprietor's wife is Cantonese. It's also a particularly good spot for an evening nargile (₺10). Daily 8am–midnight.

ŞİRİNCE

★**Ocakbaşı** Just uphill from the basilica ☎0232 898 3094, ⓦsirinceocakbasi.com. This is where the locals come to dine out. Everything's phenomenal value, and the *meze* – starting at ₺4 and all made with local ingredients – are simply out of this world. Try the samphire (*deniz börülce*) or stuffed pumpkin flowers (*kabak ciceği dolma*). Daily 8.30am–11pm.

4 Kuşadası and around

Brash and mercenary it may be, but **KUŞADASI** holds a perennial charm for groups of mostly boozy Brits, Irish and Australians – most of whom end up calling the place "koo-sa dar-sy", rather than the more correct "koo-sha-da-suh". In just three decades its population has swollen tenfold, and the scrappy, bustling conurbation now extends several kilometres along the coast and inland. The town is many people's first taste of Turkey: efficient ferry services link it with the Greek island of Sámos, while the resort is an obligatory port of call for Aegean **cruise ships**. These disgorge vast crowds in summer, who delight the local souvenir merchants both before and after a visit to the ruins of **Ephesus** just inland (see p.239). **Dilek National Park** (see p.248) is a quick trip away by minibus, and the ruins of **Priene** (see p.249), **Miletus** (see p.255) and **Didyma** (see p.253) are also within easy day-trip range.

This slew of nearby attractions makes Kuşadası as popular with independent travellers as it is with cruise ships. And while the city mainly caters to the latter, it's an attractive place in its own right, with hundreds of good bars, restaurants and shops dotting the central **Kale** area, as well as excellent connections to nearby **beaches**.

The town centre

There's not too much to actually see in town, though themed "Turkish Nights" concerts are held in its most beautiful building – the sixteenth-century **Öküz Mehmet Paşa Kervansaray**, now restored as a hotel (see p.251). This backs on to a pleasing pedestrian precinct, within which you'll find a little **stone tower** and other remnants of the town's medieval walls.

Güvercin Adası

Off Güvercinada Cad · Daily 8am–8pm · Free

Just west of the centre, a causeway leads to **Güvercin Adası**, a small islet poking out of the surf. Otherwise known as "Pigeon Island", it presents a series of landscaped terraces within its fortifications – there's nothing in particular to get your teeth into, though the place does provide a leafy respite from the bustle of town. The causeway itself is also the launching point for boat trips around the bay (see p.248).

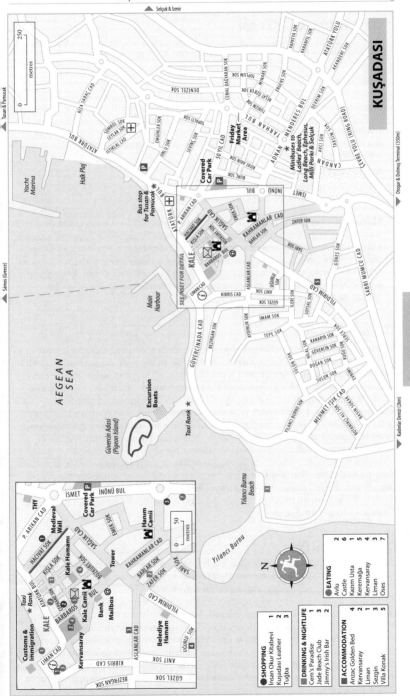

KUŞADASI

WATERY FUN IN KUŞADASI

The main appeal of Kuşadası is that the sea is right next to it. Besides the posse of **beaches** that fringe the city (see below), two huge **waterparks** lie just to the north, and it's also possible to organize short **boat trips** around the bay.

BOAT TRIPS

A clutch of boats lies in wait just off Pigeon Island (see p.246), their skippers eagerly drumming up custom in the morning, then again in the evening for the next day's venture. Most offer a similar itinerary, leaving at 9.30am, visiting three isolated beaches and returning by 4.30pm. The price hovers around ₺40 including lunch; chat with the skippers before you make your choice. There are also bargain sunset trips available – just ₺5 per person for a boat ride and predictably beautiful views.

WATERPARKS

Both the large waterparks off Tusan Beach run regular shuttle buses from Kuşadası, and are also accessible on Selçuk-bound minibuses. Both offer discounts for minors.

Adaland Off Tusan Beach ☎0256 618 1252, ⓦ adaland.com. An absolutely brilliant waterpark, with quirky rides including loop slides (you plummet through a trapdoor, then do a loop-the-loop) and a "water coaster" which sends you skittling uphill. Park entry costs ₺75, the dolphin section an extra ₺45 (₺300 extra if you want to swim with them). Daily 10am–6pm.

Aquafantasy Off Tusan Beach ☎0232 893 1111, ⓦ aquafantasy.com. Also a hotel, this waterpark boasts a mind-boggling array of zany rides – not as much fun as Adaland, but a great place nonetheless, and usually much less crowded. Entry ₺75; ten percent discount for online bookings. Daily 10am–6pm.

The beaches

Sun and sand are what most of the city's visitors are here for, and there are a number of decent **beaches** to choose from. First up is **Halk Plaj** in the town centre itself, though it's not terribly appealing. **Yılancı Burnu** is the closest "real" beach to town, and far more pleasing; it's within walking distance of the centre (though you'll have to navigate a small hill), or failing that, jump on any minibus heading that way. Some 3km southwest of town, **Ladies' Beach** is Kuşadası's most famous stretch of sand and very popular in summer, but a rather scrappy affair; there are regular dolmuşes from town. One cove further along from Ladies' Beach, and accessible on the same minibuses, **Paradise Beach** is smaller and quieter, with fewer bars.

There are also options north of town. **Tusan Beach** is a nice, long stretch of hard-packed sand, 5km north of Kuşadası, and famed for its adjacent waterparks (see above). Some 10km further is **Pamucak Beach**, the best in the whole area, though the sea can be rough on windy days; there are regular minibuses from both Kuşadası and nearby Selçuk.

Dilek National Park

28km south of Kuşadası • Spring & autumn daily 7am–5pm; summer daily 8am–6.30pm; winter closed • ₺5, cars ₺10 • Take a minibus from Kuşadası – signed for the Milli Parkı, and continuing as far as Karasu Beach (every 30min; 45min; ₺7)

Looming from the sea like a giant crocodile, the imposing outline of **Samsun Dağı** dominates the skyline south of Kuşadası. It's the central feature of **Dilek National Park** (Dilek Yarımadası Milli Parkı), a peninsular tract set aside in 1966 for, among other reasons, the protection of its thick forest and diverse **fauna**, said to include rare lynx, jackal and wild cats. However, you're unlikely to see any of those species, as much of the 28,000-acre park is an off-limits military zone; indeed, most visitors go no further than the pleasant **beaches** on the north side of the peninsula. The park has no facilities for overnight stays, but the village of **Güzelçamlı**, 1km from its main entrance, holds several **pansiyons**.

Dilek's beaches

The most visited portion of the unrestricted zone of Dilek National Park consists of a 10km stretch of mostly paved road beyond the entrance and four good, but often windswept, beaches along it. Just beyond the gate, **İçmeler** is a popular hard-sand beach shaded by plane trees. Next come the pebble beaches of **Aydınlık** and **Kavaklı**, but it's best to continue to the last and prettiest one, **Karasu**, where the minibuses stop. This 700m-long stretch of gravel is perfect for swimming; stand in the sea for long enough and fish will nibble at your toes. Each beach has its own small snack bar or drinks kiosk operating in high season, as well as toilets, barbecue areas and a small café.

Cave of Zeus

A short walk back down the road from the park entrance, the **Cave of Zeus** is a water-filled grotto in which it's possible to swim in summer (though the water is still freezing cold). Though beautiful, the cave is highly popular with local visitors and often fills up with cigarette smoke.

The summit ridge

The best access to the **summit ridge** east of Samsun Dağı (1237) is via a trail from **Eskidoğanbey**, a village to the south. It's an all-day outing, best done in spring or autumn to avoid the heat. Chances of spotting wildlife, particularly badgers, jackals and birds of prey, are higher here than within the confines of the national park on the other side of the mountain. Since the closure of most short-term accommodation in Eskidoğanbey, walkers tend to take an early dolmuş to one or other of the trailheads, hike over the mountain, and take an evening dolmuş back to Söke or Kuşadası from the walk's end point.

Priene

35km south of Kuşadası • Daily: summer 9am–7pm; winter 9am–5.30pm • ₺5 • Accessible by dolmuş from Kuşadası or Söke, or on tours or chartered taxi from Kuşadası (see p.251) and Selçuk (see p.245)

The ancient Greek city of **Priene** represents the best-preserved Hellenistic townscape in Ionia, without any of the usual Roman or Byzantine additions. It also occupies perhaps the finest location of any such city – perched on a series of pine terraces graded into the south flank of Samsun Dağı, this compact but exquisite site enjoys a situation to bear comparison with that of Delphi in Greece. Despite all this, and the fact that it's just 35km south of Kuşadası, Priene remains far less visited than Ephesus – even in summer, you'll largely have this wonderful place to yourself, and there are a couple of accommodation options for those seeking a break from city life.

Visitors to Priene who are dropped by dolmuş at the western edge of the strung-out village of **Güllübahçe** face an uphill walk to the site ticket office, and then another good steep walk up the hill to the northeast gate into the city itself. Beyond that, the ruins are strewn over a wide area, and all major points of interest have English-language information boards.

Brief history

The original settlement of Priene lay elsewhere in the Meander basin. Following the receding shoreline, however – now just visible to the west – its inhabitants re-founded the city on its present site during the fourth century BC, just in time for **Alexander** to stop in and finance the cost of the principal temple of Athena. The town was set up along a grid pattern made up of various *insulae* (rectangular units), each measuring roughly 42m by 35m. Within each rectangle stood four private dwellings; a public building had its own *insula*, sometimes two. Priene enjoyed little patronage from Roman or Byzantine emperors – which, of course, adds to its modern-day appeal.

Bouleuterion and around

Take the uphill path from the ticket office and the first civic monument you're likely to come across is the square **bouleuterion**, a former council chamber that's more or less in the centre of the site. The most intact such monument in Turkey, it consists of seats on three sides enclosing the speakers' area, together with a sacrificial altar. Beside the bouleuterion lie the scantier remains of the **prytaneion**, or town administration offices, with traces of a dining area for the highest municipal officials.

Sacred stoa, agora and Temple of Zeus

On the terrace immediately below the bouleuterion, the **sacred stoa** was originally graced by outer and inner series of Doric and Ionic columns. One step further down and you'll find the **agora** and the **Temple of Zeus** (still known as such, though it's actually the sanctuary of Asclepios, the god of healing). Little is left of these, but the commanding views suggest that this was the heart of public life in the city.

Gymnasium and stadium

Clearly visible below the Temple of Zeus, reached by way of a stairway from the agora, are the **gymnasium** and **stadium**, with nearby **bathing basins**, complete with gutters and lion-head spouts, for use after athletics. On the west side of the stadium there are a few sets of **starting blocks** for foot races; spectators watched from the north side of the 190m-by-20m area, where some seats are still discernible.

Residential district

Priene's densest surviving **residential district** lies west of the central street, down a gentle slope. Its thick walls stand up to 1.5m in some places. Just west are the remains of what was once a **fish and meat market**. Continue west for the city's **west gate**, which marks the end of the main street; a wonderful walking trail lies beyond.

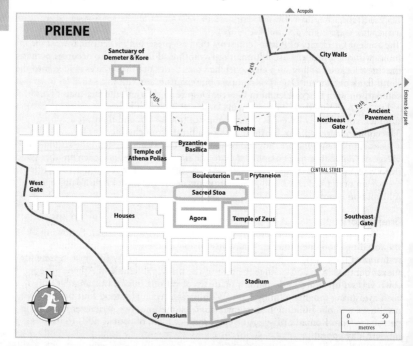

Temple of Athena Polias

The most conspicuous monument in Priene, the **Temple of Athena Polias**, stands two terraces above the main residential street, its fallen columns strewn around like gigantic cogs. The temple took more than two centuries to complete and, in its time, was considered the epitome of Ionic perfection; a manual written by its designer Pytheos was still considered standard reading in Roman times.

Theatre and Byzantine basilica

Priene's old **theatre** remains in an excellent state of preservation, its layout and seating (for five thousand, the entire population) unchanged from the Hellenistic original. Most prominent are five larger-than-average marble thrones for the municipal dignitaries. The stage buildings were extensively modified during the second century AD – virtually the only Roman tampering with Priene's public buildings. Just behind them are the remains of a **Byzantine basilica**, its entrance and columns clearly visible.

Acropolis

If you're keen on scrambling and the weather is not too hot, take the path beginning above the theatre to the **acropolis**; allow an extra hour and a half for the round trip.

ARRIVAL AND DEPARTURE   KUŞADASI

By plane The closest major airport is in İzmir. Taxis charge ₺140 to get into town, and there are bus connections, too (every 2hr; 90min; ₺10). Taxis to Bodrum airport cost in the region of ₺250.

By bus or dolmuş The long-distance *otogar*, where arrivals from the south are dropped, is 2km south of the old town, just past the end of Kahramanlar Cad. Local dolmuşes, labelled "Şehir İçi", connect with the centre of town, stopping at the corner of Atatürk and İnönü buls. You can pick up minibuses to all nearby destinations, including Ephesus, the Milli Parkı and Söke, at the junction of Adnan Menderes and Candan Tahran buls, 600m southeast of the old town.

Destinations Aydın (hourly; 1hr 30min); Antalya (2 daily; 8hr); Bodrum (4 daily; 2hr); Istanbul (12 daily; 9hr); İzmir (every 30min; 2hr); Selçuk (every 20min; 30min).

By ferry Arriving by ferry from the Greek island of Sámos, you'll exit customs directly onto Liman Cad. Tickets to Sámos (1hr 30min) are available from any travel agent in town, with two alternative services: the Turkish boat (one-way €35, day return €40, open return €55) leaves at 9am daily, and a Greek one (one-way €45, open return €75) at 5pm daily except Mon and Fri. For the Turkish boat, you usually have to buy tickets and register your passport the day before.

By car Car rental offices (including Avis and Europcar) cluster along İnönü and Atatürk buls; standard walk-in rates of around €60 a day can be bargained down to under €40 at slack times. Car parks in the centre of town cost around ₺4 for up to three hours, ₺8 for the entire day.

INFORMATION AND TOURS

Tourist office Liman Cad 13, opposite the ferry terminal (Mon–Fri 8am–12.30pm & 1.30–5pm; ☎0256 614 1103). They can offer maps and general advice, but can't book hotels.

Tours and travel agencies Most hotels can get you on day-tours to Ephesus, Pamukkale and combined trips to Didyma, Miletus and Priene, for around €35/person. Recommended travel agents include Peron Tour, İsmet İnönü Bul 12 (☎0256 614 3450, ⓦperontour.com).

ACCOMMODATION

There are hotels and *pansiyons* all over Kuşadası, particularly along the **seafront**, but note that accommodation can get pricey in summer – if this bothers you, or pink-faced, beer-guzzling holiday-makers leave you cold, you might prefer Selçuk (see p.237) as a base from which to explore the fascinating hinterland. If you're set on Kuşadası, you should be able to find a room quite easily at all times of the year. The major out-of-town beach resorts are aimed squarely at package tourists, and not good value if you try to book independently.

Anzac Golden Bed Aslanlar Cad, Uğurlu Sok 1 ☎0256 614 8708, ⓦanzacgoldenbed.com. Signposted from Yıldırım Cad, this quiet, laidback *pansiyon* is nicely decorated with kilims and home furnishings, and has a well-used barbecue area. There are good views from the rooftop breakfast terrace. Book ahead. ₺95

Kervansaray Kale ☎0256 614 2225, ⓦkusadasi hotelcaravanserail.com. Occupying much of the *Öküz Mehmet Paşa Kervansaray*, this showstopper is built around an elegant courtyard-cum-restaurant, which is where

4

you'll also take breakfast. Rooms boast period furniture, parquet floors and lofty ceilings. ₺200

★ **Liman** Kıbrıs Cad, Buyral Sok 4 ☎ 0256 614 7770, ⓦ limanhotel.com. Run by the ebullient "Mr Happy", this is hands down the most popular place in town among independent, budget-minded travellers. In addition to exceptionally friendly service, they provide fair-sized rooms with a/c and tiled bathrooms – some face the sea. And even if your room doesn't, you'll get grand views from the rooftop bar-restaurant (see below). ₺120

Sezgin Aslanlar Cad 68 ☎ 0256 614 4225, ⓦ sezginhotel.com. This well-run backpacker favourite has a leafy garden, large pool, satellite TV, basic double rooms and a wide range of other services including airport pick-up and discounts for various Turkish baths. ₺100

★ **Villa Konak** Yıldırım Cad 55 ☎ 0256 614 6318, ⓦ villakonakhotel.com. Lovely converted old house with delightful rambling gardens, thick with magnolia and citrus trees. Rooms are big and stylish, with antiques; there's also a pool table and a hammock. ₺180

EATING

Although the vast majority of **restaurants** in Kuşadası are indifferent, aimed squarely at the package-holiday/cruise-liner crowd, authentic local cuisine can be found, and usually at cheaper prices. Almost all places are licensed. A fair few **cafés** strung along the promenade serve juice, coffee and desserts by day, then cocktails at night. Lastly, be sure to try the **mussels**, stuffed with rice and with a squeeze of lemon juice, sold by hawkers along the seafront – large ones cost ₺1 each, the runts ₺0.50.

RESTAURANTS

Avlu Cephane Sok 15a ☎ 0256 614 7995, ⓦ avlu restaurant.com. You'll do no better for traditional Turkish food than at this ever-popular place with rear-courtyard seating and a few tables out on one of the centre's more chilled alleys. It serves low-priced grilled kebabs (from ₺14), and *pide* for half that. Daily 8am–midnight.

Castle Kaleiçi Camikebir Mahallesi Tuna Sok 35 ☎ 0256 614 7787, ⓦ castlerestaurant.com.tr. A touch touristy, but with a divine location underneath a leafy trellis in the middle of the Kale. The seemingly endless menu is strong on soups and steaks (₺30), with a long list of beers, wines and rakı to accompany. Daily 9am–1am.

Kazım Usta Overlooking customs port ☎ 0256 614 1226. Seafood restaurant where you can sup rakı overlooking the boats that bring in the fish. They'll happily cook up anything that you buy at the small fish market a stone's throw away, but the regular menu is fine too – a whole fish will set you back around ₺50, and stuffed calamari are a bargain at ₺10 a pop. Daily 8am–1am.

Liman Kıbrıs Cad, Buyral Sok 4 ☎ 0256 614 7770, ⓦ limanhotel.com. The rooftop restaurant of this hotel (see above) makes an excellent place to eat whether you're staying here or not – try a mixed *meze* platter (₺10), grab a shot of rakı, and watch the sunset together with the departing cruise ships. Daily 10am–10pm.

Oses İsmet İnönü Bul 8 ☎ 0256 612 2202. If you've yet to try *çiğ köfte*, this is your chance – ₺4 for a large wrap filled with fresh greens and a delicious spicy paste. A perfect light summertime lunch. Daily 8am–late.

CAFÉS AND ICE-CREAM SHOPS

Keremağa Barbaros H. Bul. In the middle of the main pedestrian drag, and selling sumptuous ice cream for ₺2 a scoop. Try the *karadut* (black mulberry). Daily 8am–late.

Kervansaray Kale ☎ 0256 614 2225, ⓦ kusadasi hotelcaravanserail.com. This hotel (see p.251) is also a splendid place for Turkish coffee (₺5) or a puff on a nargile (₺20). It's a popular shopping spot, too, so perhaps try to avoid the morning and evening tsunami of cruise tourists. Daily 8am–midnight.

DRINKING AND NIGHTLIFE

After-dark activity in Kuşadası is spread across dozens of **bars**, which can be clumped into distinct groups: the arty, genteel bars of the Kale district; their more energetic neighbours, featuring live music in either Turkish or English; and Irish/British pubs complete with karaoke gear and house music. The latter proliferate along **Barlar Sokak** ("Bar Street"), a side street where the

---

WHEN IN TURKEY ... HANGOVER CURES, LOCAL STYLE

As any Brit worth their salt can tell you, at the end of a night on the booze the best way to say sorry to your body is by throwing a kebab into it. A handy Turkish (and, of course, Greek) cure to an international malady, but what do Turks themselves do? One answer is **işkembe çorba**, a soup made with cow offal, often with a dash of lemon juice to cut straight through the offending alcohol. Its success as a hangover remedy may be behind the fact that, for many Turks, it's the first meal of the year, consumed just after midnight on New Year's Day. A few soup kitchens around the back of the Hanım Camii sell işkembe çorba; some stay open all night long.

> **VILLAGE FEASTS IN CHERRY VALLEY**
>
> One of the Aegean's most interesting restaurants lies just a short drive from Kuşadası, beautifully set amid the orchards in the village of **Kirazlı Köy** in "Cherry Valley", and readily accessible by minibus (40min; ₺6) from Kuşadası. While it remains all but unknown to foreign travellers, it has become hugely popular with Turkish visitors.
>
> Riding the crest of the home-cooking wave that's washing over western Turkey, **Köy Sofrası** (☎ 0256 667 1003, ⓦ koysofrasi.com.tr, daily 9am–10pm) translates as "village feast", and that's exactly what you'll find if you make your way out here. Diners are treated to round after round of superb food, using the freshest ingredients from the surrounding countryside. This is the Aegean, so a mixed *meze* plate will best showcase the area's wonderful herbs, pulses and veggies; otherwise the breakfasts are phenomenal, if you can get here early enough in the morning.

list of establishments reads like an Irish phonebook. As well as bars full of cheap booze and pelvis-thrusting Westerners, Bar Street is lined with snack-shacks doling out English-style kebabs and, somewhat worryingly, a fair few tattoo parlours.

Cem's Paradise Şafak Sok 16 ☎ 0532 732 5515. Tucked away down a side alley, this is the antithesis of most bars hereabouts, with local cool cats replacing pink-skinned tourists, chilled rock replacing Bruno Mars and reasonably priced beers replacing expensive foreign imports. Daily 3pm–late.

Jade Beach Club Yılancı Burnu ☎ 0256 612 7220, ⓦ jadebeachclub.com. Just out of town on the beach of the same name, this gigantic complex offers plenty – a swimming pool, volleyball nets, tune-spinning DJs and beachside deckchairs are all lined up for your pleasure. Daily 3pm–late.

Jimmy's Irish Bar Barlar Sok 8 ☎ 0256 612 2308. The most raucous (usually) of a glut of bars on Bar Street. If it's quiet, expect the bar staff to start a line dance in the hope that others will join in. Also the place if you've a burning desire to watch your football team in action. Daily 2pm–late.

SHOPPING

İnsan Okur Kitabevi Hacivat Sok ☎ 0256 378 8332. Small, out-of-the-way bookstore with a modest collection of English-language books (mostly secondhand) sitting in a rack out front. Daily 9am–8pm.

Kuşadası Leather Kale ☎ 0256 614 1313. A cut above the other leather-goods shops in town, with men's and women's jackets starting at around €80 – all leather used here (mostly lamb) is produce of the country, and sewn together locally. Daily 9am–midnight.

Tuğba İsmet İnönü Bul 24a ☎ 0256 614 8858. The city's best shop for Turkish delight and other sweeties. Cheery staff won't mind giving you a few samples of their delectable titbits. Daily 8am–late.

Didim and around

The resort of **DİDİM** is a curious place, sloping gently downhill from **Didyma**, an ancient **sanctuary of Apollo** from which it took its now-Turkified name. Most people are here for the beach at nearby **Altınkum** (not to be confused with the resort of the same name near İzmir) – a gently sloping expanse with no surf, it's ideal for children, although the packed-out sand and large British package presence means it's definitely not for everyone. The ruins themselves sit 5km uphill, in an area whose atmosphere is completely different – especially at night, when it makes the best place to stay for independent travellers. There are more ruins further north at **Miletus**, a tremendous site that you can hit on the way to or from Kuşadası.

Didyma: the sanctuary of Apollo

5km north of Altınkum beach • Daily 8.30am–7pm • ₺10 Accessible by dolmuş from Kuşadası or Söke, or on tours or chartered taxi from Kuşadası (see p.251) and Selçuk (see p.245)

Jutting incongruously from a dry, dusty, suburban area just north of **Altınkum** beach, the ancient Ionian sanctuary of **Didyma** (Didim in Turkish) is a real treat. Though

CONSULTING THE ORACLE OF APOLLO

Pilgrims visiting the sanctuary of Apollo would first **purify** themselves at a well below the resting place of the Medusa head, then approach the still-prominent circular **altar** to offer a sacrifice before proceeding to the steps of the **shrine** itself. As at Delphi, prophecies were formulated by proxy – supplicants would first deliver their queries to the priest of Apollo, who would disappear to consult the **priestess**, who (accounts disagree) either drank from, bathed in, or inhaled potent vapours from, the waters. Her subsequent ravings were rephrased more delicately to those waiting out front; the priest would reappear after a suitable interval on a terrace some 2m higher to deliver the oracular pronouncement. Questions ranged from the personal to matters of state; prophecies were recorded and stored for posterity.

half-ruined, its oracular **sanctuary of Apollo** rarely fails to impress, even when besieged by the tour groups that rock up throughout the day. The best time to visit is late afternoon or early evening, when the site is relatively calm, and its masonry glows in the sunset. Didyma's best-known feature is the **Medusa head** near the foot of the steps as you enter the site. Fallen from a Roman-era architrave, it's now the unofficial logo of the place, repeated ad infinitum on posters and cards all over Turkey.

Even in ruins, the **shrine** itself, which stands beyond the nearby **circular altar**, is still intimidatingly large. The surviving column stumps alone are considerably taller than a human, and in its nearly complete state it must have inspired reverence. The effect was accentuated by its position on a steep, stepped base and enclosure in a virtual forest of 108 Ionic **columns** – only three of which now stand to their original height. The remaining twelve stumps supported the roof of the entry porch, reached by a steep flight of steps, where supplicants would deliver their queries to the priest of Apollo (see box above). Only traces remain of the miniature shrine that formerly enclosed the cult statue of Apollo, his sacred laurel and the **sacred well**, but the well itself is still obvious.

Brief history

While an oracle and shrine of some sort apparently existed at Didyma long before Ionian settlers arrived in the eleventh century BC – the name itself is an ancient Anatolian word – the imported **cult of Apollo** quickly appropriated whatever previous oracle, centred on a sacred well and laurel tree, had worked here. Didyma remained a sacred precinct, under the jurisdiction of a clan of priests originally from Delphi, and was never a town as such, though it eventually became a dependency of nearby **Miletus**. Every four years the sanctuary was also the venue for the Didymeia, a festival of music and drama as well as athletics.

The archaic shrine, started during the eighth century BC, was finished within two hundred years. Though similar in design to the current structure, it was half the size. After their defeat of the Ionian revolt in 494 BC, the **Persians** destroyed this first temple and plundered its treasures, including the cult statue of Apollo. The oracle puttered along until Alexander appeared on the scene, when the cult statue was retrieved from Persia and a new temple (the one existing today) commissioned.

Despite continuing subsidy from the **Romans**, work continued at a snail's pace for more than five centuries and the building was never actually completed – not entirely surprising when you consider the formidable engineering problems it presented.

In the end Christianity put paid to the oracle, and when the edict of Theodosius in 385 AD proscribed all pagan practices, construction ceased for good, after which a medieval earthquake toppled most of the columns. At its zenith Didyma was approached not only from Miletus but also from Panormos, a cove 6km west, via a sacred way whose final stretches were lined with statuary. Neither pavement nor statues are visible today; the latter were spirited away to the British Museum in 1858.

Miletus

22km north of Didim, 55km south of Kuşadası • Daily: summer 8.30am–7pm; winter 8.30am–5.30pm • ₺5 • Accessible by dolmuş from Kuşadası or Söke, or on tours or chartered taxi from Kuşadası and Selçuk (see p.237)

Perched on an eminently defendable promontory, the ancient city of **Miletus** (Milet in Turkish) once outshone **Priene** (see p.249). However, its modern setting, marooned in the seasonal marshes of the Büyük Menderes, leaves little to bear witness to the town's long and colourful past, although the massive theatre, visible from afar, testifies to its former glories. Up close, the site is a confusing juxtaposition of widely scattered relics from different eras, often disguised by weeds, mud or water, depending on the season. Following the theft of various artefacts, the **museum**, 1km south of the main ticket booth, is no longer open; ask about the current situation when you buy your ticket.

Brief history

Miletus is at least as old as Ephesus and far older than Priene; German archeologists have uncovered remnants of a **Creto-Mycenaean** settlement from the sixteenth century BC. **Ionian** invaders made their first appearance during the eleventh century, and by the seventh century BC Miletus was in the first flush of a heyday that lasted more than two hundred years.

While not strong enough completely to avoid Persian domination, Miletus did manage to secure favourable terms as an equal, and even took the opportunity to appropriate the nearby oracle of Didyma. But with Athenian instigation, the city was unwisely persuaded to take command of the abortive **Ionian revolt** against the Persians between 500 and 494 BC, which led to large-scale destruction. Within fifty years Miletus was rebuilt some way northeast of its original site, but it was never again as great – or as independent. **Alexander** saw fit to "liberate" the city from a new, short-lived occupation by the Persians and their allies. Later it was bequeathed to the **Romans**, under whose rule it enjoyed a brief renaissance – most of what you see today is a legacy of various emperors' largesse. The Byzantine town stubbornly clung to life, producing Isidorus, architect of Istanbul's

4

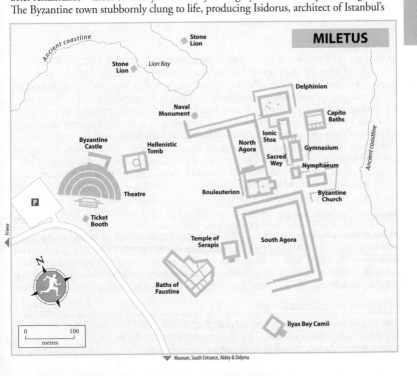

MILETUS

Ancient coastline

Stone Lion

Stone Lion

Lion Bay

Delphinion

Naval Monument

Capito Baths

Byzantine Castle

Hellenistic Tomb

Ionic Stoa

North Agora

Gymnasium

Sacred Way

Nymphaeum

Theatre

Bouleuterion

Byzantine Church

P

Ticket Booth

Priene

Temple of Serapis

South Agora

Baths of Faustina

İlyas Bey Camii

N

0   100
metres

Ancient coastline

Museum, South Entrance, Akköy & Didyma

VISITING DIDYMA, MILETUS AND PRIENE

The absorbing ruins of **Didyma** (see p.253), **Miletus** (see p.244) and **Priene** (see p.249) can all be visited on public transport. Infrequent minibuses head to all three from the town of **SÖKE**, itself very well connected to other parts of western Turkey. Most visitors, however, find it far easier to take a **tour**, which is the only realistic option if you want to see all three sites in a single day. Travel agencies in Selçuk (see p.237) or Kuşadası (see p.246) will be happy to arrange these; in general, a seat on a group **minibus** will cost ₺70–100 from either. If you're in a small group, chartering a **taxi** for the day can actually work out cheaper, at around €100 for the vehicle from either Selçuk or Kuşadası.

Aya Sofya. In the ninth century Miletus was already dwindling, and by the time the Menteşe emirs, and then the Ottomans, took control, there was little left to prize.

The theatre

Miletus' most obvious attraction lies just behind the site entrance: a **theatre**, whose Hellenistic base was modified and enlarged during the second century AD to hold fifteen thousand spectators. A stone block on the orchestra floor bears two griffins carved in relief, while the centre front row sports two pillars that once supported the emperor's canopy. Further up, the vaulted exit passageways are enormous and virtually intact.

An eighth-century **Byzantine castle** and some contemporaneous ramparts surmount the theatre, giving a marvellous 360-degree view over the flood plain, as well as the site itself.

Around the old bay

Though the waters have long since retreated, the old "Lion Bay" is one of the best sections of the site in which to get your bearings. It was so called for the two **stone lions** that guarded the entrance, now mostly embedded into the marsh silt. Easier to spot is a round base marking the remains of the **naval monument**, commemorating an unknown victory of the first century BC.

Sacred Way

In its time, the handsomely paved **Sacred Way** linked Miletus with Didyma. Standing at its north end is the sixth-century **Delphinion**, dedicated to Apollo Delphinius, patron of sailors, ships and ports. Not surprisingly in such a maritime community, this was the most important religious establishment in town, and you'll still be able to see the foundations of altars and semicircular benches, and the enclosing colonnade. On the same side of the pavement as you walk south stands a first-century AD **Ionic stoa**, which partly shields the enormous **Capito baths** and a **gymnasium** of the same era.

The most satisfying monument east of the Sacred Way is the **nymphaeum**, the largest public fountain of Miletus, once extremely ornate but now standing at barely half its original height. Just to the south are the ruins of a sixth-century **Byzantine church**, while the Roman **Baths of Faustina** (Marcus Aurelius's wife), west of here at the foot of the theatre hill, are distinctive for their good state of repair.

ARRIVAL AND DEPARTURE
DİDİM

By bus or dolmuş Services between Söke and Altınkum beach run almost directly past the ruins. These are located in Didim village, the modern name for Didyma, though confusingly the whole beach resort is often referred to as Didim too – ask to get off at Didim Köyü. To head back out to Söke or Bodrum, there's no need to make the 2km trek into Altınkum (there are regular dolmuşes, or it's a 50min walk); simply wait in the car park where you were dropped off.

By ferry Ferries head to the Greek island of Kós (June–Sept Wed & Sat; 1hr); the journey costs €40 one-way or day return.

ACCOMMODATION AND EATING

There are a few **guesthouses** near the ruins, and plenty of actual hotels near the beach. The **restaurants** around the ruins are overpriced and serve poor food, so if you're staying the night the beach is the best place to head to eat, with umpteen places serving *pide*, kebabs, English breakfasts and even Chinese food.

Medusa House Overlooking Didyma ☏ 0256 811 0063, ⓦ medusahouse.com. By far the best of the limited accommodation near Didyma, this comfortable, characterful place, run by a German-Turkish couple, features rustic rooms in two restored old buildings, separated by a lovely, rambling garden. **₺180**

Bafa Gölü

Surrounded by jagged mountains and more than 100 square kilometres in size, **Lake Bafa** – in Turkish, **Bafa Gölü** – is an entrancing spectacle. Created when silt sealed off the Büyük Menderes River's passage to the sea, it's now most famed as the site of **Heracleia ad Latmos**, a spectacularly located set of lakeside ruins.

As for Bafa itself, the water is faintly brackish and fish species include *levrek* (bass), *kefal* (grey mullet), *yayın* (catfish) and *yılan balığı* (eel). Although levels are depleting, stocks are still high enough to support the arrival throughout the year of more than two hundred species of migratory wildfowl, including the endangered **crested pelican**, of which there are believed to be fewer than two thousand left in the world.

Heracleia ad Latmos

Look across Lake Bafa from its southern shore and you'll spy a patch of irregular shoreline, and the modern village of **KAPIKIRI**, whose lights twinkle at the base of **Mount Latmos** by night. Strewn higgledy-piggledy around the village are the ruins of **Heracleia ad Latmos** (Heraklia in Turkish), one of the most evocatively situated ancient cities in all Turkey.

A settlement of **Carian** origin had existed here long before the arrival of the **Ionians**, though Latmos – as it was then known – had far better geographical communication with Ionia than with the rest of Caria. Late in the Hellenistic period the city's location was moved a kilometre or so west, and the name changed to Heracleia, but despite its numerous monuments and enormous wall it was never a place of great importance. Miletus (see p.255), at the head of the gulf, monopolized most trade and already the inlet was starting to close up.

The site

Only the retaining wall and some rows of benches survive of the second-century BC **bouleuterion** that lies 100m east of the first parking area. The **Roman baths** visible in the valley below, and a crumbled but appealing **Roman theatre** off in the olives beyond, can be reached via an unmarked trail starting between the first and second parking areas. The path up to the **hermits' caves** on Mount Latmos begins at the rear of the second parking area; stout boots are advisable. Similar cautions apply for those who want to trace the course of the **Hellenistic walls**, the city's most imposing and conspicuous relics, supposedly built by Lysimachus in the late third century BC.

The restaurant of the *Agora Pansiyon* (see p.258) looks south over the **Hellenistic agora**, now an open, grassy square; the downhill side of its south edge stands intact to two storeys,

4

ENDYMION: DEMIGOD OF THE WET DREAM

Heracleia owes its fame, and an enduring hold on the romantic imagination, to a legend associated not with the town itself but with **Mount Latmos** behind. **Endymion** was a handsome shepherd who, while asleep in a cave on the mountain, was noticed by Selene, the moon goddess. She made love with him as he slept, and in time, so the story goes, bore Endymion fifty daughters without their sire ever waking. Endymion was reluctant for all this to stop and begged Zeus, who was also fond of him, to be allowed to dream forever; his wish was granted and, as a character in Mary Lee Settle's novel *Blood Tie* flippantly observed, thus became the only known demigod of the wet dream.

complete with windows. The grounds offer a fine view west over the lake and assorted castle-crowned promontories. A box-like Hellenistic **Temple of Athena** perches on a hill west of the agora; less conspicuous is an inscription to Athena, left of the entrance.

From the agora a wide, walled-in path descends toward the shore and Heracleia's final quota of recognizable monuments. Most obvious is the peninsula – or, in wet years, island – studded with **Byzantine walls** and a **church**. A stone causeway half-buried in the beach here allowed entrance in (drier) medieval times. Follow the shore southwest, and across the way you should be able to spot the tentatively identified Hellenistic **Sanctuary of Endymion**, oriented, unusually, northeast to southwest. Five column stumps front the structure, which has a rounded rear wall – a ready-made apse for later Christians – with sections of rock incorporated into the masonry.

ARRIVAL AND DEPARTURE   BAFA GÖLÜ

The southern shore Frequent buses along the southern shore make the lake easy to see. If you'd like to get off, note that Söke–Milas dolmuşes (every 30min) are more flexible than the big coaches in terms of stopping.

The ruins Getting to Kapıkırı and the ruins is the hard bit;

if you have your own wheels, take a north turn at Çamiçi village, from where it's a juddering 8km. If you're on foot, you may find a taxi, but it's best to arrange pick-up with one of the hotels nearby (see below).

ACCOMMODATION

The highway lining the **southern shore** of Bafa has a small slew of guesthouses and fish restaurants, but staying in the village of **Kapıkırı**, at the base of Mount Latmos, provides a more relaxing stay.

Agora Pansiyon Kapıkırı ☎0252 543 5445, ⓦagorapansiyon.com. Doubles, bungalows and a rooftop restaurant, around an organic garden: they also organize boat trips, and guided hikes to cave paintings. Half board. ₺200

★**Karia Pansiyon** Kapıkırı ☎0252 543 5490, ⓦkariapension.com. Smart guesthouse with a fern-filled garden, splendidly rustic rooms and superlative lake views

from the roof. The food's wonderful, too. Half board. ₺225

Silva Oliva Southern shore ☎0252 519 1177, ⓦhotelsilvaoliva.com. This German-owned establishment has thirty large, pleasingly decorated rooms spread through nine houses, all of which have lake-view balconies. The associated restaurant serves a very broad range of dishes (all of them doused in their own home-pressed olive oil), and guided hikes of the local area are offered. ₺150

Milas and around

A small, initially nondescript town of some 35,000 people, **MİLAS**, or **Mylasa**, as it was formerly known, was an important **Carian** centre – its original location was at the nearby hill of Peçin Kale. Few foreigners stay the night, but there are some sights of interest here, and plenty within day-trip distance – the fantastic castle of **Peçin Kale**, the Carian ruins of **Euromos** and **Labranda**, and the beach resort of **Ören**.

Milas's lively tradesmen's **bazaar** covers the western slopes of Hisarbaşı hill, which has been the focus of settlement in every era. Once you get past the warren of alleys arranged perpendicular to the main street, Cumhuriyet Caddesi, veer uphill to reach the late Ottoman **Belen Camii**. Immediately to its right stands the eighteenth-century **Çöllühanı**, one of the last semi-functioning, unrestored *kervansaray*s in western Turkey.

West of town, along Kadıağa Caddesi, an elaborate early Roman tomb known as the **Gümüşkesen** (literally "cuts-silver") lies in a slight depression south of Hıdırlık hill. This landscaped site is the most impressive relic of ancient Mylasa.

Peçin Kale

5km east of Milas • Castle Mon–Wed & Fri–Sun 8.30am–5.30pm • ₺5 • Take any Ören-bound dolmuş (every 45min)

Ancient Mylasa originally stood atop the hill of **Peçin Kale** (Beçin Kale in local dialect and signposting). Mylasa's shift to its current position during the fourth century BC means that the hill is actually more interesting for its **castle**, an unmistakable fortified bluff, originally Byzantine but adapted by the Menteşe emirs during the fourteenth century.

Clearly marked 400m south of the castle, the main Menteşe buildings include the unusual two-storey **Kızıl Han**, and the fourteenth-century **Orhan Bey Camii**. Bearing right takes you to the **medrese and türbe of Ahmet Gazi**, from the same era – tombs of a Menteşe governor and his wife that are venerated as those of minor Islamic saints, with coloured rags and candles.

Labranda

15km north of Milas • Daily 8.30am–5.30pm • ₺10 • Only accessible with your own vehicle, or by taxi (₺50 including waiting time)

While it's a bit of a haul to the isolated ruins of **Labranda**, they're a real treat for fans of ancient history. Set on a plateau of sorts, on a steep, pine-lined hillside, the **sanctuary of Zeus** is arguably the most beautifully located, and least visited, archeological zone of ancient Caria. There's not too much here above human height, but still enough for you to imagine what the place must have looked like in Carian times.

Euromos

12km northwest of Milas and 1km from Selimiye village, 200m from the highway • Daily 8.30am–5.30pm • ₺10 • Accessible on any Selimiye dolmuş or Milas–Söke bus

Artefacts found on the site of **Euromos** suggest that it was already in use as far back as the sixth century BC. The impressive Carian ruins visible today include a **Corinthian Temple of Zeus**, supposedly requisitioned by Hadrian. It's thought that the structure was never realized in full, but almost half of the columns remain standing, including two near-complete sides – good photo-fodder if you've made it this far.

Iassos

15km west of Milas • Mon, Tues & Thurs–Sun, hours vary • ₺5 • Served by hourly dolmuş

Set on a headland almost completely surrounded by the Gulf of Asim, ancient **Iassos** certainly has a dramatic location. Its ruins, however, dating mostly from the Roman Imperial period of the second century AD, are only mildly diverting. The real reason to come here is to eat the delicious **seafood** caught nearby and served in the restaurants of the modern village of **Kıyıkışlacık**; *çipura* (gilthead bream) is the local speciality.

On entering Kıyıkışlacık, you first pass a Roman mausoleum, arguably more interesting than anything within the city walls and now in service as the site **museum**. Inside, the star exhibit is a Corinthian temple-tomb resting on a stepped platform.

The main highlights of the site itself are the well-preserved Roman **bouleuterion**, with four rows of seats, and a Roman **villa** with murals and mosaics. The meagre hillside **theatre**, of which only the cavea walls and stumps of the stage building remain, offers fine views over the northeast harbour. The hilltop **castle** was a medieval foundation of the Knights of St John, and after the Turkish conquest the place was known as Asimkalesi (Asim's Castle), Asim being a local *ağa* (feudal lord).

Ören

45km south of Milas • Dolmuşes from Milas (1hr) pass through the upper village then drop off at the beach

ÖREN is an endangered Turkish species – a coastal resort that's not completely overdeveloped. One of the few sizeable villages on the north coast of the Gulf of Gökova, it owes its pre-tourism history to the narrow, fertile, alluvial plain adjacent, and the lignite deposits in the mountains behind.

The **upper village**, an appealingly homogeneous settlement on the east bank of a canyon mouth exiting the hills, is scattered among the ruins of **ancient Keramos**. You can easily make out sections of wall, arches and a boat slip, dating from when the sea (now 1km distant) lapped the edge of town. The resort area down on the coast holds little in the way of relics, save for sections of column carted off from the main site by *pansiyon* owners for use as decoration. The **beach** is a more than acceptable kilometre of coarse sand, gravel and pebbles, backed by handsome pine-tufted cliffs; in clear weather you can spy the Datça peninsula opposite. A working harbour once stood at the east end of town, but what's left of the jetty now serves a few fishing boats and the occasional wandering yacht.

In the morning and late afternoon, there are great thermals on the coast – the 640m-high **Mount Koçatepe**, looming above, makes an ideal jumping-off point. **Paragliding** trips can be organized through several agencies in town.

ARRIVAL AND DEPARTURE

By plane The Havaş bus to Milas-Bodrum airport (₺5) stops at the roundabout at the end of Atatürk Bul in Milas (18km away), and is geared to the times of THY internal flights.

By bus or dolmuş Milas's *otogar* is way out on the northern edge of town. You'll be left here unless you've

MİLAS AND AROUND

come from Iassos or Ören, whose dolmuşes use a small terminal close to the town centre. To get into the centre from the *otogar*, take either a cab, a dolmuş marked "Şehir İçi" or the complimentary shuttle run by the big companies.

ACCOMMODATION AND EATING

MİLAS

Siler Halilbey Bul 121 ☎0252 513 2222. A bit far south of the centre, but worth the trek for the nicest rooms in town. The cheapest ones are a wee bit small, but they're all decorated with snazzy accoutrements and feature clean, spacious bathrooms. Good buffet breakfasts, too. ₺150

Sürücü Atatürk Bul 34 ☎0252 512 4001. A few hundred metres south of the centre, opposite the Atatürk statue, but

surprisingly large and also good value, if a little lacking in character. Students from the nearby university frequent its restaurant and café. ₺100

ÖREN

Keramos Centre of the beach area ☎0252 532 2250. The best mid-range option on this stretch of coast, with large, stylish rooms and a lovely garden. ₺200

Bodrum

It's fair to say that the coastal resort of **BODRUM** has a reputation. To many travellers, the very name conjures up images of drunken debauchery, full English breakfasts, and belly-out Europeans turning slowly pink on the beach. While there's an element of truth to that stereotype, the reality is somewhat different – with its low-rise whitewashed houses and subtropical gardens, Bodrum is the most attractive of the major Aegean resorts, given a more cosmopolitan air by the increasing number of Turkish and Arabic visitors.

The town is neatly divided into two contrasting halves by its castle, and a largely pedestrianized **bazaar** that sits immediately to its north. To the west is the more genteel area that surrounds a spruced-up yacht marina, with its upmarket hotels and restaurants, while to the east the town's party zone holds its highest concentration of bars and restaurants. The eastern zone also features a thin, scrubby strip of beach, packed with sunbathers during the day and shoreside diners in the evening.

Lastly, mention must also be made of the delightful **peninsula** that Bodrum calls home (see p.266); a tranquil and highly characterful place with beaches galore, it has recently become immensely popular with moneyed locals.

Brief history

Originally known as **Halikarnassos**, Bodrum was colonized by Dorians from the Peloponnese in the eleventh century BC. They mingled with the existing Carian population, settling on the small island of Zephysia, which later became a peninsula

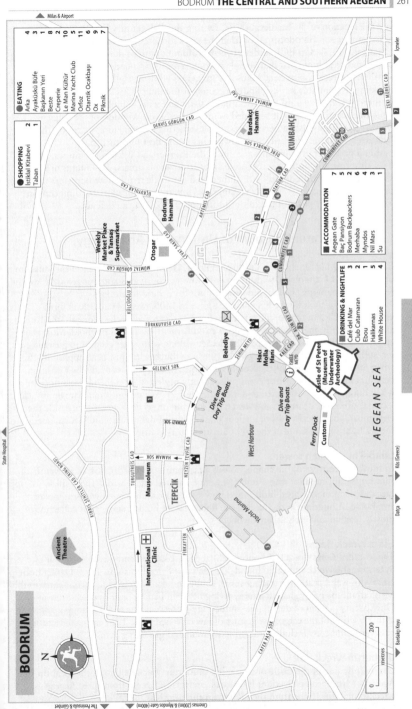

BODRUM

N

200

0

metres

● EATING

Arka	4
Ayaküskü Büfe	3
Başkanın Yeri	1
Beste	8
Creperie	10
Le Man Kültür	5
Marina Yacht Club	11
Orfoz	6
Otantik Ocakbaşı	9
Ox	9
Piknik	7

● SHOPPING

İstiklal Kitabevi	1
Taban	2

■ ACCOMMODATION

Aegean Gate	7
Baç Pansiyon	5
Bodrum Backpackers	2
Merhaba	6
Myndos	3
Nil Mars	4
Su	1

■ DRINKING & NIGHTLIFE

Café del Mar	3
Club Catamaran	2
Ebou	1
Halikarnas	5
White House	4

Milas & Airport

İçmeler

DERVİŞ GÖRGÜN CAD

MÜMTAZ ATAMAN CAD

Bardakçı Hamam

KUMBAHÇE

ÜÇKUYULAR CAD

ANTEMİS CAD

ATATÜRK CAD

CUMHURİYET CAD

ZEKİ MÜREN CAD

Weekly Market Place & Tansaş Supermarket

Bodrum Hamam

Otogar

MÜMTAZ GÖRGÜN CAD

SEVKİ SABİR CAD

KÜLCÜOĞLU SOK

TÜRKKUYUSU CAD

Belediye

ŞEHİR METD.

Hacı Molla Hanı

İSKELE METD.

DR. ALİM BEY CAD

KALE CAD

İSKELE METD.

Castle of St Peter (Museum of Underwater Archeology)

GELENCE SOK

Dive and Day Trip Boats

ÇIKMAZI SOK

West Harbour

Dive and Day Trip Boats

Ferry Dock

Customs

TURGUTREIS CAD

HAMAM SOK

NEZZEN REVFİK CAD

Mausoleum

TEPECİK

FİRKATEN SOK

International Clinic

Ancient Theatre

State Hospital

(KIBRIS ŞEHİTLER CAD (RING ROAD))

Yacht Marina

AEGEAN SEA

Kôs (Greece)

Datça

Bardakçı Koyu

Cinemas (200m) & Myndos Gate (400m)

The Peninsula & Gümbet

4

and the location of the medieval castle. During the fifth century BC, **Halikarnassos'** most famous son **Herodotus** chronicled the city's fortunes in his acclaimed *Histories*.

Mausolus (377–353 BC), leader of the **Hecatomnid satraps** dynasty, increased the power and wealth of what had already become a semi-independent principality. An admirer of Greek civilization, Mausolus spared no effort to Hellenize his cities, and was working on a suitably self-aggrandizing tomb at the time of his death – thereby giving us the word "mausoleum". **Artemisia II**, his sister and wife, completed the massive structure, which came to be regarded as one of the Seven Wonders of the Ancient World. She distinguished herself in warfare, inflicting a humiliating defeat on the Rhodians, who were tricked into allowing her entire fleet into their port.

After a period of little importance under the Roman and Byzantine empires, and brief shuffling among Selçuk, Menteşe and Ottoman occupiers, the **Knights of St John** slipped over from Rhodes in 1402 and erected the castle that is now Bodrum's most prominent landmark – indeed, the name *bodrum*, meaning "cellar" or "dungeon" in Turkish, probably pays tribute to the stronghold's subterranean defences.

Castle of St Peter (Museum of Underwater Archeology)

Tues–Sun 8am–6.30pm • ₺25

Bodrum's main landmark, the **Castle of St Peter**, is now home to the excellent **Museum of Underwater Archeology**, with its array of towers, courtyards and dungeons, as well as separate museums displaying underwater finds from various wrecks.

The castle was built by the Knights of St John in 1406, over a small Selçuk fortress. Urgently needing to replace the fortress at Smyrna destroyed by the Mongols, the Knights engaged the era's finest military engineers to construct their new stronghold. More walls and moats were added over succeeding decades, along with water cisterns to guarantee self-sufficiency in the event of siege. The finishing touches had just been applied in 1522 when Süleyman's capture of the Knights' headquarters on Rhodes made their position here untenable. Bodrum's castle was subsequently neglected until the nineteenth century, when the chapel was converted to a mosque, the keep to a prison, and a hamam installed.

Initial entrance is through the **west gate**, looking on to the water. Once inside the west moat, you'll notice bits of ancient masonry from the mausoleum incorporated into the walls, as well as some of the 249 Christian coats of arms.

Chapel and Italian tower

In the **lower courtyard**, the **chapel** houses a fascinating reconstruction of a seventh-century Byzantine ship, whose remains were excavated off Yassıada. The display, incorporating the salvaged hull, shows how such ships were loaded with cargoes of amphorae. A building at the base of the **Italian Tower** holds a small glass collection, mostly Roman and early Islamic work.

Glass Wreck Hall

The so-called **Glass Wreck Hall** houses well-labelled, climate-controlled displays on a **Byzantine shipwreck** and cargo found 33m down at Serçe Limanı in 1973. Dating from 1025, this was a peacetime trading vessel, tubby and flat-bottomed to permit entry to the Mediterranean's many shallow straits, plying between Fatimid and Byzantine territories. Only twenty percent of the original timbers are preserved. The rest is a mock-up, loaded with a fraction of the cargo: two tonnes of raw coloured glass. The personal effects of the passengers and crew include gaming pieces, tools and grooming items.

Uluburun Wreck Hall

On the east side of the castle precinct, the **Uluburun Wreck Hall** holds the local Bronze Age and Mycenaean collection. It features artefacts recovered from three Aegean wrecks, including finds from the Uluburun site near Kaş.

Carian Princess Hall

The **Carian Princess Hall** contains artefacts from an ancient tomb found miraculously unlooted during hotel construction in 1989. The sarcophagus, with its skeleton of a Carian noblewoman who died in the fourth century BC, is on view along with a few gold tomb finds – almost certainly imported, since the metal is not found locally.

English Tower

Although financed and built by English Knights during the fifteenth century, the **English Tower** now appears a bald attempt to pander to Bodrum's major foreign constituency. Around the themed cafeteria inside, assorted standards of the Order of St John and their Muslim adversaries compete for wall space with an incongruous array of medieval armour and weapons. Many visitors attempt to decipher extensive swathes of Latin graffiti incised into the window jambs by bored Knights.

Dungeon

It's certainly worth making the long, dead-end detour to the Knights' former **dungeon**, adorned with dangling chains and bathed in lurid red light. In case you missed the point, an original Latin inscription over the door reads "Here God does not exist".

Mausoleum

Turgutreis Cad, 10min walk northwest of the castle • Tues–Sun 8am–6.30pm • ₺10

Designed by Pytheos, architect of the Athena temple at Priene (see p.249), the ancient **Mausoleum** was once a whacking great structure, measuring 39m by 33m at its base and standing nearly 60m high. A colonnade surmounted the burial vault and supported a stepped pyramidal roof bearing a chariot (now in the British Museum) with effigies of **Mausolus** himself and his sister-wife Artemisia. Despite diligent work by archeologists, little is left of the original mausoleum. Visitors can examine the precinct wall, assorted column fragments and some subterranean vaults probably belonging to an earlier burial chamber. A shed east of the foundation cavity exhibits plans and models, plus copies of the original friezes.

4

Ancient theatre

Off the Ring Road • Tues–Sun 8.30am–5.30pm • Free

Bodrum's **ancient theatre** has been almost overzealously restored, though if you've been to the mausoleum it's worth the extra five-minute walk uphill. Begun by Mausolus, it was modified in the Roman era and originally seated thirteen thousand, though its current capacity is half that.

ARRIVAL AND INFORMATION   **BODRUM**

BY PLANE

Airport Milas-Bodrum airport (ⓦ bodrum-airport.com) is 35km northeast of town. Regular buses link it with Bodrum's *otogar* (₺10; 45min), off Cevat Şakir Cad; the only other option is taking a taxi, for around ₺90.

Airlines THY, Kıbrıs Şehitleri Cad 82 (ⓣ 0252 317 1203, ⓦ turkishairlines.com). Turkish Airlines ticket-holders can book here for free shuttle buses to the airport.

BY FERRY

To Datça Small ferries link Bodrum to the Datça peninsula year-round (one-way ₺30, return ₺50; 1hr 45min). They depart daily at 9.30am and 5.30pm from a pier in the west harbour; pay at the booth.

To Kós From April to Oct, daily services to the Greek island of Kós (one-way or day-trip €17, open return €30; 1hr) depart at 9.30am from the dock by the castle; in summer there's an extra sailing at 4pm. For the latest information, check the websites of the two main operators, Bodrum Express (ⓦ bodrumexpresslines.com) and Bodrum Ferryboat Association (ⓦ bodrumferryboat.com).

To Rhodes In July and Aug only, services to Rhodes (one-way €55, open return €75; 2hr 20min) depart at 9.30am on Sat and Mon from the east pier, returning at 5.30pm; buy your ticket the day before travel.

BOAT TRIPS, CRUISES AND DIVING AROUND BODRUM

Most of Bodrum's wide array of **boat trips** – well worth taking if you don't plan to tour the area by land – leave from the west harbour. A typical day out starts around 10.30am and finishes at 5.30pm, costing roughly ₺35 per person (including lunch). Boats range from sleepy fifteen-person *gulets* to wild party barges squeezing in seventy passengers (choose wisely), but itineraries vary little. First stop for most boats is the Akvaryum, a snorkellers' venue in the Ada Boğazı (Island Strait): the fish, however, have been frightened off, and are now seldom seen. Next halt is usually Kara Ada, a sizeable island southeast of town, where you bathe in hot springs issuing from a cave at the island's margin. The final moorings are often Kızıl Burnu (Red Bay) and Tavsan Burnu (Rabbit Bay).

There's also good **diving** around Bodrum. Several operators, including Aquapro (ⓦaquapro -turkey.com), offer courses and tours; hunt around the west harbour, where dive boats offer a full day out, usually including gear rental and lunch, for €45.

BY BUS

The pleasingly central *otogar*, off Cevat Şakir Cad, is an easy walk from anywhere in the city centre.

Destinations Ankara (4 daily; 11hr); Denizli, for Pamukkale (8 daily; 5hr); Fethiye (7 daily; 5hr); Istanbul (20 daily; 12hr); İzmir (hourly; 3hr 30min); Marmaris (hourly; 3hr 15min); Muğla (hourly; 2hr 30min).

BY CAR

Driving is difficult in Bodrum, made all the more so by a strict one-way system and a lack of good parking; if you do find a spot, it's generally ₺5/hr or ₺25/day. Many hotels have their own spaces. For rental, several agencies compete for customers in the area just east of the *otogar* – it's easy to haggle.

INFORMATION

Tourist office Barış Meyd (June–Sept Mon–Fri 8am–6pm, Sat & Sun 10am–6pm; Oct–May Mon–Fri 8am–5pm; ☎0252 316 1091). The moderately useful information office, near the castle, will be able to give you maps of the city, and perhaps a little advice on accommodation or onward transport.

ACCOMMODATION

Bodrum's room rates tend to be more **expensive** than elsewhere in Turkey, particularly in July and Aug, when advance reservations are recommended – book online if you can, since this is the easiest way to score a bargain when most hotels are booked solid. A/c is a necessity in midsummer, and all but the most humble *pansiyons* have it. Out of season, most hotels (except those with central heating) are closed.

★**Aegean Gate** Güvercin Sok 2 ☎0252 313 7853, ⓦaegeangatehotel.com. A wildly popular and highly recommended option, 1km past the *Halikarnas* nightclub (see p.266), boasting stupendous views over Bodrum bay. It's centred around an enchanting swimming pool, and has a minimum two-night stay. They have a couple of dogs on the premises, plus cats at cat-mealtimes – the hotel is involved in Bodrum's neutering process, the importance of which will be clear to anyone who's spent any time in Turkey. ₺**300**

★**Baç Pansiyon** Cumhuriyet Cad 14 ☎0252 313 1602, ⓦbacpansiyon.com. This luxurious boutique hotel has been going strong since 1970, and is right in the heart of the present-day action. All the stylish rooms are double-glazed, cutting out much of the noise, and those at the rear have castle-view balconies. ₺**300**

Bodrum Backpackers Atatürk Cad 37 ☎0252 313 2762, ⓦbodrumbackpackers.net. Noisy place for partying backpackers, offering clean, well-kept dorms, a few poor-value private doubles – the one single room is a steal, though, at ₺65. The bar on the roof terrace (guests only) is a great place to meet other travellers, and occasionally turns into a dorm of its own in the summer. Note that the sign is hard to see from the street. Dorm ₺**60**, double ₺**120**

Merhaba Akasya Sok 44 ☎0252 316 3978, ⓦmerhabaotel.com. Probably as cheap as you're going to want to get in Bodrum – rooms are simple, but, thanks to a quiet location, you'll get a good night's rest. The switched-on staff are another bonus, as is the simple rooftop breakfast. ₺**120**

Myndos 1017 Sok 11 ☎0252 313 4422, ⓦmyndospansiyon.com. Nice new option, tucked away into the side streets – quiet, though highly central. The atmosphere is homely, which is no surprise considering the fact that it's family-run, while little quirks – think petals on the bed, paintings and prints on the walls, and turquoise decor – add up to a pleasing whole. ₺**210**

Nil Mars Turgutreis Cad, İmbat Çıkmazı 20 ☎0252 313 8068, ⓦmarsotel.com. Owners of the popular *Mars* upped sticks and moved to this busier spot east of the castle. Rooms are simple affairs, occasionally quite large; there's also a small pool, and bicycles for rent. ₺**150**

★**Su** 1201 Sok, off Turgutreis Cad ☎0252 316 6906,

ⓦ bodrumsuhotel.com. Large, well-equipped complex laid out around one of the biggest pools in town. The cheery multicoloured rooms all have balconies overlooking the central courtyard, where there's a cute bar. The hotel is inaccessible to cars (which helps to keep the noise levels down), but has its own parking around the corner; follow the river-mosaic down a side alley. ₺200

EATING

Eating out in Bodrum can be pricey, especially if you're close to the water, though there are cheaper places on Atatürk Cad. Notable are the small restaurants in the vine-covered **Meyhanelar Cad**, part of the bazaar, which vie to offer the traditional Turkish experience.

RESTAURANTS

★**Arka** Dr Ekrem Uslu Sok 11 ☎0252 316 2857, ⓦarkabodrum.com. What a find this little Italian joint is – the location is both calm and charming, the food is tasty yet super-cheap (pizzas and pasta dishes from ₺10), and they've good coffee, or even Spritz Aperol, to have with your meal. This is all before mentioning the deliciously unhealthy *trileçe* for dessert – basically a sponge cake swamped with cream. Daily noon–11pm.

Başkanın Yeri Meyhaneler Sok 15b ☎0532 342 4525. Perhaps the pick of the market area's small restaurants, with great seafood at reasonable prices – which drop further if you get them to cook stuff you've bought yourself from the nearby stalls. They fire up their grill in the evening, though you can still get good calamari (₺24) or seafood platters (₺37) at lunchtime, when you'll have the run of the place. Daily 9am–2am.

Beste Cumhuriyet Cad 102 ☎0252 313 4647. Restaurant competition is fierce along the strip, but this stands out for cheap, well-prepared dishes served right above the beach – most *meze* are ₺7, a hearty fish soup is yours for ₺15, and there are good fish sets. Daily 8am–midnight.

Le Man Kültür Cumhuriyet Cad 161 ☎0252 316 5316, ⓦlmk.com.tr. Hugely popular with trendy young Turks from Bodrum and beyond, the menu of this seafront place is comical in more ways than one, and cheap to boot. Breakfast plates go from just ₺10, pasta and pizzas for a little more, and there's decent coffee. Daily 8am–2am.

Marina Yacht Club Neyzen Tevfik Cad ☎0252 316 1228, ⓦmarinayachtclub.com. Now here's a place to show off – eating on a rooftop, gazing down on the harbour's forest of masts. Meals range from Turkish to international – the mixed *meze* (₺37.50 will fill a hole, ₺10 more will get you a succulent salmon kebab), and elsewhere on the menu you'll find beef carpaccio, cheese platters and more. Daily noon–late.

★**Orfoz** Zeki Müren Cad ☎0252 316 4285, ⓦorfoz .net. This simple-looking restaurant enjoys by far the best reputation in town – you'll almost certainly need to reserve. There's no menu as such – most come for the superbly prepared set meals, starting with *meze* made with shellfish, proceeding through soups, mixed salads, grilled fish and more before you're finally ready to burst. Reckon on ₺80/head, excluding drinks. Daily 6pm–late.

Otantik Ocakbaşı Atatürk Cad 12B ☎0252 313 0058. Excellent *meze*, wood-fired *pide* and grilled meats (from ₺17) dished up on a breezy outdoor terrace. It's also licensed – together with the charming lighting, this means it's best to swing by in the evening. Daily 10am–midnight.

Ox Cumhuriyet Cad 155 ☎0252 313 3025, ⓦox.com .tr. Bodrum now has it's very own boutique burger bar. It's a good one too, with burgers costing ₺29–49 depending on what you'd like inside – manchego, blue cheese sauce, truffle paste, sautéed courgette and the like. They also sell breakfast omelettes for the same price as most places on the strip (₺15), but far better prepared. Daily noon–midnight.

★**Piknik** Atatürk Cad 65 ☎0252 317 7049. Lost under a sea of neon signs, this restaurant is pretty central, though far more proximate to "regular" Turkey as regards its prices, service and the size of the meals. The *adana* (₺15) may be the pick of their authentic range of kebabs, and there are good *pide* from ₺8. They also deliver. Daily 24hr.

CAFÉS AND JUICE BARS

Ayaküskü Büfe Atatürk Cad ☎0252 313 5407. Tiny place selling freshly squeezed orange juice for just ₺2.50. Apple juice is available too, and pomegranate in season. Daily 8am–3am.

Creperie By the harbour ☎0252 316 9630. One of the town's more pleasant places for coffee (from ₺6), surrounded by yachts and kept uncommonly cool in summer by the part-covered shopping arcade it lives inside. They've tasty crêpes too, as well as music most evenings. Daily 9.30am–midnight.

DRINKING AND NIGHTLIFE

Bodrum holds dozens of places to **drink and dance**, most of them lining the waterfront east of the castle. All get packed and sweaty on a summer night, with the busiest hours from 11pm to 3am. Few bars have cover charges, though drink prices are high. Anyone looking for nightlife beyond clubbing would do well to plan a visit during April, when Bodrum hosts its annual **Rocks Fest**, or during Aug for the annual **Ballet Festival** (ⓦbodrumballetfestival.gov.tr).

BARS

Café del Mar Cumhuriyet Cad ☎ 0252 316 7110. Chilled bar for lounge and deep house, selling pricey cocktails and slightly less pricey beers until late. Also a good place to puff on a nargile (₺40). Daily 8am–5am.

Ebou Uslu Sok 54. The most appealing café-bar on the strip, boasting candlelit tables on the beach so that you can drink while your feet are lapped by the waves. The inside's gorgeous too, and often hosts live music. Daily 11am–late.

White House Cumhuriyet Cad 147. Appealing bar with a clutch of outdoor seats (some on the beach), long happy hours, and sports on the TV. It's perhaps the best place for a dance, since the floor is up a level and indoors – safer for your belongings, in other words. Daily 8am–4am.

CLUBS

Club Catamaran ☎ 0252 316 3600, ⓦ clubcatamaran .com. Bodrum's prime piece of partyware: a disco-boat that leaves port at 10pm and glams it up on the ocean waves until dawn. Regular shuttles to and fro ensure that you're not stranded out there. Entry ₺70. Boat leaves 1am daily; returns 4–5am.

Halikarnas Eastern end of Cumhuriyet Cad ☎ 0252 316 8000, ⓦ halikarnas.com.tr. A megaclub with room for more than five thousand people, and something of a local legend. Entry can be pricey (often ₺75), but many people hit Bodrum for this reason alone. Daily 7pm–late.

SHOPPING

İstiklal Kitabevi İstiklal Cad 5 ☎ 0252 316 0077. English-language tabloids can be bought around town, but this is best for books, with an excellent selection of secondhand titles and phrasebooks. Daily 9am–2am.

Taban Cumhiriyet Cad 69 ☎ 0252 316 1251. This rather ugly sandal shop stands out amid the area's acres of tat – and its made-to-measure goods may well come in useful for hardy travellers. Daily 9am–10pm.

DIRECTORY

Consulate Honorary British Consulate Cafer Paşa Cad 2, Emsan Ev 7 (☎ 0252 313 0021, ⓦ ukinturkey.fco.gov.uk). **Hamam** Bodrum Hamam (ⓦ bodrumhamami.com.tr) on Cevat Şakir Cad opposite the *otogar* (daily segregated bathing 6am–midnight), and Bardakçi Hamam on Dere Umurca Sok (daily 8am–8pm, usually later in summer). **Hospitals** The English-speaking International Clinic, Kıbrıs Şehitler Cad 181 (☎ 0252 313 3030) promises 24hr, seven-day attention; the State Hospital is north of the centre, off Kıbrıs Şehitler Cad (☎ 0252 313 1420). **Pharmacy** Eczane Oasis, Oasis Alışveriş Merkezi (☎ 0252 317 0507). **Police** Dr Alim Bey Cad (☎ 0252 316 1216); emergency ☎ 0252 316 1004.

The Bodrum peninsula

For anyone staying in Bodrum, it's worth making at least one day- or half-day trip across the **peninsula** it calls home. You might even consider basing yourself in one of its many relaxed villages, such as **Gümüşlük** or **Akyarlar**, rather than in hectic Bodrum. The peninsular population was largely Greek Orthodox before 1923 and villages often still have a vaguely Hellenic feel, with ruined churches, windmills and old **stone houses**. However, the area has become immensely popular with moneyed Turks of late, and whitewashed cube-buildings have proliferated – some are now appealing **boutique hotels**, others, where building projects have gone belly-up, stand eerily empty. Luxury hotels, meanwhile, are proliferating – every major world chain either has, or is about to have, a hotel open here.

The peninsula still exudes a unique charm. Its **north side**, greener and cooler, holds patches of pine forest; the **south**, studded with tall crags, is more arid, with a sandier coast. There are also plenty of serviceable **beaches**, with Bitez, Ortakent, Yalıkavak and Türkbükü, among others, currently holding Blue Flag status for cleanliness.

Note that most of the peninsula's hotels and restaurants only open from **May to October**. Travel at other times is certainly possible, though, and it's blissfully relaxing.

GETTING AROUND

THE BODRUM PENINSULA

By dolmuş Frequent dolmuşes (6am–midnight) head from Bodrum's *otogar* to all the peninsula's towns. Journeys to anywhere bar Torba take 30–50min, and typically cost ₺5–9. Getting from A to B without doubling back to Bodrum is often possible too, with hourly services between Yalıkavak and Turgutreis, and a few shorter-range hops. Services are heavily curtailed Nov–April.

By taxi You'll pay ₺110 or so from Bodrum to most of the places mentioned in our account, and in summer there will usually be plenty of taxis waiting to take you back.

By rented vehicle For visitors with the requisite paperwork, there are plenty of places offering car and scooter rental on the roads just east of Bodrum's *otogar*.

The south coast

The south coast of the Bodrum peninsula is markedly dry, but has some fantastic beaches. **Barbaros Bay**, to the east, is essentially a private hotel reserve (see p.268). Heading west of Bodrum, you'll first come to **Gümbet**, 2km away and practically a suburb of the city. Its 600m-long, tamarisk-lined, gritty beach is usually packed, with parasailing, ringo-ing and waterskiing offshore. Development is exclusively package-oriented, and the (mainly young and English) clientele rather rowdy – and the nightlife rivals that of Bodrum. **Bitez**, the next cove west, is a little more upmarket, and has become a watersports and windsurfing centre. Reasonable watering holes cater to the yachties sailing or cruising through, but the beach is tiny, even after artificial supplementing.

The road around the coast occasionally rises high above the sea on the way out west to **Kargı**, whose beach and bay are sandy and gently sloping, overlooked by the ubiquitous villas and a handful of fish restaurants. The next cove on, **Bağla**, is initially off-putting with its monotonous architecture – persevere, however, and you'll find the softest sand on the peninsula. **Karaincir**, the next bay with public access, is nearly as good – 600m of sand guarded by a pair of headlands. Canoes and windsurfing boards can be rented, and while mid-beach is completely crowded out by sunbeds and umbrellas, the south end of the strand inexplicably remains in its wild, natural state.

Nearby **Akyarlar** is more of an actual village – albeit surrounded by estates of concrete villas. Its often breezy conditions make it cooler and more comfortable in summer than

4

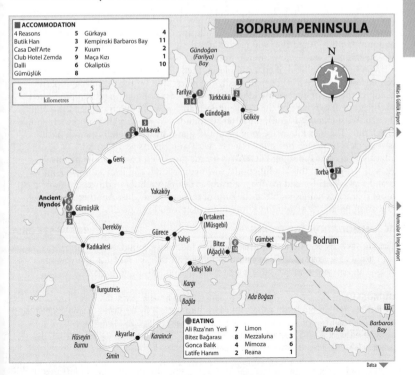

BODRUM PENINSULA

■ ACCOMMODATION

4 Reasons	**5**	Gürkaya	**4**
Butik Han	**3**	Kempinski Barbaros Bay	**11**
Casa Dell'Arte	**7**	Kuum	**2**
Club Hotel Zemda	**9**	Maça Kızı	**1**
Dalli	**6**	Okaliptüs	**10**
Gümüşlük	**8**		

● EATING

Ali Rıza'nın Yeri	**7**	Limon	**5**
Bitez Bağarası	**8**	Mezzaluna	**3**
Gonca Balık	**4**	Mimoza	**6**
Latife Hanım	**2**	Reana	**1**

sweaty Bodrum. Akyarlar's beach is small and hard-packed, mostly given over to windsurfing, but Karaincir and (in the opposite direction) the sandy cove at **Simin** are within walking distance.

ACCOMMODATION AND EATING   THE SOUTH COAST

Accommodation on the southern Bodrum peninsula is plentiful, particularly in the package resort of **Gümbet**. **Bitez** has some nice places to stay and eat, while **Akyarlar** offers some of the cheapest *pansiyons* on the peninsula, as well as some great local restaurants.

★**Bitez Bağarası** Bitez ☎0252 363 7693. The best place on the peninsula to sample Aegean cuisine, serving hearty platefuls of fish and the region's famously tasty veggies. Aegean food centres on *meze*, so order a nice mixed platter – freshly plucked samphire, stuffed pumpkin and courgette flowers, and so much more. Reservations recommended. Daily 9am–11pm.

Kempinski Barbaros Bay Barbaros Bay ☎0252 311 0303, ⍈kempinski.com. This is a great place to get away from it all, occupying a bay all to itself a 20min ride east of Bodrum. Once you're in, there's precious little reason to leave, with amenities strung down the cliff-side – the pool is up there with the largest on the Med, there's a private stretch of secluded beach, the three restaurants (seafood, Asian and Italian) are all superb and differ greatly in style, and the on-site Six Senses spa fulfils all pampering needs. Blissful. ₺600

Okaliptüs Bitez ☎0252 363 7780, ⍈okaliptus.com.tr. This well-designed four-star, nestled in a grove of tangerine trees, is the pick of Bitez's thirty-plus hotels, with its own pool and a small, private stretch of beach. Its restaurant is a winner, too. ₺250

The west coast

Less appealing than either the north or south, the Bodrum peninsula's windswept **west coast** nevertheless has a few fine beaches. The furthest south is at **Turgutreis**, the peninsula's second-largest town, though as a primarily all-inclusive resort it's not the best place to experience authentic local culture. The side road starting by its *otogar* leads north to better things, through a fertile landscape of the tangerine groves for which the region is famous. After 4km you reach **Kadıkalesı**, with its long, partly protected sand beach, and unbeatable views over to assorted islets.

If you've had a bellyful of villa complexes, then sleepy **GÜMÜŞLÜK** (2km beyond Kadıkalesi) is a refreshing change. Easily the nicest spot on the peninsula, it partly occupies the site of **ancient Myndos**, so most new development has been prohibited. Yachties are drawn here by the excellent deep anchorage between the headland and Tavşan Adası (Rabbit Island), the latter surrounded by mosaics that snorkellers should check out. The half-kilometre-long sand-and-gravel **beach** extending south of the island is less protected but still attractive, with watersports gear for rent.

Lastly, there's unappealing **YALIKAVAK** on the northwest corner of the peninsula. As with Turgutreis, this is a functional town year-round, and is most notable for its brand-new, Azeri-funded **marina** – already attracting yachties in droves (some of the more shameless names visible at the time of research were "Just Another Toy" and "Floating Asset"), it's open to visitors and makes for a lovely walk.

ACCOMMODATION AND EATING   THE WEST COAST

Gümüşlük is by far the best place to **sleep** on the west coast – Turgutreis is full of package tourists and retired Europeans, and Yalıkavak's few decent *pansiyons* are frustratingly hard to track down. For **food**, Gümüşlük wins again, though Yalıkavak has some good restaurants leading up to the marina, which itself has a few cafés and bars.

GÜMÜŞLÜK

Ali Rıza'nın Yeri On the beach ☎0252 394 3047, ⍈balikcialirizaninyeri.com. Also known as *Balıkcı*, this beachside restaurant sells fish about as fresh as fish gets – staffed by fisherfolk, it has its own private boat to supply the daily catch. Given this added luxury, prices are reasonable – try the stuffed calamari (₺20) or squash blossoms (₺15). Daily 10am–11pm.

Club Hotel Zemda On the beach ☎0252 394 3151, ⍈clubhotelzemda.com. Beachside hotel that has

APHRODISIAS (P.283) >

morphed, of late, from a watersport centre to a place for yoga, meditation and relaxation. Rooms are still a little basic, but they do the job, and the restaurant makes meals with organic food grown on the hotel farm. **₺300**

Gümüşlük Just back from the beach ☎0252 394 4828, ⓦotelgumusluk.com. This good-value hotel has large, modern rooms, and a pool surrounded by grass and deckchairs. They also rent out nearby apartments – good for long-stayers. **₺230**

Limon Above Gümüşlük town ☎0252 394 044, ⓦlimongumusluk.com. Café serving up home-grown produce in a bucolic, ruin-strewn garden setting that's up with the best on the peninsula; the same goes for the breakfasts, though they're very pricey at ₺57. It's a bit far from the beach – you'll need your own transport. Daily 8am–6pm.

★Mimoza On the beach ☎0252 394 3139, ⓦmimoza gumusluk.com. Beachside restaurant with a reputation that extends across the peninsula. Their seafood is divine, and their Aegean *meze* beyond reproach (around ₺20 each). It's particularly beautiful at sundown, when the flowers dangling over the tables fade into darkness, their role as eye-candy replaced by hanging lanterns. Daily 9am–midnight.

YALIKAVAK

4 Reasons On the hillside above Yalıkavak ☎0252 385 3212, ⓦ4reasonshotel.com. Small, friendly establishment with a secluded location overlooking Yalıkavak. It's all very informal, though certainly no slouch as far as the rooms go – some sport wood fires and gigantic balconies. **₺500**

Latife Hanım Facing the harbour ☎0252 385 2733. Designed along the lines of an Ottoman *han*, this is a real pick among the hundred-odd restaurants in this area, with tasty breakfasts and *meze* available from just ₺10, and most mains around ₺30 – all with grand views of the boats bobbing around just beyond. Daily 10am–2am.

Mezzaluna On the marina ☎0252 385 4292, ⓦmezzaluna.com.tr. Sup an espresso facing hugely expensive yachts, while wondering how life may have turned out with a few decisions made differently. With yachties themselves often popping by, prices aren't cheap – ₺16 for an espresso, and pasta for around ₺30 – but they certainly beat the ₺70 entry price at *Nobu*, just along the way. Daily 9am–11pm.

The north coast

The heavily indented **north coast** of the Bodrum peninsula hides a few picturesque bays, which would have made great pirate coves in days of yore. Starting from the west, there's **Farilya** (also known as **Gündoğan**), which is surrounded by pine forest; villas barely impinge upon its long, narrow beach, divided by a small harbour, while high winds make it a prime **windsurfing** spot. For a taste of the local Ottoman heritage, walk 1km inland to **GÜNDOĞAN village** proper, then climb to a ruined monastery.

Once-sleepy **TÜRKBÜKÜ**, one cove east, has become the St Tropez of the peninsula, losing most of its beach in the process. It's now a bit too trendy for its own good, though a fine place to go Turkish star-spotting (if you know any); if you need to come by public transport you're just not posh enough, but dolmuşes run to the nearby village of Göltürkbükü.

Lastly, there's **TORBA**, by far the closest north-coast town to Bodrum. It's a little like a budget Türkbükü, with added yachts and a decent stretch of beach.

ACCOMMODATION AND EATING   THE NORTH COAST

Much of the **accommodation** along the north coast is unashamedly luxurious and expensive, particularly in Türkbükü, though you'll find *pansiyons* on the fringes of all three villages. **Restaurants** also tend to be swanky, though in a neat reversal of global norms the cheapest options in Türkbükü are on the beach.

GÜNDOĞAN

Butik Han Sahil Seridi Emek Sok ☎0252 387 9465, ⓦbutikhanotel.com. The actual rooms at this hotel are unquestionably a little uninspired, which is all the more reason to get out and enjoy the swimming pool or sip a cocktail with superlative bay views from the beach bar. **₺250**

Gürkaya On the beach ☎0252 387 8352. Motel offering the most reasonably priced accommodation in the area – nothing special, but adequate nonetheless, and right on the beach. **₺100**

Reana Yalı Mevki Cad ☎0252 387 7117. Beautifully decorated fish restaurant with a stellar reputation – such that you may have to book ahead, particularly for a dinnertime slot. The Aegean-style *meze* are out of this world, and the prices surprisingly affordable. Daily 11am–10pm.

TÜRKBÜKÜ

Kuum Atatürk Cad 150 ☎0252 311 0060, ⓦkuumhotel .com. This architecturally adventurous space-age spa hotel enjoys a premium spot in the middle of things at Türkbükü, though thanks to a stretch of private shoreline (not actually beach in this area), you'd never know it. Comfy lounge booths gaze out to sea, as do many of the stylish rooms. **₺400**

Maça Kızı North of Türkbükü ☎0212 377 6262, ⓦmacakizi.com. Sitting in divine solitude north of Türkbükü, the "Queen of Spades" has been the talk of the peninsula – and many a Turkish celebrity – for some time. Their on-site restaurant has an equally lofty reputation – a mix of local and Mediterranean flavours, using local ingredients wherever possible. **₺800**

TORBA

Casa Dell'Arte Torba ☎0212 367 1848, ⓦcasadellartebodrum.com. Oh-so-trendy hotel in

which art plays a large role – the owners are two of Turkey's most prominent collectors, and rooms and common areas are swathed with paintings and sculptures. The rooms themselves are highly picturesque – anything from the lighting to the bed shapes can come as a surprise. **₺700**

Dalli On the coast road ☎0252 367 1076. Nice little cheapie towards the end of the stretch – basic rooms, though at this price you shouldn't expect too much. The friendly owners speak English, and whip up nice meals in the on-site restaurant. **₺180**

Gonca Balık By the beach ☎0252 367 1796, ⓦgoncabalik.com. Acclaimed seafood restaurant by the *Casa Dell'Arte*, with an array of cute blue and orange tables arranged along the beach. Fishy mains go for ₺35 and up, *meze* for ₺12 or so. Daily 11am–2am.

Marmaris

Along with Kuşadası and Bodrum, **MARMARİS** is the third of Turkey's less-than-holy trinity of hugely overdeveloped Aegean resorts. Little is left of the sleepy fishing village it used to be, mere decades ago. Development has dwarfed the old core of shops and *lokanta*s lining narrow, bazaar-like streets, an intricate warren contrasting strongly with the European-style marina and waterfront.

According to legend, Marmaris was named when Süleyman the Magnificent, not finding the **castle** here to his liking, was heard to mutter "*Mimarı as*" ("hang the architect") – a command that ought perhaps still to apply to the designers of the seemingly endless apartments and hotels. The **bazaar**, including its diminutive *kervansaray*, now rivals that at Kuşadası for its array of glitzy kitsch, and only the **Kaleiçi** district, the warren of streets at the base of the tiny castle, offers a pleasant wander.

Tucked away at the far end of town, the large **Netsel Yacht Marina** is the main base for yacht charter organizations operating on the Turquoise Coast (see box, p.294). Proximity to Dalaman airport also means that both foreign and domestic tourists pour in nonstop during the warmer months, and – the marina aside – Marmaris remains very much a package resort.

Brief history

Marmaris' **history** has been determined above all by its stunning setting, in a deep, fjord-like inlet surrounded by pine-cloaked hills. This did not seem to spur ancient Physcus, the original Dorian colony, to any growth or importance, but Süleyman comfortably assembled a force of 200,000 here in 1522, when launching the successful siege of the Knights of St John's base in Rhodes. Shortly after this campaign Süleyman endowed the old town nucleus with the tiny castle and a *han*. In 1798 Nelson's fleet sheltered here before setting out to defeat Napoleon's armada at the Battle of Aboukir Bay in Egypt.

Marmaris castle and museum

Off İskele Meyd · Daily 8am–7pm · ₺8

Built in 1522, during the reign of Süleyman the Magnificent, **Marmaris castle** has been the city's focal point for almost half a millennium, and serves as a venue during the May festival (see p.273). History aside, it's a pretty little place with an appealing **museum** showcasing local finds, and some from further along the coast.

Beaches

You don't come to Marmaris for cultural edification, and you swim off the polluted **Kordon beach** at your peril – though this doesn't seem to deter the hundreds of bathers who use it daily. It's far better to head out to **İçmeler**, 9km west of Marmaris by road and considerably less along the coastal footpath, and also served by regular dolmuşes and boat taxis. The sand is coarse but cleaner than at Kordon, as is the sea, while the old village core survives precariously at the far edge of the recently developed resort.

ARRIVAL AND DEPARTURE

MARMARIS

By plane From Dalaman airport, a full 90km east of town, Havaş airport buses (90min; ₺15; ⓦ havas.net) run every hour or two to Marmaris' *otogar*, from which a regular dolmuş service runs into town. The same buses pick up at Marmaris *otogar* 3hr before flights.

By bus or dolmuş Marmaris' *otogar* is set in a beautiful area 2km northeast of the centre on the Muğla road; most main bus companies run courtesy buses to the *otogar* to connect with their major routes. Tickets can be bought, and *servis* buses picked up, at said companies' offices at the Kordon Cad end of Ulusal Egemenlik Bul. Alternatively, there are regular dolmuşes (₺3).

Destinations Akyaka (every 30min; 30min); Ankara (14 daily; 11hr); Antalya (5 daily; 6hr); Bodrum (hourly; 3hr

15min); Bozburun (3–6 daily; 1hr); Datça (9 daily; 2hr); Denizli (8 daily; 3hr 30min); Fethiye (hourly; 3hr); Istanbul (9 daily; 13hr); İzmir (hourly; 3hr 30min).

By ferry Daily services to Rhodes in Greece leave Marmaris at 9am and return at 5pm (1hr; €40 one-way, €43 day return, €63 open return); for most of the summer there are departures each way at these times. Buy tickets from any travel agent in town.

Boat taxis Boat taxis to İçmeler and Turunç leave from outside the tourist office (₺12.50/person one-way).

By car No parking is allowed anywhere along the Kordon, but you can park at places strewn around town for ₺4 for an hour, ₺14/day.

INFORMATION AND ACTIVITIES

Tourist office By the excursion boat harbour on İskele Meydanı (Mon–Fri 8am–noon & 1–7pm, Sat & Sun 10am–noon & 1–5pm; ☎0252 412 1035). Though not terribly useful, they're able to dispense town plans, as well

as information about bus schedules and accommodation.

Vehicle rental Best Motor, Kemal Elgin Bul opposite the *Balim Otel* (☎0252 412 9436), rents bikes, mopeds, motorbikes and jeeps.

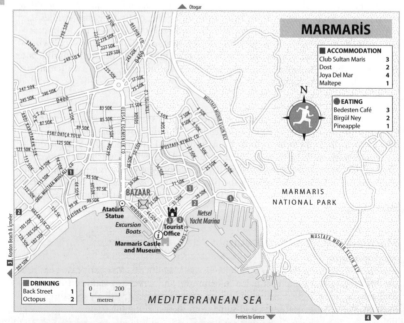

MARMARIS

■ ACCOMMODATION	
Club Sultan Maris	3
Dost	2
Joya Del Mar	4
Maltepe	1

● EATING	
Bedesten Café	3
Birgül Ney	2
Pineapple	1

■ DRINKING	
Back Street	1
Octopus	2

MARMARIS NATIONAL PARK

BAZAAR

Atatürk Statue

Excursion Boats

Tourist Office

Netsel Yacht Marina

Marmaris Castle and Museum

MEDITERRANEAN SEA

0   200
metres

Rafting Alternatif Turizm, 133 Sok 10 (☎0252 417 2720, ⊕alternatifoutdoor.com), offers regular springtime whitewater rafting trips on the Dalaman River, plus river and sea kayaking, and tailor-made Turkey-wide outdoor-sports packages.

Yachting An annual yachting and arts festival (⊕marmarisinfo.com) takes place mid-May. There's also a large yacht race in late Oct or early Nov, organized by the Marmaris Yacht Club (⊕marmarisraceweek.com).

ACCOMMODATION

Although there are very few *pansiyons* or small hotels in Marmaris, some apartment-hotels have sprung up in the area inland from the marina, while a handful of basic establishments survive in the **town centre**. Good value can be had out at the west end of the Kordon, close to where **Kemal Seyfettin Elgin Bul** splits away to run parallel to **Uzunyalı** beach. Further west, some three hundred hotels line the 5km-long, palm-fringed strip, with the luxury, all-inclusive complexes clustering at the far end.

Club Sultan Maris Yunus Nadi Cad ☎0252 417 2826, ⊕clubsultanmaris.com. A good resort-style hotel west of the main tourist action – sure, the beach is a little further away, but here you're guaranteed a more Turkish experience, and lower prices. They offer both studio rooms and one-room apartments, set around a small pool. ₺150

Dost Mustafa Muğlali Cad 74 ☎0252 412 1343, ⊕oteldost.com. This good-value spot – west of the centre, and a five-minute walk from the beach – sports comfortable rooms, all decorated with pine furniture and mint colours. Despite its professional appearance, the fact that it's family-run usually comes through loud and clear. ₺180

Joya Del Mar Adaköy Yolu 24 ☎0252 412 3947, ⊕joyadelmar.com.tr. Some way east of the centre, beyond the port, this is a very nice place to stay – as it probably should be for the price. Nevertheless, there are many similarly priced places in and around Marmaris which do not have a palm tree-studded beach, sumptuous mountain views, spiffy rooms, and a truly romantic night-time vibe – which this place has in spades. ₺500

Maltepe 66 Sok 9 ☎0252 412 1629, ⊕maltepe pansiyon.com. Reliable budget option, and about as cheap as you're going to want to go in the centre. Their cheery, blue-painted rooms are all en suite, but not all have a/c, which may come in handy during the sweltering summer – ask about this before paying. There's a back garden for relaxing, and a kitchen for guests to use. ₺75

EATING

The most popular **restaurants** with tourists are along the harbour. These change names, management and cuisine frequently and are more or less identical; a meal with wine will run to around ₺40 a head. For cheaper eats, head into the bazaar.

★**Bedesten Café** Below the mosque in the bazaar ☎0252 412 8838. A little cheesy, perhaps, but this greenery-filled courtyard is a relaxing, traditionally styled place for coffee, tea or even a beer (oddly, since it adjoins a mosque). It's especially atmospheric at night, when the air is thick with nargile smoke (₺25). Daily 8am–3am.

★**Birgül Ney** Below the castle ☎0252. Signed from the pedestrian path, this charming place is one of several restaurants on the alleys heading up to the castle – and not yet a rip-off, unlike most of its neighbours. It serves up good Turkish home cooking, with mains from ₺23 and *meze* from ₺8. Mon–Sat 10am–midnight, Sun 5pm–midnight.

Pineapple Netsel Yacht Marina ☎0252 412 0976, ⊕pineapple.com.tr. A pretty place popular with yachties, and facing a veritable forest of masts. You'd expect prices to be higher here – especially since the food is tasty too. The menu is a Turkish/English mix; they're most famed for oven-roasted lamb (₺45), with pizzas and pasta hovering at around ₺18–30. With an attached English pub upstairs, things can get a bit noisy later on. Daily 10am–11pm.

DRINKING

Most of the town's **drinking** takes place along "Bar Street" (Barlar Sok), an occasionally wild place with dozens of bars and clubs. As with restaurants, names change on a very regular basis, but you'll usually find the same old deals, such as three tequilas for ₺10.

Back Street Barlar Sok 123 ☎0252 412 4048. The most enduring bar along Bar Street, this huge place consists of two levels surrounding a pretty courtyard. Daily 6pm–late.

Octopus Barbaros Cad. For an alternative to the endless strip of places along Bar Street, head to this establishment, which faces the super-yachts next to the octopus on the waterfront (you'll see). Shots start at ₺5; if you're thirsty you might enjoy their colossal fishbowl cocktails instead. Daily 10am–late.

COASTAL EXCURSIONS AROUND MARMARIS

Chartering either a **motor schooner** (*gulet*) or a smaller **yacht** out of Marmaris will allow you to explore the convoluted coast from Bodrum as far as Kaş. Especially out of high season, the daily cost isn't necessarily prohibitive – no more than renting a medium-sized car, for example – and in the case of a *gulet*, a knowledgeable crew will be included. Virtually all the shore is accessible by boat, with abundant hidden anchorages.

You can prebook a **yacht charter** through specialist holiday operators (see p.30), or make arrangements on the spot. Prices are always quoted in euros or US dollars, but it's possible to pay in Turkish lira. Substantial deposits are required – usually fifty percent of the total price.

The best option for individual travellers or small groups is a **cabin charter**. Several companies set aside one schooner whose berths are let out individually. The craft departs on a particular day of the week with a fixed itinerary of three to seven days. Typical prices, including all food and watersports equipment, range from €330 per person per week in April, May and October, to more than €550 between June and September.

BOAT TRIPS FROM MARMARIS

Day excursions aboard a *gulet* depart from the southern end of Kordon Cad and the castle peninsula. Trips usually visit several different highlights of the bay and beyond, including a couple of swimming breaks – sights on route often include caves, Dolphin Island, Turtle Beach, the "African Queen" river, some cliff tombs, and a mud bath. In summer, boats leave around 9.30am and return before 7pm, and charge around ₺55 per person, including lunch and tickets.

You'll also see signs in Marmaris offering trips to **Cleopatra's Isle**. These actually refer to the islet of Sedir Adası (Cedar Island), near the head of the Gulf of Gökova, and said to have served as a trysting place for Cleopatra and Mark Antony. The sand on its beach was supposedly brought from Africa at Mark Antony's behest, and indeed analysis has shown that the grains are not from local strata. The tours leave between 10am and 11am from Çamlı İskelesı, and return at 4pm or 5pm; you'll pay around ₺55 per person, plus ₺15 for the entry ticket.

The Hisarönü peninsula

In ancient times the peninsula that extends from the head of the Gulf of Gökova to a promontory between the Greek islands of Sími and Rhodes was known as the **Rhodian Peraea**. This was the mainland territory of the three united city-states of Rhodes, which controlled the area for eight centuries. Despite this, there is little evidence of the long tenure. The peninsula, today known as the **Hisarönü peninsula**, was (and still is) something of a backwater. Up to now, yachts have been the principal means of getting around this irregular landmass. A proper road was completed in 1989, but the difficulty of access has so far kept development to a minimum.

Turunç

9km south of Marmaris • Easily accessible by water-taxi (₺12.5), or by dolmuş (₺6) on a twisty-turny road

Little more than a few farms and a couple of restaurants up until the late 1980s, the mini-resort of **TURUNÇ** is now an exclusive package-holiday venue – no surprise since it's stunningly beautiful, boasting a 500m beach of coarse sand backed by impressive, pine-tufted cliffs. These are dotted with hotels and villas, some of whose residents commute to sea level using cogwheel chair lifts.

A spur road heads south of Turunç, past ancient **Amos** (only Hellenistic walls and theatre remain) to **Kumlubükü**, another large bay with decent amenities. Along with Çiftlik bay, 4km southwest of here by rough tracks or paths, it's the only really big patch of sand on the whole peninsula.

Selimiye

43km southwest of Orhaniye • Dolmuş from Marmais *otogar* (9 daily; ₺9)

SELİMİYE village enjoys a truly spectacular location, at the edge of the large, mountain-lined Delikyol bay – which, from this angle, looks rather more like a lake. The clientele here is notably more diverse since the improvement of the road – no longer just yachties, but retired expats, affluent locals and a fair few independent travellers, all mixed up with a native population that remains surprisingly, and pleasingly, rural in nature.

Bozburun and around

7km from Selimiye • Dolmuş from Marmais *otogar* (9 daily; ₺12)

BOZBURUN slumbers in dusty heat six months of the year, but its setting, on a convoluted gulf with a fat islet astride its mouth and the Greek island of Sími beyond, is startling. The place is unlikely to go the way of Datça (see p.276), since there is precious little level land for villas, even less fresh water and absolutely no sand beaches. Nonetheless Bozburun has long been an "in" resort for various eccentrics – ex-journalists turned bartenders, recording executives turned restaurant proprietors, die-hard Turkish hippies – who collect in this most isolated corner of coastal Turkey.

In cool weather you could walk east one valley to SÖĞÜT, essentially a farming oasis with a minimal shore settlement boasting a few restaurants and a couple of *pansiyon*s. The dolmuş serving Söğüt terminates at TAŞLICA, a hilltop village girded by almonds and olives sprouting from what's otherwise a stone desert. From the square where the dolmuş leaves you, a three- to four-hour trail leads south to ancient **Loryma**, where a Rhodian-built fort overlooks the magnificent harbour of **Bozukkale**, which in turn holds several restaurants. If you don't want to walk back the same way, you just might be able to hitch a boat ride out from here.

GETTING AROUND
THE HISARÖNÜ PENINSULA

Overland access to the bulk of the peninsula is by way of a **paved road** that branches south from the main Datça-bound highway, 21km west of Marmaris, then hits Orhaniye and Selimiye before continuing to Bozburun. **Dolmuşes** plough this route from Marmaris, every couple of hours. Having your own transport will avoid a lot of waiting around; you'll also be able to take a different route to or from Marmaris, via Bayar, Turunç and İçmeler.

ACCOMMODATION AND EATING

TURUNÇ

Most hotels on the seafront stretch are package only, but two solid options are listed below. A handful of cheaper *pansiyons* lie back from the beach.

Diplomat ☎ 0252 476 7145, ⓦ diplomathotel.com.tr. Large, cliff-backed hotel complete with beach frontage and swimming pool. They also run a few cheaper self-catering apartments just off-site. ₺250

Zeybek ☎ 0252 476 7014, ⓦ zeybekhotel.com. This sizeable option boasts beach frontage, and tremendous bay views from its elevated swimming pool. Rooms are simple but perfectly adequate. ₺200

SELİMİYE

★ **Les Terrasses de Selimiye** Up above town ☎ 0252 446 4367, ⓦ terasselimiye.com. Classy place boasting stupendous views from its beautifully designed infinity pool. Standards have dropped slightly – and prices risen – since a change of ownership, but it's still remarkably good value for the area. ₺250

BOZBURUN AND AROUND

Aphrodite 100m along a coastal path from the south end of the quay ☎ 0252 456 2268, ⓦ hotelaphrodite .net. This vine-shaded, upmarket hotel is the nicest in town, with rooms that – while not quite plush – are a cut above the competition. Half board. ₺360

★ **Karia Bel'** Southern edge of the bay ☎ 0252 456 2056, ⓦ kariabel.com. Truly splendid place, stuck in charming isolation – you can wake up and be in the sea within one minute. Staff can organize activities including fishing, snorkelling and trekking. Half board. ₺450

Mete South end of the quay ☎ 0252 456 2099, ⓦ otelmete.com. An inexpensive family-friendly spot, complete with hammocks and a sunlounger-covered sea terrace. Half board. ₺200

Möwe Just inland from the quayside ☎ 0252 456 2526. Though apparently twice frequented by Bill Gates, this restaurant looks nothing special – their seafood, however, is pretty darn good, and not all that pricey. It also turns into a bar of sorts of an evening. Daily noon–11pm.

4

Yılmaz On the seafront road ☎ 0252 456 2167. Rose-scented garden? Check. Sea views over breakfast? Check.

Luxurious rooms? Not quite… but they're a/c, and about as cheap as you'll get in Bozburun. ₺120

The Datça peninsula

Slithering into the Aegean like a long, skinny snake, the elongated **Datça peninsula** is talked about in hushed tones by those from elsewhere along the coast. This is one part of the Aegean that has stubbornly refused to morph into a package-holiday destination: little **Datça** town, itself quite twee in an urban way, is the only place with any bustle about it. On the way into the peninsula, you'll hit the original settlement first – **Eskidatça**, now little more than a twee village, and a lovely base if you're looking to get away from it all. Once past Datça town, the road is narrow and twisting, and probably not a good idea to drive on at night. Daylight will, in any case, allow you to see more of the wonderful view – naught but pine-speckled mountains, groves of almond and olive trees, flowers, and a sea occasionally thrusting in at little **coves**. At the very western end of the cape is **Knidos**, an ancient site best viewed on a **boat tour** from Datça town.

Eskidatça

2km north of Datça town, back on the road towards Marmaris • All peninsular buses (see opposite) will be able to drop you within walking distance, or it's a short cab ride from Datça town

Cute little **ESKIDATÇA**'s sleepy maze of alleys – often used by cows – and ancient stone-built farmhouses have lately become a haven for artists and writers, who have renovated many of the dilapidated country homes. Though getting more commercial, especially on one little stretch that acts as the centre of the village, it's still just the right side of pretentious, and makes a nice place to stay – there are enough places to eat and drink to avoid making repeat trips to and from Datça town.

Datça

Too built-up and commercialized to be the backpackers' haven it used to be, **DATÇA** is still infinitely calmer than either Bodrum or Marmaris. And partly due to the basic accommodation on offer, as well as the difficulty of access, prices are noticeably lower than in those two places.

Life in and around Datça mostly boils down to a matter of picking your swimming or sunbathing spot. The **east beach** of hard-packed sand, known locally as Kumluk, is oversubscribed but has some shade. The less crowded **west beach**, mixed pebble and sand and called Taşlık, is acceptable and gets better the further you are from anchored yachts.

The south coast coves

Coves accessible by dolmuş from Datça town (5 daily; fewer outside summer); taxis around ₺110 one-way; also accessible on boat tours (see box opposite)

This peninsula's ultra-relaxed south coast coves were once accessible only by boat, but even now that there's a road they remain dreamily quiet places to stay. Bar a spot of swimming in the sea, there's nothing much going on, and that's precisely the point of a visit. Head from east to west and the first cove you'll hit is the pretty shore hamlet of **HAYİT BÜKÜ**. It doesn't have such a great beach, but the bay itself is well protected by a scenic, claw-like headland to the west. Accordingly, it sees lots of boat traffic and there's a large dock, a few restaurants and some relatively upmarket **guesthouses**. Within walking distance west, **MESUDIYE BÜKÜ**, also known as Ova Bükü, has a far better beach and is more geared towards camping.

The 9km stretch of rough coast road that links Mesudiye with **PALAMUT BÜKÜ** makes a fairly tricky prospect without your own transport. The stark setting is balanced by a kilometre-long beach of tiny pebbles lapped by brisk, clear water, with an islet offshore.

If you're headed this way, stock up on **cash** before you leave Datça town – there are no banks or ATMs elsewhere on the peninsula.

Knidos

40km west of Datca • Daily 8.30am–7pm • ₺10 • Best by far visited on a boat tour from Datça town (see opposite); the dolmuş ride is long and painful (daily 10.30am & noon), and taxis cost at least ₺200

Out on wind-lashed Tekir Burnu, **Knidos** was one of the most fabled and prosperous cities of antiquity. With its strategic location astride the main shipping lanes of the Mediterranean, it was a cosmopolitan city, and many illustrious personalities hailed from here. However, the city was most notorious for an inanimate object – the **cult statue of Aphrodite** by Praxiteles, the first known large-scale, freestanding nude of a woman. Modelled by the famous Athenian courtesan, Phryne, this adorned the new city from its earliest days and became Knidos's chief source of revenue; it's long gone, of course. In fact, very little at all remains of this former greatness, and it's probably not worth punishing any vehicle for the full distance from Datça in order to see it.

Hellenistic Knidos was laid out in a grid pattern, and most of its public buildings were on the mainland side. The **Hellenistic theatre**, overlooking the south anchorage, is the best preserved, while two **Byzantine basilicas**, one huge with extensive mosaics, overlook the north harbour.

4

ARRIVAL AND DEPARTURE

DATÇA

By bus Buses stop at, and depart from, the Pamukkale office on the main drag. In high season, there are services to a few cities around western Turkey, but even at these times you might be best off taking a short-hop dolmuş to Marmaris, which offers more frequent onward departures.

Destinations Ankara (2 daily; 12hr); Istanbul (3 daily; 16hr); Marmaris (hourly; 1hr 30min).

By ferry Ferries to and from Bodrum (2 daily; 1hr 45min) use a pier in Körmen Limanı, 9km north of Datça town. Arriving, you'll be plopped onto a free shuttle bus to Datça town; going back out, the same bus will pick you up if you arrange this when buying your ticket (from any travel agency in Datça town; one-way ₺35, return ₺55). It's worth taking the boat in at least one direction to avoid duplicating the long bus journey in from the east. Small charter boats in Datça also offer trips to Knidos (see box below).

ACCOMMODATION AND EATING

ESKIDATÇA

Eskidatça Pansiyon Can Yücel Sok 5 ☎ 0252 712 2432, ⓦ eskidatcapansiyon.com. A good choice for eating and sleeping alike, this simple guesthouse has rooms that are more than acceptable for the price, all with wooden flooring and modern bathrooms. The café-restaurant on ground level is one of the more calm, secluded spots in the village, its air often given a stir by staff playing gently on the guitar; breakfast will cost you ₺15, and it's ₺8 for a glass of home-made lemonade. **₺160**

★ **Olive Farm** Resadiye Mahallesi 30 ☎ 0252 712 4151, ⓦ guesthouse.olivefarm.com.tr. Snazzy boutique hotel, tucked into a bucolic village a few kilometres north of Eskidatça. More famous for the eponymous line of olive-oil cleansing and beauty products (which you'll find in the bathrooms, and most likely use every showertime), it is indeed set on a richly beautiful olive farm – one also boasting a pool, sauna and tennis court. Breakfast is wonderful, too, and entirely organic. **₺330**

BOAT TRIPS AROUND THE DATÇA PENINSULA

Local **boat trips**, as advertised on Datça's west harbour, make a good day out. Groups generally depart between 9am and 9.30am, returning between 5pm and 6pm. Standard stops include Palamut Bükü, Domuz Çukuru, Mesudiye Bükü and ancient Knidos. The going price per person, excluding lunch (usually in a restaurant at Palamut Bükü) and allowing three swim stops, is around ₺50 as far as Knidos, and ₺40 as far as Mesudiye Bükü – cheaper than taking a taxi, in any case.

DATÇA

Unlike most of the Aegean coast, Datça town has a fair few budget places, along with some higher-end choices. However, it has to be said that if you've come this far, there's little point staying in town – press on that little bit further to one of the coves (see opposite). A clutch of nice café-restaurants overlooks the beach; they're also the best places to head for a beer.

Ev Yapımı On the beach. Perhaps the only beachfront place popular with locals as well as tourists and out-of-towners. Many are here for the *çibörek* (fried dumplings; ₺9), and *meze* such as *dolma sarma* (₺8). Daily 8am–11pm.

Maradona On the beach ☎ 0252 712 4005. There's precious little to choose between the beach restaurants, but this is a good pick, with some seating on the beach itself. The seafood *meze* are tasty, though you'll feel a bit cheated for the amount you get – the grilled fish are better value at around ₺30. Daily 10am–11pm.

Tunç Pansion Iskele Mah ☎ 0252 712 3036. Just about the cheapest option in town, yet surprisingly nice – on entry, it feels almost like a 1970s hotel with its lobby bar and breakfast tables. Rooms are a little spartan, but their worn charm somehow seems to suit the town itself. ₺50

Villa Tokur Up on the hill, south of town ☎ 0252 712 8728, ⓦ hoteltokur.com. Run by a Turkish-German family, this is possibly the smartest choice near town, with unparalleled views of the beach, as well as a pool and nicely tended garden. ₺250

THE SOUTH COAST COVES

There's no real luxury accommodation around the coves, and prices at the *pansiyons* are pretty standard, with doubles varying from ₺100 to ₺150. Many places, especially those on Mesudiye, allow campers to pitch tents, though pitches vary from well-tended grass to spaces between cars in the car parks (not an exaggeration). Most places shut down over the winter. As regards eating, each cove has a shop and snack-shack, and most *pansiyons* double as restaurants.

Bük At the far eastern end of the bay, Palamut Bükü ☎ 0252 725 5136. The most appealing *pansiyon* on the strip, with lovingly decorated rooms and a good on-site restaurant. ₺150

★ Ortam Hayit Bükü ☎ 0252 728 0228, ⓦ ortamdatca .com. The cheapest rooms in this cove, especially if you've a group large enough to fill their ₺250 room, which sleeps five. Some rooms are a mere 10m from the beach and their on-site restaurant is superb. ₺150

Ova Pansiyon Mesudiye Bükü ☎ 0252 728 0105, ⓦ ovapansiyon.com.tr. Relatively new hotel set in a pleasantly green complex, with a couple of hammocks to swing on. Their restaurant is also the best on the strip, with food served from a swish kitchen. ₺180

★ Zephyros Mesudiye Bükü ☎ 0252 728 0330, ⓦ zephyrosdatca.com. Set in the hills some way above the beach, this is a real get-away-from-it-all spot, with lush gardens, a delightful infinity pool, and an excellent restaurant (thank goodness for that, since there's precious little else in the area). Rooms are plain in a good way – sleek and pretty, but with no unnecessary frills. ₺380

Pamukkale

As you approach the UNESCO World Heritage Site of **PAMUKKALE** from Denizli, 20km south, a long white smudge along the hills to the north suggests a landslide or mine. Getting closer, this clarifies into the edge of a plateau, more than 100m above the valley and edged in white **travertine terraces**. The Turks have dubbed this geological fairyland *Pamukkale*, or "Cotton Castle". This incredible natural phenomenon was created by the hot spring waters that gush up at the centre of the ancient city of **Hierapolis**, whose blissfully located ruins would merit a stop even if they weren't coupled with the stunning terraces.

Only a fraction of the huge number of daily visitors to Pamukkale stay the night. Most foreign travellers who do so stay in **PAMUKKALE KÖYÜ**, a sleepy village at the base of the cliff that's still, by and large, a rural settlement – you'll see more tractors than cars on its outskirts, and its main "drag" holds only a small concentration of shops, restaurants and travel agencies. Accommodation is cheap, and almost all hotels feature spring-water swimming pools. Despite the incredible draw of Hierapolis and the travertines, it's one of western Turkey's best places to chill out for a few days.

Brief history

The therapeutic properties and bizarre appearance of the hot springs were known for thousands of years before an actual town, **Hierapolis**, was founded here by a Pergamene king during the second century BC. After incorporation into the Roman Empire in 129 BC,

BATHING IN PAMUKKALE'S SPRINGS

Pamukkale's spring waters have been seducing visitors – including certain Roman emperors (see below) – for thousands of years. Three different options are available. For the first, you don't even have to leave town: just off the main road, the **Natural Park** (24hr; free) is a newish complex set around a lake. Natural attractions here include piped music and swan-shaped pedalos whose LEDs glow at night, as well as a couple of fake travertine terraces – whatever, the water is real enough, and the park is actually a nice place to spend the evening. The second option is also free, once you've bought your ticket to Hierapolis (see below) – as you head up the **travertine paths**, you can wade in the pools on the way.

However, if you want to take a proper bath in the springs, visit the **Pamukkale Thermal Baths** up on the plateau (daily 8am–7.30pm; ₺32), which encloses the sacred pool of the ancients, with mineral water bubbling from its bottom at 36°C. Changing rooms are available, as are drinks and snacks – many visitors choose to relax by the pool, coffee in hand, for an hour or more.

Hierapolis enjoyed considerable imperial favour, especially after catastrophic earthquakes in 17 AD and 60 AD – no fewer than three emperors paid personal visits, stimulating local emperor-worship alongside the veneration of Apollo and his mother Leto, who was venerated in the guise of Cybele.

The presence of a flourishing Jewish community aided the rapid and early establishment of **Christianity**. Hierapolis is mentioned in Paul's Epistle to the (neighbouring) Colossians, and Philip the Apostle was martyred here, along with his seven sons. However, as at Aphrodisias, paganism lingered well into the sixth century, until a zealous bishop supervised the destruction of the remaining ancient worship sites and the establishment of nearly one hundred churches, several of which are still visible.

Hierapolis slid into obscurity in late Byzantine times, nudged along by Arab and Turcoman raids. After the Selçuks arrived in the twelfth century, the city was abandoned, not to figure much in the Western imagination until Italian excavations began in 1957.

Hierapolis and the travertines

Daily 24hr, though only the south gate is open around the clock; other gates open 8am, though you can exit at any time • ₺25 •
ⓦ pamukkale.org.tr • Regular shuttle buses (₺2) from north entrance to baths

The combined site of ancient Hierapolis and the travertines has three entrances. The first, the signposted "Güney Kapısı" or **South Gate**, is at the end of a 2km road describing a lazy loop up from the village. Here you'll find the visitor centre, plus a ticket booth and car park, followed by a long, shadeless walk to the ruins and terraces. Most tour buses use the **North Gate** (where there's another ticket booth and visitor centre) for access to the central car parks next to the museum. Independent travellers usually use the **travertine path** up from the village itself – a fifteen-minute hike, more if you fancy a quick splash in one of the pools (see box above). However, nothing beats having the place to yourself, and this is quite possible if you get up super early (5am or before) and hike to the south entrance (a thirty-minute walk from town); time it right and you'll have seen the ruins and had a natural hot-spring bath before the crowds start to pour in at 8am.

Be sure to bring a **hat**, as much of the site is shadeless; once up on top, you'll be able to buy food or drink from stalls. You won't need to worry too much about **footwear** – you'll have to take it off when walking on the travertines, in any case.

The travertines

A 500m-long section of calcium deposits heads up from the village to the plateau. It takes you through a collection of **thermal pools**, where visitors are welcome to wallow. If you do plan to do so, wear appropriate clothing, and bring a small **towel** or flannel. Shoes are forbidden along the entire tract, so a **bag** in which to put your shoes would also come in handy. For the most part, the calcium surface makes for smooth and pleasant navigation. Pamukkale's hotels once siphoned off the precious mineral waters for their own heated pools; the waterflow is now strictly rotated in order to preserve the site and allow more diminished deposits to "regrow".

Deriving from a bubbling spring at the foot of Çal Dağı, this stunning natural wonder has been created over millennia. As thermal water surges over the edge of the plateau and cools, carbon dioxide is given off and hard chalk – also known as **travertine** – accumulates as a solidified waterfall, slowly advancing southwest. At sunrise or sunset, subtle hues of ochre, purple and pink are reflected in the water, replacing the dazzling white of midday.

The museum

Tues–Sun 9am–5.15pm • ₺5

One of the first things you'll see if you come up the travertine path is the **museum**, housed in restored second-century AD baths. Its gardens, visible without a ticket, are beautifully laid out. Indoors, the collection consists primarily of statuary, sarcophagi, masonry fragments and smaller items recovered during excavations at Hierapolis.

Temple of Apollo and the Plutonium

Besides the museum and baths, a few ruins are worth tracking down in the area bounded by the city walls. The **Temple of Apollo** in its present, scanty form dates from the third century AD, though built on a second-century BC foundation. The adjacent **Plutonium** is of more interest – dedicated to the god of the underworld, this grotto is today a small, partly paved cavity beyond which you can hear rushing water and an ominous hissing: the emission of a highly toxic gas, probably a mixture of sulphurous compounds and carbon dioxide. In ancient times the eunuch priests of Cybele were reputedly able to descend into the chasm with no ill effect; today, a formidable metal cage-grille keeps daredevils out. Before this was installed, two Germans died attempting to brave the cave.

Nearby you'll also be able to find the **nymphaeum**, or fountain-house, and a large sixth-century **basilica** – probably the Byzantine-era cathedral, with two aisles sandwiching the nave. On the other side of the Temple of Apollo is a well-preserved **Roman theatre**, dating from the second century AD. Performances are held here during the **International Pamukkale Song Festival** in late June (🌐turkcevizyon.com): the 46 rows of seats are still capable of accommodating up to seven thousand spectators comfortably, which compares surprisingly well to its original capacity of ten thousand.

The colonnaded street

Arguably the most interesting part of Hierapolis, the **colonnaded street** once extended for almost 1km from a gate 400m southeast of the sacred pool to another breach in the north wall. This thoroughfare, parallel to the plateau's edge, unevenly bisected the grid plan of the Hellenistic city and terminated at each end in monumental portals a few paces outside the walls. Only the northerly one, a **triple arch** flanked by towers and dedicated to the Emperor Domitian in 84 AD, still stands.

Basilica and necropolis

The squat bulk of some second-century AD baths, which were converted two hundred years later into a **basilica**, is easily distinguishable from the colonnaded street. Closer to the archway, west of the asphalt, stands the elaborate **Tomb of Flavius Zeuxis**, a prominent Hierapolitan merchant. This counts as the first of more than a thousand tombs of all shapes and sizes which together constitute the **necropolis**, the largest in Asia Minor. The entire complex extends for nearly 2km along the road. Many of the most sumptuous tombs bear epitaphs or inscriptions that warn transgressing grave-robbers of the dire fate that awaits them, while forecourts hold benches that were used for visits by the deceased's relatives.

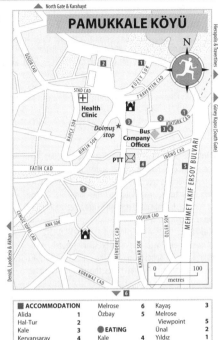

PAMUKKALE KÖYÜ

■ ACCOMMODATION		Melrose	6	Kayaş	3
Alida	1	Özbay	5	Melrose	
Hal-Tur	2			Viewpoint	5
Kale	3	● EATING		Ünal	2
Kervansaray	4	Kale	4	Yıldız	1

4

ARRIVAL AND DEPARTURE

PAMUKKALE

To get to Pamukkale by public transport, you're likely to have to head first to the major city of **Denizli**, 20km south – an ugly place where you won't want to linger. If you've booked in advance, you'll find that many of the recommended *pansiyons* are able to fetch you for free.

By plane Few travellers use Denizli Çardak airport, a full 70km east of Denizli, but it does have a few daily services to and from Istanbul and Ankara. Airport shuttle buses head to and from Pamukkale (5 daily; ₺30).

By bus or dolmuş The huge new Denizli *otogar* is well served by long-distance buses. If you've booked to Pamukkale, most companies will lay on a free *servis* to the town; going back, you'll be picked up outside your company's office at an appointed time. Otherwise, take a dolmuş from Denizli *otogar* (every 15min, 6am–11.30pm; ₺3.50; it leaves from platform 76 on the basement level).

Destinations Antalya (14 daily; 5hr); Bodrum (6 daily; 4hr 30min); Istanbul (15 daily; 10hr); İzmir (hourly; 4hr); Konya (several daily; 7hr 15min); Marmaris (8 daily; 3hr 30min).

By train Trains ply the route to Denizli from İzmir (7 daily; 4hr 30min), stopping at Selçuk along the way (7 daily; 3hr). There's also a line heading to Kütahya (1 daily; 6hr 20min), which takes longer than the bus but avoids changes and has a lovely restaurant car. Getting to Pamukkale from the station, you'll have to hit the *otogar* – turn left out of the station, and it's the giant, red building across the main road.

ACCOMMODATION

Although Pamukkale is one of Turkey's most visited destinations, few visitors stay the night, and fewer still stay longer. That's a great pity – not only is the town a rural charmer, but its accommodation is excellent value, particularly since most lodgings (even the real cheapies) boast a natural mineral-water **swimming pool**.

ACTIVITIES IN PAMUKKALE

Visitors to Pamukkale need not confine their enjoyment to the travertines (or the ancient city, or the Asian cuisine, or the serenity or brilliant views, or the hot-spring pools in most hotels, or…), for there are a few activities to take part in. **Hot-air ballooning** has, well, ballooned in recent years, with the skies over Cappadocia essentially full, and money still to be made from travellers – one session will cost around ₺330 from various agencies in town, including hotel pick-up. Then there's the opportunity to go tandem **paragliding** – cheaper at ₺180. Reliable **agencies** include Pamukkale Hijackers (Atatürk Cad 11; ☎0258 272 3222, ⓦpamukkalehijackers.com) and T4T (Cumhuriyet Meyd 7; ☎0258 272 2829, ⓦtours4turkey.com).

Alida Off Mehmet Akif Ersoy Bul ☎0258 272 2602. This lemon-coloured hotel is a great budget option, its rooms arrayed around a courtyard in the style of a *kervansaray*. It's very close to the main road and therefore good for the travertines, but still quiet enough to get a peaceful night's sleep. ₺120

Hal-Tur Mehmet Akif Ersoy Bul 45 ☎0258 272 2723, ⓦhaltur.net. One of the most prestigious hotels in the village, directly opposite the terraces, with immaculate a/c rooms – some face the travertines, though you'll pay a fair bit extra for those. All have satellite TV, and there's also a swimming pool and good restaurant. ₺220

Kale Atatürk Cad 16 ☎0258 272 2607, ⓦotelkale.com. On the "restaurant" road, this simple place is worth considering if you're after a dorm bed – or a Korean meal from the downstairs restaurant (see below). Staff aren't exactly switched on, and the rooms are occasionally scruffy, but it'll do. Dorm ₺27, double ₺80

Kervansaray İnönü Cad ☎0258 272 2209, ⓦkervansaraypension.com. A long-standing favourite, owned by the welcoming Kaya family. Many of the centrally heated rooms overlook creek greenery, and there's a pool and a rooftop café-restaurant (though this is closed in winter). ₺105

★**Melrose** Vali Vekfi Ertürk Cad 8 ☎0258 272 2250, ⓦmelrosehousehotel.com. A short walk south of the action, this is a truly wonderful place, with plush rooms, a nice pool, excellent food from a real wood oven, and the friendliest owners in town – no wonder so many people come back year after year. In fact, its popularity has been such that they've built another hotel nearer the centre – *Melrose Viewpoint*, also an excellent place, with superb views from its restaurant (see below). ₺120

Özbay Mehmet Akif Ersoy Bul 43 ☎0258 272 2126, ⓦozbayhotel.com.tr. Popular with backpackers and budget travellers, this family-run hotel stares straight at the travertines – and, unfortunately, the main road and its swarm of tour buses. Rooms are more than OK for the price, and though the dorms are often female-only, single rooms are very cheap at half the price of a double. Dorm ₺35, double ₺120

EATING

Your hotel or *pansiyon* will probably be able to whip up some food for you, though you'll find a few restaurants on the main drag; thanks to Pamukkale's popularity with Asian tourists, many offer their own takes on **Japanese** and **Korean** dishes.

Kale Atatürk Cad 16 ☎0258 272 2607. Of all the places serving Korean food on the strip, this hotel (see above) is by far the most authentic – its interior isn't very pretty, so try to grab one of the outdoor tables. Try the *bibimguksu* (cold noodles in a spicy sauce; ₺16), *bibimbap* (greens, spices and a fried egg on top of rice; ₺15) or Japanese staples including *tori-no-karaage* (fried chunks of battered chicken; ₺16). Daily 8am–11pm.

Kayaş Atatürk Cad. Popular with backpacker types, this is a café, bar and restaurant all rolled into one. Meals include grills, pizza and cheap omelettes. A Turkish coffee will set you back ₺4, a beer ₺7 and a cocktail ₺15. Daily 8am–8pm.

Melrose Viewpoint Kadıoğlu Cad, Çay Sok 7 ☎0258 272 3120, ⓦmelroseviewpoint.com. Set atop the newer branch of the *Melrose* hotel (see above), this restaurant has superlative views of the travertines and Pamukkale's rural surrounds – non-guests are almost as common as guests

here, and the Turkish dishes (mains from around ₺17) are great. Daily 10am–8pm.

Ünal Atatürk Cad ☎0258 272 2451. One of the few "real" restaurants in town – in other words, it's popular enough with villagers not to need to chase foreign customers (though it's popular with them too). Most come for the cheap grills, but don't miss the delectable *mantı* (ravioli-like dumplings; ₺14); alternatively, you can fill up on cheapies like omelette and *sarma* (stuffed cabbage) from just ₺6. Daily 9am–late.

Yıldız Atatürk Cad 32 ☎0535 311 9168. Of the strip's few rather hassly restaurants boasting views of the travertines, this is the least annoying for two reasons. Firstly, they offer some good-value items (such as Turkish coffee or egg and sausage for just ₺5). Secondly, their single treehouse table is the best place in town for a nargile smoking session (₺25). Daily 8am–midnight.

Around Pamukkale

Even when you've had your fill of Hierapolis and the travertines, there's plenty to see **around Pamukkale**. Just to the south, and accessible off the Pamukkale–Denizli road, are the ruins of **Laodicea**, not yet on the tourist trail. More popular, but much further away, is the superlative site of **Aphrodisias**, whose setting is just as much of a draw as the excellently preserved ruins. Most visit the latter as part of a day-trip from Pamukkale, though Laodicea is reachable on public transport.

Laodicea

Daily 8am–6pm • ₺10 • 1km from Pamukkale–Denizli dolmuş route

A short bus ride from Pamukkale lies a great site in the making. This is **Laodicea**, whose ruins are almost visibly in the process of rising from the ground – just a few years ago, there was little of interest to see, but it's now a real feast for the eyes, even if some ruins have been somewhat crudely restored.

While Pamukkale up the road catered for pleasure, Laodicea was an important trading centre, thanks to its position at the junction of two major trade routes. Originally hosting a large Jewish community, in time it became a highly important Christian base – in fact, it was one of the **Seven Churches of Asia** mentioned in the Book of Revelation.

Most of the sights, including **temples**, a **nymphaeum** and an unusually square **agora**, are arrayed off a colonnaded thoroughfare now known as Syria Street – religious tours make a bee line for a cross near its far end. Also of interest are the two fantastic **theatres** north of the site, each vaguely facing Pamukkale – one had room for eight thousand people, the other twelve thousand.

Aphrodisias

70km west of Pamukkale • Daily: summer 8am–6.30pm; winter 8am–5.30pm • ₺10 • Tour buses from Pamukkale (₺40) generally depart at 9.30am

Situated on a high plateau more than 600m above sea level, ringed by mountains and watered by a tributary of the Büyük Menderes, **Aphrodisias** is one of Turkey's most isolated and beautifully set archeological sites. Acres of marble peek out from among the poplars and other vegetation that cloaks the remains of one of imperial Rome's most cultured Asian cities. Late afternoon visits have the bonus of often dramatic cloud formations, spawned by the elevation, and the attendant dappled lighting.

It's quite easy to find your way around – most of the site's main features are accessible on a path that loops around the complex, maps are dotted around, and all signage is in English as well as Turkish. In general, it's best to follow a **clockwise** route, which will allow you to finish your visit in the air-conditioned cool of the museum What's more, that route means that the short climb to the theatre will come when you're fresh, at the start, rather than adding to the sweat at the end.

Brief history

Aphrodisias was one of the earliest occupied sites in Anatolia. Neolithic and Bronze Age mounds have been found here, and there has been some sort of **fertility cult** here for just as long. The Assyrian goddess of love and war, Nin, became meshed with the Semitic Ishtar, with the Hellenic Aphrodite eventually assuming the goddesses' combined attributes.

Despite a strategic position near the meeting point of ancient Caria, Lydia and Phrygia, and its proximity to major trade routes, for many centuries Aphrodisias remained only a shrine. However, during the second century BC, its citizens were rewarded for their support of the Romans during the Mithridatic revolt. Imperial favour bestowed, various emperors patronized the burgeoning city. Aphrodisias became particularly renowned for its school of sculpture, sourcing high-grade marble from nearby quarries, and local works soon adorned every corner of the empire, including Rome itself.

Perhaps because of this fixation with graven images, paganism lingered here for almost two centuries after Theodosius banned the old religions. The reputation of its Aphrodite love cult had served to protect Aphrodisias since its inception, but by the fourth century AD, two earthquakes and sundry raids began to take their toll, and decline was the dominant theme of Byzantine times. The town was abandoned completely during the thirteenth century, its former glories recalled only by the Ottoman village of Geyre – a corruption of "Caria" – among the ruins.

Only since 1961 has work by a New York University team permitted a fuller understanding of the site. The intention is to render Aphrodisias on a par with Ephesus and the eventual results will certainly be spectacular, though for now some of the more interesting areas remain off-limits.

The Sebasteion, theatre and agora

The ornate **Sebasteion**, the first stop for many Aphrodisias visitors, consists of two parallel porticoes erected in the first century AD to honour the deified Roman emperors. From here, it's a stiff climb to the large, and virtually intact, **theatre**. Founded in the first

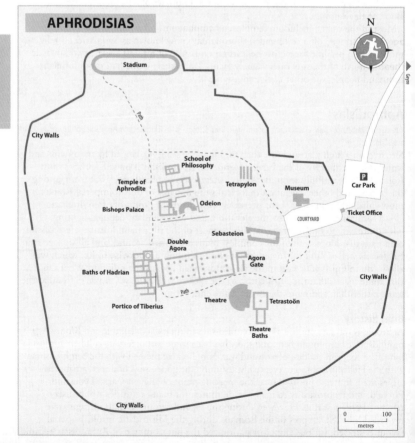

APHRODISIAS

century BC, it was extensively modified by the Romans for their blood sports three centuries later. At the rear of the stage building is a large square, the **tetrastoön**, originally surrounded by colonnades on all sides, while a large **baths complex** lies to the south.

Heading back downhill you'll pass the **double agora**, consisting of two squares ringed by Ionic and Corinthian stoas, though these are filled with vegetation, and fenced off. The **Portico of Tiberius** separates the agora from the fine **Baths of Hadrian**, preserved right down to the floor tiles and the odd mosaic; it is, however, expected to be under renovation until 2016 at the earliest.

Bishop's Palace and Odeion

North of the baths, several blue-marble columns sprout from a multi-roomed structure commonly known as the **Bishop's Palace**, from its presumed use during Byzantine times. East of here huddles the Roman **odeion**, with nine rows of seats.

Temple of Aphrodite

Only fourteen columns survive of the city's principal sanctuary, the **Temple of Aphrodite**. The Byzantines converted it to a basilica during the fifth century, so considerable detective work was required to re-establish the first-century BC foundations. Even these were laid atop at least two older structures, with evidence of mother-goddess worship extending back to the seventh century BC. The Hellenistic/Roman sanctuary had forty Ionic columns arranged eight by thirteen, with the cult image erected in the main hall. The Byzantines removed the columns at each end of the temple, fashioning an apse to the east, an atrium and baptistry on the west, and it's this architectural pastiche you see today. Immediately north is the so-called **School of Philosophy**, tentatively identified (like the bishop's palace) on the basis of resemblance to other such structures elsewhere.

The stadium and tetrapylon

The northernmost feature of the site is the thirty-thousand-seat **stadium**, among the largest and best preserved in Anatolia. A version of Delphi's Pythian Games was held here, featuring sporting, musical and dramatic events.

When you return to the main loop trail, the last thing you'll notice before exiting onto the museum square is the re-erected **tetrapylon**, a monumental gateway with two double rows of four columns, half of them fluted, supporting pediments with intricate reliefs. This second-century AD edifice is thought to mark the intersection of a major north–south street with a sacred way heading toward the Aphrodite shrine.

The museum

Same times and ticket as site

Aphrodisias' wonderful (not to mention wonderfully air-conditioned) **museum** houses a wide array of sculpture recovered from the ruins. Given that Aphrodisias met most of the demand for effigies under the empire, even what remains after the loss of originals and the spiriting away of works to city museums is considerable. Highlights here include the "Aphrodite Hall", containing statuary related to the cult, with a rendition of the goddess, much defaced by Christian zealots, occupying the position of honour. There's also the "Imperial Hall", its walls lined with superb reliefs.

The Turquoise Coast

KAŞ THEATRE

5

The Turquoise Coast

Noted for its fine beaches and stunning mountainous scenery, Turkey's southwesternmost shore has long been dubbed the Turquoise Coast, thanks to the hues of its horizons and the sea. It's dominated by the Baba, Akdağ and Bey mountains, which drop precipitously to the main coastal highway that often skims just above the water. Known in ancient times as Lycia, the region was home to an independent people whose most obvious legacy is the distinctive rock tombs that litter the landscape. Despite much recent development, many attractive coves and islets remain inaccessible to vehicles, so yachting and *gulet* trips are popular. Fortunately, the impact of ever-increasing visitor numbers has been minimized by restrictions on construction height and by special protection for archeological sites and wildlife habitats, leaving much of the region relatively unspoiled.

The usually excellent **Highway 400** between Marmaris and Antalya offers intermittent views, and connects several major sites along the way. The coast is best approached via **Dalaman airport**, busy with direct international flights most of the year, as well as domestic flights from Istanbul.

At the far west of the region, **Dalyan** is an attractive small resort noted for its languid river, sandy beach – a sea-turtle nesting ground – and the ruins of **Kaunos**. East of here, **Fethiye**, despite its paucity of beaches, is the Turquoise Coast's oldest resort and largest town; along with **Ölüdeniz** lagoon, it's handy for spectacularly sited Lycian ruins such as **Oenoanda**, **Kadyanda** and **Tlos**, in dramatic mountainous locations. Further southeast, **Patara** abuts one of Turkey's best beaches, making it easy to combine sea and sun with cultural forays to the **Letoön** sanctuary, **Pınara**, **Sidyma** and **Xanthos**. Other convenient bases include the nearby resorts of **Kalkan** and **Kaş**, smaller than Fethiye and pitched at rather different clienteles. The spectacular mountainous hinterland is also well worth exploring, especially with your own wheels, with dramatic ancient **Arykanda** the most obvious target.

Beyond the yacht-harbour-dominated town of **Finike**, east of Demre, the scenery becomes increasingly impressive as you enter conifer forests on the slopes of **Tahtalı Dağ**, officially designated a national park, before passing ancient **Olympos** – plus more good beaches at **Adrasan** and **Çıralı** – and ancient **Phaselis**. Further east, a string of characterless resorts devoted to German and Russian holiday-makers lines the approach to Antalya.

THE LYCIAN WAY

Highlights

❶ **Kaya Köyü** This abandoned Greek Orthodox village near Fethiye is an emotive relic of the 1923 population exchange. **See p.298**

❷ **The Lycian Way** This waymarked long-distance trail – linking coves, ruins and mountains – is ideal in low season. **See p.303**

❸ **Dalyan river life** Whether watching the waters slide by or being ferried downstream to a glorious beach, the river makes Dalyan the resort it is. **See p.306**

❹ **Tlos** Perhaps the most dramatically sited of Lycia's numerous ancient cities. **See p.312**

❺ **Patara** Roman ruins behind a great sweep of sandy beach that's among the longest strands in the entire Mediterranean. **See p.321**

❻ **Kaş** Set opposite the Greek islet of Kastellórizo, this is one of the most congenial resorts on this coast. **See p.326**

❼ **Kekova** Eerie seascapes and submerged ruins make these inlets an ideal arena for sea kayakers. **See p.332**

❽ **Çıralı** A paradise for nature lovers, with a turtle-nesting beach and an ancient city, backed by the spectacular foothills of Mount Tahtalı. **See p.345**

HIGHLIGHTS ARE MARKED ON THE MAP ON P.290

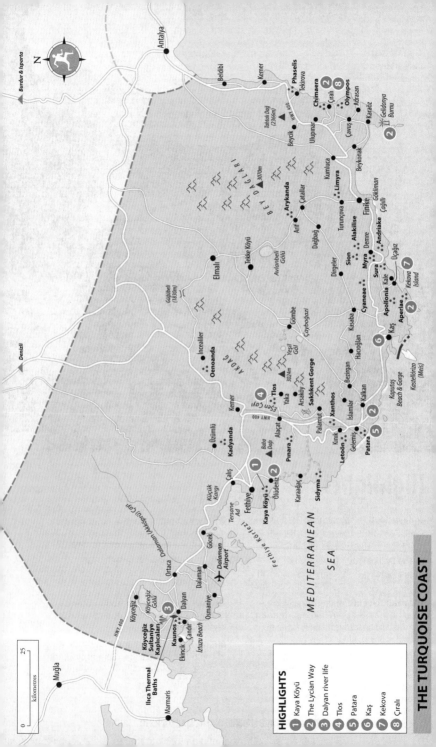

THE TURQUOISE COAST

HIGHLIGHTS

1. Kaya Köyü
2. The Lycian Way
3. Dalyan river life
4. Tlos
5. Patara
6. Kaş
7. Kekova
8. Çıralı

Brief history

Mountainous, rugged **Lycia** (*Likya* in Turkish) lies south of a line drawn roughly between Antalya and Köyceğiz Gölü. At the core of the territory, the Bey Dağları and Akdağ, each exceeding 3000m elevation, isolate it from the rest of Anatolia. Relatively secure in their mountain fastness, the fiercely independent ancient Lycians – probably an indigenous, pre-Hittite people – organized their main cities and conurbations of smaller towns as the democratic **Lycian Federation**, with 23 voting units. This elected municipal and federal officials and, until imperial Rome assumed control, made decisions of state. Homer's *Iliad* mentions the Lycians as allies of the Trojans; later, in the sixth century BC, the region was subdued by the Persians, but then largely left to govern itself.

From 454 BC, after the Athenian general Cimon had expelled the Persians from the Mediterranean coast, the Lycians became members of the Athens-dominated Delian League. The League ceased to exist after the Peloponnesian War and Lycia again fell under Persian domination. Alexander the Great arrived in 333 BC and, after conquering Halikarnassos, secured the region's surrender; following his death, Lycia was ruled by his general, Ptolemy, also king of Egypt. During the third century BC, under Ptolemaic rule, Greek displaced the native Lycian language and Lycian cities adopted Greek constitutions. The Ptolemies were defeated by Antiochos III in 197 BC, himself bested in 189 BC by the Romans, who handed the kingdom over to the Rhodians. The Lycians bitterly resented Rhodian control and succeeded in 167 BC in having this administrative relegation revoked.

Thereafter, the Lycians enjoyed over two centuries of semi-independence under a revived federation. After they resisted the Pontic king Mithridates in 88 BC, they were rewarded by Rome for their loyalty. During the Roman civil wars, Lycian reluctance to assist Brutus caused the destruction of Xanthos, and in 43 AD it was joined to Pamphylia in a larger Roman province. **Roman imperial rule** saw Lycia reach its maximum ancient population of 200,000, a figure not again equalled until the twentieth century, and the cities were graced by the Roman civic architecture that constitutes most of the ruins on view today.

During the fourth century the province was divided by Diocletian. A period of Byzantine-supervised decline followed, abetted by Arab raids in the seventh and e ighth centuries. From then on, the area's history resembled that of the rest of western Anatolia, where, after Selçuk Turk sovereignty during the eleventh and twelfth centuries, and an interlude of minor emirates, the **Ottomans** installed a more durable Anatolian Muslim state. They continued a pattern of moving nomadic Turkic tribes into the Lycian uplands, leaving the coast to pirates and local chieftains, until in the eighteenth century the sultan ordered its settlement by more tractable, productive Greek Orthodox colonists from the offshore islands.

Fethiye

FETHIYE is the fulcrum of the Turquoise Coast, and a hub of its property industry. It remains, however, a lively market town of 145,000-plus souls, sprawling north along the coastal plain, and the transport and marketing of oranges and tomatoes is still important to its economy. Fethiye occupies the site of ancient **Telmessos**, and some impressive rock tombs are an easy stroll from the centre. It also makes a convenient base for the nearby **beaches** of Ölüdeniz and Kıdrak, while a short drive or long walk out of Fethiye brings you to the atmospheric ghost village of **Kaya Köyü**. Much of the nearby coastline is accessible only by sea, and with the **Gulf of Fethiye** speckled with twelve islands, one- to four-day boat tours from Fethiye harbour are popular, aiming for secluded coves in which to swim, fish and anchor for the night.

5

Brief history

Little is known about the early years of ancient **Telmessos**, except that the city wasn't originally part of the Lycian Federation, and, in the fourth century BC, actually resisted it. A Lycian ruler later subdued the Telmessans, and during the Roman imperial era it formed part of the Federation, albeit unique in maintaining good relations with Rhodes.

During the eighth century, the city's name was changed to **Anastasiopolis** in honour of a Byzantine emperor. This became **Makri** in the following century (*Meğri* in Turkish). Finally, a thousand years later, and following the expulsion of the predominantly Greek Orthodox population, it was changed once again during the 1930s to Fethiye, in honour of Fethi Bey, a pioneering pilot who was killed during World War I.

That little now remains of the medieval town is largely due to two immense **earthquakes**, in 1857 and 1957, which toppled most of its buildings; the rubble lies compacted beneath the present quay and shoreline boulevard. Another, lesser quake in the spring of 2012 did little damage, but nonetheless had a significant impact on domestic tourism to the town and its environs.

The Amyntas Tomb

115 Sokağı • Daily 8.30am–sunset • ₺8

The remains of ancient **Telmessos** are obvious as soon as you arrive. Several **Lycian rock tombs** are located above the bazaar, strikingly close to town. Most notable is the **Amyntas Tomb**, so called because of the Greek inscription *Amyntou tou Ermagiou* (Amyntas son of Hermagios) on its wall. To get there, take any of the lanes leading south from Kaya Caddesi (also negotiable by car). These give on to 115 Sokağı, which runs along the base of the fenced-in archeological area.

The tomb porch consists of two Ionic columns surmounted by a triangular pediment. Carved in imitation of a temple facade – right down to the bronze nails on the doorframes – it gives an excellent impression of how wooden temple porches would have looked. The tomb itself would have been entered through the bottom right-hand panel of the doorway, which was broken by grave robbers long ago.

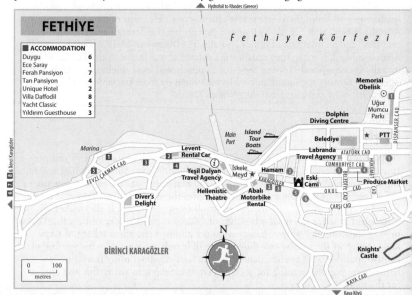

FETHİYE

ACCOMMODATION
Duygu	6
Ece Saray	1
Ferah Pansiyon	7
Tan Pansiyon	4
Unique Hotel	2
Villa Daffodil	8
Yacht Classic	5
Yıldırım Guesthouse	3

5

Çalış Beach

Minibuses to the beach (daily 7am–11pm every 20min; ₺3) depart from the Şehir *otogar*, Sokak 97, east of the centre off Atatürk Caddesi

Around 5km northeast of the centre, **Çalış** is Fethiye's only beach. Gravelly and backed by hotels, it's nothing special, but it is the town's closest place to swim. Sunbeds and umbrellas are available to rent, and there are plenty of places to eat and drink behind the promenade.

Knight's Castle

On the hillside behind the bazaar • Daily 24hr • Free

The path up to Fethiye's so-called **Knight's Castle** leads through the backstreets from Çarşı Caddesi, affording good views of the town on the way. Although the fortress is attributed to the Knights of St John, its wide range of architectural styles suggests handiwork on the part of Lycians, Greeks, Romans, Byzantines and Turks.

Fethiye Museum

Okul Sok • Daily: June–Sept 8am–7pm; Oct–May 8am–5pm • ₺5

Compact it may be, but **Fethiye Museum** is well worth seeing if you want to flesh out your knowledge of the nearby sites. Its most compelling exhibit is a **stele** found at the Letoön (see p.316), dating from 358 BC; the trilingual text, in Lycian, Greek and Aramaic, was vital in deciphering the Lycian language. It's now located in a room to the left of the ticket desk, along with Bronze, Archaic and Classical age pottery, as well as some fine Roman-era statuary from Tlos (see p.312) and Kaunos (see p.309).

The room to the right of the entrance holds more finds from Kaunos, including a fascinating **statuette of Kybele** complete with symbolic scorpion and deer motifs, and incredibly detailed, larger-than-life statues of the Roman emperors Hadrian and Antoninus Pius, both from Tlos. The **garden** is also worth a look, with its fine collection of sarcophagi lids and a Roman-era olive pressing stone, whose cut-channels look remarkably like a peace symbol.

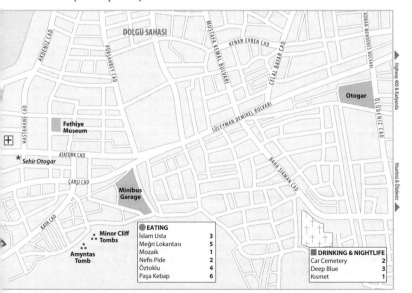

EATING	
İslam Usta	3
Meğri Lokantası	5
Mozaik	1
Nefis Pide	2
Öztoklu	4
Paşa Kebap	6

DRINKING & NIGHTLIFE	
Car Cemetery	2
Deep Blue	3
Kismet	1

5

Hellenistic Theatre

Fevzi Çakmak Caddesi • No public access

Fethiye's conspicuous Hellenistic **theatre**, sprawling behind the main quay, has only been excavated since 1994. Much of its masonry was carted away after the 1957 earthquake for construction material, but much restoration work has been done in recent years, giving it a less than antique appearance. Restoration was ongoing at the time of writing, and the theatre can only be viewed from the road.

ARRIVAL AND DEPARTURE   FETHIYE

By plane Havaş buses (12–15 daily 1.30am–7.15pm; ₺10) between the *otogar* in Fethiye and Dalaman airport, timed to coincide with incoming flights.

Tickets Labranda Tourism, opposite Belediye at Atatürk Cad (☎0252 614 7500, ⊛labrandatour.com), handles tickets for all airlines.

By bus Short-haul dolmuşes run almost constantly from Fethiye's *otogar*, over 2km east of the town centre at the junction with the Ölüdeniz road, to the accommodation district of Karagözler. Other dolmuşes to Ölüdeniz, Göcek, Faralya, Saklıkent and Kaya use the minibus garage, on 136 Sokağı south of Çarşı Caddesi, 500m east of the central market area. In season, the Patara Ko-op runs a 24-seat minibus service along the coast between Fethiye and Finike.

Destinations Antalya (10 daily; 3hr inland, 6hr 30min by coast); Bodrum (6 daily; 4hr 30min); Denizli (6 daily; 4hr express, 6hr normal); Kabak (12 daily; 1hr 20min); Istanbul (5 daily; express 12hr, 15hr normal); İzmir (every 30min; 7hr); Kaş (15 daily; 2hr); Marmaris (hourly; 3hr); Ölüdeniz (27 daily; 45min); Pamukkale (several daily; 5hr); Patara (15 daily; 1hr 30min).

By car Park near the museum (tickets either from a parking warden or pay-and-display machines), or use one of the handful of fee-paying *otoparks*.

By hydrofoil Between late May and early October, hydrofoils run almost daily from the main jetty to Rhodes in Greece (June–Sept Mon & Wed–Fri at 9am; return from Rhodes at 4pm; 1hr 30min; €50 single, €60 return). Ferries are operated by Yeşil Dalyan travel agency (☎0252 612 4015, ⊛yesildalyantravel.com), facing the jetty at Fevzi Çakmak Cad 168, but tickets can bought from any agency.

GETTING AROUND

By taxi The main taxi ranks are near the PTT, and in front of the ancient amphitheatre.

Car rental Levent, Fevzi Çakmak Cad, Yat Limanı Gümrük

Karşısı no. 37/B (☎0252 614 8096, ⊛leventrentacar.net).

Motorbike rental Abalı, just behind the theatre roundabout (☎0252 612 8812).

BOAT TOURS AND CRUISES FROM FETHIYE

Standard-issue, multi-island, one-day **boat tours** from Fethiye cost around ₺50 per person; just turn up at the quayside for daily departures between May and October, usually leaving at around 10am and returning at 6pm. Tours with Kardeşler, a reliable outfit (☎0252 612 4241, ⊛kardeslerboats.com), depart daily 10.30am, and return at 6.30pm.

However, these one-day trips take in a set repertoire of relatively spoiled islands, with little time at each; it's far better to charter your own crewed boat to stop at just one or two selected islands. If you've more time, sign on for one of the **cabin cruises** that usually depart several times per week in season. A typical four-day, three-night itinerary heads east, overnighting near or at Gemiler Adası, Kalkan and Kekova before a final minibus shuttle from Andriake to the backpacker lodges at Olympos. Shorter cruises take in Aya Nikola, Ölüdeniz and Butterfly Valley. Paying a bit over the cheapest option, and boarding only owner-operated craft, is recommended to ensure quality; also make sure that you check the vessel carefully before paying, and talk to returning clients.

Before Lunch ☎0535 636 0076, ⊛beforelunch .com. A well-established, Australian/Turkish-run Fethiye outfitter that generates consistently positive feedback. Noted for good food, they're at the high end of the price spectrum, and run a new 25m-long boat that has six double cabins, and one family-sized one. A leisurely four-day, three-night Fethiye-to-Fethiye cruise taking in the twelve islands costs €275 per person in low season, €350 in high season.

Tribe Travel (My Blue Cruise) ☎0252 614 4627, ⊛tribetraveltours.com. Professionally run by Ömer Yapış, owner of the *Yıldırm Guesthouse*, and offering a four-day, three-night cruise on the roomy *Seaborn Legend* from Fethiye to Olympos, for €255 per person in low season, €295 in high season, starting every Tues, Thurs & Sat.

INFORMATION AND ACTIVITIES

Tourist information The office is at İskele Meydanı 1, near the harbour, but is pretty useless (May–Sept Mon–Fri 8am–noon & 1–7pm, Sat & Sun 10am–noon & 1–5pm; Oct–April Mon–Fri 8am–noon & 1–5pm; ☎0252 614 1527).
Scuba diving Though lacking fish, the gulf offers reasonable visibility, coral and caves plus submerged ruins.

Outfits include Dolphin Diving Centre, its boat moored behind the post office (☎0535 717 3130, ⱳdolphindiving.com.tr), and Diver's Delight, Dispanser Sok 25/B, Cumhuriyet Mahallesi, near the memorial obelisk (☎0252 612 1099, ⱳdiversdelight.com). One-day introductory courses cost around £35, PADI four-day courses £265.

ACCOMMODATION

Fethiye has lodging for all tastes and budgets; unlike other coastal resorts, you should find something even in high summer. Unless otherwise stated, recommended accommodation is open (or claims to be open) year-round. Divided into Birinci (First) and İkinci (Second), the quiet, desirable **Karagözler** neighbourhood supports the oldest cluster of hotels and *pansiyons*, with most premises enjoying a bay view. The only drawback is remoteness from transport terminals and restaurants, but parking is easier than in the centre. Fethiye's **bazaar area**, extending two blocks to either side of Çarşı Caddesi, can be noisy even at night, and now holds very few accommodation options.

Duygu Pension Karagözler Ortayol 54 ☎0252 614 3563, ⱳwww.duygupension.com. Situated on a pleasant residential street just behind the waterfront, the *Duygu* is the only Fethiye pension to have its own pool. The eleven en-suite rooms have a/c, and a nice roof terrace enjoys sea views. ₺100

Ece Saray Marina quay, Birinci Karagözler ☎0252 612 5005, ⱳecesaray.net. Indisputably the top lodging in central Fethiye, this mock-traditional low-rise hotel occupies impeccably landscaped grounds in a quiet corner of the shore esplanade. All the plush rooms enjoy sea views, while common facilities include a spa, fitness centre, infinity pool, two bar/restaurants and a private marina. Good value for the facilities on offer. €140

Ferah Pansiyon (Monica's Place) 16 Sok 21, İkinci Karagözler ☎0252 614 2816, ⱳferahpension.com. Part of a chain of Turkish backpackers' hostels, with dorm beds or basic en-suite doubles, pick-up service from the *otogar*s and optional evening meals. Some sea views, despite the location one block inland. Dorm ₺40, double ₺120

Tan Pansiyon Eski Karagözler Cad 41, Birinci Karagözler ☎0252 614 1584, ✉tanpansiyon@hotmail.com. Good budget option run by a friendly Turkish family. The bathrooms are on the small and eccentric side. The four roof-terrace units are the best (though the hottest in summer), with wonderful views across the bay from the terrace. ₺90

★**Unique Hotel** Karagözler 30, Sok 43/A Cad 41, Birinci Karagözler ☎0252 612 1145, ⱳhotelunique turkey.com. At last Fethiye has a boutique hotel worthy

of the name. Cleverly terraced into the steep hillside close to the marina, each of the nineteen stylish yet homely rooms has a sea view and balcony. Architecturally it's a clever mix of the old and new, with 150-year-old beams and re-used stone beautifully complementing the contemporary blue-painted shutters and ornately carved doors. With a restaurant, lovely designer pool, chic bar and lushly landscaped terraces, there's no need to head into town. €135

Villa Daffodil Fevzi Çakmak Cad 115, İkinci Karagözler ☎0252 614 9595, ⱳvilladaffodil.com. Overtly yellow, mock-Ottoman structure in one of the quieter shoreline corners, with a pool, on-site restaurant, hamam and landscaped grounds, as well as fair-sized pine- and white-tile rooms, making it a prime mid-range option. ₺180

Yacht Classic Hotel Birinci Karagözler ☎0252 614 1530, ⱳyachtclassichotel.com. A self-contained seaside resort opposite the yacht marina, with private jetty, lush bayside breakfast garden and good-sized pool. Rooms have recently been given a revamp in the neo-modernist style: think clean white lines and a stylish lack of clutter. ₺400

Yıldırım Guesthouse Fevzi Çakmak Cad 53, ☎0252 614 4627, ⱳyildirimguesthouse.com. Backpackers' favourite run by the friendly Ömer, who takes guests on free guided walks from Ovacık to Faralya on request. Plain but tidy carpeted rooms are enhanced by the opportunity to make free tea or coffee all day. There are three dorm rooms, one male, one female and one mixed, as well as private double rooms. Ömer apart, the best thing about this place is the generous breakfast. Dorm ₺35, double ₺100

EATING AND DRINKING

One of the best options for eating in Fethiye is to head for the central courtyard of the **fish and produce market**, and buy the fish of your choice (best selection before 7pm) from the central stalls, then take it to be cooked at one of several *meyhanes* around the perimeter (₺8 basic fee); however, expensive drinks and accompanying *meze* are the norm here, so maybe carry on into the vegetable section and eat your fish at the *Öztoklu* diner there. Otherwise the eating scene largely consists of basic Turkish with an admixture of British/Turkish crossover joints. Most of Fethiye's drinking **bars** are in the old bazaar, especially on Hamam Sokak.

5

RESTAURANTS AND CAFÉS

İslam Usta Belediye Cad 12 ☎0252 612 9487. This friendly, long-running, female-run *börek* place has a few outside tables, and is recommended for its flaky *kol boreği* (₺5 a portion) and cheesy *talaş* (puff-pastry) triangles – all best washed down with a glass of fresh black tea. The cakes here are delicious too – look out for the *portakal kek*, made with fresh oranges. Daily 7am–10pm.

Meğri Lokantası Çarşı Cad 30 ☎0252 614 4047, ⓦmegrirestaurant.com. The doyenne of local restaurants, *Meğri* is equally popular with locals and tourists alike for home-style Turkish food. Pleasantly located on a lively corner in the backstreets. Mains around ₺25. Daily 8am–2am.

★**Mozaik** Sok 2/A ☎0252 614 4653. This Turkish-English place behind *Domino's Pizza* brings the spicy taste of southeast Turkey to Fethiye. Try the mixed *meze* platter for two (₺18), which includes dips such as *cevizli biber* (spicy walnut, pepper and bread paste) and hummus. Kebabs and casseroles are from ₺22, a good-value bottle of wine ₺40. Daily 10am–2am.

Nefis Pide Eski Cami Sok 9 ☎0252 614 5504. One of the best-value options in town, with *pides* from ₺8 and kebabs from ₺18. There are a few tables out on the street, and unusually for a *pide* place, it's licensed. Daily 9.30am–midnight.

Öztoklu Meyve Pazarı (fruit market). Buy fresh fish from the adjacent fish market (the waiters will go with you) and bring it here to be cooked for a mere ₺8, which includes salad, bread or garlic bread and a special sauce. The advantages of this joint over those congregated in the adjacent fish market are the quiet, and the more delicate, non-fishy aromas. Drinks are only slightly overpriced. Daily noon–midnight.

Paşa Kebap Çarşı Cad 42 ☎0252 614 9807, ⓦpasakebap .com. The *Paşa* may be a typical kebab restaurant, but it's a notch up on most of its rivals. Try the *soslu beyti* (spiced mincemeat baked in a wrap and served with tomato sauce and yoghurt; ₺20). They also serve *pides* from ₺7 and pizzas from ₺15, as well as *meze*. Licensed. Daily 9am–1am.

BARS

Car Cemetery Bar Hamam Sok 25 ☎0252 618 7872. A well-established favourite at the south end of Hamam Sokağı, which puts on live rock music most weekends and has big-screen sports whenever there is something major on. You can toke on a nargile if you're in the mood to relax. Daily 10am–4am.

Deep Blue Hamam Sok 23 ☎0252 612 1008. Almost adjacent to the *Car Cemetery Bar* on this narrow street; watch the world go by from a comfortable couch, cool beer in hand (₺12). Daily 10am–3am.

Kısmet Uğur Mumcu Parkı Yanı ☎0543 227 2325. Run by personable gay couple Nigel and Ian, this down-to-earth bar overlooking a newly revamped park area is a good place to meet local expats, as well as being one of the cheapest places for a drink, with beers at ₺9. Its current location was faced with possible demolition at the time of writing, but the bar is likely to reappear in the replacement structure. Daily 1pm–late.

DIRECTORY

Hamam Hamam Sok 2 (daily 7am–midnight, mixed-sex); usually lukewarm and touristy, and not a particularly good introduction to Turkish baths despite the building's purported sixteenth-century vintage. Bath, soap and scrub ₺50.

Post office Atatürk Cad (Mon–Sat 8am–midnight, Sun 9am–7pm).

Shopping Fethiye's central food market is between Cumhuriyet Cad and Tütün Sok. The adjacent district offers plenty of fake (plus a few real) designer clothes and perfume; safflower marketed as saffron and adulterated honey abound too. Main market day is Tuesday, when local villagers flood into town with their produce; peak hours are 10.30am–1pm. The place to hunt for carpets, leather goods and jewellery is Paspatur district, especially to either side of Hamam Sok.

Around Fethiye

Despite the overdevelopment that has taken place in the hills south of Fethiye, notably the mass-market British-orientated resorts of Ovacık and Hisarönü, there are still some notable attractions set in beautifully unspoiled locations. The best of these are the appealingly remote ancient city of **Kadyanda**, and the abandoned Greek village of **Kaya Köyü**, which is set in a pretty valley and holds plenty of accommodation options suited to those seeking a peaceful retreat.

Kadyanda

Around 25km north of Fethiye • Daily 24hr; unfenced • ₺8 when warden present • Frequent public transport to Üzümlü, from where you can either take a taxi or walk the direct path (1hr 30min up, 1hr down); if driving, turn left at Üzümlü onto a narrow 3.5km paved road that crosses a mountain pass, then turn right and follow 5km of improved dirt track

The ruined mountaintop city of **Kadyanda** dates back at least 2500 years. The attractive village of **Üzümlü**, 16km north of Fethiye along a broad, well-marked road, makes little of its proximity to the site, other than a basic restaurant opposite the mosque and a low-key trade in its fine *dastar* cloth. At the site itself, 9km further by road, an arrow points towards a self-guided circular walking trail. First bear south, past the vaulted tombs of the **necropolis**, then keep close to bits of the **city wall** on the left, followed by a climb to a false summit with a long, partly preserved **agora**, and views of Fethiye. The site's highlight is at the true highest point: a long, narrow **stadium**, with seven rows of seats surviving. Steps in the seats climb to a huge jumble of masonry, all that's left of a **temple** to an unknown deity. On the opposite side of the stadium stand substantial **Roman baths**, with their polygonal masonry and entry archway. At the northeast edge of the stadium, a flat expanse is pierced by the mouth of a deep cistern that supplied the city with water – one of many, so beware holes in the ground.

Finally, the path angles south to the best-preserved stretch of **city wall**, punctuated by windows and affording fine views of distant ridges and forested valleys in between. Crossing the top of a square bastion, you look down into the **theatre**, which retains its

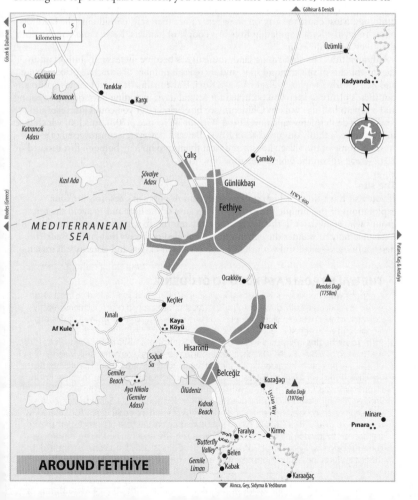

AROUND FETHIYE

5

stage wall and rear-facing wall, plus many of its seats – though like most of Kadyanda it's only partly excavated. The descent to the road completes a leisurely 45-minute walk through superb mountain scenery –reason enough for a visit.

Kaya Köyü

Daily 8.30am–6.30pm • ₺5

The atmospheric ghost village of **KAYA KÖYÜ**, whose Greek Orthodox Christian inhabitants were forced to leave their homes in the compulsory exchange of populations between the newly created Republic of Turkey and Greece in 1923 (see p.660), stands roughly 9km southwest of Fethiye. The roofless remains of the six hundred or so houses that comprised this three thousand-strong community are arrayed in tiers up a pine-scented hillside. They stand above a pastoral idyll of a valley which has, so far, escaped the excesses of tourist development that have swamped nearby Ovacık and Hisarönü.

While the population of Kaya Köyü, or Levissi as it was known to Greek inhabitants, was being shipped west, Macedonian Muslims were sent to occupy the abandoned buildings. Most chose to carry on elsewhere rather than stay, considering the land too poor. Today the local population lives in a couple of hamlets, Keçiler and Kınalı, set in the valley below the ruins.

Although this is fertile farming land, tourism has become increasingly important to the inhabitants of this tranquil spot, and there are a number of attractive places to stay and eat. Clearly the ghost village of Kaya Köyü is the main attraction for most visitors, but there's plenty to keep you occupied for several days, including horseriding, kayaking and a superb half-day walk to Ölüdeniz (see box below). Or you could just relax and read Louis de Bernières' epic novel *Birds Without Wings* (see p.700), much of which is set in Eskibahçe, a thinly disguised Kaya Köyü. Beware, however: a controversial plan to "restore" some of the village houses and turn them into holiday homes – first mooted in 2012 – was still on the table at the time of writing.

The site

If you visit Kaya Köyü in high season – July and August – it's best to start your explorations of this unique site early, both because of the heat and to avoid the tour groups who arrive later in the day from nearby resorts. To get a flavour of the place, it's enough simply to wander the lichen-crusted cobbled pathways that cut between the derelict houses – most still with their fireplaces, earth-closets and cisterns still intact –

THE WALK FROM KAYA KÖYÜ TO ÖLÜDENIZ

A popular **walk** from Kaya Köyü leads along a spectacular coastal path, affording great views out to sea and, eventually, down onto Turkey's most photographed beach, Ölüdeniz. Mostly downhill, it takes between ninety minutes and two hours to reach the northwest shore of the lagoon, and another half-hour or so to the main dolmuş stop.

The **route begins** in Kaya at the easterly Taksiarhis church (aka Yukarı Kilise). Although it's fairly well marked by red-and-yellow blazes, it's essential to take care, as you could easily wander off-trail into potentially hazardous gully and cliff terrain. Ignore blue or rust-red paint blobs that would lead you over the pass that features a windmill, chapel and Turkish flag. The proper path climbs somewhat faintly to a plateau within 15min, then levels out through pine woods for another 20min, before reaching fine overviews of Aya Nikola and Soğuk Su, and a stretch of well-engineered, cobbled descending path. This ends at some charcoal-burners' flats, with a less distinct path to a large rectangular cistern just beyond, before the head of a ravine. Here the trail appears to split; the left-hand option is easier going. Just under an hour along, both routes converge before you reach an obvious pass with some pine-studded rocks on the right, affording the first eyeful of the lagoon. From here you've an uncomplicated, if sharp, drop to the shore.

and try to imagine the village as it might have been a hundred years ago, with workers on their way home from the fields, or dressing up in their Sunday best, ready for church. If you want more of a focus, head to the small, barrel-roofed and whitewashed **chapel**, clearly visible on a hilltop just above the town, which affords splendid views back over the settlement and, in the opposite direction, over the sea.

A more sizeable church dating to 1888, that of **Panayia Pyrgiotissa**, stands a couple of hundred metres above the road in the west of the village. Its red roof-tiles, like those of many other buildings here, were imported from Marseille, a testament to the prosperity of the place prior to the expulsion of its inhabitants. The **Taksiarhis** church, in the east of the village, was restored in 1910, with a pretty courtyard floored with a black-and-white pebble mosaic.

ARRIVAL AND INFORMATION ‖ KAYA KÖYÜ

By dolmuş Dolmuşes run to Kaya from Fethiye (daily 7am–10pm, every 30min in summer, hourly in winter; ₺5).

On foot A paved 9km road – complemented by a largely intact cobbled path that makes a significant short cut – climbs to Kaya Köyü from behind the castle in Fethiye. The walk is marked and takes about 2hr, but don't underestimate it; some visitors get lost after leaving too late in the day.

Activities Seven Capes Sea Kayaking (ⓦ sevencapes.com) is now based in Kaş (see p.326) but many of its exciting tours and other get-wet experiences take place in the sea around Kaya Köyü.

ACCOMMODATION

★ **Gunay's Garden** Gümrük Sokak, Kaya Köyü ☎ 0252 618 0073, ⓦ gunaysgarden.com. This beautifully landscaped villa complex on the very edge of Kaya Köyü offers superb accommodation in its six villas, some two-bedroom, some three. Be warned, it is often fully booked a year in advance – it's that kind of place. Weekly rate for two-bed villas **£795/€1100**

Keçiler Villas Keçiler ☎ 0044 118 932 1866, ⓦ turkeyvillas.com. Three high-standard two- and three-bedroom villas, arrayed around a pool, in the same hamlet as *Misafir Evi*; help finding flights and rental cars is available. Weekly rate for two-bed villas **£595/€822**

Misafir Evi Keçiler ☎ 0252 618 0162, ⓦ kayamisafirevi .com. An excellent upmarket choice in Keçiler, on the valley's north slope, this boutique hotel offers nine tasteful, wood-trimmed rooms, a well-regarded restaurant and a large pool. Rates include breakfast; half board costs ₺30 extra per person. **₺140**

Villa Rhapsody Kınalı ☎ 0252 618 0042, ⓦ villarhapsody .com. Substantial white house with dark-wood trim set in a pretty garden with pool. Well run by fluent English-speaker Attilla and his wife, it has simple but comfortable carpeted rooms. Closed Dec–March. **£42.50/€57.50**

★ **Village Garden Pension** Kınalı ☎ 0252 618 0259. One of the best-value establishments in the valley, comprising four tidy studios, 1.5km from Kaya's central teahouse at the eastern edge of Kınalı. Run by the friendly Temel and his wife Ebru, with excellent breakfasts taken in a small, rustic eating-place just behind the accommodation, where excellent evening meals are available (see below). Temel also has a nearby detached villa sleeping 6–7 for a good-value ₺500. Pension double **₺110**

EATING

★ **Cin Bal** Kayaköy ☎ 0252 618 0066. This popular year-round barbecue joint has pleasant tables under the trees in summer and a welcoming, open-fire-warmed stone dining room for winter. Buy a kilo of lamb for ₺60 and grill it to your taste over charcoal, or for ₺75 buy lamb more suited to roasting in the wood-fired oven. *Meze* ₺5–6, beer ₺9, glass of wine ₺14. Daily noon–midnight.

İzela Gunay's Garden Gümrük Sokak, Kaya Köyü ☎ 0252 618 0073. Attached to the upmarket *Gunay's Garden* villa complex, this is the place to head for a secluded, romantic meal in a lovely shaded courtyard. Chef and owner Tolga knows his stuff, producing some excellent Turkish and French-inspired dishes; try the Anatolian lemon chicken for ₺38, or lamb shank for ₺51. Daily noon–midnight.

Levissi Garden Kaya Köyü ☎ 0252 618 0173. Atmospheric eating place in an old Greek house at the edge of the ghost village. Try the local cheese platter with Turkish wine followed by a lamb sauté main for ₺22. A log fire provides warmth in the chilly winter months, while the breezy terrace is cool in the summer. Daily 11am–midnight.

Village Garden Gemiler Yolu, Kınalı ☎ 0252 618 0259. Even if you don't stay at the *Village Garden* pension it's worth coming here for a delicious home-cooked Turkish meal in simple rural surroundings. The fixed-price menu (₺45–50) is very popular, comprising a tasty array of *meze*, a fish, lamb or *köfte* main with salad, rice or chips, and a freshly prepared dessert. Daily 11am–10pm.

5 Ölüdeniz

Ölüdeniz, the "Dead Sea", lies 12km south of Fethiye, below the ugly, sprawling resorts of Ovacık and Hisarönü. This azure lagoon, now part of a nature park, features on countless Turkish travel posters and is one of Turkey's iconic sights. The area southeast of the lagoon, fronting onto an attractive sandy beach, has developed into the popular resort village of **Belceğiz** – though it is far more commonly referred to, even by locals, as Ölüdeniz. Belceğiz holds sufficient accommodation, cafés and bars to attract one- and two-week holiday-makers, and is also a world-ranking spot for paragliding (see box below). It's also handily located near the start of the waymarked **Lycian Way** walking trail (see p.303).

Ölüdeniz Nature Park

Daily dawn–dusk • ₺5 per person, ₺17 per car (or park on road outside for ₺5 and walk in)

Officially known as the **Ölüdeniz Nature Park** (Ölüdeniz Tabiat Parkı), the lagoon of Ölüdeniz lies just west of the resort of Belceğiz, a few minutes' walk along the road paralleling the sea, passing the PTT (Post Office) en route. Its warm – if occasionally turbid – waters make for pleasant swimming even in April or May, while in the height of summer the waters off the sand spit fronting the sea proper are more appealing. There are cafés, showers and toilets, and the views up to the dramatic pine-cloaked mountainsides are wonderful.

Kıdrak Beach

May–Oct daily 8.30am–7.30pm • ₺4.5, sunbed and umbrella ₺10

The sands at **Kıdrak Beach** (Kıdrak Plajı), 3km east of Belceğiz beside the all-inclusive *Club Lykia World*, belong to the forestry department. Cleaner and far less commercialized than Belceğiz itself, they hold no more than a small snack bar and seasonal sunbed/umbrella concession; there's also natural shade in the pines.

ACTIVITIES AND BOAT TRIPS AROUND ÖLÜDENIZ

Ölüdeniz is among the best paragliding spots in the world. The season lasts from April to November, with the best visibility in autumn. Both Belceğiz and Kıdrak serve as landing venues for paragliders, who are kitted out by several beachfront outfits for a hefty ₺200 or thereabouts and taken to a point near the summit of 1976m Baba Dağı for launching. Sky Sports (☎0252 617 0511, �🌐skysports-turkey.com) is the most heavily publicized and longest-established outfit, while Reaction Paragliding is also recommended (☎0252 617 0501, 🌐reaction.com.tr). If you want the expansive sea and mountain views but don't want to paraglide, you can get on a minibus from the seafront dolmuş stand to the summit of Baba Dağı (departing daily 10am, noon & 2pm, returning at 11am, 1pm and 3pm; ₺11.5 o/w).

BOAT TRIPS

A wide range of **boat trips** operate from Belceğiz, to some beautiful and fascinating destinations including remote coves, islets such as Gemiler, and Byzantine ruins. Among the potential pitfalls are limp lunches, bored guides and stops that are either rushed or missed out altogether.

The cheapest and most popular destination is the so-called **Butterfly Valley** (Kelebek Vadisi), a beach backed by a limestone canyon just inland (3 dolmuş boats, daily mid-May to Oct 11am–6.30pm; ₺20 return). Named after the many species that flutter about during the right seasons, it also features a waterfall, 20min inland (₺5 admission). The beach itself is frequented by an uneasy mix of day-trippers sipping overpriced beers at the café, and New Age patrons attending regular yoga, Indian dance and healing seminars while staying in basic tent or bungalow accommodation.

FROM TOP TLOS (P.312); KEKOVA (P.332) >

5

ARRIVAL AND DEPARTURE

ÖLÜDENIZ

By dolmuş Dolmuşes run to Ölüdeniz from Fethiye (summer daily 7.30am–1am, every 20min, ₺6). From Kaya Köyü, take the Fethiye-bound bus to Hisarönü (daily 7am–10pm: summer every 30min; winter hourly), from where buses to Ölüdeniz run every 10min.

ACCOMMODATION

Most accommodation clusters behind Belceğiz beach with its broad, landscaped pedestrian promenade. The bungalow-campsites popularized by hippy travellers in the 1970s have been eclipsed by **tent/bungalow/caravan sites** along the north shore of the lagoon. The former orchards behind Belceğiz and on the slopes flanking the road are now home to dozens of **hotels**, mostly in thrall to package companies, though worthwhile exceptions do exist.

Jade Residence Mid-promenade, Belceğiz ☎ 0252 617 0690, ⓦ jade-residence.com. Two pleasant, mock-colonial-style stone buildings with wooden shutters and wrought-iron grilles, set in beautifully lush landscaped gardens. There's also a nice pool complete with decking, and a good buffet breakfast. **€100**

★Oyster Residences Mid-promenade, Belceğiz ☎ 0252 617 0765, ⓦ oysterresidences.com. Atmospherically located in lush subtropical gardens, the 26 large, wooden-floored rooms here are immaculately well-presented in a charming neo-colonial style. There's a great pool with wooden decking and direct beach access, too. Sumptuous breakfast, which sources local produce wherever possible. No children under 14. **€110**

Paradise Garden Ölüdeniz Yolu ☎ 0252 617 0545, ⓦ paradisegardenhotel.com. Best of the hillside hotels, halfway back to Ovacık and set in vast grounds, with variably sized if low-ceilinged and balcony-less rooms. It's a longish walk through fifteen acres of garden to the main pool, but it's quite stunning when you get there. **€100**

Sugar Beach Club Ölüdeniz Cad 20 ☎ 0252 617 0048, ⓦ thesugarbeachclub.com. The best of the campsites fronting the east shore of the lagoon, with three grades of wooden bungalows, caravan hook-up spots and places to pitch a tent. Tent **₺20**, double bungalow **₺140**

Sultan Motel Kırancağıl Mahallesi ☎ 0252 616 6139, ⓦ sultanmotel.com. High above the beach on the fringes of the resort of Ovacık, this slightly ramshackle motel is nevertheless great value, and conveniently located at the official start of the Lycian Way. The en-suite bungalow rooms are light and bright with decent balconies and LCD TVs. Great pool, too. **€70**

EATING, DRINKING AND NIGHTLIFE

Cloud 9 Çarşı Caddesi ☎ 0252 617 0391. The best beachfront bar in Ölüdeniz, with a good mix of rock, blues and Spanish music, a bonus extended happy hour (6–8pm) and reasonably priced drinks. Daily 11am–2am.

Gözlemeci Sema 224 Sok. A 5min walk behind the seafront, this Is probably the last old-school *gözleme* place in town, and makes a refreshing change from the full-English and full-Scottish places nearer the beach, with the down-to-earth Sema feeding a steady stream of locals and a trickle of foreign visitors; try a three-dish fixed menu of home-cooked staples for ₺15, *gözleme* for ₺10 or *menemen* for ₺15. Daily 10am–10pm.

★Kumsal Pide Seyir Beach Hotel Yanı ☎ 0252 617 0058. This popular place dishes up *mezes* that are above average in quality and size; a large *pide* (₺14) easily feeds two. There's even a bowling alley in the basement and a kids' menu of chicken nuggets and the like. Daily 9am–midnight.

Secret Garden 226 Sok 5 ☎ 0252 617 0150. Hidden away like the name suggests, with a lovely quiet garden location and good service that make it a great choice for a romantic dinner. The menu features slightly unusual dishes like *tandır kebap* and sea bass baked in a salt crust, with mains starting at ₺25. Daily noon–2am.

Beyond Ölüdeniz: hamlets along the Lycian Way

South of Kıdrak, the **Yediburun** (Seven Capes) headlands constitute some of the most beautiful and least exploited coastline in Turkey, with several isolated villages lying just inland. The mountains, which reach close to 2000m in height, plunge dramatically into the sea, making road construction, and therefore tourist development, extremely difficult. What tourism there is remains low-key, with the majority of visitors either hanging out in bohemian "Butterfly Valley" or Kabak, or making the very most of the wild and picturesque seafront by walking the waymarked **Lycian Way** trail (see box opposite).

5

THE LYCIAN WAY

Inaugurated in 2000, the **Lycian Way** is a long-distance trail that runs parallel to much of the Turquoise Coast. In theory, it takes five weeks to complete the entire trail, but most walkers sample it in stages rather than tackling it all in one go.

Starting above Ölüdeniz and ending just shy of Antalya, the trail takes in choice mountain landscapes and seascapes en route, with many optional detours to Roman or Byzantine ruins not found in conventional guidebooks. Some of the wildest sections lie between Kabak and Gavurağili, above the Yediburun coast, and between Kaş and Üçağız. Elevation en route varies from sea level to 1800m on the saddle of Tahtalı Dağ. The best **walking seasons** along most of the way are October (pleasantly warm) or April and May (when water is plentiful and the days long); except in the highest mountain stages, summer is out of the question.

The **route** itself ranges from rough boulder-strewn trails to brief stretches of asphalt, by way of forested paths, cobbled or revetted Byzantine/Ottoman roads and tractor tracks. While the entire distance is marked with the conventional red-and-white blazes used in Europe, plus occasional metal signs giving distances to the next key destination, **waymarks** can be absent when you need them most. Continual bulldozing of existing footpath stretches into jeep tracks is such a major problem that the notional initial section between Hisarönü and Kirme has now ceased to exist, with most hikers starting at Faralya, while periodic maintenance (and where necessary re-routing) barely keeps pace with fast-growing scrub and rockfalls.

An unofficial "add-on" route, the **Likya Yolları**, runs from Hisarönü to Fethiye via Kaya, while loop side trails and alternative routes are being marked in different colour schemes. Kate Clow, who marked the original Lycian Way, adapted the Turkish military's ordnance survey 1:50,000 maps for her *The Lycian Way*, a **guide-booklet-with-map**, which indicates points for water, camping and (often now obsolete) overnighting indoors. The English-language version is sold at select bookshops, newsstands and travel agencies all along the coast as well as from online book retailers. Hard-wearing and waterproof, the map often saves the day, as trail descriptions can be frustratingly vague. It's also important to be aware that timings in *The Lycian Way* apply to those carrying a full pack; deduct about a quarter when doing sections as day-hikes.

A website, ⓦcultureroutesinturkey.com, offers updates on route conditions and a user forum.

Faralya

The cliff-side hamlet of **FARALYA** (officially Uzunyurt), set magnificently partway up the slopes of Baba Dağı, enjoys views across to Rhodes on clear days. Unless you're hiking the Lycian Way, there's little to do in Faralya, but a steady stream of walkers spend the night here.

Most of the accommodation options, including the three listed below, are perched just above "Butterfly Valley" (see box, p.300). A difficult trail, entirely distinct from the Lycian Way, drops to the eponymous beach in 45 minutes. Allow an hour to climb back up again, and take great care, using the rope and pegs provided for safety at the scrambly bits; the *jandarma* regularly have to be called out to rescue hapless bathers/explorers.

ARRIVAL AND DEPARTURE
FARALYA

By minibus and truck Minibuses to Kabak, on the main coast road from Fethiye, run via Ölüdeniz and Farlaya
(hourly 7am–7pm; around 40min; ₺7).

ACCOMMODATION

★**Değirmen/Die Wassermühle** Faralya Köyü Hısar Mah 4 ⓣ0252 642 1245, ⓦnatur-reisen.de. In the area's most prestigious accommodation, you'll be lulled to sleep by the sound of mill-race water. Seven comfortable apartments and two conventional rooms are grouped around a restaurant (meals usually for guests only), the restored mill and a stone-crafted swimming pool; minimum one-week stays are preferred. Closed late Oct to March. **€55**

★**George House** ⓣ0252 642 1102, ⓦgeorgehouse faralya.com. At the end of a steep dirt track some 500m northwest of Faralya centre, this well-regarded place has a user-friendly mix of camping, sleeping platforms and bungalows, as well as a small pool and decent restaurant/ bar. Set in an olive grove with superb views of sea and mountains and run by the friendly and knowledgeable Hassan, it's one of the premier places to stay along the

5

Lycian Way. All rates are half board, per person. Closed Dec, Jan & Feb. Camping ₺45, sleeping platform ₺55, waterless bungalow ₺55, en-suite bungalow ₺80

Melisa Pansiyon ☎0252 642 1012, ⓦmelisapension .com. Some 400m northwest of Faralya centre, with four

simple yet comfortable en-suite B&B rooms with verandas overlooking fruit orchards and the valley; you can also sleep camp in the orchard, and use the kitchen and cosy lounge in cool weather. Extra charge for air conditioning. Two-person tent pitch ₺20, two-person pension tent ₺40, double ₺100

Kabak

The village of **KABAK**, usually reached by bus from Fethiye, or on foot along the Lycian Way, straggles down a beautiful wooded valley from the narrow coastal road to the sea at **Gemile Liman**. While several pensions and eating options are strung along the main road, most visitors come here to chill out in one of the wooden huts/bungalows, set in the pine-forested valley behind the sand and pebble beach.

Whether you like Kabak or not is very personal. Some will find its ramshackle New Age hippy vibe a delight, others will baulk at the steep prices to stay in what is essentially a wooden hut. Either way, mosquito repellent is strongly recommended in summer.

ARRIVAL AND DEPARTURE KABAK

By minibus and truck Minibuses run to Kabak, on the main coast road, from Fethiye, via Ölüdeniz and Farlaya (hourly 7am–7pm; around 1hr; ₺7). From there, a 4WD truck ferries visitors down a horrendously dusty and steep track to the beach, stopping on request at the various

accommodation options in the woods en route (₺8–8.5 depending on number of customers).

On foot To walk to the beach from the main road, follow the eastbound Lycian Way (around 40min) from the *Olive Garden* pension/restaurant.

ACCOMMODATION AND EATING

Full Moon ☎0252 642 1081, ⓦfullmooncamp.com. Sixteen hillside chalets right at the end of the road (some en suite) and a proprietor who looks after trekkers and the local trails. There's a large hillside pool for those not up for the drop to the beach, while meals are served at the popular bar area. Half board only. ₺130, en suite ₺180

Olive Garden Kabak Köyü ☎0252 642 1083, ⓦolivegardenkabak.com. Seven well-built bungalows with the best sea views and congenial locally born management. There's also a great pool, and chef/owner Fatih is renowned for his Turkish/Mediterranean dishes, with mains from ₺20. Half board only. Restaurant daily 11am–11pm. ₺250

Reflections Camp Kabak Köyü ☎0252 642 1020, ⓦreflectionscamp.com.This well-established camp has a high ratio of toilets to accommodation and recycles its trash and grey water. Very chilled. Half board only, closed

Nov–April. Tent ₺80, waterless bungalow ₺120, en-suite rooms ₺180

Sea Valley Kabak Köyü ☎0252 642 1236, ⓦseavalleybungalow.com. This large and luxurious bungalow complex is set in landscaped gardens just above the beach. Old Kabak hands may decry its attempts to take the "community" upmarket, but its spruce en-suite bungalows are very popular despite the very high prices (which include breakfast). ₺280

Turan's Camp Kabak Köyü ☎0252 642 1227, ⓦturancamping.com. Established back in 1987, one of the first in the valley, with seven bungalows in grades from basic to balcony en suite, for twice the price. Relatively elaborate cooking, yoga programmes and a small plunge pool. All rates include half board. Waterless ₺200, en suite ₺300

Göcek

In a beautiful location at the northwest corner of the Gulf of Fethiye, **GÖCEK** is an obligatory stop on yacht or *gulet* tours thanks to its four marinas and busy boat-repair yard, and has become very trendy among both foreigners and Turks. While there's no beach to speak of, the passing boat trade means an astonishing concentration of **facilities** for such a place: supermarkets, laundries, yacht chandleries and posh souvenir shops along, or just off, the main inland commercial street, largely pedestrianized. The meticulously landscaped, lawn-fringed shore esplanade is car-free too, and the venue for a hugely popular evening promenade. For the average traveller, however, the main reason to stay here is the proximity to Dalaman airport.

ARRIVAL AND INFORMATION   GÖCEK

By dolmuş Regular dolmuşes link Fethiye with Göcek, dropping passengers at the main car park just off the inland shopping street (hourly 8am–10pm; 45min; ₺7).

Tours Visitors wanting some beach/swimming action while in Göcek usually head out to Göcek Adası, a large, pine-forested island studded with small bays. Boats for the island leave regularly from the main marina (10am–5.30pm; ₺15 return), taking around 15min each way.

ACCOMMODATION

Tufan's Çarşı Yolu ☎0252 645 1334. Handily located just 50m behind the beach and right in the heart of the village, this small pension is very good value for this upmarket resort, with eight basic rooms kitted out with pine beds. ₺100

Ünlü Çarşı Yolu ☎0252 645 1170, ⓦgocekunluotel .com. The plain, old-fashioned rooms in this bog-standard mid-range hotel, which is right in the village centre and just behind the seafront, don't excite for their style, but it's comfortable enough and all rooms have sea views. ₺180

Yonca Resort Gonca Sok ☎0252 645 2255, ⓦyoncaresort.com. Set off Atatürk Bul amid a grid of villas, well back from the waterfront in a pleasantly green suburb, this guesthouse has eight rooms, all tastefully furnished in a dark-wood antique style. There's a small pool, and if you don't want to eat out, food can be delivered from nearby restaurants. ₺225

EATING AND DRINKING

Many local **restaurants**, and especially those closer to the Port Göcek Marina, cater exclusively for the trendy set with obligatory service charges and tiny portions. Plenty of simple cafés, however, dish up standard Turkish food at prices lower than, for example, Dalyan.

Café West Turgut Özal Cad ☎0252 645 2749. International cuisine dished up in a laidback café-bar-bistro, not far from the marina. Full English and Turkish breakfasts, pasta (from ₺18), pizzas, sandwiches (from ₺15), smoothies and a wide range of coffees (from ₺8). Daily 9am–midnight.

Can Restaurant Skopea Marina ☎0252 645 1507. One of the best-value visitor-orientated places in town, despite its sea views and prime location abutting the fancy Skopea marina. *Meze* start from ₺9, a grilled sea bass will set you back a reasonable ₺28, a bottle of decent wine ₺60. Daily 9am–midnight.

★**Kebab Hospital (Antep Sofrası)** Turgut Özal Cad ☎0252 645 1873. Just inland in the pedestrian zone, this place specializes in quality kebabs (from ₺19) at affordable prices – plus *pides* from ₺10. There's seaside seating as well. Daily 9am–midnight.

Tabul Rasa off Turgut Özal Cad. Set in a narrow side street, and offering a completely different vibe to most other places in town: chilled, relaxed and studenty, with a decent snack menu including *köfte* for ₺22, beers at ₺12 and lattes at ₺10. Daily 10am–midnight.

Dalaman

The first real town west of Fethiye is dull, grid-planned **DALAMAN**. As home to the Turquoise Coast's main airport, it provides many visitors with their introduction to the region. There's absolutely no reason to stay here, however, with both Göcek (see opposite) and Dalyan (see p.306) so close at hand, and Fethiye/Ölüdeniz not much further away. For that reason, we have only supplied information on how to arrive and depart.

ARRIVAL AND DEPARTURE   DALAMAN

By plane Dalaman airport, 6km south from town (☎0252 792 5291), is not linked with the town centre by public transport; a taxi to the central *otogar* costs at least ₺40, to Dalyan ₺90. Domestic and international flights arrive at separate terminals. Havaş run regular coaches from the domestic terminal to both Fethiye (₺10) and Marmaris (₺15), with departures timed to coincide with flight arrivals. The airport has round-the-clock banking facilities, as well as three car rental booths: Avis (☎0252 792 5118), Budget (☎0252 792 5150) and Europcar (☎0252 792 5116).

Destinations Atlasjet, Onur Air, Pegasus and Turkish Airlines fly to Istanbul (Sabiha Gökçen or Atatürk) at least daily, while AnadoluJet fly to Ankara daily.

By bus The *otogar* is in the town centre, just east of the D555 highway.

Destinations Antalya (2 daily in summer; 5hr inland route); Bodrum (5 daily; 3hr 30min); Denizli (2 daily; 4hr 30min); Fethiye (every 30min; 1hr); Istanbul (2 daily; 14hr); İzmir (14 daily; 5hr); Kaş (4 daily; 3hr); Marmaris (12 daily; 1.5hr); Muğla (18 daily; 2hr); Ortaca (every 30min; 20min).

5

Dalyan and around

The growing but still beautiful riverside resort of **Dalyan**, 24km west of Dalaman, is home to around five thousand people and over three hundred tourist-orientated boats. It makes a good base for visiting nearby attractions like the ancient site of **Kaunos** across the brackish river, **İztuzu Beach** at the river mouth, and the beautiful lake of **Köyceğiz** with its shoreline hot springs.

Dalyan first came to prominence in 1986, when controversy erupted over a proposed luxury hotel on İztuzu Beach, a nesting ground for **loggerhead turtles**. Conservationists succeeded in halting the scheme, and the beach is now statutorily protected between May and October, when eggs are laid, while the town has styled itself as an eco-resort. Riverside location apart, Dalyan is little different from other mainstream resorts, with sports bars, cafés offering full English breakfasts and shops selling fake designer wares. It has a pleasantly relaxed air nonetheless, as the vast majority of visitors spend all day at either İztuzu Beach or on one of the myriad boat trips on offer. Life in Dalyan itself revolves around the **Dalyan Çayı**, which flows past the village between Köyceğiz lake and the sea. Many choice *pansiyon*s line the river's east bank, and the boats that put-put

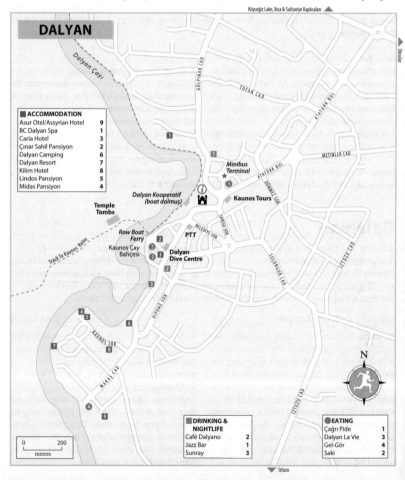

DALYAN

Köyceğiz Lake, Ilıca & Sultaniye Kaplıcaları

Okular

İztuzu

ACCOMMODATION

Asur Otel/Assyrian Hotel	9
BC Dalyan Spa	1
Caria Hotel	3
Çınar Sahil Pansiyon	2
Dalyan Camping	6
Dalyan Resort	7
Kilim Hotel	8
Lindos Pansiyon	5
Midas Pansiyon	4

Minibus Terminal

Dalyan Kooperatif
(boat dolmuş)

Kaunos Tours

Temple Tombs

Row Boat Ferry

Kaunos Çay Bahçesi

PTT

Dalyan Dive Centre

Track To Kaunos Ruins

GÜLPINAR CAD
TUFAN CAD
METİNLER CAD
ATATÜRK BUL
DÖNMEZ SOK
SABRISU SOK
BELEDİYE SOK
DİPDAŞ SOK
SULUNGUR CAD
İZTUZU CAD
KAUNOS SOK
MARAŞ CAD

N

0   200
metres

DRINKING & NIGHTLIFE

Café Dalyano	2
Jazz Bar	1
Sunray	3

EATING

Çağrı Pide	1
Dalyan La Vie	3
Gel-Gör	4
Saki	2

up and down it are the preferred means of transport to the major local sites. Craft heading downstream pass a series of spectacular fourth-century BC **"temple" tombs** in the west-bank cliffs.

ARRIVAL AND DEPARTURE
DALYAN AND AROUND

By bus and dolmuş Dalyan's minibus terminal is near the mosque, close to the centre.
Destinations from Dalyan Fethiye (2 daily; 1hr); Göcek (2 daily; 30min); Köyceğiz (1 daily; 35min); Ortaca (frequent; 20min).
Destinations from Ortaca From the town of Ortaca, on Highway 400 13km north of Dalyan, buses run to: Antalya (2 daily; 7hr coastal route); Bodrum (5 daily; 4hr); Dalaman (every 30min; 20min); İzmir (10 daily; 5hr 30min); Kaş (5 daily; 3hr 30min); and Köyceyiz (every 30min; 30min).
By boat Dolmuş boats run by Dalyan Kooperatifi run to the

river end of İztuzu Beach (₺10 return; 40min) depart from Kordon Boyu, opposite the mosque. They leave as soon as they are full (almost constantly in the summer season), returning from 1pm or so until sunset. Otherwise, peak-season minibuses ply every 30min along the 13km road to the east end of the strand. Many of the riverside *pansiyons* and hotels also have their own small motorboats providing morning service to the beach for a nominal fee. To reach Kaunos (see p.309) take the little-publicized rowboat ferry; ₺5 round trip from the jetty next to the Kaunos Çay Bahçesi riverside garden.

INFORMATION AND TOURS

Tourist office On Cumhüriyet Meydan, but only open sporadically, and of little use.
Adventure tours Kaunos Tours (☎0252 284 2816, ⓦkaunostours.com) rents cars and organizes adventure trips – canyoning, scuba diving, horseriding, mountain biking, sea kayaking and rafting on the Dalaman Çayı (aka Akköprü Çayı). Excursion days range ₺55–135.
Scuba diving Dalyan Dive Centre (☎0555 412 5438, ⓦdalyandivecentre.com) offers one-day scuba-diving taster trips (£45) as well as certification courses (£230).

Boat tours The most popular local outing is the day-tour offered by the quayside motorboat co-op. These excursions – usually departing by 10.30am – take in Sultaniye thermal springs on Köyceğiz lake, Kaunos ruins and the beach, and are passable value at about ₺30 per person. Custom-renting is considerably dearer but worthwhile if you have a large group. Riverside *pansiyons* may take you on evening boat trips to spy water snakes, and freshwater terrapins surfacing for air.

ACCOMMODATION

The most desirable *pansiyons* line or overlook the river; book well in advance in high season. **Maraş Caddesi**, which heads from the town centre to a dead end nearly 2km south, passes the junction with **Kaunos Sokağı**, home to several garden-set *pansiyons* and hotels, which serve breakfast at waterside terraces. The dolmuş boats to İztuzu Beach will usually collect passengers from riverside accommodation. If you're driving to Kaunos Sokağı, take the signposted İztuzu road from the centre, then bear right at the second junction, to get around a one-way system and nocturnal street closures. **Mosquitoes** can be a nuisance, though repellents or vaporization mats are widely sold. Most establishments close between November and Easter.

RIVER-VIEW ESTABLISHMENTS
Asur Otel/Assyrian Hotel South end of Maraş Cad ☎0252 284 3232, ⓦasurotel.com. Nicely landscaped complex, with a lawn/garden down to the river, that's popular with tour companies. Pleasant, if small and slightly dark hexagonal rooms, all with a/c and tidy en-suite bathrooms, ranged around a beautiful pool. Double ₺270, apartments per person £130
BC Dalyan Spa Gurpınar Mah 313 So 7, off Maraş Cad ☎0252 284 2101, ⓦbcspahotel.com. Lovely riverside setting just north of the town centre, with spectacular views across to a wooded spur. The real draw are the various spa treatments, vitamin bar, indoor and outdoor pool and other health/relaxation-orientated services, but the rooms are extremely well kitted out. ₺290
Caria Hotel Yalı Sok 9, off Maraş Cad ☎0252 284 5035, ⓦhotelcaria.com. This has Dalyan's best roof terrace, with

great views across to the tombs. Rooms are simple but very comfortable and many have river views. Nocturnal boat trips and barbecues are on offer, as is airport pick-up on request, but there's limited parking. ₺120
Çınar Sahil Pansiyon Yalı Sok 14 ☎0252 284 2117. Set in a small citrus grove abutting a busy part of the waterfront, and perfectly located to make the most of the bustling town centre. The rather dated but clean and airy one-, two- or three-bed rooms are nonetheless adequate and there's a rooftop breakfast terrace. ₺120
Dalyan Camping Maraş Cad 144 ☎0252 284 5316, ⓦdalyancamping.net. With its brilliant location on a bend in the river across from the rock tombs, this laid-back place offers shady spots to pitch a tent, plus four-person, en-suite pinewood bungalows with a/c, and hard-standing pitches with electric and water hook-up facilities for caravans and campervans. Wi-fi and a nice riverfront sitting area complete

5

the picture, as does chilled two owner Servent, a former musician. Tent pitch ₺30, two-person waterless bungalow ₺90, two-person en-suite bungalow ₺120

KAUNOS SOKAĞI

Dalyan Resort Kaunos Sok 50 ☎0252 284 5499, ⊚dalyanresort.com. Popular with package operators, this self-contained complex, set in lovely gardens that roll down to the riverside, offers tasteful rooms with travertine tiles much in evidence, an airy domed restaurant, rental canoes and a hamam with mud therapy offered. Suites cost €30 extra. €110

Kilim Hotel Kaunos Sok 11 ☎0252 284 2253, ⊚kilimhotel.com. Anglo/Turkish-managed, nicely overhauled 1980s hotel. Half its stall-showered rooms have balconies and/or a/c. There's a poolside lawn under palm trees, regular barbecues and snacks on request. The pleasant riverside annexe has a line of (cheaper) single rooms. €60

★ **Lindos Pansiyon** Kaunos Sok 28 ☎0252 284 2005, ⊚lindospension.com. Well-appointed bungalow rooms with both twin and double beds plus two family rooms and one four-bed studio. Pleasant library-lounge for cool weather, free canoes available, and pleasant decking by the river with atmospheric views across to the temple-tombs. Genial English-speaking owner Levent Sünger makes the hotel bar the place to be. A keen mountain biker, he rents out bikes (see box below), knows all the best routes and is involved in a project to waymark local cycling and walking routes. Closed Nov to mid-March. Double €50, family room €70

★ **Midas Pansiyon** Kaunos Sok 32 ☎0252 284 2195, ⊚midasdalyan.com. Delightful setting right on the river, with decking and a ladder allowing patrons to bathe. Rooms are on the small side and plain, but spotlessly clean and easy to cool with the a/c. The hearty breakfast is served under the graceful branches of an ancient fig tree next to the river. ₺120

EATING AND DRINKING

While Dalyan's **restaurants** tend to be bland, Anglicized and a little overpriced, several establishments offer no-nonsense Turkish cuisine at sensible prices. Restaurants line the waterfront between the jetty and Cumhüriyet Meydan, with generally cheaper options inland northeast of the square. **Nightlife** is concentrated along the upper pedestrianized reaches of Maraş Caddesi.

RESTAURANTS

Çağrı Pide Atatürk Bul ☎0252 284 3427. Inauspiciously located near the entrance to the minibus square, hidden behind ATMs and palm trees. There are a few tables set out in the street where you can enjoy *pides* from ₺7, pizzas from ₺13 plus a range of *meze* and grills. Beers cost a bargain ₺9. Daily 8am–midnight.

Dalyan La Vie Sağlık Sok 5 ☎0252 284 4142. With a touch more class than the average Dalyan restaurant, and a superb location looking over to the mysterious tombs on the opposite side of the river, this is the most central place to come for a reliable fish dinner in romantic surroundings. The delicious *güveç* (casseroles) are a reasonable ₺38 per sizzling dish; chicken meals start at ₺28, while wild-caught fish is priced per kilo. Daily 8am–midnight.

★ **Gel-Gör Maraş Mah** Dalko Karşısı ☎0252 284 5009. It's well worth the 1km stroll from the town centre to this

quietly located waterfront restaurant, Dalyan's oldest fish place, with a great terrace overlooking the river and a rustic white and blue wooden shack for cooler evenings. Fifty types of *meze* (₺8 and up), farmed sea bass and sea bream (₺25), and wild-caught red mullet charged by the kilo. Daily 9am–1am.

Saki Geçit Sok ☎0252 284 5212. Right on the river near the rowboat jetty, this small, no-menu place has some of the best traditional Turkish *meze* in town, specializing in vegetarian recipes as well as meat-based dishes. Mains from ₺18, *meze* from ₺6. April–Oct daily 10am–11pm.

BARS AND CAFÉS

Café Dalyano cnr Maraş and Davran caddesis ☎0555 597 3058. Sought out during the day for its excellent ice creams and range of coffees, and in the evening for its well-priced alcoholic drinks, with mojitos a bargain ₺17, 50cl

---

BIKE RIDES FROM DALYAN

Renting a **mountain bike** in Dalyan is an appealing option in the cooler months; they're available at better hotels and certain travel agents for around ₺15 a day, the *Lindos Pansiyon* (see above) charges ₺35 for a quality machine and also sells a good topographical 1.70,000 map of the area.

The best local ride is to **İztuzu Beach**: there's one challenging hill en route, with *ayran* and *gözleme* stalls to pause at for refreshment in the village of Gökbel. This land route is recommended at least once, as you loop around the Sulungur lake and get glimpses of marsh and mountain not possible amid the claustrophobic reed beds of the Dalyan Çayı.

beers ₺9. Decor is bright pastel, and there's good people-watching opportunities from the outside tables. Daily 9am–1am.

Jazz Bar Gülpınar Cad ☎0532 490 7161. The first live music venue in town and still the best, with live music (mainly rock rather than jazz) virtually every night in season, Fri and Sat evenings only in winter. It occupies a eucalyptus-shaded corner plot with great views across the river and cliffs rearing up beyond. Daily 2pm–2am.

Sunray Maraş Cad. This long-established café-bar is the most sophisticated in Dalyan, with coffees, fresh juices and shakes as well as alcoholic drinks. Gaze across river to the illuminated rock tombs and listen to a mix of jazz, rock, blues and Turkish pop. Daily 1pm–1am.

Kaunos

1.5km southwest of Dalyan • Daily: April–Oct 8.30am–7pm; Nov–March 8.30am–5pm • ₺8 • To get there take a tour boat (see p.311); drive from Köyceğiz via the Sultaniye baths and Çandır village, though the road beyond Sultaniye is potholed and indirect, with no parking by the upper site entrance; or cross the river from Dalyan on the rowboat ferry (see p.307), and walk 15min

Excavations at ancient **Kaunos** began in 1967 and still take place each summer under the aegis of Başkent University. While the ruins are far from spectacular, they're well labelled, and the site is among the least deservedly overlooked archeological sites on the Mediterranean coast. It's alive with herons and storks in summer, flamingoes in winter, plus terrapins, tortoises, snakes and lizards in all seasons.

Passengers arriving by **tour boat** disembark either at the fish weir (*dalyan* means weir) or at another jetty at the base of the outcrop supporting Kaunos's acropolis. The fish caught are mostly grey mullet and bass, and a Kaunos ancient inscription suggests they've been part of the local diet since ancient times. From either landing point it's a seven-minute walk up to the fenced **site**.

Brief history

Although Kaunos was a ninth-century BC **Carian** foundation, it exhibited **Lycian** cultural traits, not least the compulsion to adorn nearby cliffs with rock tombs. Kaunos was also closely allied to the principal Lycian city of Xanthos; when the Persian Harpagos attempted to conquer the region in the sixth century BC, these two cities were the only ones to resist. The city began to acquire a Greek character under the Hellenizing Carian ruler Mausolus. Subsequently, Kaunos passed to the Ptolemies; then to the Rhodians; and finally, after fierce resistance to Rhodes, it came under indirect Roman imperial administration.

Besides its fish, Kaunos was noted both for its **figs**, and the prevalence of **malaria**; excessive fig consumption was erroneously deemed the cause, rather than the anopheles mosquitoes which, until 1948, infested the surrounding swamps. Another insidious problem was the silting up of its **harbour**, which continually threatened the city's commerce. The Mediterranean originally came right up to the foot of the acropolis hill, surrounding Kaunos on all sides apart from an isthmus of land to the north; the Dalyan Çayı has since deposited over 5km of silt, leaving an expanse of marshy delta in its wake.

The site

Much of Kaunos has yet to be unearthed, despite the long-running excavations. Well-preserved stretches of **defensive wall** extend north of the city, some constructed by Mausolus early in the fourth century BC. Just below the **acropolis**, with its medieval and Hellenistic fortified area, is the second-century BC **theatre**, which is the most impressive building here. Resting against the hillside to the southeast, it's greater than a semicircle in the Greek fashion and retains two of its original arched **entrances**; in 2008 a **nymphaeum** was uncovered next to one archway. A **path** winds up to the acropolis behind the theatre, but take care as it is covered in loose stones for much of the approximately fifteen-minute ascent. There's little of real substance to be seen on the top, but the staggering bird's-eye views over the still unspoilt Dalyan delta, İztuzu Beach and Dalyan town itself more than compensate.

Northwest of the theatre, closer to the upper ticket booth, the **Byzantine basilica** and the city's **Roman baths** are also in excellent condition. A cobbled street leads downhill from the baths to an ancient **Doric temple**, consisting most obviously of an attractive circular structure, possibly an altar, sacred pool or podium, flanked by bits of re-erected colonnade. A path continues to the **agora**, on the lowest level, graced by a restored **fountain-house** at the end of a long **stoa**. The ancient **harbour** below is now the Sülüklü Gölü, or "Lake of the Leeches"; the entrance could be barred by a chain in times of danger.

The rock-cut fourth-century BC **"temple-tombs"** so clearly visible from across the river in Dalyan town lie to the northeast of the main site, close to the landing stage for the rowboats arriving from Dalyan. A special walkway has been built to take visitors up close to the tombs and, at the time of writing, a ticket office was being established and a separate charge was set to be introduced.

İztuzu Beach

Extending for 4.5km southeast from the mouth of the Dalyan Çayı • Summer daily 8am–8pm, winter open 24hr • Sunbed and umbrella rental ₺10 • Dolmuşes serve the south end of the beach in season (every 30min; ₺8); drivers face a ₺5 parking charge (May–Oct)

Tourism and turtles have been made to coexist uneasily on the beautiful hard-packed sand of **İztuzu Beach**. Be sure to look out for **turtle nests**, which can all too easily be trampled on. Turtle tracks – scrapings where the creatures have hauled themselves up onto the beach to lay their eggs – are visible in the sand during June and July. The marshes immediately behind are often alive with other wildlife too, while the approach road is lined with flowering oleander bushes and trees deformed by the high winter winds.

Lack of shade is a problem, though you can rent sunbeds and umbrellas at the river end of the beach. There are snack kiosks at either end of the beach, though they only sell crisps, ice cream, *gözleme* and *sandviç*, so it's best to bring some food. Thanks to wind exposure, the water can be choppy and murky, but the gently shelving seabed makes İztuzu excellent for children. You can also be ferried across the river mouth (don't swim, there are dangerous currents) to a smaller, more peaceful beach, shaded by some pines.

Sea Turtle Conservation Foundation

Daily 10am–5pm • Free, but donations welcome • ☎ 0252 284 2855, ⓦ dalyanturtles.com

At the southern end of the beach, just behind the car park and toilet area, the **Sea Turtle Conservation Foundation** was established by long-time British resident June Haimoff, known to locals as Kaptan June. Accustomed to wintering in Gstaad and spending summers cruising the Aegean and Mediterranean in her yacht *Bouboulina*, in 1984 this intrepid society girl pitched up on İztuzu Beach – and stayed. Over the years she has been instrumental in saving the beach from proposed tourist developments, and was awarded the MBE for her good works in 2011. The small museum to her conservation work is set in the beach hut she had built on her arrival. Inside are a few **displays** about turtles and their conservation, aimed primarily at children, and souvenirs for sale, including several books written by Kaptan June herself.

Sea Turtle Research, Rescue and Rehabilitation Centre

Daily 10am–6pm • Free, but donations welcome • ☎ 0252 289 0077, ⓦ dekamer.org.tr

At the southern end of İztuzu, and further back from the sand than the Sea Turtle Conservation Foundation is the **Sea Turtle Research, Rescue and Rehabilitation Centre**, run by Pamukkale University and dedicated to rescuing and returning to the wild baby turtles whose nests have been disturbed, and adults injured by boat propellers, fish hooks or the plastic bags turtles easily mistake for one of their natural prey, jellyfish. Inside visitors can see rescued **baby turtles** (in season), as well as the more harrowing sight of older turtles maimed by boat propellers.

Ilıca thermal mud baths

Daily 9am–7pm • ₺5 • 10min by boat upriver from Dalyan, towards Köyceğiz

The **Ilıca thermal baths** (40°C), a series of open-air mud pools, are located not far upstream from Dalyan. However, the total area is small, and in season gets packed with tour groups – best go at an odd hour, or have your skipper take you to the Köyceğiz Sultaniye Kaplıcaları (see below) hot springs, further upstream on the lakeshore itself.

Köyceğiz Sultaniye Kaplıcaları

Daily 6am–10pm • ₺5 • The springs are 7km by boat upriver from Dalyan, or 18km southwest of Köyceğiz on a paved road; if driving, head west following signs for Ekincik, then veer left following signs for Çandır

Housed in a conspicuous white-domed structure right on the lakeshore, the **main baths** at the remote hot springs known as the **Köyceğiz Sultaniye Kaplıcaları** are claimed to be open around the clock, despite the nominal posted hours. However, 10.30am to 8pm is set aside for *tur* (mixed bathing), while at other times there are roughly alternating hours for men and women. The dome shelters a large round pool with a naturally rocky, uneven bottom, from which the water wells up at 39–41°C; it's best appreciated at night or during the cooler months. Ancient masonry at the pool rim is evidence that the baths have been present in some form at least since Roman times. Three **open-air pools** are scattered around the domed structure: one hot (beside the bar), one cold, and one muddy-bottomed (beside the snack-café).

Köyceğiz

KÖYCEĞIZ, 23km north of Dalyan, is a laidback market town that has been eclipsed touristically by its rival across the lake. Its economy is based largely on cotton, olives, fishing in the brackish lake, logging and citrus cultivation, though its position on the scenic **Köyceğiz Gölü** – once a bay open to the sea – allows it to function as a resort. The centre has a certain charm, with scattered buildings from the 1920s and 1930s, an atmospheric bazaar lane lined by *pide salonları* and *hazır yemek* kitchens – some open long hours – plus a well-attended lakeshore promenade on warm nights. As well as cheaper prices than Dalyan, Köyceğiz has better **transport** connections.

ARRIVAL AND INFORMATION
KÖYCEĞIZ

By bus Dolmuşes shuttle regularly into town from the *otogar*, out towards the main highway, 2km north of the lakeshore. Destinations Dalaman (hourly; 30min); Fethiye (8 daily; 1hr 30min); and Ortaca, for Dalyan (half-hourly; 30min).

Boat tours Trips to the Sultaniye Kaplıcaları and Kaunos usually leave at 10am and return at 7pm (₺15–30).

ACCOMMODATION

Alila Emeksiz Cad ☎0252 262 1150, ✉omeroflaz38 @mynet.com. The welcoming *Alila* has plain but serviceable rooms in varied sizes (including family suites sleeping five) with small balconies that mostly face the lake, plus an outstanding ground-floor restaurant (see p.312). ₺90

★ **Flora Hotel** Cengiz Topel Cad 110 ☎0252 262 4976, ♨florahotel.com.tr. Set at right angles to the lakefront, most of the simple but comfortable a/c rooms have water views. It's a notch up on the pensions and worth the extra money, especially as free bikes and a couple of canoes are available. Course anglers may be tempted by carp-fishing tours offered by Belgian summer resident Franky Wauters. ₺120

Fulya Pansiyon Ali İhsan Kalmaz Cad ☎0252 262 2301. On the second road in from the lakefront around 600m from the town centre, the basic but very clean sixteen-room *Fulya Pansiyon* boasts a fine roof terrace and has free bikes for guests. ₺70

Kaunos Cengiz Topel Cad ☎0252 262 3730. This is a basic concrete block but has a great lakeshore position. Most of the 75 sparsely furnished but comfortable rooms (think bright walls and tiled floors) have sizeable balconies to take advantage of the views. Bathrooms are tidy with chrome shower stalls, and there's a big pool to one side. ₺200

Tango Pension Ali İhsan Kalmaz Cad ☎0252 262 2501, ♨tangopension.com. This somewhat institutionalized backpackers' favourite (cornflakes for breakfast), one block back from the water, has minimalist en-suite rooms or six-bed dorms, garden bar and roof terrace. Dorm ₺30, double ₺70

5

EATING AND DRINKING

Alila Restaurant Emeksiz Cad ☎ 0252 262 1150. Much the best lakeshore restaurant is attached to the *Alila* hotel; owner Ömer's kitchen produces unusual *mezes* to die for, like stewed artichokes, yoghurt with coriander greens and caper shoots marinated in sour pomegranate syrup, while

mains (from ₺18) are generous. Daily 10am–midnight.
Thera Cengiz Topel Cad ☎ 0541 833 6154. Reasonable fish restaurant with a fine location, separated from the lake by a narrow park. Assorted farmed (from ₺20 a portion) and wild-caught fish are on offer. Daily 9am–midnight.

The Xanthos valley

The heart of Lycia, east of Fethiye, is home to several archeological sites, including the ancient citadel-cities of **Tlos** and **Pınara**, on opposite sides of the **Xanthos valley**. Tlos had the geographical advantage, lying above a rich, open flood plain and sheltered to the east by the Massikytos range (today's Akdağ); Pınara's surrounding hilly terrain was difficult to cultivate. Even more remote and less fertile is mysterious **Sidyma**, up on the ridge separating the valley from the Mediterranean. All these cities were unearthed by the English traveller Charles Fellows between 1838 and 1842, contemporaneous with his work – or rather pillaging – at **Xanthos**, though he seems to have left the nearby religious sanctuary of **Letoön** unmolested.

Mostly following the valley of the ancient Xanthos River (now the Eşen Çayı), the road between Fethiye and Kalkan threads through an immensely fertile area that's known for its cotton, tomatoes and other market-garden crops. The fact that plans for a local airport have never materialized, in tandem with archeological restrictions, means that growth at **Patara**, the main resort, has remained modest by Turkish coastal standards. Between Tlos and Patara, the magnificent river gorge of **Saklıkent** is easily reached by dolmuş or with your own vehicle, though it's become something of a tourist circus. Fans of isolated ruins can instead visit the unpromoted, unspoiled Lycian city of **Oenoanda**, high in the mountains north of Tlos.

Tlos

Daily 8.30am–dusk • ₺8 when staff present

Among the most ancient and important Lycian cities, **TLOS** stands beside modern Asarkale village. Hittite records from the fourteenth century BC refer to it as "Dalawa in the Lukka lands", and the local discovery of a bronze hatchet dating from the second millennium BC confirms the long heritage of the place. However, little else is known about its history.

The **ruins** themselves have been much excavated over recent years, making a visit extremely worthwhile. The setting is undeniably impressive, too, on a high rocky promontory giving excellent views of the Xanthos valley. The acropolis bluff is dominated by an Ottoman Turkish fortress, home during the nineteenth century to the brigand and local chieftain, Kanlı ("Bloody") Ali Ağa, who killed his own wayward daughter to uphold the family's honour.

The site

Entry to the **main site** at Tlos is via the still intact northeastern **city gate**, next to the guard's portakabin. Cobbled stairs climb to the main **necropolis** with its freestanding sarcophagi and complex of rock-cut house-tombs, one of which was discovered intact in 2005, yielding treasure kept at the Fethiye museum. The path continues towards the summit of the acropolis for expansive views, though access to the very highest point is forbidden.

Look down and east from the top of the acropolis and you'll see the large, flat expanse of land at its feet, sandwiched by rows of well-preserved ancient stone seating: this was once the settlement's **stadium**. Beyond this and the curving onward road that cuts the site in two is the second flat area, once the **agora**, though the surviving (and today rather scruffy) remains are scant. The agora area is backed by a magnificent second-century AD **theatre**, with 34 rows of seats still intact. Its stage building holds several finely carved blocks – including one with an eagle beside a garlanded youth – and its northern section still stands to nearly full height, vying with the backdrop of mountains. The theatre was closed to visitors at the time of writing.

Several more impressive structures stand to the south of the road running through the site. The first is a large, triple aisled **Byzantine-era church**, probably the basilica of the Roman settlement; the remains of a **synthronon** (seating area) survive in the main, east-facing apse. Beyond the church, a well-preserved stepped base once supported the second-century Corinthian-style **Temple of Kronos**. The large structure beyond the temple is the main Roman-era **bathhouse**, while the slightly smaller building nearby is a smaller bathhouse and **palaestra** (exercise area). The views from here over the Xanthos valley are breathtaking.

ARRIVAL AND DEPARTURE | TLOS

By minibus Patchy public transport to Tlos is provided by Saklıkent-bound minibuses from Fethiye, which occasionally detour to the site. As Tlos is firmly established on the organized-excursion circuit, however, you shouldn't need to hire a private taxi.

By car from Fethiye Head east on the main coast road, Highway 400, and veer left (east) after 22km onto Highway 350, the Korkuteli/Antalya road. Once across the Koca Çayı bridge, bear immediately right onto the marked side road to

both Tlos and Saklıkent. After 8.5km, turn left (east) onto a paved minor road festooned with signposting for restaurants and inns; the base of the acropolis hill is 4km along.

By car from Patara At Alaçat take the eastbound road marked "Saklıkent 15km"; at a T-junction in Kadıköy, with "Saklıkent" signposted opposite a mini-market for the right turning, bear left (north) instead, following a "Tloss" sign, for just over 2km until another "Tloss" sign points up the final 4km.

ACCOMMODATION

★**Mountain Lodge** ☏ 0252 638 2515, ⓦ tlosmountain lodge.com. Choose between nicely appointed, carpeted, beam-ceilinged en-suites in the garden annexe, or luxury units in the wing overlooking the pool and bar. Engaging owner Melahat prepares fine set evening meals in an area thin on non-trout-based cuisine, served in the wood-beamed

and stone pub-restaurant. She also organizes treks in the area, and is knowledgeable about local flora. All rates are for two people, including breakfast. Half board available for €15 extra per person. It's just under 2km down the road from the entrance to the ruins. Closed mid-Nov to mid-Dec & mid-Jan to mid-Feb. **€40**

Oenoanda

Unrestricted access • Free • No public transport; turn off Highway 400 onto Highway 350 at the Kemer river bridge toward Korkuteli; after 34km, bear east on a side road marked for Seki and Elmalı; after 1.1km turn south onto a more minor road; 800m down this, veer right at an unmarked fork to proceed 1.5km further to İncealiler village, then turn right at the phone box and park by the coffee house – do not follow the river further upstream

Some 50km northeast of Tlos, ancient **Oenoanda** was among the northernmost and highest (1350–1450m elevation) of the Lycian cities. Set in wild, forested countryside, it's almost unpublicized. As an example of how all local sites used to be before tourism, however, it thoroughly rewards the effort that's required to reach it (own transport essential).

Oenoanda was the birthplace of **Diogenes**, the second-century AD Epicurean philosopher; to him is attributed antiquity's longest inscriptionary discourse, scattered in fragments across the site. First surveyed by British archeologists in 1996, Oenoanda is set for more vigorous future excavations. With luck, these will reassemble Diogenes' text to its full estimated length of 60m, and firmly identify structures. Until then, the site remains a romantic, overgrown maze of tumbled lintels, statue bases, columns, cistern mouths and buried arches, frequented only by squirrels and the occasional hunter or shepherd.

The site

From the coffee-house parking in İncealiler, head up the main pedestrian thoroughfare among village houses, then near the top of the grade bear right at heaped boulders onto a

5

narrower track which soon dwindles to a path. Continue west towards the escarpment in front of you, where the first freestanding **tombs** poke up. The path describes a broad arc south around the top of a stream valley, forging through low scrub.

Some 45 minutes from the coffee house, the trail fizzles out at the polygonal masonry of the massive south-to-north **aqueduct** that supplied the city, whose site-bluff inclines gently to the south but is quite sheer on all other sides. Slip through a gap in the aqueduct, where necropolis tombs are flung about on every side, and veer right along the ridge towards Oenoanda's massive Hellenistic **city wall**, with its arched window; the way through is left of this, by a strong hexagonal **tower** with archers' loopholes. Some fifteen minutes' walk north from here, keeping just east of the ridge line, brings you to the large flat paved **agora**; tentatively identified **baths** stand just beyond, with a surviving apse and dividing arch. Just northeast, a gate in the **Roman wall**, longer but much lower than the Hellenistic one, opens onto a vast flat area, provisionally dubbed an "**esplanade**", flanked by traces of stoas. Northwest of the presumed baths, a **nymphaeum** or small **palace** with a three-arched facade precedes the partly preserved **theatre**, its fifteen or so rows of seats taking in fine views of Akdağ.

Saklıkent gorge

Walkway Open during daylight hours • ﬨ8

The hugely popular **Saklıkent gorge**, 44km from Fethiye, is the most dramatic geological formation in the Xanthos valley, and at 20km the second-longest gorge in Europe. Its mouth is deceptively modest; to reach it leave the road bridge for a 150m pedestrian **walkway** spiked into the canyon walls, ending at the **Gökçesu/Ulupınar springs**, which erupt at great pressure from the base of towering cliffs, exiting the narrows to mingle eventually with the Eşen Çayı. It's a magical place, seemingly channelling all the water this side of Akdağ, though less impressive if you coincide with the many tour groups that come, primarily, to eat trout at several restaurants that are built on wooden platforms suspended over the water.

The water-sculpted chasm extends 18km upstream, though further progress for all except rock climbers is blocked after about 2km by a boulder slide. If you want to explore up to that point, it's initially a **wading** exercise – take submersible shoes, or rent a pair here. The entire length of the gorge was first descended in 1993 by a **canyoning** expedition that took eighteen hours, bivouacking halfway and abseiling down several dry waterfalls. This trip is now offered on a custom basis, during summer only, by Bougainville in Kaş (see p.330).

ARRIVAL AND DEPARTURE — SAKLIKENT

By minibus Vehicles marked "Kayadibi/Saklıkent" operate a regular minibus service in season, from Fethiye's dolmuş *otogar*.

By car Drive east of Fethiye on Highway 400, and veer left (east) onto Highway 350 after 22km. Cross the Koca Çayı bridge and bear immediately right onto the marked side road to both Tlos and Saklıkent. After driving 17.5km south, bear left for just over 3km to the (signed) gorge mouth.

ACCOMMODATION

Saklıkent Gorge Club Saklıkent ☎0252 659 0074, ⓦ saklikentgorge.net. Set at the mouth of the gorge near the car park, this backpacker-oriented treehouse place makes a great base if you want to explore the gorge and enjoy the ambience once the tour groups have gone. Tent pitch €10, dorm €16, treehouse double €40

Pınara

Daily 8.30am–dusk • ﬨ8 when guard present • If driving, turn right off Highway 400 and continue just over 3km to the village of Minare, from where the ruins are a 2.2km walk along a steep signposted track

Almost nothing is known about the ancient city of **PINARA**, 46km southeast of Fethiye, except that it may have been founded as an annexe of Xanthos. Later, however, Pınara

– meaning "something round" in Lycian, presumably because of the shape of the original, upper acropolis – became one of the region's larger cities, minting its own coins and earning three votes in the Federation.

Approaching the site, the **cliff** on which the city was first founded all but blocks out the horizon – indeed it's worth the trip up just to see this towering mass, its east face covered in rectangular openings, either tombs or food-storage cubicles. These can now only be reached by experienced rock climbers and it's hard to imagine how they were originally cut. As to the **site** itself, Pınara is perfect for those who like their ruins largely unexcavated, overgrown and picturesquely set. Battered metal signs take visitors in a logical order around the major remains, but it's still easy to wander off course.

The Royal Tomb

Pınara's **tombs** are its most interesting feature, especially a group on the west bank of the seasonal stream that passes the site. On the east side of the lower acropolis hill the so-called **Royal Tomb** sports detailed if well-worn carvings on its porch of walled cities with battlements, gates, houses and tombs; a frieze survives above, showing people and animals in a peaceable scene – perhaps a religious festival. Inside is a single bench set high off the ground, suggesting that this was the tomb of just one, probably royal, person.

The lower acropolis

The jumbled remains of the **lower acropolis** area sprawl across the hillside below the Royal and other tombs. Reached by a direct path north from the Royal Tomb, a house-tomb with an arched roof is topped by a pair of stone **ox horns** for warding off evil spirits. This stands near the summit of the **lower acropolis**, at the eastern edge of the presumed **agora**. Just north of the horned tomb, the massive foundations of a **temple** to an unknown god overlook the theatre. Hairpinning back south, a level path threads between the pigeonholed cliff and the lower acropolis, first past a ruinous but engaging **odeon**, then through a chaos of walls, uprights, heart-shaped column sections and tombs that clog the flattish heart of the city.

The theatre

Pınara's well-preserved **theatre**, signed northeast of the lower acropolis, is well worth seeking out. Small but handsome, it was never modified by the Romans (on-site signage to the contrary) and retains its classic Greek horseshoe shape. Its compact size gives a fair idea of just how modest the population of Pınara was.

Sidyma

Unrestricted access daily dawn–dusk

Sited halfway up the ancient Mount Kragos – the modern coastal peak of Avlankara Tepesi – **Sidyma** is the most remote of the Xanthos valley's ancient cities; indeed, it's scarcely in the valley at all. Set in a striking landscape astride the Lycian Way, it's a rewarding, understated site that was only "rediscovered" by Europeans during the mid-nineteenth century, and has never been properly excavated.

There are no accommodation options at the site, so most visitors stay at either nearby **Alınca**, a pretty village astride the Lycian Way, or head up to remote **Karaağaç**.

The site

Sidyma is one of many ancient sites in this part of the world to have been reoccupied at a much later date by local people, who have used the remains as a handy depository of ready-hewn stone blocks to build their own homes. Today's settlement is known as **Dudurga**, and the village mosque not only occupies the site of the baths but reuses pillars from the agora's stoa. Indeed the principal charm of Sidyma is how ancient masonry crops up everywhere: incorporated into house corners, used as livestock troughs, sprouting incongruously in courtyards next to satellite dishes. An exceedingly ruined **castle**, garrisoned in Byzantine times, sits on a hill to the north; scattered in the fields to the east, and requiring some scrambling over walls to reach, the **necropolis** holds various tomb types, though most have angular gabled roofs rather than the "Gothic" vaulted ones seen elsewhere.

Near the centre of the agricultural plain is a group of remarkable, contiguous **tombs**: one has ceiling panels carved with rosettes and human faces, while the adjacent tomb sports a relief of Eros on its lid and Medusas at the ends (a motif repeated elsewhere). Another spectacular cluster, including one tomb with two storeys, covers the low ridge beyond the fields.

The enormous, fairly intact, square structure in the middle of the necropolis is probably a Roman imperial **heroön** or temple-tomb. There's a walled-up doorway on its north side.

ARRIVAL AND DEPARTURE   SİDYMA

By car From Highway 400 take the turning marked for Eşen and "Sidyma, 13km", just north of a side road for Kumlova and Letoön. Turn left (south) at a junction 6km on, and it's just over 2km to the first buildings of Dodurga village, and another 3km to the road's end in Dodurga's

Asar Mahallesi, where two mulberry trees flank the ruins of the agora and a Lycian Way metal signpost.
On foot Trekking southeast on the Lycian Way, Sidyma is a day and a half's march from Kabak, via Alınca.

ACCOMMODATION

ALINCA
Dervish Lodge ☎ 0252 679 1142, ⓦ dervishlodge .com. Just off the Lycian Way at the top of Alınca village, with accommodation ranging from wooden bungalows (rates include half board) to log-house self-catering apartments (same rates, but without food), with views to die for. Non-trekkers can reach the lodge by dolmuş from Fethiye to Eşen village (30min), and also, for ₺20, be collected from it. **₺130**

KARAAĞAÇ
Black Tree Farm Karaağaç ☎ 0252 617 0045,

ⓦ blacktree.net. Some 3.5km beyond Alınca and located in extensive grounds, 1100m up and well off the trail, with rare Baba Dağı cedars nearby and a zoo's worth of animals on site. Accommodation comprises a restored trekkers' lodge with 16 dorm beds, and nine newer one- and three-bedroom cottages built in local stone and pine. There's a swimming pool, tennis courts and restaurant-bar serving simple lunches. A marked, non-Lycian Way trail links Karaağaç with Kirme, allowing the completion of circular hikes from Faralya (see p.303). Closed Nov–March. Dorm bed **€12**, one-bedroom cottage **€54**, three-bedroom cottage **€72**

The Letoön

Daily: summer 8.30am–8.30pm; winter 8.30am–5pm • ₺8 • Dolmuşes run from Fethiye to Kumluova village, 500m from the site; if driving, take a turning marked "Kumluova, Karadere, Letoön 10", turn right after 4km at another Letoön sign, and then left again after 4km more

Some 16km south of Pınara, the **Letoön**, shrine of the goddess **Leto**, was the official religious sanctuary, oracle and festival venue of the Lycian Federation, and extensive remaining ruins attest to its importance. Christianized following the demise of the federation, it was only abandoned after the Arab raids of the seventh century. The Letoön was initially rediscovered by Charles Fellows in 1840, although French-conducted digs didn't begin until 1962, since when it has been systematically uncovered and labelled.

THE LEGEND OF THE LETOÖN

In legend, the nymph **Leto** was loved by Zeus and thus jealously pursued by his wife Hera. Wandering in search of a place to give birth to her divine twins Apollo and Artemis, Leto approached a fountain to slake her thirst, only to be driven away by local herdsmen. Leto was then led by wolves to drink at the Xanthos River, and so changed the name of the country to Lycia, *lykos* being Greek for wolf. After giving birth, she returned to the spring – on the site of the existing **Letoön**, and forever after sacred to the goddess – to punish the insolent herdsmen by transforming them into frogs.

Excavations have uncovered the remains of three temples and a nymphaeum, as well as various **inscriptions**. One stipulates conditions of entry to the sanctuary, including a strict dress code prohibiting rich jewellery, ostentatious clothing or elaborate hairstyles.

The temples

The low ruins of three **temples** occupy the centre of the site, beyond the relatively uninteresting (and waterlogged) agora. The westernmost temple, straight ahead as you approach from the site gate, bears a dedication to Leto. Once surrounded by a single Doric colonnade with decorative half-columns around the interior walls, it dates from the third century BC. Three columns on the north side of the structure plus the cella (inner chamber) walls have been reconstructed; though the masonry seems jarringly garish, it was, in fact, sourced from the original marble quarry near modern Finike.

The central temple, partly carved out of the rock, is from the fourth century BC, identified by a dedication to Artemis. The easternmost temple was similar to the Leto temple. The reproduction **mosaic** on the floor – the original is now in the Fethiye museum – depicts a lyre, bow and quiver with a stylized flower in the centre. This suggests a joint dedication to Artemis and Apollo, the region's most revered deities, since the bow and quiver symbolized Artemis, and the lyre Apollo. The architecture and mosaic technique date the temple to the second and first centuries BC.

The nymphaeum and theatre

A rectangular **nymphaeum**, flanked by two semicircular recesses with statue niches, extends southwest beyond the temples. This is abutted by a semicircular paved basin 27m in diameter, now permanently flooded by the high local water table and full of ducks, terrapins and Leto's croaking victims (see box opposite). A **church** was built over the nymphaeum in the fourth century, but destroyed by Arab invaders in the seventh, so only its foundations and apse are now discernible. The notable stork mosaic on its floor is, alas, headless, though currently exposed to view.

Returning towards the car park, you'll reach a large, well-preserved Hellenistic **theatre**, entered through a vaulted passage. Sixteen plaques, adorned by comic and tragic relief **masks**, decorate the perilously collapsing northeast entrance to this passage. Nearby sits an interesting Roman **tomb**, with a carved representation of its toga-clad occupant.

Xanthos

Officially open daily: summer 8am–7.30pm, winter 8.30am–5pm; however, apart from the theatre area, the site is unfenced • ₺6 admission, plus parking fees

The remains of hilltop **Xanthos**, with their breathtaking views of the Xanthos River – now the Eşen Çayı – and its valley, are among the most fascinating in Lycia. The city was first made familiar in 1842, when Charles Fellows carried off the majority of its artworks, just four decades after the Elgin marbles had been similarly pillaged. It took two months to strip the site and load the loot onto the HMS *Beacon* for shipment to London. The most important artefact, the fourth-century **Nereid Monument**, a beautifully decorated Ionic temple on a high podium, is one of several items now in the British Museum. However, enough was left behind here to still require a two-hour visit.

Brief history

Xanthos is linked in legend with Bellerophon and Pegasus (see p.345). King Iobates – who initially set impossible tasks for Bellerophon and later offered him a share in his kingdom – ruled here, and Xanthos was the birthplace of Bellerophon's grandson, Glaukos, cited in the *Iliad* as "from the whirling waters of the Xanthos".

While the earliest archeological finds date to the eighth century BC, the city enters history in 540 BC during the conquest of Lycia by the Persian **Harpagos**, who besieged Xanthos. The Xanthians' response was the first local holocaust, in which they made a

5

funeral pyre of their families with their household goods. The women and children died in the flames while the men perished fighting, the only survivors being out of town at the time.

Xanthos subsequently shared the fate of all Lycia, with Alexander following the Persians, in turn succeeded by his general Antigonos and then by Antiochos III. After Antiochos's defeat, Xanthos was given to Rhodes along with the rest of Lycia. The second Xanthian holocaust occurred in 42 BC during the Roman civil war, when **Brutus**'s forces surrounded the city, prompting the citizens again to make funeral pyres of their possessions and immolate themselves. Xanthos prospered anew in Roman imperial times, and under Byzantine rule the city walls were renovated and a monastery built.

The site

The monumental **Arch of Vespasian** and an adjoining **Hellenistic gateway**, which bears an inscription of Antiochos III dedicating the city to Leto, Apollo and Artemis, stand alongside the access road from Kınık. East of the road, the former location of the **Nereid Monument** is marked by a plaque.

Theatre and acropolis

Xanthos's **Roman theatre**, near the summit of the access road, was built on the site of an earlier Greek structure and is pretty complete, missing only the upper seats, which were incorporated into the Byzantine city wall. Behind the theatre, overlooking the

XANTHOS

valley, lies the **Lycian acropolis**, in whose far southeastern corner are the square remains of what's probably an early Xanthian royal palace destroyed by Harpagos. Beneath protective sand, patches of sophisticated mosaic indicate Roman or Byzantine use of the acropolis. Water channels everywhere underfoot, and a huge cistern, suggest an advanced plumbing system and a preoccupation with outlasting sieges.

Pillar tombs

The **Harpy Tomb**, in front of the theatre to the north, was originally topped with a marble chamber that was removed by Fellows, and now replaced by a cement-cast reproduction. The paired bird-women figures on its north and south sides are identified as harpies, or – more likely – sirens, carrying the souls of the dead (represented as children) to the Isles of the Blessed. Other reliefs portray unidentified seated figures receiving gifts, except for the west face where they are regarding opium poppies. Beside the Harpy Tomb a third-century BC **Lycian sarcophagus** stands on a pillar. Traces of a corpse and pottery were found inside, along with a sixth-century BC relief – brought from elsewhere – depicting funeral games.

Just northeast of the Roman agora, the so-called **Xanthian Obelisk** is in fact another pillar tomb, labelled as the "Inscribed Pillar" and covered on all four sides by the longest-known Lycian inscription, 250 lines including twelve lines of Greek verse. Since the Lycian language hasn't been completely deciphered, interpretation of the inscription is based on this verse, which glorifies a champion local wrestler.

The rest of the site

East of the car park, then south through the "**late**" agora, lies a **Byzantine basilica**, fenced off but easy enough to enter – beware unauthorized guides offering incomprehensible and overpriced "tours". The basilica features extensive abstract **mosaics** – the best in western Turkey – and a synthronon (seating area) in the semicircular apse. On the **Roman acropolis** to the north are various freestanding **sarcophagi**, and above, cut into the hillside, picturesque **tombs** mainly of the Lycian house (as opposed to temple) type. A well-preserved early **Byzantine monastery**, with washbasins along one side of its courtyard, stands further north.

ARRIVAL AND DEPARTURE	**XANTHOS**

By bus Dolmuşes between Fethiye and Patara drop passengers at Kınık, less than 2km beyond the southerly Letoön turn-off, from where the site is a 20min uphill walk.

By organized tour Xanthos features on many organized excursions, usually in tandem with the Letoön.

Gelemiş

The laidback village of **GELEMİŞ**, around 75km southeast of Fethiye and 15km northwest of the resort of Kalkan, serves as the base for visitors to explore the remarkable beachfront ruins of ancient **Patara** (see p.321) and enjoy its eponymous **beach**, the longest in Turkey. Owing to the fame of the beach and ruins, Gelemiş itself is usually referred to by locals and visitors alike as Patara – though SatNav users need to enter Gelemiş rather than Patara to find the village. Set back a couple of kilometres from the beach, Gelemiş consists of a busy T-junction, with a main, crescent-shaped neighbourhood threaded by a single twisting high street extending west, and then uphill. Before 1950, the entire area was malarial – a municipal truck still sprays pesticide on spring nights – and the nomadic *Yörük*s who wintered here spent the hottest months up in the healthier mountain village of İslamlar, near Gömbe.

Over the last few years, Gelemiş has smartened itself up considerably. A decent crop of cafés, restaurants and even bars now makes it perfectly possible to enjoy a little low-key nightlife around the T-junction centre.

ARRIVAL AND INFORMATION

By bus and dolmuş Regular minibuses from Kalkan and Kaş stop in the centre near the PTT. Dolmuşes from Fethiye, long-haul buses and all intercity buses drop passengers on the roundabout on Highway 400, 3.5km from the centre, connected by dolmuş to the village every 45min.

Destinations Antalya (8 daily; 5hr); Fethiye (8 daily; 1hr 15min); Kalkan (8 daily; 30min); Kaş (8 daily; 1hr).

Activities Agencies in the village offer activities that take advantage of Patara's natural beauty, including horseriding,

GELEMIŞ

canoeing on the Eşen Çayı, scuba diving, and walking on the Lycian Way. Reputable operators include Gelemiş Turizm (☎0242 843 5257, ⊛pataraviewpoint.com/gelemis-tours .html), Kırca Travel (☎0242 843 5298, ⊛pataracanoeing .com and ⊛patarahorseriding.com), and St Nicholas Travel (☎0535 416 2416, ⊛patarabeachadventure.com).

Hamam The town's small hamam (☎0537 633 7970; daily 9am–9pm) has a good reputation, with a bath, scrub and massage for ₺40.

ACCOMMODATION

★**Akay** ☎0242 843 5055, ⊛pataraakaypension.com. Kazim and Ayşe provide keen management and excellent cooking. It's set on the right of the main road as you approach the village from Highway 400 and rooms – best facing away from the road – are plain but spotless, with orthopedic mattresses and mosquito nets. A small pool adds to the *Akay's* charm. **€38**

Bademli Apartments Tömler Sok 3 ☎0242 843 5184, ⊛apartmentsinpatara.com. Owned and very professionally run by Muzaffer and Anne-Louise of the *Patara Viewpoint Hotel*, the four apartments in this detached house with pool are all of a very high standard. The pair on the top floor have long balconies with superb views over the encircling orchards, and there are sea views from the communal terrace. Weekly rate for one-bed apartments **£400**, two-bed apartments **£500**

★**B&B Camelion** ☎0536 643 9199, ⊛bbcamelion -com.webnode.nl. Perched among olive groves at the end of a windy dirt track 6km southwest of Gelemiş village (and a 15min walk from the sea), you couldn't hope to find a more unspoiled and unobtrusive hideaway – no wonder it's called *Camelion* (chameleon). Set in a beautifully designed contemporary-style house, it's a family affair, with the Turkish-Belgian couple who run it living on the first floor, and guests in the four rooms (some en suite) on the floor above. Great pool, great vistas and good organic home cooking too. **€60**

Camel Camping ☎0538 0824 410, ⊛pataraviewpoint .com. Cheapest accommodation in town, just south of the centre and close to both its own and the other village bars, this is the impecunious backpackers' prime choice In

Gelemiş. The tiny A-framed two-person cabins are basic, the pitching ground hard, but at these prices who cares? Two-person tent pitch **₺10**, cabin **₺30**

Flower Pension ☎0242 843 5164, ⊛pataraflower pension.com. The first noteworthy *pansiyon* as you approach the village from Highway 400, with tidy bathrooms. Ayşe cooks up delicious meals (and breakfast) on the terrace overlooking a lush garden. Very popular with Lycian Way walkers, who appreciate its small pool. **₺100**

Golden Lighthouse Hotel ☎0242 843 5107, ⊛pataragoldenlighthouse.com. Quiet yet central, on the north edge of the village centre above the mosque, this hotel has large airy rooms with plain white decor, a/c and spotless bathrooms, plus an unusually large pool. Double **₺100**, four-bed family room **₺200**

Golden Pansiyon ☎0242 843 5162, ⊛pataragolden pension.com. Mayor Arif Otlu caters to budget travellers, with fairly large rooms (some balconied, all double-glazed and with a/c) near the crossroads in the village centre. The first pension to open in the village (back in 1984), it has consistently maintained its good reputation. **₺100**

★**Patara Viewpoint Hotel** Gedik Sok 11 ☎0242 843 5184, ⊛pataraviewpoint.com. Muzaffer Otlu's and Anne-Louise Thomson's hotel enjoys an unbeatable setting on the easterly ridge. The tastefully decorated and furnished rooms have mosquito nets, balconies, heating and a/c. There's a shuttle to the beach, a pool-bar where breakfast is served, a Turkish-style night-time terrace with fireplace – and even a replica Lycian stone beehive out front. Good-value weekly rates. Local history buff Muzaffer offers fascinating private tours to assorted regional sights. Closed Dec–Feb. **₺225**

EATING AND DRINKING

CAFÉS AND RESTAURANTS

Aspendos ☎0541 715 4100. This quirky rooftop place south of the village centre has a jaunty blue and white nautical theme, with lifebuoys hung from the railings. Try the baked trout for ₺17 or the *köfte* for a bargain ₺15. Daily 8am–midnight.

Patara Gözleme Evi/Esra's Pancake House The best of several simple places in the village centre, specializing in *gözleme* (₺5 and up), eaten either at small tables or

nomad-style on cushions on the floor. As well as the standard flavours, there are 11 sweet pancakes plus *menemen* and *mantı* and, bizarrely, smoothies. The home-made *ayran* is tangy and delicious. Daily 8am–10pm.

Tlos ☎0242 843 5135. One of the longest-established and still the best of the stand-alone restaurants in Gelemiş, right in the centre and serving big platters of hearty food such as *pide* (from ₺7) and *güveç* (₺18). Daily 8am–midnight.

BARS

Gypsy Bar Just south of the village centre, this funky, rustic place is constructed from dark wood and has a pleasant upstairs terrace and mock ships'-wheel light fittings. Singers of three songs on the popular karaoke nights get a free drink. Beers ₺10. Daily 9am–2am.

Medusa Alongside *Gypsy*, just south of the centre, this place has occasional live Turkish music, best enjoyed lounging on one of the kilim-cushioned benches. Beers and glasses of wine ₺10, cocktails from ₺20. Daily 9am–2am.

Sim Bar The new kid on the block, this bar is centrally located in a colonial-style bungalow next to the post office, and has special evenings such as reggae nights. Outdoor area in the summer. Beers ₺10. Daily 9am–2am.

Patara

Daily: May–Oct 7.30am–7.30pm; Nov–April 8am–5pm • ₺5; PlajKarts, valid for ten days, allow multiple entry to the site, for multiple users; 10 entries ₺7.5, 25 entries ₺15 • Served by local dolmuşes from Gelemiş in summer

Some 2km south of Gelemiş village, **Patara** was once the principal port of Lycia, famed for its oracle of Apollo, and as the birthplace in the fourth century AD of St Nicholas, Bishop of Myra (aka Santa Claus). Today, however, the area is better known for its huge sandy **beach**, a turtle-nesting area in summer that's off-limits after dark (May–Oct), while in winter the **lagoon** behind attracts considerable birdlife. Conservationists backed by the Ministry of the Environment have managed to exclude villas from the cape at the southeast end of the strand, while the area's protected archeological status has halted most new building at Gelemiş.

Brief history

Legend ascribes Greek origins to Patara, but in fact the city was originally **Lycian**, borne out by coins and inscriptions sporting an un-Hellenic PTTRA. The city was famous for its temple and oracle of **Apollo**, which supposedly rivalled Delphi's for accuracy, because Apollo was said to winter in the Xanthos valley. However, no verifiable traces of this temple have ever been found.

Patara served as a **naval base** during the wars between Alexander's successors. Later, in 42 BC, **Brutus** threatened the Patarans with a similar fate to the Xanthians (see p.317) if they didn't submit, giving them a day to decide. He released the women hostages in the hope that they would lessen the resolve of their menfolk. When this didn't work, Brutus freed all the remaining hostages, thereby endearing himself to the Patarans, who subsequently surrendered. Whatever his tactics, his chief motive was suggested by the fact that he exacted no other punishments, but merely confiscated the city's gold and silver.

The site

A gate and ticket booth controls vehicle access to both the beach at Patara and the **archeological site** beyond. Although the ruins are unfenced, visitors are not allowed in outside the official opening times. Despite ongoing digs, much of Patara remains unexcavated, and only a few paths link the individual ruins. There are no facilities or shade – bring water, stout shoes and a head covering during summer.

The city's entrance is marked by a triple-arched, first-century AD **Roman gateway**, almost completely intact. A head of Apollo has been found on a little hill just west, prompting speculation that his temple was nearby. Outside the gate, a **necropolis** is being excavated by a team from Antalya's Akdeniz University.

The Roman baths

South of the hill near the entrance to Patara there's a **baths complex**, similar to Yedi Kapı at Tlos, with arches and five rectangular apsidal windows. An exotic touch is lent to nearby foundations of either a **basilica** or an extension of the baths by a palm grove that sprouts from the floor and almost totally obscures it. West of these, tacked onto the longest surviving stretch of **city walls** – and difficult to reach – is an attractive

5

second-century **temple**. While too modest to be the famous local Apollo shrine, it has a richly decorated 7m-high doorframe – its lintel on the point of collapse – leading into a single chamber.

Further south, reached by a different track, are more **baths** built by Emperor Vespasian (69–79 AD), impressing mainly by their squat bulk. Just west of these lies a large paved main agora or a processional street, with its north end submerged by the high local water table, and a growing number of re-erected columns.

The theatre and bouleuterion

Patara's **theatre**, under the brow of the acropolis hill southwest of the baths, is best reached by a track that heads off the main road, just before the beach car park. The **cavea** has been cleaned of sand to reveal eighteen rows of seats up to the **diazoma** (dividing walkway), and a dozen more beyond. The stage building is slowly being reassembled; a Greek inscription outside ascribes its erection to a woman, Vilia Prokla, and her father, both citizens of Patara. Funding for it was approved by the Lycian Federation's assembly, which apparently met in the **bouleuterion**, between the theatre and the agora, with a horseshoe array of seating. The restoration – critics would say, rebuilding – of this fine council chamber building, which held over 1400 citizens, was completed in 2012, and it's arguably the finest example of its kind in Turkey.

The acropolis area

A reasonable path climbs uphill, south of the theatre, to reach the city's **acropolis**. At the top lurks an unusual rectangular pit, 10m across, with a pillar (for measuring water level) rearing out of the bottom and badly damaged stairs down its side. This was almost certainly a **cistern**, and not the **lighthouse** as originally supposed; that is the square, arched tower, its top collapsed, on the west side of the hill, which still has a fine view over the sea, beach and brackish swamp that was once the **harbour**. After gradually silting up in the Middle Ages, the harbour was abandoned, and is now separated from the beach by 300m-wide dunes. On the far side of the swamp, across the dunes, stand the bulky remains of **Hadrian's granary**.

The beach

Patara's fine white-sand **beach** ranks as one of the longest continuous strands in the Mediterranean: it measures 9km from the access road to the mouth of the Eşen Çayı, and then another 6km to the end. Rather than making the hot, half-hour stroll out from the centre of Gelemiş in summer, most visitors take a **beach dolmuş** or transport laid on by the hotels. Parking (free) at the road's end is limited, as the archeological authorities have refused permission to expand the space. The sole café is run by the owner (and local mayor) of the *Golden Lighthouse* and *Golden Pension* and is no more expensive than the places in the village. Local youth are employed and all proceeds go into the village community chest.

In season the immediate vicinity of the beach entrance gets **crowded**, but walking northwest past the dunes brings you to plenty of solitary spots – and a few unharassed colonies of nudists. Spring and autumn **swimming** is delightful, but in summer the exposed shoreline can be battered by body-surfable waves.

Kalkan and around

The former Greek fishing village of **Kalkan** is today a very popular upmarket resort. Its population of four thousand includes some 1500 expats, two-thirds of whom are British, and most of the small boutique hotels that used to be Kalkan's lifeblood have been converted into apartments and second homes. The surviving package-holiday trade dominates the remaining short-stay accommodation, and ensures that Kalkan remains more exclusive than nearby Kaş. Once you accept the resort's pervasive social profile, lack of a proper sandy beach and the fact that restaurants, though good, are uniformly overpriced, Kalkan makes a good base for exploring Patara and the Xanthos valley, while **excursions** east or inland might occupy another day or so.

Kalkan

Once the Greek Orthodox village of Kalamaki, **KALKAN**, 15km southeast of Patara, tumbles down a steep slope to a smart marina. Despite the rash of new villas and apartments spreading over the hillsides around, the compact centre has retained many of its nineteenth-century Greek houses, many now serving as restaurants and bars, and much of its charm. Tourism and property sales, now the town's *raison d'être*, are fairly new phenomena: until the late 1970s both Kalkan and neighbouring Kaş eked out a living from charcoal burning and olives. It's hard today to imagine it as it was in the 1980s, when its rather bohemian atmosphere contrasted starkly with the often oppressive conditions prevailing in Turkish cities after the 1980 coup.

Halk Plajı

Hire of two sunbeds and an umbrella costs ₺15

The artificially supplemented mixed sand-and-pebble **Halk Plajı** (People's Beach), just to the left of the marina entrance, is pleasant enough and has a Blue Flag rating. Unfortunately, it gets hopelessly full in summer, when the sunbeds are at a premium.

Beach clubs

The alternative to Halk Plajı beach is to take a free boat from Kalkan's marina to one of the so-called "**beach clubs**" owned and run by local hotels, where swimming is from platforms and food and watersports are on offer. There are several dotted around the bay, and all provide free boat services to their establishments from the waterfront/ marina. The *Caretta Beach Club* (☎0242 844 3435) charges ₺10, though entry sunloungers are free if you eat at their restaurant. Other clubs include *Palm Beach Club* (☎0242 844 3987, ⓦpalmbeachkalkan.com; ₺20) and the upmarket *Mahal Beach Club* (☎0242 844 3268, ⓦvillamahal.com; ₺25).

ARRIVAL AND INFORMATION   KALKAN

By bus Kalkan's *otogar* is at the very top of town, by the roundabout on the bypass road.
Destinations Antalya (7 daily; 4hr 30min); Bodrum (1 daily; 6hr); Fethiye (every 30min; 1hr 20min); Istanbul (1 daily; 15hr); İzmir (2 daily; 8hr); Kaş (every 30min; 30min); Marmaris (2 daily; 4hr 30min); Patara/Gelemiş

(14 daily; 30min).
Boat trips The other popular way to sunbathe and swim is to take a boat trip from the marina, taking in assorted islands and bays, for around ₺60 including lunch (ⓦkalkanboattrip.com).

ACCOMMODATION

A handful of surviving *pansiyons* occupy converted old buildings lining the central grid of lanes – **Yalıboyu district** – that drops from Hasan Altan Sokağı down to the harbour, and merges east into Dereboyu towards the ravine. There's also a district of newer, purpose-built hotels extending 1.5km west along **Kalamar Yolu**, towards Kalamar Bay. Most such establishments are block-booked by tour operators; larger rooms, and swimming pools, offset the disadvantage of a hefty walk into town.

Caretta Boutique Hotel İskele Sok 3 ☎0242 844 3435, ⓦcarettahotelkalkan.com. Housed in the last building on the west bay shore, 1.5km west of town via a bumpy gravel road, this cult *pansiyon*-restaurant, suffused with the character of owner/chef Gönül Kocabaş, has a loyal Turkish and UK following. Rooms are

generally bright and white, with stone floors and terraces, though those at the rear, with side-on sea views from the balcony, are a little dark. There's a swimming pool with stunning views. Closed early Nov to Easter. Rear room €65, sea-view room €90
★**Courtyard Hotel** 5 Nolu Sok ☎0242 844 3738 or

5

SCUBA DIVING NEAR KALKAN

Most of the twenty-odd **dive sites** near Kalkan are 25–40min away by boat, with many located around the islets at the mouth of the bay. Of these, beginners dive the shallows at the north tip of **Yılan Adası** (Snake Island), and almost the entire perimeter of the remoter Heybeli; another excellent novice or second-dive-of-day venue is **Frank Wall** on the east side of the bay, with spectacular rock pinnacles and plenty of fish. More advanced divers are taken to an even more dramatic wall between 20m and 50m at the south tip of "Snake", alive with barracuda, grouper and myriad smaller fish; to reefs off Heybeli and Öksüz; or to sand-bottom **caves** on the mainland with their entrances at 25m.

The most spectacular calm-weather dive site, for intermediate and advanced divers, is **Sakarya Reef**, southeast of Kalkan off İnce Burun. Here, the mangled remains of the *Duchess of York*, a North Sea trawler built in Hull in 1893 and apparently scuttled for an insurance payout sometime after 1930, lie in 15m of water. However, more interesting is the newer, larger Turkish-built *Sakarya* nearby, wrecked in the 1940s, broken into three sections at depths of 35–60m, and retaining teak-plank decking, intact winches and a vast cargo of lead ballast.

Except in the caves, fed by chilly fresh water, **water temperatures** are a comfortable 18–30°C; the sea warms up abruptly in late May or early June with a current change, and stays warm into November. **Visibility** is typically 25–30m.

The two local dive operators are **Dolphin Scuba Team**, working off its boat in Kalkan's main port (☎0242 844 2242 or ☎0542 627 9757, ⊛dolphinscubateam.com), and **Kalkan Diving/Aquasports**, at the Kalamar Beach Club (☎0242 844 2361 or ☎0532 553 2006, ⊛kalkandiving .com). **Prices** are competitive, with two-dive mornings from £45/€60, and a PADI Open Water course from £235/€310.

☎0532 443 0012, ⊛courtyardkalkan.com. Three 1920s Greek properties have been beautifully converted into six elegant a/c rooms ranged around a courtyard, which boasts pretty black-and-white pebble mosaic flooring. Bed linen is crisp and white, bathrooms luxurious and wherever possible the original wood features of the old houses has been retained. Anglo-Turkish hosts Marion and Halil are always on hand to help guests get the best from their stay. Closed early Nov to Easter. ₺448

Gül Pansiyon Şehitler Cad, Sok 7 ☎0242 844 3099, ⊛kalkangulpansiyon.com. Perched 300m above the waterfront, and enjoying expansive views from the roof terrace, this long-standing family-run pension is very good value for Kalkan. There's a mix of six a/c doubles, all with balconies, and three slightly more expensive apartments with kitchens. ₺100

★**Türk Evi (Eski Ev)** Şehitler Cad 19 ☎0242 844 3129, ⊛kalkanturkevi.com. Near the top of a lane heading up from Süleyman Yılmaz Cad in Yalıboyu, this wonderfully refurbished old house features welcoming common areas and rooms with kilims and, in some cases, fireplaces. Open in winter by arrangement (there's no other heating). ₺60

Viewpoint Villas Kalamar Yolu ☎0242 844 3642,

⊛viewpointvillaskalkan.com. Halfway along Kalamar Yolu, on the uphill side, these six villas arranged around a pool are equipped to a very high standard – jacuzzi, full kitchen, fireplace in sitting room – and each sleep four to five. Weekly rate ₺600

★**Villa Mahal** Mahal Yolu ☎0242 844 3268, ⊛villamahal.com. Kalkan's most exclusive lodging, 1.5km from town on the east bay shore, has road access, but is best approached on a free boat shuttle from the harbour. A segmented veranda wraps itself around ten irregularly shaped rooms, some with huge bathrooms and private massage rooms. Steps descend past an infinity pool to the sea and lido – one of the few in Kalkan directly linked to accommodation, though open to the public for the sake of its popular restaurant. Closed Nov–April. €220

White House Pension 5 Nolu Sok ☎0242 844 3738 or ☎0532 443 0012, ⊛kalkanwhitehouse.co.uk. With large, airy, pine- and white-tile rooms ranging from singles to quads, this is one of Kalkan's best pensions. Although only four rooms have balconies, the roof terrace is one of the best in town, with superb sea views – a great place to enjoy the wonderful breakfast. Co-hosts Marion and Halil also run the adjacent *Courtyard Hotel*. Closed early Nov to Easter. ₺269

EATING AND DRINKING

Kalkan has a ridiculous number of **restaurants** for a town this size, the majority located between the **marina promenade** and lively **Süleyman Yılmaz Caddesi**, set well above the harbour. **Bars** tend to cluster either just above the seafront or along **Hasan Altan Sokağı**, which after dark becomes the main pedestrianized drag into the village centre. Meal prices are high for Turkey, though service is usually very good.

CAFÉS AND RESTAURANTS

Aubergine İskele Sok ☎0242 844 3332. This upmarket Turkish/international restaurant offers elegant marina-front dining, with comfy bamboo chairs pulled up to white-clothed tables. Generous salads from ₺18, fajitas and pizzas ₺25 and up. More sophisticated dishes such as fish start at ₺30. Daily 8am–2am.

Hünkar Ocakbaşı Şehitler Cad 38 ☎0242 844 2077. Excellent value by Kalkan standards, this is the place to come for a superb charcoal-grilled kebab (from ₺18), served on a flatbread base and accompanied by a salad, *ezme* (spicy tomato dip) and *haydari* (yoghurt and garlic dip). It's a small place and there can be queues to get a seat. Daily 10am–midnight.

Iso's Kitchen Süleyman Yılmaz Cad 39 ☎0242 844 2415. This characterful little restaurant is tucked away at the end of an atmospheric cobbled alley that is fast becoming one of the liveliest spots in town. Try to bag a table on the terrace for sea views before settling down to an array of *meze* (₺7 and up) washed down with a cold beer (₺10), and followed by *köfte* (₺23) or fish (₺25 and up). Daily 9am–2am.

★**Korsan Meze/Korsan Balık** Atatürk Cad ☎0242 844 3622. Some 75m up and in from the harbour, this long-established and elegant pair of restaurants offer arguably the best eating in Kalkan. The kitchen is in an attractive traditional building, the terrace of which specializes in fish, with sea bream costing ₺30. The *Meze* terrace, prettily decked out in blue and white, fronts the building and overlooks the harbour. Traditional Turkish starters from ₺9. Mid-April to Oct daily 10am–midnight.

★**Salonika 1881** Süleyman Yılmaz Cad ☎0242 844 2422. Proving the old adage that small is beautiful, this cross between a traditional *meyhane* (tavern) and contemporary restaurant, fashioned from a tiny fishermens' cottage, is a great addition to Kalkan's dining scene. Experienced owner Rasul puts everything into ensuring customer satisfaction. Starters include spicy *muhammara*, made from walnuts, bread and hot pepper (₺9); for a satisfying main try the sea bass stuffed with cream, mushrooms and shrimp (₺46). Reservations advised. (Closed Jan & Feb). Daily 10am–midnight.

BARS AND CLUBS

Botanik Süleyman Yılmaz Cad ☎0535 470 9099. Set in a lush grove of olive and citrus trees, *Botanik* quite correctly advertises itself as Kalkan's last garden. It's about as bohemian as this conservative place gets, with friendly Robert Plant lookalike and former guide Namak and compadres in charge of the curved bar. Cocktails are popular, and beer drinkers get a free supply of popcorn to keep them going. Beers ₺12. Daily 11am–2am.

Mojito Lounge & Club Mustafa Kocakaya Cad ☎0242 844 3985. Kalkan's most sophisticated nightlife venue, with DJ sets every night, sometimes fronted by a saxophonist. Decor is white on white, though subdued lighting gives the place a soothing ambience. There are five varieties of mojito on offer (₺28) and other cocktails ranging from ₺26 to ₺45. Daily 7pm–3am.

Yalı Hasan Altan Cad ☎0242 844 1001. On a busy corner, with a big LCD TV out on the street, this bustling place is great for smoothies (₺12) in the day and reasonably priced drinks in the evening (beers ₺12, glass of wine ₺15). Daily 9am–2am.

İslamlar

Dramatically set, high in the mountains 8km north of Kalkan, **İSLAMLAR** has long provided a summer refuge from the steamy heat of the coast. The village's old name of Bodamya – Ottoman Greek for "rivers" – remains in use, and it is indeed alive to the sound of falling water, used to power mills and nurture various trout-farm **restaurants**. Local accommodation is partly the preserve of the more upmarket package companies and partly – appropriately enough given its name – of conservative Turkish Muslims seeking a secluded destination.

ARRIVAL AND DEPARTURE   İSLAMLAR

By car Take the Sütlüğen/Elmalı road from the town-edge roundabout, then the first unsigned left, and turn right at the top of the inclination.

EATING AND DRINKING

★**Çiftlik** ☎0242 838 6055. Budget favourite just south of the village square doing good *kızartma* vegetables with a large trout garnished with olives, peppers and *yufka* for around ₺14 a portion. Daily 10am–11pm.

Değirmen ☎0242 838 6295. Posh option with a seasonally working mill in the basement grinding locally grown sesame seeds, which you can have served with *pekmez* or grape molasses. South of the village square. Credit cards accepted. Daily 10am–11pm.

5

Bezirgan

The attractive upland pasture village of **BEZİRGAN** lies 17km northeast of Kalkan. Famous in the past for its horses, but today devoted to barley, sesame, chickpeas and orchard crops, this fertile plain was a prehistoric lake, drained finally by an ingenious Roman tunnel. The hillside holds a sprinkling of Lycian rock tombs and an ancient citadel.

By studying the Lycian Way map, you can fashion a **loop walk** with the *ova* (plain) as pivot; only 1.6km separates the two intersections of the path with the ascending road from Kalkan, and indeed this circular walk is offered as an organized outing. On your own, take a minibus from Kalkan's top roundabout to Bezirgan – there are two daily from Kınık bound for Gömbe – and then walk back to Kalkan in about three hours.

ARRIVAL AND DEPARTURE
BEZİRGAN

By car Drive north from Kalkan to join Highway 400, then follow the sign for Elmalı. Follow another sign 1km along, towards Sütleğen/Elmalı, then turn left for Bezirgan after another 10km.

ACCOMMODATION

★ Owlsland ☎ 0242 837 5214 or ☎ 0535 940 1715, ⓦ owlsland.com. Turkish Erol and Scottish Pauline's excellent and well-signposted 150-year-old village-house inn is named after the scops and little owls resident in the nearby almond trees. It lies about 600m off the Lycian Way at the northwest edge of Bezirgan, making it a logical stop on the trek; Erol is a mean cook and you're well advised to have half board. At 720m elevation, you'll need the woodstoves in the minimally restored en-suite rooms during spring or autumn. Rates include breakfast; half board available for €20 per person. Closed Dec–Feb. **€45**

Kaputaş beach

Sunbed and umbrella rental ₺10

The deep canyon known as **Kaputaş Gorge** slashes back into the cliffs on the beautiful coastal road to Kaş, just under 6km southeast of of Kalkan. Steps from the roadside parking area – where there's a *jandarma* post, and signs warning you not to leave valuables in cars (break-ins are rife when the *jandarma* aren't patrolling) – take you down to **Kaputaş beach**. This 150m expanse of pebbles and blonde sand is normally pretty packed, and has a beach café and (poor) toilets.

Kaş and around

Until 1923, **KAŞ** was a small, Greek-populated shipping port, dwarfed by the rock-cut tomb-riddled cliffs that tower behind it, and with views out to sea dominated by the nearby Greek island of **Kastellórizo** (Meis). Today, despite the fact that tourism has made inexorable inroads, with new development sprawling up every slope that's short of being totally precipitous, and the sleepy winter-time population of around eight thousand multiplying in summer, Kaş remains at heart a small town. The tombs, cliffs and views out to sea remain as lovely as ever as well, though the Greek Christians who once admired them were replaced after the 1923 population exchanges by Muslim Turks.

The fact that the local beaches are hardly stellar, along with the lack of a really convenient airport, has spared Kaş the full impact of modern tourism. However, it gets lively at night, since shops stay open until 1am in season, and bars much later still. The modern town is built atop ancient **Antiphellos**, whose remaining ruins speckle the streets and cover the base of the Çukurbağ peninsula. A handy base from which to reach Kekova and nearby Patara, Kaş has also become the "adventure capital" of the southwest Turkish coast, offering all sorts of sea- and mountain-based **outdoor activities**.

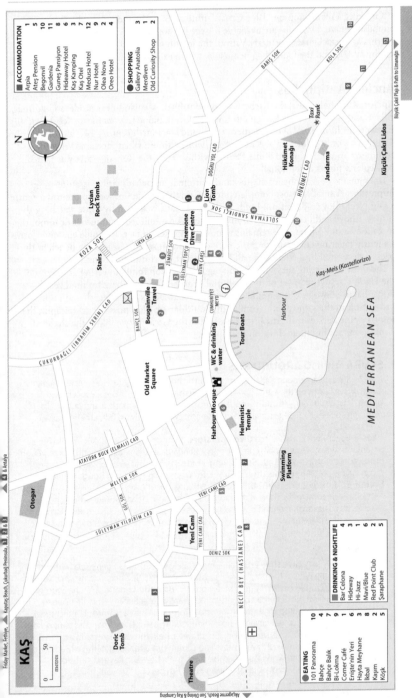

KAŞ

N

MEDITERRANEAN SEA

Kaş-Meis (Kastellorizo)

Harbour

ACCOMMODATION

Arpia	1
Ateş Pension	5
Begonvil	10
Gardenia	11
Guneş Pansiyon	8
Hideaway Hotel	6
Kaş Kamping	3
Kaş Otel	7
Medusa Hotel	12
Nur Hotel	9
Olea Nova	2
Oreo Hotel	4

SHOPPING

Gallery Anatolia	3
Merdiven	1
Old Curiosity Shop	2

EATING

101 Panorama	10
Bahçe	4
Bahçe Balik	7
Bi-Lokma	9
Corner Café	1
Enişte'nin Yeri	6
Hayta Meyhane	3
İkbal	8
Kaşım	2
Köşk	5

DRINKING & NIGHTLIFE

Bar Celona	4
Hideway	1
Hi-Jazz	3
Mavi/Blue	6
Red Point Club	2
Şaraphane	5

Lycian Rock Tombs

Stairs

KOZA SOK

LINYA CAD

ÇUKURBAĞLI (İBRAHİM SERİN) CAD

Bougainville Travel

BAHÇE SOK

Old Market Square

ATATÜRK BULV (ELMALI) CAD

MELTEM SOK

GÜL SOK

Otogar

SÜLEYMAN YILDIRIM CAD

YENİ CAMİ CAD

Yeni Cami

YENİ CAMİ CAD

DENİZ SOK

NECİP BEY (HASTANE) CAD

Doric Tomb

Theatre

Harbour Mosque

WC & drinking water

Hellenistic Temple

Swimming Platform

Tour Boats

CUMHURİYET MEYD

ZÜMRÜT SOK

SÜLEYMAN TOPÇU

UZUN ÇARŞI

Anemone Dive Centre

Lion Tomb

DOĞRU YOL CAD

SÜLEYMAN SANDIKÇI SOK

Taxi Rank

Hükümet Konağı

HÜKÜMET CAD

Jandarma

BARIŞ SOK

KOLA SOK

Küçük Çakıl Lidos

0   50
metres

5

Kaş being a major stop on "Blue Cruise" itineraries, **yacht and gulet culture** is well established here. Day-trips are available for the less well-heeled, while there's a new yacht marina at **Bucak Limanı** (formerly Vathy), the long fjord west of town, wedged between Highway 400 and the Çukurbağ peninsula, which extends 5km southwest of Kaş.

Ancient Antiphellos

Ancient **Antiphellos** was the harbour of ancient Phellos, inland near modern Çukurbağ village and one of the few Lycian cities with a Greek name (*phellos* means "cork oak"). Excavations have dated the settlement to around the fourth century BC, although Antiphellos only gained importance in Hellenistic times, when increased seagoing commerce meant it thrived while Phellos withered. By the Roman era, it was famed particularly for its exceptionally soft sponges.

The remains of Antiphellos are few and scattered, but what's visible is quite impressive. A small, almost complete Hellenistic **theatre**, 500m west of the town centre along Necip Bey Caddesi, still holds 26 rows of seats, well used by those watching the sunset. Above and behind here, 100m northeast on a hilltop, a unique **Doric tomb**, the so-called Kesme Mezar, also remains almost completely intact. Its single chamber forms a slightly tapering cube cut from the rock on which it stands; inside, the bench at the back is decorated by a frieze of small female figures performing a dance.

The most interesting surviving sarcophagus is the **Lion Tomb**, towering at the top of the Uzun Çarşı. The lower of its two burial chambers forms a base for the Lycian sarcophagus above it. On the side of the lower chamber is an undeciphered Lycian inscription in the same poetic form as the Xanthian obelisk, possibly an epitaph. The tomb's name derives from the lifting bosses for the Gothic-style lid, in the shape of lions' heads resting their chins on their paws.

SCUBA DIVING AROUND KAŞ

The Mediterranean around Kaş offers arguably the best **visibility** (up to 30m) and greatest range of sea life along the entire Turkish coast. **Fish** you're likely to see – especially in spring or late summer – include grouper, barracuda, amberjack, garfish and ray; smaller common species include cardinal fish, damselfish, parrotfish, flying fish, ornate wrasse, bream and pandora.

Kaş notionally holds around ten **dive operators**, many operating out of Küçük Çakıl hotel basements, but in terms of boat comfort, safety standards, equipment condition and thorough instruction, only three stand out: **Sun Diving**, inside *Kaş Camping* (☎0242 836 2637, ⊛sundiving.com), **Anemone**, Uzun Çarşı Sok 16 (☎0242 836 3651), and **Bougainville Diving**, Çukurbağlı Cad 10 (☎0242 836 3737, ⊛bougainville-turkey.com).

It's quite common to dive only in the morning or afternoon, so **prices** are per dive rather than per day. The recommended operators advertise single dives from €30, making Kaş the least expensive place to dive in Turkey. A PADI Open Water course costs €299, and advanced Open Water €245.

DIVE SITES

There are nearly sixty **dive sites** in the area, many along the Çukurbağ peninsula, with most others around the islets at the marine frontier with Kastellórizo. Beginners visit a tunnel at 15m and a shoreline cave fed by an icy freshwater spring in **Bayındır Limanı**, or "Stone Edge" or **Güvercin Adası** off the Çukurbağ peninsula. Moderately experienced divers are taken to "**Canyon**", where they drop through the namesake formation past a reasonably intact Greek cotton-carrying freighter that ran aground in the 1960s. This was later dynamited to remove the navigational hazard, so its stern lies in 35m of water. Next there's a traverse of a big-wall drop-off, and then a return north with prevailing currents via a tunnel system. Only advanced divers can visit a wrecked World War II bomber shot down between Kaş and Kastellórizo, resting nearly intact in 65m of water at "**Flying Fish**", just beyond "Canyon".

CANYONING ABOVE KAŞ

Most **canyoning** outings from Kaş focus on one of two stream canyons: Hacıoğlan Çayı or Kıbrıs Çayı. The former traverse, starting near **Hacıoğlan** village east of Bezirgan, makes a good beginners' spring expedition of 6hr, finishing at Dereköy, with plenty of easy slides and long swims as well as one 6m abseil about two-thirds of the way along. In summer the action shifts to **Kıbrıs Çayı**, which retains water all year and, while shorter, takes the same time to emerge at Beldibi, with two abseils and two zip-wire transits. There are several recommended agencies offering canyoning (see p.330); days out typically cost €50.

The beaches of Kaş

Considering that Kaş is a major Turkish resort, local natural beaches are surprisingly poor. In town itself, **Küçük Çakıl** has been pretty much taken over by the hotels above it, who have installed snack bar and sunbed concessions, and fitted the shoreline with flagstone or wooden-decked lidos – though the public is welcome to patronize the facilities. The only good pebble beach on Bucak Limanı is **Akçagerme**, 3km west, where the tourism school runs an inexpensive snack bar.

Büyük Çakıl, just over 1km east of town, is a small (60m wide) and often crowded shingle-and-sand cove that holds a handful of snack bars. For more space, take a water dolmuş (hourly low season, every 20min peak times; ₺15 return) to **Limanağzı**, the next, large bay to the southeast, with three tavernas and sunbeds behind each of three swimming areas.

The **Çukurbağ peninsula**, west of town, enjoys good views of the Greek island of Kastellórizo, and is lapped by clear, aquamarine water, but again has no beaches other than two pebble coves either side of the isthmus.

Kastellórizo

Regular ferries (see below) run between Kaş and Kastellórizo

The picturesque island of **Kastellórizo**, known as Meis in Turkish after the Greek alternative name (Meyísti), lies just over three nautical miles off the Turkish coast. Among the smallest inhabited islands of the Greek Dodecanese archipelago, its harbour-front, lined with pastel-coloured Neoclassical houses, is a delight. You'll find complete coverage in *The Rough Guide to the Greek Islands*, but it's worth saying that there are at least two weekly onward boats to Rhodes most of the year, plus several inexpensive weekly flights on a small aircraft. If you just miss a departure, a day or two on Meis will be well spent, with affordable seafood, walking opportunities and adequate nightlife.

Kaş and Meis have since 2006 hosted an annual, late June, port-to-port **swimming and kayak race** in the interests of peace and friendship between Greece and Turkey, winked at thus far by both customs authorities as passport controls for all concerned are dispensed with.

ARRIVAL AND INFORMATION   KAŞ

By bus and dolmuş All buses and dolmuşes arrive at the *otogar* at the top inland end of Atatürk Bulvarı (alias Elmalı Caddesi). The schedules below are greatly enhanced in season by Batı Antalya Ko-op minibus, which shuttles almost constantly between Kaş and Antalya.

Destinations Antalya (18 daily; 3hr 30min); Bodrum (3 daily; 6hr); Fethiye (10 daily; 2hr); Istanbul (2 daily; 14hr); Kalkan (20 daily; 30min); Marmaris (4 daily; 5hr).

By ferry Boats to Kastellórizo sail from the harbour, just east of Cumhüriyet Meydanı (Mon–Fri April–Oct, minimum

10am departure and 4pm return, extra departures by demand; winter usually Fri only, depending on number of customers, departing 10am, returning 4pm; 20min; €25 one-way, €25 day return, €35 open return). The most reliable company is Meis Express (☎0242 836 1725, ⊛meisexpress.com). You'll need to surrender your passport to customs the night before returning to Kaş from Kastellórizo.

Tourist information The office at Cumhuriyet Meyd 5, on the waterfront (May–Oct Mon–Fri 8.30am–noon &

5

1–7pm, Sat & Sun 10am–noon & 1–7pm; Nov–April Mon–Fri 9am–noon & 1–5pm; ☎0242 836 1238), has glossy brochures and hotel lists, but little other information.

GETTING AROUND

By bus Minibuses labelled "Yarımada–Şehiriçi" operate a shuttle service around the Çukurbağ peninsula's loop road (at least hourly, until midnight in summer).

Taxis Ranks in the old market square, and base of the jetty.

TOURS AND ACTIVITIES

Boat tours Boatmen at the harbour offer standard full-day tours (depart 10am, return 6pm) to either Kekova or Patara (from ₺60 per person, including lunch).

Bougainville Travel Çukurbağlı (officially İbrahim Serin) Cad 10 ☎0242 836 3737, ⓦbougainville-turkey.com. The foremost adventure-travel agency in the area, long-established and British/Turkish-run, Bougainville offers diving, mountain treks, mountain biking, canyoning, sea kayaking and paragliding, as well as more conventional excursions.

Dragoman Uzun Çarşı 15 ☎0242 836 3614, ⓦdragoman-turkey.com. This Francophone-orientated agency offers a wide range of high-quality outings, including yoga and wine tasting, and sea-level "coasteering".

Fly Lycia İlkokul Sok 4 ☎0242 836 2581, ⓦflylycia .com. The cliffs above Kaş are beginning to rival Ölüdeniz as a paragliding venue, with flights from €80, and this, alongside Bougainville (see above) is one of the more reliable operators.

Seven Capes ☎0252 618 0390, ⓦsevencapes.com. Intrepid Brit Dean Livesley lives in a sustainable eco-house above Kaş, and offers well-priced sea kayaking and SUP tours in the Fethiye area and other prime spots on the Lycian coast, plus tailor-made walks around Kaş and along the Lycian Way.

ACCOMMODATION

Kaş's nocturnal rhythms make it worth staying away from the centre for calm, views and privacy. The highest concentration of desirable hotels and *pansiyons* within the town limits lies east of the centre, above **Küçük Çakıl**. There's also an enclave of budget lodgings west of Atatürk Bulvarı, along **Necip Bey Caddesi** (alias Hastane Caddesi) and around the hilltop **Yeni Cami**, formerly a Greek church. Few of the multi-starred hotels on the **Çukurbağ peninsula** deserve their ratings. Most in-town accommodation is open all year, while Çukurbağ establishments close Nov–April. All have a/c unless otherwise stated.

NECİP BEY CADDESİ AND AROUND YENİ CAMİ

Ateş Pension Yeni Cami Cad 3 ☎0242 836 1393, ⓦatespension.com. This backpackers' favourite is the only place in town with dorm rooms. The pension comprises two connected buildings; rooms in the rear section benefit from newly renovated bathrooms. Pleasant host Ayşegül dishes up a fifty-dish breakfast spread as well as *meze* and charcoal-cooked grills; evening meals are on the roof terrace. Dorm bed ₺50, double ₺150

Gülşen Pansiyon Necip Bey Cad 21 ☎0242 836 1171. Basic but right on the seafront, with access to the water from the very pleasant garden and breakfast area. Rooms are en suite; lucky balconied rooms face the sea. ₺130

★**Hideaway Hotel** Eski Kilise Arkası 7 ☎0242 836 1887, ⓦhotelhideaway.com. Owners Ahmet (Turkish) and Marie (Belgian) are very engaging, multilingual hosts in this ever-evolving establishment, which is always one step ahead of its rivals. Great quiet location by the ancient theatre, expansive views from the brilliant rooftop terrace, library/TV room, free tea and coffee all day, a small pool and modestly priced morning yoga sessions. Rooms are bright, airy and very comfortable – choose from the smaller, slightly darker economy rooms, brighter standard doubles or luxury suites with jacuzzi. Economy €55, standard room €65, suite €80

Kaş Otel Hastane Cad 20 ☎0242 836 1271, ⓦmyhotelkas.com. Spartan but superbly located, right on the seafront with its own sunloungers and a ladder into the sea. Try to get a balconied room near the water; the ones behind have no views to speak of. ₺120

Oreo Hotel Yaka Mahallesi ☎0242 836 2220 or ☎836 3737. This high-standard hotel north of the town centre is managed by Bougainville Travel (see above), so it's often occupied by adventure sports groups. Over half the rooms have sea views, there's a big pool and adjacent shady garden for breakfast. €60

KÜÇÜK ÇAKIL

Begonvil Hotel Koza Sok ☎0242 836 3079, ⓦhotelbegonvil.com. Boutique hotel with cheerful small-to-medium-size rooms sporting tile mosaics, wrought-iron touches and floral curtains. All but three have sea views from small balconies, and some have double beds. Rooms and bathrooms were renovated to a good standard in 2015. Buffet breakfast taken in the courtyard. €70

★**Gardenia** Küçük Çakıl shore road ☎0242 836 2368, ⓦgardeniahotel-kas.com. Boutique hotel with just eleven quite different rooms and suites over four storeys (beware, no lift) with Philippe Starck decor and marble floors, and oriental art in the common areas. Proprietors Ömer and Nevin speak American English. No children under 12, sea-view rooms cost €30 extra. Closed Nov–April. **€90**, suites **€130**

Medusa Hotel Küçük Çakıl shore road ☎0242 836 1440, ⓦmedusahotels.com. Well-equipped, well-run three-star hotel with a pool and lido, though standard rooms – some with double beds and island views – are rather small. Four-person family suites on the roof offer a bit more space. **€80**, suite **€115**

Nur Hotel Küçük Çakıl shore road ☎0242 836 1203, ⓦnurapart.com. The 18 rooms of this modish contemporary hotel are suitably white and bright, apart from the heavily grained laminate floors. All have big LCD TVs, and range from standard doubles to four-bed family suites costing €40 extra. There's a good-sized pool out front and a bizarre parking area in the downstairs reception. **€110**

ÇUKURBAĞ PENINSULA

Arpia North-shore loop road ☎0242 836 2642, ⓦclubarpiahotel.com. Well-positioned on the steep slopes of the west side of the peninsula, 7km out of town, with a nicely terraced pool and restaurant/breakfast area,

and a lido area below. Rooms are pleasantly shaded, plain and simple yet comfortable, and there's a tranquil feel to the place unimaginable in nearby Kaş. Bookable direct or through the Bougainville Travel agency in town (see opposite). **€60**

Olea Nova Demokrasi Cad 43, 3.5km out ☎0242 836 2660, ⓦoleanova.com.tr. Arguably the most stylish hotel out on the peninsula, *Olea Nova*'s uber-white decor works perfectly on this sun-kissed, azure-sea-skirted peninsula. Rooms are on the compact side and only the few at the front have expansive sea views, but the stunning terrace with its sleek kidney-shaped pool more than makes up for this, with stunning views across to Kastellórizo island. A short walk down to the sea reveals the hotels private, terraced lido. Closed Nov–April. **€120**

CAMPING

Kaş Kamping Necip Bey Cad ☎0242 836 1050. Well-located, quiet seafront campsite, 1km west of town, past the theatre, with a swimming platform, lively bar-restaurant and a popular caravan space. Note that to reach *Kaş Kamping* by car you need to turn off the main road by the new marina, initially following signs for the Çukurbağ peninsula. Also has its own diving school (see p.328). Closed Nov-March. Tent pitch **€16**, waterless A-frame cabin **€37**, en-suite chalet **€80**

EATING, DRINKING AND NIGHTLIFE

Kaş has several excellent **restaurants**, but few actually face the waterfront, and some that do are prone to scams and rip-offs. The varied, crowded, sometimes high-decibel **nightlife and café society** is easily the best on the Turquoise Coast.

RESTAURANTS

101 Panorama Hükümet Cad 102 ☎0242 836 3688. A hop and skip away from the busy centre in terms of distance but miles away in character, this sophisticated eating place has a lovely terrace with great views right across the marina – ideal for a quiet cocktail watching the sun go down while choosing from a good selection of seafood, steaks and other grills, plus an array of tempting puddings. Good wine list too. Mains from ₺26. Daily 10am–midnight.

★**Bahçe** Uzun Çarşı ☎0242 836 2370. The broadest range of hot and cold *mezes* in town, served in the garden (*bahçe* in Turkish) and incuding okra in oil (in season) and the delicious courgette fritters *mücver*. Mains, which include kebabs and stews (from ₺22) are by comparison almost incidental, though their *ayva tatlısı* (quince dessert) makes a fitting finale. May–Oct daily 10am–midnight.

Bahçe Balık Süleyman Sandıkçı Sok 18 ☎0242 836 2779. The seafood annexe of nearby *Bahçe* serves *mezes* such as shrimp pie (₺15) and mains including grilled sea bass (₺70 a kilo). Even more popular are the *balık köfte* (breaded fish balls). Booking essential in season. May–Oct daily 10am–midnight.

Bi-Lokma Hükümet Cad 2 ☎0242 836 3942. A Kaş institution, located a short stroll uphill east of the harbourfront, this is the place to come for well-priced fish mains from ₺25, delcious *mantı* (Turkish ravioli) for ₺20 and competitively priced drinks, with beers at ₺11 and wine by the glass at ₺15. They also rustle up the tastiest and most abundant breakfast spread in town. Daily 8am–1am.

Corner Café İbrahim Serin Cad 20 ☎0242 836 3661, ⓦcafecornerkas.com. *Corner Café* has made a successful transition from a cheap and cheerful snack place to a well-regarded restaurant, serving up a good mix of traditional Turkish and international dishes, with mains priced ₺22–45. Try the mixed *meze* platter to start. Daily 10am–2am.

Enişte'nin Yeri Necip Bey Cad ☎0242 836 3212. Unlicensed restaurant, nicely located on the waterfront just west of Cumhuriyet Meydan, which dishes up plenty of Turkish favourites including soups (₺6), *pide* (₺9) and kebabs (from ₺18). There's a nice air-conditioned covered garden room out back. Daily 9am–midnight.

★**Hayta Meyhane** Zumrut Sok 5. This charming tavern in an old Greek house is a great place to try the Turkish aniseed spirit rakı with simple *meze* and grilled-fish mains

5

(from ₺18). It's named after the resident golden retriever Hayta, who greets guests with a friendly wag of his tail. Daily noon–10pm.

★ **İkbal** Süleyman Sandıkçı Sok 6 ☎ 0242 836 3193. This atmospheric Turkish/German-run restaurant, with a lovely vine- and bougainvillea-shaded veranda, is rightly regarded as one of Kaş's best eating places. Does a nice mix of traditional Turkish dishes and more international fare, including steaks. The slow-roast lamb is particularly good. Mains from ₺25. Daily 10am–midnight.

Kaşım Öztürk Sok 15 ☎ 0242 836 2052. The best of several options on this inland pedestrian lane, with a mix of affordable *hazır yemek* (from ₺7 per portion), kebabs (from ₺18) and tasty puddings. Unlicensed, but very popular at lunch. Daily 7am–midnight.

Köşk Gürsoy Sok 13 ☎ 0242 836 3857. Well-regarded rustic-style restaurant with a dark-wood dining room warmed by an open fire on winter evenings, and tables out on the narrow street in summer. Starters (from ₺7) include hummus; mains such as kebabs cost ₺20 and up, and they also offer seafood. Wine is a reasonable ₺45–60 per bottle. Daily 10am–midnight.

BARS AND CAFÉS

Bar Celona Gursoy Sok 2/A ☎ 0242 836 4490. This lively place, set on a busy people-watching corner, usually keeps the party going until the early hours, attracting a good mix of locals, expats and holiday-makers. Owner Haldun is an engaging host, the beers are well-priced (₺12) and the cocktails delicious. Great place for a fun night out or as a last-gasp watering hole. Daily 10am–late.

★ **Hideway** Cumhuriyet Cad 16/A ☎ 0242 836 3369.

Easily the coolest garden bar/café in town, set just off the square. Vintage rock, reggae and blues soundtrack, divan and table seating, romantic lighting and ever-popular Sunday breakfast. Beers ₺11. May–Nov daily 4pm–2am.

Hi-Jazz Zümrüt Sok 3 ☎ 0242 836 1165. This trendy L-shaped bar is at its best in winter, when the open fire is blazing and the mellow sounds of soul and jazz soothe the ear. A few tables outside in summer. Beer, and wine by the glass, ₺15. Daily 5pm–2am.

Mavi/Blue Cumhuriyet Meyd ☎ 0242 836 1834. The oldest bar-café in town, right on the harbour. Three decades ago it was a coffee house where retired fishermen played backgammon; now it's favoured by Kaş's young moneyed locals who are happy to pay ₺9 for a beer. Less well-off locals and visitors buy beer from the off-licence and drink it on the harbour wall opposite. Daily 10am–2am.

★ **Şaraphane** Hastane Cad, Yeni Cami Sok 3 ☎ 0242 836 2715. A few minutes' walk from the town centre and tucked up a quiet side street leading to the Yeni Cami, this mellow wine bar is the perfect place to share a tasty cheeseboard (₺20) and bottle of locally produced Likya Vineyard wine (a bargain ₺30). They also do decadent mains from ₺20. Daily 10am–midnight.

CLUBS

Red Point Club Süleyman Topçu Sok ☎ 0242 836 1165. Kaş's premier after-hours dance club, set in an old barn and packed solid after midnight despite a fairly spacious dancefloor on account of the DJ-spun rock and soul. Tables out in the lane during summer. Daily 5pm–3am.

SHOPPING

The **Uzun Çarşı** (Long Market) is precisely that – an uninterrupted bazaar of antique and designer clothing shops with stock (and prices) matching European city-centre malls. The **antique shops** are all of similar quality, with few worth singling out: carpets, jewellery, metal antiques and kitsch knick-knacks. Better are the Turkish-made **textiles** such as *peştemals* (bath wraps) and towels.

Gallery Anatolia Hükümet Cad 2 ☎ 0242 836 1954, ⓦ gallery-anatolia.com. Original hand-painted ceramics are the mainstay here, and they make a refreshing change from the gimcrack mock-İznik wares on sale in most other shops. It's not cheap but these are one-off pieces and the designs a refreshing mix of traditional Turkish and contemporary. Mon–Sat 9am–9pm.

Merdiven İlkokul Sok 4/B ☎ 0242 836 3022. Small bookshop selling new and used paperbacks and a few new dictionaries and guidebooks. Daily 9am–10pm.

★ **Old Curiosity Shop** Lise Sok. Cornucopia of a place off Uzun Çarşı stocking a unique selection of objects in all sizes – and at a fair price. Mon–Sat 10am–9pm.

The Kekova region

Some of the most beautifully situated ruins on the Turquoise Coast are in the **Kekova** area, named for the eponymous offshore island. This stretch of rocky shore is littered with the remains of Lycian settlements, some now submerged under the translucent waters of the calm, shallow, almost landlocked gulf here. Land access – both by road

KEKOVA & AROUND

and by the Lycian Way – has improved considerably, so the region is no longer the exclusive preserve of boat and yacht tours. Many monuments are easily visited from **Üçağız** on the inlet shore by boat tour – the main activity at this beachless place – while inland lie the neglected remains of **Apollonia**, a dependency of coastal Aperlae, and the substantial ruins of **Cyaneae**.

Üçağız

The central village of the Kekova region, **ÜÇAĞIZ**, is 38km southeast of Kaş and connected to Highway 400 by a surfaced 20km road. Thus its quiet days are past: bus parks for coaches have been built right by the harbour and on the approach to the hamlet; carpet, antique and jewellery shops have sprouted; and boat-trip touts swarm around you on arrival. However, the fact that most of the surroundings have been designated as an archeological site protects Üçağız from unseemly concrete expansion; indeed, some illegal buildings have been demolished. And its essential village identity has yet to be completely supplanted – out of season the place is still idyllic.

ARRIVAL AND DEPARTURE   ÜÇAĞIZ

By bus or dolmuş One daily dolmuş (₺7), geared towards villagers not tourists, heads from Demre to Üçağız at 5pm, and leaves Üçağız at 8am. To get here from Kaş, catch an Antalya-bound bus along the coastal highway and then hitch from the turning, or take a taxi all the way (around ₺90). One daily Batı Antalya dolmuş departs at 8am for Antalya, which is useful if you're heading to Çıralı/ Olympos as well as Antalya itself.

ACCOMMODATION AND EATING

Üçağız's **pansiyons** are simple, but often overpriced considering the remote location and lack of a beach. Note, however, that prices drop by up to half in winter. Although fresh water has been piped in from Gömbe, hot showers can still be erratic, but on the positive side all places offer free boat trips to beaches on Kekova island. For something more upmarket it's worth considering staying in the hills to the northeast of Üçağız, in the village of **Kapaklı köy**. Most visitors tend to eat in their pension, as the village **restaurants** are undistinguished and geared up for day-trippers.

5

SEA KAYAKING AND BOAT TOURS AROUND KEKOVA

Kayaking day-tours in the Kekova area make a wonderful, low-impact way to appreciate the eerie seascapes. They have the further advantage of allowing you to approach the shoreline, and the Batık Şehir in particular, much closer than the glass-bottomed cruise boats, and also to use narrow, shallow channels off-limits to larger craft. So long as your head is covered and you bring enough water, you'll tolerate all but the hottest summer days, even wrapped inside a life vest.

The principal operators are **Bougainville** and **Dragoman** in Kaş (see p.330). Trips may begin with a motorized tow from Üçağız to the starting point of your choice, for example Tersane; outings can be as long or short as stamina allows. The typical cost, including a transfer from Kaş to Üçağız and a picnic lunch, is €30 per person.

To avoid the ubiquitous touts offering **boat trips** from Kekova (the waterfront is jam-packed with moored vessels), most visitors arrange a tour through their pension. The most popular combine both Kekova island and Kale for around ₺60 per person assuming a reasonable number of passengers, considerably more if you have to charter a boat specially. The tours allow time to explore Simena and its castle and admire the underwater remains, and usually stop at a small beach for sunbathing and swimming.

Ekin Hotel Üçağız ☎ 0242 874 2064 or ☎ 0534 936 7783, ⓦ ekinpension.com. This well-established place has clean, spacious rooms in a waterfront building, and larger ones (for €10 more) in a smarter extension at the back separated from the original by a pleasant garden, with insect screens and a/c. There's also a posh new bungalow with four rooms and its own veranda. Excellent evening meals are available, with eight kinds of *meze* followed by a grill. ₺30

Kekova Pansiyon Üçağız ☎ 0242 874 2259, ⓦ kekovapansiyon.com. This attractive stone-clad building, located at the western end of the village and a few metres back from the water, has eight palatial a/c rooms and a shared wraparound balcony on the first floor with sea views. Add another ₺40 for half board. ₺120

★ **Lykia Yolu Palas** Kapaklı Köyü 44 ☎ 0242 874 2222, ⓦ likyayolupalas.com. Wonderful five-room boutique hotel around 20km by road northeast of Üçağız, with sweeping views down to the sea and easterly tip of Kekova island, and its own pool. Owner Orhan is a keen walker and mountaineer – and cook – so expect some great food, perhaps while listening to his extensive collection of vinyl "classics". Good value for the individually decorated and furnished rooms. €100

Theimussa Pension Üçağız ☎ 0532 272 6407, ⓦ thiemussa.eu. Üçağız's smartest accommodation, in a great location at the very eastern edge of the village, abutting the necropolis. The eight rooms in this 80-year-old building are simple but immaculately presented, with tiled floors, white walls, comfy beds and a/c, and small bathrooms with quality fittings. A pleasantly landscaped area outside, complete with banana tree and breakfast room/bar, fronts the sea. ₺250

Around Üçağız

Üçağız means "three mouths", in reference to the straits at each end of the island opposite, plus the entry to the lake-like gulf, at whose rear the village is situated. Several small **islands**, quarried in ancient times to near sea level, dot the bay. Until the road was built, the **Lycian remains** around Üçağız were visited by few apart from hardy goats and archeologists. **Teimussa** – and if you like walking, **Simena** and **Aperlae** – can be reached on foot from the village, though most visitors, especially in summer, opt for a **boat excursion** instead (see boxes above and opposite).

Kekova island

The most romantically situated local ruins are submerged along the northern coast of **Kekova island**. Known locally as Batık Şehir (Sunken City), they have not yet been identified with any ancient city. The underwater remains of stairs, pavements, house walls and a long quay wall can all be seen; however, snorkelling or even just swimming are banned to prevent the removal of antiquities. Most boatmen won't approach the rocky shoreline, but you can get the best views from a kayak (see above).

Near the southwest tip of the island, at the spot called Tersane (Dockyard), looms the apse of a long-vanished church, in whose shadow bathers spread their towels on a fine-shingle beach; unhappily, much of the apse collapsed during a particularly violent storm in 1996.

Teimiussa

The acropolis and necropolis of ancient **Teimiussa** are just a few minutes' walk east of Üçağız, reached by passing through the grounds of the waterfront *Theimussa* pension. While nothing is really known about its history, inscriptions indicate occupation in the fourth century BC. The site, apparently a settlement without walls and few or no public buildings, consists mainly of scattered rock tombs. Some have semicircular benches cut into their bases – convenient for pondering mortality as you stare out to sea, and used by the ancients when visiting their deceased relatives with *nekrodeipna* (food for the dead). On the hill above squats a house-sized fort or tower, while at sea level there's a tiny, rock-cut landing stage.

Kale

A ruined castle of the Knights of St John, visible on the horizon from Üçağız – and the village of **KALE** below it – can be reached on foot or via a ten-minute boat ride. The secluded village is the haunt of Rahmi Koç, scion of a wealthy industrialist family, who donated a school while restoring an old house here as a holiday retreat. Even for lesser mortals, Kale makes a lovely place to stay – it's a protected archeological zone, with no new buildings permitted – though some rustic-looking **pansiyons**, overlooking the sea and a marooned sarcophagus, are pricey for what you get.

The acropolis of Simena

Daily: April–Oct 9am–7.30pm; Nov–March 8am–5pm • ₺8 when warden present

The steep but brief climb up to the **acropolis** of ancient Simena is worth it both for the views and for the medieval **castle** itself, whose ramparts are in good condition, partly resting on ancient foundations. Inside the Knights' castle, a 15m-wide **theatre** is carved into the living rock, large enough for perhaps two hundred people. Some well-preserved **sarcophagi** stand on the eastern slopes of the hill, off the path. Brace

---

WEST ALONG THE LYCIAN WAY: APERLAE AND APOLLONIA

Ancient **Aperlae** lies on the far side of a peninsula southwest of Üçağız, astride the Lycian Way. Access most comfortably involves a 40min boat ride to a landing stage that's home to a couple of restaurants, followed by a half-hour walk. It's a remote site, and practically deserted, though there's a cluster of modern houses at Sıcak İskelesı, beside the ruins. The **city walls** are fairly well preserved, enclosing a rectangular area with the sea lapping the southern side; the **necropolis**, typically, lies almost entirely outside the walls. As at Kekova, subsidence has submerged the harbour quarter, but swimming and snorkelling here are unrestricted. If you follow the line of the old **quay**, now in 1–2m of water and indented at 15m intervals for the mooring of ships, you'll see heaps of pottery shards, amphora necks, terracotta tiles and shell-middens from the ancient murex-dye industry, all encrusted together.

If Aperlae is neglected, unexcavated **Apollonia** is even more so. It can be reached on foot, either from Boğazcık, via a spur from the Lycian Way, or from Aperlae (2hr 15min), or partway by a 2km track from the modern village of **Kılınçlı** (alias Sıcak) on the Üçağız-bound road. Apollonia is remarkable for its superb **necropolis**, which spikes the lower northeast slope of the hill on which the city is found, facing Kılınçlı. There is one conventional sarcophagus with extravagant Gothic-type details, but most distinctive are a half-dozen **pillar tombs**, considered the ur-burial method of the ancient Lycians, and proving Apollonia's antiquity. Isolated from the other tombs, at the west end of the hill facing Boğazcık, stands an unusual **carved tomb** on two levels. There is more to see in the acropolis, at the east end of which sits a much older stockade inside a Byzantine citadel. Particularly on the southwest flank, the **city walls** – made of unusually large quadrangular and pentagonal blocks – are pierced by windows and a gate.

5

yourself for being followed by children peddling printed headscarves, and village women pressing oregano into your hands or offering guiding services.

ARRIVAL AND DEPARTURE

On foot The best way to reach Kale/Simena is to walk, which takes 45min via a clear track that runs east, then south, of Üçağız village.

By boat Boat tours from Kekova (see box, p.334) run to Kale and Simena, and you can negotiate one-way fares. Pensions will arrange a free boat transfer for guests.

ACCOMMODATION AND EATING

Although **accommodation** is uniformly overpriced in high season (July & Aug), Kale is a special place, and a night or two here well worth the experience. Most of the half-dozen waterfront **restaurants**, which have had a long and jading acquaintance with the tour-boat trade, offer a set-price, fill-your-plate *meze* buffet; you're better off sticking with what's on offer at the pensions.

Kale Pansiyon ☎0242 874 2111, ⓦkalepansiyon .com. Simple but comfortable nine-room pension, in an old waterfront house. Plain whitewashed walls, kilim-decked wooden floors, and great island-view balconies. €80
Mehtap Pansiyon ☎0242 874 2146, ⓦmehtap pansiyon.com. Set back and up the hill from the water, the

Mehtap has eight plain but a/c wood-floored rooms in a lovely period house set in a sea of citrus, banana, carob, olive and palm trees. It also has camping space available, and good suppers served on the terrace. Friendly owner-manager Saffet will collect/return you from/to Üçağız by boat. Tent pitch ₺20, room ₺250

Cyaneae

Unrestricted access • Free • A signposted 2km path leads to the site from Yavu village centre – 45 minutes of extremely steep hiking; rather easier is an unmarked 4km dirt road that takes off from the north side of Highway 400, precisely 1km west of the side road to Yavu; the last stretch is rough, but negotiable with care in an ordinary car

The wild, inhospitable countryside east of Üçağız is amenable these days only to herds of sheep and goats. In antiquity, however, this region was scattered with small settlements, of which the most interesting is **CYANEAE** (Kyaneai in Turkish signage), 23km east of Kaş above the village of Yavu. The name Cyaneae/Kyaneai derives from the ancient Greek for "dark blue" – also the origin of the word cyanide – but it's uncertain why the place was so named. The Lycian and Roman **sarcophagi** here are the most numerous of any local site, and the main reason to visit. Cyaneae was the most important Roman town between Myra and Antiphellos (modern Kaş), and linked by a direct road to Teimiussa port, 12km away.

The site

Some of Cyaneae's oldest, most interesting **tombs** lie along the path up from Yavu, flanking what may have been part of the ancient road. The most impressive – a sarcophagus carved completely from the rock on which it stands – lies south of the road. Two lions' heads project from each side of the Gothic-arch "lid", cut from the same piece of rock. Near the top of the path, there's a subterranean shrine or tomb with six columns.

Below the city, fairly inaccessible on the south face of the hill, stands an impressive **temple-tomb** whose porch has a single freestanding column and, unusually, a recess above the pediment with a sarcophagus. An inscription states that this was reserved for the heads of the household, while the rest of the family were buried in the tomb.

The **acropolis** is surrounded on three sides by a wall; the south side is too precipitous to need protection. The buildings inside are ruined and cloaked with vegetation, but a library, baths and two Byzantine churches (one with a lengthy inscription) have been identified. A tomb near the summit bears a relief of a charioteer driving a team of four horses. The city had no natural spring nearby, so vaulted cisterns and reservoirs square-cut into the rock are ubiquitous.

West of the summit beyond the parking area is a **theatre** that retains 23 rows of seats. Those above the diazoma make ideal vantage points over the acropolis walls,

Kekova inlet, and sarcophagi flanking an ancient path linking the theatre and the acropolis. Mainly Roman, these are mostly simple, with rounded lids and crests, but some have lion-head bosses.

Demre and around

East of Yavu, Highway 400 swoops down in a well-angled arc towards **DEMRE**, a rather scruffy river-delta town. The main local businesses are citrus fruit and tomatoes, whose greenhouses – spread below as you descend the escarpment to the west – make Demre seem bigger than it really is. Unlike other nondescript towns along the coast, which juggle sun-and-wave motifs in their municipal logos, Demre is unequivocal about its self-image: a giant tomato occupies most of its coat of arms.

As ancient Myra, Demre was the adult home of **Saint Nicholas**, a major Orthodox saint, and the **central church** honours him. Father Christmas has therefore crept in here, and the town centre is absolutely overrun with **Santa kitsch**, as well as considerable midday groups of Russian pilgrims, catered to by a huge number of icon stalls. In fact so many Russians visit the church that this is Antalya province's most visited site – incredible given the wealth of fabulous Greco-Roman remains hereabouts. Nearby attractions include the site of **Myra** just north, the ancient harbour of **Andriake** and the beach at **Çayağzı**.

Brief history

An important member of the Lycian Federation, Myra remained important throughout the Byzantine era through its association with Bishop, later Saint, **Nicholas**, aka **Santa Claus** (see box, p.338). Some associate the city's name with the Greek for myrrh, a plant resin used in the production of incense, but there's no evidence it was made here, and Myra is probably a corrupted Lycian place name. When the bishop's tomb was opened by eleventh-century grave robbers, however, they were supposedly overwhelmed by the smell of myrrh.

Despite its later fame, Myra wasn't heard from before 42 BC, when the city displayed typical Lycian defiance by refusing to pay tribute money to **Brutus**. Brutus's lieutenant had to break the chain closing off the mouth of Andriake harbour – Myra's port – and force his way in. Subsequently, Myra had an uneventful if prosperous history until abandonment in the fourteenth century, was treated well by its imperial overlords, and became **capital** of Byzantine Lycia in the fifth century.

Church of St Nicholas

Müze Cad • Daily: May–Oct 9am–7pm; Nov–April 8.30am–5pm • ₺10

The **Church of St Nicholas** dominates central Demre, on the right of the pedestrianized Müze Caddesi as you head west. Despite the unsightly synthetic protective canopy on one side, the building remains evocative of its patron saint. Nicholas was beatified after visitors to his purported tomb reported miracles, and Myra soon became a popular focus of **pilgrimage**; even after the Bari raiders stole his bones, the pilgrimages continued. Monks from a nearby monastery simply designated another tomb as the saint's, pouring oil through openings in the top and collecting it at the bottom, to sell to pilgrims as holy secretions.

The contemporary church – basically a three-aisled basilica, with a fourth added ater – has little in common with the fourth-century original, having been rebuilt in 1043 after its destruction by occupying Saracens and again in 1862 by Russian Tsar Nicholas I, who installed a vaulted ceiling instead of a cupola in the central nave, along with a belfry. Turkish archeologists have carried out more recent protective modifications, such as the extra small stone domes in the narthex.

5

ST NICHOLAS – THE ORIGINAL SANTA CLAUS

Myra's prestige was greatly enhanced by the reputation of one of its citizens, namely **St Nicholas**, born in Patara in 270 AD and later appointed local bishop. The Orthodox patron saint of sailors, merchants, students, prisoners, virgins and children, his Western identity as a genial old present-giver is perhaps more familiar, based on the story of the three daughters of a poor man who were left without dowries. Nicholas is credited with throwing three purses of gold coins into the house by night, enabling them to find husbands instead of prostituting themselves. Many posthumous miracles were attributed to the saint, but little is actually known about the man. However, after his death he was probably buried in the church in Demre that's now dedicated to him, and it is also widely believed that in 1087 his bones were carried off to Italy by a group of devout raiders from Bari.

Demre still banks heavily on its connection with St Nicholas (**Noel Baba** or "Father Christmas" in Turkish); a special mass is held here on his main feast day, December 6, attracting Orthodox and Catholic pilgrims, while others take place on random Sundays throughout the year.

The most typically Byzantine feature is the **synthronon** (bishop's throne) in the apse, rarely found *in situ* since most were removed when Anatolian churches were converted into mosques. Among the patchy interior **frescoes**, the best and clearest – in the dome of the north transept – is a *Communion of the Apostles*. **Mosaic floor-panels**, mainly geometric designs, adorn the nave and south aisle, while masonry fragments near the entrance include one carved with an anchor – either symbolic of Christian faith, or Nicholas as protector of sailors. His purported **sarcophagus**, in the southernmost aisle as you face the synthronon, is not considered genuine. The saint's bones were reputedly stolen from a tomb under a pavement – and, more significantly, on this one there's a relief representation of a married couple on the lid.

Myra

Daily: April–Oct 8.30am–7.30pm; Nov–March 8.30am–5pm • ₺15 • The site is 2km north of Demre's town centre; there's no public transport so either walk or take a taxi for around ₺10

As one of the most easily visited Lycian sites, ancient **Myra** is packed with tours even in the off season. In summer, it's best visited early or late in the day, though you'll still run a gauntlet of overwhelming tourist tat lining the approaches, plus kids selling oregano and unnecessary guide services.

Apart from a large theatre and some of the finest house-style rock tombs in Lycia, most of the city is still buried. The **theatre** was destroyed by an earthquake in 141 AD but rebuilt shortly afterwards; two concentric galleries cover the still-intact stairs by which spectators entered the auditorium. The substantial chunks of carving lying around the orchestra and just outside, which once decorated the stage building, include several theatrical masks, a bust of a woman and a Medusa head.

The main concentration of **tombs** (currently off-limits during ongoing archeological excavations) stands west of the theatre. Most are of the house type, in imitation of Lycian dwelling places, even down to the wooden roof-beams. Some are decorated with reliefs, including warriors at the climax of a battle, a naked page handing a helmet to a warrior, and a funerary scene.

A second group of tombs, called the **river necropolis**, is around the side of the second long ridge on the right as you stand with your back to the theatre stage. To get there, leave the main site, turn left off the final access drive onto the main approach road, and continue inland for 1.5km. Here the "**painted**" **tomb** (though it is no longer pigmented) features the reclining figure of a bearded man and his family in the porch, and outside on the rock face what's presumed to be the same family, in outdoor apparel.

Andriake

Unrestricted access • Free • No public transport; head west out of Demre towards Kaş then bear left, and where the main highway starts to tackle the slope on the right bank of the stream leading down to the sea, turn left again at a black-on-yellow sign

Set astride the Androkos River 2.5km southwest of Demre and almost 5km from Myra itself, **Andriake** was ancient Myra's port and the site of Hadrian's granary. This was vital to the whole Roman world, since its contents were sent to Rome to be distributed around the empire. The substantial remains of this building can still be seen south of today's river, which runs parallel to the road between Demre and the beach.

Built at Hadrian's behest in 119–139 AD, and very similar to the one at Patara, the **granary** consists of eight rooms constructed of well-fitting square blocks. Above the main central gate are busts of Hadrian and possibly his wife, the empress Sabina. Another decorative relief on the front wall, near the second door from the west, depicts two deities of disputed identity, one flanked by a snake and a griffin, the other reclining on a couch. The granary has been reconstructed, with a new roof and smart wooden doors, and at the time of writing was in the process of being turned into the site's museum. In front of it, in the reed-fringed marshes of the river estuary, a replica Roman-era ship complete with an elegant swan-neck figurehead has been built, along with the assorted winches and trailers used in the loading/unloading of grain ships.

Back towards the site entrance are the ruins of a **Byzantine church**, easily identified by its apse. More impressive is a large open space measuring some 60m by 40m, flanked by colonnaded rooms on three sides. This was once the Plakoma, Andriake's **agora**. At its centre are the remains of a large cistern, some 7m deep. Recent excavations have shown that murex, a sea snail much prized in the ancient and Byzantine worlds for the purple dye that could be extracted from it, was processed on an a large scale here.

Çayağzı

1km southwest of Andriake, 3.5km southwest of Demre • Boat trips to Kekova from Çayağzı to (3–4hr; ₺200 for the boat) include the standard tour of the underwater ruins around the island and of Simena; journey time to Kekova is 45min

Modern **Çayağzı** ("Rivermouth") anchorage, is a major jumping-off point for boat tours to Kekova (see p.332). A new harbour wall shelters dozens of boats awaiting customers, mainly coached in from nearby holiday villages.

The only other reason to come here is for a swim. The adjacent **beach** is fairly short, if broad and duney – though also trash-strewn and prone to algae slicks, which, together with the Kaş–Demre highway passing just overhead and the area's status as an archeological zone, accounts for the minimal development here. However, the beauty of the skyline to the west cannot be underestimated, where parallel ridges – just like in a Japanese print – march down to Kekova.

ARRIVAL AND INFORMATION

DEMRE AND AROUND

By bus and dolmuş Buses and dolmuşes drop passengers at Demre's *otogar*, close to the centre.
Destinations Antalya (at least 15 daily; 2hr 30min);

Fethiye (6 daily; 4hr); Finike (for Arykanda; hourly; 30min); Kaş (hourly; 1hr); Üçağız (1 daily; 45min).

ACCOMMODATION AND EATING

Camping & Café Andriake Çayağzı ☎ 0242 871 3130, ⓦ andriake.com. In addition to tent camping, this green and attractive campsite on the beach/river mouth at Çayağzı, 3.5km southwest of Demre, holds a café that offers a wide range of food, including barbecued fish. Tent pitch ₺15

Kent İlkokul Cad, Myra ☎ 0242 871 2042,

ⓦ kentpansiyon.com. Very friendly and family run, and used mainly by trekkers on the Lycian Way, this is still the only accommodation option worth recommending in Demre. The rooms are simple but spacious and have a/c, and there's a basic bungalow in the leafy garden as well. Bungalow ₺70, double ₺100

5

Arykanda

Daily: April–Oct 8am–7pm; Nov–March 8am–5pm • ₺10 • The site is 60km northeast of Demre, 34km north of the Highway 400 town of Finike; catch a frequent Antalya–Kaş bus to Finike's *otogar*, then an Elmalı-bound dolmuş as far as Arif, a 1km signposted walk from Arykanda

Set in a breathtaking location, high in the mountains on a steep, south-facing hillside that overlooks the main valley between the Akdağ and Bey mountain ranges, **Arykanda** is a fabulous ancient site that's comparable with Delphi in Greece. Its individual monuments are scattered, often only partly excavated and unlabelled, but there are good site plans by the entrance and the acropolis. While finds date to the fifth century BC, the typically Lycian "anda" suffix suggests that the city was founded a millennium earlier. Arykanda was a member of the Lycian Federation from the second century BC, and remained inhabited until the eleventh century.

The site

A pronounced ravine and power pylons divide the site of Arykanda roughly in two. The function of the complex structure dubbed **Naltepesi**, entered by a right-angled stairway beside the parking area, is not yet completely understood, but you can make out a small bathhouse and presumed shops. North of the parking area, a large **basilica** holds extensive mosaic flooring under tin-roof shelters posed over each aisle, and a semicircular row of benches (probably a synthronon or bishop's throne) in the outer apse; a more colourful mosaic just below features two birds. Another, smaller basilica just inside suggests eighth-century destruction and more modest rebuilding. The most impressive sight, however, looming on the east, is the 10m-high facade of the **main baths**, with numerous windows on two levels, and apsidal halls at each end. The westerly one holds a still-intact plunge pool, and the easterly one has stacked hypocausts.

Other constructions worth seeking out include a small **temple** or tomb above the baths complex (one of three "monumental tombs" on the site plan), adapted for Christian worship. There are more Roman or Byzantine mosaics in the tombs or temples immediately east of the Christianized one. West of the ravine and power lines, and above the **agora** – whose engaging **odeion** has been defaced by horrible new marble cladding – an impressive, six-aisled **theatre** retains twenty rows of seats plus a well-preserved stage building. Above this sprawls a short but attractive **stadium**, with several rows of seats exposed.

The coast to Olympos

East of Finike, which is noteworthy only for its yacht marina, Highway 400 runs dead straight before turning ninety degrees to enter the high-rise market town of Kumluca. Beyond that, it curls up through the **Beydağları National Park**, a spectacular sequence of densely pine-forested ridges and precipitous bare cliffs. Two relatively unspoiled beach resorts, **Adrasan** and **Olympos/Çıralı**, lie hidden at the mouths of canyons that plunge to the sea. If you're heading towards either by your own transport, leave the main highway for the narrow but paved side road that veers off east of Kumluca, signposted "Beykonak, Mavikent". This short cut roller-coasters through forested valleys and along dramatic coastline to **Gelidonya Burnu**, with its lighthouse and scenic sections of the Lycian Way, before emerging at Çavuş, the nearest proper village to Adrasan and Olympos. The only trick en route involves turning left (north) at a signposted junction near the outskirts of Karaöz, the last bay and village before Gelidonya Burnu.

5

THE LYCIAN WAY AT GELIDONYA BURNU

From the small pebbly beach at Karaöz, an obvious dirt road heads south along the coast towards the cape. Roughly 6.5km along, leave the track in favour of the marked **Lycian Way**, now a steadily rising path through oaks and pines. From the trailhead, a round trip of just under an hour (with a daypack) will take you to the photogenic **lighthouse** just above Taşlık Burnu (as **Gelidonya Burnu**, "Swallow Cape", has been officially renamed). Built by the French in 1936, the lighthouse is not currently inhabited, but a keeper cycles out from Karaöz at dusk to light the lamp. The treacherous **Beş Adalar** (Five Islands) that straggle beyond the cape are shipping hazards that have caused many a wreck, including an ancient one that yielded a huge amount of treasure to archeological divers during the 1960s.

North of the lighthouse, the Lycian Way threads deserted hillside between the sea and a high ridge on its 6hr course to Adrasan (path or cross-country except for the final hour). This dramatic stretch has become a popular organized group target, so you'll probably have company.

Adrasan

Nestling in the shadow of pointy Musa Dağı (Mt Moses), **ADRASAN** is an attractive beach resort with a pretty curving beach bookended by pine-forested limestone spurs. It's more mainstream and less hip than nearby Çıralı (see p.345) and there's none of the backpacker scene so prevalent at Olympos (see opposite), a day's walk north along the Lycian Way. The resort is very popular with Turks, especially in July and August, while in spring and autumn it's an overnighting spot for trekkers following the Lycian Way. Though falling within national park boundaries, development (including second-home building) is proceeding slowly.

ARRIVAL AND DEPARTURE
ADRASAN

By bus Adrasan is tricky to reach on public transport. Catch one of the very frequent coastal highway buses south and west from Antalya (₺12) or east and north from Kaş (₺18) as far as the turn-off, 13km north of the resort, and catch a minibus from there (every 2hr in season; ₺6). Most hotel/pension owners will collect guests – call ahead.

By car If you're driving, look out for a steep road that descends right to Çavuş village and the bay of Adrasan, 12km beyond Kumluca on Highway 400. Whether you arrive from this direction, or from Mavikent, turn east in Çavuş village centre (at the bank ATM) onto the seaward road (marked "Sahil"), following hotel placards for 4km.

ACTIVITIES

Boat trips Ceneviz Limanı, a cliff-girt bay beyond Musa Dağı and inaccessible on foot, is the most popular outing, costing ₺50–60 including lunch.
Scuba diving Diving Center Adrasan on the central

beachfront (closed Feb to late March ☎0242 883 1353, ⓦ diving-adrasan.com) offers beach dives (€30), boat dives (€40) and CMAS/PADI certification (from €360).

ACCOMMODATION, EATING AND DRINKING

Two dozen *pansiyons* and hotels are scattered inland from the long beach, or along the stream meeting the sea at its north end. The fancier **hotels** – though the term is only relative – overlook the south end of the bay, near the jetty. There are several independent **restaurants** on the east bank of the watercourse, reached by wobbly suspension bridges and with diners seated on platforms in the stream, where hundreds of ducks come to cadge your spare bread. All are very Anglicized in menu, clientele and price, and none is really worth singling out. In addition, several perfectly adequate, and more traditionally Turkish, restaurants back the beach; expect to pay ₺18 and up for kebabs, ₺25 and up for grilled fish.

★**Aybars** ☎0242 883 1133 or ☎0532 314 1887, ⓦ aybarshotel.com. The pick of the riverside accommodation, set at the far north end of the beach and reached via a suspension bridge. Large, a/c, balconied rooms, renovated in 2012, overlook lush grounds and an in-river restaurant. Aysın, on the mobile number given, speaks good English. Closed Dec–March. Rates include half board. ₺210

Ford ☎0242 883 1098, ⓦ fordhotel.net. With a nicely landscaped pool and its own phalanx of beach sunbeds, this upmarket place at the very southern end of the beach has 29 rooms (including three family suites) in two wings, with hillside or sea views. Rates (for two) include breakfast. Closed Nov–March. ₺230

Olympos

Around 60km northeast of Demre, a spectacular wooded cleft, the **Olympos valley** runs down to a shingle beach and the sea. This valley is home to the atmospheric ruins of the ancient Lycian city of **Olympos**, virtually lost in thick scrub by a reed-fringed river, along with a veritable "village" of wooden huts and treehouses that has become a staple on Turkey's backpacking circuit. As well as backpackers, summer weekends see the place busy with young folk from Antalya escaping the heat, and on major holidays with groups of university students from elsewhere in the country; the period around ANZAC day is often bristling with Australians and New Zealanders. Throw in an increasing number of Russian tourists seeking a break from the all-inclusive hotels down the coast, and it's easy to see why Olympos enjoys a reputation as the liveliest "alternative" party-time resort on the Turkish coast.

Brief history

Although nothing is known about the origins of Olympos, the city presumably took its name from **Mount Olympos**, present-day Tahtalı Dağ, 16km north – one of over twenty mountains in the ancient world that bore the name Olympos. The city made its historical debut during the second century BC, minting its own coins; within a few decades Olympos was one of six cities in the Lycian Federation to possess three votes, confirming its importance.

The principal deity of Olympos – **Hephaestos** (the Roman Vulcan), god of fire and of blacksmiths – was considered native to this region, and traces of a temple dedicated to him exist near the Chimaera. During the first century BC, the importance of his cult diminished when pirates led by **Zeniketes** overran both Olympos and nearby Phaselis, and introduced the worship of the Indo-European god Mithras. Zeniketes made Olympos his headquarters, but in 78 BC he was defeated by the local Roman governor, and again in 67 BC by Pompey, after which Olympos became public property. The city's fortunes revived after it was absorbed into the **Roman Empire** in 43 AD, and Christianity became prominent. Olympos was later used as a **trading base** by the Venetians and Genoese – hence Ceneviz Limanı (Genoese Harbour) just south – but was abandoned after the Ottomans dominated the Mediterranean.

Olympos valley

The Olympos valley is quite beautiful in its own right; the vast majority of visitors are content to admire the scenery, chill in the treehouses, and swim or explore the ancient site that lies between the accommodation area and the beach.

More **active pursuits** include hikes along the Lycian Way, south over Musa Dağı to Adrassan (see opposite) or north to the flames of the Chimaera (see p.345) and, beyond, ancient Phaselis (see p.348). In addition, various agencies offer, usually through the pensions, activities such as jeep safaris, boat tours, sea kayaking, diving and rock climbing. The drawback to basing yourself in Olympos, as opposed to neighbouring Çıralı (see p.343), is that you're quite a way from the beach and have to negotiate the ancient site (see below) on each trip. In winter, moreover, the secluded valley gets much less sun than its less confined neighbour and can be pretty cold.

The site of Olympos

Daily: April–Oct 8am–7pm; Nov–March 9am–5.30pm • ₺5; PlajKarts, valid for ten days, allow multiple entry to the site, for multiple users: 10 entries ₺7.5, 25 entries ₺15

Potentially, the site of **Olympos** should be idyllic, set on the banks of an oleander- and fig-shaded stream that runs between high cliffs. Alas, years of visitors littering or sleeping rough here, despite notices forbidding both, have seen the water muddied or worse, and the turtles, ducks and frogs that may still live here now make themselves scarce. The scanty ruins line the banks of the stream, which rarely dries up completely in summer, owing to three freshwater springs welling up on the north bank, close to the ocean.

5

The site has two entrances. One is inland, at the end of the southerly approach road; the other, which is often unmanned, and thus allows free access to the site, is fifteen minutes' walk south along the beach from Çıralı's river mouth. As at Patara, nocturnal "raids" of the ruins are expressly forbidden.

Extensive **Byzantine-Genoese fortifications** overlook the beach from each creek bank, just 25m up the crags. At the base of the north-bank fort are two "**harbour tombs**", one of which has a touching epigraph on a ship captain translated for visitors. Further along the south bank stands part of a quay and an arcaded **warehouse**; to the east on the same side lies a Byzantine **church**; while in the river itself is a pillar from a vanished **bridge**. In the undergrowth there's a **theatre**, its seats mostly gone.

The most striking ruins are on the stream's north bank. East of the path to the beach looms a well-preserved marble **doorframe** built into a wall of ashlar masonry. An inscribed statue base at the foot of the carved doorway is dedicated to Marcus Aurelius, dated 172–175 AD. East of the portal, a Byzantine **aqueduct** that once carried water to the heart of the city overlaps the outflow of one of the aforementioned springs. Head upstream to reach a mausoleum-style **tomb**, and a Byzantine **villa** with mosaic floors.

ARRIVAL AND INFORMATION   OLYMPOS

By bus and minibus Minibuses bound for Kumluca or Kaş from Antalya *otogar* pass the Olympos turn-off (every 20–30min; daily 6am–9pm; ₺10), where waiting minibuses ferry travellers the 9km down to Olympos (₺8) approximately half-hourly. Between November and April, you may have to wait a while before the driver deems he has sufficient customers. Minibuses leave Olympos for the main road every hour. Note that there is no ATM in Olympos, though most places accept card payments.

Activities Most accommodation options organize a range of activities and excursions. *Kadir's Top Tree Houses* (☎ 0242 892 1250, ⓦ kadirstreehouses.com) has the most comprehensive programme on offer with their Olympos rock-climbing centre; they also operate their own scuba-diving outfit and offer sea-kayak tours, canyoning, rafting, jeep safaris, mountain biking and trekking.

Festivals The annual rock-climbing festival (ⓦ olympos rockclimbing.com/festival) is held in Olympos at the end of October.

ACCOMMODATION

Bayram's ☎ 0242 892 1243, ⓦ bayrams.com. The closest option to the ruins, set in an orange grove, this well-run place has standard, a/c, all-wood treehouse-bungalows, with friendly and helpful staff. The youthful clientele lounge about the cushioned garden. Rates per person, including breakfast and evening meal: six-bed dorm ₺60, bungalow ₺100, bungalow ₺150

Kadir's Top Tree Houses ☎ 0242 892 1250, ⓦ kadirstreehouses.com. The original backpacker's lodge, furthest from the ruins. Quirky stilt-bungalows are its main appeal, but there's also a lively bar. In the summer heat the walk to the beach seems a whole lot longer. Rates per person, including breakfast and evening meal: dorm ₺40, treehouse (five-person) ₺45, bungalow ₺65, a/c bungalow ₺85

Şaban ☎ 0242 892 1265, ⓦ sabanpansion.com. One of the quieter establishments, near the stream ford opposite the *Türkmen*. It doesn't play constant music, but does have better-than-average food, lower-density treehouses (some en suite) and more personable management in Ali and Meral. Their shop next door sells a wide range of imported beers. Rates per person, including breakfast and evening meal: dorm ₺35, treehouse ₺60, bungalow ₺80

Türkmen ☎ 0242 892 1249, ⓦ olymposturkmen treehouses.com. The largest and most overtly commercial outfit, set near the stream ford between *Kadir's* and *Bayram's*, with "bloks" (sic) of standard hotel rooms as well as densely sown cabins. It attracts a substantial Turkish clientele and serves some of the best food in the valley. Rates per person, including breakfast and evening meal: treehouse (2–5 person) ₺60, a/c bungalow ₺45, luxury a/c bungalow ₺65

DRINKING AND NIGHTLIFE

Olympos now has something of a reputation as a party spot, with several places offering local **live music**. Many of the treehouse hostels have their own laidback **bars**, too.

Bull Bar Kadir's Top Tree Houses ☎ 0242 892 1250. The in-house bar attached to behemoth *Kadir's Top Tree Houses* opens up its doors to all, though there's a ₺10 entry fee for non-residents in July and August. The big attraction here is the large fire pit. Daily 4pm–2am.

Cactus Café ☎ 0242 892 1055, ⓦ olymposcactus.com.

With live music nightly, this is the place to come for funk, reggae and pop – especially after 11pm, when it really gets going. Daily 1pm–2am.

Eski Yeni ☏ 0242 892 1342, ⓦ eskiyeni.com.tr. This dedicated live music venue draws some surprisingly well-known Turkish bands to its stage, with an emphasis on world music old and new. Daily noon–2am.

Çıralı

The laidback resort of **ÇIRALI**, shrouded in citrus groves, is situated on a narrow plain between the mountains and a long, curving, 3km-long shingle **beach**. Less oriented towards backpackers than neighbouring Olympos, and more family-friendly, it's located in a valley that runs parallel to Olympos on the south side of a mountain spur. Its major attraction is the natural phenomenon known as the **Chimaera**, an area of flames erupting from the ground on a pine-forested hillside. It's also possible to walk along the beach for around half an hour to the ruins of ancient Olympos (see p.343), and there are longer **hikes** on the Lycian Way, which blazes its way through the settlement. Apart from a surprising amount of accommodation tucked beneath the trees – six hotels and around a hundred *pansiyon*s – there's little here bar a beachfront strip of restaurants and, just over the river bridge as you enter the settlement, a short parade of basic shops and cafés.

Locals and the government are currently in dispute over the future of Çıralı, as many of its pensions and other buildings have been built on what's either wholly or partly state forestry land. Some people claim that only ten to fifteen percent of its buildings are legal, and a few have been demolished as a result. However, the fact that Çıralı is safeguarded by various Turkish bodies for its unique **ecology**, along with its designation as a protected area by the WWF, has enabled threatened loggerhead and green sea **turtles** to continue laying their eggs here. Don't dig up, litter or nocturnally illuminate the beach during the summer nesting season.

The Chimaera

Daily 24hr • ₺3.5 • The car park/ticket kiosk is 40min walk north of Çıralı along the road that skirts the mountains; to reach the flames themselves, walk another 20min up the steps

Named after a mythical fire-breathing monster supposed to have inhabited these mountains, the eternal flames of the **Chimaera** (alias Yanartaş) are fed by natural gases emanating from the ground. The climb up to the flames is most rewarding (and coolest) at dusk, since the fire is best seen after dark.

No one really knows what causes the phenomenon of clustered flames that sprout from cracks on the bare hillside. Analysis reveals traces of methane in the gas, but otherwise its make-up is unique. The flames can be extinguished temporarily if covered, when a gaseous smell is noticeable, but will spontaneously re-ignite. They have been burning since antiquity, and inspired local worship of Hephaestos (Vulcan), generally revered wherever fire or lava issued forth. The region was also home to a fire-breathing monster with a lion's head and forelegs, a goat's rear end, and a snake tail: the **Chimaera**. Close to the flames are a small **Byzantine chapel** and the **tholos of Hephaestos**.

BELLEROPHON AND PEGASUS

In legend, **Bellerophon** was ordered by Iobates, king of Xanthos, to kill the Chimaera in atonement for the supposed rape of his daughter Stheneboea. Astride the winged horse **Pegasus**, Bellerophon succeeded, dispatching the beast from the air by dropping lead into its mouth. Later, Bellerophon was found to have been falsely accused, and avenged himself on Stheneboea by persuading her to fly away with him on Pegasus and flinging her into the sea. Retribution came when he attempted to ascend to heaven on Pegasus, and was flung from the back of the magical horse. Lamed and blinded, Bellerophon wandered the earth as a beggar until his death.

5

YOGA IN ÇIRALI

Çıralı is increasingly becoming a destination for **yoga**, with many pensions and hotels offering daily classes in their grounds or on the beach; those at *Myland Nature* (☎0242 825 7044, ⓦmylandnature.com) are open to non-residents as well as residents. The annual week-long **Rainbow Yoga Festival** (ⓦrainbow.yogafest.info/turkey/yoga-rainbow-çıralı), which celebrates its tenth anniversary in Çıralı in 2016, takes place at the start of May in conjunction with a number of establishments in the village.

ARRIVAL AND DEPARTURE
ÇIRALI

By bus and minibus Kumluca- or Kaş-bound minibuses from Antalya *otogar* pass the Çıralı turn-off, signed "Çıralı, Yanartaş, Chimaera" (every 20–30min; daily 6am–9pm;

₺10). Between May and Oct, minibuses wait at the turn-off to make the 7km trip down to Çıralı (₺5); services are infrequent during the rest of the year.

TOURS

Boat tours make a popular way to break up the beach routine; they generally head south to explore the dramatic cliffs and bays around Ceneviz Liman (Porto Genoese) or the opposite direction to Phaselis (see p.348).
Çıralı Beach ☎0242 825 7188, ⓦciralibeach.com. Reliable boat-tour agency, set just behind the beach, where the main road in sweeps left. Tour prices start at €25 per person. Cars (from €30/day) and bikes (₺15/day) are

also available for hire.
Yanartaş ☎0242 825 7188, ⓦyanartas.net. On the road connecting the village centre to the beach, this popular agency rents out bikes for ₺15 per day, and offers daily boat trips from the beach (from ₺70), scuba diving, airport transfers, and excursions (from ₺50) to sites such as Phaselis, Arykanda and the Tahtalı mountain cable car.

ACCOMMODATION

Çıralı's accommodation Is uniformly low-key. The many **pansiyons** either line the beachfront track or dot the citrus grove behind it, and there are also a handful of **campsites**, all tucked away at the quieter north end of the beach.

Azra Villas ☎0535 367 7120, ⓦazravillas.com. On the Yanartaş road, 1.5km north of the village centre, these eight self-catering wooden bungalows are delightfully set among pomegranate trees, with raised verandas looking out over a sea of orange groves. Each bungalow sleeps two to six, and all come with a/c, a fully equipped kitchen and LCD TV. There are picnic tables and hammocks in the garden to the rear, below the limestone cliffs, and guests get free use of the in-house bikes, several of which have child seats. **€75**
Barış Pansiyon ☎0242 825 7080. Set just behind the beach near the restaurants, with a choice of spartan, older en-suite rooms, a new wing of part-balconied upper-floor units (₺20 extra), and three wooden chalets, plus ample parking. Double **₺110**, chalet **₺150**
★**Cemil's Pansiyon** ☎0242 825 7063, ⓦcemil pension.com. Located at the junction of the beach and Chimaera road, *Cemil's* is run by a charming family. The six rooms, part of a long, low terrace, are simple but have a/c and good-quality en-suite bathrooms. The buffet breakfast is eaten in the shade of spreading mulberry trees. The best rooms are, however, in the family farmhouse, fronted by its own orange orchard, just down the road. **€50**
Emin Pansiyon ☎0242 825 7320, ⓦeminpansiyon .com. A mix of stone- and wood-built chalets, with plenty of orchard and/or lawn between the rows. It's on the beach road, 80m beyond *Odile Hotel*, and is popular with yoga and

Lycian Way walking groups. Friendly family management, ample parking and superior breakfasts. **₺130**
Güneş Pansiyon ☎0242 825 7161, ⓦgunespansiyon .com. Friendly owner Recep presides over this laidback place at the start of beach road, inland from the restaurants. Each with its own little veranda fronting onto the citrus grove at the heart of the complex, the series of bungalows are solidly built and simply but nicely decorated, with good bathrooms, fridges and TVs. There are a couple of apartments available, sleeping up to five, and an on-site restaurant. Bungalow **₺200**, apartment **₺450**
★**Myland Nature Pansiyon** ☎0242 825 7044, ⓦmylandnature.com. Better-than-average wooden chalets set in 15 acres of orchard at the north end of the beach strip, beyond the *Odile Hotel*. Pınar and Engin, refugees from the urban rat-race, are your fluent English-speaking hosts. The upscale restaurant features organic food. Free use of the in-house bicycles and sunloungers on the beach out front, and massage and other therapies available. Closed early Nov to late March. **₺280**
★**Odile Hotel** ☎0242 825 7163, ⓦhotelodile.com. Set in lush, beautifully landscaped gardens just past the middle of the beach, with 36 a/c rooms and self-catering bungalows. Rooms all have their own terrace and small garden, and the bungalows are well-equipped, with the kitchen containing a fridge, hob and kettle. There are two

pools and a small bar serving drinks and snacks. Breakfast is generous, and there's complimentary afternoon tea/coffee and cakes. Closed mid-Nov to mid-April. Standard room **€75**, two-person bungalow **€120**

Oleandro Pension 0242 825 7213, oleandro pension.com. One of Çıralı's most stylish pensions, set on the road that runs from the village centre to the beach, opposite *Güneş Pansiyon*. All the ten en-suite rooms in the main building, and two lovely rustic/contemporary bungalow rooms, are elegantly decorated in plain wood, with white walls and white linen, and very tidy en-suite bathrooms. A major plus is the shady garden and delightful

attached restaurant. **€65**

Olympos Lodge 0242 825 7171, olymposlodge .com.tr. Set in 20,000 square metres of lush, semi-tropical gardens at the south end of the beachfront road, next to the river, this is Çıralı's most exclusive accommodation. The bungalows here are extremely comfortable and tastefully fitted out, with natural wood floors, soothing white decor and, out front, a veranda for relaxing as you watch the resident peacocks strut their stuff. A vast breakfast is laid out in a lovely glass gazebo, and evening meals are available. **€190**

EATING AND DRINKING

★**Aubergine** Cemil's Pansiyon 0242 825 7063, cemilpension.com. Traditional Turkish home cooking at its best, plus a few innovative flourishes: you won't find such things as feta cheese, walnut and orange salad in many other places here, nor delicious deep-fried carrots. More familiar is the delicious *testi* kebab, slow-cooked in a sealed pot in the restaurant's own wood-fired oven. There are plenty of fish dishes to choose from too, as well as a handy all-inclusive kids' menu. Mains from ₺20. Decent wine list too. Daily 11am–11pm.

Oleandro Oleandro Pension 0242 825 7213,

oleandropension.com. Formerly the best restaurant on the beach strip, *Oleandro* has maintained its high standards now that it has moved to be a part of the eponymous pension (see above). There's a small, stylish dining room looking out onto elegantly draped tables on wooden decking beneath the greenery. Food, overseen by the relaxed but very professional Cemal, is Turkish/international and very good value for the quality. The tasty grilled steak with spinach is ₺22, chicken with halloumi cheese ₺18, and wine ₺9 a glass; they also serve a decent latte. Daily 9am–11pm.

Beycik

The village of **BEYCİK** spreads out amid pleasant orchards, almost in the shadow of 2366m Mount Olympos (Tahtalı Dağı). At over 1000m above sea level, it has become something of a refuge for both Turks and foreigners to escape the humidity of the coastal belt in the summer months. Many have bought property here to enjoy the cool air and superb views over forest and mountain, though in truth there's not much to do bar relax or walk.

As the inland variant of the **Lycian Way** links Beycik with Çıralı, the village makes a logical staging point on the traverse to Yayla Kuzdere and Gedelme along the Lycian Way, crossing over the cedar-clad saddle of Mount Olympos at 1800m. Keen walkers can enjoy a long hike from Beycik to the summit of **Mount Olympos**; allow ten hours for the full round trip.

Tahtalı 2365 cable car

Daily: May–Sept 9am–7pm; Oct–March 10am–6pm; cars run every 30min • ₺50 return • olymposteleferik.com

The peak of Mount Olympus is now crowned by a bunker-like restaurant, and can also be reached much more easily via a **cable car** that ascends via unsightly pylons from Tekirova. Known as **Tahtalı 2365**, the cable car runs through a supposedly protected national park, and can be reached via a side road that loops right from the main coastal highway 2km north of Phaselis.

ARRIVAL AND DEPARTURE
BEYCİK

By car Beycik is a 45min drive southwest of Antalya, and some 17km above and northwest of Çıralı. To reach it, drive

7km inland from Highway 400, up a side road just east of the Ulupınar turning.

ACCOMMODATION AND EATING

Rivera Yukarı Beycik 0242 816 1005. Far better than the more famous places down on the coastal highway at

Ulupınar, this quirky place dishes up sizzling trout oven-baked in clay dishes, accompanied by tender roasted

5

onions and potatoes – all for ₺18. Just as big a draw is the setting, a series of wooden decks at different heights built into the spreading boughs of an ancient, monumental plane tree. Daily 11am–midnight.

★ **Villa il Castello** Beycik Köyü ☎0242 816 1013,

🌐villa-castello.com. Extremely attractive Turkish-German-run place, set around a neat pool in immaculately landscaped grounds. The nine large, well-appointed suites provide space for two kids and two adults and, at 1000m elevation, are heated but not air-conditioned. ₺250

Phaselis

Daily: summer 8.30am–7pm; winter 9am–5.30pm • ₺8, plus parking fee

Heading north from Olympos, there's scant pretext to stop before Antalya. The overdeveloped, overpriced package resorts along this coast – Tekirova, Kemer, Göynük and Beldibi – leave much to be desired. Lying 1km off Highway 400, 3km north of Tekirova, only ancient **Phaselis**, with its superb swimming opportunities, will tempt you off the main road. Founded by Rhodian colonists in 690 BC, Phaselis, almost in Pamphylia, was not always Lycian. The Phaselitans were great **traders**, sailing as far as Egypt, and their coins were decorated with ships. Along with most of Asia Minor, Phaselis was overrun by the Persians in the sixth century, and not freed until 469 BC, when Athenian general Cimon "liberated" them with some difficulty, enrolling the reluctant city in the Athenian maritime confederacy along with Olympos. A century later, Phaselis helped Mausolus, satrap of Caria, attempt to subdue Lycia, while in 333 BC Phaselitan sycophancy continued: not content with merely surrendering to Alexander the Great, the city also proffered a golden crown.

Phaselis finally became part of the Lycian Federation during the second century BC, but was soon, like Olympos, occupied by Zeniketes' **pirates**. Although it rejoined the federation afterwards, the pirates had devastated the city. Under imperial Rome, Phaselis distinguished itself with yet more obsequiousness: when touring Emperor Hadrian visited in 129 AD, statues were erected, and a gateway dedicated to him.

The site

The **ruins** of Phaselis flank three small bays, providing ample opportunity to contemplate antique monuments while lying on the beach. While they can't compare with some sites east of Antalya, or nearby Arykanda, there's certainly enough to see at Phaselis, where *Jason and the Argonauts* was filmed in 1999. The natural beauty and clear sea make for a rewarding half-day outing – bring a picnic if you don't fancy the car-park snack-caravans.

The access road passes under a bluff that holds a **fortified settlement** enclosed by a Hellenistic wall, including a tower and three archery slits. The most obvious landmark, behind a helpful map placard and the first car park, is the substantial, elegant Roman **aqueduct**. Said to have been among the longest in the ancient world, it carried water from a spring inside the northern fortifications almost as far as the south harbour.

The harbours

Arrayed around the promontory behind which most of the fan-shaped city stood, Phaselis's three **harbours** are obvious, and ideal for orientation. The north harbour was too exposed to be used except in very favourable conditions, but traces of the ancient **south quay** remain. It made an easy landing point for aggressors, however, so was fortified with a 3m-wide wall – now submerged, but still intact. The middle harbour also had a strong sea wall, and its 18m-wide entrance could be closed off; today it's a shallow cove with a small beach that's wonderful for swimming (and snorkelling out to explore the Roman breakwater).

The largest, **southwest port** (with its own parking and ticket booth for boat arrivals) was protected by a 180m-long breakwater, now mostly submerged. It sheltered the largest trading vessels, and now sees numerous pleasure craft calling for the sake of its fine, large beach.

The ancient city centre

Between the harbours, the promontory **acropolis** is covered with overgrown ruins of dwellings and round cisterns. The city's main axis is the **paved avenue** across the neck of the promontory, linking the south and middle harbours; a rectangular plaza partway along is thought to be the heart of the **agora**. At the southern-harbour end, only the foundations and tumbled marble masonry survive of the monumental **gateway** constructed to honour Hadrian's visit.

The well-preserved **theatre**, dating from the second century AD, looks towards Tahtalı Dağ from between the acropolis and the main street, and held around 1500 people. Three large doors above what's now ground level probably led to the stage; below these, five smaller doors would have opened into the orchestra, and may have been used to admit wild animals.

ARRIVAL AND DEPARTURE **PHASELIS**

By bus Buses along the coastal highway from Antalya (frequent; 1hr; ₺5) drop passengers at the clearly marked turn, a pleasant pine-shaded walk from the site and beach.

The Mediterranean coast and the Hatay

KIZKALESI

The Mediterranean coast and the Hatay

6

Turkey's Mediterranean coast, where the Toros (Taurus) mountain range sweeps down to meet the sea, broadly divides into three parts. The stretch from Antalya to Alanya is the most accessible tourist region, although intensive agriculture, particularly cotton growing, and package tourism have taken a toll on the environment. East of Alanya, the mountains meet the sea head-on, making for some of Turkey's most hair-raising roads, curving around jagged stretches of coastline. As a result, this is the least developed and unspoilt section of the Mediterranean shore. Further east the mountains finally recede, giving way to the flat, monotonous landscape of the Ceyhan river delta. South and east of here, turning the corner towards Syria, the landscape becomes more interesting, as the Amanus mountain range dominates the fertile coastal plain, with citrus crops and olives the mainstay of the economy.

The bustling, modern city of **Antalya** is the prime arrival and junction point. East of here, in the ancient region of Pamphylia, the ruins of three cities – **Perge**, **Aspendos** and **Side** – testify to the sophisticated civilization that flourished during the Hellenistic period, and are well-established day-trip destinations from Antalya. The more isolated **Termessos**, a Pisidian city north of Antalya, is the most spectacularly sited, with its rugged hilltop terrain peppered with stone ruins.

Seventy kilometres east along the coast from Side, the former pirate refuge of **Alanya** – now a bustling package-tour destination – is set on and around a dramatic headland topped by a Selçuk citadel. As you continue east, the best places to break your journey are **Anamur**, where a ruined Hellenistic city abuts some of this coast's finest beaches, and **Kızkalesi**, whose huge Byzantine castle is marooned 200m off the shore of a sandy bay. Kızkalesi also makes a good base from which to explore the ancient city of **Uzuncaburç**, a lonely ruin perched high in the Toros Mountains.

Beyond Kızkalesi, in the fertile alluvial delta known as the **Çukurova**, the Ceyhan River spills down from the mountains and meanders sluggishly into the eastern Mediterranean. This end of the coast – characterized by concentrations of industry and low-lying cotton plantations – has very little to recommend it. **Mersin** offers regular ferry connections to Northern Cyprus; **Tarsus**, the birthplace of St Paul, holds a few surviving reminders of its long history; and **Adana**, one of the country's largest urban centres, is a hectic staging post for journeys further east.

From Adana, routes head north to the central Anatolian plateau, or east to the Euphrates and Tigris basins; this chapter turns its attention south, towards the area formed by the curve of the coast down towards Syria. This is the **Hatay**, a fertile, hilly region where different cultures have met – and often clashed – in their efforts to dominate the important Silk Route trade. **Antakya**, the Hatay's main centre, is the best starting point

ANTALYA HARBOUR

Highlights

❶ Kaleiçi Antalya's old quarter, clustered around a charming harbour, is great for nightlife and shopping. **See p.355**

❷ Köprülü Kanyon Spanned by a graceful Roman bridge, the Köprülü river gorge is ideal for novice whitewater rafters. **See p.364**

❸ Termessos Arguably the most dramatically situated of all Turkey's ancient sites, perched on the edge of a precipitous gorge. **See p.364**

❹ Aspendos Stunningly preserved Roman theatre, and the impressive venue for an annual opera and ballet festival. **See p.368**

❺ Uzuncaburç Wander along the streets and through the temples of the ruined city, now a sleepy mountain village. **See p.384**

❻ Kızkalesi Recline on the sandy Mediterranean beach and ponder the serenity of the offshore Maiden's Castle. **See p.385**

❼ Antakya's Archeological Museum Don't miss the immaculately preserved collection of Roman mosaics. **See p.400**

❽ Regional cuisine For a taste of the Hatay, try the unique fiery *muhammara*, served with flatbread and a chilled beer. **See p.403**

HIGHLIGHTS ARE MARKED ON THE MAP ON PP.354–355

for explorations, though cosmopolitan **İskenderun** makes for a surprisingly agreeable base. Antakya has frequent dolmuş connections to **Harbiye**, site of the Roman resort of Daphne, and to the town of **Samandağ**, from where you can visit Armenian **Vakıflı**.

Antalya to Alanya

The stretch of coast between **Antalya and Alanya** is among the most developed in Turkey. With a four-lane highway running right behind many beaches, flanked by all-inclusive hotels and holiday-village complexes, it's hard to imagine that this was once ancient **Pamphylia**, a loose federation of Hellenistic cities established by incomers from northern Anatolia. Home to a busy international airport, the booming city of **Antalya** is the gateway to the region. Now a fully fledged resort, it is worth visiting for its restored old town and marvellous Archeological Museum. The nearest (and most fascinating) ruined city is **Termessos**, perched on the saddle of Mount Solymos overlooking the Antalya gulf. East of Antalya, the surviving ruined cities of Pamphylia also rival the beaches as tourist attractions, with **Perge** and **Aspendos** the best-preserved and most evocative sites. Further along the coast, **Side** is a major resort, though the striking ruins of its ancient city are fast being overshadowed by package-tourist facilities. **Alanya**, the next sizeable centre, has also seen an explosion of hotel building and tourism-related commerce over the last few years, but has retained an attractive old quarter.

Antalya

One of Turkey's fastest-growing cities, **ANTALYA** is blessed with an ideal climate (excluding the searing heat of July and Aug) and a stunning setting atop a limestone plateau, with the formidable Beydağları looming to the west. In the heart of town, the pretty yacht harbour huddles below the Roman walls, while the crescent of Konyaaltı bay curves to

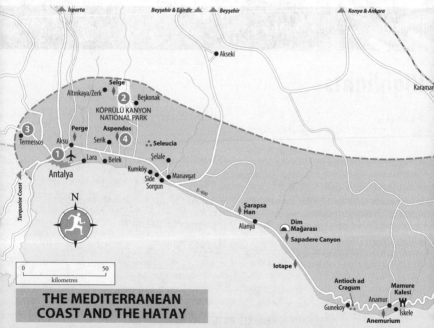

THE MEDITERRANEAN
COAST AND THE HATAY

the industrial harbour 10km west. Interest for tourists is largely confined to the relatively tiny and central old quarter within the Roman walls, known as the **Kaleiçi** (or "within the castle"). The city's renowned **Archeological Museum**, however, west of the old town, is home to one of the finest collections in the country, and a crop of new attractions have sprung up around it, most notably the sizeable **Antalya Aquarium**.

Brief history

Antalya was founded as late as the second century BC by Attalus II of Pergamon, and named **Attaleia** in his honour. The Romans only consolidated their hold on the city and its hinterland during the imperial period, following successful campaigns against local pirates. Christianity and the Byzantines had a similarly slow start, though because of its strategic location and good anchorage Antalya was an important halt for the Crusaders. The Selçuks supplanted the Byzantines for good early in the thirteenth century, and to them are owed most of the medieval monuments visible today (albeit some built on Byzantine foundations). Ottoman Antalya figured little in world events until 1918, when the Italians made it the focus of their short-lived Turkish colony.

6

Kaleiçi

The best place to start exploring Antalya's old town, **Kaleiçi**, is from the redeveloped **old harbour**, where the once-crumbling quays have been rebuilt, gardens laid out and the harbour walls restored. Popular with tourists and locals alike, the quayside is now clustered with restaurants, cafés and clubs, while pirate boats, charter *gulets* and fishing boats are moored along the waterfront, offering day-trips to the caves and islands along the coast. A new **glass lift** runs between the harbour (to the left of the Toy Museum) and Cumhuriyet Caddesi (a short walk from the Atatürk statue) above, offering panoramic views and a welcome alternative from the steep cobblestone lanes of Kaleiçi. At the top of the lift, the vast public square has been redeveloped, with ample picnic spots, grassy areas and cafés perched on the cliffs overlooking the harbour.

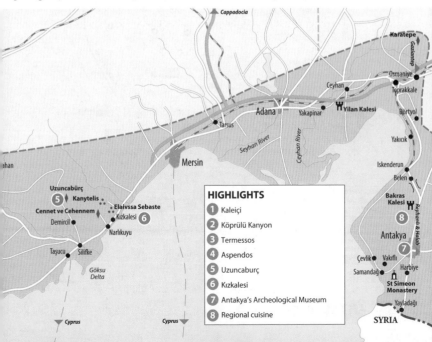

HIGHLIGHTS

1. Kaleiçi
2. Köprülü Kanyon
3. Termessos
4. Aspendos
5. Uzuncaburç
6. Kızkalesi
7. Antakya's Archeological Museum
8. Regional cuisine

Ankara, Termessos & Otogar (7km)

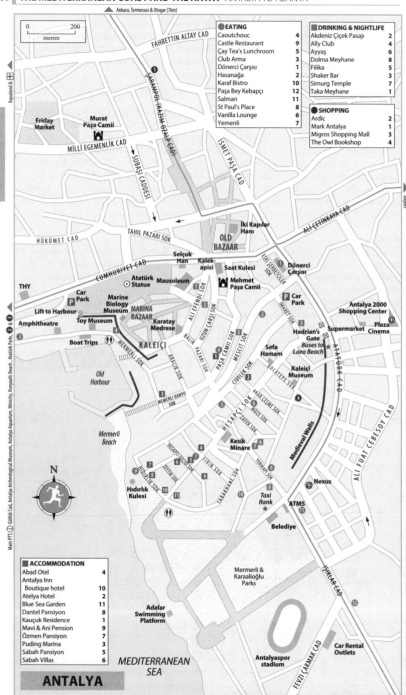

0 200 metres

EATING
Caoutchouc	4
Castle Restaurant	9
Çay Tea's Lunchroom	5
Club Arma	3
Dönerci Çarşısı	1
Hasanağa	2
Karaf Bistro	10
Paşa Bey Kebapçı	12
Salman	11
St Paul's Place	8
Vanilla Lounge	6
Yemenli	7

DRINKING & NIGHTLIFE
Akdeniz Çiçek Pasajı	2
Ally Club	4
Ayyaş	6
Dolma Meyhane	8
Filika	5
Shaker Bar	3
Simurg Temple	7
Taka Meyhane	1

SHOPPING
Ardic	2
Mark Antalya	1
Migros Shopping Mall	3
The Owl Bookshop	4

ACCOMMODATION
Abad Otel	4
Antalya Inn Boutique hotel	10
Atelya Hotel	2
Blue Sea Garden	11
Dantel Pansiyon	8
Kauçuk Residence	1
Mavi & Ani Pension	9
Özmen Pansiyon	7
Puding Marina	3
Sabah Pansiyon	5
Sabah Villas	6

FAHRETTIN ALTAY CAD

SARAMPOL (KAZIM OZALP CAD)

İSMET PAŞA CAD

MİLLİ EGEMENLİK CAD

Friday Market

Murat Paşa Camii

SUBAŞI CADDESİ

HÜKÜMET CAD

TAHİL PAZARI SOK

OLD BAZAAR

İki Kapılar Hanı

ALİ ÇETİNKAYA CAD

CUMHURİYET CAD

Selçuk Han

Kalek-apisi

Saat Kulesi

Dönerci Çarşısı

ESKİ SEBZECİLER SOK

THY

Atatürk Statue

Mausoleum

Mehmet Paşa Camii

Car Park

Car Park

Antalya 2000 Shopping Center

Marine Biology Museum

MARINA BAZAAR

Karatay Medrese

Hadrian's Gate

Supermarket

Plaza Cinema

Lift to Harbour

Amphitheatre

Toy Museum

Boat Trips

KALEİÇİ

MERMERLİ SOK

ARKLIK SOK

BALIK PAZARI SOK

ALİ EFENDİ SOK

UZUN ÇARŞI SOK

PAŞA CAMİİ SOK

MESCİT SOK

İMARET SOK

Sefa Hamam

Buses to Lara Beach

ATATÜRK CAD

Kaleiçi Museum

Old Harbour

Mermerli Beach

MEMERLİ BANYO SOK

HESAPÇI SOK

CİVELEK SOK

AKAR ÇEŞME SOK

LOCATEPE SOK

Kaleiçi Museum

N

HESAPÇI ÇIKMAZ

ZAFER SOK

MÜZE SOK

Kesik Minare

YENİKAPI SOK

Medieval Walls

ALİ FUAT CEBESOY CAD

ZEYTİN SOK

FIRIN SOK

HIDIRLIK SOK

ZABERHANE SOK

Hıdırlık Kulesi

Taxi Rank

Nexus

ATMS

Belediye

Mermerli & Karaalioğlu Parks

Adalar Swimming Platform

MEDITERRANEAN SEA

Antalyaspor stadium

Car Rental Outlets

FEVZİ ÇAKMAK CAD

IŞIKLAR CAD

ANTALYA

Aqualand &

Main PTT, Güllük Cad, Antalya Archeological Museum, Antalya Aquarium, Minicity, Konyaaltı Beach, Atatürk Parkı,

Airport

Lara & Düden Waterfalls

To explore on foot from the harbour, head uphill along Uzun Çarşi Sokak, past the eighteenth-century **Mehmet Paşa Camii**, to **Kalekapısı** (Castle Gate), the main entrance to the old town. Nearby, the **Saat Kulesi** (Clock Tower), a Selçuk tower with inset Roman column drums, is built into a section of the old walls. Kalekapısı is overlooked by the **Yivli Minare** or "Fluted Minaret", erected during the thirteenth-century reign of the Selçuk sultan, Alâeddin Keykubad, and today something of a symbol of the city. Facing the Yivli Minare is an early, plain **Selçuk han** whose crumbling walls have been "restored", a rather grand term for encasing the ruins in glass and filling the interior with souvenir shops. Above this area, but accessed from Cumhuriyet Caddesi, is an old baths, and a pyramidal **mausoleum** from 1377.

Bearing right onto Atatürk Caddesi, you'll soon come across the triple-arched **Hadrian's Gate** (Üç Kapılar), recalling a visit by that emperor in 130 AD. Hesapçı Sokak, the quietest entry to Kaleiçi, begins here; it's a cobbled street of restored Ottoman houses that now holds assorted pensions, trinket shops, restaurants and bars. About halfway along, the tower and attendant buildings known collectively as the **Kesik Minare** (Broken Minaret) form an architectural anomaly that's done successive duty as temple, church and mosque.

Kaleiçi Museum

Kocatepe Sok 25, off Hesapçı Sok • Daily except Wed 9am–noon & 1–5pm • ₺3 • ☎ 0242 243 4274, ⓦ kaleicimuzesi.org

Set in two restored Ottoman houses, the **Kaleiçi Museum** showcases traditional Turkish interiors and cultural heritage items. The first house depicts life in the nineteenth century, with costumed mannequins portraying scenes of daily life, but the second is arguably the most interesting, containing a marvellous library. Here, treasures include original editions of the engravings made by the archeologist-cum-explorer **Texier** when he investigated Asia Minor for the French government in the 1840s. Behind the houses, the restored **church of St George** is used for exhibitions of items from the private collection of the Koç family, who sponsor the institute.

Mermerli beach

By the harbour • Day pass ₺15 • Accessible via a private staircase from the *Mermerli* restaurant

The only city-centre beach, **Mermerli**, just by the harbour, is, not surprisingly, packed. Sunbeds and parasols are cramped along a mere sliver of sand; it's hardly idyllic, but this is one of the only places to catch some rays and take a dip without having to travel out of town.

Toy Museum

On the harbour • Tues–Sun 10am–12.30pm & 1.30–5pm • ₺6, children under 12yrs ₺3.5 • ☎ 0242 248 4933

Out of a number of small museums that have sprung up in recent years around the waterfront, the quirky **Toy Museum** (Oyuncak Müzesi) is notable. The displays, dating back to the 1960s, include a sassy collection of Barbie dolls as well as a colourful array of well-loved wooden toys, tin cars and action figures from all over the world.

Marine Biology Museum

Iskele Cad • Tues–Sun 9.30am–6.30pm • ₺6 • ☎ 0242 248 3941

East of the Toy Museum, at the entrance to the Marina Bazaar, the **Marine Biology Museum** (Deniz Biyolojisi Müzesi) is worth a look. Inside is a small but significant

---

THE PARKS OF ANTALYA

The **Mermerli** and **Karaalioğlu** parks, just east of **Kaleiçi**, offer some well-needed shade and contain a number of pleasant tea gardens, with views stretching along the coast. In the northwestern corner, the **Hıdırlık Kulesi**, a round Roman tower, is the best place in town to watch the frequently spectacular sunsets over the snowcapped mountains and the gulf of Antalya.

Atatürk Parkı, 2km west of the centre, is a clifftop park and a favourite spot for joggers, roller-bladers and Sunday strollers, with tea gardens and children's playgrounds on site.

collection of preserved specimens with English descriptions and a focus on local sea life, including various fish, squid, rays, crabs and sharks.

The bazaars

Antalya's **Old Bazaar**, at the southeast corner of Şarampol, sells mainly gold, clothes and shoes. Of the daily bazaars throughout the city, the most interesting is the **Friday Market** (Cuma Pazarı), with local produce stalls and clothing vendors packed into the streets west of Murat Paşa Camii.

Antalya Archeological Museum

At the far end of Konyaaltı Cad, on the western edge of town • Tues–Sun: April–Oct 9am–7.30pm; Nov–March 8.30am–5pm • ₺20 • Take bus #8 or any "Müze" or "Liman" dolmuş from the city centre – departing from one of the "D" signs along Cumhuriyet Cad – or catch the westbound tramway to its last stop, Müze (₺2)

The one must-see attraction in Antalya, well worth a few hours of your time, is the **Antalya Archeological Museum** (Arkeoloji Müzesi), which ranks among the top five archeological collections in the country. The galleries are arranged both chronologically and thematically. Standing out among the early items is a cache of **Bronze Age** urn burials from near Elmalı. Dating from the seventh and sixth centuries BC, they include several silver and ivory Phrygian figurines sporting droll yet dignified expressions and silver *paterae* (plates for wine libations).

It's quite a jump in time to the next galleries, which contain second-century AD **statues from Perge**: a complete pantheon in unusually good condition has been assembled. Best exhibits of the adjoining sarcophagus wing are two almost undamaged coffers depicting the **labours of Hercules**. The corner hall leads into a gallery dedicated to **friezes** and statues from Perge's theatre. It's a marvellous display, including statues of gods and emperors and a frieze showing battles between heroes and giants.

The upstairs galleries are devoted to coinage and **icons** recovered after 1922 from various local churches, including a reliquary containing what are purported to be the bones of **St Nicholas of Myra** (see p.338). There's also a bookshop, a **café** and a pleasant shady garden scattered with fine overspill sculptures and tombs.

Konyaaltı beach

Free entry; loungers and umbrellas ₺10–15 • Catch a taxi (around ₺30), take bus #5 from Cumhuriyet Cad or ride the west-bound tram to the terminus, then walk 5min downhill

Antalya's lengthy western beach, **Konyaaltı**, now spruced up, is finally beginning to live up to its dramatic situation between Antalya's cliffs and the Beydağları mountains. Shingle rather than sand, it's clean and well maintained. Visitors with children should be aware that the beach shelves quite steeply, and there's a slight tow from west to east. A pleasant **promenade** lined with palm trees and cafés backs the beach, behind which the recently redeveloped area is home to a number of family attractions (see box opposite).

Lara Beach

10km southeast of Antalya • Parasol and sunbed ₺10 • Catch bus #8 or a dolmuş along Atatürk Cad

Lara Beach, with its long stretch of fine sand, runs east of Antalya's cliffs, just past the popular **Lower Düden waterfall**. It combines both free and pay areas; the gentle waves make for some great swimming spots.

Adalar swimming area

Day pass ₺10

Reached via steep steps from Karaalioğlu Park, the **Adalar** swimming area, with decking on the rocks and ladders running into the sea, offers a worthy alternative to the beach. The staff are friendly, drinks and snacks reasonably priced, and the views across the bay magnificent.

ANTALYA FOR KIDS

Behind Konyaaltı beach are a number of child-friendly attractions to keep the whole family occupied. **Antalya Aquarium** (daily: 9.30am–11pm; adult €32 or €85 including other parks, children 3–12yrs €26 or €65 including other parks, under 3yrs free; ☎0242 245 6565, ⊛antalya aquarium.com), has the world's biggest tunnel aquarium (an impressive 131m long) and forty themed areas. The complex is also home to a 4-D **cinema**, the **Wildpark** (devoted to insects and reptiles) and an **indoor snow park**. Be aware that **prices** for the Aquarium do vary throughout the year, and many visitors complain of being overcharged, or the stated price changing on arrival. The safest option is to pre-purchase tickets through your hotel or a tour agency – make sure you confirm which areas your tickets provide access to and whether transfers are included.

Next door are the **AquaLand** and **DolphinLand** waterparks (see p.360) and **Antalya Minicity** (daily 8am–7pm; ₺5; ☎0242 229 4545, ⊛minicitypark.com), which has 1:25 scale re-creations of some of Turkey's most iconic landmarks, including Haghia Sophia, Pammukale, the Aspendos theatre and the Temple of Artemis at Ephesus.

The **Toy Museum** (see p.357) at Antalya's harbour also provides a fun distraction from the beach.

6

ARRIVAL AND DEPARTURE ANTALYA

BY BUS OR DOLMUŞ

Otogar On the Ankara road, 7km north of town, and used by both buses and inter-town dolmuşes. There's a 24hr left-luggage office marked "Emanet" (from ₺10). To reach the town centre, catch either the bus companies' own *servis* buses, or the blue-and-white municipal bus #83 (₺2). Alight near the Atatürk statue on Cumhuriyet Cad for accommodation on the west of the old city, or at the Belediye (Town Hall) corner for the east side. The AntRay tramline also runs from the *otogar* to the centre of town – take the southbound tram towards Meydan.

Tickets Pensions in the old town sell or book tickets for direct buses from Antalya *otogar* to almost all Turkey's provincial capitals. Major companies, such as Kamil Koç, Akdeniz and Metro, have ticket offices in town, mostly on Subaşı Cad.

Destinations from Antalya otogar Adana (13 daily; 12hr); Afyon (hourly, 5hr); Alanya (every 30min; 2hr); Ankara (every 30min; 10hr); Antakya (14 daily; 14hr); Denizli (5 daily; 5hr 30min); Diyarbakır (5 daily; 16hr); Eğirdir (8 daily; 3hr); Fethiye, by inland route (6 daily; 4hr); Isparta (hourly; 2hr 30min); Istanbul (every 30min; 12hr); İzmir (hourly; 9hr 30min); Konya (15 daily; 5hr 30min); Manavgat/Side (every 20min; 1hr 30min).

Destinations in the southwest Buses leave from the *otogar*. Fethiye by coastal route (8 daily; 8hr); Finike (8 daily; 2hr); Kalkan (8 daily; 5hr); Kaş (8 daily; 4hr 30min); Kemer/Beldibi/Göynük (every 30min; 1hr).

BY FERRY

Ferry harbour The main ferry harbour and dock where fortnightly ferries arrive from Venice is west of Konyaaltı Beach, 10km from the centre of town. There is no dolmuş service, so you'll have to take a taxi to the centre (from €20). **Tickets** Turkish Maritime Lines office, Konyaaltı Cad 40/19 (☎0242 241 1120).

BY PLANE

Airport Antalya's lushly landscaped airport is 12km east of the city, at the centre of a maze of motorways (general info ☎0242 330 3030, flight enquiries ☎0242 330 3600; ⊛aytport.com). Official taxis (☎0242 330 3108; ⊛antalyaairporttaxi.net), available outside the terminal, can be booked online. Expect to pay around €20 per car to get into town during the day, or €30 midnight–6am. If you flag a taxi, drivers may tell you that your chosen hotel has closed, and offer to take you to another. If this occurs, be insistent. Municipal bus #600 connects the airport with the *otogar* (every 30min; 30min), but check with your flight company, as many offer free shuttles to the city centre or *otogar*.

Airlines THY, Konyaaltı Cad 24, Antmarın İş Mer-kezi (☎0242 243 4383, reservations ☎0212 444 0849); Onur Air, Çağlayan Mah, 2055 Sok 20, Barınaklar (☎0242 324 1335, reservations ☎0212 444 6687); Atlas Jet, Antalya Airport (☎0242 330 3900, reservations ☎0242 444 3387).

Domestic destinations Ankara (3 daily; 1hr); Bodrum via Istanbul (5 weekly; 6hr); Istanbul (15 daily; 1hr–1hr 20min); İzmir via Istanbul (1 or 2 daily; 3hr 40min).

International destinations East Midlands (1 weekly in season; 4hr 30min); Glasgow (2 weekly in season; 4hr 50min); Leeds Bradford (2 weekly in season; 4hr 30min); London Gatwick (daily; 4hr 10min); London Luton (2 weekly in season; 4hr 20min); Manchester (5 weekly; 4hr 35min); Newcastle (1 weekly in season; 4hr 35min).

BY CAR

Car rental Kaleiçi has numerous car rental agencies, and there are many more on Fevzi Çakmak Cad, near Antalyaspor's stadium. In July and Aug, book your car well in advance; at other times, bargain hard. Alternatively, try the *Özmen Pension* (see p.361), Mithra Travel (see p.360), or Hertz (☎0242 330 3848) out at the airport.

6

GETTING AROUND

By dolmuş Frequent dolmuşes run around the city, as well as to nearby towns and beaches, and can (in theory) be flagged down at any point en-route. However, many routes have now been replaced by minibuses (often still referred to as dolmuşes by locals) that stop only at scheduled points. If in doubt, wait at one of the marked bus stops.

By tram Antalya has two tramlines: the AntRay line runs from north of the *otogar* to Meydan, via Atatürk Cad and Kaleiçi (₺5 for three rides), and the Nostalji Tramway runs from Antalya Museum, via Kalekapısı, to Lara Beach (₺2 for a single fare). Plans are also underway to extend the AntRay line to the airport, which may come to fruition at some point in 2016.

INFORMATION

Tourist office Currently the city's only tourist office is inconveniently located on Güllük Cad, 100m north of the main PTT (daily: summer 9am–6pm; winter 8.30am–5.30pm; ☎0242 241 1747), but plans are underway to open information points and wi-fi hubs in Kaleiçi; check with your hotel before heading out. Most

Kaleiçi pensions will provide free maps and information on tours and transport.

Useful Website "Kaleiçi Old Town" (ⓦ kaleicioldtown .com) has excellent English-language information. They are also in the process of launching an iPhone and Android app for visitors; keep your eye on the website for details.

TOURS AND ACTIVITIES

Bike tours A new bike route runs along the entire coastline from Konyaaltı beach to Lara Beach and the Düden waterfalls – E-Bike Antalya (☎0552 213 1513, ⓦ ebikeantalya.com) offer tours by electric bike.

Boat tours Tours offered from the harbour in Kaleiçi range from 45min to a full day, with various pirate boats, yachts and *gulets* available. Full-day tours take in the best views of the Düden waterfalls, cascades that end at Lara Beach, plus a combination of local beaches, swimming, cruising the gulf and a barbecue lunch. Expect a 2hr trip to cost from ₺25 per person, and an evening cruise with entertainment from ₺50, but be sure to negotiate.

Hiking Mithra Travel (Hesapçı Sok ☎0242 248 7747, ⓦ mithratravel.com), in the old city, organize one- or two-day treks (from around €25/person/day) in the limestone massifs overlooking Antalya, and can also arrange self-guided walks.

Scuba diving Assorted diving spots along Antalya's coastline include the possibility to try wreck diving or even diving to a sunken plane. Akdeniz Diving (at the harbour

right next to the amphitheatre – look for the signs; ☎0242 248 1257, ⓦ akdenizdiving.com) offer PADI dive courses, try-dives and more challenging excursions for experienced divers. A day's diving for beginners, including training and two full-length dives, costs around €65.

Waterparks AquaLand, next door to the Antalya Aquarium (May–Oct daily 10am–6pm; adults ₺47, children ₺28; ☎0242 249 0908, ⓦ aqualand.com.tr), has a range of giant slides, chutes and wave pools, while the adjoining DolphinLand offers daily dolphin shows for an extra cost (adults ₺40, children ₺27) as well as the chance to swim with them (from ₺270).

Whitewater rafting A full-day excursion on the Köprülü river, with a day's rafting, plus transfers and meal, costs from €35 from Antalya. Book through Antalya travel agents or one of the Kaleiçi *pansiyons*.

Yachting Some yachts are open to charter for groups of four to twelve. Ask around at the harbour during the slow spring season and you could get a bargain overnight cruise for the same price as hotel bed and board.

ACCOMMODATION

All accommodation listed below is in the walled quarter of **Kaleiçi**. Heavily discounted rates can be negotiated off season.

Abad Otel Hesapçı Sok 65 ☎0242 248 9723, ⓦ antalyahostel.com. Friendly and well-run *pansiyon* with simple yet impeccably clean rooms, with crisp white linens and a/c. *Abad*'s biggest selling point is that guests have free access to the pool and terrace at the nearby *Blue Sea Garden* hotel (see below), giving it an edge over other budget options. Prices drop considerably out of season. ₺90

★ **Antalya Inn Boutique Hotel** Hıdırlık Sok 41 ☎0242 241 5242, ⓦ antalyainnhotel.com. Matching marble and hardwood floors with cast-iron furniture and beautifully restored stone-brick walls, this self-effacing hotel offers a romantic retreat at a fraction of the price of most boutique

hotels. The rooftop terrace restaurant is the icing on the cake, where you can tuck into delicious *mezes* and fresh juice with a spectacular view over the Med. ₺160

Atelya Hotel Civelek Sok 21 ☎0242 241 6416, ⓦ atelyahotel.com. A delightfully restored Ottoman house in a central location, set around an attractive courtyard bar and open-air swimming pool. The rustic decor is delightful – the walls are hung with bright kilim, black-and-white photographs, and quirky antiques. €60

Blue Sea Garden Hesapçı Sok 64 ☎0242 248 8213, ⓦ hotelblueseagarden.com. The undeniable highlight of *Blue Sea Garden* is the idyllic central courtyard with its swimming pool and sunloungers shaded by orange trees and towering palms – the perfect setting for breakfast or evening drinks. Rooms overlook the garden and are modern and comfortable; some have a sea view. The adjoining *Blue Sea Garden Family* offers excellent-value family rooms and apartments, with exquisite decor and brand-new bathrooms. ₺150

Dantel Pansiyon Zeytin Geçidi 4 ☎0242 247 3486, ⓦdantelpension.com. Charming staff and well-furnished rooms combine to produce a favourable budget option in this seafront location. The cheerful rooms feature bold-coloured bedspreads and kitsch black chandeliers, livening up an otherwise clean and functional abode. €45

Kauçuk Residence Paşa Camii Sok 22 ☎0242 244 2377, ⓦkaucukotel.com. Named after the rubber tree that sprouts over its walls and masterfully restored with handcrafted wood- and ironwork, *Kauçuk* is a boutique hotel in the true sense of the word. English-speaking owner Rengin has painstakingly designed each of the eleven rooms, which are named after important women in her life, and her subtle style lends them a calm elegance. The on-site restaurant (see below), open-air swimming pool and palm-fringed sun terrace further add to the experience, as does the tasty home-cooked breakfast. €85

★Mavi & Ani Pension Tabakhane Sok 13, 19, 23 ☎0242 247 5676, ⓦmaviani.com. It's the warm welcome at *Mavi & Ani* that wins rave reviews from guests, and this homely pension offers a quiet haven for road-weary travellers. The English-speaking hosts have stamped their personal touch on the traditional Anatolian residence, with rich wood fittings, crisp white sheets and unique artworks adding a splash of colour – plus there's a sizeable terrace. The family rooms with mezzanines are particularly good value, but there's also a selection of new, well-kitted out luxury apartments (from €70). €45

Özmen Pension Zeytin Çıkmazı 5 ☎0242 241 6505, ⓦozmenpension.com. One of the friendliest and most reliable of Kaleiçi's many pensions, *Özmen* is run by English-speaking couple Deniz and Aziz, who will go out of their way to make you feel at home. Rooms are simple but comfortable, with a/c throughout, but the highlight is the sea-view rooftop terrace, where you can tuck into the excellent breakfast buffet or chill out with a sundowner. Tours, airport/*otogar* pick-ups and free parking are also available. €35

Puding Marina Mermerli Sok 15 ☎0242 244 0730, ⓦpudinghotels.com. Fresh, contemporary design alongside a luxurious spa/hamam and gourmet cuisine make this one of the trendiest hotels in town. Funky mirrored panels, marble floors and purple overtones throughout the rooms liven it up, while the incredible pool bar and terrace (including a fully equipped outdoor gym) are strewn with beautiful people. If you have money to burn, you may want to try the opulent designer accommodation at the ajoining *Puding Marina Suites* (from €100) – truly showstopping. €62

★Sabah Pansiyon Hesapçı Sok 60 ☎0242 247 5345, ⓦsabahpansiyon.com. Run by three friendly English-speaking brothers, *Sabah* has a reputation for being Kaleiçi's most popular backpacker hub, and deservedly so. Rooms are sunny, comfortable and spotless, the vibe is relaxed and convivial, and there's always an interesting mix of travellers passing through. They also offer good-value car rental, tours, free luggage storage, parking, cheap beer and satellite TV, plus there's a small guest pool. €30

Sabah Villas Hesapçı Sok 60 ☎0242 247 5345, ⓦsabahpansiyon.com. Opposite the *Sabah Pansiyon* and operated by the same team (reception is at the *pansiyon*), these modern two-storey villas offer great value for families or groups. The spacious apartments each feature two large rooms (a double and twin), a fully equipped kitchen, lounge with movies-on-demand TV, and an enclosed courtyard area with a small pool. Ask about deals for longer stays. €100

EATING

Antalya is full of **cafés and restaurants**, with excellent choices in Kaleiçi, Atatürk Parkı and along Atatürk and Işıklar cads. For the local speciality – *tandir kebap*, clay-roasted mutton – visit Eski Serbetçiler İçi Sokak, a narrow street down the side of the *Dönerci Çarşısı* (see p.362), crammed with restaurants.

KALEIÇI

★Caoutchouc Paşa Camii Sok 22 ☎0242 244 2377, ⓦkaucukotel.com. The in-house restaurant of the elegant *Kauçuk Residence* (see above) is an enchanting spot, set between a leafy lantern-lit courtyard and a beautifully restored stone-brick dining hall, displaying an ever-changing exhibition of Turkish contemporary art. The cuisine, created in-house by hotel owner Rengin, is an innovative blend of Mediterranean and Anatalion traditions with fresh, locally sourced ingredients. The menu changes daily, but staples include shrimp casserole, lemon chicken tabbouleh and buffalo-milk ice cream (mains from ₺24). Reservations recommended. Closed Jan & Feb. Daily midday–11pm.

Castle Restaurant Hıdırlık Kulesi Sok 48 ☎0242 248 6594. In the shadows of the old castle tower, this elegant bar-bistro benefits from a dramatic setting, perched on the clifftop at the edge of Karaalioğlu Park. Tuck into dishes like grilled calamari (₺25) or beef stroganoff (₺28) accompanied by a selection of mezes (from ₺5), and enjoy the sunset over the coast. Daily 9am–1am.

Çay Tea's Lunchroom Hıdırlık Sok 3 ☎0544 233 4464, ⓦcay-teas.com. If you want proof that European café

6

culture has made it to Turkey, look no further than *Çay Tea's*, where grown-up hippies come to sip hot chocolate, catch up over cappuccinos, or cool off with home-made lemonade. The interior is charmingly eclectic, decked out with shabby-chic furniture, vintage candlesticks and kitsch buddhas, and the menu includes an array of cakes, pancakes and light bites (from ₺8). Daily 9.30am–11.30pm.

Club Arma İskele Cad 75 ☎0242 244 9710, Ⓦclubarma.com.tr. Transformed from oceanside club to upmarket restaurant, *Club Arma* boasts stylish surroundings and spectacular views over the harbour, with price tags to match. There's an impressively varied range of inventive Turkish-fusion dishes, including fresh seafood and elaborate sushi plates (ranging from a reasonable ₺16 to a whopping ₺100), but best of all is the indulgent dessert menu, spanning two long pages. Daily 11am–11pm.

★**Hasanağa** Mescit Sok 15, near Hadrian's Gate ☎0242 247 1313. With tables set out under a canopy of citrus trees in a charming courtyard garden, this is a popular local haunt, with authentic Turkish cuisine at competitive prices. The open buffet dinners (from ₺15) present an array of regional specialities – try the spicy red-cabbage soup followed by fresh *hamsi* (sardines) – and there's live folk music and dance every Fri. Daily 6–11pm.

Karaf Bistro Sakarya Sok 2 ☎0242 242 8081, Ⓦkarafbistro.com. Housed in a 120-year-old Ottoman building, *Karaf* is a romantic addition to Kaleiçi's dining scene, with candlelit tables hidden behind a striking stone-brick and wood facade. There's a limited menu of pasta dishes and grills, but the real highlight is the extensive wine list – order one of the excellent cheese plates (from ₺19) and pair it with a glass of local wine (around ₺14). Wine tastings and workshops are also available on request. Tues–Sun 3pm–1am.

St Paul's Place Yenikapi Sok 24 ☎0242 247 6857, Ⓦstpaulcc-turkey.com. It may be attached to the American-run evangelical church, but Paul's Place is more arthouse café than church hall – there's an extensive library for guest use, slick cherry-wood furnishings and a pleasant courtyard out back. Sip a café latte (₺5) accompanied by your choice of delicious home-made cookies and cakes (from ₺3). Mon–Fri 9am–6pm.

Vanilla Lounge Hesapçı Sok 33 ☎0242 247 6013, Ⓦvanillaantalya.com. The flowery, stone-brick courtyard here is idyllic in summer, while the plush armchairs, ambient lighting and roaring open fire indoors make for a cosy hideaway in winter. The stylish cuisine is beautifully presented, with dishes like wild mushroom gnocchi (₺29), white bean and tahini soup (₺16) and Indian-spiced chicken (₺39.50), as well as some decent pizzas. Head there between 4.30 and 6pm for happy-hour prices on beer, wine and cocktails. Daily 11am–midnight.

Yemenli Hesapçı Sok 66, opposite Sabah Pansiyon ☎0242 247 5346, Ⓦyemenlicafe.com. With friendly service and authentic home cooking, *Yemenli* is one of the best spots in the old town to sample local dishes at reasonable prices, with generously portioned kebabs (from ₺17.50) and *köfte* (₺19). There's also a range of casseroles, steaks and burgers, a vegetarian option that changes daily and a pleasant courtyard, where live music is hosted in summer. Daily 8am–11pm.

ATATÜRK CADDESİ AND IŞIKLAR CADDESİ

Dönerci Çarşısı Cnr of Atatürk & Cumhuriyet cads. The cheapest place to grab a mid-sightseeing bite, this "*Döner*-sellers' market" is devoted to food stalls hawking kebabs, *köfte* and *kokoreç*, as well as *midye* (mussels) in season. A meal here should cost less than ₺10, but select carefully; not all places are clean. Daily 8am–late.

Paşa Bey Kebapçı Gençlik Mah, off Işıklar Cad ☎0242 244 9691. Crammed with locals, this smart dinner spot offers delicious *güveç* (casseroles, from ₺15), a generous *meze* selection – the *kısır* (lightly spiced bulgar and peppers) and *baba ganush* (mashed aubergine) are scrumptious – and warm, freshly baked breads. No alcohol. Daily 8am–midnight.

Salman Işıklar Cad ☎0242 244 1455, Ⓦsalman patisserie.com. Anyone with a sweet tooth will be spoilt for choice in this heavenly patisserie, where you'll find row upon row of hand-crafted chocolates, bite-size biscuits, gooey *baklava* and *poğça* (plain and filled savoury breads), alongside a range of continental-style pastries, cakes and tarts. Smuggle a bag of treats (₺25 per kg) or a home-made ice cream (₺2 a scoop) down to the nearby park for a sea view. Daily 7am–10pm.

DRINKING AND NIGHTLIFE

Much of Antalya's **nightlife** is concentrated in Kaleiçi, with its myriad bars, clubs and discos, and there are also plenty of places to listen to live **Turkish music**, particularly *halk*, *türkü* and *özgün*.

BARS

Dolma Meyhane Yenikapı Sok 11 ☎0242 247 4050. A laidback, modern bar, with street-side seating during the warmer months, *Dolma Meyhane* offers well-priced drinks and cheap eats, plus daily happy-hour prices 3–8pm. There's live music a few times a week too, and a good mix of locals and expats. Daily 11am–midnight.

Filika Mescit Sok 46 ☎0554 854 0224. With tables spilling out onto the streets, arty black-and-white photographs and painted silhouettes of jazz musicians on the walls, this laidback bar-bistro is ideal for whiling away the evening hours. A varied roster of live rock, jazz and blues performed on its small stage draws in a mixed crowd of locals. Beers start at ₺9. Daily 11am–1am.

Shaker Bar Hadrian's Gate ☎ 0541 403 7270. Perched in a prime location right next to Hadrian's Gate, this modern café-bar serves up frothy cappuccinos (₺8) by day and classic cocktails by night (from ₺25). Happy-hour prices last all day until 7pm, so get there early and snag a seat on the terrace. Daily 9am–1am.

Taka Meyhane İzmirli Ali Efendi Sok 2 ☎ 0532 387 6322. With its gingham tablecloths, nostalgic movie posters and quirky cartoon-character memorabilia, this fun café-bar is a hit with local students and hipsters. There's a range of cheap eats (try the grilled sardines) and drinks (from ₺8) on offer, plus live music and DJs most nights of the week. Daily 10am–4am.

CLUBS AND LIVE MUSIC

Ally Club Sur Sok 4/8 ☎ 0242 244 7704, ⓦ ally.com.tr. With pinging lasers, podium dancers and Top 40 hits at ear-splitting volumes, this open-air club is one of Antalya's top party hubs. Entry is ₺15–65 (usually including a drink) depending on the night, though women often get in free. Don't bother arriving before midnight. Daily 10pm–5am.

★ **Simurg Temple** Hamam Sok 2 ☎ 0242 244 5105, ⓦ simurgtemple.com. With live pop and rock bands almost every night of the week, and an atmospheric beer garden out back, this is one of Antalya's coolest gig venues. Come in the day to enjoy a nargile, or after hours to tackle one of the enormous beer kegs (₺43). Daily 10am–4am.

SHOPPING

Atatürk Cad, Işıklar Cad and Cumhuriyet Cad are the main shopping areas outside of Kaleiçi, where you'll find everything from designer clothing and gold jewellery to traditional handicrafts and carpets.

Ardic Seleker Mall, Güllük Cad 66-67 ☎ 0242 247 0356, ⓦ ardickitabevi.com.tr. This is the best place in Antalya to buy English-language guides or novels. Mon–Sat 9am–6pm.

Mark Antalya Kazım Özalp Cad 88 ☎ 0242 244 6666, ⓦ markantalya.com. This gigantic shopping mall opened in 2013 and has over 150 shops, a large food court and a multiplex cinema. Daily 10am–10pm.

Migros Shopping Mall Atatürk Bulvarı 3 ☎ 0242 230 1111, ⓦ antalyamigros.com. Located next to Antalya Aquarium in Konyaaltı, this modern mall has around 130 shops, an enormous Migros supermarket and an 8-screen cinema. Daily 10am–10pm.

The Owl Bookshop Kocatepe Sok 9 ☎ 0532 632 3275. This friendly bookshop in a rustic building in the old town has an excellent selection of mainly English-language secondhand books. Mon–Sat 9am–7pm.

TURKISH MUSIC VENUES

Akdeniz Çiçek Pasajı Uzun Çarşısı Sok 24–26 ☎ 0242 243 4303. The best place to catch live Turkish music, a couple of hundred metres down from the clock tower, this popular local haunt has tiered seating areas surrounding a central well where the musicians play, and a small terrace with views over Kaleiçi and the bay. Daily 7pm–late.

Ayyaş Hamam Sok 16 ☎ 0542 783 6164. Music wafts into the small square in front of this chilled-out bar, where a bohemian mix of patrons sip beers (₺8 a bottle) at alfresco tables. Live music is provided by local classical Turkish musicians, with an open-air stage in summer. Daily 6pm–midnight.

DIRECTORY

Banks and exchange Banks with ATMs and *döviz* offices are scattered throughout the city. Most operate Mon–Sat 9am–7pm, but some *döviz* offices on Şarampol open on Sun. You can also exchange currency at the PTT.

Cinemas The Plaza cinema in the Antalya 2000 building, 100m northeast of Hadrian's Gate (☎ 0242 312 6296), is the most convenient cinema, or head to the Cinemaximum (☎ 0242 242 4141) in the Mark Antalya centre (see p.363).

Consulate UK, Gençlik Mahallesi, 1314 Sok, Elif apt 6/8 (☎ 0242 244 5313), to the right of and behind the *Talya Hotel*, off Fevzi Çakmak Cad.

Hamams In Kaleiçi, the historic Sefa Hamam (Kocatepe Sok 32; daily 10am–8pm; ☎ 0242 241 2321), dates back to 1450, and offers full bath, soap massage and oil massage packages for ₺80.

Hospital State Hospital (Devlet Hastane) and outpatients' clinic, Soğuksu Cad ☎ 0242 241 2010;

GOLDEN ORANGE FILM FESTIVAL

Antalya's Altın Portakal or **Golden Orange film festival** runs for a week each autumn, usually at the start of October. It's a major international film event, screening around 150 films throughout the week. Events culminate with an award ceremony at the Atatürk Kültür Merkezi, where golden statuettes of Venus carrying an orange are handed out. All week, directors, screenwriters and producers of Turkish and Eurasian cinema hold panel discussions and workshops, and parties take place across the city. All films are subtitled in English as well as in Turkish. For the full festival programme, visit ⓦ altinportakal.org.tr.

University Teaching Hospital (Tip Fakultesi), Dumlupınar Bul ☎ 0242 227 4480.

Laundry Several places around the Kesik Minare offer laundry services, as do many *pansiyons*.

Police Tourist Police, Emniyet Müdürlüğü, Yat Limanı, Kaleiçi ☎ 0242 527 4503.

Post office The main PTT is at Güllük Cad 9 (daily 9am–5pm for exchange and letter service; 24hr for phones).

Köprülü Kanyon National Park

90km northeast of Antalya • Little public transport apart from one afternoon dolmuş to nearby Selge; without your own transport, it's far easier to access as part of a tour

The **Köprülü Kanyon National Park** (Köprülü Kanyon Milli Parkı) makes a good full-day outing from Antalya. Many companies operate half-day **rafting trips** (see p.360) down the Köprülü River, allowing time for a stop en route for a swim and lunch. Be warned that in peak season, thousands of rafters are bussed into this area each day, making both the road and river very crowded places – serious rafters should look elsewhere.

Selge

100km northeast of Antalya, 12km west of Köprülü Kanyon • Daily 24hr • One afternoon dolmuş runs to Selge/Zerk, returning early the next morning, but it's best reached by hiring a taxi and guide from Antalya (€100–150 for the day)

The ancient city of **Selge** lies at an altitude of 900m above sea level. As you climb up the steep road to reach it, the panoramas become more sweeping, the thickly wooded countryside more savage, and the 2500m Kuyucak range ahead more forbidding. The site itself is scattered around the hamlet of **ZERK** (also known as Altınkaya). Little is known for certain of the origins of Selge; it only entered history – and the Roman Empire – in the first century AD. The city was inhabited until early Byzantine times and must have been abandoned when the aqueduct supplying it with water collapsed.

The ten-thousand-spectator theatre that dominates **ancient Selge** is impressive, even though the stage building was pulverized by lightning some decades ago. Close by is the ancient **agora** with its part-visible paving, jumbled masonry and chunks of unexcavated inscriptions. The foundations of a **Byzantine church** sit up on a hill to the southeast and enjoy panoramic views down the valley and up to the snow-streaked peak of Bozburun, while the jumbled remains of a temple of Zeus and a large water cistern lie northwest along the ridge. From here you can catch views to the ruined temple of Artemis and old city wall to the northwest, and to the stoa in the valley below. Returning to the main track, you'll pass the **stadium**, of which only the western ranks of seats are left; the sporting area itself is now a wheat field.

Termessos

Situated more than 1000m above sea level, the ancient site of **Termessos**, 30km northwest of Antalya, is one of Turkey's prime attractions. Its dramatic setting and well-preserved ruins, tumbling from the summit of the mountain and enclosed within a national park – Güllük Dağ Milli Parkı – merit at least an afternoon of exploration.

Despite its close proximity to Lycia, Termessos was actually a Pisidian city, inhabited by the same warlike tribe who settled in the Anatolian Lakeland, around Isparta and Eğirdir, during the first millennium BC. The city's position, commanding the road from the Mediterranean to the Aegean, enabled Termessos to extract customs dues from traders; a wall across the valley is believed to be the site of their customs post. Later, in 70 BC, Termessos signed a treaty with Rome, under which their independence was preserved – a fact the Termessians proudly expressed by never including the face or name of a Roman emperor on their coinage. The city must have been abandoned quite early, probably after earthquake damage in 243 AD, and has only been surveyed, never excavated.

The site

Daily: April–Oct 9am–7pm; Nov–March 8.30am–5pm • ₺5

A thorough exploration of the **ancient site** can be quite strenuous; steep climbs are necessary to reach many of the key sights. Bring sturdy footwear and lots of water – there's nowhere to buy supplies beyond the park entrance – and time summer visits to avoid the midday sun. After checking the site map at the car park, you'll need to climb a good fifteen minutes to reach the first remains of any interest. On the way, you'll pass a number of well-labelled, though mainly inaccessible, ruins, including the aqueduct and cistern high on the cliff face to the left of the path.

The King's Road and city walls

The second-century AD **King's Road** was the main road up to Termessos, close to which the massive lower and upper **city walls** testify to a substantial defence system. The central part of the city lies beyond the second wall, to the left of the path. Its surviving buildings, formed of square-cut grey stone, are in an excellent state of repair, their walls standing high and retaining their original mouldings. In part, this is due to the inaccessibility of the site; it's hard to imagine even the most desperate forager coming up here to pillage stone.

Gymnasium and theatre

While the first building you come to once you pass through Termessos' mighty walls is the well-preserved **gymnasium** and bath complex, this is far overshadowed by the nearby **theatre**. One of the most magnificently situated in Turkey, it's set on the edge of a steep gorge, with a backdrop of staggered mountains. Greek in style, it had seating space for 4200 spectators, and although some seats are missing, it's otherwise in an excellent state of preservation.

The agora, Corinthian temple and Odeon

At the far end of the open grassy space of the **agora**, west of the theatre, a **Corinthian temple** is approached up a broad flight of steps, with a six-metre-square platform. The smaller theatre or **Odeon** on the far side of the agora was, according to inscriptions, used for horse and foot races, races in armour, and, more frequently, wrestling. The walls of the building rise to almost 10m, surrounded by four **temples**. Only one – that of Zeus Solymeus, god of war and guardian of the city of Termessos – is in a decent state of repair.

The necropolis

Uphill from the Odeon, Termessos' **necropolis** holds an incredible number of sarcophagi dating from the first to the third centuries AD. Most are simple structures on a base, though some more elaborate ones were carved from the living rock, with inscriptions and reliefs.

Tomb of Alcatus

Set in a dramatic mountaintop location, the so-called **Tomb of Alcatus** is widely accepted as the mausoleum of the general, a pretender to the governorship of Pisidia. The tomb itself is cave-like and undistinguished, but the **carvings** on its facade are remarkable, particularly one depicting a mounted soldier, with a suit of armour, a helmet, a shield and a sword – the armour of a foot soldier – depicted lower down to the right of the figure.

ARRIVAL AND DEPARTURE   TERMESSOS

By car To drive to Termessos from Antalya, take the Burdur road, then turn left after 11km towards Korkuteli. From the left turning to Termessos, marked another 14km along, a track climbs 9km up through the forested national park to the site.

By bus and taxi Catch a Korkuteli-bound bus (hourly) from Antalya's *otogar* to the start of the forest track, where taxis tout for business (₺40–50, including waiting time and return to main road).

6

Yeşil Vadi Just off the main road near the park entrance ☎0242 423 7555. This perfectly located restaurant makes a popular stop-off for a cold beer (₺7) before the journey back to town. Simple but tasty food, with meat and vegetable *güveç* (casseroles, from ₺15) and assorted kebabs. They also run a no-frills pension (₺80), and there are camping spots available. Daily 8am–10pm.

The Pamphylian cities

The twelfth century BC saw a large wave of Greek migration from northern Anatolia to the Mediterranean coast. Many of the incomers moved into the area immediately east of Antalya, which became known as **Pamphylia**, meaning "the land of the tribes", reflecting the mixed origins of the new arrivals. Although Pamphylia was a remote area, cut off from the main Anatolian trade routes by mountains on all sides, three great cities grew up here – **Perge**, **Aspendos** and **Side**.

Most of Pamphylia fell to Alexander the Great in the fourth century BC. After his death the region became effectively independent, though nominally claimed by the various successor kingdoms that inherited Alexander's realm. During the first century BC, the **Romans**, annoyed by the Cilician pirates operating from further along the Mediterranean, took control of the coast. Their rule ushered in three centuries of stability and prosperity, during which the Pamphylian cities flourished as never before. In later years, Mark Antony was sent to take charge of the region, treating it as his personal domain until defeated by Octavius at the battle of Actium in 31 BC, after which Pamphylia was formally absorbed into the Roman Empire.

GETTING AROUND   THE PAMPHYLIAN CITIES

By taxi A guide and driver to visit the main Pamphylian sites in a single day should cost around €100 from most tour operators. Hiring a taxi for the trip may be marginally cheaper – check the wooden board at the rank at the southern end of Atatürk Bulvarı in Antalya, which lists prices for various destinations.

By bus tour Bus tours (around €50) organized by agents in Antalya's Kaleiçi district seldom include Selge – instead they usually feature tedious stops at out-of-town gold and carpet shops.

Perge

15km east of Antalya • Daily: April–Oct 9am–7pm; Nov–March 8.30am–5pm • ₺20 • From Antalya, take a dolmuş (frequent) or *Belediye* bus (every 20min) from the *otogar* to the village of Aksu (around 35min) on the main eastbound road, then walk 15min to the site itself

Founded around 1000 BC, **Perge** ranked as one of the great Pamphylian trading cities, despite the fact that it's nearly 20km inland. Its defensive siting was deliberate, to avoid the unwanted attentions of the pirate bands that terrorized this stretch of the Mediterranean. Later, when Alexander the Great arrived in 333 BC, the citizens of Perge sent out guides to lead his army into the city. Alexander was followed by the Seleucids, under whom Perge's most celebrated ancient inhabitant, the mathematician Apollonius, lived and worked. Most of the city's surviving buildings date from the period of Roman rule, which began in 188 BC. After the collapse of the Roman Empire, Perge remained inhabited until Selçuk times, before being gradually abandoned.

The site

Perge's **theatre**, just outside the site entrance, has been closed for excavation for several years. Originally constructed by the Greeks, it was substantially altered by the Romans in the second century AD. Capable of accommodating 14,000 people on 42 levels, it was the venue for theatrical entertainment, poetry contests and musical concerts. To the northeast, Perge's massive horseshoe-shaped **stadium** was at 234m by 34m the largest in Asia Minor, with a seating capacity of 12,000. It was used not only for chariot races, but also wild beast hunts, public executions and gladiator spectacles.

Beyond the site entrance, stretches of the Seleucid walls have survived, giving some indication of the extent and ground plan of the original city. Just in front of the outer gates stands the **Tomb of Plancia Magna**, a benefactress of the city. Passing through the **Roman gate**, you'll see a ruined **Byzantine basilica** on the right, beyond which lies the fourth-century AD **agora**, centred on a ruined temple.

Southwest of the agora, in the excavated **Roman baths**, a couple of the pools have been exposed. Across the cracked surface of the inlaid marble floor, the original layout of frigidarium, tepidarium and caldarium can – with the help of a few signs – still be discerned. Also visible in places are the brick piles that once supported the hypocaust floor of the baths, enabling warm air to circulate underneath.

Perge's **Hellenistic Gate**, at the northwest corner of the agora, is with its two mighty circular towers the only building to survive from the Hellenistic period. Behind, the horseshoe-shaped court and ornamental archway were both erected at the behest of Plancia Magna. The former was once adorned with statues, the bases of which were found during mid-1950s excavations. Beyond is the start of a 300m-long **colonnaded street**, with a water channel running down the middle and the shells of shops to either side. Walking along it, you'll be able to pick out the ruts made by carts and chariots in the stone slabs of the roadway. Also visible are reliefs near the tops of the columns, just beneath the capitals. One depicts Apollo, while another shows a man in a toga, offering a libation at an altar.

From the **nymphaeum**, an ornamental water outlet at the end of the street, a stream splashes down into the water channel below. Above here is the **acropolis**, probably the site of the original defensive settlement, of which little has survived, while the nearby **palaestra** was an open-air exercise area surrounded by changing rooms. To the west, outside the city walls, is the **necropolis**, but its most impressive tombs and sarcophagi have been removed and are now on display in the **Antalya Archeological Museum** (see p.358).

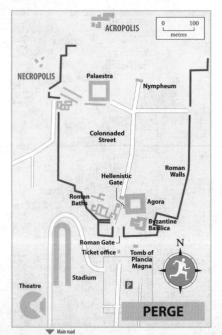

Aspendos

46km east of Antalya, 1km northeast of the village of Aspendos • Daily: April–Oct 9am–7pm; Nov–March 8.30am–5pm • ₺20 • Take a bus from Antalya's *otogar* to Serik, 6km southwest of Aspendos (every 2hr; 45min), then a dolmuş to Aspendos (15min)

Still used to stage the annual Aspendos Opera and Ballet Festival (see box opposite), the theatre of **Aspendos** is among the best preserved in Asia Minor and made it onto the UNESCO World Heritage Tentative List in 2015. Aspendos changed hands regularly in ancient times between the Persians, Greeks and Spartans, before coming under the control of Alexander the Great around 333 BC. After his death, Aspendos became part of the Seleucid kingdom and was later absorbed by the kings of Pergamon. In 133 BC, the city became part of the Roman province of Asia. Roman rule consisted mainly of successive consuls and governors demanding protection money and carting off the city's treasures. Only with the establishment of the Roman Empire did the city prosper, growing into an important trade centre, its wealth based on salt from a nearby lake.

Aspendos remained important throughout the Byzantine era, although it suffered badly from the Arab raids of the seventh century. During the thirteenth century the Selçuks arrived, followed a couple of hundred years later by the Ottomans, who ruled here until the eighteenth century, when the settlement was abandoned.

The theatre

The Aspendos **theatre** was built in the second century AD by the architect Zeno. He used a Roman design, with an elaborate stage behind which the scenery could be lowered, instead of allowing the natural landscape behind the stage to act as a backdrop, as had been the custom in Hellenistic times.

The **stage**, **auditorium** and **arcade** above are all intact, as is the several-storey-high **stage building**. What you see today is pretty much what the spectators saw during the theatre's heyday. A dubious legend relates that the theatre was built after the king of Aspendos announced that he would give the hand of his beautiful daughter to a man who built some great work for the benefit of the city. Two men rose to the challenge, one building the theatre, the other an aqueduct (see below). Both finished work simultaneously, so the king offered to cut his daughter in two, giving a half to each man. The builder of the theatre declared that he would rather renounce his claim than see the princess dismembered and was, of course, immediately rewarded with the hand of the girl for his unselfishness. Later, the theatre was used as a Selçuk *kervansaray*, and restoration work from that period – plasterwork decorated with red zigzags – is visible over the stage.

The acropolis

A path leads up from the right of the theatre entrance at Aspendos to the **acropolis**, built on a flat-topped hill. The site is a little overgrown, but some substantial buildings are still in place. Foremost among them are the **nymphaeum** and **basilica**, both 16m in height, while sections of the main street and a drainage system also remain in good condition.

The aqueduct

The aqueduct and towers can be reached from the acropolis or by car – take a left turn down a paved path just outside Belkis, skirting around the western side of the hill

A Roman **aqueduct** stretches northwards across the plain below the acropolis. Originally 15km long, it brought water to Aspendos from the mountains above and

---

ASPENDOS OPERA AND BALLET FESTIVAL

The **Aspendos Opera and Ballet Festival** is staged in the Aspendos theatre every year, over a three- to four-week period starting in mid-June. Both Turkish and foreign companies perform, and the programme consists of popular and experimental opera, ballet and classical concerts (*Madame Butterfly* and *Swan Lake* feature regularly). With an inflow of choreographers and musicians from Russia and Eastern Europe, Turkish opera and ballet companies have improved out of all recognition, and stage design and costumes match the standard of the performers.

Tickets (around ₺50 for foreigners, less for Turks) are available both in advance and on the night from the theatre, and you can also buy them in Antalya and Side, though the booking office seems to switch venues each year – ask at the tourist office and check ⓦaspendosfestival .gov.tr for programmes. Cheap shuttle buses run to the theatre from Antalya and Side on performance nights and most festivalgoers bring along dinner to while away the time before the start of the 9.30pm performance, as well as cushions to sit on, and an umbrella or waterproof in case of a thunderstorm.

A number of year-round shows, including the popular **Fire of Anatolia** (ⓦaspendosfestival .gov.tr) dance troops, are performed at the Aspendos Arena, a nearby modern facility erected to help preserve the original arena. While many of these shows are excellent, if you are going in order to experience the ancient theatre, be sure your tickets are for the right place.

6

GOLF TOURISM IN BELEK

Turkey might not be your first thought as a **golfing destination**, but with its mild climate and vast acres of verdant countryside, the southern coastal region is fast gaining acclaim on the international golf scene. **Belek**, 30km east of Antalya, is the main hub of the sport, home to five golf courses. The eighteen-hole championship course at the impressive **National Golf Club** (☎ 0242 725 4625, ⓦ nationalturkey.com) is the most coveted, designed by Ryder Cup player David Feherty and host of the 2012 World Golf Final.

Luxury hotel resorts in the Belek area offer inclusive golf **packages** (check out ⓦ golfturkey .com for ideas). Even if your game isn't quite up to par, you'll be able to revel in the landscape of natural lakes, gently undulating lawns and eucalyptus forests, set to a backdrop of the snowcapped Toros Mountains.

---

incorporates an ingenious siphonic system that allowed the water to cross the plain at low level; you can still (with care) climb the towers.

Side and around

One-time trysting place of Antony and Cleopatra, **SİDE** was perhaps the foremost of the Pamphylian cities. Now, however, its impressive array of ruins form the backdrop to a modern holiday resort, set within the boundaries of the old town. Despite the recent influx of package tourists, Side remains one of the friendliest communities along the Mediterranean, home to a burgeoning number of expats and regular holiday-makers. Many of the old-fashioned charms beloved of past visitors are fast disappearing – the creaky tractors that once shunted arrivals from the *otogar* to the city walls have been replaced by air-conditioned shuttle buses, and the quaint seafront is now overrun with hawkers. However, with many of the smaller, family-run pensions in the ancient city now competing for business with the big hotels on its outskirts, Side can make an affordable base for travels around the region. Wander down the dusty backstreets or strike up a conversation with one of the friendly pension owners and you'll catch a glimpse of the old Side that travellers still rave about.

Brief history

Side (meaning "pomegranate" in an ancient Anatolian dialect) was founded in the seventh century BC by colonists attracted by the defensive potential of the rocky cape. It grew into a rich port, home to an estimated sixty thousand inhabitants during its peak in the second century AD. Initially a significant proportion of Side's wealth stemmed from the slave trade; city authorities allowed pirates to run an illegal slave market inside the city walls. After the collapse of the Western Roman Empire, Side survived only until Arab invaders put the place to the torch during the seventh century AD, and drove out the last inhabitants. Side was abandoned until Muslim fishermen from Crete settled here early in the twentieth century. Despite later attempts by the Turkish government and archeological agencies to evict them, these villagers stayed, and by the 1980s their descendants were starting to reap the rewards of Side's tourist boom.

Ancient Side

Ancient Side has been almost overwhelmed by the modern town, and becomes hideously crowded with tour groups in summer. Sadly, many areas, particularly the theatre and colonnaded street, have suffered serious damage from the sheer number of visitors. However, independent travellers who set out early in the day can still enjoy some corners of the city.

East of the badly preserved **city gate**, the old walls are in a reasonable state, with a number of towers still in place. Back at the gate, a colonnaded street runs down to the **agora**, the site of Side's second-century slave market, today fringed with the stumps of many of the agora's columns. The circular foundation visible at the centre of the agora is all that remains of a **Temple of Fortuna**, while in the northwest corner, next to the theatre, you can just about make out the outline of a semicircular building that once served as a public latrine, seating 24 people.

Side Museum

Opposite the agora • Tues–Sun 8am–6.45pm (Nov–March till 5pm) • ₺10 • ☎ 0242 753 1006

The site of Side's ancient Roman baths, restored in 1961, is now home to the small but well-executed **Side Museum**. It retains its original floor plan and contains a cross section of locally unearthed objects – mainly Roman statuary, reliefs and sarcophagi from local excavations made between 1947 and 1967.

6

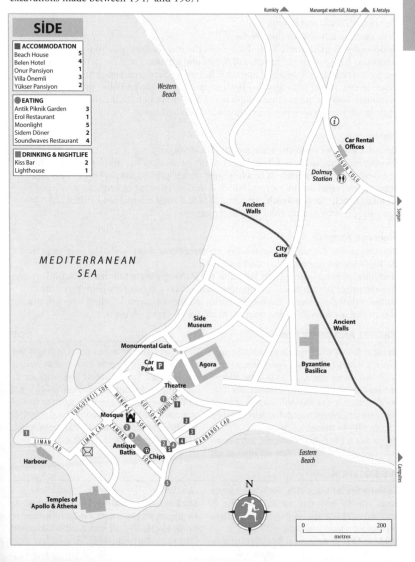

SİDE

ACCOMMODATION
Beach House	5
Belen Hotel	4
Onur Pansiyon	1
Villa Önemli	3
Yükser Pansiyon	2

EATING
Antik Piknik Garden	3
Erol Restaurant	1
Moonlight	5
Sidem Döner	2
Soundwaves Restaurant	4

DRINKING & NIGHTLIFE
| Kiss Bar | 2 |
| Lighthouse | 1 |

Kumköy

Manavgat waterfall, Alanya & Antalya

Western Beach

Car Rental Offices

SORGUN YOLU

Dolmuş Station

Sorgun

Ancient Walls

City Gate

MEDITERRANEAN SEA

Side Museum

Ancient Walls

Monumental Gate

Car Park

Agora

Byzantine Basilica

Theatre

TURGUTREIS SOK

MENEKŞE CAD

GÜL SOKAK

SÜMBÜL SOK

Mosque

ZAMBAK SOK

LIMAN CAD

LIMAN CAD

Antique Baths

@ Chips

SOK

BARBAROS CAD

Eastern Beach

Campsites

Harbour

Temples of Apollo & Athena

N

0 200
metres

6

More of the city's **antique baths** lie just off Camii Sokak, where Cleopatra is supposed to have bathed. Here, the remains include several separate rooms, baths, a garden and even a marble seat with a dolphin armrest.

Monumental gate and theatre

Just south of Side Museum • Theatre daily: April–Oct 9am–6.45pm; Nov–March 9am–noon & 1–5pm • ₺15

Side's still-intact **monumental gate** now serves as the entrance to the town's modern resort area. To the left of the gateway, an excavated monument to Vespasian, built in 74 AD, takes the form of a fountain with a couple of water basins in front. Inside the gate is the entrance to the stunning twenty-thousand-seat **theatre**, a freestanding structure supported by massive arched vaults that was the largest in Pamphylia.

Temples of Apollo and Athena

On the waterfront at Side's southern tip • Daily 24hr • Free

Modern Side's main street leads down from the monumental gate to the old harbour, and turns left towards the **temples of Apollo and Athena**. The Athena temple has been partly re-erected, and its white portico is becoming Side's trademark and a favourite place to take sunset photographs. Both temples were once partially enclosed in a huge Byzantine basilica, parts of which gradually disappeared under the shifting sand; the still-visible section now provides a home to birds and bats.

The beaches

Dolmuşes run in both directions along the coastline every 30min from Side's *otogar*

Given Side's fine sandy **beaches**, it's no surprise the resort has developed so rapidly. To the west, the 10km stretch of beach is lined with expensive hotels, beach clubs and watersports rental outfits, beyond which is the less crowded but equally developed **Kumköy beach**. **Sorgun Beach**, 3km east of Side, is well maintained by the local authority, but far quieter than its counterparts.

Manavgat Waterfall

5km northeast of town • Daily 9am–8pm, winter till 5.30pm • ₺5 • Boat cruises from Side cost around €15, but you can also get here on the "Şelale" dolmuş from Side dolmuş station (₺2 each way, 15min)

The most popular outing from Side is to the **Manavgat Waterfall**. It's a beautiful setting, but the influx of tour buses and subsequent hawkers can be overwhelming in the summer months – watch out for the pushy monkey or parrot handlers who will place the animal on your shoulder, then try to charge you for a photo.

ARRIVAL AND DEPARTURE SİDE

By bus or dolmuş Most intercity buses head to the *otogar* in nearby Manavgat, from where regular dolmuşes run to Side's small dolmuş station, just north of the old town entrance (around ₺3; some bus companies offer a free shuttle). From there it's a 10min walk into town, or you can hop on one of the free minibuses that run in season and will drop you off by the theatre.

By car Side is effectively pedestrianized. Cars can only enter the town 7–10am and 3–6pm, and after midnight (though attendants let through drivers heading to their hotels with luggage). There are a few car parks, including one just inside the monumental gate, which can be accessed all day; fees range from ₺10 for a half-day to ₺20 for 24hr. There are several car rental outlets on the road approaching the main town entrance: Europcar (☎0242 753 1764, ⓦ europcar.com) is next to the *Asteria Hotel*; Avis is on Atatürk Bulvarı (☎0242 753 1348, ⓦ avis.com).

INFORMATION

Tourist office The tourist office, 10min walk from the *otogar*, on the main road out of town (Mon–Fri 8am–12.30pm & 1.30–5pm; ☎0242 753 1265), has good city maps and regional pamphlets.

Banks and PTT On the square at the southern tip of the promontory.

Bike & motorbike rental Dozens of outlets, mostly outside the city gates, rent bikes or motorbikes. Donatello, just before the gate (☎0242 753 1234), offers mountain bikes (around €15/day), as well as Yamaha mopeds and quad bikes.

ACCOMMODATION

Few towns can claim to have such genuinely friendly and generous hosts across the board, and Side's abundant family-run **pensions** form a huge part of the town's charm. For the most atmospheric options, in and around the ruins and never more than a few minutes' walk from the beach, give the package hotels on the outskirts a miss, and head inside the ancient city walls. Even in high season, when booking is strongly advised, you're still likely to stumble across available rooms in the smaller and slightly shabbier pensions.

Beach House Hotel Barbaros Cad ☎ 0242 753 1607, ⓦ beachhouse-hotel.com. With its flower-filled courtyard weaving around the remains of a Byzantine villa, and an eclectic collection of animal residents including a party of free-roaming tortoises, there's no place quite like the *Beach House Hotel*. Rooms are clean and airy, with plenty of natural light, and all have balconies looking out over the ocean, plus there's a peaceful rooftop terrace. Closed Nov–March. **€55**

★**Belen Hotel** Lale Sok 12 ☎ 0242 753 1043, ⓔ birdenbire74@hotmail.com. It's impossible not to be charmed by the boho-country-garden vibe at *Belen*, located right opposite *Villa Önemli* (see below); the palm-shaded courtyard is overflowing with flowers, twee ornaments and colourful windmills. Rooms are clean yet simple, but it's the details that make this such good value – spacious balconies, a/c, fast wi-fi and individual safes available downstairs. The pair of attic rooms make a quirky choice for families or couples, and it's €5 extra for a sea view. **€35**

★**Onur Pansiyon** Karanfil Sok 5/1 ☎ 0242 753 2328, ⓦ onur-pansiyon.com. Pretty bedspreads and plump pillows lend this cosy pension a home-away-from-home feel, an atmosphere underpinned by the friendly English-speaking staff and home-cooked breakfasts. The communal garden terrace is ideal for escaping the sun and mingling with other guests, making it a top choice for backpackers or families. Discounted prices available off season. **₺120**

Villa Önemli Lale Sok ☎ 0242 247 6714, ⓦ hotelvilla onemli.com. In a beautiful wood-and-stone manor house set around a palm-fringed courtyard, this attractive hotel offers excellent value for money. Deluxe suites have their own kitchenette with washing machine, fridge-freezer and stove, but you'll pay extra for a sea view. **€70**

Yükser Pansiyon Lale Sok 10 ☎ 0242 753 2010, ⓦ yukser-pansiyon.com. A charming, family-run abode, with simple, good-value rooms, jazzed up with colourful paintings and brightly patterned rugs. The garden courtyard is the main highlight, where you can meet other guests or doze off in a hammock. **₺100**

EATING

Side has plenty of places to eat; the main challenge is to walk past them without being dragged inside by the smooth-talking hustlers. For vastly cheaper and often tastier food, opt for the less pushy establishments or small **local options**, tucked away in the tumbledown backstreets.

★**Antik Piknik Garden** Zambak Sok 35 ☎ 0242 753 5033, ⓔ side_piknikgarden@hotmail.com. This bohemian hideaway couldn't be further removed from the pushy salesmen and high prices of the seafront eateries, with its artfully ramshackle garden courtyard dotted with rustic hut-like huts (doubles €30 with breakfast). The home-cooked food is also a hit, and while it lacks the showmanship of its peers, it's tasty, hearty and a fraction of the price. Tuck into a clay-pot casserole (₺17) or chicken şiş (₺13) and couple it with a cold Efes beer (₺9). Daily 8am–midnight; closed in winter.

Erol Restaurant Liman Mah, Sümbül Sok ☎ 0242 753 2826. Just across the street from *Onur Pansiyon* (see above), this no-frills eatery serves up tasty Turkish staples and feeds a steady stream of locals throughout the day. There's a variety of food on offer, including soups, rice, meat dishes and salads, and you'll get a full meal for less than ₺15. Daily 9am–11pm.

Moonlight Barbaros Cad 49 ☎ 0242 753 1400. A romantic venue, with a large, lantern-lit terrace overlooking the ocean, an impressive wine list and excellent service. A good range of *mezes*, casseroles and kebabs pad out the menu, but the emphasis is on fresh fish and seafood. Mains start from €11. Daily 9am–2am.

Sidem Döner Hanımeli Sok, opposite the mosque entrance ☎ 0242 753 1315. Escape the seafront tourist haunts for a cheap and tasty ₺5 *döner* at this humble local joint. There's a small but pleasant seating area out the back, or they'll wrap up your pitta to go. Daily 9am–11pm.

Soundwaves Restaurant Barbaros Cad ☎ 0242 753 1059. Long-established restaurant run by the *Beach House Hotel* proprietors (see above; guests get a discount), this is one of the most reliable of the beachside options, benefitting from a serene sea view and offering access to the hotel's private beach. There's an excellent selection of fresh, seasonal seafood, with mains around ₺35, but there are some cheapies on the lunch menu too (burgers from ₺7) and some inspiring vegetarian options. Daily 8am–midnight.

6

DRINKING AND NIGHTLIFE

For the best of Side's nightlife, head to the strip along the **harbour**, where bars and nightclubs open their doors in summer months, and penny-pinchers can cruise the staggered happy hours that run between 6pm and 9pm.

Kiss Bar Barbaros Cad 64 • 0242 753 3182. Friendly, unobtrusive staff, quirky mannequins and a varied soundtrack of current pop hits and old classics make this one of the better choices for an evening out. The bar is well stocked, and there's a decent range of cocktails for €5 (₺15). Daily 4pm–4am.

Lighthouse Just west of the harbour • 0242 753 3588. If strobe lighting, thumping techno music and scantily clad podium dancers are your idea of a good night, *Lighthouse* is the place for you. You won't be alone, either – it's the best and busiest club in town, in a good harbour-front location and, as a bonus, entrance is free. April–Nov daily 11pm–5am.

Alanya

With vast swathes of golden sand hugging a ragged sea cliff, ample hiking possibilities and the smooth waves of the Mediterranean lapping beneath a looming fortress, it's easy to explain **ALANYA's** booming popularity among tourists. The beachside sprawl of uninspiring yet all-encompassing restaurants, shops and nightclubs serves merely as a colourful fringe to the charismatic old city. Peel yourself away from the watersports and overpriced cocktails, and you'll find a city heaving with historical gems, atmospheric places to eat, and charmingly chaotic bazaars.

Brief history

Little is known about Alanya's early **history**, but it's thought to have been founded by Greek colonists who named it Kalonoros, or "beautiful mountain". Things were pretty quiet until the second century BC, when Cilician pirates began using the town, known by now as Coracesium, as a base to terrorize the Pamphylian coast. Eventually, the Romans decided to put a stop to things and sent in Pompey, who destroyed the pirate fleet in a sea battle off Alanya in 67 BC. In 44 BC, Mark Antony gave the city to Cleopatra as a gift. Romantic as this might sound, there was a practical reason for his choice: this area was an important timber-producing centre, and Cleopatra needed its resources to build up her navy. In 1221, the Byzantine city fell to the Selçuk sultan Alâeddin Keykubad, who gave it its present name and made it his summer residence. Most buildings of historical importance date from that era.

Kızılkule and around

West end of the harbour • Museum: summer daily 9am–7pm; winter Tues–Sun 8am–5pm • ₺9 • 0242 513 3255

Guarding the harbour on the east side of the promontory, the **Kızılkule** – the "Red Tower" – is a 35m-high defensive tower of red stone. Built by Alâeddin Keykubad in 1226 and restored in 1951, it now houses a small **ethnographic museum** and offers impressive views along the coast.

Old wooden houses cling to the slopes above, and you can follow the old coastal defensive wall along the water's edge to the **Tersane**, an Ottoman shipyard, where five workshops are linked by an arched roof. Beyond here is a small defensive tower, the **Tophane**.

Alanya castle

Grounds open daily 24hr • Free • Tour buses head up almost every hour, and taxis are available behind the tourist office (10min; ₺20 per person); you can also walk, following the road that climbs the hill behind Kızıkule (1hr) or the main road from Damalataş Cave (1.5hr) – both routes are signposted • 0242 511 3304

No trip to Alanya would be complete without a visit to its crowning spectacle, reached by a winding path which climbs uphill southwest of town. The sprawling fortification system of its **castle** makes a fascinating alternative to the beach, with spectacular views to boot. The castle grounds are free and easy to explore on foot, but wear sturdy shoes if you plan to wander off-path. The castle walls are the best aid to navigation; they snake right around the upper reaches of the promontory and are linked by a network of overgrown footpaths.

The main route is well waymarked, with plenty of restaurants and little cafés to stop off at. If you get lost, keep heading up and you'll eventually hit signs for the **İç Kale** (**Inner Fortress**). On the way, you'll pass the **Aksebe Türbesi**, a distinctive thirteenth-century tomb, half-restored but still with its original minaret (kids will enjoy clambering the stairwell inside, although there's no view) and surrounded by clusters of wild thyme.

In among the foliage off the main road, in an area known as **Ehmediye**, lies a small village of a few old Ottoman houses. They're clustered around the dilapidated sixteenth-century **Süleymaniye Camii** – only open at prayer times – and a *kervansaray*.

Inner Fortress

Daily 9am–7pm • ₺15 • Parking ₺4

The **İç Kale**, or **Inner Fortress**, of Alanya castle was built by Keykubad in 1226. The interior is pretty much intact, with the shell of a **Byzantine church**, decorated with

6

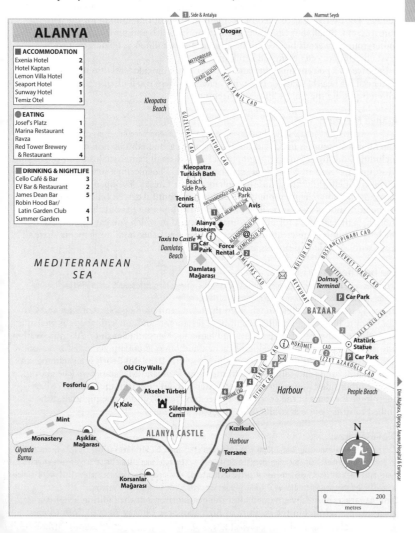

6

fading frescoes, in the centre, and wooden-decking pathways making it easy to pick through the finds. Look out for the **cisterns** that supplied the fortress with water and to which it owed much of its apparent impregnability.

A **platform** in the northwest corner of the fortress gives fine views of the western beaches and the mountains. It originally served as a point from which prisoners were thrown to their deaths on the rocks below. These days tour guides assure their charges that it's customary to throw a rock from the platform, attempting to hit the sea rather than the rock below – an impossible challenge supposed to have been set for prisoners as a chance to save their necks.

Damlataş Mağarası

Behind *Damlataş Restaurant* on Damlataş Beach • Daily 10am–sunset • ₺5 • ☎ 0242 513 1240

The aptly entitled "Cave of Dripping Stones", or **Damlataş Mağarası**, casts an eerie silhouette with its peculiar assemblage of stalagmites and stalactites drooping from the ceiling. The cave was discovered by accident in 1948 during mining for the harbour construction. Small, but easily accessible from the beach and undeniably dramatic, the underground cavern is believed to be around fifteen million years old, formed by crystallized limestones from the Permian era.

The cave's 95 percent humidity and higher carbon dioxide levels are supposedly beneficial for health, so it's dotted with benches, where you'll often see local asthma sufferers passing the time – and even sleeping.

Alanya Museum

On the corner of İsmet Hilmi Balcı Cad and Damlataş Cad • Tues–Sun: summer 9am–7pm, winter 8am–5pm • ₺5 • ☎ 0242 513 1228

The **Alanya Museum** is filled with local archeological and ethnological ephemera, including finds from (and photographs of) several small Pamphylian sites in the region. Most unusual is an inscription in sixth-century BC Phoenician, a sort of halfway house between cuneiform writing and the alphabet as the Greeks developed it. There's also a mock-up Ottoman living room complete with a beautiful carved ceiling, shutters and cupboards, and a model of a village wedding. The best thing about the museum, though, is the garden, a former Ottoman graveyard in which you can take refuge from the heat in summer; re-creations of grape presses and other farm implements share space with a gaggle of peacocks and chickens.

The beaches

City beaches can all be reached on foot from the harbour, and dolmuşes run along the coast to beaches further afield from the dolmuş terminal – the numbered route maps on display make it easy to plan your route

Alanya's extensive **beaches** stretch from the town centre for a good 3km west and 8km east. They're lined with a multitude of bars, restaurants and souvenir shops as well as a surprising number of tattoo parlours and hamams. **Kleopatra Beach** on Alanya's western side is the most popular of the local beaches, and offers abundant activities in season (see box opposite). At the southern tip of Kleopatra, **Damlataş Beach** is a sheltered cove with pristine sands and calm waters fronting the Damlataş Mağarası cave (see above). On the other side of town, **People Beach** stretches out east from the harbour, where boats leave for **tours** of the coastal caves (see box, p.378) and, come nightfall, lithe-limbed tourists pour out of the thumping bars and clubs.

Dim Mağarası

11km east of the town centre • Daily 9am–7.30pm, winter till 5.30pm • ₺ 15 adults, ₺ 7.50 children • ☎ 0242 518 2275, ⓦ dimcave.com .tr • Dolmuş #10 from the dolmuş station runs hourly in season (40min; ₺2); by car, continue past the Dimçay bridge for a few hundred metres, make a U-turn through a gap in the central reservation, then head back to the bridge and take the right turn just before it – follow this road for 3km, then turn right and follow a track for a further 5km through increasingly attractive scenery

Dim Mağarası (Dim Cave, named after the nearby river, not the lighting level) is a spectacular cavern set in the mountains high above the **Dimçay River**. A 360m-long

ACTIVITIES AT ALANYA'S BEACHES

KLEOPATRA BEACH

During warmer months, sunbeds and parasols are available on Kleopatra Beach (from ₺5), and kids can try **go-karting** (€10) on the promenade or visit **SeaLanya seapark** (May–Oct daily 10am–5pm; €60, children 4–9yrs €50, under-3s free; ☎0242 543 1139, ⍟sealanya.com) which puts on dolphin and sea-lion shows, and offers the chance to swim with dolphins (€120). Active types can sample a range of **watersports**: jet-ski rental, waterskiing and banana-boat rides are all available, and **paragliding** (try Ulusky, ⍟ulusky.com; or Trikeforce, ⍟trikeforce .com; from €60) is growing in popularity. The end nearest the castle has **mini golf** (€5), **beach volleyball** nets, **basketball** courts and **tennis** courts (from €10), as well as beachside **massage** huts (€15 for 40min).

PEOPLE BEACH

At People Beach you can take **Segway tours** (⍟segwayalanya.com) or book a **scuba-diving** trip to local dive sites which include wrecks and caves (see below).

6

walkway leads through the well-lit cavern itself, with a series of limestone formations providing interest en route to the prime attraction, a lovely crystal-clear pool. A small café-restaurant at the entrance offers great views over the heavily wooded mountains. Alternatively, stop beside the river itself, and either join in the riverside activities or eat out at one of the many trout restaurants scattered along the banks.

ARRIVAL AND DEPARTURE   ALANYA

By bus Alanya's *otogar* is a 30min walk north of the town centre; plenty of *servis* minibuses and municipal buses shuttle passengers to and fro. Most of the many buses to destinations east and west start their journeys elsewhere, so book your departure seat well in advance.
Destinations Adana (2 daily; 9hr); Ankara (7 daily; 9hr); Antalya (every 30min; 2hr); Diyarbakır (1 daily; 19hr); Istanbul (4 daily; 18hr); Konya (6 daily; 5hr); Manavgat

(10 daily; 1hr); Mersin (8 daily; 8hr); Samsun (3 daily; 15hr); Silifke via Taşucu (5 daily; 6hr).
Car rental Alanya has several outlets; prices are higher than in Antalya, so shop around, and bargain hard. Big names include Avis, just off the western end of Damlataş (☎0242 513 3513), and Europcar, at Hasan Akcalioglu Cad 34 (☎0242 513 1929). Force Rental, at Damlataş Cad 68/A (☎0242 511 4243), is cheaper.

INFORMATION, TOURS AND ACTIVITIES

Tourist office Opposite the Alanya Museum on Damlataş Cad, the tourist office (Mon–Fri 8am–12.30pm & 1.30–5pm; ☎0242 513 1240) offers excellent booklets and maps on the region. There's also a tourist information booth (summer daily 9am–5pm) on Bostancıpınarı Cad 1, where you can pick up town maps and get information on the city sights.
Dive operators Dolphin Dive, overlooking the harbour at İskele Cad 23 (☎0242 512 3030, ⍟dolphin-dive.com), has PADI-certified instructors and day-trips for beginners

starting from €62 (including lunch and two dives), as well as numerous options for certified divers.
Tours and travel agents Timeless Travel, Damlataş Cad 27 (☎0242 512 0539, ⍟famtouralanya.com) offer trips to Cappadocia, Pamukkale or the Pamphylian cities (from €30 per person, including hotel pick-up), as well as jeep safaris, boat tours and trips to the Manavgat waterfalls and Sapadere Kanyonu (around €30; see p.380).

ACCOMMODATION

Despite the boom in package tourism, rooms are easy to find in Alanya, even in high season, and the competition has kept the prices manageable (although they can almost double come the end of June). Keykubat Caddesi, the extension of Atatürk Caddesi, leading off to Mersin and backing the eastern beach, is Alanya's out-of-town resort strip, lined with upmarket hotels and all-inclusive resorts.

AROUND İSKELE CADDESİ

Exenia Otel Damlataş Cad 52 ☎0242 512 2729, ⍟exeniaotel.com. This recently renovated hotel offers simple, spotless rooms, with spacious balconies and

welcoming staff. It's in a great location for access to both parts of town, and prices are always negotiable, with some good deals on family and triple rooms, making it a top choice for those on a budget. **₺100**

6

COASTAL CAVE TOURS FROM ALANYA

Entrepreneurs in Alanya offer **boat tours** to several caves dotted along the waterline at the base of the promontory. Trips leave from the harbour and cost from ₺20 per person for one hour, or from ₺30 for longer excursions that include dolphin watching. If you want to go inside the smaller caves, make sure you take a small boat tour; the bigger ships will just pull up outside.

The first stop is usually the **Fosforlu** (Phosphorus Cave), where the water shimmers green; then it's on round the **Cilyarda Burnu**, a long spit of land that's home to a ruined monastery and former mint. It's not possible to go ashore.

On the other side of the skinny peninsula, according to a bizarre local story, a German woman and her Turkish boyfriend were stranded for three months in 1965 in the **Aşıklar Mağarası** (Lovers' Cave), while the police and army mounted searches for them.

More credibly, the **Korsanlar Mağarası** (Pirate's Cave), a little further round, is said to be where the pirates of yesteryear used to hide out. You will also be taken to **Kleoptra Mağarası** (**Cleopatra's Cave**), where legends claim the queen used to descend to bathe while staying here with Mark Antony.

Hotel Kaptan İskele Cad 70 ☎0242 513 4900, ⓦkaptanhotels.com. *Kaptan's* identikit balcony rooms might favour substance over style, but the newly renovated pool and bar area, the pleasant rooftop restaurant and good ocean views more than make up for it. There are options for B&B or half board, and it's just a few minutes' stroll from the bars and restaurants of the harbour. ₺200

★**Lemon Villa Hotel** Tophane Cad 20 ☎0242 513 4461, ⓦlemonvilla.com. With its patchwork stone walls, ocean-view balconies and pretty flower-lined courtyard framed by tall lemon trees, *Lemon Villa* is a pocket of calm set on the hill above the harbour. The nine individually tailored rooms feature antique furnishings, exquisite bathrooms and comfy beds, scattered with luxe cushions, and guests are greeted with freshly squeezed lemonade on arrival. €80

Seaport Hotel İskele Cad 82 ☎0242 513 6487, ⓦhotelseaport.com. In a prime location above the harbour, this swish hotel offers impeccable service,

well-soundproofed rooms and free parking. Rooms are classically decorated with dark wood and charming anchor-print bedspreads, but the highlight is the view from the balconies. Rates include breakfast and dinner. ₺240

Temiz Otel İskele Cad 12 ☎0242 513 1016, ⓦtemizotel .com.tr. If you're after a budget room in the heart of the action, *Temiz* makes a worthy contender, where the spick-and-span rooms are well-equipped and tastefully decorated. A balcony view over the harbour is tempting, but if you prefer peace and quiet, ask for a room at the back to escape the thumping music from the bars below. €30

KLEOPATRA BEACH

Sunway Hotel Bebek Sok 4 ☎0242 511 1880, ⓦalanyasunwayhotel.com. Popular with tour groups, this lively family-run hotel always has a varied mix of guests, and its live music nights are good fun. Rooms are well-equipped and cheerful, and the English-speaking staff go above and beyond. Closed Nov–Feb. €30

EATING

Though the overpriced and heavily westernized restaurants that clog the beachfront might make you doubt Alanya's culinary abilities, the city has a trove of quality options if you can tear yourself away from the main strip. Many restaurants offer free taxis to and from hotels, so it's worth calling ahead to book a table. A weekly **market**, with masses of fresh provisions, is held every Fri, next to the dolmuş station, north of İsim Tokuş Bulvarı.

Josef's Platz Demir Sok 5 ☎0242 513 9296. Grilling the self-proclaimed best steaks in Alanya since 1980, *Josef's Platz* might serve more tourists than locals these days, but fortunately the boost in custom hasn't seen a loss in quality. Splash out on the house speciality, "Josef's Südsee special steak" (from ₺53) and watch it cooked right in front of you on an enormous stone grill. Licensed. Daily 9am–midnight.

Marina Restaurant At the east side of the harbour ☎0242 513 1034. Rare among the waterfront restaurants, *Marina* doesn't need to pester passers-by for business,

what with their quietly sophisticated environment, huge rooftop terrace and reliably good cuisine – choose from a good mix of international and Turkish dishes (mains from ₺26). Families can make the most of the small children's play area too. Licensed. Daily 9am–1am.

★**Ravza** Zambak Sok 16, off Gazipaşa St, just before the park ☎0242 519 0862, ⓦravza.com.tr. Packed with locals and a smattering of in-the-know tourists, *Ravza* offers an authentic but unintimidating introduction to Turkish cuisine, with traditional dishes for half the price of the beachside haunts. Located at the entrance to the maze-like bazaar, the age-old recipes are whipped up with fresh, local produce, and the bread is kneaded and baked in front of you. Kebabs start from ₺12, but the sizzling clay-pot casseroles (from ₺17) are the real speciality – try the *osmanish* (meat and vegetables, topped with cheese) or the *karides güveç* (shrimp pot). No alcohol. Daily 9am–2am, winter till 11pm.

Red Tower Brewery & Restaurant İskele Cad, above the harbour ☎0242 513 6664, ⊛redtowerbrewery.com. The brainchild of local entrepreneurs, this mega-restaurant not only houses its own unique microbrewery (try the refreshingly light home-brewed lager), but the city's first and foremost sushi bar (prices start around ₺20 for a six-roll plate), a menu of Turkish and international favourites and one of the best rooftop views in town. Daily 10am–midnight.

DRINKING AND NIGHTLIFE

A veritable circus of flashing neon and pop music pumping at ear-popping volumes, Alanya's coastal strip comes alive after dark with bars, discos and clubs geared towards the package tourist masses. Several out-of-town mega-discos also open their doors in summer (with free all-night buses to and from the city).

Cello Café & Bar İskele Cad 36 ☎0242 511 4290. With its rustic wooden panelling and walls hung with bongos and banjos, this dimly lit tavern has barrel-loads of character. The varied set of live folk and ethnic music, from 9.30pm nightly, makes a refreshing change from the throbbing beats that seep up from the waterfront. Daily 11am–11pm.

EV Bar & Restaurant Atatürk Cad 8, opposite Atatürk statue ☎0242 511 1051. Away from the hard-partying crowds of the harbour, *EV* is a more grown-up affair, with live guitar music drawing in a laidback mix of locals, expats and travellers. The set lists mix traditional numbers with classic crowd-pleasers, and at ₺15 the cocktails are considerably cheaper than the bigger clubs. Daily 10am–1am.

James Dean Bar Rıhtm St (on the harbour) ☎0536 724 2992. James Dean might turn in his grave at the sight of the mini-skirted tourists knocking back cocktails (from ₺22) in his name, but while cheesy music and skin-baring Europeans reign here, the place itself has a quirky rock'n'roll vibe. Red and black interiors, reminiscent of a 1950s' diner, are decorated with a collage of images and memorabilia of the man himself. Daily 9pm–3am.

Robin Hood Bar/Latin Garden Club & Restaurant Rıhtm St (on the harbour) ☎0242 511 2023. Sherwood Forest gets a neon-dream makeover at this sprawling three-floor club, right on the harbour. If the ear-splitting playlist of pop and dance gets too much, head to the rooftop *Latin Garden Club & Restaurant*, where you can swing your hips to latino grooves with a view of the ocean instead. Daily 10pm–3am.

Summer Garden 10km west of town on Konakli Kasabasi ☎0242 565 0059, ⊛summer-garden.com. The best of Alanya's megaclubs is decked out like a Mediterranean fantasy, with strobe-lit palm trees, man-made waterfalls and gyrating podium dancers. Several dancefloors, a VIP area and a mix of Turkish pop and R&B should distract you from the pricey ₺29 cocktails. Look out for the daily event flyers along the beachfront and hop on the free shuttle bus from the harbour. Daily: restaurant 7–11pm, club 7pm–5am.

SHOPPING

Touristy **silverware** and **carpets** are sold in İskele Cad, and there are yet more shops on the side streets between Gazipaşa and Hükümet cads. **Fake designer-label clothes** are ubiquitous, and if you're looking to add to your collection of replica soccer shirts, Alanya is the place to do it.

DIRECTORY

Banks and exchange Several banks with ATMs can be found on Atatürk and Hükümet cads, and there are plenty of stand-alone ATMs along the beachfront.

Cinema Örnek Sinemaları, on Damlataş Cad opposite the museum (☎0242 513 2671, ⊛orneksinemalari.com), shows some films in English with Turkish subtitles.

Hamams Kleopatra Turkish Bath (Güzelyali Cad; ☎0242 519 2505, ⊛kleopatra.com.tr), opposite Kleopatra Beach, offers a traditional hamam experience and a range of massages and spa treatments from €20.

Hospital The State Hospital (Devlet Hastane) is on the bypass, east of the centre.

Internet Damlataş, on Gemicioğlu Sok, just off Damlataş Cad.

Post office The main PTT is on Atatürk Cad, opposite Kültür Cad (daily 24hr), sells phonecards. PTT caravans are scattered about town in summer.

East of Alanya

The region between Alanya and Adana formed ancient **Cilicia**, and was settled by refugees from Troy at the same time as Pamphylia further west. Its remoteness and rugged, densely wooded coastline made it a haven for pirates, which eventually spurred the Romans into absorbing Cilicia into the empire in the first century BC. Today, the region retains a wild appearance, and travel involves frighteningly daring drives along winding mountain roads that hug the craggy coastline. All this is worth it if you're trying to escape the crowds further west, as far fewer people make it here.

Immediately east of Alanya, roads scallop the coastal cliffs, occasionally dipping inland through verdant banana plantations and passing little wayside restaurants, sheltered but hard-to-reach sandy bays, and the odd camping ground. Decent stretches of beach around **Anamur** are overlooked by an Armenian castle and a partially excavated Greek site, while in the mountains above **Silifke** the abandoned city of **Uzuncaburç** is perhaps the most extensive of the region's ancient remains. The up-and-coming seaside resort of **Kızkalesi** is intent on earning its stripes as a summer holiday destination, with its impressive castles breaking up the shoreline and a mixed bag of historical sites and day-hikes on its doorstep.

A miscellany of marginally interesting ruins and lesser-frequented beaches runs down the coast until the outskirts of **Mersin**, where ferries head to Northern Cyprus. A little further on, **Tarsus**, birthplace of St Paul, plays host to some significant Christian sites, although its modern aspect does little to betray its former historical importance. **Adana**, Turkey's fourth-largest city, contains few remains of any era despite its venerable history, but does have excellent market shopping.

Sapadere Kanyonu

40km east of Alanya • Daily 9am–7.30pm, winter till 5.30pm • ₺9 adults, ₺4.50 children; or book a full-day tour from Alanya (see p.377) • ☎ 0242 543 1212, ⊛ sapaderekanyonu.com

If you're looking to escape Alanya's sweltering city heat for an afternoon, you'll find that the sleepy village of **Sapadere** makes a popular picnic spot. The **Sapadere Kanyonu** itself, just outside the village, is a 750m canyon that reaches heights of 400m, winding through rocky coves, shallow rock pools and gushing waterfalls, before opening out into a sizeable pool, where the water remains cool even in summer. A network of wood-and-steel walkways has been erected, making it an easy stroll, and there's a café-restaurant on site.

If you have time, head back to the village to take a peek at the watermill, or visit the small **silk factory**, to watch the villagers raising silkworms and spinning silk threads.

Iotape

45km east of Alanya • Daily 24hr • Free

Oddly situated on a rocky peninsula between the road and sea, the ancient site of **Iotape** was named after the wife of the Commagenian king Antiochus IV (38–72 AD), and struck its own coins from the reign of Emperor Trajan until that of Emperor Valerian. The ruins are very tumbledown, apart from a fairly impressive triple-arched bathhouse. Closer inspection uncovers drainage and heating systems. The acropolis is on the promontory out to sea, while a colonnaded street runs east–west to the mainland. The **beach** below Iotape is idyllic: with luck, you might get it to yourself.

İskele and around

Originally just a small harbour suburb of the unexciting town of **Anamur**, 4km northwest, **İSKELE**, which means "quay", has developed into a fully fledged, but unpretentious, resort. In summer, when holidaying Turks descend on the coastline, it's heaving with life. Its two beaches are sliced in half by a pier from which regular ferries run to Cyprus.

Mamure Kalesi

2.5km east of İskele • Closed for renovations at the time of writing, but normally daily: April–Oct 9am–7pm; Nov–March 8.30am–5pm • ₺3 • From İskele, either walk along the seashore, which involves a ₺5 ferry ride across the Dragon River, or catch a taxi for ₺10 per person

Closed for renovations at the time of writing, the forbidding castle known as the

Mamure Kalesi was built by the rulers of the Cilician kingdom of Armenia, on the site of a Byzantine fort. The castle was later occupied by Crusaders, who had established a short-lived kingdom in Cyprus and used the castle as a kind of bridgehead in Asia. Used by successive local rulers to protect the coastal strip, it was most recently garrisoned by the Ottomans, who reinforced it after the British occupied Cyprus in 1878, and maintained a strong presence here during World War I. Constructed directly above the sea, its stark facade of crenelated outer walls and watchtowers is certainly impressive. The languorously decaying buildings in its interior have formed a backdrop to many Turkish films.

6

Anemurium

6km southwest of Anamur • Tues–Sun: April–Oct 9am–7pm; Nov–March 8.30am–5pm • ₺5 • No dolmuş service, but a taxi from İskele costs ₺15 per person; be sure to arrange a pick-up time

The ancient settlement of **Anemurium**, at its peak during the third century AD, stands on the eastern side of a headland where the Toros Mountains jut out into the sea. As you approach, you'll see two parallel **aqueducts** running north to south along the hillside to the right. Below these, a sun-baked **necropolis** contains numerous freestanding tombs whose cool interiors harbour murals of mythological scenes. To the right of the road, the hollow ruins of three **Byzantine churches** are starkly silhouetted against the blue backdrop of the Mediterranean.

Further down towards the beach, you'll see the crumbling remains of a **bath complex**, a desolate **palaestra** or parade ground, and a ruined but still identifiable **theatre** set into the hillside. Above the theatre, some of the ruined houses still have intact vaulted roofs, while to the east, the shell of a building holds sixteen curved rows of seating and a mosaic floor. It's thought to have been either a **council chamber** or a **concert hall**, or possibly both. If you have time, you might want to clamber up the scrubby slopes of the headland to what was once Anemurium's **acropolis**. The promontory is **Turkey's southernmost point**, and on a clear day gives views of the mountains of Cyprus, 80km south.

ARRIVAL AND DEPARTURE   İSKELE AND AROUND

By bus From Anamur's *otogar*, where the main street meets the coast road, dolmuşes and city buses run southeast to İskele (daily every 30min, summer 7am–midnight, winter 7am–8pm). Taxis from the *otogar* to

İskele cost around ₺10.
Destinations from Anamur Alanya (6 daily; 3hr); Silifke (6 daily; 3hr).

ACCOMMODATION

Accommodation in the İskele region is refreshingly cheap compared with resorts further west; the three places listed here are all in İskele.

Eser Pansiyon İnönü Cad 6 ☎0536 217 9878. This humble eleven-room hotel is the cheapest in town, and while the rooms are a little timeworn, they are still clean, tidy and many have balconies. There's no breakfast, but guests are welcome to use the kitchen and washing machine, plus there's a small garden with hammocks out the back. ₺50
Tayfun Hotel Yolu Yunuslu Kavşak 176 ☎0324 814 1161. Guests are greeted with a smile from English-speaking owner Tayfun at his namesake hotel. It's good

value for money, with comfortable, spacious rooms and a/c throughout, and he puts on a well-stocked breakfast buffet, including eggs, fresh fruit and cappuccinos. ₺110
Yan Hotel Yalıevleri Mah ☎0324 814 2123, ⊕yanhotel.com. Run by a friendly elderly couple, *Yan* makes an affordable choice if you want a quiet bed to rest your head. Opt for a room with a balcony and take your breakfast in the flower-filled atrium below. ₺100

EATING

All the listings below are in İskele, home to several simple restaurants, all of which seem incredibly cheap after the overpricing so prevalent further west. Make sure you pick up some of the region's famed **miniature bananas** too, as featured on one of the town's principal statues. Market stalls abound with the yellow fruits, and restaurants offer creative banana-centred desserts.

Efsun İskele Köyu Yolu ☎ 0535 331 7740. A simple family establishment with cheap eats and good, friendly service; you can pick up a tasty fish sandwich for as little as ₺5, and *gözleme* from ₺6. Daily 7.30am–10.30pm.

Tayfun Restaurant Yolu Yunuslu Kavşak 176 ☎ 0324 814 1161. Flavoursome, home-cooked food is on offer at this friendly hotel restaurant, with generous portions and a selection of salads and *mezes* to choose from. There's no menu, but staples sich as *adana kebap* or chicken *şiş* will set you back less than ₺15, with all the trimmings. Daily 8am–10pm.

6 Taşucu

Crammed with European birdwatchers in springtime, the small but charming port town of **TAŞUCU** makes a pleasant base from which to explore the nearby **Göksu Delta**. There are few attractions in the town itself, but its frequent ferry and hydrofoil services to Cyprus make it a popular transport hub. A stroll around the pretty marina makes a pleasant way to kill time, and there are some excellent fish restaurants along the main strip. You can take a dip in the water from the tiny **pebble beach** before the harbour; the nearest **sandy beaches** are a kilometre-walk beyond the marina, heading south.

Amphora Museum

Cumhuriyet Meydanı • Mon & Fri–Sun 9am–5.30pm • ₺2

Despite its diminutive size – a mere three rooms – the **Amphora Museum** manages to cram in a trove of wacky curiosities. Its unassuming entrance, next door to the *Deniz Kizi Restaurant* (see below), belies its quirky appeal. It holds a fascinating collection of Hellenistic, Roman and Byzantine amphorae, mostly from locally salvaged wrecks, and a small but beautifully embellished assortment of antique dresses. A makeshift encampment is set up in one corner, with a *Yörük* tent, some traditional leather saddles hung with tribal tassels, and an old spinning wheel.

ARRIVAL AND DEPARTURE | TAŞUCU

By minibus Frequent minibuses run to and from Silifke, 10km west (20min; ₺2). The pick-up and drop-off point in Taşucu is at the top of İnönü Cad, where it meets the main road.

By ferry & hydrofoil From Taşucu you can get ferries and hydrofoils to Girne in Northern Cyprus (see box opposite).

ACCOMMODATION

Hotel Fatih Atatürk Bul 199; follow signs from near the museum ☎ 0324 741 4125, ⓦ hotelfatih.net. Fatih's gregarious English-speaking owner, Abdullah, is a talented painter whose colourful creations make a striking first impression, hung up around the lobby. Upstairs, the compact, a/c rooms benefit from glorious ocean views, but this is still a budget hotel – the bathrooms are looking a bit worn, plus there's no breakfast. **₺120**

Lades Otel İnönü Cad 45 ☎ 0324 741 4415, ⓦ ladesotel .com. Once the town's premium hotel, the standards have slipped somewhat at *Lades*, but the corresponding price drop might still tempt you to stay. Rooms are simple and outdated, although there are some more recently renovated options available where there's a notable jump in quality. The helpful staff and huge terrace swimming pool overlooking the Med are worthy compensation. **₺90**

EATING

Baba İnönü Cad 43 ☎ 0324 741 5991. With stunning views over the marina, *Baba* makes a scenic pit stop, and serves up plenty of fresh-caught fish and seafood (from ₺15). Finish it off with a scoop of home-made pistachio gelato. Daily 11am–midnight.

Deniz Kizi Restaurant İnönü Cad 62 ☎ 0324 741 4194. Hands down the town's best restaurant, *Deniz Kizi* (meaning "Mermaid") is fittingly decked out with fish murals and dangling seashell mobiles. Grab a table on the atmospheric rooftop terrace and order the house speciality, *balik buğulama* (₺22), a fish stew made with onions, tomatoes and potatoes. Daily 11.30am–midnight.

Silifke

SİLİFKE, 10km east of Taşucu, was once ancient Seleucia, founded by Seleucus, one of Alexander the Great's generals, in the third century BC. Nowadays, it's a quiet, fairly

---

FERRIES AND HYDROFOILS TO CYPRUS

The cheapest way to get to the **Turkish Republic of Northern Cyprus (TRNC)** from Turkey's Mediterranean coast is by boat; regular ferries and hydrofoils run from both Taşucu and Mersin.

FROM TAŞUCU

By ferry For anyone travelling with a **car**, the quickest way to get to Northern Cyprus is by taking the ferry to **Girne** on the north coast (Mon–Thurs & Sun 10am & midnight; 7hr; ₺65 one-way per person, from ₺75 for a car with one passenger). These are packed with heavy lorries and their drivers, so solo women travellers may feel uncomfortable.

By hydrofoil On calm seas at least, hydrofoils (*deniz otobüsü*) to Girne make a quicker and more pleasant alternative to the ferries for foot passengers (daily 10.30am; 2.5hr; ₺65 one-way).

Tickets Akgünler, on the main road opposite the waterfront (☎0324 741 4033, ⓦakgunler .com.tr) sells tickets for both ferries and hydrofoils.

FROM MERSİN

By ferry Ferries sail from Mersin to Gazimağusa (Famagusta) in Northern Cyprus (Mon, Wed & Fri 8pm; 12hr; one-way adult ticket ₺105, car with driver ₺315).

Tickets Buy tickets from the Cyprus-Turkish Shipping Company (ⓦkibrisdeniz.net) or directly from the harbour, at the east end of İsmet İnönü Bulvarı.

ENTRY REQUIREMENTS

To enter the TRNC, EU, US, Canadian and Australian citizens require only a valid passport, holding an unexpired Turkish entry visa. It's not possible to enter southern (Greek-speaking) Cyprus from the TRNC.

6

undistinguished town where only the occasional tourist passes through, typically en route to the ruins at Uzuncaburç.

Silifke Kalesi, a Byzantine castle, dominates the local skyline. A twenty-minute walk southwest of town, it looks a lot less spectacular close up. On the way up you'll pass an old **cistern** – the so-called *tekir ambarı* or "striped depot" – that kept Byzantine Silifke supplied with water. Other sights include the second-century AD **Jupiter Tapınağı** (Temple of Jupiter) on İnönü Caddesi, which comprises little more than a pile of stones and one standing pillar topped by a stork's nest, and the early Christian site of **Aya Tekla**, 5km west of town off the road to Taşucu, where there's little to see except an underground chapel (take a torch).

Incidentally, it was near Silifke that **Frederick Barbarossa**, the Holy Roman Emperor, met his end: he drowned while fording the Calycadnus (now Göksu) River about 9km north of town, en route to Palestine with the Third Crusade. A plaque now marks the spot.

Archeological Museum

On the main road to Taşucu and Antalya, signposted from the town centre • Tues–Sun 8am–noon & 1–5pm • Free

Silifke's **Archeological Museum** (Arkeoloji Müzesi) contains the finds from excavations at Meydancıkale, a fourth-century BC temple site in the mountains above the coast. Relics include two enormous caryatids; huge, shapeless stone blocks with human-looking feet carved into the bases; and a hoard of 5200 silver coins dating from the reigns of Alexander and his generals in Egypt, Syria and the province of Pergamon.

ARRIVAL AND INFORMATION	**SİLİFKE**

By bus The *otogar* is a 15min walk east of the town centre, on İnönü Cad.

Destinations Adana (every 15–20min; 2hr); Alanya (8 daily; 7hr); Antalya (8 daily; 9hr); Konya (8 daily; 5hr); Mersin (every 20min; 2hr); Taşucu (minibuses every 30min; 20min).

Tourist office Veli Gürten Bozbey Cad 6, on the road opposite the *Göksu Hotel* (Mon–Fri 8am–noon & 1.30–5pm; ☎0324 714 1151). Look out for the yellow signs as you cross the bridge.

6

WILDLIFE IN THE GÖKSU DELTA

The **Göksu delta** and its **Kuşcenneti bird reservation** are of outstanding environmental importance, boasting a tremendous variety of native flora and fauna. The best place to start an exploration is Akgöl, the westerly lagoon, where pygmy cormorants, Dalmatian pelicans, marbled and white-headed ducks and even the practically extinct black francolin and purple gallinule feed. The sand spit is a nesting ground for loggerhead and green turtles as well as a home to sea daffodils and Audouin's gulls. East of this, reached by an access road halfway between Taşucu and Silifke, are extensive ditches where you'll see kingfishers (including the rare chestnut brown and white Smyrna variety), coots, wagtails, spoonbills, egrets and grey, purple and squacco herons. Still further east, the huge natural fishpond of Paradeniz lagoon and the flats beyond it harbour waders, ospreys and terns.

Nesting and migration seasons are in the spring (with a peak between late March and early April), and in October. Information leaflets and maps of the delta are available from the **Özel Çevre Koruma Kurumu** (Special Environmental Areas Protection Agency; ☎0324 714 9508), 5km west of Silifke, who can also arrange an English-speaking guide for group trips. Alternatively, hire a taxi from your hotel to the **Göksu delta birdwatching tower**, on the south bank of the Akgöl lagoon (daily 5am–9pm; free). Make sure to take your own water and supplies, as no cafés or facilities are available.

ACCOMMODATION AND EATING

Hotel possibilities are limited, but there are some passable budget options close to the *otogar*. For eating, there are plenty of basic food stalls and teahouses, but most close after dark, leaving you with very few options for an evening meal – try to arrange dinner at your hotel if possible.

Arısan Otel İnönü Cad 81; turn left out of the otogar ☎0324 714 3331. The cheery proprietor doesn't speak a word of English, but this is still a safe bet for budget travellers. While the rooms could definitely do with an update, there is reliable a/c, and many have balconies from which you can see the Silifke Kalesi. There are also good-value family rooms and cheaper options with shared bathrooms. No breakfast. **₺70**

Göksu Hotel Atatürk Bul 20 ☎0324 712 1021. The best-positioned hotel in town, on the northern riverbank, with great views over the river, bridge and castle, and free parking. The carpeted rooms are spacious, with TVs and fridges, but are in dire need of a lick of paint. Dinner available on request. **₺140**

Otel Ayatekla Mirzabey Cad, next to the otogar ☎0324 715 1081. In prime location right by the *otogar*, this two-star hotel is the obvious choice for a pit stop, although don't expect more than your money's worth. Rooms are basic and dimly lit, albeit comfortable enough for a night, and a simple breakfast is provided. **₺80**

Özkaymak Pastaneleri İnönü Cad 130, opposite the otogar ☎0324 714 8183. Although this bakehouse is best for desserts – the ₺6 *şübiyet*, a kind of *baklava* with cream, is particularly good – it also serves a range of savouries, including decent sandwiches and burgers (from ₺12). Daily 8am–9pm.

Uzuncaburç

30km north of Silifke • Daily 24hr • ₺5 • Uzuncaburç-bound dolmuşes leave from 50m west of Silifke's tourist office (every 2hr Mon–Fri 9am–7pm, Sat & Sun 3 departures daily; last dolmuş back to Silifke normally around 5pm; 1hr)

The ancient city ruins at **Uzuncaburç** (Olba and Diocaesarea), a spectacular one-hour drive from Silifke through a jagged gorge, make a worthwhile day-trip. A small, rural **village** has sprung up in haphazard fashion around the ruins, with makeshift stalls flogging leather bags and handmade rugs (known as *çul*), and local teahouses where you can try regional specialities like *kenger kahvesi* (coffee made from acanthus) and *pekmez* (grape molasses).

While the main **site** of Uzuncaburç lacks the size and scale of Perge and Aspendos, it's atmospheric enough in its own way, if only because of its relatively neglected state. Although the area was first settled by the Hittites, they left little behind; the most impressive ruins that survive date from Hellenistic times.

Theatre and monumental gateway

The best place to start exploring Uzuncaburç is the overgrown Roman **theatre**, overlooked by a couple of beautiful houses whose walls are choc-a-bloc with Classical masonry. From here, pass through an enormous five-columned **monumental gateway** to reach a colonnaded street, once the city's main thoroughfare. Keep your eyes open for what look like small stone shelves on the columns, which once supported statues and busts.

Nymphaeum

A **nymphaeum**, now dried up, on the northern side of Uzuncaburç's colonnaded street once formed part of the city's water-supply system. This was part of a large network of pipes and tunnels, built by the Romans nearly two thousand years ago, that still supplies water to the modern village and others around.

Temple of Zeus Olbios

The columns of the **Temple of Zeus Olbios**, south of the nymphaeum, feature one of the earliest examples of the Corinthian order, erected during the third century BC by Seleucus I. Only the fluted columns now remain intact. Look out for the fine sarcophagus carved with three Medusa heads, and a sarcophagus lid depicting three reclining figures.

Temple of Tyche and city gate

The **Temple of Tyche** stands at the western end of Uzuncaburç's colonnaded street. Dedicated to the goddess of fortune, it's believed to date from the second half of the first century AD. Five Egyptian granite columns still stand proud, joined by an architrave bearing an inscription stating that the temple was the gift of a certain Oppius and his wife Kyria. From here a right turn leads to a large three-arched **city gate**, which dates from the fifth century AD and is home to nesting birds.

Tower

North of the main ruins; turn right at the Ak Parti office

The 22m-high, five-storey Hellenistic **tower** once formed part of the city wall and gives its name to the modern town (*Uzuncaburç* means "high tower"). In addition to playing a defensive role, it's believed that this tower also formed part of an ancient signalling network, whereby messages were relayed by flashing sunlight off polished shields.

Alahan

110km northwest of Silifke • Daily 8am–sunset • ₺5 • Buses along Hwy 715 between the coast and Konya drop passengers at a turning (around 1.5hr from Silifke), which is a steep 2km walk from the site; taxis are often available at the bottom. A taxi and driver from Silifke will cost around €100

Reached by a dramatic road that cuts through the Toros Mountains en route for Konya, the Byzantine site of **Alahan**, a well-preserved monastic complex, stands at a height of 1200m, overshadowing the idyllic Göksu Valley. Despite being listed as a UNESCO World Heritage Site, it remains a little-visited treasure – more due to its isolated location and awkward transport links than any lack of impressive sights – and it's well worth a visit if you're passing through.

The **monastery buildings**, believed to date back to 440 AD, include two late fifth- and sixth-century basilicas (one sporting elaborate relief sculptures of the Evangelists and the two archangels), and a baptistry with a cross-shaped font. Christian tombs and some impressive owl and fish carvings and Bible inscriptions are dotted around the three main structures.

Kızkalesi and around

Midway between Silifke and Mersin, **KIZKALESİ** ("Maiden's Castle") is the longest-established resort along the Eastern Mediterranean coastline, with its lively beaches

6

burrowed between a pair of looming Byzantine castles. While Turkish families have been descending en masse for years, international tourists are still a relatively new phenomenon, and the genuine, unobtrusive hospitality of the locals makes a welcome relief from the tourist-packed haunts further up the coast. Fine sandy **beaches** and shallow waters make the resort an excellent choice for children, and there's everything from jet-skiing to paragliding on hand to keep the rest of the family entertained.

With its improved transport links and tour possibilities, Kızkalesi also makes a great base for exploring the surrounding area, like the popular **Cennet ve Cehennem** (caves of heaven and hell), the dramatic chasm of **Kanlıdıvane**, or the mosaic-floored **Bath of Poimenius** in Narlıkuyu. If you have a special interest in exploring off-the-beaten-track ruins, buy Celal Taşkiran's *Silifke and Environs*, an exhaustive guide to all the sites between Anamur and Mersin, available for €10 from Rain Tour & Travel Agency (see p.388).

Brief history

Known as Corycus in ancient times, Kızkalesi changed hands frequently until the arrival of the **Romans** in 72 BC. It then prospered to become one of the most important ports along the coast. Roman-era relics still survive in the area, notably a series of mysterious rock reliefs north of town and the carvings at the chasm at Kanlıdivane to the east. Kızkalesi continued to thrive during the Byzantine era despite occasional Arab attacks – against which its defences were strengthened by the construction of two **castles** during the twelfth and thirteenth centuries – before falling to the Ottomans in 1482.

Sea castle

On an island 300m offshore • Daily dawn–dusk • Boats run from the pier at the west end of the beach; ₺10 per person return

Kızkalesi's most compelling feature is its eponymous twelfth-century **sea castle** and the *Kızkalesi* (Maiden's Castle) makes an imposing sight floating on the horizon out to sea. According to a legend also found elsewhere in Turkey, a medieval Armenian king had a beautiful daughter. After it was prophesied that she would die from a snakebite, the king had the castle built and moved the girl out to it for safety. One day, however, an adviser sent a basket of fruit out to the island for the girl, out of which slid a snake that killed her. Locals say the snake still lives there so the only people who venture out to the island are tourists, for whose benefit boat services operate; you can also hire a pedalo and go it alone. The unadorned walls and sturdy towers still stand, but apart from masonry fragments and weeds there's little to see within.

Land castle

At the eastern end of the beach, opposite the sea castle • Daily: April–Oct 8am–8pm; Nov–March 8.30am–5pm • ₺5

The overgrown ruins of Kızkalesi's mighty **land castle** (Korkyos Kalesi) are easily explored, while its battlements make a good venue for watching the sunset. The main gate, constructed from ancient stones, bears various Greek inscriptions, whereas the western gate was a third-century Roman structure that was later incorporated into the castle. The complete lack of restrictions on where you can walk means kids might need some supervision, but those happy to scramble a few rocky verges are rewarded with some wonderful lookout points.

Necropolis

Immediately northeast of Kızkalesi, across the main road from the land castle

Dating from the fourth century AD, Kızkalesi's **necropolis** contains hundreds of tombs and sarcophagi, some of them beautifully carved. Many of the epitaphs give the jobs of the occupants – weavers, cobblers, goldsmiths, vintners, olive-oil manufacturers, ship-owners and midwives, who all had their last resting places here. Also scattered around this area are the remains of several Byzantine churches and cisterns. Explore these out-of-town areas at your own risk, as they are scattered throughout overgrown fields and farmers' plots.

Beaches

Kızkalesi's **main beach**, west of the land castle, is the most popular and is equipped with sunbeds, parasols, children's playgrounds and plenty of options for eating and drinking. Between mid-June and mid-Sept (and on many weekends throughout the year), the main beachfront plays host to all sorts of watersports and activities, including paragliding, jet-skiing and pedalo rides.

A smaller and less populated beach, to the east, offers quieter swimming areas but considerably fewer facilities.

6

Narlıkuyu

5km west of Kızkalesi

The small coastal village of **NARLİKUYU** lies on the fringe of a rapidly developing bay that's home to several decent fish restaurants. Next to the little car park in the village centre, the remains of the Roman **Bath of Poimenius** hold a fine mosaic floor depicting the well-rounded nude forms of the Three Graces and the daughters of Zeus. Poimenius' bath was fed from the limestone caves above by an ancient Roman spring that supplied a celebrated fountain, drinking the waters of which was said to confer wisdom.

Cennet ve Cehennem

5km northwest of Kızkalesi and around 1.5km north of Narlıkuyu • Daily dawn–dusk • ₺5 • From Narlıkuyu you can either hike, take a taxi (around €10 one-way) or join a tour (see p.388)

Cennet ve Cehennem, or the "Caves of Heaven and Hell", the most popular local sight, can be reached on a pleasant walk from Kızkalesi, winding through the olive grove hills north of **Narlıkuyu**. The three main caves here, including the cave of Heaven and the menacing chasm of Hell, rank among the most impressive of the many limestone caverns scattered along this coast.

Cennet Deresi (Cave of Heaven)

The large and impressive cave known as **Cennet Deresi** – Cave of Heaven – is located at the end of a 70m-deep canyon, entered via 452 steps cut into the rock. The culmination of the descent is the **chapel of the Virgin Mary**, a well-preserved Byzantine church built over the former temple of Zeus and still containing a few frescoes. Next to the church and part of the Cave of Heaven is the entrance to a smaller cave, **Tayfun Mağrası** (Cave of Typhon), which is reputed to be one of the gateways to Hades. Typhon, an immense hundred-headed fire-breathing lizard, was the father of Cerberus – the three-headed guard dog to Hades.

Down here you can also hear the start of the **underground river**, which flows downstream to meet the sea at Narlıkuyu.

Cehennem Deresi (Cave of Hell)

A hundred metres north of the Cave of Heaven

The **Cehennem Deresi** – Cave of Hell – is little more than a chasm, but considerably easier to reach than its counterpart. It's impossible to enter, as its sides are practically vertical, although you can teeter on the edge of a fenced platform and gaze, supposedly, into the depths of hell. Legend dictates that Typhon, the huge many-headed lizard, was once temporarily imprisoned here.

Dilek Mağarası (Wishing Cave)

The opening of the third cave at Cennet ve Cehennem – the **Dilek Mağarası** or Wishing Cave, 500m west of "Heaven" – has been widened, and a spiral staircase provided for ease of access. Down below, solid pathways connect a number of subterranean halls, with a total length of about 200m. The main chamber is filled with stalactites and stalagmites, and the air is supposed to be beneficial for asthma sufferers.

6

Adamkayalar rock reliefs

6km north of Kızkalesi; the turning is near the PTT

An intriguing side trip from Kızkalesi leads to the **Adamkayalar rock reliefs**. These consist of a series of seventeen Roman men, women and children (plus a mountain goat), carved into niches in the wall of a valley. It's not clear who the figures are, or why they might have been constructed, and the fragmentary inscriptions below most of them offer few clues. Unfortunately, severe damage has been caused to one figure by treasure hunters, who blew up the statue in the hope of finding booty secreted inside.

Kanlıdivane

10km northeast of Kızkalesi • Head 7km east from Kızkalesi, then follow a signposted turn-off 3km north

The village of **KANLIDIVANE**, which means "place of blood" or "place of bloody madness", owes its name to legends that describe condemned criminals being thrown into a huge gorge to be devoured by wild animals. If you come to see the chasm, it's worth taking a little extra time to visit some of the other sights in town, such as the impressive 17m-high **Tower of Zeus Olbios**, which bears an inscription on its southwest corner alongside a three-pronged triskele, a symbol that links the region to the nearby state of Olba. Various large Byzantine **basilicas** nearby survive in assorted states of collapse, while a cluster of **tombs** to the northeast includes numerous ancient sarcophagi, and a mausoleum dedicated by a woman to her husband and two sons, who probably fell victim to the plague.

The chasm

Daily 8am–7pm • ₺5

Kanlıdivane's dramatic **chasm** stood at the core of the ancient city of **Kanytelis**, and remains terrifying to this day. Measuring 90m by 70m, the hole reaches a depth of 60m, while its red-rock walls lend it a menacing aura. From the car park and ticket-seller's hut that mark the entrance to the chasm, visitors can descend an eroded staircase to see several carvings set into niches.

ARRIVAL AND INFORMATION   KIZKALESİ AND AROUND

By bus Buses plying the coastal road between Mersin and Silifke drop passengers in Kızkalesi centre, an easy walk from the numerous hotels.

Tours Rain Tour & Travel Agency, Barbarossa Cad 15D (March–Nov daily 8am–6pm; ☎0324 523 2784, Ⓦoztoprain.com), Kızkalesi's only tour agency, doubles as a one-stop tourist information centre offering impartial advice, maps and transport information. They also organize day-trips to surrounding sights, and try to make up groups to keep costs low (around €35 per person).

ACCOMMODATION

While shabby **cheaper options** line the side streets near the main road, Kızkalesi's **best hotels** are at the western end, just over the bridge. Street names appear redundant in these parts so look out for signs for your chosen hotel and book ahead for July and Aug. Considerable bargains can be had outside peak season. All the following listings are in Kızkalesi.

Barbarossa Club & Hotel Çetin Özyaran Cad ☎0324 523 2364, Ⓦbarbarossahotel.com. This sprawling four-star hotel checks all the boxes: indoor and outdoor pools, a gym and spa, and a range of stylish rooms and suites. The beachfront garden bar is the highlight, dotted with swinging settees, plump beanbags and sunloungers, and drawing a lively crowd in the evenings. ₺200

★**Rain Hotel** Ahmet Erol Cad ☎0324 523 2782, Ⓦrainhotel.com. Nothing is too much effort at this exceedingly friendly family-run hotel, whether you want scrambled eggs whipped up for breakfast, off-street parking or help booking tours and activities. Just a short stroll from the beach but away from the noise of the beachside bars, the a/c rooms are sunny and peaceful, and many of them have balconies. Owner Şirin speaks fluent English, and his knowledge and enthusiasm for the region's sights makes this an ideal spot from which to plan your onward trip, while the breezy terrace is a good place to meet other travellers. Call ahead in season, as it can get busy. ₺140

Yaka Hotel Avcılar Cad ☎0324 523 2444, Ⓦyakahotel .com.tr. A cheerful ambassador for Kızkalesi's outstanding hospitality, owner Yakup likes guests to feel they are part of the family, and entertains visitors with his quick wit in any of four languages, including English. The motel-style rooms are clean and comfy, with a/c and tea- and coffee-making facilities, plus there's a pleasant garden. €45

EATING, DRINKING AND NIGHTLIFE

Kizkalesi's places to **eat and drink** line the beach, and the area is constantly undergoing new developments. Summer nights see many beachside venues converted into **bars and clubs** with booming music and lengthy cocktail lists, but the classiest place to drink is at the *Barbarossa Club & Hotel* with its enormous garden, beachside bar and beanbags laid out for you to watch the tide coming in.

Albatros Beach Club & Restaurant On the pier, at the far western end of the beach ☎ 0536 676 3902, ⊛ albatrosbeachclub.com. If you want to party with the locals, this is the place to do it. A night at *Albatros* is quite an experience, and the party often spills over onto the waterfront. You may need some stamina to bear the cheesy pop and dance music. June–Sept daily: restaurant 8am–10pm; club 10pm–4am.

Marin Restaurant At the western tip of the beach, past the pier and Albatros Club ☎ 0324 523 2515. Hands down the best-located restaurant in town, the recently opened *Marin* has a terrace perched on the waterfront, with tables set right up to the sea's edge and a view across to the castle. There's a great selection of food, including an excellent steak (₺28) and some delicious kebabs and salads (from ₺15). Wash it down with a cold Efes (₺10). Daily 8am–11pm.

Mersin

From the flower-filled parks and palm-tree-lined walkways that stretch along its waterfront to the spirited bustle of its daily fish bazaar, **MERSİN** is a model example of contemporary Turkish urban planning, and living proof that modernization can flow alongside tradition. Turkey's largest Mediterranean port, and home to 1.5 million people, Mersin has, thanks to rapid industrial growth and its role as an international free-trade zone, become an important trade and transport hub.

Despite being inhabited since Hittite times, however, the city retains little of historical interest, and aside from its regular ferries to Cyprus (see p.383), there are few attractions to draw travellers in. That said, the harbour city makes a pleasant stop-off along the coast, and the opening of an impressive new marina has given rise to a new area of development, with hip bars and restaurants sprouting up along the waterfront.

Mersin Museum

Atatürk Cad • Tues–Sun 8.30am–12.30pm & 1.30–5.30pm • ₺5 • ☎ 0309 309 0850

The **Mersin Museum** (Mersin Müzesi), in the heart of town, is home to a small but well-presented collection of local **archeological finds** from Neolithic times to the Byzantine era. Its chief highlight is an assortment of Roman clay sarcophagi, some with lift-off lids, others with sliding ones.

Marina

8km west of the old city • Catch one of the frequent westbound blue buses on İsmet İnönü Bulvarı (10min)

Mersin's lively **marina** is the largest on Turkey's Mediterranean shores. An impressive yacht harbour with berths for around five hundred boats now brightens up the coastline, while a number of trendy bars and restaurants make it the liveliest place to spend an evening. There's also a new sports centre with outdoor swimming pools and sunbeds, two shopping malls and a two-thousand-seat amphitheatre.

Bazaar

Between İstiklâl Cad and Uray Cad

While the goods on sale are nothing to rival Istanbul's bazaars, an hour or two spent sidling through the cobbled streets of Mersin's old-town **bazaar** makes for a good introduction to the local medley of inhabitants. Most famous is the **fish bazaar**, a dimly lit street wriggling with live seafood and crammed with tiny, backstreet food stalls where you can tuck into a grilled-fish sandwich fresh off the boat.

ARRIVAL AND INFORMATION

MERSİN

By bus From Mersin's *otogar*, just off Gazi Mustafa Kemal Bulvarı northeast of the centre, frequent minibuses run to İsmet İnönü Bulvarı in the centre, stopping outside the tourist office, and close to most of the bus companies' offices. Minibuses run to local destinations from here.
Destinations Adana (hourly; 1hr); Alanya (8 daily; 8hr); Silifke (every 20min; 3hr).

By train Mersin's train station is a 2min walk north of the tourist office, on İstiklal Cad.
Departures Adana (every 30min; 50min).

By ferry Ferries sail from Mersin to Gazimağusa (Famagusta) in Northern Cyprus (see box, p.383).

Tourist office The office is at Uray Cad 15/A; follow the signs from the east end of İsmet İnönü Bulvarı (Mon–Fri 8.30am–5.30pm; ☎ 0324 237 1900, ⓦ mersinkulturturizm.gov.tr). Staff can give you an annotated city map and help book ferry tickets, but they speak little English.

Car rental Companies include Hertz, at Adnan Menderes Bulvarı, in the *Hilton Hotel* (☎ 0322 458 5062).

ACCOMMODATION

As an important port, Mersin has plenty of accommodation, most of it concentrated on İstiklâl and Soğuksu caddesis, and all of it aimed at business travellers.

Mersin Hotel İsmet İnönü Bulvarı 62 ☎ 0324 238 1040, ⓦ mersinoteli.com.tr. Towering over the waterfront, with incredible views of the marina and Atatürk Park, this huge hotel has long been a popular choice for tradesmen. Rooms are well-sized and modern, with lots of natural light, balconies and cosy duvets. **€80**

Nobel Oteli İstiklâl Cad 73 ☎ 0324 239 0000, ⓦ nobeloteli.com. An elegant hotel befitting its four-star status, the spacious carpeted rooms are adorned with luxe bedsheets, plump pillows and modern bathrooms, alongside a well-stocked minibar and complimentary tea and coffee. Welcoming, English-speaking staff are another plus. **€90**

EATING AND DRINKING

Mersin has no shortage of eating choices, with a host of fresh seafood on offer, and kebab houses just about everywhere you turn. For an alternative, head to the marina, where a row of floating restaurants serve everything from pizza to more upmarket options.

Deniz Yıldızı Restaurant Uray Cad ☎ 0324 237 9633. One of the best of the fish restaurants dotted around the entrance to the fish bazaar (see p.389), where friendly, English-speaking waiters will talk you through the best catches of the day. *Levrek* (sea bass) and sea bream are always available; otherwise, the menu depends on the fishermen's luck (mains from ₺12). Wash it down with rakı (₺12 for a double) for the full experience. Daily 7am–9pm.

Gattini Bistro Adnan Menderes Bulvarı 160 ☎ 0324 326 9695, ⓦ gattinibistro.com. This stylish bistro-café serves up a range of creatively presented cuisine, from fresh

fettucini to delicious stuffed sea bass (mains from ₺16). The decadent dessert menu also has an international slant, with fruit tarts, cheesecakes and profiteroles too tempting to pass over. The garden seating is particularly atmospheric in the evening. Daily 9.30am–late.

Nobel Café & Restaurant İstiklâl Cad 73 ☎ 0324 239 0000. Adjoining its namesake hotel, the *Nobel Café* serves up tasty sweets and pastries (from ₺4) in modern, a/c surrounds. For something more substantial, the restaurant offers both a cafeteria and à la carte options, with a mix of Anatolian and international cuisine (mains around ₺20). Daily 7am–10pm.

Tarsus and around

TARSUS, the birthplace of St Paul, and the city where Cleopatra met Mark Antony and turned him into a "strumpet's fool", lies about 30km east of Mersin, across the factory-dotted cotton fields of the Çukurova. St Paul was born as Saul in Tarsus about 46 years after the meeting between Cleopatra and Antony. He returned after his conversion on the road to Damascus, fleeing persecution in Palestine. Proud of his roots, he is described as having told the Roman commandant of Jerusalem "I am a Jew, a Tarsian from Cilicia, a citizen of no mean city."

Nowadays, the **Antik Şehir** or "old city" has been exposed by excavations, but although there remains a good section of black-basalt main street and some underground stoas and temples, only a few reminders of the town's illustrious past survive.

FROM TOP ROMAN THEATRE AT ASPENDOS (P.368); MOSAICS IN ANTAKYA'S ARCHEOLOGICAL MUSEUM (P.400) >

Cleopatra's Gate

On a roundabout, near the main bus drop-off point

The **Kancık Kapısı** ("the gate of the bitch") is a Roman construction, also known as **Cleopatra's Gate**. Although it doesn't actually have any known connection with the Egyptian queen, she is thought to have come ashore for her first meeting with Mark Antony, back in 40BC, somewhere in the vicinity. At that time Tarsus was linked to the sea by a lagoon, which has since silted up.

Tarsus Museum

From Cleopatra's Gate, head south to a roundabout flowing with fountains and turn right; the museum lies 100m west • Tues–Sat 9am–5pm • ₺5

The **Cultural Centre** (Kültür Merkezi) houses the **Tarsus Museum**, an eclectic collection of objects uncovered in regional excavations with pieces from the Neolithic period onwards. The "Tarsus house corner" focuses on the lifestyles and culture of the Çukurovan nomads, and there's a wide collection of stoneworks, coins and jewellery collections. Most inexplicably of all, you'll also see the mummified lower arm of an unnamed woman.

St Paul's well

5min signposted walk from the centre of town • ₺5

St Paul's well, or "Sen Pol Kuyusu", may be something of a disappointment, since it's just a borehole in the ground covered by a removable lid. However, it's said to be built on the site of St Paul's house and attracts a trickle of visitors who pay to sip water from a bucket hauled up from the depths.

Roman road

15km north of Tarsus • No public transport

The remains of a limestone paved **Roman road** run for around 2km along the hills above the village of **Sağlıklı**. Thought to have been constructed in the first century AD, and used until the middle of the fourth century, the road is mostly well preserved, featuring a monumental gate and vehicle entrance and exit points.

ARRIVAL AND DEPARTURE   TARSUS AND AROUND

By bus Tarsus's *otogar* is 2km east of town, but minibuses to and from Mersin (40min) and Adana (50min) stop near   Cleopatra's Gate, right in the centre.

ACCOMMODATION

Cihan Palas Otel Mersin Cad 21 ☎ 0324 624 1623. A short walk from Cleopatra's Gate, this budget hotel is well located, but while rooms are clean, you still only get what you pay for. Ask for one of the recently refurbished rooms with a/c. ₺**100**

Konak Efsus Kizilmurat Mah Tarihi Evler 31–33

☎ 0324 614 0907, ⓦ konakefsus.com. A short walk from Atatürk Bulvarı, this is head and shoulders above the competition – easily the best of Tarsus's slim pickings. Housed in a 170-year-old mansion, it's been lovingly restored with cherry-wood fittings and stone-brick walls, and the seven themed rooms are huge. €**60**

Adana

ADANA, Turkey's fifth-largest city, with more than 1.5 million inhabitants, sprawls 40km east of Tarsus. A modern place, which has grown rapidly since the 1990s, Adana continues to owe much of its wealth to the surrounding fertile countryside of the Çukurova. Its textile industry has grown up on the back of the local cotton fields.

The city itself is divided by the E5 highway into the swanky north, with its cinemas and designer malls, and the more traditional bustling south, centred around the markets, mosques and hotels of the old town. As there are few pedestrian bridges and underpasses, you have to negotiate mind-blowing traffic to reach many of the local sights.

Brief history

Despite its contemporary, metropolitan feel, Adana has historical roots going back to 1000 BC. The arrival of the Greeks precipitated an on-off power struggle with the powerful Persian Empire that was to last for a thousand years, ending only when the Romans arrived during the first century BC. Under the Romans, the city became an important trading centre, after which it passed through various hands before falling to the Ottomans in the sixteenth century.

Archeological Museum

On the north side of the D-400 • Closed for renovations at the time of writing • ₺5

Adana's small **Archeological Museum** (Arkeolji Müzesi) is home to an intriguing collection of predominantly Hellenistic and Roman statuary, plus some fine sarcophagi

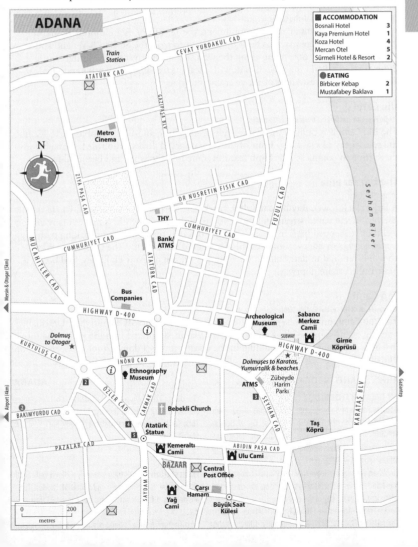

ADANA

ACCOMMODATION

Bosnali Hotel	3
Kaya Premium Hotel	1
Koza Hotel	4
Mercan Otel	5
Sürmeli Hotel & Resort	2

EATING

| Birbicer Kebap | 2 |
| Mustafabey Baklava | 1 |

and Hittite statues. At the time of writing, the museum was in the process of moving to a new, as-yet undisclosed location, and is set to reopen in late 2016.

Sabancı Merkez Camii

On the north side of the D-400, next door to the Archeological Museum

With a capacity of 28,500 and the highest dome in Turkey, the **Sabancı Merkez Camii** is a testament to the continued strength of Islam in the southeast. A stunningly photogenic construction, it has gold trimmings, marble entrance arches, six towering minarets and beautiful İznik tile-work inside. It was built mainly by subscription, but finished with the aid of the Sabancı family – hence the name. These local boys made good and are now the second-richest family in Turkey.

Taş Köprü and around

100m southeast of the Sabancı Merkez Camii

Adana's most substantial ancient monument, the **Taş Köprü**, is an impressive sixteen-arched Roman bridge that was built by Hadrian to span the Seyhan River and still carries heavy traffic. Stretching along the west side of the river by the bridge, the **Zübeyde Harim Parkı** is a shaded park with pleasant tree-lined walkways and picnic areas that afford great views of the river and mosque.

Ulu Cami

Abidin Paşa Cad, not far from the bridge in the centre

The **Ulu Cami** was built in the Syrian style, using white-and-black marble, in 1507. It's the sole legacy of Halil Bey, Emir of the Ramazanoğlu Turks, who ruled Adana before the Ottoman conquest. His **tomb** features some fine tile-work and beautiful mosaics.

The bazaar area

South of Ulu Cami

A large clock tower, **Büyük Saat Kulesi**, marks the start of the **bazaar area**, where the narrow, barely paved streets and the echoing clink of metalworkers makes many visitors feel they've stepped back in time. A wander through the labyrinth of snaking pathways is a good way to uncover some of the intrigues of the old city. The **Çarşı Hamam** (see above) is reputed to date back to the time of Piri, son of Emir Halil Bey, and boasts a beautifully ornate doorway.

Yağ Cami

Just southeast of the central Atatürk statue

The **Yağ Cami**, on the west side of the bazaar, is accessed across a courtyard. Unusually, one bay of the mosque was a church until it was incorporated into the main structure in 1502. A peculiar square building in the courtyard has a domed roof supported by a line of slabs with Selçuk decoration, although its original purpose is unknown.

ARRIVAL AND INFORMATION
ADANA

BY BUS OR DOLMUŞ

Otogar Frequent dolmuşes run from Adana's *otogar*, 5km west of town on the E5 (also known as Cemal Beriker Bulvarı), to the town centre. In addition, most bus companies lay on *servis* minibuses to and from their central offices, most of which are on Ziya Paşa Cad, just north of the E5. When you want to leave town, buy a ticket from one of these and a *servis* bus will take you to the *otogar*, connected with virtually every city in the country.

Destinations Adıyaman (10 daily; 6hr); Afyon (4 daily; 7hr); Alanya (2 daily; 9hr); Ankara (hourly; 10hr); Antalya (13 daily; 12hr); Diyarbakır (10 daily; 10hr); Gaziantep (12 daily; 4hr); Istanbul (hourly; 12hr); Kayseri (14 daily; 7hr); Konya (5 daily; 7hr); Malatya (8 daily; 8hr); Şanlıurfa (4 daily; 6hr).

BY TRAIN

Train station Adana's train station is a 20min walk north of the centre, at the northern end of Atatürk Caddesi. There are dolmuşes from town, or you can flag a taxi (less than ₺15).

Destinations Ankara (1 daily, overnight; 14hr); İskenderun

(3 daily; 2hr 30min); Kayseri (daily; 6hr); Mersin (Every 30min between 6am–11.30pm; 50min).

BY PLANE

Airport Adana Airport Meydan Cad (☎ 0322 435 0380) is 4km west of the centre. To get into town, it costs double to catch an airport taxi from outside the door; instead, walk another 50m to the street and either catch a dolmuş or a normal taxi. A shuttle bus leaves the city-centre THY office 1hr 30min before departure, and in theory a THY bus awaits arrivals.

Airlines THY, Prof Dr Nuşret Fişik Cad 22 (☎ 0322 457 0222), for flights to Ankara, Istanbul and İzmir; for flights to Istanbul, contact Onur Air's office at the airport (☎ 0322 436 6766). Domestic destinations Ankara (2 daily; 1hr); Antalya (daily; 1hr); Ercan (2 daily; 50min); Istanbul (9 daily; 1hr 20min); İzmir (2 daily; 1hr 30min); Van (daily; 1hr 20min).

BY CAR

Car rental Avis (Ziyapaşa Bul, Nakipoglu Apt 9/A; ☎ 0322 453 3045); Europcar (at the airport; ☎ 0322 433 2957); and Talay Turizm (Resatpasa Mah Bul 46/B; ☎ 0322 459 6448).

INFORMATION

Tourist office The office is at Atatürk Cad 7, on the south side of the E5 Highway, next to the AK Bank (Mon–Fri 8am–5pm; ☎ 0322 363 1448). A second tourist information point is located at the junction of Ziya Paşa Cad and İnönü Cad (Mon–Fri 9am–5pm).

ACCOMMODATION

Adana's accommodation options have undergone some changes in the last few years. **Boutique hotels** have sprung up, and many new, swisher hotels have replaced their outdated predecessors. Plenty of **budget options** still survive on and around Saydam and Özler caddesi.

Bosnali Hotel Seyhan Cad 29 ☎ 0322 359 8000, ⓦ hotelbosnali.com. With its cream facade and quaint wooden shutters, this elegantly renovated nineteenth-century mansion offers unfussy luxury in a prime location, overlooking the river and the Sabancı Merkez Camii. Plush, dark-wood interiors, roomy bathrooms and a tranquil rooftop terrace add to the effect. €60

★**Kaya Premium Hotel** Turhan Cemal Beriker Bul 16/A ☎ 0322 888 0336, ⓦ kayapremium.com. A show-stopping homage to Ottoman-era extravagance, few boutique hotels could get away with such decadent interiors (think rich velvets, Baroque armchairs and lashings of gold paint) without appearing ostentatious, but *Kaya* strikes the perfect balance between style and comfort. Each room is individually designed, with ornate headboards, embossed wallpapers, glittering chandeliers and a dazzling array of antique telephones. €50

Koza Hotel Özler Cad 31 ☎ 0322 352 5857, ⓦ otelkoza.com. Excellent value and surprisingly quiet considering its central location, *Koza* has undergone a recent facelift. Inspired by the Ottoman era, rooms feature gold or silver furnishings, fabric wallpapers and vintage lamps, but combined with wooden floors and crisp white linens, it's just the right amount of glitz. ₺100

Mercan Otel Ocak Meydanı 5 ☎ 0322 351 2603 ⓦ otelmercan.com. Tucked down a side street just west of the Atatürk statue, this cheerful family-run hotel makes a good budget choice, with cheaper rates out of season. Rooms are simply designed but spotless, all with TVs and tea-making facilities. €40

Sürmeli Hotel & Resort Özler Cad 49 ☎ 0322 352 3600, ⓦ surmelihotels.com. One of Adana's most upmarket options, this enormous hotel has everything you'd expect from a five-star resort, including an impressive swimming pool and waterfall, a Turkish hamam and spa, and all the mod-cons, although service is predictably impersonal. €100

EATING

Although the local speciality is the spicy **Adana kebap** – minced lamb and pepper wrapped around a skewer and grilled – frankly, you can eat better ones elsewhere. Pavement **food stalls** selling sandwiches and pastries abound, as do hole-in-the-wall *börek* and kebab places near the bazaar and central PTT.

Birbicer Kebap Bakimyurdu Cad ☎ 0322 365 1444, ⓦ birbicer.com. Always crammed with locals, this humble kebab house is the best place to tuck into an *Adana kebap*, but the real highlight is the *ciğer şiş* (liver kebab). Generously portioned mains start from around ₺12 and come with heaped salad and fresh bread. Daily 9am–11pm.

Mustafabey Baklava Ziyapaşa Bul ☎ 0322 363 2737, ⓦ mustafabeybaklava.com. With row upon row of glistening *baklava*, piping-hot *halka tatlısı* (sweet, fried pastries) and pistachio-dusted *künefe*, this patisserie is a dessert-lover's nirvana. A bite-size sugar fix starts from as little as ₺1, and there's seating upstairs overlooking the street. Daily 7am–11.30pm.

DIRECTORY

Banks and exchange Most banks are near the tourist office. There are also several *döviz* offices around Saydam and Özler cads.

Cinema Metro Cinema a couple of blocks south of the train station.

Hamam Çarşı Hamam, Büyük Saat Civari (daily: women 9am–3pm, men 4–9.30pm; from ₺15 depending on level of service).

Hospital State Hospital (Adana Devlet Hastane), on Riza Cad ☎ 0322 321 5752.

Post office The main PTT office (8.30am–9pm), on Ulu Cami, the street parallel to Abdin Paşa Cad, sells phonecards and *jetons*.

East of Adana

A number of interesting ancient sites line the road that parallels the final eastern stretch of the Mediterranean coast, before it turns irrevocably southwards. Splendid castles watch over the towns of **Yakapinar** and **Toprakkale**, while the much older remains of a Hittite palace can still be seen at **Karatepe**, inland.

Yılan Kalesi

Follow signs from Yakapinar, 35km east of Adana, to Yılan Kalesi, 3km south of the main road • Daily 24hr • ₺3

From the first town along the road to İskenderun, **Yakapinar**, the **Yılan Kalesi**, or "Snake Castle", is clearly visible, peering down on the town from the top of a mountain. So called because of the legend that it belongs to the king of the snakes, it's actually an Armenian castle, dating from the eleventh century. There's still plenty left to see, including seven horseshoe-shaped towers, but it's worth the hike (or drive) just to admire the view of the meandering Ceyhan River below.

Toprakkale Kalesi

Toprakkale, 85km east of Adana, just off the main highway

The town of Toprakkale is dominated by a towering black basalt castle, **Toprakkale Kalesi**. Much fought over in medieval times by the Armenians and Crusaders, it has been abandoned since about 1337. If you do visit Toprakkale, be careful – much of it is unstable, with numerous concealed cisterns waiting for unwary people to fall into them.

Karatepe Aslantaş National Park

Tues–Sun 8.30am–noon & 2–5.30pm • ₺5; from the car park (₺3), walk up to the gatehouse to buy a ticket and join a tour • Head to Osmaniye, 95km east of Adana, then follow signs 30km north across the Ceyhan River, beyond the Hellenistic ruins of Hierapolis Castabala

If you're heading down towards the Hatay and have your own transport, you might want to consider a 70km detour to the **Karatepe Aslantaş National Park** (Karatepe Arslantaş Milli Parkı), where the wooded hillsides overlooking the **Arslantaş dam** provide the perfect picnic venue. **Karatepe** is thought to have been a frontier castle or summer palace of the ninth-century BC neo-Hittite king Asitawanda. Today, little of the building complex remains, but the eloquent stone carvings arranged around the two entrance gates of the former palace are exquisite.

The Hatay

Extending like a stumpy finger into Syria, the region known as the **Hatay** has closer cultural links with the Arab world than with the Turkish hinterland, and its multi-ethnic, multi-faith identity gives it an extra edge of interest. **Antakya** (ancient Antioch), a cosmopolitan city and gastronomic centre set in the valley of the Asi River, and **İskenderun**, a heavily industrialized port, are the two main destinations, and the majority of people here speak Arabic as well as Turkish. Arab influence in the Hatay goes back to the seventh century AD, when Arab raiders began hacking at the edges of the collapsing Byzantine Empire. Although they were never able to secure long-lasting political control over the region, the Arabs did establish themselves as permanent settlers, remaining even when the Hatay passed into Ottoman hands.

The region only became part of modern Turkey in 1939, having been apportioned to the French Protectorate of Syria following the dismemberment of the Ottoman Empire. Following the brief-lived independent **Hatay Republic** of 1938 it was handed over to Turkey after a plebiscite. This move, calculated to buy Turkish support, or at least neutrality, in the imminent world war, was successful. It was Atatürk, in a move to "Turkify" the region, who dreamt up the name "Hatay", supposedly based on that of a medieval Turkic tribe.

For some time relations between the two countries improved dramatically and there was even some backing for union with **Syria**, but the civil unrest in Syria in 2012, and President Assad's refusal to listen to Turkish calls for reform, meant that friction once again escalated. At the time of writing, Syria was embroiled in a complex civil war, with refugees fleeing to Turkey and Turkish military presence mounting around the border regions. With the situation looking increasingly unstable, the UK Foreign and Commonwealth Office (FCO; ⓦgov.uk/foreign-travel-advice) had issued warnings on travelling in the region at the time of writing (see box below).

İskenderun

İSKENDERUN was founded by Alexander the Great to commemorate his victory over the Persians at the nearby battle of Issus, and, as Alexandria ad Issum, it became a major trade nexus during Roman times. Under the Ottomans, İskenderun became the main port for Halab (Aleppo), now in Syria, from where trade routes fanned out to Persia and the Arabian peninsula. Known as Alexandretta during the French-mandate era, the town is now an industrial, military and commercial centre. Although there is little of historical interest left to see, İskenderun's coastal strip is visually appealing, with its broad promenade and magnificent backdrop of the Amanus Mountains and glistening ocean. İskenderun's numerous **churches** include the Catholic **St Mary's**, a sizeable nineteenth-century building, close to the tourist office; the pastel-coloured Greek Orthodox church of **St Nicholas**, built in 1876, on Şehit Paşa Cad; and the atmospheric **St George's** on Denizciler Cad, with its walled garden of palm and cypress trees.

Seafront park

Don't leave İskenderun without a stroll along its landscaped **seafront park**, where kiosks, palm-tree-lined canals and gardens partially shield the industrial landscape

---

TRAVELLING TO SYRIA AND THE HATAY

At the time of writing, **Syria** was in the midst of a **civil war**. The **border** to the east of Antakya at Cilvegözü/Baba al Hawa was closed to travellers, and controlled on the Syrian side by the Islamic Front. As of 2015, almost two million Syrian **refugees** had crossed the border into Turkey, thousands of whom were housed in camps in the Turkish border regions, and many of these in the Hatay province. Turkish military presence along the border was also increasing.

The UK Foreign and Commonwealth Office (FCO; ⓦgov.uk/foreign-travel-advice) currently advises against all travel to within 10km of the Syrian border and all but essential travel to the Hatay province. **Flights and buses** are still running as normal to Antakya and İskenderun, and travellers have reported visiting without problems. However, it's imperative to get up-to-date information before travelling, so be sure to check the latest government travel advice. It's also worth noting that most **travel insurance** companies will not insure travellers going against government-issued travel advice.

As and when Syria does reopen to travellers, the situation regarding visas and border crossings is very unlikely to be the same as it was before the war, so seek up-to-date advice from local tourist offices before heading out.

across the bay and provide a lovely atmosphere for a picnic. **Boat trips** on the Mediterranean run from near the Atatürk monument area in season; a twenty-minute trip costs around ₺5 per person, a half-day tour with lunch around ₺50 per person.

ARRIVAL AND INFORMATION ISKENDERUN

By bus Buses from the *otogar*, a 15min walk north of the seafront, run to all major towns. Frequent minibuses to Antakya also leave from near the junction of Şehit Pamir and Prof Muammer Askoy Cad.
Destinations Adana (hourly; 2hr); Antakya (every 20min; 40min); Antalya (2 daily; 13hr).
By train İskenderun's station, 1km east of the centre, is reached by following 5 Temmuz Caddesi and then Bahçeli Sahil Evler Caddesi.

Destinations Adana (3 daily; 2hr 30min); Mersin (3 daily; 3hr 30min).
Tourist office On a side street off Şehit Pamir Caddesi (Mon–Fri 8.30am–noon & 1–5pm; ☎ 0326 614 1620). Follow yellow signs off Atatürk Bulvarı to a slightly ominous-looking building, and take the lift to the second floor, where you can pick up some decent city maps and other information.

ACCOMMODATION

Altındişler Oteli Şehit Pamir Cad 11 ☎ 0326 617 1011, ⓦ altindislerotel.com. Among the more chic budget options, this place offers spotless a/c rooms with dark wood furnishings and newly tiled bathrooms. Rooms facing Şehit Pamir Caddesi can be noisy, so ask for one round the back. **₺100**

Sun Otel Muammer Aksoy Cad 31 ☎ 0326 613 5500, ⓦ suninnotel.net. Uninspiring but well-equipped rooms and a decent on-site restaurant make this a satisfactory stopover. Prices are always negotiable; even bigger discounts are available in low season. **₺150**

EATING AND DRINKING

The promenade area is home to several *gazinos* where you can enjoy a beer overlooking the sea, but İskenderun's restaurants are mostly uninspiring.

Emirgan Bulvar Café Atatürk Bul 2 ☎ 0326 613 3131. Well-positioned waterfront café, with stunning views over the ocean and generous portions. Tuck into *köfte* (from ₺10) accompanied by freshly squeezed pomegranate juice (₺5), or join locals to smoke a nargile (₺12, various flavours). Daily 8am–midnight.

Petek Pastaneleri Mareşal Çakmak Cad 16 ☎ 0326 617 8888, ⓦ petekpastanesi.com.tr. Dating back to 1942 and claiming to be the oldest patisserie in the Hatay, there's no better place to overindulge. Specialties include *künefe*, walnut-stuffed *nokul* (pastries) and *şambalı* (honey-soaked semolina cake). Daily 7am–1am.

Belen and around

The road southeast from İskenderun climbs up into the mountains to reach the small hill town of **BELEN**, 13km southeast of İskenderun (and also accessible by dolmuş from Antakya). From here, the road strains and curves through the **Belen pass** (Belen Geçidi) – of great strategic importance during Roman times, when it was known as the *Pylae Syriae* or "Gates of Syria". For a week or two in early October (if the winds are right), Belen becomes the most important **migration route** on the western Palaearctic corridor for birds of prey.

Bakras Kalesi

5km south of the D817 highway, on the way to Belen • From Bakras village, which is served by regular dolmuşes from Antakya and İskenderun, the castle is a 15min uphill drive

Bakras Kalesi is an imposing **medieval castle** first erected by the Arabs during the seventh century and destroyed during the First Crusade. Later, the Knights Templar built a new fortress, which became an important link in their defensive system, and forms the basis of the impressive remains you see today. It was repeatedly fought over; in 1156, a bloody battle took place here between the Templars and the soldiers of Thoros, ruler of Cilician Armenia. The castle fell to Arabs in 1188, but possession was fiercely contested until the Ottomans took over during the sixteenth century.

Antakya and around

The city of **ANTAKYA**, 45km south of İskenderun, stands on the site of ancient Antioch. Its laidback pace, cosmopolitan outlook and subtly Arab atmosphere make it a unique destination. Flanked by mountains to the north and south, it sits in the bed of a broad river valley planted with olive trees – a welcome visual relief after travelling from the drab flatlands around surrounding Adana.

Antakya is split in two by the **Asi River**, known in ancient times as the Orontes. Recent developments along the riverbank are slowly transforming the stretch into a fetching (if traffic-ridden) thoroughfare, bordered by flowerbeds, palm trees, fountains and cafés. The eastern bank is home to **old Antakya**, a maze of narrow streets that still offer glimpses of traditional Turkish life – clusters of men perched on low stools in their doorways sipping tea, and the odd scruffy horse dragging a ramshackle cart laden with goods. Best of all is the **food**, which thanks to the city's Arab heritage is among the best, and most varied, in Turkey.

Brief history

Antakya was founded as **Antioch** in the fourth century BC by Seleucus Nicator, one of the four generals among whom the empire of Alexander the Great was divided. By the second century BC it had developed into a multi-ethnic metropolis of half a million –

6

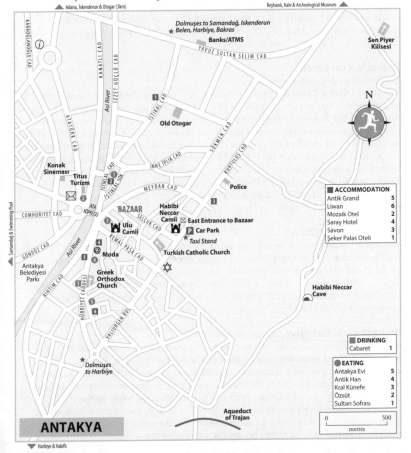

Adana, İskenderun & Otogar (3km)

Reyhanlı, Kale & Archeological Museum

Dolmuşes to Samandağ, İskenderun
Belen, Harbiye, Bakras

Banks/ATMS

Şen Piyer
Kilisesi

YAVUZ SULTAN SELIM CAD

KARAOĞLANOĞLU CAD

KANATLI CAD

IZZET GÜÇLÜ CAD

Asi River

İSTİKLAL CAD

Old Otogar

SOKMEN CAD

KURTULUŞ CAD

ATATÜRK CAD

INNE IPLIK CAD

N

Konak
Sineması

Titus
Turizm

MEYDAN CAD

İSTİKLAL CAD
İSTİKLAL SOK

Police

CUMHURIYET CAD

ATA
KÖPRÜSÜ

BAZAAR

Habibi
Neccar
Camii

East Entrance to Bazaar

Car Park

Taxi Stand

Samandağ & Swimming Pool

GÜNDÜZ CAD

Asi River

Ulu
Camii

SELCUK CAD

KEMAL PAŞA CAD

Moda

Turkish Catholic Church

Antakya
Belediyesi
Parkı

RIHTIM CAD

Greek
Orthodox
Church

Habibi Neccar
Cave

HÜRRIYET CADDESİ

YALILIDÜKEN BUL

Dolmuşes
to Harbiye

Aqueduct
of Trajan

0   500
metres

ANTAKYA

Harbiye & Vakıflı

ACCOMMODATION	
Antik Grand	5
Liwan	6
Mozaik Otel	2
Saray Hotel	4
Savon	3
Şeker Palas Oteli	1

DRINKING	
Cabaret	1

EATING	
Antakya Evi	5
Antik Han	4
Kral Künefe	3
Özsüt	2
Sultan Sofrası	1

one of the largest cities in the ancient world and a major staging post on the newly opened **Silk Road**. It also acquired a reputation as a centre for all kinds of moral excess, causing **St Peter** to choose it as the location of one of the world's first Christian communities, in the hope of exercising a restraining influence. Indeed, the patriarchy of Antioch became one of the five senior official positions in the early Christian Church.

Despite being razed by **earthquakes** during the sixth century AD, Antioch maintained its prosperity after the Roman era. Only with the rise of Constantinople did it begin to decline. In 1098, after a vicious eight-month siege and a savage massacre of Turks, the Crusader kings Bohemond and Raymond took the city in the name of Christianity. They imposed a **Christian rule** that lasted until Antioch was sacked by the Mamluks of Egypt in 1268. By the time the Ottomans, under Selim the Grim, took over in 1516, Antioch had long since vanished from the main stage of world history. At the start of the twentieth century, the city was little more than a village, squatting amid the ruins of the ancient metropolis. After World War I, Antakya, along with most of the rest of the Hatay, passed into the hands of the **French**, who laid the foundations of the modern city.

Bazaar

North of Kemal Paşa Cad, running west–east just northeast of the main bridge, Ata Köprüsü

It's worth spending an hour or two wandering around Antakya's **bazaar** and market areas. Although many of the traditional stores have given way to clothing, household goods and cheap jewellery sellers, there are still plenty of ogling opportunities, with colourful spice stalls, home-made soap sellers and small wood workshops squeezed in alongside the obligatory Turkish-delight sellers.

Habibi Neccar Camii

At the junction of Kemal Paşa Cad and Kurtuluş Cad

The **Habibi Neccar Camii** is a mosque incorporated into the shell of a former Byzantine church, which was in turn built on the site of an ancient temple. Its distinctive pointed minaret, added during the seventeenth century, is not – as you might be tempted to imagine – a former church tower. From the southeast corner of the yard, a door leads downstairs to the tomb of the prophet Habibi Neccar. While very little is known about the prophet or exactly what became of him, he was allegedly violently done to death by Christians, some time during the first century AD. If you believe the legends, only his head is buried here, while his body lies in the **Habibi Neccar cave** (Habibi Neccar Mağrası) on the hillside 1km east. A minor Muslim holy place, the cave was once home to the solitary prophet and exists now as a shrine.

Greek Orthodox Church

Corner of Hurriyet Cad and Gazipaşa Cad • Two daily masses Mon–Sat, one on Sun

Numerous churches, synagogues and mosques dotted throughout Antakya bear witness to the Hatay's long history of toleration. Some four thousand Christians live in the region, 1500 of them in Antakya itself. The majority are Greek Orthodox, and their substantial nineteenth-century **church** is one of the more impressive of Antakya's remaining religious buildings, containing some beautiful Russian icons.

Archeological Museum

Around 4km north of Antakya centre off the D420/Reyhanlı road • Tues–Sun: summer 8.30am–7pm; winter 8.30am–5pm • ₺8

Antakya's **Archeological Museum** (Arkeoloji Müzesi) ranks among Turkey's biggest and most impressive, now situated in a brand-new purpose-built museum located just out of town. Opened in 2015, the state-of-the-art 50,000-square-kilometre museum includes 5000 square kilometres of exhibition space devoted solely to the collection of locally unearthed **Roman mosaics**, the largest of its kind in the world. Still in almost pristine condition, they make for an impressive display and now include many previously unseen pieces, finally brought out of the archives.

Most of the mosaics were uncovered in the suburb of **Daphne** (now Harbiye), which was Antioch's main holiday resort in Roman times. That origin is reflected in the sense of leisured decadence that pervades many of the Greco-Roman mythology scenes. A good example is the so-called **Buffet Mosaic** (no. 4), a vivid depiction of the rape of Ganymede, abducted by Zeus in the form of an eagle, and a banquet scene showing different courses of fish, ham, eggs and artichokes. Other memorable images include a fine portrait of **Thetis and Oceanus** (no. 1); an inebriated **Dionysos**, too drunk to stand (no. 12); **Orpheus** surrounded by animals entranced by the beauty of his music (no. 23); and a fascinating depiction of the **Evil Eye** (no. 6) – a superstition that still has remarkable resonance.

After the dramatic mosaics, the rest of the museum can seem a little mundane, although the modern backdrop breathes new life into the old exhibitions, and the collection now features many items not displayed at the former museum. Stand-out pieces include two **stone lions**, which served as column bases during the eighth century BC, and the **Antakya sarcophagus**, where the remains of two women and a man, as well as the fine gold jewellery with which they were buried, are displayed.

Sen Piyer Kilisesi

At the northeast edge of Antakya • Tues–Sun: summer 9am–6.30pm; winter 8.30am–12.30pm & 1.30–5.30pm • ₺8 • 40min walk or 10–15min drive, signposted from the centre – head 2km northeast on Kurtuluş Cad, then turn right and keep going for about 400m to the church; you can also catch a dolmuş as far as the turn-off on Kurtuluş Cad

Recently reopened after extensive renovations, **Sen Piyer Kilisesi** is the famous **cave-church of St Peter**, from which it's said that the apostle preached to the Christian population of Antioch. Whether the tale is true remains open to question, as does the matter of the exact dates of his stay in the city. Theologians do seem to agree, however, that he spent some time in Antioch between 47 and 54 AD, founding one of the world's first Christian communities with Paul and Barnabas.

Inside the church, water drips down the cave walls, and the cool atmosphere provides a welcome break from the heat of summer. Beneath your feet you'll be able to discern traces of fragmentary **mosaic** thought to date from the fifth century AD, while a kind of font set in the floor, to the right of the altar, is fed by a spring said to have curative properties.

Carved into the mountainside above the church (ask for directions at the ticket office), there's a relief thought by some to depict Charon, ferryman of the River Styx at the entrance to the underworld.

Harbiye

10km south of Antakya • Catch a minibus from Antakya's *köy garaji*, or flag down a dolmuş travelling southwest along Kurtuluş Cad (30min)

HARBİYE, a short way south of Antakya, is a beautiful gorge to which revellers and holiday-makers flocked in Roman times, drawn by shady cypress and laurel groves dotted with waterfalls and pools. The Romans built a temple to Apollo here, since it was held to be the setting for the god's pursuit of Daphne. According to the myth, Daphne, when seized by amorous Apollo, prayed for deliverance; in answer to her prayers, Peneus transformed her into a laurel tree. Another legend relates that Harbiye was where Paris gave the golden apple to Aphrodite, and indirectly precipitated the Trojan War. Later, and possibly with more basis in fact, Mark Antony and Cleopatra are said to have been married here.

Today, Harbiye makes for a pleasant **day-trip** from Antakya, especially for those with their own transport, and is famous for its Daphne (Defne) soap – a natural toiletry made from the scented fruit of the laurel tree, sold in regional bazaars.

Vakıflı

26km southwest of Antakya • Regular dolmuşes run from Antakya's *köy garaji* to Samandağ on the coast, where you can catch dolmuşes to Vakıflı

The tiny village of **VAKIFLİ**, with its mix of dilapidated mud-brick and timber houses and modern concrete villas, may not look impressive at first glance, but it possesses unique cultural significance. In fact, the unassuming community, set amid orange groves on the lush lower slopes of Musa Dağı, is Turkey's sole surviving **Armenian village**, founded almost two thousand years ago. The villagers held out against the Turkish forces during the 1915 Turkish deportations and massacres of the Armenians, until they were evacuated to Port Said by French and British warships. Most returned in 1919 when the Hatay became part of French-mandated Syria. When the Hatay joined the Turkish Republic in 1939, the majority of of the region's Armenians fled, but the majority of Vakıflı's inhabitants chose to stay.

While the village holds few sights of interest, or many residents aged under 60, its original architecture and traditional lifestyles provide a fascinating peek into community life. If you do choose to visit the village, be respectful – while locals are welcoming of visitors, remember that this is a living community, not a mere curiosity.

Saint Simeon monastery

29km southwest of Antakya • Daily 24hr • Free • No public transport – a day-trip by taxi from Antakya will cost around ₺150; to drive, turn south at Uzunbğ, just beyond Samandağ, continue uphill for 4km, then branch right along a dirt track for another 2km

One of the more bizarre aspects of early Christianity was the craze for sitting on pillars. Emerging in Antioch in the fourth century, the art was perfected by **Simeon Stylites the Younger**, whose **monastery**, listed as a UNESCO World Heritage Site in 2011, perches on a high ridge southwest of Antakya. Simeon the Younger first chained himself to a rock in the wilderness in an act of ascetic retreat, then ascended progressively higher **pillars** before reaching a final height of some 13m. He lived chained to the top of this pillar for 25 years, meditating and sporadically castigating the citizens of Antioch for their moral turpitude. The base of the pillar still remains, surrounded by the octagonal layout of the monastery that grew up around Simeon as curious pilgrims flocked to share his enlightenment. You can climb onto the diminutive stump, which is just wide enough to lie down and reap the same views of the Orontes valley and Mount Cassius looming out of the Mediterranean that Simeon must have enjoyed over fifteen centuries ago.

ARRIVAL AND INFORMATION
ANTAKYA AND AROUND

The Syrian border, 50km east of Antakya, was closed to travellers at the time of writing (see box, p.397).

By plane Antakya's airport (often listed as Hatay Airport), 19km north of the centre, is connected by the Havaş shuttle bus (timed to meet arrivals; ₺10) with İnönü and Atatürk Cad in the town centre. A metered taxi from the airport costs around ₺50 (25min, traffic dependent).
Destinations Istanbul (3 daily; 1hr 45min).

By bus Antakya's new *otogar*, 4km north of the town centre, is served by municipal buses from the centre (₺2). Most bus companies offer free shuttle buses direct to central hotels, and if you buy tickets from the bus company offices in the centre, they typically include free shuttles to the new *otogar*. Regular minibuses run from the *köy garaji*

(village garage) to İskenderun, Harbiye, Samandağ, Belen, Bakras and other destinations.
Destinations Adana (hourly; 3hr); Ankara (9 daily, 13hr); Antalya (14 daily; 14hr); Gaziantep (every 30min; 4hr); İskenderun (every 20min; 1hr); Istanbul (5 daily; 22hr); Konya (5 daily; 15hr); Samandağ (hourly; 1hr).

Car rental Titus Turizm, under the *Büyük Antakya Oteli*, Atatürk Cad 8 (☎ 0326 213 9141), plus there are several companies at the airport.

Tourist office Inconveniently located on a roundabout at the end of Atatürk Cad, a 10min walk northwest of the museum (Mon–Fri 8am–noon & 1.30–5pm; ☎ 0326 216 6098).

ACCOMMODATION

Antik Grand Hürriyet Cad 10 ☎ 0326 215 7575, ⍟ antikgrand.com. While the shabby facade with its blacked-out windows may not be particularly enticing, the interior of this hotel is surprisingly stylish, with deep-red furnishings and spacious rooms. There's also a generous buffet breakfast of *mezes* and Turkish breads. **₺150**

Liwan Hotel Silahli Kuvvetler Cad 5 ☎ 0326 215 7777, ⍟ theliwanhotel.com. This 1920s residence, set around a central courtyard, has everything you'd expect from a

boutique hotel, with individually designed rooms, strewn with antique furnishings, plump cushions and all the mod-cons. The atmospheric stone-brick bar, open fireplace and wooden shutters make it particularly cosy in the winter months, while the shaded location ensures the rooms stay cool and airy throughout the summer. **€90**

Mozaik Otel Silahli İstiklâl Cad 18 ☎ 0326 215 5020, ⍟ mozaikotel.com. From the jaunty mosaics adorning the walls to the gaudy bows jazzing up the breakfast hall, there's no denying that an effort has been made at this well-priced hotel, and it largely falls on the right side of kitsch. Rooms vary wildly, so ask to see a few others if hot-pink bedspreads aren't to your taste, and don't be afraid to negotiate the price in low season. ₺140

Saray Hotel Hürriyet Cad 3 ☎ 0326 214 9001. Cheap and cheerful, if you can get over the drab furnishings and sickly peach-painted hallways, this friendly place is a great-value budget option, with a/c rooms and standard breakfasts. Call ahead if you're arriving late, and they'll meet you at the door. ₺75

★ **Savon Hotel** Kurtuluş Cad 192 ☎ 0326 214 6355, ⓦ savonhotel.com.tr. Housing a soap factory until the 1960s, this stone-vaulted complex has since metamorphosed from industrial warehouse to elegant, upmarket hotel. The pretty courtyard and striking entrance hall with its domed ceilings, ornate candlesticks and rich pink upholstery are highlights, while rooms offer a laidback luxury, with balcony views over the mountains. €100

Şeker Palas Oteli İstiklâl Cad 79 ☎ 0326 215 1603. With singles from as little as €25, this hotel is undeniably good value and a decent choice for budget travellers. Rooms are clean, basic and sparsely furnished; the cheapest have shared bathrooms. The friendly proprietor does his best to liven things up with his eclectic collection of knick-knacks on proud display around the hotel. €50

EATING AND DRINKING

Antakya's renowned food shows its Arab influence in many **regional specialities**. Dishes to look out for include *Ispanak borani*, a soup-like stew of spinach, chickpeas, shredded meat, yoghurt and lemon juice; *serimsek börek*, a sort of chicken-filled samosa; and *kağıt kebap*, kebabs cooked in greased-paper packages.

Antakya Evi Silhali Kuvvetler Cad 3 ☎ 0326 214 1350. A pocket of tranquillity just off the busy central shopping streets, this well-turned-out Turkish restaurant has a good range of kebabs for around ₺10 and a pretty stone courtyard dominated by a tribe of free-roaming tortoises. Try the *Antioch kebap*, a *köfte* of minced lamb stuffed with cheese, walnuts and olives, washed down with a cold glass of Efes (₺7). Daily 9am–midnight.

★ **Antik Han** Hürriyet Cad 19 ☎ 0326 215 8538, ⓦ antikhan.com.tr. An underwhelming entrance stairwell opens out into an elegant stone courtyard and rooftop terrace reminiscent of an Italian villa. The varied menu features *ızgara* (grills) from ₺12, and an impressive array of *mezes* (₺7 each) including regional specialities *muhammara*, a fiery purée of walnuts, hot pepper and wheat, and *bakla*, a purée of broad beans, garlic, tahini and parsley. No alcohol. Daily 7am–midnight.

Cabaret Hürriyet Cad 26 ☎ 0326 215 5540. Climbing the crumbling staircase from the main street transports you into a dimly lit music grotto, with old gramophones, amps and record covers adorning the walls, a well-stocked bar and twinkling sitars seeping from the stereo. Head to the courtyard around the back for cheap and tasty eats throughout the day (including a ₺10 kebab, salad and drink meal deal) or come in the evening to enjoy live performances by local rock bands. Daily 7am–2am.

Kral Künefe Ulucami Mevki ☎ 0326 214 7517, ⓦ hataykralkunefe.com.tr. This long-established pudding shop is a great place to try the ubiquitous *künefe* (₺5), a regional favourite of shredded wheat and soft, mild cheese that's far sweeter and tastier than its ingredients suggest, or *haleb burmasi* (Aleppo roll, ₺2.50), a sweet confection stuffed with pistachios. The outdoor seating is crammed with locals come lunchtime, so grab a takeaway bag and wander out to the benches on the street. Mon–Sat 8am–10pm.

Özsüt Cumhuriyet Alanı 2 ☎ 0326 213 5000. With plenty of balcony seating overlooking the river and the Ata Köprüsü bridge, this popular dessert bar is the perfect place to tuck into some traditional Turkish desserts – try the *muhallebi* (₺5.50), a creamy rice-flour and milk pudding, or the *kadayıfı*, a sweet bread-based dessert (₺5). The real showstopper, though, is the location – the restaurant is housed in the Gündüz building, an impressive Art Deco cinema with geometric friezes and porthole windows that once served as the parliament building for the Hatay Republic. Daily 8am–1am.

Sultan Sofrası İstiklâl Cad 20/A ☎ 0326 213 8469. A tour-group favourite for good reason, where a hearty array of regional specialities is laid out for your delectation; there's no menu, but the affable, English-speaking staff will happily talk you through the options. Expect to pay around ₺10 for a meat dish – *aşur*, a stringy stew of chickpeas, meat, walnuts and wheat, is a good choice, but even a side of rice and chickpeas is delicious. Mon–Sat 11am–9.30pm.

DIRECTORY

Banks and exchange İstiklâl and Atatürk cads hold several banks, and you can change money at the weekends at the *döviz* on Kurtuluş Cad.

Hospital The Devlet Hastane (State Hospital) is a couple of kilometres northwest of the centre.

Internet Modanet, on Hürriyet Cad (☎ 0326 216 5290).

Police Selçuk Cad; emergency number for foreigners ☎ 0326 213 5953.

Post office Northwest of the roundabout at the western end of the Ata Köprüs bridge (daily 9am–8pm).

Swimming There's an open-air pool on Gündüz Cad next to the municipal park (summer daily 10am–3pm).

South Central Anatolia

HOT-AIR BALLOONING IN CAPPADOCIA

South Central Anatolia

At first sight, the central Anatolian plateau seems an unpromising prospect. A large area is virtual desert, while much of the central plateau is steppe, blitzed by cold and heavy snowfall in winter and suffering water shortages in summer. Yet this region holds two landscapes any traveller to the country should visit – the azure Lakeland, where the lakeside village of Eğirdir is a popular starting point for hikers following the St Paul Trail, and the unique rock formations of Cappadocia, one of Turkey's highest-profile tourist attractions.

7

In **Cappadocia**, between the extinct volcanoes of Erciyes Dağı and the Melendiz range, water and wind have created a land of fantastical forms from the soft rock known as tuff, including forests of "fairy chimneys", table mountains, canyon-like valleys and castle-rocks. From the seventh to the eleventh centuries AD, this was a place of refuge for Christians during Arab and Turkish invasions into the steppe. Churches and dwellings carved into the rock, particularly by monastic communities, and unearthly landscapes make it an irresistible tourist draw. At its northwest fringes, the modern city of **Kayseri**, set below the imposing volcanic peak of Mount Erciyes, harbours a wealth of towering fortresses and venerated tombs. Of the region's other cities, **Konya**, once the capital of the Selçuk Empire, is perhaps the most intriguing, home to the **Whirling Dervish** sect, the Mevlevî, and the epicentre of Sufic mystical practice and teaching throughout the Middle East.

Lakeland

After years of isolation, Turkish **Lakeland** has been discovered by birdwatchers, trekkers and skiers, and many tourists now stop off en route from Cappadocia and Konya to the south coast around Antalya or Fethiye. Facilities are quickly improving, especially in **Eğirdir**, but the area as a whole remains unspoiled by tourism, making it ideal for quiet, unhurried holidays away from the seething coastal resorts. As well as the eye-catching **lakes** themselves, it holds the remains of Pisidian cities (notably at **Sagalassos** and **Antioch ad Pisidiam**), and the provincial town of **Afyon**, a popular winter destination with its acclaimed thermal spa hotels.

Brief history

Despite Lakeland's inhospitable landscape, it has been populated as long as anywhere in Anatolia. In early Paleolithic times, the lakes provided a livelihood for primitive

WHIRLING DERVISHES, KONYA

Highlights

❶ **Sagalossos** Perched high above Lakeland, these remote ruins are among the most beautifully sited in Central Anatolia. **See p.414**

❷ **Eğirdir** Tuck into fillets of crisply fried lake fish as the sun sets over Lake Eğirdir. **See p.414**

❸ **St Paul Trail** Follow in the footsteps of the apostle over the Toros Mountains, to reach stunning Lake Eğirdir. **See p.418**

❹ **Whirling dervishes, Konya** Watch the dervishes whirl each December in their spiritual home. **See p.424**

❺ **Göreme Open-Air Museum** The frescoes inside Göreme's cave churches are a vibrant

reminder of the region's Christian past. **See p.434**

❻ **Hot-air ballooning** Witnessing the sunrise over Cappadocia's fairy-tale landscape from the basket of a balloon is an unforgettable experience. **See p.439**

❼ **Mustafapaşa** One of Cappadocia's most attractive villages, sporting a wonderful concentration of old Greek houses. **See p.447**

❽ **Ihlara valley** Don't miss the natural beauty of this fertile gorge, enhanced by its rock-cut Byzantine churches. **See p.452**

HIGHLIGHTS ARE MARKED ON THE MAP ON PP.408–409

hunters and fishermen, and during the Bronze Age, the **Hittites**, a race who once rivalled the Egyptians, chose the plateau as their homeland.

By the early historical period, northern Lakeland had been settled by the **Pisidians**, mountain people who sold their services as mercenaries throughout the eastern Mediterranean. Their strategically situated settlements were difficult to subdue, and Xenophon described them as perennially obstinate troublemakers, who succeeded in keeping their towns independent despite the continuing encroachments of the Persian Empire.

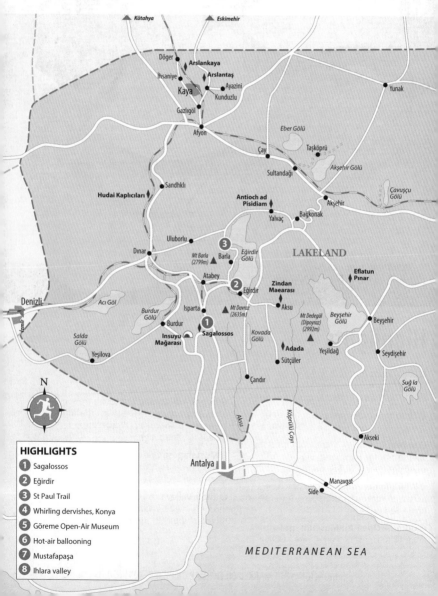

HIGHLIGHTS

1. Sagalossos
2. Eğirdir
3. St Paul Trail
4. Whirling dervishes, Konya
5. Göreme Open-Air Museum
6. Hot-air ballooning
7. Mustafapaşa
8. Ihlara valley

Afyon and around

Dominated by an ancient citadel, built atop a tall, dark and imposing rock, **AFYON** certainly makes an impact, and remains impressive on closer inspection. Clean and relaxed, it retains much interesting Ottoman architecture as well as some attractive mosques. Until recently, the city bore the resounding name of Afyon Karahisar, or "**Opium Black Fortress**", thanks to its long history of opium production (see box, p.411). First fortified by the Hittites, the towering rock was later occupied by the Romans. The Byzantines built most of the present-day fortress, which served as an

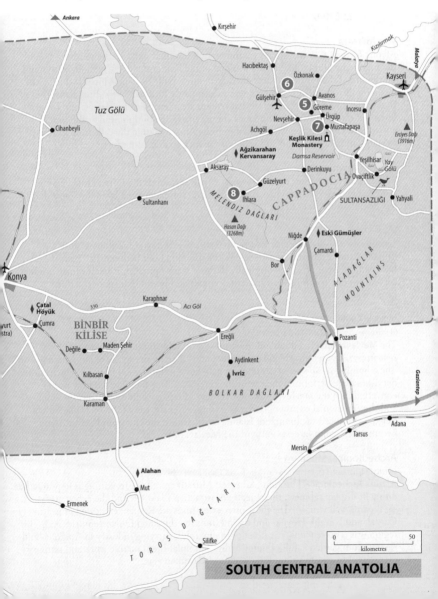

SOUTH CENTRAL ANATOLIA

imperial treasury for both Selçuks and Ottomans. For three weeks leading up to August 26, 1922, Afyon was Atatürk's headquarters, prior to the last, decisive battle of the independence war fought against the Greeks at nearby Dumlupınar.

Aside from the region's many **thermal baths** (see box, p.412), the most interesting side trip from Afyon is to a series of sixth-century **Phrygian sites** (Frig Vadisi). There are also several areas of rock formations similar to those in Cappadocia, and some rock-cut churches, promoted by the local tourism authorities as the Afyon Turizm Kuşağı (**Afyon Tourism Route**). As village roads are badly signed, and the locals unused to giving directions, the easiest way to make the trip is to form a group and rent a **taxi** for the day (around €100).

The fortress

Afyon's **fortress** (220m), scaled via some seven hundred steps on the southern face of the rock – the 20min hike is best avoided in the heat of the day – is thought to stand on the site of the Hittite fortress of Khapanouwa, built by King Mursil II during the second millennium BC. The rock was subsequently fortified by the Phrygians, the Byzantines and the Turks, but all that remain are a few crenellated walls and towers. Look out on the way up for hoopoes among the varied birdlife, and at the top for votive rags, representing wishes, tied to trees. At prayer time the calls from as many as eighty minarets resound and echo off the rock to dramatic effect.

The old town

A warren of tiny streets, the **old town** of Afyon surrounds the fortress rock. Several remarkably preserved mosques stand near here, complemented by many somewhat less distinguished ones in the bazaar area.

Ulu Cami

Opposite the base of the steps leading up the side of the rock • Outside of prayer time, wait for the caretaker to let you in

The **Ulu Cami**, a typically square Selçuk construction built between 1272 and 1277, has been restored. While its originally flat roof is now pitched, it retains forty original carved wooden columns with stalactite capitals and beams that support a fine geometric ceiling.

Mevlevî Camii

Slightly downhill from Ulu Cami • Open at prayer times

The **Mevlevî Camii** is a double-domed mosque notable for its pyramid-roofed *son cemaat yeri*, a porch in which latecomers pray – literally the "place of last congregation". The adjoining *semahane*, or ceremonial hall, has a walnut-wood floor on which Mevlevî dervishes once performed their whirling ceremony. This building has now been converted into the **Mevlevî Museum** (Mevlevî Müzesi), exhibiting musical instruments and the ceremonial costumes of the dervishes. After the son of the Mevlâna, Sultan Veled, introduced the branch of Islamic mysticism to the city from Konya, Afyon became the second-largest centre of the Mevlevî order.

Archeological Museum

Kurtuluş Cad, 1km east of the centre • Tues–Sun 8am–noon & 1.30–5.30pm • Free • ☎ 0272 215 1191

Afyon's **Archeological Museum** (Arkeoloji Müzesi) is well worth visiting. Despite rather dimly lit display cabinets, the objects are attractively laid out and the explanatory signboards well written. The most interesting finds are Roman, excavated at nearby Çardalı and Kovalık Höyük, and dating from the third and fourth centuries AD. This region was (and remains) the heart of the marble-quarrying industry in Anatolia, and the museum garden is full of noteworthy (but unlabelled) marble work and statuary from the Roman, Phrygian, Byzantine and Ottoman eras.

THE OPIUM POPPIES OF AFYON

A quarter of the world's legal production of **opium** is harvested from the poppy fields surrounding Afyon. While the authorities are reluctant to tout the city's eponymous enterprise as a tourist attraction, there are still tell-tale signs of civic pride in the traditional industry: a close look at the fountain in the town square reveals that it is a graceful bronze sculpture of poppy seed pods.

If you want to take a look at the crop, in May/June head out of town for around 5km on the Sandıklı road; the open fields of poppies are clearly visible from the road. Much more grows around Yalvaç and in the Toros Mountains. The fields are regularly patrolled by officials, who check whether the seed heads have been illegally "bled" for heroin.

Gedik Ahmet Paşa Külliyesi
Kurtuluş Cad, near the centre in its own patch of parkland

The **Gedik Ahmet Paşa Külliyesi** was built for one of the viziers of Mehmet the Conqueror in 1477. Adjoining it are a stone *medrese* and a functioning hamam – the original marble floors are in good condition, but it's otherwise in a bad state of repair. The complex's mosque, identified as the **İmaret Camii**, has a fluted minaret dashed with zigzagging blue İznik tiles.

Museum of Victory
Milli Egemenlik Cad • Daily 8.30am–noon & 1.30–5.30pm • ₺2

The **Museum of Victory** (Zafer Müzesi) is a museum that commemorates Atatürk's brief stay in Afyon, housed in the building in which he planned his victory at Dumlupınar in the summer of 1922. His office has been preserved, and weapons and other paraphernalia from the war, as well as old photos of Atatürk and Afyon, are on show.

Kaya
32km north of Afyon; turn left off the minor Afyon–Eskişehir road, north of the turn for Ayazini • Best reached by taxi (see p.410)

The most noteworthy of several **Phrygian ruins** near the village of **KAYA** are the rock-cut tomb of **Arslantaş** (Lion Stone), flanked by another relief of lions, two enormous beasts snarling at each other with bared teeth, and the nearby cult monument called **Arslankaya** (Lion Rock), featuring a high relief of the goddess Cybele flanked by two more enormous lions. Close to Arslankaya is Lake Emre, set in the village of **DÖĞER**, where the remains of a fifteenth-century Ottoman *kervansaray* can also be found.

Ayazini
33km north of Afyon; turn right off the minor Afyon–Eskişehir road at Kunduzlu • Best reached by taxi (see p.410)

The modern village of **AYAZİNİ** is home to some remarkable Phrygian remains. As you approach the village, **cave houses** and a well-preserved ninth-century **Byzantine church** are visible across fields of opium poppies. Closer observation reveals lion reliefs and the scars from excavations by locals and archeologists, who have found coins and other objects in the rooms.

ARRIVAL AND DEPARTURE   AFYON

By train The station is at the far north end of Ordu Bul, about 500m east of the centre.

Destinations Adana (1 daily; 11hr); İstanbul (1 daily; 8hr 30min); Konya (2 daily; 6hr).

By bus or dolmuş The otogar, 500m east of town on the çevre yolu (ring road), is linked to the middle of town by a dolmuş service marked "Sanayi/PTT". Free servis buses run from the otogar to Hükümet Meydanı, the main square. To reach the *otogar* from the town centre, take bus #9 from behind the post office.

Destinations Adana (10 daily; 7hr); Alanya (5 daily; 6hr 30min); Ankara (21 daily; 4hr); Antalya (hourly; 5hr); Aydın (4 daily; 5hr); Bursa (6 daily; 4hr); Fethiye (2 daily; 7hr); Isparta (6 daily; 2hr); İstanbul (20 daily; 8hr); İzmir (4 daily; 6hr); Konya (14 daily; 3hr); Kuşadası (2 daily; 7hr); Kütahya (6 daily; 1hr 30min); Marmaris (2 daily; 9hr).

7

THERMAL TOURISM

Thanks to its natural thermal waters, the Afyon region has become synonymous with **thermal tourism**. Hot springs, whose waters bubble up to temperatures of 50–80°C and have a high content of fluoride, bromide and calcium salts, are located in four different districts of the city. Marketed for their curative properties, the natural springs have given rise to assorted spa hotels and treatment centres providing hydrotherapy exercise pools, whirlpool massage and therapeutic mud baths, used to treat muscular disorders, injuries and even neurological issues, as well as for pain relief and rehabilitation. Even drinking the water supposedly reaps health benefits, and mineral water from this region is bottled and sold all over Turkey.

If you don't fancy visiting one of the region's spa hotels (see below), consider trying the deep mineral **mud baths** at Hudai Kaplıcıları (48km south of Afyon, beyond Sandıklı off the Denizli road), which are accessible for a ₺4 cover charge.

7

INFORMATION

Banks The major banks and ATMs are on Banklar Cad.
Tourist information A booth in Hükümet Meydanı (Mon–Fri 8.30am–noon & 1.30–5.30pm; ☎ 0272 215 7600) hands out town maps and a brochure covering the "Afyon Tourism Route" (see p.410), north of the city.

ACCOMMODATION

HOTELS

Çakmak Marble Hotel Süleyman Gonçer Cad 2, just east of Hükümet Meyd ☎ 0272 214 3300, ⓦ cakmak marblehotel.com. Favoured by Turkish travellers and wedding parties, *Çakmak* is the most upmarket of the central hotels, and it's a comfortable stay, if you can handle the garish tangerine colour scheme. Rooms are clean and well furnished, and there's an excellent breakfast buffet, but the basement hamam could do with some TLC. **₺230**
Hotel Soydan Karagözoğlu Sok 2 ☎ 0272 215 6070, ⓦ soydanhotel.com. Ideally located by the tourist information booth and run by amiable staff, this place could do with a revamp, but it's nonetheless clean and cosy. Ask to see the rooms before you check in as they vary in quality. **₺120**

SPA HOTELS

Hüdai Termal Otel 45km southwest of Afyon ☎ 0272 535 7327, ⓦ hudai.sandikli.bel.tr. Comfortable rooms and an attached treatment centre, with mud baths that reach up to 50°C, a naturally heated thermal pool and spring-water baths each with individual curative properties. **₺80**
Termal Resort Oruçoğlu 14km north of Afyon, on the Kütahya road ☎ 0272 251 5050, ⓦ orucoglu.com.tr. Part of the Ömer/Gecek Kaplıcıları hot springs complex, with accommodation ranging from simple chalets to half- and full-board suites with thermal water on tap. Use of the hamam, sauna, indoor and outdoor pools is included, and massages and treatment packages are available. Half board. **₺259**

EATING AND DRINKING

İkbal Lokantası Close to Hükümet Meyd on Uzun Çarşı ☎ 0272 215 1205. Established in 1922, this local favourite is charmingly old-fashioned, with a snaking Art Deco staircase leading up to the grand family dining area. The grills are excellent (from ₺15) but the best part is the puddings (from ₺7), all served with a generous slice of thick Afyon cream – delicious. Daily 8am–10pm.

İnyo Café Ordu Bul 10 ☎ 0272 213 0133. This surprisingly modern café, one of the few places you can grab a decent cappuccino (around ₺5), sticks out amid the drab city sprawl. A range of lunchtime eats are on offer and there's plenty of shady outdoor seating. Daily 8am–10pm.

Isparta

The largely modern town of **ISPARTA** is set on a flat plain that's dominated by 2635m Mount Davraz to the south. Its only hint of romantic appeal lies in its chief industries: rosewater and rose oil, distilled here for more than a century, and carpets, manufactured in industrial quantities. While the lakeside town of Eğirdir, 12km east, makes a more appealing base from which to explore the region (see p.414), Isparta's surrounds bloom with colour come the annual rose harvest.

The Greek quarter

Until the 1923 exchange of populations many **Greeks** lived in Isparta, and their old residential quarter is a fifteen-minute walk southwest from the town centre, near the State Hospital (Devlet Hastanesi). The once handsome lath-and-plaster houses are now crumbling, but there are a couple of restored nineteenth-century churches to admire.

Archeological Museum

Kenan Evren Cad, 500m northeast of the Belediye building • Tues–Sat 8.30am–5pm • Free • ☎ 0246 218 3437

Isparta's **Archeological Museum** (Arkeoloji Müzesi) holds a reasonable collection of local finds, including some fine Roman grave stelae, plus assorted items from a nearby Bronze Age burial site. The ethnography section includes a wonderful felt-and-reed yurt, which, along with some fine old carpets and kilims, attests to the region's bygone nomadic culture.

ARRIVAL AND INFORMATION ISPARTA

By train At the time of writing, no trains were running to Isparta.

By bus or dolmuş The *otogar* is a few kilometres northwest of town on Süleyman Demirel Bul – free *servis* buses run into the centre and to the minibus terminal (*köy garajı*) in the middle of town, 500m southwest of Kaymakkapı Meydanı, from where you can take a dolmuş to Burdur, Eğirdir, Ağlasun or Atabey, all around 40min away (around ₺5). There have been tales of travellers being ticketed to Eğirdir but left stranded in Isparta's *otogar*; if this

happens to you, head for the *köy garajı* and onto Eğirdir by dolmuş (20min, last bus leaves around 7.30pm).

Destinations Afyon (6 daily; 2hr); Antalya (hourly; 2hr 30min); Beyşehir (6 daily; 2hr 30min); Kayseri (5 daily; 9hr); Konya (4 daily; 4hr).

Tourist office On the fifth floor of the elaborate Vali Konağı, or governor's building, next to the main square (Mon–Fri 8am–noon & 1.30–5pm; ☎ 0248 232 2210). Largely unhelpful staff offer a town map and English-language brochure, but little else.

ACCOMMODATION

Hotel Artan Cengiz Topel Cad 12/B ☎ 0246 232 5700, ⓦ hotelartan.com. A good budget option, tucked away in a quiet side street off the main square, this place is clean and well-equipped, with polite, English-speaking staff. Rooms have a dated 1980s feel, but are clean and functional. **₺150**

Basmacıoğlu Hotel Süleyman Demirel Bul 81

☎ 0246 223 2700, ⓦ basmacigluotel.com. Once the swankiest hotel in town, *Basmacıoğlu* is looking a little worn around the edges these days, but the rooms are still comfortable enough for a night or two. There's a range of standard, deluxe and suite rooms available and rates are often negotiable. **₺150**

EATING AND DRINKING

Isparta's *fırın* kebabs (or *tandır kebap*), in which the meat – traditionally lamb or goat – is cooked in deep clay ovens throughout the summer, are delicious, while its largely alcohol-free restaurants serve huge jugs of **Üzüm Hoşafı** (sweet grape juice) with their meals.

ISPARTA: THE ROSE CITY

Endearingly nicknamed the **Rose City**, Isparta ranks among the world's biggest growers of the renowned Damascena rose, and exports rose oil all around the globe. Eco-friendly British brand Lush are buyers, and the rosewater is shipped out to the grand mosque at Mecca. With a two-hundred-year history of rose oil distillation, **harvest time** in Isparta (May/June) is more than just a boost to the economy (a mere 1kg of rose oil retails for around €8000, making it a profitable venture). It's also a time of celebration for the villagers, with the two-day **Isparta Rose Festival**, and a plethora of home-made rose marmalades, ice creams and cosmetics on sale.

Essential Travel (ⓦ essentialtravel.nl), founded by Dutch rose specialist Joanne Klein Wolterink in conjunction with Isparta's Sebat Rose factory, runs small-group **rose harvest tours** (from €25 for a half-day tour, with lunch; local homestays can also be arranged). The tours include the chance to help villagers with the morning rose harvest; explore the factory, with a demonstration of a traditional distillation kettle; sample organic rosewater cosmetics; and, most entertainingly, frolic on a 30cm-thick "bed" of roses. Tours can also be arranged for the **lavender** harvest (July/Aug) and the **chamomile** harvest (April/May) on request.

★**Ferah** Üzüm Pazarı 1, next to the main square ☎0246 218 1270. One of the best local restaurants, this place is a dab hand at *fırın* kebabs (around ₺20), and they'll happily let you peek into their traditional clay oven, just by the entrance. Squeeze in between the regulars and sip some of the town's best Üzüm Hoşafı (₺2.50), served in traditional copper jugs and swimming with sugary raisins.

Mon–Sat 11am–8pm.

Kebabçı Kadir Hukumet Meydani 8 ☎0246 218 2460. An atmospheric option for an evening meal, with garden seating right on the main square, this family-run place offers a wide range of *fırın* kebabs (₺10–20), and specializes in home-made *helva* (₺5), which they also sell boxed to take away. Daily 10am–10pm.

Sagalassos

30km south of Isparta, 55km southwest of Eğirdir • Daily 7.30am–6pm • ₺10 • ⓦ sagalassos.com.tr • Dolmuşes run from Isparta to Ağlasun, from where taxis run 7km uphill to the site (around ₺20 return, including wait) or tours cost around ₺75/person from Egirdir Outdoor Centre (see p.417)

Identified as the first Pisidian city, the striking ruins of **Sagalassos** were discovered in 1806. The population of Termessos (see p.364) probably moved here in 244 AD after an earthquake, but it was abandoned soon after, with the population moving downhill to the present town. Wear sturdy shoes if you visit, as the site is quite rugged and steep.

The site

The **site** of Sagalassos is well labelled, with illustrations that show the buildings in their original state. The 96m-wide **theatre**, to the right of the entrance, remains much as the 244 AD earthquake left it, with seating mostly in place, but the stage building rather more wrecked. Two restored **nymphaea** (fountain-houses) here have retained their floor mosaic almost intact, along with the alcoves and a major inscription. Walking west you come to the **upper agora**, of which the second, huge nymphaeum formed one side. Two ceremonial arches opened off, and a pagoda-like monument stood in the centre.

Just above, north of the upper agora, a Doric **temple** of the second century BC is incorporated into the city walls. As you walk down from the upper agora, you'll see fragments of beautiful Roman friezes laid out like a giant jigsaw. Below the main track is the **lower agora** and adjacent baths; earthenware pipes and hypocausts reveal how water was distributed and heated. A temple with Corinthian columns dedicated to Antonius Pius stands beyond this area, while straight ahead down the steps are the **necropolis** and a hill that locals say is the site of an Alexander monument – they believe a gold statue dedicated to Alexander is waiting to be discovered.

Eğirdir

Few places enjoy as idyllic a setting as **EĞİRDİR**, with its glistening blue lake framed by undulating mountains. Long heralded by locals as Anatolia's best-kept secret, this humble lakeside town has a reputation for enticing travellers to stay a lot longer than they'd intended. That's not surprising when you consider the plethora of **hikes** – Eğirdir is a major stop on the acclaimed long-distance **St Paul Trail** (see box, p.418) – bike routes and watersports in close proximity.

A kilometre-long causeway divides the town, separating the mainland market town (the **Kale**), with its historical sites and harbour filled with colourful fishing boats, from **Yeşilada**, a tiny island reached by a sliver of land running out onto the lake, which is home to most of the local pensions and lakeside restaurants. Aside from its scenic vistas and outdoor activities, Eğirdir's real charm lies in its endearing indifference to modern tourism. You're more likely to find restaurant proprietors sipping tea on the terrace than rustling up business on the streets below, so take heed of the slower pace of life and relish lazy evenings relaxing by the lakeside.

Brief history

Founded by the **Hittites**, Eğirdir was taken by the Phrygians in 1200 BC. Not until Lydian times, however, when it straddled the so-called King's Way from Ephesus to Babylon, did the town become famous for its recreational and accommodation facilities.

Early in the thirteenth century, the town came under the control of the Konya-based Selçuks, who refortified it in its role as a gateway to Pisidia. Shortly thereafter the city reached the height of its fortunes as capital of the **emirate of Felekeddin Dündar**, remaining prominent during the reign of the Hamidoğlu clan. The Byzantines knew the place as **Akrotiri** ("promontory" in Greek) after its obvious geographical feature. That name was originally corrupted in Ottoman times to **Eğridir** (meaning "it's bent"), but was changed again in the mid-1980s to **Eğirdir**, meaning "s/he's spinning", which officialdom thought more dignified.

Eğirdir Lake

At a vast 488 square kilometres **Eğirdir Lake** is Turkey's second-largest freshwater lake, and its cool clear waters offer ample swimming spots. Come summer, it also plays host to **watersports** such as kayaking and windsurfing, as well as **boat tours** with local fishermen (around ₺60/half-day, including lunch), who will point out all the best swimming, fishing and barbecue spots.

Hızırbey Camii

Adjoining the Dündar Bey Medresi

Notable for its unique walk-through minaret, the **Hızırbey Camii** has been tastefully restored, with its roof supported by Selçuk wooden pillars, an ornately carved door, wooden porch and İznik-tiled *mihrab*. The earliest building in the *medrese* complex, dating back to 1202, is Eğirdir's six-domed **bathhouse** (daily 8am–10pm), which retains its sixteen original washing basins.

Yeşilada

15min walk across the causeway • Buses (8 daily) from the central *otogar*, the last at 9pm

The island of **Yeşilada** boasts the twelfth-century Byzantine church of **Ayios Stefanos**, now re-roofed but still awaiting internal restoration. The remaining Greek houses are mainly set in the centre of the island in walled gardens dominated by mulberries and grapes, accessed by tiny cobbled lanes. The small pebble **beaches** that border the island are hard on the feet, but the convenience of being able to take a dip from your pension before breakfast compensates.

Beaches

Belediye Plajı on the mainland, 750m northwest of the town centre in the Yazla district, is Eğirdir's least attractive beach. Sandy **Altınkum**, as you head towards the west shore of the lake, is much better, and great for children thanks to its shallow waters; it

---

THE MARKETS OF EĞİRDİR

Eğirdir's **weekly market** is held each Thursday. Locals from the surrounding areas pour into the mainland town centre, selling fresh produce, clothing, rosewater soaps from Isparta and just about everything else you can imagine. If they're in season make sure you pick a bag of deliciously sweet locally grown cherries.

Between the end of July and October, a special series of Sunday Pinar Pazars, or **Yörük Markets**, is held for the *Yörük* mountain tribes to trade produce and stock up for the winter. Single women should take care if they attend the women-only market that precedes the tenth and final market; legend has it that this is the negotiation ground for mothers to discuss potential marriage matches for their sons or daughters.

7

EXCURSIONS FROM EĞIRDIR

Despite its comparatively small tourism industry, Eğirdir makes a great base from which to explore the region. The local pensions are well organized, with tours, guides, maps and independent travel information all easily available, and it's often possible to team up with other travellers and split costs.

HIKING TRAILS

While the **St Paul's Trail** (see p.418) is the region's most famous long-distance walking trail, numerous trekking routes have been mapped out and independent hiking is easy. These range from half- or full-day walks, to multi-day trips such as the hike to Barla (25km) and the overnight trips to the summits of Mount Dedegöl and Mount Davraz. The **Eğirdir Outdoor Centre** (see opposite) can tailor routes to your requirements and arrange transport (around ₺3/km), guides (around ₺100/day), camping equipment and packed lunches.

CYCLING ROUTES

Potential **bike routes** vary from easier circuits around the region's many lakes, or the mostly flat terrain leading to Kovada National Park (54km round trip), to more challenging routes like the hilly climbs to Barla village (46km round trip) or the mountainous course to Zindan Cave (50km round trip).

KOVADA NATIONAL PARK

The lake, marshland and forests of **Kovada Gölü** form a carefully tended and hardly visited national park. Its animal population includes wolves, bears and wild boars, and the lake itself, teeming with fish, receives the outflow of Eğirdir Gölü. The limestone shore is harsh and the lake is tinted green by its sediment, so it's not a particularly enticing swimming spot, but the largely untouched wildlife makes for some great walking and birdwatching opportunities.

ÇANDIR/CANYONS/KING'S WAY

Many tours of Kovada National Park continue 30km south on the main road through a gorge towards **Çandır** (signed Yazılı Kanyonu), passing a series of icy but scenic pools and waterfalls, crisscrossed by bridges, and best sampled in high summer. Well-preserved stretches still survive of the ancient **Kral Yolu**, or "King's Way", a road that threaded through Pisidia.

SKIING

Between December and the end of March, the northern slopes of the 2635m **Mount Davraz** (a 30min drive from Eğirdir) offer decent downhill skiing and snowboarding, and the views from the slopes down to Lake Eğirdir are superb. Conditions are fairly reliable, though the limited runs won't satisfy everyone. The **Eğirdir Outdoor Centre** (see opposite) and the **Davraz Ski Centre** (Ⓦ davraz.com) rent skis (from ₺30) and snowboards (from ₺35), and a weekday lift pass costs from ₺30.

also offers umbrellas, pedaloats and camping. However, its charm is diminished by a holiday-camp ambience and the modern housing development that backs it.

Sivri Dağı

The most popular hike close to Eğirdir scales the heights of **Sivri Dağı** (Needle Mountain), whose rugged peak dominates the skyline to the west of the lake. The nomadic village of **Akpinar**, 7km – or less than two hours' walk – south of town, makes a popular stop-off, part of the way uphill. It consists of just fifty houses clustered around a yurt (*Yörük* tent), selling *gözleme* and *ayran*, and a small apple orchard, peering down over the lake below.

ARRIVAL, INFORMATION AND TOURS   EĞIRDIR

By bus Eğirdir's very central *otogar* is south of the Hızırbey Camii. Eastbound buses stop opposite the Hızırbey Camii, not in front of the *otogar*. Many local pensions offer free pick-ups; call to let them know you're coming.

Destinations Ankara (4 daily; 7hr); Antalya (8 daily; 3hr); Beyşehir (12 daily; 1hr 30min); Denizli (4 daily; 3hr); Göreme (2 daily; 8hr); Istanbul (1 daily; 10hr); Konya (4 daily; 4hr).

Tourist office The well-meaning but largely unhelpful office is at 2 Sahil Yolu 13, a 5min walk west of town on the Isparta road (Mon–Fri 8.30am–noon & 1.30–5pm; ☎0246 311 4388).

Tours and trekking Eğirdir Outdoor Centre, opposite the harbour on the mainland (daily 7am–11pm; ☎0246 311 6688, ⓦegirdiroutdoorcenter.com). Run by İbrahim and the team from *Lale/Charley's* pensions, this rental outlet offers bikes, skis and full trekking kits including backpacks, sleeping bags and tents. Doubling as a coffee house, book exchange and travellers' meeting place, they also offer free information and maps, and organize tours, drivers and pick-ups for hikers.

ACCOMMODATION

THE KALE

★**Charly's Pension** Cami Sok 2 ☎0246 311 4611, ⓦcharlyspension.com. Hosting a cosmopolitan mix of travellers and trekkers, and run by Lakeland experts İbrahim and Muslum, *Charly's* offers a home from home from which to explore the surrounding area. Rooms are clean and cosy, the home-cooked dinners are excellent and camping is available, but the real highlight is the breezy terrace perched high above the lake. It can get busy in season, so book ahead and secure a free pick-up from the *otogar*. Camping €15, double €35

Fulya Pension Cami Sok 9; reception at Charly's Pension (see above) ☎0246 311 2175, ⓦfulyapension .com. The latest venture from the *Charley's Pension* crew is a beautifully remodelled boutique hotel with stone-brick walls and fireplaces, carved wood furniture and spacious bathrooms. The spectacular rooftop terrace is currently being renovated, so watch this space. €45

★**Lale Pension** On the hillside; reception at Charly's Pension (see above) ☎0246 311 2406, ⓦlalehostel .com. Set on the hillside with sweeping views of the lake, *Lale*, run by the same team as the nearby *Charly's Pension*, is a sanctuary for road-weary travellers, with sunny rooms and comfy beds padded out with plump duvets and a mound of pillows. There's also a good lounge and breakfast terrace. €40

YEŞILADA

★**Ali's Pension** East side ☎0246 311 2547, ⓦalispension.com.tr. One of the most popular hotels on Yeşilada for good reason. *Ali's* bright red facade fronts a homely pension, with simple but spotless rooms. The English-speaking owners offer a warm welcome and can help you plan your trip, while the pretty garden out front is the perfect spot for breakfast. €35

Choo Choo Pension South side ☎0246 311 4926, ⓦchoochoopension.com. A simple, well-run family pension with a great lakeside location and a friendly atmosphere. The cheerful, light-filled rooms are well furnished and spacious, and there's a superb restaurant right on the waterfront. €50

Göl Pension South side ☎0246 311 2370, ⓦgolpension.com. A long-established pension run by a mother and her daughters, where the warm welcome transcends the language barrier. Rooms are modest, but exceptionally clean, and a hearty breakfast is served on the pretty terrace. ₺150

Sehsuvar Peace Pension Up the hill just behind Ali's Pension ☎0246 311 2433, ⓦpeacepension.com. A charmingly traditional pension, with spick and span rooms and a country-cottage feel. The hosts are exceedingly friendly, but speak no English, making communication difficult, but it's still among the cheapest options in town and a quieter alternative to the lakefront pensions. ₺90

EATING AND DRINKING

Fresh-caught **lake fish** – especially carp (*sazan*), zander and crayfish – figure prominently on local menus, presented either as batter-fried fillets, grilled, or poached in tomato sauce (*buğulama*). Most restaurants serve **alcohol**.

THE KALE

Günaylar Opposite the Hızırbey Camii ☎0246 311 2899. Decent kebabs (from ₺10) and *pides* at local prices are the mainstay of this bustling joint, and it's always full of hungry patrons. The *menemen* (a breakfast dish of eggs, tomatoes, onions and peppers; ₺6) is particularly delicious. Daily 6am–11pm.

İrfando Dondurmaları Cami Mahallesi 3, opposite the Atatürk statue ☎0246 311 4888. This humble hole in the wall serves up delicious ice creams (₺3 for a massive three-scoop cone) in a myriad of flavours. There's chocolate, caramel, blackberry, lemon and mango, but best is the unique home-made *gül* (rose) ice cream. May–Oct daily 10am–midnight.

Meşhur Köfteci Güngör Uzun Çarşı. Local chef Güngör Gül serves up home-made tahini from a secret recipe and delicious grilled *köfte* (meatballs) at this Eğirdir institution. A full meal will set you back less than ₺20. Daily 8am–11pm.

YEŞILADA

Big Apple West side of the island ☎0246 311 4555. Easily spotted right on the waterfront as you enter the island, this is a reliable choice, with fish dishes from ₺14 and *köfte* at ₺16. The portions are generous, the beer is cold and there's plenty of shaded seating right by the water. Daily 8am–midnight.

Big Fish West side of the island, next door to the Big Apple ☎0246 311 4413. A cheerful family-run restaurant that dates back to 1983 and remains a hit with locals, *Big Fish*

7

7

THE ST PAUL TRAIL

Opened in 2004, the rugged **St Paul Trail** offers over 500km of trekking in the spectacularly beautiful Toros Mountains. Waymarked to international standards, with red and white flashes on rocks and trees, it allows relatively easy exploration of a remote, unspoiled area of Turkey. A detailed guidebook (which includes a map), written by Kate Clow, covers the trail – the Eğirdir Outdoor Centre (see p.417) will let you photocopy pages if you don't have your own.

The twin starting points of the route are the ancient cities of **Perge** (see p.366) and **Aspendos** (see p.368), on the Mediterranean coastal plain. It was from Perge that St Paul set out, in 46 AD, on his first proselytizing journey. His destination was the Roman colonial town of Antioch ad Pisidiam (see below), where he first preached Christ's message to non-Jews. En route from the Mediterranean to the Anatolian plateau, the trail crosses tumbling mountain rivers, climbs passes between limestone peaks that soar to almost 3000m, dips into deeply scored canyons and weaves beneath shady pine and cedar forest. It even includes a boat ride across the glimmering expanse of Lake Eğirdir.

Hikers interested in archeology can discover remote, little-known Roman sites and walk along original sections of Roman road. Active types can raft the Köprülü River, scale 2635m Mount Davraz and 2799m Mount Barla (ascents of both appear in the trail guidebook; for more information check ⓦtrekkinginturkey.com), or even tackle the mighty Dedegül (2992m).

PRACTICALITIES

Eğirdir (see p.414) makes an ideal base for forays along the trail. The town's pension owners will be able to help you sort out the relevant dolmuşes, negotiate car or taxi rental and let you store unwanted gear until your return from the hills. **Guides**, camping equipment, pick-ups and luggage storage can be arranged by İbrahim at the Eğirdir Outdoor Centre (see p.417).

---

is, unsurprisingly, best known for its fish. Trout and lake bass (mains from ₺15) are the main specialities, accompanied by salad, *meze* and bread. Daily 8am–midnight.

Felekabad Northeastern tip of the island ☎0246 311 5881, ⓦfelekabad.com. Friendly, family-run and excellent value, serving tasty *gözleme* (from ₺6) and a range of fresh fish and Turkish staples. There's no alcohol, but the huge covered terrace on the lakefront offers a prime view even when it's raining. Daily 7.30am–midnight.

DIRECTORY

Banks The town centre holds a couple of ATMs, plus several banks.

Car parks There are two car parks at the north and south of the mainland; many pensions offer limited parking spaces.

Hamam Behind the post office on Çay Boyu Sok 1 (daily 7am–11pm; Thurs & Fri women only; ☎0246 311 3618). Expect to pay around ₺35 for a scrub and massage.

Police Next door to the tourist office.

Antioch ad Pisidiam

75km northeast of Eğirdir, 2km from modern Yalvaç • Tues–Sun 8.30am–5.30pm • ₺5 • Catch a minibus from Isparta (via Eğirdir) to Yalvaç (12 daily in summer; 1hr 30min), then walk or take a taxi

The ancient city of **Antioch ad Pisidiam** is where the apostle **St Paul** first attempted to convert pagans to Christianity. Originally a Hellenistic foundation of the late third century BC, the city peaked as the capital of the Roman province of Pisidia, and remained important well into Byzantine times.

The most unusual surviving remains are of the sizeable **temple**, at the highest point of the city, built in a semicircular colonnaded precinct in honour of the Emperor Augustus. Below this is the toppled three-arched **propylon** (gateway) dedicated to Augustus, where the Tiberius and Augustus squares meet. Even more substantial are the remains of the **baths** fed by an **aqueduct** and surviving sections of a flagged Roman **street**. At the lower end of the site, a few courses of monumental stone blocks belonging to the fourth-century **Church of St Paul** (on the site of the synagogue) still stand, but little else can be seen except for the ground plan and some small areas of mosaic floor.

Adada

Signposted off the Aksu road, 65km southeast of Eğirdir • Free

Cut from grey stone, the ancient town of **Adada** lies along both sides of a minor road. The site has never been excavated, and history books are strangely silent about it, but judging from coins found hereabouts, it was thriving during imperial Roman times. Visible remains include a particularly well-preserved Corinthian temple, plus two other small temples, a forum with unusual seating along one side, a badly preserved theatre, a church and various Hellenistic buildings.

If you follow the stream bed between the acropolis hill and the adjacent hill, heading southwest behind the forum, it's possible to trace the original Greco-Roman road from the south. This is almost certainly the original road that St Paul walked on his first missionary journey from Perge to Antioch in Pisidia.

Beyşehir

The town of **BEYŞEHIR**, on the eastern shore of Beyşehir Gölü, sees a lot of through traffic, and its attractive lakeside position and historical legacy make it a good prospect for at least a day-trip.

Judging by Neolithic remains, there has been human settlement here since the sixth or seventh millennium BC, and evidence exists of Hittite settlement around the lake. The town itself was originally Byzantine, known as Karallia, and in Selçuk times acquired a citadel, mosques and hamams. The most notable monument is the distinctive **Eşrefoğlu Camii**, dating back to the Eşrefoğlu dynasty (1277–1326), but there's also a lovely weir-bridge, built by German workers in 1902, from where you can watch locals throwing their nets out for the evening catch of *sazan* (carp).

Eşrefoğlu Camii

Off Türbe Sok in the centre of town • Open at prayer times

The **Eşrefoğlu Camii**, Beyşehir's finest monument, was built by Eşrefoğlu Seyfeddin Süleyman between 1297 and 1299. A large, flat-roofed stone building, surmounted by a typical Selçuk flat-sided cone, it's an exceptional example of a medieval wooden *beylik* mosque. (The *beylik*s were the minor Turkish principalities that ruled Anatolia before the Ottomans gained supremacy.) Restoration carried out in the 1950s explains the ugly concrete blocks at the base of the minaret, but otherwise the mosque is in a remarkable state of preservation.

The effect inside is incredibly forest-like: not only are the columns and capitals wooden, but also the rafters, galleries, furniture and balustrades. Dappled light plays on the columns from a central aperture, now glassed over, and from high-set windows. Below this is a deep pit, which once held ice for preserving food and cooling the mosque. The *mihrab* is decorated in typical Selçuk style, its turquoise, black and white tiles being almost the last surviving of their type, and the *mimber* is also a lovely period piece of woodcarving, echoing the star motif apparent throughout the mosque.

The conically roofed building attached to the east side of the mosque, the **Eşrefoğlu Türbesi**, was built in 1302 to commemorate Eşrefoğlu Seyfeddin Süleyman who died in that year. Ask the imam if he'll open it up for a look at its beautifully tiled interior, one of the most ornate surviving examples of its type.

Beyşehir Gölü

Religious and civic architecture aside, the most obvious attraction near Beyşehir is the shallow, freshwater **Beyşehir Gölü**, one of Turkey's largest lakes at 650 square kilometres. The number of its islands is a hotly disputed topic among the locals, hindered by the fact that smaller ones appear and disappear according to the water level (averaging a mere 10m in depth). Roughly twenty, however – mostly those that hold ruined Byzantine monasteries – have names.

7

Boat trips (around ₺10) take in several, including the formerly magnificent Selçuk island palace of **Kubadabad**, whose unique tiles can be seen in the Karatay museum in Konya (see p.423). Pedalos are also available for rent (around ₺5), while tiny cafés serve fish sandwiches by the lakeside; some offer seating on harboured boats.

The best **beach** on the lake is **Karaburnu**, signposted 500m off the Yeşildağ road, 18km west of Beyşehir.

Eflatun Pınar

On Beyşehir Gölü's east shore, on the main road towards Eğirdir • Turn right 15km northwest of Beyşehir, just before a petrol station; follow a paved side road for 5km, then bear left for another 2km, along a dirt track

The **Eflatun Pınar** (Violet Spring) is a Hittite shrine that dates from the thirteenth century BC. On its outskirts, a large, walled pond filling a natural depression receives the flow of vigorous springs. Huge carved blocks at one corner bear four relief figures with winged sun discs (symbols of royalty) carried by semi-human monsters, with statues of seated divinities to either side. Excavations by the Konya museum have revealed a row of mountain gods with holes in their skirts that once gushed water, and a large stone block with bull reliefs.

ARRIVAL AND DEPARTURE

BEYŞEHİR

By bus *Servis* buses connect Beyşehir *otogar*, 2km north of town, with the centre (every 20min), dropping passengers near the weir-bridge.

Destinations Alanya (6 daily; 4hr); Ankara (4 daily; 5hr); Antalya (5 daily; 4hr); Eğirdir (12 daily; 1hr 30min); Isparta (6 daily; 2hr 30min); Konya (hourly; 1hr 30min).

ACCOMMODATION AND EATING

Adana Sofrasi Overlooking the weir at Çarşı Camii yanı ☎ 0332 512 4535. The best place to eat in Beyşehir, this modern restaurant sprawls along the weir, with plenty of outdoor seating and a spotless open kitchen. A decent kebab or fish meal will set you back a very reasonable ₺12–15 but, like everywhere in town, they don't serve alcohol. Daily 8am–10pm.

Ali Bilir Bilir Sok 1, visible from the weir ☎ 0332 512 0455, ⊛ alibilirotel.com. The best of Beyşehir's slim pickings is a modern and friendly choice, with a beautifully situated terrace restaurant overlooking the lake. Be sure to negotiate the room rates, especially in low season. ₺150

Beyaz Park Overlooking the weir at Atatürk Cad 1 ☎ 0332 512 3865. If you're looking for the cheapest room in town, this is it, but keep your expectations low. That said, the hosts are friendly, there's a decent restaurant overlooking the weir and it's clean enough for a night's stay. ₺60

Konya

KONYA, the medieval Selçuk capital, is a place of pilgrimage for the Muslim world, and a city that holds pride of place in the hearts of all pious Turks. This was the adopted home of Celaleddin Rumi, better known as the Mevlâna (Our Master), the Sufic mystic who founded the **Whirling Dervish** sect, the Mevlevî (see box, p.422); his writings helped reshape Islamic thought and modified the popular Islamic culture of Turkey. Konya today has a reputation as one of the country's most religious and thus conservative cities. That said, most visitors are surprised by its modern and bustling city centre, with monumental landmarks sandwiched between fashion stores and towering flat blocks.

Turkey's seventh-largest city is surrounded by some exceptionally fertile countryside, and its many parks – in particular, the central hillock of **Alâeddin Parkı** – add a splash of green to the ubiquitous light-coloured stone.

Brief history

Konya's history is as long and spectacular as that of any Turkish city. The earliest remains discovered date from the seventh millennium BC, and the acropolis was inhabited successively by Hittites, Phrygians, Romans and Greeks. **St Paul** and **St Barnabas** both delivered sermons here after they had been expelled from Antioch, and in 235 AD, one of the earliest Church councils was convened in the city – known then, under the Byzantines, as Iconium.

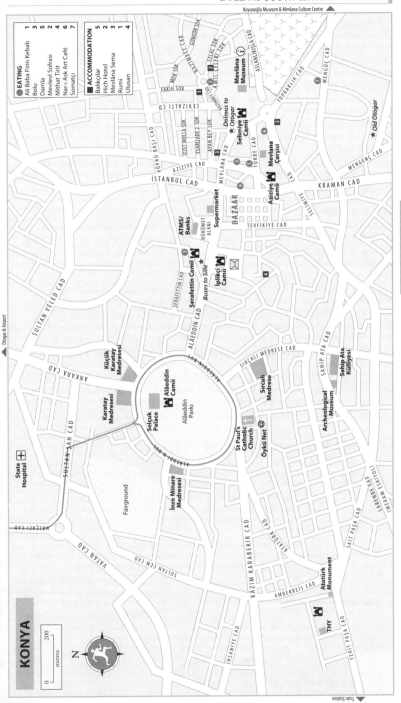

KONYA

0	200
metres	

N

State Hospital

Otogar & Airport

Fairground

Karatay Medresesi

Küçük Karatay Medresesi

Selçuk Palace

Alâeddin Camii

Alâeddin Parkı

İnce Minare Medresesi

St Paul's Catholic Church

Öykü Net @

Sırçalı Medrese

Archeological Museum

Sahip Ata Külliyesi

Atatürk Monument

THY

Serafettin Camii

Buses to Sille

ATMS/ Banks

Supermarket

HÜKÜMET ALANI

BAZAAR

İplikçi Camii

Azîziye Camii

Mevlâna Çarşisi

Selimiye Camii

Mevlâna Museum

Dolmus to Otogar

Balıkçılar

Koyunoğlu Museum & Mevlana Culture Centre

Old Otogar

Train Station

EATING

Ali Baba Fırın Kebab	1
Bolu	3
Damla	5
Mevlevî Sofrası	2
Mithat Tirit	2
Nar-ı Aşk Art Café	6
Somatçı	7

ACCOMMODATION

Balıkçılar	5
Hich Hotel	2
Mevlâna Sema	3
Rumi	1
Ulusan	4

SULTAN VELED CAD

ANKARA CAD

SULTAN ŞAH CAD

VATAN CAD

NALÇACI CAD

SULTAN CEM CAD

İHSANİYE CAD

KÂZIM KARABEKİR CAD

ATATÜRK CAD

AMBERREİS CAD

FERİT PAŞA CAD

LÂRENDE CAD

(MERAM ESKİ YOL)

SALİT PAŞA CAD

SAHİP ATA CAD

SIRÇALI MEDRESE CAD

ALÂEDDİN CAD

ALÂEDDİN BUL

SERAFETTİN CAD

KÖPRÜ BAŞI CAD

AZİZİYE CAD

İSTANBUL CAD

MEVLÂNA CAD

CEVİZALTI CD

İZZET MOLLA SOK

ESERİZADE 2 SOK

AYAN BEY SOK

FAKİH SOK

MOR SOK

NAZIMBEY CAD

GÖNGÖR SOK

CELAL SOK

ÂMİL ÇELEBİ SOK

NİMBER SOK

ASLANLIKIŞLA CAD

TOPRAKLIK CAD

MENGÜÇ CAD

TÜRBE CAD

MENGENE CAD

KRAMAN CAD

TEVFİKİYE CAD

SELİMİYE

7

It also took a central role during the era of the western Selçuks, becoming the seat of the **Sultanate of Rum**. After they had defeated the Byzantine army at the Battle of Manzikert in 1071, the Selçuks attempted to set up a court in İznik, just across the Sea of Marmara from Istanbul. They were expelled from there by the combined Byzantine and Crusader armies, but still ruled most of eastern and central Asia Minor until the early fourteenth century.

While the concept of a fixed capital was initially somewhat alien to the Selçuks, Konya became the home of their sultans from the time of Süleyman Ibn Kutulmuz, successor to Alparslan, the victor at Manzikert. **Alâeddin Keykubad**, the most distinguished of all Selçuk sultans, established a court of artists and scholars in Konya early in the thirteenth century, and his patronage was highly beneficial to the development of the arts and philosophy. Many of the buildings constructed at this time are still standing, and examples of their highly distinctive tile-work, woodcarving, carpet making and masonry are on display in local museums.

7 Mevlâna Museum

Eastern end of Mevlâna Cad • Daily 9am–7pm; last admission 30min before closing • Free, English-language audioguides ₺10

A visit to the **Mevlâna Museum** (Mevlâna Müzesi) is among Turkey's most rewarding experiences; the stunning manicured gardens and colourful rose bushes framing the central courtyard are an attraction in themselves. Try to arrive early or late in the day, however, to avoid the crowds.

Housed in a former *tekke*, the first lodge of the Mevlevî dervish sect, the museum is most easily found by locating the distinctive fluted turquoise spire that rises directly above Celaleddin Rumi's tomb. The *tekke* served as a place of mystical teaching, meditation and ceremonial dance (*sema*), from shortly after Rumi's death in 1273 until 1925, when Atatürk banned all Sufic orders. Over the centuries the various dervish orders had become highly influential in political life, and thus posed a potential threat to his secular reforms.

Most of the **buildings** in the compound, including the *tekke* and *semahane*, were built late in the fifteenth and early in the sixteenth centuries by sultans Beyazıt II and Selim I. Along the south and east sides of the courtyard, the **cells** where the dervishes prayed and meditated now hold waxwork figures dressed in the costume worn during the whirling

---

THE LIFE AND TEACHINGS OF THE MEVLÂNA

Celaleddin Rumi, later known as the **Mevlâna**, was born in the central Asian city of Balkh in 1207. At the age of 20, having received a warning vision, the young man convinced his father to flee with him for western Asia, which they did just in time to avoid being massacred with the rest of Balkh by marauding Mongols. They settled in Konya, where the reigning sultan Alâeddin Keykubad received them cordially. The city had a cosmopolitan population, whose beliefs were not lost on the young man, and it was here that he emerged as a leading heterodox mystic or **Sufi**.

During the 1250s, Rumi completed a masterpiece of Persian devotional **poetry**, the *Mathnawi*. A massive work covering several volumes, it concerns the soul's separation from God – characterized as the Friend – as a consequence of earthly existence, and the power of a mutual yearning to bring about a reunion, either before or after bodily death. The Mevlâna – as Rumi was by now widely known – himself died on December 17, 1273.

On a practical level, the Mevlâna instructed his disciples to pursue all manifestations of truth and beauty, while avoiding ostentation, and to practice infinite tolerance, love and charity. He condemned slavery, and advocated monogamy and a greater prominence for women in religious and public life. The Mevlâna did not advocate complete monastic seclusion – the Mevlevîs held jobs in normal society and could marry – but believed that the contemplative and mystical practices of the **dervish** would free them from worldly anxieties. Although his ideas have never been fully accepted as Islamic orthodoxy, they still attract Westerners and liberal Muslims alike.

ceremony. Next to the quarters of the *şeyh* (head of the dervish order), today the museum office, a **library** preserves five thousand volumes on the Mevlevî and Sufic mysticism.

The mausoleum

The main building of the Mevlâna Museum is the **mausoleum** that contains the tombs of the Mevlâna, his father and other notables of the order. Slip the plastic bags provided at the entrance over your shoes and shuffle along in a queue of pilgrims, for whom this is the primary reason to visit. Women must cover their heads; regardless of gender, if you're wearing shorts you'll be given a skirt-like affair to cover your legs. The measure of devotion still felt toward the Mevlâna is evident in the weeping and impassioned prayer that takes place in front of his tomb, but non-Muslim visitors are treated with respect and even welcomed. This is in strict accordance with Rumi's own dictates on religious tolerance. If you're a lone *gavur* (infidel) in a centre of Islamic pilgrimage, this sentiment is surely to be cherished.

The semahane

Adjoining the mausoleum is the original **semahane** (the circular hall in which the *sema* was performed), considered the finest in Turkey. Exhibits include musical instruments belonging to the original dervishes, including the *ney* (reed flute), silk and woollen carpets and the original illuminated *Mathnawi* – the long devotional poem of the Mevlâna. One 500-year-old silk carpet from Selçuk Persia is said to be the finest ever woven, with 144 knots to the square centimetre; it took five years to complete.

The latticed gallery above the *semahane* was for women spectators, a modification introduced by the followers of the Mevlâna after his death. The heavy chain suspended from the ceiling, and the concentric balls that hang from it, were carved from a single piece of marble. In the adjoining room, a casket containing hairs from the beard of the Prophet is displayed alongside finely illuminated medieval Korans.

Alâeddin Parkı

Modern Konya stretches out from the **Alâeddin Parkı**, at the end of Mevlâna/Alâeddin Caddesi. Despite the encircling traffic, it's a lovely wooded place for a stroll, and holds many outdoor cafés. The site of the original acropolis, the *tepe*, has yielded finds dating back to 7000 BC, as well as evidence of Hittite, Phrygian, Roman and Greek settlers; most are now in the museum in Ankara. The scant remains of a **Selçuk palace** survive at the foot of the hill to the north.

Alâeddin Camii

Alâeddin Parkı • Daily 8.30am–5.30pm • Free

The eye-catching centrepiece of Alâeddin Parkı is the imposing **Alâeddin Camii**, started by Sultan Mesut I in 1130 and completed by Alâeddin Keykubad in 1221. Its typically plain Selçuk interior contains 42 ancient columns with Roman capitals supporting a flat roof, and there's a small domed area over the *mihrab*. Dated 1155, the beautiful carved ebony *mimber* is the oldest inscribed and dated Selçuk work of art in existence.

Karatay Medresesi

Ankara Cad • Tues–Sun 9am–noon & 1–5.30pm • ₺5

The restored **Karatay Medresesi** is a major Selçuk monument. Built in 1251, the *medrese*, or school of Islamic studies, now houses a museum of ceramics, but the building itself provides greater interest. Its main **portal** is a fine example of Islamic art at its most decorative, combining elements such as Arabic striped stonework and Greek Corinthian columns with a structure that is distinctly Selçuk: a tall doorway surmounted by a pointed, stalactite arch, resembling the entrance of a tent.

Inside the *medrese* the most attractive exhibit is again part of the building itself. Excavations beneath the floors reveal the building's terracotta hydraulic system,

7

KONYA'S DERVISH FESTIVAL AND DANCES

Since Konya is the spiritual and temporal home of the whirling dervishes, the city plays host to the annual **dervish festival**, held between December 7 and December 17, during the week prior to the anniversary of the Mevlâna's death. Unfortunately, with sub-zero temperatures, doubled hotel rates and shops full of whirling dervish kitsch, this is not the best time to witness a dervish rite. In fact the most authentic place to watch a ceremony is in the restored *semahane* in Istanbul, the Galata Mevlevîhane (see p.104). Unlike the dancers in Konya, its members are also practising dervishes who live according to the teachings of the Mevlâna. Alternatively, **free sema performances** are staged in the gardens of Konya's Mevlâna complex every Thursday in July and August, while the **Mevlâna Culture Centre**, 500m up the road from the Mevlâna Museum, hosts shows every Saturday night year-round, except during the festival period (May–Oct 9pm; Nov–April 7pm; free).

The **whirling ceremony** – the *sema* – for which the Mevlevî dervishes are renowned, is a means of freedom from earthly bondage and abandonment to God's love. The **clothes** worn by the Mevlevîs during the observance have symbolic significance. The camelhair hat represents a tombstone, the black cloak is the tomb itself, and the white skirt the funerary shroud. During the ceremony the cloak is cast aside, denoting that the dervishes have escaped from their tombs and from all other earthly ties. The **music** reproduces that of the spheres, and the turning dervishes represent the heavenly bodies themselves. Every movement and sound made during the ceremony has an additional significance – for example, the right arms of the dancers extend up to heaven while their left arms point to the floor, denoting that grace is received from God and distributed to humanity.

uncovered in 2008. The symmetrical tiling of the famed **dome of stars** is a stylized representation of the heavens in gold, blue and black monochrome tiles. Painted Ottoman tiles from İznik and Kütahya appear clumsy in contrast with those of this delicate mosaic.

Selçuk **ceramics** on display in the galleries bear witness to the fact that pious concerns were overruled by secular taste – not to mention the contributions of conquered Christian and pagan subjects – even in medieval times. The striking images of birds, animals and angels would have been strictly forbidden in more orthodox Islamic societies.

İnce Minare Medresesi

West side of Alâeddin Parkı, by the tramway stop • Daily: May–Oct 8.30am–12.30pm & 1.30–5pm; Nov–April 8am–noon & 1–5pm; last entry 15min before closure • ₺5

Behind its fine Selçuk portal, the **İnce Minare Medresesi**, or "Academy of the Slender Minaret", is now a lapidary and woodcarving museum. The minaret from which it takes its name was severely truncated by lightning in 1901; its most exquisite feature is now the **portal**, even more ornate than that at the Karatay Medresesi.

Most of the museum's exhibits, like the ceramics in the Karatay Medresesi, came from the ruined Selçuk palace across the way. The finest individual items are Selçuk stone reliefs, explicitly showing the influence of Byzantium. Most prominent are winged angels, bestiary pediments and a two-headed eagle relief, said to be from the vanished walls of the medieval city and now the official logo of the modern town.

Sırcalı Medrese

A short walk southeast of Alâeddin Parkı, along Ressam Sami Sok • Daily: May–Oct 8.30am–12.30pm & 1.30–5.30pm; Nov–April 8am–noon & 1–5pm • Free

The thirteenth-century **Sırcalı Medrese** now houses government offices. Highlights of the building, mostly restored in harsh brick, are the fine blue-glazed tile-work in the rear porch, all that remains of what was once a completely ornamented interior, the handsome portal and a collection of tombstones – all visible even when the gate is locked.

Archeological Museum

Sahip Ata Cad 91 • Tues–Sun: May–Oct 8.30am–12.30pm & 1.30–5.30pm; Nov–April 9am–noon & 1–5pm • ₺5

Konya's small **Archeological Museum** (Arkeoloji Müzesi) contains the only pre-Selçuk remains in the city. These include the few Hittite artefacts from the nearby site of Çatal Höyük (see p.427) that have not been relocated to Ankara, and six well-preserved Roman sarcophagi from Pamphylia, one of which depicts Hercules at his twelve labours. Note how the hero's beard grows as his labours progress. Just northeast of the museum is the thirteenth-century **Sahip Ata Külliyesi**, which is semi-ruined, but retains its beautiful brick and stone entrance portal, plus a tiled minaret.

Around the bazaar

The north edge of Konya's weekday **bazaar**, on Hükümet Alanı, 100m from the Mevlâna Museum, is marked by the brick **İplikçi Camii**, Konya's oldest mosque (1202) to survive intact and still be in use; legend claims that the Mevlâna preached and meditated here. Look out, too, for the **Aziziye Camii** in the bazaar, an Ottoman mosque easily recognized by its unusual (for Turkey) Moghul-style minarets.

The bazaar, like the city itself, is very traditional and surprisingly relaxed, but keep an eye out for pickpockets. You'll probably also see alternative healing remedies on sale, from daisy water to leeches.

7

ARRIVAL AND INFORMATION
KONYA

By plane Konya's airport, 17km northwest, is linked with the city centre by THY shuttle buses, which leave from Alâeddin Cad to connect with all departures. Check in advance at the THY office on Amberreis Cad (☎ 0332 239 1177).
Destinations Istanbul (6 daily; 1hr 10min).

By bus To reach the city centre from Konya's *otogar* (luggage lockers available), inconveniently located 15km north, catch tram #2 (signposted "Tramvay" from the *otogar*) to Alâeddin Parkı at the end of the line (buy tram passes from the ticket booth on the platform; they cost ₺5 for two fares, so hold on to your ticket). From there, either walk or take a dolmuş to the main street, Mevlâna Cad. Dolmuşes also connect the *otogar* with the Mevlâna Museum (₺2). Taxis will cost around ₺30.
Destinations Afyon (14 daily; 3hr); Alanya (6 daily; 5hr); Ankara (hourly; 3hr); Antalya (8 daily; 5hr); Beyşehir (hourly; 1hr 15min); Bursa (8 daily; 10hr); Göreme (6 daily; 3hr); Isparta (4 daily; 4hr); Kayseri (8 daily; 4hr); Silifke (8 daily; 5hr).

By train The station is at the far end of Ferit Paşa Cad, 4km from the centre and connected by dolmuş or by taxi (less than ₺10).
Destinations Adana (3 weekly; 8hr); Afyon (1 daily; 6hr); Ankara (8 daily; 1.5hr).

By car Rental cars are available from Avis, Nalçacı Cad, Acentacılar Sitesi, B-Blok 87 (☎ 0332 237 3750); Rüya Turizm, Zafer Meydanı (☎ 0332 352 7228); and Selen, Aziziye Cad (☎ 0332 353 6745).

Tourist office Aslanlıkışla Cad 5, just down from the Mevlâna Museum (Mon–Sat 8am–5pm, ☎ 0332 353 4021). Helpful English-speaking staff will weigh you down with brochures and up-to-date city plans. They also take bookings for the December dervish festival (see box opposite) and weekly dervish concerts, and can help with local transport. Note that many old city maps still mark the former tourist information centre on Mevlâna Cad; it no longer handles tourist information.

ACCOMMODATION

Balıkçılar Mevlâna Karşısı 2 ☎ 0332 350 9470, ⊕ balikcilar.com. Timeless grandeur without a hint of ostentation is the order of the day at this four-star hotel. Rooms are spotless and refined, with all the home comforts you'd expect, but it's the dramatic spiral stairwell with its stone mosaic walls and neon strip lighting that really ups the atmosphere. **€120**

★ **Hich Hotel** Aziziye Mah Celal Sok 6 ☎ 0332 353 4424, ⊕ hichhotel.com. The painstaking attention to detail makes this designer hotel a truly unique find, marrying Sufi-inspired decor with all the trimmings of a luxurious modern hotel. Housed in a grand 200-year-old building in a prime

location opposite the Mevlâna Museum, the thirteen themed rooms feature hand-woven rugs, romantic drapes and wrought-iron furniture, as well as iPad docks, espresso machines and minibars. Even the breakfast is a cut above, with fresh-squeezed juice and a huge buffet spread served in the wood-beamed basement or the flower-filled garden. Enthusiastic, friendly staff are the icing on the cake. **€70**

Mevlâna Sema Mevlâna Cad 67 ☎ 0332 350 4623. This central hotel could do with an update, but it's good value and the whirling dervish mosaics in the lobby add a cheerful vibe. Rooms are a bit drab but well-equipped and the breakfast buffet is well stocked. **₺100**

7

Rumi Fakih Sok 3, behind the Mevlâna museum ☎ 0332 353 1121, ⓦ rumihotel.com. Behind its unmistakable aqua-blue facade, *Rumi* offers smart, comfortable rooms, room service and all mod cons. The central yet quiet location, helpful English-speaking staff and generous breakfast buffet served on the rooftop terrace are additional pluses. ₺150

★ **Ulusan** Çarşı PTT Arkası (on a side street behind the PTT building) ☎ 0332 351 5004. Make no mistake, this is a humble, no-frills hotel, but it's ideal for anyone on a budget and brightened up with homely trinkets. The English-speaking host takes great care of his guests, cooking up toasted sandwiches for breakfast and dishing out city maps and advice. Rooms are clean, comfortable and quiet, and the shared bathrooms are well maintained. ₺90

EATING

While Konya's innate religious conservatism has hampered the development of an "eating out" culture and restaurants serving alcohol are few and far between, there are still some excellent restaurants and a range of **traditional dishes** to sample.

Ali Baba Firin Kebab Şeref Şirin Sok ☎ 0532 581 5601, ⓦ alibabafirinkebap.com. A long-established local joint specializing in Konya's signature dish – *firin* kebab, lamb slow-cooked in a traditional wood-fired oven and served with onion and *pide*. Eat it as the locals do – scoop up the lamb with the bread and wash it down with a glass of *ayran*. Price is by grams, starting around ₺12. Mon–Sat 10am–5pm.

Bolu Aziziye Cad, a few doors up from Damla ☎ 0332 352 4533. A Konya institution serving an excellent *etli ekmek* (the city's signature thin-crust *pide* topped with ground meat and finely diced peppers) and *ayran* for around ₺9. Always packed with locals. Daily 10am–9pm.

Damla Türbe Cad 59 ☎ 0332 352 0881. This smart and spotless kebab *salonu* is a cut above the rest, and one of the best (and most popular) places to try the city's staple foods – tuck into some delicious *bamya* (okra soup), tender *firin* kebabs (₺15) or crispy *etli ekmek* (₺8). No alcohol. Daily 8am–9pm.

Mevlevî Sofrası Amil Çelebi Sok 1, north side of the Mevlâna complex ☎ 0332 353 3341, ⓦ mevlevisofrasi .com. With its terrace offering serene views over the Mevlâna rose gardens, this is the obvious choice for post-sightseeing dining, but surprisingly, the tourist crowds don't come with the typical price bump or drop in quality. Try the hearty *güveç* (a slow-cooked meat casserole, ₺15) followed by *höşmerim* (a sweet doughy dessert, ₺8). Daily 9am–10pm.

★ **Mithat Tirit** Yusufaga Sok 21 ☎ 0332 350 7298. The Konya speciality *tirit* kebab (₺22) is the sole dish on offer here, and unsurprisingly it's cooked to perfection. The rich dish of broth-soaked bread, onion, lamb and tomatoes comes with a topping of yoghurt and sumac and will fill you up for the day. Combine it with a fresh carrot juice and finish with *zerde* (sweet saffron-infused rice pudding). Daily 10am–6pm.

Nar-ı Aşk Art Café Mimar Sinan Sok 6 59 ☎ 0532 337 6070. Swirling with felt whirling dervish mobiles and painted with bold stencils, this kitsch café is crammed with quirky handmade souvenirs. Head downstairs to the cushioned courtyard area for a *turk kalvesi* (Turkish coffee, ₺4) and ask the friendly hosts to read your coffee cup fortune once you've finished shopping. Daily 10am–10pm.

★ **Somatçı** Mengüç Cad 36 ☎ 0332 351 6696, ⓦ somatci.com. *Somatçi's* inspired menu of ancient Ottoman, Sufi and Seljukian dishes and its romantic setting in a beautifully restored townhouse make a winning combination – there's truly nowhere else like it. Expect surprising flavours and traditional ingredients, with highlights including apricot-stuffed chicken, veal and plum pottery kebabs, *badem helvası* (almond *helva*) and *kremalı incir* (stuffed figs with cream). Mains cost around ₺20 and there's no alcohol, so wash it all down with a glass of *sherbet* (a sweet drink favoured by the dervishes) instead. Daily 7.30am–10pm.

DIRECTORY

Banks and exchange There are several *döviz* offices and ATMs on Hükümet Alanı.

Hamam The hamam behind Şerafettin Camii on Hükümet Alanı is everything you could ask of a Turkish bath: all white stone and marble, with traditional tiny round skylights striping the steam with rays of sunlight, and skilled and thorough masseurs (separate wings for men and women; daily 6am–midnight; from ₺18 for a scrub and massage).

Internet Öykü Net, opposite the front entrance of the Catholic church, off Alâeddin Bul.

Police Ferit Paşa Cad (☎ 0332 353 8141).

Post office Kurşuncular Sok (daily 8.30am–midnight).

Around Konya

Konya's tourist office is well geared towards organizing day-trips to the area's more remote archeological and historical remnants. The highlights are **Çatal Höyük**, possibly Anatolia's earliest settlement; the ancient site of **Kilistra**; and the ruined Byzantine churches and monasteries of the **Binbir Kilise** region. Minor sites, like the beautiful crater lake of **Acı Göl** or the isolated ancient ruins of **İvriz**, make pleasant stop-offs en route to Cappadocia, but are hardly worth rerouting for.

Çatal Höyük

58km southeast of Konya • Daily 8.30am–5.30pm • Free • Catch the Karkin minibus from the old *otogar* on Fergandede Cad (Mon–Fri noon; 1hr 10min; ₺5); hire a taxi (₺130–150 return, but be sure to agree a price up front, including wait time); or drive from Konya on the Karaman/Silifke road, Highway 715, then take a left to Çumra 2km before İçeri Çumra, and follow signs

Discovered by the British archeologist James Mellaart in 1958, and added to the UNESCO World Heritage list in 2012, the important Neolithic site of **Çatal Höyük** consists of twin, flattened hills that are supposed to resemble the shape of a fork – hence the name, which means "Fork Tumulus". An international team, resident on site in summer, continues to excavate the prehistoric tumuli here. Summer is the best time to visit, but bear in mind that you'll need a lively imagination, as there's little to see.

Exciting discoveries at Çatal Höyük have provided significant clues about one of the world's oldest civilizations, dating from 6800 BC. Evidence pointed to entire complexes of houses, crammed together without streets to separate them, and entered through holes in the roof. Also found were murals of men being eaten by vultures, animal-head trophies stuffed with squeezed clay, and human bones wrapped in straw matting and placed under the seats in a burial chamber. There is also the world's first landscape painting, a mural depicting the eruption of a volcano, presumably nearby Hasan Dağa.

Most famous of all are the statuettes of the **mother goddess**, supposed to be related to the Phrygian goddess Cybele and her successor Artemis. The baked earthenware or stone figures are 5–10cm tall and show a large-breasted, broad-hipped woman crouching to give birth. While the most interesting pieces are now in Ankara's Museum of Anatolian Civilizations (see p.471), a small **museum** near the site entrance houses some less remarkable finds.

Binbir Kilise

Directly north of Karaman, 107km southeast of Konya • Take a paved road 21km north from Karaman via Kılbasan, then turn left (northwest) and follow a rougher dirt track for 10km towards the village of Maden Şehir

Scattered across the base of the extinct volcano Kara Dağ, the remote region known as **Binbir Kilise**, or "A Thousand and One Churches", does indeed hold close to that number of ruined churches and monasteries. Most date from the ninth to the eleventh centuries, when the area was a refuge for persecuted Christians.

The village of **MADEN ŞEHIR**, in the middle of one of the main concentrations of basalt-built chapels, is all that's left of a substantial, unidentified town that flourished from Hellenistic to Byzantine times.

Kilistra

Gökyurt, 45km southwest of Konya • No public transport

The ancient site of **Kilistra**, established in Hellenistic and Roman times, remains something of an enigma. It's said to be one of a handful of "hidden cities" that were built by the first Christian settlers in Anatolia, and carved into the rocks in a similar architectural style to the cave dwellings of Cappadocia. The site lies on the famous King's Road, and St Paul supposedly stopped by here en route to nearby Lycia. That claim is loosely supported by an area of the city named **Paulönü**, and the **Sünbül church** (a possible translation of St Paul).

Today the site lies within the traditional farming village of **GÖKYURT**, renowned for its so-called "black-hive honey". It contains the well-preserved remains of a meeting hall, antique tombs, numerous cave dwellings and the intriguing **Sandikkay chapel** carved from a single piece of rock.

Cappadocia

The unique landscape of **Cappadocia** has become one of the star attractions of Turkey. Despite being plastered across tour brochures, however, it still retains much of the mystique that makes it so enchanting. While the dryness and omnipresent dust give an impression of barrenness, the volcanic tuff that forms the land is exceedingly fertile, and the peculiar formations of soft, dusty rock have been populated for millennia. The area's major appeal has to be its startlingly dramatic vistas – light dancing over fields of **fairy chimneys** and still-inhabited **rock caves** dotted throughout modern villages. Both local **wine**, produced since Hittite times, and the renowned **pottery** works fashioned from the clay of the Kızılırmak River, are still key crafts. In addition, the **horses** from which the region takes its name – Cappadocia translates from Hittite as "land of the beautiful horses" – still play a big role in local life, and make a popular way for visitors to explore the region.

The most famous sites are located within a triangle delineated by the roads connecting Nevşehir, Avanos and Ürgüp. This region holds the greater part of the valleys of fairy chimneys; the **rock-cut churches** of the **Göreme Open-Air Museum**, with their beautiful frescoes; and the **Zelve Open-Air Museum**, a fascinating warren of troglodyte dwellings and churches. **Nevşehir**, the largest town, is an important travel hub, while **Ürgüp** and its neighbouring villages, **Göreme**, **Çavuşin**, **Uçhisar** and **Ortahisar**, all make attractive bases for tours of the surrounding valleys. **Avanos**, beautifully situated on the Kızılırmak River, is the centre of the local pottery industry.

A little further out, the underground cities of **Derinkuyu** and **Kaymaklı** are astonishingly sophisticated labyrinths that attest to the ingenuity of the ancient inhabitants. The **Ihlara** valley near **Aksaray**, a red canyon riddled with churches cut into its sides, is perhaps the

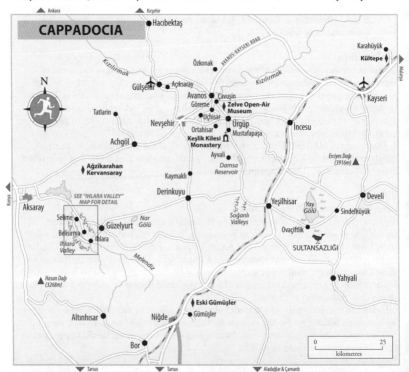

THE GEOLOGICAL FORMATION OF CAPPADOCIA

The peaks of three **volcanoes** – Erciyes, Hasan and Melendiz Dağları – dominate Cappadocia. It was their eruptions, which covered the former plateau of Ürgüp in ash and mud some thirty million years ago, that provided the region's raw material: **tuff**, formed by compressed volcanic ash. Erosion has worked on this soft stone ever since, to form the valleys and curious fairy chimney rock formations for which the region is so famous.

The original eruptions created a vast **erosion basin**, dipping slightly towards the Kızılırmak River, which marks an abrupt division between the fantasy landscapes of rocky Cappadocia and the green farmland around Kayseri. Where the tuff is mixed with rock, usually basalt, the erosion process can result in the famous cone-shape chimneys: the tuff surrounding the basalt is worn away, until it stands at the top of a large cone. Eventually the underpart is eaten away to such an extent that it can no longer hold its capital: the whole thing collapses and the process starts again.

In the **Cemil valley**, near Mustafapaşa, the cones give way to tabular formations – table mountains – caused by the deep grooves made by rivers in the harder geological layers. Another important region lies northwest of the Melendiz mountain range – the valley of the Melendiz Suyu, or **Ihlara valley**. The most individual feature of this region is the red canyon through which the river flows, probably the most beautiful of all the Cappadocian landscapes.

7

most spectacular sight not to have yet felt the full force of tourism. **Kayseri** has long been a quiet provincial capital, recommended for its Selçuk architecture and bazaars, and side trips out to the ski resort on Erciyes Dağı and the Sultansazlığı bird sanctuary. To the south, attractions around the town of **Niğde** include the **Eski Gümüşler** monastery, whose frescoes rival the more famous examples in Göreme.

Brief history

The earliest known settlers in the Cappadocia region were the **Hatti**, whose capital, Hattuşaş, was located north of Nevşehir. The growth of the Hattic civilization was interrupted by the arrival of large groups of Indo-European immigrants from Western Europe, the **Hittites** (see box, p.491). After the fall of the Hittite Empire, around 1200 BC, the region was controlled to varying degrees and at different times by its neighbouring kingdoms, Lydia and Phrygia in the west, and Urartu in the east. This continued until the middle of the sixth century BC, when the Lydian king Croesus was defeated by the Persians under Cyrus the Great.

Saved from Persian rule by the arrival of **Alexander the Great** in 333 BC, Cappadocia subsequently enjoyed independence for 350 years, until it became a Roman province with Kayseri (Caesarea) as its capital. Despite this nominal annexation, effective **independence** was ensured in the following centuries by the relative lack of interest of the Roman and Byzantine rulers, whose only real concerns were to control the roads (and thereby keep open eastern trading routes), and to extort tributes. Meanwhile the locals existed in much the same way as they do now, living in rock-hewn dwellings or building houses out of local stone, and relying on agriculture, viniculture and livestock breeding.

This neglect, combined with the influence of an important east–west trading route, enabled various faiths, creeds and philosophies to flourish. **Christianity** was introduced in the first century by St Paul; suffering from increasingly frequent attacks by Arab raiders, the new Christian communities sought refuge in the hills, where they carved out dwelling places, churches and monasteries.

The **Selçuk Turks** arrived in the eleventh century, quickly establishing good relations with the local communities and channelling their energy into improving trade routes and building the *kervansarays* that are strung along these roads to this day. After the Selçuk Empire was defeated by the **Mongols** in the middle of the thirteenth century, Cappadocia was controlled by the Karaman dynasty, based in Konya, until it was incorporated into the Ottoman Empire in the fourteenth century. The last Christian Greeks left the area in the 1920s, during the exchange of populations by the Greek and Turkish governments.

Nevşehir

Home to Cappadocia's main airport, **NEVŞEHIR** is an important transport hub, but hardly a place to linger. It consists of a couple of scruffy streets (**Atatürk Bulvarı** and **Lale Caddesi**) with no real centre or monumental architecture.

Since the *otogar* lies just 1km north of the town centre, it's easy to make a quick foray downtown; if you do stay, you'll find that dolmuş side trips to the monastic complex at Açıksaray are also straightforward.

Although the long walk up to the remains of the Ottoman **kale** (castle) in the heart of the old city is pleasant enough, once you get there, there's little left apart from a few crenellated walls.

Damat İbrahim Paşa Camii

On the side of the citadel hill

Completed in 1726, the **Damat İbrahim Paşa Camii** is still the most imposing building in Nevşehir, with its *medrese* and library above it and a tea garden directly below. Its construction stone is an attractive, unadorned yellow, while its internal painting, especially under the sultan's loge and around the casements, is delightful.

Nevşehir Museum

Yeni Kayseri Cad • Tues–Sun 8am–5pm • Free

Nevşehir Museum (Nevşehir Müzesi) is well worth the fifteen-minute walk from the tourist office. Its comprehensively labelled exhibits include three terracotta sarcophagi, dating from the third to fourth centuries AD, which resemble abstract mummy cases with little doors inserted at face and knee level. Finds from the Phrygian and Byzantine periods include mirrors, pins, spoons, terracotta pots and the like; upstairs is an exhibition of Turkish carpets and kilims, and the looms on which they were made, as well as lovely old silver Ottoman jewellery.

ARRIVAL AND DEPARTURE
NEVŞEHIR

By plane The airport is 30km northwest of the town centre. You can arrange for an Argeus tour-agency minibus (☎0384 341 4688, ⓦcappadociaexclusive.com) to meet Turkish Airlines flights and take you to the village of your choice in Cappadocia.
Destinations Istanbul (2 daily; 1hr 20min).
By bus or dolmuş Nevşehir *otogar* is 1km north – a short dolmuş or city bus ride – from the town centre. Most

minibuses running to and from Göreme, Avanos and Ürgüp drop off and pick up on Hafız İnce Kara Cad in the centre.
Destinations Adana (3 daily; 5hr); Ankara (7 daily; 4hr 30min); Antalya (3 daily; 11hr); Fethiye (1 daily; 11hr 30min); Göreme (every 30min; 15min); Hacıbektaş (4 daily; 1hr); Istanbul (3 daily; 10hr); Kayseri (8 daily; 2hr); Konya (6 daily; 3hr); Mersin (3 daily; 5hr); Ürgüp (every 30min; 30min).

INFORMATION

Tourist office Atatürk Bul, on the right as you head downhill towards Ürgüp (daily 8am–5.30pm; ☎0384 213 3659).

Post office Lale Cad, near the top of Atatürk Bul.

ACCOMMODATION

Hotel Şems Atatürk Bul 27 ☎0384 213 3597, ⓦsemshotel.com. A friendly and comfortable enough option for if you find yourself stuck in town. Rooms are

clean and have en-suite bathrooms with guaranteed hot water, but are sparsely furnished; ask for a quieter room at the back. ₺80

Açıksaray and around

19km north of Nevşehir • Served by Gülşehir dolmuşes from Nevşehir's *otogar* (every 30min)

Açıksaray is a sixth- to seventh-century monastic complex, carved out of fairy chimneys and tuff cliffs. The abandoned remains include living quarters, stables and some decorative church facades, stretching around a square kilometre.

Far more rewarding is the nearby **church of St John**, 2km north towards Gülşehir (daily 8.30am–5.30pm; ₺5), and home to some of the most vibrant **frescoes** in Cappadocia, rescued from beneath the soot in 1995. As it is so rarely visited, you have time and space to appreciate the poignant biblical scenes, including the *Last Supper* and the *Betrayal by Judas*.

Hacıbektaş

45km north of Nevşehir • Catch an Ankara-bound bus from Nevşehir, or a dolmuş from Gülşehir, 20km north of Nevşehir

The small town of **HACIBEKTAŞ** was chosen by one of the greatest medieval Sufic philosophers, Hacı Bektaş Veli (see box below), as the location of a centre of scientific study. It was renamed in his honour after his death, and his tomb is located within the **Hacı Bektaş monastery complex**. The main part of the complex, however, dates from the Ottoman period, when it was the headquarters of a large community of Bektaşi dervishes.

Hacıbektaş is also well known for its **onyx**, by far the cheapest in the region – shops are dotted along the street that leads up to the monastery.

7

The monastery complex

Tues–Sun 8am–5pm • ₺8

Construction of the **monastery complex** started during the reign of Sultan Orhan in the fourteenth century, and it reopened as a **museum** in 1964. It comprises three courtyards, the second of which contains the attractive Aslanlı Çeşmesi, the **lion fountain**, named after a lion statue brought from Egypt in 1853. The sacred *karakazan* or **black kettle** (actually a cauldron) can be seen in the kitchen to the right of the courtyard. Important to both the Bektaşi sect and the janissaries, the black kettle originally symbolized communality, with possible reference to the Last Supper of the Christian faith.

To the left of the courtyard, the **Meydan Evi**, where formal initiation ceremonies and acts of confession took place, bears the earliest inscription in the complex, dated 1367. Its beautifully restored timber roof shows an ancient construction technique that's still in use in rural houses in central and eastern Anatolia. It's now an exhibition hall containing objects of significance to the order, including musical instruments and a late portrait of Hacı Bektaş, apparently deep in mystical reverie.

The third courtyard holds a **rose garden** and a well-kept **graveyard**, where the tombs bear the distinctive headwear of the Bektaşi order. The **tomb of the sage** is also located

---

THE LIFE AND TEACHINGS OF HACI BEKTAŞ VELİ

While little is known about the life of **Hacı Bektaş Veli**, he is believed to have lived from 1208 to 1270. Like other Turkish intellectuals of the time, he was educated in Khorasan, where he became well versed in religion and mysticism. After journeying with his brother, he returned to Anatolia and lived in Kayseri, Kırşehir and Sivas. Eventually he settled in a hamlet of seven houses, Suluca Karahöyük, the present-day location of the monastery.

Hacı Bektaş's **teachings**, on the other hand, are well known. His great work, the *Makalat*, gives an account of a four-stage path to enlightenment or *Marifet* – a level of constant contemplation and prayer. The faults that grieved him most were ostentation, hypocrisy and inconsistency: "It is of no avail to be clean outside if there is evil within your soul." This could be the origin of the unorthodox customs of later followers of the **Bektaşi sect**, which included drinking wine, smoking hashish, eating during Ramadan and – for women – uncovering the head outside the home. Hacı Bektaş's widely quoted dictum on women was unequivocal: "A nation which does not educate its women cannot progress."

The teachings reverberated throughout the Muslim world, and sects including the Bektaşi, the Alevi and the Tahtacı still follow traditions that originated in his doctrines. These now form an important counterbalancing force to Islamic fundamentalism in Turkey.

An annual **festival**, held in Hacıbektaş on August 16–18, celebrates the philosopher's life.

in the third courtyard, entered through the Akkapı, a white-marble entranceway decorated with typical Selçuk motifs including a double-headed eagle. A small room off the corridor leading to the tomb is said to have been the cell of Hacı Bektaş himself.

Underground settlements

Among the most extraordinary phenomena of the Cappadocia region are the remains of **underground settlements**, some of them large enough to have accommodated up to thirty thousand people. Around forty such settlements, from villages to vast cities, have been discovered, but only a few have so far been opened to the public. The best known are **Derinkuyu** and **Kaymaklı**, on the road from Nevşehir to Niğde. There are no fairy chimneys here, but the ground consists of the same volcanic tuff, out of which the beleaguered, ever-resourceful Cappadocians created vast subterranean cities that are almost completely unnoticeable from ground level.

Brief history

The underground cities are thought to date back to **Hittite** times at least (1900–1200 BC). Hittite-style seals have been found during excavations, and other Hittite remains, such as a lion statue, have turned up. The subterranean rooms may have served as shelters during the attacks of 1200 BC, when invaders from Thrace destroyed the Hittite Empire. Later the complexes were enlarged by other civilizations, and the presence of missionary schools, churches and wine cellars would seem to indicate that they were used by **Christian communities**.

Derinkuyu

29km south of Nevşehir • Daily: May & June 8am–6pm; July–Sept 8am–7pm; Oct–April 8am–5pm • ₺20 • Dolmuşes from Nevşehir otogar (every 30min)

Derinkuyu, the most thoroughly excavated of the underground cities, is so popular with tour groups that it's advisable to get there before 10am. The city is well lit and the original ventilation system still functions remarkably well, but some of the passages are low and narrow and can feel claustrophobic. The lowest floor in particular is reached by a very shallow passageway, best avoided by anyone with back problems.

The area cleared to date occupies 1500 square metres and consists of a total of eight floors reaching to a depth of 55m. On the first two floors, you'll see stables, winepresses and a dining hall or school with two long, rock-cut tables; on the third and fourth floors, living quarters, churches, armouries and tunnels; and on the lower levels, a crucifix-shaped church, a meeting hall with three supporting columns, a dungeon and a grave. A circular passageway in a room off the meeting hall is believed to have been a confessional.

The city takes its name, meaning "deep well", from the 52 large **ventilation shafts** and **deep wells** that drop between 70m and 85m, far below the lowest floor level. A number of escape routes connect different floors, while passages lead beyond the city; one is thought to have gone all the way to Kaymaklı, 9km away. The walls of the rooms are completely undecorated, but chisel marks are clearly visible and give some idea of the work that went into the creation of this extraordinary place. Most evocative are the huge **circular doors** that could be used to seal one level from another. Virtually impregnable from the outside, these doors would have been closed with a pole through the circular hole in their centre. Once the door was secure, arrows could have been shot through the hole.

Kaymaklı

On Nevşehir–Niğde highway, 9km north of Derinkuyu • Daily: March–Sept 8am–7pm; Oct–Feb 8am–5pm • ₺20 • Dolmuşes from Nevşehir's otogar (Mon–Fri every 15min, Sat & Sun every 30min)

The underground city of **Kaymaklı** is slightly smaller, and thus less popular, than Derinkuyu. While only five of its levels have been excavated to date, there's still plenty to marvel at. The layout is very similar to Derinkuyu, and showcases such ingenuities as the winery, with its 30m-deep winepress, and the 60m-deep ventilation shaft (peek inside to see the footholds along the wall). Small living spaces open into underground plazas with various functions, the more obvious of which are stables, smoke-blackened kitchens and storage spaces. Most adults have to duck to get through the low passageways.

Kaymaklı's small size means that the streets are easy to navigate without a guide, but the added information you get from a tour certainly helps to bring the place to life.

Uçhisar

Uçhisar, 7km east of Nevşehir, is the first truly Cappadocian village en route to the centre of the region from Nevşehir. Much quieter than neighbouring Göreme, it's extremely popular with French visitors, who have been coming here for decades. Its stunning hillside residences are home to some of the region's most luxurious **accommodation**.

Uçhisar Castle

Daily 7am–8.15pm • ₺6.5

Uçhisar's imposing, 60m-high **rock/castle** dominates the modern town and makes a striking introduction to Cappadocia's extraordinary geology – it's riddled with abandoned caves and tunnels that once housed the entire village. The best time for a visit is at sunset, when the views of the surrounding countryside, including Erciyes Dağı to the east and Melendiz and Hasan Dağları to the southwest, are particularly alluring.

7

ARRIVAL AND DEPARTURE   UÇHISAR

By bus or dolmuş Dolmuşes run approximately every 30min from Nevşehir (15min), Göreme (10min) and Ürgüp (30min), dropping visitors in the upper village, just west of the centre. Regardless of what overzealous taxi drivers may say, you can also flag down a dolmuş from anywhere along the main road to Göreme, below the village.

ACCOMMODATION

The old village on the hillside is home to an array of **plush hotels** and restaurants, which have engulfed many of the charming village pensions and left budget options few and far between.

Binbir Gece (1001 Nuits) Orhan Gök, just off the main square in the upper village ☎0384 219 2293. This humble pension is looking a little faded and could do with a lick of paint, but it's among the cheapest you'll find in Uçhisar and boasts a first-class view from its spacious terrace. **₺80**

Kaya Pension Below the rock/castle ☎0384 219 2441, ⓦkayapension.com. The best of the lower-priced options, this homely pension is quirkily decorated, with traditional musical instruments hung up around the restaurant area and hallways strewn with brightly patterned kilims. Rooms are simple, but clean and well furnished, and the terrace area has a relaxed vibe. Don't confuse it with the decidedly more pricey *Kaya Hotel* nearby. **₺50**

Millstone Cave Suites Divanlı Sok 20 ☎0384 219 2288, ⓦmillstonecavesuites.com. An impressive architectural feat with a warren of thirteen rooms sculpted from stone, marble and original tuff, *Millstone* has an industrial chic feel. The sleek interiors are seamless, from the repurposed teak furniture to the spacious stone bathrooms to the specially designed *Millstone* coffee filters. **₺150**

★**Rox Cappadocia** Koyun Yolu Sok 11 ☎0384 219 2406, ⓦroxcappadocia.com. With its enthusiastic welcome, charmingly eclectic decor and rooftop terrace overlooking the valleys, *Rox*, the latest addition to Uçhisar's growing collection of boutique hotels, makes guests feel instantly at home. English-speaking owner Arda is hands-on in both design and service, and the result is both eye-catching and functional. The highlights are in the details – the six individually styled rooms have huge comfy beds and espresso machines, the breakfast is excellent and the hanging "nests" on the terrace offer a romantic hideaway from which to watch the sunset. **₺110**

Taşkonaklar (Rocky Palace) On the cliff-side road as you head down to the lower village ☎0384 219 3001, ⓦtaskonaklar.com. If self-effacing luxury is what you're after, this stunning boutique hotel ticks all the boxes. It's an architectural accomplishment in itself, with its beautifully preserved rock dwellings embellished with arched ceilings, uniquely shaped alcoves and original chimneys dating back 150 years. Antique furnishings, a chic garden terrace bursting with roses and perhaps the best views in town make this a classy choice. **₺120**

EATING AND DRINKING

Lil'a Museum Hotel, Tekelli Mah 1 ☎0384 219 2220, Ⓦlil-a.com.tr. Acclaimed for its creative, all-organic Turkish cuisine, *Lil'a* is the ultimate spot for a romantic dinner, with plush furnishings, candlelit tables and stunning views. It's best to reserve a table in advance, and the dress code is strictly smart, with no shorts, trainers or T-shirts allowed. The restaurant also runs cooking classes and cooking tours to those interested in learning about local cuisine. Daily 7–10pm.

Seki Restaurant Argos Hotel ☎0384 219 3130, Ⓦseki.com.tr. The showstopping building and cliff-side location makes a dramatic first impression, but this upmarket restaurant manages to be hip without being pretentious. The menu is ideal for those with a curious palate, adding a contemporary twist to traditional dishes, although you'll pay for the privilege, with mains costing upwards of ₺32 and a 10 percent service charge added. Try the duck *confit* with pumpkin purée and ginger sauce (₺90) followed by home-made fig sorbet. Daily 7.30am–midnight.

DIRECTORY

Banks ATMs are located in the main square, but there are no banks.

Internet The Uçhisar internet café is just off the main square.

Post office Just east of the main square.

Göreme

The village of **GÖREME**, just 3km northeast of Uçhisar, is one of few remaining Cappadocian settlements whose rock-cut houses and fairy chimneys are still inhabited. These, along with the village's celebrated **open-air museum**, make it a hugely popular tourist destination. The honeycomb of cave dwellings etched into the landscape not only provides visual intrigue, but is well-equipped to provide for everyone from budget backpackers to luxury holiday-makers, and there are carpet shops, *pansiyon*s, tour companies and restaurants everywhere.

While the influx of visitors has enabled the local economy to boom, the fragile environment is under increasing pressure, and prolific construction has pushed out most local residents. Despite the **commercialization**, however, Göreme has held on to a degree of authentic charm, and a short stroll off the main street or into the nearby valleys will still take you up into tuff landscapes, vineyards that the locals cultivate for the production of *pekmez* (grape molasses), and the occasional rock-cut church, unknown to the crowds who frequent the nearby museum.

Churches of Göreme

Signposted off Uzundere Cad

Two ancient Christian **churches** are located in the hills above Göreme. Believed to date from the seventh century, **Kadir Durmuş Kilisesi** has a cave house with rock-cut steps next door to it, clearly visible from the path across a vineyard. It's not painted, but it has a fascinating and unusual upstairs gallery, and cradle-shaped tombs outside.

The eleventh-century **Yusuf Koç Kilisesi**, or "church with five pillars", boasts two domes, one of which has been damaged in the past to accommodate a pigeon coop, and frescoes in very good condition. Among them are the *Annunciation*, to the left; saints George and Theodore slaying the dragon, to the right; and *Helena and Constantine* depicted with the True Cross beside the door. The dome above the altar holds the *Madonna and Child*, while below, beside the altar, are the *Four Evangelists*.

Göreme Open-Air Museum

1.5km southeast • Daily: summer 8am–7pm; winter 8am–5pm; last entry 45min before closing • ₺20 including Tokalı Kilise, Karanlık Kilise ₺8, audioguide ₺10

The **Göreme Open-Air Museum** is the best known and most visited of all the monastic settlements in the Cappadocia region. It's also the largest of the religious complexes, and its **churches**, of which there are more than thirty, contain some fascinating frescoes.

FROM TOP GÖREME OPEN-AIR MUSEUM (ABOVE); LAKE EĞİRDİR (P.414) >

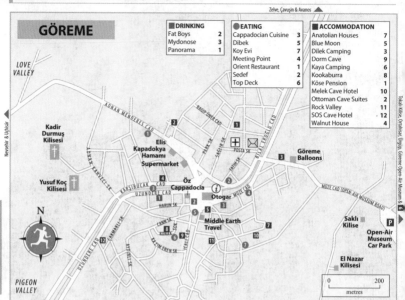

GÖREME

DRINKING
Fat Boys	2
Mydonose	3
Panorama	1

EATING
Cappadocian Cuisine	3
Dibek	5
Koy Evi	7
Meeting Point	4
Orient Restaurant	1
Sedef	2
Top Deck	6

ACCOMMODATION
Anatolian Houses	7
Blue Moon	5
Dilek Camping	3
Dorm Cave	9
Kaya Camping	6
Kookaburra	8
Köse Pension	1
Melek Cave Hotel	10
Ottoman Cave Suites	2
Rock Valley	11
SOS Cave Hotel	12
Walnut House	4

Virtually all date from the period after the Iconoclastic controversy, and mainly from the second half of the ninth to the end of the eleventh century.

The three columned churches

The best-known churches in the main complex of Göreme are the three eleventh-century columned churches: the **Elmalı Kilise** (Church of the Apple), the **Karanlık Kilise** (Dark Church; separate entrance fee of ₺8) and the **Çarıklı Kilise** (Church of the Sandals). All were heavily influenced by Byzantine forms: constructed to an inscribed cross plan, the central dome, supported on columns, contains the Pantocrator above head-and-shoulders depictions of the archangels and seraphim. The painting of the churches, particularly of Elmalı Kilise, is notable for the skill with which the form and movement of the figures correspond to the surfaces they cover, and their features are smoothly modelled. The intricately carved facade of the restored Karanlık Kilise is painted an expensive blue colour, obtained from the mineral azurite.

Barbara Kilise

The open-air museum holds various late eleventh-century single-aisle churches that are covered in crude geometric patterns and linear pictures, painted straight onto the rock. The **Barbara Kilise** (Church of St Barbara) in this style is named after a depiction of the saint on the north wall. Christ is represented on a throne in the apse. The strange insect-figure for which the church is also known must have had a symbolic or magical significance that is now lost.

Yılanlı Kilise

The **Yılanlı Kilise** (Church of the Snake) is most famous for the depiction of St Onophrius on the west wall of the nave. St Onophrius was a hermit who lived in the Egyptian desert, eating only dates, with a foliage loincloth for cover. Opposite him, Constantine the Great and his mother St Helena are depicted holding the True Cross. Between the Yılanlı and the Karanlık churches is a **refectory** with a rock-cut table designed to take about fifty diners.

Tokalı Kilise

50m before museum ticket office • Use museum ticket to gain entrance

The best-preserved and most fascinating of the churches on the road back to Göreme village from the open-air museum is the **Tokalı Kilise** (Church with the Buckle). Different in plan to others in the area, it features a transverse nave and an atrium hewn out of an earlier church, known as the "Old Church". The **frescoes** here, dating from the second decade of the tenth century, are classic examples of the archaic period of Cappadocian painting: the style is linear, but like the mosaics of Aya Sofya in Istanbul, the faces are modelled by the use of different intensities of colour. The paintings in the New Church are magnificent examples of tenth-century Byzantine art, with scenes of the Passion and Resurrection: the Descent from the Cross, the Entombment, the Holy Women at the Sepulchre and the Resurrection.

Saklı Kilise

Halfway between museum and village

The **Saklı Kilise** (Hidden Church) uses Cappadocian landscapes complete with fairy chimneys as a background for biblical scenes. It lives up to its name, so ask the keyholder to show you the way. You can find him in the shop Hikmet's Place.

Hiking to Uçhisar

The most rewarding **walk** in the Göreme region is the 4km, two-hour hike to the picturesque village of **Uçhisar**. Starting above the *Ataman Hotel*, the path heads through the Uzundere valley, passing through rock-cut tunnels into the heart of the Cappadocian countryside. Good shoes are essential, and the final descent into Uçhisar is precipitous, with narrow stretches, but it's an easy route to follow. Minibuses run the route frequently, so you can easily catch a ride back to Göreme.

ARRIVAL AND DEPARTURE — GÖREME

By bus Göreme's *otogar* is in the town centre. Cappadocia Express (☎ 0384 271 3070, ⦿ cappadociatransport.com) runs airport shuttle buses to Nevşehir (₺20) and Kayseri (₺25), with hotel pick-up.

Destinations Alanya (2 daily; 12hr); Ankara (5 daily; 4hr); Antalya (2 daily; 10hr); Denizli (2 daily; 10hr); Eğirdir (2 daily; 8hr); Istanbul (3 daily; 11hr); İzmir (1 daily; 11hr 30min); Kayseri (hourly; 1hr 30min); Konya (4 daily; 3hr); Marmaris (2 daily; 15hr); Nevşehir (hourly; 30min); Ürgüp (hourly; 20min).

Car and bike rental Several companies around the *otogar* rent out cars, mountain bikes and scooters, the most reliable being Öz Cappadocia (cars from ₺120/day; jeeps from ₺200/day; bikes from ₺40/day; mopeds from ₺45 for 2hr; ☎ 0384 271 2159, ⦿ ozcappadocia.com).

INFORMATION AND TOURS

Tourist office In the centre of the village, next to the *otogar* (daily 5am–8pm; ☎ 0384 271 2558).

Tours Reputable tour companies include Middle Earth Travel (☎ 0384 271 2528, ⦿ middleearthtravel.com), Neşe (☎ 0384 271 2525, ⦿ nesetour.com) and New Göreme (☎ 0384 271 2166, ⦿ newgoreme.com). All offer daily tours from €35/person including the Ihlara valley, Soğanlı and the underground cities.

ACCOMMODATION

With tourism booming in Göreme, entrepreneurial locals are developing hotels on every available plot of land. While the desire for authentic cave dwellings is at least keeping the landscape attractive, many of the cheap and cheerful pensions beloved by backpackers are being transformed into **luxury suites** with price tags to match.

CAMPSITES

Dilek Camping Müze Cad 11 ☎ 0384 271 2395. A short walk from the town centre, with basic but clean washing and cooking facilities, free wi-fi in communal areas and a pool, restaurant and tour company on site, this is a good budget option for campers. There's a range of powered campsites and simple wooden cabins, plus breakfast available (₺10/person). The rates here are for two people/night, but weekly rates are available. Tent ₺35, cabin ₺100

Kaya Camping 2.5km southeast on Ortahisar road ☎ 0384 343 3100 ⊜ kayacamping@gmail.com. A

OUTDOOR AND ADVENTURE TOURISM IN CAPPADOCIA

ATV SAFARIS

ATV safaris have become hugely popular in recent years, but be careful to choose a company with a record for safety, which provides proper instruction and takes precautions to limit environmental damage.

Oz Cappadocia Uzundere Cad, Göreme ☎ 0384 271 2159, ⊛ ozcappadocia.com. Offers a range of ATV safaris; ₺80 for an hour including guide, helmet and practice time at their off-road racecourse before heading out.

HIKING

While there are plenty of **hiking trails** through the valleys, so far only basic sketch maps are widely available, and signposts sparse. The trails through the Ihlara Gorge (see p.452), and from Göreme to Uçhisar through Pigeon valley, are among the most popular routes with independent walkers.

Kirkit Voyage Atatürk Cad 50, Avanos ☎ 0384 511 3259, ⊛ kirkit.com. Guided hikes with English-speaking guides, from €50/day including lunch.
Middle Earth Travel Göreme ☎ 0384 271 2559, ⊛ middleearthtravel.com. From €60/person for hikes in the Ihlara valley; from €190 for two-day climbs up Erciyes Dağı or Hasan Dağı; from €590 for a one-week trek, including accommodation and meals.
Walking Mehmet ☎ 0532 382 2069, ⊛ walking mehmet.net. Local guide Mehmet knows the area inside out and speaks English fluently; group hikes for €80 a day.

HORSERIDING

With its wide-open spaces, gaping canyons and jutting mountain paths, Cappadocia evokes the Wild West, and **horseriding** makes a natural way to explore. Several ranches have opened up, but be wary of so-called "Turkish cowboys" or "horse whisperers", with no track record of safety and horse welfare – tales of mistreated, untrained horses and unsafe tack are common. Both companies below are long-standing and reputable, with excellent safety equipment and genuine horses for all levels.

Akhal-Teke Gesteriç Sok, Avanos ☎ 0384 511 5171, ⊛ akhal-tekehorsecenter.com. Modern stables housed in a beautiful garden and restaurant complex, with lessons also available in their arena. Rides start at €20 for an hour, but there are also a range of multi-day treks.
Kirkit Voyage Atatürk Cad 50, Avanos ☎ 0384 511 3259, ⊛ kirkit.com. A well-regarded stable with well-trained horses, tours to suit all abilities, and friendly, knowledgeable guides. This place featured on the US TV series *Equitrekking*, and has great options for more experienced riders too. Two-hour treks from €40; half-day, day and multi-day treks (up to nine days) also possible.

---

friendly, spacious campsite shaded by apricot and cherry trees, with all facilities including a small shop selling necessities, wi-fi and electricity throughout, and a huge swimming pool. The rates here are for two people/night, but weekly deals are available. Tent €20, caravan €22

BACKPACKERS/PENSIONS

Blue Moon Müze Yolu 24 ☎ 0384 271 2433, ⊛ bluemooncavehotel.com. An easy stroll from the *otogar*, with sunny, tastefully decorated rooms equipped with TV, kettle and minibar. The huge terrace makes a lively spot to spend the evening, welcoming a mixed bag of backpackers, families and older travellers. €60
Dorm Cave Efendi Sok 4 ☎ 0384 271 2770, ⊛ travellerscave.com. The latest addition to the ever-growing Cappadocian chain of *Traveller's Cave* hotels, this is a reliable budget choice, run by young, English-speaking staff. The fourteen- and sixteen-bed dorms are basic, but

have everything you need for a comfortable stay – proper duvets, clean bathrooms and breakfast included. There's also a four-bed female dorm, doubles and triples. Dorm €10, double €30
Kookaburra Konak Sok 10 ☎ 0384 271 2549, ⊛ kookaburramotel.com. Comfy beds, clean, spacious bathrooms and a nice quiet location make this the perfect place for budget travellers to enjoy home comforts. Lovably eccentric owner İhsan is Göreme-born and will be happy to share his vast local knowledge over a beer on the idyllic rooftop terrace; his eclectic collection of antiques includes traditional Cappadocia clothing, musical instruments and a kilim loom. Dorm €10, double €40
Köse Pension Just off the Avanos road, near the post office ☎ 0384 271 2294, ⊛ kosepension.com. Run by the hospitable Mehmet and Dawn, this travellers' favourite offers a choice of dorm beds, doubles with and without bathrooms, wooden huts and simple singles, all clean, snug

HOT-AIR BALLOONING

The region's canyons and fairy chimneys take on dazzling hues at sunrise and **hot-air balloon** trips have become ubiquitous. Hundreds of balloons take to the skies early each morning, so you won't be alone, but it's nevertheless an unmissable adventure. Be sure to pick a reputable company; very cheap prices may indicate that the company scrimps on safety. Check what the policy is if you can't fly, too – flights cancelled due to bad weather should be refunded or rearranged free of charge.

Butterfly Balloons Uzundere Cad, Göreme ☎ 0384 271 3010, ⓦ butterflyballoons.com. Reliable, safety-conscious and uncrowded, with daily flight departures; prices from €175/hr, including transfer, breakfast and champagne on landing.
Kapadokya Balloons ☎ 0384 271 2442, ⓦ kapadokyaballoons.com. The original operator, with twenty-five years' experience and highly professional pilots. Standard flights (1hr) begin at dawn and cost €175/person, including transfers, insurance and champagne breakfast.

MOUNTAIN BIKING

Cappadocia appears tailor-made for **mountain biking** with its hilly terrain, plunging valleys and far-reaching networks of dirt tracks running between the many villages and valleys. The region also hosts the annual Cappadocia Mountain Bike Festival, which attracts top bikers from around the world.

Kirkit Voyage Atatürk Cad 50, Avanos ☎ 0384 511 3259, ⓦ kirkit.com. Top-quality mountain-bike rental at €20 a day, and day-tours from €70 including lunch.
Middle Earth Travel Göreme ☎ 0384 271 2559, bikinginturkey.com. Guided and self-guided bike tours from €70 depending on group size, plus mountain-bike rental.

SKIING AND SNOWSHOEING

Between Christmas and early March, winter snows give the Cappadocian landscape a hauntingly beautiful appearance, and snowshoeing treks are a unique way to soak up the scenery. The resort on the flank of Erciyes Dağı (see p.460) has reliable snow and reasonable facilities for downhill skiing.

Argeus İstiklal Cad 7, Ürgüp ☎ 0384 341 4688, ⓦ cappadociaexclusive.com. This ski-touring and mountaineering operator organizes all-inclusive guided tours.
Kirkit Voyage Atatürk Cad 50, Avanos ☎ 0384 511 3259, ⓦ kirkit.com. Snowshoeing treks for €50 a day including lunch.

and cheerfully decorated. There's also a pleasant garden, swimming pool and home-cooked breakfast (extra charge) and dinners on request. Dorm ₺20, double ₺120
Rock Valley Isali Mah, Iceri Dere Sok ☎ 0384 271 2831, ⓦ rockvalleycappadocia.com. Although the interiors are looking a little shabby these days, this pension still makes a worthy choice for those on a budget, thanks to its large swimming pool and lively communal areas. The cheapest doubles share bathrooms, while there are various dorms, including a female-only option. Dorm ₺35, double ₺110
★ **Walnut House** Uzundere Cad 6 ☎ 0384 271 2235, ⓦ walnuthousehotel.com. A delightful family-run pension in the village centre, flanked by beautiful rose gardens and walnut trees; this place instantly feels like home. The simple yet stylish rooms are the masterpiece of the architect owner, and feature walnut and wrought-iron furnishings, fluffy duvets and pillows, plenty of natural light and heated marble floors throughout. The backyard vegetable garden supplies the home-made breakfasts. €40

HOTELS

★ **Anatolian Houses** Garferli Mah ☎ 0384 271 2463, ⓦ anatolianhouses.com.tr. Built around five natural fairy chimneys and sculpted from pristine white stone, this stunning hotel has a range of individually designed cave rooms and suites to choose from, plus two restaurants serving Anatolian and Indian cuisine. Most impressive is the heavenly courtyard, where the pool, waterfall and wine fountain lead through to an underground spa, a work of art in glistening marble, with a large indoor pool and hamam. €100
Melek Cave Hotel Cevizler Sok 28 ☎ 0384 271 2223, ⓦ melekcave.com. A quiet, leafy courtyard, stone stairwells and hobbit-hole doorways lead into a warren cave and stone-arch rooms. The rooms themselves are

sparse, albeit homely and good value, while the affable staff go above and beyond. ₺**100**

★**Ottoman Cave Suites** Avcilar Mah, Okul Sok 6 ☎0384 271 3090, ⓦottomancavesuites.com. Regal opulence meets caveman chic, with thirteen exquisite cave and stone rooms set around an atmospheric courtyard. It's the details that will win you over – helpful English-speaking staff, a fresh and varied breakfast buffet and complimentary tea, coffee and bottled water. It's worth splashing out on a suite – undeniably romantic with their king-size round beds, sumptuous furnishings and gigantic marble-floored bathrooms. €**70**

SOS Cave Hotel Just off Uzundere Cad ☎0384 271 2134, ⓦsoscavehotel.com. This humble and incredibly welcoming hotel has been open for more than 25 years and offers great-value rooms (including nine authentic cave rooms). The genuinely friendly staff can provide a wealth of honest information about local sights and tours – to top it all, there's a spacious terrace and free pick-up from the *otogar*. €**50**

EATING

★**Cappadocian Cuisine** Uzundere Cad ☎0536 964 6225. Local food at local prices is the order of the day here, and while they might serve more tourists than locals these days, they haven't lost sight of their roots. Kebabs and casseroles start from ₺15 and include generous heaps of rice and salad. Owner Hatice also invites small groups into her traditional cave house nearby, where she'll cook up her most delicious dishes in her own kitchen for around ₺20/person; bookings essential. Daily 6.30am–10.30pm.

★**Dibek** On the main square ☎0384 271 2209, ⓦdibektraditionalcook.com. With its lantern-lit vaulted caves, polished oak beams and kilim-strewn alcoves, this 475-year-old cave dwelling oozes atmosphere. Settle onto traditional floor cushions and tuck into local speciality *testi kebab* (a meat or vegetable dish slow-cooked in a sealed clay pot; ₺42, preorder, as they take 3hr to cook) – *Dibek* is one of few places that actually cooks them within the clay pots. Accompany it with a glass of the home-made house wine and village dessert *aside* (an oddly more-ish sweet made from flour, oil and grape molasses; ₺8). Daily 8am–late.

Koy Evi Aydınkırağı Sok 40 ☎0384 271 2008, ⓦcappadociakoyevi.com. On a mission to bring "village food" to the masses, *Koy Evi* is deservedly popular with tour groups. The signature "village soup" is delicious, the *meze* varied and the bread is baked fresh in the outdoor *tandir* (stone oven) – for the full effect, opt for the four-course menu for a very reasonable ₺35. Daily 8am–1am.

Meeting Point Müze Cad 34 ☎0535 894 9436. Once the go-to spot for fresh fruit smoothies, this easy-to-find café has recently changed hands and turned its attention to more traditional fare. It's still a lively spot, with a rooftop terrace and cheap eats like *gözleme* (₺8) and *tantuni* (*lavaş*

wraps, from ₺7). Daily: summer 8.30am–11.30pm; winter 9am–9pm.

Orient Restaurant Adnan Menderes Cad ☎0384 271 2346, ⓦorientrestaurant.net. One of Göreme's longest-running restaurants, dating to 1986, *Orient* has a romantic ambience, with candlelit tables in its leafy courtyard. There's a wide selection of Turkish and international cuisine, using ingredients sourced from their organic vegetable garden out the back, plus an extensive wine list and four-course set menus for ₺35. Daily 9am–midnight.

Sedef Bilal Eroglu Cad ☎0384 271 2356, ⓦsedefrestaurant.com. An excellent choice for authentic, reasonably priced Turkish cuisine, with a good mix of both locals and tourists. The sizzling casseroles (from ₺22) are always a hit, but it's the extras that make the difference – mounds of well-seasoned salad, scrumptious *meze* and a huge slab of fresh-baked *lavaş* bread. Daily 8am–midnight.

★**Top Deck** Efendi Sok 15 ☎0384 271 2474, ⓔtopdeckcave@yahoo.com. A truly family-run affair, with owners Mustafa – Mr Top Deck himself – and his South African wife Zaida bringing barrel-loads of personality and enthusiasm to the table. Welcomed into their cosy cave home, guests sprawl on plump floor cushions, dine by the flicker of candlelight and feast on flavoursome *meze* and *börek* (from ₺8.50). Mains start from ₺22 and can be tailored for vegetarian or other dietary requirements, and desserts are served with a gigantic scoop of home-made ice cream. Dinner is by reservation only; it's best to book three days in advance, especially in high season. Cooking classes are also possible. June–Sept Mon–Thurs, Sat & Sun 6–10pm; Oct–May Tues–Sat 6–10pm.

DRINKING

Göreme's once-thriving **bar scene** has been somewhat put to rest by the soaring popularity of hot-air ballooning. With many visitors heading to bed early in preparation for a 4am start, there's little market these days for partying.

Fat Boys Belediye Cad ☎0536 936 3652. Long-established pub run by Turkish-Australian couple Yilmaz and Angela, and serving a steady stream of backpackers. There's a relaxed vibe, with board games and international football on TV, a range of local and imported beers (from

₺9) and cheap eats. Daily 9am–late.

Mydonose Müze Cad 18 ☎0384 271 2850. A reliable spot for light bites and drinks, with an excellent selection of American-style coffees (including cream-topped hot chocolates and frappuccinos, from ₺6). The lively rooftop terrace has a good mix of people, great views and comfy seating, and there's a cocktail menu for when you prefer something a little stronger. Daily 8am–2am.

Panorama Uzundere Cad ☉0384 271 2494. This popular backpacker haunt offers a chilled-out vibe, with

bohemian decor, a rainbow of comfy beanbag chairs and cheery staff. There's also free wi-fi, various flavours of water pipes (₺15) and cheap beer (₺10 for a beer and plate of chips). Daily 6am–2am.

DIRECTORY

Banks There are several ATMs near the tourist office.
Hamam Elis Kapadokya Hamamı (☉0384 271 2975) is an immaculate and unintimidating tourist-orientated hamam that offers excellent traditional services, perfect for those

new to the experience. An all-in package costs ₺75 including soap massage/scrub, sauna and swimming pool, while an oil massage is an extra ₺30 for 20min.

Çavuşin and around

A small village set beneath the abandoned cave dwellings of its old town, **ÇAVUŞIN** stands 6km north of Göreme, off the road to Avanos, which lies 4km further north. While rock falls have rendered these caves uninhabitable, and villagers have gradually moved to the other side of town, the area is wonderful to explore – hire a local guide to make the most of it (and avoid crumbling pathways). That said, many of the original caves are in the process of being sold off and with new hotels springing up each year, the peaceful surrounds of the tiny village may not remain much longer.

While Çavuşin is often overpowered by tour groups during the day, its unique landscape and great central location on hiking routes make it an appealing place to stay, at least if you have your own transport.

The best approach is to walk from Göreme through the fabulous tuff landscapes of the **Rose valley**. Follow the path for about forty minutes, and where it takes a helter-skelter bend through a tuff tunnel to the left, follow the vertiginous path to the right, heading down into the Kızılçukur valley: this will bring you to Çavuşin in another thirty minutes or so.

Church of St John the Baptist

Daily 8am–5pm, last entry 4.30pm • Free

A large basilica with a colonnaded and moulded facade set up on the cliff face, the **Church of St John the Baptist** was thought to have been a centre of pilgrimage, most probably constructed in the fifth century. Inside is a votive pit, the only one in

CHRISTIANITY IN CAPPADOCIA

Cappadocia today holds more than a thousand churches, dating from the earliest days of Christianity to the thirteenth century. For many centuries the religious authority of the capital of Cappadocia, Caesarea (present-day Kayseri), extended over the whole of southeast Anatolia, and it was where Gregory the Illuminator, the evangelizer of Armenia, was raised. The region also produced some of the greatest early ecclesiastical writers, including the fourth-century **Cappadocian Fathers**: Basil the Great, Gregory of Nazianzen and Gregory of Nyssa.

By the start of the eighth century, the political power of Cappadocia's increasing number of monks was beginning to cause concern, leading to the closure of monasteries and confiscation of their property. The worst period of repressive activity occurred during the reign of Constantine V, marked by the **Iconoclastic Council** of 754. All sacred images, except the cross, were forbidden, a ruling that had a profound effect on the creative life of the region's churches.

After the restoration of the cult of images in 843, the religious activity of Cappadocia saw a renewed vigour. The wealth of the Church increased to such an extent that in 964 monastery building was prohibited, an edict only withdrawn in 1003. Meanwhile, the religious communities were brought to heel, controlled to a greater extent by the ecclesiastical hierarchy. Even though Cappadocia continued to be a centre of religious activity well into the Ottoman period, it had lost the artistic momentum that had produced the extraordinary works of earlier centuries.

Cappadocia, that is thought to have contained the hand of St Hieron, a local saint born a few kilometres away.

The Pigeon House

The church known as the **Pigeon House**, located in a tower of rock, is renowned for its frescoes, which commemorate the passage of the Byzantine emperor Nicephoras Phocas through Cappadocia in 964–965, during his military campaign in Cilicia. He's thought to have been making a pilgrimage to the church of St John the Baptist, nearby.

Paşabağı

The most picturesque of all the Cappadocian valleys, **Paşabağı**, between Zelve and Çavuşin, makes a pleasant hour's walk from the village. As a favourite place of retreat for stylite hermits who lodged in the abundant fairy chimneys, it was once known as "Valley of the Monks". One of the triple-coned chimneys contains a **chapel** dedicated to St Simeon Stylites, hollowed out at three levels, with a monk's cell at the top. A hundred metres east of the chapel, a **cell** bears the inscription "Receive me, O grave, as you received the Stylite."

ARRIVAL AND DEPARTURE   ÇAVUŞIN

By dolmuş The regular Göreme-Avanos dolmuş stops at Çavuşin (less than 10min).

ACCOMMODATION AND EATING

Panorama Pansiyon & Restaurant Set back from the road, towards the bottom of the village ☎0384 532 7002. This reliable family-run café-restaurant makes a popular pit stop for hungry trekkers and sightseers. Excellent value, with *gözleme* from ₺8, casseroles from ₺15 and beers from ₺8.

Turbel Cave Hotel Behind the Panorama ☎0384 532 7084, ⓦturbelcavehotel.com. French-speaking owner Mustafa welcomes guests with a smile and the four guestrooms have wooden floors, marble-floored bathrooms and attractive furnishings. Original cave structures and wrought-iron bedframes add to the cosy effect. ₺120

Village Cave Hotel Nestled beneath a cliff at the head of a small valley ☎0384 532 7197, ⓦthevillagecave .com. An intriguing building full of original cave features and eerie lantern-lit tunnels, this is a great option if you fancy a taste of authentic cave life. There's bags of atmosphere, but be aware that these are traditional dwellings; while they're comfortable, rooms can be dark and a bit musty. ₺220

Zelve Open-Air Museum

3km off the Avanos–Çavuşin road • Daily: May–Oct 8am–6.30pm; Nov–April 8am–4.30pm; last entry 15min before closing • ₺10 • Dolmuşes from Avanos, Göreme and Ürgüp (every 2hr)

A fascinating remnant of Cappadocia's troglodytic past, the deserted city that spreads across the three valleys of **Zelve** makes up the **Zelve Open-Air Museum**. The valley was inhabited by Turkish Muslims until 1952, when rock falls, which still occur, made it too dangerous to remain. Areas are frequently closed off due to unstable surrounds, and it's essential to heed the warning signs.

To explore the complex, bring a torch and old clothes, along with a considerable sense of adventure. At the top of the right-hand valley, on the right as you go up, a honeycomb of rooms is approached up metal staircases. Some are entered by means of precarious steps, others by swinging up through large holes in their floors (look for ancient hand- and foot-holes). Old stables, pigeon houses high up on the walls, an old mill, still with its wheel stone intact, and a large number of chapels and medieval oratories, many decorated with carved **crosses** and well-preserved altars, are scattered up and down the valleys. The few **painted images** found in Zelve are in the churches of the third valley, and nearby, the twin-aisled **Üzümlü Kilise** has grapevines painted in red and green on the walls, and a cross carved into the ceiling.

Ortahisar

The friendly little village of **ORTAHİSAR**, off the road between Göreme and Ürgüp, retains a degree of charm and innocence absent from many of Cappadocia's more touristed areas. Its chief attraction is the staggering, fortress-like 86m-high **rock** that once housed the entire village, which is now in precarious shape and should be explored only with extreme caution.

Pancarlık church and monastery complex

3km south of Ortahisar • Daily: summer 8am–7pm; winter 8am–5pm • ₺10 if the warden is around • Follow the road marked "Pancarlık Kilise" off the second square to reach the valley of the Üzenge Çay

Hardly visited due to the difficulty of access, the **Pancarlık church and monastery complex** holds some excellent frescoes in good condition – even their faces are intact. They include the Baptism of Christ and the Annunciation, and, to the left of the altar, the Nativity.

ARRIVAL AND DEPARTURE ORTAHİSAR 7

By bus or dolmuş Regular *Belediye* buses run from Avanos direct to Ortahisar, or an Uçhisar–Ürgüp dolmuş will stop on the Nevşehir–Kayseri road, leaving you a 20min downhill walk to the village.

ACCOMMODATION AND EATING

Alkabris Ali Reis Sok 23 ☎0384 343 3433, ⓦalkabris .com. Tucked away in a peaceful warren of old dwellings behind the village rock, this elegant hotel is run by a friendly Turkish couple who speak some French and English. The immaculate white stone en-suite rooms are beautifully decorated, with colourful handmade mosaics adorning walls, curtains and tabletops. There's parking outside, but the steep rocky roads can be quite difficult to navigate. **€100**

Culture Museum & Restaurant Cumhuriyet Meyd 15 ☎0384 343 3344, ⓦculturemuseum.com. Dinner by reservation only. Standing out amid Ortahisar's slim pickings, this historic restaurant offers a wide range of local favourites, with mains starting from ₺15 and a pretty good wine list. It's most notable though, for its quirky "culture museum" (free to diners, ₺2 otherwise), a series of fun, if slightly kitsch, installations showcasing traditional Cappadocian lifestyles. Daily 9am–6.30pm.

★**Hezen Cave Hotel** Tahir Bey Sok 87 ☎0384 343 3005, ⓦhezenhotel.com. This tranquil haven set high in the hills above Göreme is one of Cappadocia's most distinctive and inspired boutique hotels. Acclaimed interior designer Halide Didem has modernized the beautifully preserved cave interiors with creative furnishings and splashes of colour, and it's a striking result. Each of the fifteen cave rooms is unique, with cosy alcoves, spotlit wall holes and quirky cave wardrobes, while the *hezen*-roofed lobby and dreamy breakfast terrace are showstopping. Best of all, with its friendly staff and welcoming, non-pretentious vibe, the place hasn't traded cordiality for style. Closed Nov–March. **US$180**

Ürgüp

With its clusters of stately cave hotels nuzzled in the tuff cliffs of the **Esbelli district**, and a burgeoning population of bars and restaurants, **ÜRGÜP** makes a worthy rival to Göreme as the destination of choice for visitors to Cappadocia. Before 1923, Ürgüp had a largely Greek population, so many distinctive and beautiful houses of Greek (and Ottoman) origin are still scattered around the town.

The old village

Despite its rather incongruous modern central square, Ürgüp retains much of its rural village charm. Men and women in traditional working clothes, leading horse-drawn vehicles and donkeys out to the surrounding vineyards, orchards and vegetable gardens, are not an unusual early-morning sight. This is the time to explore the **old village**, whose buildings appear to be slowly emerging from the rocky hills into which they have been carved. Some feature stylish pillared and decorated facades of the same stone; others are simple caves with doors and windows cut into the cliffs themselves.

7

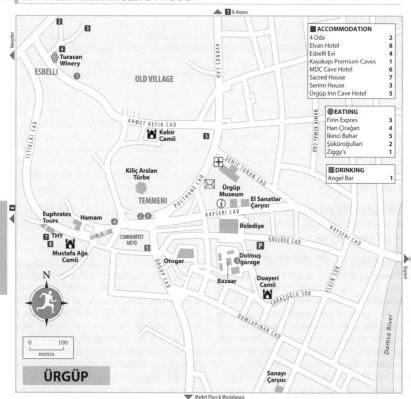

Temmeni

Daily 8.30am–6pm • Free

The walk up to the central park known as **Temmeni** ("Hill of Wishes") starts with a flight of steps opposite the thirteenth-century **Kebir Camii**, and includes a 700m-long tunnel, which leads to a "balcony", furnishing panoramic views of the town and surrounding countryside. Continuing uphill, past the former troglodyte town dwellings (now mainly used for storage or abandoned altogether), brings you to the park itself, where a Selçuk tomb, the **Kılıç Arslan Türbe**, dating from 1268, is open to visitors. A small, renovated *medrese* from the same period now serves as a café.

Ürgüp Museum

Kayseri Cad • Tues–Sun 8am–12.30pm & 2.30–5.30pm • Free

The **Ürgüp Museum** is tiny and not particularly well labelled, but the helpful staff are prepared to explain the exhibits. These include a selection of prehistoric ceramics, figurines, lamps, stelae, statues and ornaments found during excavations in the area.

ARRIVAL AND GETTING AROUND   ÜRGÜP

By bus or dolmuş The *otogar* is in the centre of town. Destinations Adana (4 daily; 5hr); Ankara (6 daily; 5hr); Antalya (2 daily; 10hr); Denizli (2 daily; 12hr); Göreme (hourly; 20min); Istanbul (3 daily; 13hr); Kayseri (hourly; 1hr 30min); Konya (8 daily; 3hr); Marmaris (2 daily; 15hr); Mersin (3 daily; 5hr); Nevşehir (hourly; 30min).

Bike rental Argeus, İstiklal Cad 7 (☎0384 341 4688, ⓦcappadociaexclusive.com), rents mountain bikes from around €20/day.

Car rental Avis, İstiklâl Cad 19, Belediye Pasajı (☎0384 341 2177); Alpin, Cumhuriyet Meyd 32 (☎0384 341 7522).

INFORMATION AND TOURS

Tourist office Kayseri Cad 37, next to the museum, in a park with tea garden (daily: May–Sept 8am–6pm; Oct–April 8am–5pm; ☎0384 341 4059).
Tours Euphrates Tours, İstiklâl Cad 59 (☎0384 341 7487, ⓦcappadociatours.com). An excellent range of tailored

cultural tours with the best local guides and some unique itineraries. A Turkish Village Life and Culinary tour includes visits to local wineries and orchards, followed by a cooking class with a local family (€75).

ACCOMMODATION

CENTRAL ÜRGÜP

Elvan Hotel Barbaros Hayrettin Sok 11 ☎0384 341 4191, ⓦhotelelvan.com. A well-run budget choice, with recently renovated rooms set in a characterful old house just a short walk from the centre of town. Opt for one of the stone rooms, where the arch ceilings offer a natural alternative to a/c and be sure to check out the cool, semi-underground lounge area. ₺100
Kayakapı Premium Caves Kuşçular Sok 43 ☎0384 341 8877, ⓦkayakapi.com. A sprawling complex so vast that golf buggies are needed to transfer guests to their rooms, *Kayakapı* is one of Cappadocia's most breathtaking hotels, perched high on the hilltop above Ürgüp. Part of a unique project to restore the UNESCO-listed Kayakapı cave village, there's nowhere quite like it in Cappadocia. Thirty-two luxurious rooms have been renovated so far, with lounge areas, hamams and private terraces, while there's also a restaurant, spa and swimming pool overlooking the valleys. ₺230
★Sacred House Barbaros Hayrettin Sok 25 ☎0384 341 7102, ⓦsacredhouse.com.tr. Twenty-one individually designed concept rooms in a beautifully restored mansion, featuring plush furnishings, antiques and religious, Gothic and medieval themes throughout. It's a remarkable work of design and each room tells a story – choose from masterpieces like the romantic "Fairy's Nest", the bewitching "Shaman", the opulent "King's Ego" or the whimsical "Harem". There's also a spa and hamam. €200

★Ürgüp Inn Cave Hotel Mescit Sok 22 ☎0384 341 4147, ⓦurgupinncavehotel.com. An excellent budget option in the town centre, run by the friendly and accommodating Ömer. Rooms are clean, quiet and comfortable, with genuine cave features and bags of character; breakfast is served beneath a flower-filled pergola. €45

ESBELLI DISTRICT

4 Oda Esbelli Sok 46 Cad ☎0384 341 6080, ⓦ4oda .com. The perfect blend of comfort and cool, with five – not four, despite the name – authentic cave rooms. The wood-floored guestrooms each have their own unique touch, with traditional artworks and grand oak furniture, while the cosy lounge and flower-filled courtyard make guests feel right at home. ₺300
Esbelli Evi Esbelli Sok 8 ☎0384 341 3395, ⓦesbelli .com. Owner Suhu has managed to create a tranquil space that's simultaneously luxurious, inviting and affordable. The spacious cave rooms offer privacy, alongside some unique design features, and the airy lounge areas, colourful rose gardens and delicious fruit-filled buffet breakfasts lend themselves to a more communal vibe. Rooms range in size, but the impressive en-suite bathroom and kitchen facilities in some far surpass expectations for the price range. US$150
MDC Cave Hotel Karağandere Mah. Sok 37 ☎0384 341 4415, ⓦmdchotel.com. A majestic strip of Greek Ottoman mansions in the heart of the valleys, this is a tranquil retreat

CAPPADOCIAN WINE

With its cool mountain climate and fertile volcanic soils, Cappadocia is blessed with the ideal climate for growing grapes. **Wine making** here dates back four thousand years, and many vineyards remain small and family-run. Their crops are used for both wine and grape juice, as well as being boiled to produce *pekmez*, a sweet grape syrup. Local wines are celebrated at Ürgüp's **International Wine Festival**, held each October, and can be sampled on vineyard tours.

Kocabağ Kav Butik Uçhisar ☎0384 219 2979, ⓦkocabag.com. A popular wine house offering free samples of their award-winning wines (try the fruity white Narince) in an atmospheric traditional cave room. By request, Kocabağ also offers guided tours of their wine production outlet, 45km out of town. Daily: summer 8am–8pm; winter 8am–6pm.
Turasan Yunak Mah, Tevrik Fikret Cad, Ürgüp

☎0384 341 4961, ⓦturasan.com.tr. Cappadocia's oldest wine producer, established in 1943, produces some of the region's finest wines and has an annual output of 2,161,000 litres. The upmarket winery offers free tastings and guided tours, and the extremely knowledgeable, English-speaking staff make this a great place to start your wine education. Be sure to sample the crisp Emir and fruity, deep red Öküzgözü. Daily 8am–6pm.

far removed from the bustle of the village. The 39 dazzling rooms and suites boast original cave features including winepresses, fireplaces and inscriptions, while the traditional decor and grand bathrooms, adorned with marble and onyx, add an air of timeless luxury. Breakfast is served on the expansive garden terrace, overlooking the orchard, and a rooftop swimming pool is in the offing. **€120**

★**Serinn House** Esbelli Sok 36 ☎0384 341 6076, ⓦserinnhouse.com. Five ultramodern rooms, decked out with sleek industrial design pieces whose clean lines create a beautiful contrast with the soft curves of the caves, and resonate character. The delightfully welcoming owner Eren bakes delicious goodies for breakfast, served on the panoramic terrace. **US$150**

EATING

Firin Expres Ürgüp Cad ☎0384 212 0053, ⓦfirinexpres.com. A modern, European-style café, where you can indulge in decadent desserts, sip cappuccinos (₺7) and fruit smoothies (from ₺9) or tuck into delicious *pide* (from ₺7) and burgers. Head up to the rooftop terrace for the best views. No alcohol. Daily 8am–1am.

Han Çirağan Cumhuriyet Meyd 4 ☎0384 341 2566, ⓦhanciragan.com. Set in a distinctive 150-year-old house, this restaurant started life as Ürgüp's very first teahouse, as depicted in the old black-and-white photos on the walls. The extensive menu features regional dishes like *düğün çorbası* (wedding soup), *saç tava* (wok-fried lamb in tomato sauce) and *mantı* (Turkish ravioli; ₺18.50), plus a good selection of local wines (from ₺55). Daily 10.30am–midnight.

İkinci Bahar Merkezi Karşisi 14 ☎0384 341 3133. Catering mostly to local families, this long-established kebab joint is a reliable choice for those on a budget, with a wide range of grills, *köfte* and *kebabs* (mains from ₺15). There's also an English-language menu and vegetarian options, but no alcohol. Daily 7am–11pm.

Şüküroğulları Cumhuriyet Meyd 10–12 ☎0384 341 8375. From its grand stone atrium to its glass-floored rooftop terrace, this local favourite is instantly impressive, with cosy lounge areas, a funky bar and a formal dining room. The menu (in English) is all-encompassing, with a mouthwatering range of Turkish and international cuisine. Head here for lunch and choose from well-priced toasties, *gözleme*, burgers, wraps and crêpes (mains from ₺9), accompanied by fresh juices or a range of coffees. No alcohol. Daily 9am–midnight.

★**Ziggy's** Tevfik Fikret Cad 24 ☎0384 341 7107, ⓦziggycafe.com. A living tribute to its namesake, the owner's dog (himself named after Ziggy Stardust), whose adorable logo adorns mugs, signs and lampshades, *Ziggy's* strikes just the right balance between cute and cool. Opt for the taster menu (₺60/person) and dive into a generous spread of *meze*, perfectly baked *börek* and tender *şiş* kebabs, followed by the cinnamon-laced signature dessert "Sweet Ziggy". There's also a varied cocktail and wine list, and a shop downstairs crammed with exquisite handicrafts and handmade jewellery. Daily noon–11pm.

DRINKING

Angel Bar Cumhuriyet Meyd 3 ☎0384 341 6894. Right on the main square, this lively spot blasts out an eclectic mix of music into the early hours and there's a good cocktail menu (from ₺25). Sink into one of the bright red beanbags strewn around the outside seating area and watch the world go by. There's a good range of light bites and coffees, too. Daily 9am–2.30am.

DIRECTORY

Banks Garanti Bank on Kazım Karabekir Cad 7 has an English-speaking manager, while the Ziraat Bankası on Atatürk Bul has a 24hr currency exchange machine.

Hamam İstikal Cad 18, mixed men and women (daily 7am–11pm; ₺35 including massage).

Hospital Posthane Cad (☎0384 341 4031).

Pharmacy Elif Eczanesi, Kayseri Cad, across from the tourist office, is friendly, with some English spoken.

Police Opposite the post office in the centre, on Posthane Cad.

Post office Posthane Cad (daily 9am–5pm).

Mustafapaşa and around

The village of **MUSTAFAPAŞA**, 6km south of Ürgüp, makes for a pleasant excursion or, with your own transport, a good base for explorations. It has a clutch of surprisingly good hotels, making it a worthy alternative to the central villages. The charm of the place lies largely in its concentration of attractive *konaks* with carved house facades, which date back a century or so to the era when the village was known as Sinasos and home to a thriving Greek community.

Mustafapaşa is also central to a cluster of little-visited **churches**. Its main square holds the **Aios Konstantine Eleni Kilisesi** (daily: summer 8am–7pm; winter 8am–5pm; ₺3), dedicated to Constantine and his mother St Helena, while a monastery complex across the village, reached via streets of houses cut into the tuff cliffs, includes the churches of **Aya Nicolas** and **Aya Stefanos**.

Ayios Vasilios

1km north of Mustafapaşa; pick up key from the guardian at the Konstantinos-Eleni Church in central Mustafapaşa • Daily: summer 8am–7pm; winter 8am–5pm • ₺5

The church of **Ayios Vasilios**, overlooking the Üzengı Dere ravine, holds some well-preserved frescoes, although the faces are damaged, as well as four rock-cut pillars. Below it, pre-Iconoclastic and tenth-century paintings in the partly rock-cut **Holy Cross** church include an attractive Christ of the Second Coming.

Keşlik Kilesi monastery complex

3km south of Mustafapaşa • April–Oct daily 9am–7.30pm; Nov–March by appointment only • ₺5 • ☎ 0536 887 5517

7

Along the Soğanlı road south from Mustafapaşa, the fairy chimneys give way to a table-mountain formation that is no less fantastic and surreal: the red canyon ridge that the road follows could be a backdrop for *Looney Tunes*' Road Runner.

Out here, the **Keşlik Kilesi monastery complex**, believed to be one of the earliest communal monastic establishments in Cappadocia, consists of three churches, a winepress and a refectory. The first church, named after a prominent picture of the archangel Gabriel, includes depictions of the Last Supper, the Annunciation and the Flight to Egypt, all badly damaged and soot-blackened (a torch is essential). The church of St Michael has a wine cellar downstairs, while the most beautiful of all, the church of St Stephen (seventh or eighth-century), is unusually decorated with stylized foliage and interlaced patterns reminiscent of Turkish kilims.

ARRIVAL AND INFORMATION | **MUSTAFAPAŞA**

By dolmuş Regular dolmuşes connect the 6km between Mustafapaşa and Ürgüp (10min).

Tourist office On the main square (daily: summer 8am–7pm; winter 8am–5pm).

ACCOMMODATION AND EATING

Mustafapaşa has some very good **places to stay**, with a particularly good line in friendly, family-run hotels and **restaurants**.

★**Hanımeli Restaurant** Yılmaz Sok 4 ☎ 0384 353 5203. A short walk south of Mustafapaşa, this exceedingly friendly, family-run restaurant serves excellent home-cooked dishes, with an emphasis on traditional Turkish cuisine. Opt for the ₺50 menu, which includes soup (the lentil is particularly good), an array of tasty *meze*, a meat or vegetarian main (*testi* kebab is popular), dessert (the cinnamon-dusted rice pudding is divine) and Turkish tea. Cooking classes are also available. Daily 9.30am–midnight.

Monastery Cave Hotel In the centre ☎ 0384 353 5005, ⓦ monasteryhotel.com. Friendly, family-run hotel with recently restored cave rooms, each with TV, fridge and an intriguing collection of antiques. There's also a café-restaurant on site, mountain bikes for rent and traditional live music nights. €45

Pacha Kale sok, in the centre ☎ 0384 353 5331,

ⓦ pachahotel.com. Run by brothers Ismail and Özgür, this hospitable hotel has the air of a family home, with the dining area dotted with trinkets and the flower-filled courtyard climbing with mulberry vines. The fourteen cosy rooms are jazzed up with embroidered bedspreads and bold kilim, and a home-cooked dinner is available on request. ₺100

★**Perimasalı Cave Hotel** Sehit Aslan Yakar Sok 6 ☎ 0384 353 5090, ⓦ perimasalihotel.com. A magnificently renovated Greek mansion provides the setting for this exquisite boutique hotel, which does its best to live up to its name, meaning "fairy tale". The indiviually designed rooms feature sculpted stone headboards, velvet chaise longues and candlelit jacuzzi baths, while the terrace restaurant offers dramatic views. Don't forget to ask the owner to make you a cup of his favourite *menengiç* coffee too – a delicious traditional drink made from roasted pistachios. €120

Ayvalı

With its jumble of largely unexplored caves and rock-cut churches, stunning topography, and daily market brimming with locally harvested fruits, the traditional Anatolian village of **AYVALI**, 12km south of Ürgüp, is an alluring spot.

Since being chosen as a "sample village" by the Ministry of Tourism in 2005, this humble harvest village has embarked upon a unique approach to tourism. Well-executed tours allow residents to open their homes to tourists – guests can learn the art of cooking Cappadocian cuisine in a local home; witness the ritual of a wedding ceremony; help with the fruit harvest; or learn to cook up grape molasses, a local speciality. Even the premier boutique hotel not only employs many local workers, but funds community projects, creating as close to a **sustainable tourism** model as you'll find in Cappadocia.

So far, tourism has done little to change Ayvalı. While it holds a cluster of attractions, and trekking routes circle the centre, the real delights are found in the simplicity of everyday life. Rooftops are blanketed with apricots drying in the sun; villagers collect water from the communal fountain; the local teahouses bustle with quickfire gossip; and the scent of bread wafts from the street-side stone ovens.

ARRIVAL AND DEPARTURE
AYVALI

By dolmuş While public transport to Ayvalı is scarce – dolmuşes only run as far as Mustafapaşa – the *Gamirasu Cave Hotel* offers free transfers for its guests.

Tours Euphrates Tours, İstiklâl Cad 59 in Ürgüp (☏0384 341 7487, ⓦcappadociatours.com), offers tours to Ayvalı.

ACCOMMODATION

★**Gamirasu Cave Hotel** Ayvalı Köyü Ürgüp ☏0384 354 5815, ⓦgamirasu.com. The brainchild of local-boy-done-good İbrahim, *Gamirasu* offers the ultimate in guilt-free luxury, a deservedly popular boutique hotel at the heart and soul of Ayvalı village. It's undeniably atmospheric, with a honeycomb of cave rooms carved into the tiered tuff and lamp-lit stairwells snaking up to the terrace restaurant. Choose from elegant stone-vaulted rooms, homely cave suites or the lavish King suites, complete with hamam, 24hr butler service and beds that could sleep an army. €185

The Soğanlı valleys

40km south of Ürgüp • Daily: summer 8am–6pm; winter 8.30am–5pm • ₺6 entrance to the churches • No public transport

The little-visited **Soğanlı valleys** make a spectacular diversion as you head south of Ürgüp. **SOĞANLI** itself is an attractive village in two parts, Yukarı (upper) and Aşağı (lower) Soğanlı, set into the side of a tabletop mountain. In winter, it's often completely cut off by snowdrifts.

As you face Yukarı Soğanlı, the most interesting local churches and monasteries are in the valley to the right. To reach the two-storey **Kubbeli Kilise** (Church with the Dome), follow the footpath across a stream bed from the village square, and proceed uphill through the village and along the side of the valley. This has perhaps the most striking exterior of all the Cappadocian rock churches, its form – a conical dome that's the tip of a fairy chimney, resting on a circular drum – being an imitation of a masonry structure. The **Saklı** (Hidden) **Kilise**, holding frescoes of the Apostles, stands 100m before the Kubbeli Kilise, its door facing into the valley.

Go down to the road, then head up the other side of the valley to reach the **Meryem Ana Kilisesi** (Church of the Virgin), which has four apsidal chapels with frescoes and Iconoclastic decoration. The **Yılanlı Kilise** (Church of the Snake) is best seen using a torch, as it is blackened and damaged by Greek and Armenian graffiti. It derives its name from an eleventh-century painting of St George slaying the dragon, to the left of the entrance.

On the way back towards the village, you'll find the **Karabaş Kilise** (Church of the Black Head), with two adjoining apsidal chapels. In the first, well-preserved tenth- and eleventh-century frescoes depict scenes from the life of Christ.

Avanos and around

The old city of **AVANOS** clambers up the hills overlooking the magnificent **Kızılırmak River** (or "Red River") – the longest in Turkey and named for the distinctive red clay mined from its banks. Famed for its earthenware **pottery**, Avanos remains a characterful town that's delicately poised between the modern and the traditional, and its authenticity is steadily stealing visitors away from the tourist-ruled Göreme. Cobbled backstreets and tumbledown Ottoman, Armenian and Greek buildings climb the hill north of Atatürk Caddesi, while the Friday **market** is Cappadocia's biggest and liveliest, and pottery workers still employ techniques dating back to Hittite times. Yet there's no shortage of progress, with the recently redeveloped **waterfront** now juggling a clutch of modern restaurants, a tranquil grassy promenade and a noisy parade of jet boats, as well as a rather dizzying suspension bridge. Exploration of the fields and hills around the town reveals further attractions: a tiny *kervansaray*, and even an underground city, 14km away at **Özkonak**.

Pottery shops

Most of Avanos's **pottery shops** are located just off the main street, a few minutes' walk east of the prominent **potter's monument**, which is sculpted from clay. The potters' square and the streets that surround it contain numerous tiny workshops where local techniques can still be observed or even attempted. A top choice is **Le Palais du Udu** (Yukarı Mah 68; daily 10am–6pm; ☎0537 471 1428), where local artist Mehmet crafts quality ceramic-based drums, vases and jugs.

Chez Galip Pottery and Hair Museum

Town centre, near *Kirket Pension* • Daily 8.30am–8.30pm • ☎ 0384 511 4240, ⓦ chezgalip.com

One of Avanos's most unusual pottery stores, **Chez Galip Pottery**, is renowned for its bizarre **Hair Museum**. Inspired by the owner's French lover, who left behind only a lock of her hair, its incredible collection contains locks of hair from thousands of women around the world, each taped to a handwritten note from its benefactor and hung from every nook and cranny of the room. It's featured in the *Guinness Book of Records*, and fans of the eccentric will surely find it irresistible.

Despite its quirky claim to fame, the pottery store itself houses plenty of well-crafted and reasonably priced souvenirs (₺15 and up for hand-painted crockery), alongside some incredible works of art with price tags to match. They'll happily showcase traditional pottery making and even let you have a go. And women visitors – don't forget to snip off a lock of your hair for the museum.

Saruhan Kervansaray

New Kayseri road, 6km east of Avanos • ₺3

The Selçuk-era **Saruhan Kervansaray** is well worth a visit. Built in 1238, it features five naves, a courtyard and the remains of what was once a hamam. Beautifully restored, it offers evocative evening performances by a troupe of **whirling dervishes** (schedules vary, so ask locally; tickets are typically €25).

Özkonak

Off Kayseri road, 14km north of Avanos • Daily: summer 8am–7pm; winter 8am–5pm, last entry 30min before closing • ₺8 • Hourly dolmuşes from the *otogar*

The most interesting excursion from Avanos is to **Özkonak**, one of Cappadocia's least known and least excavated underground cities. While in its present state it's not as interesting as Derinkuyu or Kaymaklı, but, by the same token it's not as crowded.

The city was discovered in 1972 by a *muezzin*, Latif Acar, who was trying to find out where the water disappeared to when he watered his crops. He found a subterranean room, which, later excavation revealed, belonged to a city where sixty thousand people could exist underground for three months. Its ten floors descend to a depth of 40m, but at present only four are open, to 15m. The first two levels were used for food storage and wine fermentation, and a press and reservoir are labelled, as are mangers for stabled animals. Another typical feature is the thick sandstone doors, moved by wooden levers; above them was a small hole, through which boiling oil would have been poured on an enemy trying to break in.

ARRIVAL AND DEPARTURE   AVANOS

By bus or dolmuş Avanos's *otogar* is 250m south of the river, across the bridge from the town centre.
Destinations Göreme (hourly; 30min); Nevşehir (hourly; 40min); Özkonak (every 30min; 30min); Uçhisar (hourly;

35min); Ürgüp (every 2hr; 30min).
By plane Shuttle buses run to Nevşehir (₺20) and Kayseri (₺25) airports, with hotel pick-up – book at your hotel or at Kirkit Voyage (see below).

INFORMATION, TOURS AND ACTIVITIES

Tourist office Next door to the *Sofa Hotel*, Atatürk Cad (summer Mon–Fri 8.30am–noon & 1.30–7pm; winter Mon–Fri 8.30am–noon & 1.30–5pm; ☎ 0384 511 4360).
Tours Kirkit Voyage, Atatürk Cad 50 (☎ 0384 511 3259, ⓦ kirkit.com), is a reliable and long-established tour operator that runs horseback treks, canoeing trips and bike and snowshoe tours all over Cappadocia, with English-speaking guides. Kapadokya Jet Boat & Gondola, on the riverbank (☎ 0384 511 3459, ⓦ kapadokyajet.com), offers

adrenaline-fuelled jet-boating tours (€40/person for 20min) and more peaceful gondola tours (€10/person for 20min) along the river.
Hamam Alaaddin Turkish Bath, Orta Mahalle Peker Sok 6 (☎ 0384 511 5036) is friendly and accustomed to tourists; it's a good option for first-timers (€25 for a scrub, soap massage and refreshments). Be aware that this is a mixed hamam – enquire about women-only hours if you're not comfortable with that.

ACCOMMODATION

Ada Camping South bank of the Kızılırmak ☎ 0384 511 2429, ⓦ avanosadacamping.com. This excellent campsite has good facilities, including a basic but clean kitchen, wi-fi in communal areas, a huge pool (also open to non-guests) and plenty of lush grass to set up on. Staff are friendly and tents are also available to rent for ₺5/night. Rates are for two people. Tent or caravan **₺30**
★ **Kirkit Pension** Off Atatürk Cad ☎ 0384 511 3148, ⓦ kirkitpension.com. Owned by the eponymous tour company, this homely pension immediately welcomes guests into the Kirkit family and you'll experience the full breadth of Turkish hospitality. Rooms are clean, comfortable and full of character, with beautiful embroidered bedsheets, sandstone interiors and antique curiosities dotted throughout, while the owners join guests for dinner around a communal table in the courtyard. Delicious traditional cuisine, multilingual

conversation and impromtu live music and dancing is all part of the experience. Lunch or dinner costs €10 extra. **€55**
Sofa Hotel Orta Mahalle Gedik Sok 9 ☎ 0384 511 5186, ⓦ sofa-hotel.com. An imposing neo-Ottoman mansion, put together from fifteen redesigned Ottoman houses, this sprawling abode is effortlessly chic and timeless. Rooms are immaculate, with stunningly carved wooden furnishings, restored beams and traditional decor, and there's a delightful terrace and garden courtyard. **€100**
Venessa Pansiyon Just off Atatürk Bul on Hafızağa Sok 20 ☎ 0384 511 3840, ⓦ venessapension.com. A friendly and reliable budget option with some unique underground caves and a spacious terrace from which to watch the sunset. The comfy stone rooms are let down by somewhat shabby bathrooms, but they're nonetheless clean and functional. **₺120**

EATING AND DRINKING

Dayının Yeri Atatürk Cad, next to the main bridge ☎ 0384 511 6840, ⓦ dayininyeri.com.tr. This long-established kebab house is always packed with locals and the food doesn't disappoint. The şiş kebabs are cooked on an open coal grill, but for something a little different, try the *dayı* special, an *Adana*-style kebab oven-baked with melted cheese, or a *beyti* kebab, made of ground lamb wrapped in *lavash*. Mains from ₺15; no alcohol. Daily 8am–midnight.
Mado Café Bahçelievler Mah, on the riverfront by the footbridge ☎ 0384 511 5022, ⓦ mado.com.tr. A recently opened addition to Mado's far-reaching franchise, this

modern café occupies a prime spot right along the riverfront. Head here to sample the signature home-made ice cream (from ₺10), accompanied by an iced mocha (from ₺7) or a generous slab of *baklava*, and watch the jet boats zip by from the sunny waterfront terrace. Daily 7am–11pm.
Sofra Çarşı içi 3 ☎ 0384 511 6777, ⓦ sofrarestaurant .com. A popular local haunt known for its delicious slow-cooked *testi* kebabs (₺60 for two people), and a wide range of kebab-based meals from around ₺16. Head out the back, where a large covered terrace area teems with local families, and the lively atmosphere is infectious. No alcohol. Daily 6.30am–10pm.

Tafana Pide Salonu Atatürk Cad 31 ☎0384 511 4862, ⓦtafanarestoran.com. A colourful *pide* house, filled with decorative pottery and photos and news clippings from the elderly owner's extensive world travels, this place is brimming with character. *Pides* (₺15) come with a variety of toppings, but there are also some great salads and a delicious *firinda kuru fasulye* (white bean casserole cooked in a stone oven; ₺7). Wash it down with a glass of *şalgam suyu* (beetroot juice; ₺3). Daily 8am–midnight.

Southern Cappadocia

As most visitors to Cappadocia never get beyond the well-worn Nevşehir–Avanos–Ürgüp triangle, **southern Cappadocia** is far less charted and trampled. There's a reason for its obscurity – the two major towns, **Aksaray** and **Niğde**, leave a lot to be desired as tourist centres, and much of the scenery is a depressing mixture of scrub or barren steppe. That said, the area does have its fascinations – most notably, the **Ihlara valley**, between Aksaray and Niğde, where the Melendiz River has carved a spectacular narrow ravine with almost vertical walls. Also easily accessible from Niğde is a small enclave of beautifully painted rock-cut churches belonging to the **Eski Gümüşler** monastery. South and east of Niğde, the spectacular limestone spires of the **Aladağlar Mountains** rear from the plateau, affording excellent trekking and climbing.

Niğde and around

Despite a long history spent guarding the important mountain pass between Cappadocia and Cilicia, the small provincial town of **NIĞDE** holds few remaining monuments, aside from a Selçuk fortress perched above the main street. While Niğde feels as if it's been thrown together by people more interested in nomadic wandering than town planning, the nearby **Eski Gümüşler** monastery complex, with its remarkably preserved frescoes, makes it a popular stopover en route to the Aladağlar Mountains.

Eski Gümüşler monastery

Off the Kayseri road, 9km east of Niğde • Daily: summer 9am–6pm; winter 9am–12.30pm & 1.30–5pm • ₺8 • Hourly Belediye buses from Niğde's *otogar*

Rediscovered in 1963, the **Eski Gümüşler monastery** has a deserved reputation for the excellent preservation of its paintings. The **main church**, with its tall, elegant pillars, is entered through an almost circular arched doorway opposite the entrance to the courtyard. Decorated with black-and-white geometric designs, it contains beautiful frescoes in the most delicate greens, browns and blues. These include a Nativity scene complete with tiny animal heads peering in at the swaddled Jesus and the Magi, off to the left, and a tall, serene Madonna, framed in a rock-cut niche. The upstairs **sleeping quarters** hold rock-cut beds, and the walls are decorated with hunters with bows and arrows and a Roman soldier. Outside in the central courtyard there's a skeleton in its grave, protected under glass, and a kitchen and underground baths reached down a set of steps, while below ground level are various chambers and a water reservoir.

ARRIVAL AND DEPARTURE   NIĞDE

By bus and dolmuş Niğde's *otogar* is on Emin Eşirgil Cad, off the Nevşehir–Adana highway, 1km north.
Destinations Aksaray (8 daily; 1hr 30min); Alanya (1 daily; 12hr); Ankara (10 daily; 4hr 30min); Antalya (2 daily; 12hr); Çamardı (summer 4 daily; 1hr); Derinkuyu (hourly; 45min); Istanbul (3 daily; 12hr); Kayseri (hourly; 1hr 30min); Konya (8 daily; 3hr 30min); Mersin (5 daily; 4hr); Nevşehir (hourly; 1hr 30min); Sivas (1 daily; 6hr).

By train To reach the town centre from the station – right on the highway, within sight of the citadel's clock tower – cross the road and walk 10min along İstasyon Cad.
Destinations Adana (2 daily; 4hr); Kayseri (2 daily; 3hr).

INFORMATION AND ACTIVITIES

Tourist office Atatürk Meyd 16, in the town centre (Mon–Sat 8.30am–noon & 1.30–5.30pm).
Trekking Sobek Travel, Bor Cad 70/16 (☎0388 232 1507, ⓦsobekculture.com), a reputable company that deals mainly with package groups, can arrange treks in the Aladağlar Mountains.

ACCOMMODATION

Grand Hotel Niğde Hükümet Meyd ☎ 0388 232 7000, ⓦ grandhotelnigde.com. Clean, modern lines are the name of the game at this stylish hotel, with a sauna, hamam, fitness centre and restaurant on site. ₺130

Aladağlar Mountains

The **Aladağlar Mountains** form part of the Toros range, at the point where it swings north of the Mesopotamian plain. The isolated gorges and lakes of the Aladağlar, a paradise for **birdwatchers**, are at their best during the autumn migration, when the snow has melted and access is easier. *Yaylas* (mountain pastures) are used after snowmelt by nomad families and their flocks, and black tents dot the upper valleys from June to September.

The best **trekking season** is May to June, followed by September, when the weather is at its most dependable – enquire at your *pansiyon* or the tourist office in Niğde (see p.451) for maps and a guide. By far the most popular way up to the peaks is via the **Emler valley**, where, in season, Sobek Travel (see p.451) run permanent base camps. From here you can take day-walks up many of the peaks, and also cross into the **Kokorot valley** on the east, or walk the north–south section of the range, emerging on the **Acıman plateau**.

ARRIVAL AND DEPARTURE — ALADAĞLAR MOUNTAINS

By bus In summer, minibuses run from Niğde's *otogar* to Çamardı, 7km northwest of Aladağlar (4 daily; 1hr). Ask for the Demirkazık road, or the driver will automatically drop you at the *Şafak Pansiyon*.

ACCOMMODATION

Aladağlar Camping Çamardı 465 ☎ 0534 201 8995, ⓦ aladaglarcamping.com. A perfect base for hikers, this homely campsite has a friendly, communal vibe. Food is served on site, or else the kitchen is available for use; breakfast costs €7. The knowledgeable owner is full of advice on trekking in the region, and can organize guided trips (€130/day), transport and luggage transfers. Tent €7, cabin €24, bungalow €30

Demirkazik Just outside Çamardı ☎ 0536 464 5168, ⓦ demirkazik.net. This twenty-bed pension offers transfers to trekking routes, as well as organizing trekking groups and guides. Cool and comfortable, it's excellent value, with exceedingly friendly staff. ₺60

Aksaray

Huddled in a riverside oasis on the far side of the Melendiz mountain range from Niğde, **AKSARAY** is a market town of little interest except as a base for reaching the Ihlara valley. It is perhaps best known for its namesake suburb in Istanbul, founded by people from here after the fall of Constantinople in 1453. Of marginal interest are the thirteenth-century **Eğri Minare**, the **Ulu Cami** on Banklar Caddesi, and the main square with its Atatürk statue and restored public buildings.

ARRIVAL AND INFORMATION — AKSARAY

By bus Aksaray's *otogar*, 6km west, is linked to the town centre by *servis* buses and a blue *Belediye* bus.
Destinations Konya (6 daily; 1hr 45min); Nevşehir (3 daily; 1hr 30min); Niğde (6 daily; 2hr).

Tourist office Kadioğlu Sok 1, in a restored Ottoman building a 2min walk from the main square (Mon–Fri 8am–noon & 1.30–5.30pm; ☎ 0382 213 2474).

ACCOMMODATION

Otel Yuvam Next to the Kurşunlu Camii at Eski Sanayı Cad ☎ 0382 212 0024. The best bet in town, occupying a renovated old townhouse; rooms are well furnished and clean, with modern bathrooms. ₺60

The Ihlara valley

Daily 8am until 1hr before sunset • ₺10

A fertile gorge cut by a deep green river between red cliffs, the **Ihlara valley** is an astonishingly beautiful natural landscape. Add some of the most attractive and

OPPOSITE IHLARA VALLEY (ABOVE) >

7

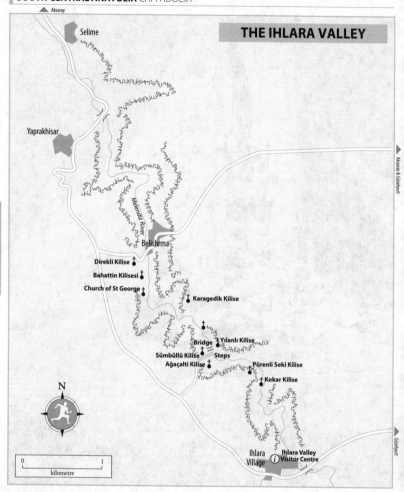

interesting **churches** and **rock-carved villages** in Cappadocia, and it's easy to see why the valley has become the highlight of the south.

Three villages offer ticketed entry points to the valley: **Selime**, **Belisırma** and **Ihlara village**. Most visitors come on day-trips from Ürgüp or Göreme; to appreciate the valley at its best, however, it's satisfying to do the trip independently, and to spend a night in either Ihlara village or Selime.

The 6km **walk** from Selime to Belisırma takes around three hours, while you'll need a further three hours to complete the 10km walk to Ihlara village. There are places to eat en route, in Belisırma, and one or two river-pools to swim in for when it's hot.

Selime

The beautiful troglodyte village of **SELIME**, en route to Ihlara and the valley entrance, is often overlooked in favour of the busier Ihlara village area. Several of the massive, squat **fairy chimneys** that dot the valley here contain churches; there's even a rock-cut cathedral, divided into three aisles by irregular pillars. The village takes its name from a Selçuk **mausoleum** in its cemetery, with a pyramidal roof inscribed "Selime Sultan".

Belisırma

The troglodyte village of **BELİSIRMA**, three hours' walk from either Selime or Ihlara village, blends into the tawny rock face from which it was carved to such an extent that in a bad light it can all but disappear from view. Its tranquil riverside location provides the opportunity to enjoy a meal at one of the simple tree-shaded restaurants on the west bank.

The eleventh-century **Direkli Kilise** (Church with the Columns) holds some very fine Byzantine frescoes, including a beautiful long-fingered Madonna and Child on one of the columns from which the church takes its name, and a picture of St George fighting a three-headed dragon.

The **church of St George**, 50m up the cliff-side, 500m south of Belisırma and 3km from the stairs at the main entrance, was dedicated to the saint by a thirteenth-century Christian emir, Basil Giagoupes, who was in the army of Mesut II. It bears an inscription expressing Christian gratitude for the religious tolerance of the Selçuk Turks. St George is depicted in armour and cloak, holding a triangular shield and flanked by the donor and his wife Tamara, who is handing a model of the church to the saint. To the right, St George can be seen in action, killing a three-headed serpent, with an inscription above that reads "Cleanse my soul of sins".

Ihlara village

At the valley's southernmost point, the **Ihlara village** offers two separate entrance points to the valley. One is in the village itself, and the other at the **Ihlara Valley Visitor Centre**, a car park and information point around halfway along the main road between Ihlara and Belisırma. This latter entrance provides direct access to the area that holds most of the valley's churches, via a precipitous but manageable descent of several hundred **steps** that plummet 150m to the valley floor. Walking from either village to this point offers a tremendous sense of solitude; easy trails run in both directions, each taking about one and a half hours.

Ihlara valley churches

The monastic occupation of the Ihlara valley, or **Peristrema** as it was originally known, seems to have been continuous from early medieval times until the fourteenth century. It would seem from the decoration of the churches, whose development can be traced through pre- and post-Iconoclastic periods, that the valley was little affected by the religious disputes of the period; the paintings show both Eastern and Western influences.

The most interesting of the churches are located near the small wooden **bridge** at the bottom of the steps from the visitor centre. A plan down here shows all the accessible churches, most of which are easy to find. To the right of the bridge, on the same side as the steps, is the **Ağaçaltı Kilise** (Church under the Tree). Cross-shaped with a central dome, the church originally had three levels, but two have collapsed, as has the entrance hall. The magnificent frescoes inside depict the Magi presenting gifts at the Nativity, Daniel with the lions (opposite the entrance in the west arm) and, in the central dome, the Ascension.

The **Pürenli Seki Kilise** – 500m beyond, 30m up the cliff-side, also on the south bank – can be seen clearly from the river below, although its frescoes, mainly depicting scenes from the life of Christ, are badly damaged. Another 50m towards Ihlara, the **Kokar Kilise** is relatively easy to reach and showcases the Annunciation, the Nativity, the Flight into Egypt and the Last Supper in the main hall. In the centre of the dome, a picture of a hand represents the Trinity and the sanctification.

Perhaps the valley's most fascinating church is located across the wooden footbridge, 100m from the entrance. The **Yılanlı Kilise** (Church of the Snakes) contains unusual depictions of sinners suffering in hell. Four women are being bitten by snakes, one of them on the nipples as a punishment for not breast-feeding her young. Another is covered in eight snakes, while the other two are being punished for slander and not heeding advice. At the centre of the scene, a three-headed snake is positioned behind one of the few Cappadocian depictions of Satan; each of its mouths holds a soul destined for hell.

Another church worth exploring is **Sümbüllü Kilise** (Church of the Hyacinths), just 200m from the entrance steps. Its attractive facade is decorated with horseshoe niches, while its badly damaged frescoes show Greek influence.

Güzelyurt

With its still-inhabited troglodyte dwellings, and old Greek houses with beautifully carved facades, **GÜZELYURT**, the nearest small town to the Ihlara valley, 13km northeast of Ihlara village, offers a chance to catch a glimpse of the old, untouched Cappadocia.

The religious community was established by St Gregory of Nazianzen in the fourth century, and a newly renovated church (**Kilise Camii**) dedicated to him. The golden bell given to the church by a Russian Orthodox community in Odessa is now in Afyon museum, but other items of interior decor, such as a carved wooden iconostasis and chair, gifts from Tsar Nicholas I in the nineteenth century, can still be seen *in situ*.

The most breathtaking sight in the Güzelyurt area has to be **Monastery valley** below the town, approached by taking a right turn out of the village after the Cami Kilise. The valley is riddled with more than fifty rock-cut churches and monastery complexes, some dating from the Byzantine era. The most attractive, the nineteenth-century **Yüksek Kilise** (High Church), is dramatically located on a high rock. A walk along its entire 4.5km length takes about two and a half hours, and brings you to the village of **Sivrihisar**. From there, a signposted fifteen-minute walk south leads to a freestanding church of note, the sixth- or seventh-century **Kızıl Kilise** (Red Church), one of the few remaining churches containing masonry in the whole of Cappadocia.

ARRIVAL AND DEPARTURE   IHLARA VALLEY

By minibus or dolmuş Minibuses to Ihlara village leave Aksaray's *otogar* (3 daily; 50min), passing Selime and the turn-off to Belisırma, and returning the same day. Dolmuşes run from Aksaray to Güzelyurt (6 daily; 1hr), and there are frequent dolmuş connections between Güzelyurt and Ihlara (15min). Groups can rent a whole minibus from Aksaray or Ürgüp; you'll need about ten people to make it viable.

By taxi A taxi from Aksaray to Ihlara (around 40min) costs in the region of €25.

ACCOMMODATION AND EATING

SELIME

Çatlak Hotel 1km from Selime entrance to the valley ☎0382 454 5006, ⊛catlakturizm.com.tr. This homely spot might be in need of an update, but its quirky stone mosaics and varnished driftwood walls add a spark of creativity, and it has bags of rustic charm. Rooms are simple but clean, and free transport is provided to the same-name restaurant (see below) at any time of day. €40

Çatlak Restaurant Directly opposite Selime entrance to the valley ☎0382 454 5006, ⊛catlakturizm.com.tr. Resembling a castle flanked by giant plastic fairy chimneys, this fun restaurant is hard to miss, and it's a reliable choice, with seating on the riverfront. Portions are well sized and a set menu with soup, main and dessert will set you back a mere ₺25. Daily 9am–1am.

BELISIRMA

Anatolia Valley Restaurant & Camping Along riverfront ☎0382 457 3040. Lounge around *sofra* tables on the floating river platforms, and enjoy live music in the evenings at this conveniently located restaurant. Camping spots are good, with power supplies for caravans and clean shower blocks, and the restaurant (daily 8am–11pm) offers good casseroles (from ₺15), including vegetarian options. Rates are for two people. Camping ₺25, caravan ₺35

IHLARA VILLAGE

Akar Pansiyon Atatürk Cad ☎0382 453 7018, ⊛ihlara-akarmotel.com. A good-value stopover for trekkers, this friendly *pansiyon* offers clean, carpeted rooms that are comfortable albeit basic. There's also free parking and free shuttles to and from the valley entrance. ₺100

Star Restaurant Pansiyon Ihlara Çarşı ☎0382 453 7020. Set by the river in the centre of the village, with a relaxing garden full of ducks and lovely views over the river from the balcony rooms. The ten rooms are a little run-down but clean enough and good value, plus there's camping and a decent restaurant (daily 8.30am–11pm). Tent (per person) ₺15, caravan ₺35, double ₺80

GÜZELYURT

Güzelyurt Pide Salonu Just off main square ☎ 0382 451 2397. This unassuming *pide* house welcomes a steady stream of locals. The food is reliably cheap and tasty, with freshly made *pides* from ₺7 and hearty casseroles from ₺12.50. Daily 7.30am–10pm.

Kalvari Restaurant On main square ☎ 0535 512 7448. Grab a chair out on the main square and join the throngs of locals that frequent this inviting kebab house. Staff speak minimal English but are so friendly it doesn't matter. Popular dishes include *Adana kebap* (₺15) and *şac tava* (lamb, ₺20). Daily 9am–1am.

★ **Hotel Karballa** Just up from main square ☎ 0382 451 2103, ⓦ karballahotel.com. Run by the team behind the *Kirkit Pension* in Avanos, this wonderfully rustic hotel is housed in an arresting nineteenth-century Greek monastery. The nuns' quarters are now cosy bedrooms, with spiral staircases leading to the top-floor rooms, and traditional decor, while the historic refectory has been transformed into a grand dining hall where dinner is available by reservation. There's even an open-air swimming pool overlooking the hills. €45

Yilmaz Traditional Home Pension Ortaokul Sok 6, signposted from main road ☎ 0382 451 2693, ⓔ kadeh-68@hotmail.com. With three basic but spacious rooms in a genuine Turkish home, *Yilmaz* offers a unique alternative to the region's other pensions. The host family speak little English, but their warm smiles and home-made breakfast make up for it. ₺70

Kayseri

Green fields, wooded hills and a snowcapped volcano surround the modern-looking concrete city that is today's **KAYSERİ**, encircling an old Selçuk settlement of black volcanic stone. While it has a reputation for religious conservatism and ultra-nationalism, most visitors find the locals welcoming and accepting of foreigners. It's also a thriving business centre, where traditional commerce, particularly raw textiles and carpets, still flourishes in the medieval *hans*. Kayseri's long history and strategic importance have left it littered with striking monuments, while two nearby attractions, the bird sanctuary of **Sultansazlığı** and **Mount Erciyes**, are ideal for picnics in summer and skiing in winter.

Part of the delight of Kayseri is that its beautiful old buildings still play an important role in everyday life, their very existence witness to the social conscience of the Selçuks. Koranic teaching forbade excessive concern with private houses, so public figures poured money into buildings for public welfare and communal activities.

Brief history

Originally called Mazaka, what's now Kayseri gained importance under the Phrygians. In 17–18 AD, renamed **Caesarea** in honour of Tiberius, it became the capital of Roman Cappadocia. As part of the Byzantine Empire, Caesarea was relocated 2km north of the ancient acropolis, allegedly around a church and monastery built by St Basil, the founder of eastern monasticism. Strategic in terms of both trade and defence, it soon became a cultural and artistic centre, though always vulnerable to attack from the east. The Arab invasions of the seventh and eighth centuries were particularly threatening, and in 1067 it finally fell to the great Selçuk leader Kılıç Arslan II. The Crusaders (from 1097) and the Mongols (from 1243) both briefly enjoyed possession before it became part of the Ottoman Empire in 1515, under Selim the Grim.

The citadel

Life in Kayseri centres around the towering crenellated walls of the **citadel** (*iç kale*), built from black volcanic rock. A sixth-century fortress erected in the reign of the Emperor Justinian once stood here, but the citadel you see today was built in 1224 by the Selçuk Sultan Keykubad. Naturally it has been much restored since, particularly by Mehmet II, who also built the **Fatih Camii**, the small mosque near the southwest gate.

Hunat Hatun Külliye

Opposite the citadel at the top of Seyyid Burhanettin Bul • Free

Construction of **Hunat Hatun Külliye** began in 1239, making it the first mosque complex to be built by the Selçuks in Anatolia. It consists of a mosque and *medrese*, the

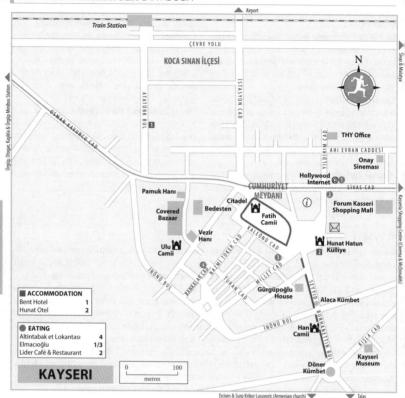

KAYSERI

■ **ACCOMMODATION**
| Bent Hotel | 1 |
| Hunat Otel | 2 |

● **EATING**
Altıntabak et Lokantası	4
Elmacıoğlu	1/3
Lider Café & Restaurant	2

latter ranking among the most beautiful examples of Selçuk architecture in Turkey. This former theological college has an open courtyard and two *eyvan*s (vaulted chambers open at the front). A wooden box containing a hair reputed to be from the Prophet Mohammed is located near the beautifully decorated *mihrab*.

Covered markets

Kayseri's three central **covered markets**, all dating from different periods, remain integral to the city. The **Bedesten**, built in 1497 and originally used by cloth-sellers, is now a carpet market, while in the **Vezir Hanı**, built by Damat İbrahim Paşa in 1727, raw cotton, wool and Kayseri carpets are sold, and leather is prepared for wholesale. The beautifully restored **covered bazaar**, built in 1859, holds five hundred individual shops.

Ulu Cami
Beyond the market area, south of the covered bazaar

The first of several ancient mosques in Kayseri, the **Ulu Cami**, or Great Mosque, was constructed under the Danişmend Turkish emirs in the first half of the thirteenth century. Still in remarkable condition, the mosque can be entered from three sides. Its roof is supported by four rows of stone pillars with assorted marble capitals, and it retains its original carved wooden *mimber*, although the central dome is modern.

Mausoleums

Thanks to its large number of tombs, Kayseri has been described as the **city of mausoleums**. Curious, squat, beautifully carved bits of masonry known as *kümbet*s, dating from the thirteenth to fifteenth centuries, can be found scattered in the most unlikely places – there are a couple on traffic islands on the main highway to Mount Erciyes.

The best-known mausoleum in Kayseri is the **Döner Kümbet**, "turning tomb", a typical example probably dating to the mid-thirteenth century, built for Shah Cihan Hatun. The tomb, west of the Kayseri Museum, is decorated with arabesques and palmettes, and a tree of life with twin-headed eagles and lions beneath.

Gürgüpoğlu House

Off Turan Cad, just inside the city walls • Tues–Sun 8am–5pm • Free

The **Gürgüpoğlu House** (Gürgüpoğlu Konağı), a half-timbered fifteenth-century Ottoman family home, is now a museum of ethnography, complete with wax dummies. Its first room is a typical Turkish salon, the walls intricately painted using natural dyes, with models seated on low divans, holding musical instruments. Upstairs, the rooms have beautifully carved and painted wooden ceilings; displays include wedding objects such as headdresses, make-up applicators and masterfully crafted silver belts. One room holds Selçuk tiles from the Hunat Hatun and glass nargiles, while the landing has a *topak ev*, or nomad's tent.

Kayseri Museum

Kışla Cad • Tues–Sun 8am–5pm • ₺3

The **Kayseri Museum** (Kayseri Müzesi) contains important finds from Kültepe (see p.461), and is well labelled in English. Its first room deals with the Hittites, their cuneiform writing and hieroglyphics, and includes a fascinating Hittite rock-relief from Develi and the head of a sphinx. Items from Kültepe include early Bronze Age depictions of the mother goddess, Assyrian bowls and jugs in the shape of animals, dating from the second millennium BC, and a collection of clay tablets in their clay envelopes – essentially small cheques – from the same period.

In the second room are finds from around Kayseri itself, including Hellenistic and Roman jewellery, and grave gifts from a Roman tumulus, among them highly worked pieces in gold and silver. In the garden, a pair of lovely seventh-century BC Hittite lions still have their teeth intact.

Surp Krikor Lusuvoriç

30min walk south of town on the Hacılar/Erciyes road

The domed Armenian church of **Surp Krikor Lusuvoriç** is a final architectural reminder of Kayseri's importance in the Byzantine Christian world. Dating from 700 AD, it's one of Turkey's largest consecrated churches, with room for a thousand worshippers. Surp Krikor (St Gregory), the first bishop and official founder of the Armenian Church, spent much of his early life here. To gain entry, ring the bell; the caretakers will be happy to let you look around.

ARRIVAL AND DEPARTURE   KAYSERI

By plane Kayseri's airport, 10km north of the centre, is connected to the centre by municipal buses (every 20min). On request, minibuses run by the Argeus tour agency (☎0384 341 4688, ⓦargeus.com.tr) or the Göreme-based Neşe (☎0384 271 2525, ⓦnesetour.com) will meet Turkish Airlines flights and take you to any village in Cappadocia. Expect to pay around ₺20/person to reach Ürgüp, for example. THY (Turkish Airlines) has an office in Istasyon Cad 48 (☎0352 222 3858).

Destinations Istanbul (6 daily; 1hr 30min); İzmir (1 daily; 1hr 35min).

By bus Kayseri's *otogar*, 2km west of the centre on Osman Kavuncu Cad, stands alongside a new minibus station used by minibuses to and from Ürgüp, Aksaray and Nevşehir. To reach the town centre, take the "Terminal" dolmuş from the minibus station, or from the opposite side of Osman Kavuncu Cad, to Cumhuriyet Meyd, 100m northwest of the Hunat Hatun complex.

Destinations Adana (22 daily; 7hr); Adiyaman (2 daily; 8hr); Afyon (6 daily; 9hr); Ankara (hourly; 4hr 30min); Antalya (8 daily; 11hr); Bursa (4 daily; 11hr); Isparta (5 daily; 9hr); Istanbul (12 daily; 12hr); İzmir (3 daily; 12hr); Konya (8 daily; 4hr); Niğde (hourly; 1hr 30min); Ürgüp (hourly; 1hr 30min).

By train The station is 1km north of town, at the end of Atatürk Bul. Frequent "Terminal" dolmuşes run into town, or to the *otogar* in the other direction.

Destinations Adana (2 daily; 7hr); Ankara (hourly; 9hr); Diyarbakır (4 weekly; 20hr); Istanbul (2 daily; 12hr); Kars (1 daily; 24hr); Malatya (2 daily; 6hr); Van (1 daily; 22hr).

INFORMATION

Tourist office Just north of Hunat Hatun complex on Sivas Cad (Mon–Sat: summer 8am–5.30pm; winter 8am–noon & 1–5pm; ☎0352 222 3903). Friendly, English-speaking staff can provide city and regional maps and information, and help book trips to the Mount Erciyes ski resort.

Internet Hollywood Internet Café, Sivas Cad 15.

ACCOMMODATION

Kayseri is well served by **chain hotels** like Ibis, Novotel, Hilton and Radisson Blu and there are few budget options.

Bent Hotel Atatürk Bul 40 ☎0352 221 2400, ⊛benthotel.com. A stylish choice right in the centre, offering well-sized a/c rooms with parquet floors, elegant furnishings and minibars. There's also a decent breakfast buffet and choice artworks dotted throughout. ₺170

Hunat Otel Zengin Sok 5, behind the Hunat Hatun complex ☎0352 232 4319. It's a shame that this place couldn't fork out for a cleaner, as it's the cheapest option in town and in an excellent location. The welcoming owner will be happy to show you the rooms before you decide – worthwhile, as some are notably more hygienic than others. Shared bathrooms, no breakfast. ₺50

EATING

While Kayseri is more famous for its spicy, garlicky *pastırma* (cured meat), *sucuk* (a kind of sausage-like salami) and *mantı* (Turkish ravioli) than for its actual **restaurants**, it does hold a few decent places to eat.

Altıntabak et Lokantası Bankalar Cad 16 ☎0352 222 2522. A stylish local haunt with waiters kitted out in traditional uniforms, this is an atmospheric place to tuck into traditional soups or a generous bowl of *mantı* (₺12), served with a healthy dollop of fresh yoghurt. Daily 8am–10pm.

Elmacıoğlu Millet Cad 5/Sivas Cad ☎0352 222 6965, ⊛elmaciogluiskender.com. This popular café-restaurant has two branches in the city centre, with pleasant a/c surroundings and plenty of generously portioned traditional dishes. For the best value, opt for one of the meal deals like an *Iskender kebap* or *köfte* with fries, salad and *ayran* for ₺19. Daily 8am–9pm.

Lider Café & Restaurant Opposite tourist office at Sivas Cad 6 ☎0352 232 1530, ⊛liderunmamulleri .com.tr. Immaculate and a/c, this modern café serves *pides* (from ₺5), reasonably priced kebabs (from ₺10), omelettes and desserts, with pleasant views across to Mount Erciyes. Head to the open-air downstairs area to tuck into the wide range of ice-cream flavours. Daily 24hr.

Erciyes Dağı

25km south of Kayseri · Catch a Develi-bound dolmuş, near the Han Camii on Talas Cad (every 10min)

Visiting **Erciyes Dağı**, the 3916m-high extinct volcano that dominates Kayseri to the southwest, is one of the greatest pleasures of a trip to this region. If you have transport, take a packed lunch and head for its foothills, a twenty-minute drive from town. Otherwise, the city dolmuş will take you to Tekir Yaylası, at an altitude of 2150m. Hiking, mountain biking and horseriding tours are also available in summer.

During the **ski season**, between December and May, eight lifts provide access to heights of up to 3000m. It's a little barren, but snow conditions are often very good, and several winter sports are gaining popularity – snowrafting, snowshoeing and snow tubing are all possible. The Kayseri tourist office (see above) has full information on mountain activities, and can help book tours and accommodation. Erciyes Ski Center offers **equipment rental** (skis cost around ₺30/day; a ski pass ₺40 for one day; ⊛kayserierciyes.com.tr).

Sultansazlığı

50km southwest of Kayseri · ₺5 · Catch a Yahyalı bus from the *otogar* to Ovaçiftlik (daily 8am–5pm, every 30min; 1hr), 1km walk from the water

You might assume that the flat, dull steppe that lies beyond Erciyes Dağı, around the Kayseri–Niğde road, was bereft of bird or plant life. Consequently, the oasis of the

Sultansazlığı bird sanctuary, now a national park, is easy to miss, but it's worth the effort of hunting out.

The five thousand acres of freshwater marshes here, also known as **Kuş Cenneti** (Bird Paradise), stand at the crossroads of two migration routes, making it an extremely important wetland for breeding migrant and wintering birds. Visiting species include flamingoes, pelicans, storks, golden eagles, herons, spoonbills and cranes. As the best time to spot birds is at dawn, it's worth staying **overnight**.

In an effort to preserve the wildlife, access is supposedly only possible with an accredited **park guide** (expect to pay around ₺100 a day), although at the time of writing it was still possible to visit independently. The *Sultan Pansion* (see below) can advise you on the current situation; all their tours are accredited so you won't have to pay extra.

ACCOMMODATION

SULTANSAZLIĞI

Sultan Pansion Sultansazlığı Kuş Cenneti ☎ 0352 658 5549, ⓦ sultanbirding.com. The best choice for birdwatchers, with eighteen clean, simple en-suite rooms and ample camping space, just 200m from the marshes. Knowledgeable, English-speaking staff can arrange everything you need for your trip, including binoculars, guides and boat and jeep tours. Breakfast is included and the on-site restaurant also serves lunch and dinner (call ahead to be sure, especially if you're traveling in a large group). €50

Kültepe

22km northeast of Kayseri • Tues–Sun 8am–noon & 1–5pm • Free • Catch a Bünyan-bound bus, from Sivas Cad in Kayseri; the site is signposted, near a petrol station, after 20km, but it's a 2km hike from the bus stop

The important **archeological site** of the ancient city of Kanesh is now known as **Kültepe**. Some fifteen thousand clay tablets and a well-preserved selection of household furnishings, including human and animal statuettes, were discovered here – the best are housed in Kayseri and Ankara museums. The site itself has been well excavated and gives some idea of building plans and street layouts, as well as construction techniques that are still prevalent in Anatolia.

Brief history

The city's golden age was in the second millennium BC. At that time, the nearby *karum* of **Kanesh** – the most important of nine Assyrian *karum*s (trade centres) in Anatolia, importing tin and textiles in exchange for cattle, silver, copper and skins – was inhabited by the Assyrian trading colony and the lower classes, while Kanesh itself was reserved for royalty of Anatolian stock. The thin layer of ash covering the site dates from two massive conflagrations, the first in around 1850 BC, and the second around 1200 BC. The city lost its importance during the Hittite age, but was still occupied during the Hellenistic and Roman periods.

The sites

Excavations labelled "level II", from the second millennium BC, dominate the upper site of Kanesh, especially the Large Palace, which covered an area of 3000 square metres and included a paved central courtyard, and the **Palace of Warsana**, king of Kanesh. Walls were generally of large mud bricks with stone foundations, though the Large Palace held long storage rooms with stone walls.

The **Karum** is five minutes' walk further down the country lane that leads past the entrance to Kanesh. Here, excavations have revealed the foundations of shops, offices, archives and storerooms, all packed closely together inside a defensive wall. The dead were buried together with precious gifts under the floors of their own houses in stone cist graves, some of which can be seen on site.

North Central Anatolia

AMASYA

North Central Anatolia

When the first Turkish nomads arrived in Anatolia during the tenth and eleventh centuries, the landscape – rolling grassland dotted with rocky outcrops – must have been strongly reminiscent of their Central Asian homeland. Any visitors who choose to trek through the region today are in some respects an equally hardy bunch, braving long journey times, occasionally tricky roads and seasonal temperature extremes to visit towns, cities and sights far less heralded than their counterparts in South Central Anatolia. However, visitors prepared to do a little digging will find beguiling ancient cities, Selçuk ruins and clutches of picture-perfect Ottoman housing, scattered hither and thither around what counts as one of Turkey's most rewarding and undiscovered quarters – somewhat surprising, since it's also home to Ankara, the Turkish capital and the second-largest city in the land.

8

From northern Anatolia in general, most roads lead to **Ankara**. A provincial town that found itself suddenly elevated to become capital of the entire country, it feels surprisingly tourist-free despite being the political and social centre of modern Turkey. Its nightlife isn't a patch on that in Istanbul and the coastal resorts, but perhaps a welcome change if you've been in the provinces for a while; in addition, it boasts the best museum in the country.

West of Ankara lie two cities typical of the region – off the tourist radar, but perfect opportunities to take Turkey's true pulse. First up is **Eskişehir**, a lively, student-filled city whose own crop of Ottoman buildings has been painted in attractive pastel tones; the place is known to pipe-puffers worldwide for meerschaum, a local rock famed for its smoke-cooling properties. Then comes salt-of-the-earth **Kütahya**, an initially scruffy-looking place where, if you peer a little harder, you'll find some of Turkey's most delightfully located museums, as well as whole streets of buildings swathed with the city's famous glazed tiles. Some way to the northeast, there are even more beautiful Ottoman buildings on show in charming **Safranbolu**, deservedly one of the most tourist-oriented towns in the region, and something of a national must-see.

In the northeast of Ankara, the former Hittite capital of **Hattuşa**, with its temples and fortresses, is simply jaw-dropping – one of the most distinctive ancient cities in the land. Pressing further on you'll soon come to **Amasya**, a very pleasant city boasting a collection of tombs dug into the steep cliffs overlooking its centre, along with yet more tranches of Ottoman buildings. A road heads southeast to **Tokat**, home to the biggest **kebabs** in Turkey, and the Selçuk treasure-troves of **Sivas** and **Divriği**.

SİVAS

Highlights

❶ Museum of Anatolian Civilizations, Ankara A treasure-trove of artefacts from around the country, in one of Turkey's most prestigious museums. **See p.471**

❷ Kütahya Fantastic little museums, an incredibly appealing old town, superb food … and not a tourist in sight. **See p.481**

❸ Stay the Ottoman way in Safranbolu This small town's laidback nature is best appreciated in its wonderfully restored Ottoman houses – many are now hotels, featuring low-slung beds, creaky floorboards and authentic antiques. **See p.485**

❹ Hattuşa Former Hittite capital in a magnificently bucolic setting – even more reason for a 6km trek around the old city walls. **See p.490**

❺ Rock tombs of Amasya The highlights of this spellbinding city are the massive rock tombs of the Pontic kings – carved into a cliff face and lit up at night to great effect. **See p.494**

❻ Tokat kebap Every Turkish city has its own kebab, but Tokat's is truly unique – not least because it's about twice the size of any other. **See p.499**

❼ Selçuk monuments in Sivas At the centre of this intriguing city you'll find superlative examples of Mongol-inspired architecture, with highly decorative facades and beautiful mosaic work. **See p.500**

HIGHLIGHTS ARE MARKED ON THE MAP ON P.466

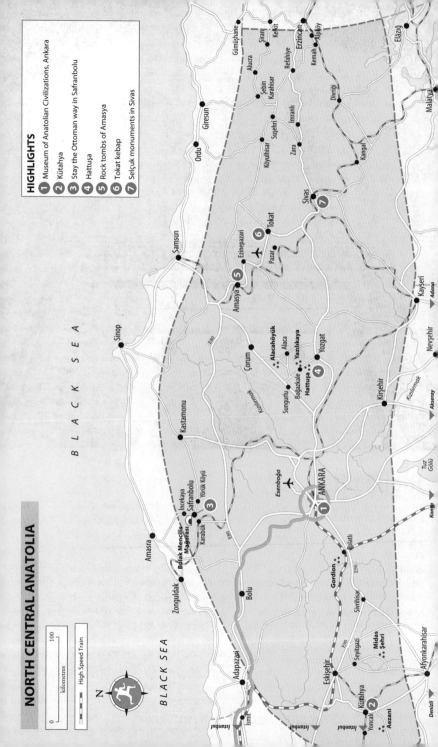

NORTH CENTRAL ANATOLIA

N

BLACK SEA

0 kilometres 100

— — High Speed Train

HIGHLIGHTS

1 Museum of Anatolian Civilizations, Ankara
2 Kütahya
3 Stay the Ottoman way in Safranbolu
4 Hattuşa
5 Rock tombs of Amasya
6 Tokat kebap
7 Selçuk monuments in Sivas

BLACK SEA

Sinop
Amasra
Zonguldak
Adapazarı
İstanbul
İzmit
İstanbul
Bolu
Eskişehir
İstanbul
Kütahya
Yoncalı
Aezani
Denizli
Afyonkarahisar
Midas Şehri
Seyitgazi
Sivrihisar
Gordion
E90
Polatlı
ANKARA
Esenboğa
Konya
Kastamonu
Safranbolu
İncekaya
Yörük Köyü
Bulak Mencilis Mağarası
Karabük
E80
Kızılırmak
Çorum
Sungurlu
Boğazkale Hattuşa
Alacahöyük
Alaca
Yazılıkaya
Yozgat
Kırşehir
Kızılırmak
Tuz Gölü
Aksaray
Nevşehir
Adana
Kayseri
Samsun
Ordu
Giresun
Amasya
Ezinepazarı
Pazar
Tokat
Sivas
Köyulhisar
Suşehri
Zara
İmranlı
Gümüşhane
Alucra
Şiran
Şebin Karahisar
Refahiye
Kelkit
Erzincan
Kemah
Alpköy
Divriği
Kangal
Malatya
Elazığ
E90

Ankara and around

Few cities have changed so much, so quickly, as the Turkish capital of **ANKARA**. When Atatürk declared it capital of his nascent republic in 1923, it was little more than a small provincial town, known chiefly for its production of angora, soft goat's wool. Fast-forward to the present day, and it's a bustling, modern city of well over four million souls, its buildings spreading to the horizon in each direction across what, not too long ago, was unspoiled steppe. This was, of course, Atatürk's vision all along – a carefully planned attempt to create a seat of government worthy of a modern, Westernized state.

Many visitors to Turkey believe Istanbul to be the nation's capital, and comparisons between the two cities are almost inevitable. While Ankara is never going to be as attractive a destination, it certainly holds enough to keep you occupied for a few days – diverting sights, good restaurants and pumping nightlife. Most visitors' first taste of Ankara is **Ulus**, an area where a couple of **Roman monuments** lurk beneath the prevailing modernity. Heading east you'll pass the superb **Museum of Anatolian Civilizations** before heading up to **Hisar**, the oldest part of the city. Here, the walls of a Byzantine **citadel** enclose an Ottoman-era village of cobbled streets; climbing on up will buy you a jaw-dropping city view. Heading south of Ulus you'll soon come to studenty **Kızılay**, filled with bars and cheap restaurants; real-estate values increase exponentially as you move south again towards **Kavaklıdere** and **Çankaya**, where the cafés and restaurants are somewhat more salubrious.

Thanks to its extensive bus, plane and train connections, many use Ankara as a springboard for other sights in Northern Anatolia. The most notable place within day-trip range is **Gordion**, an ancient site particularly notable for its connections to King Midas and his reputedly golden touch.

8

Brief history

After the **Hittites** founded Ankara around 1200 BC, naming it Ankuwash, the town prospered due to its position on the royal road running from Sardis to their capital at Hattuşa. Their successors, the **Phrygians**, called the city Ankyra, and left behind a huge necropolis that was uncovered near the train station in 1925. They, in turn, were followed by the **Lydians** and the **Persians**. Alexander the Great passed through on his way east, while in the third century BC invading **Galatians** (Gauls) held sway for a while.

By the start of the first century BC, the **Romans** had made substantial inroads into Asia Minor. In 24 BC Ankara was officially absorbed into the empire under Augustus and renamed Sebaste (Greek for Augustus). The city thrived under the Romans, but the later Byzantine era ushered in a period of decline. Arabs, Persians, Crusaders and Mongols stormed the city en route to greater prizes, but only the **Selçuks** were to settle, taking control in 1071. By 1361 Ankara had been incorporated into the burgeoning **Ottoman state** and went into another decline; only its famous wool stopped it disappearing altogether.

After Atatürk's final victory, despite being little more than a backward provincial centre Ankara was made the official **capital of the Turkish Republic** – an attempt by the revolutionaries to distance themselves from the perceived corruption of Ottoman Constantinople, and gain pan-national favour with a new central location. Turkey's vociferous pro-Istanbul lobby, however, was dismayed by this choice, and many foreign governments initially baulked at the idea of establishing embassies here (though there are plenty today, often running in tandem with consulates in Istanbul). Meanwhile, people were drawn to Ankara from the Anatolian countryside in search of work and a higher standard of living, and the city's **population** of thirty thousand swiftly swelled.

With great power, however, comes great responsibility – present-day Turkey has its fair share of ethnic, religious and political tension, and while Istanbul has played host to most of the recent anti-government protests, Ankara occasionally bears witness to civil strife. October 2015 saw the deadliest bomb attack in recent Turkish history, with

ANKARA

0   500
metres

N

EATING

And Cafe	5
Bedesten	7
Bolulu	11
Büyükşehir Market	4
Cafémiz	13
Can Balık	9
Enver Simit Sarayı	10
Günaydın	14
Kınacızade Konağı	6
Mado	2
Muhabbet	8
Şehzade Ocağı	1
Sushico	15
Tevhid	3
Tunalı Balıkçısı	12

SHOPPING

Antiques Alley	2
Büyükşehir Market	1
D&R	4
Dost	3

DRINKING & NIGHTLIFE

Bilim Ve Sanat	3
Eski Yeni	1
Hayyami	4
Up Lost	2

ACCOMMODATION

Angora House	5
Berlitz	3
Çevikoğlu	1
Deeps Hostel	8
Divan	6
Golden Boutique	12
Gordion	9
Gülpınar	2
Mostar	7
Radisson Blu	4
Sheraton	11
Tunalı	10

ANKARA ORIENTATION

Ankara is neatly bisected along its north–south axis by the 5km-long **Atatürk Bulvarı**, and everything you need is in easy reach of this broad and busy street. At the northern end is **Ulus Meydanı** – usually known simply as **Ulus** ("Nation") – a large square that has lent its name to the surrounding area. While it's not particularly attractive, it's where you'll probably gravitate on arrival as it holds cheap hotels and is well positioned for both sightseeing and city transportation.

Heading south down Atatürk Bulvarı from Ulus brings you to the main west–east rail line, and beyond that **Sıhhıye Meydanı**, an important junction that marks the start of **Yenişehir** ("New City"). A 10min walk south of Sıhhıye brings you to **Kızılay**, the busy square that's the main transport hub of the modern city. At the bottom of Atatürk Bulvarı, **Çankaya** is Ankara's most exclusive suburb and location of the **Presidential Palace**.

---

more than one hundred killed at a **peace rally**. At the time of writing no group had taken responsibility for the blasts.

Ulus

One of Ankara's busiest neighbourhoods, teeming **Ulus** neatly tells the story of the city – and served as the birthplace of modern Turkey itself. The area is home to an appealing smattering of sights dating back to **Roman** times, including an ancient temple, stone column and bathhouse. **Ottoman** Ulus has largely been extinguished by the mania for concrete, but the intriguing new developments around the Hacı Bayram mosque give a Disney-fied impression of the era. Then, of course, there are the sights pertaining to the **Republic**: at Ulus Meydanı, a towering equestrian **statue of Atatürk** – flanked by threatening bronze soldiers in German-style coal-scuttle helmets – gazes out over the building that once housed his Grand National Assembly, and is now the **Museum of the War of Independence**. Lastly, attractive **Gençlik Parkı**, with its fairground rides and fancy tearooms, will bring you racing into the modern day.

Temple of Augustus

Off Hacı Bayram Veli Cad

The remains of the **Temple of Augustus** constitute Ankara's most important ancient monument. Built in honour of Augustus between 25 and 20 BC, after Ankara was made the provincial capital of Galatia, its main claim to fame is an inscription on the outer wall. Detailing the Res Gestae Divi Augusti (Deeds of the Divine Augustus), this was the emperor's political testament, carved on every temple of Augustus after his death. The Ankara version is the only one to survive in its entirety. The temple, whose walls alone have endured, was converted into a Christian church around the fifth century AD, and during the fifteenth century became the *medrese* of the Hacı Bayram mosque (see below).

Recently, the whole area surrounding the temple, and the mosque next to it, was fully gentrified with a swathe of **mock-Ottoman buildings**. It remains debatable whether the Ottomans also enjoyed gawping at gaudy fountains, riding escalators or shopping for chandeliers, but the overall effect is pleasing, featuring a couple of **miniature mosques** with wooden minarets, and even a couple of mock-Ottoman guesthouses (see p.476).

Hacı Bayram Camii

Off Hacı Bayram Veli Cad • Free

The hilltop **Hacı Bayram Camii** was named after **Bayram Veli**, Ankara's most celebrated Muslim saint, who founded the Bayrami order of dervishes at the start of the fifteenth century. His body is buried in the tomb in front of the building. Visit at prayer time and you'll hear some of Turkey's most distinctive **muezzins** at work; at other times you'll have to content yourself with superb views over the city.

8

Column of Julian

Hükümet Meyd

The **Column of Julian** commemorates a visit to Ankara by the Byzantine emperor Julian the Apostate, chiefly remembered for his short-lived attempt to revive worship of the old Roman gods in the fourth century. The column's stonework is characterized by a strange, layered effect rather like a long, cylindrical kebab – almost exactly like a vertical *kokoreç*, in fact.

Roman baths

Off Çankırı Cad • Daily 8.30am–7pm • ₺5

Dating back to the third century AD, the **Roman baths** (Roma Hamamları) are set in a large palaestra (exercise field) that's scattered with overgrown truncated columns and fragments of cracked masonry. Of the baths themselves, the only extant features are the brick pillars that supported the floors, allowing warm air to circulate and heat the rooms above.

War of Independence Museum

Ulus Meyd • Tues–Sun 8.45am–7pm • ₺1

The modest late Ottoman schoolhouse building that's now home to the **War of Independence Museum** holds a special place in Turkish hearts. Atatürk and his Nationalist supporters convened their provisional parliament here on April 23, 1920, while three years later it was also the venue for the **declaration of the Turkish Republic**, serving as the parliament building until 1925.

Today's museum is devoted to the military struggle that preceded the foundation of the modern republic. An extensive collection of photographs, documents and ephemera covers every detail of the various campaigns. All the captions are in Turkish, but much of the material speaks for itself. Visitors can also view the chamber where delegates sat in small school desks, illuminated by candlelight and oil lamps, with Atatürk overseeing from the vantage point of a raised platform.

Gençlik Parkı

Talat Paşa Bul • Daily 24hr • Free

Filling most of the gap between Ulus Meydanı and the train station, **Gençlik Parkı** (Youth Park) was built on the orders of Atatürk to provide a worthy recreational spot for the hard-toiling citizens of his model metropolis. The park is often packed with families strolling around the artificial lake, and hosts occasional outdoor concerts. Its southern section features **fairground rides**, while near the eastern gate you'll find the **State Opera House** (Devlet Opera; see p.478). Looking like a dark pink, Art Deco underground station, this was built at Atatürk's behest – he developed a taste for opera while a military attaché in Sofia in 1905.

Ethnographic Museum

Türkocağı Sok, off Talat Paşa Bul • Tues–Sun 9am–noon & 1–5pm • ₺5 • ⓦ etnografyamuzesi.gov.tr

Just south of Ulus, the **Ethnographic Museum** is housed in a grandiose white marble building that was the original resting place of Atatürk before the construction of the Anıt Kabir mausoleum (see p.473). It holds an extensive collection of folk costumes and artefacts from Selçuk times onwards, and some fine Selçuk woodcarving.

The old town

Ankara's **old town** is set within the inner walls of the **Hisar**, a Byzantine **citadel** whose walls enclose the city's original settlement. Of all Ankara's districts, this Ottoman-era village of cobbled streets and ramshackle wooden houses most fully rewards a relaxed and aimless stroll. Most of the area remains defiantly unrestored, but many grand Ottoman mansions have been renovated, decked out with carpets and antiques, and

GECE KONDU

From the upper fortifications of Ankara's **citadel**, you'll see the city spread out in all its glory. Many of the nearby buildings look less than glorious, however – these are referred to by locals as **gece kondu**, which loosely translates as "built overnight". Though likely put together over more than a day, their hasty construction is all too apparent: after Ankara was declared national capital, Anatolians moved to the city in droves, and many erected their own houses around the citadel. Effectively **shanty towns**, these have remained the most impoverished parts of the city ever since; Ankara's present-day rulers would, of course, prefer to see the back of them, and bit by bit, the old buildings are being replaced with rows of ugly high-rises. Mercifully, the former residents of the *gece kondu* are being moved here, rather than flung to the outskirts of the city.

transformed into restaurants or carpet shops geared towards the tourist trade. On the way up here, you'll walk past the wonderful **Museum of Anatolian Civilizations** – an absolute must-see for those wanting to make sense of Turkey's multifaceted history.

Museum of Anatolian Civilizations

Opposite southern end of İnönü Parkı • Daily 8.30am–6.45pm • ₺15, audioguides ₺5

Whenever you see a replica artefact at an archeological site in Turkey, you can bet that the original lies under the protective wings of the unmissable **Museum of Anatolian Civilizations**. For most visitors, its outstanding archeological collection, documenting the peoples and cultures of Anatolia from the late Stone Age through to Classical times, is the high point of a visit to Ankara.

The museum is housed in a restored fifteenth-century *bedesten*, which fell out of use after a catastrophic fire in 1881. Its vast cache of artefacts is laid out in chronological order, clockwise from the entrance, with large stone reliefs dating from the Hittite and Phrygian periods in the central chamber. Most exhibits are clearly labelled in English.

From the Paleolithic to the Bronze Age

The museum's first four sections move visitors through Turkey-time from the Old Stone Age to 2000 BC. The **Paleolithic** section features assorted bone fragments and primitive stone tools and weapons from a cave site at Karain, 30km northwest of Antalya, while objects found at Çatal Höyük, a settlement of New Stone Age mud-brick houses 52km north of Konya, have yielded significant evidence about the **Neolithic** period (7000–5500 BC). The importance of agriculture in this era may account for the abundant fertility-goddess figures – represented by baked-clay female forms of ample proportions – that appear throughout the museum.

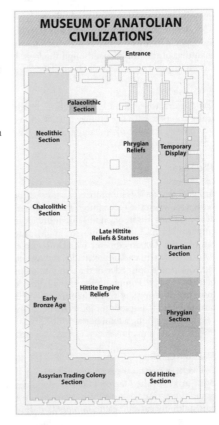

MUSEUM OF ANATOLIAN CIVILIZATIONS

8

Entrance

Palaeolithic Section

Neolithic Section

Phrygian Reliefs

Temporary Display

Chalcolithic Section

Late Hittite Reliefs & Statues

Urartian Section

Hittite Empire Reliefs

Early Bronze Age

Phrygian Section

Assyrian Trading Colony Section

Old Hittite Section

Most of the objects in the **Bronze Age** section (3000–2000 BC) come from Alacahöyük; among the most striking exhibits are the pieces of gold jewellery unearthed in the royal tombs. There then follows a small **Assyrian Trading Colony** section (1950–1750 BC), with the most notable exhibits being well-preserved cuneiform tablets that rank among Anatolia's earliest written records.

Hittite sections

The **Hittites** (1700–700 BC) left spectacular sites at Boğazkale and nearby Yazılıkaya, east of Ankara (see p.489). Most of the objects here are from Boğazkale and Alacahöyük, with the most sophisticated example being a vase with a relief depicting a lively wedding procession. Stelae carved with hieroglyphs have proved a valuable source of information about the **Old Hittite kingdom** (1700–1450 BC).

There's even more to see from the **Hittite Empire** (1450–1200 BC) itself. Elaborate reliefs from Alacahöyük indicate the sophistication of Hittite culture during this time, while if you're planning to visit Hattuşa, look out for the lion and sphinx figures from the city gates. The originals are here, replaced with replicas at the site itself.

Phrygian and Urartian sections

Most of the museum's **Phrygian** objects (1200–700 BC) were recovered from the royal tumulus at Gordion (see p.474), capital of Phrygian Anatolia after the fall of the Hittites. The timber-framed chamber at the heart of the tumulus has been re-created and objects from it are on display nearby. Most impressive are a wooden table of intricate design and skilfully wrought bronze vessels.

Modern knowledge of the **Urartians** largely derives from clay tablets listing military successes. On the evidence of such artefacts here, their culture was less sophisticated than that of the Phrygians, though the large bronze cauldron resting on a tripod with cloven bronze feet is austerely beautiful.

Ankara section

Downstairs, towards the exit, a section details finds from **Ankara** itself. While it can't really compete with the bounty upstairs, the collections of Roman coins are of interest – as are the remains of Ankarapithecus, a 9.8-million-year-old ape named after the city of its discovery.

The Hisar

Daily 24hr • Free

Ankara's **city walls** were probably first constructed by the Hittites over three thousand years ago, when they recognized the defensive potential of the citadel outcrop. The walls of the existing **Hisar**, or citadel, are more recent, built on the orders of the Byzantine emperor Michael III (remembered as "Michael the Sot") in 859, who updated defences built by the Roman emperor Heraclius atop earlier Galatian fortifications.

At the northern end of the citadel, the **Ak Kale**, or "White Fortress", presents tremendous views. The northeast edge of the city, just about visible, is the approximate site of the battlefield where Pompey defeated the Pontic king Mithridates the Great in 74 BC. Rising from the eastern walls is **Şark Kulesi**, a ruined tower whose panoramic outlook makes it a favourite kite-flying spot for local children. Lastly, the **Güney Kapı** (South Gate) has two vast towers flanking a twin portal; embedded in the wall connecting the towers are various fragments of Roman masonry, including altars supported by recumbent statues of Priapus.

Alâeddin Camii

Just inside the Hisar's western gate • Free

Built in 1178, the **Alâeddin Camii** is the oldest mosque in Ankara, albeit much restored since its creation. Its exterior is pretty, if unexceptional; duck inside and you'll find a painstakingly carved Selçuk *mimber* (a pulpit from which the imam delivers homilies).

Aslanhane Camii

Aslanhane Sok • Free

An unadulterated example of Selçuk architecture lies a few streets southeast of the Hisar, in the shape of the **Aslanhane Camii** or "Lion-House Mosque", whose interior is by far the most impressive in Ankara. It's known as a "forest mosque" on account of the 24 wooden columns that support the intricately carved wooden ceiling. The astonishingly detailed walnut *mimber* dates back to 1209 and is one of the last examples of Selçuk decorative carving.

The new town

South of the railway tracks, you'll find the bulk of what passes for Ankara's **new town**. The land slopes uphill for several kilometres towards the Presidential Palace, and on the way you'll notice things becoming progressively more affluent and orderly. The first area of note is **Kızılay**, which is Ankara's main shopping and nightlife zone – department stores, chain restaurants and suchlike. To its west is **Atatürk's mausoleum**, Anit Kabir, while just to the southeast is the **Kocatepe Camii**, the biggest mosque in Anatolia. There are few sights at all around the rich, café-strewn neighbourhoods of **Kavaklıdere** and **Çankaya**, though they're worth hitting for what may be a sneak preview of Turkey's future.

Kocatepe Camii

Off Esat Cad • Free

The minarets of the massive **Kocatepe Camii** loom a few blocks east of Kızılay's array of cheap restaurants. Ankara's largest mosque by far, and indeed one of the biggest in the world, this neo-Ottoman structure was completed in 1987, and has a shopping centre and car park underneath.

Anıt Kabir

Anıt Cad; rear entrance on Akdeniz Cad • Daily 9am–5pm • Free, though bring photo ID • Ankaray (LRT) train, or bus #265 from Ulus Meydanı, to Tandoğan; free shuttle buses every 5min from main entrance

The mausoleum of **Anıt Kabir** is a national shrine to **Mustafa Kemal Atatürk**, the man who shaped modern Turkey (see p.662). Both shrine and man are tremendously important to locals – the level of reverence inspired here is almost dictatorial, though nobody is forced to come, and you can be sure that the emotions are real. As with similar facilities in Pyongyang, Hanoi and Beijing, the complex has a larger-than-life air intended to convey a sense of power and majesty.

Approaching from the main (northern) entrance, you'll find yourself on **Lion Road**, a 260m-long pedestrian thoroughfare flanked with lion statues. At the end of this is a courtyard, with the **mausoleum** itself lying at its head – look for a squared-off Neoclassical temple with huge bronze doors. Visitors wearing hats must remove them as they enter; soldiers ensure that everyone shows the appropriate respect. The mausoleum interior is almost completely bare – the only decoration is some discreet mosaic work – so that all attention is focused on the plain sarcophagus. Atatürk's body was brought here in 1953 from its original resting place in what's now the Ethnographic Museum.

Three large halls are positioned around the courtyard. The largest houses the **Atatürk Museum** in which you'll find everything from Atatürk's evening dress to the rowing machine he used for exercise. Among the most eye-catching exhibits are a gun disguised as a walking stick, of which Ian Fleming would have been proud, and the gifts of a diamond-encrusted sword from the shah of Iran and an elegant toilet set from the king of Afghanistan. Lastly, note that a highly picturesque **changing of the guard** takes place hourly on the main courtyard.

8

Gordion

92km southwest of Ankara, and 18km northwest of Polatlı • Polatlı best accessed by high-speed train from Ankara (10 daily; 35min); onward dolmuşes are very infrequent, so catch a taxi (at least ₺120 return, including waiting time)

After the collapse of the Hittite Empire, the Phrygians briefly dominated Anatolia. Their capital, **Gordion**, is one of western Anatolia's most important archeological sites – albeit hard to reach without your own transport. It's a name of much resonance, associated not only with the eponymous knot, but also with King Midas and his golden touch (see box below). The first things you'll see as you approach are the immense royal tumuli, scattered across the drab, steppe-like landscape. Inside these, archeologists found stunning artefacts that testified to the sophisticated nature of Phrygian culture. Nearby, the foundations of the Gordion acropolis have been uncovered.

Brief history

The original settlement at Gordion dates back to the Bronze Age, and the site was certainly occupied during the Hittite period. The Phrygians arrived during the ninth century BC, and a hundred years later the settlement became capital of the empire founded by the Phrygian king **Gordius**. Gordion, like the Phrygian Empire itself, experienced a brief flowering, followed by destruction and protracted decline.

There's little left in the records, save for the myths and legends associated with the empire, though some concrete information survives about its final king, Mitas (Midas) of Mushki, who is thought to have reigned from 725 BC to 696 BC.

It was invading **Cimmerians** who laid waste to the Phrygian Empire, destroying Gordion, and though the Phrygians made a comeback and rebuilt their capital, their power had been irreversibly reduced. The city was occupied in 650 BC by the **Lydians**, fell in turn to the **Persians** just over a century later, and in 333 BC welcomed **Alexander the Great** for wintertime during his great march east. The arrival of the **Galatians** (Gauls) in Asia Minor in 278 BC was the final chapter in the long decline, precipitating the flight of Gordion's population.

THE MYTHS AND LEGENDS OF GORDION

The name **Midas** is inextricably associated with Gordion. Several Phrygian kings bore this name, and over the centuries a kind of composite mythical figure has emerged. The best-known legend, of Midas and the **golden touch**, tells how Midas captured the water demon, Silenus, after making him drunk by pouring wine into his spring. As ransom, Midas demanded of Dionysos the ability to turn all he touched into gold. After Dionysos granted this wish, Midas was dismayed to find he had been taken literally, and his food and even his own daughter were transformed. He begged Dionysos for release from the curse, and was ordered to wash his hands in the River Pactolus. The cure worked, and thereafter the river ran with gold.

According to another tale, Midas was called upon to judge a musical contest between Apollo and the satyr Marsyas. Midas decided in favour of Marsyas and in revenge Apollo caused him to grow the ears of an ass. (Marsyas came off even worse – the god skinned him alive.) To hide his new appendages, Midas wore a special hat, revealing his ears only to his barber who was sworn to secrecy on pain of death. Desperate to tell someone the king's secret, the barber passed it on to the reeds of the river, which ever after whispered, "Midas has ass's ears."

Another story may have some basis in reality. During the reign of Gordius, an oracle foretold that a poor man who would enter Gordion by oxcart would, one day, rule over the Phrygians. As the king and nobles were discussing this prediction, a farmer named Midas arrived at the city in his cart. Gordius, who had no heirs, saw this as the fulfilment of the prophecy and named Midas his successor. Subsequently, Midas had his cart placed in the temple of Cybele on the Gordion acropolis, where it was to stand for half a millennium. Somehow the belief arose that whoever untied the intricate knot that fixed the cart to its yoke would become master of Asia. During his stay in the city **Alexander the Great** decided not to untie the **Gordian knot**, but to slice through it with his sword. The phrase "cutting the Gordian knot" is still used today, to describe solving any intractable problem in one swift move.

Royal tombs and museum

Yassıhüyük • Tues–Sun 8am–5pm • Combined ticket ₺5

Of the main concentration of the huge and inscrutable tumulus **tombs** of the Phrygian kings, only the **Midas Tümülüsü** (Royal Tomb), conveniently located in the village of Yassıhüyük, just short of the site itself, is likely to attract your attention. Measuring 300m in diameter and over 50m high, it's thought to be the burial chamber of an unidentified Phrygian king, buried, curiously, without weapons or ornaments. The tumulus was excavated during the 1950s, when American archeologists bored a 60m **tunnel** through to its centre and discovered the intact wooden chamber. Inside they found the skeleton of a man in his 60s on a wooden couch surrounded by grave objects. Among these were three exquisitely crafted wooden tables, inlaid screens, large numbers of bronze clasps for garments and 178 bronze vessels, including three large cauldrons; now, the chamber is all you'll see.

The worthwhile **museum**, across the road, contains items recovered from the tombs, and some attractive mosaics. However, the best of the finds are, inevitably, in Ankara's Museum of Anatolian Civilizations (see p.471).

Acropolis

2km south of Yassıhüyük

An easy-to-spot raised area, south of the village, is the site of an eighth-century BC **acropolis**. The heart of the city, this was the location of the royal palace, temples and administrative buildings, the foundations of which have been revealed by excavations.

Substantial remains of the huge Phrygian-era **town gate** survive on the southeastern side of the acropolis. This must have been a formidable structure: even in its present truncated state it's more than 10m high, making it one of the largest surviving pre-Classical buildings in Anatolia. The outer portal was flanked by twin towers, from which defenders would have been able to inflict heavy casualties on attackers in front of the gate.

Fencing keeps visitors away from the central **palace**, which consisted of four megara, or large halls with vestibules, each featuring wonderful mosaics. The fourth megaron was probably a temple to Cybele, the Phrygian incarnation of the mother goddess. If that's the case, then it was here that Alexander the Great cut the Gordian knot.

ARRIVAL AND DEPARTURE

ANKARA

BY PLANE

Ankara's Esenboğa Airport is 33km north of the city (☎0312 398 0100, ⊚esenbogaairport.com). At the time of writing, the Havaş buses connecting it with 19 Mayis Stadium in Ulus had been discontinued; private services are likely to pop up even if the original ones (every 30min; 45min; ₺12) are not replaced. A taxi from the airport to the centre will cost around ₺75, or more between midnight and 6am.

Destinations Adana (3–6 daily; 1hr); Antalya (6–9 daily; 1hr); Bodrum (2–5 daily; 1hr 20min); Dalaman (2 daily; 1hr 15min); Diyarbakır (4 daily; 1hr 20min); Elazığ (2 daily; 1hr 15min); Erzurum (2–3 daily; 1hr 25min); Gaziantep (2 daily; 1hr 10min); Istanbul (1–2 hourly; 1hr); İzmir (8–10 daily; 1hr 20min); Kars (1–2 daily; 1hr 35min); Malatya (1 daily; 1hr 10min); Mardin (2 daily; 1hr 35min); Şanlıurfa (2 daily; 1hr 20min); Trabzon (4 daily; 1hr 20min); Van (3 daily; 1hr 35min).

BY TRAIN

The train station (☎0312 311 0602) is close to the heart of things at the bottom of Cumhuriyet Bul; at the time of writing, a colossal new terminal was being built alongside to handle the inevitable large future increase in rail traffic. Frequent buses head from the main entrance to Ulus (also within easy walking distance) and Kızılay, or you can walk through the tunnel under the railway line to Maltepe Ankaray (LRT) station.

Destinations Adana (1 daily; 11hr 30min); Divriği (1 daily; 13hr); Diyarbakır (1 daily; 20hr 30min); Erzurum (1 daily; 20hr); Eskişehir (11 daily; 1hr 25min); Istanbul (Pendik station; 6 daily; 4hr); İzmir (1 daily; 15hr); Kars (1 daily; 24hr); Konya (7 daily; 1hr 45min); Malatya (2 daily; 15hr); Sivas (3 daily; 10hr).

BY BUS

The city *otogar* (known as Aşti) is in the western suburbs; free *servis* minibuses run to the centre from the car park out front. Some go to the plush hotels in Kavaklıdere, and others to Ulus station; alternatively, catch the Ankaray light rail (every 15min; 20min; ₺3).

Destinations Adana (10 daily; 7hr); Amasya (hourly; 6hr); Antalya (12 daily; 7hr); Bodrum (10 daily; 12hr); Bursa (hourly; 6hr); Diyarbakır (6 daily; 12hr); Erzurum (4 daily;

8

15hr); Eskişehir (6 daily; 3hr); Gaziantep (12 daily; 10hr); Istanbul (every 30min; 4hr 45min–6hr); İzmir (hourly; 8hr); Kayseri (14 daily; 5hr 30min); Konya (hourly; 3hr 30min); Kütahya (7 daily; 5hr); Mardin (3 daily; 16hr); Nevşehir (12 daily; 5hr); Safranbolu (16 daily; 3hr 30min); Samsun (10 daily; 6hr 30min); Şanlıurfa (4 daily; 12hr); Sivas (hourly; 7hr 30min); Sungurlu (hourly; 2hr 30min); Tokat (12 daily; 6hr 30min); Trabzon (5 daily; 13hr).

GETTING AROUND AND INFORMATION

Tickets Ankara's public transport is pretty good, with tickets costing ₺3/journey – valid on buses and the metro lines, you can buy them at metro stations or street kiosks (you'll need one before boarding a bus). If you're in town for a while, consider buying a transport card (₺5), which will knock ₺1 off each journey.

By bus Buses run the length of Atatürk Bul from Ulus to Kızılay, and then either branch off to Maltepe under a tunnel or continue to Çankaya via Kavaklıdere; there are too many routes to mention, but all buses have their main destinations on the front.

By metro Four modern metro lines run efficient, regular trains until around 10.30pm. One light-rail line (green on the system maps), called the Ankaray, heads from the *otogar* to join both line 1 (red) and line 2 (yellow) at Kızılay. Line 3 (blue) starts at the western end of line 1, and you're unlikely to need it; lines 4 and 5 will follow in due course.

By taxi Plentiful taxis can be flagged down just about anywhere (minimum fare ₺4, higher from midnight to 6am). A trip from Ulus to Kavaklıdere, for example, costs around ₺20.

Car rental Avis, airport (☎0312 398 0315) and Tunus Cad 68, Kavaklıdere (☎0312 467 2313); Best, Büklüm Sok 89/9, Kavaklıdere (☎0312 467 0008); Budget, Tunus Cad 39, Kavaklıdere (☎0312 417 5952); Europcar, airport (☎0312 395 0506) and Koza Sok 154, Gaziosmanpaşa (☎0312 398 0503); Hertz, airport (☎0312 398 0535) and Atatürk Bul 138, Kavaklıdere (☎0312 468 1029).

Tourist office There's a small, near-useless office in Gençlik Parkı, just downhill from the entrance opposite the *Radisson Blu* (Mon–Fri 8.30am–5pm; ☎0312 324 0101), and a more helpful one at the airport (daily 9.30am–6pm; ☎0312 398 0348); there's also a small branch in the Hisar (daily 10am–5pm).

ACCOMMODATION

Finding a room in Ankara is rarely a problem, given the relative lack of tourists. Most of the cheaper hotels are in **Ulus**, though lone women may not feel comfortable in the very cheapest places. The few hotels in and around the **Hisar** make by far the quietest after-dark options. Moving down into **Sıhhıye** and **Kızılay** takes you up another notch or two, and prices and standards steadily increase towards **Kavaklıdere**, further south.

ULUS AND AROUND

★**Berlitz** Hükümet Cad 4 ☎0312 324 5316, ⓦberlitzhotel.com. One of the area's newest hotels, with surprisingly swish rooms decked out in a gold-maroon-brown colour scheme, featuring perfectly clean bathrooms. Those at the front have small, semicircular balconies. ₺150

★**Çevikoğlu** Çankırı Cad, Orta Sok 2 ☎0312 310 4535. Clean option whose backstreet setting cuts out a lot of noise. Curved furnishings provide retro chic in the clean, simple rooms, which also feature TVs and a minibar. Perhaps the cheapest safe option for lone females – single rooms can usually be haggled down to ₺45, including a tasty buffet breakfast. ₺80

Gülpinar Hacı Bayram Cad 6 ☎0312 311 5998. As cheap as Ankara gets, especially for single travellers (₺35). Beyond its mock-Ottoman facade, it sports cell-like rooms and just-about-clean shared facilities; it's so close to Hacı Bayram mosque that, unlike other places of this price, prostitution doesn't appear to be a problem. No wi-fi. ₺55

Mostar Opera Meyd, Tavus Sok 6 ☎0312 310 6242, ⓦmostarhotelankara.com. Sitting pretty in a pleasantly earthy area, this hotel sports clean and bright rooms with spacious tiled bathrooms. There's a 24hr restaurant on the premises. ₺180

Radisson Blu İstiklal Cad 20 ☎0312 310 4848, ⓦradissonblu.com. The only "proper" hotel in the area, with well-appointed rooms, huge buffet breakfasts and a largely business clientele. Try to get a park-facing room. ₺400

THE OLD TOWN

★**Angora House** Kalekapısı Sok 11 ☎0312 309 8380, ⓦangorahouse.com.tr. It's well worth splashing out for a stay at this boutique hotel, set inside a 200-year-old house. The Hisar location is perfect and the service first class, but best of all are the individually styled rooms – carved wooden ceilings, quality linen, large bathrooms and arty flourishes. Only six rooms, so book ahead. ₺200

★**Divan** Depo Sok 3 ☎0312 306 6400, ⓦdivan.com.tr. Luxurious hotel set in a converted *han* – a bit of a trend across Turkey, but this is one of the better conversions, bar the ugly scaffolding that protects its large courtyard. Rooms are slick and charmingly decorated, and there are a couple of places to eat on the fringes of the complex. Best rates are available online. ₺375

THE NEW TOWN

★**Deeps Hostel** Atac Sok 2 ☎0312 213 6338, ⓦdeepshostelankara.com. Ankara's first hostel is a friendly, brightly painted affair with a wider range of rooms than the small lobby might suggest. Singles are good value at ₺55, and if there are enough willing participants, staff have been known to lead guests on bar crawls. Dorm ₺27, double ₺85

Golden Boutique Boğaz Sok ☎0312 426 0111, ⊛goldenboutiquehotel.com.tr. Golden? They're not kidding… from the sofas to the shower fittings, gold hues are absolutely all over the place in this hotel. On the plus side, staff are extremely friendly, the location is nice and quiet and the rates are as cheap as the area gets. ₺180

Gordion Büklüm Sok 59 ☎0312 427 8080, ⊛gordionhotel.com. At the upper end of middle-range, this hotel has large, comfortable rooms, all decorated in a tasteful, classical style. There's also a pool on site, and candlelit massages on offer in the health club. ₺350

Sheraton Noktalı Sok ☎0312 468 5454, ⊛sheraton.com. Enjoy a pampered existence in this cylindrical concrete monolith. There's a friendly atmosphere for a five-star hotel, a great view of the city from the top, plus various restaurants, a pool and two cinemas. ₺800

Tunalı Tunalı Hilmi Cad 119 ☎0312 467 4440, ⊛hoteltunali.com.tr. A good upper-mid-range option, run by the same family for two generations; cheaper than most places in Kavaklıdere, it's close to all the nightlife. Rooms are ordinary but functional, with fridge, satellite TV and huge windows overlooking the busy street. Coffee shop and formal dining room attached. ₺260

EATING

If you're looking for cheap eats, **Ulus** is your best bet. **Kızılay** has most of the mid-range places (particularly on and around Karanfil and Selanik sokaks), while classier restaurants can be found in **Kavaklıdere** and **Çankaya**. The exceptions to this general rule are the restaurants in the Hisar's restored Ottoman houses.

ULUS AND AROUND

Büyükşehir Market Hal Sok. This excellent market (see p.479) is as good for budget dining as it is for self-catering. Though establishments change like the wind, you should be able to track down some *kokoreç* (something like Turkish haggis in a bun) or *cupra levrek* (fried fish and salad in a bun) for less than ₺6. Opening times vary.

Mado İşhani 1 ☎0312 310 1717. Part of a nationwide chain serving expensive (but delectable) traditional Turkish desserts, often with a contemporary twist. A round of *baklava* and ice cream will set you back around ₺16. Daily 8am–10pm.

Muhabbet Gençlik Parkı ☎0312 310 6778. The best of Ankara's many park-based tearoom-cafés, tucked into an area near the train station – and therefore ideal when waiting for your train, or recovering from a long journey. Despite the location, it's not too dear – ₺3.50 for lemonade, a little more for coffee, or ₺14 for a nargile. Daily 8am–10pm.

Şehzade Ocağı Opposite Hacı Bayram Camii. Small café, with some outdoor seats facing directly onto the Temple of Augustus. Augustus didn't specify which ice-cream flavour he liked on the List of Achievements he left there (see p.469), but there are plenty to choose from (₺4). Daily 8am–9pm.

Tevhid Anafartlar Cad 10 ☎0312 310 4851. One of those restaurants that looks nothing out of the ordinary from the outside, but serves phenomenal food. Justly famed for its *İskender kebap* (₺16), which is up there with the best in the land – the lamb is sliced from the skewer with almost surgical precision. They also do good *pide* from ₺7. Daily 7am–10pm.

THE OLD TOWN

And Cafe Just uphill from Alâeddin Camii ☎0312 312 7978, ⊛and-cafe.com. Just inside the Hisar, this open, elegant place serves Turkish coffee (₺7), "Early Grey" tea (₺5.50) or a slice of cake (₺6 and up), all enjoyable over a commanding view of the city. It's a restaurant too, but the food is overpriced. Tues–Sun 9am–10pm.

Bedesten Opposite Aslanhane Camii. Rickety teahouse meets oversized treehouse: have a good clamber around before settling on a place to sit, squat, lie or lounge. The coffee's good too (₺4), but best of all you can buy anything you see hanging around the place. Tues–Sun 9am–9pm.

★ **Kınacızade Konağı** Kalekapısı Sok 28 ☎0312 324 5714, ⊛kinacizadekonagi.com. Set in a wonderful Ottoman house, this restaurant also has history to its credit – Atatürk himself swung by when it was still a home. The owners now whip up some great meals, though are proudest of their huge village breakfasts (₺60; feeds two). Regular breakfasts, or hot dishes such as clay-baked trout or sizzling lamb, go for around ₺20, and the honey walnut *gözleme* just beg to be tried. Daily 8am–midnight.

THE NEW TOWN

Bolulu Tunalı Hilmi Cad 79 ☎0312 444 4248, ⊛bhu.com.tr. The best ice cream in Ankara, and a fancy-looking place to boot, with coffee-coloured chairs and smart light fittings. Their delectable gelato costs just ₺2 a scoop – try a mulberry-pistachio combo, a local mix giving you a blend of the tart and the creamy. Daily 9am–10pm.

Cafémiz Arjentin Cad 19 ☎0312 467 7921, ⊛cafemiz.com.tr. The best of the wider Kavaklıdere area's glut of cafés, a trendy spot with semi-enclosed seating areas, floral prints on the walls and cushions, and cherub prints on the lampshades. A breakfast omelette will set you back around ₺16, burgers and salads go for a little more, and their range of coffees and teas start at ₺9. Daily 8.30am–midnight.

8

Can Balık Sakarya Cad 13/F ☎0312 431 7870. Most evenings, the queues go around the corner at this eat-on-the-street snack-restaurant, which serves quality seafood at low prices – a plate of calamari, *alabalık* (trout) or *hamsi* (anchovy) will get you change from ₺10, with a piece of bread to scoff it down with (this is Turkey, after all). Also good beer-food if you're doing a round of the area's bars. Daily 10am–10pm.

Enver Simit Sarayı Ziya Gökalp Cad ☎0312 431 0807. Just around the corner from *Deeps Hostel* (see p.476), this is a good place to fill up on cheap grub – try *çiğ köfte* (a wrap filled with cold, spicy paste and greens) and an *ayran* for just ₺3, have a chicken *döner* for ₺3.50, or get a full half-litre of freshly pressed orange juice for ₺4. Daily 24hr.

Günaydın Arjentin Cad 18 ☎0312 468 5353, ⓦwww.gunaydinet.com. A steak place on "Argentina Road" ... you couldn't make it up. This classy restaurant has an almost religious following among expats and well-off locals alike, and the fact that meats are cured in-house lends the place the air of an upscale butcher's – choose your table carefully. Daily 11am–11pm.

Sushico Arjentin Cad, Attar Sok 10 ☎0312 444 7874, ⓦsushico.com.tr. Ankara's Asian restaurants are typically drab affairs serving food that can hardly be called authentic. What a pleasant change this highly attractive place is, serving well-prepared Japanese, Chinese and Thai dishes – try a bento set (from ₺28), crispy duck (₺32) or a green curry (₺28). Daily 11am–11pm.

Tunalı Balıkçısı Tunalı Hilmi Cad 106 ☎0312 426 2728, ⓦtunalibalikcisi.com.tr. Fresh-looking fish restaurants are the latest trend to hit Ankara, with at least a dozen of them strewn around the city's wealthier areas, all painted a fetching baby blue. This one is an airy spot also good for people-watching, with great lunch deals – just ₺20 for grilled fish with salad and soup. Daily 9am–midnight.

DRINKING AND NIGHTLIFE

For a good night out you're best advised to avoid Ulus and head south – the student district of **Kızılay** is the obvious starting point. Ankara is pretty progressive, so female visitors shouldn't attract too much unwelcome attention. For something more trendy head for the bars of Kavaklıdere. The **clubbing** scene is improving but don't expect too much; some student late-night venues are hidden away in the backstreets of the university district, Cebeci, but you really need a local to guide you to them.

Bilim Ve Sanat Konur Sok 6, Kızılay. More chilled than most of its neighbours in this busy area, with a wraparound balcony and dangling vines, and a great view of Ankara's most vibrant street. Beers ₺10 for a half-litre. Daily 10am–3am.

★**Eski Yeni** İnkılap Sok 6, Kızılay ☎0312 433 0701, ⓦeskiyenibar.com. With draught beer at ₺10 for a half-litre, shots from ₺7 and a heaving dancefloor, this is a great place to have a drink and throw some shapes on a weekend evening. The bar's name translates as "Old New", which is rather apt: the happy, easy-to-please crowd squeals in delight when the latest "Ankara house" hit comes on, then does exactly the same thing for Annie Lennox or Simply Red. Daily 3pm–late.

Hayyami Bestekar Sok 82, Kavaklıdere ☎0312 466 1052, ⓦhayyamisarapevi.com. Cosy, laidback wine-bar-cum-restaurant, where the Italian dishes play second fiddle to an excellent selection of booze (₺45 and up for a bottle, or ₺15 and up for a glass). Pop by for live music in the evenings. Daily 11am–late; music Wed–Sun.

Up Lost Bayındır Sok 17, Kızılay ☎0312 432 4919. Grungy yet somehow homely, this sixth-floor bar is a friendly place with live music and karaoke sessions on weekend evenings – they'd be more than pleased to see a foreigner grabbing the mic. Mon–Sat 6pm–late.

ENTERTAINMENT

Once Ankara was made capital of the new republic, the city had to become the cultural capital of Turkey, supported by the opera-loving Atatürk. **Concerts**, and in particular **opera**, are well worth attending if you can. A visit to Ankara's **Opera House** is a unique experience, while classical music performances by the State Orchestra take place at the State Concert Hall and other venues. The atmosphere is refreshingly informal, and thanks to government subsidies tickets are cheap. The main season starts in earnest in Oct and runs through to March, and monthly programmes are listed in the Sun edition of the *Turkish Daily News*. Recent international **films** are usually shown in their original language with Turkish subtitles; tickets cost around ₺18, with discounts before 6pm.

CLASSICAL MUSIC AND OPERA

State Opera Atatürk Bul ☎0312 324 2210, ⓦdobgm.gov.tr. Classics such as *Tosca*, *La Bohème* and *Madame Butterfly*, as well as occasional piano recitals and classical concerts. Tickets (₺25 and up) are available from the box office in season (9.30am–5.30pm, 8pm on performance days), up to a month in advance and from the Dost bookshop in Kızılay (see opposite).

State Orchestra Talat Paşa Bul 38, just south of the Opera House and Gençlik Parkı ☎0312 309 1343. The Presidential Symphony Orchestra performs here twice weekly, showcasing classical music by Turkish and foreign

FESTIVALS IN ANKARA

Ankara Film Festival ⓦfilmfestankara.org.tr. The city's main film festival, taking place over ten days each March.

Ankara Music Festival ⓦankarafestival.com. Now well over thirty years old, this major classical music festival takes place in the spring (usually April), and is spread across three weeks or so.

Büyük Ankara Festival ⓦankara.bel.tr. A fun, family-friendly series of events taking place over one week each July – ask at a tourist office (see p.476) for the latest plans.

Flying Broom ⓦfestival.ucansupurge.org. Women's film festival hosted by a feminist organization, taking place each May.

International Cartoon Film Festival ⓦankara.bel.tr. Cartoon festival aimed at children, but inevitably enjoyed by older folk too. It runs for a few days each April – ask at the tourist office for information.

composers. Tickets sold by the State Opera box office (see above), ₺15 and up. Thurs & Fri 8pm, plus occasionally Sat 11am.

FILM

Megapol Konur Sok 33, Kızılay ☎0312 419 4493. More arty than the *Metropol*, which it backs onto, screening anything from Japanese to Eastern European films. Look out for occasional English-speaking classics.

Metropol Selanik Cad 76, Kızılay ☎0312 425 7479. Hugely popular multiscreen cinema showing new releases and special screenings of classic movies and foreign films. There's a coffee shop inside, a beer garden outside and any number of cafés and bars along this street.

SHOPPING

Antiques Alley Outside Hisar. A collection of shops in an atmospheric little alley near the citadel. You'll find all sorts of quirky goods here – marble-print clothing, artsy glassware, cool wall hangings and sweet candleholders. Come out of the *Divan* hotel (see p.476) and swing a right; it's right there on your left. Most shops daily 9am–6pm.

Büyükşehir Market Ulus. This atmospheric market is heaven for self-caterers – fruit, veggies and honey from all over the country, including scrumptious olives from İzmir and *beyaz* (yellow) cherries from Konya, are on offer. The market's butchers sit uncomfortably close to a few pet shops outside, though mercifully these only trade in birds. Daily 6am–6pm, restaurants open later.

★ **D&R** İran Cad 7, Kızılay ☎0312 478 0777, ⓦdr.com .tr. Great bookstore with a decent English-language selection on the fourth floor – grab a coffee from the ground-level café before you head up, and mull over your purchases on a comfy chair. Daily 9am–10pm.

Dost Karanfil Sok 11, Kızılay ☎0312 425 2464, ⓦdostyayinevi.com. Central bookstore with English novels in the basement, alongside a good selection of pricier coffee-table books. Mon–Sat 9.15am–9.35pm, Sun noon–7pm.

DIRECTORY

Banks and exchange Banks and ATMs are all over the city, especially south of Ulus along Atatürk Bul. The airport also has several places to change money.

Embassies Australia, Nenehatun Cad 83, Gaziosmanpaşa (☎0312 459 9500); Canada, Cinnah Cad 58 (☎0312 409 2712); Iran, Tehran Cad 10, Kavaklıdere (☎0312 468 2820); New Zealand, İran Cad 13, Kavaklıdere (☎0312 467 9054); Russian Federation, Karyağdi Sok 5, Çankaya (☎0312 439 2122); USA, Atatürk Bul 110, Kavaklıdere (☎0312 455 5555); UK, Şehit Ersan Cad 46/A, Çankaya (☎0312 455 3344).

Hamams Karacabey Hamamı, Talat Paşa Bul 101, Ulus, is the oldest in town, built in 1445 (daily 10am–10pm; ₺25). A little cheaper are the baths at the *Sürmeli Hotel*, Cihan Sok 6, Sıhhıye (daily 10am–10pm; ₺15; ☎0312 231 7660) and Eynebey Hamamı, Adnan Saygun Cad 11 (daily 24hr; ₺19; ☎0312 309 6865).

Hospitals Hacettepe Hastanesi, just west of Hasırcılar Cad in Sıhhıye (☎0312 466 5858 or ☎0312 466 5859), should have an English-speaking doctor available at all times. You may be treated more quickly at one of Ankara's private hospitals: Çankaya, Bülten Sok 44, Çankaya (☎0312 426 1450), is the most central.

Pharmacies In each neighbourhood, pharmacies take turns in providing a 24hr service called *Nöbetçi*, with the location of the relevant branch posted on the window of the other pharmacy shops. Most central is Ülkü, Meşrütiyet Cad 23, Kızılay.

Police The tourist police (☎0312 384 0606) are located in Ankara's main police station (Emniyet Sarayı) in the district of Akköprü, a short walk south of the Akköprü metro station.

Post office Ankara's main PTT is on Atatürk Bul in Ulus (daily 24hr; ☎0312 509 5000). There's also a PTT at the train station (daily 7am–11pm) and smaller branches dotted around town.

8

Eskişehir and around

Handily positioned on the high-speed train line linking Istanbul and Ankara, the modern university town of **ESKİŞEHİR** makes a potential stopover on the way from Istanbul, especially if you want to buy trinkets made from **meerschaum** (see box below) or are heading to the charming village of **Seyitgazi**.

Eskişehir's energetic mayor has, since the turn of the century, implemented such reforms as pedestrianizing much of the centre, gentrifying the (now very attractive) **canal area**, and inaugurating a flashy new tram system. An appealing crop of **Ottoman houses** in the **Odunpazarı** district, just south of the centre, has also been restored – imagine a miniature, pastel-painted version of Amasya or Safranbolu.

Seyitgazi

45km south of Eskişehir • Direct buses from Eskişehir (hourly; 1hr; ₺6)

Little **SEYİTGAZİ** sits in a fertile valley set incongruously amid the rolling Anatolian steppe. Despite its beautiful location and its status as a diverting historical attraction, visitors are rare and your arrival may take the tractor-driving locals by surprise – the ability to string a sentence together in Turkish will likely see you afforded hero status, and bought some tea.

Türbe-tekke complex

On the valley slopes, above town • Daily 8am–6pm • Donations suggested for main hall

Seyitgazi takes its name from Şehit Battal Gazi, the commander of an Arab army that forayed into Anatolia during the eighth century. An unlikely legend relates that he was killed during the siege of Afyon and buried with a Byzantine princess who had pined away through love for him. The site of their resting place was revealed to the mother of the Selçuk sultan Alâeddin Keykubad, who promptly built a *türbe* (tomb) for the *gazi*. It became a popular place of pilgrimage, and during the thirteenth century Hacı Bektaş Veli, founder of the Bektaşi dervish order (see box, p.431), established a *tekke*, or monastery, here.

The **Türbe-tekke complex** itself is roughly horseshoe-shaped, open towards the slope and with a Byzantine church and a Selçuk mosque by the entrance. The former is a reminder that a Christian convent originally stood on the site, while the latter contains the outsized sarcophagus of Şehit Battal, just under 7m in length. Next to it is the more modest sarcophagus of his princess.

Midas Şehri

30km south of Seyitgazi • No public transport

The wonderful valley that stretches between Seyitgazi and Afyon is filled with eerie rock formations, and dotted with **Phrygian tombs**, temples and fortifications. **Midas Şehri** ("City of Midas" in Turkish, though there's no specific Midas connection) is by far the most accessible and substantial Phrygian sight, though you'll need your own transport to

---

MEERSCHAUM

Literally "sea foam" in German, **meerschaum** is a porous white stone, large deposits of which are mined in the villages that surround Eskişehir. While wet, the soft stone is carved into all manner of ornaments, but the smoke-cooling properties of a meerschaum pipe make that the most highly prized item. Several shops in Eskişehir work the mineral, and with a little haggling it's usually possible to pick up a bargain – prices tend to range from ₺30–90, and there are cute little shops dotted around the Odunpazarı district. **Bay Pipo** (daily 8am–9pm; ☎0532 761 9180) by the mosque, has a particularly wide and fairly priced selection.

get here – it's on a lovely route used almost exclusively by tractors. The cave-pocked site, too, is a beauty – it's as if Midas had touched Cappadocia and made it not gold, but green.

The **site** itself comprises the sketchy ruins of a Phrygian city atop a 30m-high plateau whose steep rock sides have been carved with elaborate decorative facades. The one on the northwest face of the plateau has come to be known as the **Midas tomb**; heading west from here leads to more niches carved in the rock, a number of rock tombs and an incomplete relief. Access to the upper part of the plateau and the remains of the Phrygian **citadel** is via a flight of steps on the eastern side. Near the top of the steps, some of the many altars and tombs bear inscriptions and decorative reliefs.

In the southwestern part of the citadel is a **rock throne**, a kind of stepped altar on which the figure of a deity would have been placed. Its upper part holds a clear **inscription** and crude decorative scratchings. Elsewhere a few fragments of the citadel's defensive wall survive.

ARRIVAL AND DEPARTURE ESKİŞEHİR

By train Hosting an ever-increasing number of high-speed services, Eskişehir's train station is on the northwest edge of the centre, an easy walk along the nearby canal. Destinations Ankara (11 daily; 1hr 25min); Istanbul Pendik (8 daily; 2hr 40min); Kütahya (6 daily; 1hr 20min).

By bus The colossal *otogar* is 3km east of town, a distance usually spanned by *servis* minibus, though it's also linked to the centre by tram (every 10min; ₺2.40). Destinations Ankara (6 daily; 3hr); Bursa (6 daily; 2hr 30min); Istanbul (4 daily; 5hr); Kütahya (11 daily; 1hr 20min).

ACCOMMODATION

Abacı Konak Türkmen Hoca Sok 29 ☎0222 333 0333, ⊛abaciotel.com. The only option in the old town area is less a hotel than a miniature village of faux Ottoman housing – rooms are as comfortable as they are charming, and the grounds make a wonderful spot for coffee in the morning, or a glass of wine after dark. **₺260**

Ada Life Adalar Sok 2 ☎0222 233 7711, ⊛adalifeotel .com. Decent business option, more or less overlooking the canal; if your room doesn't have a view, you'll still, be able to soak one up over a superb rooftop breakfast. **₺180**

EATING AND DRINKING

The canal banks are lined with places to eat and to sup coffee – mostly cheap, since this is a university town. The local dish, **çi börek** – a kind of fried, half-moon dumpling with mincemeat and onions inside, always bought in rounds of five – is a Crimean Tatar delicacy; many locals, especially in the old town, are of similar stock. Eskişehir is quite conservative, so despite its huge student population, it's hard to find a place to **drink**.

★**Kasr-ı Nur** Kocamüftü Sok 7 ☎0222 230 5703, ⊛kasr -inur.com. This is by far the best place to eat in the old town: it's family-run and set in the area's most attractive square – at least eight different pastel hues on view, and not that many cars. All foods are organic and handmade – try the village-style breakfast (*köy kahvaltısı*; ₺20), a gigantic affair with loads of jams, olives and cheeses, mainly from İzmir (like the family). Later in the day, a round of *çi börek* (₺10) may be in order, and there's always good coffee and tea on offer. Daily 8am–10pm.

Travelers' Cafe Under Ada Life hotel, Adalar Sok 2 ☎0222 230 3011, ⊛travelerscafe.com.tr. Youthful restaurant-bar serving global food including pad thai (₺15), as well as pasta, fajitas and burgers at similar prices, all under a ceiling of international football shirts. In the evenings, most are here for the beer, sangria and caipirinhas (most cocktails ₺18). Daily 9am–midnight.

Kütahya and around

Tiles, tiles and more tiles. That's what you'll see when strolling around **KÜTAHYA**, a likeable, working-class city, halfway between İzmir and Ankara, in which a substantial number of buildings are swathed in decorative **glazed products**. Even the main square is distinguished by a fountain that centres on a huge ceramic vase. Kütahya tiles are used throughout Turkey, especially in restoration work on Ottoman mosques – İznik may be more famous (see box, p.165), but in reality much of the industry has moved here.

Most travellers whoosh straight past Kütahya, but those who choose to stay a night are usually glad: the town boasts an array of pleasing little **museums**, each housed in a superb piece of architecture, as well as Ottoman remains including a **fortress** and a crumbling swathe of old town. Throw in some value-for-money restaurants, a chance to visit the splendidly isolated Roman ruins of **Aezani** and a near-total absence of tourists, and you're onto an off-the-beaten-track winner. You'll also be able to take some of the famed tile-work home with you – **ceramic shops** on virtually every street sell tiles, dinner services and vases ... not to mention toilets, of which Kütahya is the nation's largest producer.

All the city sights are within easy walking distance. Several well-preserved Ottoman-era houses lie near the main square, **Belediye Meydanı**, with the bulk of the museums and mosques at the end of **Cumhuriyet Bulvarı**, a pedestrianized road to the west. The action starts just past the little roundabout with a **rotating dervish** at its centre. (One can only hope that this feature takes hold across Turkey.) The fortress is a little further along, and visible from a distance.

Brief history

Kütahya enjoyed its golden age as a **tile-making centre** under the Ottomans, after Sultan Selim I forcibly resettled tile-workers from Tabriz here after defeating the Persians at Çaldıran in 1514. Contemporary Kütahya tiles look a little garish and crude in comparison with Ottoman-era examples – the secrets of the pigment blends that gave the original Kütahya tiles their subtle and delicate lustre have been lost with the centuries.

During the War of Independence, the Greek army were defeated twice in battles at the defile of İnönü, northeast of Kütahya, in January and April 1921. They managed to break out that same summer, capturing Eskişehir and Afyon and launching an offensive that took them to within striking distance of Ankara. The following year the Turkish offensive that was to throw the Greeks out of Anatolia once and for all began at Dumlupınar, midway between Kütahya and Afyon.

Archeological Museum

Off Cumhuriyet Cad, just past the dervish roundabout · Daily 8.45am–12.30pm & 1.30–7pm · ☎ 0274 224 0785 · ₺5

Set alongside the Ulu Camii, an attractive but unexceptional fifteenth-century mosque, Kütahya's **Archeological Museum** houses finds from the area, including a beautiful **sarcophagus** from Aezani depicting a heroic battle between the Greeks and Amazons. The contents of the museum are considerably less interesting than the building itself, the **Vacidiye Medresesi**, a fourteenth-century seminary built by the Germiyanid emir Bey Bin Savcı as an astronomical observatory and school of science and mathematics. The high point of the interior is the central marble pool, beneath a dome with glass skylights.

Tile Museum

Behind the Ulu Camii · Tues–Sun 8.45am–12.30pm & 1.30–7pm · ₺5

Splendidly set inside an old mosque just behind the Ulu Camii, Kütahya's small **Tile Museum** focuses on **local tiles** from across the ages. The various plates, vases and wall-tiles are mostly local, though there are a few works from rival tile-city İznik, too; they fill four small alcoves, surrounding a dome-covered fountain.

Kossuth Evi

Gediz Cad, signed "Macar Evi" · Tues–Sun 8.45am–12.30pm & 1.30–7pm · ☎ 0274 223 6214 · Free

Tucked away in a side street, the charming Ottoman building known as the **Kossuth Evi** was once home to **Lajos Kossuth** (1802–94), a Hungarian patriot who fled to Turkey after the failure of the 1848 uprising against Habsburg rule. The immaculate house has been preserved much as it must have been when he lived there in 1850–51. It's the nineteenth-century Ottoman ambience of the rooms, rather than the Kossuth connection, which will be of interest to most visitors.

FROM TOP OTTOMAN HOUSE, SAFRANBOLU (P.485); HATTUŞA (P.490) >

Kütahya fortress

Several access points; simplest is Etek Sok, which starts as Kutup Hane Sok behind the Ulu Cami • Daily 24hr • Free

Kütahya fortress – or **kale** – towers above town; signposts point you in the right direction should you wish to wander up to the summit, which offers predictably impressive views of the city below. The hilltop fortress was originally built by the Byzantines and extended by their successors, but these days only the western walls survive in anything like their original state. It's a steep walk up, but there are a couple of places to eat and drink near the entrance.

Aezani

60km southwest of Kütahya • Daily 9am–6pm • Temple ₺5 • Buses from old *otogar* to Çavdarhisar village, 1km southeast (every 30min; 1hr)

Roman **Aezani** is famed for its atmospheric **Temple of Zeus**, built by Hadrian in 125 AD and one of Anatolia's best-preserved Roman buildings. The temple occupies a commanding position atop a large, rectangular terrace. On its north and west sides, double rows of columns topped by a pediment survive, but elsewhere the columns have largely collapsed, and broken fragments are scattered nearby.

At the heart of the temple, the **inner sanctum** was originally dominated by a magnificent statue of Zeus. Its walls, made of rectangular stone blocks, are largely intact, but the roof has long since caved in. A subterranean **sanctuary** beneath is dedicated to Cybele; the affable site attendant opens it on request. Back outside, just northeast, a fallen but well-preserved bust of Cybele – not, as locals will tell you, Medusa – surveys the landscape.

From the temple, you can walk north past the baths to the remains of the uniquely combined **stadium-theatre**. Paths lead from the fine inscriptions of the southern gate, up between ruined stadium seats, to the backdrop wall of the theatre and the fallen remains of its marble facade. East of the temple stand the arches of the ruined **agora**. The old ceremonial road leads south from here, over a second Roman bridge, to the enigmatic **macellum** (marketplace), whose walls carry a fourth-century decree from Emperor Diocletian fixing market prices in an attempt to stop rampant inflation.

Complete your circuit by heading back to the first Roman bridge, and ask the site guardian to open up the nearby second set of **baths**, with their satyr mosaic and statue of Hygeia, goddess of the baths.

ARRIVAL AND INFORMATION
KÜTAHYA

By bus Kütahya's *otogar* is 3km northeast of the centre, along a road that eventually morphs into Atatürk Bul; *servis* buses connect most arrivals to the centre. The old *otogar*, a tile-swathed building on Atatürk Bul just northeast of the centre, is now a fire station, but some local services start from outside.

Destinations Afyon (14 daily; 1hr 45min); Ankara (7 daily; 6hr); Antalya (5 daily; 5hr); Bursa (12 daily; 3hr); Eskişehir (11 daily; 1hr 20min); Istanbul (14 daily; 6hr);

İzmir (12 daily; 6hr).

By train The small station, 1km east of the main square, is best used for the short hop to Eskişehir – other destinations are usually far faster by bus.

Destinations Ankara (3hr–4hr 20min); Denizli (1 daily; 6hr 20min); Eskişehir (6 daily; 1hr 20min); Istanbul (1 daily; 4hr 40min).

Tourist office There's a booth on the main square (Mon–Fri 9am–noon & 1–5pm; ☎0274 223 6213).

ACCOMMODATION

Gül Palas Belediye Meyd ☎0274 216 1233, ⊛gulpalas .com. There are tiles all over the place at this mid-range option, which provides excellent value. Tiny lifts squeak up to rooms that are comfortable enough, with cute shower areas. The hotel sign is actually above the decrepit *kösk* (pavilion); head next door to the tiled building. ₺100

★**Hilton Garden Inn** Atatürk Bul ☎0274 229 5555, ⊛hilton.com. If you can afford to stay here, do – three-star prices for what, in essence, approximate five-star

rooms. Such savings come because services are pared down to a minimum, with little more than a fitness centre, bar and restaurant, though all these are excellent. ₺200

Yüksel Belediye Meyd 1 ☎0274 212 0111, ⊜otelyuksel@hotmail.com. The pick of the budget hotels, clean and about as central as you could hope for. Pastel-painted rooms feature colourful bedding straight from the local market. No wi-fi. ₺70

EATING AND DRINKING

Kütahya has some excellent places to eat. Its working-class character, and lack of foreign tourists, keep prices low. Cheap snack-shacks do good trade around the main square; there are also a couple of **bars** on Atatürk Bul.

Antepli Seyfi Cumhuriyet Cad ☎0274 216 4326. Good central option for *pide* (from ₺11) or *çiğ köfte* (spicy wrap; ₺3), its indoor seats augmented by a couple of outdoor tables. Daily 9am–11pm.

Karavan Cumhuriyet Cad ☎0274 226 0626. Occupying a charmingly gloomy old building, this café is popular with locals, who come for cheap eats – there are all sorts, from simple breakfasts (₺7.50) to gloopy chocolate *gözleme* (₺4.50), as well as coffee and tea, and nargiles to puff on

outside. There are also some Ottoman clothes to try on, if you so desire. Daily 8am–11.30pm.

★**Mülayimoğulları** Atatürk Bul 11B ☎0274 224 9203. Attractive kebab house with the friendliest staff in the city. All of their grills are great, but try the *yoğurtlu köfte* (₺14.50), a round of super-succulent meat rissoles served on yoghurt-cooked bread, served with a huge salad. Daily 9am–11pm.

Safranbolu and around

Little **SAFRANBOLU** is, quite possibly, the one place in Turkey where you'll be glad your hotel room has a squeaky floor. Over one thousand of the **whitewashed, half-timbered houses** built here during **Ottoman** times (see box, p.486) have survived to the present day, with around a tenth of these now functioning as guesthouses. With few modern buildings to speak of, it's essentially an entire village where architectural time seems to be standing still – an old-world feeling heightened by its setting in a gorgeous rural valley. Such charm has endowed Safranbolu with a near-constant stream of "Ottomania"-seeking domestic tourists, and a growing number of foreign adventurers. Perhaps significantly, it's especially popular with visitors from China and Korea, two countries where traditional wooden housing has largely gone the way of the dodo.

Despite Safranbolu's popularity, its old way of life stays remarkably intact. Apart from a bazaar of souvenir shops, few concessions have been made to the twenty-first century. Most of the town remains slightly, and very pleasingly, run-down – heaven for the swallows that squeal and wheel their way from eave to wooden eave. A short walk in either direction from the centre will soon see you in the countryside, while even in

8

Aquaduct, Bulak Mencilis Mağarasi, Kıranköy, Karabük & 2

SAFRANBOLU

0 — 200 metres

Clock Tower
Museum
Ziraat Bank
Kazdağlı Camii
Dolmuş stop
Cinci Hamamı
Dolmuş stop
HÜKÜMET SOK
Mümtazlar Konaği
Belediye
Arasta (bazaar)
Köprülü Mehmet Paşa Camii
Cinci Han
Kaymakamlar Evi
Hıdırlık Parkı
İzzet Mehmet Paşa Camii
Kileciler Paşa Evi

● SHOPPING

| Blacksmiths' District | 2 |
| Imren | 1 |

● EATING

Arasta Kahvesi	4
Berketet Sofrası	2
Hoş Şefa	1
Kazan	6
Nil	5
Nostalji Café	3
Taşev	7

■ ACCOMMODATION

Efe	4
Gül Evi	3
Havuzlu Konak	2
Kahveciler Konaği	1

town the backstreets – particularly those that head up to the park – are home to real people living real lives, away from hotels and scented souvenirs.

In addition, the presence of a modest clutch of sights in the vicinity of town make a good excuse to stay on for more than a night. Public transport is nonexistent, but the tourist office can help with tours (see p.484). Most visitors head east to **Yörük Köyü** village – the best of the sights – before hitting the Byzantine-era **aqueduct** in **İncekaya**, and the cave network of **Bulak Mencilis Mağarası**.

Ottoman mansions

Three **Ottoman mansions** have been restored for visitors. Built in 1727, the **Kaymakamlar Evi** (daily 9am–5.30pm; ₺4), or "Lieutenant Colonel's House", is the most popular. Its ground floor, devoid of external windows, served as a stable, while on the upper floors the *selâmlık*, overlooking the street, would have been divided from harem quarters, with a separate entrance and lattice windows looking onto interior courtyards. Each room has a distinctively carved wooden ceiling, and furniture would have been sparse, with personal items stored in decorative wall-niches, and bedding in cupboards doubling as bathrooms.

On the other side of town, **Mümtazlar Konağı** (daily 9am–5.30pm; ₺4) needs a little more love; its exhibits seem like modern-day cast-offs, and dusty rugs make it look like a house under construction. To the south of town, coffee-coloured **Kileciler Paşa Evi** (daily 9am–5.30pm; ₺4) has been more attractively renovated and is more worthy of a visit; its rooms are filled with Ottoman antiques, many of which are explained on the free information sheet you receive on entry.

Cinci Hamamı

Adjoining the town square • Daily: men 6am–11pm; women 9am–10pm • ₺30 • ☎ 0370 712 2103, ⓦ tarihicincihamam.com

The seventeenth-century **Ottoman baths** known as the **Cinci Hamamı** stand right in the centre of Safranbolu, where the buses drop off. They've been fully restored so that you can relax in comfort, surrounded by their marble splendour – they're arguably up there with the best hamams in the land.

The bazaar and around

The courtyard of the unexceptional seventeenth-century **Köprülü Mehmet Paşa Camii** leads to a restored **arasta** (bazaar) where day-trippers are brought to browse at

---

OTTOMAN HOUSES

Whitewashed **wooden houses** are a distinctive and enduring legacy of **Ottoman** rule. Many Turkish towns feature a smattering of such buildings, while sizeable clutches can be found as far afield as Albania and Bosnia. The houses were often masterful pieces of design, exhibiting a flair for function and a use of space that prompts some to draw comparisons with Japanese design of the time – think built-in cupboards, carved ceilings and central heating, as well as plumbing systems able to draw cooking, cleansing and waste-disposal processes from a single stream of water. Safranbolu's own town-wide plumbing system was only decommissioned in the 1970s, but is still visible in part today – you'll notice distinctive paving stones running down the centre of many streets, which is where much of the water passed after leaving the homes.

Larger Ottoman **mansions** would have three or more levels and over a dozen rooms. The ground floor was often used as stable space, though thanks to ingenious design the smell would not waft through to the upper floors, which were themselves split into male (*selâmlık*) and female (*haremlik*) quarters. Other features to look out for are interior courtyards, revolving cupboards and conical safe-rooms, as well as one innovation found in many Safranbolu hotels: tiny bathrooms located inside what appears to be a cupboard.

well-stocked souvenir and antique shops. The bazaar is completely covered by a magnificent vine, which in season dangles grapes so close to your head that you'll be tempted to pick them – notices warn you not to. South of the *arasta*, in the old **bazaar district**, traditional stalls of blacksmiths, cobblers, leatherworkers, tanners and saddlemakers still work away – or, as is more common these days, sell items made elsewhere.

A short walk south is the **İzzet Mehmet Paşa Camii**, an elaborate, late eighteenth-century mosque. Beyond here, the town slides into dilapidation, with a ravine now used as a household dump and, further downstream, women washing clothes in the stream. If you walk down here, though, there's a stunning view back towards the mosque, whose domes and minarets seem to hover above the surrounding houses; the walk is also a real beauty at night, just as Safranbolu is readying itself for sleep.

Hıdırlık Parkı

Kalealtı Sok • Daily 6am–midnight • ₺3, though the ticket booth isn't always manned

Superb views of Safranbolu can be had from **Hıdırlık Parkı**, a hilltop park that looks out over town from the southeast. The Ottoman buildings appear at their best in the late afternoon light, a view that can be enjoyed with tea or coffee from the small on-site café.

The museum and around

Kalealtı Sok • Tues–Sun 9am–5.30pm • Combined ticket with clock tower ₺4

The old Governor's House, a palatial-looking edifice that replaced what was once a castle, now holds a so-so **museum**. Apart from the photos of "old Safranbolu" upstairs, which show just how little things have changed since the 1920s, the general layout is pretty slapdash. The modern mannequins, all too obviously lifted straight from some high-street clothing store, may give you a laugh.

Head around the back of the museum and you'll find yourself in a curious park, featuring miniature versions of famous buildings from all over Turkey. Here, surrounded by mulberry trees, you'll find an Ottoman-era **clock tower** whose mechanism was imported from London in the 1760s – clamber up for a grand view of town.

Bulak Mencilis Mağarası

8km northwest of Safranbolu • Daily: summer 9am–6.30pm; winter 10am–4pm • ₺4

Set on a beautiful mountain slope, the small network of **caves** known as **Bulak Mencilis Mağarası** is a joy to visit. The location is quite spectacular, and the walk to the mouth – a steep climb of more than 150 steps – will give your calf muscles some definition. You'll soon get the chance to cool down, since the temperature in the caves is 10–15°C year-round; there's no real need for special clothing, since only 500m (out of a total of around 4km) is open for viewing. As with cave systems across Asia, your guide will compare some of the more distinctive formations to animals or religious figures.

Yörük Köyü

Think of a smaller, more remote version of Safranbolu, minus the tourists and polished Ottoman renovations, and you're already halfway to imagining the tiny village of **YÖRÜK KÖYÜ**, 16km east of its more illustrious neighbour. Most villagers here follow the moderate **Bektaşi** sect of Islam, in which alcohol is allowed in moderation, and Ramadan only lasts twelve days. Women also have greater equality and the right to choose whom they marry – note the statue of Leyla Gencer, a noted intellectual born here.

The village's one concession to the tourist trade – along with a little hotel – is the **Sipahioğlu Evi** (daily 9am–6pm; ₺2/section), an eighteenth-century mansion that feels even more authentic than its counterparts in Safranbolu. Owned by the same family for almost three centuries, it's now split in two by feuding sons – each half with its own entry ticket. It's a bit of a slog to the *kule* on top, though the views are superb and you'll even find a handy stand on which to pop your fez.

ARRIVAL AND INFORMATION

SAFRANBOLU

By bus From Safranbolu's *otogar*, up in the new town, most companies lay on a *servis* to the old town area, known as Eski Safranbolu. You can also take a dolmuş, bus (both ₺1.50) or taxi (₺15) down, or even enjoy a delightful 40min walk down into the valley.

Destinations Amasya (1 daily; 6hr); Ankara (16 daily; 3hr 30min); Göreme (daily, 8hr); Istanbul (15 daily; 6hr 30min); İzmir (daily; 12hr).

Tourist office In Safranbolu's main square, next to the Kazdağlı Camii (daily 9am–5.30pm; ☏ 0370 712 3863).

Quite helpful for a provincial tourist office, they can often reserve bus tickets.

Tours Touts just outside the tourist office offer golf-buggy tours of Safranbolu (₺20–35/person), with taped information delivered in squawky English. Of more interest are the half-day taxi-tours to sights around town, organized by the tourist office for ₺60/carload, including entry fees and guide; ask at your accommodation and you may get a cheaper quote.

ACCOMMODATION

Safranbolu's old **Ottoman houses** provide some of Turkey's most atmospheric accommodation. Prices might be a little higher than you may be used to (and bathrooms necessarily smaller), but there are options to suit all budgets. Be sure to avoid any of the places starting with "Yıldız" – the owner is on record as saying that Westerners are not welcome.

SAFRANBOLU

Efe Kayadibi Sok ☏ 0370 725 2688, ⓦ back packerspension.com. The best of the several places offering dormitory accommodation in town – not saying a great deal, admittedly. Here you'll find clean rooms, occasionally friendly service, and a bright dining area; call from the bus station and they'll come to pick you up. Dorm ₺30, double ₺90

★**Gül Evi** Hükümet Sok 46 ☏ 0370 725 4645, ⓦ gulevisafranbolu.com.tr. Refurbished by an amiable local architect, this boutique hotel is the best in town. Rooms are traditionally styled but feature modern tweaks like large bathrooms – rare in Safranbolu's space-conscious old buildings – and comfy beds. Check out the old safe-room, now a tiny, atmospheric bar. ₺300

Havuzlu Konak Çelik Gülersoy 18 ☏ 0370 725 2883, ⓦ havuzluasmazlar.com. Very appealing option, set in a

splendid 1820s building just outside the centre of the old town. The four corner rooms are best, but all are immaculate and well laid out, with brass fittings and thin rugs. The eponymous indoor pool (*havuz*) provides a superb setting for breakfast or coffee. ₺200

★**Kahveciler Konağı** Mescit Sok 46 ☏ 0370 725 5453, ⓦ kahvecilerkonagi.com. The nicest of the mid-rangers in town, with polite-to-a-fault service augmenting rooms decorated in a style that somehow contrives to be both modern and traditional. The garden is an ideal breakfasting spot, too. ₺150

YÖRÜK KÖYÜ

Yörük Evi Yörük Köyü, 16km east of Safranbolu ☏ 0370 737 2153. Anyone who fancies spending a night in isolated splendour should hunt down signs for this place, where the rooms are rustic but comfortable enough. ₺120

EATING

While Safranbolu's old town has several places to **eat**, prices are a little high, not always with the quality to match. One thing is conspicuous by its absence – there are almost no snack-stands in the old town.

RESTAURANTS

Berketet Sofrası Pazar Yerı ☏ 0370 712 8656. One of the cheapest places to eat in town, with *lokanta* dishes going for around ₺6, and chicken kebabs for around the same (with a free *ayran*). Ignore the saffron-flavoured items, made with no saffron whatsoever. Daily 8am–9pm.

Kazan Celal Bayar Cad ☏ 0370 712 5960. Tatar by name, Tatar by nature, this restaurant whips up tasty Turkish regulars, as well as Crimean specialities – order the *peruhi* (dumplings; ₺10), or a giant breakfast (₺20), then eat

upstairs on the terrace, from where you'll catch the breeze and hear the muted rushing of an adjacent stream. Daily 8am–10pm.

★**Nil** Cinci Han Arkası Sok ☏ 0370 712 1830. Easily locatable on the main square, this is the best all-round place in town for hungry souls. The menu's full of good old-fashioned home cooking – dishes like *mantı* (₺12) and *sucuklu menemen* (eggs, tomato and sausage; ₺8), together with a few quirky items like the "red" *ayran*. The indoor tables are often graced with fresh herbs. Daily 9am–11pm.

8

PUTTING THE SAFRAN INTO SAFRANBOLU

Safranbolu is famed for growing **saffron** – indeed, it even took its name from the precious herb. Although production fell to almost nothing before a recent **revival**, it's now quite possible to buy some to take home, or sample its taste in locally made sweets such as *safran lokum* and *helva*. You can purchase them – or munch free samples if you're feeling cheeky – in the ubiquitous **pastanes**. A number of local restaurants claim to serve meals made with saffron, but beware – many simply colour the food (and, in many cases, "saffron" tea) with Indian Yellow dye.

Taşev Hıdırlık Sok 14 ☎0370 725 5300, ⊛eng .tasevsanatvesarapevi.com. Relatively upmarket place, and one of the few restaurants in town to serve alcohol. Steaks cost around ₺25, and cheese plates, usually enjoyed with a nice bottle of local wine, much the same. Choose from a table in the garden, or a balcony seat with a city view. Daily 10am–midnight.

CAFÉS AND TEAROOMS

★**Arasta Kahvesi** Arasta Bazar, beside the mosque. Vine-covered café in the eponymous mosque-side bazaar (see p.487), notable for its *közde* coffee (₺7.50) – the *cezve* is placed directly onto hot coals, then served with sweets and, if you're in luck, mulberry syrup. Daily 8am–10pm.

Hoş Sefa Next to the clock tower. The town prison until 1994, this is now a café. The interior is, understandably, a little plain – all the more reason to head outside to drain a tea (₺2.50) under the mulberry trees, while drinking up great views. Daily 8am–8pm.

Nostalji Café Opposite Cinci Han entrance ☎0370 725 4500. The café component of Imren, the best shop for Turkish sweets in town (see below). You'll get a free cube of their tasty *lokum* to enjoy with your Turkish coffee (₺5), under the vines outside. Daily 8am–11pm.

SHOPPING

Blacksmiths' District By the İzzet Mehmet Paşa mosque. Not a shop but a whole area of blacksmiths, selling far better souvenirs than the tat you'll find in the bazaar (see p.486). Metalware has been made and sold here since Ottoman times, and though much of the production itself has moved elsewhere, you're still likely to hear clanging emanating from various shops. Coffee sets are a popular purchase – they start at ₺30–40 for the moulded variety, or up to ten times that if they're carved from pure copper. Most shops daily 8am–7pm.

Imren Opposite Cinci Han entrance ☎0370 725 4500. Of the many Turkish sweet shops strewn across town, this is the one locals themselves rave about – one big reason is that they use powdered sugar rather than plain glucose. A box of forty sweets goes for around ₺17. Daily 8am–11pm.

8

Boğazkale and the Hittite sites

The **Hittite sites** centred on the village of **Boğazkale**, 150km east of Ankara, are the most impressive and significant in the whole of Anatolia, and are appropriately located amid rolling countryside that has changed little through the centuries.

This area was once the heart of the Hittite Empire, with **Hattuşa**, spread south of the modern village, as its capital. The temple site of **Yazılıkaya** is a few kilometres east, while remote **Alacahöyük**, 25km north, is worth the trip if you have your own transport.

Excavation on these sites began in earnest in 1905, and many of the objects unearthed are now housed in Ankara's Museum of Anatolian Civilizations (see p.471). If you've already seen the museum, a visit to the original excavations is doubly interesting; if not, a quick visit to the new archeological museum in nearby **Çorum** is definitely worthwhile.

BOĞAZKALE itself is a modern village, with the ancient Hittite capital of Hattuşa fanning out from its southern rim. Finding your way around is fairly straightforward, as it basically consists of one street, running up a hill to the main square.

Boğazkale Museum

On the main approach road to town • Daily: summer 8am–7pm; winter 8am–5pm • ₺5

The only attraction in the village itself is the **Boğazkale Museum**, located on the way up to the village square. Though small, it's superbly laid out, boasting a little collection of cuneiform tablets, pottery and other objects from the former Hittite capital. The other bonus is that you're most probably going to have all of these antiquities to yourself.

Hattuşa

Just southeast of modern Boğazkale • Daily: summer 8am–7pm; winter 8am–5pm • ₺8 joint ticket with Yazılıkaya (see p.492) • Accessible on foot from Boğazkale, though it's large enough that on a hot day you might want to explore it by taxi

Enclosed by 6km walls, **Hattuşa** was, by the standards of its era, an immense city, and its scale is still awe-inspiring today. The site, on a steeply sloping expanse dotted with rocky outcrops, was originally occupied by the Hatti, who established a settlement here around 2500 BC. The Hittites moved in after their conquest of central Anatolia, and made it their capital from about 1375 BC onwards, as their empire was reaching its greatest extent. Archeologists unearthed the Hittite city during the first half of the nineteenth century. Of the numerous buildings once scattered over a wide area, only the limestone foundation blocks survive. The vulnerable upper parts, originally consisting of timber frames supporting clay brick walls, have long since vanished.

Büyük Mabet

The largest and best-preserved Hittite temple to survive at Hattuşa, the **Büyük Mabet**, or "Great Temple", stands immediately beyond the ticket office. Built around the fourteenth or thirteenth century BC, and one of an original seventy on the site, it was dedicated to the storm god **Teshuba** and the sun goddess **Hebut**. It consisted of a central temple building, surrounded by 78 storage rooms laid out in an irregular plan.

BOĞAZKALE AND HATTUŞA

You approach it between two large stone blocks, remnants of the **ceremonial gateway**. A stone lion nearby originally formed part of a cistern, while a large, green **cubic stone** a little further on was reputedly a wedding present from Ramses II of Egypt, who married a Hittite princess. In Hittite times the king and queen, in their roles as high priest and priestess, would have led processions through here on holy days. Most visitors now follow the same route, along a clearly defined processional way of uneven slabs.

The **temple** consisted of about twelve small chambers around a central courtyard, with the rooms that would have contained the cult statues of Teshuba and Hebut at the northeastern end – the god on the left and the goddess on the right.

Just below the Büyük Mabet, archeologists have identified an early Assyrian **merchant quarter**. This held the Hittite equivalent of the Rosetta Stone, a parallel Hittite hieroglyph and Akkadian inscription that was instrumental in the final cracking of the hieroglyphic code, and is now in Ankara's Museum of Anatolian Civilizations.

THE HITTITES

The **Hittites** appear to have been an Indo-European people who moved into Anatolia around 2000 BC, and entered the territories of the indigenous Hatti. Where exactly the Hittites came from remains unclear; possibilities include the Caucasus and the Balkans. Neither do records survive of how the Hittites rose to dominance. Layers of burned material found in most Hatti settlements suggest at least some degree of violence was involved, but the Hittites also absorbed important elements of Hatti culture, so a more complex interaction may have taken place.

While **Hattuşa** is by far the most famous, the Hittites actually set up a number of **city-states**, drawn together during the mid-eighteenth century BC under King Anitta. He transferred his capital from the city of Kushara (possibly modern Alişar) to Nesha (Kültepe), and destroyed Hattuşa, cursing any Hittite king who might attempt to rebuild the place. A century or so later his successor Labarna returned to Hattuşa and did just that. The Hittites came to regard Labarna and his wife Tawannanna as founders of the Hittite kingdom, and their names were adopted as titles by subsequent monarchs.

In 1595 BC, Mursili I succeeded in capturing distant Babylon, but his successor (and assassin) Hantili lost many previous gains. Stability was restored when Tudhaliyas II re-established the Hittite state as an empire, around 1430 BC. An important period of expansion followed under King Suppiluliuma (1380–1315 BC), who secured the northern borders and conquered the Hurrian kingdom of Mitanni. This achievement raised the Hittites to superpower status, equal with Egypt, Assyria and Babylon. The Egyptians even asked Suppiluliuma to send one of his sons to marry the widow of Tutankhamun, but the boy was murdered en route, and the union never took place. Hittite expansion continued after Suppiluliuma's death. In 1286 BC, during the reign of Muwatalli II, a Hittite army defeated the Egyptians, commanded by Ramses II, at the **Battle of Kadesh**. Events from the battle can be seen carved into the columns at Luxor in Egypt.

Following the conflict, peace between the two empires was established, cemented by the marriage of one of the daughters of Ramses II to Hattuşiliş III. However, the Hittite Empire had less than a century left. The arrival of the Sea Peoples in Anatolia ushered in a period of instability that was to erode Hittite power, culminating in the **destruction of Hattuşa** around 1200 BC, at much the same time as the fall of Troy. The Phrygians replaced the Hittites as the dominant power in central Anatolia, taking over the ruins of Hattuşa and other Hittite cities.

Hittite civilization was highly advanced, with a complex **social system**. While the Hittite kings were absolute rulers, an assembly called the *panku* appears at times to have wielded considerable influence. The major division in Hittite society was between free citizens – including farmers, artisans and bureaucrats – and slaves, who, while they could be bought and sold, were probably entitled to own property and to marry.

Hittite **religion** seems to have been adopted from the Hatti, with the weather god Teshuba and the sun goddess Hebut as the two most important deities. As the Hittites were in the habit of incorporating the gods of conquered peoples into their own pantheon, up to a thousand lesser gods also played a role in their beliefs.

8

Aslanlıkapı

The **Aslanlıkapı**, or "Lion Gate", takes its name from the two stone lions that flank the outer entrance (one an all too obvious replica), symbolically guarding Hattuşa from attackers and evil spirits. It also marks the start of a surviving section of dry-stone **city wall**, which runs along the top of a massive sloping embankment that's 10m in height and surfaced with irregular limestone slabs.

Yerkapı

The **Yerkapı**, or "Earth Gate", along the embankment from the Aslanlıkapı, is more popularly known as the Sphinx Gate after the two huge sphinxes that once guarded its inner portal; one was returned in 2011 to the Boğazkale museum (see p.489).

The most striking feature of the Sphinx Gate is the 70m **tunnel** that cuts through from the city-side of the walls to the exterior. It was built using the corbel arch technique, a series of flat stones leaning towards each other creating its triangular profile. Some archeologists argue that it enabled the defenders of the city to make surprise attacks on besieging enemies. Others, citing the tunnel's obvious visibility from the outside – and the presence of two sets of monumental steps leading up the embankment – suggest that it had a more ceremonial function.

Kralkapı

The **Kralkapı**, or "King's Gate", east of the Sphinx Gate, is named after the regal-looking figure carved in relief on the left-hand pillar of the inner gateway. This actually represents the god Teshuba, and shows him sporting a conical hat while raising his left fist in the air as though holding an invisible sword. What you see is a copy – the original is in Ankara's Museum of Anatolian Civilizations.

Nişantepe and around

The **Nişantepe**, down the hill from the Kralkapı, is a rocky outcrop with a ten-line Hittite inscription carved into its eastern face, alternately reading right-to-left and left-to-right. Enough of the badly weathered, 30cm hieroglyphs have been deciphered to suggest that it's a memorial to Suppiluliuma II, last of the Hittite kings. Immediately southwest is the **Sarıkale**, the foundation of a Phrygian fort built on the site of an earlier Hittite structure.

Büyük Kale

The **Büyük Kale**, or "Great Fortress", down the road from the Nişantepe, served the Hittite monarchs as a fortified palace during the fourteenth and thirteenth centuries BC. The palace consisted of three courtyards, each higher than the previous one, meaning that any attacker would have had to capture it piecemeal. The lower and middle courtyards are thought to have been given over to servants and aides of the royal family, while the upper courtyard was the palace proper. It's easy to see why they chose to reside at this wild and windswept location on the very eastern edge of Hattuşa. In effect, it was a citadel within the city, protected on all flanks by steep drops. Three thousand **cuneiform tablets** found on the site of a building near the southeast entrance have yielded important clues about Hittite society. Among them was the Treaty of Kadesh, signed in around 1270 BC by the Hittite king Hattuşiliş II and Ramses II of Egypt, the earliest surviving written treaty between two nations.

Today only the lower parts of walls and some masonry fragments survive of the Büyük Kale, but it's worth coming up here to wander among the weather-battered remnants and take in the stunning view of the Great Temple.

Yazılıkaya

3km northeast of Hattuşa • Daily: summer 8am–7pm; winter 8am–5pm • ₺8 joint ticket with Hattuşa (see p.490)

Although archeological evidence suggests that a temple of some sort existed on the site of **Yazılıkaya** as early as 1500 BC, not until the thirteenth century BC were the two small ravines that cut into a rocky outcrop here decorated with reliefs (hence Yazılıkaya, Turkish for "inscribed rock"). At roughly the same time a **gateway** and the **temple buildings** were constructed. Today, only a few sketchy foundations remain of these ancient structures, and attention is focused on the two "galleries" of reliefs that depict nearly a hundred figures, mostly gods from the vast array of Hittite deities.

The reliefs

The entrance to the **larger ravine** at Yazılıkaya is on the left behind the temple foundations. Its left-hand wall is lined with images of gods moving from left to right, and the right-hand one with goddesses wearing identical long, pleated dresses and conical headgear. Several figures on the male side stand out, in particular the group of twelve war gods bringing up the rear of the procession. Further along, two figures have human bodies and bulls' heads. The deities seem to rise in rank as the procession progresses, and towards the front are the conspicuous figures of the moon god Kusuh, with a crescent moon, and the sun god, seemingly balancing a winged sun symbol on his head. The two lines of deities meet on the far wall of the ravine, where a scene depicts Teshuba, astride a couple of mountain peaks, facing Hebut, who is standing on a panther.

The **smaller ravine**, over to the right, can be reached via a short flight of steps that leads up to a cleft in the rock. The entrance is guarded by two sphinx reliefs, which can be hard to spot, while a group of twelve figures armed with swords lines the left-hand wall. Similar to the warrior-god figures in the first ravine, these are much better preserved. Opposite this group are two separate reliefs. One shows an unusual figure that has come to be known as the "Sword God", a blade with a human torso and head where the handle should be. To add to the already strange effect, lions' heads, instead of arms, sprout from the torso shoulders. This vaguely disturbing image is thought to represent Neargal, the Hittite god of the underworld.

Alacahöyük

25km north of Boğazkale • **Site** Tues–Sun 8am–5pm • **Museum** Tues–Sun 8am–noon & 1–5pm • ₺5 joint entry

After Hattuşa, **Alacahöyük** is the most important Hittite site in existence. Originally a major Hattic settlement, it was taken over by the Hittites during the early stages of the second millennium BC, and later, like Hattuşa, by the Phrygians as well. Most of the ruins that remain are Hittite, but archeologists have unearthed a vast array of Hattic artefacts, including standards featuring stags, bulls, sun-discs and statues of the earth goddess, from various tombs.

The site

The site of Alacahöyük is entered via the southern **Sphinx Gate**, named after the large sphinxes that guard it. These eerily impressive figures, stained ochre by lichen, have blunted faces with empty eye sockets, and sweeping headdresses. Either side of the gate are **reliefs** (copies of originals now in Ankara), depicting religious ceremonies. The left-hand section, the more lively of the two, shows a procession moving towards the god Teshuba – shown here as a slightly comical-looking bull with outsized sex organs. Approaching him are a king and queen, followed by sacrificial animals and priests, with a group of what look like acrobats bringing up the rear.

The Sphinx Gate opens onto a pathway with excavated areas on either side, all signed in English. Immediately behind the gate are vast irregular blocks, the remnants of the city walls, followed by the foundations of storage buildings. Beyond the storage areas, a few metres below ground level to the left of the path, are thirteen **tombs**. These date from the Hattic period and yielded much of the vast hoard that's now in the Bronze Age section of Ankara's Museum of Anatolian Civilizations. Judging by the opulence of the grave goods, these were the tombs of Hatti monarchs. The small on-site **museum** is well worth investigating; it has some striking Hattic standards and elegantly designed pottery.

ARRIVAL AND GETTING AROUND   BOĞAZKALE

By bus or dolmuş Public transport to Boğazkale is far from straightforward and can be incredibly frustrating. You'll first have to get to the small town of Sungurlu, just off the main Ankara–Samsun road. Buses leave Sungurlu's *otogar* for Boğazkale at 7.30am and 5.30pm (having left Boğazkale 30min earlier); otherwise, you'll have to catch a Boğazkale-bound dolmuş (weekdays only, no fixed schedule; 30min; ₺5). You just might find one waiting at the *otogar*, but you're more likely to have to head 1km north into Sungurlu itself (taxi ₺5), where dolmuşes leave from alongside the park. If you get stuck in Sungurlu, you'll find that it holds plenty of cheap hotels.

By taxi A taxi from Sungurlu to Boğazkale costs ₺125 off the meter, one-way; you'll most likely be able to haggle it to ₺70 or so.

Getting to the sites It's as easy as pie to walk from Boğazkale to Hattuşa, and Yazılıkaya isn't all that hard either. Taxis are the only easy way of getting to Alacahöyük, though, and Hattuşa is large enough to tire your legs on hot days – drivers will charge around ₺125 (try to haggle) to show you around Hattuşa, Yazılıkaya and Alacahöyük, while paying a little more will get you dropped back in Sungurlu for an onward bus.

ACCOMMODATION

The hotels listed here are also the only options in the village for **eating and drinking**. If you're here in **winter**, note that heating and hot water is far from reliable in the village, so come prepared.

Başkent Yazılıkaya Yolu Üzeri ☎0364 452 2037, ⓦbaskenthattusa.com. The newest and most presentable hotel in the area. All its large rooms hold one double and one single bed; try to get one facing fields, rather than the hotel car park. ₺140

★ **Baykal** Next to the PTT on the village square ☎0364 452 2013. Also known as the *Hattuşaş Pension*, this option offers two types of accommodation: clean and spacious

pansiyon rooms, mostly with showers (discounts for those without), and comfortable en-suite rooms in the hotel at the back. The restaurant serves up tasty and economical dishes. Pension ₺75, hotel ₺120

Kale Yazılıkaya Yolu Üzeri ☎0364 452 3126. Family-run hotel in a pretty location, with simple whitewashed rooms and adequate bathrooms, but little atmosphere. ₺140

Amasya

Occupying the narrow valley of the **Yeşilırmak River**, and blessed with a super-abundant historical legacy, **AMASYA** is one of the high points of northern Anatolia. Most visitors come to see the **rock tombs** hewn into the cliffs above the town by the kings of Pontus, more than two thousand years ago, but Amasya also harbours some truly beautiful Selçuk and Ottoman architecture and a multitude of restored nineteenth-century **wooden houses**. Many of the latter are now authentic and atmospheric antique shops, *pansiyons* and restaurants, in keeping with the general Ottoman theme.

Brief history

Amasya was once part of **Pontus**, one of several small kingdoms to spring up following the death of Alexander the Great, which survived for two hundred years. Its downfall began when Mithridates VI Eupator reputedly ordered the massacre of eighty thousand Romans in a single day and plunged his kingdom into a series of wars, which culminated in its being absorbed by Pompey into the Roman sphere of influence around 70 BC.

Under the Romans, and through the succeeding centuries of Byzantine rule, the town prospered, and it continued to do so after falling to the **Selçuks** in 1071. In the late thirteenth century, Amasya became part of the burgeoning **Ottoman** state. It became a training ground for crown princes, who would serve as governors of the province to prepare them for the rigours of statesmanship at the Sublime Porte. Amasya then became a vital staging post en route to the creation of modern Turkey: it was here that, on June 21, 1919, Atatürk delivered a speech that was in effect a call to arms for the coming **War of Independence**.

North and west of the river

Amasya's finest sights, including the **rock tombs** and the vast majority of its **Ottoman buildings**, are on the north bank of the Yeşilırmak. The **kale** is further up again, though access is on the other side of the mountain.

Rock tombs

Entrance on Tevfik Hafız Sok; duck under the rail tracks • Daily 8am–7.30pm • ₺5

The massive **tombs** of the Pontic kings are carved into the cliff face on the northern bank of the Yeşilırmak – there's little to see bar the holes, although the **city views** from here are spellbinding. Do note that the paths can be a little **slippery**, and not all of them have fences to guard against falls; as well as bringing decent, sturdy footwear, in summer you're advised to visit in the evening, when the cliff-side is in welcome shadow.

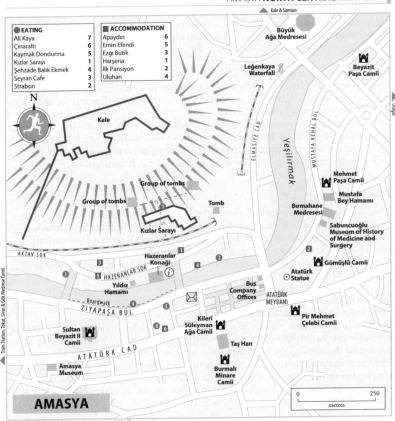

There are **two main clusters** of tombs. Where the path splits above the entrance, bearing left will bring you to two large tombs; beside the entrance to one of them is the mouth of a tunnel, thought to lead to the river. Bearing right instead, then passing the **café**, will bring you to a less accessible group slightly sullied by graffitied love declarations. More tombs can be found with a bit of effort – there are eighteen throughout the valley.

Hazeranlar Konağı

Hazeranlar Sok • Tues–Sun 8am–7pm • ₺5

Amasya's half-timbered **Ottoman houses** make an enormous contribution to the atmosphere of the town. A good starting point for explorations is the nineteenth-century **Hazeranlar Konağı**, an imposing riverside mansion. Its heavily restored interior has been turned into a convincing re-creation of a nineteenth-century family home, liberally decked out with carpets, period furniture and domestic artefacts. It incorporates typical features of the time: wall niches for oil lamps, bathrooms secreted away behind cupboard doors and *sedirs* (cedars) or divan seating running along the walls.

Büyük Ağa Medresesi

Off Zübeyde Hanım Cad • Free

Across the road from the small Leğenkaya waterfall is the **Büyük Ağa Medresesi**, a **seminary** that was founded in 1488 by the chief white eunuch of Beyazıt II. A roughly octagonal structure, it's now a Koranic school. It's not officially open to the public, but no one seems to mind if you take a look inside the courtyard.

The kale

2km uphill from Büyük Ağa Medresesi • ₺15 for a taxi up; around ₺30 return including waiting time

Amasya's sprawling citadel, or **kale**, dates back to Pontic times, though the surviving ruins are of Ottoman vintage. While it's difficult to reach, it's well worth the effort for the stupendous views of the town below.

At the top, the outer walls of the kale have been rebuilt in bright, modern stone, but beyond you'll find the crumbling remains of the Ottoman-era fortress. Nothing is signposted and there are no clear paths through the ruins, so much of the time you'll find yourself scrambling over rocks and rubble and through undergrowth.

The east bank

Amasya's relatively under-explored **east bank** holds a smattering of delightful mosques, a worthwhile museum, and the atmospheric **Sıhhı Mustafa Bey Hamamı**. The northernmost mosque is the fifteenth-century **Beyazıt Paşa Camii**, whose leafy riverbank location enhances the quiet beauty of its architecture. Further down, the sizeable **Mehmet Paşa Camii** was constructed in 1486, and boasts a *medrese* and finely decorated marble pulpit.

Sabuncuoğlu Museum of History of Medicine and Surgery

Mehmet Paşa Cad • Daily 9am–noon & 1–6pm • ₺4

Phew, what a mouthful – but at least one is left with no illusions about the contents of the **Sabuncuoğlu Museum of History of Medicine and Surgery**. While its contents are not terribly interesting, the building itself is a stunner. It was built by the Mongols in 1308 as a **lunatic asylum**, and both its function and structural beauty go rather against the popular image of the Mongols as a brutal, destructive people. The Mongols used music therapy to pacify the patients; it was, in fact, used as a **music school** for centuries, and only opened as a museum in 2011.

Gümüşlü Camii

Atatürk Cad, by the Atatürk statue • Daily 9am–noon & 1–6pm • ₺4

The creamy yellow **Gümüşlü Camii**, or "Silvery Mosque", was originally built in 1326 but has been reconstructed at various intervals since. Its almost pavilion-like oriental exterior and carved wooden porch overlook the river, and there's an unusual tall brick minaret.

The south bank

At the centre of Amasya, the riverfront **Atatürk Meydanı** commemorates Atatürk's 1919 visit with an equestrian statue of the hero surrounded by admirers. A short way west is the **Kileri Süleyman Ağa Camii**, an imposing Ottoman mosque built in 1489. The south bank also has a **pedestrian promenade**, which is immensely popular with local youths.

Sultan Beyazıt II Camii

Between Ziyapaşa Bul and Atatürk Cad • Free

Set in a spacious rose garden, the **Sultan Beyazıt II Camii**, Amasya's largest mosque, was built in 1486. It's laid out on a symmetrical plan, with two large central domes flanked by four smaller cupolas and two slightly mismatched minarets. Though some of Amasya's other mosques beat it for sheer whimsy, none can quite match its structural harmony. It's best appreciated from the front, where it faces the river, flanked by two plane trees thought to be as old as the mosque itself.

Amasya Museum

Atatürk Cad • Tues–Sun 8.30am–7pm • ₺5

A real gem, the **Amasya Museum** holds archeological finds dating back as far as the Bronze Age, which is represented by some practical-looking pottery and a case full of rather unwieldy tools. Hittite relics include beak-spouted jugs, some with what look like built-in filters, and there's also a bronze statue of the storm god Teshuba. On the second floor you'll see the original door of the **Gök Medrese Camii** (a thirteenth-century mosque, a five-minute walk west), a riot of arabesque geometrical patterns enclosing lattice reliefs.

Most visitors, however, head straight to the eight **mummies**, six of whom were family: the eldest, Cumudar, was a Selçuk minister apparently drowned in 1297. His son Izzettin Mehmet – a former governor of Amasya executed during a rebellion against the Mongols – is also here, together with four of his children and a concubine.

ARRIVAL AND INFORMATION

AMASYA

By train Amasya's little-used train station, hosting very slow services from Samsun (1 daily; 5hr) and Sivas (1 daily; 7hr 30min), is 1km west of the centre, and connected by regular dolmuşes.

By bus The *otogar* lies a whopping 7km north of the centre. This arrangement can add more than an hour to your travel time – buses from points south go right through the city centre but will refuse to let you off, meaning that you'll have to wait for, then double back on, a *servis* minibus to the bus company offices facing Atatürk's statue (the reverse is true if you're heading south).

Destinations Ankara (hourly; 6hr); Istanbul (12 daily; 12hr); Kayseri (3 daily; 8hr); Malatya (5 daily; 9hr); Safranbolu (1 daily; 6hr 30min); Samsun (10 daily; 3hr); Sivas (10 daily; 4hr); Tokat (10 daily; 2hr).

Tourist office Inside the dull Ottoman Selçuk museum, off Hazeranlar Sok – don't expect too much (Tues–Sun 9am–5pm; ☏ 0358 212 4059).

ACCOMMODATION

Amasya's most appealing accommodation options are the clutch of antique-decorated, kilim-strewn **pansiyons** in restored Ottoman houses. Rates are reasonable so it's well worth splashing out, particularly given that the city's budget options are less than salubrious. Note that very few of the city's hotel staff speak English.

Apaydın Atatürk Cad ☏ 0358 218 1184. If you're on a shoestring, this very basic hotel on the main road is the place for you – some rooms are en suite, but all are a bit grubby. No wi-fi. **₺80**

Emin Efendi Hazeranlar Sok 73 ☏ 0358 212 0852. Friendly *pansiyon*, spread over a few buildings; opt for a room overlooking the river. If you're lucky, you may be treated to a little evening music in the attractive vine-shaded courtyard. **₺180**

Ezgi Butik Hazeranlar Sok 56 ☏ 0358 218 7311, ⓦ ezgikonaklari.com. Rooms in this restored Ottoman house have pleasing modern flourishes, but it's otherwise a

simple affair with a thoroughly relaxing atmosphere. It's also good for singles, for whom rooms can go for less than half the doubles price. **₺150**

Harşena Tevfik Hafız Sok ☏ 0358 218 3979, ⓦ harsenaotel.com. Stunning former Ottoman residence with creaky floorboards and rooms furnished with period antiques, lace and linen, and low-slung Ottoman beds. Some overlook the river, where you can breakfast on the balcony, but the best are at the back beneath the floodlit rock tombs where you can sleep to the sounds of gentle guitar music from the garden below. **₺180**

İlk Pansiyon Hitit Sok 1 ☏ 0358 218 6277,

GETTING STEAMY IN AMASYA

Amasya boasts a couple of wonderfully atmospheric **hamams**, each of them centuries old – stay here a few days and you'll be able to take them in at your leisure.

Mustafa Bey Hamamı Mustafa Kehal Bul ☏ 0358 218 3461. Sandwiched between a mosque, a museum and the river, this hamam is very old but very much in use, as the wreaths of vapour emerging from its chimneys testify. Entry ₺15, same again for massage. Daily: men 7–10am & 5–11pm; women 10am–5pm.

Yıldız Hamamı On the north bank, next to the Hazeranlar Konağı. According to the plaque outside, this hamam was constructed "in the mid's of the 13th contray and rebult in the 16th countruy". Mercifully the interior beats the spelling hands down. Entry ₺15, ₺7 extra for a sponge-down or massage. Daily 6am–midnight.

8

ⓦ ilkpansiyon.com. Faultlessly restored eighteenth-century Armenian mansion, retaining much of the original decor and period antiques. Reservations advisable; there are just six rooms. **₺150**

★ **Uluhan** Tevfik Hafız Sok ☎ 0358 212 7575,

ⓦ oteluluhan.com. Right under the rock tombs, this hotel sports some of the nicest rooms in town, many of them carpeted affairs with fancy wallpaper – not exactly Ottoman stylings, but pleasing nonetheless. The garden area is also a great place for breakfast or coffee. **₺160**

EATING

With a riverside setting and the rock tombs above lit up at night, dining out in Amasya provides unbeatable atmosphere. *Lokanta*-style joints around Atatürk Cad, south of the river, offer cheap eats, or you can enjoy a traditional meal in the Ottoman-house **restaurants** on the north side. Note that there aren't many **bars**, and given the number of mosques in the centre it's even hard to find shops serving alcohol.

RESTAURANTS

Ali Kaya On the hill on the south side of town; look up and you'll see the sign ☎ 0358 218 0601. Magnificent views, attentive service and tables under shady pine trees, with meals clocking in at around ₺60 including drinks. Best of all, they usually provide a free transport service – just ask at your hotel reception. Daily 11am–11pm.

Çınaraltı Ziyapaşa Bul 5 ☎ 0358 218 5692. Popular place with outdoor seating. Inexpensive and piping hot stews, soups, *pide* (from ₺7.50) and kebabs (from ₺13), including a gut-busting *Tokat kebap* (see box opposite) for ₺35. It's also *the* place to head for breakfast – laid out buffet style, and therefore all you can eat, for just ₺10. Daily 7am–11pm.

Şehzade Balık Ekmek Pedestrian promenade, off Ziyapaşa Bul. The only boat on the river (so far) has been converted into a sort of floating snack-shack serving delicious rounds of fried fish in bread for ₺6. Daily 9am–9pm.

Strabon Tevfik Hafız Sok ☎ 0358 218 1515. River-view restaurant that gets the basics right – good, cheap, filling

meals, most of which are pictured on the menu. Though it's not actually on the menu, you're best off asking for a *meze* platter (*karışık mezeler*; ₺15), and perhaps a shot of rakı; alternate suggestions include catfish (₺18) and Albanian liver. Daily 9am–11pm.

CAFÉS AND ICE-CREAM PARLOURS

Kaymak Dondurma Ziyapaşa Bul 35a. A well-located local favourite for ice cream; ₺2 and a smile for a few scoops. Daily 8am–10pm.

Kızlar Sarayı By the rock tombs ☎ 0358 218 6366. A lovely watering hole (good for coffee or tea, too) for those who have taken the short, yet steepish, walk up to the rock tombs. There's seating inside the charming wooden building, although grab a table outside to make the most of the sweeping views. Daily 8.30am–5pm.

Seyran Cafe Hazeranlar Sok ☎ 0358 218 0211. The pick of Amasya's many cafés, a fun but relaxing place in which you can sip a coffee (though avoid the cappuccino like the plague), suck on a nargile (₺15) or simply enjoy a river view. Daily 9am–11pm.

Tokat

TOKAT clusters at the foot of a jagged crag, with a ruined Pontic fortress on top. Despite its undeniably dramatic setting – and richly colourful history – it lacks the appeal of Amasya or even Sivas, the two cities between which it's stuck, and most travellers whoosh straight past, seeing only the *otogar* en route.

However, there are certainly enough sights to justify at least a half-day stop – especially since the city's famed **kebab** (see box opposite) is large enough to count as one. More conventional attractions include some excellent Ottoman buildings, a **Selçuk seminary** and a superb museum – more than enough to work off the kebab's calories.

Brief history

Tokat first came to prominence as a staging post on the Persian trans-Anatolian royal road, running from Sardis to Persepolis. Later it fell to Alexander the Great and then to Mithridates and his successors. In 47 BC, **Julius Caesar** defeated Pharnaces, son of the Pontic king Mithridates VI, earlier Eupator, who had taken advantage of civil war in Rome to attempt to re-establish the Pontic kingdom as an independent state. Caesar's victory in a five-hour battle at Zile, just outside Tokat, prompted his immortal line "Veni, vidi, vici" (I came, I saw, I conquered).

Under **Byzantine** rule, Tokat became a frontline city in perpetual danger of Arab attack. That state of affairs continued until the Danişmend Turks took control of the city after the battle of Manzikert in 1071. Less than one hundred years later the İlhanid Mongols arrived, then Tokat was briefly transferred to the Ottoman Empire before a second great Mongol wave under **Tamerlane**.

With the departure of the Mongols and return of the **Ottomans**, life returned to normal, and prosperity ensued. In time, though, trade patterns shifted, the east–west routes to Persia lost their importance and Tokat became the backwater it remains today.

Tokat Museum

Sulusokak Sok; take the side road immediately south of the Taş Han, and zigzag left then right at the top • Tues–Sun 8am–5pm • ₺5

Set in the old **Arastalı Bedesten**, the **Tokat Museum** is a smart repository for local archeological finds. Its ethnographic section features examples of local yazma-making – printing with wooden blocks on cloth, to produce colourful patterned handkerchiefs, scarves and tablecloths – but perhaps of more note are the unusual relics collected from the churches that served the town's sizeable Greek and Armenian communities before World War I. Typical of these is a wax effigy of Christina, a Christian martyred during the rule of the Roman Emperor Diocletian.

Latifoğlu Konağı

Gazi Osman Paşa Bul, 660m south of the Taş Han • Tues–Sun 9am–5pm • ₺5

Assorted Ottoman-era half-timbered houses survive in the side streets of Tokat. While most are in states of advanced decrepitude, one exception is the heavily restored **Latifoğlu Konağı**. With its plain white walls, brown-stained woodwork and low-pitched roof, it stands in dramatic contrast to the surrounding modern buildings. The interior is opulent almost to the point of tastelessness, but gives a good impression of how a wealthy nineteenth-century family would have lived.

ARRIVAL AND INFORMATION

TOKAT

By bus The *otogar* is just north of the centre. Most bus companies run a *servis* into town, otherwise it's ₺5 by taxi, or an easy walk: head left down the main road, then turn left onto Gazi Osman Paşa Bul after 300m, and walk a further 10min south. If you're only making a day-trip, ask your bus company to keep your bags at the *otogar* while you see the sights.

Destinations Amasya (12 daily; 2hr); Ankara (12 daily; 6hr 30min); Erzurum (2 daily; 9hr); Sivas (10 daily; 1hr 45min).

Tourist office You'll need a phrasebook to extract any information from the tiny office, set into the Taş Han off Gazi Osman Paşa Bul (daily 8am–6pm), and there are no maps or leaflets to collect.

ACCOMMODATION

★**Tower** Gazi Osman Paşa Bul 172 ☎ 0356 212 3570, ⓦ cavusoglutowerhotel.com. A relatively new, swanky option, on a street that boasts a clutch of establishments. Cheery youthful staff will proudly show you around the

spa, terrace café and top-floor pool; the rooms themselves are large with funky lighting, and have been nicely decorated with a monochrome colour scheme. Expect prices to rise. <u>₺200</u>

CONQUER A TOKAT KEBAB

Julius Caesar uttered his famous "I came, I saw, I conquered" in Tokat, and unsubstantiated rumours suggest that he did so after sampling the huge local **kebab**. You can do the same on your visit to the city, though be warned that it's a beast – a mouthwatering (and very filling) combination of roast lamb, potatoes, aubergine, tomato and peppers, grilled beneath a whole bulb of garlic, whose juices permeate the meal. Amazingly, this style has yet to take hold anywhere further than Amasya, and almost faded out in Tokat itself before making a recent comeback. Prices are in the region of ₺25, and if it takes less than twenty minutes to land on your table, it's not the real deal.

Yücel Meydan Cad 22 ☎0356 212 5235, ⓦyucelotel .com. Located on a pleasant side street, this welcoming hotel has fresh-looking rooms, some with mosque views (and, of course, the attendant noise). There's also a hamam in the basement. **₺100**

EATING

★**Pirhan** Camii Yanı Meyd ☎0356 232 0033. The swishest restaurant in town, set in a *han*-style building. It's the best place to head for the local speciality, *Tokat kebap* (see p.499), which is not too dear at ₺30 – when you see the size of the dish you'll know you've got yourself a deal, but the fact that they serve it with full rounds of salad and bread is almost too much. From the Taş Han, head down the side street across the main road; it's a little way down, by the mosque. Daily 24hr.

Sedirhan Meydan Camii Yanı. Near the *Pirhan*, and similarly attractive, this is a good place for coffee or snacks; they also have no fewer than seventeen different nargile flavours. Daily 9am–11pm.

Taş Han Gazi Osman Paşa Bul. The Taş Han, originally called the Voyvoda Han, was built in 1631 by Armenian merchants. A large, rectangular building of two storeys, its courtyard houses some shabby shops and makes a great place for tea, as long as the music isn't on full blast (which it usually is). Daily 8am–11pm.

Sivas

An orderly city of around 200,000 people, **SİVAS** figures on few visitors' itineraries – a pity, since it's an immensely likeable place, with a concentration of **Selçuk monuments** that are up there with the finest in existence. Most were built during the Sultanate of Rum, and the period of Mongol sovereignty that followed under the İlhanids; with their highly decorative facades and elaborately carved portals, they epitomize architectural styles of the era. Most of these buildings are conveniently grouped together in **Selçuk Parkı**, in the very centre of town. The other sights are all within easy walking distance – as are all the good places to stay and eat.

Brief history

Sivas has been settled since Hittite times, and according to local sources was later a key centre of the Sivas Frig Empire (1200 BC), which seems to have been consigned to historical oblivion. The town's real flowering came during **Selçuk** times, after the Battle of Manzikert (1071). Sivas intermittently served as the Selçuk capital during the Sultanate of Rum in the mid-twelfth century, before passing into the hands of **İlhanid Mongols** during the late thirteenth century. The **Ottomans** took over in 1396, only to be ousted by the Mongols four years later under **Tamerlane**, who razed much of the city after an eighteen-day siege, and put its Christian inhabitants to the sword. The Ottomans returned in 1408 and Sivas pretty much faded out of history until a nineteenth-century reawakening.

Selçuk Parkı

Selçuk Parkı, set in a small, central area just off **Konak Meydanı**, wouldn't fit most people's expectations of a park, even if does sport a few odd patches of green. The buildings here are all architectural stunners, and though none count as "sights" as such, the whole is so much more than the sum of its parts – they make for a wonderful walk around.

Most notable, perhaps, is the **Bürüciye Medresesi**; founded in 1271 by the İlhanid emir Muzaffer Bürücirdi, it consists of a series of square rooms laid out to a symmetrical ground plan around a central courtyard. As you pass through the entrance, the *türbe* of the emir and his children is to the left. Directly opposite the entrance is the **Kale Camii**, which dates from 1580. As a straightforward Ottoman mosque, it's an oddity in this area.

Next comes the stunning **Çifte Minare Medrese**, or "Twin Minaret Seminary", which also dates from 1271. Its facade alone still stands, adorned with tightly curled relief filigrees, and topped by two brick **minarets**, which are speckled with pale blue tiles. Behind, only the well-defined foundations of student cells and lecture halls survive.

Lastly, there's the **Şifaiye Medresesi** – built in 1217 on the orders of the Selçuk sultan Keykavus I, it went on to function as a **hospital** and **medical school**. All three places mentioned here now function as richly distinctive places to take tea, but this is just about the pick of the bunch (see p.502).

Ulu Cami

Off Cumhuriyet Cad • Free

The **Ulu Cami** is the oldest mosque in Sivas, built in 1197. Step inside its northern entrance, and you enter the subterranean cool of an interior supported by fifty wooden pillars. The peaceful silence is broken only by the murmur of boys reading from the Koran.

Gök Medrese

Off Cumhuriyet Cad

Famed for its ornate tile-studded minarets, the stunning **Gök Medrese Camii**, or "Blue Seminary", was undertaking substantial renovation at the time of writing. It was built in 1271 by the Selçuk grand vizier Sahip Ata Fahrettin Ali, who was also responsible for buildings in Kayseri and Konya.

ARRIVAL AND INFORMATION   **SİVAS**

By train The train station is 2.5km west of town – easily walkable, or you could hop on one of the municipal buses or dolmuşes that run down İstasiyon Cad (later İnönü Bul) to Konak Meydanı.

THE SIVAS MASSACRE

Mention Sivas to any Turk, and you may well receive an abbreviated account of the events of **July 2, 1993** – a tragic massacre that has given the city an enduring notoriety, especially given the current friction between the country's secular and religious elements.

A group of **Alevi intellectuals** had gathered inside the Madımak Hotel for a small festival, celebrating the work of a sixteenth-century Alevi poet. One of their number, **Aziz Nasin**, had recently published translated extracts from Salman Rushdie's *The Satanic Verses*, and a vengeful mob of more than a thousand Islamic fundamentalists gathered outside in protest after Friday prayers. The hotel was set alight, and 37 perished, including hotel guests and employees. Aziz himself managed to escape. Many of the protagonists were rounded up and charged – 87 went to jail, including 33 whose death sentences were commuted to life imprisonment when Turkey abolished the death penalty in 2002.

Destinations Ankara (3 daily; 10–11hr); Divriği (3 daily; 2hr 40min); Diyarbakır (1 daily; 10hr); Erzurum (1 daily; 10hr); Kars (1 daily; 14hr 30min).

By bus Buses from Ankara and beyond arrive at the *otogar*, 1.5km south of town. From here *servis* buses run to the centre, taking an indirect route along İnönü Bul.

Destinations Amasya (10 daily; 4hr); Ankara (hourly; 6hr 30min); Divriği (4 daily; 3hr); Diyarbakır (12 daily; 8hr); Erzurum (12 daily; 7hr 30min); Kayseri (10 daily; 3hr); Malatya (12 daily; 4hr 30min); Tokat (10 daily; 1hr 45min).

Hamam The Meydan Hamamı, up a side street off Atatürk Cad, has been hissing and steaming for over four centuries, and is still going strong (daily 7am–10.30pm; ₺15 for bath).

ACCOMMODATION

Büyük İstasyon Cad ☎0346 225 4767, ⓦsivas buyukotel.com. Monolith of a hotel trying desperately to cling onto its class. Bedrooms are large and soulless, but also note the typical Sivas mini-tiling around the base of its exterior. ₺300

Eray Eski Belediye Sok 12 ☎0346 223 1647. A few apartment rooms trying their best to function as a youth hostel. Dormitory beds are comfy enough; single travellers are likely to get the room to themselves for the same price. Dorm ₺35, double ₺80

Köşk Atatürk Cad 7 ☎0346 255 1724, ⓦkoskotel.com. Beautifully decked-out contemporary hotel, complete with fitness centre. All rooms are spacious and spotless, with excellent showers, and there's a buffet breakfast. Often full, but you're still likely to slash a fair bit from the rack rates. ₺220

Sultan Eski Belediye Sok 18 ☎0346 221 2986, ⓦsultanotel.com.tr. Swish, very good value, contemporary hotel. While the rooms don't quite live up to the promise of a semi-opulent lobby, they're clean, cosy and quiet. ₺230

EATING

Cheap **kebab places** line the road behind the PTT; keep an eye out for the flat *Sivas köfte*, which are essentially miniature burgers. Precious few places serve **alcohol**, though there are a couple of dull bars on Atatürk Cad.

Elif Kebap Atatürk Cad 2 ☎0346 224 6770. Clean, friendly and popular, this two-level restaurant doles out round after round of excellent kebabs (including *Sivas köfte*, ₺15) and some very lengthy *pide* for a little less. Daily 9am–10pm.

Hakan Bistro Atatürk Cad 22 ☎0346 225 0666. Presentable place whose upper floor is a great option for breakfast – ₺13 for the regular plates, and ₺17.50 for the village feast with cheeses from all over Eastern Anatolia. International dishes include chow mein, quesadillas and salmon – just the thing if you've been travelling a while – plus some of the best *baklava* and desserts in town. Daily 7.30am–10pm.

Kahvemiz Behind Büyük Otel. This café is popular with Sivas trendies, and local women: it's a relaxed, funkily designed place serving Turkish coffee (₺6) in a proper *cezve*

(coffee pot). They usually throw in some chocolates, *lokum* and lemon-mint water for good measure – sugar overload for sure, yet some people even order cake on top. Wi-fi available. Daily 11am–11pm.

★Şifaiye Medresesi Selçuk Parkı. Gulp a coffee back (₺1.50) in the superb setting of this *medrese* courtyard (see p.501), which also functions as a swallow's playground. Also a great place to suck on a nargile (₺10). Daily 8am–11pm.

Sosyal Tesisleri On the main square ☎0346 223 4764. This new venture is wildly popular with locals (especially the outdoor seats by the water feature), and makes a perfect stop-off while touring the sights. Try the *Sivas köfte* (₺13), or some tasty *içli köfte* (₺9), essentially meatball dumplings in a casing of cracked wheat. Daily 8am–midnight.

Divriği

Stuck in the middle of a mountainous nowhere, on a hill overlooking a tributary of the young Euphrates, sleepy **DIVRIĞI** merits a visit for the sake of a single monument – the whimsical and unique **Ulu Cami** and its dependency, the **Darüşşifa**. These date from the early thirteenth century, when the town was the seat of the tiny **Mengüçeh** emirate. The Mongols, who evicted the Mengüçehs in 1252, demolished the castle but left the religious foundations alone, and the place was not incorporated into the Ottoman Empire until 1516.

Divriği retains a ramshackle bazaar area, crisscrossed by cobbled lanes and grapevines. It also sports distinctive wooden **minarets** and old houses with inverted-keyhole windows, neither of which are seen elsewhere in Anatolia. The conspicuous **mosque** and **sanatorium**, joined in one complex at the top of a slope 250m east of town, command a fine view.

The town is some 175km from Sivas, on a series of twisting roads. Better by far to come by train – it's a slow but stunning journey, following the river rather than the road.

Ulu Cami

Easily visible from town; entrance on Canlar Sok

Dedicated in 1228 by a certain Ahmet Şah, the **Ulu Cami** is remarkable for its outrageous external **portals**, most un-Islamic with their wealth of floral and faunal detail. Far-fetched comparisons have been drawn to Indian Moghul art, but a simpler, more likely explanation is that Armenian or Selçuk craftsmen had a hand in the decoration.

The north door, festooned with vegetal designs, is the most celebrated, although the northwest one is more intricate – note the pair of double-headed eagles, not necessarily copied from the Byzantines since it's a very old Anatolian motif. Inside, sixteen columns and the ceiling they support are more suggestive of a Gothic cloister or Byzantine cistern. There's rope-vaulting in one dome, while the northeast one sports a peanut-brittle surface.

8

Darüşşifa

Easily visible from town; entrance on Canlar Sok • Theoretically open daily 8.30am–5pm, but you may have to find the caretaker to gain admission

The **Darüşşifa**, like the Ulu Cami, was built in 1228 by Adaletli Melike Turan Melek, Ahmet Şah's wife. Its portal is restrained in comparison to the mosque, but still bears medallions lifted almost free from their background. The interior is asymmetrical in both ground plan and ornamentation, and even more eclectic than the mosque. The fan-reliefs on the wall behind this once formed an elaborate **sundial**, catching rays through the second-floor window of the facade.

ARRIVAL AND DEPARTURE   DIVRIĞI

By train Divriği's train station is down by the river, a 20min walk from the bazaar; taxis meet most arrivals and won't cost more than a few lira.
Destinations Erzurum (1 daily; 6hr 45min); Sivas (3 daily;

2hr 40min).
By bus The *otogar* is 400m south of town on the road to Elazığ, but for once in rural Turkey, travel times are far longer than by train – don't bother.

ACCOMMODATION AND EATING

Divriği holds very few places to **stay**, though you'll see a clutch of simple guesthouses as you approach town from the train station. **Eating** options are certainly better, with cheap restaurants and snack bars concentrated around the bazaar area.

Konak On the way up to the mosque. Citadel views and the best *kahvaltı* in these parts (₺15), as well as succulent kebabs. Daily 7am–10pm.
Ninni Sivas Divriği Yolu. Simple hotel that has renovated its lobby in recent years. They've still got a little way to go

with the rooms, however. ₺70
Özkanlar Pansiyon Sivas Divriği Yolu ☎ 0346 418 1742. Consisting of a few rooms above an internet café; "en-suite" options have a shower and urinal. ₺90

The Black Sea coast

SUMELA MONASTERY.

9

The Black Sea coast

From the northern end of the Bosphorus just east of Istanbul to the frontier with Georgia, the Black Sea region is a real anomaly, guaranteed to smash any stereotypes you may hold about Turkey. The combination of damp northerly and westerly winds, confronting an almost uninterrupted wall of mountains south of the shore, has created a relentlessly rainy and riotously green realm. That said, while the coastline may have cooler water temperatures and cloudier skies, semi-tropical heat still sets in during July and August. The Black Sea (Karadeniz in Turkish) was – and indeed still is – an important maritime route; the ancient civilizations who ruled the waters left behind castles, churches, monasteries and mosques. Alongside these, the region's charm lies in its craggy beauty, empty beaches, vibrant seaside towns unspoilt by tourism, and its low-key vibe.

Although the region's characterless central portion is dominated by the hulking port of **Samsun**, the coast west of the strikingly sited town of **Sinop**, towards the Byzantine/Genoese harbour of **Amasra**, is filled with attractive villages and deserted beaches. To the east of Samsun are the old mercantile towns of **Ünye** and **Giresun**, and the ancient port city of **Trabzon** (Trebizond), which has more historical attractions than any other destination on the Turkish Black Sea, including the spectacular nearby **monastery of Sumela**.

Emerging north of Ankara as mere humps, the coastal **mountain ranges** attain world-class grandeur by the time they reach the Georgian border. Until recently they made land access all but impossible and provided refuge for a complex quilt of ethnic subgroups, pockets of which still exist among the **Hemşin valleys** and the **Kaçkar Mountains**. Today these regions provide excellent trekking opportunities and rural retreats among the misty forests, glassy lakes and babbling streams.

Black Sea **cuisine** is strongly influenced by geography and climate. The Black Sea anchovy (*hamsi*) has a cult-like fan base as far as Istanbul, and the region produces excellent dairy and locally grown hazelnuts, walnuts and cherries.

With the exception of the winding and slow western section between Sinop and Amasra, bus and dolmuş links are excellent along the D010 coastal highway.

Brief history

The ancient Greeks ventured onto the Black Sea, or as they called it, the Pontos Euxine, at the start of the first millennium BC. They fought with the local "barbarians" and occasionally, as in the semi-legendary tale of Jason and the Argonauts, got the better of them. Between the seventh and fourth centuries BC, the Aegean cities founded numerous colonies. These became the ancestors of virtually every modern Black Sea town, whose names as often as not are Turkifications of their ancient monikers. The region made its first brief appearance on the world stage when a local Pontic king, **Mithridates IV Eupator**, came close to expelling the Romans from Anatolia.

UZUNGÖL

Highlights

❶ Driving from Sinop to Amasra Cruise the little-used coast road from Sinop to Amasra, where sharp switchbacks lead to peaceful bays and long beaches. **See pp.511–516**

❷ Amasra Enjoy the small-town charm and historical pedigree of Amasra, with its old cobbled streets, Byzantine gateways and Genoese castle walls. **See p.514**

❸ Ordu cable car For sweeping Black Sea and mountain views, ride the gondola 550m above Ordu. **See p.518**

❹ Trabzon The heart of this relaxed city features historical neighbourhoods and sophisticated shopping streets radiating off an

atmospheric central square. **See p.519**

❺ Sumela Climb to this cliff-clinging thirteenth-century monastery in a superb forested setting. **See p.528**

❻ Uzungöl Large natural lake in the foothills of the Kaçkar Mountains, the focus of a popular resort. **See p.530**

❼ Hemşin valleys This lushly forested district is home to a colourful, outgoing people with their own tenaciously preserved culture. **See p.531**

❽ Tea Taste the nation's favourite drink and watch the leaves being picked from the hillsides surrounding Rize. **See p.535**

HIGHLIGHTS ARE MARKED ON THE MAP ON PP.508–509

9

With the arrival of Christianity, relations between natives and imperial overlords hardly changed at all. Only the Byzantine urban centres by the sea became thoroughly Hellenized. The Byzantine defeat at Manzikert in 1071 (see p.650) initially meant little to the Black Sea, safe behind its wall of mountains; the fall of Constantinople to the Fourth Crusade in 1204 had far greater immediate effects, prompting the Black Sea's second spell of historical prominence. For two and a half cultured (and ultimately decadent) centuries, the empire-in-exile of the Komnenos dynasty, centred on **Trebizond** (today's Trabzon), exercised influence grossly disproportionate to its size.

After Manzikert, Turkish chieftains had begun to encroach on the coast, especially at the gap in the barrier ranges near Sinop and Samsun. The Trapezuntine dynasty even concluded alliances with them, doubtless to act as a counter to the power of the Genoese and Venetians who also set up shop hereabouts. Most of this factionalism came to an end under the **Ottomans**, though even they entrusted semi-autonomous administration of the Pontic foothills to feudal *derebeys* ("valley lords") until early in the nineteenth century.

The equilibrium was upset when the Black Sea area entered the history books for the third time, as a theatre of war. Imperial Turkey and **Russia** clashed four times between 1828 and 1915, and the Tsarist regime gave aid and comfort to various regional separatist movements after 1877. Between 1918 and 1922, Greeks attempting to create a Pontic state fought with guerrillas loyal to Atatürk's Nationalists. Following the victory of the **Republic**, the Greek merchant class was expelled, and the Black Sea experienced temporary economic disarray, verging on famine during the 1930s.

Most of the credit for the modern decades of **recovery** must go to *hamsi* (the Black Sea anchovy caught here in large numbers during winter) and hazelnuts – Turkey meets some 75 percent of the world demand for hazelnuts, and the Black Sea coast is the principal area of production.

The most visible sign of the post-Soviet era, since Turkey's eastern border opened up in the early 1990s, is a coastal highway and a further bout of urbanization. The Black Sea and its six bordering countries – Bulgaria and Romania to the west, Ukraine to the north, Russia and Georgia to the east, and Turkey to the south – today is a major trade hub, with a bottleneck exit point through the Bosphorus Strait.

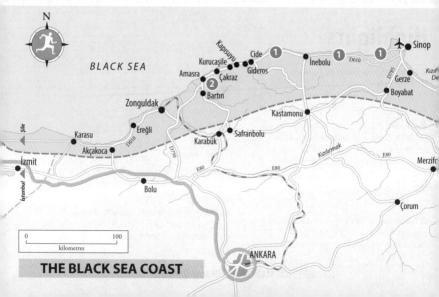

THE BLACK SEA COAST

The western Black Sea

Without any specific attractions, the coast from Samsun west to Amasra is perhaps the least visited part of the entire Turkish shoreline. **Samsun** makes a dreary gateway to the region, but matters improve as you head northwest to **Sinop**, more interesting than your average Black Sea town. West of Sinop, the coast road is tortuous and slow, with sparse bus and dolmuş schedules. However, the weather is drier here than further east, and the scenery is spectacular, dappled with fig trees and olive groves and interspersed with unspoiled **beaches** and small, pretty ports. The only place that sees visitors in significant numbers is picturesque **Amasra**, an old medieval stronghold at the western end of this beautiful stretch.

Samsun

Because of its strategic location midway along the Black Sea coast, **SAMSUN** changed hands frequently over the centuries. It was besieged, captured (and usually sacked) by the Pontic kings, Romans, Byzantines, several tribes of Turks and the Genoese, who had a major trading station here until 1425, when they torched the town rather than hand it over to Ottoman control. When the advent of the railway facilitated the transport of tobacco to Ankara and beyond, Samsun's flagging fortunes revived, and by 1910 it was a thriving city of 40,000 inhabitants. The port city gained a place in Turkish folklore when then Mustafa Kemal, under the guise of "Inspector General of the Ottoman forces in Anatolia", arrived in 1919 by steamship from Istanbul and quietly began to sow the seeds of independence among the local Turk population.

Today's Samsun, with a population of about 600,000, is a thoroughly modern city, laid out on a grid plan with endless suburbs stretching 30km along the east–west coast road. Until recently, the centre was rather scruffy and uninspiring, but it has become a little more appealing since the municipality began a programme of civic refurbishments in 2012, including new public spaces and a tram network. It now holds a couple of hours' worth of interesting sights, plus a fair amount to offer in terms of food and lodgings, should you need to spend the night.

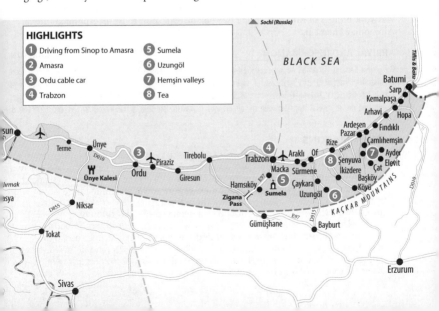

HIGHLIGHTS

1 Driving from Sinop to Amasra
2 Amasra
3 Ordu cable car
4 Trabzon
5 Sumela
6 Uzungöl
7 Hemşin valleys
8 Tea

9

Atatürk Bulvarı (the D010 coastal highway) runs through the city centre, and parallel to it is now an impressively **landscaped waterfront**. The main square, **Cumhuriyet Meydanı**, has a statue of Atatürk on horseback, and you can ride around town in a horse-drawn carriage (*fayton*), groups of which wait at Cumhuriyet Meydani or Atatürk Bulvari (around ₺20/hr).

Archeology and Ethnography Museum

19 Mayıs Bul 5 • Daily 8am–7pm, Nov–March till 5pm • ₺5 • ☎ 0362 431 6828, ⓦ muze.gov.tr

Samsun's **Archaeology and Ethnography Museum** (Arkeoloji ve Etnografya Müzesi) is well laid out and worth visiting for its main exhibit, a Roman mosaic found in Karasamsun, site of an ancient acropolis that juts out to sea 3km west of town. The museum's grounds are also beautifully landscaped. A life-sized installation marks the spot where Atatürk arrived on May 19, 1919, to take control of the local anti-Greek forces.

Gazi Museum

Gazi Cad, off 19 Mayis Bul • Tues–Sun 8am–5pm • ₺5 • ☎ 0362 435 7535

Housed in the former *Mintika Palas Hotel* (1902), the **Gazi Müzesi** commemorates Atatürk's 1919 visit to Samsun. On this first and most historic visit (the first of several), he only stayed six days before moving on to Havza, 85km inland and away from the watchful eye of British warships. Scores of photos, letters, clothing and even the trademark hats from the great man are on display.

Amisos Tepesi and Batı Park

3km west of the centre, off Atatürk Bul • **Cable car** Daily 9am–10pm • ₺5 each way • **Amazon waxworks** Daily 8am–7pm • Free • Take the tram from the Cumhuriyet stop and get off at the Baruthane stop

A visit to **Amisos Tepesi** (Hill) and the surrounding **Batı Park** (West Park) is worthwhile to ride the 323m cable car and enjoy a spectacular view of the Black Sea before wandering around the hilltop Hellenistic-era tombs. The lower station of the cable car, **Samsun Amisos Tepesi Teleferik Hattı**, is in the park (north of Atatürk Bulvarı). It takes less than five minutes to get to the top, depositing passengers in front of the pleasant *Amisos Café*.

Also in Batı Park, a huge **new statue** facing out to sea represents the figure of a fierce female warrior, flanked by two buildings designed to look like crouching lions, with waxwork models of **Amazons** inside (see box below), soon to be incorporated into an Amazonian theme park.

ARRIVAL AND INFORMATION
SAMSUN

By plane Samsun Çarşamba Airport (☎ 0362 844 8830, ⓦ carsamba.dhmi.gov.tr) is 23km east of town. Havas (☎ 0362 844 8856, ⓦ havas.net) buses meet all incoming flights, and run to several stops between the airport and

Cumhuriyet Meyd in the centre, from where they also depart 2hr before flight departures. Car hire companies at the airport include Avis (☎ 0362 844 8657, ⓦ avis.com.tr), Budget (☎ 0362 844 8898, ⓦ budget.com.tr), Sixt (☎ 0362 444 0076,

---

THE AMAZONS

Just east of Samsun, the Black Sea coastal plain, watered by the Yeşilırmak delta, widens to its broadest extent. According to ancient Greek history, the area was once thought to be the land of the **Amazons**, a semi-mythical fierce tribe of women – there's no real evidence to support their existence except in legends depicted in classical art, poems, statues and ancient oral tales. They supposedly founded their capital **Themiskyra** in the pre-Pontic period near the mouth of the Terme River, at or near modern-day Terme, 58km east of Samsun.

According to the legends, these warriors had their right breasts cut off in childhood to facilitate **spear throwing** and **arrow shooting**. They only coupled with men during two months of the year, after which the unfortunate fellows would be killed, and any male babies abandoned in the wilderness. The females were brought up by their mothers, and were trained in agricultural skills, hunting and the art of war.

@ sixt.com.tr) and Europcar (☎ 0362 266 6555, @ europcar
.com.tr).

Destinations Ankara (2 daily; 1hr); Istanbul Atatürk (4–6
daily; 1hr 50min); Istanbul Sabiha Gökçen (4 daily; 1hr
50min).

By bus Samsun's otogar, 4km south of the centre on the
D010 towards Trabzon, is connected by servis buses and
frequent dolmuşes to the bus companies' ticket offices on
the southeast side of Cumhuriyet Meyd.

Destinations Afyon (8 daily; 11hr); Amasya (hourly; 2hr);
Ankara (hourly; 6hr 30min); Artvin (3 daily; 8hr 45min);
Balıkesir (2 daily; 14hr 30min); Batumi, Georgia (5 daily;
10hr); Erzurum (4 daily; 11hr); Giresun (10 daily; 4hr);
Istanbul (10 daily; 11hr); Rize (hourly; 7hr); Sinop (every

30min; 3hr); Sivas (10 daily; 5hr 30min); Trabzon (hourly;
5hr 30min); Van (3 daily; 12hr).

By train The train station is halfway between the otogar
and the centre, 2km south of Cumhuriyet Meyd. However,
the Samsun–Sivas (via Amasya) line is closed till
(estimated) 2018 for improvements; once complete, the
upgrade will reduce journey times from 9hr to 5hr on the
370km route – check the TCDD website for progress
(@ tcdd.gov.tr).

Tourist office The reasonably helpful (though little
English is spoken) tourist office is on the first floor of the
Atatürk Kültür Merkezi (Atatürk Cultural Centre), Atatürk
Bulvarı (Mon–Fri daily 9am–6pm, Oct–May till 5pm;
☎ 0362 431 1228).

GETTING AROUND

By tram Samsun's new urban tram network runs between
the train station in the southeast and the university

stations in the northwest, including a useful section more
or less parallel to Atatürk Bulvarı (tickets from ₺3).

ACCOMMODATION

Otel Necmi Kale Mah 6, Bedesten Sok ☎ 0362 432
7164, @ otelnecmi.com.tr. Super-friendly, well-located
hotel – look out for signs on Kazımpaşa Cad – with compact
a/c rooms, all with shared bathrooms, accessed up a steep
staircase; some will fit three beds at a squeeze (₺125).
Breakfast is served in a ground-floor living room. **₺90**

Samsun Park Cumhuriyet Cad 38 ☎ 0362 435 0095,
@ samsunparkotel.com. A short walk from Cumhuriyet
Meyd, this shiny hotel has all-white decor and modern,

mostly tiny rooms, all with a/c, TV and fridge; those on the
top floor have sea views. The staff are generally friendly, and
breakfast is served in a spotless dining room. **₺130**

Yafeya Otel Cumhuriyet Meyd 4 ☎ 0362 435 1131,
@ yafeyaotel.com. Housed in an imposing tower on the
corner of the square, and a short walk from the museums,
the Yafeya boasts 96 comfortable rooms with large
windows, some with glimpses of the sea. There's a large
buffet-style restaurant and spacious a/c lobby. **₺220**

EATING AND DRINKING

Oskar Restaurant Şeyhhamza Sok 3, off Belediye
Meyd. Friendly, 60-year-old family-run restaurant,
recommended for its surroundings, service and good
selection of traditional Turkish-only food; mezes, meat and
fish dishes, plus traditional desserts such as bafra nokul, a
flavoured sweet pastry. Mains ₺9–20. Daily noon–10pm.

★Samsun Balık Restaurant Kazımpaşa Cad 20
☎ 0362 435 7550. Aptly named place in a welcoming brick
house, where diners select their fish downstairs and have it
brought to them in the refined upstairs dining room. Non-
fish eaters can ask for vegetarian meze (₺7). Mains from
₺15. Licensed. Tues–Sun 7–11pm.

Sinop

Perched on Anatolia's most northerly point, **SINOP**, 160km west of Samsun, is blessed
with a fine natural harbour that was the biggest shipyard in the Black Sea during Ottoman
rule. Renowned as one of the prettiest towns along the coast, it's home to a fine clutch of
monuments, though most visitors are content to relax along the café-lined compact
waterfront, where bobbing boats supply the day's catch to the line of restaurants behind.

Brief history

Sinop takes its name from the mythical Amazon queen **Sinope**. The daughter of a
minor river god, she attracted the attention of Zeus, who promised her anything she
desired in return for her favours. Her request was for eternal virginity; Zeus played the
gentleman and complied.

   After a wealthy period of Roman rule, Sinop declined during the Byzantine era,
while Persian and Arab raids thwarted sixth- and seventh-century attempts to revive its
fortunes. The Selçuks took the town in 1214, converting churches into mosques and

9

Map of SİNOP showing:

EATING
Saray	2
Sinop Örnek Mantı	1

ACCOMMODATION
Otel 57	2
Bossinop	4
Mola	1
Reis	3
Yilmaz Aile Pansiyonu	5

DRINKING & NIGHTLIFE
Kale Burç Café	2
Liman Café/Bar	1

erecting a *medrese*, but after the Mongols smashed their short-lived state, Sinop passed into the hands of the İsfendiyaroğlu emirs of Kastamonu. After Ottoman annexation in 1458, the town was rarely heard of until November 30, 1853, when the Russians destroyed an Ottoman fleet anchored off Sinop, triggering the **Crimean War**, and again on May 18, 1919, when Atatürk passed through en route to Samsun on May 18, 1919. Sinop also played a front-line role during the **Cold War**, when it was the location of a US-military listening post, closed in 1992.

The city walls

Although time has inevitably taken its toll, Sinop's prominent **city walls** remain by far its most compelling feature. Opposite the old fortress and prison the bulky **Kumkapı** juts out bastion-like into the sea on the northern shore, while down near the harbour a hefty square tower offers good views out to sea and pleasant strolls along the nearby sections of wall.

Sinop Kale Cezaevi and Tarihî Sinop Kapalı

Gelincik Mahallesi Yolu • Daily 8am–7pm, Nov–March till 5pm • ₺5 • ☎ 0368 261 3023, ⓦ muze.gov.tr

The first thing you'll notice on entering Sinop is its old fortress, **Sinop Kale Cezaevi**, parts of which date to 1215 and served a defensive purpose for the initial settlement. A citadel, which the Ottomans used as a shipyard, was added a year later during the Selçuk era. It was then converted into a **prison** in 1887 – now called the **Tarihî Sinop Kapalı** (Historical Sinop Prison) – and housed convicts for the next hundred years. A wander round the old cells and a peek into the grim dungeons will reveal why this was one of Turkey's most notoriously archaic prisons.

Alâeddin Camii

Sakarya Cad

Sinop's oldest mosque, the thirteenth-century Selçuk **Alâeddin Camii**, is five-domed and set in a rectangular plan. It lies within a tree-shaded, high-walled courtyard with a

9

central *şadırvan*, where a blue-painted porch lets onto a plain interior enlivened by a fine *mimber*.

Alaiye Medresesi
Batur Cad, behind the mosque

The mosque's **Alaiye Medresesi**, dating from the 1260s, is also known as the **Pervane Medresesi** after its founder, Mu'in al-Din Süleyman Pervane. Its most notable feature is a marble-decorated entrance portal, relatively restrained by Selçuk standards. The former pupils' rooms with a small courtyard now house cafés and craft shops selling locally made embroidered linen.

Sinop Museum
Okullar Cad 2 • Daily 8am–7pm, Nov–March till 5pm • ₺5 • ☎ 0368 261 3023, Ⓦ muze.gov.tr

The Sinop Museum has an array of objects from the Bronze Age onwards, including the relatively recent Independence War. Many of its oldest exhibits were unearthed at Kocagöz, an archeological site a few kilometres southwest. The museum grounds hold the Aynalı Kadın Tomb, built in 1335, and the sparse remains of the Hellenistic **Temple of Serapis**, excavated in 1951.

Balatlar Kilise
Corner of Kaynak and Tarakçi Cads

The Byzantine **Balatlar Kilise** church is thought to have been built during the seventh century, atop the remnants of a Roman bathhouse. Only its northern and southern walls are still standing, while inside, traces of frescoes depicting Jesus and Mary are suffering from exposure to both the elements and graffiti taggers.

The town beaches
Dolmuşes connect Kumsal and Karakum via the *otogar* and town centre (every 30min)

Sinop's main beaches are **Kumsal**, less than 1km southwest of the bus station, and a pay beach at **Karakum**, on the southern side of the peninsula, 3km east of the harbour. Kumsal beach is smaller, but the sand is lighter and the sea rather more enticing than at Karakum, whose name, meaning "black sand", is a fairly true description.

Akliman
Sinop-Akliman Yolu; the main picnic area is 9km from town • Dolmuşes run hourly, more frequently in summer (20min)

The best beach on the northwest side of Sinop is **Akliman**, where a 7km-long fine stretch of white sand begins 2km from town and runs along the seaward side of the airport. It's backed by pine forests and picnic areas but is less frequented than the other beaches, as unpredictable currents make swimming here dangerous.

ARRIVAL AND INFORMATION **SİNOP**

By plane The small Sinop Airport (☎ 0368 271 5608, Ⓦ sinop.dhmi.gov.tr) is 5km west of the centre and only served by one daily THY flight (☎ 0368 271 5628) to/from Istanbul. An airport bus meets arrivals and goes to the main PTT on Atatürk Cad, from where it departs 1hr 30min before departure. A taxi to town should cost around ₺25. KRL Rent-A-Car is the only agency at the airport (☎ 0538 546 5757).
Destinations Istanbul Atatürk (1 daily; 1hr 15min).

By bus and dolmuş Sinop's *otogar*, 3km southwest of town, on the D010 towards the airport, is connected with the centre by bus company *servis* buses and dolmuşes that run along Sakarya Cad. Note that buses to Amasra use the faster inland road via Kastamonu (where you'll need to change). Most local dolmuşes gather at the dolmuş terminal on Cumhuriyet Cadi, by the fortress.
Destinations Ankara (2 daily; 13hr); Istanbul (6 daily; 10hr 30min); Kastamonu (9 daily; 3hr 30min); Samsun (every 30min; 3hr); Trabzon (2 daily; 8hr).

By car Allow a full day to drive the 300km or so along the scenic coast road from Amarsa to Sinop.

Tourist office Just south of *Kale Burç Café*, on İskele Cad (daily June–Sept 8am–7pm, Oct–May 9am–5pm; ☎ 0368 261 5298). There is also an irregularly manned booth at the Pervane Medresesi.

9

ACCOMMODATION

Sinop has a great selection of central hotels, mostly in the streets behind the harbour, and many small *pansiyons* have sprung up at Karakum beach on the southern side of the peninsula, 3km east of the centre.

Otel 57 Kurtuluş Cad 29 ☎ 0368 261 5462, ⓦ otel57 .com. Standard business-class place, within strolling distance of the water. The comfortable and modern rooms have wood-panelled floors, TV, a/c, heating and balconies, and the higher ones have sea views. Free parking nearby and a generous buffet breakfast. ₺**190**

Bossinop Uğur Mumcu Meyd 37 ☎ 0368 260 5700, ⓦ bossinopotel.com. Overlooking the town's main roundabout, with glimpses of the sea and castle, the *Bossinop* offers spacious rooms (some triples) with large sliding doors leading onto French balconies and good-sized bathrooms. Breakfast is served on a glassed-roof terrace with views, and parking can be arranged. ₺**220**

Mola Kurtuluş Cad 34 ☎ 0368 261 1814, ⓦ sinopmolaotel.com.tr. In a great location across from the harbour, this modest hotel offers ageing but comfortable rooms, some with balconies and sea views

— those without both are considerably cheaper. Good buffet breakfasts are taken in the pleasant garden courtyard set into the fortress wall. ₺**155**

★**Reis** Kurtuluş Cad 19 ☎ 0368 260 4020, ⓦ sinopreisotel.com. The friendly and well-managed *Reis*, overlooking the harbour, has simple yet stylish rooms with large windows and smallish bathrooms. The rooftop terrace has great views and serves buffet breakfasts and à la carte dinners. ₺**225**

Yılmaz Aile Pansiyonu Tersane Çarşısı 11 ☎ 0368 261 5752 or ☎ 0532 616 9777. Family-owned and -run, this is the best-value budget option close to the water's edge. The twelve small, clean rooms mostly share basic but acceptable bathrooms, and there's one en-suite double. Breakfast is not included, but there's a kitchen for guest use, and the welcoming owners also run the downstairs café. ₺**80**

EATING

Saray İskele Cad 18 ☎ 0368 261 1729, ⓦ sarayrestaurant.com.tr. Located on a floating pier, this is one of the most popular fish restaurants along the harbour-front, despite its sometimes slow service. The fish is often farmed rather than wild; expect ₺18–25 for fresh mackerel or sea bass. Daily noon–11pm.

Sinop Örnek Mantı İskele Cad 1/A ☎ 0368 261 7341. Friendly place with fast service, popular with locals for light, delicious breakfast pastries. You can ask for *paket servis* (takeaway) to enjoy in any of the local teahouses or while strolling along the harbour-front. Daily 7.30am–11.30pm.

DRINKING AND NIGHTLIFE

Kale Burç Café Sinop Kalesi, İskele Cad ☎ 0507 637 5707. Enjoying glorious sea views from atop the massive stone tower by the waterfront, the mostly outdoor *Burç* is a popular place for both a cold beer (₺7) and live (late) music, especially from local folk bands. Daily 8am–2am.

Liman Café/Bar İskele Cad 20 ☎ 0368 264 7821. This

picturesque teahouse, one of many in Sinop, is set in a restored stone house with chairs on the waterfront and a fine view of the boats in the harbour. As well as traditional tea, they serve beers, cocktails and wine, plus there's live music on summer evenings. Beer ₺8. Daily 11am–midnight.

Amasra

AMASRA brazenly flaunts its charms to new arrivals. Approached from any direction, the town suddenly appears below you, swarming up onto a rocky headland sheltering two bays. A narrow stone bridge links the main town to the island of **Boztepe** further out, while the headland shelters the east-facing **Büyük Liman** (Big Harbour) on one side and the west-facing **Küçük Liman** (Little Harbour) on the other. As the beaches at both are at best average, it's best to regard Amasra as a base for forays to better beaches further east.

Amasra's historical pedigree and colourful atmosphere make it worth at least an overnight stop. During the day it's a quiet place, full of shady corners; by night it's much livelier, but it doesn't lose its small-town charm.

Brief history

Mentioned as Sesamus in the *Iliad*, Amasra was colonized by Miletus in the sixth century BC. The name derived from Queen Amastris, a lady of the court of Alexander the Great, who, after the death of her husband, acted as regent for her

9

young son, only to be repaid with murder at his hands. Avid letter-writer Pliny the Younger was appointed Rome's special commissioner to this region in 110 AD. After the ninth century, following a barbarian attack, the town declined in importance, though the Byzantines maintained a garrison here. The Genoese took over when Byzantine strength declined, and held the city until the Ottomans assumed control in 1460.

Byzantine fortifications

Both Amasra itself and Boztepe island are scattered with stretches of ancient fortifications from two Byzantine/Genoese **castles** near the tip of the peninsula. One is situated in the modern town above Büyük Liman, where a short walk above the *Timur Otel* (see p.516) reveals old cobbled streets straddled by Byzantine gateways. The other castle is reached by following Küçük Liman Caddesi across the bridge to Boztepe, where a ruined watchtower on a piece of land jutting out into the harbour is still visible.

Boztepe's heavy-duty **walls**, pierced by several gates, remain largely intact. The **inner citadel** is studded with towers and the Genoese coat of arms. Of the two **Byzantine churches** that you can hunt down in the maze of alleys on Boztepe, the larger was converted to a mosque after the Ottoman conquest, while the ruined smaller one was in use until 1923.

Amasra Museum

Çamlık Sok 4, at the western inland end of Küçük Liman • Tues–Sun 8am–5pm • ₺15 • ☎ 0378 315 1006, ⓦ amasramuzesi.com

The high-quality **Amasra Museum** contains locally unearthed archeological finds including a beautiful selection of Roman sculptures discovered in nearby Bartın. Pride of place is given to the torso of an emperor, with Romulus and Remus carved on his tunic, discovered in the citadel area in 1995.

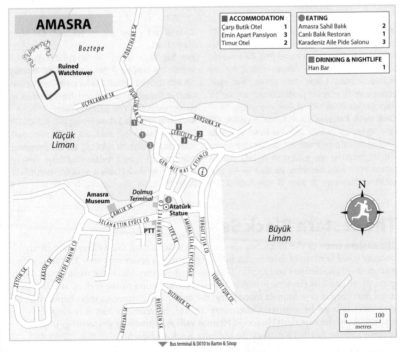

ACCOMMODATION		EATING	
Çarşı Butik Otel	1	Amasra Sahil Balık	2
Emin Apart Pansiyon	3	Canlı Balık Restoran	1
Timur Otel	2	Karadeniz Aile Pide Salonu	3

DRINKING & NIGHTLIFE	
Han Bar	1

AMASRA

Boztepe

Ruined Watchtower

Küçük Liman

Büyük Liman

Amasra Museum

Dolmuş Terminal

Atatürk Statue

PTT

N

0   100
metres

▼ Bus terminal & D010 to Bartın & Sinop

9

By bus or dolmuş The dolmuş terminal is opposite the Atatürk statue on Cumhuriyet Cad, in the central part of the headland. Some long-distance buses use a terminal on the southern end of town; irregular *servis* buses connect the two. Note, however, that most long-distance buses arrive and depart at Bartın, 16km south of Amasra; frequent dolmuşes run from the terminal in Amasra to the Bartın *otogar* (40min). Buses use the faster inland route via Kastamonu to Sinop. If you use the point-to-point dolmuşes east along the winding D010 coast road to Sinop (322km), leave early and allow a full day.

Destinations from Amasra Ankara (5 daily; 5hr); Bartın (hourly; 40min); Istanbul (8 daily; 9hr); Sinop via Zonguldak (hourly; 1hr 40min).

Destinations from Bartın Amasra (hourly; 40min); Ankara (7 daily; 4hr); Istanbul (8 daily; 8hr); Kastamonu (10 daily; 4hr 30min); Samsun (2 daily; 9hr); Sinop via Kastamonu (6 daily; 7hr 30min).

By car Allow a full day to drive the quiet, rather lovely scenic coast road between Amasra and Sinop.

Tourist office A small information kiosk at Büyük Liman opens irregularly in summer (ⓦ amasra.net).

ACCOMMODATION

Çarşı Butik Otel Çekiciler Cad 23 ☎0378 315 1146, ⓦ carsibutikotel.com. Centrally located but surprisingly quiet, the wooden bungalow-style rooms here have individual entrances and patios, with spacious a/c interiors though tiny bathrooms. Good breakfasts, and the English-speaking owner is friendly and helpful. ₺210

★ **Emin Apart Pansiyon** Çekiciler Cad 52 ☎0378 315 1676, ⓦ eminapartpansiyon.com. This tall, narrow *pansiyon* offers a varied range of rooms, all with wood-panelled floors, a/c and modern bathrooms, some with balconies and one with its own kitchen. Breakfast and cold drinks are served by the friendly staff in a pleasant rear courtyard full of plants. ₺235

Timur Otel Çekiciler Cad 53 ☎378 315 2589, ⓦ timurotel.com. One block back from the seafront with a can't-miss red facade, this popular well-priced hotel offers 21 simply furnished rooms with a/c, TV, thick windows and small bathrooms. A creaking lift climbs to the top floor, where breakfast with a view is served. Some triples and quads available. ₺190

EATING AND DRINKING

After dark the town takes to the streets along both harbour-fronts, especially Küçük Liman, which holds a string of very good, licensed fish restaurants.

★ **Amasra Sahil Balık** Küçük Liman 15 ☎0378 315 3465, ⓦ amasrasahil.com. This stylish restaurant offers tables right by the water on a small jetty. The wonderful setting is matched by the cuisine; excellent fish and seafood including lobster, tiger prawns and squid, accompanied by *meze* and salads. Licensed, and the bar stays open late. Mains ₺15–35. Daily noon–2am.

Canlı Balık Restoran Küçük Liman 8 ☎0378 315 2606, ⓦ amasracanlibalik.com. Also known as *Mustafa Amca'nin Yeri* and popular with both locals and tour groups, this fish restaurant was established in 1945 and has terraces on the water overlooking the Black Sea – a great sunset-watching spot. A plate of *istavrit* (Black Sea

mackerel) and a beer will set you back ₺30. Daily 11am–11pm.

Han Bar Küçük Liman Cad 17 ☎0378 315 2775. Amasra's late-night bar of choice, a typical low-lit smoky den with scattered loungers and bar stools. There's always plenty of drinking and dancing, and there's live music on summer nights. Beer ₺10. Daily 7pm–late.

Karadeniz Aile Pide Salonu Eyiceoğlu Cad 25 ☎0378 315 1543. Popular little place, just off the main street, renowned for piping-hot *pide* (₺8), and also serves soup, grilled meats, fish and a few breakfast dishes. There are usually enough shaded tables to go round. Mains ₺7–11. Daily 9am–10pm.

The eastern Black Sea

The **eastern coast** of the Black Sea sees far more visitors than the western half, partly because it holds more of interest, and partly because it's easier to access. **Trabzon**, with its romantic associations and medieval monuments, is very much the main event. With good plane and bus services, it makes a logical introduction to the region, and is the usual base for visits to **Sumela Monastery**, the only place covered in this chapter that is ever overwhelmed by tourists. Other forays inland, however, are just as rewarding – particularly the superlatively scenic **Hemşin valleys**, home to a welcoming, unusual people, and the northern gateway to the lofty Kaçkar Dağları.

East of Samsun: the coast to Trabzon

Beyond Samsun, and thanks to a new series of long and impressive tunnels, the main D010 coastal highway heads well inland in parts, through an especially fertile stretch of Turkey's interior, thus bypassing rocky peninsulas and the deathly slow coastal road. The highway does veer back towards the coast, however, to **Ünye**, **Ordu** and **Giresun**, all attractive seaside towns flanked by reasonable beaches and served by endless relays of buses and dolmuşes. The road then leads on to the metropolis of Trabzon, the most noteworthy city on the Black Sea coast.

Ünye

You could miss the small, friendly **ÜNYE** (ancient Oinaion), 90km east of Samsun, altogether thanks to a new bypass, but it makes a thoroughly pleasant overnight stay. It still holds a few grand buildings from its eighteenth-century heyday as a regional port, including a former Byzantine church on the main square (Cumhuriyet Meydanı) which now serves as a hamam (see below).

As one of the flatter (and less wet) areas of the Black Sea coast, Ünye profits from its reputation as a **beach resort**. The town promenade is home to a leafy park, a pedalo hire station, and a pier that was built for leisure rather than commerce or fishing – a rarity in these climes. The best strands lie to the west, where the highway is lined by ranks of motels and *pansiyon*s reminiscent of the Aegean or Marmara regions. The best of these overlook aptly named **Uzunkum** (Long Sand) beach, which is thought to be the longest stretch of sand on the Black Sea, though signs warn you not to bathe when the water is rough.

Ünye Kalesi

5km inland, 2km off the D850 to Niksar and Tokat • Take a dolmuş and ask to be dropped off at the signpost – you'll have to hike the final 2km to the gate; alternatively, take a taxi from Ünye (around ₺25–30 round trip, but you'll have to negotiate waiting time too)

The medieval fortress of **Ünye Kalesi** crowns a natural pinnacle inland from the coast. The Byzantine ramparts around the south-facing gateway have been restored, but the adjacent rock-cut tomb, of Roman or Pontic-kingdom vintage, suggests that one or other culture was originally responsible for fortifying the site. Beyond the gate little remains intact, though you can follow a slippery, usually damp path almost to the summit for views south over an exceptionally lush valley, and north to the coast. The final approach to the very top is for competent climbers only.

ARRIVAL AND INFORMATION
ÜNYE

By bus Ünye's minuscule *otogar* is at the eastern edge of town, by the road to Niksar; some bus companies also operate from offices along the main seafront highway (D010).

Destinations Giresun (18 daily; 2hr 30min); Ordu (every 30–45min; 1hr 15min); Samsun (hourly; 1hr 30min); Trabzon (16 daily; 3hr 30min).

Hamam Eski Hamamı, in an old church, is on the main square (daily 5am–midnight: women Tues, Fri & Sat 11am–5pm; men only all other times; ₺18).

ACCOMMODATION AND EATING

Sebile Hanim Konağı Cubukcu Arif Sok 10 ☎0452 323 7474, ⓦsebilehanimkonagi.com. This friendly, restored stone-and-wood Ottoman mansion is 200m uphill from the water, with fourteen en-suite rooms, including some attic-level singles. There's also a very good restaurant (open to non-guests) and a lovely shaded courtyard. ₺145

Sofra Belediye Cad 25 ☎0452 323 4083. In an atmospheric stone building with a beamed ceiling, this stalwart of the local dining scene is often full, especially at lunchtime, with locals who come for the home-styled cooking. The menu offers grills, *mezes*, *pide* and kebabs, as well as an excellent *sutlaç* (rice pudding) topped with hazelnuts and pistachios. Mains ₺8–18. Daily 7am–10pm.

★**Yalıhan Arı** Devlet Sahil Yolu 443 ☎0452 324 2470, ⓦyalihanariotel.com. Neat, modern and well-priced, this slender seafront tower hotel has sixteen airy rooms with a/c, TV and balconies with terrific views over the boats bobbing in the bay. There's a buffet breakfast, 24hr bakery next door and parking spaces on the main road out front. ₺185

9

Ordu

Lying 61km east of Ünye, **ORDU** occupies the site of the Ionian settlement of Kotyora, though all hints of a grand past have long since disappeared, and today it's a fast-growing modern city of 200,000 residents. The area is a significant hazelnut-growing centre: roughly 75 percent of the world's **hazelnuts** (*findik*) come from the coastal area from Samsun to Georgia, and one-third of that emanates from Ordu's lush green hills. During late July and August you'll see vast mats of them, still in their husks, raked out to dry.

Ordu's pleasant seaside boulevard is lined with parks, the old Greek district with its timber-framed houses lining narrow alleyways has plenty of character, and there are good sweeps of sand both to the east and west of town.

Ordu Boztepe Teleferik Hattı

Lower station at Atatürk Bulvarı • Mon–Thurs 10am–9pm, Fri–Sun 9am–10pm • ₺8 return • ☎ 0452 225 1456

For outstanding panoramic views over Ordu, the hazelnut groves and the Black Sea, head for the new **Ordu Boztepe Teleferik Hattı**, a cable car that takes visitors from the seafront up to the Boztepe hilltop (550m), where there are a couple of cafés and shady picnic spots. Views are superb; on clear days you can admire the surrounding mountains, which are snowcapped in winter.

Paşaoğlu Mansion and Ethnography Museum

Taşocak Cad, 500m uphill from Cumhuriyet Meyd • Tues–Sun 9am–noon & 1.30–5pm • ₺5 • ☎ 0452 223 2596

An excellent example of regional Ottoman architecture, the fine **Paşaoğlu Mansion** (Paşaoğlu Konağı), built by wealthy merchant Pasaoglu Huseyin Efendi in 1896, houses Ordu's small **Ethnography Museum**. The dusty ethnographic exhibits don't amount to much, but the elaborate furnished upstairs rooms show the sophisticated style in which the upper classes lived towards the end of the Ottoman era.

ARRIVAL AND DEPARTURE

ORDU

By plane The Ordu Giresun Airport, 19km east of the city, opened in 2015 and is located on a purpose-built artificial island – the world's only such facility outside of the Far East – just off the coast at Gülyalı. At the time of writing THY (ⓦ turkishairlines.com) operated flights to/from Istanbul and the number of flights and airlines is expected to increase. Havas (☎ 0555 985 1196, ⓦ havas.net) operates *servis* buses to/from the airport to town.

Destinations Istanbul Atatürk (1 daily; 1hr 45min); Istanbul Sabiha Gökçen (2 daily; 1hr 50min).
By bus and dolmuş Regular dolmuşes run along the coastal D010 highway to/from nearby towns. Long-distance buses go from the *otogar*, 5km east of town.
Destinations Giresun (hourly; 1hr); Samsun (14 daily; 2hr 20min); Trabzon (16 daily; 3hr); Ünye (every 30–45min; 1hr 15min);

ACCOMMODATION AND EATING

Evimiz Butik Sıtkı Can Cad 64 ☎ 0452 666 7575, ⓦ evimizbutikhotel.com. This boutique hotel is an architect's modern interpretation, rather than an authentic restoration, of two of Ordu's old Ottoman houses. On the hillside above the main coastal road, the five rooms are super-stylish, with plenty of glass, steel and clean lines. The restaurant has a lovely terrace garden with sea views. ₺280
Sinema Atatürk Bul 13 ☎ 0452 352 5252, ⓦ sinemahotel.com.tr. Right in the heart of the city, this smart newly built hotel has 62 rooms with a/c, TV and

balconies, and a rooftop restaurant with sea and mountain views. Directors' chairs and portraits of movie stars in the lobby pay tribute to the building's former life as a cinema (hence the name). ₺170
Derin Balık Lokantası Yükçülük Sok 3, off Atatürk Bulvarı ☎ 0452 223 4435. Behind the town hall, this is one of Ordu's most popular fish restaurants and a good place to try Black Sea grilled *hamsi* (anchovy) and sea bass. The outside tables are on a cobbled lane, and there's a modern stylish interior, but no alcohol. Mains ₺12–25. Daily 11am–10pm.

Giresun

Founded in the second century BC by the Pontic king Pharnaces, **GİRESUN** derives from the word for "cherry", batches of which have been exported from here since Roman times, though hazelnuts are now the main event in the area. In town, a pleasant seafront square leads to the cobbled hilly main street, Gazi Caddesi, offering a welcome respite from the noise and pollution of the coastal D010 highway.

Giresun Adası

2km offshore from Giresun • Arrange boat trips at Giresun harbour (around ₺70–90)

Giresun Adası is the only major island in the Black Sea. In pre-Christian times it was called Aretias, and was sacred to the Amazons who dedicated a temple to the war god Ares on it. Jason and his Argonauts supposedly stopped here to offer sacrifice, but were attacked by vicious birds.

ARRIVAL AND DEPARTURE   GİRESUN

By plane The new Ordu Giresun Airport (see opposite) is 25km west of Giresun.

By bus and dolmuş The *otogar* is 4km west of the centre, but most buses also drop off and pick up at the bus

company offices on Alpaslan Cad, near the town hall.

Destinations Ordu (every 30–45min; 1hr); Samsun (14 daily; 4hr); Trabzon (hourly; 2hr); Ünye (18 daily; 2hr 30min).

ACCOMMODATION AND EATING

Damcilar Fatih Cad 16 ☎0454 201 2828. Centrally located, 100m back from the seafront, the reasonably spacious, contemporary-styled rooms here have earthy neutral tones, modern compact bathrooms, fridges, a/c and the higher rooms with balconies have sea views. ₺**240**

Kittur Arif Bey Cad 2 ☎0454 212 0245, ⌨otelkittur .com. Just off the main coastal highway, within a bland, ageing exterior lies this well-managed hotel, offering comfortable rooms (some triples; ₺200) with a/c and TV.

There's a large top-floor restaurant as well as a rooftop terrace, perfect for a sunset beer. ₺**160**

Yetimoğulları Köprülü Han Sok, off Gazi Cad ☎0454 212 0839, ⌨yetimogullari.com.tr. The pick of central Giresun's many *pide* and kebab houses, this friendly restaurant with decent service boasts menus – a rarity hereabouts – offering a range of soups, appetizers, pizzas and meats cooked over hot coals, as well as a few salads. Mains ₺8–15. Daily 9am–10pm.

Trabzon

No other Turkish city except Istanbul has exercised such a hold on the Western imagination as **TRABZON** (ancient Trebizond). Travel writers from Marco Polo to Rose Macaulay have been enthralled by the fabulous image of this quasi-mythical metropolis, long synonymous with intrigue, luxury, exotic customs and fairy-tale architecture. Today, the celebrated gilded roofs and cosmopolitan texture of Trebizond may be long gone, but the bustling, modern Turkish provincial capital of over 750,000 people is worth a visit for its decidedly relaxed atmosphere and easy access to several regional sights.

While modern Trabzon sprawls in all directions, its heart remains **Meydan Parkı**; a pleasant plane-tree-shaded square with the obligatory Atatürk statue, always thronging with people and ringed with tea gardens, restaurants and patisseries. It's now closed to traffic on three sides and has been expanded to include the İskender Paşa Camii on the northwest corner. An easy stroll to the west will take you to the two areas most worthy of exploration: the **bazaar area** and the Ortahisar district or **old town**. A poke around their cobbled alleyways will unearth tangible evidence of Trabzon's former splendour.

Brief history

Trabzon was founded during the eighth century BC by colonists from Sinope and Miletus, attracted by the readily defensible high plateau or *trapeza* ("table" in ancient Greek) after which it was first named "Trapezus". Although the city prospered under both the Romans and Byzantines, Trabzon's romantic allure derives almost exclusively from its brief, though resplendent, golden age during the thirteenth and fourteenth centuries, when, after the sacking of Constantinople, it became the capital of the breakaway **Trapezuntine Empire**. Its wealth grew when the main Silk Route was diverted this way because Mongol raiders controlled territory further south.

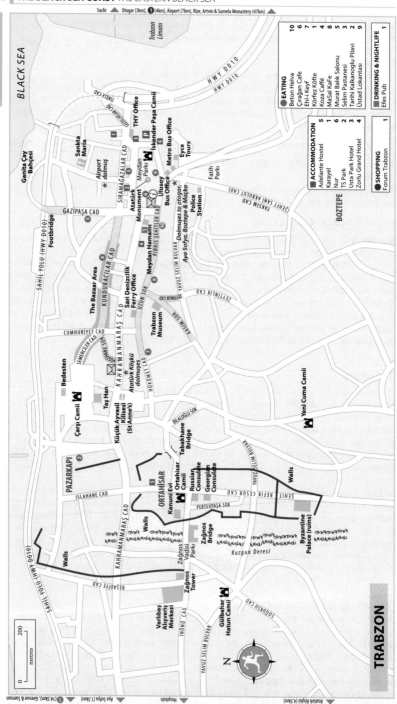

Sochi ▲ Otogar (3km), ⓵ (4km), Airport (7km), Rize, Artvin & Sumela Monastery (47km) ▲

BLACK SEA

Trabzon Limanı

HWY D010

HWY D010

Ganita Çay Bahçesi

Sankta Maria

Airport dolmuş

İSKELE CAD

GÜZELHİSAR CAD

THY Office

İskender Paşa Camii

Metro Bus Office

SIRAMAĞAZALAR CAD

Eyce Tours

GAZİPAŞA CAD

Meydan Parkı

Atatürk Monument

Ulusoy Bus Office

Fatih Parkı

Police Station

TAKSİM CAD

ŞEHİT SANİ AKBULUT CAD

BOZTEPE

SAHİL YOLU (HWY D010)

Footbridge

The Bazaar Area

KUNDURACILAR CAD

Meydan Hamam

KIBRIS ŞEHİTLER CAD

Sarı Denizcilik Ferry Office

UZUN SOK

Dolmuşes to otogar, Aya Sofya, Boztepe & Maçka

YAVUZ SELİM BULVAR

ZEYTİNLİK CAD

CUMHURİYET CAD

KAHRAMANMARAŞ CAD

SEMERCİLER CAD

POSTAHANE SOK

Trabzon Museum

KASIM SOK

Bedesten

Taş Han

Çarşı Camii

Küçük Ayvasıl Kilisesi (St Anne's)

Atatürk Köşkü dolmuşes

HÜKÜMET CAD

Yeni Cuma Camii

BİLALOĞLU SOK

Tabakhane Bridge

PAZARKAPI

ISLAHANE CAD

Ortahisar Camii

Kanuni Evi

Russian Consulate

Georgian Consulate

PERTEVPAŞA SOK

ZİNDAN

ŞEHİT REFİK CESUR CAD

Walls

ORTAHİSAR

Walls

Walls

Zağnos Vadisi Parkı

Zağnos Bridge

Byzantine Palace (ruins)

Kuzgun Deresi

SAHİL YOLU (HWY D010)

REŞADİYE CAD

KAHRAMANMARAŞ CAD

İNÖNÜ CAD

Zağnos Tower

Varlıbaş Alışveriş Merkezi

Gülbahar Hatun Camii

SÖĞÜKSU CAD

YAVUZ SELİM BULVAR

N

TRABZON

200 metres
0

● EATING
Beton Helva	10
Çırağan Cafe	6
Ehl-i Keyf	7
Körfez Köfte	1
Koza Caffè	4
Maşal Kafe	8
Murat Balık Salonu	5
Selim Pastanesi	3
Tarihi Kalkanoğlu Pilavı	2
Üstad Lokantası	9

■ ACCOMMODATION
Adelante Hostel	5
Karayel	1
Nur	6
TS Park	2
Usta Park Hotel	3
Zorlu Grand Hotel	4

■ DRINKING & NIGHTLIFE
Efes Pub	1

■ SHOPPING
Forum Trabzon	1

Someone had to transport all the goods that accumulated at Trebizond's docks, and this turned out to be the **Genoese**, followed soon after by the Venetians as well. Each demanded and won the same maritime trading privileges from the Trapezuntine Empire as they received from the re-established empire at Constantinople. Western ideas and personalities arrived continually with the boats of the Latins, making Trebizond an unexpected island of art and erudition in a sea of Turkish nomadism, and a cultural rival to the Italian Renaissance city-states of the same era.

Unfortunately, the empire's factional politicking was excessive even by the standards of the age. One civil war in 1341 completely destroyed the city and sent the empire into its final decline. It was Mehmet the Conqueror, in a campaign along the Black Sea shore, who finally put paid to the self-styled empire; in 1461 the last emperor, David, true to Trapezuntine form, negotiated a more or less bloodless surrender to the sultan.

In late Ottoman times the population and influence of the city's Christian element enjoyed a resurgence. The presence of a rich merchant class ushered in a spate of sumptuous civic and domestic building. But it was a mere echo of a distant past, soon ended by a decade of world war, the foundation of the Republic, and the steady transference of trade from ship to rails.

Today, Trabzon benefits from the major Black Sea exports of hazelnuts (*fınkık*) and tea through its modern port, and the transhipment of goods by truck to the Caucasian republics and onwards to Russia. The city is also flourishing as a weekend destination for Istanbulites, thanks to its less humid summer weather and low-cost flights from the capital.

The bazaar
Usually entered via the pedestrianized Kunduracılar Cad, northwest of Meydan Parkı

Trabzon's crowded bazaar streets are perfect for aimless wandering, with their interesting mix of rickety wooden shops, air-conditioned Western-style shops, and the odd restored old building. Despite the name, just about everything *except* shoes can be found on "Shoemakers' Street", **Kunduracılar Caddesi**, with a special emphasis first on pharmacies and doctors, then gold jewellery. As you walk from east to west, once you cross Cumhuriyet Caddesi, Kunduracılar veers right to become **Semerciler Caddesi** (Saddlers' Street), which is devoted to a mix of factory-made clothing and bedding.

Sooner or later you'll stumble upon the monumental heart of the bazaar, and the **Çarşı Camii**, Trabzon's largest mosque, which has a handsome exterior and late Ottoman interior. Just behind it is the sixteenth-century **Taş Han**, a rather standard tradesmen's hall that still holds retail outlets and (inside the courtyard) tailors' workshops.

Bedesten
Just north of and below the mosque

The **Bedesten** was built by the Genoese in the fourteenth century, and revamped by the Ottomans. After decades of dereliction, it has been restored as a somewhat touristy crafts bazaar mostly selling the vibrantly coloured, striped *keşans* (shawls) and *peştemals* (loincloths) that were once worn by local women, but these are days are more likely to be incorporated into jaunty headscarves and cushion covers.

Trabzon Museum
Zeytinlik Cad 10, just south of Uzun Sok • Daily April–Oct 9am–6pm, Nov–March 8.15am–5pm • ₺5 • ☎ 0462 326 0748, ⊕ muze.gov.tr

One of Trabzon's finest *belle époque* mansions, the Italian-designed (and originally Greek-owned) Kostaki Theophylaktos Konağı, built in 1900, now houses the **Trabzon Müzesi**. The ground- and first-floor rooms, with their parquet floors, painted ceilings, fancy drapes and plush armchairs, give a wonderful idea of life among the Ottoman bourgeoisie with displays of glitzy furniture, silverware and antiques. Pride of place in the basement, which is devoted to a mildly interesting archeological collection, belongs to a complete but slightly crushed bronze, human-sized statue of Hermes unearthed in 1997.

9

Yeni Cuma Camii

Camii Sok, 300m south of Yavuz Selim Bulvar

The thirteenth-century mosque of **Yeni Cuma Camii** was formerly the church of St Eugenius, patron saint of Trabzon. Mehmet the Conqueror offered up his first Friday prayers here after capturing Trabzon in 1461, and immediately re-consecrated the church and added its minaret. Built of a faded white ashlar stone, it has a graceful cupola and a floor of exquisite mosaic tiling. Its high vantage point offers splendid views over Trabzon's old town.

The old town and Ortahisar

West of the pedestrianized Uzun Sokak, the gorge known as the **Tabakhane Deresi** (Tannery Ravine) is spanned by a namesake bridge offering access to Trabzon's fortified **old town**. The best place to get a sense of the city's history – the heart of the old town – is the **Ortahisar** (Middle Castle) quarter. The birthplace of Suleyman the Magnificent, the neighbourhood is built over two tunnels that date back to Byzantine times, and is dotted with fine examples of Ottoman houses, many of which have been restored. The walls are in variable condition but at their crenellated and vine-shrouded best give some idea of Trabzon's skyline in its heyday.

Ortahisar Camii

Corner of İnönü and Şehit Refik Cesur cads

Also referred to as the Fatih Camii, the golden-domed **Ortahisar Camii** was formerly the church of Panayia Khrysokefalos. As the main cathedral of the Trapezuntine Empire, this was the venue for most royal weddings, funerals and coronations. While a church almost certainly stood on this site from the third century, the present building dates mostly from the thirteenth, with major renovation after a fire during the 1341 civil war. Some fine Byzantine opus sectile stonework (similar to mosaic) remains visible in the apse, but it's the sheer volume of the soaring basilica, with its massive interior columns, that impresses.

Kanuni Evi

Off İnönü Cad · Closed for restoration at the time of writing

Just west of Ortahisar Camii is a shady square with a sprawling tea garden, flanked by **Kanuni Evi**, a fine nineteenth-century house presently being restored into a museum to celebrate Ottoman sultans, particularly Suleyman the Magnificent, otherwise known as Kanunî ("Lawgiver"). Kanunî was born in Ortahisar in 1494, and went on to become sultan of the empire in 1520. Outside the building is a fine statue of his father, Sultan Selim the Grim, on horseback, who served as Trabzon's governor between 1490 and 1512.

Zağnos Bridge

Built by a Greek convert who was one of Mehmet the Conqueror's chief generals, the **Zağnos Bridge** leaves Ortahisar across the Kuzgun ravine, where down below, the municipality has laid out the **Zağnos Vadisi Parkı**, an attractive park studded with picnic spots, teahouses and an amphitheatre.

Zağnos Tower

On the far side of Zağnos Bridge, **Zağnos Tower**, the southernmost dungeon in Ortahisar's outer boundary walls, sports the ornate, late Ottoman Abdullah Paşa fountain at its base. Today, the tower is a **library**, standing in stark contrast to its thoroughly modern neighbour, the Varlıbaş Alışveriş Merkezi, which is a shopping mall.

Gülbahar Hatun Camii

Junction of Şenul Güneş Cad, Soğuksu Cad and Yavuz Selim Bul

The **Gülbahar Hatun Camii**, the most important Ottoman monument in Trabzon, squats across busy İnönü Cadessi and a swathe of parkland from the Zağnos Tower and

Varlıbaş Alışveriş Merkezi. Sultan Selim the Grim built this mosque in 1514 in honour of his mother, once a Byzantine princess. It was originally part of a greater complex that included a *medrese*, soup kitchen and hamam, but only the last of these is easily distinguishable today, located under the largest of the building's five domes. Entered through a portico with marble columns, the prayer hall includes a simple altar and pulpit made from marble, while a minaret outside has an unusual eight-sided base.

Atatürk Köşkü

Soğuksu Cad, 6.5km southwest of Meydan Parkı • Daily 8am–5pm • ₺3 • ☎ 0462 231 0028 • Catch a dolmuş marked "Köşk" from outside the PTT on Kahramanmaraş Cad

Set in immaculate gardens in the cooler, higher reaches above Trabzon, the **Atatürk Köşkü**, or Atatürk Mansion, began life in 1903 as the property of the Greek banker Karayannidhis, who was obliged to abandon it two decades later. Atatürk stayed here on the first of three occasions in 1924, and the city formally presented it to him a year before his death. As an example of patrician Black Sea architecture, the whitewashed, wooden mansion is more compelling than the contents – which include a bevy of photos of Atatürk, plus a map bearing his strategic scribbles during the Kurdish Dersim revolt of 1937. A tea garden within the grounds offers splendid views.

Aya Sofya

D010 coastal highway, 3km west of the centre • Catch a dolmuş marked "Aya Sofya" from under the flyover on the northwest corner of Meydan Parkı

The former monastery church and now functioning mosque of **Aya Sofya** (Haghia Sophia; Church of Divine Wisdom) ranks among Turkey's most romantic clusters of Byzantine remains and one of Trabzon's principal sights. It seems certain that there was a pagan temple here, and then an early Byzantine chapel, long before Manuel I Komnenos commissioned the present structure between 1238 and 1263.

The building is laid out along a greatly modified cross-in-square scheme, with a dome supported by four columns and three apses at the east end of the triple nave. The ground plan and overall conception were revolutionary at the time, successfully assimilating most of the architectural trends, Christian and Muslim, prevalent in contemporary Anatolia.

Converted to a mosque after 1461, Aya Sofya subsequently endured leaner and more ignominious times as an ammunition store and then as a hospital during the Russian occupation in World War I, before it was restored in 1964 to a church again and as the **Trabzon Aya Sofya Museum**. However, in 2013 it was transformed once again back into a **mosque**, after the Presidency of Religious Affairs (Diyanet İşleri Başkanlığı) successfully filed a lawsuit against the Ministry of Culture and Tourism, claiming that the Ministry had been illegally occupying the church.

Although non-Muslims are allowed to enter the mosque, a tent-like veil now covers the fantastic apse frescoes, and its floor of inlaid pictorial coloured stone has been carpeted. The west entrance, originally the main entrance to the church via the narthex, has been locked, and the north entrance is now used for access to the mosque, as it's opposite the *mihrab* (prayer niche) which orients worshippers south toward Mecca.

Despite the restricted access, this impressive building is still worth a visit, if you concentrate instead on admiring the finely sculpted, albeit weatherworn, frieze illustrating Adam and Eve in the Garden of Eden on the **south portal**; the frescoes in the **narthex** (see p.524), which is outside the worship area; the ensemble of sunken **masonry** in the grounds that was once the baptismal font; the tall square **belfry**, which was a 1443 afterthought to the building; and the fine Black Sea **views** from the garden.

The frescoes

In their fluidity, warmth and expressiveness, Aya Sofya's original **frescoes** represented a drastic break with the rigidity of earlier painting, and compare well with the best work

9

of their century. The most impressive frescoes, now covered, are in the central **apse** where a serene *Ascension* hovers over *The Virgin Enthroned* between the two Archangels, and there's a dramatic scene of *The Miraculous Draught of Fishes*. The **north portico**, now out of bounds for non-worshipers, is taken up mostly by Old Testament scenes, including *The Sufferings of Job* and *Jacob's Dream*. The ceiling of the **narthex** – still accessible to visitors – is almost wholly devoted to scenes from the life of Christ. These include miraculous episodes such as *The Wedding at Cana*, a decidedly adolescent *Child Jesus Teaching in the Temple, Healing the Blind Man at Siloam* and *Healing the Canaanite's Daughter* (complete with vomited demon), *Feeding the Five Thousand* and *Calming the Storm on the Lake of Galilee*.

The shoreline

Trabzon's **shoreline** is accessible down the hill from Meydan Parkı, via the northern end of Gazipaşa Caddesi, which crosses the busy the D010 double-lane coastal highway. On the other side is the **Ganita Çay Bahçesi**, a hilltop tea garden and small park on the west flank of the old Genoese castle ruins. With the rest of the city isolated up on its elevated plateau, this seems to be Trabzon's sole acknowledgement of its seafront location.

Boztepe

1.5km south of Meydan Parkı, off Taksim Cad · Catch a dolmuş marked "Boztepe" from the flyover dolmuş stop

Boztepe, the hill that dominates Trabzon to the southeast, has always been held in religious esteem. In ancient times, it was holy to the amalgamated cults of the Persian sun god Mithra and the Hellenic deity Apollo – ironic when you consider how little unfiltered sun this coast receives. That reverence persisted into the Christian era, when the hill was studded with churches and monasteries. Near the park's summit are an appealing **picnic park**, a **tea garden** and restaurant that share the view over the city with a military base, and the locked **mosque and tomb of Ahi Evren Dede**, a target of pilgrimage for Trabzon's faithful.

ARRIVAL AND DEPARTURE   TRABZON

BY PLANE

Airport Trabzon airport (☎0462 328 0940, ⊛trabzon .dhmi.gov.tr) is 7km east of the centre and served by taxis (₺30) and frequent dolmuşes. In town, airport dolmuşes arrive/depart one block north of Meydan Parkı, just off Sıramağazalar Cad. A Havas shuttle bus (☎0462 325 9575, ⊛havas.net) meets all incoming flights, departing 25min after each flight's arrival, and runs to several city stops along Yavuz Selim Bulvarı.

Tickets Borajet (☎0850 222 2672, ⊛borajet.com.tr), Onur Air (☎0462 3256 292, ⊛onurair.com), Pegasus (☎0888 228 1212, ⊛flypgs.com) and THY (☎0462 325 6738, ⊛turkishairlines.com) have desks at the airport. THY also has a town office in front of the Usta Park Hotel (İskenderpaşa Mah 6–8; ☎0462 325 7536).

Destinations Adana (1 daily; 1hr 30min); Ankara (5 daily; 1hr 20min); Istanbul Atatürk (up to 12 daily; 1hr 50min); Istanbul Sabiha Gökçen (up to 10 daily; 1hr 50min); İzmir (1 daily; 2hr 10min).

BY BUS

Bus terminal Trabzon's *otogar*, 3km east of the centre, is served by dolmuşes to the stop under the flyover just

south of the Meydan Parkı (marked "Meydanı"). Both Metro (☎0462 444 3455, ⊛metroturizm.com.tr) and Ulusoy (☎0462 325 9368, ⊛ulusoy.com.tr) have offices next to each other on İskenderpaşa Cad on the southeast side of Meydan Parkı (opposite the flyover dolmuş stop) where you can book tickets and use the free *servis* buses to/from the *otogar*.

Destinations Ankara (18 daily; 11hr 30min); Batumi, Georgia (5 daily; 3hr 30min); Bayburt (7 daily; 4hr 30min); Erzurum (10 daily; 5hr); Giresun (hourly; 2hr); Hopa (hourly; 2hr 30min); Istanbul (20 daily; 16hr); İzmir (5 daily; 21hr); Of (hourly; 45min); Rize (every 30min; 1hr); Samsun (hourly; 6hr 30min).

BY CAR

Parking Parking is a trial anywhere in congested Trabzon – the closest car park to Meydan Parkı is behind the İskender Paşa Camii.

Car rental There are at least two dozen local companies with offices in and around Meydan Parkı, and rental can be as cheap as ₺100 per day; book in advance in summer. There are also several agencies at the airport, including Avis (☎0462 325 5582, ⊛avis.com.tr); Cande Rent A Car

FROM TOP RIZE TEA FIELDS (P.535); COASTAL DRIVE SİNOP (PP.511–516) >

9

(☎0462 328 0204, ⊕canderentacar.com); Europcar (☎0462 325 3424, ⊕europcar.com.tr); and Sixt (☎0530 178 8456, ⊕sixt.com.tr).

BY FERRY

Ferry services A car-and-passenger ferry between Trabzon and Sochi, Russia, is operated by Sari Denizcilik (Sultan Sok 10, off Uzun Sok; ☎0462 326 4484, ⊕saridenizcilik.com). In theory the ship makes two round trips per week (departing Trabzon Fri and sometimes Tues), departing from each at 7pm and taking 12hr, but schedules are erratic, so check with the office (one-way: US$120 reclining seat, US$150 basic sleeper compartment, from US$500 for a car depending on size). The Trabzon port is 1km east of Meydan Parkı; turn off the D010 at the base of the hill. At present, all non-Turkish foreign travellers need a visa for Russia (see opposite).

INFORMATION AND TOURS

Tourist office On the south side of Meydan Parkı (July–Sept daily 9am–5pm, Oct–June Mon–Fri only; ☎0462 326 4760). The excellent fold-up map of Trabzon, which you can pick up at the tourist office, is just as helpful as the (mostly) English-speaking staff.

Tours Bus companies Metro (☎0462 444 3455, ⊕metroturizm.com.tr) and Ulusoy (☎0462 325 9368, ⊕ulusoy.com.tr), as well as tour operator Eyce Tours (☎0462 326 6337, ⊕eycetours.com), have offices on İskenderpaşa Cad on the southeast side of Meydan Parkı. Each organizes day-trips using the same local drivers. They run day-trips to several places including Sumela Monastery (see p.528), Uzungöl (10am–5pm; ₺40), Rize and Ayder (9am–7pm; ₺45), and to Batumi in Georgia (Sat and Sun 7am–8pm; ₺80).

ACCOMMODATION

Meydan Parkı, at the heart of Trabzon, is home to many hotels, cafés and restaurants. If you have transport, you might consider more peaceful stopovers on the way to Sumela or at Uzungöl, or one of the chain hotels on the D010, such as the *Hilton* to the west or the *Novotel* to the east. Book ahead in midsummer, when Trabzon swarms with weekenders and locals returned from northern Europe.

Adelante Hostel Çiftehamam Sok 1, Ortahisar ☎0462 544 4344, ⊕trabzonhostel.com. This new and super-friendly hostel, the only backpackers' in Trabzon, is just north of the Ortahisar Camii and very handy for the Russian and Georgian consulates. It offers three bunk-bed rooms (each sleeping eight), spotless shared bathrooms and a kitchen. A small breakfast is included and taken on the lovely roof terrace. Dorm **₺70**

Karayel Iskenderpasa Mah 8 ☎0462 321 2528, ⊕karayelotel.com. Friendly and well-priced mid-range hotel, down a surprisingly quiet side street but still very close to the action. The 29 a/c rooms – some with balconies – have TV, modern decor and wood-panelled floors, plus there's a good buffet breakfast and on-site parking. **₺207**

Nur Cami Sok 15 ☎0462 323 0445. The popular *Nur* offers small but well-equipped rooms with a/c, TV and fridge, and a couple are economical quads (₺440); request one on the upper floors to evade the street noise. The affable English-speaking management are a good source of information, and breakfast is served on the roof terrace. **₺140**

★**TS Park** Meydan Cad 5 ☎0462 323 3141, ⊕facebook.com/tsparkotel. Located in a renovated eighteenth-century building right on Meydan Parkı, some of the walls of the luxurious and spacious a/c rooms here have been stripped back to reveal the original stonework. Breakfast is served in a small, wood-panelled restaurant with an open balcony, and nearby parking can be arranged. Triples (₺400) and four-bed family rooms (₺500) available. **₺300**

Usta Park Hotel İskenderpaşa Mah 6–8 ☎0462 326 5700, ⊕ustaparkhotel.com. Large, plush hotel with impressive plasma-screened lobby and workmanlike, rather than friendly, staff. The comfortable rooms are pricey, but discounts are easily negotiable out of peak season. There's an impressive buffet breakfast, basement parking, and the top-floor *Sunset Restaurant* has sea views. **₺290**

Zorlu Grand Hotel Maraş Cad 9 ☎0462 326 8400, ⊕www.zorlugrand.com. Suitably plush rooms, with marble-clad bathrooms, but you're really paying for the facilities, like an opulent atrium, two restaurants, an "English pub", a nightclub, gym, very small indoor pool and valet parking. Rack rates are massively overpriced, but advance booking or/and bargaining may produce discounts. **₺625**

EATING

Central Trabzon holds plenty of good places to eat, though alcohol in this conservative town is very hard to come by, as is – surprisingly for a port – fish. However, dessert-lovers will be in heaven, and Trabzon is well-known for its **confectioners**.

RESTAURANTS

★**Körfez Köfte** Sahil Yolu Cad, Liman Mevki, Akçaabat ☎0462 228 0150, ⊕korfezkofte.com.tr. This local legend, 16km west of Meydan Parkı, serves up authentic "Akçaabat *köfte*" in classy, easy-to-find surroundings overlooking the sea. They serve *köfte* by the kilo, accompanied by crispy salads and fresh bread, though lots of other meat and fish dishes are available too. There are plenty of tables and a small children's playground, and the service, location and cuisine are worth the effort to get here. Regular dolmuşes run along the D010 between Trabzon and Akçaabat. Mains ₺8–28. Daily 11.30am–10pm.

Murat Balık Salonu Meydan Parkı ☎ 0462 322 3100. On the square's northern edge, this tiny hole-in-the-wall fish restaurant displays the day's catch in a glass cabinet. The bright green interior houses a few tables, often busy with locals enjoying an inexpensive and quickly served meal. Mains ₺6–15. Daily 11am–9pm.

Tarihi Kalkanoglu Pilavi Tophane Hamam Sok 2, Pazarkapı ☎ 0462 321 3086. Always full of locals and worth seeking out in the narrow lanes of the western bazaar district, this historic simple wooden lunchtime restaurant is famous for its delicious plates of Central Asia-style *pilav* rice served with either bean or meat sauce and pickles (₺12). It's hard to imagine eating half a kilo of rice, but it's delightful, especially washed down with *ayran*. Daily 11am–5.30pm.

Üstad Lokantası Meydan Parkı ☎ 0462 321 5406. One of the number of lively joints that line the eastern edge of the square with outside tables, always popular with locals looking for a quick meal of typical *lokanta* fare – meatballs, kebab and bean stew – from ₺6 per dish. Daily 10am–10pm.

CAFÉS AND CONFECTIONERS

Beton Helva Uzun Sok 21 ☎ 0462 321 2550, ⊛ betonhelva.com.tr. A Trabzon institution, established in 1953, ever popular despite the somewhat off-putting name, meaning "Concrete *Helva*". Huge blocks of *helva* (₺15–20/kg) are on display, and also on offer is tasty *dondurma* and *sıra* (half-fermented grape must), in wonderfully retro surroundings. Daily 9am–9pm.

Çırağan Café Meydan Parkı ☎ 0462 323 2424. Dominating the square with tables scattered beneath the trees around the shiny bronze Atatürk statue, this is a perfect place to people-watch with a cappucino, ice cream or *sütlaç*. Coffee ₺8. Daily 7am–11pm.

Ehl-i Keyf Cemul Sok 2, off Uzun Sok ☎ 0462 321 3044. Popular with Trabzon's young things, this classy café's welcoming interior includes comfortable couches and antique- and art-adorned walls. Breakfasts and light meals are served, nargiles are available, and live acoustic music is played most evenings. Coffee ₺6, mains ₺6–12. Daily 9am–1am.

Koza Caffé Kunduracılar Cad, Sanat Sok 1 ☎ 0462 321 0225. A first-floor café with a small balcony, serving a surprising array of coffees and teas (₺6) as well as flavoursome sandwiches and pizza (₺7). Despite the ersatz castle interior, it's a warm and welcoming place to while away a few hours. Daily 11am–11pm.

★ **MaSal KaFe** Uzun Sok 89 ☎ 0462 322 3857. An artsy first-floor hangout serving Trabzon's best coffee (₺7) and comfort food, such as burgers and fries (₺8–15), in comfortable surroundings, with colourful feature walls, high-backed leather-studded chairs and low-lying loungers. There's also a small balcony overlooking busy pedestrianized Uzun Sok below. Daily 10am–11pm.

Selim Pastanesi Gazipaşa Cad 11/A ☎ 0462 326 2420. This modern and airy *pastanesi* sports leather sofas and is a pleasant place to stop for *dondurma*, milk-based sweets, pastries and *boza* (a millet-based drink). The menu also offers a few heartier options, such as grilled chicken. Desserts ₺3–7, mains ₺8–15. Daily 8am–11pm.

DRINKING AND NIGHTLIFE

Trabzon's very few bars are significantly male-dominated and football-related – women may feel more comfortable going to a hotel bar for a drink; try the English Pub at the *Zorlu Grand Hotel* (see opposite).

Efes Pub Maraş Cad 5 ☎ 0462 326 6083. A surprisingly accurate, not to mention pleasant, rendition of an English pub on a busy side street off Meydan Parkı. Great for enjoying both a draught beer and with a good view of the streets below from the upstairs shaded balcony. Draught beer ₺9. Daily noon–midnight.

SHOPPING

Forum Trabzon Off the D010, 4km east of Meydan Parkı towards the airport ☎ 0462 377 0200, ⊛ forumtrabzon.com. Trabzon is home to the largest modern shopping mall on the Black Sea coast. The Forum Trabzon has 160 quality shops, a Migros hypermarket, eight-screen cinema, food court, cafés and restaurants. Dolmuşes marked "Migros" go from under the flyover on the edge of Meydan Parkı. Daily 10am–10pm.

DIRECTORY

Consulates The consulates for Georgia (Pertevpaşa Sok 10; ☎ 0462 326 2226 ⊛ trabzon.mfa.gov.ge) and Russia (Şehit Refik Cesur Cad 6; ☎ 0462 326 2600, ⊛ www.turkey .mid.ru) back onto each other near the Ortahisar Camii. Most nationalities do not need a visa for Georgia (see box, pp.536–537), but all non-Turkish travellers need one for Russia. Note, however, that you should apply for a Russian visa from your country of citizenship before you leave home. Despite this, the Trabzon consulate does issue visas to EU citizens, but no one else unless they have Turkish residency. At the time of writing, visas cost US$60 (3-day wait) or US$75 (next working day); you need one blank page in your passport, proof of medical insurance and an invitation or accommodation reservation.

9

Hamam The most central and friendliest is Meydan Hamami, just west of Meydan Parkı; the women's entrance is in an alleyway off Kahramanmaraş Cad (daily 8am–8pm; ₺23, exfoliating mitt (*kese*) ₺7, massage ₺8; ☎ 0462 323 0362, ⓦ meydanhamami.com).

Hospitals The best private hospital is Medical Park Karadeniz (Reşadiye Cad; ☎ 0462 229 7070, ⓦ www .medicalpark.com.tr/karadeniz), which is out near the Aya Sofya. The biggest local hospital is Tıp Fakültesi Hastanesi

(☎ 0462 325 3011), opposite the airport on the D010 – buses and dolmuşes marked "KTÜ" run there from the centre.

Police The main police station is on Taksim Cad, under the flyover by Meydan Parkı (☎ 0462 321 2998).

Post office PTT is at Posthane Sok, corner of Kahramanmaraş Cad (daily 8am–7pm); there's also a booth at the southwest corner of Meydan Parkı next to the tourist office (daily 8am–7pm).

Sumela Monastery

Closed for restorations till Sept 2016 (see box below), but normally daily 9am–6pm, Nov–March till 4pm • ₺15 • ☎ 0462 326 0748, ⓦ muze.gov.tr

At the start of the Byzantine era, a large number of monasteries sprang up in the mountains behind Trabzon. The most important and prestigious – and today the best preserved and impressive – was **Sumela Monastery** (Sümela Manastiri), which clings to the cliff face of Karadağ Mountain nearly a thousand feet above the Altındere valley, 47km south of Trabzon, in precisely the sort of setting that has always appealed to Greek Orthodox monasticism. Despite the usual crowds, often rainy or misty weather, and the rather battered condition of its frescoes, Sumela justifiably rates as one of the mandatory excursions along the Black Sea coast, and it attracts more than one million visitors per year.

The monastery is linked to the valley floor by a 3km scenic, winding paved road through the **Altındere Vadisi Milli Parkı** (Altındere Valley National Park). However you arrive (see opposite), the final part of this drive provides a stunning approach to the monastery; as you climb, the habitual cloud ceiling drifts down from the dense fir forest to greet you. In exceptional circumstances, you may catch an advance glimpse of the monastery's faded, whitewashed flank soaring above the trees at the top of the valley, at an altitude of 1200m.

Aim to spend at least three hours at the site, allowing for a good look around and a spot of lunch by the **rapids** which flow through the valley below.

Brief history

The name "Sumela" is a Pontic Greek shortening and corruption of *Panayia tou Melas* or "Virgin of the Black (Rock)". She has been venerated on this site since at least 385 AD, when the Athenian monk Barnabas, acting on a revelation from the Mother of God, discovered an **icon** here said to have been painted by St Luke. He and his nephew Sophronios found the holy relic on a site that matched the one in his vision – a cave on a narrow ledge, part way up the all-but-sheer palisade – and installed it in a shrine inside.

A **monastery** supposedly grew around the image as early as the sixth century, but most of what's visible today dates from the thirteenth and fourteenth centuries. Over the years the

---

SUMELA: CLOSED FOR RESTORATION

Turkey's Ministry of Culture and Tourism closed **Sumela Monastery** in September 2015, purportedly for a year, to undertake essential **renovations**. Sumela underwent restoration from 1991 till 2007, and while the surviving frescoes have been consolidated and cleaned, it has since transpired that some of this previous work actually damaged the building structure. Incorrect stones were used in the walls, and modern concrete was poured onto the monastery's floors, which were originally bare, levelled rock. The new US$1.3 million project aims to rectify these issues and mitigate the risk of rock (and ice) fall from Karadağ Mountain above the monastery. The information here (see above & opposite) about visiting the monastery was correct just before its closure; in theory it should reopen in **September 2016**, but check first at ⓦ kultur.gov.tr or ⓦ muze.gov.tr.

icon was held responsible for countless **miracles**, and the institution that housed it shared its reputation, prompting even Turkish sultans to make pilgrimages and leave offerings.

Sumela was hastily evacuated in 1923, along with all other Greek Orthodox foundations in the Pontus, when the new Turkish Republic founded by Atatürk prompted the population exchange between Greece and Turkey (see p.684). Six years later, the monastery was gutted by fire, possibly started by careless squatters. In 1931, one of the monks returned secretly and exhumed various treasures, including the revered icon of the Virgin, now housed in the new monastery of Sumela in northern Greece. From 1991 to 2007, **restoration** projects were carried out on the monastery. However, a scientific committee concluded that some of the restoration used faulty methods which harmed the original structure (see box opposite), leading to the site's closure at the time of writing.

The site

The **building** itself occupies a far smaller patch of level ground than its five-storey facade would suggest. A climb up the original entry **stairs** – lacking hand rails and slightly hazardous after rain – followed by an equivalent drop on the far side of the gate, deposits you in the central courtyard, with the monks' cells and guest hostel on your right overlooking the brink, and the chapel and cave sanctuary to the left.

The main grotto-shrine is closed off on the courtyard side by a wall, from which protrudes the apse of a smaller chapel. A myriad of **frescoes** in varying styles covers every surface, the earliest and best dating from the fourteenth or fifteenth centuries, with progressively less worthwhile additions and retouchings done in 1710, 1740 and 1860. Although the most famous frescoes have been cleaned up considerably in recent restorations, the appalling degree of vandalism is still highly evident: sophisticated art thieves were caught levering away large slabs of the frescoes in 1983, and any pictures within arm's reach have been obliterated by graffiti.

Fortunately, the highest cave paintings are in good condition – **ceilings** being harder to vandalize – though the irregular surface makes for some odd departures from Orthodox iconographic conventions. The Pantocrator, the Mother of God and various apostles seem to float overhead in space; on the south (left) wall is an archangel and various scenes from the Virgin's life (culminating in *The Virgin Enthroned*), while *Jonah in the Whale* can be seen at the top right.

Outside on the **divider wall**, most of the scenes from the life of Christ are hopelessly scarred. Among the more distinct is a fine *Transfiguration*, about 3m up on the right; just above sits *Christ in Glory*, with two versions of the *Ascension* nearby. At the top left is *Christ Redeeming Adam and Eve*. On the apse of the tiny chapel, the *Raising of Lazarus* is the most intact image. Next to it is the *Entry into Jerusalem*, with the *Deposition from the Cross* just right of this. On the natural rock face north of all this appears the *Communion of Saints in Paradise*.

When craning your neck to ogle the surviving art gets too tiring, there is (mist permitting) always the spectacular **view** over the valley – and the process of imagining what monastic life, or a stay in the wayfarers' quarters, must have been like here in Sumela's prime.

ARRIVAL AND DEPARTURE   SUMELA MONASTERY

The main, **top car park** is below the monastery, 43km from the coastal junction of highways D010 and E97, which is 3.5km east of central Trabzon. The car park has souvenir shops, restaurants and a picnic area, all scattered around the teeming rapids that mark the valley floor. A 3km tarmacked winding road continues to the **bottom car park**, with lovely vistas; however, it gets busy with vehicles, especially as they pull over at the viewpoints. Once at the top car park, it's a 300m (mostly uphill) walk to the ticket kiosk, situated at the foot of the stairs up to the monastery gate.

On a tour Daily minibuses leave at 10am from outside the offices of Metro, Ulusoy and Eyce Tours (see p.524) in Trabzon, from where it's about 1hr 15min to the top car park. The buses get back to Trabzon at around 2pm, allowing for an hour at the restaurants at the bottom car park on the way out (₺30, not including Sumela entry fee).

By dolmuş Dolmuşes run from under the Trabzon flyover (opposite the bus offices) to Maçka, 29km from Trabzon and 16km from Sumela, from where you'll need to change to Sumela (no more than ₺5 per dolmuş). Note, however, that dolmuşes are only permitted to go as far as the bottom car park, from where you can either walk up via the steep woodland trail (see below) or the 3km road.

By car Driving from Trabzon takes an hour. Turn off the E97 at Maçka, 29km southwest of Trabzon, and follow the Altındere valley upstream for 16 km. About 2km before you reach the bottom car park, a tollbooth signifies the start of the national park (₺6 per car).

By taxi Taxis are permitted to drive all the way to the top car park. A taxi from Trabzon is around ₺160 return for four people (1hr each way), and you will also need to negotiate an additional waiting time fee. A return taxi from Maçka (20min each way), with waiting time, should cost around ₺80.

On foot You can walk from the bottom car park to the top one via a steep and often slippery woodland trail, which rises 300m and takes around 45min.

ACCOMMODATION AND EATING

Most visitors come from Trabzon on a day-trip, but there is the option of staying overnight in **Maçka**, 16km away, which has a few decent hotels and restaurants. In addition, the road from Maçka up to Sumela is littered with trout farms and campsite-cum-restaurants, including *Camping Sumelas*, *Sumela Camping* and *Sümela-s Camping*.

Büyük Sümela Atatürk Cad 8, Maçka ☎0462 512 3540, ⊛sumelaotel.com. Maçka's main hotel has good standards and facilities, with over a hundred spacious rooms, an indoor swimming pool and rooftop restaurant, though the faux-antique decor throughout borders on garish. You can hire bikes here to ride to Sumela or explore the countryside. Service in their other licensed restaurant over the bridge can be abrupt, but the fish, *meze* and meat dishes (₺9–23) are reasonable and tasty, perhaps surprisingly so, given how many tour groups pass through. **₺220**

Inland: the Eastern Kaçkar foothills

While Sumela is a hard act to follow, several other enticing destinations lie scattered in the **foothills** of the **Kaçkar Mountains** (Kaçkar Dağları) which stretch inland between Trabzon and Rize. The valleys that lead to and past them also make useful alternative routes toward Erzurum, avoiding some or all of the often congested E97 highway. The mountains are part of the Pontic range, also known in Turkish as the Kuzey Anadolu Dağları (North Anatolian Mountains); the highest peaks are covered in the Northeastern Anatolia chapter (see p.554).

The coastal starting point for excursions up the valley of the Solaklı Çayı is the unprepossessing **OF** (pronounced "oaf", the ancient Ophis). Both Of and **Çaykara**, 27km south, the unexciting main town of the lower valley, are renowned for their devoutness, with the highest ratio of *kuran kursu*s (Koran schools for children) per capita in the country.

Uzungöl

45km south of Of • Frequent dolmuşes make the trip south from Of on the D915 road (1hr 30min); alternatively, Trabzon bus companies Metro and Ulusoy, as well as Eyce Tours (see p.528) organize daily minibus transport from Trabzon (departing 10am, returning 5pm; ₺40)

The trip to **Uzungöl** (Long Lake) is the second most popular excursion out of Trabzon after Sumela. The touristy but incredibly scenic lake is surrounded by lush green mountain scenery – awash with wildflowers in spring and snow-covered in winter – best seen by renting a mountain bike from one of the teashops. Were it not for the mosques, you could be in Switzerland. The main village, dotted with hotels and a souvenir-shop bazaar, is at the lake's southern end.

Treks

Uzungöl makes an ideal base for rambles southeast up to the nearby peaks of **Ziyaret** (3111m) and **Halizden** (3376m), with a chain of glacier lakes at the base of the latter. It's a very long day's hike there and back – though you can go part way by car to save time – so take a tent and food for two days if at all possible.

There are at least a couple of dozen hotels, all similar in both style – easy-on-the-eye wooden exteriors – and value, as well as a handful of *pansiyons*. In line with its mushrooming popularity with Arabic-speaking tourists, most don't serve alcohol. Summer weekends and school holidays get very busy, so book ahead.

Ensar Motel Fatih Cad 18 ☎0462 656 6321, ⓦensarotel.com. One of the more upmarket hotels, with a welcoming feel, friendly management and good traditional cuisine. Choose from wooden bungalows (sleeping 4–6; ₺255) with balconies, separate bathroom and living room, or en-suite doubles with (you guessed it) wooden interiors. ₺220

İnan Kardeşler Tesisleri Uzungöl Golbasi Cad ☎0462 656 6260, ⓦinankardeslerotel.com. The oldest hotel in town but refurbished in a modern style, and a pretty combination of trout farm, restaurant and resort, offering spacious all-wood rooms with balconies or chalet-style bungalows (₺305). The à la carte restaurant offers a good selection of traditional dishes including *muhlama* (cheese fondue) and *lahana sarması* (meat-stuffed cabbage leaves) from ₺12 and overlooks a gurgling stream. ₺210

The İkizdere valley

About 60km east of Uzungöl as the crow flies • Driving from Uzungöl, head north on the D915 up to Of, turn right onto the D010 heading east for 14km, then take the right-hand turn (southbound) onto the D925 (well-signposted to Erzurum); a varying number of daily minibuses connect İkizdere with both Of (1hr) and Rize (1hr 15min) – once the tunnel is open, more direct buses from the eastern Black Sea towns are expected to use the D925 to Erzurum

The **İkizdere valley** follows the often-raging waters of the İkizdere River and holds no specific attractions, but the scenery along the way is memorable, and it serves as an alternative route to Erzurum (see p.543). Beyond **İKİZDERE**, the main town in the valley, the D925 soon finds itself between jagged peaks and high sheep pastures at the 2640m **Ovitdağı Pass**. In winter, the pass is usually blocked by heavy snow and closed off, though the new Ovit Dağı Tüneli (Mount Ovit Tunnel) is due to open soon. With its length of 14.7km, it will be Turkey's longest tunnel, and the sixth-longest road tunnel in the world.

On the way up the valley, you'll pass various grill and trout restaurants overlooking the river.

Ridos Termal Otel Beside the river, 800m above town ☎0464 416 2150, ⓦridosotel.com.tr. In a lovely forested spot in the valley, by a natural thermal spring, this large spa hotel offers well-appointed rooms in either the main block or separate villas with fantastic views from the balconies. There are indoor and outdoor thermal pools and a spa centre, plus you can arrange hiking, fishing and bike trips. An excellent base to explore the area. ₺390

The Hemşin valleys

The most scenic and interesting of the foothill regions east of Trabzon are the valleys of the **Fırtına Çayı** and its tributaries, which tumble off the steepest slopes of the Kaçkar Dağları. Between the sea and these higher peaks lie a few hundred square kilometres of rugged, isolated territory known simply as **Hemşin**. This is Turkey's dampest and mistiest region – 500cm of rain falls annually in some parts – resulting in gorgeous, lush forest vegetation, with moss-fringed firs and alders, and creeping vines clinging to the slopes.

Çamlıhemşin

ÇAMLIHEMŞİN, 28km upstream from the mouth of the Fırtına Çayı at coastal Ardeşen, may be too low at 300m to give a real feel for the Hemşin country, but still offers a hint of what's to come. The last proper town before the mountains, it's utilitarian and busy. A constant chaos of minibuses and shoppers clogs its single high street.

To either side of Çamlıhemşin, along both the main stream and the tributary flowing down from Ayder, you begin to see some of the two dozen or so graceful humpbacked **bridges** that are a regional speciality.

9

THE HEMŞINLIS AND YAYLAS

With their fair skin and strong features, the people of the Hemşin valleys, the **Hemşinlis**, tend to look more Caucasian than Turkish. According to competing theories, these outgoing, gregarious people are either ethnic Armenians who arrived here at or before the time of the Georgian kingdoms, or natives descended from the Heptacomete tribesmen of old, who, through contact with "true" Armenians, adopted their dialect and were nominally Christian or pagan until the early nineteenth century. Although most Hemşinlis are now Muslim, they wear their religion lightly: you're unlikely to hear a call to prayer, and the men are prodigious drinkers.

This is a fairly low-income district; most people live from forestry, beekeeping or herding animals. Successive generations have migrated to the cities where their uncanny and renowned brilliance in pastry- and pudding-making has been gratefully received: the top **sweet shops** (*pastanes*) of major Turkish cities are usually owned and/or staffed by natives of these valleys.

To fully understand the Hemşin traditional way of life, you need to visit at least one **yayla**, or summer pastoral hamlet. *Yaylas* are found in highlands throughout Turkey, but in the Kaçkar region – and especially Hemşin – they're at their best. Tightly bunched groups of dwellings, usually stone-built to waist height, and chalet-style in timber thereafter, albeit with metal roofs, they begin just at the tree line and recur at intervals up to 2700m. They're inhabited only between late May and early September, when the snow recedes. Traditional **activities** include making yoghurt, butter and cheese, and (increasingly) catering to trekkers' needs.

The Fırtına valley

As you head up to **Şenyuva**, 7km south of Çamlıhemşin along the main branch of the Fırtına Çayı, the road steadily worsens while the scenery just as relentlessly grows more spectacular. Below, the water roils in chasms and whirlpools that are irresistible to the lunatic fringe of the **rafting** fraternity – as well as the central government which, in the face of local opposition, is currently diverting the river's flow into assorted hydroelectric projects. (The massive Yusufeli Dam project on the Çoruh River deeper in the Kaçkar Dağları will affect the flow of Fırtına; see box, p.550).

Zilkale

The single-towered castle of **Zilkale**, improbably sited by either the Byzantines or the Genoese to control a decidedly minor trade route, appears at a bend in the track 5km beyond Şenyuva. This tree-tufted ruin, more often than not garnished with wisps of mist, now dominates one of the most evocative settings in the Kaçkar.

Çat and around

ÇAT, 16km worth of violent abuse to your vehicle's suspension beyond Zilkale, is a classic base for rambles in the western Kaçkar. At an elevation of 1250m, the village itself is made up of just a few scattered buildings and an exquisite bridge where the upper reaches of the Fırtına divide. The road that runs parallel to the main fork of the river heads 30km due south to Ortayayla or Başhemşin. On the way is Zilkale's sister fort of **Varoş** (Kale-i-Bala) at Kaleköy, where yet another side road winds up to an alternative trailhead for the western Kaçkar mountains at Kale Yayla.

Elevit

The village of **ELEVIT** (1800m), 5km east of Çat along a perennially poor road, makes a good trek from Çat, and has good hiking opportunities in the surrounding area (see box opposite). It's also the end point for ordinary cars; only daily minibuses and 4WD vehicles can continue east to Karunç, Tirovit and Palovit.

Ayder

The tollbooth for the Kaçkar Dağları Milli Parkı (Kaçkar Mountains National Park) is just under 5km before Ayder, if you're coming from Çamlıhemşin • ₺10 per car

The busiest road above Çamlıhemşin ends after 17km at **AYDER**, the highest permanently inhabited settlement in the Hemşin valley system. Having long since abandoned the struggle to be a genuine village or *yayla*, Ayder revels in its role as a mountain-ringed tourist **spa resort**, packed with river-terrace restaurants and charming wooden bungalows. Of its two small *mahalles* or districts, **Birinci** (Lower) Ayder, at about 1250m, holds the spas, a handful of restaurants and most of the considerable high-season noise and congestion. İkinici (Upper), better known as **Yukarı Ambarlık**, at about 1350m elevation, is much calmer and has most (but not all) of the more desirable accommodation.

While the surrounding **scenery** – a narrow, sharply inclined valley with waterfalls pouring off the sides – has always been the main attraction, roads are being pushed ever higher, so Ayder no longer rates as a genuine trekking trailhead. Every walk necessitates a minibus transfer: the two most important are the day-jaunt to the Çengovit lakes above the *yayla* of Yukarı Avusor, and the three lakes above Kavron.

The hot-spring complex

Ayder Kaplıcaları Cad • Daily 8am–7pm • ₺12; private family tub rooms ₺40 • ☎ 0464 657 2102, ⓦ ayderkaplicalari.com

Ayder boasts an old *kaplıcalar* or sulphurous modern **hot-spring complex**, a big crowd-puller for the town. It's fed by a communal *havuz* (pool) from which scalding water (close to 60°C) is piped into rectangular tiled pools. Separate sections cater for men and women, and more expensive private family tub rooms are available.

ARRIVAL AND INFORMATION   **THE HEMSİN VALLEYS**

ÇAMLIHEMŞİN

By dolmuş Frequent dolmuşes come up from the coastal towns of Ardeşen and Pazar to Çamlıhemşin (hourly in summer; 30min); in summer there are also a few from Rize (1hr).

Services The main street has a bank with an ATM, a PTT, and stores for last-minute hiking supplies.

FIRTINA VALLEY

By dolmuş Despite the dreadful road, a fairly regular dolmuş service – at least daily in the morning and more in summer – connects Çamlıhemşin with Çat (45min) and Elevit (1hr).

AYDER

By bus and dolmuş Frequent dolmuşes connect Ayder with the coastal towns of Ardeşen and Pazar in season (both 1hr), though you may have to change vehicles in Çamlıhemşin. Out of season the link from Çamlıhemşin (30min) is less frequent – usually just a couple head to Ayder in the morning, returning late afternoon. To catch the dolmuşes up the Fırtına valley to Çat and Elevit from Ayder, you'll need to be in Çamlıhemşin by noon at the latest.

By taxi A taxi between Çamlıhemşin and Ayder costs around ₺40.

Services Birinci (Lower) Ayder has some small supermarkets, a PTT booth and ATMs on the main street.

TOURS

Türkü Tourism İnönü Cad 35, Çamlıhemsin ☎ 0464 651 7230, ⓦ turkutour.com. This agency, based in Çamlıhemsin, has been owner-managed since 1993 by Mehmet Demirci, the region's most genial and knowledgeable mountain guide. With a team of local guides, including daughter

Güneyce, Mehmet offers assorted year-round multi-day treks, either tent-based (camping equipment provided), farmhouse-based or *pansiyon*-based, as well as day-tours around Ayder and various themed tours, such as 4WD, photography and wildlife.

TO THE STARRY LAKE AND BEYOND

The most rewarding of several possible **day-hikes** that start near **Elevit** is the three-hour walk up to **Yıldızlı Göl** (Starry Lake), at the top of the vale that opens up to the south. You won't appreciate the name unless you camp overnight there: just after sunrise little scintillating points of light flash briefly – for perhaps twenty minutes – on the surface of the water. With more substantial equipment, you can continue along a superb **three-day traverse** southwest across the western Kaçkar, taking in Başyayla, Çiçekliyayla, the 2800m-high lakes at the base of Tatos and Verçenik peaks – all potential campsites – and finishing at Başhemşin at the head of the Fırtına valley. If necessary, you can "bail out" at Çiçekliyayla, where there's a road.

ACCOMMODATION AND EATING

ÇAMLIHEMŞİN

★ Ekodanitap Asagi Camlica Mah, off the northern entrance to Çamlıhemşin **☎**0464 651 7787, **W**ekodanitap.com. Owned by Mehmet Demirci of Türkü Tourism (see p.533), this peaceful set-up in the hills below Çamlıhemşin has a choice of solar-powered accommodation in heated wooden bungalows with balconies sleeping up to four, or cheaper two-person "treehouses" (traditional Hemşin cabins on stilts) with shared bathrooms. Meals are provided fresh from the organic garden, served in a communal open-sided terrace with stunning views. Bunglaow **₺310**, treehouse **₺180**

★ Moyy Mini Otel & Café İnönü Cad 35, **☎**0464 651 7497, **W**moyyminiotel.com. A charming wooden building and one of the oldest in the village. The six rustically boutique en-suite rooms here have kilims scattered on the floors and good views from the shared balconies, which look straight onto the rushing river below. The menu in the downstairs café (open to non-guests daily 7am–8pm) is a little more contempory than most and does decent coffees. **₺280**

THE FIRTINA VALLEY

Cancık Pansiyon In the centre of Çat **☎**0464 654 4120, **W**cancikpansiyon.com. The most conspicuous building in the village is a surprisingly good hotel-restaurant and general store/souvenir shop, with six clean wood-trimmed rooms upstairs, several bungalows and a simple trout and grilled meat restaurant. Half board only. **₺140**

Fırtına Pansiyon Northern end of Şenyuva **☎**0464 653 3111 or **☎**0532 783 2708, **W**firtinavadisi.com. Located on a bend of the gurgling river, this welcoming, family-run *pansiyon* is housed in a former schoolhouse. Various different-sized rooms and bungalows are spread around the property; all are simply furnished but exceptionally clean, as are the shared bathrooms. Home-cooked meals are offered; half board only. **₺180**

Toşi Pansiyon 1km downstream from Çat **☎**0464 654 4002 or **☎**0533 484 1456, **W**bit.ly/Tosipansiyon. The best fallback if the *Cancık* is full, this has nine rooms, one double in the attic of the main building, plus double, triple and quad en-suite cabins along the river. There's a terrace restaurant, though it can get packed out by organized trek groups. Half board only. **₺170**

AYDER

Many accommodation options in Ayder are only open between April and Oct, though the ones listed here are open year-round; book ahead in Aug. As for food, most visitors arrange half board, and although local cuisine tends to be repetitive, that's no bad thing as it's based largely on trout, salad and *muhlama* (a fondue-like dish of cheese, butter and cornflour), the latter scooped up with corn bread.

Ayder Sofrası Ayder Yaylasi Yolu, between Birinci and Yukarı Ambarlık **☎**0464 657 2974. Owned by the *Haşimoğlu* (see below), this large, central restaurant is one of the few to serve alcohol, and the wooden tables on the outside stone-walled terrace is a lovely place to be, overlooking the river and with sweeping mountain views. There's a breakfast buffet (₺8) and an à la carte menu that includes the regional specialities of trout, *muhlama* and *labana sarması* (stuffed cabbage). Mains ₺5–18. Daily 9am–10pm.

Haşimoğlu Otel Ayder Kaplıcaları Cad, Birinci Ayder **☎**0464 657 2037, **W**hasimogluotel.com. Large, smart and friendly hotel where the wood-lined rooms and bungalows come in assorted sizes and have TVs and balconies; a river view costs extra. There's a restaurant as well as cosy communal areas with fireplaces, and even a jacuzzi. It's a short walk to the kaplıcalar. Half board only. **₺240**

★ Kalegon Butik Otel Ayder Yaylasi Yolu, near the top of Yukarı Ambarlık **☎**0464 657 2135, **W**ayderkalegon .com. A notch up from most hotels in Ayder, the *Kalegon* offers slick, Swiss-style wood-panelled rooms with heating and TV. Open to non-guests, the restaurant serves an impressive menu of trout, salads and lamb (daily noon–10pm; mains ₺6–17), while the small bar can get lively, especially when there's live folk music. In winter the restaurant is cosy, with an open fire, while in summer diners sit at the outdoor terrace. **₺290**

Kuşpuni Dağ Evi Ayder Yaylasi Yolu, signposted before Yukarı Ambarlık **☎**0464 657 2052. Ayder's cutest establishment, the family-run "bird's nest" is more of a *pansiyon* than a hotel, with basic low-ceilinged rooms that vary from doubles to family suites, all with heating and ageing bathrooms. The kitchen serves up delicious regional food in the stove-heated lounge or on the outside terrace. Half board only. **₺175**

Serender Otel Near top of Yukarı Ambarlık **☎**0532 162 5883, **W**ayderserender.com. Another cosy, *pansiyon*-style place with en-suite wood-trim heated rooms in varying formats. Located in a peaceful corner of the village, *Serender* has a restaurant and several common sitting areas with chess and backgammon sets. **₺160**

The coast east of Trabzon

The coast **east of Trabzon** gets more extreme as you approach the Georgian border – if the Black Sea coast as a whole is wet, here it's positively soggy. The mountains, shaggy with tea plants and hazelnut trees, begin to drop directly into the ocean – imposing natural defences which led to the development of ethnic groups such as the **Laz** (see box opposite).

9

THE LAZ

The Black Sea's most celebrated minority group, descended from the ancient Colchians (from whom Jason supposedly stole the Golden Fleece), the **Laz** are a distinctively Caucasian people, often with reddish hair. They accepted Christianity in the sixth century under the Byzantine Empire and the Kingdom of Georgia, but the Ottomans induced conversion to Islam early in the sixteenth century. Today's Laz are well integrated into the national fabric, and many have migrated to cities in western Turkey. Their language, Lazuri, is most closely related to Georgian; small pockets of Lazuri-speakers remain around Pazar, Ardeşen, Fındıklı, Arhavi and Hopa.

Sadly, this section of the coast has remarkably little to offer travellers. The first decent, unpolluted beaches east of Trabzon are found between **Arakli** and **Sürmene**, towns which are nothing to write home about. The same goes for the boatyards with their colourful, top-heavy *taka* fishing boats at **Çamburnu**, 3km east. A much-touted pay beach is tucked at the base of the cliff just beyond the port, but equally good, or better, free beaches line the road to Of.

Rize

A modern Turkish city of 105,000 inhabitants and the capital of the province of the same name, **RİZE** sits in a grand setting around a bay backed with mountains. Though not the hottest tourist spot in Turkey, the name will at least be a familiar one to every traveller who's bought a souvenir box of "Rize Turist Çay" to brew back home. Of its ancient history as Rhizos nothing survives, and of its role as the easternmost outpost of the Trapezuntine Empire, hardly more than a tiny, eighth-century castle pays tribute. The local university is named after President Recep Tayyip Erdoğan, who was born in the nearby village of Güneysu.

Rize has two main streets, Atatürk Caddesi (inland) and Cumhuriyet Caddesi which runs parallel to the sea; the town square, **Belediye Parkı**, lies between them. The PTT here has been decorated with wooden trimmings, complementing the two nineteenth-century restored **wooden houses** on the hill behind, one now housing a mildly interesting museum. East of the square, Rize's major **tea garden** is, not surprisingly, the focus of the town's social whirl. Surrounding shops sell Rize tea in every conceivable packaging, plus the unlikely spin-off product of tea cologne.

Sarı Evi Museum

Antika Sok 4, uphill from the northwest end of Atatürk Cad • Tues–Sun 9am–noon & 1–4pm • Free • ☎ 0464 214 0235

The "Yellow House", a restored Ottoman mansion known locally as the Tuzcuoğulları Konağı, now holds the **Sarı Evi Museum**, focusing on local life. The upstairs rooms are

TEA

Thanks to the moist and moderate climate, **tea** (*çay*) is king east of Trabzon. The tightly trimmed bushes are planted everywhere between sea level and about 600m, to the exclusion of almost all other crops. Picking the tender leaves is considered **women**'s work, and during the six warmer months women can be seen carrying enormous loads of leaves in back-strap baskets. Each year, nearly a million raw tonnes of tea is sent more or less immediately to the cutting, fermenting and drying plants whose stacks are recurring regional landmarks.

Oddly enough, tea is a very recent introduction to the Black Sea, the pet project of one Asim Zihni Derin, who imported the first plants just before World War II to a region left badly depressed following the departure of its substantial Christian population in 1923. Within a decade or so, tea became the mainstay of the local economy, overseen by **Çaykur**, the state tea monopoly. Despite the emergence of private competitors since 1985, and the Chernobyl accident, which spread radiation over the 1986 crop, Çaykur is still a major player in the domestic market. Export, however, seems unlikely, as supply can barely keep pace with domestic demand.

9

VISITING BATUMI, GEORGIA

The 540km Black Sea coastal highway continues for a final 20km beyond the industrial port of Hopa to the **Turkish–Georgian frontier**. Set by the Turkish and Soviet revolutionary governments in 1921, the crossing was virtually inactive between 1935 and 1988, a casualty of Stalinist, then Cold War, paranoia. Since the gates have opened, and especially since a 2011 agreement that allows Georgian and Turkish citizens to cross passport-free, it has become a busy 24-hour crossing. Furthermore, citizens of most countries, including Australia, Canada, EU, New Zealand and the US, may enter Georgia visa-free.

A gleaming white futuristic-looking tower now marks the border at **Sarp**. Built in 2011, it was conceived to represent Georgia as a progressive boom country bursting with energy and creativity. This is certainly true of **Batumi** (also spelt Batum in Turkish), 17km beyond the border; a visit to this extraordinary city makes a very worthwhile excursion from northeastern Turkey.

BORDER PRACTICALITIES

Getting to Sarp and across the **border** is very straightforward. There are a few direct buses from Trabzon to Batumi (3hr 30min), stopping at Rize and Hopa on the way. Another option is to take the more frequent dolmuşes from Trabzon – or anywhere along the D010 coastal highway – as far as Sarp and take onward transport from there. For either option, once in Sarp you'll have to walk through the impressive tower building via the immigration and customs desks for each country; the process rarely takes more than 30min.

On the Georgian side, the arrivals hall has ATMs and a tourist information desk for *Go Batumi* (🌐 gobatumi.com) where the friendly, English-speaking staff will give you an excellent map and brochure for the city. Outside are small shops, cafés, exchange bureaus (which change most currencies to Georgian Lira, GEL), and vehicles waiting to take arrivals the 17km to Batumi. The #44 minibus goes direct to the centre of Batumi and costs 4 GEL ($1.70); expect to pay no more than 15 GEL ($6.30) for a taxi (20–30min).

SIGHTS

Batumi was once a typically grim Soviet-era Black Sea holiday resort, but, thanks to recent public and private **investment** from Georgia, Russia and Turkey, the town has had a dramatic metamorphosis. The old quarter has been renovated such that its charming cobbled streets

lavishly decorated in the opulent Western style of the later Ottoman bourgeoisie, and there are also some interesting displays on the traditional dress of the coastal Laz (see box, p.535) and the inland-dwelling Hemşinlis (see box, p.532).

A *serander*, traditionally used to store grain safely out of reach of rats, stands alongside the museum. Beside that, another restored mansion houses an uninteresting display on the machinations of tea production.

Tea Research Institute

Narenciye Sok, Ziraat, 1km south and uphill from central Rize • Daily 9am–10pm • Free; tea ₺2 per cup • Served by "Ziraat" buses from Sarı Evi Museum (Mon–Fri 7am–noon, hourly on the hour) • ☎ 0464 213 0241

If the sight of all the surrounding tea fields has you hankering for a cuppa, then the **Tea Research Institute** ("Çay Araştırma Enstitüsü") – part botanical garden, part tasting and sales outlet – is the best reason to pause in Rize. Beneath grand magnolia trees, all manner of tea is served by a *çaycı* (tea-waiter) from heated *samovars*, while you take in sweeping views of Rize and the Black Sea.

ARRIVAL AND INFORMATION   RİZE

By bus and dolmuş Rize's *otogar* is 800m west of town; *servis* buses connect with the centre. Dolmuşes heading east and west also leave from the main shorefront D010 highway.
Destinations Ankara (12 daily; 13hr); Batumi, Georgia (5 daily; 2hr); Erzurum via İspir (11 daily; 7hr); Hopa (hourly;

1hr 15min); İkizdere (hourly; 1hr); Istanbul (11 daily; 20hr); Samsun (hourly; 7hr); Trabzon (every 30min; 1hr).
Tourist office The helpful office is on Atatürk Cad on the north side of Belediye Parkı, near the mosque (Mon–Fri 8.30am–5pm; ☎ 0464 213 0408).

now feature upmarket boutiques, stylish hotels and swish apartments, popular with wealthy Muscovites and Ukrainians. The promenade alongside the pebbly beach has been paved and landscaped into the 7km-long Batumi Boulevard, with parks, piers and cafés, and sprinkled with thought-provoking modern statues. A cable car is another recent addition, and it whisks visitors up the hills above the city for Black Sea views.

Must-sees in Batumi include the well-laid-out **Batumi Botanical Garden**; the **Dancing Fountains** along the boulevard; the **Monument of Medea** in Europe Square; and the lovely **Piazza Batumi**, with its numerous restaurants and nightly live music. The **Gonio-Apsaros Fortress** – the oldest fortification in Georgia – is another highlight, and there are plenty of museums, churches, art galleries and theatres to keep you occupied. If you've ever had the desire to watch a Russian film noir, then the delightful 1911 **Apollo cinema**, recently restored to its former Art Nouveau glory, is worth a visit.

GETTING AROUND

Municipality **buses** run frequently throughout the day and are an efficient way of travelling around the city. There's also a useful city **bike-sharing scheme**, accessed with smartcards. Information for both can be found at ⓦ batauto.ge.

ACCOMMODATION

Accommodation varies from backpackers' hostels and self-catering holiday apartments to boutique hotels in the old quarter and beachfront casino-and-spa resorts. **Go Batumi** has a full list on their website (ⓦ gobatumi.com), and they also operate several tourist information kiosks around the city.

RETURNING TO TURKEY

The **#44 minibus** goes to the Sarp border; once back on Turkish soil, you can pick up dolmuşes heading west along the D010 coastal road. Alternatively, through-minibuses depart from Batumi's bus station on Shavsheti Street in the centre and cost around 30 GEL ($12.60) to Trabzon. THY (ⓦ turkishairlines.com) run a daily flight (2hr 5min) between Batumi and Istanbul Atatürk. Or, of course, if your appetite has been whetted, you can see more of Georgia and move on to the capital, **Tbilisi** (6hr bus from Batumi) where there are more flight options back to Turkey.

ACCOMMODATION

Milano Cumhuriyet Cad 115 ☎ 0464 213 0028. Close to the main square, shops and restaurants, this well-established hotel in a seven-storey block offers good-value, though ageing, rooms with a/c, fridges, TVs and sound-proofed windows, plus there's a buffet breakfast. Parking is usually available down the nearby side streets. ₺130

Rize Dedeman Alipaşa Koyu, 5km west of Rize on the D010 coastal highway ☎ 0464 223 4444, ⓦ dedeman .com. Head for this large, four-star chain hotel for comfortable, contemporary-styled rooms with all mod cons; the suites (₺410) have separate living areas and sea views. The restaurant serves decent buffets, and there's a lobby bar, gym and private beach. ₺280

EATING AND DRINKING

★**Dergah Pastanesi** Deniz Cad ☎ 0464 217 9898. This large, cheerful café serves delicious cakes, chocolate mousse and *baklava*, plus cappucinos, ice cream and savoury dishes such as filled baked potatoes and *meze* platters. There are balcony tables and free wi-fi. Desserts ₺4–7, mains ₺5–10. Daily 8am–11pm.

Evval Zaaman Piri Çelebi Mahallesi, 50m uphill from the southeast side of Belediye Parkı ☎ 0464 212 2188, ⓦ evvelzaman.com.tr. Located within a restored Ottoman mansion and with a leafy garden patio, "Past Times" is almost part museum, part restaurant, with memorabilia

scattered throughout its two floors. The house speciality is a very tasty *muhlama* (cheese fondue), and it's a popular hangout for a slightly artsy university crowd. Mains ₺9–15. Daily 9am–11pm.

Liman Lokantası Deniz Cad ☎ 0464 217 1568. Rize's best-known and most popular *lokantası* won't disappoint, with waiters ready to help newcomers choose from a plethora of ready-made meat and vegetable dishes, including the regional *kuru fasuliye* (beans) dish. Mains ₺5–12. Daily 10am–10pm.

Northeastern Anatolia

KAÇKAR DAĞLARI

Northeastern Anatolia

10

Turkey's northeast is, quite simply, the most visually arresting part of the country: whitewater rivers rush through valleys dotted with distinctive wooden houes, and there are dramatic mountains every which way you look. In addition, an almost bewildering array of ruins showcases this area's heritage as part of the ancient kingdoms of Georgia and Armenia – eagle-eyed travellers will spy castle after castle crumbling away on inaccessible peaks. The region itself is easily accessible by bus, train or plane, though still maintains an air of remoteness – tell a big-city Turk you plan to visit the northeast, and you'll likely provoke astonishment, followed by a wistful admission that they'd love to visit. For the few foreign travellers who make it this far there's plenty to see and do, including tremendous skiing and hiking opportunities for active sorts.

Much of northeastern Anatolia is a high, windswept plateau segmented by ranks of eroded mountains. Four great **rivers** – the Çoruh, Kura, Aras and Euphrates – rise here, starting courses that take them to scattered ends in the Black, Caspian and Persian seas. Despite ambitious development projects, much of the area remains poor – horse-drawn ploughs are still a common sight, as are stacks of cow dung used for fuel; indeed, some of the more remote farm communities, and even whole villages, live partly underground in burrow-houses. These provide insulation against the area's fierce winters, which drag on far longer than one would expect of Turkey – with numerous passes approaching 3000m above sea level, you may well see patches of ice from the roadsides well into June. In comparison, the relatively prosperous and forested valleys around Yusufeli and Artvin have a lighter atmosphere and quasi-Mediterranean climate, as a tangible Caucasian influence begins to be felt.

However you approach – from central Anatolia, the extreme southeast of Turkey or the Black Sea – your first stop is likely to be **Erzurum**, long a goal of armies and merchants and the only real urban centre. Today it's the main jumping-off point to just about anywhere else, and also holds a clutch of post-Selçuk Turkish monuments. North of Erzurum, the **valleys of early medieval Georgia** hide dozens of little-visited churches and enchanting ruined castles, dotting a chiselled landscape more redolent of modern Georgia than "regular" Turkey. Place names, too, betray Georgian lineage – most commonly in the form of the common prefix "Ar-", equivalent to "-ville" or "-burg". North of Erzurum lie the southern valleys, home to the churches of **Haho** and **Öşk Vank**. Without your own transport, you'll find it easier to tour the western valleys, where the main town, **Yusufeli**, has reasonable transport links and accommodation, and also provides a good base from which to organize a tour of the stunning **Kaçkar Dağları** mountain range, or spectacular ruins such as **İşhan**. To the north, the unlovely city of **Artvin** is the best base for a tour of the churches and castles of the northern valleys, or to continue on to Georgia proper.

PAMAKKULE

Highlights

❶ Palandöken Just south of the gritty city of Erzurum, Palandöken is Turkey's best ski resort by far, and also a great place for coffee in summer. **See p.548**

❷ Yusufeli With its dramatic setting above a churning river and beneath craggy mountaintops, the village of Yusufeli makes an appealing base for hikers. **See p.549**

❸ İşhan The most magnificent of the area's many ancient Georgian churches, and the most exciting to get to – it's a steep ride along a hair-raising mountain road, with spectacular views at every turn. **See p.553**

❹ Kaçkar Dağları The glacially sculpted, wildflower-carpeted Kaçkar Mountains rank as the most versatile and popular alpine trekking area of Turkey. **See p.554**

❺ Kafkasör festival One of the most authentic folkloric expressions in the country, this picturesque event is celebrated outside Artvin in early summer. **See p.560**

❻ Ani An absolute must for anyone visiting eastern Turkey, this ruined medieval capital boasts the region's densest concentration of Armenian ruins, plus a jaw-dropping location. **See p.566**

HIGHLIGHTS ARE MARKED ON THE MAP ON P.542

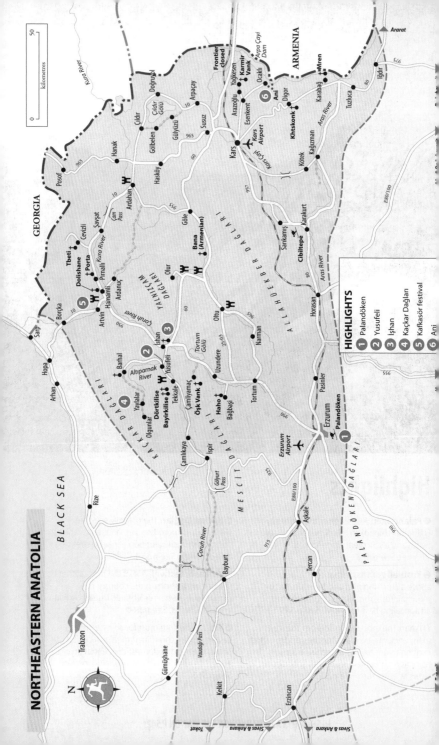

NORTHEASTERN ANATOLIA

HIGHLIGHTS

1. Palandöken
2. Yusufeli
3. İşhan
4. Kaçkar Dağları
5. Kafkasör festival
6. Ani

East of Erzurum, **Kars** is the last major town before the Armenian frontier, and serves as the base for visits to the former Armenian capital of **Ani** – justifiably the best-known complex, and certainly up there with the best ruins in all Turkey, it now possesses an isolated, decaying grandeur carrying subtle echoes of former glories. Buildings here, as well as many of the less heralded **Armenian churches** and **castles** you may come across, are made from a peach-coloured stone known as *duf.* There's also good skiing, at **Palandöken** near Erzurum, and **Cibiltepe** on the way to Kars – your photos will likely astonish any friends or family who assume Turkey to be all beaches and bazaars.

10

Brief history

Thanks perhaps to its discouraging climate and meagre resources, this corner of the country was thinly settled until the second millennium BC. The **Urartians** had their northernmost city at today's Altıntepe, near Erzincan, between the ninth and sixth centuries, but the next imperial power to make an appearance was the **Roman Empire**, succeeded by the Byzantines and **Armenians**. The eleventh-century undermining of the Armenian state and the Byzantine defeat at Manzikert marked the start of a pattern of invasion and counterattack that continued until 1920. The **Selçuks**, their minor successor emirates and the newly ascendant **Georgian** kingdom jockeyed for position until swept aside by **Mongol** raids in the early thirteenth century and Tamerlane's juggernaut two hundred years later; the **Ottomans** finally reasserted some semblance of centralized control early in the sixteenth century.

Just as the northeast had been a remote frontier of the Byzantines, so it became the border of this new Anatolian empire, confronting an expansionist Tsarist Russia, which effectively ended what remained of Georgia's autonomy in 1783. As the Ottomans declined, **Russia** grew bolder, advancing out of its Caucasian fortresses to lop off slices of the region on several occasions during the nineteenth century, though they got to keep their conquests only in 1829 and 1878. Nearly half the sites described in this chapter were under Russian rule until 1914, with additional conquests up to 1917 nullified by the Bolshevik Revolution and the collapse of the Caucasian front. Between 1915 and 1921 the area was the scene of almost uninterrupted **warfare** between White Russian, Armenian Dashnakist and Turkish Nationalist armies, and of massacres among the mixed civilian population that had historically been over a third Armenian and Georgian-Christian.

By 1923 the northeast was all but prostrate, with ninety percent of its former population dead or dispersed. The present international boundaries between Turkey and Georgia or Armenia are the result of treaties between Atatürk and the **Soviet Union** in March and October 1921, and don't necessarily reflect historical divisions – indeed, as late as 1945 Stalin was still demanding that Kars and Ardahan be returned to the "Russian motherland".

Erzurum

One of eastern Turkey's few large cities, **ERZURUM** sits almost 2000m above sea level on the slopes of a burly mountain range, some of whose peaks poke at least another kilometre higher. It's fair to say that the city's reputation fails to live up to these lofty heights – Turks from elsewhere deride Erzurum as too conservative and too prone to earthquakes, while travellers tend to use it as a place in which to break long journeys, or start mountaineering and rafting expeditions bound for the **Kaçkar Dağları**. However, the city's **devout** nature is a large part of what makes it interesting: mosques here are not only fancy but full of worshippers night after night, while many local women wear the black chador – a cultural import from nearby Iran – or the *çarşaf*, a full-length hooded robe tinted the same dun colour as the surrounding steppe. Add to this a compact group of very early Turkish **monuments** – all handily lined up along the

THE GEORGIANS

Georgians have lived in the valleys of the Çoruh, Tortum, Kura and Berta rivers, now in Turkey, since the Bronze Age. Like the neighbouring Armenians, they were among the first Near Eastern nations to be evangelized, and were converted rapidly to Christianity by St Nino of Cappadocia in the mid-fourth century. Unlike the Armenians, they never broke with the Orthodox Patriarchate in Constantinople, and maintained good relations with Byzantium.

THE GEORGIAN KINGDOMS

An effective Georgian state only entered the local stage early in the ninth century, under the auspices of the **Bagratid** dynasty. This clan contributed rulers to both the Georgian and Armenian lines – hence the partial overlap in the medieval history of the two kingdoms. They claimed direct descent from **David** and Bathsheba, which explains a preponderance of kings named David, a coat of arms laden with Old Testament symbols, and curiously Judaic stars of David embossed on many of their churches.

Ashot I Kuropalates began the first stages of territorial expansion and church-building in the area, under the guidance of the monk Gregory Khantzeli. Ashot's descendants included David "the Great" Magistros of Oltu (see p.547), as well as Bagrat III, who in 1008 succeeded in unifying the various Georgian principalities into one kingdom. The Selçuks arrived in 1064, ravaging Georgia and all of eastern Anatolia, but as soon as they turned to confront the Crusaders a Bagratid revival began. David the Restorer managed to expel the Selçuks by 1125, moved the Bagratid court to newly captured Tblisi, then reunited the various feuding principalities ruled by minor Bagratid warlords.

Under the rule of David's great-granddaughter **Tamara**, medieval Georgia acquired its greatest extent and prestige, controlling most of modern Georgia, Armenia and Azerbaijan, as well as the ancestral Georgian valleys. A formidable military strategist and shrewd diplomat, the queen displayed a humanity and tolerance unusual for the era. Many churches and monasteries were repaired or re-endowed under Tamara; despite being a woman and a non-Muslim, her name still elicits respect from local Turks.

After Tamara died, the Georgian kingdom began a slow but steady decline, effectively partitioned between the Ottoman and Persian empires. The rise of imperial Russia signalled the end of any viable Georgian state, and the last semi-independent king effectively surrendered to Catherine the Great in 1783.

GEORGIAN MONUMENTS

The Bagratids were a prolific bunch, who erected **castles** on just about every height; generally you'll have to be satisfied with a passing glance, since access to many of these eyries has long been impossible other than for technical climbers. The most remarkable examples are the early Bagratid monastic **churches**, all dating from before the move northeast to the Caucasus proper, and most sited amid oases at the heads of remote valleys. The Georgians borrowed many of the architectural features of Armenian churches. It takes a trained eye to distinguish the two styles, though in general the Georgians rarely attempted the rotundas or multi-lobed domed squares beloved of the Armenians.

There's not been nearly the degree of official stonewalling about Georgian Christians as there is concerning Armenians, and the churches have become recognized as tourist attractions. Almost all have suffered damage from dynamite- and pickaxe-wielding **treasure hunters**: the locals have an unshakeable conviction that all the Christians who left the area in 1923 secreted precious items in or under their churches, in the mistaken belief that they'd eventually be able to return.

same road – and a city centre recently beautified with fountains, small parks and the like, and you may even find yourself wanting to stay longer.

As the highest city in Turkey, Erzurum endures **winters** that are both long and hard – temperatures often plunge below -30°C. Keeping local homes warm at these times is a matter of survival, rather than comfort, and even some of the city's more modern apartment blocks sport wood-fire niches on their balconies. Despite the brutal wind and bone-chilling temperatures, however, winter is high season: tourists aplenty (mostly Turks and Russians) arrive to use the excellent **skiing** facilities at **Palandöken**, just south.

Brief history

Because of a strategic location astride the main trade routes to Persia, the Caucausus and western Anatolia, Erzurum's sovereignty has always been contested. Although the site had been occupied for centuries before, a city only rose to prominence here towards the end of the fourth century AD, when the Byzantine emperor Theodosius II fortified the place and renamed it **Theodosiopolis**. Over the next five hundred years the town changed hands frequently between Constantinople and assorted Arab dynasties, with a short period of Armenian rule.

After the decisive battle of Manzikert in 1071, Erzurum – a corruption of Arz-er-Rum, or "Domain of the Byzantines" in Arabic – fell into the hands of first the Selçuks and then the Saltuk clan of Turks. These were in turn displaced by the İlhanid Mongols during the fourteenth century, forerunners of Tamerlane himself, who used the city as a springboard for his brief blitzkrieg into western Anatolia. Erzurum was incorporated into the Ottoman Empire by Selim I in 1515, where it remained securely until 1828, after which the Russians occupied it on three occasions. Finally, the 1970s saw Erzurum become a bit of a hippy hub, thanks to its location on the way east to Iran, Afghanistan and India – travellers of a certain vintage still remember it rather fondly.

Yakutiye Medresesi

Off Cumhuriyet Cad • Museum daily 8am–7pm • ₺5

Work on the appealing **Yakutiye Medresesi** was started in 1310 by Cemaleddin Hoca Yakut, a local governor of the İlhanid Mongols. With its intricately worked portal, and

truncated minaret featuring a knotted lattice of tile-work, it's easily the most fanciful building in town. The minaret in particular seems displaced from somewhere in Central Asia or Persia – not such a far-fetched notion when you learn that the İlhanids had their seat in Tabriz, in the northwest of present-day Iran.

The beautiful interior of the *medrese* now holds the excellent **Museum of Islamic and Turkish Arts**, nicely arranged around the students' cells. Exhibits include displays of local *oltu taşı* jewellery (see opposite), various dervish accessories, *ehram* (woven waistcoats for pilgrims to Mecca) and some interesting old prints of Erzurum.

10

Ulu Cami

Off Cumhuriyet Cad • Free

The large, ornate **Ulu Cami** was erected in 1179 by Nasirüddin Muhammed, third in the line of Saltuk emirs. Like most mosques of that age, it's a big square hall, with dozens of columns supporting bare vaults; the one note of fancy is a wedding cake of stalactite vaulting, culminating in the central skylight.

Çifte Minareli Medrese

Off Cumhuriyet Cad, next to the Ulu Cami

The "double-minaretted" **Çifte Minareli Medrese** – the literal translation of the seminary's name – is Erzurum's main tourist attraction and most picturesque feature, thanks in part to the sumptuous mountain backdrop visible behind the two ribbed, 30m-high minarets that rise from its northern flank. There is some dispute about the structure's vintage, but majority opinion holds that Hüdavend Hatun, daughter of the Selçuk sultan Alâeddin Keykubad II, commissioned it in 1253. In conception the Çifte Minareli was the boldest and largest theological academy of its time, but was never finished.

At the time of writing the *medrese* was in the early stages of a major reconstruction – completion was initially scheduled for 2015, but it should now be finished by 2017, when the courtyard is likely to revert to its previous function as an occasional marketplace. Until then, you'll have to content yourself with a visit to *Tebrizkapı*, an excellent café-tearoom behind the *medrese* (see p.548).

Üç Kümbetler

250m south of Çifte Minareli Medrese • Daily 8am–5pm • Free, though there are plans to introduce a ₺5 ticket

The cluster of mausoleums known collectively as **Üç Kümbetler** dates back to the early twelfth century. The oldest of the three tombs – and the most interesting by far – is that of the first Saltuk emir. Its octagonal base of alternating light and dark stone, breached by half-oval windows, demonstrates the mutual influence of Georgian, Armenian and early Turkish architecture.

The citadel

Just north of Cumhuriyet Cad • Daily 8am–5pm • ₺5

While Erzurum's **citadel** – or *kale* – is no longer the highest point in town, it still lends the best view over the city, and the great, intimidating vastness of the plateau beyond. Its huge rectangular bulk was originally laid out by Emperor Theodosius II.

The adjacent freestanding **Tepsi Minare** now doubles as a clock tower. Like the Ulu Cami mosque (see above) nearby, it's mostly twelfth century, though the superstructure (which can be climbed) was added by the Russians during one of their occupations. Stairs on the east side lead up to the ramparts.

Rüstem Paşa Bedesteni

Off Menderes Cad • Most shops open daily 8am–5pm • Free

Süleyman the Magnificent's grand vizier endowed Erzurum with the **Rüstem Paşa Bedesteni**, an enchanting covered bazaar, in the sixteenth century. The city owed much of its wealth to transcontinental trade routes; right up until the nineteenth century, some forty thousand laden camels passed through the city every year.

Trade in the bazaar today is almost totally monopolized by **oltu taşı**, an obsidian-like material mined near Oltu, 150km northeast, that's most frequently made into *tespih* (prayer beads), *kolye* (necklaces) and *küpe* (earrings).

10

ARRIVAL AND DEPARTURE ERZURUM

By plane The airport, 10km northwest of town, is connected by hourly buses (₺3) with a stop opposite the train station; taxis charge ₺50 for the trip.

Destinations Ankara (5 daily; 1hr 30min); Istanbul (7 daily; 2hr); İzmir (1 daily; 2hr).

By train The station is around 1km north of the centre, near a cluster of inexpensive accommodation options.

Destinations Ankara (1 daily; 20hr); Divriği (1 daily; 6hr 40min); Kars (1 daily; 4hr 30min); Sivas (1 daily; 9hr 30min).

By bus The long-distance *otogar* is 3km northwest of the centre, and connected by several bus routes (₺2.25) as well

as taxis (₺12). Some long-distance buses also pick up and drop off at the small Gölbaşı Semt Garajı, conveniently situated just over 1km northeast of downtown, which is also the starting point for some dolmuşes to Yusufeli and Artvin.

Destinations Ankara (8 daily; 13hr); Artvin (5 daily; 4hr); Doğubeyazit (4 daily; 4hr); Kars (hourly; 3hr); Rize (2 daily; 6hr); Sivas (12 daily; 6hr 30min); Trabzon (3 daily; 6hr); Van (2 daily; 6hr); Yusufeli (3 daily; 3hr).

Car rental Avis, airport and Terminal Cad, Blok 5 (☎ 0442 233 8088); Palandöken, Çaykara Cad (☎ 0442 235 4524).

ACCOMMODATION

The supply of **accommodation** in Erzurum usually exceeds demand, and as long as you're not too fussy you should have no trouble finding a room in the area just uphill from the train station. Higher-end choices are all south of town at the base of **Palandöken** ski resort (see box, p.548), about 5km south; in summer, when the few hotels there slash their rates, they can prove far better value than the motley hotels in the centre.

CITY CENTRE

Kral Erzincankapı 18 ☎ 0442 234 6400, ✉ kralhotel @gmail.com. This oddball hotel is a real love-it-or-hate-it affair. Some rooms have been intriguingly designed – the most striking feature is mock İlhanid-Mongol decor in their mosaic-tiled baths – but the bed linen can be tatty, while service standards are not always sky-high. ₺120

Polat Kâzım Karabekir Cad 2 ☎ 0442 235 0363, ⓦ www.otelpolat.com. Central hotel whose rooms are simple, but fair value for the price. Staff are amiable, and the rooftop breakfast room is a bonus – start your day with a buffet meal and a valley view. ₺120

★**Rafo** Milletbahçe Sok 19 ☎ 0442 235 0225, ⓦ rafootel.com. Newer than most of the nearby competition, this sleek boutique hotel inspires confidence all the way from its snazzy lobby. The rooms themselves sport purple trim, spotless bathrooms and comfortable beds – all in all, a splendid place to stay. ₺200

Yeni Çınar Ayazpaşa Cad 18 ☎ 0442 213 6690. Friendly, comfortable and with extremely low prices, this is about as far downmarket as you'll want to go in Erzurum – an extra ₺20 will get you an en suite. The establishment itself is fine for single females, though

the dark alley on which it's located does not encourage wandering around at night. ₺60

PALANDÖKEN

Dedeman 3km uphill from the resort entrance ☎ 0442 316 2414, ⓦ dedeman.com. Four-star hotel, in an alpine bowl 2450m above sea level, and aimed at doorstep skiers who want to be right at the heart of the action. Large (if spartan) rooms and wood-lined, mock-chalet common areas. They also run the smaller *Ski Lodge* nearby, which some may find more likeable. Closed mid-May to Nov. ₺350

Polat Renaissance By the resort entrance ☎ 0442 232 0010, ⓦ marriott.com. This five-star is a bit remote from most of the ski slopes – a private chair lift bridges the gap – but compensates with cheerful, fair-sized rooms. Palatial common areas include a pleasant indoor pool, hamam and gym. ₺400

★**Xanadu Snow White** By the resort entrance ☎ 0442 316 6851, ⓦ www.xanaduhotels.com.tr. Forget the cheesy name – this is by far the most luxurious accommodation in Palandöken, with classy rooms and common areas, ultra-efficient staff, and fantastic views over Erzurum – not to mention a café-bar with very fair prices. Rates drop by more than half in summer. ₺500

EATING

Erzurum's **restaurants** tend to offer good value, with a concentration of sorts on or around Cumhuriyet Cad and the central park – there is a glut of cheap spots, but for a few lira more you can eat somewhere truly special. Licensed places are rare in this devout town, as are shops selling alcohol, but there are a couple of **bars** on Mumcu Cad. The most famous local dish is **cağ kebap**, a peppery lamb-meat variant cooked horizontally and served on small skewers; you'll find it at simple restaurants all over the city centre, and the quality is uniformly high.

★ Emirşeyh Tebrizkapı Cad 172 ☎ 0442 213 9292, ⓦ emirseyh.com.tr. The most attractive restaurant in town, with some rather lovely paintwork and fixtures on the various levels of its large interior. Most people, however, head straight up to the rooftop for enchanting views of Erzurum's monuments and mountainous surroundings – it's a fantastic place at sunset, when encircling swallows lend their shrill cries to proceedings. Meat's the word here – they're justly proud of their signature *köfte* (₺12) and *sarma beyti* (₺15) – though a fair few veggie dishes, including an odd "peanut kebab", peek out from the wide-ranging menu. Daily 8am–11pm.

Erzurum Evleri Yüzbaşı Sok 18, south of Cumhuriyet Cad ☎ 0442 213 8372. Eight old dwellings knocked together to make an institution that's equal parts amusement-park maze, folklore museum and restaurant. Antique displays feature everything from Ottoman houseware to 1950s portable gramophones. The food's merely OK – ₺25 for a huge breakfast, or more like ₺15 for *sarma* or *mantı* – but the cushion-seats in secluded alcoves are highly atmospheric, so at least stop by for an *ayran* (₺3). Daily 7am–11pm.

★ Gel-Gör İstasyon Cad 4 ☎ 0442 234 2122, ⓦ gelgorcagkebabi.com. The best place to sample Erzurum's signature dish, *cağ kebap* (₺7.50/skewer), for which lamb meat is marinated with onions and black pepper, then grilled on a horizontal, rather than vertical, skewer. Doesn't sound all that different? Taste it for yourself – it's fantastic, and they won't stop bringing you meat until you ask them to. Daily 9am–11pm.

Kılıçoğlu Sütiş Cumhuriyet Cad 20 ☎ 0442 444 1495. The main branch of three in town for this premier pudding shop and nemesis of dieters: two dozen flavours of *dondurma*, plus profiteroles, biscuits and every imaginable sort of oriental sticky cake. They've also got good coffee and orange juice. Daily 9am–11pm.

★ Tebrizkapı Behind Çifte Minareli Medrese ☎ 0442 214 1413. Ambitious new café-cum-tearoom behind the Çifte Minareli Medrese, which acts as a backdrop to the outdoor seats – they're on a lawn-like expanse, which means that you can kick off your shoes and get some grass in between your toes as you drink, or puff on a nargile (₺15). The lengthy interior is lovely too, curling through ninety degrees and featuring some opulent-looking private rooms. Daily 8am–11.30pm.

DIRECTORY

Consulate Iran, Emniyet Sok 26 (☎ 0442 315 9983). If you plan to cross into Iran, it's important to know what you're doing before you leave Erzurum (see p.543); however, plenty of travellers (from countries other than the UK and USA) have acquired visas here of late.

Hamam Boyahane Hamamı (daily 5.30am–midnight; ₺14), just across the road from the Rüstem Paşa Bedesteni, is both historic and salubrious.

Supermarket The Migros by the train station is good for stocking up with trek-suitable food.

SKIING AT PALANDÖKEN

Palandöken, the resort that stretches away 5km south of Erzurum, offers far and away the best **skiing** in Turkey – more than adequate compensation for being stuck in Erzurum during its habitually arctic winters. With largely north-facing slopes ranging from 2300m near the *Palan Hotel* up to Point 3140 on Mount Ejder, excellent conditions (essentially nice dry powder on a 2m base) are just about guaranteed. Pistes total 45km, with eight chair lifts, two drag lifts and a tele-cabin giving access to eight easy, six intermediate and two advanced runs, as well as four recognized off-piste routes.

Palandöken is easily reached by taxi from Erzurum, for a fare, depending on your precise destination, of around ₺25. Bus #5G (₺2.25) also heads this way from various points in the city centre, though since it stops a full 10min uphill walk short of the resort, it's not worth considering unless you're really strapped for cash. The handful of good hotels in the resort (see p.547) are your best bets for equipment rental, which costs from ₺70 per day.

Note that there's also good winter skiing at **Sarıkamış**, west of Kars (see box, p.570).

Yusufeli

Squeezed into a tight valley on the banks of the Çoruh, and surrounded by knobbly crags on which trees struggle to gain a roothold, gritty little **YUSUFELİ** enjoys a truly spectacular location. Despite the Georgian ruins and Black Sea-style wooden dwellings on its periphery, the town itself is somewhat old-fashioned – no great surprise, given the fact that it remained on civic death row for several decades (see box, p.550). The fact that it was granted a new lease of life is a boon to travellers to northeastern Turkey, since Yusufeli is both a charming place to hunker down for a few days, and an ideal gateway to a series of nearby attractions. Although lauded as one of the best **rafting** spots on earth, general tourism has never really taken off here, and the stark simplicity of local facilities will appeal mostly to hardier travellers. You'll need a steady hand at the wheel – or, if you're a minibus passenger, a strong stomach – for the steep, and often bumpy, rides out to the trailheads or Georgian churches.

10

ARRIVAL AND DEPARTURE

YUSUFELİ

By bus and dolmuş Yusufeli can be a little tricky to get to on public transport – the only regular buses are from Artvin. There are a few morning departures from Erzurum, though if you can't get a direct bus try hopping on one linking Erzurum and the coast, then ask to be set down at Su Kavuşumu junction on the main highway, 10km below the centre; connecting taxis from there cost around ₺15. Yusufeli also marks the start of dolmuş routes to villages further upriver, including Barhal, Yaylalar and Olgunlar,

though services to these three high settlements adhere to a somewhat informal schedule. Vehicles leave for Barhal at 1pm if there are enough people, and also at 3pm if there's sufficient demand. The same goes for access to Yaylalar and Olgunlar – you may have to offer over the odds if it's just you who wants to head that far.

Destinations Artvin (hourly; 1hr 45min); Barhal (1–2 daily; 1hr 30min); Erzurum (3 daily in the morning; 3hr); Tekkale (1–3 daily; 15min); Yaylalar and Olgunlar (1–3 daily; 3hr).

INFORMATION AND ACTIVITIES

Tourist office Just up the road from the *otogar* (☎ 0466 811 4008); staff often seem much keener to sell tours than give general travel advice.

Banks Several banks on Yusufeli's main drag have reliable ATMs; make sure to stock up on cash here if you're headed to the mountains or anywhere remote.

Rafting Most of the outfits that used to ply the local rapids have closed down. Probably your best bet is the *Greenpeace* guesthouse (see below), which still arranges rafting trips most weeks – it'll cost around €100/person, four people minimum.

ACCOMMODATION

★**Almatur** Beside the river, in the town centre ☎ 0466 811 4056, ⓦ almatur.com.tr. By far the most appealing option in town, this three-star hotel has excellent little rooms, many with river and/or mountain views. They also offer superb breakfasts on the uppermost level – which will taste even better if you've managed to score one of the sizeable discounts usually available on the rack rate. ₺**140**

Baraka Beside the river, in the town centre ☎ 0466 811 3403. On the main-road side of the pedestrian suspension bridge, this place has small, cleanish en-suite

rooms that are deservedly popular with backpackers. Go for those that overlook the river. No wi-fi. ₺**50**

Greenpeace Across the river, 500m upstream ☎ 0466 811 3620, ⓦ birolrafting.com. Particularly popular with travellers who are visiting Yusufeli with a rafting excursion in mind (see above), this simple, friendly place is ideally located just outside town – easy to access, but far away enough to foster a feeling of remoteness. Rooms are clean, if a bit small; camping is also available for ₺15/ person, and the in-house restaurant can knock up a tasty fish supper. ₺**60**

EATING

★**Almatur** Beside the river, in the town centre ☎ 0466 811 4056, ⓦ almatur.com.tr. Breakfasts at this hotel's top-floor restaurant are gargantuan, and great value at just ₺10; pasta dishes and the like are served through the day. Daily 7am–10pm.

Çoruh Pide Just over the road-bridge from the town

centre ☎ 0466 811 2870. The best spot to load up on its namesake flatbreads (*pide* from ₺8), though it often closes earlier than its quoted hours. Daily 10am–9pm.

Hacıoğlu On the main road ☎ 0466 811 3009. This restaurant has the best location in town, with tables on a large terrace abutting the river. The food's not bad either;

their signature dish is *cağ kebap* (lamb marinated with onions and black pepper; ₺10), a speciality of nearby Erzurum (see p.543), though there are some good *lokanta*-style dishes available too. Daily 9am–9pm.

Around Yusufeli

10

Yusufeli is the gateway to the **western Georgian valleys**. Set around the confluence of the Barhal and Çoruh rivers, these are scenically and climatically some of the most favoured corners of the northeast. During the balmy summers, all sorts of fruits ripen, and you're treated to the incongruous spectacle of rice paddies (and further downstream, olive groves) by the Çoruh, within sight of parched cliffs overhead. In their lower reaches they offer **Georgian churches** near **Tekkale** and **Barhal**, plus trekkers' trailheads not only at Barhal but also higher up at **Yaylalar** and **Olgunlar**. All these places have simple **accommodation**.

GETTING AROUND

You'll need your own vehicle, or a lot of time for walking and hitching, to visit most of the sights around Yusufeli – even if you rent a car or hire a taxi, you'll need at least three days to see all the monuments described in our account.

By bus Bus services, where they exist, usually arrive near the sights in the afternoon and depart for the nearest town in the morning – exactly the opposite of most tourist schedules.

By taxi Some roads are in bad shape, but if you can get a group together and find a willing taxi driver, travelling by taxi can end up being far cheaper than renting a vehicle in Erzurum (see p.543) or Trabzon (see p.519).

Tekkale and around

7km southwest of Yusufeli • Dolmuşes from Yusufeli (1–3 daily; 15min); alternatively, taxis cost around ₺12, or it's 1hr 30min on foot

There's little to see in sleepy little **TEKKALE**, one of the most popular trailheads for the **Kaçkar Dağları** (see p.554), though there are a couple of fantastic Georgian ruins hereabouts. Do, however, keep your eyes peeled on the road in from Yusufeli – you'll pass two ruined chapels (one perched above the Çoruh in Yusufeli town, the second 2km upstream on the far side of the river) and a vertiginous castle guarding the valley road, before curving the last 2km into the village.

THE DAMMING OF THE ÇORUH

Anyone lucky enough to have visited Yusufeli in May or June will have seen, and certainly heard, the **Çoruh River** pounding along at a quite incredible speed, emitting a roar that's audible all along the valley – the result of the melting of winter snow in the Kaçkar Mountains (see p.554). The area's enormous **hydroelectric** potential is now being tapped at long last – of major importance in a country accustomed to importing costly fossil fuels. The first schemes to **dam** the Çoruh were drawn up in the 1970s; thanks to poor planning, environmental lobbying and retracted investments, they were torn up and put back together many times in the following decades.

Little Yusufeli bore the brunt of this uncertainty – under the initial plans, and many subsequent ones, the town would have been the largest of eighteen settlements swallowed, either in whole or in part, by the highest major dam. This lingering Sword of Damocles ensured that, for decades, nothing new was built in Yusufeli. In 2011, the pendulum swung back towards the creation of a series of smaller dams further up the river – the town received a reprieve, though the local **rafting** industry (see p.549) has been affected.

The gigantic **Deriner Dam** near Artvin was sealed in 2012, and it will slowly start to produce electricity as the waters rise. At the time of writing, the whole area around the dam was a vast, post-apocalyptic mess scratched with ugly construction tracks – however, as the terrain beds in, the new roads linking Artvin with Yusufeli and Ardahan are becoming highly scenic driving routes.

Dörtkilise

6.3km upstream from Tekkale • Follow a dirt road uphill from *Cemil's Pansiyon*; ignore the first two bridges that span the stream to the right – the church is on a grassy hillside to the left, just beyond the third bridge

Domeless, with a steep gabled roof and relatively plain exterior, **Dörtkilise** is a twin of the church at nearby Barhal, though built several decades earlier and later renovated by David Magistros (see box, p.544). Despite its name – meaning "Four Churches" – only one remains intact, but it's very fine and unlike most other Georgian places of worship.

As Dörtkilise is 3km from the nearest village, it was never reconsecrated as a mosque, and is now home only to bats, swallows and occasionally livestock. Inside, a double line of four columns supports the barrel ceiling hiding under the pitched roof; some fresco traces persist in the apse, while an unusual choir takes up much of the west end. The large half-ruined building to the northeast, arcaded and double-vaulted, was the monastery refectory, joined to the main body of the church by an equally decrepit gallery that served as a narthex.

Bayırkilise

5km walk beyond Dörtkilise • Follow the broad path from a jeep "ramp" and culvert beside a power pylon, 150m north of Dörtkilise; it dwindles as it climbs, changing banks of the adjacent stream, and fizzles out completely after 45min; the final 30min is a steep, trackless walk on an unstable surface; bring insect repellent

The remote church of **Bayırkilise** – outrageously perched on a seemingly inaccessible pinnacle rearing above the canyon – remains in distant view of Dörtkilise just long enough to give you bearings. In fair to middling condition, Bayırkilise has a gabled roof like its lower neighbour, with a single barrel vault and traces of frescoes inside; the views, and the sense of accomplishment in arriving, are the main rewards.

Up the Altıparnak River

The **Altıparnak River** wends upwards from Yusufeli to the Kaçkar Dağları, and the road running alongside it is one of the best forms of access to those mighty peaks. Even if you're not planning to hike or camp, it's still worth heading this way in order to view terrific scenery and a life little changed in decades – the hamlets of **Barhal**, **Yaylalar** and **Olgunlar** all have accommodation options, and make grand places to get away from it all.

Barhal

29km north of Yusufeli • Take a dolmuş from Yusufeli (see p.542)

The most popular route out of Yusufeli follows the valley of the Barhal Çayı north through a landscape straight out of a Romantic engraving, complete with ruined Georgian castles on assorted crags overlooking the raging river. After 18km of one-lane asphalt, the road surface changes to dirt at river-straddling Sarıgöl; **BARHAL** (1300m), officially renamed Altıparmak after the mountains behind, is 11km beyond, ninety minutes' drive in total from Yusufeli. With its scattered wooden buildings peeking out from lush pre-alpine vegetation, Barhal conforms well to idealized notions of a mountain village, and makes a popular starting point for high-altitude treks in the **Kaçkar Dağları** (see p.554).

Church of Barhal

20min walk upstream from Barhal; follow signs to *Karahan Pansiyon*

The tenth-century **church of Barhal** (Parkhali) is the final legacy of David Magistros. Set in a hillside pasture next to the *mahalle*'s school, it's virtually identical to Dörtkilise (see above), except for being somewhat smaller – and in near-perfect condition owing to long being used as the village mosque. It's now only opened for Friday prayers, but it's worth securing admission to appreciate the sense of soaring height in the barrel-vaulted nave – and the debt European Gothic owed to Georgian and Armenian architects. You'll have to track down the imam for keys – the *Karahan Pansiyon* (see below) will be willing to give him a call.

Yaylalar

50km north of Yusufeli • Take a dolmuş from Yusufeli (see p.549)

Formerly known as Hevek, and still occasionally shown as such on maps, **YAYLALAR** lies 21km southwest of Barhal, along a scenic dirt road. Yaylalar is one of the most popular trailheads for high-altitude treks in the **Kaçkar Dağları** (see p.554), and at an elevation of over 2000m, you'd expect the setting to be spectacular. It doesn't disappoint – jagged peaks muscle their way into the distance, and life dawdles by at a pedestrian pace. Architecturally the village varies from new concrete to century-old houses, and though the only specific sight is an Ottoman **bridge** just downstream at the mouth of the Körahmet valley, it's a pleasure simply to amble around.

Olgunlar

3km north of Yaylalar, 53km north of Yusufeli • On request, the daily dolmuş to and from Yaylalar (see above) will continue to, or start from, Olgunlar

The tiny road's-end village of **OLGUNLAR**, once known as Meretet, is surrounded by gorgeous mountains on all sides. At 2200m this is the highest trailhead for the **Kaçkar Dağları** (see p.554), and while Barhal and Yaylalar are great places to stay, Olgunlar beats them hands down – it's smaller and more pastoral, the views are more spectacular, and there are some fine accommodation options. It's not a year-round settlement, and only really functions from April to October – other than the guesthouse owners, pretty much all villagers are farmers, many living in charming wooden houses at the top end of the settlement.

ACCOMMODATION AND EATING UP THE ALTIPARNAK RIVER

BARHAL

Barhal holds three good accommodation options, for which advance booking is strongly advisable in July and Aug. Village facilities are completed by a bakery, a few well-stocked shops, a restaurant and a well-attended teahouse.

Barhal Pansiyon At the entrance to Barhal village ☎0466 826 2031. This simple guesthouse is a perfectly acceptable choice, with a varied range of pleasant, pine-clad rooms and a homely atmosphere. You'll eat well here, too, if you opt for breakfast (an extra ₺15/person) or half board (an extra ₺50). No wi-fi. **₺80**

Karahan Pansiyon 1.2km upstream from the village, next to the church ☎0466 826 2071, ⓦkarahanpension .com. The most characterful option, with treehouse-style chalets and views that get better as you climb up the various layers of rooms. Given the remote location, it may be wise to convert to half board for an extra ₺20/person. **₺100**

Marsis Village House Just upstream from Barhal Pansiyon ☎0466 826 2026, ⓦmarsisotel.com. Three-storey building with clean double/triple/quad rooms (sharing bathrooms), and a *teleferik* that hoists your bags up the slope from the roadside. Suppers are large and strictly vegetarian, with beer available. You'll wake early here, as every footfall reverberates from the upper floors to the lower ones. **₺100**

YAYLALAR

Yaylalar's two decent accommodation options, facing each other, belong to the same owner. You're likely to see him around quite a bit during your stay, since he also runs one of the town's few shops and the village bakery, rents out mules and arranges trekking expeditions – and occasionally drives the dolmuş in from Yusufeli.

Altunay Pansiyon Entrance to Yaylalar village ☎0466 832 2001, ⓦkackar3937.com. The cheaper of Yaylalar's two guesthouses, with 25 beds spread across a large, rambling building. Shared facilities, and no wi-fi. Half board **₺120**

Çamyuva Pansiyon Entrance to Yaylalar village ☎0466 832 2001, ⓦkackar3937.com. Newer and slightly more luxurious than the *Altunay*, with good, en-suite rooms, an open kitchen and a sitting room. The four-person chalets (₺90/person) are great value, and if demand is low you may be able to take the whole thing for the price of a single. No wi-fi. **₺160**

OLGUNLAR

★**Kaçkar Pansiyon** Next door to the Deniz Gölü ☎0466 824 4432, ⓦkackar.net. Rambling affair with large en-suite rooms, a communal TV area and shared kitchen. It's the village's best option for food – try a trout straight from the farm. In addition, you can rent tents and other trekking equipment here for around €10/day, and the owner is able to help with trekking plans. **₺200**

Olgunlar Pansiyon Not far beyond the Kaçkar Pansiyon ☏ 0466 832 2105. Set in a rather garish pink building, this is by some stretch the most basic option in the village; that said, these are by far the cheapest rooms this side of Yusufeli. Breakfast costs a little extra, and there's no wi-fi. **₺50**

Along the Tortum River

Between Yusufeli and Erzurum, a series of stupendously attractive valleys branching off from the **Tortum River** marks the southern extent of **medieval Georgia** (see box, p.544); the superlative churches on this stretch include **İşhan**, **Öşk Vank** and **Haho**. Though our account follows the river down from Yusufeli, the most atmospheric approach is actually from Erzurum – about 70km out, you'll spy a pair of **castles** crumbling away atop dramatic pinnacles, announcing the southern frontier of ancient Georgia more effectively than any signpost ever could.

Access is tricky on public transport, and there are no real travellers' bases in this area; most visit the sights in a rented car, en route between Erzurum and Yusufeli. However, simple **accommodation** near Haho and right next to İşhan makes it tempting to stay the night in these rarefied surroundings.

İşhan

23km east of Yusufeli • One daily minibus from Yusufeli to the church (4pm; returning 7am the next morning); if you're staying at the guesthouse (see p.554), they'll pick you up from the turn-off on Highway 60, 6km east of the main Erzurum–Artvin highway, where the steep, part-paved 5.7km track to the church begins

Far and away the most spectacular church in the western valley, **İşhan** enjoys a truly magnificent mountain setting. The road up – not recommended for vertigo sufferers – weaves a lonely course through a heavily eroded, lifeless moonscape, which makes it all the more surprising when you arrive at the church and its surrounding apple, mulberry and walnut groves. This is charming **İŞHAN** village, which despite its beauty seems to be in near-terminal decline – since the 1980s, when its one school had more than 130 students, the number has dwindled to just eleven. Surprisingly, the village is served by occasional public transport, and even boasts a simple guesthouse.

The imposing **church** itself was originally dedicated to the Virgin, and constructed in stages between the eighth and eleventh centuries, ranking it among the oldest extant sacred Georgian architecture. The semicircular colonnade that lines the apse, with superb carved capitals, is the earliest surviving portion of the building, and was modelled consciously after the church at Bana (see p.562). Great chunks of the roof are now missing, so the 42m-high dome, constructed much like that at Öşk Vank, rests in isolation on four columns. The acoustics, however, remain superb, as you can hear for yourself if you stand directly beneath the dome, and some patches of fresco can be seen high up on the surviving walls of the south transept.

Tortum Gölü

36km south of Yusufeli • Accessible on all Artvin–Erzurum buses

Tortum Gölü, beside the highway between Erzurum and Artvin, is a highly picturesque lake that's almost entirely surrounded by chunky, unspoiled mountains, their steep, diagonal strata giving hints as to the area's creation. The views are magnificent from the road, which is forced up onto a corniche bypass above the western shore – you may also be able to see a couple of Cappadocia-style rock chimneys on the eastern side of the lake.

Created when a landslide blocked the north end of the valley a couple of centuries ago, the lake now measures roughly 10km long by 1km wide. The famous *şelale* or **falls of Tortum** are today its natural outlet, accessible by a signposted side road 12km north of the Öşk Vank turning. To get a good look at the 48m cascade, you'll have to scramble down a path; to be honest, though, it's only spectacular when the falls are at their fullest, in May and June. The road heading north to Yusufeli, on the other hand, is scenic in the extreme – corrugated walls of rock close in from both sides until you're spat out of a giant gate of rock.

Öşk Vank

7.2km west of Highway 950, 54km in total south of Yusufeli • Turn west off the highway just south of Tortum Gölü, and follow a direct, mostly paved road up the valley to Çamlıyamaç

The most elaborate example of Georgian Gothic architecture in the western valleys, the monastery church of **Öşk Vank** (Oshkhi) is set in the pretty village of **ÇAMLIYAMAÇ**, which holds a couple of shops and simple places to eat. Founded by David Magistros in the late tenth century, Öşk Vank represents the culmination of Tao Georgian culture before the Bagratid dynasty's move northeast and the start of the Georgian "Golden Age" after 1125. The interior colonnade – with no two columns alike – exudes a European Gothic feel with its barrel-vaulted, coffered ceiling; halfway up the south transept wall, the vanished wooden floor of the mosque that once occupied the premises acted as protection for a stretch of **frescoes**, the best preserved in any of the Turkish Georgian churches.

Haho

7.2km west of Highway 950, 75km in total south of Yusufeli, or 90km north of Erzurum • There are no direct services to or from Yusufeli, but minibuses run from Erzurum's Gölbaşı Semt Garajı (4 daily; 1hr; ₺9); by car, turn west from the highway over the humpback bridge, then bear left, past a modern mosque – a few minutes later you pass through a large village, after which you need to take a right towards Bağbaşı at the next, well-marked junction (Haho is listed here as "Taş Camii")

Tucked away in a small, wooded valley, just outside the large village of **BAĞBAŞI**, 8km west of Highway 950, the tenth-century church of **Haho** owes its excellent state of repair to its continuous use as a mosque since the eighteenth century. Entry is only possible around prayer time, or by tracking down the key-keeper in the village. Most of the monastery complex – the boundary wall and gate, and three satellite chapels – is in good condition, the effect spoiled only by aluminium corrugated sheets on the roof, though the conical-topped dome is still covered in multicoloured tiles.

ACCOMMODATION AND EATING

ALONG THE TORTUM RIVER

İŞHAN

Little House Next door to the church, İşhan village ☏ 0533 500 0128. This basic guesthouse, which feels more like a mountain-based youth hostel, has four simple twin rooms. Oddly, the only double beds sit happily in the dorm; toilets are shared, and a little far away from the bedrooms. Whichever bed you sleep in, the price is same, and includes a delicious breakfast. No wi-fi. Per person ₺35

TORTUM GÖLÜ

İskele Alabalık Tesisleri 8km north of the Öşk Vank side road, Tortum Gölü. This is the best lunch option while touring the churches, located at the far end of a little peninsula jutting into the lake. Simple but salubrious, it serves salad, trout and nothing else, and it's a great place to pitch your tent for the night – the scenery around here is out-of-this-world good, though marred slightly by the new roads. No wi-fi. Camping per person ₺15

HAHO

Pehlivanlı 3km west of Highway 950 on the Haho road ☏ 0442 772 2054. A delightful little guesthouse on the way up to Haho, snuggled in between cliff faces; you'll need your own transport to get here. The rooms are surprisingly well-appointed given the location; the owners can also whip up small meals for guests and visitors alike, including trout from the on-site farm. No wi-fi. ₺80

The Kaçkar Dağları

Making a formidable barrier between the northeastern Anatolian plateau and the Black Sea, the **Kaçkar Dağları** are the high end of the Pontic coastal ranges – and comprise Turkey's most rewarding and popular trekking area. Occupying a rough rectangle that measures 70km by 20km, the Kaçkars extend from the Rize–İspir road to the Hopa–Artvin highway. The more abrupt southeast flank is lapped by the Çoruh River, while the

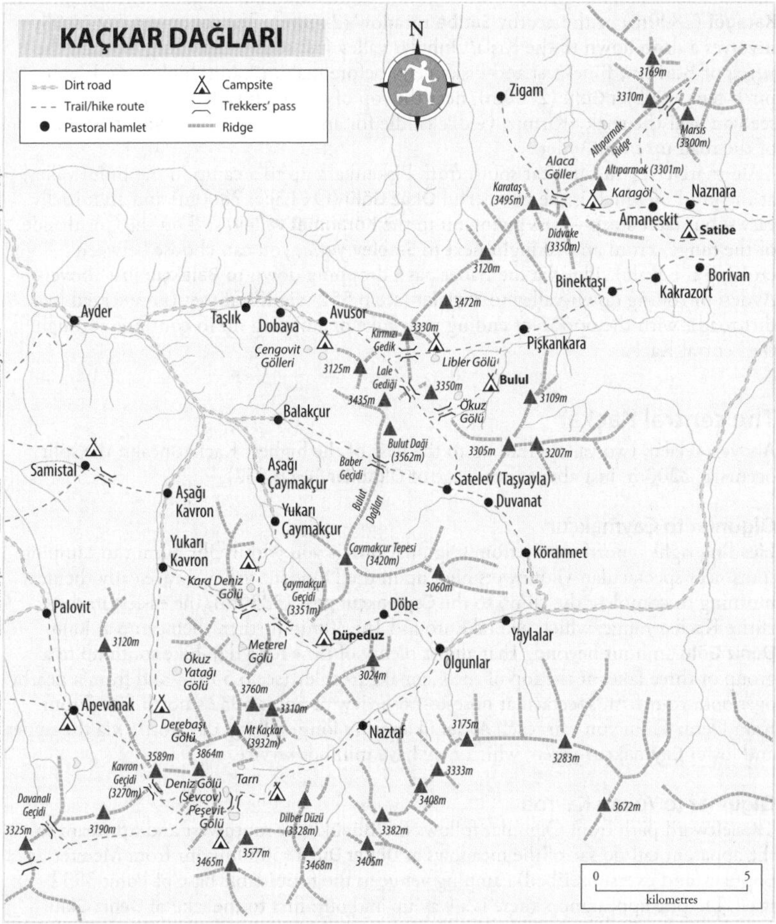

KAÇKAR DAĞLARI

Legend:
- Dirt road
- Trail/hike route
- Pastoral hamlet
- Campsite
- Trekkers' pass
- Ridge

10

gentler northwest folds drop more gradually to misty foothills. At 3932m, their summit ranks only fourth highest in Turkey, but in scenic and human interest they fully earn their aliases "Little Caucasus" and "Pontic Alps". Besides the principal summit area, several other major massifs are recognized: the Altıparmak and Marsis groups of about 3300m, at the north end of the Bulut ridge, which links them with Point 3932; and the adjacent Tatos and Verçenik systems of about 3700m, at the extreme southwest of the chain.

Partly due to intensive human habitation, the high Kaçkars support relatively few large **mammals**; bear and boar prefer the forested mid-altitude zones, while wolves and ibex are ruthlessly hunted in the treeless heights. **Birds** of prey and snow cocks are more easily seen and heard, while the summer months witness an explosion of **wildflowers**, butterflies – and vicious deer flies.

The northern Kaçkar: Barhal to Avusor

Starting from **Barhal** (see p.551), at 1300m, most trekkers head west to the top of the valley walled off by the Altıparmak chain, finishing a tough first day either near

Karagöl (2800m) or the nearby **Satibe** meadow (2450m). The following day usually involves a drop down to the Kışla/Önbolat valley just south, threading through the *yaylas* of Borivan, Binektaşı and Pişkankara before making camp higher up. If you pitch tent at **Libler Gölü** (2700m), near the top of the main valley, the next day will see you over the tricky Kırmızı Gedik saddle for an easy descent to **Avusor**, at the end of the road up from Ayder.

Alternatively, you can bear south from Pişkankara up to a camp in the Bulul valley, at the head of which is the wonderful **Öküz Gölü** (Ox Lake; 2800m) and an initially easy – but later steep – pass giving on to the **Körahmet valley**, still on the Çoruh side of the range. From an overnight next to **Satelev** *yayla*, you can choose between crossing the Bulul ridge via the Baber pass, dropping down to **Balakçur** just above Ayder; or rolling down-valley to **Yaylalar** (see p.552) via Körahmet (now served by a dirt road), with the option of ending your hike or stocking up to continue through the central Kaçkar.

The central Kaçkar

Above Yaylalar, two valleys lead up to the base of the highest Kaçkar peaks; the split occurs at 2200m, just above the village of **Olgunlar** (see p.552).

Olgunlar to Çaymakçur

Heading right – northwest – from Olgunlar brings you within 3hr 30min to camping spots near spectacular wildflowers high up in the Düpedüz valley. Leave early the next morning to complete the climb to the **Çaymakçur pass** (3230m), the easiest in the entire Kaçkar range, which will take around 1hr 30min further, then camp at **Kara Deniz Gölü** an hour beyond. That allows plenty of time for a day-hike south up to a group of three lakes at the top of the Cennakçur valley (see p.558) – and from a nearby overlook, your first, spectacular nose-to-nose view of Point 3932's north face. From Kara Deniz Gölü you can reach **Ayder** in another long walking day north, via the upper and lower **Çaymakçur** *yaylas*, which may have minibus service.

Olgunlar to Yukarı Kavron

The leftward path from Olgunlar follows the Büyük Çay southwest and upstream to the apparent cul-de-sac of the meadows at **Dilber Düzü** (3050m; 3hr from Meretet), a popular (and oversubscribed) camping venue at the formidable base of Point 3932 itself. Despite appearances there is a way up and out: first to the lake of **Deniz Gölü** (also known as Sevcov; 3400m; 1hr 45min more), with just two or three cramped sites for tents, and then over the low crest just south to **Peşevit Gölü** (Soğanlı; 3377m; 2hr 15min from Dilber Düzü), a lake with much better camping.

Try to get an early enough start out of Olgunlar to reach one of the lakes before dark, in preference to Dilber Düzü. Deniz Gölü, where ice floes last into August during many summers, is the veering-off point for the moderately difficult, five- to six-hour return climb north to the **summit**, where the climbers' register is hidden underneath a rubble cairn.

From Peşevit lake you've a pathless scree-scramble west up to a false pass, then an even more miserable scree descent, another climb and a final drop to some water meadows near the top of the **Davali valley**, where a faint cairned path takes you up to the **Kavron pass** (3310m; 2hr 45min from Peşevit). Because of the rough terrain, no organized expeditions or pack animals come this way, and you'll need walking poles to save your knees – and yourself, from a nasty fall.

Once on the Black Sea side of the pass, the most popular route follows the distinct path north an hour to another col (3200m) overlooking the **Kavron valley** – and allowing superb afternoon views of Point 3932's west flank. The trail, fainter now,

OPPOSITE ANI (P.566) >

drops within 45 minutes to **Derebaşı lake** (2885m), where it's advisable to camp. There are limited sites at the inflow, and a few better ones by the lake's exit, where you scout around for the easiest cross-country route down to the floor of the U-shaped, glacial Kavron Deresi. After two hours' walk along a clear, right-bank trail, you'll reach a roadhead at the busy, electrified *yayla* of **YUKARI KAVRON** (2350m), a substantial place with a central teahouse where you can get basic supplies, and also some simple accommodation.

From just past the *Şahin Pansiyon* on the access road, a sporadically cairned route leads west-southwest up the **Çennakçur valley** to the lakes at its head (2hr 30min; c.2900m). There are at least three lakes here – **Kavron Gölü**, right by the path with emergency camping, and **Büyük Deniz** and **Meterel** off to one side – Meterel is the highest and, in summer, often the driest. Another hour over a saddle behind Kavron Gölü will take you to Kara Deniz Gölü, and usually a lot of company. From here it's simple enough to reverse the directions given above for traversing the Düpedüz valley and Çaymakcur pass from Olgunlar, and complete a three-day, three-night circuit around Point 3932 – an excellent plan if you've left a vehicle or stored extra gear in Olgunlar or Yaylalar.

Another possibility from the ridge above Derebaşı lake is to veer west, initially cross-country, to Apevanak *yayla*, which is linked by path or track to the *yaylas* of Palovit and Tirovit; the latter gives access to the western Kaçkar.

The western Kaçkar: Elevit to Çat or İkizdere

Elevit *yayla*, roughly halfway between Tirovit and Çat, is the starting point for the march up to **Yıldızlı Gölü** ("Star Lake"; a place with good camping), just across the top of the valley from Haçevanag *yayla*. The nearby, gentle Capug pass allows access to the headwaters of the Fırtına Çayı, though the onward route is briefly confused by the maze of bulldozer tracks around Başyayla (2600m) and Kaleyayla. At the latter, bear south up toward campsites by a lake at the foot of Tatos peak; the following day you'd cross a saddle to another lake, Adalı, at the base of 3711m Verçenik.

From this point you'd either descend to **ÇAT** via Ortaköy and Varoş, using a morning bus if possible part of the way, or continue walking west for another day, past other lakes just below the ridge joining Verçenik to Germaniman peak. A final 3100m pass just north of Germaniman leads to the valley containing Saler and Başköy *yayla*s, linked by daily bus to **İkizdere** (see p.531).

The southern Kaçkar: Tekkale to Yaylalar

Starting from **Tekkale** (see p.550), the same dirt road that serves Dörtkilise continues another 3km to Bölükbaşı *yayla* and the start of a two- to three-day traverse finishing in the Yaylalar valley. The weather is more reliable (and also hotter) than elsewhere in the Kaçkar, but this route is thus far relatively unspoiled.

From **Bölükbaşı** (1400m), a path heads west via the *yayla*s of **Kusana** (1630m) and **Salent** (2400m), before reaching a pair of **lakes** (imaginatively dubbed Küçük – "little" – and Büyük – "big"), below a 3300m pass. It would be prudent to overnight east of the pass, possibly beside **Büyük Gölü** (2900m), before descending a valley northwest to **Modut** *yayla* (2300m) and then **Mikeles** (1700m), about 5km downstream from Yaylalar itself.

ESSENTIALS   THE KAÇKAR DAĞLARI

Seasons The main trekking season is June to Sept, with the mists less of a hazard as autumn approaches; if you show up earlier than late July, you may need crampons and an ice axe to negotiate some of the higher passes. Note that it gets warm enough in midsummer for a quick swim in most of the lakes.

Trailhead villages The six most popular trailhead vilages are Çat and Ayder on the Black Sea slopes, and Barhal (see p.551), Yaylalar (see p.552), Olgunlar (see p.552) and Tekkale (see p.550) on the Çoruh side.

Itineraries In terms of potential itineraries, the Kaçkars are infinitely versatile. Manic or pressed-for-time hikers cross from Yaylalar to Ayder via certain passes in two gruelling days, but there's little pleasure in that. A more reasonable minimum time to switch sides of the mountains would be three or four days, and most visitors are happy to spend a week or even ten days trekking around. The approach from the Black Sea hills is gentler than that on the Çoruh side, with clearer trails, but the paths and villages can be crowded, and the almost daily mist rising up to 2900m is a problem. Meanwhile, although the weather is more dependable on the Çoruh flank, hiking grades are tougher.

Equipment There are few suppliers in the area, so you will need to bring a full trekking kit: high-quality walking boots, wool socks, a waterproof jacket and trousers or gaiters, a backpack cover and a proper, freestanding tent. A camp stove and ample backpacking food are also essential – and carry ten to twenty percent more supplies than you think you'll need for the projected length of the trek, in case you're stuck for an extra day by thick mist. Pure water, available everywhere from springs, is never scarce.

Maps The lack of good-quality, large-scale maps is a major drawback, but some thorough route descriptions are available in mountaineering books (see p.699). A GPS device will also come in handy. Paths are not waymarked or signposted, but cairns may be present at ambiguous points.

Dangers Aside from unmarked paths, there are few specific dangers, apart from the absolute necessity of crossing all tricky passes early in the day – certainly by noon – before they're shrouded in mist or storm cloud. Territorial domestic bulls are also a nuisance, far more likely to charge a tent than any wild beast.

10

GUIDES

If you'd rather go with a guide than alone, you'll be able to find helpful individuals in Ayder, Şenyuva, Yusufeli, Yaylalar and Olgunlar. Otherwise, try one of the following adventure travel companies running Kaçkar group itineraries – these cost more but guarantee an English-speaking guide, and include transfers too.

Ararat Expedition ☎0472 312 5232, ⓦararat expedition.com. Week-long trips, between July and Sept, starting in Barhal, overnighting in Yaylalar, ascending the main peak, then heading back down on an alternative route. The last day is spent seeing a couple of Georgian monuments, before you're dropped back into Erzurum; it'll all cost around ₺1200.

Arcadia Mountain Travel ☎0537 600 7835, ⓦarcadiamountaintravel.com. Operator offering a choice of three week-long itineraries between July and Sept, all starting in Trabzon and costing $925/person.

Artvin and around

What an absolute pummelling man has given nature in the area around **ARTVİN**. Arrayed in sweeping tiers across a steep, east-facing slope, it should possess one of the finest views in Turkey. Sadly, though, poorly planned development makes good views scarce, while the valley-junction it calls home has in any case been turned into a quarry of sorts, in order to facilitate construction of the gigantic **Deriner Dam** down the road (see box, p.550) – on the way here you'll gawp at the steep, forested mountain scenery, but grimace at the wounds inflicted on this landscape. Travellers usually stay in Artvin out of necessity rather than choice, since it's one of the few bases between Yusufeli and the Black Sea coast; however, like a bad joke you eventually come to love, there is a certain gritty appeal to walking the winding, heavily trafficked main road that wends its way through the city from bottom to top. In addition, Artvin becomes a destination in its own right when the **Kafkasör festival** comes to town (see box, p.560).

Artvin also makes a good base for exploring the northerly Georgian valleys, and a series of **churches** dotted along the **Berta River valley** and its tributaries. **Dolishane**, **Porta** and **Tbeti** are the most important; individually these are not as impressive as their southern relatives, but their situations are almost always more picturesque. Except for the Kaçkars, nowhere else in Turkey do you feel so close to the Caucasus: ornate wooden domestic and religious architecture, with lushly green slopes or naked crags for a backdrop, clinch the impression of exoticism. Here, too, you may actually encounter native **Georgian speakers**, though they're mostly confined to the remote valleys around the towns of Camili, Meydancık and Posof, and the immediate

10

THE KAFKASÖR FESTIVAL

One of the best times to visit Artvin province is in early summer when the fantastic, multi-day **Kafkasör festival** takes place at an eponymous *yayla* (village) above town. The highlight has traditionally been the pitting of bulls in rut against each other, but since the opening of the nearby frontier the event has taken on a genuinely international character, with wrestlers, vendors, jugglers, musicians and dancers from both Turkey and Georgia appearing among crowds of more than fifty thousand.

The festival is one of the last genuine folk fairs in the country, so be there if you can. It usually takes place for several days over the third or fourth weekend in **June**, but in recent years has occasionally been brought forward as far as late **May**.

---

surroundings of Şavşat. Public transport is both sparse and unreliable in this area, so having your own vehicle is a near necessity. Drawing a lazy parallel with the Berta, Highway 10 links Artvin (see p.559) and Şavşat, though all three churches lie a significant distance away from the road.

Dolishane

28km east of Artvin • Regular dolmuş service

The dome of the tenth-century church of **Dolishane** looms above the lush vegetation of the oasis village of **HAMALI**. The interior was, for decades, used as an agricultural tool shed, but has now been cleared – a good job, since patches of fresco remain visible. The exterior is even more rewarding, the south facade window surrounded by such reliefs as the Bagratid builder-king Smbat I (954–958) offering the church to Christ; a Star of David; and an archangel.

Porta

Pırnallı village, 48km northeast of Artvin

The ninth-century monastery of Khantza is now known as **Porta** to the Turks. Its main church is still impressive despite gaping holes in the dome and walls, but the walk up is of greater reward: from the sign on Highway 10, it's an enjoyable but steep 45-minute climb up to the Bağcılar district of **PIRNALLI** village. The slippery track makes good footwear an absolute necessity.

Tbeti

Cevizli village, 75km northeast of Artvin • Turn off the Artvin–Şavşat road at Söğütlü Kale, following signs for Veliköy, and follow the valley for 7km to Ciritdüzü, then another 3.5km

The tenth-century monastic church of **Tbeti** peeks out of the trees at the head of a beautiful valley. Its remains are visible at a distance to the sharp-eyed, though up close the building has suffered extensive damage from local treasure hunters. The paved but one-lane side road up to it leaves the Artvin–Şavşat road at the compact fortress of **Söğütlü Kale**.

ARRIVAL AND DEPARTURE
ARTVİN

Getting to and from Artvin is likely to take longer than you'd expect given the distance and how far it looks on a map – roads hereabouts rarely run in straight lines. That said, thanks to recent damming projects (see box, p.550), views from the various roads into and out of town often provide stunning views, which is some compensation for the time spent travelling.

By bus Artvin's *otogar* sits below town at the bottom of the valley – frustrating if you want to stay here, but handy if you're merely obliged to change buses. A regular dolmuş connection links the *otogar* with the city centre (15min; ₺2.25).

Destinations Ardahan (10 daily; 2hr 30min); Erzurum (5 daily; 4hr 30min); Kars (1 daily; 4hr 30min); Rize (hourly; 2hr 45min); Trabzon (8 daily; 4hr); Yusufeli (hourly; 1hr 45min).

ACCOMMODATION AND EATING

Things have improved slightly since the 1990s, when Artvin ranked as the prostitution capital of Turkey, but it still pays to be vigilant when selecting a place to stay. At the time of writing the **Grand Artvin** was going up just downhill from the centre – it will most likely become the town's nicest place to stay.

Çoruh Pide Selimiye Sok ✆ 0446 212 2244. Set into the pedestrianized parade abutting the Merkez Camii, this *pide* place is one of the more acceptable restaurants in town, serving up decent Turkish pizza from ₺8.50. Daily 8am–10pm.

Kat 5 Hamam Sok ✆ 0446 212 6595. Just along from the Merkez Camii, this café has a major draw – it's one of the few places you can enjoy views with your food. The panoramas of Artvin's arresting scenery are quite superb from some tables and, rarely for provincial Turkey, the clientele is mainly female. Daily 8am–11pm.

Sabah Hamam Sok ✆ 0446 212 8400. Staring straight at the Merkez Camii, the town's main mosque (and therefore occasionally noisy on that side), this cheapie has decent-enough rooms, with squat-only shared facilities. No wi-fi. ₺50

Sadıkoğlu Oteli Cumhuriyet Cad ✆ 0446 212 2162. One of the newer options in town, and certainly one of the few with an English-speaking owner. Rooms are fair value but can be a trifle stuffy, and don't quite live up to the promise of the small, spick-and-span lobby. ₺120

Ardahan and around

Faintly reminiscent of Kars (see p.562) with its Russian grid plan and *fin-de-siècle* architecture, **ARDAHAN** is one of the smallest Turkish provincial capitals. There's nothing in particular to see, except a fine old **bridge** over the Kura River, just opposite the massive **citadel**, originally Georgian but restored by Selim the Grim early in the sixteenth century. It's still an army camp, so no photography is allowed.

There are a few things to see in the area surrounding Ardahan. The **eastern Georgian valleys** ripple their way across one of Turkey's most pristine and least visited corners – here unspoiled countryside, rather than ancient ruins, is the main attraction. Some mountain passes edge towards 3000m in altitude, and you'll see patches of ice through to June. One of the main routes to and from Kars passes **Çıldır Gölü**, a lake that's worth a look. Another route heads via Göle, from which you'll be able to make a small detour to see the fantastic Armenian ruins at **Bana**, though in this case access is even tricky *with* your own wheels.

Çıldır Gölü

The slate-like expanse of **Çıldır Gölü**, nearly 2000m up, is the primary source of the Arpa Çayı/Ahuryan River, and the highest sizeable lake in Turkey. Only during the summer, when hay and grain grow by the shore, is there a hint of colour. Men on horseback, wielding scythes, rakes and other farming implements, canter splendidly across the steppe against the backdrop of 3197m-high Kısır Dağı, but their families live like moles, with houses burrowed even deeper than the norm for this province.

Abundant birdlife, fishing boats and changeable weather give the shallow lake an air redolent of a Scottish highland loch. Frozen for six months of the year, it becomes an important **bird habitat** during the warmer months, when handsome falcons and hawks swoop over your vehicle, while migrating waterfowl include pelicans and more mundane gulls.

Around the lakeshore

Doğruyol, Djala in Georgian, is the only substantial town on the lake's eastern shore; its thirteenth-century hilltop church masqueraded until recently as a mosque. There are other eleventh- to thirteenth-century churches on the lake's southwest shore at the villages of **Gülyüzü** (Pekreşin; badly ruined) and **Gölbelen** (Urta; in a better state, still used as a mosque).

ON TO GEORGIA

While most visitors cross from Turkey to Georgia through the Black Sea ports of Sarp and Batumi (see p.536), adventurous travellers can make use of an inland border post linking **Posof** and **Akhaltsikhe**. At the time of writing, citizens of most countries could get a free visa on arrival, but double-check with your nearest Georgian embassy.

ARRIVAL AND DEPARTURE

Buses run from **Kars** and **Ardahan** to the cute Turkish border town of Posof; there's nothing to see there, but the lofty views may even entice you to stay the night. The border is 12km away and accessible by taxi (₺30); you'll pay around the same for the remaining run to Akhaltsikhe (drivers will accept euros and Turkish lira), a pleasant Georgian town with banks, hotels and good links to Tbilisi and Batumi. Alternatively, there are direct daily buses from Ardahan to Tbilisi, via Akhaltsikhe and Borjomi.

The unprepossessing town of **Çıldır** is north of, and out of sight of, Çıldır Gölü. Its single commercial street is hard-pressed to muster a proper restaurant, and the one grubby "hotel" is best left unpatronized. Çıldır serves as the theoretical jumping-off point for **Şeytan Kalesi** (Satan's Castle), a brooding medieval keep and watchtower perched on a gorge, but local taxis are pricey and it's best visited on a tour from Kars.

Bana

84km southwest of Ardahan, or 115km west of Kars • No public transport; leave Highway 60 at a hard-to-spot turn-off 28km northeast of Oltu or 37km southwest of Göle, then continue through Penek and branch left 2.8km from the highway; depending on ruts and mud an ordinary car can drive with care almost all the way up

Perched on a knoll surveying water meadows, and dominated in turn by tawny crags, the seventh-century Armenian church of **Bana** enjoys a commanding position. A century after local Christians abandoned it, the Ottomans fortified Bana during the Crimean War, adding the crude bulwark still visible on the south side. The Russians blasted the upper levels off during the 1877–78 war, and later carted away much of the masonry to build a church in Oltu. Of an originally three-storeyed, vast rotunda, one floor remains, half-submerged in its own ruins. Even before you take into account the church's magnificent views of the surrounding countryside, its beauty fully justifies any trouble you may take to reach it.

ARRIVAL AND DEPARTURE

ARDAHAN

By bus Buses to and from Erzurum and Yusufeli use the *otogar* near the citadel, while dolmuşes for Kars, Artvin and Çıldır use the central depot. There are a few morning dolmuşes for Posof, near the Georgian border, and a daily service all the way to the Georgian capital of Tbilisi, via Akhaltsikhe and Borjomi.

ACCOMMODATION

Ardahan is not somewhere you'd want to stay for long, and its few simple hotels, many of which are occupied by prostitutes, are less than inviting.

Kafkas Ari Cumhuriyet Cad 87 ☎ 0478 211 3680. One of the only acceptable places to stay in town – indeed, it can come across as rather luxurious in relation to its surroundings. Tasty breakfasts, too. **₺100**

Kars and around

Most visitors come to **KARS** with but one purpose in mind – a visit to the fantastic ruins of the former Armenian capital of **Ani**, one of the most visually pleasing ancient cities in a country chock-full of them, and within easy day-trip distance to the east. However, this once-ugly city may make you want to linger longer – hidden in a natural basin on the banks of the Kars Çayı, it's an oddly attractive place, unusual in Turkey thanks to a few incongruous terraces of Russian *belle époque* buildings (see box, p.565).

The central streets are clean, and many have been repaved with cobbles or bricks (though watch out for some near-invisible steps on the pavements). Ordu Caddesi is the best street for strolling, and lined with some fantastic **Russian architecture**, while the winding road to the citadel above town is dotted with appealing pre-Ottoman structures. Kars is also famed across Turkey for its **cheese** and **honey** – which may become mouthwateringly evident at breakfast time. You may find yourself confronted with a dozen different varieties of cheese – time to learn your *tulum* from your *dil*.

Although a couple of hundred metres lower than Erzurum, the **climate** is even more severe; winters are fierce, while when it rains, which it often does, the outskirts become a treacherous swamp. Appropriately enough, perhaps, it has also found fame as the setting for the novel *Snow*, by Nobel Prize winner Orhan Pamuk (see p.694).

Meanwhile, if Ani has piqued your interest, and you have your own transport, or a good hitch-hiking thumb and lots of time, you could also consider making a trip from Kars to some less-heralded **Armenian ruins**. **Khtskonk** and **Mren** – perhaps even more architecturally and historically significant than those around Ani – lie near the uninspiring town of Digor.

Brief history

Kars was originally founded by the Armenians, who knew it as Kari. It became the capital of their **Bagratid dynasty** early in the tenth century, when the citadel that still dominates the town was substantially improved. Later that century, the main seat of Armenian rule was transferred to nearby Ani, and Kars lost importance. The **Selçuks** took it along with almost everything else in the area during the mid-eleventh century, but devastating **Mongol** raids made a mockery of the new overlords' plans. In 1205 the **Georgians**, profiting from the waning of both Selçuk and Byzantine power, seized the town and held it for three centuries until displaced by the **Ottomans**.

The **Russians** tried repeatedly during the nineteenth century to capture what they saw as the key to Anatolia. Sieges in 1828 and 1855 – the latter during the Crimean War, when a British and Turkish garrison was starved out of the citadel after five months – were successful, but on both occasions Kars reverted to the Ottomans by terms of peace treaties. Not so in 1878, when, after a bloody eight-month war between the two powers, the city was finally awarded to the Tsar. It only returned to Turkish rule following the **Treaty of Kars** in 1920. In the immediate aftermath of World War II the Soviet Union made unsuccessful attempts to overturn the treaty and reclaim the city.

THE ARMENIAN ISSUE

The **Turkish-Armenian border** has been closed since 1993, when politicians in Ankara chose to side with their Turkic brethren in Azerbaijan over the conflict in **Nagorno-Karabakh**, a majority-Armenian area that lies in Azeri territory, and now forms a de facto independent state. Complicating matters were decades of ill feeling surrounding the fate of the Ottoman Empire's ethnic Armenians in the years following World War I: a hugely contentious issue on both sides of the border. The events are viewed by Armenia – and most international historians – as the world's first orchestrated genocide, a term that the Turkish government has repeatedly refused to accept (see p.682).

Turkish **Prime Minister Recep Erdoğan**'s 2009 visit to Baku came during a political thaw, and at one stage the border seemed likely to reopen, but relations have since frosted over once again. The Kars–Yerevan rail line may one day reopen, but for now the fastest overland route from Turkey to Armenia is through Georgia, via the border crossing near Posof (see p.562).

10

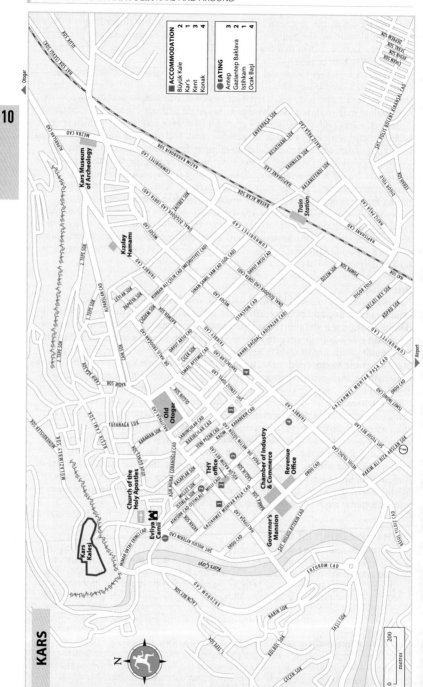

KARS

ACCOMMODATION
Büyük Kale 2
Kar's 1
Kent 3
Konak 4

EATING
Antep 3
Gaziantep Baklava 2
Istihkam 1
Ocak Başı 4

N

0 200 metres

HUNTING DOWN THE BELLE ÉPOQUE IN KARS

Kars' period under Russian rule, between 1878 and 1920, explains both the unusual **grid layout** of the city centre, and its incongruous **belle époque buildings**. Most of these structures were made from basalt and sport elaborate street facades and iron roofs; rainwater is often channelled onto the ground with decorative (often animal-shaped) spouts.

The best place in which to hunt for these architectural treasures is the stretch of Ordu Caddesi north of Faikbey Caddesi, along which three superb examples surround a small park which really, really would offer visitors somewhere to sit and have tea. Approaching from the north, the first *belle époque* beauty you'll come across is the old **Governor's Mansion**, a large, lemon-coloured structure built in 1883; this is where the Treaty of Kars was signed in 1921. Just southeast, the squat **Chamber of Industry and Commerce** sports decorative motifs on its front walls. Further south again is the peach-coloured **Revenue Office**, a large structure with false columns and some wonderfully elaborate balconies (you certainly wouldn't want to take tea on any of these – they all look set to drop off at any second).

Church of the Holy Apostles

Just north of the Kars Çayı • Free

The **Church of the Holy Apostles** was erected between 930 and 937 by the Armenian king Abbas I. Crude reliefs of the twelve Apostles adorn the twelve arches of the dome, but otherwise it's a squat, functional bulk of dark basalt; the belfry and portico are relatively recent additions. A church when Christians held Kars, a mosque when Muslims ruled, it briefly housed the town museum before being reconsecrated in 1998 as the Kümbet Camii. Just before or after prayer times (evenings are the most atmospheric), you can slip inside to view the elaborately carved altar-screen.

Kars Kalesi

Daily 9am–7pm • Free

Kars' lofty citadel, **Kars Kalesi**, is now open as a park, after decades spent off-limits as a military reserve. Locals come to enjoy the panoramic view, but there's little else to see other than the black-masonry military engineering.

A fortress of some kind has overlooked the river confluence from the hill for around two millennia. The Armeno-Byzantine structure was maintained by the Selçuks but levelled by the Mongols; the Ottomans rebuilt it as part of their late sixteenth-century urban overhaul, only to have the Russians blast it to bits, then put it back together again during the nineteenth century. On October 30, 1920, an Armenian Dashnakist army besieged in the castle surrendered to Turkish general Halitpaşa, and with that went any hopes of an Armenian state straddling both banks of the Ahuryan River.

Kars Museum of Archeology

Mezra Cad • Daily 8.30am–5pm • Free

The excellent **Kars Museum of Archeology**, set over two levels in a quiet part of town, ranks among its finest attractions. The downstairs is given over to ancient pottery, and ecclesiastical artefacts of the departed Russians and Armenians, particularly a huge church bell inscribed "This Tolls for the Love of God". The upper floor hosts a less interesting collection of woven material and firearms, while the outside yard contains gravestones from various historical periods – more interesting than it may sound.

Ani

45km southeast of Kars, just beyond Ocaklı village • Daily 7am–8pm • ₺8 • No buses; ₺120 for a 4hr return trip by taxi including 2hr at the site; minibus tours (organized through some hotels) typically cost ₺65/person

Once the capital of Bagratid Armenia, **Ani** is today a melancholy, almost vacant triangular plateau, divided from Armenia by the stunning **Arpa Çayı** (Ahuryan River) gorge and all but separated from the rest of Turkey by two deep tributaries.

While the site now consists of little more than an expanse of rubble, from it rise some of the finest examples of ecclesiastical and military architecture of its time. The Armenians were master stoneworkers, and the **fortifications** that defend the northern, exposed side of the plateau, and the handful of **churches** that lie behind, are exquisite compositions in a blend of ruddy sandstone and darker volcanic rock. Recent mining of the same materials has resulted in a few unsightly scars on the Armenian side of the border – which is surely the result of spite, given their positioning. However, the gently undulating landscape remains every bit as evocative as the ruins: it's inconceivable to venture east of Erzurum or Artvin without fitting Ani into your plans.

Ani's vast tenth-century walls, studded with towers, are visible from afar, as you approach past villages teeming with sheep, buffalo, horses, donkeys and geese. **Aslan Kapısı**, site of the **ticket office** and named for a sculpted Selçuk lion on the wall just inside, is sole survivor of the four original gates. Once beyond the inner wall you're confronted by the forlorn, weed-tufted plateau, dotted with only the sturdiest bits of masonry that have outlasted the ages. **Signposted paths**, many of them remnants of Ani's former streets, lead to or past all of the principal remains.

Be sure you're prepared for a trip to Ani. Midsummer is usually very hot, so you're advised to bring a hat, sun cream and water to tour the site, as well as snacks. Note also that the site itself nudges up against the highly sensitive **Armenian border** (see box, p.563) and whole areas remain out of bounds. The *jandarma*, who patrol the site continuously, will let you know which areas to avoid.

Brief history

Ani first came to prominence after the local instalment of the Armenian **Gamsarkan** clan during the fifth century. Situated astride a major east–west caravan route, the city prospered, receiving fresh impetus when Ashot III, fifth in the line of the Bagratid kings of Armenia, transferred his **capital** here from Kars in 961. For three generations the kingdom and its capital enjoyed a golden age. Beautified and strengthened militarily, with a population exceeding one hundred thousand, Ani rivalled Baghdad and Constantinople themselves.

By the middle of the eleventh century, however, **wars of succession** took their toll. The Byzantine Empire annexed the city in 1045, but in the process dissolved an effective bulwark against the approaching Selçuks, who took Ani with little resistance in 1064. After the collapse of the Selçuks, the Armenians returned in less than a century. The Pahlavuni and Zakhariad clans ruled over a reduced but still semi-independent Armenia for two more centuries, continuing to endow Ani with churches and monasteries.

The Mongol raids of the thirteenth century, a devasting earthquake in 1319 and realigned trade routes proved mortal blows to both Ani and its hinterland; thereafter the city was gradually abandoned, forgotten until noticed by European travellers of the nineteenth century.

Church of the Redeemer

The **Church of the Redeemer** (Prkitch) was built between 1034 and 1036. In 1957, half the building was sheared away by lightning, so that the remainder, seen from the side, looks uncannily like a stage set, albeit one with carved filigree crosses and Armenian inscriptions. Three metres up on the exterior wall you can see a frieze of a cross on an ornate rectangular background; this is a fine example of the typically

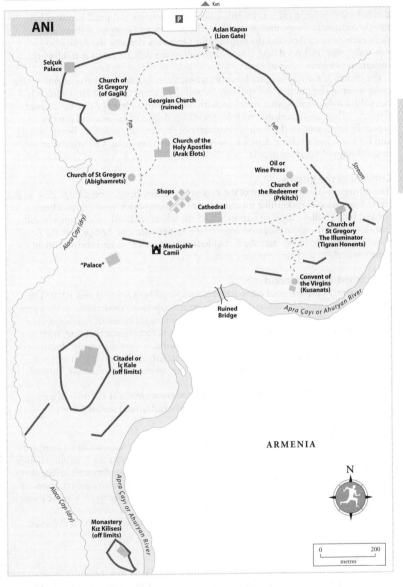

Armenian *khatchkar* (literally "cross-stone") carvings that gave their name to the Kaçkar Mountains.

Church of St Gregory the Illuminator (Tigran Honents)

The charming monastic **Church of St Gregory the Illuminator** (Tigran Honents), Ani's best-preserved monument, is somewhat confusingly one of three dedicated to the saint who brought Christianity to Armenia at the start of the fourth century. The pious foundation of a merchant nobleman in 1215, it's unusually laid out in a rectangle divided width-wise in three (though a colonnaded narthex and small baptistry have mostly collapsed). Its ground plan reflects the prominent Georgian influence in thirteenth-century Ani, and the fact that the Orthodox rite, not the Armenian Apostolic, was celebrated here. The church still sports delicate exterior relief-work, including extensive avian designs.

The church is most rewarding for its **frescoes**, the only ones to survive at Ani, which cover most of the interior and spill out around the current entrance onto what was once the narthex wall, giving the church its Turkish name *Resimli Kilise* or "Painted Church". They are remarkable both for their high degree of realism and fluidity – especially compared to the static iconography of the contemporaneous Byzantines – and for the subject matter, depicting episodes in early Armenian Christianity as well as the doings of ordinary people.

Convent of the Virgins

The thirteenth-century **Convent of the Virgins** (Kusanats) perches on a ledge close to the river. A minuscule, rocket-like rotunda church, contemporary with Tigran Honents, is flanked by a smaller chapel or baptistry, and the whole enclosed by a perimeter wall. Just downstream are the evocative stubs of the ruined medieval **bridge** over the Arpa, though it's unwise (if not actually forbidden) to approach it – the Turkish bank of the river is stoutly fenced and probably mined as well.

The cathedral and around

Ani's elegantly proportioned **cathedral** was completed between 989 and 1010. The architect, one Trdat Mendet, could present rather impressive credentials, having very recently completed restoration of the earthquake-damaged dome of Aya Sofya in Constantinople. However, this is a surprisingly plain, rectangular building, with just the generic blind arcades of Armenian churches and no external apse; the dome, once supported by four massive pillars, has long since vanished. The main entrance was – unusually – not to the west, opposite the apse, but on the side of the nave, through the south wall.

A **replica** of this church was in the early stages of construction at the time of writing, across on the Armenian side of the river, and clearly visible (and audible) from Ani itself.

Menüçehir Camii

Just beyond an excavated area that's thought to have been a medieval street lined with shops, the **Menüçehir Camii** is billed as the earliest Selçuk mosque in Anatolia, though its lack of *mihrab*, alternating red and black stonework and inlaid mosaic ceiling invite suspicions of mixed antecedents. Certainly the view from the ornate gallery across the frontier river fits more with use as a small palace. Slightly southwest, the foundations of a purportedly verified "**palace**" have been exposed.

Beyond the mosque, you'll probably meet the friendly *jandarma*, who will prevent you from wandering any further.

The citadel and Kız Kilisesi

Although Ani's inner **citadel**, or İç Kale, has long languished in a forbidden zone and is likely to remain so, a few travellers – and occasionally entire groups – are lucky enough to sneak through.

Also off-limits is the fairy-tale monastery of **Kız Kilisesi**, spectacularly sited above a sharp curve in the river gorge and originally accessed by a tunnel carved into the rock that has long since eroded.

Church of St Gregory (Abighamrets)

The second **Church of St Gregory** (Abighamrets) in Ani was begun in 1040 by the same individual responsible for the Church of the Redeemer. This rotunda is like no other on the site – instead of just blind arcades in a flat surface, the twelve-sided exterior is pierced by functional recessed vaults, which alternate with the six rounded interior niches to lend extra structural stability.

Church of the Holy Apostles

Ani's so-called "Kervansaray" began life as the eleventh-century **Church of the Holy Apostles** (Arak Elots). Despite ruinous first impressions, it proves a rewarding hybrid Selçuk-Christian monument. At first the church seems to have an odd south-to-north orientation, with a rounded apse at the north end. Then you realize that this is the *kervansaray* part, added at a later date, and that the western half of the church nave is three-quarters crumbled but still discernible. Copious Armenian inscriptions confirm the building's original use, while overhead in the nave, superb four-way ribbing arcs cross an intricate ceiling in a two-colour mosaic pattern, culminating in a stalactite-vaulted dome.

Church of St Gregory of Gagik

The sparse ruins of a third **Church of St Gregory of Gagik**, northwards on the main circuit beyond the Church of the Holy Apostles, was started in 998 by Trdat, architect of the cathedral. Intact, it would have been one of the largest rotundas in medieval Armenia proper, based on the three-storey, seventh-century rotunda at Zvartnots in Armenia. However, it collapsed almost immediately, and today only man-high outer walls, bases of the dome piers and giant column-stumps remain.

Selçuk Palace

Before completing your tour at the Aslan Kapısı, you can stop in at the **Selçuk Palace**, the only indisputably Islamic item at Ani, tucked into the northwest extremity of the ramparts. Since 1988, this has been meticulously rebuilt – the only structure to receive any degree of archeological investigation and maintenance, and a striking example of ultra-nationalist archeology in action.

Karmir Vank

48km east of Kars, towards Oğuzlu • Drive 4.5km east from the junction at Başgedikler, then loop to the right around the hamlet of Bayraktar, fork left and continue another 3.2km to Yağkesen

The region around Ani holds countless remote **churches and castles** – mostly Armenian – besides those at Ani itself, a few of which can be visited with your own transport or a cooperative taxi. The most fascinating is **Karmir Vank** (*Kızıl Kilise* in Turkish – both mean "Red Monastery"), a real beauty and remarkably intact for a thirteenth-century **church**. It's stunningly located to boot, with hay and *tezek* (dung) patties stacked to one side and the land sloping gently down to a stream on the other.

Khtskonk

1hr on foot up the gorge from Digor village, 40km southeast of Kars • Digor is served by fairly frequent dolmuşes, but holds few amenities

The dramatically located church at **Khtskonk** is the closest monument to Digor, just a few kilometres upstream along the Digor Çayı. There were originally five churches (hence the Turkish name, *Beşkilise*) perched on the rim of the narrow canyon, but the rotunda of **St Sergius**, founded in 1029, is the sole survivor. All five were restored in 1878, but at some time between 1920 and 1965 the other four were destroyed either by rolling boulders onto them or with explosives. St Sergius's side walls are rent by fissures, but the dome is still intact and the west wall is covered in intricate Armenian inscriptions, making it the equal of any single monument at Ani.

Mren

71km southeast of Kars on Highway 70 • Around 21km southeast of Digor (itself 50km from Kars), look out for a dirt road heading east, signed for the village of Karabağ; park there, and walk another 50min (4.5km)

The seventh-century cathedral of **Mren** (Mirini), atop a very slight rise near the confluence of the Digor and Arpa streams, was once the focal point of a fair-sized town. That town was abandoned at some point in the fourteenth century, amid İlhanid Mongol raids, but its rubble still litters the immediate surroundings. The cathedral was completed in 640 by David Saharuni, Prince of Armenia, and is one of Turkey's earliest examples of Armenian architecture. Built of alternating red and dark basalt blocks, it weathered the centuries remarkably well before 1920, though the southwest corner and south transept vault have collapsed since then.

The most outstanding **decorative features** include numerous, extravagant *khatchkar*s on the inner and outer south wall. The outer apse and north wall are by contrast featureless, except for a somewhat defaced lintel relief over the north door, showing the *Restoration of the Cross* at Jerusalem in 630, following its removal by the Persians in 614.

ARRIVAL AND INFORMATION

KARS

By plane Kars' airport is 6km south of town. Shuttle buses (₺10) meet Turkish Airlines flights; they can be picked up 1hr 30min before flight time in front of Sınır Turizm, Atatürk Cad 86 (☎0474 212 3838) or Atlas Jet on Faikbey Cad 66 (☎0474 212 4747). A taxi there or back costs around ₺30, and a minibus swings by some hotels for ₺5 (ask at your reception).

Destinations Ankara (2 daily; 1hr 50min); Istanbul (2–3 daily; 2hr 30min).

By train The train station lies 1km southeast of the centre, off Cumhuriyet Cad, on the way to the museum. A taxi to hotels in town should cost around ₺10.

Destinations Ankara (1 daily; 24hr); Erzurum (1 daily; 4hr 30min); Sivas (1 daily; 15hr).

By bus and dolmuş The long-distance *otogar* lies 5km northeast of the centre – *servis* buses link it with bus company ticket offices, most of which can be found on Faikbey Cad, around the nexus with Atatürk Cad. The old *otogar*, on Küçük Kâzımbey Cad, now houses only dolmuşes to nearby Yusufeli, Ardahan, Posof (for Georgia) and Iğdır (change for Doğubeyazıt).

Destinations Ankara (5 daily; 16hr); Ardahan (hourly; 1hr 30min); Artvin (1 daily; 4hr 30min); Çıldır (2 daily; 1hr 30min); Digor (hourly; 45min); Erzurum (hourly; 3hr); Iğdır (hourly; 3hr); Trabzon (2 daily; 8hr).

Tourist office Hakim Ali Rıza Arslan Sok 15 (daily 8.30am–5.30pm; ☎0474 212 2179); it is only really worth visiting for its maps.

SKIING AT CIBILTEPE

Surrounded by conifers, 55km west of Kars, **SARIKAMIŞ** is the coldest town in Turkey. Thick seasonal snow supports the very good **Cibiltepe ski resort**, 3km back east towards the main highway. Facilities comprise just two chair lifts from 2150m up to 2700m, serving two advanced runs, two intermediate ones and one novice piste threading the trees.

Equipment rental is cheap at around ₺35 per day – this, as well as the arrangement of lift passes and instruction, is cheapest at the lift offices rather than the resort's few hotels.

Note that there's also excellent skiing at **Palandöken**, near Erzurum (see box, p.548).

CIBILTEPE ACCOMMODATION

Çamkar At the foot of the lifts ☎0474 413 5259. This ostensibly three-star hotel offers medium-sized, standard units in a chalet-style structure with a sauna and licensed restaurant. Half board ₺280

Toprak At the foot of the lifts ☎0474 413 4111, ⚲toprakhotels.com. Relatively new hotel that's by far the most appealing option in the resort. It's dear but

still good value, with attractive rooms exuding a sort of watered-down Alpine feel. ₺350

Turistik Sarıkamış Halk Cad 64, Sarıkamış ☎0474 413 4338. Though not in the resort itself, this simple hotel in Sarıkamış is the cheapest option if you intend to ski at Cibiltepe, with a funky rustic-style lobby and spacious rooms. ₺100

ACCOMMODATION

Accommodation options in Kars have improved immeasurably of late, thanks to the construction (or renovation) of a swathe of **mid-range** facilities. Some cheaper establishments remain beyond the pale – if you're really keen to save a few lira, you'll find the very cheapest in the grimy streets surrounding the market.

Büyük Kale Atatürk Cad 60 ☎0474 212 6444, ⓦbuyukkalehotel.com. Swish affair with large, well-appointed rooms that provide excellent value. Breakfasts are prodigious, often featuring no fewer than twelve kinds of local cheese, and are taken with a commanding view of the city. ₺200

Kar's Halitpaşa Cad 79 ☎0474 212 1616, ⓦkarsotel .com. A boutique hotel in eastern Anatolia – wonders will never cease. It's a highly atmospheric place, if rather pricey; the eight muted-grey rooms feature flatscreen TVs, super-comfy beds and powerful showers. There's also an excellent restaurant downstairs. ₺420

★**Kent** Bakırcılar Cad 72 ☎0474 223 6666, ⓦhotelkentani.com. Good budget choice by the market, with pleasant, clean rooms and English-speaking management. Breakfast is served on a terrace that provides castle views – if you like the honey, ask at reception for a jar of the stuff, yours for ₺35/kilo and made by their very own pet bees (which live in the countryside, not at the hotel). ₺100

Konak Faikbey Cad 79 ☎0474 212 3332, ⓦkarskonakotel.com. Strengthening the case for what appears to be an addiction to alliteration among Kars hotel owners, this relatively new spot makes an excellent mid-range option. Not all rooms have windows, but even if that's your only choice, the darkness is compensated for by pleasing decor and spacious bathrooms. ₺140

EATING

Fortunately the **restaurant** scene in Kars is excellent, and much better than its accommodation. One Russian legacy remains – despite the city's far-flung location, it's surprisingly easy to get **alcohol** with your meal, while most shops are also licensed. There are also a couple of dull bars on Atatürk Cad.

★**Antep** Atatürk Cad 7 ☎0474 223 0741. This rather ordinary-looking restaurant is known for doling out extraordinarily good *pide* for ₺10 and up – they're simply delectable, which goes some way to account for the fact that there are now two smaller branches elsewhere in town. Why not go the whole hog and savour these takes on Turkish pizza – if you're brave enough – over a glass of spicy turnip juice (₺2.50).

Gaziantep Baklava Atatürk Cad 39 ☎0474 223 2954. The most appealing *pastane* in town, a tiny place serving small rounds of *baklava* and ice cream for just ₺6. Ask nicely and you may get a couple of extra pastry-sweets for free. Daily 7am–10pm.

Istihkam By the Kars Çayı. A terrific escape from Kars' often grimy streets, this relaxed, outdoor café allows you to drain a tea (₺1) or suck on a nargile (₺10), with a splendid view of the citadel from some seats. Snack food also available. Daily 8am–11pm.

★**Ocak Başi** Atatürk Cad 156 ☎0474 212 0056, ⓦkaygisizocakbasi.com. The more appealing of two identically named restaurants on Atatürk Cad, notable for its mock-troglodytic style. Prices are surprisingly reasonable, and portions large – try the superb *patlıcan kebap* for ₺18 or give the *çiğ köfte* (spicy paste in a wrap) a whirl. Daily 10am–10pm.

DIRECTORY

Consulate Azerbaijan, Ordu Cad 9 (Mon–Fri 9am–4pm; ☎0474 223 1361).

Hamam The Kızılay Hamamı (men 6.30am–11pm; women noon–5pm; ₺15) is northeast of the town centre on Faikbey Cad.

Post office The main PTT branch (open late into evenings) is next to the tourist office; there's a useful, more central *çarşı* branch on Kâzımpaşa Cad.

10

The Euphrates and Tigris basin

NEMRUT DAĞI

The Euphrates and Tigris basin

The mountain-rimmed basin of the Euphrates and Tigris rivers is perhaps the most exotic part of Turkey, offering travellers a heady mix of atmospheric ancient sites and bustling Middle East-style towns. Forming the northern rim of ancient Mesopotamia (literally "between two rivers"), the region has been of importance since the Neolithic period. The eastern boundaries of the Roman and Byzantine empires lay here, and the two rivers were crossed by Arab Muslim invaders from the south and east after the birth of Islam in 632 AD. Thereafter, almost everybody of any import in Middle Eastern affairs seems to have passed through the region: Crusaders, Armenians, Selçuks, Turcomans, Mongols and finally the French, who invaded southeastern Turkey in World War I.

Arab influence is strong in the region, but even here **Kurds** predominate and ethnic Turks are in a distinct minority. Traditionally, smallholding farmers and herdsmen scratched a living from this unrewarding land, though the new dams of the **Southeastern Anatolia Project** (see p.579 & p.616) have dramatically improved the fertility of the area. However, the economic fortunes of much of the region have been seriously affected by the ongoing war in bordering **Syria**, where Syrian Kurds and Islamic State (ISIS) battled for control of Syrian lands bordering Turkey throughout 2014 and 2015. Many **refugees** fleeing the conflict have been housed in camps along the border, while others have swollen the population of cities such as Gaziantep and Şanlıurfa. The ongoing civil war in Syria and the separatist sympathies of some Kurds means there is often a security presence in the area and a possibility of unrest – particularly in the frontier zone, so it makes sense to investigate the current situation before you decide to travel here. The British Foreign and Commonwealth Office and the foreign offices of many other countries have issued **travel warnings** to the region (see box, p.577); the Crime and Personal Safety section of this guide (see p.58) also offers additional information.

However while you should exercise caution, you may well find that this fascinating region feels welcoming and pleasantly threat-free once on the ground. First stop coming from the west is the city of **Gaziantep**, booming on its new-found industrial wealth. East of here, the road shoots across the plain to cross the River Euphrates at bleached **Birecik** before cutting through rocky uplands to the pious town of **Şanlıurfa** – well worth a couple of days' sightseeing. It's also a good base for exploring **Harran**, an evocative village of beehive-shaped houses, and the extraordinary Neolithic temple complex of **Göbekli Tepe**.

Northeast of Gaziantep, the spectacular mountaintop funerary sanctuary of **Nemrut Dağı** fully justifies a pilgrimage, though the main base for reaching it from the south is scruffy **Kahta**. Malatya, to the north, makes for a more attractive gateway to Nemrut, and boasts the nearby attractions of **Eski Malatya** and **Aslantepe**.

Highlights

❶ **Zeugma Mosaic Museum** A magnificent collection of Roman-era mosaics, rescued from the drowned site of Zeugma and displayed in a state-of-the-art museum in Gaziantep. **See p.578**

❷ **Şanlıurfa Archeology and Mosaic Museum** Cavernous, cutting-edge museum showcases incredible finds from Göbekli Tepe and beautiful mosaic floor panels displayed in situ. **See p.587**

❸ **Göbekli Tepe** This unique hilltop Neolithic temple complex, with its intricately carved T-shaped monoliths, challenges established views of human development. **See p.589**

❹ **Nemrut Dağı** One of the classic images of Turkey – massive stone heads of Hellenistic deities glare out from a remote mountaintop

sanctuary. **See p.594**

❺ **Diyarbakır** Walk around the mighty basalt walls of this predominantly Kurdish city, high above its medieval alleys. **See p.599**

❻ **Syrian Orthodox churches** Catch a service in Diyarbakır, Mardin or Midyat, and experience a liturgy that has remained virtually unchanged for 1500 years. **See p.604, p.609 & p.614**

❼ **Mardin** This hilltop town of beautiful Arab-style houses and graceful mosques affords stunning views over the Mesopotamian plain. **See p.607**

❽ **Hasankeyf** A dam-threatened medieval city, spectacularly situated on a soaring cliff overlooking the green Tigris. **See p.615**

HIGHLIGHTS ARE MARKED ON THE MAP ON P.576

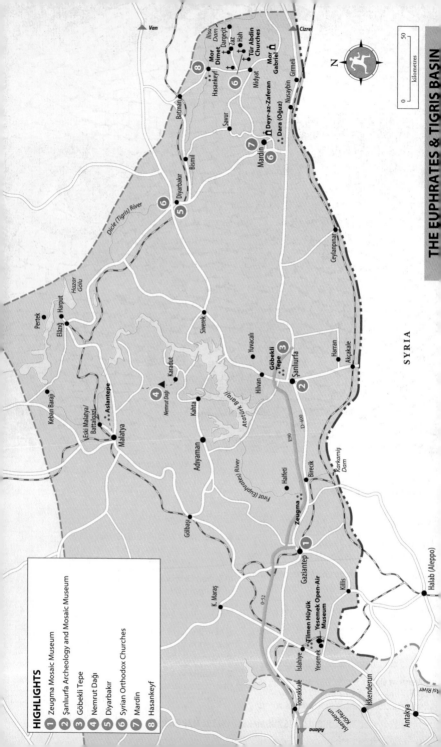

THE EUPHRATES & TIGRIS BASIN

N

0   50
kilometres

HIGHLIGHTS

1. Zeugma Mosaic Museum
2. Şanlıurfa Archeology and Mosaic Museum
3. Göbekli Tepe
4. Nemrut Dağı
5. Diyarbakır
6. Syrian Orthodox Churches
7. Mardin
8. Hasankeyf

SYRIA

Van

Cizre

Ilısu
Dam

Mor
Dimet
Dargeçit
Hah
Zaz

Tür Abdin
Churches

Mor
Gabriel

Midyat

Deyr-az-Zafaran

Dara (Oğuz)

Nusaybin   Girmeli

Hasankeyf

Batman

Savur

Bismil

Mardin

Diyarbakır

Dicle (Tigris) River

Hazar
Gölü

Pertek

Harput

Elazığ

Keban Barajı

Eski Malatya/
Battalgazi

Aslantepe

Malatya

Karadut

Nemrut Dağı

Kahta

Adıyaman

Atatürk Barajı

Fırat (Euphrates) River

Gölbaşı

K. Maraş

İslahiye

Toprakkale

Yesemek

Tilmen Höyük

Yesemek Open-Air
Museum

Gaziantep

Kilis

Halab (Aleppo)

Asi River

İskenderun

İskenderun
Körfezi

Antakya

Adana

Siverek

Yuvacalı

Göbekli
Tepe

Şanlıurfa

Harran

Akçakale

Ceylanpınar

Hilvan

Birecik

Halfeti

Karkamış
Dam

D-400

E90

D-52

TRAVEL WARNINGS

Owing to the civil war in nearby **Syria**, and clashes between the Turkish security forces and **PKK** (Kurdish Worker's Party) supporters or their affiliates, the foreign offices of many countries have issued **travel warnings** for several places covered in this chapter. At the time of writing, the British Foreign and Commonwealth Office warned against all travel to within 10km of the **Syrian frontier**, a zone which includes Tilmen Hüyük and Yesemek Open-Air Museum (see p.582), Harran (see p.590) and Dara (see p.613). They also advised against all but essential travel to **Gaziantep**, **Mardin** and **Şanlıurfa** provinces, as well as **Diyarbakır**. During the update of this guide, all these places were relatively peaceful, but you should think carefully before travelling around this region. Bear in mind, too, that things can and do change very quickly in this part of the world, and an area that was off-limits one month may well be visitable the next – and vice versa. If you do travel here, it's critical to **do some research before you go**: read all you can about the current situation, check the relevant advisories, and make sure that your travel insurance will cover your trip. We have given a wider coverage of security issues in Turkey in this guide's Basics section (see p.58 & p.59), and explored the political and social background to the situation in Contexts (see p.674 & p.678).

11

From either Şanlıurfa or Malatya, it's a journey of half a day or less to **Diyarbakır**, Turkey's most overtly Kurdish city, on the banks of the River Tigris. Famed for its 6km black-basalt city walls, added to the UNESCO World Heritage site list in 2015, Diyarbakır is also peppered with fine mosques and churches. To the south lies the region's tourist "capital", **Mardin**, with its atmospheric collection of vernacular houses set on a crag overlooking the Syrian plain. East of here, the **Tür Abdin** plateau, scattered with monasteries and churches, is home to the remnants of Turkey's Syrian Orthodox Christian population. At its heart lies **Midyat**, a town of elegant mansions and churches that still draw small congregations, their faith kept alive largely by the monastery of **Mar Gabriel** to the south. Between Midyat and Diyarbakır are the evocative ruins of **Hasankeyf**, breathtakingly sited on the Tigris, but set to disappear beneath the waters of the İlisu Dam by 2018 (see p.616).

Getting around is easy, with good bus links between all the major towns and new motorways like the 0-52 and 0-54 and E-90, which will speed things up dramatically. Decent **accommodation** is available virtually everywhere, but bear in mind that summers are scorching – you'll want to have air conditioning in your hotel room.

Gaziantep

Rapidly expanding **GAZIANTEP**, with a population approaching a million and a half, is the wealthiest city in the region. A principal beneficiary of the GAP project, it derives its income largely from textile production and agriculture (and is especially famed for its **pistachio nuts**). There's lots on offer for visitors here: many of the city's beautiful, pale-stone historic buildings have been restored and made accessible, with explanatory display boards in English, and Gaziantep is also touted as Turkey's foodie capital. The **Zeugma Mosaic Museum**, whose collection rivals the best in the world, is simply stunning; it alone would make a trip here worthwhile. However, Gaziantep's role as a major trade entrepôt and tourist destination has been adversely affected by the civil war in nearby **Syria** – Aleppo, Syria's second city, is just 100km away. With ISIS operating just across the frontier at the time of writing, cross-border trade had virtually dried up, while visitor numbers plummeted by some eighty percent in 2015, thanks in part to FCO warnings against all but essential travel to the city (see box above). Nonetheless, life here continues as normal, and the city's population remain very welcoming to visitors.

Gaziantep has been successively **occupied** by the Hittites, Assyrians, Persians, Hellenistic Greeks, Romans, Selçuks, Crusaders, Byzantines and Arabs. Locals still

call it "Antep", a corruption of the Arab *ayn teb* ("good spring"); the prefix "Gazi" ("warrior for Islam") was added to honour the Turkish Nationalist forces who withstood a ten-month siege by the French in 1920. For centuries Gaziantep held a mixed **Muslim** and **Christian Armenian** population. The Armenians were expelled during the vicissitudes of World War 1, but their attractive old quarter remains on a hill above the prominent city-centre Atatürk statue. The traditional Muslim **bazaar quarter**, centred on the castle, lies a short walk northeast of the Atatürk statue.

Zeugma Mosaic Museum

Haci Sani Konukloğlu Bul • Tues–Sun: April–Oct 8am–6.30pm; Nov–March 9am–5pm • ₺10 • Catch bus #5 from in front of the Yaşar Büfe on İstasyon Cad (₺2.25)

The superb **Zeugma Mosaic Museum**, located on the ring road north of the city centre, exhibits a superb collection of mosaics rescued from the once-opulent Hellenistic/Roman border city of **Zeugma** (see p.583), now virtually submerged by the Birecik dam on the Euphrates. It's well worth catching the free, 15-minute **video** on the history of Zeugma, shown at regular intervals to the left of the entry turnstiles.

On the **ground floor**, where visitors enter, arrows direct you along the best route around an incredible array of mosaic floor panels, taken from the houses of wealthy citizens at Zeugma. Particularly impressive are the re-creations of Roman peristyle villas, complete with their original mosaic flooring and wall frescoes. The mosaics themselves, most of which portray scenes from Classical Greek mythology, including Perseus and Andromeda, Eros and Psyche, and Pasiphae and Daedelus, are well labelled in English.

Below ground level, a section is devoted to the bathhouse of a gymnasium complex, including mosaics, water pipes, toilets and the under-floor heating system – and a magnificent bronze statue of the god of war, Mars. The **first floor** holds yet more wonderful mosaics, including a superb scene of Zeus kidnapping Europa. The mosaic panel that has become a symbol of today's city, the enigmatic face of a young female known as the "Gypsy Girl", gets a darkened room all to itself.

The Kale

Castle Closed at time of writing • **Panorama Museum** Daily 8.30am–4.30pm • ₺1

An imposing **kale** (castle) dominates Gaziantep from the eastern hill, which is itself a partly artificial mound dating back to at least 3600 BC. The structure, with its twelve bastions, probably started to take its present form during the Roman period, and was certainly enlarged by Justinian in the sixth century. What you see today, though, is largely Mamluk.

Although the castle itself was closed for renovation at the time of writing (work was slated to be completed by 2017), the **Panorama Museum**, housed in an approach tunnel adjacent to the main gateway, remains open. It gives a vivid (if very one-sided) portrayal of the successful Turkish defence of the city against the French and Armenian irregulars who attempted to take Antep in 1920.

11

The bazaar quarter

Gaziantep's **bazaar** area, north of the *kale*, is home to several *hans*, including the attractive **Zincirli Han**, now given over to tourist-orientated shops, and the over-restored **Şira Han**. Between them lies a more interesting collection of lanes and alleys, lined with stalls piled high with pungent spices, the ubiquitous pistachio, decorative strings of the dried vegetables so crucial to Gaziantep's famous cuisine (peppers, aubergine and okra), and more unusual items such as *tarhana* (dried yoghurt used for soups) and *meyan* (liquorice root used in sherbet).

There are also some attractive mosques, with Syrian-style enclosed balconies atop the minarets. Look out in particular for the nineteenth-century **Alauddevle Camii**, south of the castle, with its bands of contrasting black and white stone, designed by an Armenian architect. The Ottoman-era **Tahtani** and **Şirvani** mosques, south and west of the *kale* respectively, are also worth seeking out. Many of these fine buildings have been restored over the last few years, with handy explanatory signboards in Turkish, Arabic and English. Craftsmen still manufacture furniture inlaid with *sedef* (mother-of-pearl) and beat copper in the bazaar.

THE SOUTHEASTERN ANATOLIA PROJECT (GAP)

The colossally expensive Güneydoğu Anadolu Projesi (GAP), or **Southeastern Anatolia Project**, was begun in 1974 with the aim of improving economic conditions in Turkey's impoverished southeast. Centred on the massive **Atatürk Dam**, the fourth largest in the world, the US$32 billion scheme has diverted waters from the Euphrates and Tigris to irrigate vast swathes of previously barren land and generate much-needed hydroelectric power.

In terms of the local benefits of GAP, the improvement to **agriculture** is apparent from the main road: eastwards from Gaziantep, new pistachio and olive plantations flourish, and cotton is being grown around Harran. While this has benefitted large landowners able to secure state bank loans to buy fertilizer and machinery, however, smaller farmers have seen few improvements. Many have given up agriculture altogether and migrated to the cities to work as unskilled labourers.

Environmentalists point out the scheme's other pitfalls, including local **climate change** caused by evaporation from the reservoirs; depletion of the soil from the overuse of artificial **fertilizers**; the lowering of the **water table**; and severe loss of **wildlife habitats**.

The region's **archeological** heritage has been hit, too. While some artefacts have been painstakingly excavated and relocated – note especially the wonderful finds from Zeugma now on display in Gaziantep – much has vanished forever beneath the waters.

Medusa Museum

Şakır Sok 9 • Daily 9am–6pm • ₺4

Set in a pretty old courtyard house just west of the castle, the **Medusa Glass Artefacts and Archeology Museum** (Medusa Cam Eserler Arkeoloji Müzesi) displays a private collection of artefacts, spanning several millennia. Exquisite objects on show include a beautiful Islamic-period gold deer figurine; toy terracotta war chariots from the Hittite-era; and gorgeous Greek and Roman figurines. Among the more mundane items is a Roman bread-marking stamp, while there's plenty of Roman glass in the upstairs room. The courtyard holds a welcome café, where you can watch caged monkeys tumble and listen to the cooing of ornamental pigeons.

Emine Göğüş Culinary Museum

Karagöz • Daily 9am–6pm • ₺1

Housed in an old stone dwelling tucked into the backstreets south of the *kale*, the **Emine Göğüş Culinary Museum** (Emine Göğüş Mutfağı Müzesi) gives a fascinating insight into Gaziantep's cuisine, with excellent display boards in English which explain the ingredients that give the local food its distinctive flavours, and what implements are used to prepare the region's famous dishes.

The former Armenian quarter

Gaziantep's former **Armenian Christian quarter** stretches down a hill west of the Atatürk statue. It boasts a large number of old courtyard houses, each with its own well, food cellars and stabling. Many are now trendy cafés and boutique hotels, with a few former churches sprinkled among them.

Hasan Süzer Ethnography Museum

Hanifioğlu Sok 64 • Daily 8am–noon & 1–5pm • ₺3

The **Hasan Süzer Ethnography Museum** (Hasan Süzer Etnografi Müzesi) freeze-frames the life of an upper-class Antep family in the 1930s. Successive rooms are laid out in traditional style, though the effect is somewhat spoiled by the incongruous mannequins. A basement below the courtyard was originally used to store food, while above it there's a German-made motorcycle that's said to have belonged to Lawrence of Arabia.

Kurtuluş Camii

The monumental **Kurtuluş Camii** (Independence Mosque), perched near the top of the hill, is claimed to be the largest Armenian church in the Middle East. Built in 1892 as the Church of the Virgin Mary, it features black-and-white stone trim, and restrained carvings around the windows. Ongoing restoration is scheduled for completion in 2016.

Gaziantep City Museum

Atatürk Bul • Tues–Sun 9am–6.30pm • Free

In the state-of-the-art **Gaziantep City Museum** (Gaziantep Kent Müzesi), assorted exhibits, mock-ups and video presentations offer valuable background information on the city's recent history, culture and economy. Interesting, mannequin-filled tableaux depict bygone artisans at work. Headsets with English-language commentary are available. The attractive courtyard behind the museum is home to the tempting *Beyazhan* restaurant (see p.582).

ARRIVAL AND DEPARTURE   **GAZIANTEP**

By plane From Sazgan airport, 20km southeast of Gaziantep, taxis (₺50) or Havaş buses (₺10) run (daily 2am–10pm) to a spot just west of the Büyükşehir Belediyesi (Municipality Building), 500m northwest of the city centre. The THY office is at the airport (☎0342 582 1045). Most travel agencies sell tickets for all domestic carriers – try

Fırsat Turizm on Suburcu Cad 16/A (☎ 0342 232 8825). Destinations Ankara (3 daily with Anadolujet; 1hr 10min); Antalya (3 weekly direct with Sunexpress; 1hr 15min); Istanbul (3 daily direct with Anadolujet, 1hr 40min; 1 daily with Onurair, 1hr 35min; 5 daily with THY, 1hr 50min); İzmir (6 weekly with Sunexpress; 1hr 50min).

By bus Gaziantep's *otogar*, 5km northwest of the centre, is served by free service buses, blue or yellow minibuses (₺2.5) and taxis (₺25) into town. Get off at Hükümet Konağı, near the junction of Suburcu and Hürriyet caddesis, close to most of the hotels and restaurants.

Destinations Adana via Mersin (10 daily; 4hr); Adiyaman (for Kahta/Mt Nemrut; 8 daily; 2hr 30min); Ankara (12 daily; 10hr); Antakya (8 daily; 4hr); Diyarbakır (8 daily; 5hr); Malatya (5 daily; 4hr); Mardin (5 daily; 6hr); Şanlıurfa (11 daily; 2hr 30min).

By train The train station stands at the north end of İstasyon Cad, 2km north of the centre. In theory, dolmuşes and trams run into town (both ₺2.5), but train services were suspended at the time of writing due to major works and the Syrian conflict.

Car rental Car rental outfits abound on Ordu Cad. One reliable outfit is Maksi, Ordu Cad 13/A (☎ 0342 336 2694) with rates from ₺65 per day.

INFORMATION

Tourist office In a dark-glass block in Yüzüncü Yıl Parkı (Mon–Fri 8am–noon & 1–5pm; ☎ 0342 230 5969); good town maps plus lots of other literature. The main PTT is just west of the *Adliye* building.

11

ACCOMMODATION

Gaziantep holds a healthy mix of business-orientated and boutique-style hotels, but there's less choice at the budget end of the market. The **boutique hotels**, all housed in period Ottoman or Armenian dwellings, are either in the former Armenian quarter or the bazaar.

★**Anadolu Evleri** Köroğlu Sok 6 ☎ 0342 220 9525, ⓦ anadoluevleri.com. The most authentic of the boutique hotel conversions, with high-ceilinged old rooms lined with period fitted cupboards. Bathrooms are cavernous and the collection of old phones, radios and carpets is a delight. There's a cosy bar off the courtyard, plus bags of atmosphere, and the castle is just a few minutes' walk. Single rooms cost little more than half the doubles. ₺**180**

Evin Kayacak Sok 11 ☎ 0342 231 3492. Cheapest of several budget options on this quiet street, handily situated close to the modern centre yet on the fringes of the former Armenian quarter. It's a friendly place, with small but passable en-suite rooms in an older building. Great value. ₺**60**

Hidiroğlu Konak Hidir Sok 19, Şahinbey ☎ 0342 230 4555, ⓦ hidiroglukonak.com. This mid-range boutique hotel, set in a a period house on the edge of the former Armenian quarter, has just six individually sized and priced rooms set around a pleasant courtyard. More expensive rooms have offshoot living rooms, all boast stone floors and high wooden ceilings. It's very friendly, though bathrooms are small and it is difficult to keep the floors dry. ₺**180**

Princess Çamurcu Sok 26 ☎ 0342 231 6565, ⓦ Gaziantepprincesshotel.com. The best thing about this standard three-star place is its rooftop restaurant, which has a great view across to the (very) nearby castle and of the city roofscape. The rooms are underwhelming but tick all the boxes in terms of comfort, making it good value for what it is. ₺**120**

Tepebaşı Konakları Prof Dr Metin Sözen Cad 17 ☎ 0342 231 0122, ⓦ tepebasikonaklari.com. A fine 28-bed boutique hotel, in an excellent elevated location on a hill behind the former Armenian Church of St Mary's (Kurtuluş Camii). Tastefully furnished with period pieces, it boasts natural wood floors, exposed stone walls and a/c. The only letdown is its exposed courtyard. ₺**135**

Tuğcan Atatürk Bul 34 ☎ 0342 220 4323, ⓦ tugcanhotel.com.tr. Plush five-star establishment, with spacious rooms tastefully furnished in contemporary style – and a pillow menu for the fussy sleeper. Perhaps the main reason to stay is the fancy spa and indoor pool, and the fact that standard rates are quite reasonable at slack periods. ₺**180**

★**Zeynep Hanım Konağı** Eski Sinema Sok 17 ☎ 0342 232 0207, ⓦ zeynephanimkonagi.com. Fourteen rooms set around the small courtyard of a former Armenian house provide compact and comfy accommodation in this atmospheric part of town. The composite stone cladding applied to many interior walls jars a little, but that's a small gripe, compensated for by the tea- and coffee-making facilities, flatscreen TVs, friendly, professional staff – and the chance to explore the cave-like cellars hollowed from the natural rock. ₺**150**

EATING AND DRINKING

Gaziantep is unrivalled in Turkey for **sweets**, particularly pistachio-based pastries like *baklava* and *fıstık sarma*. Not surprisingly given the proximity of Syria, much of its cuisine is Arab-influenced, with many savoury dishes spicier and more sour than western Turkish dishes – the pizza-like *lahmacun* here is the best in the land.

RESTAURANTS

Bayazhan Atatürk Bul 119, Şahinbey ☎0342 221 0212, ⓦbayazhan.com.tr. Located in the large, airy courtyard of an historic *han* behind the Gaziantep City Museum, this is actually an eating complex, including a *meyhane* where you get an alcoholic drink with your meal; a cavernous restaurant; and the *SPR* pub. Turkish and regional specialities are served in all, and prices are quite reasonable. Try the stuffed dried aubergine (₺10) or creamy hummus (₺12). Daily11am–midnight.

★**İmam Çağdaş** Kale Cıvarı Uzun Çarşısı 49 ☎0342 231 2678, ⓦimamcagdas.com. This long-established traditional kebab-cum-*lahmacun* restaurant is best at lunchtimes, when it's thronging with local shopkeepers, craftsmen and shoppers. The *lahmacun* are spicy, huge and delicious (₺3), and the *ayran* is served up in a tinned copper bowl. Its *baklava* is famed even in Gaziantep, the home of the stuff. Daily 11am–10pm.

Kadir Usta Eyüpoğlu Mah Eblehan Cad 25 ☎0342 220 6839. Close to the Kurtuluş Camii, this cheap and cheerful place was established in 1966. Despite its humble origins, some of Turkey's top celebrities have eaten here, choosing from *lahmacun*, kebabs, or the local meaty soup, *beyran*. Some outside tables, and a pleasant roof terrace for warm summer evenings. Daily 7am–10pm.

Katmerci Zekeriya Usta Körükçu Sokak, Hilmi Gecidi 16, Şahinbey ☎0342 230 0971. Gaziantep is renowned nationwide for its delicous *katmer*, a concoction of thin layers of pastry dough filled with locally grown pistachios, cream and syrup. One thick, tortilla-wrap sized *katmer* (₺10) is enough for two people – most locals head here for breakfast, but it makes a great mid-morning snack too. Daily 6am–noon.

Yörem Lokantası Sok 15, Ali Api Apt. İncili Pınar Mah

☎0342 220 4609. Run by an Antep émigré returned from Europe, this place has a more refined decor and ambience than the average Gaziantep restaurant. Wooden blinds, a high ceiling, white tablecloths and the like complement the delicious regional food such as *firik* (a smoked bulgar wheat dish), served up by smartly attired waiters. Prices are great too, with kebabs from ₺12. No alcohol. Daily 10.30am–11pm.

BARS AND CAFÉS

Ekim 29 Çekemoğlu Çıkmaz, Gaziler Cad ☎0342 220 4885. This old Armenian stone dwelling, set around a shady courtyard, is the place to come for a refreshing cold beer and to listen to recorded or live (mainly weekend nights) Turkish folk music. Beers are ₺10 – though watch out for the price of the snacks, which are brought to your table (without your being asked) to go with the drinks. Daily noon–midnight.

Papirus Noter Sok 10 ☎0342 220 3279. Among the first of the rash of nargile cafés in the former Armenian quarter, this has a great vine-shaded courtyard that's always busy with middle-class locals and students. The empty upstairs rooms hold some peeling, over-the-top nineteenth-century European-style murals. Be sure to try the *menengiç* (wild pistachio) coffee for ₺17. Daily 10am–10pm.

Tahmiş Kahvesi Elmacı Pazarı Civarı ☎0342 232 8977. The city's oldest coffee house dates back to the seventeenth century. Dark wood ceilings and polished wood floors set the traditional tone of the place, as do the old boys playing *tavla* (backgammon) under the incongruously large TV. A range of traditional coffees (from ₺6) and herbal teas, plus local delicacies such as *içli köfte* and *yuvarlama*. Daily 9am–10pm.

DIRECTORY

Hamam The Ottoman-era Naib Hamam, tucked beneath the northern face of the *kale*, offers an atmospheric cleanse for ₺16; scrub and massage an extra ₺14 (daily: women 9.30am–5pm, men 6pm–midnight).

Hospital Housed in old American mission buildings, the Sev Amerikan Hastanesi on Yuksek Sok 3, Tepebaşı Mah (☎0850 222 2224) is the city's best hospital.

Southwest of Gaziantep

A couple of important archeological sites southwest of Gaziantep, **Tilmen Hüyük** and **Yesemek Open-Air Museum**, can only be visited by car. The best opportunity to do so comes if you are travelling to or from Antakya (see p.399), but check the latest **travel advice** (see p.577) as both sites are very close to the Syrian frontier.

Tilmen Hüyük

90km southwest of Gaziantep and 10km east of İslahiye • Daily dawn–dusk • Free

Close to the Syrian border, **Tilmen Hüyük** – a *hüyük* is a settlement mound – is rich in material from the late Chalcolithic, Bronze and Iron ages. An important Hittite settlement between the eighteenth and fifteenth centuries BC, it's set beside a lazy, reed-fringed and frog-filled river in a broad valley that's actually a northern extension of the African Rift Valley. Unlike so many of the settlement mounds that litter Turkey's Syrian borderlands, this one has been lovingly excavated and interpreted, with informative **display boards** to explain the surviving walls, steps and other features.

Yesemek Open-Air Museum

22km south of İslahiye, beyond Tilmen Hüyük · Daily dawn–dusk · ₺2

Between the fourteenth and seventh centuries BC, the remarkable **Yesemek Open-Air Museum** (Yesemek Açık Hava Müzesi) was a quarry-cum-workshop that churned out monumental statuary to be distributed around the Hittite world. Most common are sphinxes and lions (the latter of which often flanked temple doorways), but there are many other statue types as well.

The statues, which weigh many tonnes, were only quarried and roughly carved here before being transported to their destination to be finished off. Those left have been attractively lined up on a green hillside above a stream. The modern village of **Yesemek** lies beyond the café at the entrance.

East of Gaziantep: towards Şanlıurfa

The newly completed 0-52 toll motorway and the old D-400 link Gaziantep with the next destination for most travellers, **Şanlıurfa**. Either en route, or using Gaziantep as a base, it's worth also trying to see the site of **Zeugma**, where the magnificent mosaics on display in Gaziantep were found, and the relaxed village of **Halfeti**, on the banks of the Euphrates.

Zeugma

50km east of Gaziantep, 7km north of the village of Dutlu · Daily 8am–5pm · Free

For anyone intrigued by the incredible mosaics showcased in the Zeugma Mosaic Museum (see p.578), it's worth – assuming you have your own transport – visiting the waterside excavations at Hellenistic/Roman **ZEUGMA**, where they were found. In 2000, shortly before the Birecik Dam waters submerged most of the ancient villas here, an international archeological rescue mission recovered many of the mosaics that are now displayed in Gaziantep. A couple of villas left above the new waterline, named after the scenes depicted on their major mosaics – Dionysus and Danae – have been excavated, and are now housed under an impressive steel-and-mesh building. There's a café and toilets at the site entrance, pleasantly set above the reservoir.

Birecik

40km east of Gaziantep · Served by dolmuşes to and from Gaziantep's *otogar* (₺7), and Şanlıurfa (₺8)

The D-400 crosses the broad Euphrates River at **BIRECIK**. Set on a rise below the striking pale limestone bluffs backing the river, Birecik's **castle** was founded during the eleventh century, and served as a frontier outpost for the Crusader state of Edessa. Birecik is also the hub for onward transport to atmospheric Halfeti (see below).

Halfeti

The spectacular old village of **HALFETI**, 110km east of Gaziantep, is now partially submerged beneath the waters of the Birecik dam, set in a gorge carved by the Euphrates. Most visitors come to take one of the regular boat trips upstream (see below), along the dramatic dam-flooded gorge, to see the impressive remains of the medieval castle of **Rumkale** (closed for restoration at the time of writing).

Halfeti has a few simple pensions and makes for a pleasantly relaxed hangout after the rigours of city-to-city travelling in the southeast. Enjoyable restaurants line the palm-fringed waterfront in Halfeti itself, most serving charcoal-grilled *şarbot*, a kind of catfish caught in the river. Behind the waterfront, lost in a canopy of mulberry, walnut, fig, olive and pomegranate trees, lie old honey-coloured houses once inhabited by Armenians.

ARRIVAL AND INFORMATION   HALFETI

By dolmuş Halfeti is served by regular dolmuşes from Birecik (daily 7.30am–7pm; ₺6).
Boat trips Boat trips from Halfeti to Rumkale cost round

₺60 per boat-load; there are no set times, with boats departing as soon as they're full.

ACCOMMODATION

Fırat Pansiyon ⊕0530 886 4945, ⊛halfetifirat pansiyon.com. Moderately upmarket seven-room pension with individually furnished en-suite rooms complete with LCD TVs and a/c. There's a nice courtyard terrace to sit out in, with views of the dammed Euphrates and town. **₺120**

Şitamet Pansiyon ⊕0535 706 6029. This rudimentary but charming pension consists of a few simple rooms in the home of (basic) English-speaker Aydın. Find him at the municipally run local produce store Turizm Satış Noktaları, opposite the Atatürk statue. **₺50**

Şanlıurfa and around

The name of **ŞANLIURFA**, or "Glorious Urfa" – most locals just say Urfa – commemorates resistance to the French invasion and occupation of 1918–20. A place of pilgrimage for many religions, and the reputed birthplace of the prophet Abraham, its chief attraction until recently was its beautiful **mosque** complex, reflected in the limpid waters of a sacred pool. Opened in 2015, the city's cutting-edge **Archeology Museum** should prove just as compelling an attraction, splendidly displaying as it does the remarkable finds from the prehistoric temple-sanctuary of nearby **Göbekli Tepe**.

Urfa has a distinctly Middle Eastern atmosphere. Much of the population is Kurdish, a significant minority Arab, and you'll find the bazaars full of veiled, henna-tattooed women, and men wearing baggy trousers and traditional headdresses. Although one of Turkey's fastest-growing cities, thanks largely to the money generated by the GAP project, Urfa still ranks very low in terms of socio-economic development, and agriculture remains the major industry. The influx of huge numbers of refugees from the **conflict** in nearby Syria has inevitably exacerbated matters, as has the instability in the border region, highlighted by a major ISIS suicide-bomb attack on Suruç, 43km southwest of Urfa, in July 2015. As a consequence the FCO and others have warned against all but essential travel to Şanlıurfa (see box, p.577).

Hotels, money-exchange and ATMs are all found on the main street of **Köprü Başı/ Sarayonu Caddesi**, which links, via Divan Caddesi, with the bazaar quarter and Pools of Abraham to the south and west.

Brief history

The **Hurri**, members of one of Anatolia's earliest civilizations, built a fortress on the site of Urfa's present citadel around 3500 BC. Later came the Hittites and Assyrians, but only after the city was re-founded as **Edessa** by Seleucus Nicator in 300 BC did it eclipse nearby Harran. It later became an important eastern outpost for the Romans against Persia.

From the second century AD, Edessa was a thriving centre of **Christianity**, and Abgar IV (176–213) made it the world's first Christian kingdom. The city changed hands between Byzantine and Arab several times; according to Syrian Orthodox legend it was once ransomed for the "*mandalyon*", a handkerchief bearing the imprint of Christ. As Byzantine control ebbed, the **Arabs** moved in, staying until the eleventh century. During the First Crusade, a French count, **Baldwin of Boulogne**, stopped off en route to Tripoli and the Holy Land to establish the county of Edessa, a short-lived Christian state. In 1144 the Arabs recaptured Edessa, giving the rulers of Europe a pretext to launch the Second Crusade. After being sacked by the Mongols in 1260, Edessa never recovered. The city was eventually absorbed as Urfa into the Ottoman Empire in 1637.

Old Urfa

Urfa's vibrant historic core holds a number of fascinating sights. On Divan Caddesi is the twelfth-century **Ulu Cami**, a typical Arab design based on the Grand Mosque in Aleppo, Syria. Its courtyard boasts a massive octagonal minaret (originally the belfry of the fifth-century Church of St Stephen) and graves, though the interior is

11

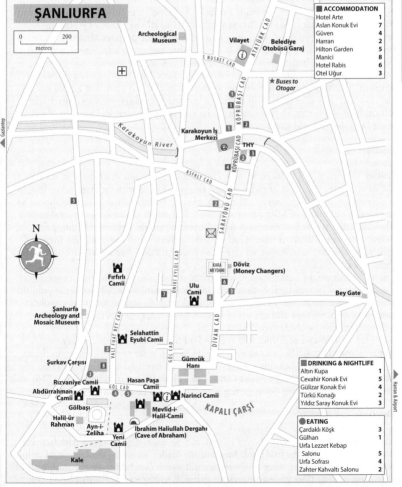

Otogar, Mardin, Diyarbakır & Göbekli Tepe

ŞANLIURFA

0 ———— 200
metres

Gaziantep

Harran & Airport

Archeological Museum
Vilayet
Belediye Otobüsü Garaj

S NUSRET CAD
ATATÜRK CAD

★ Buses to Otogar

KÖPRÜBAŞI CAD

Karakoyun River

Karakoyun İş Merkezi
@ THY

ASFALT CAD

SARAYÖNÜ CAD

N

ONİKİ EYLÜL CAD

Fırfırlı Camii

KARA MEYDANI
Döviz (Money Changers)

Ulu Cami

Bey Gate

Şanlıurfa Archeology and Mosaic Museum

VALİ FUAT BEY CAD

Selahattin Eyubi Camii

GÖL CAD

Gümrük Hanı

DİVAN CAD

Şurkav Çarşısı

Rızvaniye Camii
Abdürrahman Camii

GÖL CAD
Hasan Paşa Camii

Narinci Camii

KAPALI ÇARŞI

Gölbaşı
Mevlid-i-Halil-Camii

Halil-ür Rahman
Ayn-i-Zeliha
İbrahim Haliullah Dergahı (Cave of Abraham)
Yeni Camii

Kale

■ ACCOMMODATION	
Hotel Arte	1
Aslan Konuk Evi	7
Güven	4
Harran	2
Hilton Garden	5
Manici	8
Hotel Rabis	6
Otel Uğur	3

■ DRINKING & NIGHTLIFE	
Altın Kupa	1
Cevahir Konak Evi	5
Gülizar Konak Evi	4
Türkü Konağı	2
Yıldız Saray Konuk Evi	3

● EATING	
Çardaklı Köşk	3
Gülhan	1
Urfa Lezzet Kebap Salonu	5
Urfa Sofrası	4
Zahter Kahvaltı Salonu	2

unexceptional. Old stone-built houses, many of them once owned by the city's long-departed Armenian community, sprawl either side of the main drag.

The **Gümrük Hanı**, at the end of Divan Caddesi, is a magnificent late sixteenth-century *kervansaray*. Its plane tree shaded courtyard is taken up by the tables of teahouses, making it a great place to watch old-timers enjoy a game of dominoes or backgammon. Surrounding it is a warren of narrow, covered streets – the **Kapalı Çarşı**, or covered bazaar. Stalls and hole-in-the-wall shops sell everything imaginable, from green Diyarbakır tobacco to the lilac headscarves that are the favoured attire of traditional locals, male and female alike.

Turning right out of the Gümrük Hanı brings you to the *bedesten* next door, beyond which lies the **Hacı Kamil Hanı** and the coppersmiths' bazaar. Further west lie the **Sipahi** and **Hüseyniye** bazaars, both left over from the time when camel caravans moved regularly between Urfa and Aleppo, Palmyra, Mari and Baghdad.

İbrahim Halilullah Dergahı

West of the bazaar • Daily 8am–5.30pm • Free, donations welcomed

Named after the "Prophet Abraham and Friend of God", the colonnaded mosque and *medrese* complex that holds the **İbrahim Halilullah Dergahı** or "Cave of Abraham", attracts numerous pilgrims. According to local legend, the prophet **Abraham** was born here, spending the first ten years of his life in hiding because a local Assyrian tyrant, Nemrut (Nimrod), had decreed that all newborn children be killed.

As Abraham is recognized as a prophet by Muslims, his birth-cave is a place of worship. The majority of pilgrims are women, who throw a coin into a pool inside the cave and pray that their wish (often to become pregnant) will be granted. The atmosphere is reverential; there are separate entrances for men and women, dress must be respectful and shoes removed.

Gölbaşı

Open access • Free

Gölbaşı – literally "at the lakeside" – is a beautifully green and shady park at the foot of the *kale*, centred on a pair of mosques and two pools filled with fat carp. According to a continuation of the local legend, Abraham, after he emerged from his cave, became an implacable opponent of King Nemrut and tried to smash the idols in the local temple. The displeased tyrant had Abraham hurled from the citadel battlements into a fire below. Abraham was saved when God turned the flames into water and the firewood into carp. The carp are considered sacred, and local folklore has it that anyone who eats them will go blind.

Shady teahouses and cafés stand beside the first pool, the **Ayn-i-Zeliha** (named after the daughter of Nimrod). The elongated **Halil-ür Rahman** or Balıklı Göl is the pool that saved Abraham from a fiery end; it's surrounded by stone arches, its banks usually swarming with pilgrims and the water seething with fish (you can feed the carp with bait bought from poolside vendors).

The far western end of Balıklı Göl is closed off by the seventeenth-century **Abdürrahman Camii**. The present mosque replaced an older twelfth-century building whose square minaret, possibly once a church belfry, has survived. The north side of the pool is flanked by the **Rizvaniye Camii**, built by an Ottoman governor in 1716, with intricately carved wooden doors giving onto its peaceful courtyard.

The kale

Tues–Sun: April–Oct 8am–7pm; Nov–March 8am–5pm • ₺5

Urfa's massive **kale**, looming above Gölbaşı, can be reached via a signed path between the new mosque and the first pool. Much of the castle's surviving structure is Mamluk, but the interior has long since vanished; it's still worth clambering up the multitude of steps, and passing through the impressive gateway, to be rewarded with a bird's-eye view over Urfa. The two massive Corinthian columns at the top are thought to be the lone remnants of the palace of a second-century Christian king, Abgar; one sports crudely carved Syriac inscriptions. You can descend via an old tunnel or retrace your steps down the path.

Archeology and Mosaic Museum

Daily: April–Oct 9am–7pm; Nov–March 8am–5pm • ₺5

Opened in the spring of 2015, Urfa's superb and extensive new **Archeology and Mosaic Museum** is one of the most important collections in the country thanks to the significance of the finds on display; leave yourself half a day to do it justice. The **ground floor** is devoted to vivid tableaux depicting the lives of our hunter-gatherer ancestors, as well as case after case of beautifully displayed artefacts uncovered at the unique Neolithic temple complex of **Göbekli Tepe** (see p.589), and at other nearby sites. These include a 12,000-year-old life-sized stone statue of a man, complete with eerily blank obsidian eyes, found just down the road from the museum. Another highlight is a 2m tall "totem pole" depicting a composite human/animal figure apparently giving birth. There are also dozens of stone-carved wild animals such as boar and frogs alongside more everyday objects such as grinding stones, bowls, pestle and mortars, flint spearheads and bead necklaces.

Centrepiece of the **first floor** is a life-sized re-creation of one of the largest temple enclosures at Göbekli Tepe. Staring up at the 5m-high T-shaped monoliths that comprise the circular temple really brings home what early man achieved at this site some 12,000 years ago. Also on this floor is a replica of a temple from **Nevalı Çori**, now under the waters of the Atatürk Dam, and some more **statuary**, including a human head adorned with a lizard.

The **second floor** is devoted to objects from the Chalcolithic era through to the Iron Age, including some fine Babylonian relief-carved stelae. There's a small café at the end of the floor – take the lift opposite it back down to the ground floor, where the chronologically arranged tour continues through the Hellenistic, Roman and Islamic periods.

Haleplibahçe Mosaics

Tickets for the Archeology Museum also cover the fabulous **Haleplibahçe Mosaics**, housed in situ beneath a state-of-the-art steel and glass domed canopy just to the south. Unearthed by accident during demolition work in 2008, the **mosaics** almost certainly formed part of a Roman-era palace and date to between the third and fifth centuries AD. Very different stylistically to those from Zeugma (see p.578), the scenes depicted are stunning, especially those showing an African male leading a vibrantly executed but grumpy-looking zebra, and the centaur Chiron learning how to fight.

ARRIVAL AND DEPARTURE ŞANLIURFA

By plane Urfa's airport, 40km north, is served by a Havaş bus (₺10; 45min) into the centre. The Turkish Airlines (and Sunexpress) ticketing office is in Kaliru Turizm, Sarayönü Cad 74 (📞 0414 215 3344, 🌐 kaliruturizm.com.tr).

Destinations Ankara (Anadolujet 1 daily; 1hr 20min); Antalya (Anadolujet 1 daily, via Ankara; 6hr 50min); Istanbul (Anadolujet 1 daily; Pegasus 1 daily; THY 1 daily; 1hr 55min).

By bus Urfa's *otogar* is 5km north of the centre, above the provincial dolmuş garage, for transport down to Harran. Public buses to the *otogar* depart from the Belediye Otobüs Garaj; you have to pre-buy an Urfakart ticket for ₺3 (valid for two journeys) from the kiosk before boarding. The usual

eastern bus companies have offices all around town, especially on Sarayönü Cad, and provide service buses to the *otogar*. Harran Nemrut Tur at the *Aslan Konuk Evi* pension (see p.588), and some hotels, will book tickets. Taxis to and from the *otogar* cost ₺15.

Destinations Adana (7 daily; 5hr); Adıyaman (6 daily; 2hr 30min); Ankara (5 daily; 13hr); Diyarbakır (8 daily; 3hr); Gaziantep (8 daily; 2hr 30min); Harran (hourly 7am–7pm; 1hr); Mardin (6 daily; 2hr 30min).

Car rental Try Harran Nemrut Tur at the *Aslan Konuk Evi* pension (📞 0414 215 1575, 🌐 aslankonukevi.com; see p.588); Ruha, just off Sarayönü Cad on Bağdat Pasajı, rent cars for ₺70 and up daily.

INFORMATION AND TOURS

Tourist Information A useful kiosk (daily 9am–5pm) positioned at the eastern entrance to the Gölbaşı pools and garden complex hands out maps and other info; some English is spoken.

Tours Harran Nemrut Tur at the *Aslan Konuk Evi* pension (☎0414 215 1575, ⓦaslankonukevi.com; see below) runs full-day trips to Harran, including Şuayb and Soğmatar (₺125, min three people), as well as to Nemrut Dağı (₺150, min three people) and Göbekli Tepe (₺35 per person, including guide). Mustafa at the *Uğur* hotel (☎0414 313 1340, ⓔmusma63@yahoo.com; see below) has his own a/c minibus and arranges one-day trips to Nemrut, including all subsidiary sites (₺150 per person), and trips including Harran, Şuayb, Soğmatar (₺100 per person, min 3 people) and Göbekli Tepe (₺35 per person).

ACCOMMODATION

★**Hotel Arte** Atatürk Bul/Sinema Sok 7 ☎0414 314 7060, ⓦotel-arte.com. Good-value designer hotel, very well located in the central business/tourist area around Köprübaşı, with simple but stylish rooms boasting laminate parquet floors, a/c, flatscreen TVs and beer in the minibar. **₺130**

Aslan Konuk Evi Demokrasi Cad, Sok 10 ☎0414 215 1575, ⓦaslankonukevi.com. Run by the loquacious Özcan Aslan, a middle-school teacher and fluent English-speaker, this converted Armenian courtyard house is a backpackers' favourite. The breakfast is copious, there's use of a washing machine, and the owner can (and will) offer to sign you up for one of his tours (see above). Dorm **₺35**, double **₺130**

Güven Sarayönü Cad 133 ☎0414 215 1700, ⓦhotelguven.com. This solid three-star hotel is a safe bet for a comfy night or two. While rooms are a tad on the small side, the big, firm beds and crisp white linen compensate, as do the gleaming bathrooms with their travertine floors and chrome fittings. Another plus is the top-floor breakfast room (with a decent open-buffet spread) overlooking the Ulu Cami and the *kale*. **₺130**

Harran Atatürk Cad ☎0414 313 2860, ⓦhotelharran .com. The best feature of the reasonable-value, four-star *Harran* is its large outdoor swimming pool, very welcome in Urfa's summer heat. The rooms are comfortable and bathrooms spotless, but ask for one in the newer B block, which is quieter. **₺180**

Hilton Garden Nisan Fuar Cad 54 ☎0414 318 5000, ⓦhilton.com. Handily located close to the Archeology/ Haleplibahçe museum complex, this latest addition to the Urfa hotel scene offers all the standardized comfort you'd expect of the Hilton chain – the pool is particularly tempting during a summer visit. Those with kids may be interested in the well-appointed family rooms, and plentiful special offers can make a stay surprisingly good value. **₺160**

Manici Hotel Şurkavi Alışveriş Merkezi 6 ☎0414 215 9911, ⓦmanici.com.tr. Successor to the now defunct *Edessa*, this opulent (some might say over-the-top) hotel is well located right opposite Balıklı Göl. Rooms feature elaborately hand-painted furniture and chintzy soft furnishings as well as standard features like a/c, TV and en-suite bathrooms with tubs. Cheaper accommodation can be found in the adjoining *Narlı Evi*, an old courtyard house run by the same company. **₺150**

Hotel Rabis Sarayönü Cad, PTT Karşısı ☎0414 216 9595, ⓦhotelrabis.com. Spotlessly clean and comfortable contemporary-style hotel, with a/c, flatscreen TVs and minibar. While not quite as stylish as the *Arte*, it's just as comfy, and boasts a breakfast terrace overlooking the old city. **₺160**

Otel Uğur Köprübaşı Cad 3 ☎0414 313 1340, ⓔmusma63@yahoo.com. The distinctly old-school *Uğur* is Urfa's cheapest decent option. Rooms are basic and garish, but are clean and have a/c and comfy beds. All are waterless, but the shared showers and loos are kept very clean. The helpful owner Mustafa can arrange Harran Nemrut tours (see above). No breakfast. **₺70**

EATING AND DRINKING

Urfa is the home of the **Urfa kebap** (spiced minced meat on a skewer), and **lahmacun** (a thin, wrap-like bread topped with spicy lamb). Numerous simple eateries offer other **local specialities** based on bulgur (cracked wheat), notably *çiğ köfte*. Ciğer (liver) kebabs are big business too, eaten accompanied by lashings of raw onion and hot pepper; *şıllık*, a local *baklava*, is made with walnuts and cream. Travellers seem to suffer more from stomach bugs and food poisoning in Urfa than elsewhere in Turkey; be extra careful, especially during the hottest months.

CAFÉS AND RESTAURANTS

Çardaklı Köşk Balıklı Göl Cad 40 ☎0414 217 1080. Set in the mock-period hotel/shopping complex overlooking the gardens and pools, this place is more about its splendid views and relaxed ambience than the average food. That said, for a peaceful *pide* (₺12) or kebab (₺17 and up) away from the hustle of bustle of Urfa's standard eating places, it's a decent choice and only marginally overpriced. Daily 11am–11pm.

★**Gülhan** Atatürk Bul Akbank Bitişiği ☎0414 312 2273. Highly recommended, particularly for the lunchtime *sulu yemek*, with vegetable dishes from₺7, meat-based

---

SIRA GECELERİ – A NIGHT OUT IN URFA

Sira geceleri (literally "nights by turn") were originally informal gatherings of male friends at one of their homes, where a meal and conversation were accompanied by traditional live music. The idea was picked up by several Urfa restaurants (each invariably sited in an old courtyard house), and now "guests" pay for the experience, sitting cross-legged at a low *sofra* table and tucking into a banquet of speciality local dishes while being serenaded by a traditional band. Three of the best venues are listed below.

Cevahir Konak Evi Selahhattin Eyyub Camii Karşısı ☏ 0414 215 9377, ⓦ cevahirkonukevi.com. Probably the best, and certainly the dearest, at ₺65 for the set menu of eight different dishes. Wed, Fri & Sat from 8pm.

Gülizar Konuk Evi Sarayönü Cad, İrfaniye Sok ☏ 0414 215 0505. Lovely old mansion set below the towering Ulu Cami minaret, with an ₺40 set menu and, usually, two *sira geceleri* each week. Wed & Sat from 8pm.

Yıldız Saray Konuk Evi Yorgancı Sok ☏ 0414 216 9494, ⓦ yildizsarayikonukevi.com. Courtyard mansion with a good reputation; ₺40 for the set menu. Performances usually Wed, Fri & Sun from 8pm.

---

ones from ₺10. Kebabs range from ₺18 for a standard kebab to ₺36 for the mixed-grill-style house special. A bowl of complimentary raw onion and fresh hot peppers comes with each dish. Also does good *pide*, as well as pizzas and burgers. Well frequented by the local middle classes, its bustling nature ensures a fast turnover and fresh food. Daily 10am–10pm.

Urfa Lezzet Kebap Salonu Akarbaşı Göl Cad 31. What looks like a hole-in-the-wall kebab joint at street level actually boasts a dining room one floor up, and a pleasant roof terrace above that. Right on the edge of the bazaar, this is as local as it gets in Urfa, with cheap kebabs (₺10), *lahmacun* (₺2.5) and lentil soup. Daily 8am–10pm.

Urfa Sofrası Balıklı Göl Girişi, Hasan Paşa Han Yanı ☏ 0542 247 9766. In the same strip as the *Urfa Lezzet Kebap Salonu*, and offering many of the same dishes, this place is worth trying for its tender *ciğer* (liver) *kebaps* (₺9). The upstairs room is very popular with couples and familes, who head here after a stroll around the pools and gardens. Daily 8am–10pm.

Zahter Kahvaltı Salonu Köprübaşı Cad 17 ☏ 0414 312 8628. Spotless, semi-basement breakfast emporium facing the main street, with pine tables and a venerable, cross-vaulted high ceiling. A decent-sized breakfast plate of tender flatbread, cheese, olives, tomatoes and the like is ₺7.5, and a generous helping of honey and clotted cream is ₺6.5. Handily located near the breakfastless *Uğur* hotel. Daily 6am–8pm.

BARS

Male-dominated **bars** dotted along a terrace on Atatürk Cad, opposite the *Harran* hotel, serve beer or rakı (but not during Ramadan), as well as snacks such as fruit and nuts. The only alternatives for alcoholic drinks are the upmarket bars at the *Harran* and the *Dedeman* hotels, or the *Türkü* bar (see below).

Altın Kupa Off Atatürk Cad. At the end of a short strip of bars opposite the Karakoyun İş Merkezi, the "Golden Cup" is set in an old stone building with a vaulted ceiling. Its big advantage over its competitors is the quiet adjoining beer garden. Beers cost ₺7, and they'll send out for kebabs. Not recommended for female travellers without a male companion. Daily noon–2am.

Türkü Konağı Sarayönü Cad, Vatan Sok 7 ☏ 0414 216 9786. Atmospheric bar with live *Türkü* music nightly. Set in the old camel stables of a *kervansaray*, it's very atmospheric on the right evening. Beers are a reasonable ₺8, wine ₺11 per glass – but watch out for the price of *çerez* (nibbles). Daily noon–midnight.

DIRECTORY

Banks and exchange A couple of convenient *döviz* offices, and many ATMs on Sarayönü Cad.

Hospital Devlet Hastane ve Polikliniği (State Hospital), Hastane Cad ☏ 0414 313 1928 or ☏ 0414 313 1220.

Police station Sarayönü Cad.

Post office Sarayönü Cad (Mon–Sat 9am–noon & 1–5pm for money exchange and mail; 24hr for telephones).

Göbekli Tepe

15km northeast of Urfa • Daily 8am–7pm • ₺5 • The round-trip taxi fare from Urfa is ₺80, including waiting time; to drive, follow the Mardin road (E-400) for 10km, then turn left (north) at a brown-on-white sign – Göbekli Tepe is another 11km

Set where the southern foothills of the Toros Mountains fade into the scorching flatlands of upper Mesopotamia, **Göbekli Tepe** (Hill of the Navel) is Turkey's most intriguing archeological site. Here, on a hilltop 870m above sea level, stands a man-made mound some 300m in diameter and 15m high, containing a series of circular enclosures, carbon-dated to between 10,000 and 7500 BC.

The **enclosures** have burnt-lime floors and are lined with stone benches, but most remarkably contain a series of T-shaped **monoliths**, the tallest of which are 5m high. Clearly anthropomorphic, many of the monoliths are liberally covered with incredible relief carvings of wild animals, from scorpions and snakes to lions and wild boar. The enclosures were almost certainly used for cult purposes and the site is much hyped as the "world's first temple". Göbekli Tepe also appears to disprove the theory that only settled societies were capable of producing monumental buildings and sophisticated art. Most of the work here was done when man was still in the hunter-gatherer stage of development – no evidence has been found of human settlement.

A wooden walkway, protective canopy and supports for the monoliths and ancillary structures have helped to protect the site, though they make photography more difficult than in the past. A **visitor centre** complex was under construction at the time of writing, some way below the summit area.

Harran

The beehive-style houses of **HARRAN**, 45km southeast of Urfa, are part of a village that has grown up within the crumbling remnants of the old 4km circumference walls of a settlement once much more important than Urfa. Harran has strong biblical links, too: according to Genesis 11:31 and 12:4, the patriarch **Abraham** dwelt here before moving onto Canaan. The stone-built, mud-covered buildings owe their distinctive beehive shape to the fact that no wood is used as support. Virtually all are now used for storage or animal – not human – habitation.

These days, Arabs and a few Kurds live amid the ruins of old Harran, surviving by farming the newly irrigated fields, though the presence of the Syrian border, 10km south, was a major cause for concern at the time of writing, especially given the **travel warnings** issued by the foreign offices of many countries (see box, p.577).

Brief history

Harran is thought to have been continuously inhabited for at least six thousand years. It became a prosperous **trading** town under the Assyrians, who turned it into a centre for the **worship** of Sin, god of the moon; there was a large temple here, later also used by the Sabians. Planet worshippers, they stand accused in some accounts of holding lurid orgies and carrying out human sacrifice, and with the arrival of the Arabs were given the choice of conversion to Islam or death. In 53 BC the Roman general **Crassus** was defeated here, crucified and had molten gold poured into his mouth by the Parthians. Despite this, the Romans later converted Harran into an important centre of **learning**, a role it continued to play under the Byzantines, then the Arabs, first under the Umayyad dynasty, then the Ayyubid. However, the arrival of the Mongols during the thirteenth century meant devastation.

The site

Dwarfing the beehive dwellings, Harran's enigmatic ruins exude tragic grandeur. Near the *jandarma*, an artificial tumulus marks the site of the original settlement; excavations underway here have revealed the remains of an Umayyad palace. North of the mound is the massive **Ulu Cami**, the first mosque ever built on what is now Turkish soil. Its substantial square minaret, originally built in the eighth century, was mistaken for a cathedral belfry by T.E. Lawrence when he passed through in 1909. The layout of the mosque, much rebuilt under the Ayyubid dynasty in the twelfth century, can be made out clearly, though only fragments of its structure survive relatively intact.

The eleventh-century **citadel**, in the southeast corner of the old walled city, is possibly built on the site of the ancient temple of the moon god Sin. Three of its four polygonal towers have survived reasonably well, but take care scrambling around as there are several holes in the upper part of the structure.

ARRIVAL AND DEPARTURE HARRAN

By dolmuş Dolmuşes run hourly from Şanlıurfa *otogar* to Harran (₺6); the last returning dolmuş leaves at 7pm.

By taxi A taxi for the trip to and from Şanlıurfa, with waiting time, should cost around ₺140.

ACCOMMODATION

Harran Kültür Evi ☏ 0414 441 2477. Staying in this atmospheric complex of restored beehive dwellings, right amid the ruin, you'll sleep on mattresses on the floor, but the place is scrupulously clean, the food good, and owner Reşat (the village headman) friendly and resplendent in his flowing Bedouin robes. Rates include half board (for two), and cover two people. **€30**

Kahta

The drab and dusty town of **KAHTA** is the most commonly used gateway to Nemrut Dağı and its spectacular mountaintop sanctuary. Many travellers arrive from elsewhere in Turkey at the provincial capital of **Adıyaman**, 25km west, though several intercity bus companies have services direct to Kahta. There is nothing of interest in the town, but it's only 1km from the Atatürk Baraji reservoir, where there are a few pleasant waterside restaurants and picnic spots.

ARRIVAL AND DEPARTURE KAHTA

By plane Adıyaman airport, 20km west of Kahta, is served by Havaş bus (₺5) or taxi (₺25).
Destinations Ankara (Anadolujet 2 daily; 1hr 20min); İstanbul (1 daily via Ankara; 2hr 55min).
By bus Services to and from Ankara (1 daily; 12hr); İstanbul (2 daily; 20hr); Şanlıurfa (3 daily; 2hr 30min) stop at the town-centre *otogar*.
By dolmuş Adıyaman (every 10min, daily 6am–8pm; ₺4); Karadüt (hourly in season; 30min; ₺6); Siverek, for Diyarbkır (several daily; 2hr; ₺9). Dolmuşes also run from Adıyaman to Şanlıurfa (hourly 6am–6pm 2hr; ₺15). The dolmuş garage is just north of the central crossroads.

ACCOMMODATION AND EATING

Hotel Kommagene ☏ 0416 725 9726, ✉ kommagenem @hotmail.com. Rebuilt in wood and styling itself "boutique", the *Kommagene* is not bad value, despite its unpromising location on a major crossroads (the junction of Kahta's main street and the road up to Nemrut); guests can use the kitchen and washing machine for free. However, by staying here you are by no means obliged to go on their tours to Nemrut, and you should take their advice on other accommodation options up in the mountains with a pinch of salt. **₺80**
Neşetin Yeri ☏ 0416 725 7575. Located 2km east of town, overlooking the Atatürk lake, and much better than the cheap and basic restaurants on Kahta's main street, with excellent-value lake fish (₺20) and grills (from ₺18) served on terraces with a view of the mountain and lake. You'll need your own transport or a taxi to get here. Daily noon–11pm.
Zeus Hotel ☏ 0416 725 5694, ⊕ zeushotel.com.tr. Kahta's best hotel, with a prettily landscaped, good-sized outdoor swimming pool and a bar-restaurant, plus spacious rooms with a/c and flatscreen TVs. It gets plenty of groups so be prepared for lots of noise as they ready to depart for Nemrut summit for dawn. Bathrooms are a tad tired and cramped. **₺140**

The road to Nemrut Dağı

The 75km paved road from Kahta to the sanctuary atop **Nemrut Dağı** (Mount Nemrut) is easily done with your own transport, but make sure you fill up with fuel in Kahta. Visitors intending to reach the summit sanctuary in time for dawn go up the quick way (via Narince), and return via the subsidiary site route, while those aiming for a sunset visit to the top usually take in the lesser sites en route.

Karakuş tumulus

9km north of Kahta • Unrestricted access • Free

The huge **Karakuş tumulus**, said to be the funeral mound of Antiochus' wife, rises up dramatically by the roadside, just past a small oil-drilling field. It's adorned by three separate groups of three **columns**, each surmounted by either an animal statue or a relief carving. The best preserved is the eagle that gives the site its name – "black bird". There's a small café-cum-souvenir shop on site, plus toilets.

Cendere Köprüsü

18km north of Kahta, 9km beyond Karakuş tumulus • Unrestricted access • Free

The **Cendere Köprüsü** is a monumental Roman bridge built between 193 and 211 AD, during the reign of Emperor Septimius Severus. Its graceful single arch spans the mouth of a spectacular gorge carved by the Cendere, a tributary of the Euphrates River. Originally a pair of columns stood at either end of the bridge, but now only three of them survive. The fourth, dedicated to Severus' younger son Geta, was removed when his eldest son, Caracalla, had his brother put to death in a successful bid to become sole emperor. Cendere Köprüsü is closed to traffic; to reach its western end, take the signed but badly potholed stretch of road that branches left from shortly before the new bridge.

Eski Kahta

25km north of Kahta; turning 6km beyond Cendere Köprüsü

The traditional hillside village of **ESKİ KAHTA** is dominated by the **Mamluk Yeni Kale**. The castle is spectacular when viewed from a distance, but few people have the time or nerve to explore its precipitous heights. Indeed the best place to view it is from the heights above the Hercules and Antiochus relief at Arsameia (see below).

Arsameia

25km north of Kahta; just off the main road 1km south of Eski Kahta • Daily 8am–7pm • ₺12 combined ticket with Nemrut Dağı summit, paid at the Nemrut Dağı Milli Park gates (see box, p.595)

The ancient site of **Arsameia**, the summer capital of the ancient Commagene kingdom, was excavated during the 1950s. From the shop/café/toilet block area at the site entrance (where it's also possible to camp), take the lower path to a truncated **relief-stele** of the god Mithras. Head up the steps to join the main path, then continue to reach a man-made **cave**, in which a tunnel runs down to what's thought to be a Mithraic cult chamber. A damaged stele below the cave entrance depicts Mithridates I Callinicus, and his son, Antiochus I, the founder of the complex at Nemrut Dağı.

Heading back a short distance then taking the path up the hillside will bring you to the highlight of the site: a fabulous, perfectly preserved **relief** depicting **Hercules and Antiochus I** shaking hands – as impressive, if not more so, than anything you'll see on the top of Nemrut Dağı itself. Above the entrance to a tunnel alongside, which leads down to another cult chamber, a huge, 25-line Greek inscription tells you that Mithridates I Callinicus, father of Antiochus, is buried in the vicinity, and that the site is consecrated to him.

A short way above and beyond the relief of Hercules and Antiochus, a plateau holds the remnants of a funerary/cult **sanctuary complex** that must once have rivalled that on Nemrut. Little remains, but the views across the mountains and down over Yeni Kale are spectacular. A road cuts across the mountains, via Kayadibi village, to join the major summit road just above the *Çeşme pansiyon* in upper Karadut.

Karadut

KARADUT village probably makes for the most relaxing approach to Nemrut. Some 800m above sea level, with grand views over terraced fields, a plunging valley and limestone peaks, it's a lovely cool place named after the black mulberry trees that grow here among the apricot groves. Most of the pensions in Karadut will arrange to collect you for free from Kahta's dolmuş garage if you ring in advance.

The **Nemrut Dağı Milli Park** gate (see box, p.595), where you pay the park entry fee, is around 2km north of the village.

ARRIVAL AND DEPARTURE KARADUT

By bus Karadut is served by local dolmuşes from Kahta (hourly Mon–Fri 6am–6pm, less at weekends; 1hr).

ACCOMMODATION AND EATING

Çeşme ☎ 0416 737 2032, ⓦ cesmepansiyon.com. A couple of kilometres higher up the mountain than Karadut's other options, this laidback pension/restaurant offers tasty meals and expansive views. Rooms are plain and the plumbing temperamental, but it's cosy enough and there's a veranda where you can sit and watch the sun go down. Owner Mustafa will pick you up from lower Karadut and/or deposit you there to catch the dolmuş down to Kahta. Rates include half board for two. **₺80**

Hotel Euphrat ☎ 0416 737 2175, ⓦ nemruteuphrathotel.com. Long-established, recently refurbished hotel, just above the village and below the *Kervansaray Nemrut*. The rooms are ranged around a stone-built, U-shaped single-storey building (with outdoor pool), and there's a great terrace outside the restaurant with splendid mountain views. Rooms and bathrooms are on the small side, but fittings are good quality. Easily the most comfortable base in Karadut; the downside is that it is very group orientated. **₺150**

Karadut Motel Pansiyon ☎ 0416 737 2169. This group-orientated place just above the village offers basic but comfortable en-suite rooms, a friendly atmosphere and good home-cooked food (₺20 extra for a five-course dinner). The rooms on the first floor are cheerier than those on the dark ground floor. **₺70**

Kervansaray Nemrut ☎ 0416 737 2190, ⓦ nemrut kervansarayhotel.com. Just above the village, this appealingly situated single-storey, L-shaped hotel is very similar to the *Euphrat*. It gets generally positive feedback, has a pool and great views, and the two local guys who run it are very charming. Also offers hikes up to Nemrut (3hr). Rates include half board. **€60**

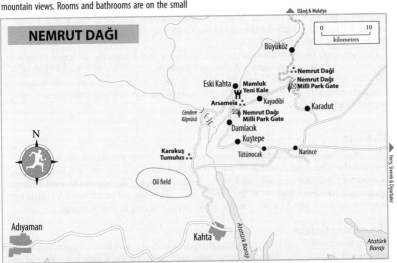

Nemrut Dağı

₺12 combined ticket with Nemrut Dağı summit, paid at the Nemrut Dağı Milli Park gates (see box opposite)

Listed as a UNESCO World Heritage site in 1987, the remote, grandiose mountain-top sanctuary at **Nemrut Dağı** is unforgettable, while the mighty stone heads that adorn the temple and tomb of King Antiochus are one of Eastern Turkey's most potent images.

Most visitors want to get here **before dawn**, in order to watch the sunrise. The majority of the available minibus tours (see box opposite) are therefore geared up to suit those timings, despite the drawback of making such an early start – between 2am and 4am, depending on season – and the crowded and chilly conditions at the summit, which is 2150m above sea level. Between late October and April, there's often snow on the ground. Minibus tours also target **sunset**, when it's not so cold, and the setting sun bathes the western terrace in a warm glow. A daytime visit means fewer visitors and the chance to explore the sanctuary at leisure and in the warmth.

At the time of writing, a new **visitor centre** was approaching completion some 2km below the summit. The "original" car park/café/souvenir stall and toilet, however, was still in use at the time of writing. From the latter, it's a twenty-minute walk up a well-paved path to the east terrace of the complex. Access may change once the visitor centre is completed.

Brief history

The result of one man's delusions of grandeur, the great tomb and temple complex of Nemrut Dağı was built by **Antiochus I Epiphanes** (64–38 BC), son of Mithridates I Callinicus, the founder of the Commagene kingdom. A breakaway from the Seleucid Empire, covering only a small territory from modern Adıyaman to Gaziantep, the **Commagene dynasty** wouldn't rate much more than a passing mention in histories of the region had Antiochus not chosen to build this colossal monument to himself. Having decided he was divine in nature, or at the very least an equal of the gods, he declared: "I, the great King Antiochus have ordered the construction of these temples… on a foundation which will never be demolished… to prove my faith in the gods. At the conclusion of my life I will enter my eternal repose here, and my spirit will ascend to join that of Zeus in heaven."

Antiochus claimed descent from Darius the Great of Persia and Alexander the Great, but eventually he went too far, siding with the Parthians against Rome, and was deposed. This was effectively the end of the Commagene kingdom, which afterwards passed into Roman hands.

The sanctuary lay **undiscovered** until 1881, when Karl Puchstein, a German engineer, located it while making a survey. Although he returned in 1883 with Karl Humann – the man who removed the Pergamon altar to Berlin – to carry out a more thorough investigation, only in 1953 did a comprehensive American-led archeological survey of the site begin.

The site

The actual tomb of Antiochus has never been found, but is thought to lie buried beneath the 60m-high **tumulus** of small rocks that completely covers the natural summit of the mountain. It's rated by the *Guinness Book of Records* as the world's largest man-made mound, covering an area of 7.5 acres. The colossal **heads** for which the site is renowned are ranged in two groups, to the west and east of the tumulus.

The eastern terrace

The **eastern terrace** comprises six decapitated seated statues, measuring several metres tall. Lined up in front of these truncated figures are the much-photographed

VISITING NEMRUT DAĞI

Nemrut's summit sanctuary, and the subsidiary site of Arsameia, both lie within the **Nemrut Dağı Milli Park** (Mt Nemrut National Park). Visitors using their own transport rather than an organized excursion should note that ₺12 entry to the park covers both the summit and Arsameia. There are two **gates to the park**, one southwest of the summit, a couple of kilometres below Arsameia, the other a few kilometres above Karadut village, south of the summit. The southwest gate is officially open daily 8am–7pm, while the Karadut gate (south of the summit) opens around an hour before dawn and stays open until around an hour after sundown, to allow sunrise and sunset visits to the sanctuary.

However, the vast majority of visitors come here by way of organized **minibus trips to Nemrut Dağı**, which run in summer from Kahta, Malatya and Şanlıurfa. Given the distances involved, they are about the only way to get there if you don't have your own transport. Note that the summit road is usually only open from April 15 until the first snowfall of winter, but outside the peak summer months (July & Aug) there may well be insufficient demand to make up groups each day. For more on the best time of day to visit the site, see opposite.

FROM KAHTA AND KARADUT

In season, there are sunrise or sunset tours from **Kahta** (see p.591) – sunset trips leave around 2pm and return at 10pm; sunrise tours leave at around 2am, returning at 10am. Best arranged by the transport cooperative – see Bayram Çınar at the Karadut market, opposite the dolmuş garage, or Ramazan Dışkaya, usually to be found around the dolmuş garage (or on ☎0532 437 2724) – the trips cost ₺150 for the dolmuş, irrespective of numbers, with the entrance fee extra. They should include the subsidiary sites of the Karakuş tumulus, Cendere bridge and the ancient Commagene capital of Arsameia.

Don't be bludgeoned into booking a tour before you check various options – indeed, assuming you arrive in time to catch the last dolmuş (6pm), it's far better to head straight up to the lovely village of **Karadut** (see p.593). All the accommodation options here arrange summit tours – a taxi to the summit costs around ₺45, a minibus around ₺60 (regardless of numbers, entrance extra); tours including the subsidiary sites are ₺125. Sunrise tours see the subsidiary sites on the return, sunrise tours en route.

FROM MALATYA

Tours from **Malatya** (see p.596), on the north side of the range, may look more expensive, but if you count in the night's stay virtually at the summit, the difference is negligible. The main disadvantage is that you miss out on Nemrut's subsidiary sites, but on the other hand you view both sets of heads at sunrise and sunset, and tours include a stay at the welcoming stone-built *Güneş Hotel* (☎0422 323 9378), which has clean and cheerful en-suite rooms and good food. Visitors arriving with their own transport can usually find a (double) room at the *Güneş* for around ₺80. A Kurdish *yayla* (summer tent encampment) lies a few minutes' walk away.

Bookings are best made the day before, either at Malatya's tourist office or the tea garden to one side. Departures are usually at noon, reaching the summit in good time for sunset; the return trip starts at about 7am, allowing time to admire the sunrise, and reaching Malatya at about 11am. The ₺120 fee per person includes transport, lodging and two meals, and trips run even if there's only one taker; the entrance fee is extra. If it suits your onward travel plans, after viewing the sanctuary at sunrise you could walk over to the south side of Nemrut and join one of the groups seeing the subsidiary sites on the way back to Kahta.

FROM ŞANLIURFA

Visiting Nemrut from **Şanlıurfa** (see p.584) has the advantage of cutting out Adıyaman and Kahta, and can include a trip to see the Atatürk Dam, but the 420km (14hr) round trip takes in lots of uninteresting scenery.

11

---

detached heads, each a couple of metres high. From left to right they represent: Antiochus I, Fortuna (symbol of the Commagene kingdom), Zeus, Apollo and Hercules. Scattered around them lie the remains of massive stone eagles and lions – one of each creature originally stood, as symbolic guardian, at either end of the royal line-up.

The anthropomorphic statues were meant to incorporate several similar deities drawn from different cultures, according to the principle of syncretism, which Alexander the Great had promoted in order to try to foster a sense of unity among the disparate peoples of his empire. On the date of Antiochus' birthday and the anniversary of his coronation, the Commagene people would file up to the mountaintop to witness the dawn sacrifice and make offerings, carried out in strict accordance with the Greek inscriptions carved onto the back of the royal statues. The stepped, sandstone sacrificial **altar** still stands in front of the statues.

The western terrace

Follow a path around the northern base of the tumulus to reach the **western terrace**, lined by slabs that were once decorated with reliefs. None of the western statues is even partially intact, but there are more of them – a complete set of five, plus two eagle-heads to flank them – and the dispersed **heads** here are much less weathered than those on the east.

The alignment of statues was originally the same as on the east side, but these heads have not been lined up in front of their "bodies". A well-paved path coils west then south from here back to the car park, so you don't have to retrace your steps around the tumulus.

Malatya and around

The largest producer of apricots in the world, **MALATYA** is a seldom-visited city of nearly half a million people, set in a broad green valley around 60km north of Nemrut Dağı. Despite a long history going back over five thousand years, during which the Assyrians, Hittites, Romans, Selçuk Turks and Ottomans all held sway, there's little of any significant age left to see within the city. Nonetheless it makes a pleasant overnight stop before tackling Nemrut Dağı, while very close at hand, the old town of **Eski Malatya** offers an interesting diversion, as does **Aslantepe** (Lion Hill), a millennia-old settlement mound that's been newly interpreted for visitors.

Scratch beneath the surface in Malatya, and an uneasy mix of Turkish nationalists, devout Sunni Muslims, Alevis and Kurds soon becomes apparent. Always a political town, it's the home of two former presidents of the Republic, General İsmet İnönü and part-Kurdish Turgut Özal. It is also the birthplace of Armenian-Turk Hrant Dink, slain by an ultra-nationalist Turkish teenager in 2007 (see p.681), and Mehmet Ali Ağca, the man who almost succeeded in assassinating the pope in 1981 (see p.698).

The old **Şire Pazarı** market (daily 9am–8pm) in the city centre, between Atatürk Bulvarı and the ring road, is devoted to local agricultural produce, namely cherries, mulberries, apples, walnuts and, especially, apricots. There's an **apricot festival** (second week in July) at Mişmiş Parkı, 5km east of the centre.

Malatya museum

Hasan Varol • Tues–Sun 8am–5pm • ₺3

The small but excellent **Malatya museum** (Malatya Müzesi) concentrates on finds from nearby **Aslantepe** (see p.598). The room to the left as you enter holds fine pottery and copper swords from 3000–3400 BC, plus reconstructions of graves from Aslantepe. Upstairs are more artefacts from the settlement mound, plus a glass case devoted to decorative seals, used to guarantee the integrity of goods in containers; the most common motifs being deer and antelope. The pick of the exhibits are three neo-Hittite relief-carved blocks depicting winged demons and an eagle-headed human.

Malatya Ethnographic Museum

Sinema Cad • Tues–Sun 8am–5pm • Free

Several traditional houses, of mainly mud-brick and timber construction, have been restored on Sinema Caddesi. One now holds the **Malatya Ethnographic Museum** (Malatya Beşkonaklar Müzesi). Labels are in English, and there's a series of upstairs rooms devoted to blocks for hand-printing cloth, muskets, pipes, hamam utensils and looms.

ARRIVAL AND DEPARTURE   MALATYA

By plane From Malatya's airport, 26km northwest of the city, a Havaş shuttle bus (₺10) meets THY flights and ferries passengers to the centre; get off on Atatürk Cad. Buy tickets for domestic flights from Bertaş, Sivas Cad, Semercioğlu Apt Alt (☎0422 326 0037).

Destinations Ankara (1 daily with Anadolujet; 1hr 20min); Antalya (1 daily via Ankara with Anadolujet); Istanbul (1 daily with Anadolujet; 2 daily with THY; 1hr 45min); İzmir (1 daily via Ankara with Anadolujet).

By train Malatya's train station, 2km west of the centre on the Çevre Yolu (ring road), is served by the Maşti bus from opposite the *Vilayet*; buy a ticket for ₺3 (two-use) from the booth here before boarding.

Destinations Adana (daily; 8hr 30min); Ankara (daily; 20hr); Diyarbakır (5 weekly; 6hr 30min); Tatvan via Elazığ (2 weekly; 10hr 30min).

By bus The *otogar* is 7km west of the centre on the Çevre Yolu (ring road). It's served by the Maşti bus from opposite the *Vilayet*; you can only buy a two-use ticket (₺3), available from the booth before boarding.

Destinations Adana (5 daily; 7hr 30min); Adıyaman (hourly; 2hr 30min); Ankara (8 daily; 11hr); Diyarbakır (4 daily; 4hr); Erzurum (1 daily; 7hr); Gaziantep (5 daily; 4hr); Istanbul (5 daily; 14hr).

Car rental Bizim Rent a Car, Kanalboyu 30/1 (☎0533 282 1363).

INFORMATION

Tourist office In the *Vilayet* (governor's office) building, behind the statue of İnönü in the main square, İnönü Meydanı (Mon–Sat 9am–noon & 1–5pm; ☎0422 323 3025). Its main function is to sign visitors up for a trip to Nemrut Dağı (see p.594); ask the helpful Bülent for advice. There's also a small information office on Sinema Cad (Mon–Fri 9am–5pm; ☎0422 323 3205), next to the Ethnographic Museum (see above).

ACCOMMODATION

Double Tree by Hilton İnönü Cad 174 ☎0422 377 7000, ⊛hilton.com.tr/malatya. This monumental new block towers over the city, affording excellent views from floor-to-ceiling windows in the stylish rooms. There's a fitness centre, outdoor sun terrace and indoor pool. Worth considering for the comfort, especially as there are plenty of deals available at certain times. ₺220

★**Hanem** Fuzuli Cad 13 ☎0422 324 1818, ⊛hanemhotel.com. Malatya's most stylish hotel features bleached wood-effect flooring, curvaceous Art Deco-style furtniture and gleaming chrome bathrooms, as well as big, comfy beds with crisp linen. Nice touches include free tea- and coffee-making facilities and a big-screen TV. ₺190

Malatya Büyük Hotel Yeni Cami Karşısı ☎0422 321 1400, ⊛malatyabuyukotel.com. Offering good views of the pretty, early twentieth-century Yeni Cami, this friendly hotel is tastefully done out with Scandinavian-style pale wood furniture, cream walls and flatscreen TVs. Bathrooms gleam with chrome. Serves up an excellent buffet breakfast. ₺120

Otel Park Atatürk Cad 17 ☎0422 321 1691, ⊜parkotelmalatya@mynet.com. A good budget option, with plain, pastel-hued rooms and tiled floors. Some rooms are fully en-suite, others just have showers and shared (squat) toilets down the hall. No breakfast. ₺70

Yeni Otel Yeni Cami Karşısı ☎0422 324 1424, ⊛malatyayenihotel.com. A good mid-range option, this two-star has all conveniences – a/c, TV, minibar etc – and a decent buffet breakfast. The soft furnishings in the rooms are a little garish, though. ₺100

EATING AND DRINKING

While Malatya holds plenty of **cafés and restaurants**, none is outstanding. In Kanalboyu, on the south side of the city at the end of Fuzuli Cad, a strip of pleasant cafés aimed at Malatya's middle classes line twin cobbled streets running either side of a watercourse. Dozens of specialist city-centre stores sell apricots, plain, sun-dried or rolled in chocolate, or chocolate-covered marzipan goodies made from apricot kernels.

RESTAURANTS

★**Beşkonaklar Malatya Mutfağı** Sinema Cad 13 ☎0422 326 0051. Malatya's most atmospheric restaurant, set in a traditional house with a nice, green and shady garden out back. The specialities are *köfte* of various sorts, including some vegetarian options such as *patlıcan köftesi* (balls of aubergine, chickpea and bulgur served in a piquant tomato sauce; ₺12). Unlicensed. Daily noon–10pm.

Cici Kebap Salonu Yeni Hamam ☎0422 324 2319. Rated one of Turkey's top-ten kebab joints by a leading daily newspaper, this down-to-earth *esnaf lokanta* dishes up the city's tastiest kebabs at bargain prices (from ₺16). Great for soups, too. Daily 11am–10pm.

Mangal Vadisi Turfanda Sok 1 ☎0422 326 2200. An *ocakbaşı*-style restaurant where you can watch your meat being grilled over charcoal. Kebabs or grills (from ₺14) are preceded by free *lavaş* bread and accompanying *meze*. Cheese *pides* are available, too. Daily noon–10pm.

BARS AND CAFÉS

Nostalji Mucelli Cad ☎0422 323 4209. The wooden house that holds this laidback café, more or less opposite the five-screen Yeşil Sineması, dates back to 1840. It's a great place to sample local specialities such as *analı kızlı köfte*, laze over a Turkish coffee or ₺12 breakfast spread – or just puff on a nargile. Daily 9am–10pm.

VIP Café Hüriyet Parkı ☎0533 511 4780. This shady tea garden/café, next to the *Vilayet* building and tourist office, is an ideal place to hang out in the heat of the day. It has a surprisingly broad menu, with big salad bowls, *börek* (pies) and chicken wings etc, as well as the usual teas and coffees. You can also try a nargile (₺12). Daily 8am–9pm.

Aslantepe

17km northeast of Malatya • Tues–Sun 8am–5pm • Free • Orduzu-bound buses, from the junction of Buharı and Sarıcıoğlu caddesis, stop 500m along a signed street from the site

Meticulously excavated for fifty years by Italian archeologists, the 16,000-square-metre settlement mound at **Aslantepe**, dating back to the fourth millennium BC, is a fascinating open-air museum. At the entrance stand newly carved copies of some of the monumental neo-Hittite **statuary** found here, including the god Tarhunzas and two grinning lions – after which the site was named when the originals were discovered in the nineteenth century. There's also the reconstruction of a typical mud-brick **Bronze Age house**.

A signed **walkway** leads visitors through the various layers of this complex but fascinating site, which has seen occupation in the Chalcolithic era (fourth millennium BC), the Bronze Age, the Hittite era, and finally the Roman and medieval periods. You can walk through the mud-brick remains of a palace dating from 3000 BC and a temple built circa 3500 BC. In the latter, archeologists found over a thousand pottery bowls – evidence of very early mass production. Everything is well explained by a series of informative display boards. The top of the mound offers fine **views**, across a veritable sea of apricot trees, to the distant mountains.

Eski Malatya (Battalgazi)

12km north of Malatya • Catch a bus in front of Ziraat Bank on Atatürk Cad in Malatya, having bought a "smart" ticket from the booth on Fuzuli Cad, just east of the *Vilayet* building

The ruined Roman/Byzantine/Selçuk/Ottoman town of **Eski Malatya**, or "Old Malatya", north of modern Malatya, has been engulfed by the modern settlement of **BATTALGAZI**.

From the main square where buses arrive, which holds plenty of shady *çay* places as well as a few basic restaurants, a 200m walk southwest brings you to a massive seventeenth-century *kervansaray*, the **Silahtar Mustafa Paşa**. The building has been so heavily restored it looks like new, but the *kışlık* (winter room), with its fine cross-vaulted ceiling and rows of fireplaces, is impressive.

The wonderful **Ulu Cami**, a huge mosque complex commissioned by Selçuk sultan, Alâeddin Keykubad, is a five-minute walk south. Built around a central courtyard, it comprises both summer and winter mosques. The latter consists of plain stonework with massive pillars, and the former of a central bay with a soaring domed roof flanked by two wings.

Diyarbakır

Superbly positioned on a bluff above a great loop in the Tigris, the old city of **DİYARBAKIR** shelters behind massive medieval walls of black basalt, enclosing a maze of cobbled streets and alleys that hold some fine mosques, churches and courtyard houses, many of which have been restored, as well as plenty of decent accommodation and a number of atmospheric cafés and restaurants. The city's tourism industry received a major boost in the summer of 2015 when its iconic **walls**, and an ancient, fertile stretch of land either side of the Tigris below them, the **Hevsel Gardens**, were added to **UNESCO's World Heritage Site** list.

Diyarbakır struggled to cope with an influx of Kurdish refugees fleeing the state–PKK war in the 1990s, many of whom now occupy old houses in the very heart of the walled city. As a result, this is now the most proudly and most overtly Kurdish city in Turkey: the Kurdish New Year (Newroz) celebrations here on or around March 21 are the biggest in the country, notices from the municipality are usually in both Turkish and Kurdish, and the local football team, Diyarbakırspor, has been re-branded Amed (the Kurds' name for the city), as can be seen on the distinctive green-on-red shirts for sale around town.

Be aware, however, that Diyarbakır has a definite "edge". Demonstrations leading to **violent clashes** between radicalized nationalist Kurds and the police are common, and the FCO warn against non-essential travel to the city as a result (see p.577). More prosaically, watch out for pickpockets and the odd stone-throwing youngster, though the old Arab saying "Black the walls, black the dogs, and black the hearts in black Diyarbakır" seems rather harsh, to say the least.

Brief history

Diyarbakır dates back at least five thousand years to the **Hurrian** period. Later subject to successive periods of Urartian, Assyrian and Persian hegemony, it fell to Alexander the Great and his successors, the Seleucids, in the late fourth century BC.

The Romans, who knew Diyarbakır as **Amida**, appeared on the scene in 115 AD. Over the next few centuries they and their successors, the Byzantines, struggled violently over the town with the Sassanid Persians. It was the Romans who built the first substantial walls around the city in 297 AD, though those visible today are the result of Byzantine and Arab rebuilds. The threatening basalt bulwarks gave the place its popular ancient name – Amid the Black – which is still used in the Kurdish language. The modern name comes from the Arabs: in 638 the Bakr tribe of Arabs arrived and renamed the city Diyar Bakr, or "Place of the Bakr". With the decline of Arab influence, Diyarbakır became a Selçuk, then an Artukid, and finally an Ottoman stronghold.

The city's position on the banks of the fertile Tigris encouraged fruit growing, particularly **watermelons** which are still cultivated here. In the old days they are said to have weighed 100kg, and had to be transported by camel and sliced with a sword.

The walls

Diyarbakır's 6km-long **city walls**, breached by four huge main gateways plus several smaller ones, are punctuated with 72 defensive towers. Much of what can be seen today dates from the eleventh-century Artukid kingdom of Malık Salih Şah. If you explore the walls in hot weather, be sure to bring water and a head covering. A torch is handy for the darkened interiors of the gate-towers.

Be warned that many sections of the walls lack either an external or internal parapet wall or rail, and can be just a couple of metres wide. The odd street urchin, especially if he is out of sight of adults, may find a visitor walking the walls a tempting target at which to throw stones, so be careful.

Exploring the walls – Mardin Kapısı to Urfa Kapısı

The best stretch of Diyarbakır's walls to walk lies between Mardin Kapısı and Urfa Kapısı. From **Mardin Kapısı**, turn right and follow the inside of the wall for 400m, at which point some steps lead up to the battlement walkway. Turn left and head back to Mardin Kapısı, threading through a vaulted passageway en route to an excellent viewpoint, then retrace your steps west along the ramparts. The first point of interest is the **Yedi Kardeş Burcu** (Seven Brothers Tower), a huge circular bastion decorated with Selçuk lions and a double-headed eagle. Not far beyond, the **Melikşah Burcu** (also known as the Ulu Badan) is also decorated with Selçuk motifs.

The views from the walls and towers over the Tigris are superb. Allow around thirty minutes to reach **Urfa Kapısı**. Follow the steps down into the (rather smelly) gate-tower and take care, as finding the next set of steps down to street level is not easy in the semi-darkness. It's possible to continue along the walls to just beyond **Çift Kapı** gate, but beyond it razor wire blocks access.

Keçi Burcu

11

The **Keçi Burcu** or "Goat's Tower" – the oldest, largest and best-preserved tower on the wall, just southeast of Mardin Kapısı – is by far the most popular location from which to admire the view down over the Tigris valley. It's especially busy around sunset on warm evenings, when locals and visitors alike come to drink tea purchased from a café on the battlements. From here you can clearly see the **Hevsel Gardens**, a lush strip of riverside poplar stands, vegetable-yielding fields and orchards covering around 1000 acres and said to date back some 8000 years. Also visible is the ten-arched **Ongözlü Bridge**, Byzantine in origin, spanning the turbid river.

It's possible to follow the line of the walls anticlockwise towards the Citadel (İç Kale, see below), though there are few places to scramble up on top. Instead, take advantage of the various gaps in the walls to take in views of the Tigris below, but be aware that this is one of the poorest neighbourhoods in the city.

İç Kale

Daily 9am–11pm

The **İç Kale** (Citadel), located in the northeast corner of Diyarbakır's walls, is best reached by walking west along İzmet Paşa Caddesi and entering through the impressive **Saray Kapısı**. Formerly a military zone, complete with one of Turkey's most notorious prisons, it is now open to visitors and home to an **Archeology Museum** and restored Byzantine **church**. The first point of interest is the black stone **Hazreti Süleyman Camii**, built in 1160 by the Artukids and boasting a huge square minaret. It comes alive on Thursdays, when hundreds of female pilgrims arrive to pray for their wishes to be granted.

Archeology Museum

İç Kale • Tues–Sun: April–Oct 8am–7pm; Nov–March 8am–5pm • ₺5 • ☎ 0412 228 2215, ⓦ muze.gov.tr

Set in a converted late nineteenth-century courthouse at the eastern edge of the Citadel, the main building of the city's **Archeology Museum** holds a thoughtfully arranged and lit collection, with superb explanations in excellent English on both signboards and video displays. The **ground floor** displays finds from prehistoric sites in the Tigris valley – Kortik Tepe, Kenan Tepe and Karavelayan – as well as the text-book site of Çayönü (approximately 7500–6000 BC), generally thought to be the place where pigs were first domesticated. Head **upstairs** and forward in time to see finds from various *hüyüks* (settlement mounds) in the Tigris valley, as well as objects discovered within the confines of the citadel itself, many of which are from the Islamic era. The pick of these is a beautiful turquoise-glazed tile depicting an Artukid double-headed eagle. A second building, which will house a thematically arranged collection, was under renovation at the time of writing.

11

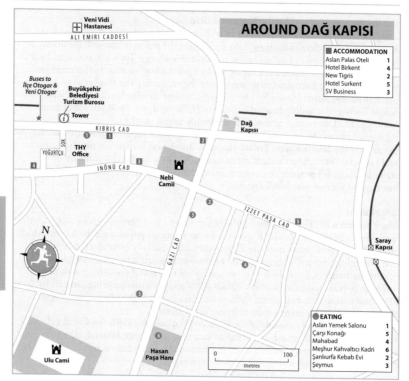

Church of St George

İç Kale • Daily 9am–5pm

Just north of the Archeology Museum is the substantial **Church of St George**, probably dating back to the early Byzantine period. Structural changes suggest that it was subsequently used as a palace by the Artukid rulers of the city. It has retained one of its original twin domes, with attractive exposed brickwork that would originally have been covered with mosaics. Next to the church is a decent café with a rear terrace affording great views over the green Tigris valley and sun-bleached uplands beyond.

The old city

The **old city**, within the city walls, holds virtually all the sights worth seeing in Diyarbakır. Just inside Dağ Kapısı, the north gate piercing the walls, is the attractive **Nebi Camii**, or Mosque of the Prophet. Founded in the late fifteenth century by the Akkoyun Turcomans, it's attractively built of contrasting bands of black basalt and white limestone – a common style in Diyarbakır. Both stones are quarried locally, and their combination is considerably less threatening than the unrelenting black of the walls.

Further down Gazi Caddesi, on its eastern side, the late sixteenth-century **Hasan Paşa Hanı** holds some decent cafe-restaurants (see p.607), plus carpet, jewellery and souvenir shops. The city's **main bazaar** area occupies the narrow, twisting streets around it.

The Ulu Cami

The gatehouse of Diyarbakır's most important mosque, the beautifully renovated **Ulu Cami**, stands opposite the *han*. The first of Anatolia's great Selçuk mosques, it's thought to have been built at the time of the Arab conquest in 639, on the site of, and using masonry from, the Byzantine church of St Thomas. It was probably extended in 1091 by Melik Şah, the Selçuk conqueror of the city, before being extensively refurbished after it was gutted by fire in 1155.

Beyond the entrance portal, decorated with bull and lion motifs, a large and singularly impressive **courtyard** holds two *şadırvan*s (ritual fountains). The north and south sides of the courtyard sport arcades, constructed using pillars salvaged from ornate late Roman and Byzantine buildings. The wing to the east and above the arch is a library, incorporating a much earlier colonnade beneath it. At the northeast corner of the courtyard, you'll find the locked entrance to the **Mesudiye Medresesi**. Built in 1198 by the Artukids, this became the first university of Anatolia, and is still in use as a Koranic school.

The prayer hall is a triumph of Islamic restraint, its simple white interior and supporting arches enlivened by a superbly decorated carved-wood roof and a white *mimber*. The banded minaret is tall and angular, like many such structures in Diyarbakır.

Diyarbakır's subsidiary mosques

The stunning fifteenth-century **Safa Camii**, west of the Ziya Gökalp Museum, is a mosque of notably graceful design and construction. Its tall, cylindrical minaret, a departure from the city norm, still bears traces of blue tile-work on its white, relief-worked surface.

Some way southeast across Melik Ahmet Caddesi is the **Behram Paşa Cami**, Diyarbakır's largest mosque. Built in 1572 by Behram Paşa, it's among the most important Ottoman-era mosques in southeastern Anatolia.

Also worth seeking out, east of Gazı Caddesi on Yenikapı Caddesi, is the early sixteenth-century **Kasım Padişah Camii**, virtually the last Akkoyun monument built before the Ottomans took over. Its tall, square detached minaret, set on four 2m basalt pillars, is known colloquially as the Dört Ayaklı Minare, or "Four-Legged Minaret". According to legend, if you walk around the minaret seven times and make a wish, it will be granted.

Diyarbakır's churches

Despite the fact that virtually the entire non-Muslim population of Diyarbakır – who formed around a third of the total early in the twentieth century – has gone, the city promotes itself as a multicultural, multi-faith destination, and several **churches** are open to visitors.

Keldani Kilisesi

Dicle Sokak • To get here on foot, walk past the Kasım Padişah Camii and turn left down an alley, then immediately right

The **Keldani Kilisesi** was founded by the Chaldeans, a schismatic Catholic group that broke away from the Nestorian church. The church and its bell tower date from 1602; the spacious, arched interior contains a rather garish altar with a crucifix and icons.

Surp Giragos Kilisesi

Özdemir Sokak • To get here on foot, turn right as you leave Keldani Kilisesi, then almost immediately left onto an alley; at the end of this turn right, then first right, and follow the signs

Until the major renovation programme that enabled the **Surp Giragos Kilisesi** (Church of St George) to reopen in 2011, it was a roofless shell. The restorers have done a superb job, and what is reputed to be the largest Armenian church in the Middle East now has its traditional flat roof, supported by rows of black basalt arches decorated with white limestone trim, back in place. The Armenian population of Diyarbakır has shrunk from a quarter of the population in 1915 to just a few individuals, but the Armenian community in Istanbul, as well those from the diaspora, use it on special occasions.

11

Meryamana Kilisesi

Ana Sokak, Lalebey • Mon–Sat 9am–noon & 2–5pm, Sun 2–5pm

Southwest of the Behram Paşa Camii in Diyarbakır's Syrian Orthodox compound, a small door in the **Meryamana Kilisesi** (Church of the Virgin Mary) leads on to a paved courtyard surrounded by buildings that were once part of a seventh-century monastery. The church itself dates from the third century, making it one of the oldest in the world. It was reconstructed after a fire a couple of centuries ago, and has been much renovated recently, the funding coming from the sizeable Syrian Orthodox diaspora. In addition to the official opening hours, visitors may be allowed to attend the services, which are conducted in either Syriac (a form of Aramaic) or Turkish at 8am each Sunday morning. Contributions are welcome, as only five Syrian Orthodox families remain in the city.

Diyarbakır's houses

Several of the city's distinctive houses have been turned into museums or cultural centres. **Esma Ocak Evi**, an attractive courtyard house near Surp Giragos Kilisesi, was built in 1899 and belonged to a wealthy Armenian family. Well-known Turkish writer Aydın Esma Ocak bought the house in 1990, using it as a base to write several books, among them a biography of Ziya Gökalp (see below); the house is now a pleasant tea garden.

Ziya Gökalp Museum

Çağın Sokak, Ziya Gökalp Mah • Tues–Sun 9am–5pm • Free

Tucked away behind the Ulu Cami, in a black basalt courtyard house constructed in 1806, the **Ziya Gökalp Museum** is devoted – ironically enough in what is today such an overtly Kurdish city – to the architect of Turkish nationalism, Ziya Gökalp, who spent many of his early years here in the late nineteenth century. Exhibits include period photographs of Gökalp and the books from his personal library.

Dengbej Evi

Kilicci Sok 4, near Behram Paşa Camii • Tues–Sun 9am–6pm • Free

The **Dengbej Evi** cultural centre is the best place in town for visitors to see and hear the traditional Kurdish folk art of **dengbey**, the telling of traditional tales through a cappella chants. It's pot luck as to how many performers will be on when you visit, but the shady courtyard of this hundred-year-old house is an atmospheric place to immerse yourself in traditional Kurdish culture for a while.

ARRIVAL AND DEPARTURE   DIYARBAKIR

By plane Kaplaner airport is 3km southwest of town; there's no public transport into Diyarbakır, but taxis to the centre cost ₺15.

Destinations Ankara (4 daily with Anadolujet; 1hr 30min); Antalya (6 weekly direct with Sunexpress; 1hr 40min or 3 daily via Ankara with Anadolujet); Istanbul (11 weekly direct with Sunexpress, 2 daily with Pegasus, 1 daily with Onurair, 2 daily with THY; 2hr); İzmir (2 daily with Sunexpress; 2hr 5min, several daily via Ankara with Anadolujet).

By train The train station is 1km west of town, at the end of İstasyon Cad.

Destinations (Güney Kurtalan Ekspresi) Ankara (Mon, Wed, Fri & Sun; 26hr 15min); Kayseri (Mon, Wed, Fri & Sun; 13hr 50min); Malatya (Mon, Wed, Fri & Sun; 5hr 35min),

Sivas (Mon, Wed, Fri & Sun; 9hr 50min).

By bus Diyarbakır's new *otogar* (Yeni Otogar) is inconveniently located 10km west of the centre – the journey can take 45min at busy periods. Buses into town run 7am–11pm (₺2) and will drop you near Dağ Kapısı (the northern gate to the old city), otherwise a taxi will set you back ₺25. Dolmuşes from Mardin, Batman and other provincial towns arrive at the dolmuş terminal (İlçe Otogar), 1km southwest of the walled city centre, from where it's a 15min dolmuş ride (₺2) into Dağ Kapısı. Eastern bus companies have ticket booths near Dağ Kapısı on Kıbrıs Cad. City buses and dolmuşes to both the Yeni Otogar and İlçe Otogar run from a stop on Kıbrıs Cad, just west of the Büyükşehir Belediyesi Turizm Burosu.

Destinations Adana (6 daily; 8hr); Ankara (8 daily; 13hr);

FROM TOP MARDİN (P.607); HASANKEYF (P.615) >

Batman (hourly; 1hr 30min); Bitlis (5 daily; 3hr 30min); Doğubeyazıt (4 daily; 9hr); Gaziantep (6 daily; 5hr); Malatya (6 daily; 4hr); Mardin (hourly; 1hr 30min); Şanlıurfa (8 daily; 3hr); Siirt (hourly, 3hr); Sivas (4 daily; 10hr); Siverek (hourly; 2hr); Tatvan (5 daily; 4hr); Van (7 daily; 7hr).

Car rental Many bus companies, with offices on Kıbrıs Cad and dotted around the old centre, also arrange car rental. Try Star Diyarbakır on Melikahmet Cad 20/B, or Avis, Elazığ Cad (☎ 0412 229 0276), or at the airport.

INFORMATION

Tourist offices Both the Büyükşehir Belediyesi Turizm Burosu on Kıbrıs Cad (Tues–Sat 9am–noon & 1–6pm), and the State Tourist Office on Gazi Cad, near *Büyük Kervansaray* hotel (Mon–Fri 9am–noon & 1–4pm; ☎ 0412 228 1295) hand out useful city information booklets in English.

ACCOMMODATION

Aslan Palas Oteli Kıbrıs Cad 21 ☎ 0412 223 6810; map p.602. A good budget choice. The small rooms have dubious diamond-checkered carpets but neat, pale furniture, a/c, flatscreen TVs and a fridge, plus crisp white sheets and firm beds. The only downside is the tiny bathrooms, which, although clean, have no shower curtains. The very cheapest rooms also lack running water, which costs ₺20 extra. No breakfast. **₺60**

Hotel Birkent İnönü Cad ☎ 0412 228 7131; map p.602. Good-value two-star place with very friendly staff. It's kept spotlessly clean, and TV and minibar are standard. With bright (and very blue) rooms, it's a good option and slightly quieter than similar establishments fronting Kıbrıs Cad. **₺80**

Büyük Kervansaray Gazı Cad, Deliller Hanı ☎ 0412 228 9606, ⊜ kervansarayotel.com.tr; map p.600. Smallish standard a/c rooms, nicely decorated and with en-suite bathrooms, set in a stunning converted *kervansaray* with a large swimming pool and hamam. The central courtyard is a double-edged sword, wonderfully quiet and relaxing – unless there's a wedding or other event on, in which case the volume pumps up and non-partying guests get irritable. **₺200**

★**Hilton Garden** Dr Şerif İnalöz Cad, Yenişehir ☎ 0412 241 1550, ⊜ hilton.com.tr/diyarbakir; map p.600. Despite its inconvenient location, tucked away behind a military hospital/military complex 15mins walk northeast of Dağ Kapısı, this place is well-worth considering for its expansive views of the lush Tıgris valley, and its decent-sized outdoor pool which, unlike many city hotels, is not overlooked. The 172 rooms have tea- and coffee-making faclities, period photos of Diyarbakır adorning the walls and all the conveniences you'd expect of a *Hilton* – and many rooms have river views. Great breakfast terrace overlooking the river, as well as safe underground parking. **₺210**

New Tigris Hotel Kıbrıs Cad 3 ☎ 0412 224 9696, ⊜ newtigrishotel.com; map p.602. While the location, on the busy corner where Gazi and Kıbrıs caddesis intersect, is not ideal from a noise point of view, it does offer sixty spotless rooms with laminated floors, tastefully muted contemporary decor, all the usual flatscreen TV, a/c et al, plus great views over the walls from the breakfast room. **₺120**

★**Hotel Surkent** Hz Süleyman Cad 19, Saraykapı ☎ 0412 228 1014; map p.602. Immaculately run hotel on a quiet(ish) street running down to the İç Kale. Conveniences include a TV, a/c and a fridge – plus it's spotlessly clean, down to the cramped en-suite bathrooms. Excellent value despite the bold pink and silver palm-leaf wallpaper. Breakfast ₺5 extra. **₺60**

SV Business Hotel İnönü Cad 4 ☎ 0412 228 1295, ⊜ svbusinesshotel.com; map p.602. You don't have to be a businessperson to stay in this smart place. Its clean, bright, ultra-contemporary lines make a refreshing change from the standard eastern-Turkish hotel, as do the free tea- and coffee-making facilities. Single rooms have extra-wide beds. There's also a free fitness centre, sauna and hamam. **₺200**

EATING AND DRINKING

Diyarbakır's **specialities** include lamb *kaburga* (ribs stuffed with fragrant *pilaf* rice), *bumbar* (stuffed intestines) and succulent *içli köfte* (meatballs in a bulgur-wheat casing), available at various restaurants in town. Liver grilled at street stalls is another local favourite, while sweet-toothed visitors should try the syrup-soaked shredded-wheat dessert, *kadayif*. Sumptuous **breakfast/brunch** spreads served up in atmospheric old courtyard houses have become very fashionable in recent years, and are especially popular on weekend mornings.

RESTAURANTS

Aslan Yemek Salonu Kıbrıs Cad; map p.602. Welcoming a/c restaurant – try the *yufkalı incik*, lamb on the bone with peas, pepper and tomato, wrapped in pastry. It also does a decent breakfast, with clotted cream, honey, bread and tea for ₺14. Daily 6am–11pm.

★**Çarşı Konağı** Gazı Cad, Çarşı Karakolu Çarşısı ☎ 0414 228 4673, ⊜ carsikonagi.com; map p.602. Set in an old Armenian courtyard house, this pleasant café/restaurant dishes up delicious *menemen* and hearty grills (from ₺12 for *köfte*) with plenty of free *meze* to begin and Kurdish coffee to finish. Also does quail and trout. Local middle-class women and families socialize here, so it's ideal for female travellers. Daily 11am–11pm.

★ **Selim Amca Sofra Salonu** Ali Emiri Cad ☎ 0412 224 4447; map p.600. A Diyarbakır institution, 5mins walk west of Dağ Kapısı, serving both chicken and lamb *kaburga* mains, *içli köfte* starters and *İrmik helvası* desserts. A fixed menu will set you back ₺27.5, good value considering the opulence of the surroundings and the quality of the food. Daily 10.30am–10pm.

Şanlıurfa Kebap Evi İzzet Paşa Cad 4 ☎ 0414 223 2690; map p.602. Very popular with the locals for its fast service, tasty food and keen prices. Watch your large *lahmacun* (₺3) or massive *pide* (₺12) being prepared in the wood-burning oven downstairs, or retire upstairs to the cooler *aile salonu*. Also serves a good range of kebabs. Daily 7am–10pm.

BARS AND CAFÉS

Büyük Kervansaray Gazi Cad, Deliller Hanı ☎ 0412 228 9606; map p.600. The courtyard of this hotel hosts the closest thing in the city centre to a nightclub; dinner is served around the pool, and there's live music and dancing some nights. One of the few licensed places in town: (small) beers are ₺12. Daily 8am–midnight.

Mahabad Yardımcı Sok 4, Liluz Hotel Yan Arkası ☎ 0412 223 6076; map p.602. Shaded by a giant mulberry tree generously adorned with glass lucky eyes, this traditional courtyard house is today a hip café named after the first (short-lived) Kurdish Republic of Mahabad, in Iranian Kurdistan. A full breakfast/brunch spread, which includes all the usual suspects (25 varieties in all) bar the cream, is ₺17.5. It also dishes up *köfte* and *menemen* as well as cheescakes and waffles. Daily 8am–11pm.

Meşhur Kahvaltıcı Kadri Hasan Paşa Hanı ☎ 0532 203 1979; map p.602. Great late breakfast or brunch spot, on a walkway around the courtyard of an atmospheric *han*. As much tea as you can drink with all the usual Turkish breakfast dishes plus clotted cream, eggs fried with tender lamb slices in a wok-like *tava*, and fiery *acar* paste (walnuts, breadcrumbs and hot pepper). Good value for the ₺17.5 set price. Daily 7am–3pm.

Samo Surp Giragos Kilisesi Arkası; map p.600. A fine period courtyard house close to the Armenian Surp Giargos Kilisesi. Given Its proximity to the Armenian church, in what used to be a Christian quarter of the old city, it's apt that *Samo* serves up glasses of red wine (₺10) produced in the Syrian Orthodox stronghold of the Tür Abdin (see p.613), rather than the glasses of tea of the Muslim neighbourhoods. Live music attracts a young and hip crowd at weekends. Daily 7am–10pm.

Şeymus Gazi Cad 25 ☎ 0412 229 4749; map p.602. This famous firm, which has many branches dotted around the city, specializes in the shredded-wheat dessert *kadayif*. Try it with *peynir* (cheese), *ceviz* (walnut) or *fıstık* (pistachio). ₺6 per portion, ₺8.5 with a generous dollop of (recommended) ice cream. Daily 7am–10pm.

DIRECTORY

Banks and exchange Most of the banks and *döviz* offices are on Gazı Cad.

Hospitals The Devlet Hastanesi (State Hospital) is north of Dağ Kapısı, or try the private Özel Veni Vidi Hastanesi (☎ 0412 229 2025) at Al Emiri Cad 1 (near Dağ Kapısı).

Police Police station on Gazı Cad, just north of the main crossroads.

Post office There is a small PTT on Yeni Kapı Cad, near the junction with Gazı Cad (Mon–Sat 9am–noon and 1–5pm for mail; 24hr for telephones). For money exchange, go to the larger PTT on Ziya Gökalp Bul, 300m north of Dağ Kapısı (same hours).

Travel agencies Diyarbakır has several reputable agencies, the best being Bat-Air, İnönü Cad 9 (☎ 0412 223 5373).

Mardin and around

Seen from the south, **MARDİN** looks spectacular, its tiered layers of vernacular houses, mansions, mosques and churches clinging to a huge citadel-topped rock that rises out of the north Mesopotamian plain. Sunset is particularly striking, with locals flying kites, a deep-blue sky filled with wheeling swifts, and shadows swallowing up the patchwork of fields on the endless plain.

The **population** is a mix of Kurds, Arabs, Turks and Syrian Orthodox Christians, the latter of whom are known in Turkey as Süriyani (see p.685). Handmade soaps are big business here, as are silver jewellery and, more prosaically, dried fruits and nuts, but Mardin's position has always made it a strategic **military outpost** – the higher of the two castellated bluffs today sports golf-ball radar domes. However, following the winding down of the conflict between the state and the PKK in these parts, Mardin became the centre of the region's tourism industry, a popular spot for well-off Istanbul Turks in search of the "quaint east", with boutique hotels opened up in the town's charming old buildings. Unfortunately, the civil war in nearby **Syria** – the more distant of the lights visible twinkling at night on the plain below Mardin's citadel rock are actually in that war-torn country – had dented tourism in the region at the time of writing, and **travel advisories** (see p.577) were warning against non-essential visits to the city and wider region.

The old town lies on the steep southern slopes below the citadel. The principal street, **Birinci Caddesi**, cuts the area in two, branching off the main road at the western end of town and rejoining it at the eastern end. North and west of the old town, the modern city, **Yenişehir**, holds nothing of interest to visitors.

Brief history

Mardin's probable **Roman** origins are lost in a welter of war and conquest, while its later history is tied up with the development of early Christianity. The first Christians to settle here were **Syrian Orthodox**, who arrived during the third century AD. Having survived the period of Arab occupation from 640 to 1104, the Christians were left alone by the Selçuk and Turcoman rulers. Today, eleven churches remain hidden away in the backstreets.

From the twelfth to the fourteenth centuries, the citadel was the capital of the **Artukid Turcoman** tribe. They beat off Arab attacks and endured an eight-month siege during the first Mongol onslaught, before falling to the second Mongol wave under Tamerlane in 1394. The **Mongols** doled out death and misery in equal measures to Christian and Muslim alike, before, in 1408, handing Mardin over to the **Karakoyun Turcoman** tribe, who built the (now ruined) palace and mosque inside the citadel walls. It became an Ottoman possession in 1517.

Before and during Turkey's War of Independence, Mardin's **Christian** population was drastically reduced by massacre and emigration. Following renewed emigrations in the early 1990s, only a few hundred practising Syrian Orthodox, Catholic and Armenian Christians remain. Fortunately, local émigrés who made good in Europe and the USA have invested heavily in the Syrian Orthodox communities in Mardin and the Tür Abdin.

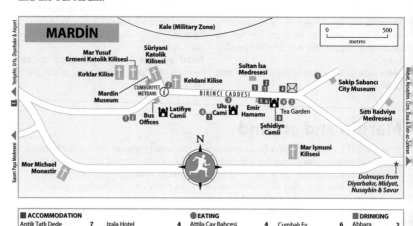

■ ACCOMMODATION				● EATING				■ DRINKING	
Antik Tatlı Dede	7	Izala Hotel	4	Attila Çay Bahçesi	4	Cumbalı Ev	6	Abbara	2
Otel Bilem	1	Reyhani Kasrı	5	Bagdadi	2	Seyr-i Mardin	3	Leylan	1
Dara Konağı	8	Şahmeran Butik Otel	2	Café del Mar	1	Yusuf Üsta'nın Yeri	5		
Erdoba Konakları Hotel	6	Zinciriye	3	Cerciş Murat Konağı	7				

Islamic buildings in Mardin

Mardin boasts some superb **Islamic buildings**. Several hundred metres east of Cumhüriyet Meydanı, the easterly of two sets of stone steps leads up from Birinci Caddesi to the **Sultan İsa Medresesi** religious school (daily 9am–6pm; free). Built in 1385, this striking structure features a magnificent doorway and fluted domes; the semi-translucent volcanic stones used in the *mihrab* of its mosque glow when illuminated with a torch.

Above the Sultan İsa Medresesi, the **kale**, or citadel, was originally built by the Romans and extended by the Byzantines. The castle itself is a forbidden military zone, but it's possible to climb part way up the *kale* hill to a cemetery and get views down over the town and plain beyond.

Below Birinci Caddesi is the **Ulu Cami**, an eleventh-century Selçuk mosque with a minaret that's attractively carved with tear-drop motifs and geometric Arabic lettering. Prominent **Şehidiye Camii**, further east on Birinci Caddesi, also has a very ornate minaret. Further on, east of the Sakıp Sabancı museum (see p.610) is the **Sıttı Radviye Medresesi**, a newly restored theological school that dates back to the late twelfth century, and contains what's believed to be the Prophet Mohammed's footprint in stone.

The **Latifiye Camii**, south of Cumhüriyet Meydanı, dates from the fourteenth century. It has a carved Selçuk-style portal, and a courtyard with a shady garden. Around here lies a maze of streets, forming part of the **bazaar**. At the western end of town, 500m south of the main road, is the (over-restored) fifteenth-century **Kasım Paşa Medresesi**, similar in design to the Sultan İsa Medresesi.

The churches of Mardin

Mardin has a vibrant **Christian heritage**, and Christians and Muslims have always intermingled rather than living in separate quarters. The Syrian Orthodox **Kırklar Kilise** (Arbin Söhad in Syriac) or Church of the Forty Martyrs, which dates back, in part, to the sixth century, is the most welcoming church to visitors. The best time to attend is Sunday morning, at around 9am, when the local Süriyani population comes to pray, though you must dress respectfully and photography is forbidden.

Next door, **Mar Yusuf Ermeni Katolik Kilisesi** (St Joseph's) serves the town's tiny Armenian Catholic population. Lacking a priest, it's usually locked, and the congregation attends services at the Kırklar Kilise.

Mardin's largest church, the **Süriyani Katolik Kilisesi** (Church of the Virgin Mary), is used by five families of Syrian Catholics, and adjoins the local museum (see p.610). On the main street, the restored **Keldani Kilise** (Chaldean Church; irregular hours; ₺2) is of considerable antiquity, though the altar, pews and other trappings are garish and modern. The **Mar İşmuni Kilisesi**, which has a typical Syrian Orthodox walled courtyard, stands at the bottom of the hill in the southeastern part of the old town.

Mardin's domestic architecture

Mardin is famed for its **domestic architecture**. The soft, pale honey-coloured local stone is easy to work, allowing for the intricate carved reliefs that embellish most of its old houses. Look out for the wonderfully ornate **post office building** on Birinci Caddesi, designed in the nineteenth century by the Armenian architect, Lole. Part of the building now belongs to Artuklu University, some of whose students train at the university-run café here. Also of note are the **abarra**, arched passageways covering the street, formed from the two houses either side. As well as providing much-needed shade, they act as cooling wind tunnels.

11

Mardin Museum

Cumhüriyet Meydanı • Tues–Sun 8.30am–4.30pm • ₺5 • ☎ 0482 212 1664

Immediately above Cumhüriyet Meydanı's two car parks, the **Mardin Museum** (Mardin Müzesi) is housed in a restored nineteenth-century mansion that was once the residence of the Syrian Catholic patriarch. It contains some impressive finds from nearby sites, from the Chalcolithic period onwards. Highlights include the burnished red **Urartian pots**, a large kneeling **Assyrian figure** carved from black basalt, and a five-thousand-year-old terracotta toy **chariot**.

Sakıp Sabancı City Museum

Birinci Cad • Tues–Sun April–Oct 8.30am–5.30pm, Nov–March 8am–5pm • ₺2 • ☎ 0482 212 9396, ⊕ sabancimuzesimardin.gov.tr

The state-of-the-art **Sakıp Sabancı City Museum** (Sakip Sabancı Kent Müzesi) is far more exciting than Mardin Museum. Housed in a lovingly restored nineteenth-century barracks on the continuation of Birinci Caddesi, beyond the post office, it offers a bold and imaginative insight into the history, culture and arts of Mardin and its surroundings. There's information on everything from Christianity and Islam through to crafts and costumes, including artefacts, photographs and video presentations. The museum's **Dilek Sabancı Art Gallery**, reached by steps from the main building, hosts top-notch temporary arts exhibitions.

ARRIVAL AND DEPARTURE   MARDİN

By plane Mardin's tiny airport is on the plain, 21km southwest. Catch a taxi for a hefty ₺50 to town, or walk to the main road and hail a Kızıltepe-bound dolmuş.
Destinations Ankara (2 daily with Anadolujet; 1hr 35min); Antalya (1 daily with Anadolujet via Ankara; 3hr 20min); Istanbul (2 daily with THY, 1hr 50min; 2 daily via Ankara with Andaolujet, 3hr 15min; 1 daily with Pegasus, 2hr 5min).

By bus The new *otogar* is inconveniently located in the middle of nowhere, northeast of old Mardin. A taxi ride to the old city is ₺20; you can also take a blue Şehir İçi city bus to the new city, then another up to old Mardin, which will drop you anywhere on Birinci Cad (₺1.5). Dolmuşes for Diyarbakır, Midyat and Nusaybin depart from the İlçe

Otogar at the east end of the old town, on the main Syria-bound road. Reach the terminal by a blue Şehir İçi bus from Birinci Cad (₺1.5). Buy intercity coach tickets from companies on Birinci Cad (near the *meydan*), or from the offices close to the *Otel Bilem* in Yenişehir (new town), reached from the old city by a blue Şehir İçi bus.
Destinations Cizre via Nusaybin (5 daily; 3hr, ₺25); Diyarbakır (25 daily; 1hr 30min, ₺12); Midyat (frequently on demand; 1hr, ₺10); Savur (10 daily; 1hr, ₺8); Şanlıurfa (3 daily, 3hr, ₺30).

Car rental There are several rental places near the *Otel Bilem* and bus agencies in New Mardin. Try Güven Vali Ozan Cad, Karataş Apt 5 (☎ 0482 212 5254).

INFORMATION

Tourist office The small tourist office, south of Birinci Cad (Mon–Fri 9am–noon & 1–5pm; ☎ 0482 212 7406), should have good street maps.

Festivals Mardin is home to the small Sinemardin film festival (⊕ sinemardin.com.tr), held towards the end of June, with the accent on Middle Eastern cinema.

ACCOMMODATION

A plethora of **boutique hotels** clusters either side of Birinci Cad. Accommodation is often booked up during spring and autumn weekends, and during Turkish national holidays, and prices tend to go up in both periods. Rooms vary markedly in size and location, so look before agreeing to take a one. Note that none of the boutique hotels has parking.

Antik Tatlı Dede 104 Sok 27 ☎ 0482 213 2720, ⊕ tatlidede.com.tr. South of the main street in a quiet backroad (noise from the nearby Ulu Cami apart), this is perhaps the most successful conversion from old house to boutique hotel in Mardin. Rooms are spacious with stone floors and barrel-vaulted ceilings, and there's a great terrace for sunset views. No a/c, fans only, as the owners reckon the stone walls keep out the summer heat. **₺130**

Otel Bilem Vali Özan Cad 72 ☎ 0482 212 5568, ⊕ bilemhotel.com. Roughly 1km northwest of, and below, the old town, the bland *Bilem*, despite its somewhat cramped bathrooms and decidedly average breakfast, still represents better value than most of the old-town hotels (particularly if you bargain), offering bright and airy rooms with a/c. Regular municipal buses to the old town run from a stop opposite the hotel. **₺80**

★**Dara Konağı** Sok 39, Şehidiye Mah ☎0482 212 3272, ⊛darakonagi.com. This Armenian courtyard house turned boutique hotel is located down a quiet alley below the landmark Şehidiye mosque. The rooms are charming, with cross-vaulted high ceilings, exposed stone walls and comfy, white-linen sheathed beds, plus a/c, a flatscreen TV and tea- and coffee-making facilities, perhaps in compensation for their small size and frosted-glass bathroom units set in the corner. Owner Burak is friendly and informative, and there are great views of the Mesopotamian plain from the rooftop breakfast terrace. ₺120

Erdoba Konakları Hotel Birinci Cad ☎0482 212 7677, ⊛erdoba.com.tr. Built in "period style" around a courtyard, the main building has an upmarket restaurant attached. A separate building lower down the hill offers rooms in a converted merchant's mansion, and there are two further annexes to the east. All rooms have a/c and are very comfortable, but the *Erdoba* has perhaps sat on its laurels a little. ₺170

★**İzala Hotel** Birinci Cad 156 ☎0482 212 7474, ⊛izalahotel.com. Nicely located next to the historic PTT building on the old town's main street, the *İzala* is arguably the best-managed hotel in town. Standard rooms have exposed stone walls, wooden furniture and flooring and all the necessary conveniences, plus generously proportioned bathrooms with rain showers. The breakfast buffet is plentiful and delicious, and roof-terrace views of the plains and citadel enchanting. ₺250

Reyhani Kasrı Birinci Cad 163 ☎0482 212 1333, ⊛reyhanikasri.net. Blithely sitting on the fence between boutique and conventional upmarket hotel, this place might upset the purist but will tick a lot of boxes for many visitors: central location in old Mardin, great views, good service and value, just enough character and all conveniences, including free tea- and coffee-making facilities. ₺170

Şahmeran Butik Otel Birinci Cad, Sok 10 ☎0482 213 2300, ⊛sahmeranpansiyon.com. Tucked up behind the main street opposite the *Erdoba Konakları Hotel*, *Şahmeran* provides the only dorm accommodation in town. It is overpriced and a bit ramshackle, but has a friendly English-speaking manager, and offers waterless and dark dorms, brighter pension rooms (aka two-person dorms), and standard en-suite double rooms. Have a good look before choosing. Breakfasts ₺5 extra. Dorm ₺30, pension bed ₺70, double ₺100

Zinciriye Medrese Mah 243, Sok 13 ☎0482 212 4866, ⊛zinciriye.com. Well placed in the old town just below the Sultan İsa Medresesi, all fifteen rooms have exposed stone walls, vaulted ceilings, tasteful furnishings and views – and there's a splendid terrace with stunning panoramas. The owners also run the nearby *Kadım*, a useful backup in busy periods. ₺150

EATING AND DRINKING

Mardin has a fabulous **local cuisine** which, unusually for Turkey, uses a lot of fruit in savoury dishes. The region also specializes in dishes such as *kaburga* (rice-stuffed rib of lamb) and *içli köfte* (dim-sum style boiled meatballs in a bulgar wheat crust). Nonetheless, Mardin's restaurants were disappointingly basic until recently, and the city's new-found popularity with well-off Turkish visitors has seen a slow improvement in the local eating scene.

RESTAURANTS

Bağdadi Birinci Cad, Vali Adil Sok 2 ☎0482 212 5555. Worthy competition for the long-established *Cercis Murat Konağı*, this white-tableclothed place, housed in a historic building with an attractive terrace and courtyard, has a number of delicious regional dishes on offer. Try the "superfood" *firik* salad, made with smoked bulgar wheat (₺12); a black plum kebab (₺25); and a stew of tender lamb, onion, garlic, plums, pomegranate sauce and chickpeas (₺25). Beer is a reasonable ₺12, wine ₺15 a glass. Daily 10am–11pm.

★**Cercis Murat Konağı** Birinci Cad ☎0482 213 6841, ⊛cercismurat.com. Set in a restored Süriyani house west of Cumhüriyet Meydanı, with great views from the terrace, this place specializes in local dishes such as *incassıye*, lamb flavoured with sweet *pekmez*, plums, chilli and tomato. A fixed-menu meal (₺50) is a worthwhile treat; the *mezes*, which appear in a panoply of silver ladles, are superb. Decent local red wine, too. Daily noon–midnight.

Cumbalı Ev Tatlıdede Konağı Karşı ☎0482 212 8484. A short walk down from Birinci Cad and opposite the *Antik Tatlı Dede* hotel, in a nineteenth-century stone house with an ornately carved bay window. More pertinently, it has a lovely little terrace where you can enjoy a glass of decent-quality Süriyani wine for ₺15, or a fixed-menu meal of regional dishes, including *kaburga*, for ₺40. There are a couple of nice indoor dining rooms for colder weather. Daily 10am–11pm.

Seyr-i Mardin Birinci Cad ☎0482 213 4741. Rooftop café above the noise and bustle of the main drag, with fabulous views to Syria. It's mostly standard Turkish dishes, with kebabs from ₺17, regional dishes from ₺10. There's an atmospheric indoor dining area too, and friendly service, but bear in mind the smoke emanating from the kitchen stove-pipes when sitting on the top terrace. Daily 9am–11pm.

Yusuf Ustanın Yeri Eski Postahane Karşısı ☎0482 212 7985. This simple, family-oriented *ocakbaşı* (charcoal grill) garden restaurant, opposite the PTT, serves delicious kebabs and *köfte*, but no alcohol. Daily 10am–11pm.

BARS AND CAFÉS

Abbara Birinci Cad, Garanti Banası Karşısı ☏ 0482 213 2231. Great views of the Mesopotamian plain from the expansive roof terrace, while inside there's live music every Wed, Fri & Sat, with Turkish, Kurdish, Süriyani and Armenian styles all on offer. Beers are a reasonable ₺10, wine (not great quality) is ₺12. Daily noon–2am.

Atilla Çay Bahçesi Birinci Cad. Mardin's oldest tea garden, opposite the PTT, affords shade and a terrace with sunset views over the Mesopotamian plain to Syria. Daily 7am–10pm.

Café del Mar Sanat Sok 17 ☏ 0482 212 7080. Located en route to the Sakıp Sabancı museum, this is the place to come if you've a craving for a latte (₺8), chocolate brownie (₺8) or other such decidedly un-Mardin-like delicacies. It also does Turkish grills, with kebabs from ₺13, plus pasta dishes from ₺13, and if you ask they'll probably find you a cold beer. More traditionally, try the wild pistachio *menengiç* coffee, or *mırra*, a bitter double-brewed local coffee. Daily 8am–10pm.

Leylan Birinci Cad ☏ 0482 212 8575. Bookshop-cum-café/bar in a fine old house all decked out with ethnic artefacts, and with a terrace overlooking the street. Good place for an early beer (₺9) and toasted-sandwich snack, with tasteful local music, mainly Kurdish, playing in the background. Daily 10pm–midnight.

DIRECTORY

Hamams The Emir Hamam on Birinci Cad is set in a splendid building, purpose-built in the thirteenth century. (Men 6.30am–noon & 6–10pm, women noon–5.30pm; ₺10).

Hospital A good bet is the private Derman Tıp Merkezi on Vali Ozan Cad, south of the *Otel Bilem*.

Deyr-az-Zaferan

6km southeast of Mardin • Daily 8.30am–noon & 1–6.30pm • ₺6 • The walk from Mardin takes 1hr 15min: follow the Nusaybin road southeast from the old town centre until you see a white-on-brown sign pointing left (east) into the hills; a taxi from old Mardin costs around ₺50 for a return trip, with waiting time

Founded in 493 AD, the Syrian Orthodox monastery of **Deyr-az-Zaferan** is known as the "Saffron Monastery", on account of the yellowish rock from which it's built. From 1160 until the 1920s, this was the seat of the Syrian Orthodox patriarch, who has since relocated to Damascus. Now the showpiece of the Syrian Orthodox Church in Turkey, it has been lovingly restored, largely with funds from the diaspora.

There's a posh gift shop and cafeteria at the entrance, and you'll be escorted, often perfunctorily, around the monastery complex by Süriyani guides. First up on the obligatory tour is an underground **vault**, topped by a stone ceiling constructed without mortar, and believed to have been a sun-worshippers' temple in pagan times. Next to it at ground level, the domed **Church of Beth Kadishe** boasts elaborately carved Corinthian capitals and a late Roman-style frieze. The remains of several metropolitan bishops and patriarchs are encased in niches lining the nave.

The domed **Church of Mor Hananyo**, immediately north, dates back to the sixth century, but has been much rebuilt. It holds some gorgeous relief-carved friezes, pretty faux-naïf altar curtains, and a rather garish 1950s altar. The last room, a chapel, contains a wooden altar from 1699, and an ancient wooden palaquin used to carry patriarchs past. This remains a working church, with one of the four metropolitan bishops of the Syrian Orthodox Church in Turkey, plus a few monks and nuns, still in residence.

Savur

45km north of Mardin • You can get here by dolmuş from Mardin (8 daily; 1hr; ₺12); if driving, follow the D-380 towards Midyat for around 8km, then turn left (north) and wind through the villages of Çınaraltı, Dereyanı, Köprülü, Pınardere and Dursu to Savur (around 36km)

Set on twin hilltops in a dramatic confluence of valleys, **SAVUR** is often referred to as "Little Mardin", and is well worth a visit if you'd like to see how Mardin used to look before it took off as the southeast's tourist capital. It has the same beautifully carved, honey-hued stone houses, a fortress atop one of its hills, and a number of the shady passages known as *abarra*. While parts of the drive to Savur are stunningly beautiful, however, it lacks the specific sights of Mardin, so the real reason to come is to stay at its only accommodation, the fascinating *Hacı Abdullah Konağı Evi*.

ACCOMMODATION SAVUR

★**Hacı Abdullah Konağı Evi** Devlet Mah, Savur
☎0482 571 2127 or ☎0533 239 7808. Fabulous
220-year-old mansion house, set on a hilltop overlooking
the town, valleys and surrounding plateau. The owner's
family trace their origins back to Hussein, grandson of the

Prophet Mohammed, and are very welcoming. Everything
is original here, from the brass beds to the kilims and
elaborately carved wooden ceilings. Bathrooms are simple
and shared. Rates include breakfast and dinner. ₺**200**

Dara

Oğuz, 30km southeast of Mardin • **Dara** Unrestricted access • Free • **Necropolis** Daily 8.30am–6pm • Free • Catch a dolmuş to Oğuz (3
daily), or take a Nusaybin-bound dolmuş as far as the turn for Oğuz, and hitch the remaining 9km east; if driving from Mardin, follow the
Nusaybin road for around 24km, then turn left (east) for Oğuz village and the site

The evocative ruins of Byzantine **Dara** (the ancient city of Anastopolis), dating from the
middle of the sixth century AD, and picturesquely set amid the houses of the traditional
Kurdish village of **Oğuz**, are difficult to access without your own vehicle. The most
extensive remains in the region, they're well worth visiting, testament to a time when
this area formed the eastern bastion of the Byzantine Christian world against the Persian
Empire. Bear in mind, however, that the site is less than 10km from the frontier with
Syria, so it's essential to check the **security situation** (see box, p.577) before heading here.

The first area of interest lies to the left of the road, just before the village. Excavations
are ongoing at the massive **necropolis**, as well as what may well be a major temple.
Excellent display boards explain the finds, while the on-site café holds a model of the
whole site, and friendly guards will point you in the right direction.

To find the obvious remains of a large **Byzantine cistern complex**, head towards
the village then turn left (north). To the south, a small, pleasant tea garden stands
at the entrance to a monumental and totally unexpected piece of architecture – an
underground (and well-lit) vaulted cistern, some 30m high. Beyond this, charmingly
scattered amid olive orchards, lie other remains of the city, including stretches of
paved road, **bridges** and parts of the city **walls** and **towers**.

The Tür Abdin plateau

The undulating plateau of the **Tür Abdin**, traditional heartland of the Syrian Orthodox
Church (see p.685), starts just east of Mardin, and is home to a dwindling number of
Christians who co-exist uneasily with the local Muslim Kurds. The rocky plateau is
more fertile than you might think if you only see it in the parched days of summer,
dotted with what appear to be little more than masses of hardy scrub oak. Grape
cultivation is a mainstay, as is lentil production, and walnut, almond, cherry, fig and
pomegranate all flourish. Olives are few and far between, however, as the winters here
are cold. **Midyat** is the western gateway to the Tür Abdin proper, where several villages
are still either wholly, or partially, inhabited by Syrian Orthodox Christians, and there
are 46 **monasteries and churches**, some recently restored. Most are tricky to reach by
public transport, so arrange either a taxi or rental car.

Given the proximity of the Syrian border, do check the **security situation** (see p.577)
before visiting this area.

Midyat

The town of **MİDYAT**, an hour east of Mardin by road, consists of two distinct districts.
The westerly portion is the modern business district of **Estel**, while the originally
Christian portion of half-abandoned medieval mansions, known as **Eski** (Old) **Midyat**,
lies 2km east. Midyat benefitted from the tourism boom in nearby Mardin, with an
influx of domestic visitors staying at newly opened boutique hotels and searching for

ASSYRISKA – A NATIONAL TEAM WITHOUT A NATION

While they lack a country of their own, Turkey's Süriyani or Assyrian population have found an unlikely rallying point: a football club in Sweden. **Assyriska**, a second-division team based near Stockholm, is made up entirely of immigrants, two-thirds of whom are Syrian Orthodox Christians who have emigrated from Turkey.

In 2006, Midyat-born journalist **Nuri Kino** brought their story to life in an award-winning documentary, *Assyriska*, charting the side's progress to a brief spell at the top of the Swedish premiership (although in 2015 they were battling for promotion from Sweden's second division). The team remain a symbol of pride for the Assyrian diaspora throughout the world, who have often been persecuted in their traditional heartlands (modern Turkey, Iraq, Iran and Syria). The documentary is controversial in Turkey, as it alleges that the massacres suffered by Assyrians at the hands of the Ottomans in World War I amount to genocide.

11

bargains (particularly *telkari* or filigree) in the multitude of silver shops for which the town is famous. However, the ongoing unrest in Syria has affected visitor numbers and, as with elsewhere in the region, you should check the latest **travel advisories** (see p.577) before heading here.

Although nearly five thousand **Syrian Orthodox Christians** still lived here in 1974, the men mostly engaged in gold- or silversmithing, the population shrank to just eighty families and one priest after the conflict in the 1980s and 1990s between the PKK and Turkish security forces. However, thanks to the changed political climate as well as economic growth, some Syrian Orthodox families are starting to return. Evidence of more recent conflicts is signalled by the presence of the **refugee camp** behind the town, home to 5000 Arab Muslim refugees from Syria and 3000 Yezidis from Iraq.

The town's **churches**, dotted among the imposing mansions built in tiers along a low ridge, are easily spotted by virtue of their graceful belfries. **Mor Barsaumo**, close to the main road and reached by an alleyway opposite the *Cihan* restaurant, was built as early as the fifth century, destroyed in 1793 and rebuilt in 1910. As the most active of the churches, this is the best to visit. It contains a small schoolroom where the kids of the remaining Syrian Orthodox families come to learn Syriac, a language closely related to the Aramaic spoken by Christ.

ARRIVAL AND DEPARTURE

MİDYAT

By bus The dolmuş *garaj* in old Midyat is a couple of hundred metres south of town on the İdil/Mar Gabriel road.

Destinations Mardin (hourly; 1hr; ₺10); Hasankeyf (6 daily; 45min; ₺9); Nusaybin (5 daily; 1hr 15min; ₺10).

ACCOMMODATION

Kasr-ı Nehroz Hotel Işıklar Mah 219, Sok 14 ☎ 0452 464 0719, ⏏ hotelnehroz.com. Converted from an old mansion house, this stunning hotel combines the best of the old with contemporary flourishes. It's as tasteful and comfortable a place as you'll stay at eastern Turkey, and far better value than Mardin's boutique hotels. It also holds a good restaurant, open to non-guests, where the menu is packed with local specialities. Prices change according to demand; low-season rates can be half those in peak season. **₺300**

★ Shmayaa Hotel Kışla Cad 126, Sok 12 ☎ 0452 464 0696, ⏏ shmayaa.com. While not quite as atmospheric as the rival *Nehroz* on the ridge-top above, this beautifully appointed 21-room boutique hotel, crafted from the traditional mansion house of a former Syrian Orthodox Patriarch, is better value. The tastefully appointed rooms are set around a courtyard, with the Gilgamesh suite room a riot of elaborate relief carving vying for attention with a massive flatscreen TV. It is also extremely well-run and friendly. **₺250**

EATING AND DRINKING

★ Cihan Lokantası Cizre Yolu Üzeri ☎ 0482 464 1566. Just south of the junction roundabout on the Mar Gabriel road, this spotlessly clean place is packed at lunchtimes for its superb *sulu yemek*, which includes tender *kaburga* (rib

of lamb) and *perde pilaf* (delicately spiced rice with shredded chicken), for ₺8. The creamy *yayık* (frothy) *ayran* is served in copper bowls. Daily 9am–10pm.

Mar Gabriel

22km southeast of Midyat, 2km east of the İdil–Cizre road • Daily 8.30am–11am & 1–4.30pm • ₺5 • ⓦ morgabriel.org • İdil-bound dolmuşes (20min; ₺4) from old Midyat's dolmuş garage drop passengers at the signed Mar Gabriel junction, 2km walk on a surfaced road from the monastery; taxis from Midyat cost around ₺35, including waiting time

Founded in 397 AD, the monastery of **Mar Gabriel** (Deyrulumur) is the geographical and spiritual centre of the Tür Abdin plateau. The oldest and most vital surviving Syrian Orthodox monastery in Turkey, it's the seat of the metropolitan bishop of Tür Abdin. A working community, set among gardens and orchards, its primary purpose is to keep Syrian Orthodox Christianity alive in the land of its birth by providing schooling and ordination of native-born monks. There are thirteen resident nuns and three monks, as well as a fluctuating number of local lay workers, guests and students.

A lay person gives visitors **guided tours** of the monastery. The glittering, mosaic-covered ceiling of the apse of the main Anastasius (512 AD) **church**, under restoration at the time of writing, is particularly memorable, though Tamerlane stripped the gold ceiling of the nave. The tour also takes in the circular **dining room**, which is surmounted by a dome donated by the Byzantine empress Theodora early in the sixth century AD, and the Church of the Mother of God, dating back some fourteen hundred years.

Hah

33km northeast of Midyat • Follow the Hasankeyf road from Midyat for 3km, then turn right for Dargeçit; after 17km turn right again (signed Meryemana/Hah); continue 6km to Hesterek village, then turn left and continue another 7km to Hah, also known as Anıtlı

Set in the fascinating village of **HAH** (Anıtlı in Turkish), the remote fifth-century **Church of the Mother of God** – İndath Aloho in Syriac, Meryemana in Turkish – is undoubtedly the most beautiful Syrian Orthodox building in Turkey. Local Süriyanis regard it as the jewel in the Tür Abdin crown. It sports a two-storey-wedding-cake-like turret with blind arches topped by a pyramidal roof; the archways and lintels are also heavily ornamented. The church has a virtually square ground plan, with a transverse nave, but what's striking about the domed interior are the gorgeously ornate Corinthian capitals and an elaborate, relief-carved frieze.

Hah itself was once the centre of a community of several thousand, with over 44 churches in the vicinity, but just sixteen families now remain. At the heart of the village, atop a small rise, is a group of fortified houses where five thousand Christians held out for months against a vastly superior Ottoman force in 1915. Downhill from here stand the remains of the church of **Mor Bacchus**, dating back to the second century, while en route back to the Church of the Mother of God is the ruined sixth-century church of **Mor Sovo**, which was destroyed by Tamerlane.

Other Syrian Orthodox churches worth seeing between Midyat and Hah include **Mor Dimet** at **Zaz**, and the important **Mar Yakoub** monastic church in Baraztepe (Salah) village.

Hasankeyf

The spectacular ruined settlement of **HASANKEYF**, an hour's dolmuş ride north of Midyat, is one of Turkey's most evocative historic sites. Poised on the very lip of a sheer cliff, carved from the mountainside by the swift-flowing waters of the Tigris, stands a remarkable series of remains of Selçuk, Arabic and Kurdish origin. Below the ruins, the Tigris is spanned by the arches of a vintage 1950s concrete bridge, itself overlooking the mighty piers of its medieval precursor. It's a photographer's dream, especially at sunset and sunrise.

11

THAT SINKING FEELING: THE DROWNING OF HASANKEYF

The remarkable historic site of **Hasankeyf** was put on the World Monuments Fund Watch List in 2008, as one of the hundred most endangered heritage sites in the world. Despite this, and a domestic and international outcry, much of the ancient city is almost certain to be drowned by the waters of the **İlisu dam** across the Tigris, part of the GAP project (see p.579).

Pledges to save key elements of the site, including for example the brick-built Zeyn El-Abdin Türbesi, and remove them to a reservoir-side open-air museum are decried by **critics**, who say the remains are far too delicate to move. The most vociferous critics of the scheme are the eighty thousand or so locals who stand to be displaced by the flood waters. Several other groups also oppose it, including those who live downstream in Iraq, who fear the dam will wipe out their already scant water resources; Kurdish nationalists, who view the dam as a deliberate attempt to wipe out their cultural heritage; and assorted national and international environmental groups. Visit ⓦ hasankeyfmatters.com for the latest news on the resistance effort.

Meanwhile, the **dam**, 70km downstream of Hasankeyf, was completed in 2015; a new, higher bridge across the river south of the town was under construction at the time of writing. Unhappy locals reckon the flood waters will subsume their homes by 2018.

11

The **modern town** of Hasankeyf is strung out either side of the road leading to the concrete bridge across the river, while a **new settlement**, visible on the flanks of the valley north of the river, is under construction and will house the entire population of the town when it is inundated by the waters of the İlisu Dam (see box above). At the time of writing, the majority of the remains of **historic Hasankeyf**, perched on the clifftop, were **closed** and are unlikely to reopen until the level of the reservoir is decided. All the same, much of the 1km road leading towards the site was still in business, its rows of souvenir stalls selling everything from tasteful, locally woven goat-hair blankets to garish wall-hangings. Its initial section, fronting the river, includes simple restaurants, some with platforms out in the water at the foot of the cliff.

Some history

While many of the four-thousand-plus **caves** in the surrounding hills were inhabited in prehistoric times, the original settlement was founded by the **Romans** as an eastern bastion of the empire, and later became the Byzantine bishopric of Cephe. In 640 AD, the conquering Arabs changed the town's name to Hisn Kayfa. During the twelfth century the Artukid **Turcoman** tribe decided to make Hasankeyf their capital, which it remained until the Mongols arrived in 1260. Hasankeyf then served as the stronghold of the **Ayyubids**, a clan of Kurdish chieftains supplanted by the Ottomans early in the fifteenth century.

Old Hasankeyf

On the approach to the Hasankeyf site, beyond the bulk of the souvenir shops, **El Rizk Camii** was built under the Ayyubids in 1409 AD, and was still open to visitors at the time of writing. According to locals, the dam waters will lap the tip of its beautiful minaret, which is decorated with *kufic* inscriptions and tear-drop patterns, and topped by a stork's nest. The building also holds useful toilets (the only ones in Hasankeyf now the main site is closed). In the town centre to the northeast is the **Eyyubi Cami**, which is of a similar age and sits in front of a cliff pocked with ancient cave dwellings, a few of them still inhabited.

Although visitors can no longer access the upper part of the site, you can at least admire the **Kücük Sarayı** or "Small Palace" from below, partly built into a spectacular promontory. Above that, probably best viewed from the north bank of the Tigris, are the assorted remains of a late medieval Islamic city. These include the **Ulu Cami**, an evocatively ruined, partially restored Ayyubid mosque built in 1305, the remains of

Lake Van
and the
southeast

MOUNT ARARAT

Lake Van and the southeast

Bordered by Iran to the east and Iraq to the south, Turkey's remote southeast is a land dominated by soaring peaks, rugged plateaux and plunging valleys. Its austere natural beauty makes the perfect backdrop for some impressive and intriguing sights, while the predominantly ethnically Kurdish population gives the region a distinctively different feel to the rest of the country. At its heart lies Lake Van, a vast inland sea ringed by snowcapped peaks. The Armenians who once lived around the lake were so enamoured with its beauty and fertility they had a saying "Van in this life, paradise in the next". North of the lake is the graceful 5137m volcanic cone of Ağrı Dağı – better known as Mount Ararat – the highest peak in Turkey, while the wild alpine range south of the lake contains lofty Reşko (4135m), the nation's second-highest peak.

Winters, starting in early November, are severe, with roads often blocked by heavy snow, but in July and August, while much of the rest of Turkey is sweltering, these highlands are relatively cool and humidity free. The road system is generally excellent, with major improvements made over recent years.

Food out here is mostly plainer than in the west of Turkey, but the local Kurdish cheeses such as *otlu peynir* are uniformly excellent, and Van's famous breakfast spread (see p.633) is now well known across the country. Until quite recently the economy of the region was largely based on nomadic pastoralism, but the lure of the big cities and the forced evacuation of hundreds of villages during the struggle with the PKK (Kurdish Workers Party) has decimated the rural population. This population decline was exacerbated in October 2011 when a massive **earthquake** struck the eastern part of the lake, causing devastation in Van city and the surrounding towns and villages.

Various cities in western Turkey offer daily flights to the regional capital, **Van** (1642km from Istanbul), on the eastern shore of the lake. Van has an ancient citadel set atop a dramatic limestone outcrop, overlooking the atmospheric but scant remains of the tragically destroyed old town. Rapidly expanding and modernizing, Van is a remarkably civilized and welcoming centre for exploration. Overland, the conventional approach is by bus from Diyarbakır (see p.599), via the old trade route through the stark valley town of **Bitlis** and dull **Tatvan**, itself a base for exploring the northwest shore of Lake Van. Alternatively, from Erzurum (see p.543), travellers can head due east to **Doğubeyazıt** and its fanciful palace below the impressive bulk of Mount Ararat. From Van, a four-hour journey leads through spectacular, if often troubled (see box, p.637), mountains to **Hakkari**.

Lake Van

Virtually an inland sea, covering almost 4000 square kilometres at an elevation of 1750m, **Lake Van** is one of eastern Turkey's most unusual features. Along with Lake Sevan in Armenia and Lake Urmia in Iran, it is one of a trio of huge upland lakes

A walk along the shore: Van İskele to Van Kalesi p.630
A forgotten Kingdom – Urartu p.635

Travel in the mountains south of Lake Van: a warning p.637
Nestorian Christians p.638

AHLAT CEMETERY

Highlights

❶ Nemrut Dağı The massive crater of this towering volcano shelters migrating birds in May and September, and in between offers the possibility of a dip in the crater lakes. **See p.626**

❷ Ahlat The eerie cemeteries of lakeshore Ahlat are home to beautifully carved, improbably angled tombstones and striking cylindrical mausoleums. **See p.626**

❸ Van Kalesi The lakeside "Rock of Van", fortified by the ancient Urartians and covered in their cuneiform inscriptions, rises above the poignant old town of Van. **See p.629**

❹ Akdamar island This picturesque islet off the southern shores of Lake Van is home to a superbly restored tenth-century Armenian church, liberally decorated with relief-carved biblical scenes. **See p.634**

❺ İshak Paşa Sarayı An ornate palace of richly carved golden limestone, nestling beneath a dramatic rocky spur above the Silk Road to Iran. **See p.640**

❻ Mount Ararat This iconic biblical peak, at 5137m the highest mountain in Turkey, rises in Mount Fuji-like volcanic magnificence above the bustling frontier town of Doğubeyazıt. **See p.642**

HIGHLIGHTS ARE MARKED ON THE MAP ON P.622

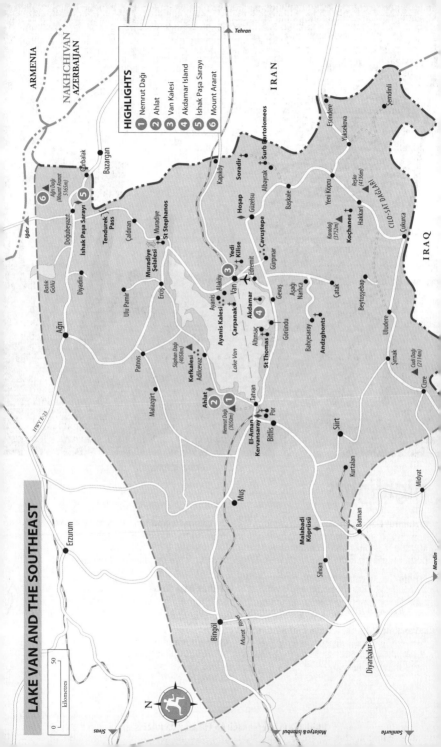

LAKE VAN AND THE SOUTHEAST

HIGHLIGHTS
1. Nemrut Dağı
2. Ahlat
3. Van Kalesi
4. Akdamar Island
5. Ishak Paşa Sarayı
6. Mount Ararat

hereabouts that lack outlets. Surrounded on all sides by a narrow but fertile plain, and then mountains, the lake – nearly 200m deep in spots – occupies what was once a lowland basin that was later dammed by lava flowing from Nemrut Dağı. Owing to rapid evaporation in this desert climate, the lake water is highly alkaline.

Although venerable **Bitlis** is a twenty-minute drive from the western shores of the lake, and set 200m below it in a narrow valley, the vast majority of visitors pass through the town en route to or from Lake Van and its immediate environs. On the west shore of the lake, workaday **Tatvan** makes a handy base for forays up impressive **Nemrut Dağı** and its crater lakes. Of interest on the austerely volcanic north shore of the lake are **Ahlat** and its incredible medieval Muslim cemeteries, while to the northwest pastoral **Adilcevaz** nestles in the shadow of 4058m Süphan Dağı. The major draw on the south shore of the lake is the beautiful island of Akdamar and its **Church of the Holy Cross**, while the east shore holds the regional capital, **Van**.

Although you can **swim** from the stony beaches on and opposite Akdamar, and along the more sparsely populated stretches of shoreline, **pollution** makes it inadvisable to bathe near Tatvan or Van. In places the shoreline is littered with plastic detritus washed up from the lake – it's a major eyesore and a public awareness campaign has had little appreciable effect.

Set on a major **bird** migration route between Africa and Russia/Central Asia, Lake Van is a magnet for serious birdwatchers. Pelican and flamingo can be seen, as well as the rare white-headed duck, velvet scoter and paddyfield warbler.

Two species of **fish** – one called *dareka* – live in the lake, but only where fresh water enters. They are caught for food during spring when, salmon-like, they migrate up incoming streams to spawn.

The fluffy **Van cat**, endowed naturally with one blue and one gold eye, is now rare, but a few specimens are still kept at local carpet shops as tourist bait, and there is a breeding station (open to visitors) on the campus of Van's Yüzüncü Yıl university.

12

Bitlis

The historic town of **BİTLİS** (1545m altitude) is reached along an attractive winding gorge dotted with *kervansaray*s and old bridges. Its lifeblood used to be its location on the main west–east transit road linking the Tigris and Euphrates basins with that of Lake Van, but Bitlis has recently been bypassed by a 4km-long tunnel. The plus side for visitors is that the once very noisy, polluted main drag is much more pleasant.

Bitlis is a fascinating and atmospheric town, ignored by most travellers in the headlong rush to Lake Van. Assuming you arrive early enough in the day, it's easy to alight here and explore before you catch one of the very frequent dolmuşes on to Tatvan. With its dark stone houses and steep valley setting, Bitlis has the feel of an isolated nineteenth-century English mill town, though it once controlled the pass from Syria to the Van region and Persia and Armenia beyond. Before World War I it was a prosperous place, and about half the inhabitants were Armenian. Today, this predominantly Kurdish town is impoverished; its last major employer, a factory that processed the famous local tobacco, closed in 2008.

Şerefiye Külliyesi
In the town centre, just south of the castle

The most notable monument in Bitlis, the sixteenth-century **Şerefiye Külliyesi** is a fine mosque/*medrese*/hamam complex. It was built in the Ottoman period, but in a distinctly Selçuk style, especially the finely carved stalactite-style portal of the mosque, enlivened by a band of black and white stone. The tombs of several dignitaries are located in the grounds.

İhlasiye Medresesi

North of the castle • Mon–Fri 8am–5pm • Free

Reached by a steep flight of steps that climbs up from the main street opposite the *Dideban* hotel, the turreted **İhlasiye Medresesi** was built in 1569 by the Kurdish emir Şerefxan. This fine theological school complex is today home to the Directory of Tourism, and boasts a beautiful minaret as well as fine views across the town to the surrounding hills.

Ulu Cami

Just west of, and below, the castle

The unusual-looking **Ulu Cami** mosque was built from the local dark stone in 1126 by the Artukids. Even by Bitlis' severe standards it's an austere structure, enlivened by zigzag motifs on the cylindrical minaret and an unusual dome on the part of the *mihrab* extending to the outside of the building.

Küfrevi Türbesi

East of the main drag, accessible via steps above the Tatvan dolmuş stop on the main street

A walled complex holds both the **Küfrevi Türbesi**, dating from 1316, and a much more modern *türbe* (tomb) built by Greek craftsmen under the orders of Sultan Abdülhamit in 1898. Together these house the tombs of six Sunni saints, who draw pilgrims from all over the Muslim world.

The citadel

Bitlis' huge **citadel**, originally built by one of Alexander the Great's generals (though the walls now visible date back only to 1530 AD), is built on a rock outcrop looming over the town. Reach it by following a road that snakes around its base to the far side, from where steps continue to the top, with great views over Bitlis. Ongoing excavations and safety work meant the castle was closed to visitors at the time of writing.

Por

9km northeast of Bitlis • Turn right, signed towards Değirmenaltı, 3km north of Bitlis on the road to Tatvan; a taxi will cost around ₺40 return, including waiting time

Although little remains of Bitlis' Armenian past, the Kurdish village of **Por** (Değirmenaltı in Turkish), beautifully situated in a lush, green valley, holds Turkey's best collection of **Armenian khatchkars**. One of these beautifully inscribed memorial stones is over 3m high. The adjoining **church of St Anania**, now used as a barn, dates back to the seventh century, and is in surprisingly good condition.

ARRIVAL AND DEPARTURE   BİTLİS

By bus and dolmuş Tatvan dolmuşes depart from a prominent minibus park situated on the main road at the western entrance to the town. Intercity buses heading to or from Van pass through Bitlis; tickets are available from several bus offices on the main drag.

Destinations Tatvan (daily 8am–6pm; 30min; ₺5); Van (several daily; 3hr; ₺20).

ACCOMMODATION AND EATING

Büryancı Vahit Usta Yeri Balıkçılar Sok 20 ☎ 0434 226 1892. One of numerous simple restaurants, tucked beneath the citadel *kale*, devoted to the local speciality, *büryan kebap*, leg of goat steamed in a *tandır* oven for four hours, and served on the bone atop a pile of fresh *pide* for a bargain at ₺12. Note that food can run out early at busy times. Daily 5am–3pm.

Çağlayan Nur Cad ☎ 0434 226 4057. If you don't fancy leg of goat, go for the standard Turkish cuisine dished up at this functional but spotless place at bargain prices, with a couple of *lahmacun* and an *ayran* for ₺5. They also serve soups, *pide* and kebab. Daily 6am–10pm.

Dideban Nur Cad 1 ☎ 0434 226 2821, ✉ didebanotel @hotmail.com. Functional, clean en-suite rooms boasting wi-fi, hairdryers and a fridge. Owner Muşfik is friendly and always pleased to see foreigners visiting his home town. ₺80

Tatvan

TATVAN, a functional town of some 70,000 souls, lodged between the mountains and lakeshore 25km northeast of Bitlis, makes a good base for exploring the surrounding sights. It has smartened up considerably in the last few years, with a couple of new shopping centres, one of which holds a cinema and bowling alley, and a promenade along the lakeshore. To the north is the massif of **Nemrut Dağı** with its crater lakes; further east around the lake are the impressive medieval remains at Ahlat (see p.626).

Tatvan's streets follow the grid layout common in new developments in Turkey, with the main street, **Cumhüriyet Caddesi**, running east to west 100m south of the lake.

ARRIVAL AND DEPARTURE

By bus and dolmuş Tatvan's *otogar* is 1km along the Bitlis road, but buses invariably drop passengers near the PTT at Cumhüriyet Meydan (Square) on Cumhüriyet Caddesi. Buses to Van usually depart from in front of the various bus company offices on Cumhüriyet Caddesi, following the main road along the beautiful south shore of the lake; Ahlat dolmuşes leave from the corner of the PTT, near Cumhüriyet Caddesi, and run along the north shore of the lake; and Bitlis dolmuşes depart from Cumhüriyet Caddesi, 400m north of the square.
Destinations Ahlat (every 45min; 45min); Bitlis (hourly; 30min); Diyarbakır (5 daily; 4hr); Van (hourly; 2hr 30min).

By train The train station is 1km northwest of the centre. The Transasya Ekspresi theoretically arrives from Ankara at 2.50pm on Fridays, though it is often subject to long delays. Only international, Iran-bound passengers can stay with the carriages as they're shipped by ferry across the lake to Van. Van Gölü Ekspresi trains arrive from Ankara on Wednesdays and Mondays.

By ferry Ferries between Tatvan and Van theoretically make at least two daily crossings (morning and afternoon). The ₺15 foot passenger fee makes for a bargain cruise, but timings are unpredictable and you may wait hours to depart.
Destinations Van (up to 3 daily; 5hr).

INFORMATION AND TOURS

Tourist office Inconveniently located in the Kültür Merkezi, 1km southwest of town on the Bitlis road.

Tours Nimetullah Özkan at the *Kardelen* hotel

(☎0532 798 2441) charges around ₺150 for a dolmuş excursion to Nemrut Dağı.

ACCOMMODATION

Dilek Hotel Yeni Çarşısı 45 ☎0434 827 1516. This friendly hotel ticks all the right boxes for the budget traveller, with tiny but clean en-suite bathrooms, small and simply furnished rooms, central heating and a quiet location just off the main drag. ₺60

Hotel Kardelen Belediye Yanı, Cumhüriyet Cad ☎0434 827 9500, ⓦotelkardelen.com. Tatvan's oldest quality hotel was upgraded in 2014, but with its flock wallpaper and dull brown and cream decor it still looks decidedly old-fashioned. A better bet is their sister *Nemrut Kardelen*, 8km away from Tatvan at the ski resort on Mt Nemrut, well worth considering if you have your own transport. *Nemrut Kardelen* is bright, clean and has superb lake views. *Tatvan Kardelen* ₺160; *Nemrut Kardelen* ₺130

★**Sahra Hotel** Cumhüriyet Cad, Sahil Yolu Üzeri ☎0434 827 6969, ⓦsahrahotel.com. The best value of Tatvan's new tranche of classier hotels, 600m south of Cumhüriyet Meydan. Singles have wide beds, all rooms are light and contemporary in style, with rug-bedecked tiled floors, white/pastel decor and crisp white bed linen. A few rooms have views down to the lake. ₺100

Üstün Otel Hal Cad 23 ☎0434 827 9014. A couple of blocks east of Cumhuriyet Cad, the *Üstün* is a basic family-run pension-style hotel that offers the cheapest suitable accommodation in town. Some of the simple but adequate rooms have their own shower, but toilets are communal; rates include a simple breakfast. ₺50

EATING AND DRINKING

Altın Kup/Deniz Kızı Just off Cumhüriyet Cad, behind Hotel Dilek. This small, kitschy male-oriented bar plays *Türkü* music and doles out cheap beer (₺7). It also serves decent grills, with *pirzola* (lamb chops) and grilled fish dishes for a reasonable ₺18. Daily 11am–midnight.

Çınar Kebab Cumhüriyet Caddesi, Özel İdare Pasajı ☎0434 827 1051. Locals swear *Çınar* has the best kebabs in town,

and they're right. Kebabs, priced around ₺16, are all served on a veritable pile of tasty flatbread, accompanied by a complimentary green salad, onion salad and two types of tomato dip – one very spicy. Choose from *adana*, *urfa*, lamb or liver. Daily 5am–midnight.

Eyvan Cumhüriyet Cad, Sok 7 ☎0432 827 6579. Tucked away on a side street behind the Bestvantur bus office on the main drag, this basic but clean restaurant offers crispy

12

lahmacun (₺2), tasty *pide* (₺7), and different types of the egg dish *menemen* (from ₺6) served up sizzling hot in a small wok-style pan – try the one dripping with *kaşar* cheese. Daily 7am–11pm.

Gökte Ada Yaşam İş Merkezi (Carrefour), Cumhuriyet Cad ✆ 0434 827 6282. This shiny, spacious place, on the third floor of the shopping centre, dishes up a wide range of kebabs, *lahmacun* and *pide*. Much favoured by the local middle classes, it's a little dearer than most, with kebabs from ₺16. Also serves good *sulu yemek* for lunch. Daily 10am–10pm.

Per 10 Near the Ahlat dolmuş stop, Cumhuriyet Cad. This small café serves a decent breakfast with flatbread, butter, honey and a large tea for ₺10. Those with a sweet tooth are in luck – it also offers Tatvan's best selection of cakes and *baklava*. Daily 6am–11pm.

Nemrut Dağı

Dolmuşes charge around ₺140 for a 3–4hr excursion from Tatvan; driving your own vehicle, join the main road to Bitlis from Tatvan, then turn right after 500m

Immediately north of Tatvan, the extinct volcano of **Nemrut Dağı** – no relation to the mountain with the statues (see p.594) – rises to 3050m. A quarter of a million years ago Nemrut is believed to have stood 4450m tall; as a result of a huge volcanic explosion, the whole upper section of the peak was deposited in the Van basin, thus blocking the natural outlet and creating the lake. The present-day volcanic cone, which is accessible after snowmelt from May or June through to November, contains three crater lakes, one of which is pleasantly warm.

From the rim, an asphalt road drops down and right towards the crater floor. To reach crescent-shaped **Soğukgöl** (cold lake), bear left on a dirt track. The lake occupies the western half of the crater, and on its east shore there are some swimmable hot springs. Better for a dip, however, is smaller **Sıcakgöl** (warm lake), connected to its partner by a narrow path leading east or a left branch off the asphalt road and heated to 60°C by ongoing volcanic activity. The 7km-diameter **crater** is lushly vegetated (beech, aspen and juniper), contrasting sharply with the bare landscape outside. In summer Kurds graze their flocks on the slopes.

A small **ski resort** on the mountain, 8km from Tatvan at an altitude of 2200m, has a smart new hotel, the *Nemrut Kardelen* (see p.625). A chair-lift ride takes visitors to the summit for ₺15, but only runs in summer for groups of ten or more. The lift goes right to the crater rim, and the views are spectacular.

Ahlat

The shabby town of **AHLAT**, which lies a picturesque drive 42km northeast of Tatvan along the north shore of Lake Van, is known chiefly for its medieval **Muslim cemetery**, holding hundreds of beautifully carved gravestones, and for its monumental **tombs**, known as *türbe* in Turkish.

The cemetery and tombs are by far the most substantial remains of a settlement that can boast a very long history. The Urartians are known to have been here in the first millennium BC, and were followed in turn by the Armenians. Ahlat fell to the Arabs during the seventh century, was retaken by the Byzantines two hundred years later, and subsequently passed to the victorious Selçuks after the nearby Battle of Manzikert in 1071. The Mongols, who arrived in 1244, were succeeded by the İlhanids a century later; by the fifteenth century Ahlat had become the main base of the Akkoyunlu Turcomans. Even after the local Ottoman conquest of 1548, real power in this remote region remained in the hands of the Kurdish emirs of Bitlis. Ahlat continued to be a populous, polyglot city until World War I.

Old Ahlat is a sprawling site, centred on a small museum, with the most visited of the monumental tombs, the Ulu Kümbet, some 300m south. The Meydan cemetery, peppered with intricately carved tombstones, is immediately north of the museum, while the Bayındır tomb lies 600m north of the museum across the cemetery. The city ruins nestle in a valley around 400m west of the Bayındır tomb.

Ahlat Museum

2km southwest of central Ahlat • Tues–Sat 8am–noon & 1–5pm • Free • Arriving from Tatvan by dolmuş, ask to be dropped here, or you'll continue to Ahlat and have to catch a town dolmuş back again

Interesting artefacts in the small **Ahlat Museum** range from the Urartian era (first millennium BC) to the medieval period, but everything is labelled in Turkish. To get an idea of the extent of medieval Ahlat, take a look at the museum's well-plotted ground plan. The museum was closed at the time of writing – it is possible that its contents will be displayed in the new museum under construction in Van (see p.629).

Ulu Kümbet (Great Tomb)

2km southwest of central Ahlat, just south of the main road opposite the museum

Ahlat's famous *kümbet* **tombs** lie scattered southwest of the town centre. The largest and most beautifully decorated of all, the **Ulu Kümbet** or "Great Tomb", built for a late thirteenth-century Mongol chieftain, now stands isolated in a field.

As is typical of local *kümbets*, which could accommodate one to four persons, it was constructed of deep brown basalt; most of the stonemasons were Armenian. The deceased was interred in an underground chamber, beneath a prayer room reached by steps from the outside. The distinctive conical style may have been inspired by the traditional nomadic tent or yurt, or by the drum and conical roof of Armenian church architecture.

Meydan cemetery

Adjacent to, and north of, the museum, 2km southwest of central Ahlat

The reason most visitors make the trek out to Ahlat is to see the **Meydan cemetery**, a wonderful collection of tilted, lichen-encrusted headstones that dates from the eleventh to the sixteenth centuries and covers almost two square kilometres. Most are covered with floral, geometric and calligraphic (Persian and Arabic scripts) decoration.

Bayındır Türbesi

Adjoining the northern rim of the Meydan cemetery

With its colonnaded upper storey, domed rather than conical roof, and small, still much-used *mescit* (prayer room), the **Bayındır Türbesi** is the most distinctive of Ahlat's *kümbets*. It was built in 1492 to house the remains of the Turcoman chief Bayındır.

Harabe Şehir

Around 400m west of the Bayındır Türbesi

The idyllic valley known as **Harabe Şehir** ("City Ruins") holds the remains of a huge mosque, a castle, rock-cut houses and the pretty fifteenth-century humpbacked bridge of Emir Bayındır. It's also alive with colourful birds such as hoopoes and bee-eaters as well as the odd tortoise. Set on a bluff above, the prominent **Hasan Padişah Türbesi**, built in 1275, stands almost 20m high, its cylindrical body topped by a pyramidal roof. North of the main city ruins, beyond the modern bridge, the valley becomes even more beautiful. Flat-roofed houses set in dense orchards on the rim of the valley were once part of the Armenian settlement of Madavanis. A waterfall plunges into the valley from the east, cave dwellings, some still used today, pepper the cliffs, and tumbled blocks of volcanic rock lay in haphazard abandon next to the tumbling stream.

ARRIVAL AND DEPARTURE   **AHLAT**

By bus and dolmuş The first daily dolmuş from Tatvan to Ahlat leaves at 7.30am. Ask to be dropped by the museum. Regular dolmuşes run from there to the town centre (₺1.5), where you can catch a dolmuş back to Tatvan (last departure 6pm) or on to Adilcevaz, or a bus on to Van. The

last of the five daily buses from Adilcevaz to Van departs at 2pm (₺15).

Destinations Adilcevaz (6 daily, 30min; ₺6); Tatvan (frequent; 45min; ₺6).

ACCOMMODATION AND EATING

Büyük Selçuklu Zübeyde Hanım Cad ☎0434 412 5695. Dark-stone place right on the shore at the extreme east end of town. The en-suite rooms are comfortable enough; get one with a lake view and you won't mind the rather garish decor too much. **₺80**

Vangölü Aşağı Çarşı PTT Yanı ☎0434 412 5500. In spanking new premises on Ahlat's main street, this excellent, scrupulously clean first-floor restaurant is always full of local teachers, women and families. *Döner* kebab and *sulu yemek* take precedence in the day, grills and *pide* in the evenings. Daily 9am–10pm.

Adilcevaz

The charming modern village of **ADİLCEVAZ**, a smaller but more pleasant place to stay than either Tatvan or Ahlat, huddles 25km north of Ahlat in a fertile valley surrounded by poplars, walnut and apricot trees. It's dominated by the shattered shell of a Selçuk fortress, which is in turn overshadowed by the 4058m volcanic peak of **Süphan Dağı**, Turkey's fourth-highest peak.

Below Adilcevaz, near the shore and constructed using the dark-brown volcanic stone typical of the area, the distinctive, multi-domed sixteenth-century **Tuğrul Bey Camii** is ascribed to the ubiquitous Sinan (see box, p.92). The lakefront near here has an attractive promenade area and a pleasant café.

A startlingly evocative shattered shell, the Armenian monastery church of **Skantselorgivank** stands high on the bare mountainside, above a small dam on the town's upper slopes. Reached via a rocky trail, it features bands of red and black stonework, *khatchkar*s (stones inscribed with crosses) and a black basalt font. Above it is the Urartian citadel of **Kefkalesi**, separated from the church by a steep, scree-strewn valley that can only be negotiated with difficulty (taxi ₺40).

ARRIVAL AND ACCOMMODATION
ADİLCEVAZ

By bus and dolmuş Adilcevaz offers connections to Ahlat and on to Van (last daily departure 2pm).
Destinations Ahlat (6 daily, 30min; ₺6); Van (5 daily; 2hr 30min; ₺20).

Cevizlibağ Otel Recep Tayip Erdoğan Cad 31 ☎0434 311 3151, ⓦcevizlibagotel.com. The best hotel in Adilcevaz is bright, new and clean, with lake views from some rooms and important features like free wi-fi, LCD TVs and central heating. It also has a decent restaurant downstairs. **₺90**

Van

Following a magnitude 7.1 earthquake in October 2011, which killed over six hundred people in the province and rendered tens of thousands homeless, the city of VAN has made a remarkable recovery. Many of the fifteen thousand or so buildings that either collapsed or were rendered unsafe by the quake have been rebuilt from scratch or made safe, and there is a new-found vibrancy about the place, especially on the main shopping streets, Cumhüriyet Caddesi and Kazım Karabekir Caddesi (marked as Maraş Caddesi on some maps). Set 4km east of Lake Van against the backdrop of the volcanic, 3200m Erek Dağı, the city continues to make a great base to explore the lake's numerous attractions. Its highlight, ancient **Van Kalesi**, is spectacularly situated 3km west by the lake, where it overlooks the poignant remains of the old city destroyed during World War I.

Most visitors reach Van by road, along the scenic **southern-shore route** from Tatvan, which initially follows a pretty willow-fringed valley before disappearing into the 2km-long Kuskunkıran tunnel and then continuing along the lakeshore, with vistas of Akdamar and Süphan Dağı reflected in the still waters.

Although Van is basically a conservative town, that's mitigated by the presence of the large student population attending Yüzüncü Yıl university. There are several bars in the centre, where it's possible to drink in mixed company, and listen to Turkish and Kurdish folk and rock music. Van is also a good place to shop, with a wide selection of local (Kurdish) tribal rugs, as well as often cheaper ones from nearby Iran.

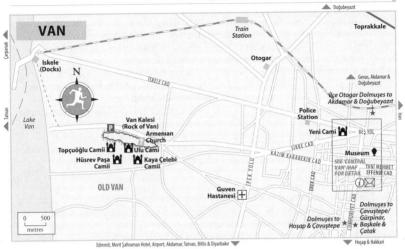

The local, predominantly Kurdish population of Van province have been increasingly asserting their **Kurdish identity** (see p.678) and in the 2015 general election Van returned four MPs from the pro-Kurdish HDP to the Turkish parliament, and two of the city's tea gardens have been given Kurdish names.

12

Van Museum

Cengiz Cad • Closed by earthquake, but likely to reopen

After **Van Museum** (Van Müzesi) was hit by the quake, all its artefacts were put into storage. Its **garden**, however, was open at the time of writing. Pride of place here belongs to the black basalt relief carving of an Urartian god, possibly Shivini, astride a bull, but it also holds a number of fine stelae, liberally covered in cuneiform Urartian inscriptions. All the artefacts from here will eventually be moved to the massive new mirrored-glass museum under construction next to Van Kalesi (see below), which is scheduled to open in 2016.

Van Kalesi: the Rock of Van

3km west of central Van • Daily 8.30am–7.30pm • ₺5 • Frequent dolmuşes (₺1.5) from Beş Yol junction drop passengers at the eastern end of the Rock; to reach the entrance, follow the road 500m towards the lake

The narrow outcrop known as **Van Kalesi** – 1.5km long, over 100m tall and perhaps 300m wide at the base – holds the nearest visitable Urartian fortification to Van. Equipped with its own spring, it was an eminently suitable stronghold. As you pass the northern face, note the arched niches, which originally belonged to an **Urartian temple**, set in the base of the cliff, behind an Ottoman-era mosque and *türbe*. These once held stelae; cuneiform inscriptions on the base of one document the life and works of a powerful Urartian king.

Entry is from the car park and **ticket booth** on the northwest side, where there's also a decent restaurant/café and a replica of an old Van house, built of mud brick. Just west of the tea gardens is a large stone platform (possibly a jetty) made of limestone blocks, some over 5m long. Two inscriptions adorn the structure, both in the Assyrian, rather than the Urartian, language, praising the Urartian king Sarduri I (844–838 BC).

From the "jetty" or ticket booth, a path ascends the gentler north face of the Rock and leads, eventually, to the citadel on top. A slight diversion south from the route leads to the single most impressive part of Van Kalesi, the rock **tomb of Argishti 1** (785–760 BC), which is set in the sheer cliff face on the south side of the Rock, west of the summit area. As the door is gated and locked, you'll need to be guided by one of the security officials who hang out near the ticket booth – expect to give a small tip. The tomb is reached by a set of worn steps, fortunately protected by metal railings. The carved rock face above the stairs is covered in well-preserved cuneiform inscriptions relating Argishti's conquests. Take a torch to explore the interior, where the fixing holes for votive plaques can still be seen. Several more anonymous rock-cut tombs are scattered on the south face of the Rock, east of the summit area, but take care – the path is badly worn, and the drops deadly.

The most prominent building on the top today is a restored **Ottoman-era mosque**. The arch-roofed building next to that is a *medrese*, while the former barracks of the Ottoman garrisons stand close by. The curious steps cut into the limestone are actually the foundation bases for cyclopean Urartian walls; the mud-brick ones visible today are much later. The new-looking sections of crenellated wall on the eastern part of the Rock are just that, but probably follow the line of ancient walling. The summit of the citadel is a popular place to watch the spectacular sunset over Lake Van.

Old Van

The destruction of **Old Van** in 1915 was so thorough that today only four mosques and fragments of an Armenian church remain. The rest is a sea of overgrown, rubble-strewn mounds where once an attractive settlement was home to eighty thousand people. Within the walls lay bazaars, churches, mosques and government offices. Nearby orchards give an indication of the once-extensive "garden suburbs" of **Aygestan**, where the bulk of the population lived in the nineteenth and early twentieth centuries. To walk through Old Van, head around the western (lake) end of the Rock and skirt the southern face of the Rock. You can exit through a gap in the fence at the southeast end of the Rock and catch a dolmuş back into Van. Alternatively, enter the ruins here and make your way through the old city to the official entrance to Van Kalesi.

The first structure as you approach from the west is the badly ruined **Topçuoğlu Camii**. The fifteenth-century **Ulu Cami** is of more interest, with an attractive brick minaret still bearing traces of faience tiles. Look due north from the mosque to see the massive fifth-century BC **cuneiform inscription** of Xerxes. Inscribed in Persian, Medean and Babylonian, and celebrating the might of the famous Persian king, it was first recorded in 1827 by the traveller/archeologist Friedrich Schulz (later murdered by Kurdish tribesmen), as he dangled on a rope from the summit.

The remains of an Armenian church, still bearing traces of frescoes, huddles right under the Rock towards its southeast corner; behind it are some *khatchkar*s inscribed onto the rock face. A pair of sixteenth-century Ottoman-era mosques near the crumbled south town wall have been recently restored/rebuilt. The easterly one is the **Kaya Çelebi Camii** (1586), while the western mosque, with attractive banded stonework and an attached tomb, is the **Hüsrev Paşa Camii** (1567), a work of the great Ottoman imperial architect Sinan (see p.92). Picnicking families descend on the grassed-over ruins on warm weekends, leaving nothing behind but their litter.

A WALK ALONG THE SHORE: VAN İSKELE TO VAN KALESİ

The construction of a new dirt road running south from Van İskele (harbour) towards the citadel has made it possible to enjoy a stroll along the lakeshore before exploring Van Kalesi. To start, take a yellow dolmuş or blue city bus from İskele Caddesi (see map, p.629) to the harbour, a scruffy area of tea gardens, cafés and a couple of funfairs, all packed with locals on warm weekends, where the railway line from Tehran terminates, at the water's edge. Couples come here after extravagant weddings to have their photos taken, providing visitors with a great chance to see a Kurdish bride in all her finery. Just before the start of the quay head south along a raised dirt road, with black volcanic sand beaches on your right, marsh and grassland grazed by copious sheep and numerous cattle on your left. The reed beds and marshes abound with wading birds, and the views of Van Kalesi and its backdrop of 3200m Erek Dağı are excellent. After about half an hour, the road ends opposite the western end of Van Kalesi; cut east across meadowland to reach the castle area in around fifteen minutes.

CENTRAL VAN

Ferry Docks, Otogar & Train Station ▲ İlçe Otogar
★ Dolmuşes to the Rock of Van
Buses to ★ İskele
✚ Hastane Hospital

İSKELE CADDESİ

Yeni Cami

BEŞ YOL

HASTANE CADDESİ

SİKKE CADDESİ

Dabakoğlu Parkı

ŞEVİT MEHMET E. CADDESİ

İRFAN BAŞTUĞ CADDESİ

KARATEKİN SOK
MENZİLCİ DEDE SOK
ZEHRA SOK
ERCİŞ EMRAH SOK
ESKİ MEYDAN SOK

Şehir Hamamı

SANTRAL 3. SOK

★ Dolmuşes to Edremit & Gevaş (Akdamar)

CUMHURİYET 1. SOK

ZÜBEYDE HANIM CADDESİ

1718. SOK

GÜNEŞ 2. SOK

MEYDAN 5. SOK

ESKİ MEYDAN SK

HAMİT PAŞA SOK

KARATEKİN SOK

ERCİŞ EMRAH SOK

CUMHURİYET 4. SOK

CUMHURİYET CADDESİ

ORDU CADDESİ

N

Dolmuş to ★ Bahçesaray

12

PTT CADDESİ

KÜÇÜK CAMİ 1. SOK

Cami

Cami

Akdamar Travel

HACI OSMAN SOKAK

MÜZE SOKAK

Feqiye Teyran Parkı

YÜZBAŞIOĞLU SOKAK

Belediye

Van Museum

CENGİZ CADDESİ

POSTA CADDESİ

THY Office

MARAŞ CADDESİ

FEVZİ ÇAKMAK CADDESİ

Bus Companies

Artoş İş Merkezi & cinema

Urartu Turizm

İNKILAP 1. SOK

ℹ️ ✉️

Dolmuş to ★ Hoşap

Star 2000

Dolmuş to Çavuştepe, Hoşap, ★ Başkale & Hakkari

0   100
metres

■ DRINKING & NIGHTLIFE
Halay Türkü	2
Hinar	4
Janya ve Şarap Evi	1
Niçhe	3

● EATING
Aişe Ev	2
Fıravin	1
Halil İbrahim Sofrası	5
People's Coffee	4
Şafak	6
Sutçu Kenan Evren Kahvaltı Salonu	3

● SHOPPING
Atsoy Gumuş	2
Galeri Kirman	1
Star 2000	3

■ ACCOMMODATION
Ada Palas	3
Büyük Asur	6
Elite World Hotel	5
Şahin	2
Side	1
Tamara	4

ARRIVAL AND DEPARTURE

VAN

By plane Van's airport, 6km south of town, is linked to the centre by dolmuş (₺1.5), though you have to walk 500m to the main road to get one, and taxis (₺30). Flights run by Anadolujet, Sunexpress and THY serve the airport.

Destinations Ankara (4 daily; 1hr 35min); Antalya (daily; 2hr 5min); İstanbul (2 daily; 2hr 5min); İzmir (1–2 daily; 2hr 20min).

By bus and dolmuş Intercity buses run to the *otogar*, around 2.5km northwest of the city centre. From the *otogar*, *servis* buses run to the busy junction of Beş Yol, at the northern end of Cumhuriyet Caddesi. Dolmuşes to Doūğbeyazıt (₺25) run from the İlçe *otogar*, 400m north of the Beş Yol junction, at 7.30am, 9am, noon, 2pm & 3.30pm. The major companies have offices clustered around the junction of Cumhuriyet/Kazım Karabekir/Fevzi Çakmak cads.

Destinations Ankara (7 daily; 22hr); Bahçesaray (3 daily; 2hr 30min); Diyarbakır (11 daily; 7hr); Doğubeyazıt (5 daily; 2hr 30min); Erzurum (4 daily; 7hr); Hakkari (hourly in daylight hours; 3–4hr); Şanlıurfa (9 daily; 9hr); Tatvan (7 daily; 3hr); Trabzon (3 daily; 15hr).

Travel to Iran Regular buses run to the Iranian border at Esendere-Sero, southeast of Van (daily 8am–5pm; 4hr 30min; ₺35), while it's also theoretically possible to cross the border at Kapıköy, reachable by dolmuş from the İlçe *otogar* (1hr). At the time of writing both borders were closed owing to PKK activity in the area.

By train Transasya Ekspresi trains to/from Tehran arrive at the station 3km northwest of the centre (Fri, nominally around 9.30pm but timetables are very erratic; 25hr); note that this train is for international (ie Iran-bound) passengers only. At the time of writing the service was suspended owing to PKK activity in the area.

By ferry The ferry port (İskele), 5km west of town, is connected with the centre by dolmuş (₺1.5).

Car rental Reliable cars are available from Europcar agents Akdamar, at Van airport (☎0532 417 9944, ⓦakdamarturizm.com) or opposite Artos shopping centre on Kazım Karabekir Caddesi in central Van.

INFORMATION AND TOURS

Tourist office Cumhuriyet Cad 127 (☎0432 216 2018).
Travel agencies Central Van is liberally dotted with travel agencies. For daily tours try Urartu Turizm, Cumhuriyet Cad

(☎0432 214 2020), who are agents for Avis and Sunexpress, Pegasus and THY.

ACCOMMODATION

Van has plenty of **hotels**, in all price ranges; and for women travelling alone staying here is safer and more comfortable than at other towns in the area. Van receives a lot of visitors from nearby Iran, keen to leave behind the strictures of the Islamic Republic, partly accounting for the number of hotels in this city that is otherwise off the beaten track.

Ada Palas Cumhuriyet Cad ☎0432 216 2716, ⓦvanadapalasoteli.com. Gleaming contemporary-styled hotel with top-notch beds and bathroom fittings, a very vibrant colour scheme plus a very cheerful breakfast room. Spotlessly clean (and with female staff on reception), this is a great choice for women travellers. Wi-fi and foreign-channel TV too. ₺140

★**Büyük Asur** Cumhuriyet Cad, Turizm Sok 5 ☎0432 216 8792, ⓦbuyukasur.com. Rooms, refurbished post-quake, are pleasantly simple and well kept, with small LCD TVs and central heating. The real bonus is part-owner Remzi (email him at ✉asur_asur2008q@hotmail.com), a qualified guide who speaks good English and offers tailor-made day-trips to the region's best sights, or simply dishes out good advice for making the best of the area. There's a well-stocked bar and free wi-fi, but the breakfast is only average. ₺120

Elite World Kazım Karabekir Cad 21 ☎0432 484 1111, ⓦbeliteworldvan.com. Van's most luxurious hotel boasts a glitteringly grand lobby area, complete with a posh coffee and cake café, a grill restaurant and, behind it, a disconcertingly dark but spacious bar. There's also a well-equipped gym and wellness centre, with a decent-sized pool. Rooms are opulently furnished in a safe, traditional style, with tea- and coffee-making facilities, LCD TVs and fancy bathrooms. East-facing rooms have views to Erek Dağı. ₺120

Merit Şahmaran Edremit Yolu ☎0432 312 3060, ⓦmeritsahmaranotel.com. If you're looking for peace and quiet, try this friendly group-oriented place on the

lakeshore 12km southwest of town, beyond the airport. The spacious rooms are tastefully decorated and the en-suites all have large baths. The buffet breakfast is excellent, there's an outdoor pool, and the views from the terrace at sunset are lovely. Make sure you get a room with a lake view. ₺200

Şahin İrfan Baştuğ Cad ☎0432 216 3062, ⓦotelsahin .com. A reliable choice. Single rooms are claustrophobically close to the next building and offer little natural light, but front rooms are spacious and, together with the rooftop breakfast room, offer views over the city. Firm beds, clean and well kept. ₺90

Side Sikhe Cad 1 ☎0432 216 6265. One advantage of staying at this budget-mid-range option is the presence of English-speaking Harun Toprak (☎0536 5772 026, ⓦararat-trek.com), who can help sort out reasonably priced tours to Mt Ararat and elsewhere, plus rental cars etc. Rooms are only average, with small en-suite bathrooms and garish bed linen, but beds are firm and comfy, and there's free wi-fi. ₺110

Tamara Yüzbaşıoğlu Sok 1 ☎0432 214 3296, ⓦtamaraotel.com. Van's first attempt at a boutique hotel works pretty well. Expect crisp white linen on firm beds, light-wood furniture, muted tones and sparkling bathrooms complete with spacious tubs, wi-fi and a/c. There's an in-house grill-your-own-meat restaurant and the *North Shield* pub. Unfortunately, it changes hands regularly, making it difficult to know how well the current owners will run it. ₺160

EATING AND DRINKING

Van's famous **breakfast salons**, most on or just off Cumhuriyet Caddesi, serve a selection of cheeses (including the mature, herb-studded *otlu peynir*), olives, honey and cream (*kaymak*) with fresh hot bread and gallons of tea. A scattering of new *ev yemekleri* (home-cooking) places has livened up a culinary scene once totally dominated by kebab and *pide* establishments.

CAFÉS AND RESTAURANTS

Aişe Ev Yemekleri Hastane 2 Cad, Özkok İş Merkezi Karşısı 5 ☎ 0432 216 1515. Traditional Turkish and Kurdish dishes served up in a spotless emporium, all cooked by a hard-working female team led by the eponymous Aişe. Mains from ₺9. Daily 8.30am–10pm.

Fıravin Hastane Cad, Nedim Odabaşı Ticaret Merkezi ☎ 0432 216 6686. Female-run home-made food joint specializing in local Kurdish dishes – try the *Çukurca köfte*, meatballs in a rice and mincemeat shell served in a yoghurt sauce – though they also serve standard Turkish dishes like *kuru fasuliye* (haricot beans in tomato sauce). Mains from ₺10. Mon–Sat 8am–8pm.

Halil İbrahim Sofrası Cumhuriyet Cad, Ziraat Bankası Yanı 62 ☎ 0432 210 0070. Spotlessly clean, prettily decorated but cavernous place, with a pleasant rear terrace. All the standard grills, *sulu yemek* dishes, *pides* etc, plus more unusual offerings (for this type of restaurant) like grilled trout and *hamsi* (anchovies). Mains from ₺9. Daily 8am–11pm.

People's Coffee Halil Cumhuriyet Cad ☎ 0538 600 0740. Shamelessly aping rather better-known chain coffee shops, this second-floor joint is the place to come if you want a bit of home comfort in Turkey's "wild east". Apart from a bewildering range of coffees, there are smoothies and shakes, plus pasta dishes, fajitas, burgers and pizzas. Decor is soothingly pastel and contemporary. Daily 9am–11pm.

Şafak Et Lokantası Yuzbaşıoğlu Sok, off Kazım Karabekir Cad ☎ 0432 216 1444. Highly recommended for the fresh *döner*, tender lamb slices served up with lashings of hot *pide* and a bowl of sumac-smothered sliced onions (₺15). Best washed down with a bowl of fresh, frothy *yayık ayran*. Daily 9am–11pm.

★ **Sutçu Kenan Evren Kahvaltl Salonu** Kahvaltıcılar Sok 7/A ☎ 0432 216 8499. On a small street devoted to breakfast places, this is the bustling best. It serves all the usual standards, with tables out on the street in the warmer months. A (very) hearty breakfast will set you back ₺18 – as an extra, try the *yumurtalı kavurma* (eggs and tender lamb served in a small wok-like dish). Daily 5am–3pm.

BARS

★ **Halay Türkü** Maraş Cad, Artoş İş Merkezi Karşısı ☎ 0432 214 8283. Trendy top-floor *Türkü* bar with live music 8pm–2am nightly, an open-air terrace and *ocakbaşı* (charcoal grill) restaurant. Beers are ₺12, grills ₺18 and up. British film director Ben Hopkins shot some of his 2008 film *Pazar* here. Daily noon–2am.

★ **Hinar** Kazım Karabekir Cad, Yüzbaşıoğlu Sok ☎ 0532 325 2447. *Hinar*, which means pomegranate in Kurdish, attracts a healthy mix of local Kurdish professionals, Turkish doctors, teachers and the like doing their obligatory work stint in the east of the country, students and the odd expat. It's a small place so soon gets jam-packed, especially at weekends. Welcoming female owner Şeyla has made this a buzzing venue. Beers ₺10 and up. Daily noon–2am.

Janya ve Şarap Evi Cumhuriyet Cad. Fifth-floor venue with live music every night at 9.30pm – mainly covers bands knocking out rock classics, but occasionally other live acts singing in Armenian, Kurdish and Turkish take the stage. Watch the action down on Van's main street from a window table. Beers ₺12, a glass of decent wine from the Tör Abdin ₺15, cocktails from ₺24. Daily noon–2am.

Niçhe (Nietzsche) Kazım Karabekir Cad, Yüzbaşıoğlu Sok ☎ 0505 903 3570. If the philosopher's main tenet had been that everyone should drink and smoke to their hearts content, he would be delighted by the number of (mainly young) people doing just that at one of Van's hippest bars. Beers ₺10, other customers' cigarette smoke free. Daily 1pm–2am.

SHOPPING

Atsoy Gumuş Maraş Cad 8/b ☎ 0432 216 1234. This jewellery shop isn't cheap but there are some beautiful silver bracelets, earrings and necklaces to be had, some based on original Urartian pieces. They have another outlet beside the ticket entrance to Van Kalesi. Mon–Sat 9am–8pm.

Galeri Kirman Müze Çarşısı, opposite the museum ☎ 0432 215 3789. A wide range of carpets and kilims at decent prices. Mon–Sat 10am–6pm.

Star 2000 YKM shopping centre, Cumhüriyet Cad 115 ☎ 0432 214 0032. Student-orientated book and music store, which also has a decent pizza/café place with a balcony overlooking the main drag. Daily 10am–10pm.

DIRECTORY

Hospitals Devlet Hastanesi, on Hastane Cad, just east of Beş Yol (☎ 0432 216 4740); Güven Hastanesi on İpek Yolu (☎ 0432 217 5900).

Police West of town on İpek Yolu.
Post office Behind the tourist office, just off Cumhüriyet Cad.

Around Van

While the main attraction near Van is the Armenian Church of the Holy Cross on **Akdamar Island**, nearby **St Thomas** and the splendidly isolated church on the island of **Çarpanak** are almost equally worthwhile. The ancient Urartian settlements at **Çavuştepe** to the south and **Ayanis** to the north also make excellent day-trips from Van. The rocky foothills to the east hold more church remains, at **Yedi Kilise**, while the landscape south of Van is the most physically impressive in Turkey, featuring rugged mountains dotted with isolated settlements such as **Bahçesaray**. The imposing castle at **Hoşap** lies en route to the wild mountain town of Hakkari.

Although it's possible to visit some of these sights by public transport, to really make the most of one of Turkey's most fascinating regions it's worth considering **renting a car** for a couple of days.

Yedi Kilise

10km southeast of Van • Around ₺60 by taxi, with waiting time

Beautifully situated in the foothills of Erek Dağı, the village of Yukarı Bakraçlı is home to the remains of the once-grand monastery of the Holy Cross, founded in the seventh century.

The locals know the village as **Yedi Kilise** (Seven Churches), or "Varaga Vank" in Armenian, as seven Armenian churches and the monastery once stood here. The thirteenth-century Church of St George has survived, but was much damaged in the 2011 earthquake. The interior, with its frescoes and crosses carved into the walls, is atmospheric. The village alone is worth the trip as it offers a genuine slice of rural Kurdish life and a great mountain location, with grand vistas down onto Lake Van.

Akdamar island

50km southwest of Van • Daily 8.30am–7.30pm • ₺5 • 20min by boat (₺15 return) from the roadside quay, which is served by dolmuşes from Van's İlçe *otogar* (daily in summer 6am–7pm; ₺7) – if they're not full of island visitors, these stop at the town of Gevaş, 5km short (₺7); a dolmuş onto Akdamar quay is ₺3, a taxi around ₺25

The tiny island of **Akdamar**, just off Lake Van's southern shore, is home to the exquisite tenth-century Armenian **Surb Khach** or Church of the Holy Cross. Restored to the tune of US$1.5 million in 2007 by the Turkish government, it stands as a glimmer of hope of reconciliation between Turks and Armenians. A metal cross has been erected on the conical dome of the church, and there's now an altar inside; occasional services are held throughout the year.

The church was erected between 915 and 921 AD, at the behest of Gagik Artsruni, ruler of the Armenian kingdom of Vaspurakan. The small building is gracefully proportioned, but what makes it so special are the **relief carvings** that run in a series of five bands around the exterior. As well as animal scenes there are several depictions of Bible stories, including Jonah appearing to dive from a boat into the jaws of a most unlikely-looking whale (south facade), and David taking on Goliath, sling in hand (south facade). King Gagik himself is carved in bold relief on the west facade, presenting a model of Surb Khach to Jesus. A number of **khatchkars** – the Celtic-looking, obsessively detailed carved crosses that the Armenians used both as celebratory or commemorative offerings and as grave markers – are also set into the facade and scattered beneath the almond trees to the east of the church.

The **frescoes** inside, formerly in a shocking state, have been sensitively restored. It's possible to make out New Testament scenes such as the Baptism of Christ, the raising of Lazarus and the Crucifixion. Outside, to the south, are the partially excavated remains of the monastery complex of which the church was once a part.

Clamber up the steep hillside behind the church for spectacular views down over the church to the lake and, beyond, to the magnificent peaks that ring the lakeshore and run all the way down to the Iraqi border. Be wary, though, of plodding tortoises, and gull-infested cliffs that drop sheer into the azure waters below.

The church of St Thomas

76km southwest of Van • 12km west of the Akdamar island quay, turn right at the first petrol station to Göründü village, 3km from the main road; continue 15km on a windy coast road to Altınsaç, and 2km after that you'll see the church on a spur to your left, a 20–30min walk from where you park

The stunningly situated monastic **church of St Thomas** (Kamrak Vank), on an isolated promontory overlooking Lake Van, is best reached with your own vehicle. The final 18km of shoreline road here is extremely picturesque.

Built to a cruciform plan, the fourteenth-century church overlooks the bay of Varış from a plateau 2km from the modern village of **Altınsaç** (formerly Ganjak). Its sparsely decorated walls uphold a twelve-sided, capped drum; the extensive covered courtyard on the west was added late in the seventeenth century.

Çavuştepe

28km southeast of Van, on the Hakkari road • Daily 24hr • ₺5 • On Başkale and Gürpınar dolmuş routes (₺6)

The **Urartian royal palace** of **ÇAVUŞTEPE** was built between 764 and 735 BC by King Sardur II in classic Urartian style, at the end of a rocky spur running down onto a plain. The quality of the masonry is incredible, with expertly cut and sited blocks that join so perfectly no mortar was necessary. Among the pick of the hilltop remains are some massive sunken pithoi (pottery storage urns), a temple with a remarkably well-preserved cuneiform inscription, some sunken cisterns and what is quite clearly a squat toilet. Below the ridge the line of the so-called Semiramis Canal can be seen, an Urartian irrigation channel that was used to take water to Van, and which still functions.

Former warden Mehmet Kuşman is one of the few people in the world who can read, write and speak Urartian, and lectures in the language at Van University. Despite his retirement, Mehmet is often on site, ready to read out the temple inscription for you and sell you attractive, if pricey, Urartian-style carvings made from basalt. Excavation work recommenced here in 2015, with archeologists uncovering a store room containing 120 giant pithoi.

12

Hoşap Kalesi

55km southeast of Van, on the Hakkari road • Daily 8.30am–noon & 1.30–5pm • ₺5 • Catch a dolmuş to Başkale, Hakkari or Yükesekova from Cumhuriyet Cad, and ask to be dropped at Hoşap/Güzelsu (₺15); the last dolmuş leaves the site around 6pm

The photogenic medieval Kurdish fortress of **Hoşap Kalesi** is an extraordinary flight of fancy, constructed in the 1640s at the behest of Sarı Süleyman Mahmudı, a local Kurdish strongman. Take a look at the pretty bridge, dating to 1671, at the foot of the castle before wending your way up. The main entrance boasts lion **reliefs**, a symbolic chain of power and a Persian inscription. Little is left of the mosques, three hamams and *medrese* inside. Best preserved is the **keep** – reached by a path from the outer

---

A FORGOTTEN KINGDOM – URARTU

Between the ninth and seventh centuries BC, the **Urartian Kingdom**, centred on Van (then known as Tushpa), encompassed most of the territory described in this chapter, plus parts of present-day Iran, Iraq and Syria.

Around a dozen Urartian **citadels** have been unearthed in modern Turkey and Armenia, always sited on naturally defensible rocky spurs or outcrops. More than a castle, they incorporated a palace, workshops, storage depots and temples.

Great engineers, the Urartians built numerous dams and irrigation channels, and their bronze-work was legendary – examples have been found in the Etruscan cities of Italy. They also planted many vineyards, and have been credited with the discovery of **wine**; curiously, their biggest rivals, the Assyrians from the flatlands of Mesopotamia to the south, were beer drinkers. Eventually, centuries of fighting with the Assyrians and later the Scythians took their toll, and the Urartian Empire went into decline at the start of the seventh century.

fortress. Looking east from the fortress you can see a skeletal line of mud defensive walls that once encircled the village.

Çarpanak Island

25km northwest of Van • 1hr 30min by boat from the docks at Van İskelesi or 2hr from the jetty opposite Akdamar island; bargaining with the help of a Turkish-speaker, you should be able to rent a boat for upwards of ₺450 – or simply chance your luck on a Sunday morning, when locals cross by boat to picnic

The well-preserved remains of the **monastery church of St John** are set on the pear-shaped island of **Çarpanak** (Ktuts in Armenian), just offshore from a promontory. The island also holds a huge Armenian gull colony.

After Akdamar's Surb Khach, this is the best-preserved Armenian church near Van. A monastery grew up here around a twelfth-century church at least as early as 1414, but a disaster befell it during the next century and the present church was heavily restored early in the eighteenth century. Despite this, it's a handsome, rectangular compound, with a shallow dome sporting a pyramidal roof, though graffiti mars some of the walls.

Ayanis Kalesi

29km northwest of Van • Come by private car or taxi (₺100 with waiting time); turn left off the main road 20km north of Van, and then turn right in the village of Alaköy 8km further on, to follow an unsurfaced road over hills to the site itself

Ayanis Kalesi, the most beautifully located Urartian site, perches dramatically above the beautiful lakeside north of Çarpanak. Dating to the reign of Rusa II (685–645 BC), this hilltop fortification is still under excavation; digs have so far revealed the perimeter walls and an impressive central **temple** compound, whose doorway bears a long cuneiform inscription.

Remarkably, the interior of the temple (only visitable when archeologists are on site, in July and early August) is decorated with stone-inlay (intaglio) designs including lions and griffins, unique in the Urartian world. The **beaches** below the site are great for a dip.

Bahçesaray

Reaching the rural town of **BAHÇESARAY**, 110km southwest of Van, involves cresting the 2985m Karabel Geçiti, the highest road pass in Turkey and usually the last to open after the winter snow, in May or June. Bahçesaray was once far more important than its present size would suggest, with a population of twelve thousand over a century ago (three times today's size). It's perfectly possible to do the round trip in a day in a hired car, but it's better to overnight if possible. The scenery is breathtaking, even better than the trip to Hakkari for the variety of scenery, vegetation and birdlife on display. Seasonally scattered **encampments** (*zoma*) of Kurdish shepherds and their flocks on the east slopes of the pass form a colourful complement to the spectacular mountain views.

In the town itself, attractive tea gardens mark the start of the single main street, which ends at a mosque and a welcoming restaurant by the stream. Still known to most locals by the Armenian name of Müküs, Bahçesaray holds the remains of a small Armenian church, called **Andzghonts**. Much damaged by fire in 1805, it still has *khatchkars* (stones inscribed with crosses) visible in the exterior walls.

Other pleasant diversions include an upstream walk to the underground source of the **Botan Çay**, a tributary of the Tigris, and, a few kilometres downstream, a single-arched, poorly restored Selçuk bridge, the **Kızıl Köprü**.

ARRIVAL AND DEPARTURE
AROUND VAN

BAHÇESARAY

By dolmuş Dolmuşes to Bahçesaray leave from outside a small teahouse on Ordu Cad in Van, a few hundred metres east of the prominent Küçuk Cami mosque.

Destinations Van (3 daily, at 10am, noon & 3pm; 2hr 30min; ₺25).

ACCOMMODATION AND EATING

AKDAMAR ISLAND

Akdamar Camping Restaurant Akdamar İskelesi Yanı ☎0432 216 1515. Attached to the restaurant opposite the quay for Aktamar, this basic campsite is well-situated for a trip out to the island and church. The friendly İbrahim will probably waive the fee providing you eat at the (reasonable) restaurant, which serves fish from the lake for ₺15. Camping per person **₺5**

BAHÇESARAY

Öğretmen Evi (Teacher's House) 1km south of the town centre. Primarily for teachers posted to this remote mountain town, but visitors can use the basic, triple-bedded rooms assuming there is space, which there certainly will be in the long summer holiday period of July and August. Note that prices are per bed – you'll have to pay the triple-bed price (₺48) if you want a room to yourself. Lunch and dinner are available for ₺5. **₺16**

Hakkari

Few travellers visit the impoverished mountain town of **HAKKARİ**, 200km south of Van along the gorge of the Zab River, reached from Van after a three- to four-hour bus trip. The town is dramatically situated high above the surging river, backed to the east by the Cilo range, which incorporates Turkey's second-highest peak, Reşko (4135m). Locals wear their Kurdish identity more openly than anywhere else in Turkey, apart from Diyarbakır. Visitors who get this far tend to spend one night here and return to Van, though a few adventurous souls, political circumstances permitting, take the checkpoint-littered road along the mountainous Iraqi border to Şırnak.

12

Koçhanes

20km north of Hakkari • Best found with the help of a taxi driver from Hakkari

The church of **Koçhanes** was once the patriarchal seat of the Nestorian Christians. Small and plain, save for some inscribed geometric designs around the doorway, it's beautifully situated on a grassy spur high above the Zab valley. The village around the church was ruined when the army forcibly evacuated it during the 1990s, but a couple of elderly watchmen and former residents still tend vegetable plots here in the summer.

A few kilometres north, the lovely, lush highland pasture of **Berçelan** is home to transhumant Kurds in summer – when they have been given permission to use it.

ARRIVAL AND DEPARTURE   HAKKARİ

By bus and dolmuş Most buses and dolmuşes arrive outside the bus offices on the main street, though the Şırnak dolmuş departs from near the Atatürk statue on the same street; book the night before.
Destinations Şırnak (daily; 6hr, ₺30); Van (hourly in daylight hours; 3–4hr).

ACCOMMODATION AND EATING

Özdamak Ocakbaşı Et Lokantası Bulvar Cad. This lively first-floor place is the best restaurant in town, serving up grills (including trout) from ₺15, and *pide* from ₺8. Daily 8am–10pm.

Şenler Hotel Bulvar Cad ☎0544 211 3808, ⓦ senlerhotel.com. Decidedly average but still the best hotel in Hakkari, with spacious, plainly decorated rooms with wi-fi, TVs and (alcohol-free) minibars. Bathrooms

---

TRAVEL IN THE MOUNTAINS SOUTH OF LAKE VAN: A WARNING

Owing to serious clashes between Turkish security forces and the PKK (Kurdish Workers Party), with the exception of Bahçesaray (see opposite) we did not visit the mountainous areas that lie south of Lake Van at the time of researching this edition (2015), including Hakkari.

This remote area is sensitively located next to the proto-Kurdish state in northern Iraq, part of which is used as a base by PKK (Kurdish Workers Party) rebels to launch cross-border raids. For more information on the security situation in the southeast see p.577 and check the latest travel advice from your home government – and keep an ear to the ground while you're travelling in Turkey.

have mosaic tiles and small baths. There's a hamam, sauna and rooftop terrace with stunning views over Mount Sümbül. **₺120**

Sibar Hotel Altay Cad 15 ☎0438 211 2505, ⓦ sibarhotel.com. Offers a similar standard of comfort to the Şenler but has flock-wallpapered rooms and garish bedspreads offset by the delights of free wi-fi and a sauna. **₺140**

Lake Van to Doğubeyazıt

Northeast of Van, the road skirts the lake before heading up into the volcanic peaks bordering Iran. The drive, over a bizarrely contorted lava landscape, is spectacular in places, especially on the 2644m Tendurek Pass. In clear weather, the views of Mount Ararat from the far side of the pass are stunning. Huddled on the plain south of Ararat, the unkempt border/garrison town of **Doğubeyazıt** is a functional base from which to visit the spectacular palace of **İshak Paşa** or, more adventurously, ascend the peak or cross into neighbouring Iran.

Muradiye waterfalls

On the west side of the main Van–Doğubeyazıt road, 20km north of the junction with the road from Tatvan/Erciş • Dolmuşes to Doğubeyazıt depart hourly from the İlçe dolmuş garage, 400m north of Beş Yol in Van, and from the northbound side of the main road in Tatvan (₺20), dropping passengers at Muradiye (₺15); after visiting the falls, take a dolmuş on to Doğubeyazıt (or on to Van if you're travelling in the opposite direction) – these are often full you may have to take a dolmuş (regular) from Muradiye to Çaldıran, a major bus garage 26km northeast, and then on to Doğubeyazıt

The roadside **Muradiye waterfalls**, particularly spectacular in the late spring and early summer snowmelt, make a welcome break en route to or from Doğubeyazıt. A rickety wooden suspension bridge crosses the Bendihmah River in front of the falls, which cascade prettily over a 15–20m-high drop. Across the bridge, you can stop for a break at a couple of cafés; *Yaşarlar Alabalık*, furthest from the falls, is best and dishes up delicious trout.

A white-on-brown sign on the main road, 1km south of the falls, points towards an old bridge known as **Şeytan Köprüsü** (Devil's Bridge) that spans the deep gorge. Further down on the far side of the river, the fairly well-preserved thirteenth-century Armenian church of St Stephanos has a spectacular location on the steep valley side, backed by basalt cliffs, overlooking the village of Muradiye itself.

NESTORIAN CHRISTIANS

The **Nestorian Church** traces its existence back to Nestorius, fifth-century bishop of Constantinople, who formulated a doctrine that Christ was predominantly human in nature. Although this was declared a **heresy** by the Council of Ephesus in 431, the faith flourished, and Edessa (Şanlıurfa), Antioch (Antakya) and Nusaybin near Mardin became important Nestorian centres. After Mongol attacks, the Nestorians fled to the Zagros mountains of western Iran and the wild mountains around present-day Hakkari. Isolated in the inaccessible mountains, they developed their own ethnic as well as religious identity, with half the population organized into tribes little different from their Kurdish neighbours.

Serious rivalries developed during the nineteenth century between the Nestorians and the Kurds, exacerbated by the British and American missionaries who were proselytizing in the region. Local Kurdish leaders massacred many Nestorian men around Hakkari, and sold the women and children into slavery. In 1915 the Nestorian patriarch sided with the World War I Allies. After the war the Nestorians, now seen as traitors, fled to Iran and then Iraq, though half their number perished in the exodus. A short-lived attempt to resettle their mountain fastnesses was crushed by Atatürk in the early years of the Turkish Republic. Today, just a few tens of thousands survive in Iraq, Iran and Syria, with the patriarchate now in Chicago.

OPPOSITE VAN KALESİ (P.629) >

Doğubeyazıt

Impoverished **DOĞUBEYAZIT**, 130km northeast of Van and just half an hour from Iran, is, thanks to its border position and largely Kurdish population, heavily militarized, with a huge army camp just outside town on the road to a spectacular ridge-top fortified place, **İshak Paşa Sarayı**. The palace apart, Doğubeyazıt's major attraction is the presence of Mt Ararat (Ağrı Dağı in Turkish), its enormous volcanic cone and summit glacier clearly visible to the north from many points in town on clear days.

In response to the blatant Turkish army presence, the truculent local council has named the main street after dissident pro-Kurdish intellectual İsmail Beşikçi. Now largely pedestrianized, this street is home to a string of basic restaurants, internet cafés, banks and shops – there's not much else to Doğubeyazıt. Once a major halt on the hippy trail to India, the town still caters to travellers heading to or from points east, but numbers fluctuate wildly according to the political climate prevailing in nearby Iran and the next country east, Pakistan.

İshak Paşa Sarayı

6km southeast of Doğubeyazıt • Tues–Sun 8am–5.30pm • ₺5 • At weekends, dolmuşes ply the route from the main road outside the old *otogar* (₺3) but are difficult to find on weekdays; a taxi from the old *otogar* in central Doğubeyazıt costs ₺40–50 return, including waiting time, or ₺30 one-way – alternatively, walk to the palace in around 1hr 30min (once past the military base the walk is very pleasant)

Overlooking Doğubeyazıt from atop a rocky promontory, the iconic **İshak Paşa Sarayı** is an overblown, impossibly romantic palace. This was once the site of a Urartian fortress; both the Selçuks and Ottomans later built castles to control traffic along the Silk Route.

The palace itself was begun in 1685 by Çolak Abdı Paşa, a local chieftain, and completed by his son, İshak Paşa, in 1784. By 1877, the complex was already in decline, being used by the Turkish army as a barracks; subsequent periods of Russian occupation set the seal on its decay. A controversial new glass and steel roof, added to preserve the walls of the crumbling palace, has spoilt the classic photograph of the palace taken from above.

The palace

The grandiose **gateway** of İshak Paşa Sarayı once boasted gold-plated doors; removed by the Russians in 1917, during their retreat from Anatolia, they're now on show at the Hermitage Museum in St Petersburg. From the outer courtyard, an ornately carved portal leads to a smaller, inner courtyard. Straight ahead is the harem entrance, while to the right is the entrance to the *selâmlık* or men's quarters. The **tombs** of İshak Paşa and his favourite wife stand in a *türbe* in one corner of the inner court.

The **harem** contains fourteen fireplace-equipped bedrooms (in which four hundred soldiers were quartered in 1877), overlooking the valley below, a kitchen and two circular bathrooms. At its centre is a colonnaded dining hall. The *selâmlık* also holds a library, bedrooms and a fine **mosque**, retaining much of its original relief decoration and ceiling painting.

Behind the palace is the picturesque, recently restored Ottoman mosque. It's possible to scramble up behind the mosque to a rock-cut **Urartian tomb** flanked by two carved relief figures. Above this, reachable only by a scramble, there's a narrow niche in the dramatic ridge-top fortress wall. Squeeze through this and you can descend to the much-visited tomb of the Kurdish poet and philosopher Ehmede Xani. His **Mem u Zin** (1692), a tale of star-crossed lovers, is *the* epic work of Kurdish literature. Drinks and souvenir stalls here cater to pilgrims. The even more energetic can climb the steep hillside east of the tomb/parking-cum-picnic area, past a seasonal shepherds' encampment, to the top of a dramatic ridge giving sensational views over a broad valley to Mt Ararat and its subsidiary cone. Allow at least two hours for the return walk, and watch out for the shepherds' dogs.

The foundations on the hillside below the palace are all that's left of **Eski Beyazıt** (Old Beyazıt), a city founded by the Urartians. It was inhabited until 1930, when – in the wake of an unsuccessful local Kurdish rebellion – it was forcibly depopulated and the new Doğu (East) Beyazıt founded in its present location.

ARRIVAL AND DEPARTURE
DOĞUBEYAZIT

By plane Ağrı airport has several flights daily from/to Istanbul with THY; service buses running from Ağrı to Doğubeyazit take 1hr 30min and cost ₺15.

By bus and dolmuş Dolmuşes from Van, and all intercity buses, drop passengers at the small new *otogar* a couple of kilometres west of the town centre. Dolmuşes to the town centre pass by on the main road next to the *otogar* (₺1) or a taxi will set you back ₺15. Dolmuşes for Iğdır, en route to Kars, depart from the town centre.

Destinations Ankara (daily; 16hr); Erzurum (10 daily; 4hr); Gaziantep (daily; 6hr); Iğdır (for Kars; every 45min; ₺15); Istanbul (3 daily; 22hr); Kayseri (daily; 10hr); Van (5 daily, at 6.30am, 8am, 9am, noon & 2pm; 3hr; ₺25).

Travel to Iran If you are considering visiting Iran, it's generally better to apply for a tourist visa in your home country. If you decide to try while you're in Turkey, the best bet is Trabzon, followed by Ankara, Istanbul and finally Erzurum – all have Iranian consulates. Ask Bilal at the *Tehran Boutique Hotel* (see p.642) for the latest information and possible visa procurement.

Transport The nearest Iranian border crossing to Doğubeyazit is at Gürbulak, 34km southeast, accessible by dolmuş from Ağrı Caddesi (regular departures until 5pm; ₺8). Iranian currency is best obtained over the border at Bazargan. From there, you can take a taxi to Maku and then an onward bus to Tabriz. Alternatively, you can cross at Esendere-Sero, southeast of Van, or Kapıköy, though neither of these crossings were functioning at the time of research (summer 2015) owing to security problems.

INFORMATION AND TOURS

Tourist office There's no official tourist office, but the various travel agents and bus companies – mainly on Belediye Caddesi (south of the Atatürk statue) – will be able to help.

Tours Tamzara Travel, Belediye Cad 16 (☏ 0472 312 2189, ⓦ mtararattour.com), run by the genuine and friendly Mustafa Arsin, is the most reliable operator for Ararat ascents and day-tours to Diyadin hot springs, the supposed

12

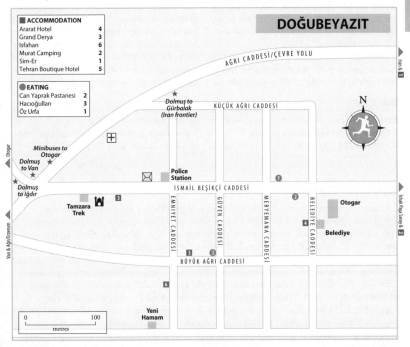

■ ACCOMMODATION
Ararat Hotel	4
Grand Derya	3
Isfahan	6
Murat Camping	2
Sim-Er	1
Tehran Boutique Hotel	5

● EATING
Can Yaprak Pastanesi	2
Hacıoğulları	3
Öz Urfa	1

DOĞUBEYAZIT

AĞRI CADDESİ/ÇEVRE YOLU

Iran

Dolmuş to Gürbalak (Iran frontier)

KÜÇÜK AĞRI CADDESİ

N

Minibuses to Otogar

Dolmuş to Van

Dolmuş to Iğdır

Police Station

İSMAİL BEŞİKÇİ CADDESİ

Otogar

Tamzara Trek

EMNİYET CADDESİ

GÜVEN CADDESİ

MERYEMANA CADDESİ

BELEDİYE CADDESİ

Belediye

İshak Paşa Sarayı

Van & Ağrı/Erzurum

Otogar

BÜYÜK AĞRI CADDESİ

Yeni Hamam

0   100
metres

"Ark" and a meteor crater near the Iranian border for €45; half-day tours €25. Zafer Onay (@zaferonay@hotmail.com) can be found at the *Tehran Boutique Hotel* (see below). A fluent and engaging English-speaker, he has worked as a guide in the area for many, many years and can help visitors with itineraries and tours of the region.

ACCOMMODATION

Ararat Hotel Belediye Cad 16 ☎0472 312 4988, ⓦhotelararatturkey.com. Well run by the owners of Tamzara Travel, the blue-themed rooms are spacious and all have balconies – some with partial Ararat views. A big plus in summer is the roof terrace where you can lounge on cushions and drink beers brought in from outside. Good value despite the average bathrooms. ₺80

Grand Derya Çarşı Cad ☎0472 312 7531. Central, friendly place, almost next door to the mosque, popular with trekking groups. The lobby area is tired looking but the rooms are cheerful enough, and there's a bar and wi-fi. Bargain if there are no groups in. ₺120

Murat Camping İshak Paşa Saray Yolu Üzeri ☎0543 635 0494. Beautifully situated on a bend in the road below the İshak Paşa Sarayı, with grand views of the plain and Doğubeyazıt, this is a cheap and cheerful option for the impecunious, with basic rooms and tent pitches. On the downside, it's something of a tea-garden-cum-kids' playground for locals, so can be noisy, especially at weekends. Room per person ₺30, pitch ₺10

Sim-Er Hotel Iran Yolu ☎0472 312 0061, @dbeyazit@simerhotel.com. Catering predominantly to coach groups, this place is really only of use if you have your own vehicle. Rooms are a little gloomy and the buffet meals very average, but the location, amid greenery a few kilometres east of town, is excellent, with the kind of unobstructed views of Mt Ararat you pray for – unsuccessfully – in the town centre. Half board only. ₺160

★**Tehran Boutique Hotel** Büyük Ağrı Cad 124 ☎0472 312 0195, ⓦtehranboutiquehotel.com. Friendly, fluent English-speaking owner Bilal has transformed the old *Tahran Oteli* into a spanking new boutique hotel that is easily the best in Doğubeyazıt. Rooms are spacious, with laminate wood floors, plain walls and stylish furnishings. North-facing rooms on the sixth floor have balconies with Mt Ararat views, as does the breakfast-terrace-cum-bar above. Bilal is a fount of knowledge about the local area and getting to Iran. ₺160

EATING AND DRINKING

Can Yaprak Pastanesi Dr İsmail Beşikçi Cad 47 ☎0472 312 6897. The best-value place for breakfasts and desserts, with everything from *simit* and *poğaça* (stuffed bread rolls) to *baklava* with glutinous ice cream. Daily 6am–10pm.

Hacıoğulları Büyük Ağrı Cad ☎0544 409 2917. Tiny place occupying a corner plot, it's good value even by Doğubeyazıt bargain standards, dishing up crisp *lahmacun*

for ₺1.5, *pide* from ₺8 and kebabs from ₺10. Daily 7am–10pm.

Öz Urfa Dr İsmail Beşikçi Cad 48 ☎0472 312 2673. This long-established place on the busy main street stands out from its competitors because of its funky first-floor dining area clad in roughly hewn pine planks. It's better than it sounds style-wise, and the *pide* (from ₺10), have a thin, crispy base with generous toppings. Daily 8am–11pm.

DIRECTORY

Banks Doğubeyazıt is well supplied with banks and *döviz*, the majority situated on İsmail Beşikçi Caddesi.
Hamam Yeni Hamam, near the *İsfahan Hotel* on İsageçit

Cad (men and women; from ₺12).
Post office On the main İsmail Beşikçi (Çarşı) Cad (Mon–Sat 8.30am–12.30pm & 1–5.30pm).

Mount Ararat

Few mountains west of the Himalayas have as compelling a hold on the Western imagination as **Mount Ararat** (Ağrı Dağı in Turkish). Traditionally, Armenian monks considered this volcanic mountain holy, and nobody was allowed to climb it; it was not until 1829 that Dr Johann Jacob Parrot, a German academic, conquered the peak. Numerous other ascents have followed, though it was forbidden by Turkish officialdom until the 1950s.

Despite the efforts of American astronaut James Irwin and others, no reliable trace of **Noah's Ark** has been found. Locals, however, insist that the oval mound of earth spotted in 1959 by a Turkish air-force pilot on a routine flight is the "Ark", which now boasts a visitor centre and is included in tours of the area. Genesis 8:4 reports the Ark as coming to rest on the "mountains of Ararat", but this is prone to misinterpretation, as Ararat was the Assyrian rendition of Urartu, the ancient kingdom centred on Lake Van, meaning the Ark could have come to rest anywhere within the bounds of the kingdom. According to the Koran, the Ark was deposited on Mount Cudi, hundreds of kilometres away near Cizre.

The ascent

Treks up Mount Ararat are normally either four- or five-day affairs, supported as far as Camp 2 by mules. From the starting point at **Eli** (2150m), 10km north of Doğubeyazıt, it's a half-day walk to **Camp 1** (3200m).

Camp 2, at 4200m, is a strenuous six-hour march higher. From Camp 2, a 1am start is needed to reach the summit (5hr) before cloud cover becomes too thick. At around 4900m the stones give way to permanent snowpack and then glacier. The views on a clear day are stupendous, compensating for the hard slog of the ascent. Winter climbs followed by ski descents have become increasingly popular for experienced mountaineers.

INFORMATION

When to visit The main climbing season is June to September.

Equipment Ararat is a serious mountain (two Italians died in a blizzard descending the peak in 2006), and you will need proper equipment, including an ice axe and crampons.

Access The mountain lies in a sensitive military zone, adjoining both the Armenian and Iranian frontiers. In the summer of 2015 permission to climb the mountain was temporarily withdrawn owing to increased PKK activity in the area, and many tours were cancelled. Permission is likely to be granted once matters settle down. Permits are essential, and best obtained through a reputable,

MOUNT ARARAT

registered travel/trekking agency (see p.641). They require a photocopy of your passport several days in advance of the mooted climb. Permits are then processed by the authorities in the provincial capital of Ağrı, usually taking around five days. Qualified guides are mandatory. Trips cost around €490 per head, ski expeditions around €680. Applicants with Armenian surnames will be denied permission to climb.

Touts Local touts in Doğubeyazit may offer to obtain a permit for you immediately, or even take you up the peak without one. If you take their advice, you risk loss of your deposit at best, and arrest at worst. That said, quite a few visitors take the chance.

12

TEMPLE OF HADRIAN, EPHESUS

Contexts

History

The present Turkish Republic is all that remains of a vast medieval empire, which at its zenith extended from the Indian Ocean almost to the Atlantic – and all of its territories contributed personalities and events. The following history covers the key events of a complex saga.

The earliest cultures

Discoveries in the heart of modern Turkey – the region known historically as Anatolia or Asia Minor – indicate settled habitation since the **Neolithic age** in the eighth millennium BC, which makes it among the oldest on earth. Excavations at Göbekli Tepe, on the northern rim of the fertile crescent, have brought to light a remarkable temple complex built by hunter-gatherer communities as early as 10,000 BC, while extensive Neolithic discoveries include entire farming communities, notably Çatal Höyük near Konya (c. 6500–5650 BC), demonstrating that early settlers lived in sizeable villages. Their tools were made from local obsidian and flint; pottery included stylized figures representing the Mother Goddess.

Influence from Upper Mesopotamia and northern Syria brought southeast Anatolia into the **Chalcolithic Age**. Sites of this period were more like fortified towns, and evidence of violent destruction suggests that they regularly waged war. More independent cultures of central Anatolia and the west Anatolian lakeland produced burnished pottery and idols of local deities.

The third-millennium BC **Bronze Age** witnessed the emergence of local dynasties ruling from fortified settlements. Sophisticated equipment found in Alacahöyük's royal cemetery suggests that early Anatolian kings benefitted from metallurgy. Religious art included standards with stylized deer and bulls, hoards of gold jewellery and musical instruments.

Meanwhile, trade was expanding along the south and west coasts. **Troy** had links with Aegean islands, mainland Greece, and other Anatolian populations in the southeast. Anatolian metals, jewellery, weapons and tableware were exchanged for lapis lazuli, rock crystal and ivory. Great wealth was amassed, as epitomized by the "Treasure of Priam", a third-millennium hoard rediscovered in the nineteenth century.

The Middle and Late Bronze Ages, during the second millennium BC, began with violent destruction and turbulence, out of which the **Hatti** emerged in central Anatolia, whose culture was later assimilated by the Hittites. Commerce took place along fixed trade routes, and many Anatolian cities were colonized by Assyrian merchants. Their meticulous records show that textiles and tin were traded for copper and ornamental pottery.

The Hittites

The first truly major civilization to emerge in Anatolia was that of the **Hittites**. They first appeared around 2000 BC, though their so-called "Old Kingdom" was founded around 1650 BC. The capital at Hattuşaş, created by Hattusilis I, was a huge city for its

10,000 BC	**2900 BC**	**1650 BC**
Hunter-gatherers build the temple complex at Göbekli Tepe in southeast Anatolia	Foundation of Troy at the mouth of the Dardanelles, northwest Anatolia	The Hittites establish an imperial capital at Hattuşaş, in central Anatolia

time, with a citadel overlooking a gorge. Hittite artistic style was a direct outgrowth of Anatolian predecessors and, unlike Syrian art, was never overwhelmed by Mesopotamian and Egyptian conventions. The principal examples are enormous rock-cut reliefs of warrior gods and stylized sphinx-like beings.

Besides their imperialist nature, the Hittite kingdoms are known for their relatively humane constitution and religion, and highly developed sense of ethics. Diplomacy was preferred to warfare, and often cemented by royal marriages. Libraries, archives and bureaucracy were central to Hittite society, and rulers were not despotic but tied to a constitution like their subjects. The Old Kingdom dynasty lasted several generations before being riven by succession struggles; the empire was re-established by Tudhaliyas II around 1430 BC, just as a rival power arose in Upper Mesopotamia. These Mitanni or Hurrians, ruled by an Indo-European dynasty, were defeated in battle by Hittite king Suppiluliumas (1385–1345 BC).

Under Muwatallis, the Hittites confirmed their military strength by defeating the Egyptians under Ramses II at the battle of **Kadesh** (1274 BC). Subsequently the two dynasties became allied through the division of Syria and the marriage of Ramses II to a daughter of another Hittite ruler. The Hittites' landlocked empire was not completely secure, however, and in the southeast Mediterranean, the Kizzuwadna region, later Cilicia, was taken by the Hurrians, who also married into the Hittite royal line.

While the west coast was not well documented in Hittite records, excavations show that Troy was rebuilt by a new dynasty, and vast supplies were amassed inside its citadel. The second-millennium Trojans were rivals to the Greeks, who eventually sacked Troy in the **Trojan War** around 1200 BC, when the Hittite Empire also collapsed.

The post-Hittite era

As more Indo-European tribes, especially the "Sea Peoples" – early Iron Age migrants from the Aegean and Balkan mainland – invaded, Hittite cities were destroyed, and Anatolia entered a long cultural Dark Age. Surviving Hittites and their Anatolian allies founded small city-states in the southeast, preserving elements of the old culture and forming a bridge between the Bronze and **Iron** ages. At these lively Neo-Hittite entrepôts, early Greek art encountered Hittite reliefs and statuary, and knowledge of oriental mythology and religion passed to Greece. They finally fell to the Arameans and the Assyrians in the eighth century BC.

To the east, the kingdom of **Urartu** was founded by descendants of the Hurrians. Their cities, including Tushpa near Lake Van, were elaborately engineered, with citadels and tunnel systems for escape or survival under attack. The Urartians expanded into central Anatolia and northern Syria before being checked, in the latter eighth century BC, by the Assyrians. The Urartians specialized in metalwork, and bronzeware was traded as far away as Greece.

To the west, a new immigrant tribe, the **Phrygians**, attained prominence; their capital was Gordion, on a strategic trading route by the River Sangarius (today Sakarya). This kingdom peaked around 725 BC under King Midas, but he committed suicide in despair when Cimmerian horsemen sacked Gordion. The southwest coast was settled during the Iron Age by Lycians, possibly the "Lukka" of Bronze Age records.

1200 BC	900 BC	725 BC
Troy sacked by the Greeks at the end of the Trojan War	Sometime around this date, the Urartian kingdom emerges in the Lake Van basin	Under King Midas, the western Anatolian kingdom of Phrygia reaches its peak

The **Lydians** occupied the Hermus valley, with their capital at Sardis. They survived the Bronze Age with an indigenous Anatolian language, emerging from the eighth century BC to dominate western Anatolia, including former Phrygian zones. Lydian luxury goods were widely exported, and their elegant art forms influenced those of Greek Ionia and even Persia.

The Persians and Alexander

Lydian power endured until 546 BC, when their king, **Croesus**, was defeated by Cyrus's ascendant **Persian Empire**. Over the next half-century, the Persians subdued the Greek coastal cities and the interior, ending Anatolian self-rule. Satraps (compliant local puppets) were enthroned but obliged to pay tribute to the Persian "Great King"; Persian allies like the Phoenicians were favoured at the expense of Greek cities as commercial intermediaries with the West. In 499 BC, western Anatolia, led by Miletus, revolted, but lacking massive aid from mainland Greece, the rebellion failed.

Enraged by even token Athenian support for the rebels, **Darius** I crossed into Greece but was soundly defeated at the battle of Marathon in 490 BC. Darius' successor, Xerxes, invaded again ten years later but was defeated at the sea battle of Salamis in 480 BC and the land battle of Plataea in 479 BC. This thwarting of Persia initially availed the cities of Asia Minor little, though they soon exploited growing rivalry between Athens and Sparta to negotiate more autonomy. By the mid-fourth century BC, some quasi-independent dynasties had arisen in western Anatolia, the most notable being the Hecatomnids at Halikarnassos, whose illustrious rulers included **Mausolus** (377–353 BC), and his wife and successor Artemisia II.

In spring 334 BC, a new power swept out of Macedonia: **Alexander**, later "the Great", equipped merely with a guiding vision and some Corinthian volunteers to supplement his small Macedonian army. Having crossed the Dardanelles, he defeated the Persians and proceeded down the Asia Minor coast via the major cities, treating them with lenience or harshness depending on whether or not they rallied to his standard. Having wintered in Lycia, Alexander and his juggernaut rolled on across Pamphylia, inland to Gordion, then over the Toros range into coastal Cilicia, intent on attacking the Persian heartland beyond Syria. **Darius III** awaited Alexander at Issos (modern Dörtyol), but was crushed by the Macedonians, despite outnumbering them two to one. This rapid conquest of Anatolia was as much indicative of Persian dynastic rottenness as of Alexander's military genius.

The prodigy swept through Persia proper as far as the Indus valley, but died of malaria – or possibly poisoning – on the return trip, in 323 BC. Following his death, Alexander's generals **divided Anatolia**: Lysimakhos took the west, while Seleukos – succeeded by Antiokhos – received most of the southeast; much of the centre and north remained independent. Lysimakhos's successor Philetaros made **Pergamon** the greatest Hellenistic city of Asia Minor; by the late second century BC, however, his heir Attalos III bequeathed it to the Romans.

Roman rule

Roman power in Asia Minor was almost immediately challenged by **Mithridates** of Pontus (ruled 110–63 BC), a brilliant, resourceful polymath; from 89 BC on, his

546 BC	**334 BC**	**89 BC**
Lydian King Croesus defeated by the Persians	Alexander the Great defeats the Persians at the battle of Granicus, northwest Anatolia	Mithridates of Pontus rebels against the Romans for the first time

rebellious campaigns kept assorted Roman generals occupied. In 72 BC, Mithridates sought refuge at the court of Tigranes the Great in the regional power, Armenia. The Romans promptly invaded, but it suited them to maintain Armenia as a buffer principality between themselves and the Parthians on the east, successors to the Persians.

First Emperor Augustus's reign marked the start of fairly durable peace and prosperity in Anatolia, as witness the numerous ruined cities dating from Roman imperial rule, many endowed by **Hadrian** (117–138 AD). Politically, however, it remained a backwater, with only the texts of Strabo and Pliny to flesh out life here – as well as the first-century AD biblical writings of St Paul during his evangelical tours of Asia Minor.

In 284 AD, **Diocletian** divided the empire into two administrative units, each ruled by an emperor (Augustus) cooperating with a designated successor (Caesar) – the so-called tetrarchy. Within forty years, however, this system collapsed into civil war. The victor, **Constantine**, moved the headquarters of the eastern portion from Salonica to the minor – but strategically located – town of Byzantium, on the western shores of the Bosphorus straits linking the Black Sea and the Sea of Marmara. This new capital, renamed **Constantinople**, was a conscious imitation of Rome. Soon afterwards Constantine began to favour Christianity, which by the end of the fourth century became the state religion of an empire that had long persecuted Christians.

A unified empire, too unwieldy to be governed from a single centre, did not survive much beyond Constantine's forceful reign. Theodosius the Great (ruled 379–395), who officially proscribed paganism in 391, was the last sovereign of a united empire, which upon his death formally split into **two realms**: the western one Latin-speaking and Rome-based, the eastern part Greek-speaking and focused on Constantinople.

The Byzantine Empire

The western provinces, always financially dependent on the east, were plagued by "barbarian" invasions from the north. The wealthier, more densely populated eastern **Byzantine Empire** had abler rulers and more defensible frontiers, but was severely weakened by religious tensions. Constantinople's writ was resented in the southeastern provinces of Egypt, Palestine, Syria and Armenia with their non-Classical indigenous cultures; moreover, their churches embraced the **Monophysite doctrine**, which maintained that Christ had a single divine nature. Until the thirteenth century, clerics in the capital persecuted the provincial "heretics", at the same time begrudging claims to papal supremacy and quarrelling over dogma with Rome. This culminated in the formal separation of the eastern **Orthodox** and western **Roman Catholic** churches in 1054.

Following the death of Justinian in 565, the empire's character changed radically. All his peripheral conquests were lost: the western realms to the Lombards and Goths, the southeastern provinces to Persians and Arabs. By 711, the Byzantine Empire consisted only of the Balkan coasts, parts of Italy, and Asia Minor. Equally significantly, it had acquired a strongly Greek character, both linguistically and philosophically, and Latin influence faded as relations with Rome worsened.

After 867, the **Macedonian dynasty**, founded by Basil I, a former stable boy who rendered Justinian's law code into Greek, reversed Byzantium's fortunes. Under Basil II

330 AD	391	527–565
The inauguration of Constantinople as a new capital of the Roman Empire	The Christian Byzantine emperor Theodosius the Great officially proscribes paganism	The reign of Justinian, the greatest Byzantine emperor after Constantine

EMPEROR JUSTINIAN

Byzantium's response to the collapse of the West after the fifth century was expansionist – or rather, nostalgic. Energetic emperor **Justinian** (ruled 527–565) attempted to recapture the glory and territory of ancient Rome in campaigns across the Mediterranean. Imperial generals Belisarius and Narses re-absorbed Italy, North Africa and southern Spain into the empire, though the Byzantines were unable to stem the flow of Slavs into the Balkans, and concluded an uneasy truce with the Persians after a long, inconclusive war.

Justinian also pursued an ambitious domestic agenda. He inaugurated a programme of public works, resulting in such masterpieces as **Haghia Sophia** in Constantinople and San Vitale in Ravenna. Justinian's streamlining of the huge, often contradictory, body of Roman law was perhaps his most enduring achievement: the new code became the basis for the medieval legal systems of France, Germany and Italy.

Justinian's reign marked the definitive emergence of a strictly **Byzantine** – as opposed to Roman – identity, with institutions that sustained the empire for the rest of its life. Having widened its boundaries to their maximum extent and established the theocratic nature of Byzantium, he can be reckoned among the greatest Byzantine emperors. Ultimately, though, many of his achievements proved ephemeral, and exhausted the empire to such a degree that it had difficulty withstanding subsequent attacks.

(976–1025), nicknamed "Bulgar-Slayer" for his ruthless campaigns against the Slavs, the empire again extended its frontiers into eastern Anatolia and up the Balkan peninsula, while Constantinople enjoyed unparalleled prosperity at the crossroads of new Eurasian trade routes. Literature and the arts flourished, and missionaries converted Balkan Slavs to Orthodoxy.

After Basil II, however, the empire began its final **decline**, slow but relentless over four centuries. For much of the eleventh century, Anatolia was wracked by civil war, with bureaucrats in Constantinople pitted against landed generals in the countryside. Each promoted their own candidates for the throne, resulting in successive nonentities as emperors. Simultaneously, the patriarchate renewed its vendetta against the Monophysite churches, whose members were concentrated in the critical eastern borderlands. The warlords reduced the free peasantry to serfdom; the bureaucrats, usually in control at Constantinople, matched their own extravagance with stinginess toward the army, increasingly staffed by unreliable mercenaries.

The first major threats came from the West. The **Normans**, greedy for Byzantine craftsmanship and splendour, invaded the Balkans late in the eleventh century, and were only repulsed with Venetian help, who in return demanded trading concessions – as did the **Genoese**. Government tolls and taxes plummeted as imperial monopolies were broken by the new Latin maritime powers, and western covetousness – which culminated in the sacking of Constantinople by the Fourth Crusade in 1204 – knew no bounds. Though able emperors emerged from the twelfth-century Komnenos dynasty and the later Paleologos clan, without consistent western aid the Byzantines were doomed to fight a long, rearguard action against enemies from the east and north. Imperial twilight was marked by a final flourishing of sacred art and architecture, as Anatolia and the Balkans were adorned with beautiful churches – this period's main legacy.

1000	1054	1071
Around this period, the first Turks begin to appear in Anatolia	Separation of the eastern Orthodox and western Roman Catholic churches	Battle of Manzikert, in which the Byzantines lose disastrously to the Selçuk Turks

The arrival of the Turks

Early in the eleventh century, a new people began to raid Byzantium from the east. They had first appeared in seventh-century Mongolia, a shamanistic, nomadic bunch whom the Chinese called "Tu-kueh" or Dürkö – **Turks** to the West. These tribes began migrating westward, encountering the Arabs by the ninth century. The latter, recognizing their martial virtues, recruited them and set about converting them to **Islam**, a process completed by the late tenth century.

One branch of the Turkish tribes, followers of the chieftain **Selçuk**, adopted **Sunni** Islam and a settled life in Baghdad. The majority, however, the so-called Turcomans, remained nomadic and heterodox, drawing on **Shi'ite** and pagan beliefs, and unamenable to state control. Selçuk rulers took advantage of their warrior zeal by diverting them into Byzantine territory.

These raiders penetrated Byzantine Armenia, and it was more to restrain them than to confront the Byzantines that Selçuk ruler Alparslan marched north from Baghdad in 1071. Meeting, almost accidentally, the demoralized armies of Byzantine emperor Romanus IV Diogenes, he defeated them easily at Manzikert. The Selçuks didn't follow up this victory, but it led to redoubled rampages by the Turcomans. The Byzantines, alternately menaced and assisted by Latin crusaders, managed to re-occupy western Anatolia, plus the Black Sea and Mediterranean coasts, by the mid-twelfth century. The Selçuk **Sultanate of Rum**, based at Konya (Iconium), consolidated the Turcoman-ravaged areas; after winning the battle of Myriokephalo in 1176, the Selçuks came to terms with the Byzantines.

Following the occupation of Constantinople by the Fourth Crusade in 1204, the Selçuks continued their good relations with the provisional Byzantine Empire of Nicaea; with peace assured, the Sultanate of Rum evolved into a highly cultured mini-empire, reaching its zenith in the first half of the thirteenth century as imposing *kervansarays*, *medreses* and other monuments adorned central Anatolia. The Selçuks also excelled in tile- and relief-work, and in the spiritual field the sultanate, despite Sunni orientation, gave refuge to many heterodox religious figures, including Celaleddin Rumi, founder of the Mevlevî dervish order.

The **Mongols** crushed the Selçuks at the battle of Köse Dağ in 1243, and although the sultanate lingered on until about 1300, the Turcoman tribes, never fully pacified, swarmed over the lands of both Selçuks and the Byzantines, who had abandoned Asia Minor after returning to Constantinople in 1261. For two centuries there was no single authority in Anatolia, but the process of Turkification and Islamization, begun in 1071, continued apace.

The rise of the Ottomans

Following the Selçuk collapse, Anatolia fragmented into mostly Turcoman **emirates**. The emirate which centred on Söğüt was not initially important; its chieftain, Ertuğrul, was a typical *gazi*, a convert to Islam, and carried the faith ever westward. His son Osman, however, head of the clan from the 1290s, gave his name to a dynasty: Osmanlı in Turkish, "**Ottoman**" to the West. This emirate began to expand under Osman's son Orhan, who by the 1330s captured Byzantine Bursa and İznik.

Anatolian culture had long been hybrid, with frequent intermarriage between Muslims and Christians, and descendants or converts bilingual in Greek and Turkish. The Bektaşi dervish order effected a synthesis between Islam and numerically dwindling Christianity.

1204	1243	1290
Decline of the Byzantine Empire is hastened by the sacking of Constantinople during the Fourth Crusade	The Mongols crush the Selçuk Turks at the battle of Köse Dağ in central Anatolia	Around this time, Osman assumes control of a tribal dynasty that will become the Ottoman Empire

As Byzantine authority diminished, the assets and facilities of Christian monasteries were appropriated by the **vakıfs**, or Islamic pious foundations; the demoralized Christian priesthood and population often converted to Islam simultaneously.

Complementing this was the *devşirme*, a fourteenth-century innovation whereby boys from conquered Christian districts were levied by the Ottomans to serve as an elite force, the janissaries. Slaves of the sultan, they were admitted to the eclectic Bektaşi order, and trained meticulously to become not only warriors but administrators. As free-born Muslims were ineligible for this corps, and promotion was by merit, the Ottoman state, up to the office of grand vizier, was run by converts. The only chance of advancement for free-born Muslims lay within the *ulema*, the Koranic sages who decreed on religious matters, or as a member of the *defterdar* (accountant) bureaucracy overseeing the empire's revenues.

While the janissaries formed a powerful praetorian guard, they were supplemented by a standing army, paid indirectly by *timar* (land grant), an adopted Byzantine practice. Conquered territory remained the sultan's property, with such grants dispensed on the understanding that the man's "salary" was the proceeds of his estate – and that he remained liable for armed service at any time. *Timar*s reverted to the crown upon the holder's death, with his sons having to re-earn their portion by service.

Despite tolerance shown to Christians, Ottoman society was hierarchical. Distinctions between Muslims and infidels were preserved in every particular from dress code to unequal status before the law. Christians were not conscripted for campaigns, and hence could not qualify for *timar*s; instead they paid a tax in lieu of military service, and congregated in towns as tradesmen.

To continue the *timar* system, more land had to be seized, and the *gazi* ethos continued. By the mid-fourteenth century the Ottomans had entered Thrace, and in 1362 **Sultan Murat I** took Adrianopolis (Edirne). Constantinople was surrounded, and the almost-vanished Byzantine Empire existed on Ottoman sufferance. With Latin and Orthodox Christians at each other's throats, Ottoman ascendancy was assured, and Murat further isolated Constantinople with new acquisitions in the lower Balkans, routing a Serbian-led coalition at Kosovo in 1389. After Murat was murdered on the battlefield by a Serbian infiltrator, his elder son and successor **Beyazıt I** established an unfortunate precedent by promptly strangling his brother Yakub to assure untroubled rule. Beyazıt, nicknamed Yıldırım (Lightning) for his swift battle deployments, defeated a Hungarian/Crusader army at Bulgarian Nicopolis in 1396, and the fall of Constantinople seemed imminent.

However, in expanding eastwards, Beyazıt – more impulsive and less methodical than Murat – provoked the great Mongol warrior **Tamerlane**. Tamerlane routed Beyazıt's armies at the **Battle of Ankara** in 1402, trundling the captive sultan about in a cage for a year before his demise, while laying waste to much of Anatolia. Even though the Mongols soon vanished, the remnant Byzantine Empire was granted a fifty-year reprieve, and for a decade the fate of the Ottoman line hung in the balance as Beyazıt's four sons fought it out. The victor, Mehmet I, and his successor, the mystically inclined Murat II, restored Ottoman fortunes.

The fall of Constantinople

The greatest prize – **Constantinople** – still eluded the Ottomans. Both symbolically, as the seat of two previous empires, and practically – as the throttle between the Black Sea

1362	1402	1453
Ottoman Sultan Murat I takes Adrianople (today's Edirne), which becomes the new capital	Tamerlane's Mongols defeat Beyazıt I at the Battle of Ankara – a major setback for the Ottomans	Sultan Mehmet II takes Constantinople, to mark the end of the Byzantine world

and the Mediterranean – its capture was imperative. **Mehmet II**, who became sultan in 1451, immediately began preparations, studding the sea approaches to the severely depopulated capital with fortresses, engaging artillery experts from Europe with an eye to breaching the city walls, and for the first time outfitting a substantial Ottoman fleet. The final siege of Constantinople, during spring 1453, lasted seven weeks, ending on May 29 when the sultan's armies finally entered the city while the last Byzantine emperor died unnoticed in the melee. Mehmet's epithet was henceforth Fatih, "the Conqueror". The capture of Constantinople confirmed the Ottoman Empire as the legitimate successor of the Roman and Byzantine ones.

The Ottoman Golden Age

Mehmet refurbished the city – which began to be known as **Istanbul** – as a worthy imperial capital, repopulating it with Muslims and Christians from rural areas, establishing public amenities and constructing a fine palace at Topkapı. The non-Muslim -communities were organized into *millets* (nations), headed by a patriarch or rabbi, answerable for his flock's good behaviour (plus tax remittances) and under whom Greek or Slavic Orthodox, Armenian and Jew were subject to their own communal laws. This system, which guaranteed more freedom of worship than in contemporary Europe, was gradually phased out in the nineteenth century.

Mop-up campaigns during 1458–60 in the Peloponnese and along the Black Sea eliminated satellite Byzantine and Genoese states. Mehmet then returned to the upper Balkans, adding Wallachia, most of Greece, Bosnia-Herzegovina and part of Albania to his domains, while expanding his navy to counter the Venetians.

Mehmet was succeeded in 1481 by **Beyazıt II**, "the Pious", who, despite that disposition, relegated Venice to secondary maritime status by enlisting pirates into the Ottoman navy. The skills of Greek renegades and Italian mercenaries were supplemented in 1493 by those of Iberian Jews, the ancestors of most contemporary Turkish Jewry, fetched by "mercy ships" sent by Beyazıt upon their expulsion from Spain and Portugal.

In 1512, Beyazıt was forced to abdicate by his son **Selim I**, vigorous like his grandfather but with an added streak of cruelty and bigotry, hence his moniker Yavuz ("the Fierce" – "the Grim" to the West). Both of Selim's predecessors had entertained Sufic and heterodox doctrines, but now religious orthodoxy was seen as vital, since neighbour Shah İsmail of Persia was promoting Shi'ism both within and without his frontiers. Selim massacred forty thousand Shi'ites in Anatolia, and then defeated the Shah at Çaldıran in 1514. Rather than continue into Persia, however, Selim turned his armies south against the Mamluks, overrunning Mesopotamia and Egypt by 1516, and occupying most of the holy cities of Islam. By capturing the caliph in Cairo and transporting him back to Istanbul, Selim became Defender of the (Sunni) Faith – and the caliphate was identified with the Ottoman sultanate.

Although the empire would reach its greatest extent after his death, **Süleyman the Magnificent** laid the foundations for this expansion during a long reign (1520–1566). The strongholds of the Knights of St John at Rhodes and Bodrum – which controlled the sea lanes to Egypt – were taken early on, as was Belgrade, leaving lands further up the Danube unguarded; by 1526 Budapest was in Ottoman hands. Campaigns in Persia and the Arabian peninsula were successful, but the **siege of Vienna** in 1529 was not – nor was

1481	1514	1516
Jews expelled from Spain are given sanctuary by the Muslim Ottoman Turks	Selim I (the Grim) defeats the Persians at the battle of Çaldıran on the Ottoman–Persian frontier	Selim I captures Cairo and Mesopotamia, and the Ottomans are seen as upholders of the Islamic caliphate

SÜLEYMAN THE MAGNIFICENT AND ROXELANA

Domestically Süleyman distinguished himself as an administrator, builder and patron of the arts; in Turkey he is known as Kanunî, "the Lawgiver". In his personal life, however, his judgement had enduringly harmful consequences. He became so enamoured of his favourite concubine Roxelana that he broke with Ottoman precedent and married her.

Scheming and ambitious, Roxelana used her influence to incite the sultan to murder his capable son and heir (by a previous liaison), Mustafa, and later her own son Beyazıt – as well as his grand vizier İbrahim. Süleyman died a lonely, morose man on his last campaign on the Danube in 1566; with the two ablest princes gone, no obstacles blocked the succession of Roxelana's first-born son, the useless Selim.

an attempt to drive the Portuguese from the Indian Ocean. Süleyman was better able to control the Mediterranean, with such admirals as Greek-born Barbaros Hayrettin (**Barbarossa**) and Turgut Reis besting Venetian/Habsburg fleets. But in 1565, the siege of Malta, where the Knights of St John had retreated, failed, marking the end of the Mediterranean as an "Ottoman lake". Nonetheless, the Ottoman Empire, however unwieldy and heterogeneous, was the leading world power of the sixteenth century.

The empire was accordingly regarded with both terror and fascination by Europe. Only the **French**, under Francis I, saw possibilities of alliance and manipulation, concluding a treaty with Süleyman in 1536. In addition to granting France trading advantages in the empire, the treaty's clauses stipulated various privileges for French nationals, the so-called **Capitulations**: exemption from most Ottoman taxes and the right to be judged by their own consuls under foreign law. What began as a stimulus to commerce became, over time, a pernicious erosion of Ottoman sovereignty, as many European nations and overseas companies secured their own capitulations, extending immunity to local employees (usually Christian) provided with appropriate passports.

Centuries of Ottoman decline

The reign of bibulous **Selim II** ("the Sot" to the West) is the best marker as the start of Ottoman decline. He was succeeded by sixteen other, generally ineffectual, sultans, of whom only bloodthirsty but resolute **Murat IV** and peace-loving aesthete **Ahmet II** did much to prevent the gradual deterioration. From Roxelana's time onwards, the **harem** was located in Topkapı palace, so the scheming of its tenants impinged directly on day-to-day government. Early in the seventeenth century the grisly custom of fratricide upon the enthronement of a new sultan was abandoned in favour of the debilitating confinement of other heirs-apparent to the so-called *Kafes* (Cage). Few sultans campaigned overseas any longer, or presided personally over councils of state, instead delegating authority to their grand viziers.

Able and honest viziers halted or reversed the downward slide of the empire, but usually nepotism and corruption flourished in the decadent palace atmosphere. The early Ottoman principle of meritocracy was replaced by **hereditary aristocracy**; the *devşirme* was all but abandoned by the late seventeenth century, and the janissary corps was no longer celibate or religiously exclusive. Sinecure passed from father to son, and the corps expanded as free Muslims enrolled. Many were artisans who only appeared to

1529	1536	1566
The unsuccessful siege of Vienna is a rare setback for the Ottoman war machine	European influence in Ottoman affairs, which will ultimately prove disastrous, begins with a treaty between the Ottomans and the French	Ottoman decline is symbolized by the accession of Selim II "the Sot"

collect pay, desire for more of which often prompted the janissaries to rebel, extorting money from hapless villagers and sultans alike, and on occasion deposing and murdering the sovereign. Similarly, land grants became hereditary, and their holders evolved into local warlords (the *derebeys*, "lords of the valley"). Revolts of idle, underpaid troops devastated Anatolia, already wracked by overpopulation and land shortage; thus began a steady rural depopulation that continues today.

More problems came from abroad. The influx into the Mediterranean of gold and silver from the New World set off a spiral of inflation, while the Age of Exploration forged new sea lanes around Africa to the East Indies, reducing the importance of overland caravan routes through Ottoman territories. Most importantly, Europe underwent the **Renaissance**, while the Ottomans remained stagnant. New, centralized nation-states in the West began to acquire well-trained standing armies and navies, equipped with new armaments, ships and navigation devices. To these manifestations of European superiority the Ottomans reacted disdainfully, seeing no reason to learn from the infidels.

External evidence of the rot took nearly a century to show: although the defeat of an Ottoman fleet at **Lepanto** (today Náfpaktos) in 1571 shattered the myth of Turkish invincibility, that victory was neutralized by their taking Cyprus from Venice the same year, and the reconquest of North Africa by 1578. The seventeenth century proceeded well, with the seizure of Crete and parts of Poland, but already the Ottomans were drafting treaties with adversaries as equals rather than, as before, condescending to suppliant Christian kings. Towards the end of the century, the most notorious of several defeats at the hands of the Austrians and allies was the bungled second siege of Vienna in 1683. Most of Hungary and other central European lands were ceded before the treaties of Carlowitz (1699) and Passarowitz (1718) stabilized the Balkan frontier for two centuries.

During the eighteenth century, most Ottoman territorial loss was to **Russia**; Russo-Turkish enmity remained a constant thereafter until the 1920s. Catherine the Great humiliated the Turks with the treaties of Küçük Kaynarca (1774) and Jassy (1792), which ceded extensive territory to the tsarina and gave Russia long-coveted access to the Black Sea – as well as the right to interfere, anywhere in the Ottoman Empire, to protect Orthodox Christians.

Reforms and Young Ottomans

The start of **Selim III**'s rule in 1789 coincided with new revolutionary regimes in France and the US – hence the name of his proposed reforms, the Nizam-i-Cedid (**New Order**). With the Napoleonic wars as a background, he hired foreign experts to set up a Western-style army. This aroused the hostility of the janissaries and the *ulema*; Selim was deposed, then murdered, in 1808, despite having dissolved the new army as a sop to the conservatives.

The new sultan, **Mahmut II**, innovated more cautiously, before being confronted by the major crisis of his reign: full-scale **Greek rebellion** in 1821. This proved impossible to crush even after the army of Mehmet Ali, semi-autonomous ruler of Egypt, was sent to the scene. The destruction of an Ottoman fleet at Navarino by French, Russian and English ships in 1827, an 1829 overland attack by Russia on Istanbul, and a treaty in 1830 created an independent Greece – the first major Ottoman loss in the south Balkans. The French simultaneously invaded Algeria, and Mehmet Ali attacked

1571	1683	1830
Ottoman military might is questioned, following the naval defeat at the Battle of Lepanto	The second siege of Vienna fails – a humiliating reverse for the Ottomans	Greece wins independence from the Ottoman Empire

Anatolia, which went unchecked until the Russians, now supporting Mahmut, landed on the Bosphorus. In consideration for services rendered, they imposed the Treaty of Hunkâr İskelesi, giving the tsar unimpeded access to the Bosphorus straits.

Mahmut had notably more success at home. In 1826 the janissaries mutinied again, but the sultan liquidated them with loyal forces in the so-called "**Auspicious Incident**". The Bektaşi sect, the janissary "house religion", was suppressed until the 1860s, and a proper army created. Prussian and Austrian advisers arrived to train it during the 1830s, starting a tradition of Teutonic involvement in Turkey's military that endured for almost a century. A formal foreign service and civil service were also established. A version of Western dress became mandatory for all except clerics – including the replacement of the turban by the more "progressive" **fez**. These centralizing reforms widened the gap between the Ottoman masses and the new elite.

Mahmut's efforts bore more fruit when his son Sultan Abdülmecit and vizier Mustafa Reşit proclaimed the **Tanzimat** (Reorganization) in 1839, an Ottoman Magna Carta that delegated some sultanic authority to advisers, ended taxation irregularities, and stipulated equal legal treatment of Muslims and non-Muslims. While this permitted the founding of newspapers and secular schools, the proposal of infidel equality deeply offended many.

Foreign economic penetration of the Ottoman Empire increased sharply, with growing commerce in port cities, and massive imports of European products; the Greeks, Armenians and foreign-Christian merchants benefitted disproportionately. Inland centres and traditional bazaar crafts declined sharply, unable to compete with industrial products.

By mid-century the empire was thoroughly enmeshed in European power struggles, since England and France had determined that the Ottomans must be propped up as a counter to Russian expansionism. Thus the empire found itself among the winners of the 1853–56 **Crimean War**, which began as a dispute between Russia and France over the protection extended by each to Christians in Ottoman Palestine. The war ended with little significant territorial adjustment, but did bring twenty years of peace for the Ottomans.

Abdülmecit, well-meaning but weak and extravagant, was succeeded in 1861 by **Abdülaziz**, who combined his predecessor's defects with a despotic manner. From among the first graduates of the empire's secular schools arose the Society of **Young Ottomans**, which advocated a constitutional monarchy; its stellar figure, poet and essayist Namık Kemal, was exiled (like others) by the sultan. Young Ottomans overseas penned reams of seditious literature, smuggled into the empire to good effect.

Faced with Abdülaziz's financial irresponsibility and his growing mental instability, together with new Russian mischief in Istanbul and brutally suppressed revolts in the Balkans, Young Ottomans among the bureaucratic elite deposed him on May 30, 1876. The sultanate was passed to Abdülaziz's promising nephew Murat, but he suffered a nervous breakdown and within months was declared unfit to rule. The next heir-apparent was Murat's brother **Abdülhamit**, an unknown quantity, offered the throne on condition that he accept various Young Ottomans as advisers and rule constitutionally.

Abdülhamit and the Young Turks

The new sultan duly presided over the first Ottoman parliament and retained – briefly – his hapless brother's advisers. But implementation of reforms was interpreted by outsiders as a sign of weakness. Accordingly, **Russia attacked** in 1877, in the Caucasus and in the

1839	1853–56	1877
The Ottoman Empire attempts to modernize with the Tanzimat reforms	The Ottomans and their allies, France and Britain, prevail against Russia in the Crimean War	The Ottomans lose a great deal of territory in the Caucasus and Balkans to imperial Russia

Balkans, with an explicitly pan-Slavic agenda. The war went badly for the Ottomans, with extensive territorial losses confirmed by the harsh peace treaty of San Stefano (at the ceasefire line near Istanbul), later mitigated by the 1878 Conference of Berlin. This provided for an independent Romania, Montenegro and Serbia; an autonomous if truncated Bulgaria; the cession of Kars and Ardahan districts to Russia; and the occupation of Bosnia and Herzegovina by Austria. **Nationalism** had been unleashed – and rewarded – in the Balkans, and would be a theme for the next forty years. Britain, as compensation for fending off further Russian advances, was given Cyprus.

During all this, the new **parliament** displayed too much independence for the sultan's liking, criticizing policy and summoning ministers to answer for their conduct. In early 1878, between the San Stefano and Berlin negotiations, Abdülhamit dropped any pretence of consultative government and dissolved the Chamber of Deputies; with all restraining influences gone, he ruled despotically and directly. Numerous spies and rigorous press censorship attended a police state and a new telegraph network helped surveillance.

After his disastrous early wars, Abdülhamit's foreign policy was xenophobic and Asia-oriented, espousing Islam as a unifying force and emphasizing his role as caliph. This didn't prevent the loss of Tunis and Egypt, along with worsening treatment of the Armenians of eastern Anatolia, who began to show the same nationalist sentiments as Balkan Christians. Abuses culminated in organized **pogroms** of 1895–96, during which nearly 150,000 Armenians died. In 1897, war with Greece and a revolt on Crete coincided; although the Prussian-trained army defeated the Greeks, the Ottomans were forced to grant Crete autonomy.

THE YOUNG TURK REVOLUTION

In 1889 the Ottoman Society for Union and Progress – later the **Committee for Union and Progress** (CUP) – arose among army doctors and the huge exile community in Europe. It took strong root in **Macedonia**, the most polyglot Ottoman province, completely infiltrating the Third Army at Salonica. Threats of intervention by European powers in Macedonia – where disorderly Greek and Bulgarian guerrilla bands rampaged – coincided with arrears in army pay, sparking the revolt of the so-called "**Young Turks**". Macedonian army units demanded by telegraph that Abdülhamit restore the 1876 constitution, or face unpleasant consequences; on **July 24, 1908**, the sultan assented. There was rejoicing in major imperial cities as mullahs fraternized with bishops, and Bulgarians walked arm in arm with Greeks.

Euphoria subsided as the **revolutionary government** fumbled for coherent policy. The coup had had as immediate goals the curbing of Abdülhamit's despotism and the physical preservation of the empire – but even these limited aims proved beyond it. By October, Bulgaria declared full independence and absorbed eastern Rumelia, while Austria formally annexed Bosnia-Herzegovina. **Elections** for the reconvened parliament were reasonably fair, and the CUP, organized as a party, gained a majority. Opposition to its Westernization and autocracy simmered, however, and in spring 1909 a **counter-revolt** of low-ranking soldiers, anti-CUP politicians and religious elements seized Istanbul. Abdülhamit, overestimating the rebels' strength, unwisely supported them. The "Young Turks" fought back from Salonica, sending Third Army general Mahmut Şevket to crush the insurrection, and then **banished the sultan** to house arrest in Salonica. His younger brother ascended the throne as Mehmet V, promising to respect the "will of the nation".

1878	1889	1895–96
Sultan Abdülhamit embarks upon a period of repressive, despotic rule	The formation of the Committee of Union and Progress (CUP) marks the start of Turkish nationalism	Massive pogroms against the Ottoman Empire's Armenian minority

Despite opposing political reform, Abdülhamit promoted technological Westernization – most famously German-built railways across Anatolia. Investment credits were extended, and a Public Debt Administration gathered revenues of state monopolies to service the enormous debt run up since the 1850s. Secular schooling and technical training were encouraged, as long as they remained apolitical – but the creation of an educated elite inevitably resulted in change.

Nationalism and the Balkan wars

Although the Young Turks managed to save the CUP revolution in 1909, there was still no agreed programme as three notions contended for supremacy. **Ottomanism** asserted that a Eurasian federal empire, in which all ethnic and religious minorities had equal rights – in return for loyalty to the sultan – was both viable and desirable. **Pan-Islamism**, Abdülhamit's pet creed, stressed the Islamic nature of the Ottoman Empire and the ties between Muslim Albanians, Caucasians, Kurds, Arabs and Turks. **Pan-Turanism**, mainly promoted by Caucasian Muslims exiled by the Russians, was more blatantly racial, dwelling on the affinities of all Turkic peoples between central Asia and the Balkans; over time it morphed into a more realistic **Turkism**, protecting the interests of Anatolia's Turkish-speaking Muslims. Although that eventually carried the day, uninhibited discussion of these alternatives – and cultural life in general – briefly flourished. Between 1908 and 1912 the CUP was hardly monolithic, and parliamentary opposition was not completely quashed until 1912.

The CUP's growing authoritarianism coincided with renewed external threats. Italy invaded Tripolitania (Libya) in 1911, and the next year took all of the Dodecanese islands. In late 1912, Bulgaria, Serbia, Montenegro and Greece united, driving Turkey out of Europe in the **First Balkan War**, even approaching Istanbul by early 1913. Enraged at attempts to limit the army's and the CUP's involvement in government, and incensed at the poor terms of a pending peace treaty, key CUP officers staged a coup, murdering the minister of war. New grand vizier Mahmut Şevket's assassination soon after allowed the CUP to suppress all dissent and establish a **military junta**.

The unlikely Balkan alliance fell apart, with Bulgaria turning on Serbia and Greece in the **Second Balkan War**, and the Ottomans regaining eastern Thrace up to Edirne. This made temporary heroes of the triumvirate junta: **Enver Paşa**, dashing, courageous, abstemious, as well as vain, ambitious and megalomaniac; **Talat Paşa**, a brutal Thracian civilian who later ordered the 1915 deportation of the Armenians (see p.681); and **Cemal Paşa**, a ruthless but competent professional soldier from an old family. They avenged the ethnic cleansing of Balkan Muslims by deporting or killing nearly half a million Greek Orthodox from Aegean Turkey in early 1914.

World War I

CUP ideology was now overtly Turkish-nationalist and secular, as well as anti-democratic – and increasingly pro-German. Public opinion, and sager CUP members, hoped that the Ottoman Empire would remain neutral in the pending conflict, but Germanophile Enver signed a secret agreement with the Kaiser on August 2, 1914. Britain committed a major blunder the same day, impounding two battleships paid for by public subscription in

1908	1912	1914
The Young Turk revolution leads to the restoration of the 1876 constitution	Balkan War is a setback for the Ottomans, who lose out to Bulgaria, Montenegro and Serbia	The CUP triumvirate that now effectively rules the Ottoman Empire decides to ally with Germany in World War I

Turkey. In response, the Germans sailed two replacement ships through an Allied blockade to Istanbul in October, presenting them to the Turkish navy – whose German commander promptly sent them to bombard Russian Black Sea ports. By November the Ottomans were at war with the Allies, though some CUP ministers resigned in protest.

The **Turkish war effort**, fought on five fronts simultaneously, was an almost unmitigated disaster. Within four years, the empire lost all its Middle Eastern domains, as Arabs backed the British on the promise of subsequent autonomy, thus proving pan-Islamism as dead as Ottomanism. Enver Paşa lost an entire army on the Russian front during winter 1914–15; the subsequent tsarist advance deep into Anatolia was only reversed after 1917. The sole Ottoman successes were bloodily defeating the British at Mesopotamian Kut, and the successful defence of **Gallipoli**, guarding the Dardanelles and the sea approaches to Istanbul. Credit for the seven-month Turkish resistance there belonged largely to a hitherto unknown Colonel **Mustafa Kemal**, later **Atatürk**. He had come of age just before the Young Turk agitation and, while an early CUP member, had opposed its autocratic tendencies and entry into the war with Germany. The Turkish public craved a hero, but jealous Enver denied them this satisfaction by shuttling Kemal between various backwoods commands, until war's end saw him overseeing a strategic retreat near Syria.

On October 30, 1918, Ottoman and British officers signed an **armistice** at Greek Límnos. Two weeks later an Allied fleet sailed into Istanbul, and occupied strategic points around the Sea of Marmara, though Turkish civil administration was allowed to continue, providing that no "disturbances" took place. Meanwhile, the CUP triumvirate had fled on German ships, and all soon met violent deaths: Talat killed in revenge by an Armenian in Berlin; Cemal assassinated in Caucasian Georgia; and Enver dying flamboyantly as a self-styled emir fighting the Bolsheviks in central Asia.

The struggle for independence

The Allies could now carry out long-deferred designs on the Ottoman heartland. By early 1919 French troops occupied southeast Anatolia, the Italians landed on the coast between Bodrum and Antalya, and the Greeks disembarked at İzmir, where Greek Orthodox formed much of the population. The British concentrated their strength in Istanbul and Thrace, and along with the other victors garrisoned in the capital dictated policy to the defeated. New sultan **Mehmet VI** was interested mainly in retaining his throne, and ready to make any necessary territorial or administrative concessions – including dissolving the Ottoman parliament.

In Thrace and Anatolia, however, various Committees for the Defence of Rights (CDRs) – patriotic guerrilla bands often led by ex-CUP personnel – had arisen, and a substantial Ottoman army survived at Erzurum, under Kâzım Karabekir. Together these would form the nucleus of resistance. Only visionary leadership, and further Allied provocations, were lacking; neither was long in coming.

Mustafa Kemal was the only undefeated Ottoman commander at war's end, and was not compromised by association with the CUP leadership. Popular and outspoken, Kemal itched to cross over to Anatolia and begin organizing **resistance**, but not without a suitable pretext. In spring 1919, he wrangled a post as a military inspector empowered to wind up the CDRs. His first destination was the Black Sea, where **Turkish guerrillas** were battling local Greeks intent on setting up a Pontic republic. On May 19, 1919, he landed at

1918	1919	1919
The Allies occupy Istanbul after the Ottoman defeat in World War I	French troops occupy southeast Anatolia, Italians the western Mediterranean region, and Greek troops land at İzmir	Atatürk lands at Samsun on the Black Sea, marking the "official" start of Turkey's War of Independence

Samsun, four days after the Greek landing at İzmir – the last straw for many hitherto apathetic Turks. Contrary to his brief, Kemal promptly began organizing and strengthening the Turkish guerrillas. The Istanbul government, realizing what he was up to, dismissed him, then ordered his arrest; he responded by resigning his commission. Kemal and Karabekir, plus other high-ranking Ottoman officers, planned resistance with support from Anatolian religious authorities. Two ideological congresses (at Erzurum in July, in Sivas in September) elected Kemal chairman, and ratified the so-called **National Pact**, which demanded Turkish borders approximating those of today, an end to the Capitulations and a guarantee of rights to all minorities. The pact also reaffirmed its loyalty to the institution of the caliphate, if not the sultan himself, deemed an Allied puppet.

The **Nationalists**, as they were soon called, began to joust with the Istanbul regime. By late 1919, they forced the resignation of the grand vizier and elections for a new parliament dominated by Nationalists, which proclaimed the National Pact. Thefts from Allied arms depots, with the connivance of the French and Italians who opposed Greek aims, became common. At the instigation of the outraged Ottoman court, the British placed Istanbul under formal occupation on March 16, 1920, raiding parliament and bundling many deputies into exile on Malta. Luckier MPs escaped to Ankara, where on April 23 the Nationalists opened the first Grand National Assembly. The sultanate secured a **fetva** from Islamic authorities sanctioning holy war against the "rebels" and condemning Nationalist leaders to death in absentia. Kemal and friends secured a counter-*fetva* from sympathetic religious figures in Ankara, and shortly after the Bektaşi dervish *şeyh* ordered his followers to help the Nationalists.

Such moral support was vital to the beleaguered guerrillas, now fighting a war on multiple fronts: against the French in the southeast, the Italians in the southwest, Armenians in the northeast, irregulars supporting the sultan in various locations, and – most dangerously – the Greeks in western Anatolia. The only consistent aid came from the young Soviet Union, which sent gold and weapons, then partitioned the short-lived Armenian republic between itself and Turkey, thus closing that theatre of war by late 1920.

The Allied governments, oblivious to all this, presented the humiliating **Treaty of Sèvres** to the Ottoman government in May 1920. By its terms, an independent Armenia and an autonomous Kurdistan were created; the Dardanelles and Bosphorus straits were internationalized; Thrace plus İzmir and its hinterland were given to Greece; France and Italy were assigned spheres of influence in Anatolia; and Turkish finances were placed under Allied supervision, with a revival of the Capitulations. By signing this document, the demoralized sultanate sacrificed its last shred of credibility, convinced waverers to back the Nationalist movement – and sparked a predictable Greek response.

The Greco-Turkish War

Greek forces, authorized by British prime minister Lloyd George, pressed inland from İzmir to capture Edirne, İzmit and Bursa, seeking to realize a "Greater Greece" on both shores of the Aegean. Only French and Italian objections halted them short of the strategic Afyon–Eskişehir railway. In early 1921, the Greeks were on the move again, but Nationalist general İsmet Paşa stopped them twice at the **İnönü** gorge, from which he later took his surname. Since the replacement of the republican Venizelos government in Greece by royalists, the Greek armies had become more corrupt, incompetently led and brutal in their treatment of Muslim civilians. Kemal's forces,

1920	1920	1921
The British formally occupy Istanbul in March	May sees the signing of the controversial Treaty of Sèvres, which, had it been implemented, would have stripped Turkey of virtually all its territory	An invading Greek army is turned back by Atatürk's right-hand man, İsmet İnönü

on the other hand, had become more cohesive and professional, with irregular bands suppressed or absorbed.

But when the Greeks advanced east once more in July 1921, they swiftly captured Afyon, Eskişehir and its vital linking railway; the Nationalists strategically retreated east of the Sakarya River, less than 100km from Ankara, to buy time and extend enemy lines. Panic and gloom reigned in Ankara, with Kemal appointed to command the defending army, and share its fate. The Greeks went for the bait, sensing an easy chance to finish off the Nationalists. But in the ferocious, three-week **Sakarya** battle that started on August 13, they failed to make further headway. Although most of the Greek army survived, anything but the capture of Ankara was a defeat. The jubilant GNA conferred on Kemal the title *Gazi*, or "Warrior for the Faith".

Sakarya greatly enhanced the Nationalists' position: both the French and Italians soon concluded peace treaties, and contributions from Muslims abroad poured in to finance the "holy war". With support for the Greek adventure evaporating, the British tried unsuccessfully to arrange an armistice. Both sides dug in until, on August 26, 1922, Kemal launched a **final offensive** to drive the Greeks out of Anatolia, at Dumlupınar near Afyon. The Greek lines crumbled, and those not taken prisoner or killed fled in a disorderly rout towards waiting boats in İzmir, committing atrocities against the Turkish population, destroying the harvest and abandoning Greek civilians to the inevitable Turkish reprisals. The latter included the **sacking and burning of İzmir** within four days of the triumphant entry of the Nationalists.

Despite this resounding triumph, ongoing conflict beckoned. A large Greek army remained in Thrace, disposed to fight on, and British contingents guarding the **Dardanelles** faced off against the Nationalist army sent to cross the straits. Some Nationalists even advocated re-taking western Thrace and Greek Macedonia, a sure path to renewed world war. Cooler heads prevailed, however, and at Mudanya on October 11, 1922, an armistice was signed, obliging the last Greek troops to quit eastern Thrace. A week later British premier Lloyd George, utterly discredited, resigned.

The fall of the sultanate and the population exchanges

There remained just one obstacle to full Nationalist control: Sultan Mehmet VI still presided over Istanbul. Few in Ankara had much time for the man himself, but many expressed reluctance to abolish his office, favouring a constitutional monarchy. The Allies helped decide the matter by extending a clumsy double invitation to a final peace conference – one to the sultanate, the other to the Grand National Assembly. The outrage this provoked in the GNA made it easy for Kemal to persuade them to **abolish the sultanate**, which took place on November 1. Within two weeks, Mehmet VI, last of the House of Osman, sneaked ignominiously out of the old imperial capital on a British warship, bound for Italian exile; his cousin Abdülmecit became caliph, but with no temporal powers.

At the 1923 Lausanne peace conference, İsmet Paşa was the sole Turkish representative. The Allies, hoping to dictate terms as at Sèvres, were quickly disappointed; the dogged İsmet reduced seasoned diplomats to despair by feigning deafness and repetitive insistence on the tenets of the National Pact. The **Treaty of Lausanne**, signed on July 24, recognized the National Pact frontiers; abolished the Capitulations; demilitarized the Dardanelles; and postponed a decision on the status of oil-rich Mosul (now in Iraq).

1922	1922	1923
The Turks win a decisive victory over Greek troops at the battle of Dumlupınar in August	An armistice is signed at Mudanya, on the Sea of Marmara south of Istanbul	The Treaty of Lausanne recognizes the boundaries won by the Turkish Nationalists in the War of Independence

More drastically, Greece and Turkey agreed to **exchange minority populations** to eliminate future communal conflict (see p.684). Lausanne marked the true end of World War I, and saw Turkey, alone of the defeated, emerge in dignity, with modest demands made of her. Compared to the old empire, this was a compact state – 97 percent Anatolian and Muslim. A new political party, the **Republican People's Party**, was formed, as was a new GNA, its members drawn from RPP ranks.

The young Republic

In October 1923 the GNA officially moved the capital to **Ankara** and proclaimed the **Republic of Turkey**; Kemal was designated head of state and İsmet prime minister. Although the sultan was gone, Caliph Abdülmecit was still around and a conspicuous public personality. That was an intolerable situation for Kemal and other westernizers; with the war over, they no longer needed the legitimizing function of Islam. In March 1924 the caliphate was abolished and all royal Osmanlıs exiled, the *medreses* and religious courts closed, dervish orders dissolved, and **vakıf** assets assigned to a new Ministry of Religious Affairs.

Many Turks, including some of his followers, were dismayed by Kemal's increasing autocracy, and some – including Kâzım Karabekir – resigned from the RPP in October to form the opposition **Progressive Republican Party** (PRP). At first Kemal tolerated it as a safety valve, but he became alarmed when PRP speakers attracted large crowds and the less supervised Istanbul press sided with them. In February 1925 the first of several twentieth-century **Kurdish revolts** – both fundamentalist Muslim and separatist-nationalist in nature – erupted; it took Ankara two months to suppress it. Kemal, demanding unity in crisis, secured the PRP's closure and established draconian Independence Tribunals; the revolt's leaders plus a few PRP members found themselves on the wrong end of a rope. By that autumn all **dervish orders** had been prohibited (though they were never completely suppressed), and pilgrimage to Sufi saints' tombs was forbidden.

Kemal's reforms re-inflamed opposition, and in mid-1926 a plot to assassinate him was uncovered. Most of the former PRR leadership, including Karabekir, were charged and tried, plus the entire surviving CUP leadership, who were hanged; even those acquitted were barred henceforth from public life. This was the last purge, however, and the feared Independence Tribunals were disbanded, having served their purpose.

Belatedly, Atatürk addressed the economy. Already weakened by ten years of constant warfare and the loss of Greek and Armenian industrial know-how, its problems were exacerbated by the 1929 crash. "**Kemalism**" stressed state-funded heavy industry with a goal of complete import substitution (except for factory equipment). Development banks had been set up in 1925, and the rail network extended, with mining, steel, cement and paper mills heavily subsidized in imitation of Italian fascism. This programme was, however, grossly inefficient, and relegated agriculture to penury until the 1950s. The east was condemned to a subsistence existence – aggravating Kurdish feelings of punitive neglect – a situation that remained unchanged until massive irrigation and hydroelectric projects during the 1970s and 1980s.

Foreign policy espoused non-interventionism and isolationism, though Turkey joined the League of Nations in 1934. Atatürk's slogan "Peace at home, peace in the world" might now seem unfortunately similar to Neville Chamberlain's utterances after

1923	1924	1925
In October, Ankara becomes the capital of the new Turkish Republic	The caliphate is abolished and all Ottoman royalty are sent into exile	The first of the Kurdish revolts that still bedevil Turkey begins

KEMAL ATATÜRK'S REFORMS

Anxious to turn his revolutionary, westernizing principles into reality, Mustafa Kemal introduced a series of far-reaching and controversial **reforms**. Traditional **headgear**, such as women's veils, the turban and the fez, were seen as reactionary; new sartorial laws outlawed them, and required the use of hated European hats. Ottoman dress had been a vital indicator of social rank, and the new regulations met with stiff resistance.

In 1926, the **Gregorian calendar** supplanted the Muslim lunar one for official use, and the **şeriat** (Islamic **law code**) was replaced by adaptations of European versions. The Jewish, Armenian and Greek minorities relinquished their communal laws; henceforth all citizens were judged by a uniform legal system. Along with a secular law code came relative **emancipation of women**: marriage and divorce became civil rather than religious or customary, polygamy was abolished, and by 1930 women were voting in local elections.

Kemal's next agenda item was **alphabet reform**. A special commission prepared a Roman script within six weeks in 1928, and by 1929 its universal use was law. The entire language was targeted over the next few years, with a language commission purging Turkish of Arabic and Persian accretions and reviving old Turkish words, coining new ones or adopting French words. Scholars now reckon the process was carried too far, as the language soon became as top-heavy with borrowed Western terms as it had been with oriental ones, but with the script change the measures substantially increased literacy and comprehension. (A deliberate side effect of language reform was to isolate Turks from their imperial past by becoming unable to read Ottoman Turkish.)

Less successful, and ultimately embarrassing, were historical "revision" programmes, variously asserting that all other languages derived from Turkish; that the Turks were Aryan (and other racial nonsense mimicking Nazi theories), or that they descended from Hittites or Sumerians. Such hypotheses, springing from feelings of inferiority and a need for political legitimacy, remained in Turkish schoolbooks until the 1970s. A more constructive 1934 move was full **suffrage for women** in national elections and the mandatory adoption of **surnames**; previously this had been discretionary. Kemal chose for himself **Atatürk**, "Father-Turk", dropping his first name, Mustafa.

Munich, but secured for Turkey years of badly needed calm. Though the RPP imitated aspects of contemporary totalitarian systems, Turkey had no wish to follow Germany, Italy and the USSR over a cliff. Atatürk removed the last irritant to Anglo-Turkish relations by renouncing claims to Mosul, but started a campaign in 1936 to annex the Hatay, part of French Syria with a large Turkish population.

Fortunately for Turkey, Atatürk had accomplished most of his intended life's work by 1938, since his health, after decades of heavy drinking, was steadily worsening. He died from liver cirrhosis in Istanbul's Dolmabahçe palace at 9.05am on November 10, 1938. Thousands of mourners bearing torches lined the route of his funeral cortege-train between Istanbul and Ankara. Fifteen years later he was interred in a mausoleum, the Anıt Kabir – designed by an Italian and a German, in monumental 1930s fascist style.

Atatürk's legacy is considerable: unlike his totalitarian peers, he refrained from expansionism and overt racial/ethnic hatred, leaving behind a compact state and a guiding ideology, however uneven, which was expressly intended to outlive him. Personally he was a complex, even tragic, figure: his charisma, energy and quick grasp of situations and people were unparalleled, but he had little inclination for methodical

1929	1934	1938
Turkey's change from the Arabic to the Roman alphabet is made law	Turkey joins the League of Nations	Atatürk dies of liver failure in Dolmabahçe Palace in Istanbul

planning or systematic study. While revered, he was not particularly lovable – despite sponsoring women's rights, he was a compulsive womanizer, with one brief, unhappy marriage. He nursed grudges that bore deadly consequences for those who might otherwise have lived to extricate Turkey from later dilemmas. Like a huge tree that allows nothing to grow underneath, Atatürk deprived Turkey of its next generation of leadership. His personality cult, obvious from the silhouettes and quotations on every hillside, is symptomatic of an inability to conceive of alternative ideologies or heroes, though since 1983 Kemalist economics has vanished completely.

World War II and after

Atatürk was succeeded as president by **İsmet İnönü**, and his Hatay policy was posthumously vindicated in 1939 with the region's annexation. France, eager for Turkish support in the imminent war with Germany, acquiesced in return for Turkey signing a vaguely worded treaty of alliance with France and Britain in 1939. But France was swiftly defeated, while German propaganda convinced Turkey that Britain was probably doomed too, and that the Axis would also dispatch Russia, the hereditary Turkish enemy. Accordingly a "Treaty of Friendship" was signed with Nazi Germany in 1941, guaranteeing at least Turkish non-belligerence. Entry into the war on either side was always doubtful, since Turkey's armed forces had become desperately antiquated; memories of World War I defeat were strong as well. Turkey remained **neutral**, but despite this fence-sitting, the country was essentially on a war footing, with mobilization, and the economy stressed by black markets and huge budget deficits.

All these, and the infiltration of Nazi ideology, provoked the 1942 imposition of the **Varlık Vergisi** ("Wealth Levy"), a crippling, discriminatory tax applied against businessmen of Armenian, Greek, Jewish and Dönme (a Judaic sect) descent. Non-payers had their property confiscated and/or were deported to labour camps in the interior, where many died. The measure, having raised very little money, was rescinded in 1944, but not before urban commerce had been set back a decade, and the Republic's reputation with non-Muslim minorities severely dented.

Even after the collapse of Italy, Turkey still declined to enter the war, despite assurances of Allied support. Turkey only declared war on Germany early in 1945 to qualify for UN membership – not soon enough to prevent the USSR from demanding the return of Kars and Ardahan, and joint control of the Sea of Marmara straits. While demurring, Turkey badly needed a protective ally, and found one in the **United States**. The 1946 arrival in Istanbul of the American warship USS *Missouri* was greeted with such euphoria that the city fathers opened the local bordellos for free to the sailors.

The first results of this mutual wooing were Turkey's participation in the Korean War and admission to **NATO**. This new pro-Western stance had other consequences, including the expulsion of numerous ethnic Turks from Warsaw-Pact Bulgaria (harbinger of an identical act four decades later), and consistently bad relations with neighbouring Arab states, particularly after Turkey recognized Israel.

At home, discontent with one-party rule, secularization and the stagnant, centralized economy coalesced when four MPs expelled from the RPP formed the **Democrat Party** (**DP**) in early 1946. Despite snap elections that summer and widespread balloting irregularities, the new opposition won fifteen percent of parliamentary seats.

1938	1942	1945
The former French-mandated province of Hatay becomes part of Turkey	Turkey introduces the "Wealth Tax", unfairly targeting its minorities	Neutral for most of World War II, Turkey finally declares war on Germany

Amazingly, this result was not reversed by force or chicanery, but a definitive showdown could not be long postponed, and campaigning for May 14, 1950 polls was unimpeded. The DP promised an end to anti-business strictures, freer religious observance, and attention to neglected farmers. Although the Democrats were sure to win, the scale of their victory – 55 percent of votes, and over eighty percent of parliamentary seats – proved a surprise. **Celal Bayar** replaced İnönü as president, while **Adnan Menderes** became prime minister.

Populist government

Among the first acts of the new government was to permit, after a seventeen-year gap, calls to prayer in Arabic; simultaneously, outbreaks of fez- or turban-wearing, polygamy and the use of Arabic script erupted in the provinces (where Atatürk's reforms had barely penetrated). With sweeping **economic reforms** Menderes effectively opened up a country where for three decades little in the way of people, ideas, capital or goods had moved in or out. However, much of this relied on unsound investment in state enterprises or patronage to supporters. Farmer-lawyer Menderes had his colossal vanity aggravated by adoring peasants who sacrificed livestock in his honour and named boy-children after him.

Bumper harvests helped keep the electorate sweet through the mid-1950s, though by 1954 enormous **national debt** and trade deficits helped put the black-market value of the Turkish lira at one-fourth the official exchange rate. But the increasingly sensitive DP would not tolerate criticism: in 1953 both the RPP and the right-wing/religious National Party, with their handful of seats, were dissolved, while repressive press laws took effect just before May 1954 elections. These the Democrats won even more easily, but instead of giving them confidence, they took this as a mandate to continue crushing dissent and to run the country even more shamelessly for their clientele's benefit. The economy kept deteriorating with rampant **inflation**, thereafter a constant of Turkish life. During 1955 the government gave tacit support to pogroms aimed at minority groups, and in particular the Greeks (see p.683).

In the wake of all this, the government lost support and, although they won the 1957 elections, these were heavily rigged, with the tally never being announced. Turkey thus approached 1960 in a parlous state, with a huge gulf between the pro-DP peasantry and the urban elite – and, more dangerously, an alienated, antagonized military.

First military coup and the 1960s

Nowhere had dismay over DP policies been keener than in the military, who considered themselves the guardians of Atatürk's heritage. On May 27, 1960, middle-ranking officers, barred from voting and fed up with the inflation that was eroding the value of their fixed salaries, staged a **coup**, announced on the radio by Colonel Alparslan Türkeş.

The putsch was bloodless, swift and complete; DP MPs and ministers were jailed as the larger cities celebrated. For the next sixteen months, a **National Unity Committee** (NUC) under Cemal Gürsel governed Turkey, while preparing a new constitution to supersede the 1924 one. The NUC, however, was a marriage of convenience between idealistic top brass, who expected the resumption of civilian rule, and junior officers

1950	**1955**	**1960**
Turkey's first truly free elections see the Atatürk-founded Republican Peoples Party replaced by the Democrat Party	Anti-Greek minority riots in Istanbul leave thousands of shops and businesses in ruins	The elected government is toppled in the country's first military coup

who desired an indefinite period of authoritarian military government. The new constitution was submitted to public referendum in July, with elections set for October.

The **referendum**, essentially a vote of confidence on the NUC, clocked just 62 percent in favour – evidence of lingering support for the Democrat Party. Leading DP members, including Menderes and Bayar, were found guilty of undermining the 1924 constitution, corruption and planning the 1955 riots. Upon the return of guilty verdicts and fifteen death sentences, the NUC hastily carried out three – against Menderes, foreign minister Zorlu and finance minister Polatkan. The three hangings just before the elections backfired badly, making Menderes a martyr and ensuring a long life for the **Justice Party** (JP), the Democrat Party reincarnated.

The elections again disappointed the NUC; neither the Justice Party nor a revitalized RPP gained a majority. The two front-runners formed a coalition, with Gürsel as president and İnönü prime minister for the first time since 1938. All this annoyed disaffected junior officers who mounted two subsequent coup attempts, one in February 1962 and another fourteen months later.

Unstable coalitions continued as NUC reforms faltered; import-substitution policies were revived, while land reform and rural development were deferred. The first wave of **emigration to Europe** acted as a social safety valve, and "guest workers" returned on holidays with consumer goods and some European notions. Independent labour unions organized, with the right to strike conferred in 1963. The urban proletariat flocked to the Turkish Workers' Party (TWP), whose very existence nudged the RPP, now led by Bülent Ecevit, leftward. **Süleyman Demirel**, among the main political figures of the next three decades, became JP leader in 1964, pushing free enterprise and foreign investment. In 1965 elections, Demirel's JP got a solid majority.

Cyprus, independent since 1960 with extensive constitutional concessions to its Turkish Cypriot minority, again intruded as the rickety set-up there collapsed in December 1963. This cued civil strife on the island throughout 1964, abetted by smuggled-in Greek and Turkish troops; a full-scale Greco-Turkish war was only avoided by US pressure. The Turkish government confined itself to retaliations against the Greeks of Turkey's Aegean islands and Istanbul (including the expulsion of 12,000 resident Greek nationals).

The spirit of 1968 was manifest in increased **anti-Americanism** and leftist sentiments, particularly at universities. Many Turks felt betrayed by the lack of US support on Cyprus, having studiously followed its foreign-policy lead since 1946. Even the government found obvious American tutelage offensive, and soon most US military installations passed to Turkish or NATO control. Demirel was returned to office in 1969 amid increased political violence. Extreme left-wing groups like Dev Sol (Revolutionary Youth) clashed with right-wing and/or Islamist activists like the Grey Wolves, their paramilitary training camps set up by Alparslan Türkeş, founder of the fascist **Nationalist Action Party** (MHP).

"Memorandum coup" and the 1970s

Faced with domestic unrest and sterile parliamentary manoeuvres, the generals acted again. Their March 12, 1971 proclamation forced Demirel out in favour of an "above-party" technocratic government. This "**memorandum coup**" kept parliament

1963	1964	1969
Turkish workers win the right to strike	Sectarian strife between Greeks and Turks on Cyprus almost leads to war between Greece and Turkey	Right- and left-wing extremists clash with depressing frequency across the nation

in session, but martial law was imposed, thousands were arrested and tried for inciting violence or class conflict, and much of the 1961 constitution was curtailed. The new government, stymied by JP MPs, resigned. The army, mindful of the hash the colonels' junta had made of neighbouring Greece since 1967, decided to let politicians take the blame for any adverse outcome here in Turkey. October 1973 elections produced a coalition of Ecevit's RPP with Necmettin Erbakan's Islamist National Salvation Party.

In July 1974, the Greek junta ousted Cypriot president Makarios, replacing him with extremists supporting union with Greece. Ecevit felt compelled to order an **invasion of Cyprus** on July 20 that ended, in August, with the Turkish army occupying the northern third of the island, which has since become the self-proclaimed Turkish Republic of Northern Cyprus. Ecevit resigned in September to seek early elections, but Demirel clung to power until 1977.

All this further polarized Turkey, which by 1980 saw escalating political violence ratchet annual death tolls up to three thousand. While extremists initially confined activities to each other, deteriorated parliamentary decorum and politicized workplaces meant that incidents became widespread. Istanbul neighbourhoods were controlled by factions – having the wrong newspaper or the wrong attire and moustache ensured trouble.

Ecevit regained power in late 1977, but proved unequal to a dire situation. In December 1978, Türkeş's MHP orchestrated bloody street battles in Maraş between fundamentalist Sunnis and left-wing Alevis; in Fatsa, an Alevi commune was smashed by army tanks. Demirel took office again in 1979, but he too failed to halt the maelstrom despite declaring martial law.

The 1980 coup and after

Turkey's importance had been underlined by the Iranian revolution and Soviet invasion of Afghanistan, and the US, keen to secure a stable Middle Eastern base, gave tacit consent to martial law and a coup. This occurred bloodlessly on September 12, 1980, to the initial relief of most Turks. The frenzied killing ceased; all political parties were disbanded, their leaders detained; all trade unions and NGOs were closed down.

It was soon obvious that this coup would not resemble the previous two. A junta of generals, not junior officers – the **National Security Council** (NSC) – controlled matters, and return to civilian rule would be long delayed. Bannings, indictments and purges proceeded apace, and while the radical right was not immune, the left bore the brunt of prosecutions. Nationalist right-wing beliefs, if not violent or fascist, were compatible with the NSC agenda – as were mildly Islamic views, as long as fundamentalists stayed out of the military.

The NSC's principal targets, relatively untouched in prior putsches, were labour unions, internationalist or separatist groups and the left-leaning intelligentsia, all crippled by show trials that dragged on so long that many defendants walked free based on time served on remand. NSP leader Necmettin Erbakan was acquitted on charges of attempting to create an Islamic state. The MHP was decimated by eight capital verdicts and dozens of prison terms – though leader Türkeş was acquitted. The military purged university staff, and all campuses were supervised by a Higher Education Council (YÖK).

A committee of carefully vetted applicants drew up a new, highly restrictive constitution in 1982, countermanding most of its 1960 predecessor. This was ratified

1971	1974	1978
The so-called "memorandum coup" brings martial law to the country	Turkey invades Cyprus, to protect the Turkish minority on the island	Civil unrest across Turkey continues, with right-wing extremists and left-wing Alevis clashing in Maraş

by ninety percent of the electorate in a coercive referendum, also an election for the presidency. No campaigning against was allowed; the only candidate was NSC chief **General Kenan Evren**, and it was an all-or-nothing package.

Return to civilian rule: ANAP

Pre-coup parties and personalities remained banned at heavily supervised November 1983 elections, but the generals' centrist slate came last, as Turgut Özal's centre-right Motherland Party (ANAP) won just under half the votes and just over half of parliamentary seats.

ANAP was a party of uneasy alliance incorporating a wide range of opinion from economic liberals to Islamists. Half-Kurdish Özal embodied these contradictions in his person: a devout Muslim, ex-member of the NSP and adherent of the still-clandestine Nakşibendi order, he had strong appetites for booze, tobacco, food and *Arabesk* tunes, while his charismatic speaking manner belied a Texan engineering degree. He juggled ANAP's technocratic and traditionalist factions while introducing sweeping economic reforms, with record export levels and six percent growth rates. Inflation and foreign debt, however, soared, as budgets were swollen.

While ANAP (and Özal) can be credited with ushering Turkey into the world economy, an ostentatious display of wealth created an ethical climate conducive to corruption. A provincial elite, sharing Özal's small-town, lower-middle-class background, earned an initial reputation of "getting things done". While trained abroad, they hadn't necessarily absorbed Western values, and when they had, their model was Texas, not Europe. English became their lingua franca, and that of many universities, which under YÖK's watchful eye became apolitical polytechnics.

Pre-coup politicians were un-banned by referendum in 1987; November parliamentary elections gave just 36 percent to ANAP but, thanks to a skewed system, nearly two-thirds of the seats. Özal's two prime-ministerial terms saw a dramatic, deliberate increase in Islamic activity, to offset Iranian-style fundamentalism and leftist ideology. The Department of Religious Affairs expanded, mandatory teaching of Islam in schools increased and *vakıfs* swelled with Saudi donations. **Kurdish separatism** resurfaced violently in the southeast, courtesy of the Kurdish Workers' Party (PKK), strengthened by overzealous reaction of the authorities (see p.678).

Ties with Greece were strained by Cyprus, disputes over Aegean airspace and territorial waters and the Greek government's harassment of ethnic Turks in Greek Thrace. Bulgarian-Turkish relations made headlines during summer 1989, as the Communist Bulgarian regime's policy of forced Slavification ultimately escalated into the largest European **mass emigration** since World War II. Over 300,000 ethnic Turks fled Bulgaria for Turkey, which initially welcomed them and tried to capitalize politically on the exodus. The numbers soon hit home, however, the border was shut by August, and in 1990 Sofia's new post-Communist government renounced the heavy-handed assimilationist campaign, while many new arrivals returned to Bulgaria or emigrated to western Europe.

In contrast to Turkey's concern for Turkish minorities abroad, **human rights violations** continued at home with inhumane prison conditions, torture of suspects and increased prosecutions of journalists and publishers testing the limits of censorship. Özal in particular reacted to even mild criticism with dozens of libel suits.

1980	**1982**	**1983**
Fed up with years of unrest, the Turkish public watch with relief as the military take power again	A new constitution is overwhelmingly approved by an undemocratic vote that also sees General Kenan Evran become president	The charismatic Turgut Özal and his moderate Motherland Party wins the first elections since the coup

Özal as president

ANAP's influence was waning due to hyperinflation and blatant nepotism benefitting Özal's cronies and extended family – including his flamboyant, cigar-smoking wife Semra. Only the second civilian president, and officially "above-party", Özal still acted as the ANAP chief. He chose the next prime minister, Yıldırım Akbulut, a lacklustre yes-man, then repeatedly undermined him.

Iraq's 1990 **invasion of Kuwait** reinforced Özal's position, and reiterated Turkey's strategic importance. Özal invited the US to use İncirlik and Diyarbakır airbases, incurred considerable financial loss by closing the pipeline shipping Iraqi oil through Turkey, and permitted coalition troops near the Iraqi Kurdish "safe haven". In return he won Bush the Elder's promise that an independent Kurdistan would not emerge from a dismembered Iraq.

1991 polls, the fairest ever, surprisingly had the right-of-centre True Path Party (**DYP**) finishing first, ANAP a strong second, İnönü's Social Democratic Peoples Party (SHP) third, and Erbakan's Islamist Welfare Party (Refah Partisi) a close fourth. A DYP–SHP coalition, with Demirel prime minister and İnönü deputy prime minister, began with both parties pledging to pull together in rescuing the economy.

There were also promises to make Turkey a *konuşan* (talking) society, where opinions were freely aired without fear of retribution. This ideal ran aground immediately when some of the 22 Kurdish HEP MPs – compelled to run on the SHP national ticket – refused to recite the standard loyalty oath upon being sworn in. An un-banning of pre-1980 parties revived the Republican People's Party (CHP).

As president, Özal delayed the signing of many bills, prompting discussion of having him impeached. He died suddenly of a heart attack on April 17, 1993, and conspiracy theories still rage as to whether he was bumped off by the "deep state".

Özal, despite his many faults, was the most eloquent and influential head of state since Atatürk. Respected by many for his energy, courage and vision, despised by an equal number for his overbearing manner and shameless self-aggrandizement, he remains an ambiguous figure.

After Özal, chaos

Demirel eventually emerged as president, while US-educated technocrat **Tansu Çiller** became prime minister in June 1993. With her assertive style and telegenic manner, her rise to power was initially viewed positively, though she soon proved woefully inadequate. Hopes of a fresh take on Kurdish issues vanished as Çiller deferred to military hardliners, the death toll in east Anatolia rocketed and the latest Kurdish-interests party (DEP) was proscribed. Inflation rocketed to 120 percent, before dipping to "only" 80 percent. Major **corruption scandals** erupted regularly; no party escaped guilt, as all had governed recently. In 1996 an Associated Press article listed Tansu Çiller among the world's ten most corrupt politicians.

The only significant foreign-policy success was the 1995 customs union with the EU. Overseas, there was stiff opposition because of Turkey's poor human rights record; domestic opponents noted that considerable import duties were being forfeited, while Turks would still not have freedom of movement in Europe. Though falling well short of EU membership, the agreement, applied incrementally between 1996 and 2000, was brandished as a triumph by the beleaguered coalition.

1989	1990	1991
Turkey welcomes 300,000 Bulgarian Muslim Turks forced out of Communist Bulgaria	Özal's Turkey offers support to the US against Saddam Hussein's Iraq following its invasion of Kuwait	Turkey's first openly Islamist party, REFAH, comes fourth in the elections

Even before Çiller's term, the coalition was becoming unpopular. Racked by dissension, the SHP dissolved in February 1995, the remnants merging with the CHP. In September, CHP leader Baykal and Çiller dissolved the coalition; elections were set for December.

The rise and fall of Refah

Islamist **Refah** shocked the establishment by garnering the most votes in the December 1995 elections, with support coming from the urban underclass, devout Kurds and disparate individuals fed up with the discredited mainstream parties. DYP leader Çiller, under investigation for corruption, negotiated a coalition with Refah provided all proceedings against her ceased. Erbakan became prime minister, with Çiller as his deputy; the NSC, at this point with mixed civilian-military membership, geared up to safeguard secularism. In June 1997, Erbakan was forced out in the so-called "**soft coup**", replaced by an unlikely ANAP–DSP coalition.

Seven months later, Refah was closed down (for "acting against the principles of the secular Republic"); the Islamists regrouped as the Fazilet party, but in September 1998 the popular Fazilet mayor of Istanbul (and future prime minister and president), **Recep Tayyip Erdoğan**, was jailed for four months for a speech the prosecution claimed "incited armed fundamentalist rebellion". He had in fact quoted from a poem by Ziya Gökalp, main architect of secular Turkish nationalism. Erdoğan was respected for both literally and figuratively cleaning up Istanbul, and his imprisonment was widely regarded as a hollow victory by a suspect establishment over an honest (if "Islamist") politician. In November, the coalition collapsed as Prime Minister Yılmaz was accused of corruption. April 1999 elections saw the DSP at the head of a weak coalition.

Earthquake – and meltdown

On August 17, 1999 a catastrophic **earthquake** struck the eastern Marmara region, killing almost 20,000. Many died trapped in shoddily built tower blocks, exposing the corruption of local authorities who had allowed building and zoning codes to be flouted. Both the shambolic emergency response and the army were criticized, with soldiers tending to their own rather than joining the rescue effort. Ironically, the earthquake had lasting positive consequences. Substantial material aid and sympathy from Greece – whose aid teams were first on the scene – heralded a sustained thaw in bilateral relations. In December 1999 Greece dropped its objections to Turkish accession and Turkey became an official candidate for eventual **EU membership**.

THE SOURCE OF ISLAMIST POLITICS

In post-1923 Turkey, "**secularism**" means the state controlling religious affairs and suppressing public expressions of Islam. An official ban on **traditional Islamic dress** in state facilities effectively bars many young people of conservative traditional background from a public career, or even admittance to university. But for most Turks, Islam remains a much stronger source of values than assertive Westernizing, and a more homespun expression of national spirit than the quasi-colonial arrogance associated with the Kemalist elite, which offers little spiritual succour.

1993	**1993**	**1995**
Özal, now president, dies of a heart attack, though conspiracy theorists cry foul	Respected journalist Uğur Mumcu dies in a car bombing	Turkey enters into a customs union with the EU

A wave of private bank failures preceded a definitive economic crash in February 2001. The Turkish lira – formerly tied to the dollar in an IMF-backed plan – was free-floated; the exchange rate (and domestic inflation) soared as the value of lira investments and wages plummeted. The crisis forced sweeping monetary reforms under the aegis of veteran World Bank supremo Kemal Derviş.

In June, Fazilet was banned for "anti-secular activities", specifically inciting protests against the prohibition of headscarf-donning by women in schools and government offices. The closure proved futile as the **AKP** (Adalet ve Kalkınma Partisi); Justice and Development Party), led by former Istanbul mayor Erdoğan, replaced it immediately.

By mid-2002, PM Ecevit was an invalid, the DSP had imploded, the economy had contracted eight percent and Turkey had become the IMF's single biggest debtor. More positively, despite the imminent end of the coalition, legislators passed several **EU-required reforms** touching on human rights and freedom of expression. The death penalty was abolished, press freedom increased and education and broadcasting in several minority languages was now theoretically permissible.

Start of the AKP era

Given the preceding stasis, the **AKP swept to power** on November 3, 2002, with 34 percent of the vote. For the first time since 1987 Turkey had a majority government. The only other parliamentary party was the CHP; all others failed to clear the ten percent nationwide minimum.

Turkey's secularist establishment suspected that the AKP would soon drag the nation into an **Islamic theocracy**; instead, given stable government, Turkey's economy revived. More remarkable was the new government's commitment to compliance with EU directives by introducing 36 reforms meeting the "Copenhagen criteria" of acceptable civic practice. Both foreign and domestic observers appreciated the irony of Turkey's EU membership quest being pursued more fervently by an "Islamic" government than by previous secularist governments.

In early 2003, Turkey declined to be used as a springboard for the **US-led invasion of Iraq**. By the time Parliament voted (on March 20, invasion day) to allow US planes to overfly Turkish airspace, Turkish–American relations had already hit an all-time low. Turkey's reluctance to be involved stemmed from fears that the war would lead to a Kurdish state, and that the country might suffer a terrorist backlash. On November 15, 2003, car bombs exploded outside Istanbul synagogues, killing 25 and injuring three hundred. Five days later, suicide car-bombers targeted the British consulate and the HSBC bank, killing thirty and injuring 450. Although the perpetrators were linked to al-Qaeda, they proved to be ethnic Kurds from the southeast.

The long-running **Cyprus problem** continued to bedevil foreign affairs and Turkey's EU quest. A UN-devised reunification scheme backed by Turkey seemed to offer hope that the long-divided island would unify under the EU umbrella. In 2004, however, despite a solid majority (65 percent) of Turkish Cypriots voting in favour, 75 percent of Greek Cypriots rejected it in the necessary referendum. A week later southern (Greek) Cyprus joined the EU on behalf of the whole island. Turks – unaccustomed to occupying the moral high ground on Cyprus – were understandably annoyed.

1995	1995	1998
Well-known left-wing novelist Yaşar Kemal is prosecuted for expressing pro-Kurdish sentiments	The pro-Islamist Refah government is forced from power in the so-called "soft coup"	Recep Tayyip Erdoğan, arguably Turkey's most successful politician since Atatürk, is elected mayor of Istanbul

On October 3, 2005, **accession talks** for Turkey's joining the EU formally began. A November EU report criticized human rights issues, military–civilian relations and inequality but, more positively, praised the "functioning market economy." The AKP government had proven a competent manager under IMF guidelines, with inflation down to single figures for the first time in decades.

AKP's second term

After a relatively quiet 2006, 2007 began tumultuously with the **assassination of Hrant Dink** (see p.681). In spring 2007, AKP nominated foreign minister **Abdullah Gül** as president over military objections, particularly as Gül's wife publicly wore a headscarf. In what became known as the "**e-coup**", the military posted an online warning, hinting they might act if Gül were appointed. Millions of secular Turks took to the streets in orchestrated rallies against Gül's candidacy and what they saw as creeping Islamicization. The threat of a coup forced an early election in July 2007, in which the AKP captured 47 percent of the vote. Ominously, the CHP lost seats to the MHP, now back in parliament along with Kurdish independents. Gül was duly elected president and attention focused on the **headscarf issue** once again, as the AKP attempted to repeal a 1998 law forbidding its wearing in universities. In response the state prosecutor filed a case against the party early in 2008 for "anti-secular activities" and the AKP narrowly avoided being closed down.

With France and Germany openly hostile to Turkish EU membership, and Erdoğan failing to implement more reforms, the **accession process** stalled. The 2008 global slump hit the economy badly; despite a banking system annealed by the 2001 crisis, the TL tumbled against other currencies, and by mid-2009 unemployment stood at over 16 percent. Erdoğan's feistiness won him admirers and critics in equal measure when he stormed out of a February Davos summit after an altercation with Israeli president Shimon Peres over Gaza.

In February 2010 AKP managed to pass crucial legislation enabling military figures to be tried in civilian courts, thus reducing the chances of a future coup. Europe approved, while the supposedly progressive CHP objected, referring the measure to the Constitutional Court. In September the AKP went even further in challenging the military/secularist establishment by organizing a national referendum on the constitution that had been in place since the 1980 military coup, and timed to coincide with its thirtieth anniversary. A massive 58 percent voted in favour of the government package, which included changes to

STREET-FIGHTING MAN – RECEP TAYYIP ERDOĞAN

The founder of the AKP, Turkish prime minister for a record three times, and finally president of this country of some eighty million, **Tayyip Erdoğan** has caught the imagination of huge swathes of the Turkish public like no politician since Turgut Özal. A pugnacious but charismatic firebrand of a leader, he was brought up in the mean streets of the gritty Istanbul dockland neighbourhood of Kasımpaşa, on the northern shores of the Golden Horn. He famously sold *simits* (sesame-coated bread rings) on the streets as a child to supplement his family's meagre income and later, a sure-fire winner in this soccer-obsessed nation, he was a semi-professional player with his local team, Kasımpaşa.

1999	2002	2003
A catastrophic earthquake in Istanbul claims the lives of more than 20,000 people	The pro-Islamic AKP sweeps to power in the national elections, with 34 percent of the vote	Al-Qaeda terrorists bomb Istanbul synagogues, the HSBC bank and the British Consulate

the judicial system. Crucially, it permitted generals involved in past coups to be put on trial, retrospectively, for their actions. Opponents claimed the AKP were simply attempting to fill the judiciary with pro-Islamists and pave the way for Islamic rule; the vast majority of "no" votes were cast in the traditionally secularist Aegean and Mediterranean coastal belts.

Relations with Israel, already at an all-time low following Erdoğan's altercation with Peres at Davos in 2009, plummeted even further in May 2010 after Israeli commandos stormed the *Mavi Marmara*, a Turkish ship taking aid to Gaza, killing nine Turkish citizens, and Turkey's once buoyant Israeli tourism trade slumped. The understanding between these two countries, once at least nominally allies, was hardly helped by AKP support of Hamas.

The rise and rise of the AKP

In June 2011, for the first time in the history of the Turkish Republic, a party was elected for a **third consecutive term**. This time, although the AKP garnered fifty percent of the vote, the number of seats they had in parliament dropped slightly, making it more difficult for the party to push through reforms without consulting the opposition.

A major reason for the AKP's repeated electoral success was not its Islamic conservatism but the fact that the country began a period of sustained economic growth. In part this was because the AKP were prepared to do business with everyone, from pariah regimes such as Syria and Libya through to Saudi Arabia, Russia and China. Foreign capital flowed into the country, not least from the oil-rich Gulf states. Tourism incomes were booming too, with over thirty million visitors in 2011.

Turkey, under the urbane Foreign Minister Ahmet Davutoğlu, also introduced a grandiose "zero problems with neighbours" policy. This was primarily aimed at increasing trade and influence in the former Ottoman lands, from the mainly Arab Middle East and North Africa to the Balkans. The "**Arab Spring**" that began in early 2011 placed Turkey in a new role in the region, as a beacon of democracy (and global capitalism) amid a sea of dictatorial and protectionist regimes – or that's how some in the West wanted to see the country. Indeed, many of the poor majority in countries like Egypt saw Turkey, with its booming economy and democratic-secular system being steered by a conservative Muslim government, as the ideal alternative to their own despotic regimes.

In late 2011, with Israel still refusing to apologize for the *Mavi Marmara* deaths, Turkey downgraded its relations with Israel, expelling high-ranking diplomats and cutting military ties. Such actions made the tough, hard-talking and pious Erdoğan a well-known and popular figure to the Arab man in the street, although cynics at home saw his moves as cheap populism at best, dangerous neo-Ottomanism (that is, a bid to regain influence in lands once under Ottoman control) at worst. Turkey's "zero problems" policy was soon sorely tested, however, as the collapse of governance in Syria sent thousands of refugees pouring over the border into Turkey, and unrest in Libya forced thousands of Turks working in the oil and construction industries to return home.

In 2012, Turkish relations with Syria, fostered so carefully over the previous decade and a half (border minefields were cleared, Syrian and Turkish citizens could travel visa-free to each other's countries), collapsed as Assad refused to heed Erdoğan's calls

2004	**2005**	**2007**
After a referendum dashes hopes of reunification, southern Cyprus alone joins the EU	Formal accession talks for Turkey's long-awaited EU membership finally begin	Leading Turkish-Armenian activist Hrant Dink is shot dead by an ultra-nationalist teenager in Istanbul

for the Syrian leader to institute massive reforms. With the opposition Syrian National Council setting up a government in exile in Istanbul, and Turkey overtly supporting Syrian rebels, relations between the two countries foundered. In June 2012, the Syrians shot down a Turkish military jet just south of the Turkish province of Hatay, escalating tensions yet further. By October, with Syria in the throes of a devastating civil war and almost 100,000 refugees finding safe haven in Turkey, as well as a de-facto Kurdish enclave (see p.680) emerging on the Syrian side of the 900km-plus border, the situation in Turkey's southeast was becoming very tense.

Gezi Park and a new authoritarianism

Equally worryingly, the AKP, boosted by its third electoral success and the lack of a viable opposition, began to act in an increasingly authoritarian manner at home. Nowhere was this more evident than in the government's heavy-handed reaction to protests against the planned re-development of **Gezi Park** in Istanbul's iconic **Taksim Square** (see box, p.105). What started in May 2013 as a small-scale sit-in by a few protestors to prevent trees being cleared to make way for a government-backed shopping mall erupted into an anti-government occupation of the park. Scenes of Taksim Square and adjoining streets filled with baton-wielding riot police beating protestors and water cannons knocking people off their feet, set against a backdrop of clouds of tear-gas billowing over the square, were broadcast around the world.

Talk of a "**Turkish Spring**" by the sensationalist element among the international media proved far-fetched, but were used by Erdoğan to back claims that "foreign enemies" were behind the riots, always a sure-fire winner with a sometimes xenophobic Turkish public. A large proportion of the protestors were a new voice in Turkey. Young, urban, educated and media-savvy (social media platforms such as Twitter played a huge part in coordinating, disseminating and publicizing the protests), they had benefitted from the AKP's economic "miracle" but felt excluded from its vision of a more conservative and pious Turkey. Inevitably, many other groups who felt estranged from the "new" Turkey joined in, including Alevis (see box, p.682), Kurds, members of the LGBT community, the fans of Istanbul's "Big Three" football clubs and many more well-meaning protestors, as well as a few less savoury radical leftists and anarchists. Protests spread to many cities across the country, and the government's disproportionate response, which resulted in eleven deaths and eight thousand people injured, drew condemnation at home and abroad.

Taksim Square was eventually cleared of protestors, but the divisions in Turkish society seemed deeper than ever. Rumours that Haghia Sophia (Aya Sofya; see p.72) would become a mosque again, new restrictions on the sale of alcohol, and the tightening of abortion laws hardly helped dispel fears of creeping Islamism among the near fifty percent of the populace who didn't vote for the AKP, nor did carefully orchestrated pro-government rallies held in the wake of Gezi Park. As 2013 drew to a close, the government became mired in a major corruption scandal, with several AKP ministers and their offspring, including Erdoğan's own son, implicated in the bribery accusations. The PM put the blame for the scandal on the powerful Turkish Islamic scholar/community leader **Fetullah Gülen**, and the government began purging the police and judiciary of Gülen's supporters.

2007	2009	2010
The AKP increase their majority in national elections in July	PM Erdoğan storms off stage in Davos after a row with Israel's Shimon Peres	Nine Turkish citizens die when Israeli commandos attack the *Mavi Marmara*

Despite this Islamist in-fighting, the March 2014 local elections saw the AKP win 42 percent of the vote, while the biggest opposition party, the CHP, received only 26 percent. Buoyed by yet another electoral success, Erdoğan continued with his heavy-handed approach to governance. The PM was defiant in the face of protests following the loss of 301 workers in the country's biggest-ever mining disaster at Soma in May 2014. He reacted angrily to accusations of government negligence, more or less saying "these things happen in mining". That Turkey has the worst work-safety record in Europe is perhaps understandable, that it has the third-worst in the world is a scandal. Tellingly, a 2013 OECD (Organization for Economic Cooperation and Development) "happiness" report revealed that Turkey came bottom out of 36 industrialized countries in terms of life satisfaction, with Turks working the longest hours and receiving the lowest pay of the countries under consideration. Despite this, Erdoğan's stranglehold on power in Turkey was reaffirmed when he became the country's new president in August 2014. For the first time in Turkey's history, a president had been elected by **popular vote**, with Erdoğan receiving the support of almost 52 percent of the electorate.

2015: general elections strike twice

The run-up to the June 2015 general elections was dominated by several major issues, including the slowing economy, the 2013 corruption scandal that had implicated Erdoğan's son, the government's fall-out with the powerful Gülen faith movement, the so-called "peace process" with the country's Kurds (see p.678), and the ever deteriorating situation in war-torn Syria. The AKP, led by PM Ahmet Davutoğlu, won a record fourth term in the **June 2015 general election**, but with a much-reduced majority, garnering a little over forty percent of the vote. This meant a hung parliament, and Erdoğan's plans to push through a constitutional change to bring presidency from a ceremonial to an executive role had to be put on the back burner. The main opposition, CHP, won almost 25 percent of the vote, the ultra-nationalist MHP 16 percent and the pro-Kurdish HDP some 13 percent. The latter were seen as the biggest winners – for the first time, a mainly Kurdish party had representation in parliament. Efforts to form a coalition were doomed from the start. The ultra-Turkish nationalist MHP refused to countenance working with the pro-Kurdish HDP, and Erdoğan was incensed that the Kurds refused point blank to support his desire to introduce an executive presidency.

Whether the **post-election instability** that gripped Turkey was an inevitable result of a weakened government struggling to cope with the ongoing crises both at home and in the wider region, or was allowed to happen by Erdoğan in order to bring about snap elections with an outcome more favourable to his party is debatable, but – regardless – the country was certainly rocked by what happened next. Following months of American pressure to provide more support in the war against **ISIS** (Islamic State of Iraq and Syria), Turkey suddenly opened up the **İncirlik airbase**, near Adana, to the US military. Although Turkey announced its intention to bomb ISIS itself, it first turned its attention to the **PKK** (Kurdish Workers Party), launching raid after raid on its bases in Iraqi Kurdistan, as well as clamping down at home. The "peace process" with the Kurds was over, for the time being at least (see p.679). The Turkish Lira, already struggling, plunged even further against the major currencies.

2010	2011	2011
The Turkish economy is ranked as the seventeenth largest in the world	The AKP wins a record third general election	So-called "Arab Spring" casts Turkey as icon of democratic stability in a region swept by turmoil

In August, Erdoğan killed off any notion of a coalition and set fresh elections for November 1. The instability continued, however, and between the two elections PKK attacks against Turkish security forces in the southeast resulted in some 150 deaths. According to official sources, Turkish military reprisals resulted in the deaths of 2000 PKK combatants. **Lack of press freedom** dominated the build-up to the elections, culminating in October when a publishing group opposing the AKP, Koza Ipek, was stormed by police and the company taken into "trusteeship" by the state. Turkey's worst-ever **terrorist attack** took place at a rally in Ankara on October 10, when twin suicide bombers killed over 100 demonstrators, most of whom were leftist and Kurdish. Critics, who had long accused the government of turning a blind eye to ISIS activities, if not actually supporting them, were up in arms. Government responded by claiming that it was a joint PKK-ISIS attack, despite the fact that the two groups are sworn enemies, actually fighting each other in northern Syria.

Turkish citizens who opposed the AKP entered the polls on November 1 with justifiable trepidation. Their worst fears were confirmed when the AKP stormed to victory yet again, winning almost fifty percent of the vote. The HDP just scraped over the controversial ten percent barrier, the MHP saw a substantial decline in its share of the vote, though the CHP's vote remained stable. Despite nearly a ten percent increase in their share of the vote from June, the AKP still lacked the majority to push though constitutional changes without consulting the other parties in parliament.

The re-elected government was immediately faced with a host of challenges. In late November, Turkey downed a Russian jet over the Turkish–Syrian border, sparking a major diplomatic incident. Meanwhile, curfews were installed in the southeast of the country while security forces attempted to "cleanse" towns and cities of Kurdish militants, resulting in scores of deaths, including civilians. Then, on January 12 2016, an ISIS member of Syrian origin blew himself up in the historic Hippodrome, in Istanbul's tourist heartland of Sultanahmet. Ten foreign tourists, mainly German, were killed and another fifteen injured. Critics who had accused the government of long turning a blind eye to militant Islam appeared to be vindicated, and the damage to Turkey's crucial tourism industry risked a major blow to the country's economy.

Trends for the future

Thus far the AKP has successfully challenged the so-called "**White Turks**" – mostly of Balkan descent – comprising the army, academia, civil service, big business and much of the media, who have run the Republic since 1923. Despite being mostly devout and lower-middle-class, the AKP and its supporters ostensibly view EU entry as the best way to raise their voters' standard of living and promote reform. The burning question is whether the AKP is genuinely liberal, or merely introducing Islamic theocracy by the back door, as their opponents assert. The fact that EU accession reforms had petered out completely by 2010 suggest that Turkey and its current government do not value membership as highly as it once appeared to do – hardly surprising, given the economic and other crises affecting the union in 2012.

A substantial body of European opinion views Turkey as a developing Muslim country inherently unsuitable for membership in a "white, Christian" club that would be overwhelmed by Turkey's geographically lopsided development and demographic

2011	2012
Turkey is now attracting more than thirty million foreign tourists per year	Turkish and Syrian relations are in tatters after Syria downs a Turkish military jet close to the border

SURGE, FLOOD, DELUGE: TURKEY'S SYRIAN REFUGEES

In April 2011, intensive fighting in northwest Syria caused several thousand civilians to flee over the border into Turkey. It marked the start of a crisis which by 2014 saw 1.6 million **Syrian refugees** in Turkey, partly prompted by the inexorable rise of ISIS, making it the largest host nation to refugees in the world. By summer 2015, the Turkish government acknowledged that the country had taken in over two million refugees from its still-war torn neighbour; unofficial estimates put the figure closer to three million. Turkey's response to the crisis has been admirable, and its open-door policy has undoubtedly saved the lives of tens, if not hundreds of thousands, of Syrian lives. The camps built to house the refugees, mostly close to the country's near 900km-long border with its southern neighbour, are state of the art and extremely well-run by the Turkish governmental disaster and relief agency **AFAD** (W afad.gov.tr).

The **cost** of looking after such large numbers of refugees was put at a colossal $7.6 billion, no mean sum for any country to bear. Additionally, the influx has put many other strains on Turkey, especially as many of the refugees are likely to stay for years, if not decades. The camps are home only to 200,000 or so Syrians, the rest live in cities scattered across the country, which has inevitably raised **social tensions** in some neighbourhoods. Forced to work in the black economy as they have no work permits, Syrians are accused of taking "Turkish" jobs and driving down wages. Rents have been driven up in some areas by Syrian families seeking accommodation, much to the chagrin of less well-off locals. In some places, such as Kilis, on the border south of Gaziantep, the population is today more than half Syrian. In many major Turkish cities, most obviously Istanbul, poor Syrian families can be seen begging on the streets, presenting a heart-rending picture, especially on a cold, rainy winter's day.

The **future** is uncertain, especially as the war in Syria shows no signs of abating. One problem is that technically the Syrians who have fled into Turkey are not officially refugees, but "guests", as according to the 1951 Geneva Convention on refugees, signed by Turkey, the country is only obliged to offer official status to refugees from Europe, not the East. Furthermore, even Syrians who have been in Turkey for more than two years are denied the right to apply for asylum. So despite Turkey's great generosity in looking after such a massive influx of people, it's no wonder that many Syrians are looking to continue their flight westwards into Europe in the hope of securing a future for themselves and their families. The exodus from Turkey had become so great by the summer of 2015 that in October of that year a panicking Angela Merkel, Germany's PM, began engaging in some unseemly horse-trading with Turkey over the refugees, promising to ease visa restriction on Turks visiting Europe, open up new EU accession chapters and hand over a substantial sum of money if Turkey would stem the tide of Syrian refugees from its soil. This cynical realpolitik was played out against a backdrop of Syrian families capsizing in flimsy rafts en route from the Turkish mainland to beleaguered Greek islands, and a drowned Syrian Kurdish toddler, Aylan Kurdı, washed up on the beach of the Turkish holiday resort of Bodrum.

profile. One excuse used to block Turkey's accession is its refusal to recognize Greek Cyprus, thus blocking Turkey from fulfilling 14 of 35 accession criteria. This in turn has sparked resentment among many Turks, and support for accession has dropped.

Turkey's **economy** is far more resilient than formerly, with consumer spending steady and foreign investment flooding in – especially since 2002 – from the Gulf states (but also through the purchase of second homes by Europeans). Particularly important is the country's role as an oil and natural gas conduit, with pipelines from Russia, Azerbaijan and Kazakhstan all crossing Turkish territory. In 2009 a deal was signed to

2012

2013

With refugees streaming into southeast Turkey, the Kurdish community across the border in Syria approaches effective autonomy

The protests in Istanbul's Gezi Park demonstrate government unpopularity among many sectors of Turkish society

pipe gas from Iran to Western Europe. **Tourism** is also crucial, with annual visitor numbers reaching 37 million in 2014. Unemployment, exacerbated by rural depopulation, remains stubbornly high, especially among the young people who constitute such a large part of the population. The over-centralized educational system, undergoing constant tinkering, cannot produce sufficient well-trained workers. Despite lip service to the Islamic tenet of alms-giving, the AKP has done little to reduce the massive gap between rich and poor.

Turkey is rapidly becoming a major regional power, with its moderate Islamist government viewed as a bulwark against Islamic extremism. Initially anxious about the emergence of an independent Kurdish entity in northern Iraq, Turkey is now happy to do business with the oil-rich enclave. Despite the "Arab Spring", links with the Arab world have improved. Egypt and Libya in particular look to Turkey as a role model, and many wealthy Arabs from the Gulf states now holiday and invest in the country. On the downside, the civil war in Syria, and Turkey's poor relations with the Shia-dominated government in Iraq, have led to very strained ties with these two important neighbours. What could make things even worse is a "water war": the Euphrates and Tigris rivers have their headwaters in Turkey, and the dams (some complete, others still projected) of the gigantic GAP project (see p.579) threaten water supplies in both Syria and Iraq. Turkey is also extremely concerned about the rise of a proto-Kurdish state (Rojava to the Kurds) in northern Syria, especially as the dominant political force there, the PYD, is linked to the PKK. The Syrian crisis looks set to run for years, with Russia seriously entering the fray in 2015 in support of Assad. This is anathema to Turkey, which refuses to countenance a Syria with Assad in control. The longer the war in Syria continues the more refugees are going to flood into Turkey (see box opposite).

In the Caucasus, Turkey assiduously cultivates **Azerbaijan**, a nation not only ethnically Turkish (albeit Shi'ite rather than Sunni), but also petroleum-rich. This precludes meaningful links with **Armenia** following its occupation of the ethnically Armenian Azerbaijani enclave of Nagorno-Karabagh in 1992 (see p.683). Turkey has also shown increased interest in its former Balkan territories, especially those retaining Muslim populations. Albania has received military training and civilian advisers, and Turkey was among the first countries to recognize Macedonia. Perhaps the biggest surprise is strong links with **Greece** in trade, banking and tourism, offset by the total inability to come to a solution over Cyprus.

There is no doubt, however, that Turkey has been transformed economically under the AKP. Major new highways lace the mountainous Anatolian interior, high-speed train links are being forged between major cities, and cheap domestic air travel is booming. Along with Brazil, Russia, India and China, Turkey has become a major emerging economy, ranking seventeenth in the world in 2015. This new-found economic wealth has given the nation a confidence it has lacked for decades, and it is far less likely to take heed of foreign powers when making decisions affecting its future. Whether taking the West to task for hypocrisy in painting ISIS as evil incarnate while turning a blind eye to the PKK, or berating Europe for criticizing Turkey for its human rights record while putting up the barriers to refugees from countries it (and the US) have helped destabilize in the first place, Turkey seems set to continue as an independent yet major regional player in a geopolitically crucial part of the globe.

2014	2015	2016
May's mining disaster at Soma, where over three hundred miners died, highlights Turkey's atrocious record of workplace safety	After a hung parliament in the June general election, in November snap elections confirm the AKP as the nation's government for a fourth time	ISIS suicide bomber kills ten tourists in an explosion in Sultanahmet, Istanbul

The peoples of Turkey

Thanks to its long history, and repeated waves of migration over many millennia, modern Turkey is home to many distinct population groups. The roots of the Turks themselves are described on p.10 & p.650, while you'll find accounts of two distinctive peoples who live on the Black Sea coast, the Hemşinli and the Laz in, in other parts of the guide (see boxes, p.532 & p.535). This section details some of the country's most obvious minority groups, from the Muslim Kurds to the Syrian Orthodox Christians.

The Kurds

Although the **Kurds** inhabit several Middle Eastern countries, including Iran, Iraq and Syria, the largest population is in southeast Turkey. Present in Anatolia long before the Turks, they are of Indo-European origin and language, and until the twentieth century were largely a tribal, nomadic people. Their dominant faiths are the same as the Turks – Sunni Islam, with significant numbers of Alevi (see box, p.682). As Kurds are not recognized as a minority by Turkey, accurate figures are debatable, but at least twelve million (and up to twenty) of the country's eighty million population are ethnically Kurdish.

A history of rebellion

Relations between the Ottomans and the Kurds were generally good. Successive sultans allowed the Kurds, split into semi-autonomous federations, to act as a buffer between the Ottoman Empire and Russia or Persia. After the collapse of the Ottoman Empire, most Kurds supported Kemal's Nationalists in the independence struggle; following the Republican victory, however, relations began to sour. Many Kurds had backed the Turkish nationalists as co-religionists, but they were outraged when Atatürk abolished the caliphate in 1924, especially as all institutions of a specifically Kurdish nature were also closed down.

The initial response was a revolt under Said, a Nakşibendi dervish *şeyh*; then a more overtly nationalist insurrection broke out near Mount Ararat, which wasn't quelled until 1929. A 1936 rebellion further west in the Alevi Kurdish heartland of Dersim, modern Tunceli, lasted two years. The Turkish state crushed each uprising with executions, expulsions to western Anatolia, and the suppression of all expressions of ethnic identity. The entire southeast became a military zone, closed to foreigners until the 1960s, with a backward, stagnant economy.

The PKK and its guerrilla war

Inevitably, an extremist organization – the **PKK** (Kurdish Workers' Party) – emerged in 1978 in reaction to forced-assimilation policies. Its founder, political-science student **Abdullah Öcalan**, set up a nominally Marxist guerrilla group intent on independence for Turkey's Kurds. The PKK's appeal cut across traditional tribal loyalties, offering something to those at the very bottom of the clan hierarchies, and it thrived in the repressive atmosphere after the 1980 coup. In 1984, from Syrian bases, the PKK started to launch attacks against the *jandarma* and army; later it targeted civil servants, especially teachers.

PKK power peaked in the mid-1990s, with over 15,000 guerrillas in the field. The state barely controlled some parts of the southeast as the PKK encouraged mass civil disobedience; schools closed as teachers refused to operate in the danger zone; and the army forcibly evacuated thousands of settlements to stop villagers (willingly or unwillingly) aiding the PKK. Successive pro-Kurdish political parties, accused by the state (sometimes correctly) of being fronts for the PKK, were closed down, and their leaders imprisoned. By 1998, the army's superior tactics and weaponry began to tell; after being expelled from his base in Damascus, Öcalan was captured in Kenya with CIA and Mossad aid in 1999. Convicted of treason and murder, he was imprisoned on İmrali island in the Sea of Marmara, where he still languishes.

Despite these setbacks, the PKK had succeeded in placing Turkey's Kurdish issue on both the domestic and world stages. In 2005, PM Erdoğan departed from the official doctrine that there were no Kurds in Turkey – "mountain Turks" were historically the code words – by referring, in a speech in Diyarbakır, the unofficial "capital" of Turkish Kurdistan, to the "Kurdish problem". Prohibitions on the public use of Kurdish were lifted, private courses in the language permitted, and in 2008 a state-broadcast Kurdish channel opened to great fanfare (and controversy).

In 2009 the AKP government announced the "**Kurdish Initiative**", aimed at solving the long-standing problem. Universities were permitted to teach Kurdish-language courses, human rights laws were changed, and settlements in the southeast were allowed to use Kurdish names. There was even an attempt to "bring home" PKK fighters from northern Iraq, by offering amnesties to those who had not been involved in attacks resulting in the deaths of Turkish soldiers or civilians.

Behind the scenes, the government at least tried to make progress, almost certainly carrying on secret talks with jailed PKK leader Öcalan. Then, in 2011, news leaked that Turkish and PKK representatives had engaged in secret talks in Oslo. Unfortunately for the initiative, however, the pro-Kurdish DTP (Democratic Society Party) was closed down by the courts in December 2011; it quickly morphed into the BDP (Peace and Democracy Party), but the damage was done.

Meanwhile, the cycle of **PKK attacks** and **Turkish military reprisals** continued; a particularly bloody PKK attack resulted in the deaths of 13 Turkish soldiers near Diyarbakır in June 2011, and mutual mistrust was reinforced later that year when a Turkish military aircraft struck a convoy of what they thought were PKK terrorists near Uludere, and killed what turned out to be 34 smugglers. PKK attacks escalated in 2012, and violence flared to levels not seen since the 1990s, with over 400 PKK and in excess of 100 Turkish security forces killed in the first nine months of the year. Semi-clandestine negotiations continued, however, between the government and the PKK. This so-called "peace process" resulted in a self-declared **ceasefire** by the PKK. But trust between the interlocutors began to dissolve in the autumn of 2014, when the Turkish government appeared to do nothing to help the beleaguered Kurds of Kobane, just across the border from Turkey in Syria, as they desperately battled besieging ISIS forces. Violent protests by Kurds erupted in Turkey's southeast, leaving over thirty people dead. The government accused the HDP (People's Democratic Party, founded in 2012 and successor to the BDP) of inciting the civil disobedience which rendered some towns no-go areas for the Turkish security forces for several days. Many Kurds were convinced that the Turkish government was more interested in stopping a Kurdish autonomous region emerging across the border in Syria than in fighting ISIS. Others believed the Turks were actively aiding ISIS.

Matters were further complicated in the **June 2015 general election** when, for the first time ever, a pro-Kurdish party, the **HDP**, passed the ten percent electoral threshold. Turkish president Recep Tayyip Erdoğan's hopes of enlisting Kurdish support for constitutional amendments which would have strengthened the role of the president were quickly dashed. Having negotiated behind the scenes with jailed PKK leader Öcalan, the government now found its ambitions being thwarted by a democratically elected pro-Kurdish party led by the dashing Selahattin Demirtaş.

Following an **ISIS suicide bombing** in July 2015 that killed over thirty young people readying themselves to help reconstruct Kobane, the PKK retaliated by killing two Turkish policeman in their sleep. Violence then escalated on both sides, as a still-smarting Erdoğan brought an end to the "peace process". Turkey began bombing PKK positions in the Kandil mountains in Iraqi Kurdistan and the PKK launched numerous deadly attacks on Turkish security forces, remotely detonating mines when military vehicles were passing and opening fire on police stations and military checkpoints. Acts of civil disobedience also became widespread, with PKK supporters declaring "self-governance" in cities such as Cizre and Nusaybin. By the end of October, just before the elections, security forces casualties numbered 150, and the government claimed 2000 PKK had been killed in air strikes and ground operations.

Relations with Iraqi Kurdistan and Syria

Ironically, Turkey now enjoys far better relations with virtually autonomous Iraqi **Kurdistan** than with its own Kurds. High-level visits between leaders of Turkey and the booming, oil-rich proto-state are common, and Turkish companies are doing big business in the region. Turkey appears to have accepted the de facto Kurdish state in northern Iraq.

What's more worrying for Turkey is the situation in **Syria**, which also holds a very sizeable Kurdish minority. Given the bloody chaos continuing (at the time of writing in the winter of 2015) to ensue from the civil war in Syria, the Kurds there have understandably begun to establish their own "safe zone", or proto-state, right along the Syrian side of the Turkish frontier. Given that the main Kurdish power in Syria, the PYD (Democratic Union Party) is organically connected with the PKK in Turkey, alarm bells began ringing loudly in Ankara – not least because the armed wing of the PYD, the **YPG** (People's Protection Units), won Western acclaim for their successful defence of Kobane against ISIS in the autumn of 2014. The Turkish state, fearful that the PKK could take advantage of Western support of the PYD, whose armed wings appear to be the only effective on-the-ground force fighting ISIS, arguably led to the Turkish government finally agreeing to take an active part in the struggle against ISIS in July 2015.

Prospects for the future

The bloody struggle between Turkish forces and the PKK has indisputably polarized Turkish society. Many Turkish families have lost sons, and the sight of weeping crowds as the flag-draped coffin of the latest loved one is borne through the streets of his home town has become depressingly familiar on TV. The less scrupulous media exploit this to stoke nationalist feelings, and most processions are accompanied by chants of "Martyrs don't die, the homeland can't be divided". In fact, however, most of the 45,000-plus estimated casualties of the conflict are of Kurdish origin – and the Kurds too mark the deaths of their "martyrs" with flamboyant funerals.

Although the PKK has only around 5000 combatants based on Mount Kandil in Iraqi Kurdistan, there seems to be an inexhaustible supply of new recruits to keep those numbers steady. Inevitably, the conflict has left the southeast **impoverished**, and many Kurds have migrated west for work. This has led to resentment on the part of some Turks, while many Kurds feel they are discriminated against. Indeed, a 2012 survey found that over half of all Turks would not want a Kurdish neighbour, which has led to the ethnic "**ghettoization**" of big cities such as Istanbul.

The ending of the "peace process" in July 2015 was undoubtedly a massive setback for rapprochement between Turkey and its large Kurdish minority. But some grounds for **optimism** remain. The ethnic genie is out of the bottle, and the Kurdish question can, and is, discussed widely. Turks seem more willing to accept the distinct identity of the Kurds, and a fair number actually voted for the HDP in the June 2015 election, even if it was solely to prevent the AKP getting the majority they needed to introduce constitutional amendments. The fact that there is now a party representing the Kurds in parliament is a promising development in itself, though how the democratically elected HDP juggles its role with that of the Marxist-Leninist PKK (deemed a terrorist organization by the US and EU as well as Turkey) remains to be seen.

The big game-changer, of course, may well be what is happening on Turkey's southern borders. There is no doubt that the Kurds in Turkey look with some envy at the

proto-Kurdish state in Northern Iraq. They are even more supportive of the Kurdish zone, known by the Kurds as Rojava, in northern Syria, especially given the brave fight put up by the YPG militia against ISIS. The meltdown of Iraq and Syria has given the Kurds there the opportunity to stake their claim for statehood – the Kurds in Turkey are watching developments with great interest. However, if Turkey can get back on track with its EU-orientated reforms, the Kurds and Turks may yet coexist peaceably in a more inclusive, fully democratic Turkey.

Let's hope so, as with more than half of Turkey's ethnically Kurdish population living outside the southeast – over three million of them in Istanbul, far more than in any other single city worldwide, including all those in their "homeland" – any attempt to separate the country into Turkish and Kurdish zones would probably result in a bloodbath.

The Armenians

The **Armenians** (Ermeni in Turkish) have been present in and around eastern Anatolia since the Urartian empire collapsed, in around 600 BC. Attempts to form their own state have, however, invariably been short-lived – at least until an independent Armenian state emerged in the southern Caucasus after World War I. Under the Ottoman Turks, the Armenians generally prospered as a loyal and favoured Christian *millet* (nation), but during the early twentieth century they fell victim to the competing nationalisms that tore the Ottoman world asunder.

Armenian history and Christianity

The Armenians gradually developed their own identity after their arrival in Anatolia in the seventh century BC. That process crystallized with the advent of Christianity, which they fervently embraced. Towards the end of the third century, Armenia became the first nation to officially adopt the new faith, thanks mainly to the efforts of St Gregory "the Illuminator". The invention of the Armenian alphabet in 404, by Mesrop Mashtots, furthered the Armenians' view of themselves as a distinct race.

This separate identity was further strengthened when the **Armenian Apostolic Church** refused to accept the ruling of the Byzantine Council of Chalcedon in 451, which declared that Christ had two equal and coexistent natures. By retaining their monophysite views – that is, believing that Christ had a single, divine nature – the Armenians cut themselves off from the mainstream Byzantine Orthodox Christian world, which held that Christ combined both human and divine natures.

During the ninth and tenth centuries, Armenian culture flowered, especially in the Van basin under the Artsruni dynasty, and under the Bagratid dynasty around Ani. The arrival of the Selçuk Turks and other Turcoman groups in the eleventh century, however, heralded a decline in their fortunes.

HRANT DINK – "WE ARE ALL ARMENIANS"

In January 2007, 100,000 Turkish citizens marched down Istanbul's İstiklal Caddesi to protest their solidarity with slain Armenian-Turkish journalist and human rights campaigner **Hrant Dink**, chanting "We are all Armenians". While some of the protesters were Istanbul's Armenians, the majority were Turks marching in sympathy.

Dink had been shot dead earlier that month in the street in broad daylight in the prosperous Istanbul business district of Sisli, close to the offices of the Armenian-Turkish newspaper **Agos**, which he co-founded and worked for as editor-in-chief. His killer was a Turkish ultra-nationalist teenager, but many believe the assassin was part of a broader, ultra-nationalist "deep state" conspiracy designed to foment unrest. To put the sympathy shown for Dink in the march in context, it's noteworthy that the assassin, following his capture, was photographed posing beneath a picture of Atatürk, holding a Turkish flag and flanked by smiling security officials.

THE ALEVİS

Cutting awkwardly across Turkey's ethno-religious divisions, the **Alevis** form up to twenty percent of the total population. Although they're officially classed as Muslims, their faith, a curious hybrid of shamanism and Shi'ism, is viewed with suspicion by many of the country's mainstream Sunni Muslim majority – not least because men and women worship together and alcohol is tolerated. Whereas Sunni Islam is the state religion, and imams are government employees whose sermons are centrally checked, Alevis are neither recognized by, nor receive funding from, the state, and worship semi-clandestinely in prayer halls known as *cemevis*. To complicate matters further for this little-understood group, they can be drawn from either the ethnically Turkish or ethnically Kurdish population, and in order to avoid Sunni Muslim bigotry, virtually all are staunch supporters of the secularist/Kemalist regime.

The Ottomans finally took control of Armenia during the fifteenth and sixteenth centuries. Ottoman rule benefitted the Armenians who, like the other non-Muslim minorities, were conceded substantial control over education and family law, and even earned for themselves the epithet of *sadık millet* (loyal nation). During the nineteenth century, however, as the Ottoman Empire declined, some Armenians (along with other Christian groups in Anatolia) developed nationalist aspirations – often encouraged by the Russians, bent on fragmenting the Ottoman Empire.

The Armenian deportations

For the Armenians of the Ottoman Empire, **April 24, 1915** was a fateful day. Acting on plans finalized in March, the CUP authorities disarmed all Armenians serving in the Turkish army, and rounded up Armenian civilians from Anatolian cities, towns and villages; only Istanbul and İzmir were exempted, for economic and public-relations reasons. During ten months of deportations, Armenian men were usually shot immediately by gendarmes, Kurdish irregulars or bands of recruited thugs, while women and children were forced to march hundreds of kilometres towards concentration camps in the Mesopotamian desert. Estimating total casualties is controversial, but Ottoman and foreign censuses around 1900 counted nearly 1.5 million Armenians living in Anatolia. Allowing for about half a million refugees who managed to hide in Turkey or escape abroad, most of the remainder can be assumed to have perished, making it the first deliberate, large-scale **genocide** of the twentieth century. In 1919 the Ottomans themselves admitted 800,000 killed.

The genocide issue

The above scenario has been hotly disputed by more recent Turkish governments, which have consistently denied that any officially approved, systematic expulsion or killing occurred. They have conceded a maximum of 300,000 Armenian fatalities, while implying that most were combatants in treasonous alliance with Russia or France. While it is true that many Armenians, particularly in Van, Kars and Adana, sided with those two powers in the hope of securing a postwar state for themselves, this happened after the deportation and massacre orders were issued, and could be construed as legitimate self-defence.

The "so-called genocide" issue, as the Turkish press describes it, continues to poison relations between modern Turkey and the tiny Armenian state – soon subsumed by Soviet Russia – that emerged in the aftermath of World War I, and also with the large and powerful Armenian diaspora. It bedevils relations between two peoples who, although they may have different religions, share much in common culturally, socially and historically. The issue is a PR nightmare for Turkey, which constantly lobbies other countries not to officially acknowledge the "genocide".

The Armenian lobby in the USA continually presses the administration to recognize the massacres of World War I as genocide. The pressure has been resisted, largely because Turkey remains a vital US ally in the Middle East. While running for the presidency,

Barack Obama confirmed his support for the Congressional passage of the Armenian Genocide Resolution, but once elected he failed to fulfil his promise. France, however, which holds an Armenian community of some 300,000, passed a bill recognizing the genocide in 1998, while in Switzerland it is a criminal offence to deny it. Relations between Turks and Armenians deteriorated even further following a two-year war between Caucasus rivals Armenia and Azerbaijan (1992–94) when Armenia occupied Nagorno-Karabagh, Azeri territory but with an overwhelmingly Armenian population. Turkey, in support of its co-Turkic brethren in Azerbaijan, broke off diplomatic relations with Armenia, and the land border between the two countries remains closed.

The Armenians in Turkey today

It's estimated that up to two million "Turks" today have Armenian blood. During the deportations and massacres of 1915 and later, many local Kurdish and Turkish families and individuals took in Armenian children, who were raised as Muslim Turkish citizens. Later generations were usually completely unaware of their origins – read *My Grandmother* by Fethiye Çetin (see p.698).

Only in Istanbul, however, did a sizeable Christian Armenian community survive. Under the 1923 Treaty of Lausanne, they were protected as an official minority, like some other non-Muslim groups, by international law. Now estimated at between forty and seventy thousand, Istanbul's Armenians have their own spiritual leader and a patriarchal church at Kumkapı on the Sea of Marmara below Sultanahmet, as well as many others scattered across the city, plus their own schools, newspapers and business organizations. Unfortunately, they are all too often misunderstood and viewed with suspicion by the majority Muslim Turks, who see them as potential fifth-columnists for outside powers, unfairly prosperous and simply not "real" Turks. The strenuous and unflagging efforts of the Armenian diaspora and their brethren in Armenia itself to have the "genocide" recognized internationally (including by Turkey) put them in a very difficult position, and they are often the target of discrimination, both from officialdom and the Turkish public. In 2011, for example, an Armenian-Turk conscripted into the Turkish army was shot in suspicious circumstances by a fellow soldier on the day Armenians commemorate the "genocide" (April 24). The mistrust is not all one-way, however; in 2010 a Christian Istanbul Armenian shot his sister and her new Muslim Turkish husband for marrying across the religious and ethnic frontier.

Some attempts at rapprochement have been made – the Turkish government's restoration of the long-neglected Armenian church on Akdamar island (see p.634) at least represents a start. Even if no Turkish government, fearful of demands for reparations, is likely to accept the events of 1915 as genocide, an increasing number of Turkish journalists, academics and ordinary citizens are prepared to acknowledge the events as ethnic cleansing. With the commemorations in April 2015 to mark the centenary of the "genocide", however, atop a hundred years of mutual suspicion and Armenia's refusal to withdraw from Nagorno-Karabagh, things are unlikely to get easier for Turkey's remaining Armenian community any time soon.

The Greeks

Mycenaean **Greeks** started to colonize Anatolia's Aegean coast as early as 1500 BC, so they can probably claim to be the oldest of the ethnic groups who have survived to the present day on modern Turkish soil. During the Byzantine Christian era, the Greeks were the dominant grouping in what's now Turkey. Now, referred to by Turks as **Rum**, they number under three thousand – a precipitous decline.

Greek history in Anatolia

From 1500 BC onwards, Greek-speaking peoples colonized first the Aegean coastline of Anatolia, and, later, parts of the Mediterranean and Black Sea coasts as well. Greek domination of the Aegean coastal belt was curbed by the Persians during the sixth century BC, but in the fourth century BC the victories of Alexander the Great helped to spread Greek culture throughout Anatolia and beyond. While Rome progressively annexed the region from the second century BC onwards, Greek language and culture remained dominant in the Greek city-states that the Romans absorbed into their empire. The Byzantine Empire subsequently developed as a Christian, Greek-speaking entity, with its capital in Constantinople.

It is to these Byzantine, eastern Orthodox Christian roots that today's tiny minority Greek Orthodox population – most of whom live either in Istanbul or on the Aegean islands of Gökçeada (Imbros) and Bozcaada (Tenedos) – look back. The inexorable Byzantine decline started as early as the seventh century, but the balance of power truly tilted with the arrival of the Muslim Turks in Anatolia following their crushing victory at Manzikert in 1071. As the Turks gradually brought Anatolia under their control, more and more Orthodox, Greek-speaking Christians converted to Islam and intermarried with their conquerors. The Ottoman Turkish capture of Constantinople in 1453 finally extinguished Christian power in Anatolia, but the Christians – Orthodox Greeks, Armenian and Syrian Orthodox among others – were allowed to run their own affairs through the *millet* (nation) system.

From the Capitulations to the population exchange

Following the introduction of the Capitulations in the sixteenth century (see p.653), the European traders who became increasingly influential in the Ottoman economy tended to favour their Christian brethren – and especially the Greeks. Although this arguably marked the start of Muslim-Turkish resentment, Turks and Greeks continued to get along, even after Greece itself won independence from the Ottoman Empire in 1830.

During World War I and its aftermath, the Greek presence in Anatolia was fatally compromised by the idea of a **Greater Greece**, to include not only the Greek state that had emerged in 1830, but also much of the Aegean and Black Sea coastline of Anatolia, where millions of Greeks still lived. A British-backed invasion by a Greek army ended in disaster for the Greeks from both Greece and Anatolia following a decisive victory for Turkish nationalists at Dumlupınar in 1922. The Treaty of Lausanne, signed on July 24, 1923, recognized the frontiers won by the Turks in the War of Independence.

There was no place for the Greeks in the new Turkish Republic. Some Pontic Greeks from the Black Sea had rebelled, other Greeks had agitated for independence from Ottoman Turkey. Now all were deemed treacherous and untrustworthy. In the internationally mediated **population exchange** of 1923, nearly all the Greek Orthodox Christians left in Turkey (some 1.3 million) were sent to Greece, while the Muslim Turkish population of Greece was sent to Turkey. Only the Greek Orthodox population of Istanbul was exempted, due to the importance of the Greek Orthodox Patriarchate in Istanbul.

The Greeks today

Istanbul held an estimated 297,000 Greeks in 1924. Many left after the Wealth Tax of 1942 unfairly targeted Turkey's minorities, while in 1955, looking for a distraction from the country's economic woes and with tensions high over Cyprus, Turkish PM Menderes deemed Istanbul's Greek minority a suitable scapegoat. Government-sponsored demonstrations soon got out of hand, and mobs ransacked Greek property. The police, apparently under orders not to intervene, stood and watched the mayhem. The riots were the beginning of the end for the city's Greek Orthodox Christian minority, many of whom left in the immediate aftermath. A further major exodus followed in 1964, again against the backdrop of nationalism inflamed by events in Cyprus, and by 1965 the Greek population was down to 48,000.

Today the 2500 or so Greek Orthodox Turkish citizens left in Istanbul are elderly, and their remaining churches virtually empty. Like the Armenians, under the Treaty of Lausanne they are recognized as an official minority and have their own schools, a newspaper and other organizations, but all of these are in severe decline. One remaining source of pride is the Greek Orthodox Patriarchate. Set on the banks of the Golden Horn in the Istanbul district of Fener, it's still, by tradition at least, the spiritual centre of the entire Eastern Orthodox Christian world.

The Syrian Orthodox

Adherents of the **Syrian Orthodox** Church (Süriyani in Turkish), who form a distinct, if much reduced, ethno-religious group of their own, are found mostly in the Syrian borderlands of southeast Turkey. Their origins lie with Jacobus Baradaeus, appointed bishop of Edessa in AD 543. A native of Mesopotamia, he was locked in a century-old theological dispute with the patriarchate in Constantinople about the divine nature of Christ. The ecclesiastical Council of Chalcedon (451 AD) ruled that Christ had both a human and a divine nature, but dissenting bishops throughout the Middle East held that Christ had only a divine nature – a creed known as monophysitism, whose adherents risked condemnation as heretics and excommunication.

An energetic proselytizer throughout what is now the Hatay and Syria, Baradaeus helped to revive his church as it suffered determined attack by the agents of Constantinopolitan orthodoxy. Under Arab dominion in the seventh century, Syrian Orthodox Christians enjoyed considerable religious freedom. By the time of the First Crusade, at the end of the eleventh century, the Tür Abdin in particular encompassed four bishoprics and eighty monasteries, the ruins of which remain dotted across the plateau. Ironically, the Christian Crusaders persecuted the "heretical" Syrian Orthodox Church, while the Mongols later massacred its adherents and pillaged its properties.

The Syrian Orthodox community enjoyed a long period of tolerance and stability under Ottoman rule. During World War I, though, tainted by association with Allied plans to dismember the Ottoman Empire, they suffered widespread persecution and massacre, a fate they shared with the Armenian and Greek minorities. Of today's global population of seven million Syrian Christians, only a few thousand are now left in Turkey, served by the bishoprics of Tür Abdin (Midyat/Mar Gabriel), Mardin (Deyr-az-Zaferan), Adıyaman and Istanbul. Many have emigrated to Europe (notably Sweden) and North America, but the seat of the patriarchy is in Damascus.

The Jews

There have been **Jews** in Anatolia since the fifth century BC. By and large they were tolerated by the Greeks, the Romans and, later, the Christian Byzantine Empire. Following the capture of Constantinople by the Ottoman Turks in 1453, many Jews from elsewhere in the Ottoman Empire were compelled to move to, and help regenerate, the new Ottoman capital. The Ottomans were incredibly tolerant in comparison to standards then prevalent in Western Europe; during the late fifteenth century, they gave sanctuary to over 150,000 Jews escaping persecution in Spain, most of whom settled in Salonika and Constantinople.

Like other non-Muslim minority groups within the Empire, the Jews prospered in their own partly self-governing *millet* (nation). By the eighteenth and nineteenth centuries, however, their wealth decreased, as the Greeks especially made the most of their Christian links with the European powers. During the early period of the Turkish Republic, the Jews did reasonably well, while Atatürk gave sanctuary (and employment) to Jewish academics expelled from Nazi Germany in the 1930s. Like all non-Muslim minority groups, the Jews fell victim to the unfair Wealth Tax of 1942, and many left following the creation of the state of Israel in 1948. The recent rift between an AKP-led Turkey and Israel in the wake of the *Mavi Marmara* (Gaza Flotilla) incident, and Turkish support for the Palestinians, has already resulted in increased emigration of Turkish Jews to Israel. The population has dropped from 23,000 to 17,000, the vast majority of whom live in Istanbul.

Turkish cinema

Turkey has had a moderately successful film industry since the 1950s, when corny rural-boy-meets-rural-girl melodramas provided escapism for Anatolian villagers. The outside world took little notice until the 1970s, when a few maverick film-makers took Turkish cinema in a more radical direction.

1971–99: early successes

Although imprisoned for his leftist leanings several times during the 1970s and 1980s, popular actor-turned-director **Yılmaz Güney** produced a series of hard-hitting films in the years around the coups of 1971 and 1980. The best were *Sürü* ("The Herd"), which follows a Kurdish shepherd and his family taking their flock to sell in distant Ankara, and *Yol* ("The Road"). Written from the confines of his prison cell, with the outside directorial assistance of **Derif Gören**, *Yol* takes an allegorical look at the state of the nation (then still under martial law) by following the fortunes of five prisoners who have been allowed a week's parole. That the film was banned in Turkey only served to bring it to the notice of the international community, and in 1981 *Yol* was joint winner of the Palme d'Or. The film finally made it onto the country's cinema screens in 1999, when it played to packed houses. Güney died of cancer in 1984, aged 46, the year after the release of his last film, *Duvar* ("Wall"), an unrelentingly gloomy critique of the country's overcrowded and brutal prison system.

With the exception of 1983's visually stunning *Hakkâri'de Bir Mevsim* ("A Season in Hakkâri"), examining the experiences of a young teacher sent to staff the local school in a remote Kurdish village, Turkish films in the 1980s made little impact on the outside world. Despite a lack of financial backing, the 1990s proved kinder, and in 1994 **Erden Kıral**'s *Mavi Sürgün* ("The Blue Exile") was nominated for an Academy Award. In 1995, **Mustafa Altıoklar**'s *Istanbul Kanatlarımın Altında* ("Istanbul Beneath my Wings"), set in the seventeenth century during the reign of tyrant **Murat IV**, drew critical acclaim and was a box-office hit. **Hamam**, made in 1998 by **Ferzan Özpetek**,

---

BOX-OFFICE SUCCESS

As in every country, what the critics adore, the vast majority of the public ignore. Ceylan's arty **Uzak** attracted some 20,000 cinema-goers within Turkey, whereas 2008's **Recep İvedik**, director Şahan Gökbakar's tale of an uneducated burping, farting and spitting taxi driver let loose in a five-star hotel, grossed $24 million domestically. Equally successful was 2006's ultra-nationalistic **Kurtlar Vadisi – Irak** ("Valley of the Wolves – Iraq"), a huge box-office action-thriller hit, in which the Turks get their fictional revenge for the real-life arrest of some of their military boys by the Americans in northern Iraq in 2003. Both films have spawned equally popular formulaic sequels.

Production in Turkey has boomed in recent years, with more and more films hitting the country's big screens (invariably today in shopping malls), and Turkish cinema is by far the most profitable in the Muslim world. Home-produced films are proving extraordinarily popular, taking a 55 percent slice of the domestic market. All the top five films in 2011 were Turkish productions, including glossy thriller *New York'ta Beş Minare* ("Five Minarets in New York"), which co-starred several Hollywood actors. Budgets are growing ever bigger as well, culminating in 2012's *Fetih 1453*, a CGI-filled sword-and-turban blockbuster about the siege and conquest of Constantinople by the Ottoman Turks in 1453. Its $17 million budget was huge by Turkish standards, but by April 2012 it had already repaid the investors' faith by grossing over $34 domestically – making it the most watched Turkish movie ever.

CRITICAL ACCLAIM: THE FILMS OF NURİ BİLGİ CEYLAN

Despite graduating from university with a degree in electrical engineering, **Nuri Bilgi Ceylan** has become Turkey's most acclaimed film director. He first came to prominence with **Uzak** ("Distant") in 2002, a beautifully crafted, Istanbul-set film of urban alienation which won the Grand Prix at Cannes. In 2006, the critically admired but rather self-indulgent **İklimler** ("Climates") was released, an existentialist tale of a failing relationship starring Ceylan and his wife Ebru. The director returned to top form in 2008 with **Üç Maymun** ("Three Monkeys"). Telling a familiar story of how power corrupts, the film won the prestigious Best Director Award at Cannes. In it, a powerful politician involved in a hit-and-run incident escapes justice by sending his driver to prison in his place; he then begins an affair wtih the driver's wife. Ceylan cemented his reputation in 2011 with the epic **Bir Zamanlar Anadolu'da** ("Once Upon a Time in Anatolia"), a powerful thriller set on the austere Anatolian plateau. With nods to sources as diverse as Chekhov and Sergio Leone, the film was joint winner of the Grand Prix at Cannes. In 2014, Ceylan went one better with **Kış Uykusu** ("Winter Sleep"), scooping the coveted Palme d'Or for his atmospheric tale of an ex-actor turned hotelier in remote Central Anatolia. Signalling his disquiet about Turkey's increasingly authoritarian government, Ceylan dedicated his award to those who had died in the Gezi Park protests of 2013 (see p.673). Fittingly, he received the Palme d'Or on the one hundredth anniversary of Turkish cinema.

sees an Italian star inherit a run-down Turkish baths in Istanbul. Through his efforts to restore it, he discovers his own sexuality, making this one of the few Turkish films dealing with gay relationships to have gone on general release.

2000–2010: a worthy decade

The new millennium has seen Turkish cinema hit new heights. Leading the way is **Nuri Bilgi Ceylan** (see box above). **Fatih Akın**, a German-born and -bred Turk, had both Turkey and Germany claiming his 2004 Golden Bear winner, *Duvar Karsısı* ("Head On"), as their own. Personalities and cultures clash in this sometimes brutal tale of ill-matched Turkish–German lovers. Akın's 2005 documentary *Crossing the Bridge: The Sound of Istanbul*, made with **Alexander Hacke**, has won many recent plaudits, and makes an unparalleled introduction to this great city's music scene (see p.691). *Yaşamın Kıyısında* ("Edge of Heaven"), 2007, won the best screenplay award at Cannes, and five awards at Turkey's equivalent of the Oscars, Antalya's Golden Orange festival. Shot in Germany, Istanbul and the eastern Black Sea city of Trabzon, it traces the interconnecting lives of four Turks and two Germans, touching on issues of cultural estrangement, family relationships, lesbianism and political activism. *Aşkı Ruhunu Kat* ("Soul Kitchen"), a 2009 comedy-drama set in a Greek-run Hamburg taverna, was a deliberate move to "lighten up", but in 2012 Akın got back down to the serious stuff with a well-received documentary charting the struggles of a Black Sea town against a municipality land-fill site, *Cenneti Kirletmek* ("Polluting Paradise"). *Kesik* ("The Cut") released in 2014, was even more controversial, a historical drama set against the Armenian genocide of 1915. Akın had problems trying to find a Turkish actor who would play the part, eventually casting French-Algerian Tahir Rahmim as the hero Nazareth. Reviews, however, were mixed.

Other Turkish films to have achieved critical accolades during the first decade of the twenty-first century include **Reha Erdem**'s 2006 *Bed Vakıt* ("Times and Winds"), which portrays the often-grim reality of growing up in an idyllic-looking Turkish village. It makes moving use of both the village's breathtaking location, overlooking the Mediterranean from a cliff-edge eyrie, and the fresh-faced innocence of its child actors. *Yumurta* ("Egg"), 2007, the first part of a trilogy directed by **Semih Kaplanoulu**, won a fistful of awards at the Golden Orange. A typically Turkish tale, it traces the life of Yusuf, a struggling poet running a secondhand bookshop in Istanbul who returns to his home town when his mother dies. The second part of the trilogy, *Süt* ("Milk"), winds back the clock to Yusuf's youth in his hometown, where he struggles financially trying to balance the family's milk business with writing poetry. *Bal* ("Honey"), from 2010, the final part of the trilogy, won a Golden Bear at the Berlin International Film Festival and is set in the wild mountains of the eastern Black Sea. Based on a true story, 2008's *Gitmek* ("My Marlon, My Brando"), the first feature from respected documentary film-maker **Hüseyin Karabey**, is the gripping story of a Turkish woman's search for her Kurdish lover, trapped in northern Iraq following the American invasion of 2003. The emotionally candid theatre actress Ayça leaves a rather grim-looking Beyoğlu, crosses snowy Anatolia and enters Iran, hoping to meet her B-movie actor lover, Hamal Ali, on the Iran–Iraq border.

Recent releases: more critical accolades

Of recent acclaimed releases, *Iki Dil Bir Bavul* ("On the Way to School"), a heartwarming documentary about the trials and tribulations of a Turkish teacher from the affluent west trying to teach in a dirt-poor village school in the ethnically Kurdish southeast, won directors **Orhan Eskiköy** and **Özgür Doğan** the best first film award at Antalya's Golden Orange Film Festival. *Çoğunluk* ("Majority"), a 2011 offering from director **Seren Yüce**, showed a side of Istanbul that few visitors are likely (or indeed want) to see. Set in unremittingly dull concrete suburbs, it tells the grubby but all-too-believable tale of a middle-class Turk, still living at home in his late twenties, attempting to subvert the brutal authority of his manipulative father by getting involved with the most "unsuitable" of women, an impoverished Kurdish waitress.

Zenne ("Zenne Dancer"), 2011, directed by Caner Alpay, won a host of domestic and international awards for its gripping tale of the murder of a male belly dancer – all the more powerful for being based on true events. The same year's *Yürüyüş* ("Walking") by **Shiar Abdi** and **Selamo**, set in the dusty, ethnically Kurdish Syrian border town of Nusaybin during the lead-up to the 1980 military coup, vividly evokes – through the eyes of a disturbed old man and a young boy – the horrors of the period.

Yozgat Blues, directed by **Mahmut Fazıl Coşkun** and released in 2013, won acclaim for a universal tale of an urbanite (in this case a musician) forced to leave the bright lights of the big city and spend some time in a remote area – in this film the drab Anatolian town of Yozgat.

Turkish music

Overseas, Turkish music was long considered mere accompaniment to belly dancing or, more recently, to Mevlevî ("Whirling") dervish ritual. But beyond these stereotypes there's far more, from refined classical to camp *Arabesk* by way of rural bards and fiery Gypsy ensembles. Turkish music is at best the millennial legacy of the many Anatolian civilizations, at worst globally marketed pop music with a bit of exotic colour. Thankfully, it has managed to maintain both its creativity and popularity – even with the younger generation – though this has not prevented the rise of a lively, Western-influenced rock, pop and even hip-hop scene.

Traditional Turkish music

Traditional sounds have more than held their own in this fast-changing country. Channel-surf Turkish TV any evening, and you're bound to hit upon a show or two devoted to native Turkish music, with a moustached bard coaxing melancholic Anatolian folk songs from his *saz* or *bağlama* (types of lute), or an orchestra of tuxedo-ed men and sombrely clad women solemnly accompanying a warbling *sanatçi* (singer of Turkish classical music). *Arabesk*, an Arab/Egyptian-influenced style of music invariably charting the singers' wretched lot in life, remains extremely popular, especially among the poor and dispossessed. Its most famous proponent, **İbrahim Tatlıses**, is a national institution, and until a drive-by shooting in Istanbul in 2010 left him paralyzed, hosted his own enormously popular TV show. *Türkü* bars (see p.127) are devoted to the various lovelorn strands of **halk muziği** – best translated as people's or folk music – and are very popular with the younger generation. The main instruments used by *halk muziği* performers are the *saz* and the *bağlama*. The very best performers are virtuosos – among them Arif Sağ and Musa Eroğlu. Female artists İlkay Akkay and Belkis Akkale possess quite beautiful voices.

Played mainly by Roma (Gypsy) bands, **fasil**, a curious but lively hybrid of Ottoman classical and folk, with violins, clarinets, *darbuka* drums and powerful, emotive vocals to the fore, is the genre of Istanbul's vibrant **meyhane** scene (see p.127). The hypnotic, spiritual strains of **Sufi** music, most often associated with the Mevlevî or "Whirling" Dervish order, and popular among world music aficionados, is very much a minority interest in its home country, though it can be heard in various places across the country wherever the dervishes "whirl" for visitors – for example at the Mevlevihanesi in Istanbul's Galata district (see p.100), in Konya (see p.420), or in Cappadocia (see p.428).

Turkish classical or **sanat** music is the most inaccessible home-grown style to foreign ears – and, despite the undoubted virtuosity of its leading musicians, the least popular domestically. Originating in the Ottoman court, this subtle, partly improvisational but often gloomy-sounding music is performed by chamber orchestras using a combination of traditional Turkish wind and string instruments backed by drums.

Many popular singers in Turkey are of Kurdish origin, though they usually perform in Turkish. Now that restrictions on singing (and speaking) Kurdish have been lifted, it's easy to obtain CDs by Kurdish artists singing in their native tongue. The doyen of Kurdish performers is **Şivan Perwer**, who chronicles the plight of his people with his powerful voice and stunning *saz* playing. Some of his CDs are still banned in Turkey because of their politics, and he lives in exile in Sweden. Other well-regarded Kurdish artists include Aynur Doğan, Ciwan Haco and Rojin.

SELECTED DISCOGRAPHY

ARABESK

İbrahim Tatlıses *Fosforlu Cevriyem* (Emre). This live recording offers a rare chance to hear what *Arabesk* sounds like in the flesh, and gives a sense of Tatlıses' phenomenal vocal presence. Includes some of his all-time favourites, plus superb *uzun hava* semi-improvisations.

FASIL

Karşılama *Karşılama* (Green Goat, Canada/Kalan). Istanbul Gypsy musicians led by Selim Sesler on G-clarinet, with locally trained Canadian vocalist Brenna MacCrimmon, interpret Roma music from western Turkey and the Balkans. Played with real panache, and it's good to have some of the vocal repertoire – gleaned from archival recordings and manuscripts – expertly showcased.

FOLK

Belkis Akkale *Türkü Türkü Türkiyem* (Sembol Plak). One of the greatest female *Türkü* singers at her earthiest, carried along by driving *saz* rhythms – plus almost all of the traditional instruments of Turkey.

KURDISH

Şivan Perwer *Zembilfroş* (Ses Plak). One of Perwer's most varied albums, partly because he is accompanied by his wife Gülistan. The vocals by the talented pair are outstanding, soaring above Perwer's insistent *saz* playing and some lush orchestration.

SUFI

Mevlâna *Dede Efendi Saba Ayini* (Kalan). A benchmark recording of a complete Mevlevî suite (*ayin*) composed by Dede Efendi. The performers read like a who's-who of early twentieth-century Turkish *sanat*, with Mesut Cemil on cello, Akagündüz Kutbay, Ulvi Erguner and Niyazi Sayın on the wind instrument known as a *ney*, Cüneyt Orhan on *kemençe* (a kind of violin) and Saadettin Heper on *küdüm* (kettle drum).

SANAT

Mesut Cemil *Early Recordings (Vol 1)* and *Instrumental and Vocal recordings (Vols 2–3)* (Golden Horn Records/US). Virtuoso musicianship and compositions from the man who ran the classical music section of TRT-Istanbul for decades.

Music documentaries

Nezih Ezen's 2008 documentary, **Lost Songs of Anatolia** (ⓦlostsongsofanatolia.com), provides the best introduction to a whole range of traditional Turkish music. A talented musician himself, Ezen's unsentimental but sensitive film was a labour of love some five years in the making. Travelling across Turkey's vast landscape, recording and filming in obscure towns and remote villages, he vividly captures the musical heritage of modern Turkey, deeply rooted in the many ethnic and cultural identities that make up the nation.

In the rain-soaked mountains of the eastern Black Sea, Laz (a Caucasian people who speak a language related to Georgian) dance the *horon* (a line dance) to the sound of the *kemençe* (upright fiddle) and *tulum* (bagpipe), while in the mountains of Bingöl a *dengbey* (Kurdish bard) uses only his voice to chart the history of his people. In an Istanbul apartment, a couple of elderly Armenian ladies sing a moving lament to an Anatolia long lost to them, while in the same city an ethnically Greek ensemble play a "Greek blues" *rebétika* number. A couple of rake-thin elderly bards in a smoky teahouse in the Armenian border town of Kars play the *saz* and battle out an instrument- and lyric-based duel; in the cotton fields of the Çukurova near Adana a group of young women from Diyarbakır, poorly paid seasonal workers, find solace from their back-breaking labour in song. The DVD is reasonably easy to obtain in Turkey but you will have to rely on the power of the songs and fabulous scenery, as there are no English subtitles.

Although much of Fatih Akın's documentary **Crossing the Bridge** concentrates on contemporary music in Istanbul, there is plenty to keep traditional music buffs happy. It features the superb vocals and even better *saz* playing of Orhan Gençbay, a legend rivalled only by İbrahim Tatlıses in *Arabesk* music, and the heart-rending voice of the young Kurdish singer Aynur Doğan. The haunting sounds of Mercan Dede, a fusion of Sufi and modern electronica and big on the world music scene, get an airing, as do the Balkan sounds of Selim Sesler, playing with an unlikely (but very talented) singer of traditional Turkish songs, Canadian Brenna MacCrimmon. Difficult to buy for a sensible price in the UK, it's far cheaper in the US. The DVD is also widely available in Istanbul, but you'll struggle to find a copy with English subtitles.

Contemporary music

Pop has a surprisingly long history in Turkey, from the Tango stars of the 1930s through to Elvis imitators in the 1950s. Not until the 1970s, though, did **rock** really take root, with the rise of the Anadolu (Anatolian) rock movement. Chief proponents of the style included long-haired, Kaftan-sporting Barış Manço, who went on to become a popular TV entertainer and even now retains a cult following among Turkish youth, and the formidable Cem Karaca, born in Istanbul of Armenian-Azerbaijani parents. Other notable stars were Erkin Koray and Moğallar, the latter still going strong today. Western-style contemporary music now forms part and parcel of the diverse Turkish music scene, especially in cosmopolitan Istanbul. The vast majority of these bands and singers perform in Turkish, which undermines their chances of achieving international success. But the best of them are worth a listen – and if you venture out into the city's labyrinthine **nightlife** scene you are bound, at some point, to have your ears assailed by familiar pop or hip-hop beats, accompanied by unfamiliar Turkish vocals.

Rock

Duman are among the most accessible of the current crop of rock bands. Erroneously labelled punk in their early days (itself indicative of the relatively conservative nature of the scene here), the Istanbul-based group are in fact a straightforward rock band, mixing up-tempo anthems with lighter-waving ballads and traditional Turkish folk songs. *Bu akşam* ("This evening") and *Belki alışmam lazım* ("Maybe I'd better get used to it") are great songs by any standards.

Pinhani shot to fame when some of their songs were used in the popular TV soap *Kavak Yelleri* ("Young and Carefree"), but don't let this put you off. Despite the number of disparate influences in their music – everything from Radiohead and the late, great Alevi troubadour Aşık Veysel to Greek *bouzouki* and Bach – their album *İnandığım Masallar* ("Fairy tales you can believe in") is a wonderfully laidback, melodic and cohesive debut. Both bands have written paeans to their hometown, Duman's *Istanbul* an angry, punky thrash, while Pinhani's *In Istanbul* drips with urban melancholia.

Fellow "Stamboul" boys **Mor ve Ötesi** formed in 1995 and have built up a huge following in Turkey – in 2003 the indie four-piece played in front of 100,000 anti-Iraq war demonstrators in Ankara. Surprisingly, given their reputation for protest, they were chosen to represent Turkey in the 2008 **Eurovision Song Contest**, with *Deli* ("Crazy") coming in seventh. Bear in mind that in Turkey the Eurovision Song Contest is not seen as the laughably kitsch endeavour it is across much of Europe – in this most patriotic of nations it's taken very seriously indeed.

Sertab Erener, the Istanbul-born belly-dancing diva who won the contest for Turkey in 2003 was, like Mor ve Ötesi, already a major star before the competition. She has recorded an album in English, and appeared in **Fatih Akın's** *Crossing the Bridge* documentary singing an orientalized version of Madonna's *Music*.

Another couple of bands who feature in Akın's *Crossing the Bridge* are **Baba Zula** and **Replikas**. Prog-rockers Replikas take extended, experimental soloing to extremes but are talented musicians with a loyal following. Baba Zula may be wacky, but their self-styled "oriental-dub" or "psyche-belly" is mesmeric live, and with their 1960s hippy-throwback looks (big beards, long straggly hair, cowboy hats), and very un-PC belly dancer, they are entertaining performers. Balkan and gypsy music has gained popularity in parts of Turkey, and Istanbul band **Luxus** incorporate these traditional sounds into their more rocky repertoire.

Far more popular is **Şebnem Ferah**. Born in Yalova, near Bursa, she is of Balkan (Macedonian) ancestry. Her goth-metal looks, powerful voice and the helping hand of that doyenne of the Turkish music scene, **Sezen Aksu** (see below), have helped secure her fame – though her brand of soft rock and power ballads will not be to everyone's taste. **Hayko Çepkin**, of Armenian origin, mixes Anatolian rock with scream metal and a lively stage act. Long-established punks **Rashit** have played with the likes of Dead Kennedys and The Offspring; their 2005 album *Herşeyin Bir Bedeli Var* was released on Sony.

Hip-hop

The roots of the **rap** scene in Turkey lie among the Turkish community in Germany. Invariably urban, often poor, disenfranchised and discriminated against, hip-hop provided a natural outlet for their anger and frustration. The movement was kick-started by the suitably controversial **Cartel** in the mid-1990s. Their debut album was banned in Turkey and the group split soon after. The scene in Istanbul really got going with another star of *Crossing the Bridge* (see p.691), the city's very own Eminem – **Ceza**. Worshipped by multitudes of the city's disaffected youth, he was born on the Asian side of the Bosphorus in Üsküdar, taking his stage name (*ceza* means punishment) from one of his early jobs – handing out fines to people who failed to pay their electricity bills. Ceza's success has bred envy, and in 2007 he was accused of lifting his beats straight from Eminem by rival Istanbul rapper **Ege Çubukçu**. Other names to look out for are **Sagopa Kajmer** and Ceza's sister, **Ayben**. Turkish vocals apart, what marks this home-grown hip-hop out from its US inspiration is the sampling of *Arabesk* and other forms of traditional Turkish music rather than Western pop.

Pop

Pop music is huge in Turkey. It's also incredibly varied – though you might not think so on a first listen. Once a teen idol, now a housewives' favourite, **Tarkan** swivels his hips and belts out dance-oriented pop with apparent abandon. A big star in Germany as well as Turkey, he has produced one album in English.

Pop rockers/balladeers **Mustafa Sandal** and **Teoman** are firm fixtures on the TV music channels, as is the chanteuse **Yıldız Tilbe**. The multi-talented queen of the Turkish pop scene, **Sezen Aksu**, has helped to preserve and build upon the best of traditional Turkish urban music, both through skilfully updated covers of old songs and with new material incorporating their best elements. Nor is she afraid of controversy, tackling feminism, human rights and ethnic cleansing in Bosnia, and singing in Ladino (the language of Turkey's Jewish population) and Kurdish as well as her native Turkish. Her albums vary enormously in style, but 1995's *Işık Doğudan Yükselir* ("The Light Rises from the East") makes a good starting point. Another queen of the scene is the incredibly well-preserved, Istanbul-schooled **Ajda Pekkan**. Born in 1946 and still touring, she has sold some thirty million albums worldwide and is a national icon.

Books

There are numerous books about every aspect of Turkey in English, many recently published or reissued. Books with Turkish publishers are rarely available outside Turkey. In the recommendations below, "o/p" means out of print, but almost all such books can be easily found through websites such as ⓦabe.com/.co.uk or ⓦbookfinder.com.

Turkish writers

Given that Atatürk's language and alphabet reforms in the early years of the Turkish Republic effectively cut off the vast majority of its citizens from the language of their Ottoman imperial past – and therefore of its literature – it's hardly surprising that it took some time for new generations of Turkish writers to establish themselves in what was a very different world.

Equally, relatively few Turkish writers have had their works translated into other languages, and today the works of only two novelists are widely available in English, Orhan Pamuk and Elif Shafak. A limited number of books by two earlier writers of note, Orhan Kemal and Yaşar Kemal, are available in English, and several Turkish publishing houses produce English-language versions of novels by Turkish authors that are generally only easily available within the country.

Orhan Kemal

Born in the then-Ottoman Turkish city of Adana in 1914, **Orhan Kemal** is sometimes viewed as a Turkish Dickens. His simply told tales, many based around his own experiences, invariably deal with the lot of the poor, the dispossessed and political dissidents. His family were affluent until his father's political opinions put him at odds with the ruling Kemalist regime, and they were forced to flee the country. An impoverished Kemal eventually returned to his beloved Turkey, where he started at the bottom of the ladder as a weaver in a cotton factory, then as a clerk. His imprisonment in 1938 for his leftist beliefs was the turning point in his life, as there he met the famous communist poet Nazim Hikmet, who encouraged his literary aspirations. Kemal struggled to make ends meet for the rest of his life, combining relatively menial office work with his writing, leaving a legacy of 38 touching stories before he died, in Sofia, in 1970.

The best introduction to Orhan Kemal's work is **The Idle Years**, which in the English version combines two semi-autobiographical tales, **My Father's House** and **The Idle Years**. The two stories recount, in deceptively simple prose, the story of the author's life from his youth in Adana, through his family's Beirut exile, to his marriage to a factory girl in Adana. Also worth reading is his account of his years of incarceration, **In Jail With Nazim Hikmet**.

Yaşar Kemal

Until the advent of Orhan Pamuk and Elif Shafak, **Yaşar Kemal** was by far Turkey's best-known novelist, in part thanks to English translations by his wife Thilda of seventeen of his titles. Indeed, so widely known was Kemal that one of his early works, **Mehmed My Hawk**, was turned into a film (1984) of the same name starring Peter Ustinov.

Although of Kurdish origins, Kemal was born (in 1923) and raised close to the cotton-growing Çukurova plain, in the shadow of the Toros Mountains, in southern Turkey. Here he witnessed first-hand the exploitation of the rural peasantry by wealthy landowners. Championing the oppressed has been a *leitmotif* of Kemal's works ever since, despite the fact that he himself escaped his family's rural origins and, following a stint at university in Istanbul, became a petition writer, journalist and, finally, author. Although he was nominated for the Nobel Prize in Literature in 1973, his nonconformist views nonetheless brought him into conflict with the state, and in 1995 he was prosecuted for his support for Turkey's Kurdish minority following an interview he gave to *Der Spiegel*.

Kemal's older books are powerful epics set in southern Anatolia and include the moving *Mehmed My Hawk* and its sequel **They Burn the Thistles** (o/p). The **Wind from the Plain** trilogy deals with similar themes and is equally hard-hitting. Later novels include **The Sea-Crossed Fishermen** (o/p), contrasting an old man's struggle to save the dolphins in the Sea of Marmara with the fortunes of a desperate hoodlum in the city, and **The Birds Have Also Gone** (o/p), a symbolic, gentle story about bird-catchers. In the more recent **Salman the Solitary**, Kemal returns to his native Çukurova with a tale of a displaced Kurdish family.

Orhan Pamuk

Most Turks just don't know what to make of their nation's first Nobel Prize-winning novelist, **Orhan Pamuk**, who was born into a wealthy family in the posh Istanbul suburb of Nişantaşı. To the liberal left, he's a talented writer who dares to challenge the Kemalist, nationalist-orientated establishment – who in turn accuse him of betraying his country. Moderates are happy to bask in the success of one of their nation's sons without questioning his beliefs too closely; many others are quick to condemn him while studiously avoiding reading any of his output.

The controversy surrounding Pamuk began in 2004, when the previously cautious novelist granted an interview to a Swiss newspaper and was reported as saying "I am the only one willing to say that one million Armenians and thirty thousand Kurds were murdered in Turkey". He was accused of "insulting Turkishness", a crime under article 301 of the Turkish Constitution. Although the accusation was subsequently dropped, in 2008 it emerged that Pamuk may have been the assassination target of an ultra-nationalist "deep state" gang working within the establishment. As a result, he now spends most of his time abroad.

What's surprising is that such a storm has broken over the head of this benign-looking, fifty-something intellectual. An urbane, cerebral author, his early works dealt with cultural and philosophical rather than political issues, and not until 2004's *Snow* did he engage in any kind of political discourse. Many Turkish cynics, however, believe that by bringing up two of the nation's "sacred cows" – the so-called Armenian genocide and the "Kurdish problem" – he was deliberately courting what they saw as the anti-Turkish West in the hope of winning the Nobel Prize. Such machinations are unlikely, although his open rejection of nationalism in a country still in nation-building mode makes him an object of suspicion.

Pamuk's enduring concerns are Turkey's often-corrosive encounter with the West, and the irrepressibility of its Islamic heritage. His debut, **The White Castle**, was an excellent historical meditation about a seventeenth-century Italian scholar enslaved by an Ottoman astronomer, but he arrived on the world literature scene with 1998's **The New Life**, which despite its unappealing narrator and slight tale had foreign critics hailing the heir apparent of Calvino and Borges. **Snow**, Pamuk's most controversial and political novel, is arguably his best. Set in bleak, northeastern Kars, it examines once-taboo topics such as political Islam and Kurdish nationalism. His mammoth **The Museum of Innocence**, published in 2008, is a fictional memoir of *amour fou* set in late 1970s Istanbul. **A Strangeness in My Mind**, published 2015, follows the love life and adventures of an Istanbul street vendor through the momentous years between 1969 and 2012. **Istanbul: Memories of a City** is a moving reflection on the author's troubled relationship with himself, his parents, and the city in which he was born and raised. For more information see Pamuk's own website, ⓦorhanpamuk.net.

Elif Shafak

Born of Turkish parents in Strasbourg in 1971, brought up from the age of one by her single mother, raised in Spain and Jordan and now, following several years in the USA, residing in London, **Elif Shafak** (⊚elifshafak.com) is very much a product of the new, fast-changing, more international Turkey. Several of her books have been bestsellers domestically, challenging the traditional male domination of Turkey's literary scene – all this from a woman who is a political science rather than a literature graduate, and who writes in English first, then has the work translated into Turkish before re-working it. The photogenic Shafak found herself, like Pamuk, a target of establishment ire for her 2007 *The Bastard of Istanbul*, and was prosecuted under article 301 for "insulting Turkishness", though the charges were eventually dropped.

The Flea Palace interweaves tragic-comic lives in a once-grand Istanbul apartment block built atop an old cemetery. **The Bastard of Istanbul** tells the tale of an exuberant, if dysfunctional, Turkish family hosting an Armenian-American girl in search of her identity. Well-drawn, strong female characters drive a narrative that inevitably delves into Ottoman Turkey's treatment of its Armenians. Shafak's critically acclaimed 2011 follow-up, **The Forty Rules of Love**, centres less controversially on a woman's search for spiritual awareness through the teachings of the thirteenth-century Islamic mysticism of the Mevlâna (Rumi) – a subject dear to the Sufi-influenced author's heart. Even better is **Honour** (2012), set in southeast Turkey, Istanbul and London, which brings to life a very real socio-cultural problem in contemporary Turkey – so-called "honour killings", the murder by a male family member of a woman deemed to have brought shame on the family. Quite different but equally engaging is **The Architect's Apprentice** (2014), a fantastical portrait of sixteenth-century Istanbul as seen through the eyes of an Indian boy apprenticed to the greatest Ottoman architect, Sinan.

THE CLASSICS

Herodotus *The Histories.* A fifth-century BC citizen of Halikarnassos (Bodrum), Herodotus – the first systematic historian/anthropologist – described the Persian Wars and assorted nations of Anatolia.

Strabo *Geography.* A native of the Pontus, Strabo travelled widely across the Mediterranean; our best (multi-volume) document of Roman Anatolia.

Xenophon *Anabasis*, or *The March Up-Country* (best as the abridged *The Persian Expedition*). The Athenian leader of the Ten Thousand, mercenaries for Persian king Cyrus the Younger, led the long retreat from Cunaxa to the Black Sea. An ancient travel classic that's still mined for titbits of ethnology, archeology and geography.

ANCIENT HISTORY AND ARCHEOLOGY

Ian Hodder *Çatalhöyük: The Leopard's Tale.* Neolithic Çatal Höyük is one of the world's earliest cities, and thus crucial to the origins of Western civilization. This reasonably accessible book, written by the principal excavator, brings it to life.

Seton Lloyd *Ancient Turkey – A Traveller's History of Anatolia.* Accessibly written by a former head of Ankara's British Archeological Institute, without sacrificing detail and research results (o/p).

J.G. Macqueen *The Hittites and Their Contemporaries in Asia Minor.* Well-illustrated general history of the first great Anatolian civilization (c.1800–1200 BC).

Antonio Sagona *The Heritage of Eastern Turkey.* Copiously illustrated guide to the archeology and history of neglected

eastern Turkey, covering everything from the Neolithic to the Selçuk periods.

Antonio Sagona and Paul Zimansky *Ancient Turkey.* Comprehensive coverage of the archeology of Turkey, from early prehistory up to the Classical era. A textbook, but a worthy and very readable one.

David Traill *Schliemann of Troy: Treasure and Deceit* (o/p). The man versus his self-promulgated myth. This portrayal of the crumbling edifice of Schliemann's reputation also helps bring the old walls of Troy to life.

Michael Wood *In Search of the Trojan War.* A very readable examination of the reality behind the legend that is Troy by one of Britain's best-known populist archeologists.

BYZANTINE HISTORY

★**Roger Crowley** *Constantinople.* Former Istanbul resident Crowley's 2005 account of the 1453 siege is more detailed than Runciman's (see p.696), but it's hugely

engaging and the pace never flags.

Jonathan Harris *Constantinople: Capital of Byzantium.* Although this very accessible book concentrates on

Constantinople circa 1200, its scope is inevitably much wider, making it a great introduction to the Byzantine city for the uninitiated.

Cyril Mango *Byzantium: The Empire of the New Rome*. Survey of daily life, economic policy and taxation, scholarship, cosmology and superstition, among other topics. The newer, more lavishly illustrated *Oxford History of Byzantium*, edited by Mango, will also appeal.

★**John Julius Norwich** *Byzantium: The Early Centuries*, *Byzantium: The Apogee* and *Byzantium: The Decline*. Astonishingly detailed trilogy, a well-informed and wittily readable account (there's a single-volume abridgement, *A Short History of Byzantium*).

Procopius *The Secret History*. Often raunchy demolition job of Justinian and his sluttish empress, Theodora, from the imperial general Belisarius's official chronicler. Belisarius, one of the greatest Byzantine generals, is (like Justinian) portrayed as spinelessly uxorious.

★**Steven Runciman** *Byzantine Style and Civilisation* (o/p). Eleven centuries of Byzantine art, culture and monuments in one small paperback; still unsurpassed. His *The Fall of Constantinople, 1453* is a classic account of the event, while *The Great Church in Captivity*, about Orthodoxy under the Ottomans, is readable if partisan.

Speros Vryonis *The Decline of Medieval Hellenism in Asia Minor and the Process of Islamization from the Eleventh through the Fifteenth Century*. The definitive study of how the Byzantine Empire culturally became the Ottoman Empire.

OTTOMAN HISTORY

★**Caroline Finkel** *Osman's Dream*. Meticulously researched yet engaging history of the Ottoman Empire, from twelfth-century origins to collapse.

Halil İnalcık *The Ottoman Empire 1300–1600*. Ever since it appeared in 1973, this has been the standard work.

Patrick Balfour Kinross *The Ottoman Centuries*. Comprehensive, balanced summary of Ottoman history from the fourteenth to the twentieth century.

Metin Kunt and Christine Woodhead *Süleyman the Magnificent and His Age*. Concise summary of the greatest Ottoman sultan's reign and its cultural renaissance.

★**Philip Mansel** *Constantinople: City of the World's Desire, 1453–1924*. Nostalgic, faintly anti-Republican popular history, organized topically as well as chronologically. The highlights of his *Sultans in Splendour – Monarchs of the Middle East, 1869–1945* are rare photos of characters from the late Ottoman Empire.

MODERN HISTORIES

Feroz Ahmad *The Making of Modern Turkey*. Not the most orthodox history: lively, partisan and full of wonderful anecdotes and quotes you'll find nowhere else. His more recent *Turkey: The Quest for Identity* updates matters to 2003.

Marjorie Housepian Dobkin *Smyrna 1922: The Destruction of a City*. This partisan (ie rabidly anti-Turkish) but scholarly and harrowingly graphic account of the sack of İzmir focuses on why the Allied powers failed to act and subsequently covered up the incident.

Michael Hickey *Gallipoli: A Study in Failure*. One of the best historical accounts of the campaign.

★**Peter Hart** *Gallipoli*. This scholarly yet eminently readable account of the conflict is particularly vivid as it includes a copious number of previously unpublished accounts of combatants from Australia, New Zealand, Britain, France and Turkey.

★**Charles King** *Midnight at the Pera Palace*. Lively and entertaining social and cultural history of Istanbul between the wars, a period when the city was busy finding a new place for itself in the world.

Sean McMeekin *The Berlin–Baghdad Express*. In this riveting cautionary tale, McMeekin shows how German attempts to expand their influence into Turkey and the Middle East, by building a railway and raising Islamic Jihad among the British Empire's Muslim subjects, have had far-reaching consequences.

★**Giles Milton** *Paradise Lost: Smyrna 1922*. Wonderful, if ultimately heartbreaking, picture of Smyrna (İzmir) at the time of its destruction, towards the end of the Turkish War of Independence.

★**Barry Rubin** *Istanbul Intrigues: A True-Life Casablanca* (o/p). Unputdownable account of Allied/Axis activities in neutral Turkey during World War II, and their attempts to drag it into the conflict. Surprising revelations about the extent of Turkish aid for Britain, the US and the Greek resistance.

Richard Stoneman *A Traveller's History of Turkey*. Easy-reading volume, updated to 2009, which touches all bases from Paleolithic times to the AKP government.

Speros Vryonis *The Mechanism of Catastrophe*. Definitive study of the state-condoned and orchestrated anti-Greek riots of 1955, which left Istanbul's İstiklal Caddesi and Greek properties across the city in ruins, and marked the start of the end for the city's Greek community.

★**Erik J. Zürcher** *Turkey, A Modern History*. If you have time for only one book covering the post-1800 period, make it this one (revised up to 2004), which breathes revisionist fresh air over the received truths of the era.

BIOGRAPHIES

İpek Çalışlar *Madame Atatürk: The First Lady of Modern Turkey.* This brave book was condemned by many in Turkey for portraying the realities of life for a remarkably modern woman who was married, for a short time, to the founder of the Turkish Republic.

Saime Göksu and Edward Timms *Romantic Communist: The Life and Work of Nazım Hikmet.* The definitive biography of Turkey's most controversial modern poet, who rubbed shoulders with Pablo Neruda, Jean-Paul Sartre and Paul Robeson. Banned and imprisoned for seventeen years at home, Hikmet spent much of his life in exile, dying in 1963 in Moscow.

Thea Halo *Not Even My Name.* Remarkable, moving story of a Pontic-Greek girl, caught up in the 1920s ethnic cleansing, who managed to escape to America. Aged 79 she returns, in the company of her daughter, the author, to her birthplace in the Black Sea mountains.

M. Şükrü Hanioğlu *Atatürk, an intellectual biography.* Intelligently written account focusing on the ideological development of Turkey's founder. If you want to know why modern Turkey is full of such paradoxes, you'll find out by reading this masterful book by a Princeton professor.

Patrick Balfour Kinross *Atatürk, the Rebirth of a Nation.* Long considered the definitive English biography – as opposed to hagiography – of the father of the Republic, and still preferred by some to the newer Mango text (see below).

Andrew Mango *Atatürk.* Does not supersede Kinross's more readable tome, but complements it. Authoritative, but also steeped in military and conspiratorial minutiae. Sympathetic to its subject, and the Turkish national project overall; the post-1922 population exchanges and the Armenian episodes rate hardly a mention.

ETHNIC MINORITIES AND RELIGION

★**Taner Akçam** *From Empire to Republic: Turkish Nationalism and the Armenian Genocide.* Brilliant study by a Turkish academic resident in the US, which shows how the ethnic cleansing of the Armenian population from 1895 to 1923, and subsequent suppression of any memory of these events, was essential for Turkish nationalism – and remains at the root of the Republic's modern problems. His more recent *A Shameful Act: The Armenian Genocide and the Question of Turkish Responsibility*, focuses more closely on how CUP nationalist ideology bred the massacres.

Peter Balakian *The Burning Tigris: the Armenian Genocide and America's Response.* As partisan as you'd expect from an Armenian-American, but nonetheless a compelling analysis of the background to, and execution of, the massacres. Strong evidence from American and European missionaries in the region; harrowing photographs.

Christopher de Bellaigue *From a Rebel Land.* The remote town of Varto in eastern Turkey sees few visitors. The brave Bellaigue spent a whole year there, exploring the often hidden relationships between the Turkish state, the area's Kurdish inhabitants and its long-gone Armenian populace.

Donald Bloxham *The Great Game of Genocide.* This scholarly and coherent historical enquiry doesn't question whether there was a genocide, but rather concentrates on explaining – in the most dispassionate way – why and how it happened.

★**Bruce Clark** *Twice a Stranger: How Mass Expulsion Forged Modern Greece and Turkey.* The build-up to and execution of the 1923 population exchanges, and how both countries are still digesting the experience nine decades on. Readable and compassionate, especially encounters with surviving elderly refugees.

William Dalrymple *From the Holy Mountain: A Journey in the Shadow of Byzantium.* Retraces a classic sixth-century monkish journey through the Near East. Section II is devoted to Turkey, and Dalrymple takes a suitably dim view of the sorry history and current poor treatment of Christians and their monuments in eastern Turkey.

John Freely *The Lost Messiah: In Search of the Mystical Rabbi Sabbatai Sevi.* Story of the millennial, Kabbalistic, seventeenth-century movement in İzmir and Salonica that engendered the Dönme, a crypto-Judaic sect disproportionately prominent in modern Turkish history.

F.W. Hasluck *Christianity and Islam under the Sultans.* Ample documentation of shrines and festivals, their veneration and attendance by different sects at the turn of the last century, plus Christian and pagan contributions to Bektaşi and Alevi rites. Great for dipping into, though a bit repetitive since edited posthumously.

Aliza Marcus *Blood and Belief: The PKK and the Kurdish Fight for Independence.* Definitive, if controversial, study on the organization; neither the Turkish state nor the PKK (especially its leader, Abdullah Öcalan) get an easy ride.

★**David McDowall** *A Modern History of the Kurds.* About a third of this book is devoted to Turkey's Kurds, the balance to those in Iran and Iraq – few states get high marks here for their treatment of Kurds, up to 2003.

Gordon Taylor *Fever and Thirst: An American Doctor Amongst the Tribes of Kurdistan 1835–1844.* The war-torn but stunningly beautiful mountains of Hakkari in southeast Turkey were once home to a remote Christian group who caught the imagination of the West. This account of an American doctor-cum-missionary working among the Nestorians is compelling reading.

VIEWS OF CONTEMPORARY TURKEY

★**Andrew Finkel** *Turkey: What Everyone Needs To Know*. Admirably succinct, well-written guide to the country, by long-term Istanbul resident and journalist Finkel. It covers everything from the role and significance of Islam in society to Turkey's position in the world – and much else besides. It's exactly what the title claims.

Tim Kelsey *Dervish: The Invention of Modern Turkey*. The troubled soul of the 1990s country, sought among minority communities, faith healers, bulging prisons, brothels and the transsexual underground, plus the mystics of the title; pitiless analysis of Turkish angst, with little optimism for the future.

Stephen Kinzer *Crescent and Star: Turkey Between Two Worlds*. Entertaining account from a former *New York Times* bureau chief in Istanbul. Whether rakı-drinking or nargile-toking with ordinary Turks, interviewing politicos, swimming across the Bosphorus or DJ-ing his own Turkish radio show, Kinzer brings the country to life.

★**Nicole and Hugh Pope** *Turkey Unveiled*. Interlinked essays, arranged topically and chronologically, by two foreign correspondents who over two decades got to understand Turkey pretty well. Good grasp of Kurdish- and Europe-related issues. Despite their affection for the country, unflinching description of its shortcomings. Updated in 2011.

Fred Reed *Ionia – Anatolia Junction*. A maze-like meander through modern Turkey by journalist Reed. Particularly enlightening on Sait Nursi, a religious figure who challenged Atatürk and his reforms and whose followers, the Nurcu, are so controversial in today's Turkey.

★**Alev Scott** *Turkish Awakening*. Scott uses her youth (under 30 when she wrote the book), gender and Anglo-Turkish origins to give a different perspective on contemporary Turkey, especially the city where she lives and works, Istanbul. At times overly chatty, anecdotal and starry-eyed about Turkey (she describes the state-sanctioned violence against Istanbul's substantial Greek minority in 1955 as "race riots" rather than the pogroms that they were), it's a great introduction to both city and nation.

★**Witold Szablowski** *The Assassin from Apricot City*. Although the title true-life tale of this gripping selection of reportage deals with the Turk who almost killed the Pope, other sections slice revealingly through the underbelly of modern Istanbul – from prostitution to "honour killings", the Turkish male's sexual psyche to the Gezi Park protests.

TRAVEL AND IMPRESSIONS

★**John Ash** *A Byzantine Journey*. Historically inclined reflections of a poet taking in all the major, and some minor, Byzantine sites in Anatolia; a lot better than it sounds.

Anastasia Ashman and Jennifer Eaton Gökmen *Tales from the Expat Harem: Foreign Women in Modern Turkey*. Collected short memoirs of female experiences; light but insightful.

Frederick Burnaby *On Horseback through Asia Minor*. Victorian officer's thousand-mile ride to spy on the Russians in the run-up to the 1877 war. Prophetically observant and inadvertently humorous; anti-Armenian, condescendingly Turkophilic.

★**Geert Mak** *The Bridge*. Quite brilliant travelogue weaving the compelling tales of the petty street-traders, hustlers, pickpockets, shoe-shiners, fishermen and other characters who frequent Istanbul's landmark Galata Bridge with a marvellously succinct, yet evocative, history of one of the world's great cities.

Mary Wortley Montagu *Turkish Embassy Letters*. Impressions of an eccentric but perceptive traveller, resident in Istanbul during 1716–18, whose open-mindedness gave her the edge over contemporary historians.

Jeremy Seal *Meander: East to West Along a Turkish River*. Seal is a witty yet perceptive writer, and this account of a journey along the famously winding course of the River Meander is every bit as engaging as *A Fez of the Heart*, in which Seal meanders around Turkey tracing the origins of that distinctive headwear.

Brian Sewell *South from Ephesus: An Escape from the Tyranny of Western Art*. Pre-touristic coastal Turkey and its ruins during the 1970s and 1980s, when vile hotels, domineering guides, patchy transport and amorous, bisexual villagers were all negotiated.

Freya Stark *Alexander's Path, Ionia – a Quest, The Lycian Shore* and *Riding to the Tigris*. All Stark's work makes great reading even today – especially if you're visiting Aegean/Mediterranean Turkey.

MEMOIRS

Fethiye Çetin *My Grandmother*. A Turkish woman discovers her secret past – a Christian Armenian grandmother. Up to two million "Turks" today share the same origins. Slim, very readable memoir by a lawyer who represented Hrant Dink.

★**Dmetri Kakmi** *Mother Land*. Moving coming-of-age memoir of the last (1969–71) days of the Greek Orthodox community on the remote Aegean Turkish island of Bozcaada (Greek Tenedos).

★**İrfan Orga** *Portrait of a Turkish Family*. This heartbreaking story follows Orga's family from idyllic existence in late Ottoman Istanbul through grim survival in the early Republican era. His *The Caravan Moves On: Three Weeks among Turkish Nomads* is a fine snapshot of the

Menderes era – and a clear-eyed portrayal of a Toros *Yörük* community, about whom reams of rose-tinted nonsense has otherwise been written.

★**Daniel de Souza** *Under a Crescent Moon* (o/p but available on Kindle). Turkish society seen from the bottom looking up: prison vignettes by a jailed foreigner, and in its compassion and black humour the antithesis of *Midnight Express*. Compellingly written.

ARCHITECTURE, ART AND MONUMENTS

Metin And *Turkish Miniature Painting – the Ottoman Period* (Dost Yayınları, Istanbul; o/p). Attractive coverage of the most important Ottoman art form, with well-produced colour plates.

Diana Barillari and Ezio Godoli *Istanbul 1900: Art Nouveau Architecture and Interiors*. Superbly researched and illustrated account of Istanbul's neglected Art Nouveau legacy, in particular works by Italian architect and resident Raimondo D'Aronco.

★**Godfrey Goodwin** *A History of Ottoman Architecture*. Definitive guide covering the whole country and providing a sound historical and ethno-geographical context for every important Ottoman construction. His *Sinan: Ottoman Architecture and Its Values Today* is also eminently readable.

Richard Krautheimer *Early Christian and Byzantine Architecture* (o/p). Excellent survey from Pelican's "History of Art" series.

Cyril Mango *Byzantine Architecture* (o/p). A complete survey of the most significant Byzantine structures, around a quarter of which fall within modern Turkey.

Gülru Necipoğlu *The Age of Sinan: Architectural Culture in the Ottoman Empire*. As it says: the master in his social context, and the best, and most recent, of several studies on the man.

★**David Talbot Rice** *Islamic Art* (o/p). Vast geographical and chronological span gives useful perspectives on Ottoman and Selçuk art forms. His *Art of the Byzantine Era* (o/p), a lavishly illustrated study in the same "World of Art" series, is unlikely ever to be superseded.

Stephane Yerasimos *Constantinople: Istanbul's Historical Heritage*. Good colour photos, with attention to mosaics and icons, plus coverage of Edirne and Bursa. The English translation of the French original via a German edition is stilted, though.

CARPETS

★**Alastair Hull and José Luczyc-Wykowska** *Kilim: The Complete Guide: History – Pattern – Technique – Identification*. Comprehensive and thoroughly illustrated survey of Turkish kilims. Hull's *Living with Kilims* (with Nicholas Barnard) is an excellent use-and-care manual.

James Opie *Tribal Rugs: A Complete Guide to Nomadic and Village Carpets*. Contains examples of Turcoman and Kurdish rugs as part of a general Central Asian survey.

Kurt Zipper and Claudia Fritzsche *Oriental Rugs: Turkish* Volume 4 of this series. Coverage of weaving techniques, symbols and rug categories, plus regional surveys of distinctive patterns.

SPECIALIST GUIDEBOOKS

Arın Bayraktaroğlu *Turkey: Culture Shock! A Survival Guide to Customs and Etiquette*. Useful, especially for a prolonged stay or business trip.

George E. Bean *Turkey's Southern Shore, Turkey Beyond the Maeander, Lycian Turkey, Aegean Turkey* (all o/p). Scholarly guides to coastal archeological sites based on Professor Bean's original research, much of it never superseded.

Everett Blake and Anna Edmonds *Biblical Sites in Turkey*. If it's mentioned in the New Testament, it's fully described here. Edmonds' *Turkey's Religious Sites* (o/p) is better produced and includes Jewish and Muslim sites.

★**Hilary Sumner-Boyd and John Freely** *Strolling Through Istanbul*. First published in 1972 and indispensable. The authors' knowledge of, and love for, the city shine through; sketch-maps and monument plans complement informative text.

Jane Taylor *Imperial Istanbul*. Excellent, stone-by-stone guide, complete with site plans, of the major Ottoman monuments in Bursa and Edirne as well as the old capital.

HIKING AND MOUNTAINEERING

Kate Clow *The Lycian Way*. Hour-by-hour, west-to-east route guide for Turkey's first officially marked long-distance trail (see p.303); supplied with folding map.

Kate Clow *St Paul Trail*. Illustrated guide to Turkey's second long-distance, waymarked trail (see p.418), loosely following in the footsteps of St Paul from Perge to Antioch in Pisidia, taking in wonderful mountain and lakeland scenery en route. GPS data and map included.

★**Kate Clow** *The Kaçkar: Trekking in Turkey's Black Sea Mountains*. Meticulously described routes in the centre of Turkey's most popular alpine range, both multi-day treks and waymarked day-walks.

Caroline Finkel and Kate Clow *The Eliviya Çelebi Way*. Guide to this long-distance cultural route in northwest Turkey, suitable for walkers, horseriders and cyclists, following in the steps of Ottoman traveller Çelebi.

Ömer B. Tözel *The Ala Dağ: Climbs and Treks in Turkey's Crimson Mountains*. More technical and less hike-orientated than the title implies, but the only volume in English.

Yunus Özdemir, Altay Özcan and Dean Livsey *Carian Trail*. The ideal companion to this exciting long-distance walking route in southwest Turkey, written by its pioneers.

TURKISH FICTION IN TRANSLATION

Sait Faik *A Useless Man*. A collection of the charming short stories of one of Turkey's most treasured writers, often compared to Chekhov, mostly set in or around Istanbul. Translated by Maureen Freely and Alexander Dawe.

Moris Farhi *Young Turk*. Ankara-born Farhi conjures thirteen interwoven short stories in this delightful evocation of Istanbul either side of World War II. Characters, whether Armenian, Greek, Gypsy, Levantine or Turkish, are lovingly sketched; the "coming of age" tales are the most convincing.

Ahmet Hamdi Tanpınar *The Time Regulation Institute*. Originally published in 1962, this highly regarded satire examines the unexpected effects that Atatürk's westernizing reforms have on the "Oriental" mind. Translated by Maureen Freely and Alexander Dawe.

Latife Tekin *Berji Kristin: Tales from the Garbage Hills*. The hard underbelly of Turkish life, in this surreal allegory set in a shanty town built on an Istanbul rubbish dump. By the same author, and similar in tone, *Dear Shameless Death* examines how rural families cope with the move to the big city.

TURKISH POETRY IN TRANSLATION

Coleman Barks (trans) *Like This*; *Open Secret*; *We Are Three*. Three of various volumes of Rumi's poetry, in lively if not literal translations.

Yunus Emre (trans Süha Faiz) *The City of the Heart: Verses of Wisdom and Love* (o/p). After Rumi, the most esteemed Turkish medieval Sufi poet. *The Drop That Became the Sea*, rendered by Kebir Helminski, will also appeal.

★**Nazım Hikmet** *Poems of Nazım Hikmet* and *Beyond the Walls*. The most easily available, reasonably priced anthologies by the internationally renowned Turkish communist poet.

FOREIGN LITERATURE SET IN TURKEY

Louis de Bernières *Birds Without Wings*. This repeats, with mixed results, the formula of his blockbuster *Captain Corelli's Mandolin*, applied to Asia Minor of the 1910s and 1920s. Most of the action occurs in "Eskibahçe", a fictionalized version of Kaya Köyü near Fethiye, though the Gallipoli set pieces are the best bits.

Jason Goodwin *The Janissary Tree*. Racy historical thriller with all kinds of skulduggery being uncovered by Yashin, a eunuch detective. A very palatable entry into a nineteenth-century Istanbul on the verge of the Tanzimat reforms, and a successful formula that has spawned three sequels, *The Snake Stone*, *The Bellini Card*, *An Evil Eye* and *The Baklava Club*.

Pierre Loti *Aziyade*. For what's essentially romantic twaddle set in nineteenth-century Istanbul, this is surprisingly racy, with good insights into Ottoman life and Western attitudes to the Orient.

Rose Macaulay *The Towers of Trebizond*. Classic send-up of Low and High Church conflict, British eccentricity and naïvety among a group travelling from Istanbul to Trebizond in the 1950s.

Barbara Nadel *A Chemical Prison*; *Arabesque*; *Harem*. Some love Nadel's Istanbul-set thrillers, where doughty, chain-smoking Inspector İkrem and associates trawl the city's underworld; others find them a tad unconvincing. But they do evoke a side of the city barely imaginable to the average visitor.

★**Edouard Roditi** *The Delights of Turkey*. Twenty short stories, by turns touching or bawdy, of rural Turkey and Istanbul, by a Sephardic Jew of Turkish descent long resident in Paris and America.

Turkish

It's worth learning as much Turkish as you can; if you travel far from the tourist centres you may well need it, and Turks always appreciate foreigners who show enough interest and courtesy to learn at least basic greetings. The main advantages of the language for learners are that it's phonetically spelled and (98 percent of the time) grammatically regular. The disadvantages are that the vocabulary is unrelated to any language you're likely to have encountered – unless you know Arabic or Persian – while the grammar, relying heavily on suffixes, gets thornier the further you delve into it. Concepts like vowel harmony further complicate matters.

Pronunciation

Mastering pronunciation in Turkish is important; once you've got it, the phonetic spelling and regularity helps you progress fast. The following letters differ significantly from English pronunciation.

Aa	short a, similar to that in **far**	**Çç**	like ch in **chat**
Ee	as in **bet**	**Gg**	hard g as in **get**
İi	as in **pin**	**Ğğ**	generally silent, but lengthens the preceding vowel, and between two vowels approximates a y sound
Iı	vowel resembling the vestigial sound between the b and the l of probable		
Oo	as in **note**	**Hh**	as in **hen**, never silent
Öö	like ur in **burn**	**Jj**	like the s in **pleasure**
Uu	as in **blue**	**Şş**	like sh in **shape**
Üü	like ew in **few**	**Vv**	soft sound, somewhere between a v and a w
Cc	like j in **jelly**		

Vowel harmony and loan words

Turkish usually exhibits **vowel harmony**, whereby words contain either so-called "back" vowels a, ı, o and u, or "front" vowels e, i, ö and ü, but rarely mix the two types. Back and front vowels are further subdivided into "unrounded" (a and ı, e and i) and "rounded" (o and u, ö and ü), and again rounded and unrounded vowels tend to keep exclusive company. A small number of native Turkish words (eg, *anne*, mother; *kardeş*, brother) violate the rules of vowel harmony, as do compound words, eg *bugün*, "today", formed from *bu* (this) and *gün* (day).

PHRASEBOOKS AND DICTIONARIES

For a straightforward **phrasebook**, look no further than *Turkish: A Rough Guide Phrasebook*, which has useful two-way glossaries and a brief and simple grammar section. For an **at-home course**, Geoffrey L. Lewis's *Teach Yourself Turkish* is best.

Among widely available Turkish **dictionaries**, the best are probably the Langenscheidt/ Lilliput in miniature or coat-pocket sizes, or the *Concise Oxford Turkish Dictionary* (o/p but sold online), a hardback suitable for serious students. The Redhouse dictionaries, produced in Turkey but marketed by Milet in the UK, are the best value, despite eye-straining fine print.

The main exceptions to vowel harmony, however, are foreign **loan words** from Arabic or Persian (plus Greek). Despite Atatürk's best efforts to substitute Turkish or French expressions (the latter again violating vowel harmony), these still make up a good third of modern Turkish vocabulary. Most words that start with f, h, l, m, n, r, v and z are derived from Arabic and Persian.

WORDS AND PHRASES

BASICS

Good morning	Günaydın	Later	Sonra
Good afternoon	İyi günler	Wait a minute!	Bir dakika bekle!
Good evening	İyi akşamlar	In the morning	Sabahleyin
Goodnight	İyi geceler	In the afternoon	Oğle'den sonra
Hello	Merhaba	In the evening	Akşamleyin
Goodbye	Allahaısmarladık	Here/there/over	Bur(a)da/şur(a)da/
Yes	Evet	there	or(a) da
No	Hayır	Good/bad	İyi/Kötü, fena
No (there isn't any)	Yok	Big/small	Büyük/küçük
Please	Lütfen	Cheap/expensive	Ucuz/pahalı
Thank you	Teşekkür ederim/	Early/late	Erken/geç
	Mersi/Sağol	Hot/cold	Sıcak/soğuk
		Near/far	Yakın/uzak
You're welcome	Bir şey değil	Vacant/occupied	Boş/dolu
How are you?	Nasılsınız? Nasılsın?	Quickly/slowly	Hızlı/yavaş
	Ne haber?	Enough	Yeter
I'm fine	İyiyim/İyilik	Mr	Bey (follows first name)
Do you speak English?	İngilizce biliyormusunuz?	Miss	Bayan (precedes first
I don't understand	Anlamadım/Türkçe		name)
(Turkish)	anlamıyorum	Mrs	Hanım (polite Ottoman
I don't know	Bilmiyorum		title follows first name)
I beg your pardon	Affedersiniz	Master craftsman	Usta (honorific title
Excuse me (in a crowd)	Pardon		bestowed on any
I'm sightseeing	Geziyorum or		tradesman; follows
	Dolaşıyorum		first name)
I'm English/Scottish	İngilizim/Iskoçyalım/		
Irish/	Irlandalıyım/	**DRIVING**	
American/	Amerikalı/	Left	Sol
Austalian	Avustralyalım	Right	Sağ
I live in…	…'de/da oturuyorum	Straight ahead	Doğru, direk
Today	Bugün	Turn left/right	Sola dön/Sağ'ta dön
Tomorrow	Yarın	No parking	Parkyapılmaz
Day after tomorrow	Öbür gün/Ertesi gün	Your car will be towed	Aracınız çekilir
Yesterday	Dün	One-way street	Tek yön
Now	Şimdi	No entry	Araç giremez

THE ORIGINS OF TURKISH

Turkish, the official language of the modern Republic of Turkey, is neither Indo-European nor Semitic in origin, but **Altaic**, a language group that includes Japanese, Korean and Mongolian as well as the Turkic languages. Turkish Turks can still communicate with their ethnic and linguistic cousins in places like Azerbaijan, Turkmenistan and Uzbekistan, even if centuries of isolation from them, and the language reforms instituted by Atatürk in the early years of the Turkish Republic, make the task difficult. Nonetheless, Turks today still feel an affinity with their Turkic kin, and the Turkish government is the first to kick up a fuss at, for example, Chinese mistreatment of its Uigur Turkish minority.

No through road	Çıkmaz sokak
Abrupt verge	Düşük banket
Slow down	Yavaşla
Road closed	Yol kapalı
Crossroads	Dörtyol, kavşak
Pedestrian crossing	Yaya geçidi

SOME COMMON SIGNS

Entrance/exit	Giriş/Çıkış
Free/paid entrance	Giriş ücretsiz/Ücretlidir
Gentlemen	Baylar
Ladies	Bayanlar
WC	WC/Tuvalet
Open/closed	Açık/Kapalı
Arrivals/departures	Varış/Kalkış
Pull/push	Çekiniz/İtiniz
Out of order	Arızalı
Drinking water	İçilebilir su
To let/for hire	Kiralık
Foreign exchange	Kambiyo
Beware	Dikkat
First aid	İlk yardım
No smoking	Sigara içilmez
Keep off the grass	Çimenlere basmayını
Stop, halt	Dur
Military area	Askeri bölge
Entry forbidden	Girmek yasaktır
No entry without a ticket	Biletsiz girmek yasaktır
No entry without a woman	Damsız girilmez
Please take off your shoes	Lütfen ayakkabılarınızı çıkartınız
No entry on foot	Yaya giremez

ACCOMMODATION

Is there a hotel nearby?	Bir yakında otel var mı?
Pension, inn	Pansiyon
Campsite	Kamping
Tent	Çadır
Do you have a room?	Boş odanız var mı?
Single/double/triple	Tek/çift/üç kişilik
Do you have a double room for one/two/ three nights?	Bir/iki/üç gecelik çift yataklı odanız var mı?
For one/two weeks	Bir/iki haftalık
With an extra bed	İlâve yataklı
With a double bed	Fransız yataklı
With a shower	Duşlu
Hot water	Sıcak su
Cold water	Soğuk su
Can I see it?	Bakabilirmiyim?
I have a booking	Reservasyonum var
Is there wi-fi?	Kablosuz var?
What's the password?	Şifre nedir?

QUESTIONS AND DIRECTIONS

Where is the…?	…nerede?
When?	Ne zaman?
What/What is it?	Ne/Ne dir?
How much (does it cost?)	Ne kadar/Kaça?
How many?	Kaç tane?
Why?	Niye?
What time is it?	(polite) Saatınız var mı? (informal) Saat kaç?
How do I get to…?	…'a/e nasıl giderim?
How far is it to…?	…'a/e ne kadar uzak?
Can you give me a lift to…?	Beni…'a/e götürebilirmisiniz?
When does it open?	Kaçta açılıcak?
When does it close?	Kaçta kapanacak?
What's it called in Turkish?	Türkcesi ne dir? or, Türkçe nasıl söylersiniz?

TRAVELLING

Aeroplane	Uçak
Bus	Otobüs
Train	Tren
Car	Araba
Taxi	Taksi
Bicycle	Bisiklet
Ferry	Feribot, vapur
Catamaran, sea bus	Deniz otobüsü
Hitch-hiking	Otostop
On foot	Yaya
Bus station	Otogar
Railway station	Gar, tren ıstasyonu
Ferry terminal/jetty	İskele
Harbour	Liman
A ticket to…	…'a bir bilet
One-way	Gidiş sadece
Return	Gidiş-dönüş
What time does it leave?	Saat kaçta kalkıyor?
Can I book a seat?	Reservasyon yapabılırmıyım?
When is the next bus/train/ferry?	Bir sonraki otobus/ tren/vapur kaçta kalkıyor?
Where does it leave from?	Nereden kalkıyor?
Must I change?	Aktarma var mı?
What platform does it leave from?	Hangi perondan kalkıyor?
How many kilometres is it?	Kaç kilometredir?
How long does it take?	Ne kadar sürer?
Which bus goes to…?	Hangi otobus…'a gider?
Which road leads to…?	Hangi yol…'a çıkar?
Can I get out at a convenient place?	Müsait bir yerde inebilirmiyim?

DAYS OF THE WEEK, MONTHS AND SEASONS

Sunday	Pazar
Monday	Pazartesi
Tuesday	Salı
Wednesday	Çarşamba
Thursday	Perşembe
Friday	Cuma
Saturday	Cumartesi
January	Ocak
February	Subat
March	Mart
April	Nisan
May	Mayıs
June	Haziran
July	Temmuz
August	Ağustos
September	Eylül
October	Ekim
November	Kasım
December	Aralk
Spring	İlkbahar
Summer	Yaz
Autumn	Sonbahar
Winter	Kış

NUMBERS AND ORDINALS

1	Bir
2	İki
3	Üç
4	Dört
5	Beş
6	Altı
7	Yedi
8	Sekiz
9	Dokuz
10	On
11	On bir
12	On iki
13	On üç
20	Yirmi
30	Otuz
40	Kırk
50	Elli
60	Altmış
70	Yetmiş
80	Seksen
90	Doksan
100	Yüz
140	Yüz kırk
200	İki yüz
700	Yedi yüz
1000	Bin
100,000	Yüz bin
500,000	Beşyüz bin
1,000,000	Bir milyon

Compound numbers tend to be run together in spelling: 50,784 Ellibinyediyüzseksendört

First	Birinci
Second	İkinci
Third	Üçüncü

TIME CONVENTIONS

(At) 3 o'clock	Saat üç(ta)
2 hours (duration)	İki saat
Half hour (duration)	Yarım saat
5.30	Beş büçük
It's 8.10	Sekizi on geçiyor
It's 10.45	On bire çeyrek var
At 8.10	Sekizi on geçe
At 10.45	On bire çeyrek kala

Food and drink

BASICS

Bal	Honey
Bulgur	Cracked wheat
Buz	Ice
Ekmek	Bread, as:
Çavdar	Rye
Kepekli	Wholegrain
Mısır	Corn
Karabiber	Black pepper
Kekik	Oregano
Makarna	Pasta (noodles)
Nane	Mint
Pilav, pirinç	Rice
Şeker	Sugar
Sirke	Vinegar
Su	Water
Süt	Milk
Tereyağı	Butter
Tuz	Salt
(Zeytin) Yağ(ı)	(Olive) Oil
Yoğurt	Yoghurt
Yumurta	Eggs
(Et)li/(Et)siz	With/without (meat)

USEFUL WORDS

Kahvaltı	Breakfast
Öğle yemeği	Lunch
Akşam yemeği	Dinner

Bakarmısınız!	Polite way of getting waiter's attention	**İşkembe**	Tripe
		Mercimek	Lentil
Bardak	Glass	**Paça**	Trotters
Başka bir…	Another…	**Tarhana**	Yoghurt, grain and spice
Tabak	Plate	**Tavuk**	Chicken
Bıçak	Knife	**Yayla**	Similar to *tarhana*, with mint
Çatal	Fork		
Kaşık	Spoon	**Yoğurt**	Yoghurt, rice and
Peçete	Napkin		celery greens
Hesap	Bill, check		
Servis ücreti	Service charge		
Garsoniye	"Waiter's" charge		

COOKING TERMS

APPETIZERS (*MEZE* OR *ZEYTINYAĞLI*)

Acı	Hot, spicy	**Antep or acılı ezmesi**	Hot chilli mash with garlic, parsley, onion
Buğlama	Steamed		
Çevirme	Spit-roasted	**Barbunya**	Red kidney beans
Etli	Containing meat	**Börülce**	Black-eyed peas, in the pod
Etli mi?	Does it contain meat?		
Etsiz yemek var mı?	Do you have any meatless food?	**Cacık**	Yoghurt, cucumber and herb dip
Ezme	Puréed/mashed dip	**Çerkez tavuğu**	Chicken in walnut sauce
Fırında(n)	Baked	**Çoban salatası**	Tomato, cucumber, parsley, pepper and onion salad
Haşlama	Meat stew without oil, sometimes with vegetables		
		Deniz börülcesi	Glasswort, marsh samphire
İyi pişmiş	Well-cooked	**Deniz otu**	Rock samphire
Izgarada(n), Izgarası	Grilled	**Haydarı**	Dense garlic dip
Kızartma	Fried then chilled	**Hibeş**	Spicy sesame paste
Kıymalı	With minced meat	**İçli köfte**	Bulgur, nuts, vegetables and meat in a spicy crust
Peynirli, kaşarlı	With cheese		
Pilaki	Vinaigrette, marinated	**İmam bayıldı**	Cold baked aubergine, onion and tomato
Pişmemiş	Raw		
Sıcak/soğuk	Hot/cold (*meze*)	**Mantar sote**	Sautéed mushrooms
Soslu, salçalı	In red sauce	**Mücver**	Courgette frittata
Sucuklu	With sausage	**Paçanga böreği**	*Pasırtma* containing, tomato and cheese
Tava, sahanda	Deep-fried, fried		
Yoğurtlu	In yoghurt sauce	**Patlıcan ezmesi**	Aubergine pâté
Yumurtalı	With egg (eg *pide*)	**Piyaz**	White haricots, onions and parsley vinaigrette
Zeytinyağlılar	Vegetables cooked in their own juices, spices and olive oil (*zeytin yağı*), then allowed to cool		
		Rus salatası	"Russian" salad – potatoes, peas, gherkins in mayonnaise
		Semizotu	Purslane, usually mixed into yoghurt

SOUP (*ÇORBA*)

		Sigara böreği	Cheese-filled pastry "cigarettes"
Düğün	Egg-lemon	**Tarama**	Pink fish-roe
Ezo gelin	Rice/vegetable broth	**Tere**	Rocket greens
		Turşu	Pickled vegetables

COMMON TOASTS

The closest equivalents to "Cheers" are: **Şeref'e, şerefiniz'e** "to your honour" and **Neşe'ye** "to joy". Otherwise there's the more formal **Sağlığınız'a** "to your health" or **Mutluluğ'a** "to happiness".

To a good cook one says: **Eliniz'e sağlık** "health to your hands". For a short grace after meals: **Allah bereket versin** ("may Allah bring blessings").

Yaprak dolması	Stuffed vine leaves, with mince
Yeşil salata	Green salad
Zeytin	Olives

MEAT (*ET*) AND POULTRY (*BEYAZ ET*)

Adana kebap	Spicy Arab-style kebab
Beyti	Minced kebab wrapped in pitta
Bıldırcın	Quail
Böbrek	Kidney
Bonfile	Small steak
Ciğ köfte	Spicy bulgur patties
Ciğer	Liver
Çöp kebap	Tiny chunks of offal
Dana eti	Veal
Dil	Tongue
Döner kebap	Rotisseried cone of fatty lamb slabs
İnegöl köftesi	Mince rissoles laced with cheese
İskender or **Bursa kebap**	*Döner* drenched in yoghurt and sauce
Kaburga	Spare ribs
Kağıt kebap	Meat and vegetables baked in wax paper
Kanat	Chicken wing
Karışık ızgara	Mixed grill
Kiremit'te kebap	Meat served on a hot ceramic tray
Köfte	Meatballs
Koyun	Mutton
Kuzu	Lamb
Keçi	Goat
Orman kebap	Roast lamb refried with vegetables
Pastırma	Cured beef
Piliç	Roasting chicken
Pirzola	Chop, cutlet
Saray kebap	Rissoles baked with vegetables
Sığır	Beef
Şiş kebap	Shish kebab
Tandır kebap	Tender, boneless lamb baked in outdoor oven
Tavuk	Boiling chicken
Tekirdağ köftesi	Finger-shaped rissoles with cumin, onion, mint
Yürek	Heart

FISH (*BALIK*) AND SEAFOOD (*DENIZ ÜRÜNLERI*)

Ahtapod	Octopus
Alabalık	Trout
Barbunya/tekir	Red mullet, small/large
Çinakop	Baby lüfer
Çipura	Gilt-head bream
Hamsi	Anchovy (Black Sea)
İskaroz	Parrotfish
İsparoz	Annular bream
İstakoz	Aegean lobster
İstavrit	Horse mackerel
Kalamar	Squid
Kalkan	Turbot
Karagöz	Two-banded bream
Karides	Prawns
Kefal	Grey mullet (Aegean)
Kılıç	Swordfish
Kolyoz	Club mackerel
Levrek	Bass; usually farmed
Lüfer	Bluefish
Mendik	Type of bream
Mercan	Pandora or red bream
Mezgit	Whitebait
Midye	Mussel
Orfoz	Giant grouper
Orkinos	Tuna
Palamut/torik	Small/large bonito
Sarıgöz	Black bream
Sarıkanat	Young *lüfer*
Sardalya	Sardine
Uskumru	Atlantic mackerel
Yayın	Catfish
Yengeç	Crab

VEGETABLES (*SEBZE*)

Acı biber	Hot chillis
Bakla	Broad beans
Bamya	Okra, lady's fingers
Bezelye	Peas
Domates	Tomato
Enginar	Artichoke
Hardal	Mustard greens
Havuç	Carrot
Ispanak	Spinach
İstifno	Boiled wild greens
Kabak	Courgette, zucchini
Karnabahar	Cauliflower
Kuru fasulye	White haricots
Mantar	Mushrooms
Marul	Lettuce
Maydanoz	Parsley
Nohut	Chickpeas
Patates	Potato
Patlıcan	Aubergine, eggplant
Roka, tere	Rocket greens
Salatalık	Cucumber
Sarımsak, sarmısak	Garlic

Sivri biber	Thin peppers, hot or mild
Soğan	Onion
Taze fasulye	French beans
Turp	Radish

SNACKS

Antep fıstığı	Pistachios
Badem	Almonds
Börek	Rich layered pastry with varied fillings
Çerez	Nibbles, usually nuts
Cezer(i)ye	Carrot, honey-nut bar
Çiğ börek	Hollow turnovers
Dürüm	Pitta-like dough roll used to to wrap meat for takeaway
Fındık	Hazelnuts
Gözleme	Village crêpe with various fillings
Kestane	Chestnuts
Kokoreç	Mixed innard roulade
Kuru üzüm	Raisins
Lahmacun	Round Arabic-Armenian "pizza"
Leblebi	Roasted chickpeas
Midye dolması	Mussels stuffed with rice and pine nuts
Pestil	Sheet-pressed dried fruit
Pide	Turkish "pizza"
Poğaça	Soft, often filled, bread roll
Simit	Bread rings studded with sesame seeds
Su börek	"Water börek" – runny cheese between filo
Yer fıstığı	Peanuts

TYPICAL DISHES

Civil	Variant of *mihlama*, served on Çoruh side of Kaçkar
Güveç	Meat and vegetable clay-pot casserole
İç pilav	Spicy rice
Karnıyarık	Aubergine and meat dish, firmer than moussaka
Lahana sarma	Black Sea *dolma*, with baby cabbage leaves
Laz böreği	Meat-filled crêpes, topped with yoghurt
Mantı	Mince-stuffed "ravioli" topped with yoghurt and chilli oil
Menemen	Stir-fried omelette with tomatoes and peppers
Mıhlama, muhlama	Fondue-like Hemşin dish of cheese, butter and corn flour
Otlu peynir	Herb-flavoured cheese, common around Van
Saç kavurma	"Wok"-fried medley
Sebze turlu	Vegetable stew
Şakşuka	Aubergine, tomato, pepper and other vegetable fry-up
Tas kebap	Meat and vegetable stew especially in eastern Anatolia
Tatar böreği	Similar to *mantı* but served with cheese and mint
Testi kebap	Stew in a sealed Avanos (Cappadocia) pot, broken at serration to serve
Türlü sebze	Alias of *tas kebap*

CHEESE (*PEYNIR*)

Beyaz	White; like Greek feta
Çerkez	Like Edam
Dil	Like mozzarella
Lor	Like ricotta
Kaşar	Kasseri, variably aged
Tulum	Dry, crumbly, parmesan-like cheese

FRUIT (*MEYVE*)

Ahududu	Raspberry
Armut	Pear
Ayva	Quince
Böğürtlen	Blackberry
Çilek	Strawberry
Elma	Apple
Erik	Plum
Hurma	Persimmon or date
İncir	Figs
(Kara)dut	(Red) mulberry
Karpuz	Watermelon
Kavun	Persian melon
Kayısı	Apricot
Kiraz	Sweet cherry
Limon	Lemon
Mandalin	Tangerine
Muşmula	Medlar
Muz	Banana
Nar	Pomegranate
Papaz/hoca eriği	Green plum
Portakal	Orange
Şeftali	Peach (June)
Üzüm	Grape

Vişne	Sour cherry
Yarma	August Bursa peach

SWEETS (*TATLILAR*) AND PASTRIES (*PASTALAR*)

Acı badem	Giant almond biscuit
Aşure	Pulse, wheat, fruit and nut "soup"
Baklava	Layered honey and nut pie
Dondurma	Ice cream
Fırın sütlaç	Baked rice pudding
İrmik helvası	Semolina and nut *helva*
Kabak tatlısı	Baked orange-fleshed squash topped with nuts and *kaymak*
Kadayıf	"Shredded wheat" in syrup
Kadın göbeği	Doughnut in syrup
Kaymak	Clotted cream
Kazandibi	Browned version of *tavuk göğsü*
Keşkül	Vanilla-almond custard
Komposto	Stewed fruit
Krem karamel	Crème caramel
Kurabiye	Almond-nut biscuit dusted with powdered sugar
Lokum	Turkish delight
Muhallebi	Milk pudding with rice flour and rosewater
Mustafakemalpaşa	Syrup-soaked dumpling
Sakızlı	Anything mastic-flavoured
Süpangile	Ultra-rich chocolate pudding, with sponge or a biscuit embedded
Sütlaç	Rice pudding
Tahin helvası	Sesame paste *helva*
Tavuk göğsü	Chicken-breast, milk, sugar and cracked rice
Zerde	Saffron-laced jelly

DRINKS

Ada çayı	Sage tea
Ayran	Drinking yoghurt
Bira	Beer
Boza	Lightly fermented millet or wheat drink
Çay	Tea
Kahve	Coffee
Maden suyu	Mineral water (fizzy)
Meyva suyu	Fruit juice
Papatya çayı	Camomile tea
Rakı	Aniseed-flavoured spirit distilled from grape pressings
Sahlep	Orchid-root-powder drink
Şarap	Wine
Şıra	Grape must, lightly fermented
Sütlü/Sütsüz	With/without milk

Glossary

Many of the Turkish terms below will change their form according to their grammatical declension (eg *ada*, island, but *Eşek Adası*, Donkey Island); the genitive suffix is appended in brackets, or the form written separately when appropriate.

GENERAL TURKISH TERMS

Ada(sı) Island.

Ağa A minor rank of nobility in the Ottoman Empire, still a term of respect; follows the name (eg Ismail Ağa).

Ahi Medieval Turkish apprentice craftsmen's guild and religious brotherhood, predecessor of the more conventional dervish orders.

Ayazma Sacred spring.

Bahçe(si) Garden.

Bekçi Caretaker or warden at an archeological site or monument.

Belediye(si) Municipality – both the corporation and the actual town hall, for a community of over 2000 inhabitants.

Bey Another minor Ottoman title like *ağa*, still in use; follows the first name.

Cami(i) Mosque.

Çarşaf "Sheet" – the full-length, baggy dress-with-hood worn by religious Turkish women.

Çarşı(sı) Bazaar, market.

Çay(ı) 1) Tea, the national drink; 2) a stream or small river.

Çeşme(si) Street-corner fountain.

Çıkmaz(ı) Dead-end alley.

Dağ(ı) Mount.

Dağlar(ı) Mountains.

Dolmuş Shared taxi system operating in larger towns.

Eski Old (frequent modifier of place names).

Ezan The Muslim call to prayer; these days often taped or at the very least transmitted up to an elevated loudspeaker.

Ferace Similar to a *çarşaf*, but less all-enveloping.

Gazi Warrior for the (Islamic) faith; also a common epithet of Atatürk.

Gazino Open-air nightclub, usually featuring live or taped music.

Gecekondu A house built quickly without proper permission. Translates as "founded-by-night" – a reference to the Ottoman law whereby houses begun in darkness that had acquired a roof and four walls by dawn were inviolable.

Gişe Ticket window or booth.

Göl(ü) Lake.

Hamam(ı) Turkish bath.

Hamsi The Black Sea anchovy; by extension, nickname for any native of this area.

Han(ı) Traditionally a tradesmen's hall, or an urban inn; now also means an office block.

Harabe Ruin; *harabeler* in the plural, abbreviated "Hb" on old maps.

Harem Women's quarters in Ottoman houses.

Hastane(si) Hospital.

Hicri The Muslim dating system, beginning with Mohammed's flight to Medina in 622 AD, and based on the thirteen-month lunar calendar; approximately six centuries behind the *Miladî* calendar. Abbreviated "H." on monuments and inscriptions.

Hisar Same as *kale*.

Hoca Teacher in charge of religious instruction.

Ilıca Hot spring.

İl(i) Province, subdivided into *ilçes* (counties or districts).

İmam Usually just the prayer leader at a mosque, though it can mean a more important spiritual authority.

Irmak River, eg Yeşilırmak (Green River).

İskele(si) Jetty, dock.

Janissary One of the sultan's elite corps during the fourteenth to eighteenth centuries; *yeniceri* in Turkish. Famous for their devotion to the Bektaşi order, outlandish headgear and marching music.

Kaplıca Developed hot springs, spa.

Kervansaray(ı) Strategically located "hotel", often Selçuk, for pack animals and men on Anatolian trade routes; some overlap with *han*.

Kilim Flat-weave rug without a pile.

Kilise(si) Church.

Konak Large private residence, also the main government building of a province or city; genitive form *konağı*.

Lokanta Restaurant; from Italian locanda.

Mağara(sı) Cave.

Mahalle(si) District or neighbourhood of a larger municipality, village or postal area.

Meydan(ı) Public square or plaza.

Meyhane Tavern where alcohol and *meze*-type food are served together.

Meze Often vegetable-based appetizer, typically fried, puréed and/or marinated.

Miladı The Christian year-numbering system; abbreviated "M." on inscriptions.

Muezzin Man who pronounces call to prayer (*ezan*) from the minaret of a mosque.

Muhtar Village headman.

Muhtarlık The office of the *muhtar*; also designates the status of any community of under 2000.

Namaz The Muslim rite of prayer, performed five times daily.

Nehir (Nehri) River.

Otogar Bus station.

Ova(sı) Plain, plateau.

Ören Alternative term for *harabe*, "ruin"; common village name.

Pansiyon Typical budget to mid-priced accommodation in Turkish resorts.

Ramadan The Muslim month of fasting and prayer; spelt *Ramazan* in Turkish.

Saz Long-necked, fretted stringed instrument central to Turkish folk ballads and Alevi/Bektaşi devotional music.

Selçuk Pertaining to the first Muslim Turkish state based in Anatolia, which lasted from the eleventh to the thirteenth centuries.

Sema A dervish ceremony; thus *semahane*, a hall where such ceremonies are conducted.

Şehzade Prince, heir apparent.

Şeyh Head of a Sufi order.

Sufi or dervish An adherent of one of the heterodox mystical branches of Islam. In Turkey the most important sects were the Bektaşi, Mevlevî, Helveti, Nakşibendi, Cerrahi and Kadiri orders.

Sultan valide The Sultan's mother.

Tatil köyü or site(si) Holiday development, usually for Turkish civil servants – not meant for foreign tourists.

Tuğra Monogram or seal of a sultan.

Ulema The corps of Islamic scholars and authorities in Ottoman times.

Vakıf Islamic religious trust or foundation, responsible for social welfare and upkeep of religious buildings.

Vezir The principal Ottoman minister of state, responsible for managing the empire.

Vilayet(i) Formal word for province; also a common term for the provincial headquarters building itself.

Yalı Ornate wooden mansion on the Bosphorus.

Yayla(sı) Pastoral mountain hamlet occupied only in summer; in the Black Sea region, may have rustic accommodation.

Yeni New (common component of Turkish place names).

ARCHITECTURAL/ARTISTIC TERMS

Acropolis Ancient fortified hilltop.

Agora Marketplace and meeting area of an ancient Lycian, Greek or Roman city.

Apse Curved or polygonal recess at the altar end of a church.

Arasta Marketplace built into the foundations of a mosque, a portion of whose revenues goes to the upkeep of the latter.

Bedesten(i) Covered market hall for valuable goods, often lockable.

Bouleuterion Council hall of a Hellenistic or Roman city.

Camekan Changing rooms in a hamam.

Capital Top, often ornamented, of a column.

Cavea Seating curve of an ancient theatre.

Deesis or Deisis Portrayal of Christ between the Virgin and John the Baptist.

Diazoma A horizontal walkway dividing the two blocks of seats in an ancient theatre.

Exedra Semicircular niche.

Eyvan Domed side-chamber of an Ottoman religious building; also applies to three-sided alcoves in secular mansions.

Göbek taşı Literally "navel stone" – the hot central platform of a hamam.

Halvet Corner room in a hamam.

Hararet The hottest room of a hamam.

İmaret(i) Soup kitchen and hostel for dervishes and wayfarers, usually attached to a *medrese*.

Kale(si) Castle, fort.

Kapı(sı) Gate, door.

Katholikon Central shrine of a monastery.

Kemer Aqueduct, or a series of vaults/arches.

Khatchkar An ornate relief carving centred around stylized crosses, on the walls of Armenian churches; also a freestanding cruciform gravestone so carved.

Köşk(ü) Kiosk, pavilion, gazebo, folly.

Kubbe Dome, cupola – as in *Kubbeli Kilise* (the Domed Church).

Kule(si) Tower, turret.

Kurna Hewn stone basin in a hamam.

Külliye(si) A mosque and its dependent buildings.

Kümbet Vault, dome; by analogy the cylindrical "hatted" Selçuk tombs of central Anatolia.

Medrese(si) Islamic theological academy.

Mescit Small mosque with no *mimber*; Islamic equivalent of a chapel; genitive *mescidi*.

Mezar(i) Grave, tomb; thus *mezarlık*, cemetery.

Mihrab Niche in a mosque indicating the direction of Mecca, and prayer.

Mimber Pulpit in a mosque, from where the imam delivers homilies; often beautifully carved in wood or stone.

Minare(si) Turkish for "minaret", the tower from which the call to prayer is delivered.

Naos The inner sanctum of an ancient temple.

Narthex Vestibule or entrance hall of a church; also *exonarthex*, the outer vestibule when there is more than one.

Nave Principal lengthwise aisle of a church.

Necropolis Place of burial in an ancient Greek or Roman city.

Nymphaeum Ornate, multistoreyed facade, often with statue niches, surrounding a public fountain in an ancient city.

Odeion Small ancient theatre used for musical performances, minor dramatic productions or civic councils.

Pendentive Curved, triangular surface, by means of which a dome can be supported over a square ground plan.

Pier A mass of supportive masonry.

Porphyry Hard purplish-red volcanic rock containing crystals.

Revetment Facing of stone, marble or tile.

Saray(ı) Palace.

Sebil Public drinking fountain, freestanding or built into the wall of an Ottoman structure.

Selamlık Area where men receive guests in any sort of dwelling.

Son cemaat yeri Literally "Place of the last congregation" – a mosque porch where latecomers pray.

Stoa Colonnaded walkway in an ancient Greek agora.

Synthronon Semicircular seating for clergy, usually in the apse of a Byzantine church.

Şadırvan Ritual ablutions fountain of a mosque.

Şerefe Balcony of a minaret.

Tabhane Hospice for travelling dervishes or *ahis*, often housed in an *eyvan*.

Tapınak Alternative term for "temple" at archeological sites; genitive *tapınağı*.

Tekke(si) Gathering place of a Sufi order.

Tersane(si) Shipyard, dry dock.

Transept The "wings" of a church, extending north and south perpendicular to the nave.

Tuff Soft rock formed from volcanic ash.

Türbe(si) Freestanding, usually domed, tomb.

Tympanum The surface, often adorned, enclosed by the top of an arch; found in churches or more ancient ruins.

Verd(e) antique Mottled or veined green serpentine.

Voussoir Stripes of wedge-shaped blocks at the edge of an arch.

Zaviye Mosque built specifically as a hospice for dervishes, usually along a T-plan.

Zhamatoun Chapter (council) hall of an Armenian church.

ACRONYMS AND ABBREVIATIONS

AKP *Adalet ve Kalkınma Partisi* or Justice and Development Party; the Islamist movement headed by Recep Tayyip Erdoğan, which has governed with a large majority from 2002 until the present.

Bul Standard abbreviation for *bulvar(ı)* (boulevard).

Cad Standard abbreviation for *cadde(si)* (avenue).

CHP *Cumhuriyetçi Halk Partisi* or Republican People's Party (RPP) – founded by Atatürk, disbanded in 1980, revived in 1992. The main opposition party at present, it also controls many municipalities.

DP *Demokrat Partisi* or Democrat Party; moderate right-of-centre party who won Turkey's first truly free elections in 1950.

DYP *Doğru Yol Partisi* or True Path Party; right of centre, conservative party founded by Süleyman Demirel in 1983.

HDP *Halkların Demokratik Partisi* (People's Democratic Party). This pro-Kurdish political party crossed the ten percent threshold in the 2015 general elections.

KDV Acronym of the Turkish VAT.

MHP *Milliyet Hareket Paritisi* (National Action Party); originally quasi-fascist group, later rebranded by new leader Devlet Bahçeli; now third party in parliament.

NSC National Security Council (*Milli Güvenlik Kurulu*); mixed military-civilian council established after the 1980 coup.

PKK *Partia Karkaris Kurdistan* or Kurdish Workers' Party, actually an armed guerrilla movement, formed in 1978 and still present in the southeast.

PTT *Post Telefon ve Telegraf*, the joint postal, telegraph and (formerly) phone service in Turkey, and by extension its offices.

Sok Abbreviation for *sokak* (*sokağı*) or street.

THY *Türk Hava Yolları*, Turkish Airways.

TIR (pronounced "turr" locally) *Transport International Routière* – large, slow trucks, your greatest road hazard.

TL Standard abbreviation for the Turkish lira, these days increasingly replaced by the typographic symbol ₺.

TRT Acronym of *Türk Radyo ve Televizyon*, the Turkish public broadcasting corporation.

Small print and index

A ROUGH GUIDE TO ROUGH GUIDES

Published in 1982, the first Rough Guide – to Greece – was a student scheme that became a publishing phenomenon. Mark Ellingham, a recent graduate in English from Bristol University, had been travelling in Greece the previous summer and couldn't find the right guidebook. With a small group of friends he wrote his own guide, combining a highly contemporary, journalistic style with a thoroughly practical approach to travellers' needs.

The immediate success of the book spawned a series that rapidly covered dozens of destinations. And, in addition to impecunious backpackers, Rough Guides soon acquired a much broader readership that relished the guides' wit and inquisitiveness as much as their enthusiastic, critical approach and value-for-money ethos.

These days, Rough Guides include recommendations from budget to luxury and cover more than 120 destinations around the globe, as well as producing an ever-growing range of ebooks.

Visit **roughguides.com** to find all our latest books, read articles, get inspired and share travel tips with the Rough Guides community.

Rough Guide credits

Editors: Helen Abramson, Samantha Cook, Emma Gibbs and Polly Thomas
Layout: Jessica Subramanian
Cartography: Swati Handoo
Picture editor: Yoshimi Kanazawa
Proofreader: Susanne Hillen
Managing editor: Andy Turner
Assistant editor: Payal Sharotri

Production: Jimmy Lao
Cover photo research: Yoshimi Kanazawa
Editorial assistant: Freya Godfrey
Senior pre-press designer: Dan May
Programme manager: Gareth Lowe
Publisher: Keith Drew
Publishing director: Georgina Dee

Publishing information

This ninth edition published June 2016 by
Rough Guides Ltd,
80 Strand, London WC2R 0RL
11, Community Centre, Panchsheel Park,
New Delhi 110017, India
Distributed by Penguin Random House
Penguin Books Ltd, 80 Strand, London WC2R 0RL
Penguin Group (USA), 345 Hudson Street, NY 10014, USA
Penguin Group (Australia), 250 Camberwell Road,
Camberwell, Victoria 3124, Australia
Penguin Group (NZ), 67 Apollo Drive, Mairangi Bay,
Auckland 1310, New Zealand
Penguin Group (South Africa), Block D, Rosebank Office
Park, 181 Jan Smuts Avenue, Parktown North, Gauteng,
South Africa 2193
Rough Guides is represented in Canada by DK Canada, 320
Front Street West, Suite 1400, Toronto, Ontario M5V 3B6
Printed in Singapore
© Rough Guides 2016
Maps © Rough Guides

728pp includes index
A catalogue record for this book is available from the
British Library
ISBN: 978-0-24124-207-0
The publishers and authors have done their best to
ensure the accuracy and currency of all the information
in **The Rough Guide to Turkey**, however, they can accept
no responsibility for any loss, injury, or inconvenience
sustained by any traveller as a result of information or
advice contained in the guide.
1 3 5 7 9 8 6 4 2

Help us update

We've gone to a lot of effort to ensure that the ninth
edition of **The Rough Guide to Turkey** is accurate and up-
to-date. However, things change – places get "discovered",
opening hours are notoriously fickle, restaurants and
rooms raise prices or lower standards. If you feel we've got
it wrong or left something out, we'd like to know, and if
you can remember the address, the price, the hours, the
phone number, so much the better.

Please send your comments with the subject line
"**Rough Guide Turkey Update**" to mail@uk.roughguides
.com. We'll credit all contributions and send a copy of the
next edition (or any other Rough Guide if you prefer) for
the very best emails.

Find more travel information, connect with fellow
travellers and plan your trip on ⊕ roughguides.com.

ABOUT THE AUTHORS

Terry Richardson Terry Richardson is based in southwest Turkey, a country he first visited in 1978. He has crisscrossed this endlessly fascinating country on numerous occasions, and wrote both the Rough Guide and the Pocket Guide to Istanbul.

Zoë Smith Zoë Smith has been enchanted by Turkey since her first visit back in 2011 and its endless charms have lured her back time and time again. She's written about Turkey for both local and international publications, and has also contributed to *The Rough Guide to Istanbul* and *The Rough Guide to France*.

Lizzie Williams Lizzie Williams has been working and travelling in Africa for more than 25 years. Starting out as a tour leader on overland trucks, her love for Turkey began in 1993 when she first led trips on the epic (and sadly no longer accessible) route between Istanbul and Cairo. Now a full-time guidebook author based in Cape Town, she's written more than fifty titles for various publishers.

Martin Zatko Martin Zatko has been travelling more or less continuously since 2002, and during that time has written or contributed to the Rough Guides to Korea, Seoul, Japan, Tokyo, China, Beijing, Vietnam, Myanmar, Morocco and Europe. A big fan of beaches, water pipes, grilled meat and aniseed-flavoured spirits, he's already looking forward to his next trip to Turkey.

Acknowledgements

Terry Richardson In no particular order, Terry would like to thank the following people for their help in getting this edition of *The Rough Guide to Turkey* together: Şeyla at the *Hinar Bar* in Van for the lowdown on that intriguing city and its hinterland, Gamze and Dom, also in Van, for their hospitality, Anne-Louise and Muzaffer in Patara and Marion and Halil in Kalkan for more hospitality and local knowledge, Phil Buckley of Bougainville Travel for the usual inside information on Kaş and around, and Cemil and family for looking after me in Çıralı. Thumbs up to long-distance walker and cycle tourer Razz for filling in some gaps in and around Olympos and inveterate traveller Rhiannon for good company on the road from Antep to Diyarbakir. Also many thanks to Mustafa of Tamzara Travel and Bilal of the *Tehran Hotel* in Doğubeyazıt for local information, and to Ismail and family, long-standing friends from Van forced to move to Ankara by the 2011 quake. In Istanbul, cheers to Erkan of Talisman tours and a tribute to a great friend and superb guide, Seyhun, who tragically died in 2015. A hearty thanks too to all the other people I met on the road exploring what remains a great and incredibly hospitable country, despite the testing political circumstances of 2015. Many thanks too for the patient and understanding work of Rough Guides editors Helen Abramson, Emma Gibbs and Polly Thomas. Finally, heartfelt thanks to the truly wonderful Lem, without whom life will never be the same.

Zoë Smith Thanks to Turan Kıraç for insider tips and unrivalled guide services in Cappadocia; Ibrahim, Muslum and Carla at *Charly's Pension* for a home away from home in Eğirdir; Tovi, Ahmet, Osman and the whole team at Kirkit Voyage, Cappadocia; Deniz, Aziz and Şehmus at *Özmen Pension*, Antalya; Şirin at *Rain Hotel*, Kizkalesi; Euphrates Travel; Tayfun Eser in Iskele; Oz Cappadocia; Sedat at *Sabah Pansiyon*, Antalya; and Ibrahim Budak at New Göreme Travel.

Martin Zatko Martin would like to thank Seda and Sophie Kim for sparing the time to hang out in Istanbul; Hasan in Kuşadası; Zeynep in Alaçatı; Idris and Gizem in Bodrum; Mehmet in Pamukkale; the *Deeps Hostel* staff in Ankara; Aram for the star-gazing in Göreme; and his sister Nicole for flying out to join for a section of the Aegean coast.

Readers' updates

Thanks to all the readers who have taken the time to write in with comments and suggestions (and apologies if we've inadvertently omitted or misspelt anyone's name):

Roger Beswick, Romano Cassar, Francesco Cisternino, Michael Hanna, Richard Hermans, Magnus Linklater, Christo Snyman and Alice Vowles.

Photo credits

All photos © Rough Guides except the following:
(Key: a-above; b-below/bottom; c-centre; f-far; l-left; r-right; t-top)

Index

Maps are marked in grey

Map symbols

The symbols below are used on maps throughout the book

✈ Airport	♜ Castle	Waterfall	Bird sanctuary
★ Bus/taxi stop	⊠ Gate	Skiing	Church (regional maps)
🅿 Parking	Mountain range	♠ Monastery	Church (town maps)
Ⓜ Metro stop	▲ Mountain peak	⊙ Statue	✡ Synagogue
Ⓣ Tram stop	Cliff	Lighthouse	Mosque
Boat	Gorge	Monument	Stadium
Point of interest	Hill Shading	Museum	Building
@ Internet access	Spa	Campsite	Park
ⓘ Tourist office	Cave	Toilet	Beach
✉ Post office	Ruins	Winery	Christian cemetery
✚ Hospital	Marshland	Wall	Muslim cemetery
Swimming pool	Mountain pass	- - Ferry route	Funicular line

Listings key

- ■ Accommodation
- ● Eating
- ■ Drinking/nightlife
- ● Shopping